Dana Facaros & Michael Pauls

SOUTH OF FRANCE

'no poodles, no shades, no attitudes...'

D0168006

CADOGANguides

1 Massif des Maures, Provence

2 Grazing sheep, Provence
3 Calanque de Sormiou, near Marseille
4 Cork oaks, Provence

4

5 Olive trees in bloom
6 Montagne Ste-Victoire, near Aix-en-
   Provence
7 Sisteron, Provence
8 Ste-Agnès, near Menton
9 Traditional *cabine*, Camargue
10 Vineyard near Châteauneuf-du-Pape
11. Mimosas

12 Pont du Gard
13 Avignon
14 Grasse
15 Les Arènes, Nîmes
16 Roman ruins, Vaison-la-Romaine

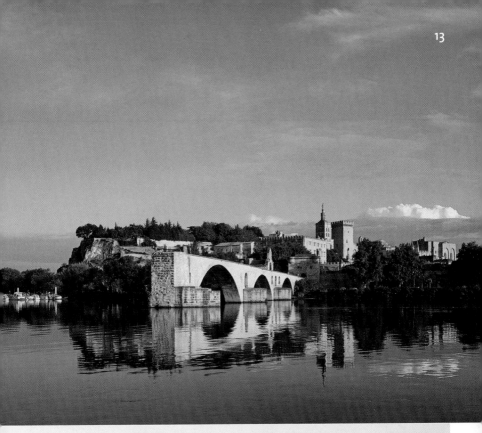

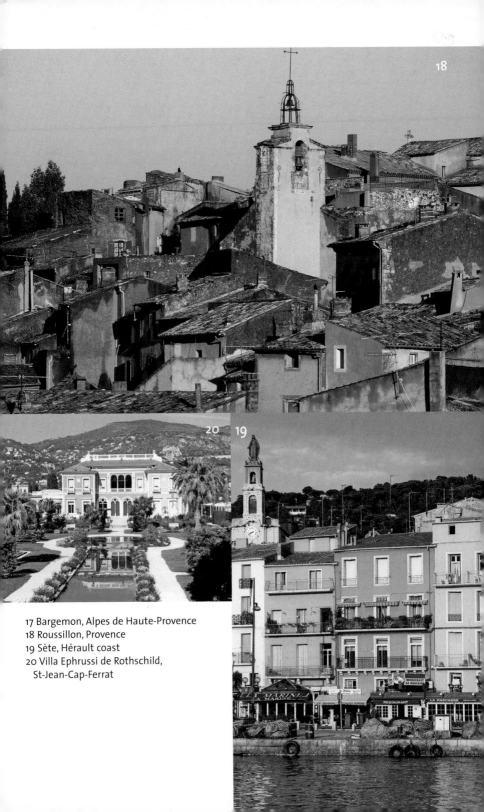

20 19

17 Bargemon, Alpes de Haute-Provence
18 Roussillon, Provence
19 Sète, Hérault coast
20 Villa Ephrussi de Rothschild,
   St-Jean-Cap-Ferrat

21 Vieux Port, Marseille

22

25

22 Hôtel Negresco, Nice
23 Vieux Nice
24 Cannes by night
25 Monpellier by night

26 Vieux Nice

About the authors

Dana Facaros and **Michael Pauls** have written over 30 books for Cadogan Guides. They have lived all over Europe with their son and daughter, and are currently ensconced in an old farmhouse in southwestern France with a large collection of tame and wild animals.

About the updaters

Jacqueline Chnéour is a freelance translator and researcher. Brought up in Paris and Nice, she moved to England in 1979 to follow a dream, and has lived in London ever since. She has updated or consulted on several guides in the Cadogan France series.

Linda Rano moved to a village near Toulouse with her French husband and two children nearly eight years ago. She regularly writes about the south of France. She is director of Couleurs de France Limited, a property agent for the southwest.

Thanks also to **Vanessa Letts** for help with the Travel and Practical chapters.

Contents

Cadogan Guides
2nd Floor
233 High Holborn
London WC1V 7DN
info@cadoganguides.co.uk
www.cadoganguides.com

The Globe Pequot Press
246 Goose Lane, PO Box 480, Guilford,
Connecticut 06437–0480

Cover and photo essay design by Sarah Gardner
Cover photographs: © Alamy/John Miller
Photo essay © John Miller
Maps © Cadogan Guides, drawn by
    Map Creation Ltd
Managing Editor: Natalie Pomier
Editorial Assistant: Nicola Jessop
Editor: Linda McQueen
Proofreading: Ali Qassim
Indexing: Isobel McLean
Production: Navigator Guides Ltd

Printed in Italy by Legoprint
A catalogue record for this book is available
    from the British Library
ISBN 1-86011-185-8

Introduction

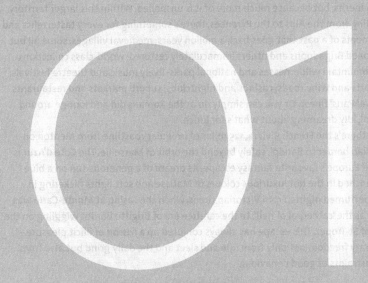

'Our nights are more beautiful than your days,' Racine boasted to his Parisian friends, writing home from Uzès, in the Gard. The nights are indeed thrilling – dry and clear and boiling with stars. After dawn, the southern sun quickens landscapes of sculpted hills and purple mountains, cypresses and lavender. Vincent Van Gogh, who saw more clearly into the heart of this extravagant world than anyone else, painted those landscapes, and especially those cypresses, as if they were moving and alive, with a lyrical and passionate intensity. Come to the hills around St-Rémy when the mistral is up and you will see nature imitating art.

We outsiders have had an on-again off-again love affair with the south of France ever since the Romans colonized it and spent their decline there. Even the medieval popes and cardinals in Avignon succumbed to its worldly temptations, its wines and the scents of its *maquis*, its roses and violets, the droning hum of the cicadas. The popes' court painters, some of the greatest artists of the 14th century, lent their radiant madonnas something of the voluptuous Mediterranean light and colour that would one day inspire Van Gogh, Cézanne, Renoir, Matisse and the Fauves, painters whose works have changed the way our eyes see not only the south of France, but the rest of our world as well.

These days, our world has decided on Provence as its possible paradise. Millions of people come here every year, hoping to catch a glimpse of it, wishing it didn't have so many second homes, holiday flats, trinket shops and traffic jams. To see the region at its best the delicate question of *when* to go becomes as important as where; in August, the worst month, even the dullest town on the coast can be as frantic as the monkey-pit in a zoo.

One reason why we've included Languedoc-Roussillon, the 'other', western half of Mediterranean France, is not only for its own considerable and undeservedly little-known merits, but because much more of it is unspoiled. Within this larger territory, extending from the Alps to the Pyrenees, there's something for every taste: relics and monuments of a past that goes back a million years; medieval villages, some all but abandoned Brigadoons and others immaculately restored; world-class collections of art; mountain wildernesses and national parks; lively music and theatre festivals; ski resorts and wine roads; casinos and nightclubs; superb markets and restaurants that rival Paris' finest. Or you can simply do as the Romans did and lounge around the pool, idly dreaming about what's for lunch.

Then there's the French Riviera, 125 miles of irregular coastline from Menton on the Italian border to Bandol, safely beyond the orbit of Marseille. The Côte d'Azur is grey old Europe's favourite fantasy escape, its dream of a generous sun on a blue sea drenched in the hot luxurious colours of Matisse and soft lights flickering in warm perfumed nights. From Victorian times, when the casino at Monte-Carlo was known as the 'cathedral of hell', to the carefree era of Brigitte Bardot wiggling on the sands of St-Tropez, this escape has always conjured up a *frisson* of illicit pleasure – temporary freedom not only from rain and sleet and the daily grind but also from the constraints of good behaviour.

These days, the glamour and lustre of flaunted wealth that made the coast sparkle in the past is concentrated on security and seclusion in private yachts and hideyhole villas. And yet the tantalizing, hedonistic vision of a fantasy escape under the palms and mimosas remains as seductive as ever. No wonder that Pope Gregory XI, who returned the papacy to Rome in 1377, took one look at the Eternal City and immediately decided to pack his bags to return to the comforts and delights of Avignon. Much to the relief of the Italians, he died before he could go.

A Guide to the Guide

Never think that this nebulous Anglo-Saxon concept 'the South of France' has any definite boundaries. Every writer who has ever covered the subject draws the line where he or she sees fit, and we must do the same. We definitely think we've given you the best of it, pushing as far inland as the Provençal Alps if something is worth the trip. The real innovation is that this book covers the entire French Mediterranean coast, offering a surprising alternative to overcrowded Provence – Languedoc and Roussillon.

For convenience's sake, the contents of this book follow a fairly strict east-to-west order, beginning on the Italian frontier with the **Eastern Côte d'Azur**. This is the French Riviera, with dramatic corniche roads and outrageous fleshpots like Monaco and Cannes, as well as great museums of modern art, music festivals and superb restaurants; here, too, is Nice, one of the most delightful cities in France.

The **Western Côte d'Azur** covers the blood-red cliffs of the Esterel, the chestnut forests of the Maures, the lovely Iles d'Hyères, the navy city of Toulon and France's beach-blanket Babylon, St-Tropez.

To the west, in **Metropolitan Provence**, lies Marseille, the metropolis of Provence, set in a coastline of dramatic cliffs and fjord-like *calanques;* here, too, are staid and elegant Aix-en-Provence, and the lovely countryside around Cézanne's Montagne Ste-Victoire.

The **Provençal Alps** chapter follows the same east–west course, but takes the inland route through the maritime Alps and their secret valleys, difficult of access but worth the trouble for the scenery – Mercantour National Park and the Grand Canyon of the Verdon – and for the art in their medieval chapels.

Next (**Northern Provence: The Vaucluse**) comes the heartland of Provence: the Luberon and Mont Ventoux, and pockets of exquisite villages full of artists and refugees from the coast.

From here we descend the Rhône, beginning in **Down the Rhône 1: Orange to Beaucaire** with Orange and its Roman theatre, through the celebrated vineyards of Châteauneuf-du-Pape and Tavel, France's finest rosé, to lively Avignon, the medieval city of the popes. As the Rhône continues south (**Down the Rhône 2: the Alpilles, Crau and Camargue**) it passes some of the south's most curious natural features: the

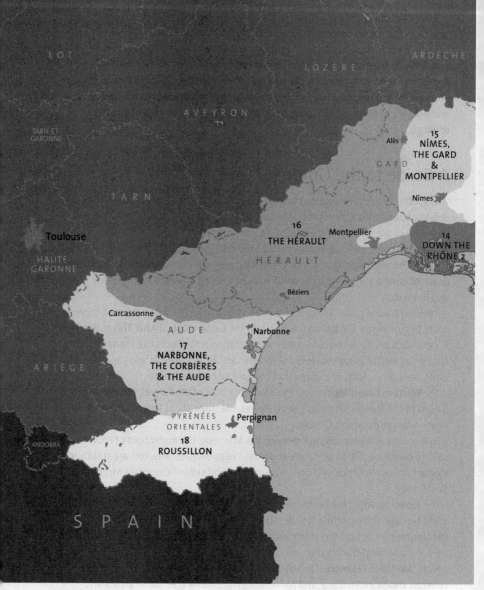

jagged Alpilles, the rock-strewn plain of the Crau and the marshlands of the
Camargue, where Provençal cowboys herd wild bulls and horses. Roman Provence is
well represented in St-Rémy and Arles, and the Middle Ages come to life in St-Gilles
and Aigues-Mortes.

West of the Rhône lies Languedoc, with all the interest of Provence and only a
fraction of the tourists – except perhaps at the magnificent Pont du Gard, one of the
three most visited sights in France. This is covered in **Nîmes, the Gard and Montpellier**,

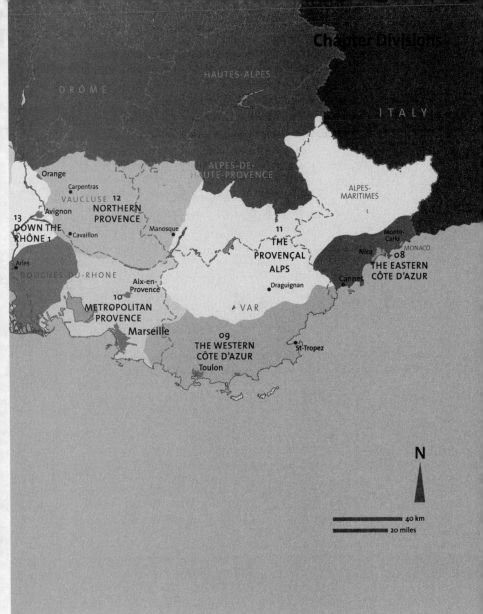

DRÔME

HAUTES-ALPES

ITALY

Orange

Carpentras

VAUCLUSE **12**

NORTHERN PROVENCE

ALPES-DE-HAUTE-PROVENCE

ALPES-MARITIMES

13 DOWN THE RHÔNE 1

Avignon

Cavaillon

Manosque

11 THE PROVENÇAL ALPS

Monte-Carlo

Nice

08 THE EASTERN CÔTE D'AZUR

MONACO

Arles

BOUCHES-DU-RHÔNE

Cannes

Aix-en-Provence

Draguignan

10 METROPOLITAN PROVENCE

VAR

Marseille

09 THE WESTERN CÔTE D'AZUR

St-Tropez

Toulon

N

40 km

20 miles

along with the art town of Uzès, Nîmes with its famous Roman monuments, and dynamic Montpellier, a university city that rivals Paris in its enthusiasm for culture and technology.

The **Hérault** introduces the biggest wine-producing region of France, with rural delights equal to those of Provence – little wine regions like the Minervois, and the serendipitous tree-lined Canal du Midi. Its coast offers long miles of open beaches and the pretty resort town of Agde, founded by the ancient Greeks.

The next *département* is the Aude (**Narbonne, the Corbières and the Aude**); here you'll find the surprising city of Narbonne, with its magnificent cathedral; Carcassonne, the biggest and best-preserved medieval fortress city in Europe; and scores of spectacular castles hanging over the lonely landscapes of the Corbières.

Last but not least, there's **Roussillon**: Catalans, sweet wines, medieval art, Pyrenean valleys and the delicious Côte Vermeille on the Spanish border.

History

02

Before starting, a little political geography might help to relieve some major confusions. In France, almost all regional names are maddeningly fluid. First of all, there is Provence, which has never had any fixed boundaries. The Romans called the southern coast their dear 'province', one of their first and most delectable conquests outside Italy. Specifically, this was the province of Gallia Narbonnensis, stretching from Toulouse to Geneva, though its rich heartland was always the coastal area from Narbonne to Marseille. In the early Middle Ages, ancient Gaul was evolving its linguistic north-south distinction between the *langue d'oc* and the *langue d'œil* (two words for saying 'yes', from the Latin *hoc* and *hoc ille*). 'Provence' came to mean the *oc* domain, the southern third of what is now France, from the Dordogne to Lyon; both troubadour poets and noblemen's secretaries enjoyed making a connection with the classical civilization that built the Pont du Gard, the arch of Orange and the amphitheatres of Nîmes and Arles.

At the same time, the political boundary of the Rhône, between lands subject to the Holy Roman Emperors and those claimed by the kings of France, was redefining the terminology. 'Provence' took on the political meaning of the semi-independent county east of the Rhône, while the rest, as far as Toulouse and Aquitaine, was grabbed by force by the French in the 13th century and took the name of Languedoc. Provence held out longer, until its union with the French crown in 1486. Today, southern regionalists call the entire south of France Occitania (a word only invented in the 17th century).

Roussillon, the modern *département* of Pyrenées-Orientales, followed an entirely different course of history: part of the Catalan nation since the 10th century, it was an essential part of the County of Barcelona and later the Catalan Kingdom of Aragon, until the French annexed it in 1559.

Under the *ancien régime*, the Revolution and all the regimes that followed it, these areas were smothered, politically and culturally, by imperialist France. The turning of the tide came only in our own time, with the election of the 1981 Socialist government and the beginnings of regional autonomy. The five *départements* east of the Rhône are now the artificially designed region of Provence-Côte d'Azur; those to the west (along with Lozère, in the Cévennes), are in Languedoc-Roussillon, still cut off from its traditional capital, Toulouse, by the intent of the Paris planners.

The First Million Years or So

The first inhabitants, with all of the Midi to choose from, not surprisingly seem to have picked the Côte d'Azur for their residence. Tools and traces of habitation around Monaco go back as far as 1,000,000 BC. The first identifiable personality on the stage, however, is 'Tautavel Man'; a remarkable recent find in the small Roussillon village of that name has unearthed hundreds of thousands of bones of a people who rate among the very first Europeans yet discovered – from at least 450,000 BC, and perhaps as far back as 680,000 BC. Someone may have been around through all the millennia that followed, but evidence is rare; more bones have been found in caves around Nice from about 200,000 BC. Neanderthal Man turns up about 60,000 BC (at Ganges, in the Hérault, and other places). The first evidence of the Neanderthals' nemesis, that quarrelsome and unlovable species *Homo sapiens*, appears some 20,000 years later.

Neolithic civilization arrived as early as 3500 BC, and endured throughout the region for the next 2,000 years. People knew agriculture and raised sheep, traded for scarce goods (obsidian from the islands around Sicily, for example), and built dry-stone houses; one of these has been reconstructed by archaeologists at Cambous, in the Hérault. The Neolithic era left few important monuments here: an impressive but little-known temple complex at Castellet, near Arles, and some large dolmens in the Minervois in the northern Hérault and the Massif des Maures. Of succeeding ages we know more about their technology than culture and changes in population: the use of copper began about 2000 BC, iron *c.* 800 BC. In both cases the region was one of the last parts of the Mediterranean basin to catch on.

By now, at least, the inhabitants have a name, even if it is a questionable one applied by later Greek and Roman writers: the Ligurians on the east coast and the Iberians in the west. There is plenty of room for confusion here; culturally and racially there may have been little difference between the two. From about 800 BC they began building their first settled villages, today called by the Latin name *oppidum*, a word you will see often in the south; it even survives in village names, such as Oppèdette in Provence. An *oppidum* is a small, fortified village, usually on a hilltop, built around a religious sanctuary or trading centre. Already, more advanced outsiders were coming to make deals with the natives: the Phoenicians, the Etruscans and, most importantly, the Greeks.

A major event of this same era was the arrival of the Celts, Indo-European cousins of the Ligurians and Iberians from the north. Beginning in coastal Languedoc in the 8th century BC, they gradually spread their conquests eastwards at the expense of the Ligurians until the 4th century. At the same time, Greek merchant activity was turning into full-scale colonization. The Ionian city-states of Asia Minor had become over-populated, agriculturally exhausted and politically precarious, and their citizens sought to reproduce them in new lands. The first was Massalia – Marseille – *c.* 600 BC. Soon Massalia was founding colonies of its own: Nice, Hyères and Agde were among the most important. Greek influence over the indigenous peoples was strong from the start; as with everywhere else they went, they brought the vine (wild stocks were already present, but the Celts hadn't worked out what to do with them) and the olive, and also their art. The Celts loved Greek vases, and had metals and other raw materials to offer in return. Increased trade turned some of the native *oppida* into genuine cities, such as Ensérune, near Béziers, and Arles.

Roman Provincia

From the start, the Greeks were natural allies of the young city of Rome – if only because they had common enemies. Besides the strong Etruscan federation, occupying the lands in between the two, there were their trade rivals, the Phoenicians (later Carthaginians) and occasionally the Celts and Ligurians. As Rome gobbled up Etruria and the rest of Italy, the area became of increasing importance, a fact Hannibal demonstrated when he marched his armies along the coast towards Italy in 218 BC, with the full support of the Celts (historians still argue over how and where he got the elephants across the Rhône).

When the Romans took control of Spain in the Second Punic War (206 BC), the coasts of what they called Gaul became a logical next step. In 125 BC, Roman troops saved Marseille from a Celtic attack. This time, though, they had come to stay. The reorganization of the new province – *Provincia* – was quick and methodical. Domitius Ahenobarbus, the vanquisher of the Celts, began the great Italy–Spain highway that bears his name, the Via Domitia, in 121 BC. New cities were founded, most importantly Aix (122 BC) and Narbonne (118 BC), which became the capital of what was now officially called *Gallia Narbonensis*. Dozens of other new foundations followed over the next century, many of them planned colonies with land grants for veterans of the legions. The Celts were not through yet, though. Two northern tribes, the Cimbri and Teutones, mounted a serious invasion of Gaul and Italy in 115 BC. They raided those areas continuously until 102 BC, when they were destroyed by a Roman army under Marius near Montagne Ste-Victoire, near Aix. Marius, later populist dictator in Rome, became a folk hero and the subject of Provençal legends ever after. Celtic-Ligurian resistance continued intermittently until 14 BC; the great monument at La Turbie, on the border of Gaul, commemorates the defeat of the last hold-outs in the Alps.

The downfall of Marseille, still the metropolis of Provence and still thoroughly Greek in culture and sympathies, came in 49 BC. Always famed for its careful diplomacy, the city made the fatal mistake of supporting Pompey over Julius Caesar in the Roman civil wars. A vengeful Caesar crippled its trade and stripped it of nearly all its colonies and dependencies. Thereafter, the influence of Marseille gave way to newer, more Romanized towns: Aix, Narbonne, Nîmes, Arles and Fréjus.

Throughout all this, Provence had been easily assimilated into the Roman economy, supplying food and raw materials for the insatiable metropolis. With Caesar's conquest of the rest of Gaul, the Rhône trade route (which had always managed to bring down a little Baltic amber and tin from Cornwall) became a busy river highway and military route. Under the good government and peace bestowed by Augustus (27 BC–AD 14) and his successors, Provence blossomed with an opulence never before seen. The cities, especially those of the Rhône valley, acquired theatres, amphitheatres for the games, aqueducts, bridges and temples. Provence participated in the political and cultural life of the Empire, even contributing one of the better emperors, Antoninus Pius (from Nîmes, AD 138–161), only obscure because his reign was so peaceful and prosperous.

Large areas of Roman towns have been excavated at Glanum and Vaison-la-Romaine, and both have turned up a preponderance of wealthy villas. This is the dark side of Roman Provence; from the beginning of Roman rule, wealthy Romans were able to grab up much of the land, forming large estates and exploiting the indigenous population. This trend was magnified in the decadent, totalitarian and economically chaotic late Empire, when, throughout Roman territory, the few remaining free farmers were forced to sell themselves into virtual serfdom to escape crushing taxation. After AD 200, in fact, everything was going wrong so that trade and the cities stagnated while art and culture decayed. The first of the barbarian raids brought Germans into Provence in the 250s, when they destroyed Glanum.

Constantine, while yet emperor of only the western half of the Empire (312–323), often resided at Arles and favoured that city; his baths there were probably the last big Roman building project in Provence. His pro-Christian policy gave the cult its first real influence in Gaul, at least in the cities; under his auspices, the first state-sponsored Church council was held at Arles in 314. Before that, Christianity does not seem to have made much of an impression (later, to make up for it, elaborate mythologies were constructed to place Mary Magdalene and other early saints in Provence after the Crucifixion; *see* the towns of Stes-Maries-de-la-Mer, pp.441–5, and St-Maximin-la-Ste-Baume, pp.330–32).

600 Years of Unwanted Guests

French historians always blame the barbarian invaders of the 5th century for destroying the cities of Provence – as if Teutonic warriors enjoyed pulling down temple colonnades on their days off. In fact, few armies passed through Provence; the Visigoths, in the early 400s, were the most notable. Though government collapsed in chaos, business went on much as usual, with the Roman landowners (and their new German colleagues) gradually making their transition to feudal nobles. Arles, untouched by the troubles, became the most important city of the west, and briefly the capital, under Constantius III in 412. The weakness of the central power brought some long-due upheavals in the countryside, with guerrilla bands and vigilante justice against the landlords. The old and new rulers soon found common cause. For a while, a clique of a hundred of the biggest landowners took over administration in Gaul, even declaring one of their own as 'emperor' in Arles (455), with the support of the Visigoths.

The Visigoths soon tired of such games, and assumed total control in 476, the year the Western Empire formally expired. They had to share it, however, with the Ostrogoths, who had established a strong kingdom in Italy and seized all of Provence east of the Rhône – the beginnings of a political boundary that would last in various forms for a thousand years. When the Eastern Empire, under Justinian, invaded Italy, the Franks were able to snatch the Ostrogoths' domain (535). They were never able to hold it effectively and the area gradually slipped into virtual independence.

The Visigoths kept their part, a distant zone of their Spanish kingdom, until the Arab invasion of the early 700s rolled over the Pyrenees. In 719 the Arabs took Narbonne. The next two centuries are as wonderfully confused as anything in prehistory. There is the legend of the great Spanish Caliph Abd ar-Rahman, defeated in battle and leaving a treasure buried somewhere in the Alpilles. And a document survives in which the bishops of Agde are rebuked by the pope for minting coins with the image of Muhammad. Charles Martel, the celebrated Frankish generalissimo who stopped the Arab wave at Poitiers, made an expedition to the southern coast in 737–9, brutally sacking Agde, Marseille, Avignon and Aix. His mission was hardly a religious crusade – rather taking advantage of the Visigothic defeat to increase Frankish hegemony in the south; the cities of Provence are recorded as petitioning the Arabs at Córdoba to help them keep the nasty Franks out.

The Arabs couldn't help; the climate was too eccentric and the pickings too slim for them to mount a serious effort in Gaul. The nascent Franks gained control everywhere, and the entire coast was absorbed by Charlemagne's father, Pépin the Short, in 759. Under Charlemagne (768–814), Occitania seems to have shared little in the Carolingian revival of trade and culture, and after the break-up of the empire (with the Treaty of Verdun in 843) its misery was complete. The 9th- and 10th-century invasions were the real Dark Ages in many parts of Europe. Provence suffered constant and destructive raids by the Normans, the Arabs again (who held the Massif des Maures and St-Tropez until the 970s), and even the Hungarians, who sacked what was left of Nîmes in 924.

The Beginnings of the Middle Ages

Even in this sorry period, the foundations were being laid for recovery. Monastic reformers in Charlemagne's time, men such as Benedict of Aniane (in the Hérault), helped start a huge expansion of Church institutions. The abbey of St-Victor in Marseille took the lead in this, founding hundreds of new monasteries around Occitania; hard-working monks reclaimed land from forests and swamps, and later they sat back and enjoyed the rents, while always keeping up the holy work of education and copying books. Pilgrimages became an important activity, especially to Arles (St-Trophime) and St-Guilhem (near Aniane), getting a sleepy and locally bound society moving again and providing an impetus to trade.

The Treaty of Verdun (see above) had confirmed the Rhône as a boundary, and politically Provence and Languedoc went their separate ways. The Kingdom of Provence (or 'Kingdom of Arles'), proclaimed by a great-grandson of Charlemagne in 879, was little more than a façade for a feudal anarchy. Though it was united with the Kingdom of Burgundy in 949, and formally passed to the Holy Roman Empire in 1032, the tapestry of battling barons and shifting local alliances continued without effective interference from the overlords. Across the Rhône it was much the same; Frankish control was almost non-existent, and the biggest power in Languedoc was that of the County of Toulouse.

The most important result of the Carolingian collapse was the birth of a new nation in the eastern Pyrenees – Catalunya. The Catalans, who spoke a language closely related to the Occitan of Languedoc and Provence, coalesced around the County of the Cerdagne, deep in the mountains. In the 10th century this dynasty became counts of Barcelona, and expanded its control into what is now Roussillon.

Occitan and Catalan Medieval Civilization

All over Europe, the year 1000 can be taken as the rough milestone for the sudden and spectacular development of the medieval world, including the Midi. Towns and villages found the money and energy to build impressive new churches. The end of foreign raids made the seas safe for merchants, from Genoa, Pisa and Barcelona mostly, but also a few from Marseille. New cities were founded, notably Montpellier, in 985. In 1002 the first written document in Occitan appeared. The great pilgrimage to Santiago de Compostela, in Spain, made what was left of the old Roman roads into busy highways once more, and along the main southern route the first of the medieval trade fairs appeared, at the new town of St-Gilles-du-Gard.

Things were on an up-swing throughout the 11th century, and the trend was given another boost by the Crusades, which began in 1095. With increased prosperity and contact with a wider world, better manners and the rudiments of personal hygiene were not slow to follow. Feudal anarchy began to look quite genteel, maintaining a delicate balance of power, with feudal ties and blood relations keeping the political appetites of rulers from ever really getting out of hand. From the more civilized East, and from nearby Muslim Spain, came new ideas, new technologies and a taste for luxury and art. As an indication of how far Occitania had come, there were the troubadours (see pp.41–2), creating modern Europe's first lyric poetry. Almost every court of the south was refined enough to welcome and patronize them.

The growing cities began to assert themselves in the 12th century, often achieving a substantial independence in communes governed by consuls: Avignon in 1129, Arles in 1132, Perpignan and Nîmes in 1198. In the countryside, successive waves of monastic reform spawned a huge number of new institutions: first the movement led from Cluny, in the 11th century, and in the 12th the Cistercians, who set up a score of important monasteries. Efficiently exploiting the lands bequeathed by noblemen made them rich, and also did much to improve the agricultural economy all round.

Probably the richest corner of the south was the Catalan Pyrenees; substantial iron deposits, and the most advanced methods of smelting them, provided the capital for a Catalan trading empire based in Barcelona and Perpignan. From then on, Catalunya's rise was dramatic. By 1125 the counts of Barcelona controlled much of Provence south of the Durance; in 1137 they became kings of Aragon, which included much of western Spain as well as Roussillon. Besides its wealth, Catalunya was characterized by its unique constitution, recognizing the interests of the new middle class as well as nobles, and writing down elaborate codes of rights called *fueros* as a check on royal absolutism.

The other leading power in the region, Toulouse, contended with the Catalans for Provence while being overlord of all Languedoc, except for Carcassonne and Béziers, ruled by the Trencavel family, and Narbonne, with its independent viscounts.

The Cathars and the Rape of Languedoc

It was a great age for culture, producing not only the troubadours but an impressive display of Romanesque architecture, and original schools of sculpture in Roussillon and at Arles. Perhaps the most remarkable phenomenon of the times was a widespread religious tolerance, shared by rulers, the common people and even many among the clergy. A long and fruitful exposure to the culture of Muslim Spain, as well as the presence of a large Jewish community, an important element in the towns since Roman times, must have helped. Still, such goodwill is hard to account for in medieval Europe. Like the troubadour poetry, it is an indication of just how advanced Occitan society was at its height in the 12th century.

Unfortunately, this tolerance was also to bring about the fall of the Occitan nation. Religious dissenters of various persuasions sprang up everywhere. Most of the new sects soon died out and are little known today, like the extremist 'Petrobrusians' of St-Gilles, who didn't fancy churches, sacraments, relics or priests, and who even had their doubts about the crucifixion of Jesus.

One sect, however, made startling inroads into every sector of society in 11th- and 12th-century Languedoc – the Cathars, or Albigensians. This Manichaean doctrine (*see* pp.36–8), obsessed with Good and Evil, had in its upright simplicity a powerful attraction for both industrious townspeople and peasants. In many ways it was the very picture of 17th-century English Puritanism, though without any of the Puritans' noxious belligerence towards the less perfect; this kept it in good standing with the worldly nobility, and also allowed Cathar and Catholic villagers to live peacefully side by side.

The Cathars were never a majority in any part of the south; in most places they never made up more than 10 per cent of the population. They might have passed on as only a curious footnote to history, had they not provided the excuse for the biggest and most flagrant land grab of the Middle Ages. The 'Albigensian Crusade', arranged after the 1208 murder of a papal legate, was a cynical marriage of convenience between two old piratical enemies, the papacy and the crown of France. One wanted the religious competition stifled, the other sought to assert its old Carolingian claim to the lands of the counts of Toulouse. Diplomacy forced King Philip Augustus to disclaim any part in the affair, but nevertheless a big army of knights from the Ile-de-France went south in 1209 to burn some heretics and snatch what they might. Their leader made the difference: too smart, too brutal and too lucky, the sort of devil that changes history – Simon de Montfort. His vicious massacres at Béziers, where the Catholic population tried to defend the heretics and were incinerated along with them inside the churches, and his taking of the impregnable fortress town of Carcassonne put the fear of God into the southerners; Montfort won battle after battle and took every town he attacked, save only Beaucaire.

In a last attempt to save their fortunes, Count Raymond VI of Toulouse and King Peter II of Aragon combined to meet the northerners. With an overwhelmingly superior force, they blundered their way to crushing defeat at the Battle of Muret in 1213. Montfort soon claimed the titles of count of Toulouse and viscount of Carcassonne and Béziers for himself. The Languedociens continued to resist until after his death in 1218; six years later, again under the pretence of a 'crusade', King Louis VIII took the matter in his own hands. Coming south with another army, he forced the annexation of all eastern Languedoc and Carcassonne, the fortress key to the Midi, in 1229. The remainder of the century saw the inexorable consolidation of French power; the building or rebuilding of gigantic fortifications, as at Carcassonne and Peyrepertuse, begun by Saint Louis (King Louis IX, 1226–70), and the new port of Aigues-Mortes, used by Louis as base for his two Crusades (1249 and 1270).

Four centuries after the fall of the Carolingian Empire, the French once again had their foothold in the south. Languedoc was through, its distinctive culture quickly snuffed out. If Montfort's men had been shock troops from France, the occupying force was made up of French bureaucrats and monks. The monks took charge of many village churches, replacing parish priests to keep an eye on the population. The Inquisition arrived to take care of the heretics – and of course anyone the northerners found politically suspect, or whose property they coveted. The last Cathar stronghold, the Château de Quéribus, fell to royal troops in 1255. The troubadours found less and less around them worthy of a song. One of the most famous, Folquet de Marseille, had already gone over to the side of France and bigotry. As a zealous convert and, later, Bishop of Toulouse, he was an extremely ferocious oppressor of the few surviving Cathars.

The Turn of Provence

Provence was still free, enjoying a prosperous era under its Catalan counts though still troubled by incessant feudal struggles, waged by such local powers as the *seigneurs* of Les Baux and Forcalquier. Count Raymond Bérenger V (1209–45) was usually strong enough to keep them in check; under him, Provence did very well, and developed a constitutional government on the Catalan model. The region managed temporarily to avert French aggression in a roundabout way. In 1246, Raymond Bérenger's daughter and heir married Charles of Anjou, Saint Louis' brother. The ambitious Angevin used Provence as a springboard to create a Mediterranean empire that, at its height in the 1280s, included southern Italy and parts of Greece.

The city of Avignon and its hinterlands, the Comtat Venaissin, loyal possessions of Toulouse, had suffered greatly at the hands of Louis VIII after the Albigensian Crusade. In 1274, Charles and Louis arranged to give the Comtat to the papacy – its discreetly delayed share of the Albigensian booty. In 1309, Pope Clement V, fleeing anarchy in Rome, installed himself at Carpentras, in the Comtat. Politically, the popes found Provence a convenient new home and decided to stay – the 'Babylonian Captivity' (as jealous Italians called it) that would last over a century. They soon moved to Avignon, purchasing the city in 1348 and conducting a worldly court that seemed a Babylon indeed to many.

The late 14th century brought hard times to Provence: first the Black Death in 1348, and then political instability under the hapless Queen Jeanne (1343–82). Once more the *seigneurs* of Les Baux and their imitators raged over the land, with bands of unscrupulous mercenaries (the *Grandes Compagnies*) to help them ravage town and country. The popes returned to Rome in 1377; they kept control of Avignon and the Comtat, though French-supported antipopes held Avignon as late as 1403. After 1434, peace had returned and Provence was ruled by Good King René (count of Provence and only 'king' from his claim to Sicily, where the Angevins had been replaced by the Aragonese after the 'Sicilian Vespers' revolution of 1282). The 'good' is equally spurious. René was open-handed to courtiers, and a patron of artists, but his futile dream of recapturing Sicily and Naples led him to wring the last penny out of everyone else.

René's successor, Charles III, lasted only a year and died without an heir in 1481, bequeathing Provence to the French Crown. It was intended to be a union of equals, maintaining Provençal liberties and institutions. As such, the Provençal Estates-General ratified the agreement. The French immediately went back on their word, attempting to govern through royal commissioners, but their attempts to swallow Provence whole had to wait. Louis XI and Charles XII needed a peaceful Provence as a bridge for their invasions of Italy; the region paid for this, with two destructive invasions in the 1520s and 30s by France's arch-enemy Charles V, Holy Roman Emperor and King of Spain. This era also saw a landmark in the cultural effacement of Occitania – the 1539 Edict of Villers-Cotterêts decreed French as the official language throughout the kingdom.

The Wars of Religion

Meanwhile, a big dose of the new Protestant heresy was floating down the Rhône from Calvin's Geneva. The Occitans received it more than warmly, and soon there were large Protestant communities in all the towns. Although this seems like a repeat of the Cathar story, the geographical distribution is fascinating – the old Cathar areas (like the Aude) were now loyally Catholic, while the orthodox regions of the 14th century now came out strongly for the dissenters; in eastern Languedoc (the Hérault and Gard) they attracted about half the population. Tolerance was still out of fashion and the opening round of a pointless half-century of religious wars came with the 1542 massacres in the Luberon mountains. The perpetrator was the Parlement in Aix (pre-Revolution *parlements* were not parliaments but powerful judicial bodies appointed by and responsible to the king), the victims mostly Waldensians (Vaudois), pre-Reformation heretics who had migrated to Provence before the union with France, to escape oppression there.

In the open warfare that followed across the south, there were massacres and atrocities enough on both sides. Protestants distinguished themselves by the wholesale destruction of churches and their art (as at St-Gilles); churches were often converted into fortresses, as can be seen throughout Languedoc. Henry IV's 1598 Edict of Nantes acknowledged Protestant control of certain areas (Nîmes, Montpellier, Uzès, Gignac, Clermont-l'Hérault, Aigues-Mortes, Sommières, Orange, Lourmarin). The French monarchy had been weakened by the wars, but as soon as it recovered new measures were introduced to keep the south in line. Under Cardinal Richelieu, in the 1630s, the laws and traditions of local autonomy were swept away; after 1639 the Estates-General of Provence was not allowed to meet until the eve of the Revolution. As insurance, scores of feudal castles (such as Beaucaire and Les Baux) were demolished to eliminate possible points of resistance.

Louis XIV's revocation of the Edict of Nantes in 1685 caused more troubles. Thousands of Protestants, the south's most productive citizens, simply left; most of the community in Orange went off to colonize new lands in Prussia. Louis' long and oppressive reign continued the impoverishment of the south, despite well-intentioned economic measures by his brilliant minister Colbert, who started new manufactures (Villeneuvette, near Clermont l'Hérault), founded the port of Sète, and helped Paul Riquet build the Canal du Midi. In the 18th century, things picked up considerably in Languedoc, with the beginnings of an important textile industry, usually promoted by the remaining Protestants: silk around Nîmes and parts of Provence (where farmers gave up their bedrooms to raise the delicate silkworms in them), and linen and cotton goods in Montpellier, Carcassonne and Orange. It was a great start, though unfortunately the English and their machines would come along to ruin Languedoc's cloth trade after 1800.

In Provence, the century told a miserable tale; economic stagnation, deforestation of mountain areas that have still not been entirely repaired today, and plagues: the biggest, in 1720, carried off almost half the population of Marseille. The one bright spot was the growing naval town of Toulon.

The Partitions of Catalunya

Roussillon had followed a quite different history, though the result was the same. Under Jaume I the Conqueror (1213–76), Aragon reached the height of its merchant empire, while keeping the French at bay along the castle-strewn Roussillon–Languedoc border. Before his death, Jaume decided to divide the kingdom between his two sons, leading to the brief but exotic interlude of the 'Kingdom of Majorca' and an equally brief golden age for Perpignan, its capital. The French tried to take advantage of the split, again shamelessly proclaiming a 'crusade' against the piously orthodox Catalans (the pope, who wanted the Aragonese out of Italy, had given his approval), but they were thrown back across the border in 1285.

Aragon was reunited in 1344, but its troubles were just beginning. After the Black Death in 1348, recessions and political strife led to a long and disastrous decline in Catalan commerce. The union of Aragon and Castile to form the Kingdom of Spain in 1492 was a disaster for the Catalans, meaning the introduction of the Inquisition, the gradual destruction of the *fueros* and a total ruin of their commerce. The long series of wars between France and Spain resulted in the ceding of Roussillon to France in 1659. Immediately, that province suffered systematic and heavy-handed Frenchification, leading to revolts in the mountain valleys that were violently suppressed. The southern angle of France's hexagon was now substantially complete; Provence, Languedoc and Roussillon would continue to be treated as conquered provinces until 1981.

The Joys of Being French

There has never been a north-south discussion, on territory currently French, except in terms of kicks in the ass: invasions, police raids, financial extortion and the squeezing of brains into the form of the Hexagon.

Yves Roquette, National Secretary of the Institut d'Etudes Occitanes

The French Revolution was largely a Parisian affair, though southerners often played important roles (such as the Abbé Sieyès and Mirabeau), while bourgeois delegates from the manufacturing towns fought along with the Girondins in the National Assembly for a liberal republic. Unfortunately, the winning Jacobin ideology was more centralist and more dedicated to destroying any taint of regional difference than the *ancien régime* had ever dreamed of being. Whatever was left of local rights and privileges was soon decreed out of existence, and when the Revolution divided France into homogenous *départements* in 1790, terms like 'Provence' and 'Languedoc' ceased to have any real political meaning.

In 1792 volunteers from Marseille had brought the 'Marseillaise' to Paris, while local mobs wrecked and looted hundreds of southern churches and châteaux. Soon, however, the betrayed south became violently counter-revolutionary. Incidents occurred like the one in the village of Bédoin, near Carpentras, in 1793: when someone cut down the 'liberty tree', French soldiers burned the town and shot 63 villagers to 'set an example'. The Catalans raised regiments of volunteers against the Revolution. The royalists and the English occupied Toulon after a popular revolt and were only dislodged by the brilliant tactics of a young commander named Bonaparte in 1793.

The south managed little enthusiasm for Napoleon or his wars. The emperor called the Provençaux cowards, goading them by saying that theirs was the only part of France that never gave him a decent regiment. Today the tourist offices promote the 'Route Napoléonienne', where Napoleon passed through on his way from Elba in 1815 to start the Hundred Days – but at the time he had to sneak along those roads in an Austrian uniform, to protect himself from the Provençaux.

After Waterloo, the restored monarchy started off with a grisly White Terror in Nîmes and elsewhere. After the revolution of 1830, the 'July Monarchy' of King Louis-Philippe brought significant changes. The old industrious Protestant strain of the south finally got its chance with a Protestant prime minister from Nîmes, François Guizot (1840–48); his liberal policies and his slogan – '*Enrichissez-vous!*' – opened an age where there would be a little Protestant in every Frenchman. Guizot's country-men were rapidly demanding more; radicalism and anti-clericalism (except in the lower Rhône and Vaucluse) increased throughout the century.

Southerners supported the revolution of 1848 and the Second Republic, and many areas, especially in the Provençal Alps, put up armed resistance to Louis-Napoléon's 1851 coup. Under the Second Empire (1852–70), France picked up yet another territory: Nice and its hinterlands (now the *département* of Alpes-Maritimes), with a mixed population of Provençaux and Italians. This was the price exacted by Napoléon III in 1860 for French aid to Vittorio Emanuele II in Italy's War of Independence.

Oppression and Resistance

The second half of the century saw the beginnings of a nationalist revival in Occitania. In Provence it was all cultural and apolitical: a linguistic and literary revival bound up with Nobel Prize-winning poet Frédéric Mistral and the cultural group called the Félibrige (*see* pp.38–9), founded in 1854. In Languedoc it was all political and unconcerned with culture, focusing on the first of modern France's agricultural move-ments. Markets since the 1800s had encouraged Languedoc to become one vast vineyard. Phylloxera hit in 1875, but the quick recovery favoured the biggest producers who could afford the new American stocks. A huge wine boom in the 1880s was followed by an even huger bust; with competition from Algeria and Italy, by 1904 prices had dropped to one-third of their 1890 levels. In 1907 the farmers went on the warpath, led by a charismatic café-keeper from the Aude named Marcellin Albert. Monster meetings in Narbonne and Montpellier attracted over 100,000 each; Paris sent troops to occupy the region, but some of the conscript regiments came close to mutiny. Finally Albert was tricked into calling off a general strike by leftist Prime Minister Clemenceau. The movement dwindled, but farmers devoted their attention to building a strong co-operative system and keeping the political pressure on by more orthodox means; French politics would never be quite the same.

To counter these advances, the post-1870 Third Republic pursued French cultural oppression to its wildest extremes. History was re-written to make Occitania and Roussillon seem eternal parts of the 'French nation'. The Occitan languages were lyingly derided as mere patois, bastard 'dialects' of French; children were punished for speaking their own language in school, a practice that lasted until the 1970s. Roussillon was not even permitted political participation – the government and parties arranged to have outsiders stand for its seats in the National Assembly.

After 1910, economic factors conspired to defeat both the political and cultural aspirations of the Midi; rural depopulation, caused by the breakup of the pre-industrial agricultural society, drained the life out of the villages – and decreased the percentage of people who spoke the native languages. The First World War decimated a generation – go into any village church in the south and look at the war memorial plaques; from a total population of a few hundred, you'll see maybe 30 names of villagers who died for the 'Glory of France'. By 1950, most villages had lost at least half their population; some died out altogether.

After the French débâcle of 1940, the south found itself under the Vichy government. German occupation came in November 1942, after the American landings in North Africa, provoking the scuttling of the French fleet in Toulon to keep it out of German hands. After 1942, the Résistance was active and effective in the Provençal Alps, the Vaucluse and the Catalan Pyrenees – not to mention Marseille, where the Germans felt constrained to blow up the entire Vieux Port area. Liberation began two months after D-Day, in August 1944. American and French troops hit the beaches around St-Tropez, and in a remarkably successful (and little-noticed) operation they had most of Provence liberated in two weeks. In the rugged mountains behind Nice, some bypassed German outposts held out until the end of the war.

The California of Europe

The post-war era was all sweetness and ice-cream and reinforced concrete, a series of increasingly passionless snapshots, the Côte d'Azur as a myth of the masses – Grace Kelly with Cary Grant in *To Catch a Thief*, later with Rainier III in Monaco; socialist Languedoc farmers on a demonstration, wondering why someone couldn't sell all the goddamned wine they grow; grey and effective political machine bosses like Gaston Deferre of Marseille (socialist), or Jacques Médecin of Nice (gastronome-fascist); Paris bureaucrats expounding the glories of the Durance hydro-electric scheme, meant to make Provence the Ruhr Valley of Tomorrow.

The changes have, in fact, been momentous. The overdeveloped, ever more schizophrenic Côte d'Azur has become the heart of Provence – the tail that wags the dog. Besides its resorts, it has the likes of IBM and the techno-paradise of Sophia-Antipolis. Above all, the self-proclaimed 'California of Europe' has money, and will acquire more;

in two or three decades it may be the first province in centuries to start telling Paris where to get off. Meanwhile, the increasingly posh Vaucluse has the highest rural crime and suicide rates in France. Those Languedoc farmers have learned their lesson; they make less wine, and much better. Their region, which stopped losing its population in about 1955, is changing fast. A typically French planning effort of 1968 has made its coastline into a growing tourist region, with new resorts like Cap d'Agde and La Grande Motte. Montpellier, inspired by its dynamic mayor Georges Frêche (1983–95), strives to become the futuristic metropolis of the Midi; jealous Nîmes bestirs itself to keep pace.

The greatest political event was the election of the Socialist Mitterrand government in 1981, followed by the creation of regional governments across France. Though their powers and budgets are extremely limited, this represents a major turning point, the first reversal of a thousand years of increasing Parisian centralism. Its lasting effects will not be known for decades, perhaps centuries. Already the revival of Occitan language and culture is resuming; indicators include such things as new school courses in the language, and some towns and villages changing the street signs to Languedocien, Provençal or Catalan. Roussillon is just beginning to feel the great upsurge of Catalan culture that began after the restoration of democracy in Spain.

Politics, quiet in most of the south, can still be primeval in Provence. Jean-Marie Le Pen and his tawdry pack of bigots found their biggest following here, riding a wave of resentment against immigrants that Le Pen himself did more than anyone else to create (although this is a Provençal tradition: there were anti-Italian pogroms in Marseille, Aigues-Mortes and other towns in the 1890s). Le Pen's Front National scared the daylights out of the French political class by winning control of four Provençal cities: Toulon, Orange and the gruesome Marseille suburbs of Marignane and Vitrolles. Since then, the party has continued to shock and upset French notions of nationality, with the first round of national elections in 2002 seeing Le Pen run a close second as the choice for president. The final round saw Jacques Chirac's centre-right RPR party take the helm, which also managed to dislodge some of the dinosaurs in the Front National strongholds of the south, such as Toulon. Despite his national loss, Le Pen carries on, especially in the south where support for the Front National has in fact grown in the past few years, with the Alpes-Maritimes and the Var regions giving the party almost 30 per cent of their vote.

Provence's political malaise isn't just about immigrants. Many Front National voters are former socialists, disgusted by the massive corruption that socialist politicians enjoyed during the Mitterrand years. In France's tightly controlled political system, where the established parties collaborate closely to monopolize power and exclude grass-roots challenges, a vote for Le Pen may seem like the only kind of protest vote available. And while Chirac seems determined to keep France's multi-ethnic pot from boiling over, only time will tell how much of a difference he can really make with his middle-of-the-road policies.

Art and Architecture

Great art and architecture in the south of France neatly coincides with its three periods of prosperity: Roman, the Middle Ages, and the mid-19th and early 20th centuries, when railways opened up the coast not only to aristocrats but to artists as well.

Prehistoric

Some of the very first art in Europe was made by Palaeolithic residents of the Riviera, who made the lumpy fertility goddesses, sea-shell bonnets and necklaces displayed in the prehistory museums of **Monaco**, **Nice** and **Menton**. Their Neolithic descendants left few but tantalizing traces of their passing: dolmens and a few menhirs (especially in the Hérault and Gard), and a tomb-temple complex at Castellet, near Arles. **Cambous**, north of Montpellier, has a reconstructed communal Neolithic house, with low walls and a thatched roof that resembles the traditional cowboy dwellings (*cabanes de gardians*) in the Camargue. The first shepherds may well have put up the dry-stone, corbel-roofed huts called *bories*, rebuilt countless times and still a feature of the landscape (most notably in the 18th-century '*village des bories*' outside Gordes). In the Iron Age (1800–1500 BC), the Ligurians or their predecessors covered the **Alpine Vallée des Merveilles**, under Mont Bégo, with extraordinary rock incisions of warriors, bulls, masked figures and inexplicable symbols. In a similar style are the statue-steles – menhirs with faces – found in Tuscany and Corsica as well as around **Nîmes** (in the Musée de la Préhistoire) and at **St-Pons** in the Espinouse mountains of Hérault.

Celto-Ligurian: 8th–3rd Centuries BC

The arrival of the Celts around 800 BC coincided with an increase in trade; Greek, Etruscan and Celtic influences can be seen in the artefacts of this age (as at the **Oppidum of Ensérune** near Béziers). The local Celts had talent for jewellery, ironwork and sculpture – and the habit of decapitating enemies and carving stone images of warriors clutching their heads. Look for them in the archaeology museum in **Nîmes**, in the Musée Granet in **Aix** (when it reopens in 2006), the Musée d'Archéologie Méditerranéenne in **Marseille** and in the Lapidary Museum of **Avignon**.

Gallo-Roman: 3rd Century BC–4th Century AD

Archaeologically, the Greeks are the big disappointment of Provence – the only remains of their towns are bits of wall at **Marseille** and at **St-Blaise** on the Etang de Berre. But what the Romans left behind in their beloved Provincia makes up for the Greeks: the **Pont du Gard**; the theatre of **Orange**, with the only intact stage building in the West; the Maison Carrée and amphitheatre in **Nîmes**; the amphitheatre and cryptoporticus in **Arles**; the elegant 'Antiques' of **St-Rémy**; the Pont Flavien in **St-Chamas**; the trophy in **La Turbie**; and the excavated towns at **Vaison-la-Romaine** and **Glanum** (St-Rémy-de-Provence).

Thanks to the Celts, Provence was the one province of the Western Roman Empire that developed a definite style of its own, characterized by vigorous, barbaric reliefs emboldened by deeply incised outlines. Battle scenes were the most popular subject, or shields and trophies arranged in the exotic, uncouth style you see on the triumphal arches of **Orange** and **Carpentras**, or in the new Musée Archéologique in **Arles**, which also has an excellent collection of models of the ancient towns and monuments of Provence. Roman landowners lived in two-storey stone houses, with their farm buildings forming an enclosed rectangular courtyard known as a *mansio*, the ancestor of the modern Provençal farmhouse, the *mas*; two large ones have been excavated in **Les Lecques**, near Bandol.

Early Christian and Dark Ages: 5th–10th Centuries

Very few places in France had the resources to create any art at all during this period; the meagre attempts were nearly always rebuilt later. The oldest Christian relics are a remarkable sarcophagus from the 2nd century in **Brignoles**, and other sarcophagi from the next century in the crypt of St-Victor in **Marseille** and in the Musée Archéologique at **Arles**, both close to Roman pagan models. Octagonal baptistries from the 5th and 6th centuries survive in **Fréjus**, **Aix**, **Riez** and **Six-Fours-les-Plages**, which also has an 8th-century Syrian-style church. Many crypts are really the foundations of original Dark Age churches, and fragments of Merovingian-era reliefs will often be found set in a later church's wall.

Romanesque: 11th–14th Centuries

When good times returned in the 11th century, people began to build again, inspired by the ancient buildings they saw around them. There is a great stylistic continuity not only from Roman to Romanesque architecture (rounded arches, barrel vaults, rounded apses), but also in the vigorous Celtic-inspired decoration of Roman Provence.

The south has four distinct varieties of Romanesque – Provençal, Lombard, Languedocien and Catalan – although the terms must be applied loosely; the enduring charm of Romanesque is in its very lack of restrictions and codes, giving architects the freedom to improvise and solve problems in highly original and sophisticated ways. Although parish and monastic churches were usually in the basilican form (invented for Roman law courts and used in Rome's first churches), masons also created extremely esoteric works, often built as funeral chapels in pre-Christian holy sites (*see* **Montmajour**, or the even odder seven-sided church at **Rieux Minervois** and a triangular one at **Planès** in the Pyrenees).

Of the four styles, the Provençal is the most austere and heaviest, characterized by simple floor plans, thick-set proportions, few if any windows, minimal if any decoration, and façades that are often blank. Churches that could double as fortresses were built along the pirate-plagued coast in the 11th and 12th centuries: **St-Honorat** in the Iles de Lérins, the basalt parish church at **Agde** and the church of **Stes-Maries-de-la-Mer** are striking examples. In the mid-12th-century, the Cistercians founded three important new abbeys in a sombre and austere style, the 'Three Sisters': **Le Thoronet**, **Sénanque** and **Silvacane**. An octagonal dome at the transept crossing is a common feature of more elaborate churches, especially **Avignon** cathedral, the Ancienne-Major in **Marseille**, **Vaison-la-Romaine**, **Le Thor** and **Carpentras** (the ruined original). The finest of the few paintings that survive from this epoch is the 13th-century fresco cycle at the Tour Ferrande, in **Pernes-Les-Fontaines**. **Ganagobie** has the only floor mosaics from the period, as well as some very good sculpture.

In general, churches in the Rhône valley are more ornate, thanks to a talented group of sculptors known as the **School of Arles**. The wealth of ruins inspired them to adapt Roman forms and decorations to the new religion, complete with triumphal arches, gabled pediments and Corinthian columns. The saints on the façade of St-Trophime in **Arles** seem direct descendants of Gallo-Roman warriors. Arlésien artists also created the remarkable façade of **St-Gilles du Gard**, portraying the New Testament – the true dogma in stone for all to see, perhaps meant as a refutation of the Cathar and other current heresies. Yet other Romanesque sculpture in the area, as at **Vaison-la-Romaine**, seems nothing but heretical.

As you move west into Languedoc, Romanesque becomes more decorative and fanciful, befitting the land of troubadours (**St-Martin-de-Londres** and the frescoed **Chapelle de Centeilles** in the Minervois). Even when the austere Cistercians built here, as at Fontfroide, the mood is much less sombre. Itinerant Lombard masons in the 12th century built Italian Romanesque churches, characterized by blind arcading and bands of decorative stonework, especially around the apse (as at **St-Guilhem-le-Désert**). The Lombard campanile, pierced with patterns of windows, was adapted by the Catalans, especially in the Pyrenees (**Elne**). But **Uzès** has something even rarer in its Tour Fenestrelle: a round, arcaded six-storey campanile, typical of Byzantine Italy.

Along with the Arles craftsmen, the **Catalans** produced the finest medieval sculpture in the south, with the school of sculptors at the magnificent 11th-century abbey of **St-Michel-de-Cuxa**. Their work is characterized by precise and fanciful detail, arabesques and floral patterns, supremely elegant without the classicizing of the Arles school; more of their best sculpture may be seen at **Serrabonne** and **Elne**, the most beautiful cloister in the Midi.

Catalunya also produced the vigorous and original **Master of Cabestany**, who in the early 12th century even went to Tuscany to teach the Italians how to sculpt. His best works in France are the tympanum at Cabestany, at **St-Papoul** (near Castelnaudary), and a pair of capitals at Rieux Minervois. Catalans could paint, too; there are rare medieval frescoes at **St-Martin-de-Fenollar**, south of Perpignan.

Although examples of medieval palaces still stand in **Brignoles**, **St-Gilles**, and **Villemagne** in the Hérault, the greatest secular architecture of the period is military, often done with surprising originality. The vertiginous castle of **Peyrepertuse** is only the most enormous example of the scores of imposing works around the Languedoc and Roussillon border – one of the very best regions in Europe for castles. Saint Louis built the walls and towers of **Carcassonne** in a romantic fairytale style that has few equals, while the king's other project, **Aigues-Mortes** (1270s), is a grid-planned, square and functional modern town encased in a perfect set of walls.

Gothic and Early Renaissance: 14th–15th Centuries

Though Gothic elements first appeared in Provence in 1150 (the façade of St-Victor in **Marseille**) and in Languedoc around 1250 (**Abbaye St-Martin-du-Vignogoul**), ogival vaulting and pointy arches belonged to a foreign, northern style that failed to touch southern hearts. Builders stuck to their Romanesque guns longer than anyone in France, and when Gothic made its final triumph it was usually a pale reflection of the soaring cathedrals of the Ile-de-France. The exceptions were built by northerners after the French conquest: the cathedrals of **Béziers**, **Carcassonne** and especially **Narbonne**, an unfinished, spectacular work that is the third-tallest Gothic church in France.

Gothic also found a home in **Avignon**, when the 14th-century popes summoned architects from the north to design the flamboyant Papal Palace, St-Pierre, the Convent des Célestines and St-Didier (other isolated examples are the Abbaye de Valmagne near **Sète**, the basilica of **St-Maximin-la-Ste-Baume**, and **Clermont-l'Hérault**). The Catalans, as ever marching to a different drum, developed their own brand of Gothic, where width and strength counted more than height. The master of the genre, Guillermo Sagrera, designed **Perpignan**'s cathedral and the complex vaulting in its Salle Capitulaire.

Painting in the south of France took a giant leap forward when the papal court in Avignon attracted some of Italy's finest *trecento* artists, especially Simone Martini of Siena and Matteo Giovanetti of Viterbo, whose frescoes inspired the graceful fairy-tale style known as **International Gothic** (*see* **Avignon** and its Petit Palais museum). A new local style developed from International Gothic, and from the precise style of the Flemish painters favoured by the last popes: the early 15th-century **School of Avignon**. The school's greatest masters were from the north: the exquisite Enguerrand Quarton (*c.* 1415–66) from Laon (**Villeneuve lez Avignon**), and Nicolas Froment (cathedral, **Aix**); also see Aix's church of the Madeleine and the Petit Palais museum in **Avignon**. King René, the great patron of the artists, built himself a fine chivalric castle in Tarascon and had a hand in the evolution of French sculpture when he invited the Italian Renaissance master Francesco Laurana to Provence (*see* 'Artists' Directory', p.32).

At the same time the **School of Nice**, led by the prolific Ludovico Brea, produced scores of altarpieces typical of northern Italian provincial styles – charming and luminous, if a good hundred years behind the Renaissance revolution going on in Tuscany. The Brea gang had some stiff competition in the early 15th century from a pair of little-known Piemontese painters, Giovanni Canavesio and Giovanni Baleison, who would be much better known had they left their charming pastel fresco cycles in less remote churches (**Notre-Dame-des-Fontaines** in the Roya Valley, and others in the nearby valleys of the Vésubie and Tinée).

High Renaissance: Late 15th–16th Centuries

Despite its promising start, subjugation by the French and the Wars of Religion made the Renaissance a non-event in Occitania. The few buildings of the day are imitative, mostly of the heavy, classicizing Roman style, as in the palace of the Cardinal Legate in **Avignon**. The best Renaissance building, the once delightful **Château La Tour d'Aigue** in the Luberon, is only a burnt-out shell, although you can get a hint of its former glory from the elegant château in nearby **Lourmarin**. Narbonne has some exquisite Flemish Renaissance tapestries. Locally, the best work of this period is minute – in the carved wooden doors and choir stalls in **Vence**, **Bar-sur-Loup** and **Fréjus**.

The Age of Bad Taste: 17th–18th Centuries

The French prefer to call this their *époque classique*, and admittedly even in the poor, benighted south many fine things were done. Towns laid out elegant squares, fountains and promenades (**Pernes-les-Fontaines**, **Aix**, **Barjols**); trees were planted on a grand scale, on market squares, along the Canal du Midi, and on the roads, especially in the western Aude, crossed with 18th-century avenues of plane trees. **Montpellier** and **Moustiers** have collections from their thriving faïence industries of the day (as does Narbonne's art museum and **Marseille**'s Musée Cantini). Southerners went ape for organs, gargantuan works sheathed in ornate carved wood. The mother of them all is in **Narbonne** cathedral; others adorn the churches in Béziers and Uzès.

But nearly everything else is all wrong. People took the lovely churches left to them by their ancestors and tinkered so much with the architecture that it's often difficult to tell the real age of anything. Aix, the capital of Provence and self-proclaimed arbiter of taste, knocked down its magnificently preserved Roman mausoleum and medieval palace of the counts of Provence just before the Revolution. The 17th- and 18th-century *hôtels particuliers* of **Aix**, **Pézenas**, **Uzès** and **Montpellier**, while lending a distinctive urbanity and ostentation to these cities, are rarely first-rate works of architecture in their own right, but rather eclectic jumbles with touches from Gothic, Renaissance and Baroque style-books. The one great sculptor and architect the south produced in the period, Pierre Puget, suffered the usual fate of a prophet in his own land, although he did manage one great project: the Vieille Charité, in **Marseille**.

In **painting**, the south produced two virtuoso court painters, Hyacinthe Rigaud and Fragonard, whose portrayals of happily spoiled, rosy-cheeked aristocrats hide the side of their personalities that provoked the Revolution. The most sincere paintings of the age are the naïve *ex votos* in many churches (some of the best are from sailors, as at Notre-Dame-de-la-Garde in **Marseille**, in Notre-Dame-de-Bon-Port at Cap d'Antibes, and Notre-Dame-des-Auzils, near **Gruissan**).

One architect who (unlike Puget) never lacked for work was Louis XIV's Maréchal Sébastien Vauban, whose forts and fortress-towns crop up everywhere; **Villefranche-de-Conflent** is a perfectly preserved example of 17th-century urban design. The next generation after Vauban produced the streamlined, modern Baroque fortresses near the Spanish border in the region around **Collioure**.

The best Baroque churches in the region are Italian: St-Michel in **Menton** and the Chapelle de la Miséricorde in **Nice**.

France's Little Ice Age: Late 18th–mid-19th Centuries
If the last era lacked vision, taste in the neoclassical/Napoleonic era had all the charm of embalming fluid. The Revolution destroyed more than it built; the wanton devastation of the region's greatest Romanesque art (begun in the Wars of Religion) was a loss matched only by the mania for selling it off in the early 20th century to the Americans. The greatest monuments of the Napoleonic era include the cold, funereal Musée Masséna in **Nice** and the paintings in many museums (especially the Musée Granet in **Aix**) by David, Ingres and Hubert Robert, the latter of whom specialized in scenes of melancholy Roman ruins in Provence and Italy, capturing the taste of the day (it was also a great age for cemeteries).

For the first time, however, there was a reaction to purposeful destruction of the past. Ruskin's contemporary Viollet-le-Duc (1814–79) restored architecture, rather than just writing about it (the walls of **Carcassonne** and **Avignon**, and the archbishop's palace of **Narbonne**). Thanks to the Suez Canal, Marseille suddenly had money to burn and tried to revive the past in its own way, with monstrous neo-Byzantine basilicas and the overripe Baroque Palais Longchamp.

Revolutions in Seeing: 1850–1939

A lady once came to look at Matisse's paintings and was horrified to see a woman with a green face. 'Wouldn't it be horrible to see a woman walking down the street with a green face?' she asked him. 'It certainly would!' Matisse agreed. 'Thank God it's only a painting!'

In the 1850 Paris Salon, hanging amongst the stilted historical, religious and mythological academic paintings were three large canvases of everyday, contemporary scenes by Gustave Courbet. Today it's hard to imagine how audacious his contemporaries found Courbet's new style, which came to be called **Realism** – almost as if it took the invention of photography by Louis Daguerre (1837) to make the eye see what was 'really' there. 'Do what you see, what you want, what you feel,' was Courbet's proto-hippy advice to his pupils. One thing he felt like doing was painting in the south of France, where his art revelled in the bright colour and light (especially his *Bonjour, Monsieur Courbet* of 1854 in **Montpellier**'s Musée Fabre). Courbet's visit was a major influence on the 19th-century painters of Provence, especially Paul Guigou and Frédéric Bazille, who painted Realist subjects drenched in southern sunlight.

In the 1860s, as physicists discovered that colour derives from light, not from form, the **Impressionists** made it their goal to strip Courbet's new-found visual reality of all subjectivity and to simply record on canvas the atmosphere, light and colour the eye saw, all according to the latest scientific theories. Although many of the great Impressionists spent time in the south, only the sensuous Renoir moved down permanently, and then only on doctor's orders (to **Cagnes-sur-Mer**, in 1895). The crucial role the south was to play in modern art dates from the 1880s, thanks to the two artists most closely associated with Provence today, Vincent Van Gogh and Paul Cézanne.

Van Gogh, one of the greatest innovators in the history of painting, was self-taught. Influenced at first by the Impressionists and Japanese prints he saw in Paris, his move to sunny Arles in 1888 thoroughly revolutionized his work: he responded to the heightened colour and light of Provence on such an intense, personal level that colour came less and less to represent form (as it did for the Impressionists), but instead took on a symbolic value; colour became the only medium Van Gogh found powerful enough to express his extraordinary moods and visions.

This revolutionary independence of colour from form was taken to an extreme by a group of painters that the critic Louis Vauxcelles nicknamed the **Fauves** ('wild beasts') for the violence of their colours. The Fauves used colour to interpret, rather than describe, moods and rhythms to the detriment of perspective and detail and even recognizable subject matter. As a movement the Fauves lasted from 1904 until 1908, but in those few years they revolutionized centuries of European art. 'Fauve painting is not everything,' Matisse explained. 'But it is the foundation of everything.'

Nearly all the Fauves – André Derain, Matisse, Maurice Vlaminck, Raoul Dufy, Kees Van Dongen – painted in St-Tropez as guests of the hospitable painter Paul Signac, and at La Ciotat, Cassis, L'Estaque and Collioure. The results paved the way for Expressionism, Cubism and abstraction – avenues few of the Fauvists themselves ever explored. For after 1908 the collective new vision these young men had shared in the south of France vanished as if they had awoken from a mass hypnosis; all went their separate ways, leaving others to carry their ideas on to their logical conclusions (the best collections are in the Musée de l'Annonciade in **St-Tropez** and the Musée d'Art at **Bagnols-sur-Cèze**).

Cézanne's innovations were as important as Van Gogh's, although his response to Provence was analytical rather than emotional, perhaps because he was born in the south. Loosely associated with the Impressionists in the 1860s and '70s, Cézanne stood apart; his interest was not so much in depicting what he saw, but in the contradiction between the eye and mind, between the permanence of nature and the ephemeral qualities of light and movement. 'Nature is always the same, but none of it lasts beyond what we perceive,' he wrote, and by the 1880s he had undertaken his stated task of 'making Impressionism solid and enduring, like the art of the museums', exploring underlying volumes, planes and structure, not through perspective, but through amazingly subtle variations of colour.

In 1908, Georges Braque and Raoul Dufy went to paint together at L'Estaque in homage to Cézanne. The beginnings of the prismatic splitting of forms are in their respective works, and when the same critic Vauxcelles saw Braque's paintings, he came up with a new name for the new art: **Cubism**. In 1912, Braque and Picasso worked together in Sorgues, near Avignon, and produced canvases that verge on abstraction. Matisse, one of the Fauves who settled permanently in Provence, kept apart from subsequent schools, and was the most outstanding among hundreds of artists who now flocked to the south.

Even Picasso, another lone genius who moved permanently to Provence after the Second World War and to whom modesty was a stranger, acknowledged Matisse as his equal, and in many ways his master. One of the great art debates of the 20th century was who was the greater artist and innovator of the two, Picasso being considered by many to have the upper hand.

In architecture, this was the opulent age of the Côte d'Azur's **Belle Epoque** confections, its Russian Orthodox cathedrals, grand hotels, villas and casinos, all done in a lavish, imaginative holiday spirit that often trod lightheartedly over contemporary rules of good taste and decorum.

Only a few buildings survive, which, along with old photographs, give a hint of what **Nice**, **Cannes**, **Monaco** and **Menton** looked like at the turn of the century. The Moorish, Bengali, Norman, Tuscan and troubadour follies that went up (nearly all built by extravagant foreigners) caused outrage when they were built, but are sorely missed now that all but a handful have been demolished.

Post-war

After the war, artists from many lands continued to pour into the hill villages of Provence: Picasso, Bonnard, Léger, Chagall, Nicholas de Staël, Max Ernst, André Masson and Vasarély, to name only the most prominent. The 1960s saw a reaction to the often precious art world in the **'second' School of Nice**, led by provocative multi-media iconoclasts like César, Arman and Ben, all displayed in a spanking new contemporary art museum in **Nice**, one of several giant projects built by the ambitious mayors of the south. None has been more ambitious than Georges Frêche, the human dynamo who ran **Montpellier** (1983–95) and chose Ricardo Bofill to create its neo-neoclassical residential quarter called Antigone.

The single most influential post-war building in the south has been Le Corbusier's Unité d'Habitation in **Marseille** (1952); if you don't care for warmed-over Bauhaus on stilts, there's the futuristic planned resort of **La Grande Motte** in Languedoc, begun in 1968 as the first post-modernist building ensemble in the south. The most artful, delightful building in recent years is the Catalan architect José-Luis Sert's Fondation Maeght, in **St-Paul-de-Vence**.

In **Nîmes**, Sir Norman Foster's glass and steel Carré d'Art was beset by criticism when it opened in May 1993, but his influence has led to a new impetus in architectural expansion in the south. New developments are planned in Nîmes, Montpellier, Aix-en-Provence and Marseille. The south, it seems, is no longer the architectural backwater it once was: indeed, as Jean Bousquet, former mayor of Nîmes, declared, its cities will soon rival Paris in the race to be a metropolis for the 21st century.

Artists' Directory

Arman (1928–): sculptor best known for his witty combinations of junk and musical instruments, who snubbed the major exhibition of his works that inaugurated the new contemporary art museum in **Nice** to protest against anti-semitic remarks by mayor Jacques Médecin. (Musée Picasso, **Antibes**; Fondation Maeght, **St-Paul-de-Vence**).

Bazille, Frédéric (1841–70). A native of Montpellier, who linked up with Monet in Paris in 1862 and, with him, was the first to paint the human figure (even nudes) out of doors, inspired by the spontaneity of photography. His career was cut short in the Franco-Prussian war of 1870. (Musée Fabre, **Montpellier**.)

Bonnard, Pierre (1867–1947). Although his early career is closely associated with the Nabis (a group of painters who rejected naturalism and natural colour), Bonnard changed gear in 1900 to become one of the 20th century's chief Impressionists, painting colour-saturated landscapes and domestic scenes, after 1939 around his villa in Le Cannet, near Cannes. (**Bagnols-sur-Cèze**; Musée de l'Annonciade, **St-Tropez**.)

Braque, Georges (1882–1963). One of Cubism's founding fathers, Braque worked so closely with Picasso (in Céret in 1911, in Borgues in 1912, and elsewhere) that their early works are practically indistinguishable. (Musée de l'Annonciade, **St-Tropez**.)

Brea, Ludovico (active 1475–1544). Leader of the International Gothic Nice School, influenced by the Renaissance in his later career. Although commissioned to do hieratic medieval-style subjects, his precise line and beautiful sense of light and shadow stand out – still, to call him the 'Fra Angelico of Provence', like some French critics, is going too far. He invented a shade of wine-red French artists still call *rouge brea*. (Franciscan church in Cimiez, **Nice**; Palais Carnolès, **Menton**; **Lucéram**; and **Monaco** cathedral.)

Canavesio, Giovanni (*c.* 1425–1500). A native of Piedmont, Canavesio collaborated with Giovanni Baleison to paint the finest Renaissance frescoes in Provence. The style is typical of North Italian early Renaissance, colourful and precise, without much of the intellectuality of Tuscan painting. (**Notre-Dame-des-Fontaines**, near La Brigue; retables at **Lucéram**; and many chapels in the Valleys of the Vésubie and Tinée.)

Cézanne, Paul (1839–1906). Born and died in Aix-en-Provence, where fellow schoolmate Emile Zola was his best friend, until Zola published his autobiographical *L'Œuvre* that thinly disguised Cézanne as the failed painter Lantier. Cézanne's painting went through several distinct periods: a sombre Romantic stage (1861–71); an Impressionistic manner, inspired by Pissarro (1872–82); a period of synthesis (1883–95), combining elements of Impressionism with an interest in volume and surface planes, and the desire to represent perspective by colour only; and lastly, his lyric period (1896–1906), where singing rhythms of colour and form are intellectually supported by the basic tenets of Cubism, where the planes and volumes are split into prisms, expressing the tension between seeing and knowing. (Musée Granet, **Aix**, *closed until 2006*.)

Chagall, Marc (1887–1985): highly individualistic Russian-Jewish painter and illustrator who drew his main themes from Jewish-Russian folklore and the Old Testament. Influenced by Cubism and Orphism (the pre-First World War movement that gave intellectual Cubism a lyrical quality with colour), his art is imbued with a distinctive fairytale, imaginative quality. After spending the war years in the USA, he moved permanently to St-Paul-de-Vence in 1950, where he became interested in stained glass. (Musée National Message Biblique Marc Chagall, **Nice**; Fondation Maeght, **St-Paul-de-Vence**; Ancienne Cathédrale, **Vence**.)

Cocteau, Jean (1889–1963). Writer, surrealist film director and illustrator, who painted pastel mural decorations in a number of chapels and town halls in the south. (Mairie and Museum, **Menton**; Chapelle de St-Pierre, **Villefranche-sur-Mer**.)

Corot, Jean-Baptiste-Camille (1796–1875). Landscape painter of ineffable charm, who made the typical French sojourn in Rome to discover the calm and tranquillity of classical landscapes. In his smaller, spontaneous sketches and private portraits his modern techniques make him a precursor of the Impressionists; painted with Ziem in Martigues. (Musée Calvet, **Avignon**; Musée des Beaux-Arts, **Marseille**.)

Courbet, Gustave (1819–77). High prince of the 19th-century Realist school, and a keen student of luminosity in nature. His journey to Montpellier in 1854 brought about a considerable lightening of his palette; his seascapes are awash in atmosphere, and his studies of skies, light and shadows inspired Monet and Bazille. (Musée Fabre, **Montpellier**; Musée des Beaux-Arts, **Marseille**.)

Daumier, Honoré (1808–79). Born in Marseille, Daumier began his career risking jail terms as a political caricaturist for a magazine. But he was also a highly original pre-Expressionist painter in the Goya mould, best known for his hypnotic, violently lit scenes based on the inherent tragedy of the human condition – a precursor of Toulouse-Lautrec, Degas and Picasso. (Musée des Beaux-Arts, **Marseille**.)

David, Jacques-Louis (1748–1825). Napoleon's favourite neoclassical painter, as cold and perfect as ice, portrayed his subjects in kitsch-Roman heroic attitudes and costumes. (Musée Granet, **Aix**, *closed until 2006*; Musée Fabre, **Montpellier**; Musée Calvet, **Avignon**.)

Delacroix, Eugène (1798–1863). Delacroix had little truck with the neoclassicism of David, and instead based his art on the chromatics and lighting of Constable. 'In painting, all is reflection,' he said; many of his landscapes and North African watercolours presaged Impressionism. (Musée Fabre, **Montpellier**.)

Derain, André (1880–1954). Along with Vlaminck, Derain was a key Fauvist painter of extraordinary innovation and originality, who took Fauvism and Expressionism to the limit before the First World War. (Musée de l'Annonciade, **St-Tropez**.)

Dufy, Raoul (1877–1953). Dufy's most original and energetic painting was as a Fauve. After a brief flirtation with Cubism with Georges Braque in L'Estaque (*see* Musée Cantini, Marseille), his style took on its characteristic graphic quality, and he spent much of his remaining life in Nice, painting pleasing lightweight decorative interiors. (Musée des Beaux-Arts (Jules Chéret), **Nice**.)

Fragonard, Jean-Honoré (1732–1806). Native of Grasse and student of Boucher, Fragonard painted frivolous rococo scenes in anaemic pastels but with a verve and erotic wit that found favour with France's spiritually bankrupt nobility, who longed to escape into his canvases. (Villa-Musée Fragonard, **Grasse**.)

Granet, François Marius (1775–1849). Native of Aix and a pupil of David. Although his canvases are run-of-the-mill academic, his watercolours and sketches reveal a poetic observation of nature that became the hallmark of the Provençal school. (Musée Granet, **Aix**, *closed until 2006*; Musée d'Art et d'Histoire, **Grasse**.)

Guigou, Paul (1834–71). Landscape painter born in Villars, in the Vaucluse. Influenced by Corot's landscapes, Guigou sought out the most arid parts of Provence, especially the banks of the Durance, for his subjects, illuminating them with scintillating light and colour. Unable to make a living in the south, he took teaching jobs in the north, where he died aged 37, just as his career was beginning to take off. (Musée des Beaux-Arts, **Marseille**; Musée Granet, **Aix**, *closed until 2006*.)

Ingres, Jean-Auguste-Dominique (1780–1867). As the most important neoclassical pupil of David, Ingres was acclaimed the master of official academic art, where he was capable of producing enormous mythological howlers. However, in his more appealing intimate subjects, especially his female nudes, he distorted proportions to achieve a sinuous eroticism and line that inspired Picasso, among other artists. (Musée Granet, **Aix**, *closed until 2006*; Musée Fabre, **Montpellier**.)

Laurana, Francesco (*c.* 1430–1502). Itinerant Istrian sculptor trained in Tuscany, best known for his precocious geometrical softening of features and forms, especially in his portrait busts. (St-Didier, **Avignon**; Ancienne-Major, **Marseille**.)

Léger, Fernand (1881–1955). Went from an early figurative manner to Cubism. Wounded in the First World War, Léger attempted to create an art that interpreted the experiences of ordinary people in war, work and play, culminating in his paintings of colourful, geometric, highly-stylized figures of workers and factories. Léger also worked in other media, especially mosaics and ceramics. (Musée National Fernand Léger, **Biot**; Fondation Maeght, **St-Paul-de-Vence**.)

Maillol, Aristide (1861–1944). Sculptor from Banyuls who spent much of his career in Paris, though he never forgot his home town, returning each summer to model female nudes on the pulchritude of the local nymphets. (Hôtel de Ville, **Perpignan**; war memorials and museum in **Banyuls**; Musée de l'Annonciade, **St-Tropez**.)

Matisse, Henri (1869–1954). A trip to the south in the 1890s converted Matisse to the vivid colours that are a hallmark of his work. After he became one of the leading Fauves, the hot colours of the south continued to saturate his ever-sensuous, serene and boldly drawn works, qualities apparent even in the paper cut-outs of his last bedridden years. After 1917 he settled in Nice. (Musée Matisse, **Nice**; Chapelle du Rosaire, **Vence**; Musée de l'Annonciade, **St-Tropez**.)

Monticelli, Adolphe (1824–86). A native of Marseille, a student of Ziem and one of Van Gogh's great inspirations. Obsessed with light ('*La lumière, c'est le ténor*,' he claimed), he conveyed its effects with pure unmixed colour applied with hard brushes; subjects dissolve into strokes and blobs of paint. (Musée des Beaux-Arts and Musée Cantini, **Marseille**.)

Picasso, Pablo (1881–1973). Born in Málaga, Spain, the 20th century's most endlessly inventive artist is celebrated for his mastery of line and his expressive power. In 1948, Picasso abandoned Paris and moved to Provence, settling first in Vallauris, then Cannes, and finally at Mougins, where he died. Living in Provence heightened the Mediterranean and pagan aspects of his extraordinarily wide-ranging work; he also loved to attend the bullfights at Arles (Musée Picasso, **Antibes**; castle chapel at **Vallauris**; Musée Réattu, **Arles**; Musée des Beaux-Arts (Jules Chéret), **Nice**.)

Puget, Pierre (1620–94). Baroque sculptor, painter and architect who began his career painting ships' figureheads before he went on to study in Rome under Bernini. Unappreciated at home, he spent much of his time sculpting enormous saints in Genoa. (Vieille Charité and Musée des Beaux-Arts, in his native **Marseille**; also the Atlantes of **Toulon**'s old Hôtel de Ville.)

Renoir, Pierre-Auguste (1841–1919). As joyful as Van Gogh was tormented. Renoir combined Impressionism with the traditional 'gallant' themes of Fragonard, updated to the 19th century: pretty girls, dances, fêtes, children, nudes, bathers, pastorals. Racked by rheumatism, he spent his last years in Cagnes, painting warm voluptuous nudes and landscapes. (Musée Renoir, **Cagnes-sur-Mer**.)

Rigaud, Hyacinthe (1659–1743). Born in Perpignan, this painter of sumptuous royal portraits was in great demand for his ability to make his subjects look lofty yet amiable, as well as for his accurate depiction of their swell get-ups. (Museums in **Perpignan**, **Narbonne** and **Aix**.)

Seurat, Georges (1859–91). Theorist and founder of neo-Impressionism, with his technique of *pointillisme* (the science of reducing a scene into dots of pure colour, juxtaposing them to achieve a greater luminosity); although he was highly influential, none of his followers could match his precision and vision. (Musée de l'Annonciade, **St-Tropez**.)

Signac, Paul (1863–1935). Georges Seurat's most faithful follower down the path of *pointillisme*. When Seurat died, Signac left Paris and discovered St-Tropez in 1892, where influenced by the Fauves he gradually abandoned his dots for a freer style. (Musée de l'Annonciade, **St-Tropez**.)

Van Dongen, Kees (1877–1968). A Fauve painter of verve and elegance, who after Fauvism became the chief chronicler of Riviera society and mores of the 1920s and '30s. (Musée des Beaux-Arts (Jules Chéret), **Nice**; Musée de l'Annonciade, **St-Tropez**.)

Van Gogh, Vincent (1853–90). Along with Cézanne, Van Gogh is most responsible for the images the outside world has of Provence – an unforgettable visionary who painted brilliantly hued land palpitating with energy. Coming from the cold, wet climes of the Netherlands and Paris, Van Gogh sought in the south 'a different light, in the belief that to look at nature under a clearer sky could give us a better idea of the way the Japanese see and draw; finally, I seek a stronger sun'. Instead, he found in the landscapes an underlying violence, tragedy and madness, which he painted with an intense lyricism that has never been equalled, in a 'research into the infinite' that ended with suicide. He sold but one painting in his short life, and ironically only one of the 800 or so canvases he painted around Arles remains in the south of France today, in the Fondation Angladon-Dubrujeaud, in **Avignon**.

van Loo, Carle (1705–65). Native of Nice and younger brother of the less successful Jean-Baptiste van Loo, Carle was a rococo painter in the 'grand style' and a keen rival of Boucher, painting hunt scenes and religious paintings, and designing Gobelin tapestries for the kings of France and Savoy. (Ste-Marthe, **Tarascon**; Musée des Beaux-Arts (Jules Chéret), **Nice**.)

Vernet, Claude-Joseph (1714–89) Born in Avignon, a landscape painter best known for his many seascapes and ports; he was also one of the first French painters interested in the play of light and water, if in a picturesque manner. (Musée Calvet, **Avignon**; Musée des Beaux-Arts, **Marseille**.)

Vuillard, Edouard (1868–1940). Like his good friend Bonnard, Vuillard began as a Nabi and later became better known for his Impressionistic, intimate domestic scenes. (Musée de l'Annonciade, **St-Tropez**.)

Ziem, Félix (1821–1911). Started off illuminating canvases with a sense of light audacious for the period; having found a successful formula, he repeated himself from then on. Much admired by Van Gogh, Ziem's favourite subjects were Venice and Martigues, where he founded an art colony with Jean-Baptiste-Camille Corot. (Musée Ziem, **Martigues**; Musée des Beaux-Arts (Jules Chéret), **Nice**.)

Topics

The Cathars

. . . because we are not of this world, and this world is nought of ours, give us to understand that which Thou understandest, and to love that which Thou lovest.

Cathar prayer

Dualism, as the philosophers call it, has always been with us. The Greek Gnostics saw Good and Evil as contending, independent forces that existed forever. Good resided somewhere beyond the stars; Evil was here and now – in fact creation itself was evil, the work not of God but of a fallen spirit, identifiable with Satan. Our duty on earth was to seek purity by refusing to have anything to do with creation. In the 3rd century AD, a Persian holy man named Mani took up the same theme and made quite a splash, and his teachings spread gradually back into the West, where the earliest Church councils strongly condemned them as the 'Manichaean Heresy'. Among other places, the Manichaeans were active in southern Gaul.

Always present in the Byzantine Empire, Manichaean ideas hit the Balkans in the 9th century; the 'Bogomil' or 'Bulgar' dualists reached a wide following, leaving hundreds of oddly carved crosses as monuments. From there, the idea spread rapidly throughout Europe. The new sect appears in chronicles of the 11th century, variously called Bulgars or Patarenes, Albigensians or Cathars (from a Greek word meaning pure). The Church was not slow to respond. In Italy and northern France the heretics were massacred and burned; in England, apparently, they were only branded with hot irons. In worldly and open Occitania, however, they gained a foothold and kept it. The new faith was popular among peasants, townspeople and even many nobles. Occitan Catharism was organized into a proper church at a council at St-Felix-de-Caraman in 1167, presided over by a prelate named Nicetas, or Nikita, from Dragovici in the Balkans.

The Cathars probably believed that their faith was a return to the virtue and simplicity of the early Church. Their teaching encouraged complete separation from the Devil's world; feudal oaths, for example, were forbidden, and believers solved differences between themselves by arbitration rather than going to law. Some features were quite modern: Cathars promoted vegetarianism and non-violence, and marriage was by simple agreement, not a sacrament, enhancing the freedom and status of women by doing away with the old Roman paternalist tradition and laws. Two other points made Catharism especially attractive to an increasingly modern society. It had a much more mature attitude towards money and capitalism than the Roman church – no condemnation of loans as usury, and no church tithes. This earned it support in the growing cities; like the later Protestants, many Cathars were involved in the textile trades. Cathar simplicity and its lack of a big church organization made a very favourable contrast with the bloated, bullying and thoroughly corrupt machinery of the Church of Rome.

Best of all, Catharism had a very forgiving attitude towards sinners. If creation itself was the Devil's work, how could we not err? Cathars were divided into two levels: the mass of simple believers, upon whom the religion was a light yoke indeed – no Mass and few ceremonies, no money-grubbing, easy absolution – and the few *perfecti*, those who had received the sacrament called the *consolament*, and were thenceforth required to lead a totally ascetic life devoted to faith and prayer. Most Cathars conveniently took the *consolament* on their deathbeds.

Catharism was a strong and growing force when the Albigensian Crusade began in 1209; the Papacy, the behaviour of which had always been a strong argument for the basic tenet of dualism, saw enough of a threat to its power to require a policy of eradication by death. The terror, enforced by French arms and overseen by the Dominicans and Cistercians, was vicious and successful. Its climax came in 1244, with the fall of the Cathar holy-of-holies, the temple-fortress at Montségur in the Pyrenees (*département* of Ariège). Cathars who survived the mass exterminations were hunted down ruthlessly by the new Inquisition; Guillaume Bélibaste, the last of the *perfecti*, was burned at Villerouge-Termenès in the Aude in 1321. Nevertheless, doctrines are always more difficult to kill than human beings, and Catharism survived its persecutors in a number of forms, especially in its influence on the later southern Protestants and on the Catholic Jansenists of the 17th century.

There are practising Cathars today; if you want to seek them out, the village of Arques, in the Aude, might be a good place to start, or else consult the worthy books (in French) of a modern-day sympathizer named René Nelli. There are probably fewer actual Cathars than books about them. Catharism did have a strong esoteric tinge to it, reserved for the *perfecti*. In the past few decades, this angle has been explored in every sort of work, from the serious to the pathetically inane, speculating on various 'treasures', real or metaphysical, that the last *perfecti* may have hidden, or connecting the sect with other favourite occult themes: the Templars (who in fact were their enemies), the Holy Grail (said to have been kept at Montségur), the Illuminati and Rosicrucians of the 15th century and onwards, and the body and possible descendants of Jesus Christ (*see* Rennes-le-Château, pp.559–60).

Nelli and other authors have some provocative things to say about the greatest and most mysterious of all the Arthurian epics, Wolfram von Eschenbach's *Parzifal* – they see the poem as a sweeping Cathar allegory, confirming Montségur as the Grail castle and identifying Parzifal with the Cathars' protector, Raymond Trencavel of Carcassonne. Trencavel's chroniclers also have an uncanny habit of comparing the viscount to Christ, especially after his betrayal and death at the hands of Simon de Montfort; his dynasty, like that of the counts of Toulouse, was quite a vortex for this sort of weirdness.

The weirdest of all modern Europe's occultist sects, the Nazis, were obsessed with the Cathars and the legends that have grown up around them. After their occupation of the south in 1942, they sealed off all the important Cathar sites and cave refuges in the Pyrenees, and Nazi high-priest Alfred Rosenberg sent teams of archaeologists to dig them up amidst the utmost secrecy. In 1944, not long before liberation, a group of local Cathars sneaked up to Montségur for an observance to commemorate the 700th anniversary of their forebears' last stand. A small German plane, with a pilot and one passenger, appeared and circled the castle. The Cathars, expecting the police, watched in amazement as the plane, by means of skywriting equipment, traced a strange, eight-branched cross over their heads, and then disappeared beyond the horizon.

Mistral and the Félibrige

The attitude of the French was best expressed by Paul Morand's speech upon being admitted to the Académie Française: 'To write in French is to see flowing the waters of a mountain stream, next to which all languages are muddy rivers; it is to live in a crystal palace.' To someone like Morand, master of *pointu*, or 'proper' French, with all its mushy slushy vowel sounds, one of the muddiest rivers was *langue d'oc*. Its demise became a priority in the 19th century; after subjugating the south politically and religiously, Paris decided to finish off the job linguistically and decreed French the sole legal language in the schools, military, government and press.

One of the strategies of the *Franchimands* (as the southerners call French-speakers) was to divide and conquer: *langue d'oc*, claimed the central Frenchifiers, was actually thousands of dialects and could never constitute a language. Even the southerners admit to seven 'grand dialects' of Occitan, three of which fall into the confines of this book: the Dauphinois of the Alpine valleys, Provençal, and Languedocien, the descendant of the troubadours' language. But it was in Provence that the reaction to the *Franchimands*' linguistic imperialism took its most curious form – in a sentimental, artificially contrived literary movement called the Félibrige.

According to legend, the idea for the Félibres was 'born of a mother's tear' when the mother of the poet Joseph Roumanille wept because she couldn't understand the French verses of her son. Not long after, on 21 May 1854, at the Château de Font Ségugne near Avignon, Roumanille, Frédéric Mistral and five other poets proclaimed the formation of a literary school to 'safeguard indefinitely for Provence its language, its colour, its easy liberty, its national honour, and its fine level of intelligence, for such as it is, we like Provence'. It was the 24-year-old Mistral who came up with the name for the school when he quoted a folk rhyme on the Seven Sorrows of Mary from his native village Maillane: *li sètt felibre de la Lèi* – the seven doctors or sages of the law. As 21 May (the day when the sun is in the constellation of the Pleiades, or Seven Sisters) was the feast day of Santo Estello, the seven-pointed star of the Cathars was adopted as one of the Félibres' symbols. In later years, after Mistral's epic *Miréio* gave the movement its lustre, 21 May would be celebrated with a Grand Félibre Banquet, when all 50 members or *majoraux* and their leader, the *capoulié* (Mistral, naturally), would pass around the *Coupo Santo*, the Félibres' Holy Grail.

The Félibres' greatest moment came in 1904, when Mistral won the Nobel Prize for Literature, the only writer in a minority language ever to be awarded a Nobel Prize. Thanks to him and the other Félibres, Provence became conscious and proud of its separate identity; the richness of the language charmed even foreigners like Ezra Pound, who wrote and translated Provençal. But in spite of these successes, the Félibrige best serves as a lesson on how *not* to revive a language. Today only a few people in their eighties in remote areas still use Provençal as a daily tool, a sorry record compared to the subsequent revivals of Irish, Catalan, Basque, Welsh and, most successful of all, Hebrew.

Where did the Félibres go wrong? Not for lack of trying: unlike the courtly troubadours, they purposely wrote in a simple style to appeal to the *paysans*. Slipshod grammar and spelling were codified in Mistral's labour of love, the *Trésor du Félibrige* (a work accused by some of passing off the rustic dialect of Maillane as the last word in Provençal). The Félibres' biggest mistake was confusing language and time, associating Provençal with folklore and the past, and shunning the necessary political fight with Paris in a romantic illusion that their poetry was powerful enough to revive a dying tongue. Mistral's powerful, mystical evocation of western Provence (the real hero of all his epics) was more of a swansong to a dying culture, not the foundation for a Renaissance of a new troubadour movement.

For nearly everything Mistral celebrated in his poetry was undergoing a sea change – Italians, Corsicans and Spaniards were moving in by the thousands and helping to build new roads and railroads, while old farming practices, rural customs, traditions and even villages were rapidly being abandoned. Mistral, for all his art, energy, charm and influence, could not turn the clock back. He even had the unique honour of attending the unveiling of his own statue in Arles – a melancholy recognition that he was dead in his own lifetime.

Hocus Pocus Popes

Filling the lifeless shell of the papal palace in Avignon with the lost trappings of the medieval popes is not an easy task for the imagination. And the more you learn, the harder it gets, for besides all the harlots, speculators, gluttons and cheats that Petrarch railed against, there seems also to have been a shocking amount of voodoo. Accusations of sorcery had already sullied the name of one Occitan pope, Sylvester II (Gerbert of the Auvergne), who reigned from 999–1003 after studying in the Islamic schools in Toledo, where he acquired a prophetic bronze head that advised him in sticky moments. Even today, his tombstone in St John Lateran is said to sweat and rattle before the death of each pope.

In 1309 the French pope Clement V moved the Papacy from Rome to Avignon, then died from eating a plate of ground emeralds (prescribed by his doctor for a stomach ache). He was succeeded by John XXII, a native of Cahors, who owed his election to a magic knife that enchanted the conclave of cardinals. This John was also a famous alchemist, and he filled the papal treasury with gold, while King Philip V gave him a pair of *languiers*, or amulets shaped like serpents' tongues, encrusted with gems that changed colour on contact with poison. They served the pope in good stead, as plenty of rivals in the Church were trying to do him in. The most notable culprits were Clement V's doctor, caught manufacturing a diabolical homunculus, and Hugues Géraud, Bishop of Cahors, who confessed in 1317 that he had tried to assassinate the pope 'by poison and by sorcery with wax images, ashes of spiders and toads, the gall of a pig, and the like substances'. John XXII ordered him burnt at the stake.

The next pope, Benedict XII, spent hundreds of thousands of florins on a new palace, and still had enough gold and precious stones left over to top up his treasury – thanks, it is said, to an elderly woman residing in Avignon's ghetto, who told him where to find the 'treasure of the Jews' buried under her hovel. And in the bitter end, just before the antipope Benedict XIII was forced to flee Avignon, he sealed up a secret room in the palace with a cache of solid gold statues, confiding the secret to his friend, the Venetian ambassador. They were never found, although in Mistral's epic *Poème du Rhône*, three Venetian ladies who inherited the secret come to the palace and remove the flagstones that cover up the secret room – only to discover a bottomless abyss.

Occitans, Catalans and Related Species

The place is Verdun, the date AD 843, and a fellow named Lothair is about to mess up European history for good. The three contentious grandsons of Charlemagne, unable to manage the Carolingian Empire peaceably, were deciding how to carve it up between them. The resulting Treaty of Verdun would be a linguistic landmark – one of the first documents issued in two new-fangled languages later called French and German. It would also determine the future map of Europe. Lothair's two brothers were more sensible: Louis took the east, the future Germany, and Charles the Bald got the western half, most of what is now France. Lothair must have thought he was the clever one. Besides the imperial title (of dubious value) and the imperial capital, Aachen, he took away the richest lands of the Empire: northern Italy, Provence, Lorraine and Burgundy, along with Switzerland and the Low Countries.

If Lothair had considered what he would be leaving to his descendants, he might have noticed that this random collection of territories could never be held together for long. If he had had any sense of historical necessity, he might have said: 'You two can keep all the northern bits; just let me have what we Franks know as Aquitania, the land that folks in a thousand years are going to call southern France and Catalunya.' It would have made sense even then, a more coherent possession both culturally and politically. In the later Middle Ages, it would have seemed the obvious choice. This is western Europe's nation that never was.

The nation would have been called Provence, most likely, as that was the name in the later Middle Ages for the Occitan-speaking lands that stretched from the Atlantic to the Alps. Its capital would probably have been Toulouse. Instead, after the speedy collapse of Lothair's and his brothers' kingdoms, the Occitan-speaking peoples south of the Loire and their Catalan cousins got centuries of a balanced feudal anarchy with no real overlord. Real power became fatally divided between two ambitious rivals, the County of Toulouse, and the new Catalan County of Barcelona, later the Kingdom of Aragon.

The Occitans didn't mind; the relative freedom gave them the chance to create their open, advanced civilization of poetry and tolerance, a March crocus heralding the blossoming of medieval Europe. The Catalans learned to sail and trade, and built themselves a maritime empire in the Mediterranean. Unfortunately, their lack of co-operation doomed the former to a brutal French military conquest followed by the near-extinction of their language and culture. The Catalans, at least those south of the Pyrenees, would later suffer the same fate at the hands of Spain.

The great castles of Languedoc and Roussillon – Quéribus, Carcassonne, Salses and the rest – are the gravestones of the Lost Nation, the sites of defeats that marked its gradual, inexorable assimilation by the power of Paris and the north. Today, if you visit them in the off season, the only other car in the car park will be likely to have a white Spanish tag with a 'B' for Barcelona. You may see the inscrutable Catalans – culturally much more alive than the poor Languedociens – picnicking in the snow at Peyrepertuse in December, or at Salses furtively taking voluminous notes on the guided tour. Catalans abroad, even when encumbered by children and small dogs, often have the raffish air of spies or infiltrating *provocateurs*; it's part of their charm. Here, they're on a real mission, piecing together the memorials and cultural survivals of a forgotten world – forgotten by everyone else, maybe, but a dream that the Catalans and France's Occitanian malcontents will never let die.

Troubadours

Lyric poetry in the modern Western world was born around the year 1095 with the rhymes of Count William (1071–1127), grandfather of Eleanor of Aquitaine. William wrote in the courtly language of Old Provençal (or Occitan) although his subject matter was hardly courtly ('Do you know how many times I screwed them?/One hundred and eighty-eight to be precise;/So much so that I almost broke my girth and harness...'). A descendant of the royal house of Aragon, William had Spanish-Arab blood in his lusty veins and had battled against the Moors in Spain on several occasions, but at the same time he found inspiration (for his form, if not his content) in a civilization that was centuries ahead of Christian Europe in culture.

The word *troubadour* may be derived from the Arabic root for lutenist (*trb*), and the ideal of courtly love makes its first appearance in the writings of the spiritual Islamic Sufis. The Sufis believed that true understanding could not be expressed in doctrines, but could be suggested obliquely in poetry and fables. Much of what they wrote was love poetry addressed to an ideal if unkind and irrational muse, whom the poet hopes will reward his merit and devotion with enlightenment and inspiration. Christians who encountered this poetry in the Crusades converted this ideal muse into the Virgin, giving birth to the great 12th-century cult of Mary. But in Occitania this mystic strain was reinterpreted in a more worldly fashion by troubadours, whose muses became flesh and blood women, although these darlings were equally unattainable in the literary conventions of courtly love. The lady in question could only be addressed by a pseudonym. She had to be married to someone else. The poet's hopeless suit to her hinged, not on his rank, but on his virtue and worthiness. The greatest novelty of all was that this love had to go unrequited.

Art songs of courtly love were known as *cansos*, and rarely translate well, as their merit was in the poet's skill in inventing new forms in his rhyming schemes, metres, melodies and images. The troubadours wrote other songs as well, called *sirventes*, which followed established forms but took for their subjects politics, war, miserly patrons and even satires on courtly love itself.

The golden age of the troubadours began in the 1150s, when the feudal lords of Occitania warred amongst each other with so little success that behind the sound and fury the land enjoyed a rare political stability. Courts indulged in new luxuries and the arts flourished, and troubadours found ready audiences, travelling from castle to castle.

One of their great patrons was En Barral, Viscount of Marseille, who was especially fond of the reputedly mad but charming Peire Vidal. Vidal not only wrote of his love for En Barral's beautiful wife, but in a famous incident even went beyond the bounds of convention by stealing a kiss from her while she slept (her husband, who thought it was funny, had to plead with her to forgive him). Vidal travelled widely, especially after the death of En Barral in 1192, and wrote a rare nostalgic poem for the homeland of his lady fair:

> With each breath I draw in the air
> I feel coming from Provence;
> I so love everything from there
> that when people speak well of it,
> I listen smiling, and with each
> word ask for a hundred more,
> so much does the hearing please me.
>
> (trans. by Anthony Bonner in *Songs of the Troubadours*)

Up Your Nose

If nothing else, Provence and Languedoc will make you more aware of that sense we only remember when something stinks. The perfumeries of Grasse will correct this 'scentual' ignorance with a hundred different potions; every *village perché* has shops overflowing with scented soaps, pot-pourris and bundles of *herbes de Provence*; every kitchen emits intoxicating scents of garlic and thyme; every cellar wants you to breathe in the bouquets of its wines. And when you begin to almost crave the more usual French smells of Gauloise butts, *pipi* and *pommes frites*, you discover that this nasal obsession is not only profitable to some, but healthy for all.

Aromathérapie, a name coined in the 1920s for the method of natural healing through fragrances, is taken very seriously in the land where one word, *sentir*, does double duty for 'feel' and 'smell'. French medical students study it, and its prescriptions are covered by the national social security. For as an aromatherapist will tell you, smells play games with your psyche; the nose is hooked up not only to primitive drives like sex and hunger, but also to your emotions and memory. The consequences can be monumental. Just the scent of a madeleine cake dipped in tea was enough to set Proust off writing *Remembrance of Things Past*.

Aromatherapy is really just a fashionable name for old medicine. The Romans had a saying *Cur moriatur homo, cui salvia crescit in horto?* (Why should he die, who grows sage in his garden?) about a herb still heralded for its youth-giving properties. Essential oils distilled from plants were the secret of Egyptian healing and embalming, and were so powerful that there was a bullish market in 17th-century Europe for mummies, which were boiled down to make medicine.

Essential oils are created by the sun and the most useful aromatic plants grow in hot and dry climates – as in the south of France, the spiritual heartland of aromatherapy. Lavender, the totem plant of the Midi, has been in high demand for its mellow, soothing qualities ever since the Romans used it to scent their baths (hence its name from the Latin *lavare*, to wash). Up until the 1900s, nearly every farm in Provence had a small lavender distillery, and you can still find a few left today. Most precious of all is the oil of *lavande fine*, a species that grows only above 3,000 feet on the sunny side of the Alps; 150 pounds of flowers are needed for every pound of oil.

For centuries in Provence, shepherds were regarded as magicians because of their plant cures, which involved considerable mumbo-jumbo about picking their herbs in certain places and at certain times – and indeed, modern analysis has shown that the chemical composition of a herb like thyme varies widely, depending on where it grows and when it's picked. When the sun is in Leo, shepherds make *millepertuis*, or red oil (a sovereign anaesthetic and remedy for burns and wounds), by soaking the flowers of St John's wort in a mixture of white wine and olive oil that has been exposed to the hottest sun. After three days, they boil the wine off and let the flowers distil for another month; the oil is then sealed into tiny bottles, good for one dose each, to maintain the oil's healing properties.

Still awaiting a fashionable revival are other traditional Provençal cures: baked ground magpie brains for epilepsy, marmot fat for rheumatism, dried fox testicles rubbed on the chest for uterine disease, and mouse excrement for bedwetting.

Wide Open Spaces

Gertrude Stein, a great fan of Provence who spent a lot of time in St-Rémy-de-Provence, once dropped a famous line about Oakland, California: 'There's no *there* there,' she concluded after a brief visit. Take an equally inscrutable modern-day rapper from Oakland out to the exact centre of Provence, around the Lac de Castillon, and you will get a neatly symmetrical opinion. Lac de Castillon, a big artificial lake behind a concrete dam, is surrounded by wrinkled hills of a grey so immaculate that it is hard to see them at all. Outside of a few dam workers and an occasional hang-glider, the whole gigantic grey place will be eerily deserted. The Lac de Castillon is nowhere, and all the villages for thirty miles or more in any direction are only variations on the theme. We like to imagine an advert in a London paper: 'Delightful farmhouse in the heart of the Provençal mountains, near mountain lake; 1hr from Cannes. Must sell.'

When you visit, take a look at the sort of Frenchman who lives in such a place: no poodles, no shades, no attitudes; even in summer, he may well be wearing a flannel shirt, which under the big moustaches will make him look entirely like one of the jolly Gaulish villagers in *Astérix*. Some of these are real frontiersmen, rough-edged, self-sufficient types whose lives revolve around hunting, gathering mushrooms and getting in wood for the winter; they grumble laconically in a tongue that is still more Provençal than French.

But we once met a picture-perfect example on the way to Draguignan. He was the baker in a village near the lake, hitch-hiking to the city with a jerry can of petrol to buy a used car (in France one never expects a used car to have any in the tank). His brother had gone off to the Harvard Business School and made it big. The baker, with his degree in cultural anthropology, preferred less stress and yeastier dough; having an assistant allowed him enough time for long, scholarly vacations in the darker corners of South America and Asia.

The moral seems to be that rural France provides some of the world's most interesting hitch-hikers. Although this is true, the point is that the English shibboleth the 'South of France' is not always what one might expect. The toadstool growth of the Côte d'Azur in the last century has entirely eclipsed the real Provence: lonely expanses of mountain and introverted villages, shepherds who still drive their flocks up to the mountains in summer on the old transhumance paths, and a traditional rural culture that, despite a great loss of population in the last century, is not yet prepared to compromise entirely with the modern world. One wild snapshot among many sticks in the mind: two Indian chiefs, Iron Tail and Lone Bear, sipping champagne with the Marquis de Baroncelli-Javon in 1889, while watching Camargue *gardians* and the cowboys of Buffalo Bill's Wild West Show compare their skills at a Provençal rodeo. The men of two worlds had a great time together, and seemed to understand one another perfectly. One young Sioux, whom the French called Pan Perdu, chose to stay behind in Provence; Frédéric Mistral met him, and thought he might be the reincarnated soul of a troubadour.

Creating the Côte d'Azur

> There was no one at Antibes this summer except me, Zelda, the Valentinos, the Murphys, Mistinguett, Rex Ingram, Dos Passos, Alice Terry, the Mackleishes, Charlie Brackett, Maude Kahn, Esther Murphy, Maquerite Namara, E. Philips Oppenheim, Mannes the violinist, Floyd Dell, May and Crystal Eastman, ex-Premier Orlando, Etienne de Beaumont – just a real place to rough it, and escape from all the world.
> F. Scott Fitzgerald, in a letter to a friend

Even though in retrospect it seems inevitable that the Côte d'Azur was destined to become a hedonistic fantasy land, it owes a good deal to the personalities, desires and imagination of its colonizers. From the word go, the climate, the primordial reason for its popularity, wasn't always as gorgeous as its propagandists claim. Statistics are coy, but many invalids who came here for a cure never went home: 'They check in, but they don't check out,' as a disgruntled resident in Nice once put it. The other striking fact about the Riviera's ascent to fame and fortune is that the locals had next to nothing to do with its creation myths: the fantasy was spun by the collective desires of strangers. Not a single person in the *dramatis personae* listed below is from the Côte d'Azur, and even the most famous native is really 'from' somewhere else: one Giuseppe Garibaldi.

The Cast

The story begins 200 years ago, when the French Riviera was a beautiful, isolated, impoverished place, best known as that rather awkward corridor to Italy a traveller had to tackle after sailing down the Rhône. Two Englishmen who stopped on the way changed all that.

Tobias Smollett (1721–71): a doctor and novelist, unforgettably nicknamed 'Smelfungus' by Lawrence Sterne for his grumpiness, Smollett spent 1763 in Nice and three years later published his best-selling *Travels through France and Italy* (with prices). He occasionally deigned to put in a good word for Nice – 'the plain presents nothing but gardens...blowing in full glory, with such beauty, vigour, and perfumes, as no flower in England ever exhibited' – while at the same time dismissing the locals as slovenly and slothful, poor and withered, or cheats, thieves and bankrupts who upped prices 30 per cent for foreigners. Seeking a cure for consumption, he shocked the Niçois by indulging in the then extraordinary practice of sea bathing, which he highly recommended, although warning that it would be difficult for women 'unless they laid aside all regards for decorum'. Typically, the more Smollett sniped at the Riviera, the more the British wanted to go there.

Henry Lord Brougham (1778–1868): ex-Lord Chancellor and the man who gave his name to a kind of carriage, Lord Brougham added an essential touch of class to the Riviera. It all happened through chance: because of a cholera quarantine on the Italian frontier (then just west of Nice) he was forced to spend a night in Cannes in 1834, where he found the climate he'd thought to find in Naples there in La Napoule. Soon afterwards he bought an estate in Cannes, and returned every winter, encouraging his friends to do the same so he'd have someone to talk to. He amazed the locals by planting a grass lawn. Within 50 years of his arrival, Cannes had 50 hotels and the most aristocratic reputation on the coast.

The die was cast. Thousands of tubercular Brits and elderly aristocrats poured down to the Riviera to die in the winter sun. The next chapter began in 1864, when the railway was extended from Marseille to Nice, putting the coast within reach of a new kind of visitor: the tourist travelling for pleasure.

Stephen Liégeard (1830–1925): a lawyer and minor poet born into a wealthy wine-growing family in Burgundy, Liégeard married the woman who owned Les Violettes, the villa adjacent to Lord Brougham's estate. He was by all accounts a most affable and charming toady of the members of the Académie Française, but they still wouldn't elect him in, and Liégeard would have been forgotten if he hadn't given the coast its name in his glowing, idolizing 1887 guidebook *La Côte d'Azur*.

Queen Victoria (1819–1901): wintered on the Riviera seven times, beginning in 1887, following a trail blazed back in 1875 by her frisky son the Prince of Wales, whose high jinks in France make the current royals look almost respectable. As the mightiest ruling monarch of the day, Victoria's diminutive presence was the best advertisement that the newly packaged Côte d'Azur could wish for (in gratitude Nice erected her statue in Cimiez, where she liked to stay; the Germans knocked it over, but it was quickly re-erected after the war). Accompanied by her Indian servants, she was popular for passing out coins to the crowds; unlike her son she studiously avoided Monaco (in London in the 1880s there was already a society for the abolition of the casino). Her grandson who abdicated, the Duke of Windsor, was to spend much of his life on the coast pursuing a rigorous social schedule with his American duchess, Wallis Simpson.

James Gordon Bennett (1841–1918): black sheep heir to the founder of the *New York Herald*, Bennett founded the *Paris Herald* (ancestor of today's *International Herald Tribune*) in 1887 and ran it from his villa in Beaulieu, using it to advertise the coast and its visitors ('Monarchs Galore!'). Bennett was one of the millionaire rogues who set the brashy tone of the Riviera in the 1880s and 1890s; if his food arrived late at a restaurant, he would buy the restaurant.

La Belle Otero (1877–1964): like Bennett, the famous *grande horizontale* Caroline Otero profited from the presence of royalty on the coast, with a list of lovers that included Tsar Nicholas II, Edward VII and Reza Shah. A stunning Andalusian gypsy dancer and child bride of an Italian nobleman, she made her fortune in Monte-Carlo in 1901 by staking her last two louis on red at *trente-et-quarante*. Knowing nothing of the game, she thought she had lost and walked away; by the time she returned red had come up 28 times and she was wealthy beyond her wildest dreams. La Belle Otero was notorious for her rivalry with the great courtesan Liane de Pougy (once in Monte-Carlo, Otero plotted to outshine Liane by making a grand entrance, blazing with every diamond she owned; Liane got word of it and followed in a simple white gown, accompanied by her dog wearing all her fabulous carats). The shape of her breasts immortalized in the cupolas of the Carlton hotel in Cannes, Otero retired in 1922 aged 45 worth 45 million francs, but gambled it away in a few years and died impoverished in a small furnished room in Nice.

The Roaring Twenties brought the first summer visitors to the Côte d'Azur. The Americans had the most money to spend and many made fools of themselves. After 1930, however, the Great Depression forced many to stay home, and in 1936 they began to be displaced by a new kind of visitor, when the French Parliament granted all workers a two-week paid holiday and cheap train tickets to the seaside. Mass tourism was on its way.

Frank Jay Gould: (1887–1956) Jay Gould, America's most famous scoundrel, robber baron and stock market manipulator, was, like James Gordon Bennett, excluded from respectable society in New York, but he left his son Frank Jay a cool $22 million when he died in 1892. Frank Jay was a drunk and a lout, and made his mark on the Côte d'Azur by acquiring even more money, by buying up the casino and building the Hôtel Provençal at Juan-les-Pins in the 1920s (getting the French army to build his roads and sewers), and by constructing the enormous Palais de la Méditerranée casino in Nice to foil his rivals. His third wife, Florence Gould, redeemed him somewhat by spending his money to become one of the most beloved and generous hostesses on the coast.

Somerset Maugham (1874–1965): the British novelist was a solid fixture of the Riviera, presiding imperially at his Villa Mauresque in St-Jean-Cap-Ferrat, where he 'lived simply' to a strict routine with 13 servants, writing in the morning and using the Riviera as a background for many of his novels (he took pride in being the last professional writer to write everything out with a fountain pen). He entertained a constant stream of celebrities – Kenneth Clark, Noel Coward and Cyril Connolly were regulars – and presided over very formal dinner parties in black tie and velvet slippers, treating his guests to his cook's secret recipe for avocado ice-cream.

Colette (1873–1954): a founding figure in St-Tropez, the only big resort on the Riviera 'discovered' by the French. (Guy de Maupassant was there first, and wrote seductively about his boat trip around the coast in *Sur l'eau*, in 1887). Colette bought a little house called La Treille Muscate in 1926, met the love of her life, Maurice Goudeket, and wrote *La Naissance du jour*, the ultimate St-Trop idyll. In 1937, a victim of her own success and tired of finding her garden full of strangers from Paris, she moved to Brittany.

Isadora Duncan (1878–1927): one of the founding mothers of modern dance, Duncan sought refuge in Nice after her children were tragically drowned in the Seine and she had separated from poet Sergei Esenin, the husband she had wed during the Russian Revolution. She opened a dance studio in Nice and was one of the most popular people on the coast. No one knew what she would say or do next, and although roly-poly, she could still enchant her audience with her unique impromptu dancing in her flowing, billowing clothes. '*Adieu, mes amis, je vais à la gloire!*' were her last words before she was driven off in a Bugatti down the Promenade des Anglais; her swirling scarf got entangled in the wheel and she died instantly of a broken neck. Although Isadora had raised funds for France during the First World War, Americans were very unpopular in France in 1927 because of the Sacco and Vanzetti case, and no one attended her funeral in Paris.

Coco Chanel (1883–1971): Isadora Duncan would have lived longer had she been dressed by Chanel. Raised in rural poverty, Gabrielle Chanel was a svelte dark beauty who got her start when her aristocratic English lover Boy Capel set her up in the millinery business. She soon displayed her gift as a designer in touch with the trends, as well as her astute canniness as a businesswoman. In 1916, inspired by Cubism, she changed the course of fashion by making austerity and simplicity elegant, '*le luxe dans la simplicité*' as she put it, creating well-cut and understated fashions and 'little black dresses' to appeal to both her *haute couture* clients and the newly emancipated working woman. A fixture of the Riviera in the '20s, with pockets full of dukes – among them Grand Duke Dimitri of Russia and the Duke of Westminster, the wealthiest man in England – she not only confirmed the new fad for sunbathing but also a whole new style of clothing: sportswear, invented for Cocteau's ballet *Le Train bleu*. Chanel set the fashion for short hair, sailor's caps and costume jewellery, and became one of the first designers to put her name to a scent when she discovered a perfumer in Grasse who produced a formula for a subtle, intriguing long-lasting fragrance, packaged in the classic No. 5 bottle.

Katherine Mansfield (1888–1923): master of the ironic, sensitive short story and married to John Middleton Murry, Mansfield spent the last five years of her life trying to find a cure for her tuberculosis, a good deal of that time in Menton. Her letters to her husband and short stories offer an evocative view of the coast at the time.

Cole Porter (1893–1964): Porter began his career as America's best-loved composer of subtle melodies and sophisticated lyrics before the First World War, when he enlisted in the French Foreign Legion and later in the French Army. In Paris in the '20s, he was commissioned by Winnaretta, Princesse de Polignac and daughter of Isaac 'Sewing Machine' Singer to write a jazz ballet called *Within the Quota*, and he hung around Paris, longing to study with Stravinsky. In the summer of 1922 he rented the Château de la Garoupe in Cap d'Antibes, invited his friends down from Paris, and convinced them that summer on the Riviera was the place to be, where, as his later musical put it, *Anything Goes*.

Aldous Huxley (1894–1963): satirical novelist Huxley spent much of his life in Sanary, near Toulon. His classic *Brave New World* (1932) was in response to the rosy ideas of H.G. Wells, who lived nearby. He moved to California during the Second World War.

F. Scott Fitzgerald (1896–1940): charter members of the Lost Generation, Scott and talented wife Zelda personified the madcap recklessness and escapades that people associated with the Côte d'Azur, both devoted – doomed almost – to maintaining a continual high of hedonism. When drunk, which was nearly always, Scott would be sawing bartenders in half, tossing full ash trays at people in restaurants or shot-putting ice-cream down the backs of ladies; Zelda liked to lie in front of cars or dance an impromptu pirouette half-naked in the ballroom at Monte-Carlo. In 1929, Zelda suffered a nervous breakdown and was diagnosed as suffering from acute schizophrenia; she never recovered.

Jean Cocteau (1889–1963): a long-time resident of Villefranche-sur-Mer, gregarious painter, poet and *cinéaste*, promoter of avant-garde musicians and artists, and a close friend of the rich and famous. Cocteau did much to define the spirit of the Côte d'Azur in its heyday, especially in *Le Train bleu*, a work evoking the carefree sporting life by the sea (named after the legendary streamlined luxury train that linked Paris to the coast), which he wrote for Diaghilev's Ballets Russes, with music by Darius Milhaud, costumes by Chanel and sets by Picasso. He would later play no small role in making sure Cannes was chosen as the venue for France's film festival, and was a frequent member of its jury.

D.H. Lawrence (1885–1930): another victim of tuberculosis and friend of Mansfield, Lawrence was only 45 when after a life of wanderings he died in Vence, dismayed by what the 'vileness of man' had wrecked on the lovely coast, but commenting on the Mediterranean in a letter shortly before he died: 'It still seems as young as Odysseus, in the morning.' Another towering figure of English literature to topple on the coast was **W.B. Yeats**, who died at Cap Martin in 1939 and was buried at Roquebrune, where rumour has it part or all of him still remains – when his relics were transferred to Ireland they got the wrong stiff. Other Irishmen who found muses on the Côte d'Azur included **James Joyce**, who claimed Nice was the first inspiration for *Finnegans Wake*, and film director **Rex Ingram**, who shot *The Four Horsemen of the Apocalypse* in Nice, based on the novel by Blasco Ibáñez.

After the war, French glumness infected even the coast, even though (with the exception of Toulon) it had escaped relatively intact. Even property prices were depressed. But it wasn't long before a new transfusion of glitter arrived and the joint was jumping all over again, although much of what seemed glamorous and carefree was now more calculated; the new movers and shakers included the likes of Greek shipping tycoon Aristotle Onassis and arms dealer Adnan Kashoggi.

Grace Kelly (1929–82): Monaco Inc. was approaching bankruptcy in 1955 and Aristotle Onassis, the majority stockholder in the Société des Bains de Mer, was manoeuvring to pull all the principality's purse strings. Prince Rainier III thwarted him by issuing more stock and marrying a glamorous American movie actress. Rita Hayworth was already spoken for: she had been living in the Château de l'Horizon in Vallauris in 1947 when she married Aly Khan, son of the Aga Khan. Rainier auditioned Marilyn Monroe for the part, but Grace Kelly won the role and the dazzling society marriage that made the daughter of a Philadelphia brick magnate into a Riviera princess took place in 1956. Perhaps appropriately enough for the star of *To Catch a Thief*, the bride's mother was robbed of her jewels after the ceremony. Monaco hasn't been in the red since.

Graham Greene (1904–91): in 1966, Greene moved to Antibes, where he wrote his autobiographical *A Sort of Life* and *Ways of Escape*. In 1982, in righteous anger, he published a booklet called *J'Accuse: The Dark Side of Nice*, lambasting the organized crime and corruption that mayor Jacques Médecin's political machine turned a blind eye to or abetted; it was and still is banned in Nice. Other writers who lived in Antibes after the war include Nikos Kazantzakis and Roland Barthes; Monaco was long the address of the English-born poet of the Yukon, Robert Service (who wrote an ode in honour of Princess Grace's wedding), and Anthony Burgess; French novelist Patrick Modiano favours Nice (his *Les Dimanches d'été* is about Nice, and *Voyages de noces* is about Jews taking refuge in the south during the war).

Dirk Bogarde (1920–99): British screen star and respected writer, Bogarde lived for many years in a villa near Grasse. His films include the at-the-time controversial *The Servant* (1963) and *Death in Venice* (1970).

Brigitte Bardot (1934–): ever since she came down with Roger Vadim to St-Tropez to film *Et Dieu créa la femme* in 1956, Bardot has personified the myth of its free, sensuous spirit. Until recently a long-time resident of the village, she married an extreme right wing politician in the '80s and now devotes her energy and formidable publicity machine to animal rights.

What new kind of Côte d'Azur, if any, may be wrought by its new glitterati – such famous names as Elton John, Luciano Pavarotti, Claudia Schiffer, Boris Becker and Joan Collins – still waits to be seen. One thing is certain, at least: property prices won't go down any time soon. Buy that dream villa now.

Food and Drink

...and south of Valence, Provincia Romana, the Roman Provence, lies beneath the sun.
There there is no more any evil, for there the apple will not flourish and the Brussels
sprout will not grow at all.
Ford Madox Ford, **Provence**

Some of the most celebrated restaurants in the world grace the south of France, but
no matter where you go, eating is a pleasure. The Mediterranean climate translates
into seafood, herbs, fruit and vegetables, often within plucking distance of the table.
The exceptional quality of the ingredients demands minimal preparation – Provençal
cooking is perhaps the least fussy of any regional French cuisine. As an added bonus,
it neatly fits the modern definition of a healthy diet. For not only is the south a
Brussels sprout-free zone, but the artery-hardening delights of the north – the rich
creamy sauces, butter, cheese and egg dishes, and mega-calorie desserts – are rare
birds in the land of olives, fresh vegetables, apricots and almonds.

Restaurant Basics

Restaurants generally serve between 12 noon and 2pm and in the evening from 7 to
10pm, with later summer hours; *brasseries* in the cities generally stay open continuously. Most post menus outside the door so you know what to expect, and offer a
choice of set-price menus; if prices aren't listed, you can bet it's not because they're a
bargain. If you summon up the appetite to eat the biggest meal of the day at noon,
you'll spend a lot less money, as many restaurants offer special lunch menus – an
economical way to experience some of the finer gourmet temples. Some of these
offer a set-price gourmet *menu dégustation* – a selection of chef's specialities, which
can be a great treat. At the humbler end of the scale, bars and brasseries often serve a
simple *plat du jour* (daily special) and the no-choice *formule*, which is more often than
not steak and *frites*. Eating *à la carte* anywhere will always be more expensive, in
many cases twice as much.

Menus sometimes include the house wine (*vin compris*). If you choose a better wine
anywhere, expect a scandalous mark-up; the French wouldn't dream of a meal
without wine, and the arrangement is a simple device to make food prices seem
lower. If service is included it will say *service compris* or s.c., if not *service non
compris* or s.n.c.

French restaurants, especially the cheaper ones, presume everyone has the appetite
of Gargantua. A full meal consists of: an apéritif (*pastis*, the national drink of the
south, is famous for its hunger-inducing qualities), *hors-d'œuvre* or a starter (typically,
soup, pâté or *charcuterie*), an *entrée* (usually fish, or an omelette), a main course
(usually meat, poultry, game or offal, *garni* with vegetables, rice or potatoes), often
followed by a green salad (to 'lighten' the stomach), then cheese, dessert, coffee,
chocolates and *mignardises* (or *petits fours*) and perhaps a *digestif* to round things off.
Most people only devour the whole whack on Sunday afternoons, and at other times
condense this feast to a starter, *entrée* or main course, and cheese or dessert.

Aïoli Recipe

This typical Provençal mayonnaise is best served with white fish such as bourride, or with snails, potatoes or soup.

Ingredients (per person)
1 clove of garlic (more if you're a garlic fiend)
1 egg yolk
extra virgin olive oil

Using a mortar and pestle, crush the garlic to a paste and add the egg yolk(s). Begin whipping the mixture with a fork or small whisk while adding good quality (extra virgin) olive oil, first drop by drop, then in a thin stream as the mayonnaise begins to set. Add salt only once all the oil has been integrated and the mayonnaise has formed.

Should the *aïoli* lack substance or the oil separate from the mixture, you can still 'save' your mayonnaise: remove the mixture and add another egg yolk to the clean mortar. Whipping constantly, reintegrate the old *aïoli* mixture and any remaining oil. This operation is called 'reconstituting' the *aïoli*.

Vegetarians usually have a hard time in France, especially if they don't eat fish or eggs, but most establishments will try to accommodate them. This is easier in the Côte d'Azur than elsewhere in France, as many of the local specialities are meat-free.

When looking for a restaurant, homing in on the one place crowded with locals is as sound a policy in France as anywhere. Don't overlook hotel restaurants, some of which are absolutely top notch even if a certain red book refuses on some obscure principle to give them more than two stars. To avoid disappointment, call ahead in the morning to reserve a table, especially at the smarter restaurants, and especially in the summer.

You'll soon notice that the Côte and big cities have a wide choice of regional and ethnic restaurants: Breton *crêperies* or *galetteries* (with wholewheat pancakes), restaurants from Alsace serving *choucroute* (sauerkraut) and sausage, Périgord restaurants featuring *foie gras* and truffles, Lyonnaise *haute cuisine,* and *les fast foods* offering *basse cuisine* of chips, hot dogs and cheese sandwiches. North African restaurants are a favourite for their economical couscous – spicy meat and vegetables served on a bed of steamed semolina with a side dish of *harissa*, a hot red pepper sauce); Asian (usually Vietnamese, sometimes Chinese, Cambodian, or Thai) and Italian are popular as well, the latter often combined with a pizzeria.

There are still a few traditional French restaurants that would meet the approval of Auguste Escoffier, the legendary chef whose birthplace has become a place of pilgrimage in Villeneuve-Loubet (*see* pp.157–8). On the whole, though, regional *cuisine de terroir,* modern Mediterranean and fusion are the rule.

The Cuisine of the South

Provence and the Côte d'Azur

Thanks to the trail-blazing work of writers and chefs like Elizabeth David and Roger Vergé, many traditional Provençal dishes will already be familiar, although even such favourites as *ratatouille* – aubergines (eggplant), tomatoes, garlic and courgettes (zucchini) which are cooked separately to preserve their individual flavour, before being mixed together in olive oil – can seem like another dish altogether when properly prepared in its native land with native ingredients. Other specialities may be less well known, such as *bagna cauda*, a dish of the southern Alps, consisting of raw vegetables dipped in a hot fondue of garlic, anchovies and olive oil.

Between November and March the olives are crushed to make the fragrant olive oil that lies at the heart of the local cuisine; during this period, a number of olive mills are open to the public (usually just in the afternoons), among them the Alziari mill in Nice (318 Bd de la Madeleine), or the mills at Grasse (Moulin à Huile Ste-Anne, 138 Route de Draguignan), Opio (Moulins de la Brague, 2 Rte de Châteauneuf), and Menton (Moulin à Huile Lottier, 102 Av des Acacias).

Many a Provençal dinner starts with an apéritif and *tapenade*, a purée of olives, anchovies, olive oil and capers served on toast. The heraldic starter on a thousand menus, the *salade niçoise*, is interpreted in a hundred different ways even in Nice, but in general it contains most of the following: tomatoes, cucumbers, hard-boiled eggs, black olives, onions, anchovies, artichokes, green peppers, croûtons, green beans, tuna and even potatoes. Another lighter speciality is *omelette de putine*, an omelette with tiny fish. In Nice pasta dishes come in all sorts of shapes, but the favourites are ravioli and gnocchi (potato dumplings), two forms served throughout Italy and invented here when Nice was still *Nizza* (the city has many other special dishes; *see* p.135). Another dish that tastes best in the summer, *soupe au pistou*, is a thick minestrone served with a fresh basil, garlic, and pine-nut sauce similar to Italian pesto.

Aïoli, a mayonnaise made from garlic, olive oil, lemon juice and egg yolks, served with codfish, snails, potatoes or soup, is for many the essence of Provence; Mistral even named his nationalist Provençal magazine after it. In the same spirit Marseille named its magazine *Bouillabaisse*, for its world-famous soup of five to twelve kinds of Mediterranean fish, flavoured with saffron; the fish is removed and served with *aïoli* or *rouille*, a sauce of fresh red chilli peppers crushed with garlic, olive oil, and the soup broth. Because good saffron costs money and the fish, especially the gruesome *rascasse* (scorpion fish) are rare, a proper *bouillabaisse* will cost at least €30. A less expensive but delicious alternative is *bourride*, a soup made from white-fleshed fish served with *aïoli*, or down a gastronomical notch is *baudroie*, a fish soup with vegetables and garlic. A very different kettle of fish is the indigestible Niçoise favourite (which the Monégasques also claim as their own), *estocaficada* – salt cod (and salt cod guts) stewed with tomatoes, olives, garlic and *eau-de-vie*. Less adventurous yet an absolutely delicious dish is *loup au fenouil*, sea bass grilled over fennel stalks.

Lamb is the most common meat dish; real Provençal lamb (becoming increasingly rare) grazes on herbs and on special salt-marsh grasses from the Camargue and Crau. Beef usually comes in the form of a *daube*, slowly stewed in red wine and often served with ravioli. A Provençal cook's prize possession is the *daube* pan, which is never washed, but wiped clean and baked to form a crust that flavours all subsequent stews. Rabbit, or *lapin à la provençale*, is simmered in white wine with garlic, mustard, tomatoes and herbs. The more daunting *pieds et paquets* are tripe packages stuffed with garlic, onions and salt pork, traditionally (although rarely in practice) served with calf's or sheep's trotters. Also look for *capoun fassum*, cabbage stuffed with sausage and rice, and *artichauts à la barigoule*, artichokes filled with pork and mushrooms.

Purely vegetable dishes, besides ratatouille, include *tian*, a casserole of rice, spring vegetables (usually courgettes) and grated cheese baked in the oven; *tourta de blea*, a sweet-savoury Swiss chard pie; stuffed courgette (zucchini) flowers; grilled tomatoes with garlic and breadcrumbs (*à la provençale*); and *mesclun*, a salad of dandelion and other green leaves. There aren't many Provençal cheeses: *banon*, nutty discs made from goat, sheep, or cow's milk, wrapped in chestnut leaves, is perhaps the best known; *poivre d'Ain* is *banon* flavoured with savory; thyme and bay add a nuance to creamy sheep's milk *tomme arlésienne*.

Languedoc-Roussillon

In France's 'culinary desert', as the region of Languedoc-Roussillon is unkindly known, they have the expression *manjar fòrça estofat* (to eat lots of stew), which describes a masochist or someone who suffers martyrdom without complaint. What more can you say about a region that goes into raptures over *cassoulet* – beans, pork, *confits* (*see* below) and sausage stewed in goose fat? In fact, in recent years, partly as a result of increased tourism in the region, the cuisine has greatly improved, with a new stylish treatment of the Catalan classics and excellent local fish, meat and fruit.

Stay away from the dreary-looking places in the towns; some of these offer cuisine on the level of the average London sandwich bar. But out in the villages, in a growing number of new hotel-restaurants with younger owners and in scores of *fermes-auberges*, you'll find something more to your liking, an honest, earthy cuisine entirely based on traditional local ingredients: game dishes, rabbit, pigeon, morels and cèpes, foie gras, occasionally truffles, Corbières wine and, in western Languedoc, plenty of duck, usually in the form of a *confit* (cooked and preserved in its own fat – much better than it sounds).

The eternal bean stew *cassoulet* (*see* Castelnaudary) is still the king of the Languedocien table, along with regional variations like the *fricassée* of Limoux; the queen, ever since the Middle Ages, has been *brandade de morue*, salt cod purée with garlic, olive oil and milk. Fresh seafood, though simply prepared, is always good along the coast; there are plenty of excellent mussels and oysters, raised in the coastal lagoons, that are one of the biggest treats the region can offer.

Some Languedocien basics have relatives in Provence. *Aïoli* (or *aïllade*) is a favourite sauce, and seafood dishes like *bouillabaisse* are similar, although here you may find ham and leeks involved. Sète is famous for its delicious *bourride*; then there's *bourboulhade*, a kind of poor man's *bouillabaisse* made of salt cod and garlic, or yet another B-soup, *boullinade*, a thicker fish soup with Banyuls wine. Sète, the seafood capital of Languedoc, also specializes in *seiches farcies*, cuttlefish stuffed with the meat of its tentacles mixed with sausage, and *langouste à la sètoise*, crawfish with cognac, tomatoes and garlic. *Escargots*, or snails, come at you in all directions, with anchovies, as in Nîmes, or grilled (*cargolade*), or even in *bouillabaisse*. Land dishes you may encounter include *mourtayrol*, a delicious chicken *pot-au-feu* flavoured with saffron, and *rouzoles*, crêpes filled with ham and bacon. When the cheese platter comes around, it may have *pelardons*, the favourite goat's cheese from the Cévennes.

The Catalans in Roussillon have many sterling qualities, but often display only the most modest ones in their restaurants. The totem fish of the *département* is the little anchovy of Collioure, which hardy souls from Spain to Marseille pulverize with garlic, onion, basil and oil to make *anchoïade*, a favourite apéritif spread on raw celery or toast. A popular starter is *gambas à la planxa*, prawns grilled and served on a 'plank', or anchovies with strips of red pepper, which is better than it sounds. Main courses include *roussillonnade*, a dish of bolet mushrooms and sausages grilled over a pine-cone fire, and *boles de Picolat*, Catalan meatballs with mushrooms cooked in sauce. The classic dessert is *crème catalane*, a caramel-covered baked cream flavoured with anise and cinnamon.

Markets, Picnic Food and Snacks

The markets in the south of France are justly celebrated for the colour and perfumes of their produce and flowers. They are fun to visit, and become even more interesting if you're cooking or gathering the ingredients for a picnic. In the larger cities food markets take place every day, while smaller towns and villages have markets on one day a week (we've listed all the ones we know in the text), which double as social occasions for the locals. Most markets finish around noon.

Other good sources for picnic food are the *charcuteries* or *traiteurs*, both of which sell prepared dishes sold by weight in cartons or tubs. Many of the local specialities lend themselves well to picnics: *pissaladière*, a cross between an onion tart and a pizza, is good hot or cold; *socca* is a kind of pancake made with chickpea flour; and the delicious *pan bagnat* is filled with all kinds of delicious fillings. You can also find counters at larger supermarkets. Cities are snack-food wonderlands, with outdoor counters selling pastries, crêpes, pizza slices, *frites*, *croque-monsieur* (toasted ham and cheese sandwiches) and a wide variety of sandwiches made from baguettes (long thin loaves of bread).

Drink

You can order any kind of drink at any bar or café – except cocktails, unless it has a certain cosmopolitan *savoir-faire* or stays open into the night. Cafés are also a home from home, places to read the papers, meet friends and watch the world go by. You can spend hours over one coffee and no one will hurry you along. Prices are listed on the *tarif des consommations*: note they are more expensive depending on whether you're served at the bar (*comptoir*), at a table (*la salle*) or outside (*la terrasse*).

French coffee is strong and black, but lacklustre next to the aromatic brews of Italy or Spain (you'll notice an improvement in the coffee near their respective frontiers).

French Menu Reader

Hors-d'œuvre et Soupes (Starters and Soups)
amuse-gueule appetizers
assiette assortie plate of mixed cold hors-d'œuvre
bisque shellfish soup
bouchées mini *vol-au-vents*
bouillabaisse famous fish soup of Marseille
bouillon broth
charcuterie mixed cold meats, salami, ham, etc.
consommé clear soup
coulis thick sieved sauce
crudités raw vegetable platter
potage thick vegetable soup
tourrain garlic and bread soup
velouté thick smooth soup, often fish or chicken
vol-au-vent puff-pastry case with savoury filling

Poissons et Coquillages (Crustacés) (Fish and Shellfish)
aiglefin little haddock
alose shad
anchois anchovies
anguille eel
bar sea bass
barbue brill
baudroie angler fish
belons flat oysters
bigorneau winkle
blanchailles whitebait
brème bream
brochet pike
bulot whelk
cabillaud cod
calmar squid

carrelet plaice
colin hake
congre conger eel
coques cockles
coquillages shellfish
coquilles St-Jacques scallops
crabe crab
crevettes grises shrimp
crevettes roses prawns
cuisses de grenouilles frogs' legs
darne slice or steak of fish
daurade sea bream
écrevisse freshwater crayfish
éperlan smelt
escabèche fish fried, marinated and served cold
escargots snails
espadon swordfish
esturgeon sturgeon
flétan halibut
friture deep-fried fish
fruits de mer seafood
gambas giant prawns
gigot de mer a large fish cooked whole
grondin red gurnard
hareng herring
homard Atlantic (Norway) lobster
huîtres oysters
lamproie lamprey
langouste spiny Mediterranean lobster
langoustines Norway lobster (often called Dublin Bay prawns)
limande lemon sole
lotte monkfish
loup (de mer) sea bass
louvine sea bass (in Aquitaine)
maquereau mackerel
merlan whiting
morue salt cod
moules mussels

If you order *un café* you'll get a small black *express*; if you want milk, order *un crème*. If you want more than a few drops of caffeine, ask them to make it *grand*. For decaffeinated, the word is *déca*. Some bars offer *cappuccinos*, but again they're only really good near the Italian border; in the summer try a *frappé* (iced coffee). The French only order *café au lait* (a small coffee topped off with lots of hot milk) when they stop in for breakfast, and if what your hotel offers is expensive or boring, consider joining them. There are baskets of croissants and pastries, and some bars will make you a baguette with butter, jam or honey.

If you want to go native, try the Frenchman's Breakfast of Champions: a *pastis* or two, and five non-filter Gauloises. *Chocolat chaud* (hot chocolate) is usually good;

oursin sea urchin
pagel sea bream
palourdes clams
petit gris little grey snail
poulpe octopus
praires small clams
raie skate
rascasse scorpion fish
rouget red mullet
saumon salmon
St-Pierre John Dory
sole (meunière) sole (with butter, lemon and parsley)
stockfisch stockfish (wind-dried cod)
telline tiny clam
thon tuna
truite trout
truite saumonée salmon trout

Viandes et Volailles (Meat and Poultry)

agneau (de pré-salé) lamb (grazed in fields by the sea)
ailerons chicken wings
aloyau sirloin
andouillette chitterling (tripe) sausage
autruche ostrich
biftek beefsteak
blanc breast or white meat
blanquette stew of white meat, thickened with egg yolk
bœuf beef
boudin blanc sausage of white meat
boudin noir black pudding
brochette meat (or fish) on a skewer
caille quail
canard, caneton duck, duckling
carré crown roast
cassoulet haricot bean stew with sausage, duck, goose, etc.
cervelle brains

chair flesh, meat
chapon capon
châteaubriand porterhouse steak
cheval horsemeat
chevreau kid
chorizo spicy Spanish sausage
civet meat (usually game) stew, in wine and blood sauce
cœur heart
confit meat cooked and preserved in its own fat
côte, côtelette chop, cutlet
cou d'oie farci goose neck stuffed with pork, foie gras and truffles
crépinette small sausage
cuisse thigh or leg
dinde, dindon turkey
entrecôte ribsteak
épaule shoulder
estouffade a meat stew marinated, fried and then braised
faisan pheasant
faux-filet sirloin
foie liver
frais de veau veal testicles
fricadelle meatball
gésier gizzard
gibier game
gigot leg of lamb
graisse or *gras* fat
grillade grilled meat, often a mixed grill
grive thrush
jambon ham
jarret knuckle
langue tongue
lapereau young rabbit
lapin rabbit
lard, lardons bacon, diced bacon
lièvre hare
maigret/magret de canard breast of duck

if you order *thé* (tea), you'll get a nasty ordinary bag and the water will be hot rather than boiling. An *infusion* is a herbal tea – *camomille*, *menthe* (mint), *tilleul* (lime or linden blossom), or *verveine* (verbena). These are kind to the all-precious *foie*, or liver, after you've over-indulged at the table.

Mineral water (*eau minérale*) can be addictive, and comes either sparkling (*gazeuse* or *pétillante*) or still (*non-gazeuse*). If you feel run down, *Badoit* has lots of peppy magnesium in it.

The usual international corporate soft drinks are available, and all kinds of bottled fruit juices (*jus de fruits*). Some bars also do fresh lemon and orange juices (*citron pressé* or *orange pressée*, served with a separate *carafe d'eau* to dilute to taste). The

manchons duck or goose wings
marcassin young wild boar
merguez spicy red sausage
moelle bone marrow
mouton mutton
museau muzzle
navarin lamb stew with root vegetables
noix de veau topside of veal
oie goose
os bone
perdreau (or *perdrix*) partridge
petit salé salt pork
pieds trotters
pintade guinea fowl
plat-de-côtes short ribs or rib chops
porc pork
pot au feu meat and vegetables cooked in stock
poulet chicken
poussin baby chicken
quenelle poached dumplings made of fish, fowl or meat
queue de bœuf oxtail
ris (de veau) sweetbreads (veal)
rognons kidneys
rosbif roast beef
rôti roast
sanglier wild boar
saucisses sausages
saucisson dry sausage, like salami
selle (d'agneau) saddle (of lamb)
steak tartare raw minced beef, often topped with a raw egg yolk
suprême de volaille fillet of chicken breast and wing
taureau bull's meat
tête (de veau) calf's head, fatty and usually served with a mustardy vinaigrette
tortue turtle
tournedos thick round slices of beef fillet

travers de porc spare ribs
tripes tripe
veau veal
venaison venison

Légumes, Herbes, etc. (Vegetables, Herbs, etc.)

ail garlic
aïoli garlic mayonnaise
algue seaweed
aneth dill
anis anis
artichaut artichoke
asperges asparagus
aubergine aubergine (eggplant)
avocat avocado
basilic basil
betterave beetroot
blette Swiss chard
bouquet garni mixed herbs in a little bag
cannelle cinnamon
céleri celery
céleri-rave celeriac
cèpes ceps, wild boletus mushrooms
champignons mushrooms
chanterelles wild yellow mushrooms
chicorée curly endive
chou cabbage
chou-fleur cauliflower
choucroute sauerkraut
choux de bruxelles Brussels sprouts
ciboulette chives
citrouille pumpkin
clou de girofle clove
cœur de palmier heart of palm
concombre cucumber
cornichons gherkins
courgettes courgettes (zucchini)
cresson watercress
échalote shallot

French are also fond of fruit syrups – red *grenadine* and ghastly green *menthe*, which are mixed with lemonade to form a *diabolo* (e.g. *diabolo menthe*).

Beer (*bière*) in most bars and cafés is run-of-the-mill big brands from Alsace, Germany and Belgium. Draft (*à la pression*) is cheaper than bottled beer. Nearly all resorts have bars or pubs offering wider selections of drafts and bottles.

The strong spirit of the Midi comes in a liquid form called *pastis*, first made popular in Marseille as a plague remedy; its name comes from the Latin *passe-sitis*, or thirst-quencher. A pale yellow 90 per cent nectar flavoured with anise, vanilla and cinnamon, *pastis* is drunk as an apéritif before lunch and in rounds after work. The three major brands, Ricard, Pernod and Pastis 51, all taste slightly different; most people drink their

endive chicory (endive)
épinards spinach
épis de maïs sweetcorn (on the cob)
estragon tarragon
fenouil fennel
fèves broad (fava) beans
flageolets white beans
fleurs de courgette courgette blossoms
frites chips (French fries)
genièvre juniper
gingembre ginger
haricots rouges kidney beans
haricots blancs white beans
haricots verts green (French) beans
jardinière with diced garden vegetables
laitue lettuce
laurier bay leaf
lentilles lentils
marjolaine marjoram
menthe mint
mesclun salad of various leaves
morilles morel mushrooms
moutarde mustard
navet turnip
oignons onions
oseille sorrel
panais parsnip
persil parsley
petits pois peas
piment pimento
pissenlits dandelion greens
poireaux leeks
pois chiches chickpeas
pois mange-tout sugar peas or mangetout
poivron sweet pepper (capsicum)
pomme de terre potato
potiron pumpkin
primeurs young vegetables
radis radishes
raifort horseradish

riz rice
romarin rosemary
roquette rocket
safran saffron
salade verte green salad
salsifis salsify
sarriette savoury
sarrasin buckwheat
sauge sage
seigle rye
serpolet wild thyme
thym thyme
truffes truffles

Fruits et Noix (Fruit and Nuts)

abricot apricot
amandes almonds
ananas pineapple
banane banana
bigarreau black cherries
brugnon nectarine
cacahouètes peanuts
cassis blackcurrant
cerise cherry
citron lemon
citron vert lime
noix de coco coconut
coing quince
dattes dates
figues (de Barbarie) figs (prickly pear)
fraises (des bois) strawberries (wild)
framboises raspberries
fruit de la passion passion fruit
grenade pomegranate
groseilles redcurrants
lavande lavender
mandarine tangerine
mangue mango
marrons chestnuts
mirabelles mirabelle plums

'*pastaga*' with lots of water and ice (*glaçons*), which makes it almost palatable. A thimble-sized *pastis* is a *momie*; mixed with grenadine it becomes a *tomate*; with *orgeat* (almond and orange flower syrup) it's a *mauresque*, and a *perroquet* is mint.

Other popular apéritifs come from Languedoc-Roussillon, including Byrrh 'from the world's largest barrel', a sweet wine mixed with quinine and orange peel, similar to *Dubonnet*. Spirits include the familiar cognac and armagnac brandies, liqueurs and *digestifs* made from walnuts, cherries, pears and herbs (these are a speciality of the Alps), and fiery *marc*, the grape spirit that is the same as Italian *grappa* (but usually better). Many Provençal villages have a special *marc* of their own; the *marc des orangers*, made in spring with orange flowers, is one of the nicest.

mûre (sauvage) mulberry, blackberry
myrtilles bilberries
noisette hazelnut
noix walnuts
noix de cajou cashews
pamplemousse grapefruit
pastèque watermelon
pêche, pêche blanche peach, white peach
pignons pine-nuts
pistache pistachio
poire pear
pomme apple
prune plum
pruneau prune
raisins, raisins secs grapes, raisins
reine-claude greengage plums

Desserts
Bavarois mousse or custard in a mould
biscuit biscuit, cracker, cake
bombe ice-cream dessert in a round mould
bonbons sweets, candy
brioche light sweet yeast bread
charlotte sponge fingers and custard cream
   dessert
chausson turnover
clafoutis baked batter pudding with fruit
compote stewed fruit
corbeille de fruits basket of fruit
coulis thick fruit sauce
coupe ice cream: a scoop or in cup
crème anglaise egg custard
crème caramel vanilla custard with
   caramel sauce
crème Chantilly sweet whipped cream
crème fraîche slightly sour cream
crème pâtissière thick pastry cream filling
   made with eggs
gâteau cake
gaufre waffle

génoise rich sponge cake
glace ice cream
macarons macaroons
madeleine small sponge cake
miel honey
mignardise same as *petits fours*
mousse 'foam': frothy dessert
œufs à la neige floating island/meringue on a
   bed of custard
pain d'épice gingerbread
parfait frozen mousse
petits fours sweetmeats; tiny cakes and
   pastries
profiteroles choux pastry balls, often filled
   with chocolate or ice cream
sablé shortbread
savarin a filled cake, shaped like a ring
tarte, tartelette tart, little tart
tarte tropézienne sponge cake filled with
   custard and topped with nuts
truffes chocolate truffles
yaourt yoghurt

Fromage (Cheese)
fromage de brebis sheep's cheese
cabécou sharp local goat's cheese
chèvre goat's cheese
doux mild
plateau de fromage cheese (board)
fromage blanc yoghurty cream cheese
fromage frais a bit like sour cream
fromage sec general name for solid
   cheeses
fort strong

Cooking Terms and Sauces
bien cuit well-done steak
à point medium steak
saignant rare steak
bleu very rare steak

Wine

One of the pleasures of travelling in France is drinking great wines for a fraction of what you pay at home, and discovering new ones you've never seen in your local shop. The south holds a special place in the saga of French wines, with a tradition dating back to the Greeks, who are said to have introduced an essential Côtes-du-Rhône grape variety called syrah, originally grown in Shiraz, Persia. Nurtured in the Dark and Middle Ages by popes and kings, the vineyards of Provence and Languedoc-Roussillon still produce most of France's wine – some graded only by its alcohol content.

aigre-doux sweet and sour
aiguillette thin slice
à l'anglaise boiled
à la bordelaise cooked in wine and diced vegetables
à la châtelaine with chestnut purée and artichoke hearts
à la diable in spicy mustard sauce
à la grecque cooked in olive oil and lemon
à la jardinière with garden vegetables
à la périgourdine in a truffle and foie gras sauce
à la provençale cooked with tomatoes, garlic and olive oil
allumettes strips of puff pastry
au feu de bois cooked over a wood fire
au four baked
auvergnat with sausage, bacon and cabbage
barquette pastry boat
beignets fritters
béarnaise sauce of egg yolks, shallots and white wine
broche roasted on a spit
chasseur mushrooms and shallots in white wine
chaud hot
cru raw
cuit cooked
diable spicy mustard or green pepper sauce
émincé thinly sliced
en croûte cooked in a pastry crust
en papillote baked in buttered paper
épices spices
farci stuffed
feuilleté flaky pastry
flambé set aflame with alcohol
forestière with bacon and mushrooms
fourré stuffed

frais, fraîche fresh
frappé with crushed ice
frit fried
froid cold
fumé smoked
galantine cooked food served in cold jelly
galette puff pastry case or pancake
garni with vegetables
(au) gratin topped with browned cheese and breadcrumbs
grillé grilled
haché minced
hollandaise a sauce of egg yolks, butter and vinegar
marmite casserole
médaillon round piece
mijoté simmered
mornay cheese sauce
pané breaded
pâte pastry, pasta
pâte brisée shortcrust pastry
pâte à chou choux pastry
pâte feuilletée puff pastry
paupiette rolled and filled thin slices of fish or meat
parmentier with potatoes
pavé slab
piquant spicy hot
poché poached
pommes allumettes thin chips (fries)
raclette melted cheese with potatoes, onions and pickles
salé salted, spicy
sucré sweet
timbale pie cooked in a dome-shaped mould
tranche slice
vapeur steamed
véronique grape, wine and cream sauce
vinaigrette oil and vinegar dressing

If a wine is labelled AOC (*Appellation d'Origine Contrôlée*) it means that the wine comes from a certain defined area and is made from certain varieties of grapes, guaranteeing a standard of quality. *Cru* on the label means vintage; a *grand cru* is a great, noble vintage. Down the list in the vinous hierarchy are those labelled VDQS (*Vin de Qualité Supérieure*), followed by *Vin de Pays* (guaranteed at least to originate in a certain region), with *Vin Ordinaire* (or *Vin de Table*) at the bottom, which is usually drinkable and cheap. In a restaurant if you order a *rouge* (red), *blanc* (white) or *rosé* (pink), this is what you'll get, either by the glass (*un verre*), by the quarter-litre (*un pichet*) or bottle (*une bouteille*). Brut is very dry, *sec* dry, *demi-sec* and *moelleux* are sweetish, *doux* sweet, and *méthode champenoise*, sparkling.

Miscellaneous

addition bill (check)
baguette long loaf of bread
beurre butter
carte non-set menu
confiture jam
couteau knife
crème cream
cuillère spoon
formule à 12€ €12 set menu
fourchette fork
fromage cheese
huile (d'olive) olive oil
lait milk
menu set menu
nouilles noodles
pain bread
œufs eggs
poivre pepper
sel salt
service compris/non compris service included/not included
sucre sugar
vinaigre vinegar

Snacks

chips crisps
crêpe thin pancake
croque-madame toasted ham and cheese sandwich with fried egg
croque-monsieur toasted ham and cheese sandwich
croustade small savoury pastry
frites chips (French fries)
gaufre waffle
jambon ham
pissaladière a kind of pizza with onions, anchovies, etc.
sandwich canapé open sandwich

Boissons (Drinks)

bière (pression) draught beer
bouteille (demi) half-bottle
brut very dry
chocolat chaud hot chocolate
café coffee
café au lait white coffee
café express espresso coffee
café filtre filter coffee
café turc Turkish coffee
citron/orange pressé(e) fresh lemon/orange juice
demi a third of a litre
doux sweet (wine)
eau (minérale, non-gazeuse ou gazeuse) water (mineral, still or sparkling)
eau-de-vie brandy
eau potable drinking water
gazeuse sparkling
glaçons ice cubes
infusion, tisane (camomille, verveine, tilleul, menthe) herbal tea (camomile, verbena, lime flower or mint)
jus juice
lait milk
menthe à l'eau peppermint cordial
moelleux semi-dry
mousseux sparkling (wine)
pastis anis liqueur
pichet carafe
pression draught
ratafia home-made liqueur made by steeping fruit or green walnuts in alcohol or wine
sec dry
sirop d'orange/de citron orange/lemon squash
thé tea
verre glass
vin blanc/rosé/rouge white/rosé/red wine

Some of Provence's best-known wines grow in the ancient places near the coast, especially its quartet of tiny AOC districts Bellet, Bandol, Cassis and Palette. But the best-known wines of the region come from the Rhône valley, under the general heading of Côtes-du-Rhône, including Châteauneuf-du-Pape, Gigondas, the famous rosé Tavel and the sweet muscat apéritif wine, Beaumes-de-Venise. Elsewhere, wine-makers have made great strides in boosting quality in the past 30 years, recognized in new AOC districts.

You can save money by buying direct from the producer (or a wine co-operative, or *syndicat*, a group of producers). Note that when you go tasting, each wine you are offered will be older than the previous one until you are feeling quite jolly and ready to buy the oldest (and most expensive) vintage. On the other hand, some sell loose wine *à la* petrol pump – *en vrac*; many *caves* even sell the little plastic barrels to put it in, so you can either bottle it yourself or take home to quaff as is (just don't leave it more than a couple of weeks, especially in the summer, or it will go off).

Travel

06

Before You Go

A little preparation will help you get much more out of your holiday in the south of France. Check the Calendar of Events (*see* pp.82–4) to help decide where you want to be and when, and book your accommodation well in advance for festival times.

If you plan to stay in one area, look on the websites of the local tourist offices listed in the text or write to them for complete lists of self-catering accommodation, hotels and campsites in their areas, or else contact one of the many companies in the UK or USA (*see* pp.91–2).

For more general information and a complete list of tour operators, get in touch with a French Government Tourist Office, or check the Maison de la France website (*www. franceguide.com*). See also *www.aito.co.uk* and *www.holidayfrance.org.uk*.

French Tourist Offices/ Maison de la France Abroad

Australia: Level 20, 25 Bligh St, Level 22, NSW 2000 Sydney, **t** (02) 9231 5244.

Canada: 1981 Ave MacGill College, Suite 490, Montreal, H3A 2W9, **t** (514) 876 9881; Maison de la France, 30 St Patrick St, Suite 700, Toronto M5T 3A3, **t** (416) 593 6427.

Ireland: 30 Merrion St, Dublin 2, **t** (01) 662 9345.

UK: 178 Piccadilly, London W1J 9AL, **t** 09068 244123 (calls charged at 60p/min).

USA: 444 Madison Ave, New York, NY 10022, **t** (410) 838 7800; John Hancock Center, Suite

Airline Carriers

UK and Ireland

Fares on low-cost carriers are highly competitive, changing frequently and at short notice depending on season, special offers or promotions. Shop around and try to book ahead; bear in mind that quoted prices usually exclude airport taxes. For price comparisons on the Internet, see *www. attitudetravel.com/france/lowcostairlines*, *www.traveljungle.co.uk, www.opodo.uk* or *www.majortravel.co.uk.*

Air France, t 0845 0845 111, *www.airfrance.co.uk.* 3–4 direct flights a day from Heathrow to Nice, and via Paris to Toulon, Toulouse and Montpellier, plus up to 3–4 flights daily from Heathrow, Gatwick and London City (with City Jet) to Marseille via Paris or Nantes.

British Airways (BA), t 0870 850 9 850, *www.ba.com.* Up to four flights a day to Nice from Heathrow, Gatwick or Manchester; up to three flights a day to Marseille and Toulouse from Gatwick; plus one flight a day to Montpellier from Gatwick, London City, Manchester and Glasgow.

British Midland (BMI), t 0870 607 0555, *www. flybmi.com.* Up to two flights a day to Nice from London Heathrow with connections via Heathrow from Belfast, Dublin, Edinburgh, Glasgow, Leeds, Manchester and Teesside. Daily flights from Manchester to Toulouse.

bmibaby, t 0870 264 2229, *www.bmibaby. com.* Two flights a day to Nice departing from Nottingham East Midlands airport, plus two flights a week to Toulouse departing from Nottingham East Midlands Airport and Cardiff.

easyJet, t 0905 821 0905 (65p/min), *www. easyjet.com.* Up to four flights a day to Nice from Gatwick, Stansted, Luton, Bristol, Newcastle, Belfast and Liverpool airports, and two a day from Gatwick to Marseille and Toulouse.

Flybe, (UK) t 0871 700 0535 (10p/min), (Ireland) **t** 1890 925 532, *www2.flybe.com.* From Southampton and Birmingham to Toulouse and Perpignan, and Bristol to Toulouse.

Flyglobespan.com, t 0870 747 3330, *www. flyglobespan.com.* Low-cost scheduled flights to Nice from Edinburgh and Glasgow, May–Oct.

Jet 2, t 0871 2261 737, *www.jet2.com.* Daily flights in summer from Leeds Bradford and Manchester to Nice.

GB Airways, t 0870 850 9 850, *www.gbair-ways.co.uk.* BA franchise flights ('in the style of' BA flights) from Gatwick to Montpellier.

Ryanair, t 0871 246 0000, *www.ryanair.com.* Regular once-daily budget flights from London Stansted to Montpellier, Perpignan and Carcassonne, and from Stansted, Luton and Liverpool to Nîmes.

3214, 875 North Michigan Ave, Chicago, IL 60611, t (312) 751 7800; 9454 Wilshire Bd, Suite 715, Beverly Hills, CA 90212, t (310) 271 6665; 1 Biscayne Tower, Suite 1750, 2 South Biscayne Bd, Miami, Fl 33131, t (305) 373 8177.

Useful Web Addresses

www.france.com
www.avignon-et-provence.com
www.provencetourism.com
www.provenceweb.fr
www.visitprovence.com
www.visit-riviera.com
www.provencebeyond.fr
www.angloinfo.com
www.hotelstravel.com
www.francekeys.com
www.frenchconnections.co.uk

Getting There

By Air

The main international airports in the south of France are at Nice, Marseille, Montpellier, Nîmes, Carcassonne, Perpignan and Toulouse. Thanks to no-frills airlines such as easyJet and Ryanair in the UK, plus deregulation and the disintegration of state monopolies, prices are becoming more competitive. Budget flights are usually cheaper if booked early and on-line – last-minute bookings don't tend to be much less expensive than flights by major carriers. Shop around and book ahead, especially in the summer and at Easter.

There are a number of charters from London to Nice and Marseille and a good selection of

Thomson Fly, t 0870 1900 737, *www.thomson fly.com*. Coventry to Marseille and Nice.

USA and Canada

Air France, USA t 800 237 2747, Canada t 800 667 2747, *www.airfrance.us*. Regular services to Paris from numerous cities.

American Airlines, t 800 433 7300, t 800 543 1586 (TDD), *www.aa.com*. Flights to Paris from Boston, Chicago, Dallas, JFK, Miami, San Diego and San Francisco.

British Airways, t 800 AIRWAYS, *www.ba.com*. Up to seven flights a day from New York to Paris via London. Up to two flights a day from San Francisco to Paris via London.

Continental, USA and Canada t 800 231 0856, t 800 343 9195 (hearing), *www.continental. com*. Flights to Paris from Houston and Newark.

Delta, USA and Canada t 800 241 4141, t 800 831 4488 (TDD), *www.delta.com*. Flights to Paris from Atlanta, Boston, Chicago, Cincinnati, Houston, Los Angeles, New York, Philadelphia and San Francisco.

Icelandair, t 800 223 5500 ext 2 prompt 1, *www.icelandair.com*. Flights to Paris from Baltimore, Boston, Minneapolis, Orlando and Philadelphia, with a stopover in Reykjavik.

Northwest Airlines, t 800 447 4747 (24hr), t 800 328 2298 (hearing impaired), *www.nwa.com*. Flights to Paris from Detroit.

United Airlines, t 800 538 2929, t 800 323 0170 (TDD), *www.united.com*. Flights to Paris from Chicago, Denver, Los Angeles, Miami, Philadelphia, San Francisco and Washington.

Charters, Discounts, Students and Special Deals

UK and Ireland

Besides saving 25% on regular flights, people under the age of 26 have the choice of flying on special discount charters. Students with the relevant ID cards are eligible for considerable reductions, not only on flights but also on trains and admission fees to museums, concerts and more.

Agencies specializing in student and youth travel can supply ISICs (International Student Identity Cards).

Check websites including: *www.cheap flights.co.uk; www.lastminute.com; www. expedia.co.uk; www.majortravel.co.uk*.

Budget Travel, 134 Lower Baggot St, Dublin 2, t (01) 631 1111 *www.budgettravel.ie*.

Club Travel, 30 Lower Abbey St, Dublin 1, t (01) 435 0016 within Eire, *www.club travel.ie*.

Europe Student Travel, 6 Campden St, London W8, t (020) 7727 7647. A small travel agent catering to non-students too.

both scheduled and low-cost flights from UK regional airports, but from most other points of departure – North America, Australia, etc. – it's often cheaper to fly to Paris, and from there catch a cheap flight or train.

There are domestic flights on Air France from Orly in Paris to Marseille, Toulouse and Nice and, less frequently, Nîmes, Perpignan, Montpellier and Hyères-Toulon. Services may be less frequent in winter.

By Train

Airport awfulness makes France's **high-speed TGVs** (*trains à grande vitesse*) an attractive (but not necessarily cheaper) alternative. **Eurostar** trains (t 08705 186 186, *www.eurostar.com*) leave from London Waterloo/Ashford International in Kent, and there are direct connections to Paris Gare du Nord (2hrs 35mins) and Lille (1hr 40mins). In summer (*July–Sept*) there are also direct Eurostar journeys from Waterloo to Avignon. The journey takes 6½hrs; fares are non-refundable and non-changeable; be sure to book ahead. As a general rule of thumb, fares on the Eurostar are cheaper if booked at least 7 or 14 days in advance, best at 21 days' notice and if you include a Saturday night away. Check in at least 30mins before departure or you will not be allowed on to the train.

In Paris, go to the Gare de Lyon for a TGV to the south. France's TGVs shoot along at the average of 180mph when they're not breaking world records, and the journey from Paris' Gare de Lyon to Marseille or Montpellier takes only 4½ hours; 3½ hours to Avignon; 6½ hours to Nice. Costs are only minimally higher

---

STA, 6 Wright's Lane, London W8 7RG, *www.statravel.co.uk*, t 0870 1 600 599, with 65 branches throughout the UK.

Trailfinders, 194 Kensington High St, London W8, t (020) 7937 1234, *www.trailfinders.co.uk*.

United Travel, 2 Old Dublin Rd, Stillorgan, County Dublin, t (01) 215 9300, *www.unitedtravel.ie*.

USA and Canada

If you're resilient, flexible and/or youthful and prepared to shop around for budget deals on stand-bys or even courier flights (you can usually only take hand luggage on the latter), you should be able to get yourself some rock-bottom prices. Check the *Yellow Pages* for courier companies.

For discounted flights, try the small ads in newspaper travel pages (for example, *New York Times*, *Chicago Tribune*, and *Toronto Globe and Mail*). Numerous travel clubs and agencies also specialize in discount fares, but they may require you to pay an annual membership fee; see *www.traveldiscounts.com* and *www.smarterliving.com*.

Airhitch, t 877 247 4482, *www.airhitch.org*. Last-minute discount tickets to Europe.

Last Minute Travel Club, USA/Canada t 800 442 0568 *www.lastminutetravel.com*. Annual membership entitles you to cheap stand-by deals, special car rental rates in Europe and Europass train tickets.

New Frontiers, 5757 West Century Bd, Suite 650, Los Angeles, CA 90045, t 800 677 0720, *www.newfrontiers.com*. Low-cost scheduled transatlantic flights, also package holidays, hotels, discount rail passes, budget car rental, etc.

STA, t 800 777 0112 *www.statravel.com*, with branches at most universities and at 10 Downing St, New York, NY 10014, t (212) 627 3111, and ASUC Travel Center, Martin Luther King Jr Building, 2nd Floor, University of California, Berkeley, CA 94720, t (510) 642 3000.

Travel Avenue, t 800 333 3335, *www.travelavenue.com*. The oldest rebate travel agency; you arrange your tour, they book it and share the commission.

TFI, 34 West 32nd St, New York, NY 10001, t 800 745 8000, *www.lowestairprice.com*. Low-cost negotiated fares, offering discounts of up to 80% on flights with Air France, Continental, Northwest, Virgin Atlantic, Northwest Airlines, US Airways and Icelandair. .

Travel Cuts, 187 College St, Toronto, Ontario ON M5T 1P7, t (866) 246 9762 or toll free t 800 592 CUTS from the USA, *www.travelcuts.com*. Canada's largest student travel specialists with branches in most provinces, plus 14 branches in the USA, including Portland, San Francisco, Stanford, LA, San Diego, New York and Seattle WA.

on a TGV. Another pleasant, if slower, way of getting south is by overnight sleeper after dinner in Paris. Some weekday departures require a very small supplement; all require a seat reservation, which you make when you buy your ticket or at the station before departure. People under 26 are eligible for a 30% discount on fares if they have an ISIC or other student ID card, and there are also discounts if you're 60 or over, available from major travel agents.

If you plan to take some long train trips, it may be worth investing in a rail pass (see *www.raileurope.co.uk/railpasses*). The excellent-value **Euro Domino** pass entitles European citizens of at least 6 months to unlimited rail travel through France for 3–8 days in a month for £138–342, or £100–196 for 12–25-year-olds.

Other alternatives include the **Inter-Rail** pass (for European residents of at least 6 months), offering 16 days' unlimited travel through France, Belgium, the Netherlands and Luxembourg (Zone E) from £159 (under-26s) or £223 (26 or over). They include 50% discounted fares on some cross-Channel ferries plus reduced fares on Eurostars (from £40 London–Calais or £50 London–Paris one way). Cards are not valid on trains in the UK.

Passes for North Americans include the **France Railpass**, giving 4 days' unlimited travel throughout the country in any one month for $218–252 (less if 2 people are travelling together) including special rates on Eurostar and an option to purchase 6 extra days if required. The equivalent **France Youthpass** entitles under-26s to 4 days' unlimited travel through France over a 1-month period including reduced rates on Eurostar, for $164–189. There's also the 6-day **Rail 'n' Drive** pass, giving 2 days' unlimited 1st-class rail travel through France and 2 days' car rental for $249–439.

Also for non-Europeans, the **Eurail Pass** allows unlimited 1st-class travel through 17 European countries for 15, 21, 30, 60 or 90 days; it saves the hassle of buying numerous tickets but will only pay for itself if you use it a lot; a 15 day Eurailpass Youth costs $414; 26-year-olds and over can get a 15-day Eurail Pass for $588, a 21-day pass for $762, 30 days for $946, or 3 months for $1,654; all fares include discounted fares on Eurostar plus free or discounted travel on selected ferries, lake steamers, boats and buses. Passes are not valid in the UK, Morocco or countries outside the European Union. There are other combinations of passes available, such as for couples travelling together. See the **Rail Europe** website for full details. Rail Europe handles bookings for all services, including Eurostar and Motorail, sells rail passes and acts for other continental rail companies.

UK: 178 Piccadilly, London W1, **t** 08708 371371 *www.raileurope.co.uk*.

USA and Canada: **t** 877 257 2887 (US), or **t** 800 361 RAIL (Canada), *www.raileurope.com*. Visitors from outside North America are serviced by general sales agents in their respective countries (see the website for more details).

Also check out the independent train travel website *www.seat61.com*.

By Coach

National Express Eurolines offers services from London to Avignon (17½hrs), Aix-en-Provence (20hrs) and Marseille (20½hrs). There are up to 4 services a week and tickets start at £66 (book 30 days ahead), £77 (book 15 days ahead) or £92 (standard return to Avignon).

Information and bookings: **t** 08705 808080, **t** (0121) 423 8479 (disabled people), *www.nationalexpress.com*

By Car

Taking your car on a **Eurotunnel** train is a convenient (if fairly costly) way of crossing the Channel between the UK and France. It takes only 35mins to get through the tunnel from Folkestone to Calais; you remain in the car, although you can get up to stretch your legs. Fares start from around £125 for a standard return in low season, rising substantially in summer and high seasons. The price for all tickets is per car less than 6.5m in length and 1.85m high, plus the driver and all passengers.

In mid-April–mid-Oct **Motorail** offers up to 6 departures a week from Calais to Avignon or Nice. Accommodation is compulsory, in a 4-berth (1st-class) or 6-berth (2nd-class) carriage. Linen is provided, along with washing facilities. Compartments are not segregated by sex.

Eurotunnel: Information and bookings t 08705 35 35 35, *www.eurotunnel.com*.

Motorail: Contact Rail Europe on t 08702 415415, *www.raileurope.co.uk/ frenchmotorail*.

If you prefer a dose of bracing sea air, you've plenty of choice, although changes and mergers may be on the horizon and crossing may cost significantly more than travelling by air or rail. The shortest ferry/ catamaran crossing from the UK is currently **Dover–Calais** with P&O Ferries, SeaFrance or (the fastest) Hoverspeed.

P&O also operates Newhaven–Dieppe; **Hoverspeed** operates a Folkestone–Bologne crossing, and **Brittany Ferries** operates between Plymouth and Roscoff in Brittany, Portsmouth–Caen, Cherbourg and St Malo, and Poole–Cherbourg. **Condor Ferries** sail between Poole or Weymouth and St-Malo, and between Poole and Cherbourg May–Sept, and Portsmouth-Cherbourg from July–Sept. **P&O North Sea Ferries** has a Hull–Zeebrugge route, which entails about a 45min drive to France.

Prices vary considerably according to season and demand so shop around for the best deal. For information and bookings contact:

Brittany Ferries, t 08703 665 333, *www.brittanyferries.com*.

Condor Ferries, t 0845 345 2000 *www.condorferries.co.uk*.

Hoverspeed: t 0870 240 8070, *www.hoverspeed.co.uk*.

P&O Ferries: t 08705 20 20 20, *www.poferries.com* (for up-to-date travel info call the weatherline, t 0871 200 2444).

SeaFrance: t 08705 711711, *www.seafrance.com*.

See also *www.ferrybooker.com* for both ferry and Eurotunnel bookings.

If you're driving down from the UK, you can either go through or around Paris, or take the A26 via Reims and Troyes. The *autoroutes* will get you south the fastest, but be prepared to pay some €50–100 in tolls; the N7 south of Paris takes longer, but costs nothing. For toll charges and route information, see *www. autoroutes.fr*. For information on driving rules and regulations, *see* 'Getting Around', p.72.

Entry Formalities

Passports and Visas

Holders of EU, US, Canadian, Australian, New Zealand and Israeli passports do not need a visa to enter France for stays of up to 3 months; most other nationals do. Apply at your nearest French consulate.

The most convenient visa is the *visa de circulation*, allowing for multiple stays of 3 months over a 3-year period. If you intend to stay for longer, the law says that non-EU citizens need a *carte de séjour*.

The creeping rise of xenophobic legislation in France means that non-EU citizens had best apply for an extended visa prior to leaving home – a complicated procedure requiring proof of income, etc. You can't get a *carte de séjour* without the visa.

Customs

Those arriving from another EU country do not have to declare goods imported into France for personal use if they have paid duty on them in the country of origin. In theory, you can buy as much as you like, provided you can prove the purchase is for your own use and not for other purposes (e.g. selling on to friends). In practice, customs will be more likely to ask questions if you buy in bulk, e.g. more than 3,200 cigarettes or 400 cigarillos, 200 cigars or 3kg of tobacco; plus 10 litres of spirits, 90 litres of wine and 110 litres of beer. Travellers caught importing any of the above for resale will have the goods seized along with the vehicle they travelled in, and could face imprisonment for up to seven years.

Travellers from outside the EU must pay duty on goods worth more than €175 that they import into France.

Travellers from the USA are allowed to bring home, duty-free, goods to the value of $800, including 200 cigarettes or 100 cigars; plus one litre of alcohol. For more information, call the US Customs Service. You're not allowed to bring back absinthe or Cuban cigars.

French Customs, *www.douane.gouv.fr*.

UK Customs, t 0845 010 9000, *www.hmce.gov.uk*.

US Customs, t (202) 354 1000, *www.customs. gov*; see the pamphlet *Know Before You Go*.

Getting Around

By Train

Call the SNCF nationwide information number, t 08 92 35 35 35 (€0.50 a minute), or go to www.sncf.com.

The **SNCF** runs a decent and efficient network of trains through the major cities of the south, with an added service called the **Métrazur** that links all the resorts of the Côte d'Azur from Menton to St-Raphaël as often as every half-hour in the peak summer season, and the SNCF's **Petit Train Jaune** from Villefranche-de-Conflent to Latour-de-Carol in the Pyrenees, with bus connections at either end to Perpignan and Andorra.

The narrow-gauge **Train des Pignes** operated by the Chemin de Fer de Provence (French rail passes are valid, other passes are granted a 50% discount) from Nice to Digne is worth taking for the mountain scenery (see p.311).

If you plan on making only a few long hauls, the **France Railpass** (*see* p.69) will save you money. Other possible discounts hinge on the exact time of your departure. The SNCF has divided the year into **blue (off-peak)** and **white (peak) periods**, based on demand: white periods run from Friday noon to midnight Saturday, and from Sunday 3pm to Monday 10am and during holidays (all stations give out little calendars; *see* box below for more on the complicated system of discounts).

Tickets must be stamped in the little orange machines by the entrance to the lines that say *Compostez votre billet* (this puts the date on the ticket). Any time you interrupt a journey until another day, you have to re-compost your ticket. Long-distance trains (*trains Corail*) have

---

Discount Rail Fares in France

Découverte discounts are free, but only available on tickets booked in advance. The annual *cartes* must be paid for. Ask about extra perks with the *cartes*, such as Avis car hire, hotel discounts, and discounts on Corsica ferries and travel to other European countries.

Découverte Enfant + This is free, issued in the name of a child under 12, and allows a 25% discount for the child and up to four other unrelated people on daytime TGVs and night berths on *trains Corail* (in any period but subject to availability); plus also seats on daytime *trains Corail*, sleeping cars and TERs departing in a *période bleue* only.

Découverte 12–25 Young people are eligible for a 25% discount on daytime TGVs and night berths on *trains Corail* (in any period but subject to limited availability); plus also seats on daytime *trains Corail*, sleeping cars and TERs departing in a *période bleue*.

Découverte Senior 25% off the journey for those over 60, on the same trains as the Enfant + and 12–25 above.

Découverte Séjour If you book a return ticket in advance, depart in a *période bleue* and travel at least 200km and stay away a Saturday night, you get a 25% discount.

Découverte à Deux If up to nine people (related or not) book a return trip together in advance, and stay away at least one night, they are eligible for a 25% discount in first or second class for journeys in blue periods.

Carte Enfant + This is bought in the name of a child under 12, and allows the child and up to four unrelated people 50% discount on daytime TGVs and night berths on *trains Corail* (in any period but subject to availablity), plus also 50% discount on seats on daytime *trains Corail*, sleeping cars and TERs departing in a *période bleue* and booked in advance; or 25% when the 50% seats are gone, or when departing in a *période blanche*, or when tickets are bought on the train. Children under 3 with this *carte* travel free and get a seat.

Carte 12–25 Gives young people aged 12–25 50% discount on daytime TGVs and night berths on *trains Corail* (in any period but subject to limited availablity), plus also 50% discount on seats on daytime *trains Corail*, sleeping cars and TERs departing in a *période bleue* and booked in advance; or 25% when the 50% seats are all gone, or when departing in a *période blanche*, or when tickets are bought on the train. This card offers 25% off journeys to 27 countries, 25% off Eurostar fares, plus other perks.

Carte Senior People over 60 can purchase an annual card offering the same discounts as the Carte 12–25 but also including reclining seats on night *trains Corail*.

snack trolleys and bar/cafeteria cars; some have play areas.

Nearly every station has large computerized **lockers** (*consigne automatique*) which take a while to puzzle out the first time; note that any threat of terrorist activity in France tends to close them down across the board.

By Bus

Do not count on seeing much of rural France by public transport. The bus network is barely adequate between major cities and towns (places often already well served by rail) and rotten in rural areas, where the one bus a day fits the school schedule, leaving at the crack of dawn and returning in the afternoon; more remote villages are linked to civilization only once a week or not at all. Along the Côte d'Azur and from towns such as Nice to Vence and Grasse the services are more efficient.

Buses are run either by the SNCF (replacing discontinued rail routes) or private firms. Rail passes are valid on SNCF lines, which generally coincide with trains. Private bus firms, especially when they have a monopoly, tend to be a bit more expensive than trains; some towns have a *gare routière* (coach station), usually near the train station, though many lines start from any place that catches their fancy.

By Car

Unless you plan to stick to the major cities, a car is unfortunately the only way to see most of Provence and Languedoc. This has its drawbacks: high car rental rates and petrol prices, and an accident rate double that of the UK (and much higher than the USA). Though **roads** are generally excellently maintained, anything of less status than a departmental route (D-road) may be uncomfortably narrow. Mountain roads are reasonable except in the vertical department of Alpes-Maritimes, where they inevitably follow old mule tracks. Shrines to St Eloi, patron of muleteers, are common here, and a quick prayer is a wise precaution.

A car entering France must have its **registration and insurance papers**. **Green cards** are no longer compulsory but are worth getting as they give fully comprehensive cover – your home insurance may only provide minimum cover. Drivers with a valid licence from an EU country, Canada, the USA or Australia don't need an **international licence**.

If you're coming from the UK or Ireland, the dip of the car **headlights** must be adjusted to the right. Carrying a **warning triangle** is not mandatory (unless you don't have hazard warning lights) but is advisable; it should be placed 50m behind the car if you have a breakdown.

Blue **'P'** signs will infallibly direct you to a village or town's already full car park. Watch out for the tiny signs that indicate which streets are meant for pedestrians only (with complicated schedules in even tinier print); and for Byzantine street **parking** rules (which would take pages to explain – do as the natives do, and be especially careful about village centres on market days).

Petrol (*essence*) is relatively expensive in France. The cheapest place to buy petrol is at the big supermarkets; the most expensive is on motorways. Petrol stations keep shop hours (*most close Sun and/or Mon, plus lunchtimes*) and are rare in rural areas, so replenish your fuel supply before making any forays into the mountains. Unleaded is *sans plomb*; diesel is *gazole* or *gasoil*. Automated machines functioning outside these hours don't currently accept foreign debit/credit cards. If you come across a garage with attendants, they will expect a tip for oil, windscreen-cleaning and air.

Speed limits are 130km/80mph on the *autoroutes* (toll motorways); 110km/69mph on dual carriageways (divided highways); 90km/55mph on other roads; 50km/30mph in an 'urbanized area' – as soon as you pass a white sign with a town's name on it and until you pass another sign with the town's name barred. Fines for speeding, payable on the spot, are high (from €200), and can be astronomical (up to €4,500) if you fail a breathalyser test.

If you wind up in an **accident**, the procedure is to fill out and sign a *constat amiable*. If your French isn't sufficient to deal with this, hold off until you find someone to translate for you so you don't accidentally incriminate yourself. If you have a **breakdown** and are a member of a motoring club affiliated with the Touring Club de France, ring the latter; if not, telephone the police (**t** 17).

France used to have a rule of giving **priority to the right** at every intersection. This has largely disappeared, although there may still be intersections, usually in towns, where it applies – these will be marked. Watch out for the *Cédez le passage* (give way) signs and be careful. Generally, as you'd expect, drive on the right, give priority to the main road, and to the left on roundabouts. When you (inevitably) get lost in a town or city, the *toutes directions* or *autres directions* signs are like Get Out of Jail Free cards.

Europ Assistance, t 0870 737 5720, *www.europ-assistance.co.uk*. Help with car insurance for abroad.

Useful Websites

Mappy route planner: *www.iti.fr*.
Autoroute information: *www.route. equipement.gouv.fr*; *www.equipement. gouv.fr* (includes information in English).
Road and traffic information: *www.asf.fr, www.autoroutes.fr, www.saprr.fr*.

Car Hire

If you plan to stay for 3 weeks or more, consider leasing a car. Car hire in France can be an expensive proposition. To save money, look into air and holiday package deals, as well as

---

Car Hire

UK

Avis, t 08700 100287, *www.avis.co.uk*.
Budget, t 08701 539170, *www.budget.com*.
easyCar, t 0906 33 33 33 3 (60p/min), *www.easycar.com*.
Europcar, t 0870 607 5000, *www.europcar.com*.
Hertz, t 08708 448844, *www.hertz.co.uk*.
Thrifty, t 01494 751600, *www.thrifty.co.uk*.

USA and Canada

Auto Europe, t 1 888 223 5555, *www.autoeurope.com*.
Avis Rent a Car, t 800 230 4898 (USA), t 800 272 5871 (Canada), t 800 331 2323 (hearing impaired), *www.avis.com*.
Europe by Car, t 800 223 1516, *www.europebycar.com*.
Europcar, t 877 940 6900, *www.europcar.com*.
Hertz, t 800 654 3131 (USA), t 800 854 3001 (international toll free number), *www.hertz.com*.

---

combination 'Train & Auto' rates. Prices vary widely from firm to firm: beware the small print about service charges and taxes. It's often cheaper to book through car hire companies in your own country before you go.

The **minimum age** for hiring a car in France is around 21 to 25, and the maximum around 70. Car hire firms are also listed for the larger towns in this book. For an instant online price comparison, log on to *www.autosabroad.com*, or call t 0870 066 77 88.

By Boat

The major towns, as well as the islands, along the Côte d'Azur are linked by regular boat services. These come in handy, especially in the summer when travelling by road is hot purgatory. Most are included in the text; just look for signs near the port for the *gare maritime*. In Languedoc, *see* the 'Getting Around' sections for Narbonne and Béziers for information on cruises and boat rentals on the Canal du Midi and the lagoons.

Yacht, motorboat and sailing-boat charters are big business, especially along the Riviera. Companies and individual owners hire them out by the hour or day (or, in the case of yachts, by the week or fortnight). The average cost per week for a 50ft yacht that sleeps six, including food, drink and all expenses is €13,700 – about what six people would pay for a week in a luxury hotel. Contact individual tourist offices for lists of firms or try Camper & Nicholsons, 25 Bruton Street, London W1J 6ZQ, t (020) 7491 2950, *www.cnconnect.com*.

Books on sailing in the area include *Reed's Mediterranean Navigator* (Thomas Reed Publications) and *South France Pilot* by Robin Brandon (Imray Laurie). For canal boats, *see* Special-interest Holidays box, p.75.

By Bicycle

Cycling spells more pain than pleasure in most French minds, and one of the hazards of driving in the Alps and Pyrenees is suddenly coming upon bands of cyclists pumping up the kinds of inclines that most people require escalators for. If you mean to cycle in the summer, start and stop early to avoid heatstroke. French drivers, not always courteous to fellow motorists, usually give cyclists a wide berth; and yet on any given summer day, half the patients in a French hospital are from accidents on two-wheeled transport. Consider a helmet. Also beware that bike thefts are fairly common, especially along the Côte d'Azur.

Getting your own bike to France is fairly easy: Air France and British Airways carry them free from Britain, for example. From the USA or Australia, most airlines will carry them as long as they're boxed and are included in your total baggage weight. In all cases, telephone ahead to the relevant airline to check on terms and conditions. On Eurostar cross-Channel trains, passengers travelling direct to Paris/ Brussels or direct to Avignon (summer only) may take a bike with them provided it can be folded and carried on board in a bicycle bag (front wheel removed, etc). The bike will count as one item of your baggage allowance; for further information see *www.eurostar.com*.

The French are keen cyclists and if you haven't brought a bike, main towns and holiday centres always seem to have at least one shop that hires them out – local tourist offices have lists. A *vélo tout terrain* (abbreviated to VTT) is a mountain bike. You may want to enquire about insurance against theft.

You can also hire bikes from most SNCF train stations in major towns; they vary in quality, so check them. The advantage of hiring from a station is that you can drop the bike back off at another, as long as you specify where when you hire it. Rates should be around €9 a day, with a deposit of up to €80 or the yielding of a credit card number. Avoid the busy N roads as far as possible.

Certain French trains (*autotrains*, with a bicycle symbol in the timetable) carry bikes for free; otherwise you have to send them as registered luggage and pay a fee of around €49, for delivery within 48hrs (though delays are common).

Maps and cycling information are available from the **Fédération Française de Cyclotourisme**, 12 Rue Louis Bertrand, 94207 Ivry-sur-Seine, t 01 56 20 88 88, *www.ffct.org*, or in Britain from the **Cyclists' Touring Club**, Cotterell House, 69 Meadrow, Godalming, Surrey GU7 3HS, t 0870 873 0060, *www. ctc.org.uk. See* also the list of special-interest holiday companies, pp.75–6.

On Foot

A network of long-distance paths or *Grandes Randonnées* (GRs, marked by distinctive red and white signs) take in some of the most beautiful scenery in the south of France. Each GR is described in a *Topoguide*, with maps and details about camping sites, refuges and so on, available in local bookshops. An English translation covering several GRs in the region, *Walks in Provence*, is available from Stanfords, Long Acre, London WC2E 9LP, t (020) 7836 1321. Otherwise, the best maps for local excursions, based on ordnance surveys, are put out by the Institut Géographique National and are available in most French bookshops.

There are 5,000km of marked paths in the Alpes Maritimes alone. Of special interest are: **GR5** from Nice to Aspremont, the Gorges de la Vésubie and St-Dalmas-Valdeblore; **GR52** from Menton up to Sospel, the Vallée des Merveilles and St-Dalmas-Valdeblore; **GR52a** and **GR5** through Mercantour National Park, both of which are open only from the end of June to the beginning of October. **GR51**, nicknamed 'the balcony of the Côte d'Azur', from Castellar (near Menton) takes in the Esterel and Maures before ending at Bormes-les-Mimosas.

In Provence, **GR9** begins in St-Tropez and crosses over the region's most famous mountains: Ste-Baume, Ste-Victoire, the Lubéron and Ventoux. **GR4** crosses the Dentelles de Montmirail and Mont Ventoux en route to Grasse; and **GR6** crosses much of the area in this book, from the Alps through the Vaucluse and Alpilles, to Beaucaire and the Pont du Gard, before veering north up the river Gard on to its final destination by the Atlantic. **GR42** descends the west bank of the Rhône from near Bagnols-sur-Cèze to Beaucaire. Most tourist information centres have maps and leaflets on walks in the area.

The Pyrenees are magnificent walking country, and the ideal way to take in the beauties of the Corbières and famous citadels of the Cathars from Padern, Peyrepertuse and Puilaurens to Montségur is by way of Le Sentier Cathare, well marked and endowed with places to eat and stay en route. The Geocentre map of Southern France is a good guide to walks in the region. Other walks in the mountains are covered in the excellent book *Randonnées pyrénéennes* by J. L. Sarret.

Special-interest Holidays

There are a number of ways to combine a holiday with study or a special interest. For information, contact the French Centre, 164–8 Westminster Bridge Rd, London SE1 7RW, t (020) 7960 2600, *www.cei-frenchcentre.com*; or the Cultural Services of the French Embassy, 23 Cromwell Rd, London SW7, t (020) 7073 1300, *www.ambafrance-uk.org*, or 972 Fifth Ave, New York, NY 10021, t (212) 439 1400, *www.info-france-usa.org*.

For language courses, see the Worldwide Classroom site at *www.worldwide.edu*.

In France

Alliance Française, 2 Rue de Paris, 06000 Nice, t 04 93 62 67 66, f 04 93 85 28 06, *www.alliance-francaise-nice.com*. French classes on all levels. Courses last a month, but they can and will tailor to your needs.

Atelier du Safranier, 2 bis Rue du Cannet, 06600 Vieil Antibes, t 04 93 34 53 72, *www.chez.com/ateliersafranier/*. Year-round courses in painting, engraving, lithography, etc., and watercolour on a boat.

Cercle d'Echanges Interculturels et Linguistiques Avignon (CEILA), 16 Impasse Jean-Pierre Gras, 84000 Avignon, t 04 32 76 39 94, *www.avignon-et-provence.com/ceila/*. Specialises in linguistics, conversational French and French as a foreign language.

Echanges Culturels Internationaux (ECI), 62 Av Maréchal de Lattre de Tassigny, 13097 Aix-en-Provence, t 04 42 21 07 68, *www.asso.fr*. As the Cercle d'Echanges.

L'Ecole du Moulin, Restaurant L'Amandier, Place Cdt. Lamy, Mougins 06250, t 04 93 90 00 91. *www.aurendezvous-mougins.com*. Week-long Cuisine du Soleil cookery courses under the auspices of Roger Vergé Inc.

Institut de Paléontologie Humaine, 1 Rue René Panhard, 75013 Paris, t 01 43 31 62 91, f 01 43 31 22 79. Palaeontology students or fans can spend a minimum of 15 or 30 days excavating caves in southeast France (address your letter to Professor Henry de Lumley).

Association Neige et Merveilles, Hameau de la Minière de Vallauria, 06430 St-Dalmas-de-Tende, t 04 93 04 62 40, *www.neige-merveilles.com*. Chalets plus occasional courses in archaeology and restoration; also pony-trekking and walks for schools.

Routes de la Lavande, 2 Av de Venterol, 26110 Nyons, t 04 75 26 65 91, *www.routes-lavande.com*. All things lavender.

Vedel – Cuisine et Tradition School of Provençal Cuisine, 11 Rue Portagnel, 13200 Arles, t 04 90 49 69 20, *www.cuisine provencale.com*. Courses in Provençal cuisine.

From the UK

ACE Study Tours, Babraham, Cambs CB2 4AP, t (01223) 835 055, *www.study-tours.org*. Tours include 'Art in the Côte d'Azur', 'Aix to Arles', and the Aix-en-Provence music festival.

Alternative Travel Group (ATG), 69–71 Banbury Rd, Oxford OX2 6PE, t (01865) 315678, *www.atg-oxford.co.uk*. Escorted walking tours tracking down the painters and gardens of Provence, or independent walking and cycling along continuous routes.

Andante Travels, Grange Cottage, The Old Barn, Old Road, Alderbury, Salisbury SP5 3AR, t (01722) 713800, *www.andantetravels.co.uk*. Archaeological and historical study tours led by experts in the field.

Arblaster and Clarke, Farnham Rd, West Liss, Hamps GU33 6JQ, t (01730) 893344, *www.arblasterandclarke.com*. Luxury tours covering all the major wine regions.

Chalfont Line Holidays, t (01895) 459 540 f (01895) 459 549 *www.chalfont-line.co.uk*. Slow-paced escorted coach or individual holidays for disabled and elderly people.

Connoisseur Holidays Afloat, t 0870 160 5648, *www.connoisseurafloat.com*. Cruises along the Camargue's Canal du Rhône and Canal de la Robine, with its pink flamingos.

Destination Provence, The Travel Centre, 5 Bishopthorpe Road, York YO23 1NA, t (01904) 622 220, f (01904) 651 991, *www.destination provence.co.uk*. Self-catering villas and hotels: special interest golf, walking, cycling, cooking and self-drive discovery tours.

Equity Total Travel, 47 Middle St, Brighton BN1 1AL, t (01273) 277 377, *www.equity.co.uk*. Group tours by coach, also tailor-made individual holidays.

Euro Academy, 67–71 Lewisham High St, London SE13 5JX, t (020) 8297 0505 f (020) 8297 0984 *www.euroacademy.co.uk*. French language courses in Nice and Antibes: also politics, art and literature, culture.

Fleur Holidays, 4 All Hallows Road, Bispham, Blackpool, FY2 0AS, t 0870 750 21213,

f (01253) 595151, *www.fleur-holidays.co.uk*. Camping and walking holidays in Provence.

French Golf Holidays, The Green, Blackmore, Essex CM4 ORT, **t** (01277) 824100, *www.frenchgolfholidays.com*. Fly-drive golf holidays.

Headwater Holidays, Old School House, Chester Rd, Castle, Northwich, Cheshire, CW8 1LE, **t** (01606) 720099, *www.headwater.com*. Cycling and walking tours, with a Luberon wine tour and a Provence coastal walk.

InnTravel, nr Castle Howard, York YO60 7JU, **t** (01653) 617788, *www.inntravel.co.uk*. Walking and riding in hilltop villages of the Luberon and Lure, plus walks, hotels and short breaks in Roman and Haute Provence.

Jacaranda Travel, **t** (01962) 776996, *www.jacarandatravel.co.uk*. Three-night motor-yacht rental on the Côte d'Azur.

Martin Randall, 10 Barley Mow Passage, London W4 4GF, **t** (020) 8742 3355, *www.martinrandall.com*. Lecturer-accompanied cultural tours.

Page & Moy, 136–40 London Road, Leicester LE2 1EN, **t** 08708 334012 **f** 08700 106 449, *www.page-moy.com*. Escorted, expert-led tours, e.g. 'Southern France – from Coast to Coast', 'Côte d'Azur and Menton'.

Peter Deilmann River & Ocean Cruises, **t** (020) 7436 2931, *www.peter-deilmann-river-cruises.co.uk*. Sailing/cruises on the Rhône.

Plantagenet Tours, 85 The Grove, Moordown, Bournemouth BH9 2TY, **t** (01202) 521 895, *www.plantagenettours.com*. Cultural tours with subjects including the Crusades, Roman remains and the troubadours.

Sherpa Expeditions, 131a Heston Rd, Hounslow, Middlesex TW5 0RF, **t** (020) 8577 2717, *www.sherpa-walking-holidays.co.uk*. Walks, cycling and treks.

Susi Madron's Cycling for Softies, 2-4 Birch Polygon, Rusholme, Manchester M14 5HX, **t** (0161) 248 8282, *www.cycling-for-softies.co.uk*. Luxurious gourmet cycling holidays in Provence and the Camargue.

Travel for the Arts, **t** (020) 8799 8350, *www.travelforthearts.co.uk*. Visits to the Aix-en-Provence music festival.

Waymark Holidays, 44 Windsor Rd, Slough SL1 2EJ, **t** (01753) 516477, *www.waymarkholidays.com*. Walking tours, centre-based in Provence and Languedoc-Roussillon.

Winetrails, Vann Lake, Ockley, Dorking, Surrey, RH5 5NT, **t** (01306) 712111, *www.winetrails.*

co.uk. Six-night walking or cycling holidays through the olive groves of Avignon to Mont Ventoux and Maussane, staying in 1- or 2-star hotels.

From the USA

Abercrombie & Kent, 1520 Kensington Rd, Oak Brook, IL 60523, **t** 800 554 7016, *www.abercrombiekent.com*. Quality city and country breaks, including 'Provence and the French Riviera', also barging and river cruises along the Rhône and rail tours along the Côte d'Azur.

Adventure Center, 1311 63rd St, Suite 200, Emeryville, CA 94608, **t** 800 228 8747, *www.adventurecenter.com*. Eight-day hiking trips for moderate walkers across the mountains of Haute Provence, taking in some rocky terrain (luggage transported).

Backroads, 801 Cedar St, Berkeley, CA 94701-1800, **t** 800 462 2848, *www.backroads.com*. Bicycling, hiking and multi-sport holidays in Provence and elsewhere.

Country Walkers, PO Box 180, Waterbury, VT 05676, **t** 800 464 9255, *www.countrywalkers.com*. Walking holidays in summer, in Provence and elsewhere, led by expert local guides; also culinary tours.

Cross Country International, PO Box 1170, Millbrook, NY 12545, **t** 800 828 8768, *www.equestrianvacations.com*. Horse-riding in Provence, including the Camargue.

Dailey-Thorp Travel, PO Box 670, Big Horn, Wyoming, 82833, **t** 800 998 4677, *www.daileythorp.com*. Luxury escorted music tours, including the music festival at Aix-en-Provence and the opera at Nice.

DuVine Adventures, 124 Holland St, Suite 2, Somerville, MA 02144, **t** 888 396 5383, *www.duvine. com*. Six-night deluxe cycling tours through French vineyards with gourmet cuisine.

Europe Train Tours, 2485 Jennings Rd, Olin, NC 28660, **t** 800 551 2085, *www.etttours.com*. Escorted tours by train and car.

Horizons New England Crafts Program, PO Box 634, Leverett, MA 61054, **t** (413) 367 9200, *http://horizons-art.com*. Week-long crafts courses in Venasque.

International Curtain Call, 3313 Patricia Ave, Los Angeles, CA 90064, **t** 800 669 9070, *www.iccoperatours.com*. Opera and music tours, including Paris–Avignon–Aix-en-Provence.

Practical A–Z

07

Climate and When to Go

Provence and Languedoc have a basically Mediterranean climate, one wafted by winds that give it a special character. The most notorious is the mistral (from the Provençal *mistrau*, or master – supposedly sent by northerners jealous of the south's climate), rushing down the Rhône and gusting east as far as Toulon and west to Narbonne, sparing the hot-house of the Côte d'Azur. On average the mistral blows 100–150 days a year, nearly always in multiples of three, except when it begins at night. It is responsible for the dryness in the air and soil (hence its nickname, *mangio fango*, or mud-eater). Houses in its line of fire are built *pointes en avant*, at an angle, the north side blank and in the shade, protected by cypresses, while on the south side plane trees protect the house from the strong sun. It blows so hard that it can drive people mad: an old law in Provence acquitted a murderer if it could be proved that he killed his victim while the mistral was blowing. But the mistral has its good points: it blows away harmful miasmas and pollution from the Rhône and makes the stars radiantly clear, as alive as in Van Gogh's painting *Starry Night*.

Besides the Master, there are 22 other winds, most importantly: the *levant*, the east or southeasterly 'Greek' wind which brings the much desired rain; the *pounent*, or west wind; and the suffocatingly hot sirocco from Africa. The region from the Spanish border to Montpellier is occasionally bulldozed by the *tramontane*, the 'Catalan wind' from the northwest.

Rainfall varies widely across the south. The Pyrenees get more rain than most places on this planet – over 2m a year (Prats de Mollo,

with 838mm in 16 hours, holds the local record) – while the Camargue barely gets 500mm a year, the least rainfall in France. In the average year, it rains as much in Nice (750mm per year) as in Brest and more in Marseille than Paris. In the heart of Provence it rains much less frequently – not at all in the summer, and violently in spring and autumn (up to 135mm in an hour) – hence the *restanques*, or terraces carved in the hills by the farmers to prevent erosion.

Each season has its pros and cons. In January all the tourists are in the Alps or Pyrenees; in February the mimosa and almonds bloom on the Côte d'Azur. In April and May you can sit outside at restaurants and swim, and within an hour's drive ski at Auron or Isola 2000. By June, the mistral is slowing down and the resorts begin to fill up; walking is safe in the highest mountains. July and August are bad months, when everything is crowded, temperatures and prices soar (Perpignan has the highest average summer temperatures in France), and tempers flare, but it's also the season of the great festivals in Avignon, Aix, Juan-les-Pins and Nice. Once French school holidays end in early September, prices and crowds decrease with the temperature. In October the weather is traditionally mild on the coast, although torrential downpours and floods are not unknown; the first snows fall in the Pyrenees and Alps. November is another bad month; it rains and many museums, hotels and restaurants close down. December brings Christmas tourists and the first skiers.

Consulates and Embassies

Canada Nice: 10 Rue Lamartine, t 04 93 92 93 22, *www.amb-canada.fr*.

Average Temperature Chart in °C (°F)

	Jan	Feb	Mar	April	May	June	July	Aug	Sept	Oct	Nov	Dec
Avignon	7 (44)	7 (44)	11 (52)	15 (59)	17 (62)	21 (70)	23 (73)	25 (77)	23 (73)	16 (61)	10 (50)	8 (45)
Nice	11 (52)	12 (54)	14 (56)	17 (62)	20 (69)	22 (72)	24 (75)	26 (79)	25 (77)	20 (69)	16 (61)	13 (55)
Perpignan	12 (54)	12 (54)	13 (55)	17 (62)	20 (69)	23 (73)	28 (82)	28 (82)	26 (79)	20 (69)	16 (61)	14 (56)

Ireland: Antibes: 'Les Chênes Verts', 152 Bd J-F
Kennedy, t 04 93 61 50 63.
UK: Marseille: 24 Av du Prado, t 04 91 15 72 10;
Nice: 26 Av Notre Dame, t 04 93 62 13 56;
www.amb-grandebretagne.fr.
USA: Marseille: Place Varian Fry, t 04 91 54
92 00; Nice: 7 Av Gustave V, t 04 93 88 89 55,
www.amb-usa.fr.
Australia: Paris: 4 Rue Jean Rey, 75724 Paris
Cedex 15, t 01 40 59 33 00, *www.austgov.fr*.
New Zealand: Paris: 7 Rue Léonard de
Vinci, 75116 Paris, t 01 45 01 43 43, *www.
nzembassy.com*.

Crime and the Police

*Everyone in Marseille seemed most dishonest.
They all tried to swindle me, mostly with
complete success.*
Evelyn Waugh

There is a fair chance that you will be had in
the south of France, though probably not in
Marseille; thieves and pickpockets go for the
flashier fish on the Côte d'Azur. Road pirates
prey on motorists blocked in traffic; train
pirates prowl the overnight compartments
looking for handbags and cameras; car
bandits just love the ripe pickings in cars
parked in isolated scenic areas or tourist car
parks (they go for expensive or rental cars, the
latter discernible by their number plates, as
most are registered in *département* 51).

In the cities, beware the bands of Gypsy
children, who push sheets of cardboard in the
faces of their victims to distract them as they
go through their pockets. Although violence
is rare, the moral of the story is to leave
anything you'd really miss at home, carry traveller's cheques and insure your property,
especially if you're driving.

Report thefts to the nearest *gendarmerie*,
not a pleasant task but the reward is the bit of
paper you need for an insurance claim. If your
passport is stolen, contact the police and your
nearest consulate for emergency travel documents. Carry photocopies of your passport,
driver's licence, etc.; it makes it easier when
reporting a loss. By law, the police in France
can stop anyone anywhere and demand to see
ID; in practice, they only tend to do it to harass
minorities, the homeless and scruffy hippy

types. If they really don't like the look of you
they can salt you away for a long time without
any reason. The drug situation is the same in
France as anywhere in the West: soft and hard
drugs are widely available and the police only
make an issue of victimless crime when it
suits them (your being a foreigner just may
rouse them to action). Smuggling any amount
of marijuana into the country can mean a
prison term.

Disabled Travellers

When it comes to providing access for all,
France isn't exactly in the vanguard, but
things are beginning to change. All SNCF TGVs
are fully equipped to transport disabled
people; alternatively you can ask for an assistant to accompany you on your journey
(although you will have to pay for the assistant). For more information contact the French
Railways office in your country, or write to
Direction Grandes Lignes, 12 Rue Traversiere,
75012 Paris, or in France call t 08 00 15 47 53, or
t 08 92 35 35 39 (provides general information
in English).

The Channel Tunnel is a good way to travel
by car; on Eurotunnel trains passengers stay in
their vehicles, while Eurostar has a special
area reserved for wheelchair users and their
assistants (who can travel at reduced rates,
t 08705 186 186 for more information).

Ferry companies offer special assistance if
contacted beforehand. Vehicles modified for
disabled people are charged reduced tolls on
autoroutes. For more information contact the
Ministère des Transports, Grande Arche, Paroi
Sud, 92055 La Défense Cedex, Paris, t 01 40 81
21 22, *www.transports.equipement.gouv.fr*.

The *Gîtes accessibles aux personnes
handicapées*, published by Gîtes de France,
lists self-catering possibilities (*see* p.91 and
www.gites-de-france.fr).

France
Association des Paralysés de France, Siège
National, 17 Bd Auguste Blanqui, 75013 Paris,
t 01 40 78 69 00, *www.apf.asso.fr*. A national
organization with offices in all *départements*,
providing local information.
**Comité National Français de Liaison pour
la Réadaptation des Handicapés**, 236B Rue

Tolbiac, 75013 Paris, **t** 01 53 8066 66. Provides info on access, and produces useful guides to various regions in France.

UK

Access Travel, 6 The Hillock, Astley, Lancashire M29 7GW, **t** (01942) 88 88 44, *www.access-travel.co.uk*. Special air fares and car hire.

Chalfont Line Holidays, 4 Providence Rd, West Drayton, Middx, UB7 8HJ, **t** (01895) 459 540, *www.chalfont-line.co.uk*. Escorted or individual travel.

Holiday Care Service, 7th Floor, Sunley House, 4 Bedford Park, Croydon, Surrey CR0 2AP, **t** 0845 124 9971, *www.holidaycare.org.uk*. Publishes an information sheet on holidays for disabled and older people (£5).

RADAR (Royal Association for Disability and Rehabilitation), 12 City Forum, 250 City Rd, London EC1V 8AF, **t** (020) 7250 3222, *www.radar.org.uk*. Some travel information.

USA

Alternative Leisure Co, 165 Middlesex Turnpike, Suite 206, Bedford, MA 01730, **t** (718) 275 0023, *www.alctrips.com*. Organizes vacations abroad for disabled people.

Mobility International USA, PO Box 10767, Eugene, OR 97440, USA, **t/TTY** (541) 343 1284, *www.miusa.org*. Information on international educational exchange programmes and volunteer service overseas for the disabled.

SATH (Society for Accessible Travel and Hospitality), 347 5th Ave, Suite 610, New York, NY 10016, **t** (212) 447 7284, *www.sath.org*. Travel and access information.

Other Useful Contacts

Access Ability, *www.access-ability.co.uk*. Info on travel agencies catering to the disabled.

Access-Able Travel Source, *www.access-able.com*. A database of information, travel operators, cruise lines, hotels, etc. for disabled travellers.

Australian Council for Rehabilitation of the Disabled (ACROD), PO Box 60, Curtin, ACT 2605, Australia, **t/TTY** (02) 62 82 43 33, *www.acrod.org.au*.

Emerging Horizons, *www.emerginghorizons.com*. An international subscription-based on-line (or mailed) quarterly travel newsletter for people with disabilities.

Global Access, *www.geocities.com/Paris/1502*. An on-line network for disabled travellers.

> ### Restaurant Price Ranges
> *very expensive* over €60
> *expensive* €30–60
> *moderate* €15–30
> *cheap* under €15

Eating Out

In this guide, price ranges have been given for the set menu for one person that almost every restaurant offers in addition to its *à la carte* menu, or for an average two-course meal for one without wine (*see* box above). For more information about food and local specialities, *see* **Food and Drink**, pp.51–64.

Electricity

French electricity is all 220V. British and Irish appliances need an adapter with 2 round prongs; North American appliances usually need a transformer as well.

E-mail and Internet

Most cities and towns now have cybercafés, or you can often e-mail from the tourist office or your hotel, and from some post offices (using a France Telecom phonecard; *see* p.86).

Most French hotels and institutions happily give out their e-mail addresses (we've included them in the text if you can't e-mail via the website), but don't rely on this as your only means of communication with them – incoming mail is not always checked daily.

Environment

'Come to the Côte d'Azur for a change of pollution,' they say. Threatened by frequent oil spills, a suffocating algae mistakenly released into the sea at the Oceanographic Institute of Monte-Carlo, too many cars and too many people, the well-named 'California of Europe', from Marseille to Menton, may be the first place in southern Europe to achieve total ecological breakdown.

As elsewhere in the Mediterranean, a sad litany of forest fires heads the television news every summer. Most forests are pine – Aleppo pines in limestone, maritime pines in the

Maures and Esterel. Here they often close roads in the summer to decrease the chance of fires. Most fires are caused by twits with matches (you'll be more careful, won't you?), though many fires are deliberately started by speculators who burn off protected forests to build more holiday villas and suchlike. Fires often lead to erosion and flooding, though the local governments now do a good job of re-forestation. The weird wasteland of Blausasc, in a valley north of Nice (caused by greedy logging in the 1800s), shows what Provence would soon look like if they didn't.

The most spectacular environmental non-issue continues to be the overbuilding of the Côte d'Azur. The damage is done; one of the most exceptional parts of the Mediterranean coast has been thoroughly, thoughtlessly, irreparably ruined. Since the war there has simply been too much money involved for governments to act responsibly; most of the buildings you'll see were put up illegally – but there they are. Although this is changing – a politically connected developer near St-Tropez was recently forced to demolish an illegal, half-built project, and many of the makeshift beach huts on St-Tropez' Pampelonne beach are not long for this world – local govern-ments continue to promote industrial and tourist growth in areas where there is absolutely no room for it. Paris bureaucrats are as responsible as local politicians; they have insisted, for example, on pushing a new TGV route around the coast, bringing even more people to the area, instead of improving local transport and cutting down on the ferocious traffic they already have. The new route is a monster, cutting across scores of scenic areas and wine regions; citizen groups in the south fought it tooth and nail but the 'biggest construction site in Europe' is well under way.

Other enemies of the Midi include: the army, which has commandeered enormous sections of wilderness (Plan de Canjuers and parts of the Crau, Ile du Levant, Roussillon's Plateau d'Opoul) and regularly blows them to smithereens in manoeuvres and target practice; the nuclear industry, with France's nuclear research centre at Cadarache and most of its nuclear missiles hidden away on the Plateau de Vaucluse; the chancre coloré, a fungus that, like phylloxera, came from the USA (on wooden crates during the Second World War) and now threatens the lovely plane trees of Provence; and, finally, the villainous national electric company, EDF, which once tried to flood the Grand Canyon du Verdon. The one genuine contemporary ecological disaster is the Etang de Berre, now entirely surrounded by the industrial and suburban sprawl of Marseille, a ghastly horror of power pylons, pollution and speculative development. Here, too, the EDF is involved: heated water, pumped from their giant power plant into the lagoon, is killing off the few remaining fish. Local groups are fighting hard to make them stop.

In August ecological dysfunction reaches its apogee on the sands of St-Tropez's crowded beaches, laced with trash, condoms and human excrement, which explains why the resort lost its blue flag last year. But there's another side to the story – over a hundred miles of clean, underpopulated beaches in Languedoc and Roussillon, and a mountainous hinterland from the Italian border to the Spanish that is still mostly pristine and delightful. Nature-lovers can find everything they desire, and much that is new and strange – as long as they avoid the Côte d'Azur.

Festivals

The south of France offers everything from the Cannes Film Festival to the village fête, with a pilgrimage or religious procession, bumper cars, a pétanque tournament, a feast (anything from sardines to cassoulet to paella) and an all-night dance, sometimes with a local band but often a travelling troupe playing 'Hot Music' or some other electrified cacophony. Bullfights (see p.87) play a part in many fêtes or ferias from Spain to the Rhône. A bravade (as in St-Tropez) entails pistol or musket-shots; a corso is a parade with carts or floats. St John's Day (24 June) is a big favourite and often features bonfires and fireworks.

At Catalan festas you're bound to see the national dance, the sardana, a complex, circular dance that alternates 16 long steps with eight short ones, properly accompanied by a cobla, a band of a dozen instruments, some unique to Catalunya. In the southern Rhône valley, people still like to celebrate with

Calendar of Events

Note that dates change every year; for complete listings and precise dates of events, pick up a copy of the annual lists, available in most tourist offices, or consult the Côte d'Azur tourist office website, *www.crt-riviera.fr* (go to 'Actualités' then 'Agenda des Manifestations'), or see *www.francefestivals.com*, *www.whats onwhen.com* and *www.culture.fr*.

January

Sun nearest the 17th *Fête de St-Marcel*, folk-dancing and singing at **Barjols**; every four years (next 2006) Barjols does an ox roast

27 *Fête de Ste-Dévote*, **Monaco**

End of month Monte-Carlo rally

February

3 *Fête de St-Blaise*, festival of olives and late golden Servan grapes, **Valbonne**

Every Sun of month *Oursinades*, sea-urchin festival at **Carry-le-Rouet**

10 *Corso du Mimosa*, **Bormes-les-Mimosas**

15 days at Carnival *Fête du Citron*, **Menton**

Carnival Nice has the most famous festivities in France; traditional celebrations during the school break in **Prats-de-Mollo**. Other towns also celebrate, including **Aix-en-Provence**, **Nîmes**, **Arles**, **Aups**, **La Ciotat** and **Marseille**

March

4–5 Reconstruction of the landing of Napoleon, **Golfe-Juan**

5 *Fête de la Violette*, **Tourrettes-sur-Loup**

6 *Sea Bataille des Fleurs*, **Villefranche-sur-Mer**

26 *Festin des Courgourdons*, folklore and dried sculpted gourds, and folklore, **Nice**

April

International show-jumping, **Monaco**

International tennis tournaments, **Monaco** and **Nice**

Throughout month New-Orleans-les-Pins Jazz Festival, **Juan-les-Pins** and **Antibes**

Mid-month Parade of vintage cars, **Menton**

Mid-month *Fête du Miel* and parade of decorated floats, **Mouans-Sartoux**

Maundy Thurs *Procession de La Sanch*, **Perpignan**, **Collioure** and **Arles-sur-Tech**

Good Fri Procession of the Dead Christ, **Roquebrune-Cap-Martin**

Good Fri–Easter Bullfights, **Arles**

Easter Flower and sweets fair, **Villefranche-de-Conflent**

12–14 *Fête Votive de la St Marc*, with shows ans free balls, **Pernes-les-Fontaines**

24 *Fête de l'Oranger*, **Le-Bar-Sur-Loup**

25 Winegrowers' festival and blessing of the vines, **Châteauneuf-du-Pape**; *Fête de St-Marc*, **Villeneuve lez Avignon**

Last Sun *Fête des Gardians*, traditional rodeo in **Arles**

Last week Wine festival, **Châteauneuf-du-Pape**

May

Third week after Easter *Bravade St-François*, **Fréjus**

Second week Cannes Film Festival

Second weekend *Fête de la Rose*, **Grasse**

Sun after the 15th *Fête de St-Gens*, costumes, pistol shots, etc., **Monteaux**

15 *Fête de Ste Maxime*

16–17 *Bravade de St-Torpes*, **St-Tropez**

21 *Fête de St-Honorat*, traditional village festival with mass, parade and a dance, **Agay**

a *farandole*, a dance in 6/8 time with held hands or a handkerchief, which may be as old as the ancient Greeks. One-man musical accompaniment is provided by a little three-holed flute called a *galoubet*, played with the left hand, and a *tambourin*, a drum played with the right. Both *farandoles* and flamenco enliven the proceedings of the 24 May pilgrimage at Saintes-Maries-de-la-Mer, by far the best attended of all popular festivities in the south.

Health and Emergencies

Ambulance (SAMU) **t 15**
Police **t 17**
Fire **t 18**

Local hospitals are the place to go in an emergency (*urgence*). Doctors take turns on duty at night and on holidays, even in rural areas: ring one to listen to the recorded message to find out what to do. To be on the safe side, always carry a phonecard (*see* 'Telephones', p.86).

Third Sun Cherry Festival, **Le Luc-en-Provence**
Ascension weekend Festival of Ochre and Colour, **Roussillon**; **Monaco** International Grand Prix
24–25 Gypsy pilgrimage, **Saintes-Maries-de-la-Mer**
10 days at Pentecost *Cavalcade*, music festival, **Apt**
Late May–mid-July International music festival, **Toulon**

June

1 *Cérémonie du St-Vinage*, **Boulbon**
First Thurs to Sun *Voiles d'Antibes*, a regatta/promenade for vintage and classic sailboats, **Antibes**
15 *Bravade des Espagnols*, **St-Tropez**
Corpus Christi *Procession dai limaça*, **Gorbio**
21 *Fête des Gênets* (broom), **Roquebrune-Cap-Martin**; *Fête de la Musique*, with outdoor concerts, celebrated all over France.
23–24 *Fête de St-Jean*, with processions in **Entrevaux**; bonfires, dancing, and fireworks in **Perpignan**, **Céret** and **Villefranche-de-Conflent**
Last Sat Folklore festival of St Jean, **Entrevaux**, **Les Baux**
Last Sun *Fête de la Tarasque*, **Tarascon**; *Fête Provençale*, with blessings of animals, **Allauch** (near Marseille)
Late June–early July Festival International de Danse, **Montpellier**
Last half of June Jazz and chamber music in **Aix-en-Provence**

July

July–Aug International Fireworks Festival, **Monaco**; Festival of Early Music, **Entrevaux**;

Nuits de l'Empéri, theatre festival in **Salon**; Modern Music Festival, **St-Paul-de-Vence**; Festival of Dance, Music and Theatre, **Vaison-la-Romaine**; *Nuits de la Citadelle*, music and theatre in **Sisteron**; Côtes du Roussillon Wine Festival, **Perpignan**; *Rencontres Internationales d'Eté à la Chartreuse*, concerts, dance and theatre, **Villeneuve lez Avignon**
All month International Music Festival, **Vence**; Music Festival, **Carcassonne**; *Rencontres Internationales de la Photographie*, **Arles**; *Cocarde d'Or* festival of music, dance and drama, **Arles**; *Festival de la Sorgue*, music, theatre and dance at **Fontaine-de-Vaucluse** and around; *Festival de Marseille*, the city's largest party
4–14 *Festival Américain*, **Cannes**
First Sun *Fête de St-Eloi*, bullfights and a decorated cart pulled by 40 horses, **Châteaurenard**
First two weeks International Folklore Festival, **Marseille**
11 International athletics, Nikaïa, **Nice**
Second Sun *Fête de St-Pierre*, with water jousts, etc., **Cap d'Antibes** and **Villefranche-sur-Mer**; choral mass and boat-burning, **Nice**
Mid-July Jazz festivals in **Nice** and **Toulon**; *Corso de Nuit* for Notre-Dame-de-Santé, **Carpentras**; *Soirées Musicales*, **St-Maximin-la-Ste-Baume**; Film Festival, **La Ciotat**
10–23 *Nuits de la Danse*, festival of ballet in **Monte Carlo**
14 Fireworks, parties, *batailles des fleurs* and big celebrations in many places for Bastille Day. Nice has a Grand Banquet serving stockfish that runs along the Promenade

---

If it's not an emergency, pharmacists are trained to administer first aid and dispense free advice for minor problems. In rural areas there is always someone on duty if you ring the bell; in cities pharmacies are open on a rotating basis on Sundays and holidays, and addresses are posted in their windows and in the local newspaper.

In France, however you're insured, you pay up front for everything, unless it's an emergency, when you will be billed later. Doctors will give you a brown and white *feuille de soins* with your prescription; take both to the pharmacy and keep the *feuille* for insurance purposes at home. British subjects who are hospitalized and can produce their E111 forms will be billed later at home for 25–30% of the costs that French social insurance doesn't cover. All EU citizens should therefore bring an E111 with them (available from post offices). In the UK, see the Department of Health website *www.doh.gov.uk/traveladvice*.

Canadians may or may not be covered by their provincial health insurance; Americans and others should check their individual policies.

des Anglais; superb shows in **Avignon** and **Carcassonne**

Last three weeks Music Festival, **Aix**

Mid-July–mid-Aug International Theatre Festival, **Avignon**; *Festival Passion*, operettas, ballet and music in **Carpentras**

Last two weeks International Jazz Festival, **Juan-les-Pins**; music festival, **Orange**; fête in **Martigues**, with theatre, seafood, music

22–23 *Fête de la Lavande*, Ste-Agnès

Last Sun Donkey races and village fête, **Lacoste**

August

All month Chamber Music Festival, **Menton**; Music and Dance Festival, **Arles**

First two weeks Music and Theatre Festival, **Gordes**

First Sun Lavender Festival, **Digne**; *Fête de la Madeleine*, with parade of flowered carts, **Châteaurenard**; Jasmine Festival, **Grasse**

5 Passion procession, **Roquebrune**

9 and 11 *Fête de St-Laurent*, with bullfights, **Eygalières**

15 Village fête and operettas, **Le Thor**

Third week Provençal Festival, with processions, *bravades* and drama, **Séguret**

First Sun after 20th *Fête du Traou*, dancing and *polenta* feasts in **Tende**

Third week Provençal Wine Festival, **Séguret**

End of August *Fête de Saint-Louis*, with historical re-enactment, **Aigues-Mortes**

September

Vintage car rally, **Monte Carlo**

First Sunday *Festin des baguettes*, **Peille**

Second Sun Last bullfights of year, coinciding with *premices du riz* (rice harvest), **Arles**

3–5 *Fête du Bois*, **St-Martin-Vésubie**

12–16 Vintage car tour, **Nice**

16–22 Royal Yacht Regatta, **Cannes**

Third weekend *Journées du Patrimoine*, special events across the region to showcase national treasures and free entry to museums

Last week–first week Oct *Nioulargue*, yacht race in **St-Tropez**

October

Throughout month *Fête de la Châtaigne*, **Collobrières** and other villages in the Massif des Maures

Thoughout month *Fête de la Châtaigne*, **St-Paul-de-Vence**

Early Oct *Fête des Vendanges* to celebrate grape harvest, various locations

Mid-Oct *Fête-Votive*, with Provençal bullfights, in **Aigues-Mortes**

November

Last Fri *Foire St-Siffrein*, with truffle market, **Carpentras**

Last Sun *Foire des Santons*, until Epiphany, in **Marseille**

December

All month Festival of Italian Cinema, **Nice**; Music Festival, **Marseille**

Last two weeks *Fête des Lumières*, **St-Raphaël**

24 Midnight Mass in **St-Maximin-la-Ste-Baume**, **Séguret** and **Fontvieille**, with shepherds at **Allauch**, near Marseille; midnight Mass in the Arènes, **Nîmes**; Fête des Bergers and midnight Mass, **Les Baux**; torchlight vigil, **Séguret**

All nationalities should consider taking out a more comprehensive travel insurance policy before leaving home. Beware that accidents resulting from sports are rarely covered by ordinary insurance.

Media

There are plenty of English-language papers available at the local *tabac*. Local papers include the *Riviera Times*, **t** 04 93 27 60 00, *www.rivieratimes.com*, and the *Riviera*

Reporter, **t** 04 93 45 77 19 (*www.riviera-reporter.com*). Riviera Radio is on 106.5 FM; and there is an English language website of the region: *www.angloinfo.com*.

Money and Banks

Euros come in denominations of €500, 200, 100, 50, 20, 10 and 5 (banknotes) and €2, €1, 50 cents, 20 cents, 10 cents, 5 cents, 2 cents and 1 cent (coins). For the latest exchange rates, see *www.xe.com/ucc*.

Travellers' cheques are the safest way of carrying money, but the wide acceptance of credit and debit cards and the presence of ATMs (*distributeurs de billets*), even in small towns, make cards a convenient alternative. Visa (Carte Bleue; a direct debit bank card in France) is the most readily accepted credit card; American Express is often not accepted. Smaller hotels and restaurants and B&Bs may not accept cards. Some shops and supermarkets have difficulty reading older UK-style, pre chip-and-pin magnetic strips; French cards contain a chip with ID information, and the holder keys in a PIN number. UK cards are switching to this model currently during 2005, but in the meantime arm yourself with cash just in case, or use the following phrase:

'*La puce n'est pas activée.*'

Some places may ask to see your passport or other ID when you pay by credit card.

Under the Cirrus system, withdrawals in euros can be made from bank and post office ATMs, using your usual PIN. The specific cards accepted are marked on each machine; most give instructions in English. Banks and credit card companies charge a fee for cash advances, but rates are often better than those at banks themselves.

Exchange rates vary, and most banks and *bureaux de change* take a commission of varying proportions. *Bureaux de change* that do nothing but exchange money, hotels and train stations usually have the worst rates or take the heftiest commissions. It's always a good idea to buy some euros before you go, especially if you arrive at the weekend.

For bank opening hours, *see* right.

Lost Cards

In the event of lost or stolen credit cards, call the following 24hr emergency numbers:
American Express, Paris, **t** 01 47 77 77 00.
Barclaycard, **t** (00 44) 1604 230230 (UK no.)
Diners Club, Paris, **t** 01 49 06 17 50.
Mastercard, **t** 0800 901387 or **t** 01 45 67 84 84
Visa (Carte Bleue), Paris, **t** 01 42 77 11 90.

Opening Hours, Museums and National Holidays

Shops: While many shops and supermarkets in Marseille, Nice and other large cities now open continuously Tues–Sat from 9 or 10am to 7 or 7.30pm, businesses in smaller towns still close for lunch from 12 or 12.30pm to 2 or 3pm (4pm in summer). There are local exceptions, but nearly everything shuts on Mon, except grocers and *supermarchés*, which open in the afternoon. In many towns, Sunday morning is a big shopping time. Markets (daily in cities, weekly in villages) usually run mornings only, except clothes, flea and antiques markets.

Banks: Banks generally open 8.30am–12.30pm and 1.30–4pm. They close on Sun, and most either on Sat or Mon as well.

Post offices: Post offices are open in cities Mon–Fri 8am–7pm and Sat 8am–noon. In villages, offices may not open until 9am, then break for lunch and close at 4.30 or 5pm.

Museums: Most museums close for lunch, and often all day Mon or Tues, and sometimes for all of Nov or the entire winter. Hours change with the season: longer summer hours begin in May or June and last until the end of Sept – usually. Most museums close on national holidays. We've done our best to include opening hours in the text, but some change their hours every month, so call in advance if you're making a special trip. Most museums give discounts on admission (which ranges from €2–10) if you have a student ID card, or are an EU citizen under 18 or over 65. National museums are free if you're under 18. The third weekend of Sept is usually the *Journées du Patrimoine*, when state-owned museums throw open their doors to the public for free (or at least reduced) entry to give everyone a taste of France's national heritage. Though queues can spiral around the museums and the hordes have to shuffle past the national treasures, everyone is very cheerful at the thought of a freebie, and nobody seems to mind not seeing very much.

Churches: Churches are usually open all day, or closed all day and only open for Mass. Sometimes notes on the door direct you to the *mairie* or priest's house (*presbytère*) to pick up the key. There are often admission fees for cloisters, crypts and special chapels.

On **national holidays** (*see* box), banks, shops and businesses close; some museums do too, but most restaurants stay open. The French have a healthy approach to holidays; if there is a holiday on a Wednesday, they often 'make a bridge' (*faire le pont*) to the weekend, and take Thursday and Friday off too.

Post Offices and Telephones

Known as La Poste, post offices (for opening times, *see* p.85) are discernible by their sign of a blue bird on a yellow background. Larger offices are equipped with special machines for you to weigh and stamp your package, letter or postcard without having to even see a real person. They are surprisingly easy to use, with an English-language option. You can receive letters *poste restante* at any post office; the postal codes in this book should help your mail get there in a timely fashion. To collect it, take some ID; you may have to pay a small fee. You can purchase stamps in tobacconists (*tabacs*) as well as post offices.

Nearly all public telephones have switched from coins to *télécartes*, which you can buy at any post office or news-stand for €7.40 for 50 *unités* or €14.75 for 120 *unités*. You can also use your credit card like a phonecard.

The French have eliminated area codes, giving everyone a 10-digit number. If **ringing France from abroad**, the international dialling code is 33, and drop the first 'o' of the number.

For **international calls** from France, dial 00 then the country code (UK 44; Ireland 353; US and Canada 1; Australia 61; New Zealand 64), and then the local code (minus the 0 for UK numbers) and number.

The easiest way to reverse charges is to spend a couple of euros ringing the number and giving your number in France, which is always posted by public phones; alternatively, ring your national operator (for the UK dial 00 33 44; for the USA 00 33 11). For **directory enquiries**, dial **t** 12, or see *www.pagesjaunes.fr* (the *Yellow Pages* website).(for the UK dial 00 33 44; for the USA 00 33 1). For international enquiries call **t** 32 12.

Mobile phones tend to work nearer the towns; in rural areas it can be difficult to get a connection. Arrange international roaming with your operator before you leave home.

Racism

Unfortunately, in the south of France the forces of bigotry and reaction are strong enough to make racism a serious concern. The rise of the National Front in France has created a particularly febrile atmosphere of late, with towns such as Orange censoring books and reducing funds to ethnic minority associations. We've heard some horror stories, especially about Marseille, Nice, Toulon and Roussillon, where campsites and restaurants suddenly have no places if the colour of your skin doesn't suit the proprietor; the bouncers at clubs will inevitably say it's really the cut of your hair or trousers they find offensive. If any place recommended in this book is guilty of such behaviour, please write and let us know; we will not only remove it in the next edition, but forward your letter to the regional tourist office and relevant authorities in Paris.

Shopping

Some villages have more boutiques than year-round residents, but their wares are rarely compelling. Traditional handicrafts have all but died out, and attempts to revive them have resulted in little model houses and *santons*, terracotta Christmas crib figures dressed in 18th-century Provençal costumes, usually as artful as the concrete studies of the

Seven Dwarfs sold at your local garden centre. Every town east of the Rhône has at least one boutique specializing in Provençal skirts, bags, pillows and scarves, printed in intense colours with floral, paisley or geometric designs. Block-print fabrics were first made in Provence after Louis XIV, wanting to protect the French silk industry, banned the import of popular Indian prints. Clever entrepreneurs in the papal-owned Comtat Venaissin responded by producing cheap imitations still known today as *indiennes*. The same shops usually sell the other essential bric-a-brac of the south – dried lavender pot-pourri, sachets of *herbes de Provence* (nothing but thyme and bay leaves) and perfumed soaps.

Big name French and Italian designers and purveyors of luxury goods have boutiques at Cannes, Monaco and Nice. Moustiers, Vallauris and Biot have hand-made ceramics, and in Provence at least a million artists wait to sell you their works. Fontaine-de-Vaucluse has a traditional paper and stationery industry; Cogolin specializes in pipes and saxophone-reeds; Grasse sells perfumes and essential oils.

The sweet of tooth will find western Provence and the Côte d'Azur heaven. Nearly every town has its own speciality: candied fruits in Apt and Nice; the chocolates and *calissons* (marzipan candies shaped like little boats) of Aix; *berlingots* (mint-flavoured caramels) in Carpentras; *nougats* in Vence; *marrons glacés* in Collobrières; orange-flavoured chocolates called *papalines* in Avignon (known as *grimaldines* in Cagnes); and creamy *Tarte Tropézienne* in St-Tropez.

In Roussillon, look out for striped, hard-wearing Catalan fabrics, especially tablecloths and napkins, and locally made espadrilles. On the coast, buy jars of Collioure anchovies.

Sports and Leisure Activities

Bullfights

The Roman amphitheatres at Nîmes and Arles had hardly been restored in the early 1800s when they once again became venues for *tauromachie*. Attempts to abolish the sport in the 1900s fell flat when the poet Frédéric Mistral, the self-appointed watchdog of all things Provençal, intervened; if anything, bullfights are now more popular than they ever were.

However, the most traditional bullfights in Provence and Languedoc are not bloody. The *courses provençales* (or *courses libres*) can be traced back to the bull games described by Heliodorus in ancient Thessaly. Played by daring young men dressed in white called *razeteurs*, the sport demands grace, daring and dexterity, especially in leaping over the barriers before a charging bull. The object is to remove a round cockade from between the horns of the bull (or cow) by cutting its ribbons with a blunt razor comb – a sport far more dangerous to the human players than the animals. The animals used for the *courses provençales* are the small, lithe, high-horned breed from the Camargue; good sporty ones retire with fat pensions.

You will see three other types of bullfight advertised. *Corrida* is the traditional Spanish bullfight, where the bull is put to death. The bullfighters are usually Spanish as well, and the major festivals, or *ferias*, bring some of the top *toreros* to France, although beware that the already expensive tickets tend to be snapped up by touts. A *novillada*, pitting younger bulls against apprentice *toreros* (*novilleros*), is less expensive, but much more likely to be a butchery void of *arte*. In a *corrida portuguaise* the bullfighter (*rejoneador*) fights from horseback, but doesn't kill the bull.

Pétanque

Like *pastis* and olive oil, *pétanque* is one of the essential ingredients of the Midi; even the smallest village has a rough, hard court under the plane trees for its practitioners – nearly all male, although women are welcome to join in. Similar to *boules*, the rules of *pétanque* were, according to tradition, developed in La Ciotat, near Marseille. The object is to get your metal ball closest to the marker (*bouchon* or *cochonnet*). Tournaments are frequent and well attended.

Rugby Union

Rugby is the national sport of Languedoc and the southwest, cradle of most of the players on the national team (although movements to change one of the Five Nations from

France to Occitania have so far fallen flat). Although the best teams lately have been Toulouse, Agen and Bordeaux, you can still see fiery matches in Béziers, long-time champions (the town has three rugby schools), and Carcassonne. Nice and Toulon also have impressive sides. In some places they play 'Cathar rugby' – 13 to a side instead of 15.

Horse-riding

Every tourist office has a list of *centres hippiques* or *centres équestres* that offer group excursions, though if you prove yourself an experienced rider you can usually head down the trails on your own.

The Camargue, with its many ranches, cowboy traditions and open spaces, is the most popular place to ride in the region, and there are increasing numbers of stables in the Alps for those who want to follow lonesome mountain trails. Most of the posher country inns can also find you a horse.

See also p.75–6, 'Special-interest Holidays'.

Skiing

Ideally, if the weather ever decides to settle down, you can do as in California: ski in the morning and bake on the beach in the afternoon. The biggest resorts in the Alpes Maritimes are Isola 2000, Auron and Valberg and, closest to Nice, Gréolières-les-Neiges. On the Mediterranean end of the Pyrenees, there's Font-Romeu, although snowfall has been just as unreliable there in recent years. Hence package deals going from abroad are practically non-existent.

Comité Régional du Tourisme Provence– Alpes–Côte d'Azur, CMCI, B.P. 46214 – 13567 Marseille, Cedex 02, t 04 91 56 47 00 *www.crt-paca.fr.*

Fédération Française de Ski, 50 Rue des Marquisats, B.P. 2451, 74011 Annecy Cedex, t 04 50 51 40 34, *www.ffs.fr.*

Association Nationale des Maires de Stations de Montagne, 61 Bd Haussmann, 75008 Paris, t 01 47 42 23 32, *www.skifrance.fr.*

Canoeing and Kayaking

The **Fédération Française de Canoë-Kayak,** t 01 45 11 08 50, *www.ffck.org,* is the national centre for information. Some of the most dramatic rafting and canoeing is down the Grand Canyon du Verdon (*see* pp.315–16), but the journey requires considerable experience and considerable portage. Another disadvantage is that the electric company may be playing with the water.

Fishing

You can fish in the sea without a permit as long as your catch is for local consumption. Freshwater fishing requires an easily obtained permit from a local club; tourist offices can tell you where to find them.

Sailing

Most of the resorts along the southern coast have sailing schools and boats to hire. You can get a complete list from the **Fédération Française de Voile,** 17 Rue Henri Bocquillon, 75015 Paris Cedex, t 01 40 60 37 00, *www.ffvoile.org.*

Water Sports and Beaches

In 1763 the consumptive English writer and doctor Tobias 'Smelfungus' Smollett tried something for his health that shocked the doctors in Nice: he went bathing in the sea. Most extraordinary of all, it made him feel better, and he recommended that people follow his example, although it would be difficult for women 'unless they laid aside all regards to decorum' – as they so often do in the most fashionable resorts. There are scores of fine, sandy beaches along the coast, although *not* on the Riviera east of Juan-les-Pins. Anyone who arrives with the idea that access to the sea is a natural God-given right will be appalled to learn that paying concessions occupy most of the Provençal shore; free, quiet beaches require more effort (the *calanques* west of Cassis, the coves below the Esterel and the Maures, the Hyères islands).

Languedoc-Roussillon is a completely different story: less glamour, but more miles of free sandy beaches than anywhere in the western Mediterranean, stretching into the horizon on either side of its scores of small resorts – until you reach the rocky Côte Vermeille, at any rate. Areas are always set aside for *les naturistes*, or nudists: Cap d'Agde and the Ile du Levant are two of Europe's biggest nudist resorts.

Every town on the coast hires out equipment for water sports, often for hefty prices. Juan-les-Pins claims to have invented water skiing. Experienced windsurfers head for Brutal Beach off Cap Sicié, west of Toulon.

The best diving is off Ile Port-Cros National Park For a list of diving clubs, contact the **Fédération Française d'Etudes et de Sports Sous-Marins**, 24 Quai de Rive Neuve, 13284 Marseille, **t** 04 91 33 99 31, **f** 04 91 54 77 43, *www.ffessm.fr.*

If you're genuinely jaded and have a weakness for medical-psychobabble, you can even indulge in *thalassothérapie* to help make you thin, fit, stress-free, or even turn you into a laid-back non-smoker.

Time

France is 1 hour ahead of GMT, 6 hours ahead of US Eastern Standard Time, 9 hours ahead of Pacific Coast Time and 9 hours behind Sydney. Summer time (daylight-saving time) begins and ends on the same dates as in Britain (end of Mar and end of Oct).

Tourist Information

Every city and town, and most villages, have a tourist information office, usually called a *Syndicat d'Initiative or Office de Tourisme* (sometimes a *Maison de Tourisme*). In smaller villages this service is provided by the town hall (*mairie*). Most offices, even in the small villages, have a website nowadays. For general information before you go, *see* the main tourist information addresses and websites listed on p.66.

Regional tourism offices, known as CDTs (Comité Départemental de Tourisme) offer very useful information:

CDT des Alpes de Haute Provence, 19 Rue Docteur Honnorat, **t** 04 92 31 57 29, **f** 04 92 32 24 94, *www.alpes-haute-provence.*

CDT de Vaucluse, 12 Rue Collège de la Croix, Avignon, **t** 04 90 47 00, **f** 04 90 86 86 08, *www.provenceguide.com.*

CDT Bouches-du-Rhône, 13 Rue Rax de Brigades, Marseille, **t** 04 91 13 84 40, **f** 04 91 33 01 82, *www.visitprovence.com.*

There are also offices for the Côte d'Azur and Provence:

CDT Côte d'Azur, **t** 04 93 37 78, **f** 04 93 86 01 06, *www.cdt.riviera.com.*

CDT Provence, **t** 04 91 56 47 00, **f** 04 91 56 47 01, *www.cdt-paca.fr.*

CDT Var, 1 Bd Foch, Draguignan **t** 04 94 50 55 50, **f** 04 94 50 55 51, *www.tourismevar.com.*

Where to Stay

Hotels

In the south of France you can find some of the most splendid hotels in Europe and some genuine scruffy fleabags of dubious clientele, with the majority of establishments falling somewhere between. As in most countries in Europe, the tourist authorities grade hotels by their facilities (not by charm or location) with stars from four (or four with an L for luxury – a bit confusing, so in the text luxury places are given five stars) to one, and there are even some cheap but adequate places undignified by any stars at all.

We would have liked to put the exact prices in the text, but almost every establishment has a wide range of rooms and prices – a very useful and logical way of doing things, once you're used to it. In some hotels, every single room has its own personality and the difference in quality and price can be enormous: a large room with antique furniture, a television or a balcony over the sea and a complete bathroom will cost much more than a poky back room in the same hotel, with a window overlooking a car park, no antiques and the WC down the hall. Some proprietors will drag out a sort of menu for you to choose the level of price and facilities you would like. Most two-star hotel rooms have their own showers and WCs; most one stars offer rooms with or without. The following guide will give you an idea of what prices to expect. The Côte d'Azur is much pricier than the rest of the region so, for example, you will pay more for a three-star hotel here than you would in Languedoc.

Hotels with **no stars** are not necessarily dives; the owners probably never bothered filling out a form for the tourist authorities. Prices are usually the same as one-star places.

Standards vary so widely that it's impossible to be more precise, but we can add a few more generalizations. **Single rooms** are relatively rare, and usually two-thirds the price of a double; rarely will a hotelier give you a discount if only doubles are available (again,

Hotel Price Ranges

*Prices listed here and elsewhere in this book
are for a double room in high season.*
  luxury €230 and over
  very expensive €150–€230
  expensive €100–150
  moderate €60–100
  inexpensive under €60

because each room has its own price). On the
other hand, if there are three or four of you,
triples or quads or adding extra beds to a
double room is usually cheaper than staying in
two rooms. Flowered wallpaper, usually beige,
comes in all rooms with no extra charge – it's
an essential part of the French experience.

Breakfast (usually coffee, a croissant, bread
and jam for €6 or €7 is nearly always optional:
you'll do as well for less in a bar. As usual, rates
rise in the busy season (holidays and summer,
and in the winter around ski resorts), when
many hotels with restaurants will require that
you take **half-board** (*demi-pension* – breakfast
and a set lunch or dinner). Many hotel restaurants are superb and non-residents are
welcome. At worst the food will be boring. In
the off-season, board requirements vanish into
thin air.

Your holiday will be much sweeter if you
book ahead, especially anywhere near the Côte
d'Azur from May to October. The few reasonably priced rooms are snapped up very early
across the board. In Provence and Languedoc,
July and August are the only really impossible
months; otherwise it usually isn't too difficult
to find something. Phoning a day or two ahead
is always a good policy, although beware that
hotels will only confirm a room with the
receipt of a cheque or credit card number to
cover the first night. Tourist offices have
complete lists of accommodation in their
given areas or even *département*, which come
in handy during the peak season; many will
even call around and book a room for you on
the spot for free or a nominal fee.

There are **chain hotels** (Sofitel, Formula One,
etc.) in most cities, but these are always dreary
and geared to the business traveller more than
the tourist, so you won't find them in this
book. Don't confuse chains with the various
umbrella organizations like *Logis et Auberges
de France*, *Relais du Silence* or the prestigious

Relais et Châteaux, which promote and guar-
antee the quality of independently owned
hotels and their restaurants. Many are recommended in the text. Larger tourist offices
usually stock their booklets, or you can pick
them up before you leave from the French
National Tourist Office, *www.tourisme.fr*. If you
plan to do a lot of driving, you may want to
pick up the English translation of the French
truckers' bible, *Les Routiers*, an annual guide
with maps listing reasonably priced lodgings
and food along the highways and byways of
France (available from Routiers Ltd., 190 Earls
Court Rd, London SW5 9QT, **t** (020) 7370 5113).

Bed and breakfast: in rural areas, there are
plenty of opportunities for a stay in a private
home or farm. *Chambres d'hôtes* are listed
separately in the tourist office brochures from
hotels, with the various *gîtes* (*see* below).
Some are connected to restaurants, others to
wine estates or a château; prices tend to be
moderate to inexpensive. Also try **BAB France,**
Rue Jacques Louvel Tessier, 75010 Paris, from
UK **t** 0871 781 0834 or from France **t** 01 42 01
34 34 (sells the Thomas Cook guide to French
B&Bs for €20), see *www.bedbreak.com*.
Fleurs de Soleil (*www.fleurs-soleil.tm.fr*)
offers *maisons d'hôtes* and B&Bs throughout
southern France.

Youth Hostels, *Gîtes d'Etape*, Refuges and *Fermes Auberges*

Most cities and resort areas have **youth
hostels** (*auberges de jeunesse*) that offer
simple dormitory accommodation and
breakfast to people of any age for around
€8.50–25 a night. Most offer kitchen facilities
as well, or inexpensive meals. They are the
best deal going for people travelling on their
own; for people travelling together, a 1-star
hotel can work out just as cheaply. Another
downside is that many are in the most
ungodly locations – in the suburbs where the
last bus goes by at 7pm, or miles from any
transport at all in the country.

For further information on youth hostels
in France, contact the **Fédération Unie des
Auberges de Jeunesse** (**t** 01 48 04 70 40,
www.fuaj.org).

In summer the only way to be sure of
getting a room is to arrive early in the day.
Most require a Hostelling International

(HI; *www.hihostels.com*) membership card, which you can usually purchase on the spot, although regulations say you should buy them in your home country.

UK: YHA, Trevelyan House, Dimple Rd, Matlock, Derbyshire DE4 3YH, **t** 0870 770 8868, *www.yha.org.uk* or **International Youth Hostelling Federation**, 2nd Floor, Gate House, Fretherne Rd, Welwyn Garden City, Herts AL8 6RD, **t** (01707) 324170.

USA: Hostelling Interational USA, 8401 Colesville Rd, Suite 600, Silver Spring MD 20910, **t** (301) 495 1240, *www.hiayh.org*.

Canada: Hostelling International Canada, 75 Nicholas St, Ottawa, ON K1N 7B9, **t** (613) 235 2595, *www.hihostels.ca*.

Australia: AYHA, 11 Rawson Place, opposite Central Station, Sydney, NSW 2000, **t** (02) 9281 9444, *www.yha.com.au*.

Another option in cities is single-sex **dormitories** for young workers (*foyers de jeunes travailleurs et de jeunes travailleuses*), which rent out individual rooms if available, for slightly more than a youth hostel.

A *gîte d'étape* is a simple shelter with bunk beds and a rudimentary kitchen set up by a village along GR walking paths (*see* p.74) or scenic bike routes. Again, lists are available for each *département*; the detailed maps listed under 'Getting Around' (*see* p.74) mark them as well. In the mountains similar rough shelters along the GR paths are called *refuges*, most of them open in summer only. Both charge around €9–15 a night.

Fermes auberges, which combine rural living with B&B comforts, are becoming a popular option. Check with the regional tourist offices for lists.

Camping

Camping is very popular, especially among the French, and there's at least one campsite in every town, often an inexpensive, no-frills place run by the town itself (*camping municipal*). Other campsites are graded with stars like hotels from four to one: at the top of the line you can expect lots of trees and grass, hot showers, a pool or beach, sports facilities, and a grocer's, bar and/or restaurant; on the coast, prices are rather similar to one-star hotels (although these, of course, never have all the extras). Beware that July and August are

terrible months to camp on the Côte d'Azur, when sites become so overcrowded (St-Tropez is notorious) that the authorities have begun to worry about health problems. You'll find more *Lebensraum* in Languedoc and off the coast. If you want to camp outside official sites, ask permission from the landowner first, or risk a furious farmer, his dog and perhaps even the police.

Tourist offices have complete lists of campsites in their regions, or if you plan to move around a lot pick up a *Guide officiel camping/caravaning*, available in French bookshops. A number of UK holiday firms book camping holidays and offer discounts on ferries:

Canvas Holidays, t 08703 667558, *www.canvasholidays.co.uk*.

Eurocamp Travel, t 08703 667558, *www. eurocamp.co.uk*.

Keycamp Holidays, t 0870 700 0123, *www.keycamp.com*.

Gîtes de France and Other Self-catering Accommodation

The south of France offers a vast range of self-catering: inexpensive farm cottages, history-laden châteaux with gourmet frills, sprawling villas on the Riviera, flats in modern beach resorts, even canal boats.

The **Fédération Nationale des Gîtes de France** is a French government service offering inexpensive accommodation by the week in rural areas. Lists with photos arranged by *département* are available from the **Maison des Gîtes de France et du Tourisme Vert**, 59 Rue St-Lazare, 75439 Paris Cedex 09, **t** 01 49 70 75 75, *www.gites-de-france.fr*, or in the UK from the **Gîtes de France** representative, **Brittany Ferries, t** 08703 665333, *www.brittanyferries.co.uk*. If you want to stay in a château, request the *Chambres d'hôtes et gîtes de prestige* list. Prices range from €175–400 a week.

Or try getting back to nature (but with a villa included), with a **Panda Gîte**, one of a network of about 250 rural *gîtes* and B&Bs in collaboration with Gîtes de France, WWF France and the Federation of French Nature Reserves. Included in the cost of your stay is a discovery pack of binoculars, local maps and guides. *See* Gîtes de France information.

Other options are advertised in the Sunday papers, or contact one of the firms listed

Self-catering Operators

In the UK

Allez France, Cutter House, 1560 Parkway, Solent Business Park, Fareham, Hampshire PO15 7AG, t 0845 330 2048 *www.allezfrance. com*. From cottages to châteaux.

Apartment Service, 5–6 Francis Grove, London SW19 4DT, t (020) 8944 1444, *www.apartmentservice.com*. Apartment accommodation in cities.

Bowhills, Mayhill Farm, Swanmore, Southampton SO32 2QW, t 0845 634 2727, *www.bowhills.co.uk*. Luxury villas and farmhouses, mostly with pools.

Chez Nous, Spring Mill, Earby, Barnoldswick, Lancashire BB94 0AA, t 0870 336 7679, *www.cheznous.com*. Over 3,000 privately owned holiday cottages and B&Bs.

Destination Provence, 49 Stonegate, York YO1 8AW, t (01904) 622 220, f (01904) 651 991, *www.destinationprovence.co.uk*. Self-catering villas and hotels.

Dominique's Villas, The Plough Brewery, 516 Wandsworth Rd, London SW8 3JX, t (020) 7738 8772, *www.dominiquesvillas.co.uk*. Large villas and châteaux with pools.

Erna Low Consultants, 9 Reece Mews, London SW7 3HE, t 0870 750 6820, *www.ernalow. co.uk*. Self-catering villas/flats in villages.

Individual Traveller Co, Manor Courtyard, Bignor, Pulborough, West Sussex RH20 1QD, t 08700 780189 *www.indiv-travellers.com*. Self-catering villas, cottages and farmhouses.

Meon Villas, Meon Villa, College St, Petersfield GU32 3JN, t 0870 909 7550, *www.meonvillas. co.uk*. Villas with pools.

Palmer and Parker Villa Holidays, Bank Rd, Penn, Bucks HP10 8LA, t (01494) 815 411, *www.palmerparker.com*. Upmarket villas with pools on the Riviera.

VFB Holidays, t (01242) 240 340, *www.vfb holidays.co.uk*. Rustic *gîtes* and luxurious farmhouses and hotels.

In the USA

At Home in France, PO Box 643, Ashland, OR 97520, t (541) 488 9467, *www.athomein france.com*. Apartments, cottages, farmhouses, manor houses and villas; moderate to deluxe.

Doorways Ltd., 900 County Line Rd, Bryn Mawr, PA 19010 2502, t 800 261 4460 or t (610) 520 0806, *www.villavacations.com*. Villas and apartments all over France.

Families Abroad, t (212) 787 2434 or t (718) 499 1977, *www.familiesabroad.com*. Apartments, villas and châteaux in Provence and elsewhere.

France by Heart, PO Box 614, Mill Valley, CA 94942, t (415) 388 3075, *www.france byheart.com*. Hundreds of properties.

Global Home Network, Bridge Street Corporate Housing Worldwide, t 800 278 7338, *www. globalhomenetwork.com*. Apartments, hotels and corporate lodging in major cities.

Heaven on Earth, 39 Radcliffe Rd, Rochester, NY 14617, t 800 466 5605, t (585) 342 5550, *www.heavenlyvillas.com*. Moderate to luxury.

Hideaways International, 767 Islington St, Portsmouth, NH 03801, t 800 843 4433 or t (603) 430 4433, *www.hideaways.com*. Villas, farmhouses and châteaux across France.

Overseas Connection, PO Box 1800, Sag Harbor, New York 11963, t (631) 725 9308, *www.overseasvillas.com*. Villas and apartments.

Vacances Provencales, 247 Davenport Rd, Suite 200, Toronto, Ontario M5R 1JT, t 800 263 7152 or t (416) 322 5565, *www.european homerentals.com*. Moderate to luxury villas, country homes, châlets and apartments throughout most of France.

Villas of Distinction, t 800 289 0900 or t (914) 273 3331, *www.villasofdistinction.com*. Private villas, cottages and châteaux.

---

below. The accommodation they offer will nearly always be more comfortable and costly than a *gîte*, but the discounts holiday firms can offer on the ferries, aeroplane tickets or car rental can make up for the price difference.

For private *gîte* rentals booked directly with the owners, try *www.frenchconnections.co.uk*, which also offers ferry discounts, and *www.abritel.fr*.

The Eastern Côte d'Azur

08

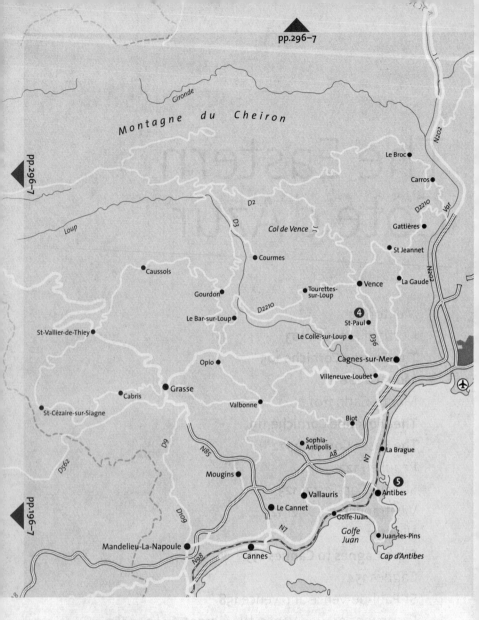

pp.296–7

pp.296–7

pp.196–7

Montagne du Cheiron

Gironde

Loup

Col de Vence

Le Broc

Carros

Gattières

St Jeannet

Courmes

La Gaude

Caussols

Vence

Gourdon

Tourettes-
sur-Loup

Le Bar-sur-Loup

4

St-Paul

St-Vallier-de-Thiey

Le Colle-sur-Loup

Opio

Cagnes-sur-Mer

Villeneuve-Loubet

Cabris

Grasse

St-Cézaire-sur-Siagne

Valbonne

Biot

Sophia-
Antipolis

La Brague

Mougins

5

Vallauris

Antibes

Le Cannet

Golfe-Juan

Mandelieu-La-Napoule

Golfe
Juan

Juan-les-Pins

Cannes

Cap d'Antibes

Var

Highlights

1 Béatrice de Rothschild's dream house, the Villa Ephrussi at St-Jean-Cap-Ferrat

2 Eze, the best-perched *village perché*

3 Nice, for a hundred reasons

4 Modern art in a transcendant setting at St-Paul-de-Vence's Fondation Maeght

5 Antibes, for its outrageous yachts, market, and Picassos

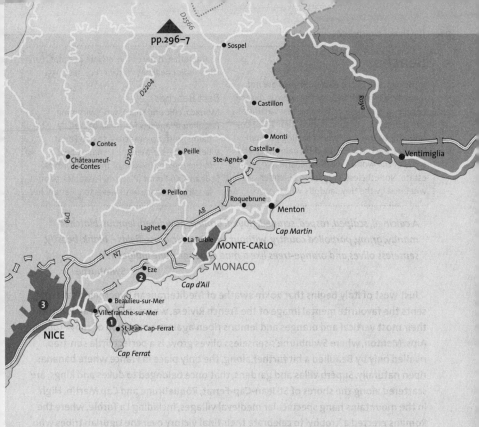

pp.296–7

Sospel

D2566

D2204

Castillon

Monti

Castellar

Ste-Agnès

Contes

Peille

Roya

Ventimiglia

Châteauneuf-
de-Contes

D2204

Peillon

A8

Roquebrune

Menton

Laghet

Cap Martin

D19

La Turbie

MONTE-CARLO

N7

Eze

MONACO

③

Cap d'Ail

②

Beaulieu-sur-Mer

Villefranche-sur-Mer

①

St-Jean-Cap-Ferrat

NICE

Cap Ferrat

N

10 km

5 miles

FRANCE

ITALY

SPAIN

Beaches

The beaches of the eastern Riviera are not renowned for their beauty. The shore is rocky – beaches are shingle, or in some cases artificial pebble. But lack of sand is more than compensated for by the spectacular settings of many beaches, backed by 650ft cliffs, palm trees and some of the world's most expensive real estate. Nonetheless, prepare to be underwhelmed by the tiny sandpits which characterize many of the 'private beaches'. For the sandier beaches west of Nice, *see* p.155.

Best Beaches

Monaco: chic and sharp; safe swimming.
Beaulieu (Plage des Fourmis): backed by palms, with a view across to Cap Ferrat.
Villefranche-sur-Mer: the trendiest beach in the region, and one of the best for kids.
St-Jean-Cap-Ferrat (Plage du Passable): popular, sloping beach with views to Villefranche.

A calcined, scalped, rasped, scraped, flayed, broiled, powdered, leprous, blotched, mangy, grimy, parboiled country, without trees, water, grass, fields – blank, beastly, senseless olives and orange-trees like a mad cabbage gone indigestible.

Swinburne

Just west of Italy begins that 20km swathe of Mediterranean hyperbole that represents the favourite mental image of the French Riviera, where the landscapes are at their most vertical and oranges and lemons ripen against a backdrop of snow-topped Alps. Menton, where Swinburne's senseless olives grow, is a perfect little sun-trap, rivalled only by Beaulieu a bit further along, the only place in France where bananas ripen naturally. Superb villas and gardens, that once belonged to dukes and kings, are scattered along the shores of St-Jean-Cap-Ferrat, Roquebrune and Cap Martin. High in the mountains hang spectacular medieval villages, including La Turbie, where the Romans erected a 'trophy' to celebrate their final victory over the Ligurian tribes who until then had effectively kept the Empire from the sweet delights of Provence.

Although first tamed by the Romans, this easternmost and tastiest morsel of the Côte d'Azur long remained a world apart, ruled until the mid-19th century by the Grimaldis of Monaco, and noted above all for its lemons and poverty. Bad relations with the French over Napoleon brought the first English and Russians, with their titles and weak lungs, to winter here, just outside France, in spite of the difficult roads. They built hotels, villas and casinos in the grand, fulsome, rococo-spa style of the period, and to this day the spirit lingers, a slightly musty violet perfume in a semi-tropical climate. Ian Fleming summed up the bygone spirit in writing about the fate of Monaco, where high class has gone high rise: 'Part of the trouble with the Monte-Carlo rooms is that they were built in an age of elegance for elegant people, and the gambling nowadays has the drabness of a Strauss operetta played in modern dress...what used to be a pastime has now become a rather deadly business of amassing tax-free capital gains.'

Even if most of the old glamour has faded, the scenery is as breathtaking as ever, one mighty mountain after another plummeting drunkenly into the sea, traced by hairpinning corniche roads that zigzag on ledges over vertiginous drops. Here, Continental hormones traditionally go into overdrive as the rich and famous in dark glasses and sporty convertibles race down to 'Monte', although not so much to gamble these days as to visit their bank managers. And the only racing that really happens is the Monaco Grand Prix; the traffic is nearly always slow and heavy – a fact that doesn't prevent some would-be James Bonds from contributing to an appalling accident rate. The worst traffic jams inch along the lowest road, the **Basse Corniche** (N98), through the seaside resorts; most of the frequent buses that ply the coast use this road, which runs parallel to the railway. To relieve the traffic, already choking in the 1920s, the most dramatic of the roads, the **Moyenne Corniche** (N7), was drilled through the rock and hung sheerly through the hills, making it the favourite for car-chase scenes. Higher up, along the route of the Roman Via Aurelia (also called Via Julia Appia), Napoleon built the **Grande Corniche** (D2564), with the most panoramic views of all.

Menton

The Côte d'Azur starts halfway between the fleshpots of Paris and Rome at Menton, right on the Italian frontier. Its history starts here as well, with the earliest traces of Riviera humans – folk who a million years ago already had the good sense to settle where a wall of mountains, still crowned with snow in April, blocks out the cold so that lemon trees can blossom all year.

Despite this early start, the Menton area wasn't inhabited again until the 10th century, when settlers clustered around the Annonciade hill, where they felt safe from Saracen pirates. The town first belonged to the counts of Ventimiglia – little better than pirates themselves – then briefly joined Provence before it was sold to Charles Grimaldi of Monaco in 1346.

The Grimaldis became rich from taxing Menton's citrus fruit and continued to enjoy the fruits of this wealth until 1848, when the town and its neighbour, Roquebrune, declared their independence. Unlike most of the revolts in Europe that fateful year, this puny one succeeded, and the Free Towns of Menton and Roquebrune endured

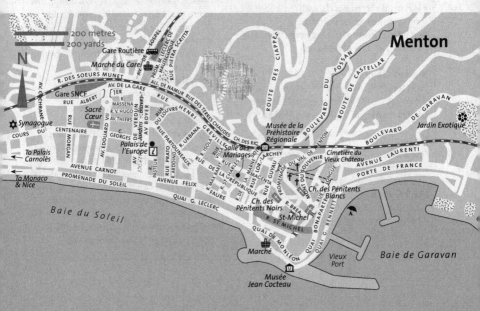

Getting There and Around

By Train

Métrazur (St-Raphaël–Ventimiglia) and all other Nice–Italy trains stop in Menton (Menton-Centre), Rue de la Gare.

There's another station – Menton-Garavan – behind the port. **SNCF, t** 08 92 35 35 35.

By Bus and Taxi

Buses for Nice (via Roquebrune-Cap-Martin and Monte-Carlo) depart frequently from the *gare routière* on Esplanade du Careï, northeast of the train station. Tickets from Monte-Carlo with the Broch and RCA bus companies, **t** 04 93 28 43 27, are valid on both. Other bus services go to Ventimiglia, Castillon and Sospel and to Ste-Agnès, Gorbio and Castellar, often in *navettes* (minibuses).

All local Menton bus lines pass by Esplanade du Careï.

There is a **taxi** rank outside the Menton-Centre SNCF station, or call **t** 04 92 10 47 00/01/02/03/04.

Tourist Information

Menton: Palais de l'Europe, 8 Av Boyer, **t** 04 92 41 76 76, **f** 04 92 41 76 58, *ot@villedementon. com, www.villedementon.com*. Open July–Aug Mon–Sat 9–7, Sun 9–1; Sept–June Mon–Fri 8.30–12.30 and 2–6, Sat 9–12, 2–6. Has details on 'passports' with reduced entrance fees for local attractions.

Post office: Corner of Cours George V and Rue Edouard VII, **t** 04 93 28 64 70.

Market Days

Every am: food market at the Halles.
Sat am: at Vieux Port (clothes, accessories).
Fri: Flea market, on the Place aux Herbes.

Festivals

Fête du Citron, Feb–Mar: floats, processions, special entrance to the gardens; call the tourist office for details.
Music Festival at Monastère de l'Annonciade, July–Aug at St-Michel. Call **t** 04 92 41 76 95 or **t** 08 92 70 52 05 for reservations.

Internet Access

Le Café des Arts, 16 Rue de la République, **t** 04 93 35 78 67.

Where to Stay

Menton ⊠ 06500

All but one of Menton's old grand hotels have been converted into flats, and no new ones have risen to take up the slack. If all below are full, you could try *www.hotel menton.com*.

★★★★**Hôtel des Ambassadeurs**, 3 Rue Partouneaux, **t** 04 93 28 75 75, **f** 04 93 35 62 32, *www.ambassadeurs-menton.com* (*luxury*). Though now a Clarion hotel, this is the last *grande dame* – gracious, spacious, pink and balconied, and slap bang in the middle of town. There's nearly every luxury, but no pool. *See also* 'Eating Out', opposite.

★★★**Hôtel l'Aiglon**, 7 Av de la Madone, **t** 04 93 57 55 55, **f** 04 93 35 92 39, *www.hotelaiglon. net* (*very expensive–expensive*). Tucked into a drowsy corner of the Parc de la Madone, this independent Belle Epoque hotel is light, stylish and very chic, with spindly antiques and high ceilings. By the pool there is a lovely arbour with wooden beams. *See also* 'Eating Out'.

★★★**Napoléon**, 29 Porte de France, **t** 04 93 35 89 50, **f** 04 93 35 49 22, *www.napoleon-menton.com* (*expensive*). This is a delight; the rooms may be decorated in comfortable dark brown like a favourite great-aunt's, but it has a pool, soundproofed, air-conditioned rooms, a private beach, and friendly, obliging staff. *Closed mid-Nov–mid-Dec.*

★★★**Royal Westminster**, 28 Av Félix Faure, **t** 04 93 28 69 69, **f** 04 93 28 60 81, *westminster@wanadoo.fr, www.hotel-menton.com/hotel-royal-westminster* (*expensive*). This upmarket chain hotel is aimed mostly at retirees; however, it is on the seafront, with quiet rooms furnished in cool sea colours, views over the bay, huddles of elderly ladies on the terrace playing poker, and a *pétanque* court on the gravel drive. *Closed Nov.*

★★**Hôtel de Londres**, 15 Av Carnot, **t** 04 93 35 74 62, **f** 04 93 41 77 78, *www.hotel-de-*

londres.com (*moderate*). Nothing is too much trouble for this hotel's cheerful host, who will even lend you a cushioned mattress for the stony beach. Rooms are simple but attractive, with air-conditioning, and some overlook the shady, flower-filled garden with its little bar and games area. *Closed end Oct–Dec.*

★★Claridge's, 39 Av de Verdun, t 04 93 35 72 53, f 04 93 35 42 90, *www.claridges-menton.com* (*moderate–inexpensive*). A slightly old-fashioned, quiet hotel on the flowery, clipped Jardin Biovès, a good 10 minutes from the sea, but very near one of Menton's local food markets and the bus station.

★Hôtel Beauregard, 10 Rue Albert Ier, t 04 93 28 63 63, f 04 93 28 63 79, *beauregard.menton@wanadoo.fr* (*inexpensive*). A sweet place with a quiet garden below the station, this is also a good bargain. *Closed Nov.*

Auberge de Jeunesse, Plateau St-Michel, t 04 93 35 93 14, f 04 93 35 93 07, *www.fuaj.org* (bus 6 from the station). *Closed Dec–Jan.*

Eating Out

Fiori, Hôtel des Ambassadeurs (*see* opposite; *expensive*). Posh nosh. *Closed Sun, Mon lunch, Sat lunch and mid-Nov–mid-Dec.*

Le Nautic, 27 Quai de Monléon, t 04 93 35 78 74 (*expensive*). Between the market and the sea, opposite the Musée Cocteau, this bright blue eatery serves up every possible fish dish, including *bouillabaisse*.

Le Riaumont, Hôtel l'Aiglon (*see* left). This hotel's restaurant (*expensive–moderate*) serves traditional regional cuisine overlooking its swimming pool in the summer. *Closed Nov–mid-Dec.*

La Coquille d'Or, on the corner of Quai Bonaparte, t 04 93 35 80 67 (*expensive–moderate*). This may be a tourist trap, complete with Gypsy strummers. but, surprisingly, it also packs in crowds of locals for the *bouillabaisse* and *paella*. *Closed Wed and Nov.*

Pierrot-Pierrette, Place de l'Eglise, Rte de Sospel, t 04 93 35 79 76 (*moderate*). Up at Monti, this restaurant complements its views with delicious fresh blue trout. *Closed Mon, Christmas and most of Jan.*

All along Rue St-Michel, in the old town, masses of restaurants vie for your attention, spilling out into the street at lunchtime with tempting displays of hot pastries and baguettes. Try the following:

Crêperie St-Michel, 5 Rue Piéta, t 04 93 28 44 64 (*inexpensive*). Tucked away off the main street, the alarmingly brisk service and odd mixture of decoration (on the mantelpiece are a sailing ship, a pair of men's shoes and a photo of Eric Cantona) make this a good lunch stop if you've a bus to catch.

Rikiki, 7 Square Victoria, t 04 93 28 27 88. (*moderate*). Away from the fray, this atmospheric and popular place serves authentic Italian dishes.

A Braijade Meridiounale, 66 Rue Longue, t 04 93 35 65 65 (*moderate*). Tucked away in the maze of alleyways near St-Michel, serving Provençal favourites. *Closed Wed.*

L'Amandine, 24 Rue St-Michel (*inexpensive*). A tempting array of nougat and all kinds of locally produced *confiserie* and *fruits confits*.

Entertainment and Nightlife

Menton isn't exactly a hopping place, but check the Menton page in *Nice-Matin* or the brochure published by the tourist office.

Clubs and Bars

The young grumble that there's nothing to do, and head west to Monaco for nightlife; **Le Casino** and its disco **Le Brummell** (t 04 92 10 16 16) are disdained as tourist ghettos.

Theatre

Théâtre Francis-Palmero, t 04 92 41 76 95, in the Palais de l'Europe, has a varied programme in French only.

Leisure

Koaland, Av de la Madone, t/f 04 92 10 00 40. Activities to keep children entertained, such as mini-golf, go-karting, etc. *Open Sept–June 10–12 and 2–7; July–Aug 10–12 and 3pm–12am; closed Tues out of season.*

until 1861, when the people voted to unite with France, and Charles III of Monaco sold his claim on the towns to Napoléon III for four million gold francs.

The following year, a Dr J. Henry Bennet wrote *Menton and the Riviera as a Winter Climate*, a book that soon attracted a community of 5,000 Brits to the town, led by Queen Victoria herself in 1883. (Her bust glowers regally from a fountain tiled like a municipal swimming pool on the Quai Bonaparte.) During the Second World War the Germans wrecked Menton's port and, when they were chased out, lobbed bombs on to it from the Italian side of the border. The damage wasn't repaired until 1956.

Nattering nabobs of negativism claim that Menton has a poor beach and as much atmosphere as your grandmother's antimacassar, a town where 30 per cent of the population are retirees (the highest percentage in France) and most of the rest are poodles. Yet Menton is magnificently situated, sprinkled with some of the coast's finest gardens, and has a healthy attitude to relaxation compared with the hardened glamour-pusses to the west. A recent influx of families and young people, mainly from nearby Italy, has begun to liven up the beaches and main streets.

Jean Cocteau, Love, and Lemons

Menton is squeezed between the mountains and a pair of shingle-beached bays: the **Baie de Garavan**, on the Italian side, where villas and gardens overlook the yacht harbour, and the **Baie du Soleil** (the Roman Pacis Sinus or Gulf of Peace), stretching 3km west to Cap Martin.

In between these two bays stands a little 17th-century harbour bastion looking out to sea that Jean Cocteau converted into the **Musée Cocteau** (*t 04 93 57 72 30; open 10–12 and 2–6; closed Tues; adm*) in the late 1950s, and which is decorated with grey and white mosaics made from seaside pebbles. The hallway is dominated by an enormous bloodthirsty tapestry, Cocteau's first, *Judith et Holopherne*, in which Judith seduces Holofernes, general of the enemy forces, in order to save her city, and then decapitates him in his sleep and slinks out looking vicious. Niches on the upper level, each with their own pebble-mosaic floor and a Cocteau-designed display case, hold the playful *Animaux fantastiques*, which Cocteau created in a burst of admiration for the colourful ceramics that Picasso was making in Vallauris in the late 1950s. Picasso's work also inspired the series of coloured pencil drawings, *Les Innamorati*, portraying the happier love affairs of the Mentonnais.

This theme of Menton's lovers was first explored by Cocteau in his decorations for the 1957 **Salle des Mariages** (*t 04 92 10 50 00; open 8.30–12.30 and 2–5; closed Sat and Sun; adm*), in the Hôtel de Ville, five minutes' walk northwest on Rue de la République. At the entrance, gilt mirrors are painted with a blowsy Marianne, symbol of the Republic, who French law insists makes it to every French wedding. The interior resembles a louche nightclub: carpeted with leopard-skin, upholstered with plush red velvet and lit with sinuous tulip-shaped lamps. A lemon-picker weds a fisherman amid rather discouraging mythological allusions: on the right wall there's a wedding party in Saracen costume, referring to the Mentonnais' Saracen blood, although among the company we see the bride's frowning mother, the groom's jilted girlfriend and her armed brother. The other wall shows Orpheus turning back to see if his beloved

Eurydice is following him out of Hell, condemning her to return there forever, while, on the ceiling, Love, Poetry (on Pegasus) and Science (juggling planets) look on.

Love was also a favourite theme of the original Riviera inhabitants, who carved the little Cro-Magnon Venuses now housed in the **Musée de la Préhistoire Régionale**, a couple of blocks north on Rue Loredan Larchey (*t 04 93 35 84 64; open 10–12 and 2–6; closed Tues*). An earnest series of dioramas recreates the area's cave interiors from the time when the furry animals people lived alongside were mammoths rather than poodles, but the star exhibit is the 30,000-year-old skeleton of Menton Man (found just over the border in Grimaldi), buried in a bonnet of seashells and deer teeth long since calcified into the bone; note, too, rock carvings from the Vallée des Merveilles, high above Menton in the Roya valley of the Alpes-Maritimes.

The 1909 **Palais de l'Europe**, west of the Salle des Mariages, on Av Boyer, was once the casino, but is now an exhibition hall (*open 10–12 and 2–6; closed Tues*) and the tourist office. In front of it is the exotic **Jardins Biovès**, the most tidied, kempt, combed and swept bit of green space you're ever likely to come across, where the elderly sit in sunshine in beige and grey to match their poodles, watching life pass by. Here the fantastical lemon-studded floats of Menton's *Fête du Citron* are parked at carnival time.

A kilometre west of the town centre, the frothy pink and white summer home of the princes of Monaco, the Palais Carnolès (1717), is now an art museum, the **Musée des Beaux-Arts du Palais Carnolès** (*3 Av de la Madone, t 04 93 35 49 71, bus 3 and 7; open 10–12 and 2–6; closed Tues; adm*). It holds a Byzantine-inspired *Virgin and Child* from 13th-century Tuscany, Ludovico Brea's luminous *Madonna and Child with St Francis*, several oils attributed to Leonardo da Vinci, and all the previous winners from Menton's very own Biennale of painting, some of which are so awful that you can only wonder what the losers were like. Other works were donated by the English landscape and portrait artist Graham Sutherland, who lived part of every year in Menton from 1947 until he died in 1980. In the grounds, a piercingly fragrant citrus fruit orchard (try to make it in the spring) doubles up as a contemporary sculpture garden; among the mixed bag of 40 pieces are Max Siffredi's languorous *Aegina* and Guy Fage's dreamy marble *Rêverie*.

Just north of here, on the route to Gorbio, is one of Menton's most romantic gardens. The **Jardin de la Serre de la Madone** (*t 04 93 57 73 90, f 06 86 37 91 49; ring for details about guided tours; closed Mon; closed 5 Nov–5 Feb; adm*) covers 15 hectares with spectacular terraces. Grottoes and nymphs sprouting from ponds with fronds of trailing ivy lend an air of enchantment and secrecy. The garden was created between 1919 and 1939 by Sir Lawrence Johnstone, another of the fervent English botanists who seemed to overrun this corner of the world in the early part of the 20th century; he was also responsible for the famous English garden at Hidcote Manor.

The Vieille Ville

The tall, narrow 17th-century houses of Menton's Vieille Ville, overlooking the Vieux Port east of the Musée Cocteau, are reminiscent of the old quarter of Genoa, knitted together by anti-earthquake arches that span stepped lanes named after old pirate captains and saints. It's hard to believe that the quiet main street, **Rue Longue** (the Roman Via Julia Augusta), was until the 19th century the main route between France and Italy. According to legend, the lady at the Palais Princier (at No.123) received a secret nocturnal visit from Casanova, who crept in through the sewers.

From Rue Longue, the shallow stairs of the Rampes St-Michel lead up to the *parvis* of the ice-cream-coloured church of **St-Michel** (1675), the largest and one of the most ornate Baroque churches of the region, decked out and made fit for the princes of Monaco by two Mentonnais artists, Puppo and Vento. A gloomy late-17th-century painting depicts Sainte Dévote looking suitably martyrish in front of the Rock of Monaco. Honoré III of Monaco tied the knot in the church in 1757 and presented the damask hangings, which are still brought out on special occasions as a celebratory gift. St-Michel's Baroque neighbour, the pert little **Chapelle des Pénitents Blancs**, was headquarters of one of the old Riviera's many religious confraternities (*see* **Nice**, p.141), and was feverishly restored in the 19th century with elaborate festooning and stucco. The three Theological Virtues glower uneasily among all the frills. The *parvis* (square in front of the church) has a pebble mosaic of the Grimaldi arms. It is used as the setting for Menton's megastar chamber music festival in August.

The **Montée du Souvenir** leads to the top of the Vieille Ville, where the citadel was replaced in the 19th century by the romantic, panoramic **Cimetière du Vieux Château** (*open summer 7am–8pm, winter 7–6*), windy and pine-scented. Curiously, it is not marked on the tourist map, but is just a quick steep haul up from those sitting out their last years below; as if a foretaste of death, it's the one place in Menton where they can't bring their poodles. Guy de Maupassant called it the most aristocratic cemetery in Europe – the venerable names inscribed on the hierarchical array of ornate tombs and little pavilions include William Webb-Ellis, the 'inventor of rugby', and a handful of Russian Grand Princes. Many immigrants, like Aubrey Beardsley, were consumptives in their teens and twenties and only came to Menton to die.

The Gardens of Garavan

From the cemetery, Boulevard de Garavan leads into the neighbourhood where this dead élite would reside if they were alive today, dotted with elegant villas amid some of the most beautiful gardens on the coast. The **Jardin Exotique du Val Rahmeh** (*entrance on Av St-Jacques, t 04 93 35 86 72; open April–Sept 10–12.30 and 3–6; Oct–Mar 10–12.30 and 2–5; closed Tues; adm; guided tours sometimes available*) was planted around the ivy-covered Villa Val Rahmeh by enthusiastic English botanists in the 1930s and has since been substantially expanded by the Natural History Museum in Paris. Now more than 700 tropical and subtropical species from around the world bloom contentedly on the garden's sloping terraces. Nearby, the drowsy **Parc du Pian** (*open daily*), an old olive orchard, is dotted with shady wooden benches perfect for afternoon siestas and secret assignations. Beyond the gardens, a road off the boulevard, Av Blasco Ibañez, was named after the author of *The Four Horsemen of the Apocalypse* (1867–1928), who lived here in the **Villa Fontana Rosa** (*contact the Service du Patrimoine, t 04 92 10 33 66, for details of guided tours*). He decorated his fantastical **Jardin des Romanciers** with colourful *azulejo* tiles from his native Valencia in the

1920s in homage to the great storytellers. Brightly tiled columns, wide shallow fountains and flower-covered walkways give way to outdoor 'reading rooms'.

Villa Isola Bella, on the other side of the Garavan station, was the home of another
victim of tuberculosis, Katherine Mansfield (1888–1923); although ailing, she was
happy here, and fictionalized her experiences in a number of short stories. To the
north of Boulevard de Garavan, the romantic red-ochre villa and gardens of the
Domaine des Colombières (*open one day a year in June, contact the Service du
Patrimoine, t 04 92 10 97 10, for details*) was the 40-year project of French artist and
writer Ferdinand Bac (1859–1952), the flamboyant and indefatigable illegitimate son
of Napoléon III. As well as designing the botanical gardens, with secret leafy
passageways dotted with statues, ponds and fountains, he painted all the paintings
and frescoes in the house himself and designed the elegant Modernist furniture. Out
almost at the town's eastern limits, on the Promenade Reine Astrid, the **Villa Maria
Serena** (*t 04 92 10 33 66; guided tours Tues 10am*) is enclosed by another lush garden,
this one devoted to an extensive collection of rare palm trees, soaking up the
sunshine in what is reputedly the most temperate garden in France.

North of Menton

Four narrow mountain valleys converge at Menton, with villages hanging over their
slopes; they are linked by bus from Menton and to each other by mule tracks. Above
the easternmost valley is **Castellar** (7km from Menton), laid out on a grid plan in 1435
to replace the original 1258 village, built by the counts of Ventimiglia high on a rocky
crag. An hour's hike will take you to the ghostly ruins of old Castellar; or take the less
strenuous walk up the Sospel road as far as the waterfall at the **Gourg de l'Oura**.
Up the second valley, the **Val du Careï**, sailors have made the little monastery of
L'Annonciade (5.5km from Menton) the focus of their May pilgrimage since the 11th
century. It has gone through countless transformations over the years and the
current building dates from the 17th century. Best of all are its grand views, from a
terrace which looks over the whole valley and out to the sea, and its *ex votos*, dating
back to the 17th century and including an unusual more recent one – a piece of a
zeppelin. Further up the Val du Careï, amid the viaducts of the old Menton–Sospel
railway, you can wander through the scented **Forêt de Menton**, then up to **Castillon**,
awaft with the scent of fresh concrete and artisan shops, and well into its third incarnation as 'the most beautiful new village in France' after being flattened by an
earthquake in 1887 and bombed in 1944.

From Menton the narrow, winding D22 noodles up to **Ste-Agnès**, at almost 2,625ft
the loftiest village on the entire coast, which huddles on the northern side of the peak
with its back to the sea. Mornings can be chilly before the sun makes its way around,
even in the height of summer. There are three buses a day from Menton, or drive up,
passing under and over the mighty viaducts of the A8, which look as insubstantial as
spider's legs once you reach Ste-Agnès. The village was founded in the 10th century,
some say, by a Saracen who fell in love with a local girl and converted to Christianity

for her sake. It certainly looks old enough – a patchwork quilt of vaulted passageways and tiny squares that have succumbed to a mild attack of trinketshopitis. When you can't look at another smirking *santon*, head up Rue Longue for a view that stretches to Corsica on a clear day, or scramble up to the ruins of the 12th-century château, which dominate the peak. It was destroyed by Louis XIV and has mouldered away ever since. The villagers have now taken over and are attempting to shore it up, but are not above putting it to practical use – in the miniature medieval garden is a patch of crazy paving and a whirling clothesline.

Ste-Agnès, perched at such a dizzying height, has always been on the defensive front line; a **fort** (*open July–Sept daily 3–6, Oct–June Sat and Sun only, 2.30–5.30; call town hall on t 04 93 35 84 58 for information about guided tours*) was gouged into the rock here in the 1930s as part of the infamous Maginot Line. Despite containing the most powerful concentration of artillery of the entire length of the Line, the fort couldn't hold out against the Germans in the Second World War; its bleak living quarters and grim cannons and mortar are still on view.

Come down the mountain at dusk if you can – it's the only safe way to see if anything's coming round those cliff-face bends, and there's the added bonus of watching Menton light up for the evening, far, far below. On foot – make sure it is a comfortably shod foot – a narrow stony path descends from Ste-Agnès to Menton in two hours or, better still, take the one-hour shortcut which forms part of the Balcon de la Côte d'Azur (the GR51) to **Gorbio** (from Menton it's 8km), passing by the tiny 17th-century Chapelle St-Lazare, abandoned and forlorn at the entrance to the village. Gorbio is just as picturesquely medieval as Ste-Agnès, with ivy-covered houses of pale honey-coloured stone and twisting vaulted streets, but has somehow been spared the trinkets. In the Place de la République, more commonly known as the Place du Village, there are a couple of terraced restaurants, a plain fountain for the gossips to collect around and an olive tree planted in 1713 (which does double service as the bus stop for Menton). The best time to visit is at Fête Dieu (Corpus Christi) in June, for the medieval Procession dai Limaça, when the village lanes are lit by thousands of flickering lamps made from snail shells filled with olive oil, set in beds of sand.

Where to Stay and Eat

Castellar ✉ 06500

*Hôtel des Alpes, Place Clemenceau, t 04 93 35 82 83, f 04 93 28 24 25, www.hotelmenton. com/hotel-des-alpes (*inexpensive*). Tidy little rooms and good food (*cheap*). Closed mid-Nov–mid Dec.

Castillon ✉ 06500

***Bergerie, t 04 93 04 00 39, f 04 93 28 02 91 (*moderate*). More upmarket, with a pool, rustic but very comfortable rooms and elaborate food. Closed mid- Oct–mid-Nov.

Le Saint-Yves, Rue des Sarrasins, t 04 93 35 91 45, f 04 93 35 65 85 (*inexpensive*). For sweet dreams, dreamy views and, most notably, courtesy. The restaurant (*moderate*), which looks out over a dramatic view of mountains and sea, serves up regional dishes such as *lapin aux herbes*. Closed mid-Nov–mid Dec.

Le Logis Sarrasin, 40 Av des Sarrasins, t 04 93 35 86 89, f 04 93 35 65 85 (*moderate–cheap*). A restaurant offering a warm welcome and more panoramic views, as well as six courses, including delicious *raviolis maison*. Closed Mon and mid-Nov–mid-Dec.

A Dip into Italy

Just over the border from Menton, in the village of Grimaldi, the beachside **Balzi Rossi** (red caves) were the centre of a sophisticated Neanderthal society that flourished c. 100,000 to 40,000 BC and produced some of Europe's earliest art, displayed in the **Museo Preistorico** (*t (00 39 for Italy, if calling from France) 0184 38113; museum open Tues–Sun 8.30–7.30; closed Mon; adm*).

The town of **Ventimiglia** has a huge market which completely takes over the town every Friday; a number of bus tours go there from Menton. Outside Ventimiglia, at Mortola Inferiore, you can visit the extraordinary **Hanbury Gardens** (*t (0039) 0184 22 95 07; open summer Thurs–Tues 10–6; winter Thurs–Tues 10–4; closed Wed; adm*), a botanical paradise of acclimatized plants from around the world, founded in 1867 by Sir Thomas Hanbury and his brother Daniel. Sir Thomas was a wealthy dealer in silks and spices from China, who fell in love with the spot during a holiday on the Côte d'Azur in 1867. The gardens fell into decay during the Second World War, but are now back in shape and managed by the University of Genoa: highlights include the Australian forest, the Garden of Scents and the Japanese garden.

If you plan to go deeper into Italy, you can save money by filling up with petrol in Menton (that's what all those Italians are doing). If you plan to feast on an excellent Italian meal, it's only 12km to **Bordighera**, where you can spend your petrol savings and your children's inheritance at the lovely, very expensive Art Nouveau **Via Romana** (*Via Romana 57, t (0039) 0184 26 66 81; www.viaromana.it; closed Wed all day, and Thurs lunch*).

The Grande Corniche

Roquebrune-Cap-Martin

Nearly every potential building site on the lush mountain shore between Menton and Monaco is occupied by Roquebrune-Cap-Martin – from old Roquebrune just beside the Grande Corniche down to the exclusive garden cape of Cap Martin. Purchased by the Grimaldis in 1355 for 1,000 florins, Roquebrune (like Menton) later revolted against Monaco and became a Free Town until joining France in 1861.

The medieval village is all steep, winding, arcaded streets with a fair number of over-restored houses, galleries and *ateliers*, culminating at the top in the **château** (*t 04 93 35 07 22; open Nov–Jan daily 10–12 and 2–5; Feb–Mar and Oct 10–12 and 2–6; April–June and Sept 10–12 and 2–6.30; July–Aug 10–12 and 3–7.30; adm*), with the oldest surviving *donjon* in France, erected in the 10th century by the counts of Ventimiglia against the Saracen threat. In the 15th century, Lambert of Monaco built much of what stands today, including the keep; in 1911, Sir William Ingram purchased the castle, planted the mock medieval *tour anglaise* by the gate, and donated it all to the town in 1921. The rooms between the ravaged 11ft-thick walls are surprisingly poky – most people have bathrooms bigger than this lordling's reception hall, which lost its roof to cannonballs in 1597. An uninspired audiovisual exhibition animates the

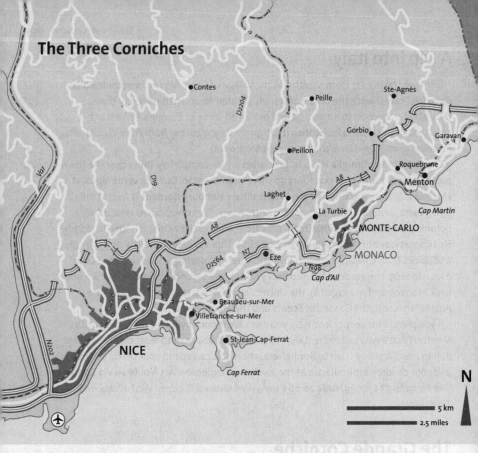

The Three Corniches

Contes

Peille

Ste-Agnès

Gorbio

Garavan

Peillon

Roquebrune

Menton

Laghet

La Turbie

Cap Martin

MONTE-CARLO

MONACO

Eze

Cap d'Ail

Beaulieu-sur-Mer

Villefranche-sur-Mer

St-Jean-Cap-Ferrat

NICE

Cap Ferrat

N

5 km

2.5 miles

prison, the archers' room and the kitchens, but the view from the top floor, huge enough for any ego, is by far the best of the castle's attractions. The castle guards lived below in picturesque **Rue Moncollet**, tunnelled out of the living rock, which leads down into Rue Grimaldi and the Place des Deux-Frères, a pretty square with a fat, attractive old olive tree, the little village *lavoir*, a sprinkling of cafés and restaurants, and a vertiginous view across the red-tiled rooftops and over the bay.

Back on Rue du Château is the pink and orange church of **Ste-Marguerite**, originally built in the 12th century but well and truly Baroqued since, which contains a *Resurrection* and *Pietà* by 17th-century Roquebrunois artist Marc-Antoine Otto. A formidable gang of village ladies maintains its current gleaming splendour. Nearby Rue de la Fontaine (turn off Rue du Château just after the post office) leads to a remarkable contemporary of the castle: a 1,000-year-old olive tree measuring 33ft in circumference, with a tangle of roots bursting out of the soil.

In 1467, as plague decimated the coastal population, the Roquebrunois vowed to the Virgin that if they were spared they would, in thanksgiving, annually re-enact tableaux of the Passion. The Virgin apparently thought it was a good deal, and the villagers have faithfully kept their side of the pact every year on 5 August, illuminating the procession with little lamps made from sea shells and snail shells. The best and most coveted of the 500 roles involved in the colourful processions are jealously 'owned' by the oldest families, who pass them down like heirlooms.

Cap Martin

In the 1890s a pair of empresses, Eugénie of France (widow of Napoléon III) and Elisabeth ('Sissi') of Austria, made Roquebrune's little peninsula of Cap Martin an aristocratic enclave, 'whispering of old kings come here to dine or die', as F. Scott Fitzgerald wrote. Churchill did the dining and Yeats, King Nikola of Montenegro and Le Corbusier the dying, the last succumbing to a heart attack in 1965 while swimming off the white rocks beside what is now the **Promenade Le Corbusier** – a lovely walk around the cape, down a succession of little ramps and stairways and past villas immersed in luxuriant pines, olives, cypresses and mimosas. Corby had been staying in one of the villas, one of the most beautiful on the Côte d'Azur, built in 1929 by furniture designer Eileen Gray; the story goes that he loved the house so

Tourist Information

Roquebrune: 218 Av Aristide Briand, t 04 93 35 62 87, f 04 93 28 57 00, *office-du-tourisme. rcm@wanadoo.fr, www.roquebrune-cap-martin.com*. Offers tours of the old town and château as well as Le Corbusier's cabin. Detailed walking maps also available. *Open Mon–Sat 9–1, 3–7, Sun 10–1, 3–7.*

Markets

Provençal market: daily am, Parking du Marché de Carnolès. *Larger on Wed.*
Roquebrune village: mid-Sept, flea market.

Where to Stay and Eat

Along the Corniches ✉ 06190

******Vista Palace Hôtel, t** 04 92 10 40 00, **f** 04 93 35 18 94, *info@vistapalace.com, www.vistapalace.com* (*luxury*). If money's no object, this is the ultimate in luxury, hanging on a 1,000ft cliff on the Grande Corniche, with a God's-eye view over Monaco; it also has a heated pool, squash, gym, sauna and famous restaurant (*see below*). *Closed Feb.*
****Westminster**, 14 Av L. Laurens, **t** 04 93 35 00 68, **f** 04 93 28 88 50, *hotel@westminster o6.com, www.westminstero6.com* (*moderate–inexpensive*). With a pretty garden terrace near the junction of the lower two Corniches. *Closed end Nov–end Dec.*

Le Vistaero, Vista Palace Hôtel (*see* above). This cliff-hanging restaurant (*very expensive*) offers some of the Côte's most talked-about cuisine under the auspices of chef Jean-Pierre Pestre. *Closed Feb.*

Roquebrune

Hôtel des Deux Frères, Place des Deux-Frères, **t** 04 93 28 99 00, **f** 04 93 28 99 10, *info@ lesdeuxfreres.com, www.lesdeuxfreres.com* (*moderate*). Looking out over Monaco, this hotel has been refurbished and is ethereally light and airy with a graceful curved stone staircase. The rooms are small, but white muslin canopies draped over the beds, whitewashed walls and endless views make up for the lack of space. Friendly, knowledge-able staff serve excellent regional dishes in the flower-edged terrace restaurant (*expensive–moderate*). *Closed mid-Nov–mid-Dec. Restaurant closed Sun night and Mon.*
Au Grand Inquisiteur, 18 Rue du Château, **t/f** 04 93 35 05 37 (*expensive–moderate*). In a former sheepfold cut into the rock, this restaurant has well-prepared Provençal dishes such as *fleurs de courgette farcies. Closed Mon and Tues lunch, and mid-Nov–mid-Dec.*
La Grotte, Place des Deux-Frères, **t/f** 04 93 35 00 04 (*moderate–cheap*). A cheaper troglodyte choice, La Grotte also has tables outside at the entrance to the Vieille Ville, and offers pizzas, pasta and a good value *plat du jour. Closed Wed and end Oct–Nov.*

much that he got a wealthy friend to buy it at auction, helping him defeat the higher bids of Aristotle Onassis by dragging the auctioneer off at a crucial moment. In a garden down by the sea, he built himself a tiny **cabin** (*guided tours Tues and Fri at 10am from the tourist office; register the previous day at the tourist office; adm*) just 12ft square, which comprised a frescoed corridor and one simple room, and wrote rapturously to a friend of the comforts of his seaside 'château'. It was built as a model of minimal accommodation based on the 'modulor', his patented system of architectural proportions, and encompassed, in his opinion at least, all a man needed to live a comfortable existence. Although unprepossessing on the exterior, each of the carefully crafted interior fittings has several ingenious functions. Le Corbusier is buried in Roquebrune churchyard, along with his wife, in a tomb he designed himself.

The spectacular path leads from Cap Martin to Monte-Carlo beach. If you walk it (about a four-hour walk), look back towards the Cap to see the ruined tower of the long-gone **convent of St-Martin**. When it was built, the men of Roquebrune vowed to protect the nuns from pirates, and one night in the late 14th century the tower's bell sounded the alarm; the Roquebrunois piled out of bed and ran down the hill to defend the good sisters, who laughingly confessed that they were just testing the bell's efficiency. A few nights later, pirates really did appear, and although the nuns rang like mad, their defenders only rolled over in bed. Next morning, in the smouldering ruins, the older nuns were found with their throats slit, while the younger, prettier ones had been carted off to the slave markets of Barbary.

Monaco

Big-time tax-dodgers agree: it's hard to beat Monaco for comfort and convenience when the time comes to snuggle down with your piggy chips. Unlike most other tax havens, the Principality is not an island, so you can purr over to France or Italy in the Lamborghini in just a few minutes. The grub is good, you can safely flaunt your jewels and there's enough culture to keep you from feeling a total Philistine; the homeless and other riffraff who might trouble your conscience are kept at bay. Security, understandably, is the prime concern: closed-circuit cameras spy over every corner; every traffic signal records every passing car. In emergencies, the whole Principality can be closed off in a few minutes.

Rainier III, chairman of the board of Monaco Inc., will probably go down in history as the Principality's greatest benefactor. Through landfill and burrowing he has added a fifth to his realm and on it built more (but certainly not better) structures than any of his predecessors, creating a Lilliputian Manhattan. Of the Principality's some 32,000 residents, only 4–5,000 are actually his subjects. To obtain one of the precious resident's permits, you have to own or rent a flat in one of these grey towers and watch your ass. Residents who still choose to work, the Luciano Pavarottis and Claudia Schiffers, are hardly ever home. Money is the main topic of conversation no matter where you go in this perfectly sanitized bolthole on the Med, where a calendar of car races, circuses, fireworks, First Division football and operas puts a glittering mask over its ghoulish, acquisitive face.

History Starts with a Stinker

Seven hundred years ago, in 1297, an ambitious member of Genoa's Guelph party, Francesco Grimaldi the Spiteful, dressed up like a friar and knocked at the door of the Ghibelline fortress at Monaco, asking for hospitality. The soldiers sleepily admitted him, whereupon the phoney friar pulled a knife from his robe, killed the soldiers and let in his men. Although Francesco was the first Grimaldi to get into Monaco, the family became lords of their rock only when they purchased it from Genoa in 1308.

Once they were rulers of a mini-empire including Antibes and Menton; today the Grimaldis' sovereign Ruritania has been reduced by the ambitions of others to a sea-hugging 194 hectares (slightly larger than half of Central Park) under the looming mountain, Tête de Chien. Here Rainier III presides as the living representative of the oldest ruling family in Europe, and Europe's last constitutional autocrat.

For centuries the Grimaldis' main income came from a tax levied on Menton's lemons and olives, and when Menton revolted in 1848 they faced bankruptcy; Monaco was the poorest state in all Europe. In desperation, Prince Charles III looked for inspiration to the Duke of Baden-Baden, whose casino lured Europe's big-spending aristocrats every summer. Monaco, Charles decided, would be the winter Baden-Baden, and he founded the **Société des Bains de Mer** (SBM) to operate a casino and tourist industry, with the Principality as the chief shareholder. The casino was built on a rock which the prince named Monte-Carlo after himself, and he hired François Blanc, the talented French manager of the Homburg Baden casino, to create a gambling city to order, 10 per cent of all profits going to the crown. Blanc was one of the most successful financiers of the day and he proved his worth. He loaned the French Government nearly 5 million francs for the completion of Napoléon III's centrepiece, the Paris Opéra, and in return assured that the French built a new railway from Nice in 1868. With transport to bring in the punters, the money poured in by the bushel; in 1870 the coffers were so full that Charles abolished direct taxation in Monaco, a state of affairs that endures to this day.

But gone are those fond days when the Monégasques could live entirely off the folly of others. France and Italy legalized gaming in 1933, ending the Principality's monopoly, and the proportion of its revenue that Monaco gleans from the tables has declined from 95 per cent to a mere 4 per cent. In the dark, bankrupt 1950s, Rainier III gave his little realm a fairytale cachet by wedding a luminous American film actress named Grace Kelly, bringing in a much-needed injection of socialites and their fat bankrolls. Since then, the Prince and the omnipresent SBM have found new ways to keep Monaco's residents from paying income tax, especially in 'offshore' banking (some 50 banks do business here), in the media (Télé and Radio Monte-Carlo), in 'business tourism' (there's a new, ultra-modern congress hall) and tourism, with no little interest fuelled by the media's scrutiny of the sadly tarnished fairytale lives of Princesses Caroline and Stéphanie.

Monte-Carlo

Set back in the sculpture-filled gardens of Place du Casino is the most famous building on the whole Côte d'Azur: the 1863 **Casino de Monte-Carlo** (*t 92 16 20 00, www.casino-monte-carlo.com*), a fascinating piece of Old World kitsch known in its heyday as the 'cathedral of hell'. Anyone over 21 in civilian clothes (no military uniforms) with a passport can visit the *machines à sous* section just inside the door, with one-armed bandits and other mechanized games. To get past the mastodons at the doorway to the glittering Salon of Europe you have to fork out €10; here, American roulette, craps and blackjack tables click and clatter away just as in Las Vegas or Atlantic City. €20 gets you into the *salons privés* (*open June–Oct, Mon–Fri from 4pm, Sat and Sun from 3pm; Nov–May daily from 3pm*), quieter and more intense, where oily croupiers, under gilt, over-the-top rococo ceilings, accept limitless bets on roulette and *chemin de fer*. In the Pink Salon Bar, where naked, cigar-chomping nymphs float on the ceiling, Charles Deville Wells celebrated his three-day gambling spree in 1891 that turned $400 into $40,000 and inspired the popular tune 'The Man who Broke the Bank at Monte-Carlo'. (Later, he spent eight years in prison after being convicted of fraud in England, but no one ever discovered the secret of his success in Monte-Carlo.)

Superstitious gamblers have used a variety of means to ensure the same success: some believed that rubbing the knee of the bronze horse bearing Louis XIV in the

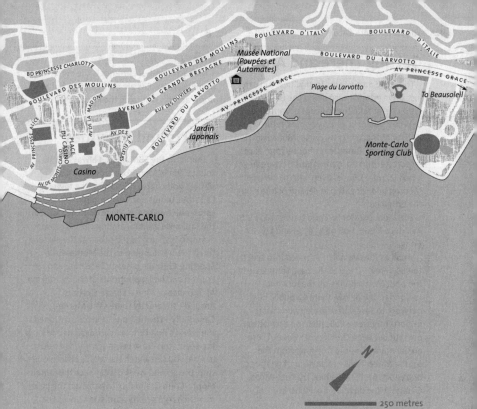

lobby of the Hôtel de Paris next door brought luck. The Prince of Nepal, whose religion only let him gamble for five days a year, had private rooms here so that he wouldn't lose a single precious second, and Cornelius Vanderbilt insisted that his entire family was present before betting a franc. Whatever you do, don't miss the thrill of flushing one of the Casino's loos.

The Casino's bijou opera-theatre, the red and gold **Salle Garnier** (*open only for performances*), was designed by Charles Garnier, his part of the payback for François Blanc's loan that completed his even more elaborate Paris Opéra. Inaugurated by Sarah Bernhardt in 1879 and backed by pots of SBM money, it became one of the most exciting theatres in Europe, especially under Raoul Gunsberg, who had been director of the Tsar Nicholas II Theatre. He commissioned operas from composers like Saint-Saëns and Massenet and, in 1911, invited Diaghilev's Ballets Russes, who became the Ballets de Monte-Carlo in 1926. Since the Second World War it's gone bland and mostly serves as an excuse for residents to put on the dog. But in the old days its gods – Diaghilev, Nijinsky, Stravinsky, and set designers Picasso, Derain and Cocteau – held court among the dukes and flukes in the café of SBM's frothy **Hôtel de Paris**, next to the Casino (*see* 'Where to Stay', p.112). Or as Katherine Mansfield put it: 'the famous Café de Paris with *real* devils with tails under their aprons cursing each other as they hand out the drinks. There at those tables sit the damned.'

Getting There and Around

There are no customs formalities; you can just **drive** into Monaco along the Basse Corniche, or take the **helicopter** from Nice airport if you're in a hurry (7mins, return €145, Héli Air Monaco **t** 92 05 00 50; Monacair **t** 97 97 39 00). **Buses** leave hourly from Nice airport (terminal 2, 9am–9pm), or you can get a **taxi** (45mins). Buses every 15mins between Menton and Nice stop at several points along the Corniche.

The Monaco/Monte-Carlo **train** station is in Av Prince Pierre, **t** 08 92 35 35 35 and **t** 93 10 60 15.

Small as it is, Monaco is divided into several towns: Monte-Carlo to the east, Fontvieille by the port, Monaco-Ville on the rock and La Condamine below; there's a **public bus** network to save you some legwork. More importantly, free **public lifts** and **escalators** operate between the tiers of streets. These are all marked on the free map from the tourist office. **Taxis** run 24 hours, **t** 93 15 01 01 or 93 30 71 63. For **bike hire**, try Auto-Moto Garage, 7 Rue de Millo, **t** 93 50 10 80.

Tourist Information

Note: If the telephone number has only eight digits, you must dial **t** 00 377 before calling from anywhere outside Monaco, even from France. If the number has 10 digits, it operates like a French number.

Monaco: 2a Bd des Moulins, Monaco, **t** 92 16 61 16, **f** 92 16 60 00, *dtc@monaco-tourisme.com*, *www.monaco-tourisme.com*. *Open Mon–Sat 9–7, Sun 10–12.*

Markets

Daily am: Marché de la Condamine, Place d'Armes.
Near Eglise St-Charles: Mon–Sat 7–1, Mon, Tues, Thurs, Fri also 4–7.30, food market.
Sat: Port de Fontieille, flea market.

Money

Monaco's unit of currency is the euro; Monégasque coins are in circulation but are rarely accepted outside the Principality.

Sports and Activities

Thanks to the SBM, there's always something to do in Monaco: a mountain-top 18-hole **golf course** high above the town at La Turbie; **tennis** and every imaginable **water sport**; one **free beach** (Plage du Larvotto, near the Japanese garden) among the exclusive paying ones, such as the beach at the eastern tip of town belonging to the **Monte-Carlo Sporting Club**; deep-sea tuna fishing and cruises; and **helicopter tours** of the coast (Héli Air Monaco or Monacair, *see* 'Getting Around'). In January there's the **Monte-Carlo Rally** – the first one in 1902 occasioned the world's first tarmac road, designed to keep the spectators from being sprayed with dust. In April you can watch the tennis championship; the second week of May sees the famous **Monte-Carlo Grand Prix** (when even the pavements charge a hefty admission price). For **football** tickets at the Louis II stadium, call **t** 92 05 40 00.

Where to Stay

Monaco ✉ 98030, **t** (00 377–)

Monaco's hotels have nearly as many stars as the Milky Way, so if you'd like one of the few more reasonably priced rooms in the summer, you can't reserve early enough.

Luxury

*****Hôtel de Paris**, Place du Casino, **t** 92 16 30 00, **f** 92 16 38 49, *www.montecarloresort. com*. A palatial residence where the tycoons check in. Opened in 1865 by the SBM for gambling tsars and duchesses, it now has direct access to the modern-day Riviera

If smug displays of wealth give you the misanthropic jitters, you can take comfort in the porcelain, metal, wood and plastic people in the **Musée National (Poupées et Automates)** (*17 Av Princesse Grace, **t** 93 30 91 26, www.monte-carlo.mc/musee-national; open Easter–Sept daily 10–6.30; Oct–Easter daily 10–12.15 and 2.30–6.30; adm*), in a luscious campanile villa designed by Charles Garnier, surrounded by rose gardens.

prerequisite, a thalassotherapy centre. Also houses the famous Café de Paris, t 92 16 20 20.

*****Hermitage**, Square Beaumarchais, t 92 16 40 00, f 92 16 38 52, *www.monte carloresort.com*. Also owned by the SBM, this Belle Epoque hotel perched high on its rock, overlooking the Port d'Hercule, has an Italian loggia and a sumptuous 'Winter Garden' designed by Gustave Eiffel.

Hôtel Columbus Monaco, 23 Av des Papalins, t 92 05 90 00, f 92 05 91 67, *www.columbus hotels.com*. Stylish boutique hotel with all the amenities, a favourite with glittering young celebs. Bar open to non-guests.

Very Expensive

***Terminus**, 9 Av Prince Pierre, t 92 05 63 00, f 92 05 20 10, *www.terminus.monte-carlo.mc*. This may be yet another concrete high-rise block, but it has been refurbished recently and to spend a night here still doesn't quite require a king's ransom.

Expensive

***Balmoral**, 12 Av de la Costa, t 93 50 62 37, f 93 15 08 69, *resa@hotel-balmoral.mc*, *www.hotel-balmoral.mc*. Next door to the Hermitage, for a fraction of the price and with a view of the sea, the old Balmoral is a top choice.

***Hôtel Alexandra**, 35 Bd Princesse Charlotte, t 93 50 63 13, f 92 16 06 48, *hotel-alexandra@monaco377.com*. More turn-of-the-last-century opulence is to be had at this gilded hotel.

Le Versailles, 4 Av Prince Pierre, t 93 50 79 34, f 93 25 53 64, *hotel-versailles@monte-carlo.mc*. A cheaper choice near the station, with a reasonable French–Italian restaurant.

Moderate

Hôtel de France, 6 Rue de la Turbie, t 93 30 24 64, f 92 16 13 34, *hotel-france@monte-carlo.mc*. A peachy building in a street full of art galleries.

Helvetia, 1 bis Rue Grimaldi, t 93 30 21 71, f 92 16 70 51, *hotel-helvetia@monte-carlo.mc*, *www.monte-carlo.mc/helvetia*. An old-fashioned place overlooking a pedestrianized shopping street lined with orange trees.

Eating Out

Very Expensive

Louis XV, Hôtel de Paris (*see above*), t 92 16 29 76. In Monte-Carlo, those who make it big at the tables, or have simply made it big at life in general, dine in the incredible golden setting of the Louis XV. This was a favourite of Edward VII when he was Prince of Wales; once, while dining here with his mistress, he was served a crêpe smothered in kirsch, curaçao and maraschino that its 14-year-old maker, Henri Charpentier (who went on to fame as a chef in America), accidentally set alight, only to discover that the flambéeing improved it a hundredfold. The Prince himself suggested that they name the new dessert after his companion, hence *crêpes Suzette*.
Under Alain Ducasse, the youngest chef ever to earn three Michelin stars, the cuisine is once again kingly – and is as sumptuous and spectacular as the setting. *Closed Tues, and Wed, also Dec and mid-Feb–mid-Mar*.

Expensive

Le Vistamar, in the Hermitage hotel (*see above*). A riotous pink and silver period piece, and a historical monument to boot, the famous Belle Epoque is now reserved for groups; in its stead, Le Vistamar, t 92 16 27 72, offers fresh fish dishes like the *pescadou à pesca du matin*, which brings the fish from the sea to your plate in under an hour at lunchtime.

L'Hirondelle, 2 Av Monte-Carlo, t 92 16 49 30. Gourmets on a diet can take solace here,

Jolliest among the exhibits is an enormous 18th-century Neapolitan *presepio*, or Christmas crib, with 250 figurines from Virgin to sausage-vendor. A smaller room holds a Josephine Baker automaton in a grass skirt and Princess Caroline's Barbie doll.

Just west of here, along Av Princesse Grace, you can unfray your nerves for free with a dose of Côte d'Azur Shintoism at the **Jardin Japonais** (*open daily 9am–nightfall*),

with lovely, light dishes accompanied by views over the sea. *Lunch only.*

Moderate–Cheap

Le St Benoît, 10 ter Av de la Costa (enter the car park and take the lift up), t 93 25 02 34. Just below the Hermitage, Le St Benoît offers superb seafood to go with the views from the terrace, high above the port. Some dishes *expensive. Closed Mon lunch and Sat lunch, and Dec.*

Loga Café, 25 Bd des Moulins, t 93 30 87 72. Sit out on the terrace and dine sumptuously on *barbagiuan* (a kind of fried cheese- and leek-filled pie) or *stocafi* (stockfish stewed with tomatoes, herbs, wine and olives), and other Monégasque specialities. *Closed Sun and Aug.*

Le Périgordin, 5 Rue des Oliviers, t 93 30 06 02. For rich duck dishes straight out of the Dordogne. *Closed Sat lunch and Sun and last 2 weeks Aug.*

Tony, 6 Rue Comte Félix Gastaldi, t 93 30 81 37. Another good choice, near the palace, with generous menus. *Lunch only. Closed Sat and Nov–Dec.*

Le Texan, 4 Rue Suffren Reymond, La Condamine, t 93 30 34 54. Come to this vivacious, rowdy, Tex-Mex joint just up from the port for the possibility of brushing shoulders with Crown Prince Albert and Boris Becker over a pizza. One of the best value places for beer. *Lunch only. Closed Sun.*

Entertainment and Nightlife

Nightlife in Monaco is a glitzy, bejewelled fashion parade catered for by the omnipresent SBM at the **Monte-Carlo Sporting Club**, Av Princesse Grace, with its summer discotheque, Las Vegas-style floor shows, dancing, restaurants and casino. There are similar offerings at **SBM/Loews**

Monte-Carlo, 12 Av des Spélugues, and at the **American Bar** at the Hôtel de Paris.

Jimmy'z, 26 Av Princesse Grace, t 92 16 22 77. Entrance is free, but the drinks require a small bank loan at Monte-Carlo's number one dance club, favourite of U2, Sting and other rich old men. Now has a Cuban cigar bar. Upstairs is the **Bar et Bœuf**, t 92 16 60 60, the Philippe Starck-designed Alain Ducasse restaurant. Open till the small hours. *Closed Nov–May.*

Le Stars n' Bars, 6 Quai Antoine 1er, t 97 97 95 95, *www.starsnbars.com.* Young people from all along the coast drive to this sports bar and club. *Closed Mon in winter.*

Flashman's, 7 Av Princesse Alice, t 93 30 09 03. A Brit-run imitation pub, open until the wee hours.

Ship and Castle, 42 Quai Jean-Charles Rey, t 92 05 76 72. Another late-running Brit-pub (which also serves food).

Opera, Circus and Fireworks

In January the **opera**, **theatre** and **ballet** season begins (t 92 16 22 99 or t 99 99 30 30 for info).

In January or February there is an excellent **Circus Festival** (t 92 05 23 45); in March, join or at least gawp at the queues of the high and mighty for the annual **Rose Ball**.

Sign up for well-attended **Concerts at the Palace** in July, August, October and December. The Monégasque **National Holiday** is 18–19 Nov.

Cinema

Cinéma d'été, t 08 36 68 00 72, 26 Terrasses du Parking des Pêcheurs. Open-air and showing a different film in its original language every evening at 9.30 from 25 June to 10 September.

Cinéma Le Sporting, Place du Casino, t 08 36 68 00 72, *www.cinemasporting.com.* Three screens.

with waterfalls, ponds and a cedar-wood Tea House. It has been blessed by a Shinto priest and the gardeners have even been taught special Eastern methods of pruning the pine and olive trees, but the calm is ruffled by the posse of boiler-suited men who ensure the rules (no picnicking, no games, no balls) are kept. Further east are beaches of imported sand, resort hotels and the élite **Monte-Carlo Sporting Club**.

La Condamine and Fontvieille

The natural amphitheatre of La Condamine, the port quarter between Monte-Carlo and Monaco-Ville, has suffered the most from the speculators, their big cement brutes dwarfing the 11th-century votive chapel dedicated to Monaco's patron saint, **Ste-Dévote**. After her martyrdom in Corsica in 305, Dévote's body was put in a boat that sailed by itself, guided by a dove that flew out of her mouth, to Monaco (still known then as Portus Herculis Monoeci, after Hercules). In the 11th century some relic pirates snatched her bones, only to be foiled when the Monégasques set their boat on fire, an event re-enacted every 26 January amidst the armada of yachts, with a big celebratory procession the next day.

From Place Ste-Dévote, Rue Grimaldi leads west to Place du Canton and the **Zoological Terraces** (*t 93 25 18 31; open daily June–Oct 9–12 and 2–7; Mar–May 10–12 and 2–6; Oct–Feb 10–12 and 2–5; adm*), used to acclimatize animals imported from the tropics, including a black panther, a white tiger and some disgruntled rhinos.

Or there's the Prince's very own **Collection de Voitures Anciennes** (*t 92 05 28 56; open 10–6; adm*), which displays over 100 vintage cars, including the 1929 Bugatti which won the first Grand Prix. At the **Musée des Timbres et des Monnaies** (*t 93 15 41 50; open daily 10–5, in summer until 6; adm*) visitors can admire the fruits of Prince Rainier III's other hobby, probably kept for rainy days: coins, bank notes, commemorative medals and a 60-year-old copper stamp press are on display with a gift of 'a free stamp for paying guests' at the end of the tour. Nearby, the **Musée Naval** (*t 92 05 28 48, www.musee-naval.mc; open daily 10–6; adm*) has more examples of earnest princely passions, this time models of famous ships from the *Titanic* to the battleship *Missouri*. The earliest were constructed by Prince Albert Ier (the 'Scientist Prince') at the end of the 19th century.

More unusual are the prickly contents of a garden near the Moyenne Corniche, the **Jardin Exotique** (*t 93 15 29 80, bus no.2; www.monte-carlo.mc/jardinexotique; open daily mid-May–mid-Sept 9–7; winter 9– 6 or nightfall; adm*), where 6,000 succulents planted in the rock face of the Tête de Chien in 1933 range from the absurd to the obscene. Footbridges dangle over 33ft African 'candelabra' cacti, which seem to be holding out their arms to catch the less-than-nimble

The same ticket admits you to the adjacent **Grottes de l'Observatoire**, one of the few places in Provence inhabited in the Palaeolithic era and, curiously, the only cave in Europe that gets warmer instead of cooler as you descend into its maw. Here, too, is the **Musée d'Anthropologie Préhistorique** (*t 93 15 80 06*), where the collection includes the bones of reindeer, mammoths and hippopotami, along with some from early editions of humankind.

To the south, between the sea and the ultra-modern **Stade Louis II** (*t 92 05 40 11; guided tours in English Mon, Tues, Thurs and Fri at 2.30 and 4pm, except during events; adm*), where AS Monaco regularly punish the rest of the French football league, stretches Fontvieille Park, where the charming **Princess Grace Rose Garden** (*open daily dawn–dusk*) is a memorial to Monaco's beloved princess, film actress and daughter of an Irish-American brick magnate in Philadelphia – the very same Kelly who supplied Ignatz mouse with ammo in George Herriman's classic comic strip *Krazy Kat*.

Near here, a **sculpture path** winds its immaculate way up from the Place du Campanile St-Nicholas. The whirling figures of Arman's *Cavalleria Eroica* and César's massive clenched fist look incongruously emotional against the fastidiously manicured lawns.

Up on the Rock: Monaco-Ville

In 1860 the Principality of Monaco consisted of 2,000 people living in this old Italian town, clinging spectacularly to a promontory 300m above the sea; they never dreamed it would turn into a shopping centre for Prince Rainier ashtrays and Princess Grace dolls. As scrubbed and cute as any town in Legoland, it offers devilries that make the Casino seem like an honest proposition: the **Historial des Princes de Monaco** (*27 Rue Basse, t 93 30 39 05; open Mar–Sept daily 9–6; Oct–Feb daily 11–5; adm*), with waxworks running the gamut from Francesco the Spiteful to Caroline and Stéphanie; the **Multi-vision Monte-Carlo Story** (*Terrasses du Parking du Chemin-des-Pêcheurs, t 93 25 32 33; showings hourly July and Aug 2–6; Jan–June and Sept–Oct 2–5; adm*), which presents 'Monaco le Film' and a mildly interesting collection of old film posters and magic lanterns; and the **Musée des Souvenirs Napoléoniens** (*Pl du Palais, t 93 25 18 31; open June–Sept daily 9.30–6; Oct daily 10–5; Dec–May Tues–Sun 10.30–12.30 and 2–5, closed Mon; adm*), with over 1,000 items connected to the little Corsican, including 'garments and toys belonging to the King of Rome!' – his ill-fated son.

Also along Rue Basse is the pink and yellow **Chapel of Mercy**, built in 1639 and disfigured in the 19th century by a sickly ceramic adoration scene above the door; inside is sculpted woodwork by Napoleon's official sculptor, François Josef-Bosio. It was the seat of the Brotherhood of the Black Penitents, whose first prior was Monaco's Prince Honoré II. In the **Musée de la Chapelle de la Visitation** (*t 93 50 07 00; open Tues–Sun 10–4; closed Mon; adm*), thanks to a sizeable private donation of sacred art, Rubens' podgy angels and Ribeira's bleeding martyrs float in the 17th-century Baroque chapel.

From June to October you can yawn your way through the plush **Palais Princier** itself (*t 93 25 18 31; open June–Sept daily 9.30–6; Oct daily 10–5; closed Nov–May; adm*) which, with its 19th-century 'medieval towers', is built around the Genoese fortress of 1215 (note the Grimaldi coat of arms, featuring two sword-wielding monks). At other times, when Rainier's at home, you'll have to be content with the rooty-toot-toot 11.55am **Changing of the Monégasque Guard**. Here, too, is Monaco's unattractive **cathedral**, built in 1875 using white stone from La Turbie, at the expense of a Romanesque chapel. From the chapel it inherited two lovely retables by Ludovico Brea from the early 16th century: *La Pietà*, over the sacristy door, and the grand *St Nicolas* with 18 panels, in the ambulatory. The more recent princes of Monaco are buried here, including Princess Grace, whose simple tomb inscribed '*Gratia Patricia Principis Rainerii III Uxor*' is often bedecked with nosegays from admirers, all waiting for the miracle that will sway the Vatican to beatify her.

Monaco's most compelling attraction is nearby: the **Musée Océanographique de Monaco** (*Av St-Martin, t 93 15 36 00, www.oceano.mc; July–Aug daily 9–8; April–June and Sept 9–7; Oct–Mar 10–6; adm*), founded in 1910 by Prince Albert Ier, who sank all of his casino profits into a passion for deep-sea exploration. To house the treasures he accumulated in his 24 voyages, he built this museum in a cliff, filling it with instruments, shells, whale skeletons and, on the ground floor, a fascinating aquarium where 90 tanks hold some of the most surreal fish ever netted from the briny deep, including a mesmerizing cylindrical tank where thousands of identical fish swim in an endless circling shoal. The rest of the building is taken up with research laboratories, which used to be headed by Jacques Cousteau, specializing in the study of ocean pollution and radioactivity. You can park directly underneath and get a lift straight up into the museum, but don't neglect to go out and look back at this remarkable Belle Epoque building clinging to its cliff, with an 250ft sheer stone façade.

Besides the path east to Cap Martin (*see* p.108), there's another trail that begins on the D53 in Beausoleil, Monaco's French suburb, and ascends to the top of **Mont des Mules**. A third path, beginning at Fontvieille's Plage Marquet, heads west along the crashing sea to the train station at **Cap d'Ail** (Cape Garlic). It continues around the cape past more snooty Belle Epoque residences, including Greta Garbo's bolthole, and then drops down a wooded slope to the little cove of **Mala Plage**.

Also out here on Cap d'Ail is another jolly Cocteau creation: the **Mediterranean Centre for French Studies** (*t 04 93 78 21 59*). A grassy path decorated with stones etched with cavorting fauns and surreal flowers leads to the open-air theatre; based on a classical Greek amphitheatre, it has bold black and white mosaic profiles in the centre of the circular stage, and a wonderful handrail formed by a sinuous gold and turquoise snake to guide the audience to their seats.

North of Monaco

From Monaco, the D53 ascends to the Grande Corniche, a road the Romans called Via Julia Augusta, built to link up the Urbs to its conquests in Gaul and Spain. Several hard campaigns had to be fought (25–14 BC) before the fierce Ligurians finally let the road-builders through, and in 6 BC the Roman Senate voted to erect a mighty commemorative monument known as the Trophy of the Alps (the Romans called it Tropea Augusti, or 'Augustus' Trophy') at the base of Mont Agel. The views are precipitous, and you can escape the crowds by venturing even further inland to Peille and Peillon, two of the most beautiful villages on the Côte d'Azur, or by following the ancient salt route up the Paillon valley to l'Escarène.

La Turbie and its Trophy

Though hemmed in by upstart mini-villas and second homes, La Turbie (a corruption of Tropea) still retains its old typical core of narrow vaulted alleys, built back in the days when it merited a mention by Dante in *The Divine Comedy*: see the relevant immortal lines proudly engraved on the tower. La Turbie also has an elliptical 18th-century church, **St-Michel-Archange**, with a sumptuous Baroque interior; the altar alone uses 17 different kinds of marble, the communion table glitters with onyx and agate and the paintings are attributed to, or by the schools of, Raphael (*Saint Mark*

Getting Around

By Bus

There are buses daily from Nice (*gare routière*) to La Turbie, continuing up to Peille (not on Sundays), and several from Monaco. Buses leave less regularly from Nice to Peillon.

By Train

Both Peillon and Peille have train stations, but they lie several steep kilometres below their respective villages.

Tourist Information

La Turbie: at the *mairie*, **t** 04 92 41 51 61, **f** 04 93 41 13 99, *accueil@ville-la-turbie.fr. Open Mon and Wed–Fri 9–12 and 2–5, Tues and Sat 9–12; closed Sun.*
Peillon: 620 Av de l'Hôtel-de-Ville, **t** 04 93 91 98 34. *In the old village. Open winter Mon–Fri 1–5; summer Tues–Sat 1–5.*
Peille: at the *mairie*, **t** 04 93 91 71 71, **f** 04 93 79 89 37. *Open Mon–Fri 9–12.*

Markets

La Turbie: Thurs am, general market.

Where to Stay and Eat

La Turbie ✉ 06320

Le Napoléon, 7 Av de la Victoire, **t 04 93 41 00 54, **f** 04 93 41 28 93 (*moderate*). Ask for a room on the top floor. You can eat good food here, too (*expensive*). *Restaurant closed Wed.*
Hostellerie Jérôme, 20 Rue Comte de Cessole, **t** 04 92 41 51 51 (*very expensive–expensive*). Simple, delicious dishes featuring regional produce. *Eves only; closed Mon and Tues.*

Peillon ✉ 06440

***Auberge de la Madone, **t** 04 93 79 91 17, *www.chateauxhotels.com/madone* (*expensive–moderate*). Just outside the walled village, this family-run inn has astonishing views over the valley. Dine out on its terrace. *Closed Jan, 20 Oct–20 Dec, and Wed.*
Auberge Lou Pourtail, **t** 04 93 79 94 58 (*inexpensive*). A cheaper but equally charming annexe to the Auberge de la Madone. *Closed Jan.*

Peille ✉ 06440

*Belvédère, Place Jean Miol, **t** 04 93 79 90 45, **f** 04 93 91 93 47 (*inexpensive*). The only hotel in the village, the Belvédère has five simple rooms with mountain views and a restaurant (*moderate–cheap; book*). *Closed Dec.*

writing the Gospel), Veronese, Rembrandt, Ludovico Brea, Murillo and Ribera (a stark *Ste Dévote*) – not bad for a village of 2,000 or so souls!

The old Via Julia Augusta (Rue Comte-de-Cessole) passes through town on its way to the **Trophy of the Alps**. This monument originally stood 147ft high, supporting a series of Doric columns interspersed with statues of eminent generals, the whole surmounted by a colossal 20ft statue of Augustus flanked by two captives; on its wall were listed the 44 conquered Ligurian tribes, and stairs throughout allowed passersby to enjoy the view. When St Honorat saw the local people worshipping this marvel in the 4th century, he vandalized it; in the dark ages it was converted into a fort; Louis XIV ordered it to be blown up in 1705, and the stone was quarried to build St-Michel-Archange. The still formidable pile of rubble that remained in the 1930s was resurrected to 114ft and its inscription replaced thanks to the patronage of a rich American, Edward Tuck. The only other such trophy to survive *in situ* is in Romania, although the base of an even older one has recently been found at Le Perthus on the Spanish border. A small **museum** (*t 04 93 41 20 84; open mid-May–mid-Sept daily 9.30–6; mid-Sept–mid-May Tues–Sun 10–1, 2.30–5; adm*) on the site has models and drawings which trace the Trophy's history, while the park behind offers magnificent views of Monaco and the coast below.

Peillon and Peille

The two villages are tiny and lovely; balanced atop adjacent hills, both require a wearying climb to reach them. But Peille and Peillon aren't quite the Tweedledee and Tweedledum of the Côte. **Peillon**, most easily reached on the D53 from Nice, is a bit posher, complete with a *foyer* – a cobbled square with fountain at the village entrance. Inside are peaceful medieval stairs and arches, which snake up through vaulted passageways to the summit and a theatrically restored Baroque parish church, the **Church of the Transfiguration**, built on the highest point of the village. But Peillon's big attraction is right at the entrance: the **Chapelle des Pénitents Blancs** (*ring the tourist office to arrange a visit, groups only*), adorned with a cycle of Renaissance frescoes on the *Passion of Christ* by the charming and vigorous Giovanni Canavesio (*c.* 1485), who would certainly be better known had he painted anything outside the valleys of the Maritime Alps. Look out for Judas, tormented by a malignant black devil who is ripping out his soul. From Peillon, there are trails that lead to country rambles.

One of those walks (*signposted near the parish church*) follows the Roman road in two hours to **Peille**, further up the D53. More isolated, Peille has more character, and its very own dialect, called *Pelhasc*. There's an ensemble of medieval streets like Peillon's and a church begun in the 12th century, with an interesting medieval portrait of Peille and its now ruined castle. Once, during a drought, Peille asked for help from a shepherd (in Provence, shepherds often moonlight as sorcerers), and he made it rain on condition that the lord of this castle give him his daughter to wed – an event remembered in a fête on the first Sunday in September. The Church may frown at such goings-on, but Peille often had its own ideas on religion, preferring twice in the Middle Ages to be excommunicated rather than pay the bishop's tithes.

The Paillon river flows up the valley to **L'Escarène**, a strategic pit stop in the days of the salt route, when salt from the marshes of Hyères and Toulon was loaded on to mules in Nice and taken across the mountains to Turin.

From the bridge, you can see the houses overhanging the river. The lovely 17th-century neoclassical church of **St-Pierre-aux-Liens** was designed by Jean-André Guibert, architect of the Cathedral Ste-Réparate in Vieux Nice. It was restored in the 19th century with admirable (and unusual) restraint, and now hosts a festival of ancient and Baroque music in the summer. Under its wings, tucked in on either side, are the twin chapels of the Pénitents Blancs, with spectacular rococo decoration, and the Pénitents Noirs.

The Moyenne Corniche

Between Monaco and Nice, the main reason for taking the middle road has long been the extraordinary village of Eze, the most perched, perhaps, of any *village perché* in France, squeezed on to a cone of a hill 1,400ft over the sea. It barely avoided being poached as well as perched in a catastrophic fire in 1986 which ravaged the pine forest that once surrounded the village.

Eze

Eze, they say, is named after a temple to Isis that the Phoenicians built on this hill. The village then passed to the Romans, to the Saracens, and so on, although rarely did Eze change hands by force; even if an enemy penetrated its 14th-century gate and walls, the tight little maze of stairs and alleys would confuse the attackers, the better to ambush them or spill boiling oil on their heads. These days, if intruders got far enough to assault what remains of the castle – 1,400ft above sea level – they would run into the needles of the South American cacti in the **Jardin Exotique** (*t 04 93 41 10 30; open daily Sept–June 9–12 and 2–6; July–Aug 9–8; adm*), a spiky paradise created on municipal initiative in 1949 by *ingénieur agronome* Jean Gastauld.

Eze's other non-commercial attraction, the cream and yellow **Chapelle des Pénitents Blancs**, built in 1766, has gathered an eccentric collection of scraps: an old model of a sailing ship is suspended from the ceiling in place of a missing chandelier, and a

Getting There and Around

Métrazur **trains** stop at Eze's coastal outpost; in summer a minibus (*navette*) will shuttle you up from the Basse Corniche to Eze-Village and Eze-Grande Corniche. It's a *very* arduous walk up otherwise, taking over an hour even for the fit. (Eze-Village is the destination you really want, for sightseeing.)

There are several **buses** a day (no.112) from Nice directly for Eze-Village. All the buses on the Nice–Menton line stop at Eze-Bord-de-Mer. Some buses from Nice to Peille stop at Eze-Grande Corniche.

Tourist Information

Eze: Place du Général de Gaulle, **t** 04 93 41 26 00, **f** 04 93 41 04 80, *www.eze-riviera.com*. Walkers can pick up an excellent little guide to walks in the area here. *Open April–Oct daily 9–7; Nov–Mar daily 9–6.30. Closed hols, and Sun Nov–Mar*. There's also a small office on the Basse Corniche, near the station. *Open April–Oct Mon–Sat 10–1 and 3–6.30.*

Shopping

Every other doorway in Eze spills over with art or souvenirs, with the usual range of quality. There are one or two more unusual places worth seeking out.

Terre de Provence, 20 Rue Principale, **t** 04 92 10 85 63, **f** 04 92 10 85 82. Whitewashed and wooden-beamed, with a selection of the best Provençal wines, regional delicacies and beautiful tableware and crystal.

La Salamandre, near the Jardin Exotique, **t** 04 93 41 19 06. A friendly shop offering soft cotton and linen clothes, mostly made in France and often dyed in sunny Provençal colours. *Closed Nov–Mar*.

Where to Stay and Eat

Eze ✉ 06360

A road links the three *corniches* at Eze, and there are hotels on each level.

Eze-Grande Corniche

****Les Terrasses d'Eze**, Rte de la Turbie, **t** 04 92 41 55 55, **f** 04 92 41 55 10, *info@ terrasses-eze.com, www.terrasses-eze.com* (*luxury–very expensive; half-board compulsory in season*). Part of the Best Western chain. The rooms are not quite as big as you might hope for the price, but the restaurant (*expensive*) offers the best views along the coast to go with the rich Mediterranean cuisine.

****L'Hermitage**, Grande Corniche, 2km from Eze village, **t** 04 93 41 00 68, **f** 04 93 41 24 05 (*inexpensive*). Two kilometres from Eze, L'Hermitage offers priceless views, traditional décor and monstrous portions

disembodied arm brandishes a 13th-century Catalan crucifix, the *Christ of the Black Death* (as is typical in medieval Catalan art, the sculptor emphasized Christ's divine nature, and he smiles, even on the Cross). Here, too, is a 14th-century *Madone des Forêts*, where baby Jesus, rather unusually, holds a pine cone.

A scenic path descending to Eze-Bord-de-Mer is called the **Sentier Frédéric Nietzsche** after the philosopher. (It starts at the entrance to the old village, down a narrow, almost hidden, path on the left, which also leads to a small observation spot.) Nietzsche, however, walked up instead of down, an arduous trek that made his head spin and inspired the third part of his *Thus Spake Zarathustra*.

He might have cleared his head up in the park which curls around the **Grande Corniche**, a speleologists' delight with caves and chasms. Nature trails, bike trails and horse trails splinter off in all directions and an orientation table surmounts a Genoese-style tower, looking across the Plateau de la Justice, where the gibbet of the Lords of Eze once stood, and out to Corsica and St-Tropez.

of startlingly good, very moderately priced Provençal food. From the hotel a footpath leads along the ancient Voie Aurélienne on to Mont Leuze, with breathtaking views. *Closed Dec–Jan; restaurant closed Thurs and Fri lunch.*

Eze-Village (Moyenne Corniche)

In Eze-Village there are two luxurious inns with only a handful of rooms each to let, but superb kitchens.

****Château Eza**, Rue de la Pise, t 04 93 41 12 24, f 04 93 41 16 64, *www.chateza.com* (*luxury*). This former prince's residence is actually a collection of medieval houses linked together to form an eagle's nest, all sharing an extraordinary perched terrace restaurant (*very expensive–expensive*). *Closed Nov–Mar; restaurant closed Nov–Christmas, and Tues and Wed in winter.*

****Château de la Chèvre d'Or**, Rue du Barri, t 04 92 10 66 66, f 04 93 41 06 72, *www.chevredor. com* (*luxury*). In a medieval castle rebuilt in the 1920s, this romantic Relais & Châteaux hotel has a small park rippling down the mountain-side, a pool and more ravishing views. Chef Jean-Marc Delacourt creates refined, light versions of the French classics (*very expensive*). *Reserve well in advance. Closed Dec–Feb.*

Le Troubadour, 4 Rue du Brec, t 04 93 41 19 03 (*expensive*). Turbot or *filet de bœuf aux cèpes* go down nicely here, and the price is nice

too. *Closed Sun and Mon lunch and mid-Nov–mid-Dec.*

Le Nid d'Aigle, Rue du Château, t 04 93 41 19 08 (*moderate*). Head to this place on the summit of the rock, next door to the Jardin Exotique, for lofty fish (*daurade au pistou*, salmon) and all kinds of Provençal staples, including *lapin à la provençale*.

Mas Provençal, Av de Verdun, t 04 93 41 19 53 (*expensive*). Just outside the tangle of medieval streets, this friendly *mas* is completely covered in flowers and ivy, and comfortably ensconced in the 19th century. Sink into plush red velvet chairs (with anti-macassars) and dine on milk-fed pig roasted on a spit, or *risotto aux cèpes*, before ordering the carriage home. *Closed Sun in winter and mid-Feb–Mar.*

Eze-Bord-de-Mer

*****Cap Estel**, t 04 93 01 50 44, f 04 93 01 55 20, (*luxury*). Set in a park, this luxurious, sparkling Riviera dream, which was originally built for a Russian princess, has two heated pools and a flight of movie-star steps down to the manicured gardens. *Ring for closing dates.*

Auberge Le Soleil, t 04 93 01 51 46, f 04 93 01 58 40, *www.auberge-le-soleil.cote.azur.fr* (*moderate*). A family-run place with well-priced rooms and gourmet dining (*expensive–moderate*). *Hotel closed Nov, restaurant closed Mon eve and Tues eve.*

The Basse Corniche

To the west of Eze-Bord-de-Mer another wooded promontory, Cap Ferrat, protrudes into the sea to form today's most fashionable address on the Côte d'Azur. The fascinating, wildly eclectic Villa Ephrussi de Rothschild and gardens crown the summit of Cap Ferrat, while the awful King Léopold II of the Belgians, Otto Preminger and Somerset Maugham had sanctuaries by the sea. To the east, the peninsula and steep mountain backdrop keep Beaulieu so sheltered that it shares with Menton the distinction of being the hottest town in France, while to the west the Corniche skirts the top of the fine old village of Villefranche-sur-Mer, with a port deep enough for battleships – grey tokens from the grey world beyond the Riviera.

Beaulieu

'*O qual bel luogo!*' exclaimed Napoleon in his Corsican mother tongue, and the bland name stuck to this lush, banana-growing town overlooking the Baie des Fourmis (Bay of Ants), so called for the black boulders in the sea. It was eccentric American millionaire and press baron James Gordon Bennett who put Beaulieu on the European tourist map; after his enforced exile from New York, he idled along the Riviera coast in his extravagant yacht and was smitten by the bay. The local fishermen refused to let him buy it and build a fabulously expensive new port, and he had to be content with establishing a coach service betweeen Nice and Beaulieu, drawn by four horses and sometimes accompanied by a brass band, to bring in the sun-seekers.

Beaulieu admits to a mere four days of frost a year and calls its steamy easternmost suburb La Petite Afrique; most of its affluent population are trying to imitate Gustave Eiffel, who retired here and lived to be 90. Beaulieu's vintage **casino** (*open daily 11am–4am, 5am at weekends*) has been renovated after years of dilapidation and is back to its former sparkling grandeur, with all the usual means of squandering fortunes, along with restaurants and a *salon* for *dîners-spectacles*. The *thés dansants* held in **La Rotonde** are a further retro attraction, but the *real* magnet is a place so retro that even Socrates would feel at home there: the **Villa Kérylos** (*t 04 93 76 44 09, www.villa-kerylos.com; bus stop Hôtel Métropole then a 5min walk; open July–Aug daily 10–7; Feb–June and Sept–Oct daily 10–6; Nov–Jan Mon–Fri 2–6, Sat, Sun and school hols 10–6; adm*), a striking reproduction of a wealthy 5th-century BC Athenian's abode, furnishings and garden, built in 1908 by archaeologist Théodore Reinach. The marble bathroom is fantastically opulent, with a submerged throne and a playful mosaic of bizarre sea creatures. The library beats most poky studies; built over two storeys, the lofty ceilings and high windows let in long shafts of natural light, along with the gentle rushing sound of the sea. Outside, the sea breeze ruffles the aromatic herbs and plants, which draw droves of giant dragonflies, buzzing like mini-helicopters. Reinach spared no expense on the marble, ivory, bronze, mosaic and fresco reproductions to help his genuine antiquities feel at home; glass windows, plumbing and a hidden piano which unfolds like a Chinese puzzle box are the only modern

Getting Around

The most amusing way to visit is by way of the Côte d'Azur's equivalent of Hollywood's 'See the Homes of the Stars' bus tours: a 'little train' starts on the quay at Villefranche and chugs around the promontory with a guide calling out, in French and abominable English, the names of the famous who live(d) in the villas.

Tourist Information

Beaulieu: Place Clemenceau, t 04 93 01 02 21, f 04 93 01 44 04, *tourisme@ot-beaulieu-sur-mer.fr, www.ot-beaulieu-sur-mer.fr. Open Sept–June Mon–Sat 9–12.15 and 2–6; July–Aug Mon–Sat 9–12.30 and 2–7, Sun 9–12.30*.

Market Days

Beaulieu: daily, fruit and vegetable market on Place du Marché. Expands to include clothes and household goods on Saturdays. An antiques (and *brocante* – 'junk') market takes place by the port on the third Sunday of each month.

Where to Stay and Eat

Beaulieu-sur-Mer ✉ 06310
****La Réserve, 5 Bd Général Leclerc, t 04 93 01 00 01, f 04 93 01 28 99, *reserve@wanadoo.fr, www.reservebeaulieu.com* (*luxury*). In the 1870s, when the wealthy James Gordon Bennett, owner of the *New York Herald* and the man who sent Stanley to find Livingstone, was booted out of New York society for his scandalous behaviour, he came to the Riviera and ran the Paris edition of his newspaper from here. It is now one of the most exclusive hotels on the Riviera and offers grand sea views, a beach and marina, heated pool and more delights, including an elegant neo-Renaissance restaurant (*very expensive*). *Closed mid-Nov–mid Dec*.

***Artemis, 3 Bd Maréchal Joffre, t 04 93 01 12 15, f 04 93 01 27 46, *www.hotel-artemis.com* (*expensive*). Near the station, this modern hotel has rooms with balconies and access to a pool at the back. *Closed Jan*.

**Le Havre Bleu, 29 Bd Maréchal Joffre, t 04 93 01 01 40, f 04 93 01 29 92, *hotel.lehavrebleu@wanadoo.fr, www.hotel-lehavrebleu.fr* (*moderate–inexpensive*). Attractive hotel with pleasant rooms, many with terraces. *Closed Dec*.

**Sélect, 1 Rue André Cane, t 04 93 01 05 42, f 04 93 01 34 30 (*inexpensive*). This small, simple place near the station is convenient yet impersonal.

*Le Riviera, 6 Rue Paul Doumer, t 04 93 01 04 92, f 04 93 01 19 31 (*inexpensive*). With pretty wrought-iron balconies, just up from the Basse Corniche. *Closed Nov–after Xmas*.

Le Catalan, Bd Maréchal Leclerc, t 04 93 01 02 78 (*moderate–cheap*). Wood-fired pizzas and delicious pasta abound round the corner from the Riviera hotel (*à la carte*). *Closed Sun*.

Le Salon des Ambassadeurs, 4 Av Fernand Dunan, t 04 93 76 48 00 (*moderate–cheap*). To dance all night with the ageing but still game local retirees, head for the casino's piano-bar and restaurant. Friday 9pm–3am.

anachronisms. And here, on a shore that reminded him of the Aegean, this ultimate philhellene lived himself like an Athenian, holding symposia, exercising and bathing with his male buddies, and keeping the womenfolk well out of the way.

St-Jean-Cap-Ferrat

Another retro-repro fantasy, the **Villa Ephrussi de Rothschild** (*t 04 93 01 45 90, www.villa-ephrussi.com, a 10min walk from the Basse Corniche, or catch the St-Jean bus which passes its entrance; open July–Aug daily 10–7; Feb–June and Sept–Oct daily 10–6; Nov–Jan Sat, Sun and school hols 10–6, Mon–Fri 2–6 state rooms and gardens only;*

Tourist Information

St-Jean-Cap-Ferrat: 59 Av Denis Séméria, t 04 93 76 08 90, f 04 93 76 16 67, *ot.saintjeancapferrat@tiscali.fr*. Can provide lists of local *chambres d'hôtes*.

Where to Stay and Eat

St-Jean-Cap-Ferrat ✉ 06230

Its villas are the most exclusive on the Riviera, and Cap Ferrat's hotels are in prce ranges to match, beginning with one of the most beautiful small hotels on the entire Côte:

****La Voile d'Or**, Av Jean Mermoz, t 04 93 01 13 13, f 04 93 76 11 17, *www.lavoiledor.fr* (*luxury*). A charming Italian villa, overlooking the marina and once owned by film director Michael Powell, who inherited it from his father (and sold it because no one ever paid their bar bills), the Voile d'Or is an ideal honeymoon hotel, with a garden hanging over the port, a heated pool and rooms with every luxury a hotel could provide. Its equally exceptional restaurant is favoured by the tanned and languid yachting set. *Closed Nov–Mar, and during Grand Prix.*

****Grand Hôtel du Cap Ferrat**, 71 Bd Général de Gaulle, t 04 93 76 50 50, f 04 93 76 04 52, *reserv@grand-hotel-cap-ferrat.com*, *www.grand-hotel-cap-ferrat.com* (*luxury*). At the very fashionable Belle Epoque Grand Hôtel the already luxurious rooms have been restored in a more airy, comfortable Riviera style, all set in acres of gardens, lawns and palms. A funicular railway lowers guests down to an Olympic-size seawater swimming pool just over the Mediterranean. Its restaurant, **Le Cap**, on a palatial terrace shaded by parasol pines, serves delicious meals (*very expensive*) decidedly unhealthy for your wallet. *Closed Jan–Feb.*

****Royal Riviera**, 3 Av Jean Monnet, t 04 93 76 31 00, f 04 93 01 23 07, *www.royal-riviera.com* (*luxury*). A sumptuous hotel in a pale pink Belle Epoque villa set, again, in acres of elegantly landscaped gardens, with the usual Riviera paraphernalia: a sandy private beach offering a wide variety of watersports; an airy, terraced restaurant serving classic French and Provençal cuisine (*expensive*); and a nearby helipad to park the runaround. *Closed Dec–19 Jan.*

More down-to-earth choices include:

***Brise-Marine**, Av Jean Mermoz, t 04 93 76 04 36, f 04 93 76 11 49, *info@hotel-brise-marine.com*, *www.hotel-brisemarine.com* (*expensive*). With a garden, terrace and large rooms, half with sea views. *Closed Nov–Jan.*

Clair Logis, 12 Av Centrale, t 04 93 76 04 57, f 04 93 76 11 85 (*expensive–moderate*). Near the centre of the Cap, this wonderful and very reasonable hotel is in a welcoming villa set back in a lush enclosed garden (*no restaurant*). *Closed Dec–Feb.*

Le Cap, Grand Hôtel du Cap Ferrat (*very expensive, see above*). Nice but pricey restaurant.

Le Provençal, Place Clemenceau, t 04 93 76 03 97 (*very expensive–expensive*). For a frisson of south-coast *hauteur*.

Around the Port de Plaisance (marina) you'll find several nautically named beaneries:

Le Pirate, t 04 93 76 12 97 (*moderate*).

Le Sloop, t 04 93 01 48 63 (*moderate*).

Skipper, t 04 93 76 01 00 (*moderate*). Best for the fish on its well-priced menus.

adm) crowns the narrow isthmus of bucolic Cap Ferrat, enjoying spectacular views over both the Baie des Fourmis and the harbour of Villefranche. The flamboyant Béatrice de Rothschild, who never went anywhere without her trunk of 50 wigs and greeted guests to her parties dressed as Marie-Antoinette, was a compulsive art collector and lover of the 18th century and, after marrying the banker Baron Ephrussi, had this Italianate villa specially built to house her treasures – a Venetian rococo room was designed for Béatrice's Tiepolo ceiling, while other rooms set off her Renaissance furniture, Florentine bridal chests, paintings by Boucher, rare Chinese screens and furniture, Flemish and Beauvais tapestries, Sèvres and Meissen porcelain,

Louis-Quinze and Louis-Seize furniture, covered Andalucían patio (a favourite location shot for films), hidden bathroom and collection of porcelain chamber pots.

To create the equally eclectic gardens, the isthmus was given a crew cut and terraced into different levels, all linked together by little pathways and stone steps. There's a French garden with a copy of the *Amour* fountain from the Petit Trianon; a Florentine garden with a white marble ephebe; a Spanish garden, with papyrus, dates and pomegranates; exotic, Japanese, English and Provençal gardens; musical fountains; and a lapidary garden decorated with Romanesque capitals and gargoyles.

For all the trouble she took to build this glorious pile, Béatrice actually spent very little time here, preferring her villa in Monte-Carlo as it was closer to the gambling tables. You can take luncheon, tea or cakes in the elegant former *salon d'hiver*, and there is a good bookshop.

Cap Ferrat, with its lush greenery, secret villas and little azure coves, is ripe territory for strolls or swims – there are a dozen small beaches, albeit of fine gravel. **Plage de Passable** along Chemin du Roy, west of Villa Ephrussi, is popular with families and scuba divers. The 'Roy' in question was bad old King Léopold II of the Belgians, whose ruthless exploitation of the Congo (see Conrad's *Heart of Darkness*) helped to pay for his luxurious life here, where he took a swim every day with his beard neatly folded into a rubber whisker-protector while his valet ironed his newspapers. His villa (Les Cèdres) is now more democratically used for a delightful **zoo** (*t 04 93 76 07 60, www.zoocapferrat.com; open daily 9.30–7 in summer; 9.30–5.30 in winter; adm*).

The former-fishing-now-yacht-port of **St-Jean-Cap-Ferrat** has the distinction of a *Salle des Mariages* painted by Jean Cocteau (without the same vigour as in Menton). A walking path circles around the dewclaw of land south of the port called **Pointe St-Hospice** where, in the 6th century, the Niçois saint Hospice had a hermitage (now marked by a 19th-century chapel). With one arm chained to the wall, Hospice lived off algae brought to him by pious souls, and uttered dire prophecies about barbarian invasions that came true, recorded by Merovingian historian Gregory of Tours.

Modern-day invasions take place at nearby **Plage de Paloma**, favourite of Italian day-trippers and millionaire pensioners, and **Plage des Fosses**. Another path, the **Promenade Maurice Rouvier**, leads from St-Jean's beach to Beaulieu, passing **Villa Scoglietto** and its sea-defying garden, where Charlie Chaplin spent his summer holidays and actor David Niven lived the last years of his life.

Villefranche-sur-Mer

In the 14th century the deep, wooded bay between Cap Ferrat and Nice was a duty-free port, hence Villefranche's name. It became an important military port for the Savoys in the 18th century, a period that saw Villefranche take on the appearance it has today: tall, brightly coloured, piled-up houses; and narrow lanes and stairs, some so overhung with houses that they're actually tunnels. An example is **Rue Obscure**, 'a good place for a knifing,' as William Sansom described it, which Cocteau used as an underworldly setting for his film *Orphée*. It also came in handy as a bomb

Tourist Information

Villefranche-sur-Mer: Jardin François Binon, t 04 93 01 73 68, f 04 93 76 63 65, ot@ville-franche-sur-mer.com, www.villefranche-sur-mer.com. Open July–Aug daily 9–7, June and Sept Mon–Sat 9–12 and 2–6.30, Oct–May Mon–Sat 9–12 and 2–6. Offers guided tours of the town.

Market Days

Villefranche: Sun, flea market in the Jardin François Binon and Av Amélie Pollonnais; Sat am, Provençal market in the Jardin François Binon and Promenade de l'Octroi.

Where to Stay and Eat

Villefranche-sur-Mer ✉ 06230

★★★Welcome, Quai Amiral Courbet, t 04 93 76 27 62, f 04 93 76 27 66, resa@welcome-hotel.fr, www.welcomehotel.fr (luxury–expensive). Just beside the port, this legendary hotel is ideally situated, although its wild days are over. The newly refurbished and finely decorated rooms are air-conditioned; those on the 5th floor are ravishing. Closed mid-Nov–22 Dec.

★★Provençal, 4 Av du Maréchal Joffre, t 04 93 76 53 53, f 04 93 76 96 00, provencal@riviera.fr, www.hotelprovencal.com (moderate–inexpensive). Unpretentious and family-run. Closed Nov–Christmas.

L'Echalote, 7 Rue de l'Eglise, t 04 93 01 71 11 (expensive–moderate). This charming restaurant has a minuscule terrace and serves excellent, and rich, Provençal dishes (themed menus change every 3 weeks). Open evenings only; closed Sun except in summer.

Le Carpaccio, Promenade des Marinières, t 04 93 01 72 97, www.restaurant-carpaccio.com (moderate). This has long been a favourite of the Rolls-Royce crowd, who travel from Monaco, yet remains affordable for the rest of us, either for a splurge or for a modest pizza.

La Belle Epoque, Place de la Paix, t 04 93 01 96 22 (moderate). As you wind your way downhill towards the sea from the Corniche, you will pass this pleasant restaurant full of locals, which serves daily lunch specials on a large covered terrace on the quiet square.

La Grignotière, 3 Rue du Poilu, t 04 93 76 79 83 (moderate). Local Niçois specialities in the old town. Open evenings only, plus all day Sun; closed Wed in winter.

Michel's, Place Amélie Pollonnais, t 04 93 76 73 24, www.michel-s.net (moderate). Michel's has a startling frieze (they are very proud of it) depicting Villefranche, a lovely terrace looking out over the bay and very friendly staff. Light, local specialities; the melt-in-the-mouth house pâté and the red pepper and aubergine terrine are especially good. A la carte only. Closed Tues.

Le Versailles, 7 Bd Princesse Grace de Monaco, t 04 93 76 52 52, www.hotelversailles.com (moderate). With suitably commanding views and kingly cuisine; the delicately prepared cod is served with the most delicious aïoli on the coast. Closed Mon except July–Aug.

Joïa, 18 Rue du Poilu, t 04 93 76 62 40 (moderate). Trendy bar/restaurant with fish dishes.

Café des Delices, Rue du Poilu (moderate). Reader-recommended friendly restaurant with good house wine, great tagliatelle au pistou and good plat du jour.

shelter in the Second World War. In the heart of the old town is the church of **St-Michel**, Baroqued with unusual restraint and containing a recumbent Christ which was carved from a fig tree by a 17th-century slave.

The streets open up to the wide quay, given over to bars and restaurants, and a fine beach with a shallow slope and calm bay that is ideal for children. The charm of the place, and the presence of so many brawny sailors from around the world on shore-leave, made Villefranche a popular intello-gay resort in the 1920s, with Jean Cocteau weaving his personal mythologies with opium, 'fluids' and his friends in the little Hotel Welcome: 'Poets of all kinds, speaking every language, lived there and by a simple contact of fluids transformed the extraordinary little town, whose steep chaos ends at the water's edge, into a veritable Lourdes, a centre of legends and inventions.' Villefranche's fishermen once stored their nets in the portside Romanesque **Chapelle St-Pierre** (*Quai Courbet, t 04 93 76 90 70; open summer 10–12 and 4–8.30; winter 9.30–12 and 2–6; adm*), and in 1957, after a protracted battle with the local municipal authorities, Cocteau, who had become fascinated by the little church three decades earlier, won permission to restore and renovate it. The fishermen resisted at first, disgruntled at the loss of a convenient storage place, and even stole his ladders when the project finally got under way. They only came round when Cocteau offered to give the proceeds of visits to the chapel to the Fishermen's Benevolent Fund. Finally let loose on the 500-year-old chapel, he began to fresco it in 'ghosts of colours' with scenes from the life of St Peter (walking on the water with an angel's help, which astounds the fish but makes Christ smile), plus images of the fish-eyed fishergirls of Villefranche, the Gypsies at Saintes-Maries-de-la-Mer, and angels from Cocteau's private heaven.

The Duke of Savoy's 16th-century **Citadelle St-Elme** has been put back to work as the Hôtel de Ville, with a few more paintings by Jean Cocteau (upstairs) and three free museums (*t 04 93 76 33 27 for general enquiries, all open June and Sept 10–12 and 2.30–6; July–Aug 10–12 and 2.30–7; Oct–May 10–12 and 2–5.30; closed Sun am, Tues and Nov*). The first, the **Fondation Musée Volti**, has voluptuous bronze, copper and terracotta female figures sculpted by Antoniucci Volti, set in an idiosyncratic series of small chambers, patios and niches. During the Second World War, Marcel Carné used them to film *Les Visiteurs du soir* and *Les Enfants du Paradis*. The **Musée Goetz Boumeester** has paintings and engravings by the American artists and collectors Henri Goetz and his wife, Christine Boumeester, along with a sprinkling of gifts to the couple from their celebrity friends, a constant parade of big stars and writers. Finally, there is the little **Collection Roux**, with ceramic figurines inspired by medieval and Renaissance manuscripts.

Nice

Other places may be fun,
But when all is said and done,
It's so much nicer in Nice.
      Sandy Wilson, *The Boyfriend*

The funny thing is, it's true. Superbly set on nothing less than the Bay of Angels, Nice has a gleam and sparkle in its eye like no other city in France: only a sourpuss could resist its lively old town squeezed between promontory and sea, its markets blazing with colour, the glittering tiled domes and creamy *pâtisserie* of 19th-century hotels and villas, the immaculate exotic gardens, and the famous voluptuous curve of the beach and the palm-lined Promenade des Anglais. It is the one town on the Côte that doesn't seem to need tourists, the one that stays open through the winter. You could go for the food alone, a seductive mix of the best of France and Italy; you haven't really had ravioli until you tuck into a plate in Nice, where it was invented.

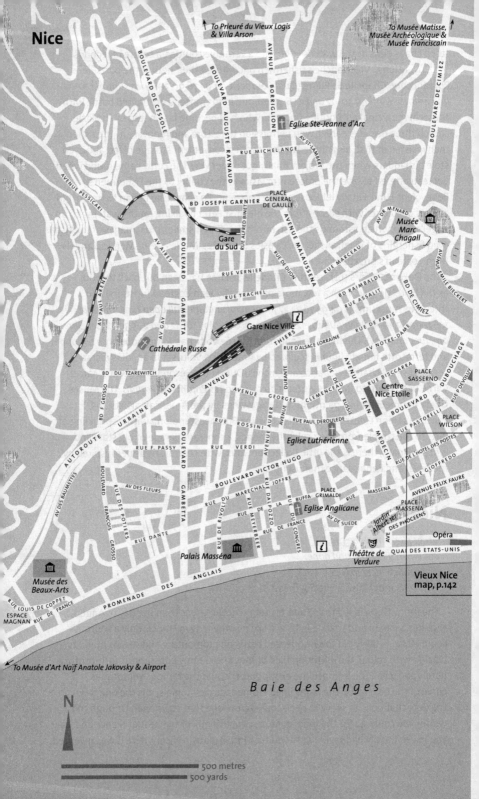

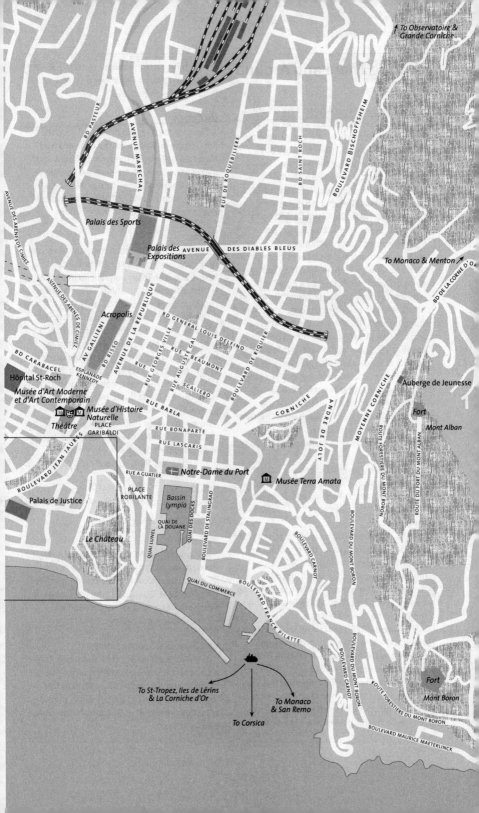

To Observatoire &
Grande Corniche

BD PASTEUR

AVENUE MARECHAL

RUE DE ROQUEBILIERE

BD SAINT ROCH

BOULEVARD BISCHOFFSHEIM

Palais des Sports

Palais des
Expositions

AVENUE   DES DIABLES BLEUS

To Monaco & Menton

BD DE LA CORNE D'O

AVENUE DES ARENES DE CIMIEZ

AVENUE DES ARENES DE CIMIEZ

Acropolis

BD GENERAL LOUIS DELFINO

AV GALLIENI

BD RISSO

AVENUE DE LA REPUBLIQUE

RUE GEORGES VILLE

RUE AUGUSTE GAL

RUE BEAUMONT

RUE SCALIERO

BOULEVARD DE RIQUIER

BD CARABACEL

ESPLANADE
KENNEDY

Hôpital St-Roch

Musée d'Art Moderne
et d'Art Contemporain

Musée d'Histoire
Naturelle

Théâtre

RUE BARLA

CORNICHE

ANDRE DE JOLY

MOYENNE CORNICHE

ROUTE FORESTIERE DU MONT BORON

Auberge de Jeunesse

Fort

Mont Alban

ROUTE DU FORT DU MONT ALBAN

PLACE
GARIBALDI

RUE BONAPARTE

RUE LASCARIS

BOULEVARD JEAN JAURES

RUE A GUATIER

Notre-Dame du Port

Musée Terra Amata

Palais de Justice

PLACE
ROBILANTE

Bassin
lympia

QUAI DE
LA DOUANE

QUAI DES DOCKS

BOULEVARD DE STALINGRAD

BOULEVARD CARNOT

BOULEVARD DU MONT BORON

Le Château

QUAI LUNEL

QUAI DU COMMERCE

BOULEVARD   FRANCK PILATTE

BOULEVARD CARNOT

BOULEVARD DU MONT BORON

BOULEVARD DU MONT BORON

Fort

Mont Boron

ROUTE FORESTIERE DU MONT BORON

To St-Tropez, Iles de Lérins
& La Corniche d'Or

To Corsica

To Monaco
& San Remo

BOULEVARD MAURICE MAETERLINCK

Getting There and Around

By Air

Nice's large, modern **Aéroport Nice-Côte d'Azur** is the second busiest airport in France, served by a wide variety of flights from around the world. For information on all the day's flights and changes for the next day, call **t** 08 36 69 55 55, *www.nice aeroport.fr.*

Airline numbers include Air France, **t** 0 820 820 820; British Airways, **t** 0 825 825 400; Delta, **t** 0 800 354 080; EasyJet, **t** 0 825 082 508; and Virgin Express, **t** 0 821 230 202.

By **helicopter**, between Nice and St-Tropez, try Nice Hélicoptères, **t** 04 93 21 34 32; between Nice and Monaco, Héli Air Monaco, **t** (00 377) 92 05 00 50 or Héli France, **t** 04 89 98 51 51.

Buses run every 12mins between the airport and Nice coach station in the centre of town, stopping along the Promenade des Anglais and at Place Masséna, while bus 23 provides links with the train station every 30mins. The bus ticket to town will also give you a free onward connection on another city bus (only valid for 1 hour). After 10pm the yellow airport bus will detour to the train station if you ask the driver, or else stops in Place Masséna, from where the night buses depart. Bus info: Aérogare 1, **t** 04 93 21 30 83, Aérogare 2, **t** 04 93 21 43 84.

There are also several buses daily from the airport to Antibes, Cannes, Grasse, Marseille, Menton, Monaco, St-Raphaël and St-Tropez.

By Train

Nice's **main train station**, **t** 08 92 35 35 35 for SNCF information, is in Av Thiers, not far from the centre of town, and has handy left-luggage lockers. Besides Métrazur trains between Ventimiglia and St-Raphaël, Nice has frequent connections to Marseille and is on the TGV route to Paris (6hrs).

The **Gare du Sud**, 4 bis Rue Alfred Binet, **t** 04 97 03 80 80, *www.trainprovence.com*, is served by the little **Train des Pignes** (*see* p.311; so called for the pine cones that the crew used to stop to collect for pine nuts). You can take an excursion on this train to Provençal towns high up the Var valley (*see* pp.311–14 – a cool and refreshing relief when the beaches

are blistering and the shopping malls pall, and you can go as far as Digne (*see* p.318) for €40 return (4 returns per day).

By Coach

The *gare routière* (coach station) is on the Promenade du Paillon, on the edge of Vieux Nice, **t** 04 93 85 61 81. There are frequent and inexpensive buses to Aix-en-Provence, Eze, Antibes, Cagnes, Cannes, Grasse, Marseille, Menton, Monte-Carlo, St-Raphaël and Vence. Bus 17 links the coach and train stations.

By Bus

Buses run by the **Sunbus** company are more than nice. Pick up a free *Guide Horaire du Réseau Bus* with maps and schedules at the tourist office or from Sunbus' information centre, 10 Av Félix Faure, **t** 04 93 13 53 13.

Several tourist tickets, called 'Sun Pass', are available from the Sunbus office and at Allô Sunbus, 29 Av Malausséna, **t** 04 93 13 53 13, *www.sunbus.com*, offering limitless rides for one, five or seven days and including one trip to the airport; they save money if you plan to make three or more bus trips a day. A one-day Sun Pass is also on sale on buses.

Buses stop early, around 9pm, and are replaced by four **Noctambus** services, all leaving from Place Masséna, in Vieux Nice, until about 1am; 8pm Sun and hols.

By Taxi

You cannot stop taxis in the street; call at a rank or call **t** 04 93 13 78 78.

By Ferry

In the summer **SNCM Ferryterranée** has frequent sailings to Corsica. For information and reservations, contact the company at the **Gare Maritime**, Quai du Commerce, **t** 04 93 13 66 66 or **t** 04 93 13 66, or contact **Corsica Ferries**, Quai Amiral Infernet, **t** 0825 095 095.

Car, Bike and Scooter Hire

Among the cheapest car-hire places is **Rent-a-Car**, opposite the train station on Av Thiers, **t** 04 93 88 69 69, **f** 04 93 88 43 36, or in the town centre, **t** 04 93 37 42 22, **f** 04 93 37 42 20, or just by the airport at 61 Route de Grenoble, **t** 04 93 19 07 07.

International car hire giant **Avis** is at the train station, **t** 04 93 87 90 11, **f** 04 93 87 32 82, or at the airport, Aérogare 1, **t** 04 93 21 36 33, and Aérogare 2, **t** 04 93 21 42 80, **f** 04 93 21 43 81. **Hertz** is at the airport, **t** 0825 342 343. Both Avis and Hertz are more expensive.

For bike/moped/scooter hire, a few options include JML, 34 Av Auber, **t** 04 93 16 07 00, **f** 04 93 16 07 48; **Nicea Location Rent**,12 Rue de Belgique, **t** 04 93 82 42 71, **f** 04 93 87 76 36; or **Arnaud**, 5 Rue François Ier, **t** 04 93 87 88 55.

Tourist Information

Nice: The main office is at 5 Promenade des Anglais, **t** 0892 707 407, **f** 04 92 14 46 49, *info@nicetourisme.com, www.nicetourisme. com; open summer daily 8–8; winter Mon–Sat 9–6.* There is also a large office on Av Thiers, next to the train station, *open summer daily 8am–8pm; winter daily 8–7.* Other offices include: airport Aérogare 1, *open summer daily 8am–10pm; winter closed Sun;* and Parking Ferber, *open summer daily 8–8 and at Carnival time daily 9–7, winter Mon–Sat 10–5.*

Museum card: A 1/3/7-day **Carte Musées Côte d'Azur** can be obtained for €8/15/25 from any museum ticket desk or the tourist office, or FNAC bookshop (Nice Etoile). There is also a 7-day **Museum Pass** (over a 15-day period) giving unlimited access to all Nice municipal museums only, for €6. On the first and third Sundays of every month, all museums in Nice are free – so everyone goes. Avoid this day unless you are hard up or it is low season.

Sightseeing: Le Grand Tour is a 1½-hour sightseeing tour in an open-deck bus with commentary in five languages (individual handsets). It runs all year round; tickets available from the bus driver, **t** 04 92 29 17 00. In summer, a dinky little white tourist train leaves from the Promenade des Anglais hourly on a trip through the old town and up to the château.

Main post office: 23 Av Thiers, near the station, **t** 04 93 82 65 22, and at Place Wilson, **t** 04 93 13 64 10, with *poste restante. Open Mon–Fri 8–7, Sat 8–12.*

Casualty wards: Hôpital St-Roch, 5 Rue Pierre Dévoluy and Rue Delille (adults only), **t** 04 92 03 33 75; **Children's Emergency:** Hôpital Lenval, 57 Av de la Californie, **t** 04 92 03 03. **24hr doctor service:** Nice-Médecins, **t** 04 93 52 42 42, and **SOS Médecins**, **t** 08 01 85 01 01. **All-night pharmacies:** 7 Rue Masséna, **t** 04 93 87 78 94, and 66 Av Jean Médecin, **t** 04 93 62 54 44. **Emergency dental care: t** 04 93 80 77 77.

Market Days

See **Markets**, p.133.

Festivals

Nice is famous for its **Carnival** in the two weeks before Lent, first mentioned in the 13th century. It died out in the 1800s, and subsequent attempts to revive it to amuse the tourists only succeeded in 1873, when the painters Alexis and Gustav-Adolf Mossa took over the show. They initiated a burlesque royal cortège to escort the figure of King Carnival, *Sa Majesté Carnaval*, down Av Jean Médecin, accompanied by comical *grosses têtes* – masqueraders with giant *papier-mâché* heads. During the subsequent parades, dances and battles of flowers and sweets, King Carnival reigns in Place Masséna, only to be immolated on the night of Mardi Gras to the explosive barrage of fireworks.

In spring there is the **Fête des Mai**, probably Nice's oldest festival, with balls, folk-dancing and picnics, and stalls around town selling lily-of-the-valley, a traditional gift.

On **Fête de la Mer** (St Peter's Day) in June, fishermen burn a boat down on the Plage des Ponchettes (opposite the old town) in honour of their patron saint, and on 14th July **Bastille Day** is marked by a huge firework display on the Promenade des Anglais and a Grand Ball on Place Masséna.

The third week of July sees the excellent **Festival de Jazz** in the Jardins Publics de Cimiez (*www.nicejazzfest.com*), and the **Nuits Musicales de Nice, t** 04 93 81 01 23, in the cloisters of the monastery in Cimiez.

From the end of July through August there is **Musicalia**, a series of world music concerts, and every two years in September there is the

Nice Military Tattoo, which brings over 1,000 military musicians to parade through the streets. Finally, on the Sunday after Christmas, revellers head off shivering for the **Bain de Noël** – a skinny-dip in the Med.

For information on all the festivals, call **t** 0892 707 407.

Internet Access

These are few and far between on the Côte d'Azur, so make the most of the facilities in Nice, most of which are off Av Jean Médecin: **Thenetgate**, 40 Rue de la Buffa, **t** 04 97 03 27 97, *www.thenetgate.it*.
3.W.O., 32 Rue Assalit, **t** 04 93 80 51 12.
Webstore, 12 Rue de Russie, **t** 04 93 87 87 99.

Shopping

The warren of streets that is **Vieux Nice** is the most attractive place to shop, and here you can browse for art, local crafts, clothes and glorious specialist foods (*fruits confits*, hand-made pasta) at the markets and local shops.

The **pedestrian zone** around Place Masséna has scores of designer clothes shops and cheap boutiques, while on **Av Jean Médecin** you'll find Nice's biggest department store, Galeries Lafayette, as well as Nice Etoile, a shopping centre with useful shops like the bookshop FNAC, **t** 04 92 17 77 77 (which also sells tickets to concerts and other events) and the Body Shop. The perfumery chain Sephora have a branch in Nice Etoile which sells its own range of stylish black-packaged toiletries.

Food and Drink

Auer, 7 Rue St-François-de-Paule, **t** 04 93 85 77 98. This Niçois landmark, in fabulously rococo premises, has been in the same family since 1820, making the region's most celebrated confectionery, jams and 'the only true' *fruits confits* for almost two centuries.
Confiserie Florian, 14 Quai Papacino, **t** 04 93 55 43 50. Offers free guided tours of the factory for its acclaimed sweets, with tastings.
Cave Bianchi, 7 Rue de la Terrasse, **t** 04 93 85 65 79. This 15th-century wine cellar benefits from an ancient underground spring that humidifies it, and has been run by the same

wine-growing family for generations. No plonk here, just the cream of France's finest wines, including the best of the Provençal region, and the charming owner will be delighted to share his extraordinary knowledge. The back room hosts modern art exhibitions.
Huilerie des Caracoles, 5 Rue St-François-de-Paule. Has a wide range of regional food products, gifts and toiletries.
Maison de l'Olive, 18 Rue Pairolière. Boasts a tempting display of olives and olive oil to take home.
Boutique Alziari, 14 Rue St-François-de-Paule, **t** 04 93 85 76 92. Many Niçois gourmets swear that the olives and olive oil from this 70-year-old shop are the best in the world (there would doubtless be many prepared to contest this claim).

Souvenirs

Among the tack in the souvenir shops you may find the occasional gem, such as big straw shopping baskets with enough room for a small dog and several baguettes.
La Maïoun, 1 Rue du Marché. A good selection.
Aux Parfums de Grasse, 10 Rue Saint-Gaétan.

Santons

La Couquetou, 8 Rue St-François-de-Paule.
Les Poupées Yolande, 4 Rue A. Gautier. A fine selection of fabrics, too.

Provençal Fabrics

Les Olivades, 8 Av de Verdun.

Antiques

For antiques, try the shops around Rue Antoine-Gautier (by the port) or the antiques market, **Village Ségurane**, at 28 Rue Catherine-Ségurane. *Open daily except Sun.*

Other Shops

BaoBab, 10 Rue du Marché. For pretty wares made from wicker and straw – from bags to hats, furniture and table goods.
Papeterie Rontani, 5 Rue Alexandre Mari. An old-fashioned, wood-floored shop which sells delicious paper of every sort, and maps a-plenty.

The Cat's Whiskers, 30 Rue Lamartine, near the train station. English language books, including second-hand.

Markets

Cours Saleya: Food and flower market – a wonderful array of herbs and every fruit you can imagine crystallized and glowing – *open Tues–Sat 6am–5.30pm, Sun 8–12*. The fresh produce is replaced by stalls selling old books, clothes and bric-a-brac on Monday. Arts and crafts appear on Wednesday afternoon and paintings on Sunday afternoons. During the summer, there is also an evening craft market daily here until midnight.

Place du Général de Gaulle: Colourful and authentically local food market, north of the train station, daily.

Place Robilante: Tues–Sat 10–6, flea market near the port.

Place St-François: Tues–Sun am, fish market.

Sports and Activities

Beaches

Many of the **paying beaches** along the Baie des Anges offer some kind of sport, including parascending, volleyball, jet-skiing and even bouncy castles. The beaches charge by the day and work out expensive if you only want a few hours' escape from the pebbles and local teenagers hogging the water's edge.

Various companies around the port offer **diving** and **snorkelling**, including:

Club Nautique de Nice, 50 Boulevard Franck Pilatte, t 04 93 89 39 78.

Locaventure, t 04 93 56 14 67. For kayaks, canoes and inflatable boats.

Nausicaa, 45 Rue de Roquebillière, t 04 93 89 04 13.

Other Activities

Golf de Nice, 698 Route de Grenoble, t 04 93 29 82 00. Golf course. *Open summer 8am–9pm, winter 8.30–6.30.*

Visiobulle, Embarcadère Courbet, Juan-les-Pins, t 04 92 00 42 30. In summer, go out into the bay in a glass-bottomed boat to revel in the submarine coastal life. 4–7 trips a day.

Trans Côte d'Azur, t 04 92 00 42 30. Offers one-hour boat tours from the Promenade des Anglais to Villefranche-sur-Mer.

To find out about **skiing** in the mountains, visit the Comité Régional de Ski, 234 Route de Grenoble, t 04 93 18 17 18.

Where to Stay

Nice ✉ 06000

Nice is packed with hotels of all categories, and in the summer most are just as tightly packed inside.

If you arrive without a reservation, the tourist office next to the station will book rooms for free. Get there by 10am in the summer, or risk joining the nightly slumber parties on the beach or in front of the station, where you'll encounter giant cockroaches from hell. Come instead in the off season, when many of the best hotels offer the kind of rates the French would call *très intéressant*.

Luxury–Very Expensive

****Negresco, 37 Promenade des Anglais, t 04 93 16 64 00 f 04 93 88 35 68, *direction@hotel-negresco-nice.com, www.hotel-negresco-nice.com*. Nice has luxury grand hotels galore, but for panache none can top the fabulous green-domed Negresco. A national historic monument, it was designed for Romanian hotelier Henri Negresco (who started his career as a Gypsy violinist) by Edouard Niermans, architect of the Moulin Rouge and the Folies Bergères. The one hotel in Nice where a Grand Duke would still feel at home, and the last independent luxury hotel on the coast, its 150 chambers and apartments have all been redecorated with Edwardian furnishings and paintings by the likes of Picasso and Léger. Don't miss the Salon Royal, lit by a Baccarat chandelier made for the Tsar and recently topped off with a contemporary sculpture by Niki de Saint Phalle, *Nana Jaune*.

****Château des Ollières, 39 Av des Baumettes, t 04 92 15 77 99, f 04 92 15 77 98, *chateaudesollieres@chateaudesollieres.com, www.chateaudesollieres.com*. A flamboyant pink, orange and yellow crenellated folly which once belonged to a Russian prince. Now it has only eight heavenly rooms, including a suite in the tower, with antique furnishings, eccentric stained glass and four-poster beds.

★★★★**Palais Maeterlinck**, 30 Bd Maeterlink, t 04 92 00 72 00, f 04 92 04 18 10, *info@ palais-maeterlinck.com*, *www.palais-maeterlinck.com*. A fastidiously refurbished pink and white palace set in beautiful gardens without so much as a pine needle out of place, with a highly acclaimed restaurant, **Le Mélisande** (*expensive*), which serves wonderfully creative Mediterranean dishes on a precipitous terrace.

★★★★**La Pérouse**, 11 Quai Rauba-Capeu, t 04 93 62 34 63, f 04 93 62 59 41, *lp@hroy.com*. Halfway up the Colline du Château, high above the hubbub, with a swimming pool and good restaurant (*moderate*). *Restaurant closed mid-Sept–mid-Mar.*

Expensive

★★★**Windsor**, 11 Rue Dalpozzo, between the station and Promenade des Anglais, t 04 93 88 59 35, f 04 93 88 94 57, *contact@ hotelwindsornice.com*. In the middle of a tropical garden, featuring a pool, an English-style pub, a Turkish-style hammam, a Thai-style sitting room and frescoes in the rooms.

★★★**Vendôme**, 26 Rue Pastorelli, t 04 93 62 00 77, f 04 93 13 40 78, *contact@vendome-hotel-nice.com*. In the centre of town, with prettily renovated, air-conditioned rooms, a superb stairway and a refreshingly peaceful garden to escape the hubbub.

★★★**Hôtel du Petit Palais**, 10 Av Emile Bieckert, t 04 93 62 19 11, f 04 93 62 53 60, *petitpalais@ provence-riviera.com*. A handsome, white Belle Epoque and Relais du Silence mansion, connected with the Best Western chain, where you can enjoy a simple breakfast on the flower-filled terrace. Rooms vary in size, but the best (at the back) look out over the rooftops of the old town to the sea.

Expensive–Moderate

★★★★**Le Grimaldi**, 15 Rue Grimaldi, t 04 93 16 00 24, f 04 93 87 00 24, *zedde@le-grimaldi.com*, *www.hotel-grimaldi-nice. cote.azur.fr*. A delightful little hotel, which has had an expensive facelift to give it an agreeable charge of Provençal colour. *Closed 10–30 Jan.*

★★★**Hôtel Suisse**, 15 Quai Rauba-Capeu, t 04 92 17 39 00, f 04 93 85 30 75. Beneath the Colline du Château, with fantastic sea views.

Moderate

★★★**Aria**, 15 Av Auber, t 04 93 88 30 69, f 04 93 88 11 35, *www.aria-nice.com*. Overlooking the Place Mozart in the musicians' quarter, a quiet residential district. Junior suites have hydro baths.

★★**Nouvel Hôtel**, 19 bis Bd Victor Hugo, t 04 93 87 15 00, f 04 93 16 00 67, *info@nouvel-hotel.com*, *www.nouvel-hotel.com*. More reasonable than some of above, this handsome Belle Epoque-style hotel has fairly bland, modern, but comfortable rooms.

For **long-term stays**, there are three comfortable apartment-hotels just off the Promenade des Anglais, run by the Citadines group, t (UK) 0800 376 3898 *www.citadines.com*.

Nice Buffa, 21 Rue Meyerbeer.

Nice Fleurs, 17 Av des Fleurs.

Nice Promenade, 3–5 Bd François Grosso.

Inexpensive

★★**Comté de Nice**, 29 Rue de Dijon, north of the station, t 04 93 88 94 56, f 04 93 87 67 40, *hotel.comte.de.nice@wanadoo.fr*. Good value rooms and apartments, if little charm and frosty staff. Avoid the noisy first-floor rooms.

★★**Floride**, 52 Bd de Cimiez, t 04 93 53 11 02, f 04 93 81 57 46, *info@hotel-floride.fr*. In quiet Cimiez, this hotel has lost some of its former charm, but is still an attractive old villa with a shady garden; each blue room has a colour TV and bath. *Closed Jan.*

★ **La Belle Meunière**, 21 Av Durante, t 04 93 88 66 15, f 04 93 82 51 76. A stone's throw from the station, this friendly place is a long-time favourite of budget travellers in Nice, especially students. It even has parking and a little garden for breakfast. *Closed Dec–Jan.*

Les Orangers, 10 bis Av Durante, t 04 93 87 51 41, f 04 93 82 57 82. A slightly downmarket, though comfy, alternative to the Belle Meunière. Most rooms have a balcony.

Auberge de Jeunesse, Rte Forestière du Mont-Alban, t 04 93 89 23 64, f 04 92 04 03 10, www.fuaj.org. The youth hostel is 4km east of town (bus 14 to the auberge; beware that the last bus leaves at 7.45pm). Closed Dec–mid-Jan.

Relais International de la Jeunesse Clairvallon, 26 Av Scudéri, t 04 93 81 27 63, f 04 93 53 35 88, CLAJPACA@cote-dazur.com. Even further afield (bus 15), although it has the added plus of a pool.

Eating Out

Although now in a solidly French-speaking corner of the Hexagon, Nice's cuisine still has a heavy Ligurian accent, with a fondness for seafood, olive oil and tiny black olives, chickpeas, fresh basil and pine nuts.

A typical first course consists of pasta (ravioli filled with seafood or artichoke hearts, or served with a walnut sauce), gnocchi or, in the winter, soupe au pistou, a hearty soup of courgettes, tomatoes, beans, potatoes, onions and vermicelli, served with pistou, a sauce based on basil, pine nuts and garlic.

Other Niçois favourites are bourride, a fish soup served with aïoli that many prefer to the more elaborate Marseille bouillabaisse, and teeny-tiny fish called poutines, by law only fished out of the sea between Beaulieu and Cagnes, which local cooks fry in omelettes or pile on top of pasta.

Another popular first course is the world-famous salade niçoise, which even in Nice is made in as many 'true and genuine' ways as bouillabaisse in Marseille – with quartered tomatoes, capers, black olives, spring onions, anchovies or tuna, green beans, and with or without hard-boiled eggs and potatoes.

Main courses are often from the sea: grilled fish with herbs or, more of an acquired taste, estocaficada, wind-dried cod and guts, stewed in eau-de-vie, with potatoes, garlic, onions and peppers. Favourite side dishes include ratatouille (another famous dish of Niçois origin) or boiled Swiss chard (blette) in vinaigrette. Snacks include socca (a sort of flat chickpea pancake), pan bagnat, pissaladière (onion tart) and stuffed vegetables or courgette flowers.

Very Expensive–Expensive

Le Chantecler, 37 Promenade des Anglais, t 04 93 16 64 00, direction@hotel-negresco.com. Gastronomic Nice is dominated by the Belle Epoque magnificence of this restaurant, which snuggles into the opulent arms of the Negresco. Here, chef Alain Llorca, successor to Dominique Le Stanc, has succeeded in seducing the Niçois with his own fabulous versions of Chantecler favourites, such as sea bass served with tomatoes and pesto, roast pigeon with foie gras ravioli, and desserts like the exotic liquorice-flavoured meringue with raspberry sorbet. Closed mid-Nov–mid-Dec.

Expensive

Chez Simon, above Nice in St-Antoine de Ginestière, 275 Rue St-Antoine de Ginestière, t 04 93 86 51 62. Chefs here have been serving up local specialities – beignets stuffed with fresh sardines or courgettes, a melting fricassée of wild cèpe mushrooms in parsley – for four generations. Rustic wood carvings, a profusion of flowers and a lovely terrace in summer. Closed Mon except for pre-booked groups, and Mar.

Auberge de Théo, 52 Av Cap de Croix, Cimiez, t 04 93 81 26 19. Genuine Italian pizzas, salads with mesclun, and Venetian tiramisù for dessert. Can be moderate. Closed Sun eve in winter and Mon all year, Christmas, New Year, and three weeks from 20 Aug.

Chez Fanny, 407 Rte de Bellet t 04 93 37 87 07. Worth a trip just outside the town centre for fresh and fun cuisine. Closed Mon and Tues, two weeks in Aug and beginning of Jan.

Moderate

The best restaurant-hunting territory in this price range is Vieux Nice and, especially for fresh fish, around Place Garibaldi and the port.

Don Camillo, 5 Rue des Ponchettes, t 04 93 85 67 95. *vianostephane@wanadoo.fr*. Opened by a former pupil of Maximin and Paul Ducasse, and already celebrated for its home-made ravioli filled with Swiss chard *en daube*, and for its desserts. *Closed Sun, and Mon lunch.*

La Mérenda, 4 Rue de la Terrasse, near the Opera House and the Cours Saleya. Join the glitterati enjoying Dominique le Stanc's celebrated idiosyncratic Niçois cuisine at this tiny bistro. *Closed weekends and school holidays. No credit cards.*

Villa d'Este, 6 Rue Masséna, t 04 93 82 47 77, *www.boccaccio.com*. The best Italian restaurant in Nice, over three floors with *trompe l'œil* Italianate décor in pretty pastel colours, attentive service and top-notch pasta. The plate of *antipasti* is a gastronomic feast. Get there early (12 noon) for lunch and watch it fill up with locals and tourists alike!

Le Pizzaïolo, 4 bis Rue du Pont-Vieux, t 04 93 92 24 79. Specialities include beef *carpaccio*, *farcis niçois* and local seafood. The surroundings may be humble, but the food ain't bad and the staff are very good-natured. *Closed Tues.*

L'Indyana, 11 Rue Delaye, t 04 93 80 67 69. World cuisine in trendy, minimalist surroundings. *Closed Sun lunch and Mon lunch.*

La Zucca Magica, 4 bis Quai Papacino, t 04 93 56 25 27. By far the best and friendliest vegetarian restaurant in Nice, with imaginative dishes that draw customers from the entire Riviera coast. Book ahead. *Closed Sun and Mon.*

Le Safari, 1 Cours Saleya t 04 93 80 18 44. Enjoying a privileged spot overlooking the water, this is one of the few restaurants on this street where the waiters don't need to entice passers-by. With wood-fired oven and terrace.

Jo L'Ecailler-Café de Turin, 5 Place Garibaldi, t 04 93 85 30 37, *cafedeturin@club-internet.fr*. Try this 19th-century café for a drink or a snack or some of the best oysters in town. *Open until 11 in summer.*

Moderate–Cheap

Voyageur Nissart, 19 Rue d'Alsace-Lorraine, t 04 93 82 19 60, *www.voyageur-nissart.com*. This is the best place near the station, with two wide-ranging menus. *Closed Mon and part of Aug.*

Hippopotamus, on the corner of Avenue Félix Faure and Place Masséna, t 04 93 92 42 77. A very central restaurant, part of a chain, but it fills up reassuringly with locals at lunchtime. Choose from several set menus or a lunchtime special of *plat du jour* and coffee.

Cheap

Chez René Socca, 2 Rue Miralheti, t 04 93 92 05 73. A self-service café offering *socca*, *pissaladière*, pizza by the slice and much more. *Closed Mon and Nov.*

Spaghettissimo, 3 Cours Saleya, t 04 93 80 95 07. Small, cheap Italian.

Pâtisserie Cappa, 7–9 Place Garibaldi, t 04 93 62 30 83. An elegant and exclusive *pâtisserie* serving afternoon tea. *Closed mid-Sept–mid-Oct.*

Fenocchio, Place Rossetti, t 04 93 80 72 52, 6 Place de la Poissonerie, t 04 93 62 88 80, 36 Rue Centrale, t 04 93 62 88 82. It's hard to beat the 99 varieties of ice cream here: lavender cream, jasmine sorbet and the bitterest chocolate imaginable make a heavenly combination.

Entertainment and Nightlife

You can find out what's happening in Nice in the daily *Nice-Matin*, although it's not much good for anything else except lining the canary's cage.

Other sources covering the entire Côte are *7 jours/7 nuits*, distributed free in the tourist offices, the *Semaine des Spectacles*, which appears Wednesdays on the news-stands, and Riviera Radio, the coast's English-language station, which broadcasts out of Monaco on 106.3 and 106.5 FM.

Local news, hours of religious services in English and more are in the monthly English-language *Blue Coast Magazine*, a glossy look at life on the Riviera, distributed in newsagents and English bookshops.

If you need a **babysitter**, try the babysitting service **Allô Mary Poppins** at 35 Rue Pastorelli, t 04 93 62 61 30, or **Association Family Jeunesse**, 4 Rue Masséna, t 04 93 82 28 22.

Film

The movie-goer in Nice is spoilt for choice:

Pathé Paris, 54 Av J. Médecin, t 0892 68 22 88.

Pathé Masséna, 31 Av Jean Médecin, t 0892 68 22 88.

UGC Variétés, 7 Bd Victor Hugo, t 0836 68 68 32.

Rialto, 4 Rue de Rivoli, t 0836 68 08 41. For films in their original language.

Nouveau Mercury, 16 Place Garibaldi, t 0836 68 81 06.

Cinémathèque de Nice, 3 Esplanade Kennedy, t 04 92 04 06 66.

Theatre, Opera and Music

Opéra de Nice, 4–6 Rue St-François-de-Paule, information t 04 93 13 98 53, reservations t 04 92 17 40 00. Puts on operas, concerts and recitals at various locations.

Acropolis, 1 Esplanade Kennedy, t 04 93 92 83 00.

Fondation Sophia-Antipolis, at Hôtel Westminster, 27 Promenade des Anglais, t 04 92 14 86 86. Organizes morning classical music concerts.

Fondation Kosma, Conservatoire de Nice, 24 Bd de Cimiez, t 04 92 26 72 20. Free classical music on Mondays at 6pm.

Concerts are also held at:

Musée Chagall, Av du Docteur Ménard, west of Bd de Cimiez, t 04 93 53 87 20 (Sept–May).

Musée des Beaux-Arts, 33 Av des Baumettes, t 04 92 15 28 28 (*Oct–May, once a month; adm*).

Musée d'Art Moderne et d'Art Contemporain, t 04 93 62 61 62, *www.mamac-nice.org*. Music, from ancient to avant-garde, and art videos.

CEDAC de Cimiez, 49 Av de la Marne, t 04 93 53 85 95. Big-league musicians and dancers, and jazz musicians twice a month.

Forum Nice Nord, 10 Bd Comte de Falicon, just off the A8 at Nice-Nord, t 04 93 84 24 37. A major venue for modern dance in July, and world music.

Théâtre de Verdure, Jardin Albert Ier. From April onwards rock, jazz and other outdoor concerts.

There are several small theatres in Vieux Nice that stage imaginative productions and some concerts:

Théâtre du Cours, 5 Rue de la Poissonnerie, t 04 93 80 12 67.

Théâtre de La Semeuse, 21 Rue St-Joseph, t 04 93 92 85 08.

For Molière and other classics:

Théâtre de l'Alphabet, 10 Bd Carabacel, t 04 93 13 08 88.

Théâtre de Nice, by the Contemporary Art Museum, t 04 93 13 90 90.

Clubs and Bars

Nice's nightlife is divided between expensive clubs, bland hotel piano bars and the livelier bars and clubs of Vieux Nice, which come and go like ships in the night. Some of the most jumping joints are the expat havens in Vieux Nice.

Cherry's Café, 35 Quai des Etats-Unis, t 04 93 13 85 45. Well-known gay club/restaurant.

Wayne's, 15 Rue de la Préfecture, t 04 93 13 46 99, *www.waynes.fr*. A British-owned pub and restaurant with live music every night. *Open noon–12.30am, reservations obligatory at weekends*).

Scarlett O'Hara's, 6 Rue Rossetti, t 04 93 80 43 22. Fiddlers fiddle in this Irish pub till 2am.

De Klomp, 6 Rue Mascoïnat, near Place Rossetti, t 04 93 92 42 85. A Dutch joint with live jazz, single malt, and a hedonistic atmosphere (not for teetotallers or anti-smokers).

Jonathan's, Rue de la Loge, t 04 93 62 57 62 Food lit by candles, and 1970s-inspired 'live' music hosted by Jonathan himself: wait long enough and he might treat you to his Rolf Harris impersonation.

Plasma Café, 11 Rue Offenbach, t 04 93 16 17 32. Juice bar and sushi bar, with Internet access. *Open till 2am.*

Vin de Bellet AOC

'The wine-merchants of Nice brew a balderdash, and even mix it with pigeon's dung and quick-lime,' wrote Tobias Smollett. But they never dared to mess with Vin de Bellet, the rare and costly elixir produced in the steep, sun-soaked hills west of Nice.

The vineyards owe their special quality to the alternating currents of sea and mountain air and to their original varieties of red grapes: braquet, folle noire and négrette de Nice, all of which combine to create a noble wine with a bouquet of wild cherry that can be aged up to 30 years. The rosés, from the same grapes, are one of the best accompaniments to *loup*, the most delicate of Mediterranean fish. Vin de Bellet blanc, reminiscent of Chablis, is a blend of rolle, spagnou, roussan and mayorquin. Only 1,200 hectolitres are produced each year, and most of it never gets much further than the cellars of the Riviera's top restaurants.

Alternatively, pick up a bottle of your own by ringing ahead and following the Route de Bellet north of Rue de France (parallel to the Promenade des Anglais) to St-Roman-de-Bellet and the 18th-century **Château de Bellet, t** 04 93 37 81 57. The second estate, **Château de Crémat**, at 442 Chemin de Crémat, **t** 04 92 15 12 15, is a fantasy castle, built in 1850 in a pseudo-medieval style called *style troubadour*.

The capital of the *département* of Alpes-Maritimes and France's fifth largest city (pop. 400,000), Nice is also the most visited after Paris. The English have been coming for well over 200 years, back when 'Nizza la Bella' still belonged to Savoy, and Russian Tsarinas and Grand Dukes fleeing winter's blasts weren't far behind. The presence of so many rich, idle foreigners who stayed for months at a time formed a large part of the city's character: corruption, reactionary politics and organized crime are part of the famous *salade niçoise*, along with a high density of apricot poodles and frown-faced poodle ladies. But Nice also has a university, big culture (over 20 museums and counting), the brilliant light that Matisse loved, and a genuine identity as a city – rough, affable and informal.

History

Nice was a hot spot even 400,000 years ago, when the hunters who tracked mammoths and learned how to make fires to grill their prey frequented the caves of Terra Amata. The Ligurians, around 1000 BC, were the first to move in permanently, constructing their *oppida* at the mouth of the Paillon river and on the hill overlooking the valley. Greeks from Marseille founded a commercial colony near the seaside *oppidum* and named it Nikaïa after an obscure military victory, or perhaps after the nymph Nikaïa. Beset by Ligurian pirates, the Nikaïans asked the Romans for aid. The Romans duly came, and stayed, but preferred to live near the hilltop *oppidum* because it was closer to the Via Julia Augusta. They named this town Cemenelum (modern Cimiez) and made it the capital of the province of Alpes Maritimae. By the 3rd century AD, Cemenelum had 20,000 inhabitants, all quickly going soft amid swimming pools and central heating.

However, by the 6th century, luxury-loving Cemenelum had collapsed with the rest of the Roman Empire, while Greek Nikaïa struggled on and regrouped itself in the 10th century around a cathedral. By the 1340s, with a population of 13,000, Nice was the third city in Provence after Marseille and Arles. The city's coat of arms had an eagle's head on it, looking to the left, to France. The Black Death and civil wars of the period soon cut it down to size, and in 1388 the city's leaders voted to hitch their wagon to a brighter star than Louis d'Anjou and pledged allegiance to Amadeus, Count of Savoy. The eagle was redrawn to look right, towards Italy.

The Savoys fortified Nice and it grew rich trading with Italy. It had its own little Renaissance, thanks to Ludovico Brea and the other members of the mid 15th-century Ecole Niçoise – Antoine and François Bréa, Jean Mirailhet and Jacques Durandi – noted for their uncluttered, simple compositions and firm sense of line. The 17th century saw the expansion of Nice outside its medieval walls, and in 1696 and 1705 came the first of several French interludes that interrupted Savoy rule – interludes that Louis XIV took advantage of to blow up the city's fortifications.

Cold Brits and Absorption into the Mystic Hexagon

Although relations remained sour with France, the Savoys became firm allies with the English, and by 1755 the first trickle of milords had begun to discover the sunny charms of a Riviera winter. Doctor and novelist Tobias Smollett spent a year in Nice in 1763, and in his singularly grouchy *Travels through France and Italy* (1766) did what Peter Mayle has since done for Provence: made the Côte, because of, or in spite of, its quaint local characters, irresistible to the British. Even though it took at least two weeks to reach Nice from Calais, by 1787 there were enough Brits wintering here to support a casino (then a fashionable Venetian novelty), an English theatre, an estate agent and a newspaper. In 1830, when a frost killed all the orange trees, the English community raised funds to give the unemployed a job: building a seafront promenade along the Baie des Anges, known to this day as the Promenade des Anglais. Part of its purpose was to keep English girls away from the riffraff, or more particularly the Niçois – along with their money, the British brought attitudes so arrogant that, as early as the 1780s, sensitive locals left town each winter to avoid being humiliated by their visitors.

In 1860, as Napoléon III's reward for promising to help Vittorio Emanuele II of Savoy create the future kingdom of Italy, a secret treaty was signed ceding Nice and Savoy to France. To keep up appearances, a plebiscite was held. Vittorio Emanuele encouraged his subjects to vote for union with France, but even more encouraging was the presence of the French army marching through Nice, and French agents bullying the majority Italian-speaking population. The final result (24,449 pro-France to 160 against) stinks even to this day. But the railway arrived shortly after and Nice settled down to its chosen vocation as the winter haven for Europe's élite. Sumptuous neo-Moorish-Gothic-Baroque follies were built to house some 20,000 wintering Britons and Russians by 1890; 20 years later the numbers of foreigners had increased to over 150,000.

Queen Victoria preferred the suburb of Cimiez; her haemophiliac son, Prince Leopold, introduced croquet to Nice before dying after slipping on the marble floor in the casino. The city even made an early bid to become the Hollywood of France, when the Victorine film studios were founded in 1911 and later purchased in 1925 by Rex Ingram, who brought in a constant parade of big stars and writers. During the war, Marcel Carné used them to film *Les Visiteurs du soir* and *Les Enfants du Paradis*.

Nice Today

Since the 1930s, many of Nice's hotels and villas have been converted into furnished flats, while the concrete mixers of destiny march further and further west and up the valleys. The Victorine studios are still there, but plagued by noise from jets landing at Nice airport, and now used mostly for television commercials. Wealthy, politically conservative retirees help support an equally right-wing *rentier* population. All this money floating about has attracted the corruption and underworld activities of the *milieu*, previously associated only with Marseille.

For decades Nice was ruled as the personal fiefdom of the right-wing Médecin family, who pretend to be related to the Medicis, although it doesn't look as if their dynasty will endure quite as long. Jean Médecin reigned as mayor from 1928 until 1965, and was succeeded by his flamboyant son Jacques, cook, crook and anti-Semitic hoster of a National Front congress no other city would have, the man who twinned Nice with Cape Town when apartheid was still on the books. Jacques Médecin had an edifice-complex nearly the size of Mitterrand's in Paris, filling Nice with huge new public complexes, and his cronies had their fingers in all kinds of pies – most spectacularly Albert Spaggiari, who got hold of the plans of Nice's sewer system in order to steal 46 million francs from the Société Générale, and was captured by the police only to escape the courtroom by jumping out of the window on to a waiting motorcycle and making a clean getaway. In 1990 the slow, grinding wheels of French justice began to catch up with Médecin, when it was discovered, among other things, that money for the Nice Opéra was being diverted into the mayor's bank account. He took to his heels and hid out in Punta del Este, Uruguay, until 1995 when he was extradited to France, where he died in 1998. His sister Geneviève narrowly defeated the National Front candidate in local government elections and took his old seat on the Conseil Général of the Alpes-Maritimes *département*; his successor as mayor of Nice, Honoré Bailet, had some troubles of his own, especially in the form of a son-in-law accused of murdering a local restaurant owner. In 1995 he was ousted by Jacques Peyrat, a friend of Le Pen and former FN member who has found a home in President Chirac's UMP. Under Peyrat, many of the FN's ideas have been implemented into city policy. He gave Médecin a funeral in Nice's city hall when the old crook died, and now there is a proposal to name a boulevard after him. Médecin's critics, noting the billion euros of debt he left the city, along with the millions he stole for himself, have proposed Rue Mozart for the honour – the street that leads to the city's prison.

Vieux Nice

Dismissed as a dangerous slum in the 1970s, Nice's Vieille Ville, a piquant quarter east of Place Masséna, is easily the trendiest part of Nice, brimful of cafés, bistros, nightclubs, designer boutiques and galleries. And the population, once poor and ethnically mixed, is now more than half French and upwardly mobile. But the shock of the new is mitigated by the tenacity of the old grandmotherly underwear, paint and stationery shops, and no-name working-men's bars, which have so far refused to budge. Picasso liked to walk here because it reminded him of Barcelona's Barrì Chino.

'Vieux' in Vieux Nice means Genoese seaside Baroque – tall, steep *palazzi*, many with opulent 17th- and 18th-century portals and windows, turning the narrow streets and steps below into chasms that suddenly open up into tiny squares, each with its chapel. To this day, the old Niçois are among the most religious people on the coast, and still join the confraternities of Penitents: lay organizations dedicated to public demonstrations of penitence, founded in Italy in the 14th century during the great Franciscan and Dominican revivals. During the Baroque period, when a number of their chapels sprang up, the brotherhoods, distinguishable by the colours of their hooded cloaks, became increasingly involved in a kind of early social work: the White Penitents cared for the sick, the Black Penitents for the dying and the Blue Penitents looked after orphans. Of the city's original seven confraternities, four still survive, all of which reside in this neighbourhood.

At its eastern end, the Vieille Ville is closed by the **Colline du Château**, the ancient acropolis of Nikaïa and site of the 10th- to 12th-century town and the cathedral of Ste-Marie. Of the latter, a few ruins remain – the Savoyards demolished it to make way for their citadel, which was in turn blown up by the congenitally suspicious Sun King, Louis XIV. Greek and Ligurian remains have been discovered beneath it. The daily cannon blast, heard across Nice at noon, booms out from up here; the tradition was begun by an Englishman, Sir Thomas Coventry, who got fed up with eating his meals at irregular hours and put a stop to it with the precisely timed firing of the cannon. You can either walk up the steps to the château, take a mini-train (€6) from the Promenade des Anglais which gives you a little tour through the flower market and around the Vieille Ville on the way, or pay a few *sous* to take the lift at the east end of the Quai des Etats-Unis, near **Tour Bellanda**, where Berlioz composed his *King Lear Overture*. From the belvedere by the artificial cascade, the real boats down below don't look much bigger than the models in the museum, and the shimmering, tiled, glazed rooftops of Nice curl into the distance around the Baie des Anges.

Among the gardens at the top of the hill are two cemeteries: in the grandiose Italian one you can find the tombs of Garibaldi's mother and of Mercedes Jellinek, who gained immortality in 1902 when her father chose her name for a new line of Daimlers. More sombrely, a reminder of the Holocaust stands just inside the gates of the Jewish cemetery: a pair of urns containing ashes from the incinerators of the concentration camps and a phial of human fat collected by the Nazis to make soap.

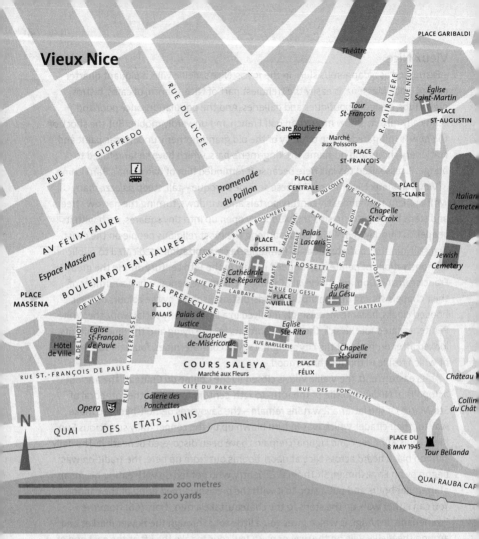

Vieux Nice

PLACE GARIBALDI

Théâtre

Tour
St-François

R. PAIROLIERE

RUE NEUVE

Église
Saint-Martin

PLACE
ST-AUGUSTIN

RUE DU LYCÉE

Gare Routière

Marché
aux Poissons

PLACE
ST-FRANÇOIS

RUE

GIOFFREDO

PLACE
CENTRALE

R. DU COLLET

RUE STE-CLAIRE

PLACE
STE-CLAIRE

Italian
Cemeter

Promenade
du Paillon

R. DE LA BOUCHERIE

R. DE LA CROIX

R. DE LA LOGE

Chapelle
Ste-Croix

AV FELIX FAURE

Espace Masséna

PLACE
ROSSETTI

R. MASCOINAT

Palais
Lascaris

R. CENTRALE

R. DE LA DROITE

R. ST-JOSEPH

Jewish
Cemetery

BOULEVARD JEAN JAURES

R. DU MARCHÉ

R. DU PONTIN

R. ST-VINCENT

Cathédrale
Ste-Réparate

R. STE-RÉPARATE

R. ROSSETTI

RUE

RUE DU GESU

Église
du Gésu

PLACE
MASSENA

DE VILLE

R. DE LA PREFECTURE

RUE DE L'ABBAYE

PLACE
VIEILLE

R. DU CHATEAU

PL. DU
PALAIS

Palais de
Justice

R. DE L'HOTEL

R. DE LA TERRASSE

Chapelle
de-Miséricorde

R. GAETAN

Église
Ste-Rita

RUE BARILLERIE

Hôtel
de Ville

Église
St-François
de Paule

PLACE
FÉLIX

Chapelle
St-Suaire

Château

RUE ST.-FRANÇOIS DE PAULE

COURS SALEYA
Marché aux Fleurs

Collin
du Chât

Opera

Galerie des
Ponchettes

CITÉ DU PARC

RUE DES PONCHETTES

N

QUAI DES ETATS - UNIS

PLACE DU
8 MAY 1945

Tour Bellanda

QUAI RAUBA CAP

200 metres
200 yards

If you descend by way of the east flank of the hill, down Montée Eberlé and Rue Catherine-Ségurane (where Nietzsche lived between 1883 and 1888), you'll end up in the wide, yellow, arcaded 18th-century **Place Garibaldi,** named after its statue of the hero of Italy's unification, who was born near the port in 1806. Once named the 'Piazza Vittorio' by the war-weary Niçois in an attempt to curry favour with King Victor Amédée III of Sardinia, it was built to both cow and flatter Sardinian sovereigns arriving from Turin. The arcades on the eastern side are now full of buzzy, lively fish restaurants. The Blue Penitents have their sombre neoclassical chapel of **St-Sépulcre** (1782) on this square, while just around the corner, facing the esplanade at 60 bis Bd Risso, is the **Muséum Barla d'Histoire Naturelle** (*t 04 97 13 46 80, www.mhnn.org; open Tues–Sun 10–6; free guided tours Wed at 3pm*), where you can ponder, among other things, a rather unusual 19th-century collection of 7,000 painted plaster mushrooms.

South of Place Garibaldi off Rue Neuve is one of the city's oldest parish churches, **St-Martin-St-Augustin**, where a monk named Martin Luther said a mass during his momentous pilgrimage to Rome in 1514. The dim interior was Baroqued in the 17th century; its treasures include a fine *Pietà* (*c*. 1500) attributed to Ludovico Brea, a tatty photocopy of Garibaldi's baptismal certificate, and a cross marking the spot where the galleys of Aladin Barbarossa sent a Turkish cannonball through the walls in the siege of 1543. Opposite the entrance to the church is a plaque to Catherine Ségurane, Amazonian heroine of that same siege, wild-eyed and wielding her washing-paddle (*see* p.146).

Further west, Rue Pairolière leads into 'Babazouck', the curious nickname for the heart of Vieux Nice, and **Place St-François**, once the terminus for the '*courreras*' (stage coaches) and now the setting for a raucous and pungent fish market which takes place every morning except Monday around a pretty fountain of entwined fish. The sad-eyed building in the northeast corner is the once-grand Palais Communal, built in 1580, now the Job Centre. South of the square, another cannonball from the Turkish siege is lodged in the plaster of a house on the corner of Rue de la Loge and Rue Droite. Continuing southeast, the **Chapelle Sainte-Croix** in Rue de la Croix is the headquarters of the Pénitents Blancs, the oldest confraternity (founded in 1306) and the most popular, perhaps because they were still into public self-flagellation in the 1750s.

Back on Rue Droite, at No.15, the **Palais Lascaris** (*t 04 93 62 72 40; open Wed–Mon 10–12 and 2–6; closed Tues and hols*) is a grand 1648 Genoese-style mansion with wrought-iron and marble balconies, hard to pick out on this dim little street. It was built for Jean-Baptiste Lascaris-Vintimille, the Duke of Savoy's brigadier, and was later sold to the counts of Peille. But its aristocratic days were numbered and it became a military garrison during the Revolution, before succumbing to the fate of most of the town's palaces and being converted into flats. It sagged into sorry disrepair until 1942, when the town bought and handsomely restored it. The ground floor contains a reconstructed pharmacy of 1738, with some of the original Delftware fittings; a fantastically opulent staircase lined with classical statues leads up to the *étage noble*, where guests would be received with suitable pomp. It is saturated with elaborate Genoese 'quadratura' (architectural *trompe-l'œil*) frescoes, Flemish tapestries, ornate woodwork and a 1578 Italian precursor of the pianoforte. The ceremonial chamber is divided with an ornamental stucco wall, supported by caryatids and atlantes and liberally sprinkled with cherubs and gilt embellishments.

The museum also holds temporary exhibitions, usually with a local or regional flavour, and has recently taken on another role as the Centre du Patrimoine, dedicated to the upkeep and restoration of the city's treasures. Craftspeople are often invited to demonstrate their arts, and there are special events for children held between 2 and 4pm most days. Baroque concerts are sometimes held here in summer; ask at the tourist information office for details of these events and activities.

Contemporary exhibitions take place at several galleries on the Rue Droite and at the corner of Rue Droite and Rue de la Loge, at the **Galerie Renoir** (*t 04 93 13 40 46; open Tues–Sat 10.30–1 and 2–6; closed Sun and Mon*). Also down Rue Droite is the

Eglise de Gésu, groaning with fake marble and oppressively ornate stucco and *putti*; it was once owned by the Jesuits, who revamped it between 1612 and 1642, producing a terrifying monument to the art of the Counter-Reformation, much envied and emulated by smaller regional chapels. The fishermen's festival (held in June) starts with a choral mass sung here, followed by a procession down to the Plage des Ponchettes (opposite the Cours Saleya), where a boat is burned in honour of St Pierre, patron saint of fishermen.

Take Rue Rossetti west to the cafés of pretty Place Rossetti, dominated by Nice's 17th-century **Cathédrale Ste-Réparate**, designed by Jean-André Guibert and crowned with a joyful dome and lantern of glazed tiles in emerald bands. The interior is extraordinary, even by the theatrical standards of Niçois Baroque: a plague of cherubim and seraphim infest the fanciful festoons around the cornice, and the chapels, each owned by an affluent family or corporation responsible for their decoration and upkeep, vie with each other in glitzy magnificence. The uncorrupted body of the young saint Réparate, a 15-year-old virgin martyred in Caesarea in the 4th century, arrived in Nice in a boat of flowers towed by a pair of angels (hence Baie des Anges).

This same Réparate was the first patron saint of Florence before the city adopted intermediaries with greater heavenly clout, and here, too, in Nice, the young virgin is currently losing a popularity contest with St Rita of Cascia, whose appeal is more contemporary. At the 17th-century **Chapelle de l'Annonciation**, which everyone calls Eglise de Ste-Rita, at 1 Rue de la Poissonnerie, her altar gets nearly all the business, possibly because her speciality is unhappy middle-aged housewives – Rita herself was burdened in the 14th century with a rotten husband, ungrateful children and a smelly sore on her forehead that just wouldn't heal.

Rita's compatriot, Paganini, who died nearby in 1840 at 23 Rue de la Préfecture, had his share of troubles too, but most of them were posthumous. Ste-Réparate's bishop was convinced that the sounds Paganini made on his violin could only have been produced by the devil incarnate (the maestro liked to startle the neighbours by making it howl like a tomcat) and refused him a Christian burial. He even wanted to toss Paganini's body into the Paillon. In the end, however, the poor dead fiddler was shunted to Cannes, and then on to Genoa and Parma, where he was finally buried in 1896. Since then he has received the acclaim he deserved.

Cours Saleya

After the dark lanes of Vieux Nice, the sun pops back into the sky over Cours Saleya, an elongated little gem of urban planning set back just a couple of blocks from the sea, where bars and restaurants line up along the famous outdoor market, over-flowing with flowers and sumptuous food displays worthy of the Riviera's gourmet vortex. Matisse lived for 17 years amid all the vivid colours that he loved, just off the Cours Saleya at **No.1 Place Charles Félix**; the brightly painted house is still there, although there is no commemorative plaque. The Cours is closed at one end by the 17th-century **Ancien Sénat**, or the old Court of Appeal, and **St-Suaire**, home of the Red Penitents, who assisted pilgrims.

But the principal focal point of the Cours is the Black Penitents' **Chapelle de la Miséricorde**, designed in 1740 by Bernardo Vittone, a disciple of Turin's extraordinary Baroque architects Guarino Guarini and Juvarra. Inside (*unfortunately locked*), it's all virtuoso Baroque geometry, a gold and stucco confection with vertiginous *trompe-l'œil* paintings in the vault. A fine, early Renaissance *Polyptique de la Miséricorde* (1430) by Jean Mirailhet hangs in the sacristy, painted for the confraternity, whose mission was to assure the dead a dignified burial.

A double row of one-storey buildings separates Cours Saleya from the Quai des Etats-Unis, where you'll find, if you look very hard, the elusive **Galerie des Ponchettes** (**t** 04 93 62 31 24; *open Tues–Sun 10–6; closed Mon*). This used to contain the exuberant paintings of Raoul Dufy and the Niçois father-and-son team Alexis and Gustav-Adolf Mossa. Although, confusingly, their names are still over the door, the paintings have been moved to the Musée des Beaux-Arts (Jules Chéret) (*see* pp.148–9) to brighten up an otherwise wan collection, leaving the Galerie des Ponchettes with little to do but display lacklustre temporary exhibitions. Stairs lead up to the roofs of the slim row of 19th-century houses which edge the seafront, where gentlefolk used to promenade before the construction of the Promenade des Anglais.

The Port, Terra Amata and Hilltop Follies

To the east, Quai des Etats-Unis circles around the wind-punched hill of the Château, where it's known as Quai Rauba-Capéu ('hat thief'), before it meets placid **Bassin Lympia**, the departure point for ferries to Corsica. The great columned edifice set into the flank of the hill is the **Monument aux Morts**, which commemorates the 4,000 Niçois who died during the First World War.

The **Place de l'Ile de Beauté**, lined with 18th- and 19th-century buildings, opens out on to the port and the imposing neoclassical church of **Notre-Dame**, topped with a statue of the Virgin Mary, where sailors still pray for full nets and a safe return. Chekhov used to saunter along the jetty opposite, where old men still sit with their papers and pooches to muse away the mornings.

East of here is the **Musée de Terra Amata** (*25 Bd Carnot,* **t** *04 93 55 59 93, www. musee-terra-amata.org, bus 32 or 14 from central Nice; open Tues–Sun 10–6; closed Mon and holidays*), rather improbably tucked into a typical Niçois *résidence,* complete with stripy blue and white awnings. Underneath, the museum comprises a cave holding one of the world's oldest 'households', a pebble-walled wind-shelter built by elephant-hunters 400 millennia ago, which was discovered in 1966. A fascinating set of models, bones and tools helps evoke life in Nice in the prehistoric era. Nor had things changed radically 200,000 years later, judging by the Palaeolithic relics left in the nearby **Grotte du Lazaret** (*for information or to arrange visits, call* **t** *04 92 00 17 37; you need to be a scholar or in a group of at least 10 people to visit, although there are also some open days every year*).

Boulevard Carnot (the Basse Corniche) continues east out of the port, up past some extravagant Belle Epoque villas gazing loftily out of the suburban sprawl, culminating in eccentricity in the **Château de l'Anglais** (*private residence, no entry*) – pink, turreted, and then crenellated for good measure. Built in 1858 by Colonel Robert Smith, a military engineer in India, the result weds English Perpendicular with mock-Mogul Palace to produce one of the best follies on the Riviera. Behind this rise the forested slopes of **Mont Boron**; off Route Forestière du Mont Boron, the magnificent **Sentier Bellevue** meanders to the top, which is capped by a fort of 1880.

A far more delightful piece of military architecture, **Fort Alban**, is just off the Moyenne Corniche, above the youth hostel (take bus 14 to Chemin du Fort or, if you're driving, turn right off Route Forestière du Mont Boron, on to Chemin du Fort du Mont Alban). Built in 1570, it bristles with four toy turrets roofed with glazed Niçois tiles. The guards could see all the way to Menton.

To the north, off the Grande Corniche, is an elegant **Observatoire** (*Boulevard de l'Observatoire, t 04 92 00 30 11, www.obs-nice.fr, bus 74 from Boulevard Pierre Sola; tours Sat at 3pm; adm*), designed in part by Charles Garnier, with a dome by Gustave Eiffel. The 59ft lens was once one of the most powerful in the world: 2,000 stars have been discovered here, which visitors can see for themselves at the annual Festival of Space and Stars in August.

Up the Paillon

In the old days, Nice's laundresses plied their trade in the torrential waters of the Paillon, and were scrubbing away in 1543 when Ottoman pirates, under the dread admiral Barbarossa, attacked. Hearing the racket on the walls, an exceptionally beefy laundress named Catherine Ségurane rushed to the highest tower, and with her hollering, enthusiasm and skilful wielding of her washerwoman's paddle galvanized the defence. When she saw that Nice was about to fall in spite of her best efforts, she climbed a ladder, bent over and dropped her drawers. The historians write that the Turks took one look at the biggest backside they had ever seen and, fearing further revelations, retreated in complete confusion and raised anchor. The often dangerous Paillon was canalized and began to vanish under the pavements in the 1830s; today it secretly flows below some of Nice's proudest showcases and prettiest gardens.

Nearest the sea, Jardin Albert Ier is the site of the open-air **Théâtre de Verdure**, and the garden also hosts free music concerts in the summer, while upstream, as it were, vast ochre-painted **Place Masséna** is generously endowed with flowerbeds and wisteria-shaded benches for Nice's sun-loving retirees. Marshal Masséna, the son of a humble Niçois wine merchant, was born in 1758, and ran away to sea. Canny and corrupt, he leapt on whichever bandwagon offered the highest price, managing to fight consecutively for Nation, Emperor and King, and scooping up a lucrative collection of titles from duke to prince during his perfidious career. Further up, the Promenade du Paillon is dominated by the dingy hanging gardens of the bus station/multistorey car park, a mini-Babylon with an unsavoury reputation for small-time vice – vice that pales in the face of ex-Mayor Jacques Médecin's pair of dreadnoughts looming beyond.

The first of these, reached by sets of Aztec temple steps, is Nice's answer to the Pompidou Centre in Paris: the 282-million-franc **Théâtre de Nice** (*t 04 93 13 90 90*) and the marble-coated **Musée d'Art Moderne et d'Art Contemporain** (*t 04 93 62 61 62;*

open 10–6; closed Mon and hols; adm). Inauspiciously inaugurated in June 1990, as the public revelations of Médecin's sins and fury over his anti-Semitism reached a pitch, the ceremony was boycotted by the Niçois art community, who convinced France's culture minister Jack Lang to stay away as well.

If you overlook the fact that the roof was already leaking four months after it was finished, or that the museum had to be closed for major repairs in December 1991 when large cracks were discovered in its foundations, the building – four concrete towers, linked by glass walkways that seem to smile and frown and afford pleasant views over the city – is an admirable setting for the works of Christo, Niki de Saint-Phalle, Warhol, Dine, Oldenburg, Rauschenberg, and other influential figures of the 1960s and '70s.

The first floor has been given over to temporary exhibitions, but the primary focus is on the artists of the 'Second School of Nice'. The most prominent of these, Yves Klein, gets a whole gallery to himself on the second floor, with paintings and sculptures like *Blue Victory of Samothrace* and *Blue Venus* electrified by his hallmark shade of 'IKB' blue. The epic *Wall of Fire* looms down from the museum's roof terraces. The New Realist concoctions of Martial Raysse, César, Arman and Swiss-born Jean Tinguely – plastic consumer junk, broken machinery, musical intruments and exploding suicide machines – and the irreverent neo-Dadaist works by the Fluxus artists like Ben, Serge III and Fillious, spoof not only society, but also the artificial, rarefied and wordy world of contemporary art – especially the push-button fun house called *Ben's Hut*. American Pop Art, which was unleashed on the other side of the Atlantic at about the same time as the New Realists were causing chaos on the French art scene, is fearsomely represented with a number of major works, from Tom Wesselman's tripartite *Still Life* – a rotary telephone, a light switch and a burning cigarette – to Jim Dine's *Hard Hearts* and Andy Warhol's serigraphed dollar signs.

The view up the Paillon is blocked by Médecin's 1985 congress and art centre and *cinémathèque* at No.1 Esplanade Kennedy, **Acropolis** (*t 04 92 04 06 66*) – a gruesome megalithic bunker of concrete slabs and smoked glass, with perfectly synchronized jet fountains spurting up soullessly at the entrance. No design could be more diametrically opposed (stylistically and philosophically) to the acropolis in Athens, and the mass of guitars in Arman's *Music Power* at the entrance hardly redeems it. Beyond this are more mastodons: a **Palais des Expositions**, which looks more like an enormous tractor shed, and the **Palais des Sports**.

West of Place Masséna and the Promenade des Anglais

The Paillon neatly divides Vieux Nice from the boom city of 19th-century tourism, full of ornate, debonair apartments, immaculate squares and hotels. Important streets fan out from Place Masséna and the adjacent Jardin Albert Iᵉʳ: Nice's main shopping street, **Av Jean Médecin**, leads up to the train station (the shops become progressively shabbier and far up towards Place du Général de Gaulle the pavement fills up with traders selling fresh fish, meat and vegetables to crocodiles of hard-eyed old ladies); **Rue Masséna** is the centre of a lively pedestrian-only restaurant and shopping zone; and the fabled, palm-lined **Promenade des Anglais** is still aglitter through the fumes of the traffic, which is usually as strangled as poor Isadora Duncan was when her scarf caught in the wheel of her Bugatti here in 1927. The pebble beach is crowded day and night in summer, when parties spontaneously erupt among the illegal but tolerated campers.

Visitors from the opposite end of the economic spectrum check into the fabled pink Belle Epoque **Hôtel Negresco** at No.37 (*see* p.133), vintage 1906, and now they can again roll snake eyes in the 1929 **Palais de la Méditerranée**, a masterpiece of French Art Deco built by Frank Jay Gould. In 1960 it was the most profitable casino in France; by 1979 it was bankrupt, thanks to the machinations of Jacques Médecin and his cronies who favoured the rival **Casino Ruhl**, all brash ferro-concrete and neon. The Ruhl reopened next to the Negresco in spring 1995, in spite of the unsolved case of the disappearance and presumed murder of Agnès Le Roux, daughter of Renée Le Roux, at the time the main owner of the Palais de la Méditerranée. Five months before disappearing in 1977, Agnès had secretly sold her share in the family business to Jean-Dominique Fratoni, owner of the Ruhl and a man with mafia and Médecin links. Meanwhile the Palais de la Méditerranée was destined for the wrecking-ball, but the speculators gave in to the protests at the last minute, on condition that the building had all its original innards removed. For years it stood, a desolate façade, increasingly a blot on the landscape and a sad reminder of glory days long past; but now it has finally been redeveloped into a new luxury hotel with a car park beneath and business spaces, plus a revamped casino.

Another gem clinging to the Promenade among the new buildings is at No.139, a flowery Art Nouveau-style villa of 1910 built by a Finnish engineer.

On the other side of the Negresco is the garden of the **Palais Masséna** (*t 04 93 88 11 34; closed for restoration, expected to re-open 2006, gardens still open*). Built in the Empire style in 1901 for Prince Victor Masséna, the grandson of Napoleon's marshal, it was left to Nice on condition that it become a *musée d'art et d'histoire*. At the entrance, a solemn statue of Napoleon tarted up in a toga sets the tone for the ground-floor *salons* – heavy and pompous and stylistically co-ordinated from ceiling stucco to chair leg. The atmosphere lightens upstairs with a pair of fine retables from the 1450s by Jacques Durandi, panels from a polyptych attributed to Ludovico Brea, ceramics, armour, and a curious 16th-century Flemish painting, the *Vierge à la fleur* with a fly in the flower, 'a symbol of death and vanity'.

The top floor displays statues of the *Ten Incarnations of Vishnu*, Spanish earrings, views of Nice and rooms dedicated to home-town boys Garibaldi and the cruel and wicked Marshal Masséna, the military genius Napoleon called '*l'enfant gâté de la victoire*', whose appetite for atrocities was matched only by his greedy plundering. Then there's the obligatory Napoleana: a billiard-ball from St Helena and Josephine's bed, with a big 'N' on the coverlet.

Fine and Naïf Arts, and a Russian Cathedral

A brisk 10-minute walk from the Masséna museum, or bus 38 from the bus station (right to the door), takes you to the handsome 1876 villa built by a Ukranian princess, enlarged by an American millionaire and now home of the **Musée des Beaux-Arts**

(Jules Chéret) (*33 Av des Baumettes,* **t** *04 92 15 28 28, www.musee-beaux-arts-nice.org; open Tues–Sun 10–6; closed Mon; adm*).

With the Matisses and Chagalls in Nice's other museums, the Musée des Beaux Arts is left with little more than the 'old masters of the 19th century' – a euphemism for tired, flabby academic paintings and portraits of Madame This and Madame That, a *Portrait of an Old Man* by Fragonard and works by Carle Van Loo, a native of Nice.

There are a few other meaty paintings: a 1615 *David* attributed to Tanzio da Varallo, a Lombard follower of Caravaggio; a self-portrait by eccentric young Russian aristocrat Marie Bashkirtseff; and a roomful of her contemporary Kees Van Dongen, including his entertaining 1927 *Tango of the Archangel*, which perhaps more than any painting evokes the Roaring Twenties on the Riviera – even the archangel, in his dinner jacket, is wearing high heels.

Picasso also gets a look-in in this room with a small collection of the ceramic pieces he created while at Vallauris (*see* p.178). Recently, the works of a much cheerier soul, Raoul Dufy, who spent his latter years in Nice producing colourful 'cafe-society' art, have been brought in to brighten the place up a bit. The handful of his early Fauve works are the most compelling, especially the remarkable 1908 *Bateaux à l'Estaque*. One room is devoted to Félix Ziem, and another to the Belle Epoque's favourite lithographist, Jules Chéret, who introduced colour posters to France in 1866, most of them decorated with his most famous creation, a pert-nosed doll-woman who became known as '*La Chérette*', caught in swirling pastel tornadoes of silly *putti*. His oil portraits decorate the walls of the upper staircase, among them portraits of Baron and Baroness Vitta, who collected Chéret's work and and then unloaded it on to the museum which now bears his name.

The florid output of Nice's carnival duo, father and son Alexis and Gustav-Adolf Mossa, has also found a home here. The collection features landscapes by Alexis, a native of Nice, who is better known for his fabulous designs for pageants and floats for the Nice Carnival, which he dragged out of obscurity in 1860. His son, Gustav-Adolf Mossa (1883–1971), painted exquisite mytho-morbid Symbolist works between 1903 and 1917, and then just stopped. He also followed in his father's footsteps and created several frothy, exuberant carnival floats.

To the west, the founder of the Monte-Carlo casino built the strawberry-pink Château de Ste-Hélène, which had a succession of owners before being bought and redesigned by the perfume magnate, Coty, in 1922. It now houses the **Musée d'Art Naïf Anatole Jakovsky** (*Av de Fabron,* **t** *04 93 71 78 33, buses 8, 9, 10, 11,11B, 12, 34, stop Fabron; open Wed–Mon 10–6; closed Tues; adm*), an offshoot of the Pompidou Centre in Paris, with a collection formed of around 600 paintings spanning the 18th to the 20th centuries, donated by Jakovsky, a tireless promoter of naïve art who became known as '*le Pape des Naïfs*'. Jakovsky met the American painter Gertrude O'Brady when they were both dabbling in Bohemianism in Paris's Latin Quarter; several of her stylized, nostalgic portraits figure here, among them one of Jakovsky himself, pipe in hand, in his plush Saint-Germain apartment. The Yugoslavs are especially well repre-sented, with an enthusiasm for the genre that perhaps in some way counterbalances the unsolvable, nightmarish imbroglio of their politics. But even among the scenes of jolly village fêtes and fairs the surreal is never far, especially in *The Clock* by Jules Lefranc, and in the funny *Sodom and Gomorrah*, where the columns go flying every which way.

Near the airport you may already have noticed the mega-greenhouse of **Parc Floral Phœnix** (*405 Promenade des Anglais*, **t** *04 92 29 77 00, bus 9, 10, 23, 24, 26; open daily summer daily 9–8; winter daily 9–5; adm*), a Disneyland for botanists or garden-lovers: its diamond dome supports 2,500 different plants in seven tropical climates. Also in the park is the austere white marble **Musée des Arts Asiatiques**, designed by Japanese architect Kenzo Tange, 'a swan that floats on the water of a peaceful lake' (**t** *04 92 29 37 00, www.arts-asiatiques.com; open May–mid-Oct Wed–Mon 10–6; mid-Oct–April Wed–Mon 10–5; closed Tues and hols; adm*). The central building is based on geometrical forms of the square and circle, symbolizing the earth and the sky, reflected in a shallow pool. Four cubes spread out over the lake contain the permanent collection: Chinese jade and bronze and Japanese lacquer and ceramics lead into Cambodian sculpture and Indian textiles. An elliptical glass staircase curves up inside to the rotunda, the 'spiritual sphere' where the up-to-the-minute multimedia displays and exhibitions with a spiritual theme round up an original collection in an original and beautiful building. Tea ceremonies – the meditative ritual of Japan or the earthier tastings of Chinese *Gong Fu Cha* (*call to reserve a place*) – take place on Thusdays and Sundays in a Japanese pavilion decorated with delicate ceramics and reached by a small footbridge.

In 1865 the young Tsarevich Nicholas was brought south to Nice and, like so many consumptives who arrived in search of health, he met the grim reaper instead. The luxurious villa where he died was demolished to construct a Byzantine mortuary chapel and the great **Cathédrale Orthodoxe Russe St-Nicolas**, known as the Eglise Russe, located a few blocks west of the train station, just off Boulevard Gambetta (*Av Nicolas II*, **t** *04 93 96 88 02, bus nos.7 or 15; open daily except Sun am and services, summer 9–12 and 2.30–6; spring and autumn 9.15–12 and 2–5.30; winter 9.30–12 and 2.30–5; no shorts or sleeveless shirts; adm*), and modelled on the five-domed church of Jaroslav near Moscow.

Tsar Nicolas II was paying the bills, so the architects bought only the best – bricks from Germany, crosses from Italy and hand-finished Russian mosaics. The design may be strictly Russian, but the colours are sublimely Mediterranean: pink Italian granite, blue terracotta tiling from Florence and palest white stone from La Turbie, its five onion domes shining with a colourful coating of glazed Niçois tiles. It was completed only five years before the Bolshevik Revolution. The interior, splayed like a Greek cross, is a sparkling wonderland of gilded frescoes, woodwork and icons, many of which were donated by the immigrants fleeing Russia in 1917.

North of here (take bus 5 – it is quite a hike) is the **Prieuré du Vieux Logis** (*59 Av Saint-Barthélémy*, **t** *04 93 84 44 74; open Wed, Thurs, Sat and first Sun of month 3–5*), an old Niçois villa which was remodelled in the 1930s to hold a collection of religious art from the 14th to the 17th centuries gathered by an obsessive forager and Dominican monk, Alfred Lemerre. The pride of the collection is a 15th-century Flemish

Pietà, but the real delight is the mellow old building itself, with its balustraded balconies and terraces and its dreamy little garden.

The Ministry of Culture sponsors the activities in the nearby 18th-century **Villa Arson** (*20 Av Stephen Liégeard, t 04 92 07 73 73, www.villa-arson.org; bus 4, 7; open summer Wed–Mon 2–7; winter Wed–Mon 2–6; closed Tues*) – not the headquarters of a pyromaniac club, but a centre for contemporary art, with students, studios for working artists, exhibitions, a library and, thankfully, a café, surrounded by 'brutalistic' buildings designed in the late 1960s by Michel Marot, and concrete terraces decorated with pebbles.

Cimiez: Chagall, Matisse and Roman Ruins

On the low hills northwest of the Paillon, where wealthy Romans lived the good life in Cemenelum, modern Niçois do the same in Cimiez, a luxurious 19th-century suburb dotted with the grand hotels of yesteryear, now genteel apartment buildings.

Bus 15 from the train station will take you to the main attractions, beginning with the **Musée National Message Biblique Marc Chagall**, at the foot of Cimiez hill (*Av du Docteur Ménard, west of Bd de Cimiez, t 04 93 53 87 20; open Oct–June Wed–Mon 10–5; July–Sept Wed–Mon 10–6; closed Tues; adm*). While Picasso, Matisse and Cocteau were all busy painting and restoring chapels (*see* pp.178, 164 and 127 respectively) dotted along the Riviera, Chagall was embarking on an integrated cycle of 17 paintings based on stories from the Old Testament. He hoped to hang them in one of a cluster of small deconsecrated 17th-century chapels just outside Vence, but, despite a lot of municipal trumpeting, nothing came of the plan. Eventually, the writer André Malraux, a friend of Chagall and erstwhile Minister of Culture, suggested that a new museum be built to hold the series, and work began in Nice. The low, unassuming building is set among a suitably biblical garden of olives and cypresses. Constructed of pale stone from La Turbie, it was dedicated in 1973 on Chagall's 86th birthday.

Temporary exhibitions, usually with a spiritual or biblical theme, take place in the niched gallery to the left of the entrance hall; to the right is the zigzag central hall, designed to allow the paintings to be viewed both as a group and individually, where Chagall's *Biblical Message Cycle* begins. The paintings are divided into three sections: *Genesis, Exodus* and the *Songs of Solomon*. They have been hung, as Chagall requested, chromatically rather than chronologically, and are paired to complement each other's rich glowing emeralds, cobalts and magentas. They leap with Chagall's idiosyncratic symbolism – tumbling flowers, fish, angels and rabbits. Best of all, in an adjacent, octagonal gallery, is the rapturous red, red, red series of the *Song of Songs* – dedicated to Vava, Chagall's wife. A small room branches off for contemplation of an exterior mosaic of *The Prophet Elijah* (Elijah soaring across the sky in his chariot of fire, surrounded by signs of the zodiac), set over a pond in order to create a kaleidoscopic, shimmering reflection.

Cimiez owed much of its original cachet to Queen Victoria, and she's gratefully remembered with a statue in front of her favourite lodging, the **Hôtel Excelsior Regina Palace** on Av Regina, off Av Reine Victoria, an unbridled effusion of ballrooms, loggias and bowed galleries. After the Second World War, the same hotel became headquarters for Henri Matisse, who died here in 1954, leaving the city a priceless collection of his works, displayed in the nearby **Musée Matisse** (*164 Av des Arènes-de-Cimiez, t 04 93 81 08 08, www.musee-matisse-nice.org, take bus 15, 17, 20 or 22 from the Promenade des Anglais or Av Jean-Médecin; open Wed–Mon 10–6; closed Tues and some holidays; adm*), a late 17th-century Genoese villa with a *trompe l'œil* façade, set in the olive-studded Parc des Arènes. The archaeological museum also used to call the Villa d'Arènes home, but was shunted to the other side of the Roman ruins in 1993 when a new, glassy modern wing, designed by Jean-François Bodin, was constructed to cope with the burgeoning Matisse collection. The extension, with the main entrance, is partly underground to the right of the villa and can be difficult to find: head down the wide flight of white steps.

Matisse's last work, the gargantuan paper cut-out, *Flowers and Fruit 1952–3*, dominates one whole side of the entrance hall. He first used this technique when designing the costumes and sets for Diaghilev's ballet *Le Chant du rossignol* (*The Nightingale's Song*) in the 1920s and returned to it increasingly, particularly in later life when his hands could no longer comfortably hold a paintbrush. He covered the walls and ceilings of his rooms at the Regina with a multicoloured world of flowers and creatures, chuckling to himself at the reactions of critics: 'Old Matisse, nearing the end of his life, is having a lot of fun cutting up paper,' he imagined them saying. He preferred to think of it as 'drawing with scissors'.

The main collection begins with some of his early bronze sculptures – among them *Le Serf* (1900), the largest of his sculptures, and the deliciously brazen *La Serpentine* (1909). There is also a lyrical series of back studies (*Dos*), an obsession to which he returned again and again throughout his career. The museum has gathered most of his sculptures and drawings, although many of his most famous paintings had already been snapped up by foresighted foreign buyers by the time Matisse really hit the big time in France. Some of his earliest paintings from the 1890s are on view in the main house, accessed by an underground passage. Even in these early works, some colours sing out, especially in the sultry *Odalisque au coffret rouge* (*Odalisque with a Red Box*, 1926); others include the soft, dreamy *Figure endormie* (*Sleeping Figure*), and the most famous painting of the collection, *Nature morte aux grenades* (*Still Life with Pomegranates*, 1947). Among the comprehensive collection of his drawings are studies for book illustrations – Joyce's *Ulysses*, Baudelaire's *Fleurs du Mal* – and a delightful series entitled *Nadia*, with every fluttering shade of the sitter's countenance recorded. There are more cut-outs, including the bright bold *Nu bleu IV* (1952) and *La Vague* (*The Wave*, 1952), plus some amusing photographs of Matisse with his hulking classical statue and a pretty lithograph series of giggling mermaids.

Upstairs, in a room specially lit to recreate the chapel light, are photographs, models and studies for the Chapelle du Rosaire in Vence (*see* p.164), which Matisse worked on – often from his wheelchair – until his death, designing everything from the lovely building itself to the wall frescoes, the stained glass windows and the priests' vestments.

Adjacent to the Matisse Museum is the new **Musée Archéologique** (*t 04 93 81 59 57; open Wed–Mon 10–6; closed Tues and some holidays; guided tours Wed and first Sun of every month; adm*), entered through the excavations of Cemenelum (*see* pp.138–9). These include the baths (hot, medium and cold, with the remnants of the heating apparatus still visible), a marble summer pool and the amphitheatre, with seating for 4,000 (unusually small for a population of 20,000, but perhaps the Romans here were too couth for gladiators). In July, Nice's jazz festival takes place here. The museum houses vases, coins, statues, jewels and models of what Cimiez looked like 2,000 years ago, with a fittingly underground section devoted to funereal steles and sarcophagi.

From the archaeological museum, it's a short walk back past the Matisse museum and across the Jardin Public to the **Musée Franciscain, Eglise et Monastère de Cimiez** (*t 04 93 81 00 04; open Wed–Sat and Mon 10–12 and 3–6; closed Tues, Sun and holidays*). The Franciscans have resided here since the 16th century, but their church was heavily restored in 1850, although it still has two beautiful altarpieces by Ludovico Brea: the *Vierge de Piété,* one of his earliest works, and a *Crucifixion* on a gold background, painted later in his life. In the cloister are other, less explicable 17th-century paintings that some scholars think may have alchemical meanings. There's a museum documenting Franciscan life in Nice from the 13th to the 18th centuries, with frescoes, engravings, sculptures and a reconstruction of the spartan cell of a poor Franciscan monk of the 17th century. Dufy and Matisse are buried in the adjacent cemetery, and there are fine views over the valley of the Paillon from the monastery garden.

From Cagnes to Cannes

The deep Greek of the Mediterranean licked its chops over the edges of our febrile civilization.
Zelda Fitzgerald

The stretch of the Riviera between Nice and Cannes is just about as dense, febrile and excessive as old Europe ever gets – 'one vast honky-tonk,' declared Noel Coward back in 1960: too many cars, villas, theme parks and marinas full of yachts the size of tankers, too many gift shops in the lovely *villages perchés*, too many Parisians and movie stars in Cannes and too many technocrats in Sophia-Antipolis, the 'Silicon Valley of the Riviera'.

The scenery, especially up around the Gorges du Loup, is decidedly excessive, and you can be bedazzled by the perfumes at Grasse and the surplus of art that crowds the coast: Renoir in Cagnes, Léger in Biot, more Matisse in Vence, Picasso in Antibes and Vallauris, and all the contemporary greats up at the dazzling Fondation Maeght. There are so many good restaurants at Mougins that you hardly dare go out.

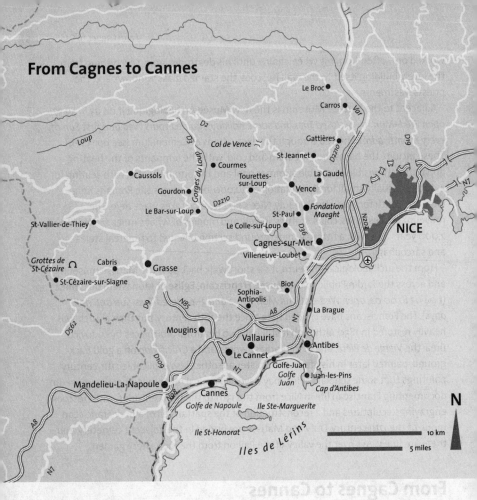

Cagnes

West of Nice runs the Var river, the wet but politically prickly border between France and Savoy, whose dukes were usually allied to France's rivals – England, Spain or Austria. As bridges over the Var were periodically blown up, for centuries people crossed the water sitting on the shoulders of two strong men. Nowadays, in the maelstrom of traffic and overbuilding, it's hard even to notice the Var at all.

Across the river lies the bloated amoeba of Cagnes, divided into three cells – overbuilt Cros-de-Cagnes by the sea, with a Hippodrome; Cagnes-sur-Mer, further up, site of Renoir's house, the happiest of all artists' shrines in the south; and medieval Haut-de-Cagnes on the hill, notorious in the 17th and 18th centuries for the indecorous pastimes and the brilliant parties held in its castle before the Revolution – beginning a long tradition of artsy decadence and futility chronicled in Cyril Connolly's *The Rock Pool* (1936), in which Zelda Fitzgerald's carnivorous Greek Mediterranean becomes merely 'the tideless cloaca of the ancient world'.

Beaches

Between Nice and Antibes the shore is as rocky as the eastern side of the Côte. Purists should make for Antibes, where the sand starts in earnest. There are two public beaches in Antibes: the best lies south of the town centre. Juan-les-Pins, blessed with fine sand, is also cursed with countless private beach clubs. Public beaches do exist here – try further west towards Golfe-Juan. Cannes has even more snooty beach clubs, but there is a public beach right in front of the Palais des Festivals. Further west towards Mandelieu, the beach is beautifully sandy – and free.

Best Beaches

Antibes: Port, and south of centre on D2559.
Cannes: Palais des Festivals and west to Mandelieu.

Cagnes-sur-Mer: The Musée Renoir

Av des Colettes, t 04 93 20 61 07; open May–Sept 10–12 and 2–6; Oct and Dec–April 10–12 and 2–5; closed Tues and Nov; adm.

There is only one thing to do in sprawling Cagnes-sur-Mer: from central Place Général de Gaulle follow Av Auguste Renoir up to Chemin des Colettes, to **Le Domaine des Colettes**, where Renoir spent the last 12 years of his life. Stricken with rheumatoid arthritis, Renoir followed his doctor's advice to move to warmer climes and chose Cagnes, where 'one's nose is not stuck in the mountains'. He rented an apartment in the old Maison de la Poste (which has since become the Town Hall) for himself, his wife and the youngest of their three sons, and then, in 1907, purchased an ancient olive grove – originally destined for destruction – with an old stone farmhouse. His wife had grander ideas and eventually Renoir built a sturdy bourgeois villa to compensate her for the years of wandering.

'The story of Cagnes and Renoir is a love story,' said his son, the film-maker Jean Renoir. Rejuvenated by the climate, Renoir produced paintings even more sensuous and voluptuous than before, and there's no contrast more poignant than that of the colour-saturated *Les Grandes Baigneuses* (in the Philadelphia Museum of Art) and the photograph in the museum of the painter's hands, so bent and crippled that they're painful even to look at. 'I pay dearly for the pleasure I get from this canvas,' he said of one portrait that he especially liked, painted with brushes strapped to his hands. It was also in Cagnes that Renoir first experimented with sculpture, by proxy, brandishing the long stick which he used as an extension of his twisted hands and dictating detailed instructions to a young sculptor, Richard Guino, a Spaniard who had been trained in Paris by Aristide Maillol. It was Maillol who urged Renoir to try sculpture when he first arrived in Cagnes, but he was only able to complete two pieces without aid before his hands failed him: *Buste de Coco* (a bust of his youngest son, Claude, nicknamed Coco) and a little medallion, *Médaillon de Claude*, both on display in the house.

In 1989 the museum's collection of portraits of Renoir by his friends was supplemented with 10 canvases the master himself painted in Cagnes, among them a later red-hued version of *Les Grandes Baigneuses*, and an affectionate portrait of Claude, with long blond hair, reading. He looks as though butter wouldn't melt in his mouth, but it is thought that Claude was responsible for the naughty handpainted tile

Getting There and Around

There are **train stations** in both Cagnes-sur-Mer and Cros-de-Cagnes (call the central number, t 08 92 35 35 35), and a continuous service of **minibuses** from Cagnes-sur-Mer bus station up the steep hill to Haut-de-Cagnes.

There's a massive **underground car park** just outside the village entrance, and restricted parking in the serpentine streets of the old village (beware of parking by the police station at the back of the château). **Buses** from Nice to Vence stop in Cagnes-sur-Mer.

There is a **free shuttle** from the bus station in Haut-de-Cagnes to the old town. For **taxis**, call t 08 02 06 60 00.

Bike Hire

Cycles Marcel, 5 Rue Pasqualini, Cagnes-sur-Mer, t 04 93 20 64 07.

Tourist Information

Cagnes-sur-Mer: 6 Bd Maréchal Juin, t 04 93 20 61 64, f 04 93 20 52 63, *info@cagnes-tourisme.com, www.cagnes-tourisme.com. Open July–Aug Mon–Sat 9–7, Sun 9–12 and 3–7; June and Sept Mon–Sat 9–12 and 2–7, Oct–May Mon–Sat 9–12, 2–6.*
Also 20 Av des Oliviers, Cros-de-Cagnes, t 04 93 07 67 08, f 04 93 07 61 59. *Open July–Aug daily 9–1 and 3.30–6.30; Sept–June Mon–Sat 9–12.*
Haut-de-Cagnes: Espace Solidor, Place du Château, t 04 92 02 85 05. *Open July–Aug daily 10–1 and 3–6.30; April–June and Sept Wed–Sun 2–6; Oct–Mar Wed–Sun 2–5.*

Market Days

Cagnes-sur-Mer: Fruit and vegetables in the Cité Marchande every morning from Tues to Sun, and in Bd Kennedy on Fri am. Bric-a-brac, clothes and almost everything else in the big car park opposite the bus station on Wed am.
Cros-de-Cagnes: Tues and Thurs am, general market, Rue des Oliviers.

Where to Stay and Eat

Cagnes-sur-Mer ✉ 06800

★★★★Le Cagnard, Rue Sous-Barri, t 04 93 20 73 21, f 04 93 22 06 39, *resa@le-cagnard.com, www.le-cagnard.com (luxury–very expensive).* The most luxurious choice on this stretch of the coast, with sumptuous comforts discreetly arranged to fit in with the 14th-century architecture. Nearly every room has a private terrace, but the largest and most magical belongs to the hotel's Michelin-starred restaurant (*expensive*), which also has a coffered Renaissance-style ceiling that opens up in summer. Among the delicacies served up beneath it are pigeon stuffed with morels and *foie gras*, and crispy red mullet with garlic and rosemary. *Restaurant closed Nov–mid-Dec, and all day Mon, Tues lunch and Thurs lunch.*
L'Oiseau d'Or, 2 Place du Général de Gaulle, t 04 93 20 80 54, *http://oiseau-d-or-chocolatier.com.* Few of the restaurants in Cagnes-sur-Mer stand out, but the 40 different kinds of fresh chocolates found here do, including *grimaldines*, flavoured with fresh orange juice. *Closed Sun and Mon.*

Villeneuve-Loubet ✉ 06270

Hôtel du Parc, 1 Av de la Libération, t 04 93 20 88 13, f 04 93 20 82 52, *www.hotelduparc villeneuve.com (inexpensive).* A simple place in the old village, with an adequate restaurant (*moderate*) and room for campers. *Restaurant closed Sun eve and Mon.*

depicting a nude on a bidet which is tucked into a discreet corner of the bathroom. The north studio, with his wheelchair and easel, looks as if Renoir might return any minute – even the chicken wire he put over the window to keep out the children's tennis balls is in place. You can wander freely through the venerable olive grove; a quiet, serene and refreshingly unkempt spot with patches of clover and violets. The only drastic change from Renoir's day is the view down to the sea.

Haut-de-Cagnes

Spared the worst of the tourist shops, intricate, medieval Haut-de-Cagnes has become instead the fiefdom of contemporary artists, thanks to the UNESCO-sponsored Festival International de la Peinture. The crenellated **Château-Musée Grimaldi** (*t 04 92 02 47 30; open summer Wed–Mon 10–12 and 2–6, winter 10–12 and 2–5; closed Tues and 3 wks Nov; enquire at tourist office for guided tours; adm*) was built by the first Rainier Grimaldi in the 14th century, at a time when there were a hundred excess male Grimaldis prowling the coast, looking for a castle to call home. This particular branch of the family held on to Cagnes until the Revolution; its most famous twig was Henri, a good friend of Louis XIII, who convinced his cousin in Monaco to put himself under the protection of France rather than Spain.

In sharp contrast with the château's dour feudal exterior, a handsome Renaissance inner courtyard is tiered with galleries to provide all the castle's light and air, shaded now by a 200-year-old pepper tree. In the vaulted halls on the ground floor there's a **Musée de l'Olivier**, where among the presses you may find a small machine for pressing coins, not olives, used by the marquis to counterfeit the king's coin (he was arrested in 1710, by Comte d'Artagnan of *Musketeers* fame). Upstairs are Henri Grimaldi's ornate reception rooms, topped by *The Fall of Phaeton* (1624) by the Genoese Giovanni Andrea Carlone, one of those hysterical *trompe-l'œil* ceiling paintings of floating horse stomachs and testicles that the Italians were so fond of. In another room, the **Donation Suzy Solidor** contains paintings donated by the free-living *chanteuse* and star of Parisian cabarets between the wars. Suzy spent the last 25 years of her life in Haut-de-Cagnes, hobnobbing with local artists and bumping up her portrait collection. There were 224 – all of herself. The 40 on display here are each by a different artist – Van Dongen, Dufy, Kisling, Friesz, Cocteau, and so on. On the next floor, the **Musée d'Art Moderne Méditerranéen** is dedicated to a rotating collection of works by the above and other painters who have worked along the coast.

Villeneuve-Loubet and Escoffier

To the southwest of Cagnes, on another hill dominated by another medieval castle, Villeneuve-Loubet is a small village known for its fishing, a visit from François Ier (where he signed a 10-year peace treaty with Charles V in 1538) and Marshal Pétain, hero of the First World War, who was working as a farmer and wine-grower before accepting the summons to govern France from Vichy. The event that really put it on the map, however, was the birth in 1846 of Auguste Escoffier, who went on to become 'the chef of kings and the king of chefs' – the king in question being Edward VII, who encouraged Escoffier and the hotelier César Ritz to move to London, thus making the Savoy and the Carlton citadels of class and cuisine. The Emperor William II gave Escoffier the title of 'Emperor of the World's Kitchens' after gorging on his creations on the imperial steamer, and France awarded him the Legion of Honour. Escoffier's birthplace is now the **Musée Escoffier de l'Art Culinaire** (*3 Rue A. Escoffier, t 04 93 20 80 51, www.fondation-escoffier.org; open summer Tues–Sun 2–7; winter Tues–Sun 2–6;*

closed Mon, hols and Nov), but don't come looking for nibbles or scratch-and-sniff
exhibits of his creations. Instead there's a 19th-century Provençal kitchen; an auto-
graphed photo of soprano Nellie Melba thanking Escoffier for calling his new peach
dessert after her (though his asparagus ice-cream never took off); a collection of the
chef's radical 'light menus', which seem incredibly elaborate nowadays; and the sugar
sculptures Escoffier loved, still prepared by local *pâtissiers* for saccharine competitions
that put the kitsch back into kitchen.

There's also a **Musée d'Histoire et d'Art** (*Place de Verdun, t 04 92 02 60 39; open
Mon–Fri 10–12 and 2–6, Sat 9.30–12.30*), with a retrospective exhibition depicting life
in Villeneuve over the last century; a modest collection of modern sculpture, painting
and photographs; and a floor devoted to sobering displays covering the biggest
conflicts of the 20th century, from the First World War to the Gulf War.

Villeneuve-Loubet-Plage is another kettle of fish, home of those concrete ziggurats
you may have already noticed, looming over the Bay of Angels with all the charm of
totalitarian Mesopotamia. They are part of the Marina Baie des Anges, built in the
1970s, before the French regulated building on the coast – too late, indeed, for the
once beautiful stretch between here and Cannes.

St-Paul-de-Vence and Vence

Inland from Cagnes are two towns as bound up with contemporary art as any in the
whole of France. St-Paul-de-Vence is the home of the wonderful Fondation Maeght,
while Vence has a unique chapel painted by Matisse.

St-Paul-de-Vence

Between Cagnes and St-Paul the D6 winds above the Loup river, passing through
La Colle-sur-Loup, a village once famous for its roses that now earns its keep from the
overspill of tourists from St-Paul-de-Vence, its mother town. For La Colle was founded
in 1540, when François Ier showed his gratitude to St-Paul-de-Vence for standing up to
the assaults of his arch rival, Emperor Charles V, by financing a rampart around the
town. Some 700 houses had to be demolished to make room for the king's gift,
obliging the displaced populace to move elsewhere.

Reduced in size, **St-Paul-de-Vence** became a *ville fortifiée*, and still preserves a *donjon*
watchtower dating from the 12th century, as well as François' costly ramparts. The
ramparts have held up for almost five centuries and St-Paul remained a military
outpost until 1868. A cannon captured from Charles V is embedded near the town
gate, a gate much more accessible these days than the simple wooden door of the
restaurant **La Colombe d'Or**, down in the square, which was built just after the First
World War. Its first owner, an unschooled farmer named Paul Roux, fell in love with
modern art and for 40 years accepted paintings in exchange for hospitality from the
impoverished artists who flocked here after the First World War – including Picasso,
Derain, Matisse, Braque, Vlaminck, Léger, Dufy and Bonnard. By the time he died he
had accumulated one of France's greatest private collections (but strictly for viewing

by those who can at least afford a meal). Just across the street, in front of the Café de la Place, is a shady *pétanque* court, dotted with moustachioed extras from a Pagnol film, where Yves Montand himself used to work off a little artistic steam.

If you're prone to claustrophobia, visit St-Paul early, before its prettily cobbled little lanes are clogged with visitors and baskets of artsy trinkets. From its ramparts, to the north you can see the odd, sphinx-shaped rock called the **Baou de St-Jeannet**, that was painted into the uncanny landscape of Nicolas Poussin's *Polyphème*. Just outside the tip of the ramparts is a tiny **cemetery**, shaded by 100-year-old cypress trees, where Chagall chose to be buried. There's a handsome urn-shaped fountain and an arcaded *lavoir* along the Rue Grande and, further up, the 12th-century *donjon* and the lovely pale stone **Chapelle des Pénitents Blancs**. Also here at the summit of the village and top of the Rue Grande is the Collegiate church of the **Conversion de St-Paul**, where you can press yourself a tin medal to commemorate your visit. It is sumptuously furnished with Baroque stuccos, woodwork and paintings – including one of *St Catherine of Alexandria* in the left aisle, attributed in part to Tintoretto. Some of its treasures are in the **Musée d'Histoire Locale** (*t 04 93 32 41 13; open daily 10–12.30 and 1.30–5.30; adm*), in the medieval residence around the corner, which tries to tempt unwary visitors with pop-eyed waxworks but actually redeems itself with a collection of celebrity photos: film stars in dark glasses and chiffon headscarves laughing over cocktails at the Colombe d'Or.

At the **Musée de St-Paul** (*t 04 93 32 86 95; open Oct–May daily 10–1 and 2–6, June–Sept daily 10–7*), next to the tourist office, artists from around the world exhibit their work, with a different artist featured each month.

Fondation Maeght

Here is an attempt at something never before undertaken: creating a world with which modern art can both find its place and that otherworldliness which used to be called supernatural.

The Foundation's inaugural speech by André Malraux, 1964

Set back in the woods up on Route Passe-Prest, the **Fondation Maeght** (*t 04 93 32 81 63, f 04 93 32 53 22, www.fondation-maeght.com; open daily July–Sept 10–7; Oct–June 10–12.30 and 2.30–6; adm*) is the best reason of all for visiting St-Paul – a vibrant and intelligently curated centre for contemporary art. Its fairy godparents, Aimé and Marguerite Maeght, art dealers and friends of Matisse and Bonnard, were struck by tragedy in 1953 when their youngest son, Bernard, died of leukaemia. When they discovered that a dilapidated chapel near their home was dedicated to St Bernard, their artist friends, among them Braque and Léger, suggested they restore it in memory of their son. The idea grew over several months and eventually the Maeghts decided they wanted to create an ideal environment for contemporary art, where they could bring together their collection and add some space for their artist friends to work and exchange ideas. They hired Catalan architect José-Luis Sert, a pupil of Le Corbusier and good buddy of Joan Miró, to design the setting – 'building' seems too confining a term for these walls that are 'a play between the rhythms of

Getting There

There are frequent **buses** from Cagnes-sur-Mer to La Colle-sur-Loup, St-Paul-de-Vence and Vence, and connections nearly every hour from Nice. La Gaude can be reached by bus from St-Jeannet and Cagnes-sur-Mer (but not from Vence); Tourrettes-sur-Loup and Le Bar-sur-Loup are on the Vence–Grasse bus route. For bus times, call SAP on **t** 04 93 58 37 60.

Tourist Information

St-Paul-de-Vence: 2 Rue Grande, **t** 04 93 32 86 95, **f** 04 93 32 60 27, *artdevivre@wanadoo.fr. Open daily June–Sept 10–7; Oct–May 10–6.*
Vence: Pl du Grand-Jardin, **t** 04 93 58 06 38, **f** 04 93 58 91 81, *officedetourisme@ville-vence.fr, www.ville-vence.fr. Open July–Aug Mon–Sat 9–7, Sun 9–1; Sept–Oct, April–June Mon–Sat 9–6, Nov–Mar Mon–Sat 9–5.*

Market Days

Vence: every am, fruit, vegetables, flowers and clothes on Place du Grand-Jardin. Wed, Flea market on Place du Grand-Jardin. Tues and Fri, market in the historical centre.

Festivals

St-Paul-de-Vence: **Fête des Châtaignes** in October.
Vence: **Fête de Pâques** in April, with parades, a *bataille des fleurs* and folk dancing. **Festival of Traditional Music** and a **garlic fair** in July.

Where to Stay and Eat

St-Paul-de-Vence ✉ 06570

To stay in St-Paul-de-Vence, you must have buckets of money and book well in advance.
★★★La Colombe d'Or, Place de Gaulle, **t** 04 93 32 80 02, **f** 04 93 32 77 78, *contact@la-colombe-dor.com, www.la-colombe-dor.com* (*luxury*). Earthy stone, low tiled roofs and rustic shutters; the rooms are full of character, the pool is heated, the stone-arcaded terrace lovely. The restaurant (*expensive*), where Yves Montand and Simone Signoret celebrated their wedding and Arnold

Schwarzenegger hosted his 1993 Cannes Film Festival bash, is more a feast for the eyes than for the stomach, but you won't go wrong with its traditional groaning platters of *hors-d'œuvre* and grilled meats. *Closed Dec–23 Jan.*

★★★★Le St-Paul, 86 Rue Grande, **t** 04 93 32 65 25, **f** 04 93 32 52 94, *stpaul@relaischateaux. com, www.lesaintpaul.com* (*luxury*). The interior designers let their hair down in this 16th-century building to create unusual but delightful juxtapositions of medieval, surreal, Egyptian and Art Deco elements. Its equally attractive restaurant (*very expensive–expensive*) is in an ancient vault, with a summer terrace settled around a stone fountain. *Closed Tues lunch and Wed lunch Nov–Mar.*

★★★La Grande Bastide, 1350 Route de la Colle, **t** 04 93 32 50 30, **f** 04 93 32 50 59, *www. la-grande-bastide.com* (*very expensive*). A stylishly renovated 16th-century manor on the hillside just outside St-Paul-de-Vence, with swimming pool, sun terrace and a very welcoming *patronne*. Hazy pastel colours brighten the rooms, some of which have private terraces leading into the gardens. No restaurant. *Closed 25 Nov–20 Dec and 12 Jan–15 Feb.*

★★★Le Hameau, 528 Rte de La Colle, **t** 04 93 32 80 24, **f** 04 93 32 55 75, *lehameau@wanadoo. fr, www.le-hameau.com* (*expensive*). One of the loveliest hotels in the area, with wide views over the orange groves from its low-beamed rooms decked out in cheery Provençal fabrics, and a small swimming pool. There is no restaurant, but two rooms have kitchenettes and there is home-made marmalade and jam for breakfast. *Closed mid-Nov–mid-Dec and early Jan–end Feb.*

★★★Les Orangers, Chemin des Fumerates, **t** 04 93 32 80 95, **f** 04 93 32 00 32, *www. stpaulweb.com/hlo* (*expensive*). Exposed beams and armfuls of flowers in a Provençal house tucked into the hillside.

★★Hostellerie Les Remparts, 72 Rue Grande, **t** 04 93 32 09 88, **f** 04 93 32 06 91, *www. stpaulweb.com/remparts* (*moderate*). Cheapest of all, with medieval nooks and crannies and antique furnishings; there's also a good, affordable restaurant with a superb terrace.

Le Sainte Claire, Espace Ste-Claire, t 04 93 32 02 02, *http://aline.gerard.free.fr* (*moderate*). Sturdy Provençal décor to match the cuisine, which is well priced and served up on a panoramic terrace a couple of minutes by car from St-Paul. *Closed Tues out of season.*

Café de la Place, Place Général de Gaulle, t 04 93 32 80 03 (*cheap*). A good lunch or coffee stop, with its own *boules* court, large covered terrace and grand Parisian-style mirrored interior.

La Terrasse, t 04 93 32 02 05 (*cheap*). Crêpes, cider and home-made cakes on a tiny, flower-filled terrace off the Rue Grande. *Closed Wed.*

Vence ✉ 06140

Vence has more choice and lower prices than St-Paul.

****Château du Domaine St-Martin, 3km from Vence on Rte de Coursegoules (Av des Templiers), t 04 93 58 02 02, f 04 93 24 08 91, *www.chateau-st-martin.com* (*luxury*). A set of villa-*bastides* built around a ruined Templar fortress. The 12-hectare park has facilities for riding, fishing, tennis and a heart-shaped pool installed at the request of Harry Truman. The restaurant is equally august, with prices to match. *Closed Oct–end Feb.*

****Relais Cantemerle, 258 Chemin Cantemerle, t 04 93 58 08 18, f 04 93 58 32 89, *info@relais-cantemerle.com, www. relais-cantemerle.com* (*very expensive*). A member of the Relais du Silence group, decorated with Art Deco bits and pieces from the gutted Palais de la Méditerranée in Nice, and very tranquil. Set in a piney garden, with terraces and a pool, the Cantemerle's restaurant (*expensive*) also serves some of the finest food in Vence. *Closed Nov–Mar.*

***Villa La Roseraie, 14 Av H. Giraud, t 04 93 58 02 20, f 04 93 58 99 31 (*expensive– moderate*). Offers a garden of magnolias and cedars, and enormous home-made breakfasts by an impeccable pool. There are

antiques, Salernes tiles aplenty and lovely ironwork. Even the bicycle provided to pedal off to the Matisse Chapel is picturesque. Beware the two topmost rooms. *Closed mid-Nov–mid-Feb.*

***Diana, Av des Poilus, t 04 93 58 28 56, f 04 93 24 64 06, *www.hotel-diana-vence. com* (*moderate*). Very reasonable single and double rooms (some with kitchenettes) in the historic centre of Vence. A tad dour on the outside, paintings and sculptures brighten up the inside and there's a library and a little breakfast terrace with a water garden.

**Le Mas de Vence, 539 Av Emile Hughes, t 04 93 58 06 16, f 04 93 24 04 21, *www. azurline.com* (*moderate*). Guests are treated like one of the family here; there is a decent pool and the restaurant is one of the best places to try real Niçois ravioli.

La Closerie des Genêts, 4 Impasse Marcellin Maurel, t 04 93 58 33 25, f 04 93 58 97 01 (*inexpensive*). Charming yet unpretentious, with quiet rooms and a shady garden where you can bring your own picnic.

Le Vieux Couvent, 37 Rue Alphonse Toreille, t/f 04 93 58 78 58 (*expensive*). Hearty helpings of locally produced, well-prepared regional dishes. *Closed Wed, Thurs lunch, and mid-Jan–mid-Mar.*

La Farigoule, 15 Av Henri Isnard, t 04 93 58 01 27 (*expensive*). Provençal cuisine and good fresh fish. *Closed Tues, Wed and Sat lunch in summer, Tues and Wed out of season.*

Auberge Les Templiers, 39 Av Joffre, t 04 93 58 06 05 (*expensive*). Elegant and traditional French style – lamb, *foie gras* and fish. Rustic Provençal surroundings and warm service. *Closed Mon lunch, Tues lunch and Wed lunch in summer, Mon and Tues out of season.*

Le Pêcheur du Soleil, Place Godeau (behind the church), t 04 93 58 32 56 (*cheap*). Right in the old town, a little place with a dazzling choice of 500 different combinations of pizza toppings. You'll need fifteen minutes just to read the menu. *Closed Sun and Mon out of season and mid-Oct–mid-Jan.*

the interior and exterior spaces', as Sert himself described them. The various levels of the building follow the changes in ground level; the white 'sails' on top collect rainwater for the fountains; 'light traps' in the roof are designed to distribute natural light evenly, although the quality of light varies from room to room. The restored chapel of St Bernard has been discreetly incorporated into the grounds, with a simple statue of the saint at its entrance. Whitewashed walls offset a restrained mosaic by Léger and a dramatic wooden 15th-century Spanish crucifix. The interior is gently illuminated by Braque's stained-glass dove and Raoul Ubac's glowing *Cross and the Rosary*.

The permanent collection, which includes around 6,000 pieces by nearly every major artist of the past century, is removed during the Fondation's frequent exhibitions of young artists and retrospectives of established ones. But you'll always be able to see the works that were incorporated into the walls and gardens from the outset: Chagall's first mosaic, *Les Amoureux*, sparkles on an exterior wall, and Miró was busy laying out the beginnings of his dreamy *Labyrinth* as the building was being raised. It has become a winding series of garden paths and terraces lined with delightful sculptures, whimsical creatures like the smooth white *Solar Bird*, gargoyle-faced fountains and a ceramic half-submerged *Egg*. Braque's blue-mosaiced fountain basin, *Les Poissons*, and Calder's *Humptulips*, with its feet in a pool, were also created specifically for the Fondation.

The works in the shady sculpture garden at the entrance to the Fondation rotate from time to time, but usually among them are Miró's great *Monument*, an airy *Stabile* by Calder, Jean Arp's *Large Seed*, and a wet and wobbling tubular steel fountain by Pol Bury. Around them, Tal-Coat's 'stone-painting' oozes earthily from the enclosing wall. On the other side of the museum, opposite the entrance hall, Giacometti's sculpture courtyard is inhabited by stick-figured animals and elongated people like his loping *Walking Man*, reminiscent of Etruscan bronzes at their quirkiest. He had to paint the bronzes in this courtyard with a wash in order to offset the blazing Mediterranean light and bring them into relief, and then, while in pragmatic mode, went on to design the quirky wrought-iron chairs and tables of the garden café. The Fondation also has a cinema and a studio for making films, plus art workshops, and one of the world's most extensive art libraries.

Vence

I live among rocks, which happy fate
Has sprinkled liberally with roses and with jasmine,
Trees carpet them from foothill to summit,
Rich orange groves blossom in the plains;
The emerald in their leaves reveals its hue,
On the fruit shines gold, and silver on the flower.

                                        Antoine Godeau, on Vence

D. H. Lawrence and Marc Chagall died in Vence, a pleasant enough old town where real people still live among the writers, artists and perfectly tanned Martians with their lifted and stretched faces.

Twin city of Ouahigouya in Burkina Faso, Vence lies 3km from St-Paul and 10km from the coast, sufficiently far to seem more like a town in Provence than a Riviera fleshpot. Roman Vintium, it kept up its regional prestige in the Middle Ages as the seat of a bishopric (the smallest in France) with a series of remarkable bishops. Two are now Vence's patron saints: Véran (449–81), an alumnus of the seminary of St-Honorat near Cannes, and Lambert (1114–54). Lambert had to confront the claims of the new baron of Vence, Romée de Villeneuve, knighted by Raymond Bérenger V of Provence after Romée arranged for Bérenger's daughters the four most strategic marriages of all time – to the kings of England, France (Saint-Louis) and Naples, and the German emperor. Although Romée earned a mention in Dante's *Paradiso* (an apocryphal story telling how he began and ended his career as an impoverished pilgrim), as baron he set a precedent of quarrelling with the bishop of Vence that lasted until the Revolution abolished both titles. Alessandro Farnese was head of Vence's see from 1508 to 1511 – one of the 16 absentee bishoprics he accumulated thanks to his beautiful sister Giulia, the mistress of Pope Alexander IV, who slept with enough cardinals to get her brother elected Paul III. But best loved of Vence's bishops was Antoine Godeau (1639–72), a dwarf famed for his ugliness, a gallant poet and 'the wittiest man in France'. Appointed the first member of the Académie Française by Cardinal Richelieu, Godeau tired of it all by the time he was 30, took holy orders and devoted himself to reforming his see.

Although a fair amount of villa sprawl extends on all sides, the **Vieille Ville** has kept most of its medieval integrity, partly because the citizens were granted permission to build their homes against the ramparts in the 15th century. Enter the walls by way of the west gate, the fortified **Porte du Peyra**. The solid, square watchtower dates from the 12th century and was annexed to the newly constucted château by the haughty Villeneuves in the 17th century, despite the heated objections of the townsfolk. It is now yet another art gallery, the **Château de Villeneuve–Fondation Emile Hugues** (*t 04 93 58 15 78; open July–Sept Tues–Sun 10–6; Oct–June Tues–Sun 10–12.30 and 2–6; closed Mon; adm*), which displays a comprehensive collection covering Hugues' fluttering career: after flirting with Abstraction, Dadaism and Realism, he finally settled on a hallucinatory mix of all three in a wide range of media. Temporary exhibitions showcase a selection of modern and contemporary paintings and sculptures, with regular retrospectives of major 20th-century artists who made the Cote d'Azur their home.

Just inside the walls, the **Place du Peyra** was the Roman forum and is still the site of the daily market. The grand, urn-shaped fountain once (with the help of the Basse Fontaine on Place Vieille at the opposite end of town) provided all the town's drinking water until the late 19th century, when the Riou river was canalized.

Roman tombstones are incorporated in the walls of the **Ancienne Cathédrale**, a rococo church full of little treasures – the pre-Christian sarcophagus of St Véran; the tomb of Bishop Godeau and St Lambert; Merovingian and Romanesque fragments of stones and birds, especially in the chapel under the belfry; a spluttery 1979 mosaic by Chagall with a flappy, beetling angel; reliquaries donated by Alessandro Farnese; and, best of all, the stalls with lace-fine carvings satirizing Renaissance customs and mores, sculpted by Jacques Bellot in the 1450s. The old cathedral had sagged into dusty decline when in 1988, in an astonishing display of collective enthusiasm, all the townsfolk got together to clean, polish and repaint it.

West, outside the walls, **Place du Frêne** is named in honour of a majestic ash tree planted here in 1538 to commemorate visits by François Iᵉʳ and Pope Paul III. Vence's Saturday market spills beyond the confines of the city into the Place du Grand Jardin, and all that's home-grown, -crafted or -made is exhibited with pride. Trawl the stalls and you may well find something way above the ordinary (Olivier de Celle hunts out his woods with the passion of a truffle-hunter, and carves them into fruits so beautiful they're hard not to touch). You'll be hurried by the crowds and the sweet stench of bakeries browning new wares, and pancakes crisping from trollies on the corners.

Matisse's Chapelle du Rosaire

t 04 93 58 03 26. From Vence, follow Av des Poilus to the route for St-Jeannet/ La Gaude. Open Tues and Thurs 10–11.30am and 2–5.30, Mon, Wed and Sat 2–5.30 (in school hols also Fri 2–5.30); closed mid-Nov–mid-Dec; adm; note there are no toilets in the chapel or nearby.

During the war, Matisse refused to leave France, but his home in Nice was dangerously near the city's arsenal and he was eventually persuaded to move to Vence in 1941 to escape the coastal bombing. Some years earlier, a young woman called Monique Bourgeois had answered an advertisement for a 'young and pretty night nurse for the painter Henri Matisse', who was recovering from a serious operation. Later, she became a Dominican nun and was sent, by an odd coincidence, to a convent opposite the villa which Matisse had taken in Vence to wait out the war. The sisters at the convent were using an old run-down garage as a chapel, but they used to daydream about the chapel they might have one day if they could get some money together. Monique, now Sœur Jacques-Marie, showed Matisse a design for a stained-glass window, which the painter promised to finance. An idea for a chapel began to develop, and with the help of a young novice priest, Frère Raysiguier, the simple **Chapelle du Rosaire**, built and designed by Matisse, came about.

Matisse worked on the project from 1946 to 1951, by now well into his 80s and using long poles to hold his brushes when he was forced to keep to his wheelchair. He insisted on designing every aspect of the chapel, from the soaring wrought-iron cross which surmounts the tiled roof, down to the priest's robes and candlesticks (chasuble designs and early models of the chapel can be seen at the Musée Matisse in Nice). He considered the result his masterpiece, an expression of the 'nearly religious feeling I have for life', the fruit 'of a life consecrated to the search for truth'. The truth he sought, however, was not in Christianity but in the essentials of line and light.

Probably the most extraordinary thing about these decorations by the most sensual of Fauves is their lack of colour, except in the geometrically patterned stained-glass windows that occupy three walls and which give the interior an uncanny, kaleidoscopic glow – at its best, Matisse considered, at 11 o'clock on a winter morning when the light is less fierce. On the west wall is *The Tree of Life*, glowing with an intense blue, green and yellow leaf motif which the sun slants through and replicates across the plain stone altar. The altar-cloth, candelabra and crucifix are all also Matisse designs. The other walls are of white faïence from Vallauris (each tile was personally examined by Matisse for evenness and luminosity), on which Matisse drew sweeping black line drawings of *St Dominic holding a Bible*, the *Virgin and Child*, the *Crucifixion* and the *Fourteen Stations of the Cross*. None of the figures has a face – except the face of Christ that appears on St Veronica's veil, which is exactly the same shape as the Tree of Life at the opposite end of the chapel – but they are powerfully drawn and compelling in their simplicity.

Excursions around Vence: the Gorges du Loup

Vence makes an excellent base for exploring the countryside, especially if you have your own car – otherwise the only connections are the once- or twice-daily buses from Nice to St-Jeannet and Gattières.

Ten kilometres beyond the Chapelle du Rosaire, the wine-making village of **St-Jeannet** balances on a terrace beneath the distinctive Baou, a sheer 1,312ft rock that dominates the surrounding countryside. The delicious local white wine is said to make the drinker hear angels. A two-hour path from the Auberge de St-Jeannet leads to the summit, with views stretching to the Alps. A narrow road continues south to the *village perché* of **La Gaude**, unspoiled and surrounded still by the vines and flowers that used to provide its livelihood, despite the giant Y-shaped IBM research centre along the way. Alternatively, continuing northeast on D2210, there are three *villages perchés* that have yet to sell their souls to Mammon: **Gattières**, surrounded by olive groves; **Carros**, on a 985ft rock over the Var crowned by a 13th-century château; and **Le Broc**, 4km up the Var on the D2209, with a Canavesio in its church.

Another excursion from Vence (take the D2 north) takes you through the austerely beautiful **Clues de Haute-Provence** by way of the **Col de Vence**, 3,200ft up and affording an incomparable, breathtaking view of the coast from Cap Ferrat to the Esterel. The D2 continues through dramatic, arid expanses of scrub and tiers of white stone to **Coursegoules**, a tiny village teetering on the brink of a ravine, popular with walkers and the perfect place to dry out after the hedonistic coast: the bar is closed on Friday and Saturday nights. The minuscule church used to hold a retable by Ludovico Brea but, to the outrage of the old lady who has become guardian of the chapel keys, it was recently stolen by some discerning art thieves.

The most popular excursion of all is to loop-the-Loup, so to speak, around the upper valley of the Loup river, starting on the D2210. On the way you can call at the **Château Notre-Dame des Fleurs**, 2.5km from Vence on Route de Grasse (*t* 04 93 24 52 00; *open by appointment only; adm*), a 19th-century castle built over the ruins of an 11th-century Benedictine abbey, which used to be home to the deliciously named Musée du Parfum et de la Liqueur, but is now sadly yet another contemporary art gallery. Still, as recompense, you can browse among works by Warhol, César and Arman, and the terraced gardens offer panoramic views over olive groves and flower plantations.

Tourist Information

Tourrettes-sur-Loup: 2 Place de la Libération, t 04 93 24 18 93, f 04 93 59 24 40, *www.tourrettessurloup. com*. Offers detailed walking guides in English, and lists of violet oil producers. *Open summer daily 9.30–12.30 and 2.30–6.30, winter Tues–Sat only.*

Gourdon: Place de l'Eglise (in the *mairie*), t/f 04 93 09 68 25, *sygourdon@wanadoo.fr, www.gourdon-france.com. Open July–Aug daily 9–7; hours vary at other times.*

Festivals

Tourrettes-sur-Loup: Fête des Violettes, Mar.

Market Days

Tourrettes-sur-Loup: Wed.

Where to Stay and Eat

Tourrettes-sur-Loup ✉ 06140

★★**Hôtel-Restaurant Les Belles Terrasses**, Rte de Vence, t 04 93 59 30 03, f 04 93 59 31 27, *bellesterrasses@free.fr (low moderate)*. Basic but pleasant rooms, with views from the hotel's terraces and a good little restaurant. *Closed mid Nov–mid Dec; restaurant closed Mon–Sat lunch and all day Mon.*

★★**Auberge de Tourrettes**, 11 Route de Grasse, t 04 93 59 30 05, f 04 93 59 28 66, *www.aubergedetourrettes.fr (expensive)*. For comfortable, clean rooms and a view of orange trees and distant sea, head here. The restaurant offers *coq au vin* and *médaillons de lotte aux légumes. Restaurant closed Mon, Tues lunch in winter, and Jan.*

Le Bar-sur-Loup ✉ 06140

L'Amiral, 8 Place Francis Paulet, t 04 93 09 44 00 *(moderate)*. Stop for lunch with local shopkeepers and *gendarmes* in this impressive 18th-century house that belonged to Amiral de Grasse. The dishes on the menu change daily, and are always spot on for freshness and value. Be sure to reserve for dinner in the summer. *Closed Sun eve and Mon, Mon lunch only July–Aug, closed Jan.*

Coursegoules ✉ 06140

★★**Auberge de l'Escaou,** t 04 93 59 11 28, f 04 93 59 13 70, *escaou@wanadoo.fr, www.hotel-escaou.com (low moderate)*. Over 3,000ft up, in the heart of the tiny village. At the restaurant *(moderate)* – outdoors under the shade of plane trees, or inside in a vertigo-inducing glassed-in terrace – try the delicious ravioli stuffed with wild mushrooms. *Closed Dec.*

Gourdon ✉ 06620

There are no hotels in Gourdon, only a few *gîtes*, but a couple of restaurants stand out. **Auberge de Gourdon**, Route de Caussols, t 04 93 09 69 69 *(moderate)*. Offers good, fresh Provençal food at reasonable prices. **Taverne Provençale**, Place de l'Eglise, t 04 93 09 68 22 *(moderate)*. Dine gazing out to the coast and as far away as Corsica on fine days. *Lunch only Sept–June; closed Jan and Mon eves in July–Aug.*

Courmes ✉ 06620

Auberge de Courmes, 3 Rue des Platanes, t 04 93 77 64 70, *www.provenceweb.fr (inexpensive)*. Booking is recommended for this charming inn, with its twisty old vine, relaxing terrace and low-beamed white-washed walls. There are just five simple rooms *(half-board compulsory for more than three nights)* and an excellent restaurant *(moderate)* serving duck with caramelized pears and other dishes from southwest France. *Closed Sun eve, Mon and Jan.*

Some essential oils, especially of violets, originate in **Tourrettes-sur-Loup**, 2.5km further on. Its medieval core of rosy golden stone has often been compared to an Algerian town, the houses knitted together so that their backs form a wall defended by the three small towers that give the village its name. Tourrettes grows more violets than any town in France, and in March all the façades are covered with bouquets for the *Fête des Violettes*, a day that ends in a public 'flower battle'. But in the summer Tourrettes turns into a veritable *souk*, where you can purchase handmade fabrics, jewellery, marionettes, ceramics, household items and more. The 15th-century village church has a triptych by the school of Ludovico Brea, a handsome carved wooden retable and a Gallo-Roman altar dedicated to Mercury, while the Chapelle St-Jean, at the village entrance, has naïve frescoes mixing biblical tales with local life, painted by Ralph Souplaut in 1959.

Before heading into the Gorges du Loup, take a short detour south at Pont-du-Loup to **Le Bar-sur-Loup**, scented by its plantations of oranges, jasmine, roses and violets. The village surrounds the château of the lords of Bar, a branch office of the counts of Grasse (one of whom grew up here to become the Amiral de Grasse who chased the British out of Chesapeake Bay so that Washington could blockade Yorktown and win the American War of Independence). Legend has it that one of his 15th-century ancestors held a wild party here in the middle of Lent, during which the guests all dropped dead. Mortified, the lord commissioned an itinerant artist from Nice to commemorate the event by painting a curious little *Danse Macabre*, now in the tribune of the church of St-Jacques: the elegant nobility dance to a drum, unaware that tiny demons of doom echo the dance on their heads. Death, grinning, mows them down, while busy devils extract their souls in the form of newborn babies and pop them into the mouth of Hell. The church also has a retable by Ludovico Brea and, on the door, beautiful Gothic and Renaissance panels representing St Jacques, carved by Jacques Bellot of Vence.

Not to be missed in **Pont-du-Loup** is the Confiserie Florian (*t 04 93 59 32 91; open daily 9–12 and 2–6*), where jams, jellied fruits, crystallized flowers, chocolates and sweets are made before your eyes, by men in white hats and blue aprons. The factory is quaint and full of antique kitchen furniture, but best is the free tasting at the end of each tour.

North of Pont-du-Loup, the D6 leads into the steep, fantastical cliffs of the **Gorges du Loup**, cooled by waterfalls (one, the Cascade de Courmes next to the road, falls a sheer 150ft) and pocked by giant *marmites*, or glacial potholes. The largest of these is up at **Saut-du-Loup**, and in spring the river broils through it like a witch's cauldron.

At Pont de Bramafan you can cross the gorge and head back south. Looming ahead is **Gourdon** (pop. 324), 'the Saracen', a brooding eagle's nest converted into yet another rural shopping-mall of crafts and goodies. Its massive, rectangular **château** was built in the 13th century over the Saracen citadel and restored in 1610. Inside are a pair of museums (*t 04 93 09 68 02, www.chateau-gourdon.com; open June–Sept 11–1 and 2–7; Oct–May 2–6 and closed Tues; adm*): the **Musée Historique**, with antique arms and armour, the odd torture instrument in the dungeon, a Rembrandt *Self-Portrait* and Marie-Antoinette's writing desk, and, upstairs, a **Musée des Arts Décoratifs et de la Modernité**. The panoramic three-tiered castle gardens were laid out by André Le Nôtre.

You can take a spectacular two-hour walk on the **Sentier du Paradis** from Gourdon to Pont-du-Loup, or sneak a preview of lunar travel by driving up the D12 (or walking along the GR4 from Grasse) on to the desolate **Plateau de Caussols**, boasting the driest, clearest air in France – hence an important observatory. Now, clouds of multi-coloured hang-gliders float over it (*www.beyond.fr/sports/hangglider.html*). French film directors often use it for Western or desert scenes, the very kind used these days for selling French cars and blue jeans.

Back Towards the Coast: Biot

Between Cagnes and Cannes, the *résidences secondaires* battle for space with huge commercial greenhouses and fields of flowers destined for the scent distilleries of Grasse, a paroxysm of fragrance and colour powerful enough to make a sensitive soul swoon. Set inland a couple of miles from the sea, Biot (rhymes with yacht) is a handsome village endowed with first-rate clay – in Roman times it specialized in wine and oil jars large enough to contain Ali Baba's 40 thieves. In 1955, Fernand Léger purchased some land here in order to construct a sculpture garden of monumental ceramics – then died 15 days later. In 1960 his widow used the land to build a superb museum and garden to display the works he left her in his will. Come late in the day if you want to see more of Biot and less of the human race.

Musée National Fernand Léger

Chemin du Val-de-Pome, t 04 92 91 50 20; open July–Sept 10.30–6; Oct–June 10–12.30 and 2–5.30; closed Tues; tours by appt for groups; adm, free 1st Sun of the month.

To the right of the entrance to Biot, the museum is hard to miss behind its giant, sporty ceramic-mosaic designed for the Olympic stadium of Hanover. Opened in 1960, the museum was the first to be built exclusively for the work of a single artist. It was enlarged in 1989 to provide more space for the 348 paintings, tapestries, mosaics and

Getting There

Biot's **train station** is down by the sea at La Brague, and you will have a steep 5km walk from here up to the village. **Buses** approximately every hour from Antibes stop at the train station en route to Biot village.

Tourist Information

Biot: 46 Rue Saint-Sébastien, t 04 93 65 78 00, f 04 93 65 78 04, *tourisme.biot@ wanadoo.fr*, *www.biot-coteazur.com*. Has lists of *chambres d'hôte* and artists' studios. *Open summer Mon–Fri 10–7, Sat, Sun and hols 2.30–7; winter Mon–Fri 9–12 and 2–6, Sat, Sun and hols 2–6.*

Market Days

Biot: Tues and Fri am, fruit and veg.

Where to Stay and Eat

Biot ✉ 06410
★Hôtel des Arcades, 16 Place des Arcades, t 04 93 65 01 04, f 04 93 65 01 05 (*moderate–inexpensive*). A delightful old hotel in a 15th-century building furnished with antiques. The popular artsy restaurant (*moderate*) below does a *soupe au pistou* and other Provençal favourites. *Closed Sun eve, and Mon.*
★★Auberge du Jarrier, Passage de la Bourgade, t 04 93 65 11 68 (*expensive*). For a special feast, reserve a table at least a week in advance in this old jar-works. A magical terrace, friendly service and a superb four-course seasonal Provençal menu. *Closed Mon and Tues out of season; closed Mon, Tues, Wed and Thurs lunch in season.*

ceramics that trace Léger's career from his first flirtations with Cubism in 1909 – although even back then Léger was nicknamed 'the tubist' for his preference for fat noodly forms. After being gassed in the First World War, he recovered to flirt with the Purist movement founded by his buddies Le Corbusier and Amédée Ozenfant around 1918, a reaction to the 'decorative' tendencies of Cubism. Purism was to be the cool, dispassionate art of the machine age, emotionally limited to a 'mathematical lyricism', and Léger's scenes of soldiers and machines fitted the bill. After teaching at Yale during the Second World War, he returned to France with a keen interest in creating art for the working classes, using his trademark style of brightly coloured geometric forms to depict factories, workers and their pastimes.

The new wing of the museum contains Léger's ceramics, mosaics and other works – most notably the tapestries called *La Création* (1922) and *Liberté*, the latter illustrating the eponymous poem by his friend Paul Eluard. The surrounding garden holds the **Bonsai Arboretum** (*t 04 93 65 63 99; open Oct–April Wed–Mon 10–12 and 2–5.30; May–Sept 10–12 and 3–6.30; closed Tues; adm*), with a collection of bonsai from all over the world.

With his bright colours and often playful forms, Léger is one artist children usually like. Afterwards you can take them to **La Brague**, by the sea, to watch the performing dolphins and other sea creatures at **Marineland**, play on the slides at **Aquasplash** and see butterflies at **La Jungle des Papillons** (*for details of these attractions and others on the Route de Biot, see p.174*).

Crafts and Arts

The presence of the museum has boosted the local ceramics and glass industries; across from the museum at **Ecomusée du Verre** (*Chemin des Combes, t 04 93 65 03 00*) you can watch workers make glass suffused with tiny bubbles (*verre à bulles*). Small workshops dotted around the big main *verrerie*, below the town walls, all sell bubbly glassware more cheaply than the museum shop. More ceramics and glass can be seen in the charming, tiny **Musée d'Histoire et de Céramique Biotoises** up in the walled town (*Rue Saint-Sébastien, t 04 93 65 54 54; open summer Wed–Sun 10–6; winter Wed–Sun 2–6; closed Tues; adm*); most of the pieces, and 400 photographs, were donated by the villagers. The town itself, and the roads leading down to the station, are crammed with art and pottery galleries, and workshops of individual artists, of widely varying quality. Even the town plan, on the wall near the bus stop, is made of glazed tiles.

Guarded by 16th-century gates, Biot itself has retained much of its character, especially around the central **Place des Arcades**. A hundred years ago, the accents in this charming square would have been Genoese – Biot's original population was almost wiped out by the Black Death and the village was only resettled in 1460, when the Bishop of Grasse invited in 50 families from Genoa.

The remains of a 13th-century Templars' chapel were demolished to create the present church, tucked among the arcades. It has two excellent 15th-century altarpieces: the red and gold *Retable du Rosaire* by Ludovico Brea, and the recently well restored *Christ aux plaies* by Giovanni Canavesio, who was married to a Biotoise.

The 17th-century gate depicts Mary Magdalene, Biot's feisty patron saint. The triangular, brightly tiled tower in the Place des Pénitents-Noirs once belonged to the chapel and now languishes picturesquely.

Antibes

*Now all the gay decorative people have left, taking with them the sense
of carnival and impending disaster that colored this summer...*

Zelda Fitzgerald, 1925

Set on the largest of the Côte's peninsulas, Antibes started out as the Greek trading colony of Antipolis, the 'city opposite' Nice. But these days it's also the antithesis of the Nice of retired folks soaking up the rays: Antibes belongs to the young, both locals, who scoot, bike and skate like their counterparts in California to *collège* and *lycée*, and visitors, who frequent the mega-white boats that measure over a hundred yards long, moored shoulder to shoulder, vying to see which has the most high-tech communications system. Here the *de rigueur* Riviera poodle has been supplanted by the seadogs' terriers, labradors and spaniels.

Antibes has been a quieter place since the Fitzgeralds and their self-destructive high jinks set a precedent no alcoholic writer or artist has been able to match. The frolicking now takes place over at Juan-les-Pins, which took off as a resort shortly after F. Scott and Zelda's holiday, leaving Antibes to tend its rose nurseries. After the Second World War, when developers cast an eye over Antibes, there were enough building restrictions to keep out most of the concrete. Even so, inlanders regard the town with jaundiced eyes: instead of 'go to hell' they say *'Vai-t'en-à-n-Antibo!'* Yet Antibes still retains an authentic vivacity all its own, drawing in crowds of bright young things who disdain the hollower charms of Juan-les-Pins.

A relic of Antibes' earlier incarnation as France's bulwark against Savoyard Nice are its sea walls, especially the massive 16th-century **Fort Carré** (*Route du Bord-de-Mer, t 06 14 89 17 45; guided tours only; Oct–May 10–4.30; June–Sept 10–6; closed Mon; adm*). Four bastions, called Corsica, France, Antibes and Nice after the places the fort was intended to protect, were added in 1565. The fort provides a decorative backdrop for Antibes' marina, big enough to moor even the 300ft behemoths of the absurdly rich.

Nicolas de Staël lived at the corner of the old port and the Rue des Saleurs ('drycurers', who made the local dried-fish preserves) before being driven to distraction by the spiky brilliance of the light and throwing himself to his death. The handsome 17th- and 18th-century houses of Vieil Antibes look over their neighbours' shoulders towards the sea, obscuring it from **Cours Masséna**, the main street of Greek Antipolis. Here, the **market** sells a cornucopia of produce, from *fromage de chèvre* to a profusion of cut flowers that leave the paintings in Antibes' galleries pale by comparison.

From Cours Masséna, Rue Sade leads back to café-filled Place Nationale and the **Musée Peynet** (*t 04 92 90 54 30; open summer 10–6; winter 10–12 and 2–6; closed Mon and hols*), housed in a 19th-century school and offering a queasy journey back to the 1960s paved with the love postcards drawn by Raymond Peynet, the father of the

Getting Around

By Train

Antibes' train station, on Place P. Semard, is out at the edge of town, about a 10-minute walk from the centre along Av Robert Soleau towards Nice, t 08 92 35 35 35. The station in Juan-les-Pins is very centrally located on Av de l'Esterel. There are frequent Métrazur and TGV trains from Antibes, Juan-les-Pins and Golfe-Juan to Nice and Cannes.

By Bus

Buses (t 04 93 34 37 60 and t 04 93 64 88 84) for Cannes, Nice, Nice airport, Cagnes-sur-Mer and Juan-les-Pins depart from Place de Gaulle in Antibes; others leave from Rue de la République. From Golfe-Juan buses leave every 20mins for Antibes. Three- and eight-day passes are available, which include round trips to Nice airport. You can get to Vallauris by bus from anywhere along the coast.

By Taxi

Antibes: t 04 93 67 67 67.
Juan-les-Pins: t 04 92 93 07 07.

Bicycle hire

Azur Bike, 33 Bd Charles Guillaumont, t 04 93 61 51 30.

Tourist Information

Antibes: 11 Place Charles de Gaulle, t 04 92 90 53 00, f 04 92 90 53 01, *accueil@antibes-juanlespins.com, www.antibes-juanlespins.com* and *www.antibes.co.uk. Open daily 9–7 in summer; winter Mon–Fri 9–12.30 and 1.30–6, Sat 9–12 and 2–6.*
Juan-les-Pins: 51 Bd Guillaumont, t 04 92 90 53 05, f 04 93 61 55 13, *accueil@antibes-juanlespins.com, www.antibes-juanlespins.com. Open daily 9–7 in summer; winter Mon–Sat 9–12 and 2–6.*
Golfe-Juan: Parking du Vieux-Port, t 04 93 63 73 12, f 04 93 63 21 07, *www.vallauris-golfe-juan.com. Open daily 9–7 in summer; winter Mon–Sat 9–12 and 2–6.*
Vallauris: Square du 8-Mai-1945, t 04 93 63 82 58, f 04 93 63 95 01, *tourisme.vgj@wanadoo.fr, www.vallauris-golfe-juan.com. Open daily 9–7 in summer; winter Mon–Sat 9–12 and 2–6.*
Internet: Accès Internet, 55 Av de Cannes, Juan-les-Pins, t 04 93 67 60 60. *Open 11am–8pm. Closed Sun.*

Market Days

Antibes: June–August daily, otherwise Tues–Sun 6am–1pm sharp, Cours Masséna, fruit and veg, flowers, rolls of fabric and wicker-work aplenty.Sat 7–6, Place Nationale, flea market. Thurs and Sat 7–6, Place Audiberti, bric-a-brac. Tues and Sat, Place Barnaud, clothes market. Thurs am, Parking de la Poste, clothes market.
Vallauris: Tues–Sun, vegetables, Place de l'Homme au Mouton.
Golfe-Juan: Fri am, vegetables, Parking Aimé Berger. Summer weekend eves, Marché Estival Nocturne.

Festivals

Jazz tops the bill in Antibes/Juan-les-Pins (the two towns melt into each other without any real boundary); there's the famous **jazz festival** in July, and the gaudy New Orleans-style **Mardi Gras parade** in February/March. Contact the Juan-les-Pins tourist office for details and ticket information.

Europe's largest harbour, the Port Vauban in Antibes, fills up with yachts in June for the celebrated **Voiles d'Antibes**, and there is more sporting fervour in October during the **Antibes Rally**.

Where to Stay

Antibes ✉ 06600

★★★Thalazur, 770 Chemin des Moyennes Bréguières, t 04 92 91 82 00, f 04 93 65 94 14, *www.thalassofrance.com (expensive).*

genre, who lived in Antibes from 1978. There are sculptures, dolls and models of some of his stage sets for true disciples of kitsch.

Back towards the sea, Tour Gilli houses the **Musée de la Tour** (*t 04 93 34 13 58; open Wed and Thurs 2.30–4.30; adm*), devoted to the costumes, furniture, household items

Combine hedonistic pleasures with thalassotherapy and beauty treatments; four heated pools, saunas and a doctor on duty (*half-board compulsory May–Sept*). *Open all year.*

★★★**Mas Djoliba**, 29 Av de Provence, t 04 93 34 02 48, f 04 93 34 05 81, hotel.djoliba@wanadoo.fr, www.hotel-djoliba.com (*expensive–moderate*). A serene *mas* in a small garden with a terrace and pool (*half-board compulsory in season*). *Closed Nov–Jan.*

Cap d'Antibes ✉ 06160

★★★★**Hôtel du Cap Eden Roc**, Bd Kennedy, t 04 93 61 39 01, f 04 93 67 76 04, www.edenroc-hotel.fr (*luxury*). Knowns as 'l'Hôtel du Cash', as credit cards are not accepted. This brilliantly white hotel is set in an idyllic park overlooking the dreamy Iles de Lérins, where the rest of the world seems very far away. No hotel on the Riviera has hosted more celebrities, film stars or plutocrats (*see* p.176). You could easily shed €150 at the exalted restaurant, the **Pavillon Eden Roc**. *Closed mid-Oct–mid-April.*

★★★★**Hôtel Imperial Garoupe**, 770 Chemin de la Garoupe, t 04 92 93 31 61, f 04 92 93 31 62, www.imperial-garoupe.com (*luxury*). A peachy villa with impeccable rooms and opulent marble bathrooms set in tranquil gardens above the sea. The staff are friendly and helpful and there is a swimming pool and a private beach. Breakfast can be enjoyed at your private terrace or overlooking the pool. There's also a restaurant (*expensive*). *Closed Nov–Mar; restaurant closed Wed Sept–June.*

★★★★**Hôtel La Baie Dorée**, 579 Bd de la Garoupe, t 04 93 67 30 67, f 04 92 93 76 39, baiedoree@club-internet.fr, www.baiedoree.com (*luxury–expensive*). Spread out across the waterfront with lovely gardens and a restaurant (*expensive*). *Restaurant closed Nov–Mar.*

★★★★**Villa Val des Roses**, 6 Chemin des Lauriers, t 06 85 06 06 29, f 04 92 93 97 24, www.val-des-roses.com (*expensive*). Pretty,

calm *chambre d'hôte* set right by a beach, 10mins' walk from Antibes, decorated in cool creams and white linen, with pool, and snacks available with drinks all day.

★★★**Hôtel Garoupe-Gardiole**, 81 Bd Francis Meilland, t 04 92 93 33 33 or t 04 93 61 35 03, f 04 93 67 61 87, www.hotel-lagaroupe-gardiole.com (*expensive*). A venerable white villa, shaded with tall cypresses and set back from the sea in a little pine wood. *Closed Nov–Mar.*

★**Nouvel Hôtel**, 1 Av du 24-Août, t 04 93 34 44 07, f 04 93 34 44 08 (*inexpensive*). Near the bus station, and with 20 soundproofed rooms which fill up rapidly in summer.

Juan-les-Pins ✉ 06160

Juan isn't exactly made for sleeping, but it makes sense to stay here if you want to join in the late-night revelry. Everything closes from November to Easter.

★★★★**Juana**, Av Georges Gallice, La Pinède, t 04 93 61 08 70, f 04 93 61 76 60, info@hotel-juana.com, www.hotel-juana.com (*luxury*). In a lovely garden facing the pines, a beautiful Art Deco hotel with a luscious white and gold façade, a private beach and heated pool and a restaurant (*very expensive*). *Closed Jan–Mar.*

★★★★**Belles Rives**, Bd Baudouin, t 04 93 61 02 79, f 04 93 67 43 51, www.bellesrives.com (*luxury*). Another palace offering de luxe rooms, vintage 1930, facing the sea. There's a private beach and jetty, and a good restaurant (**La Passagère**) with a fine view over the gulf, or you can eat on the beach. *Closed mid-Nov–Feb.*

★★★★**Hôtel Ambassadeur**, 50–52 Chemin des Sables, t 04 92 93 74 10, f 04 93 67 79 85, www.hotel-ambassadeur.com (*luxury–very expensive*). A sleekly modern thalassotherapy centre with the usual pools and doctors, as well as a private beach, piano bar and vine-covered terraced restaurant (t 04 92 93 74 52; *moderate*).

★★★**Hôtel Welcome**, 7 Av Docteur Hochet, t 04 93 61 26 12, t 04 93 61 38 04, www.

and tools of Antibes' fisher-folk of yore. But the best sea views are monopolized by the **Château Grimaldi** – a seaside castle built by the family who ran most of this coast at one time or another, and who had possession of Antibes from 1385 to 1608. It became a history museum in the 1920s, and for six months in 1946 the owner,

hotelwelcome.net (*expensive–moderate*). Lives up to its name with sunny terraces and a pleasant, well-manicured garden. *Closed Nov–Feb.*

★★Le Pré Catelan, 27 Av des Palmiers, **t** 04 93 61 05 11, **f** 04 93 67 83 11, *www.precatelan.com* (*expensive– moderate*). Quiet and set back from the hurly burly among palms, with comfortable décor of the candlewick bedspread variety, a shady terrace for breakfast and a little sitting room stuffed full of magazines and books.

★★★Hôtel des Mimosas, Rue Pauline, **t** 04 93 61 04 16, **f** 04 92 92 93 06 46, *www.hoteldes mimosas.fr.st* (*moderate*). Five hundred metres from the sea, the Mimosa's rooms have balconies overlooking the pool and garden. *Closed Oct–April.*

Eating Out

Antibes

De Bacon, Bd de Bacon, Cap d'Antibes, **t** 04 93 61 50 02 (*very expensive–expensive*). As stylish and elegant as its perfectly prepared seafood and *bouillabaisse*, at classy prices. *Closed Mon and Tues lunch, and Nov–Jan.*

La Bonne Auberge, on the N7 near La Brague, **t** 04 93 33 36 65 (*expensive–moderate*). Chef Jo Rostang's son Philippe has inherited the kitchen, and has already made a name for himself with some of the Côte's finest *nouvelle cuisine*, including his *salade de homard aux ravioles de Romans* and *mille-feuille Bonne Auberge à l'ancienne*; the lunch menu is good value. Reserve far in advance to be sure of a table.

Les Vieux Murs, Promenade Amiral de Grasse, **t** 04 93 34 06 73 (*expensive–moderate*). Cool and spacious, with wooden décor, and serving well-presented traditional food made modern.

Le Sucrier, 6 Rue des Bains, **t** 04 93 34 85 40 (*expensive–moderate*). The chef is proud to be the great-great-nephew of Guy de Maupassant, and spirits up traditional

French classics with an exotic twist in a cavernous stone setting. There is even a vegetarian menu. *Closed Tues and Jan.*

Au Pied dans le Plat, 6 Rue Thuret, **t** 04 93 34 37 23 (*moderate*). The brave can try the house speciality, *tête de veau*, otherwise there's the sublimely simple fish soup or a delicious *blanquette de noix de St-Jacques. Closing days vary; book.*

L'Oursin, 16 Rue de la République, **t** 04 93 34 13 46 (*moderate*). L'Oursin is famous for fresh fish and does particularly fine things with shellfish. *Closed Sun eve, Mon and Tues pm.*

Café Sans Rival, 5 Traverse du 24-Août, **t** 04 93 34 12 67 (*cheap*). A tiny wooden-floored shop and café fitted to the ceiling with coffee beans, teas, herb teas, rice cakes, rye breads, fat sultanas and all things wholesome and *complet.* You can perch outside, drink *real* cappuccino and eat lunch or cake. *Closed Sat and Sun.*

Juan-les-Pins

La Terrasse Morisset, **t** 04 93 61 20 37 (*very expensive*). The resort's top restaurant, in the Hôtel Juana (*see* p.143) boasts delicate dishes imbued with all the freshness and colour of Provence, and excellent wines to match from the region's best vineyards. *Closed Jan–Mar.*

Bijou Plage, Bd du Littoral, **t** 04 93 61 39 07 (*expensive*). An excellent array of sea and land dishes fill the menu, and during the Cannes festival it's a good place to find the stars tucking into a *bouillabaisse. Closed Tues eve and Wed.*

Le Grill, Av E. Baudoin, **t** 04 92 93 71 71 (*moderate*). Part of the Eden Casino. Try the excellent lunch menu, which includes daily chef's specials, coffee and wine. The delightful terrace looks out over the sea and in the evenings they hold *thés dansants.*

Le Capitole, 26 Av Amiral Courbet, **t** 04 93 61 22 44 (*moderate–cheap*). A charming welcome and generous seafood menus. *Closed Tues lunch in summer, Mon eve and Tues out of season and Nov.*

Romuald Dor, let Picasso use the second floor as a studio (although the locals say that he had discovered it years previously when it was still in ruins by following some children through a hole in the wall). Picasso, glad to have space to work in, even if it was cold and damp, quickly filled it up in a few months, only later discovering to his

Sport and Leisure

Marineland, t 04 93 33 49 49. Europe's largest marine park, with 600,000 visitors each year to see the killer whales, sea lions, sea elephants, dolphins, seals and penguins. Luc Besson filmed part of *Le Grand Bleu* here. *Open daily from 10am, performances from 10.30am; July–Aug open till midnight with nocturnal performances at 9.30pm; adm exp.* Other attractions on this site include:

La Petite Ferme: Get closer to the animals. *Open daily 10–6.*

Aquasplash: Complete with a pool with waves. *Open summer daily 10–6.*

Mini-Golf and **Adventure-Golf:** *Open mid-June–Sept daily 10–6; Oct–mid-June, Wed, Sat, Sun and hols 10–6.*

La Jungle des Papillons, t 04 93 33 55 77. A live butterfly zoo. *Open 10–6, July–Aug 10–8. Closed Jan; adm.*

Antibe Land/Luna Park, t 04 93 33 49 49. An amusement/theme park. *Open daily 10–6.*

Parc Exflora, on the N7, Rte de Cannes, Antibes. If you've lost all your money at the gaming or dining tables, this park is free.

Iles de Lérins (*see* pp.193–4). Four to five boats a day between 9am and 4pm, from Ponton Courbet, Juan-les-Pins (t 04 93 61 78 84), and Quai Saint-Pierre, Port de Golfe-Juan (t 04 93 63 45 94). The fare is €10. *Runs April–Sept.*

Visiobulle, Embarcadère Courbet, Juan-les-Pins, t 04 93 67 02 11, *www.visiobulle.com*. An hour-long boat trip to Cap d'Antibes, with underwater diving.

Entertainment and Nightlife

Antibes

The best fun to be had is in Antibes' **Vieille Ville**, full of *confiseries* and *pâtisseries*; a *mêlée* of locals, lubbers, sailors and who knows who – a mix reflected in the gamut of polyglot newspapers, which includes even the British grubbies.

Cinéma Casino, 6–8 Av du 24-Août, t 04 93 34 04 37.

Red Pier Theatre, 15 Rue Clemenceau, t 04 93 34 24 30. Theatre with some performances in English.

La Scène sur Mer, Place Nationale, t 04 93 61 27 54. Restaurant, with comedy and theatre performances on the first floor.

Geoffrey's of London, Bd Aguillon. If you're homesick, baked beans, Marmite, tea and crumpets are available here.

Antibes Books, Heidi's English Bookshop, 24 Rue Aubernon, t 04 93 34 74 11. Heidi's one-word answer to why-did-you-come-to-the-South-of-France is 'hedonism', yet she busily runs the local community centre and a tiny **theatre** below the bookshop (*open daily*). Get the best local maps here.

The nightlife in Antibes tends to keep you moving:

La Siesta, Rte du Bord-de-Mer, on the road to Nice, t 04 93 33 31 31. Operating as a beach concession by day, with activities for kids, at night this turns into an over-the-top nightclub and casino where thousands of people flock every summer evening to enjoy five dance floors, fountains and fiery torches.

Juan-les-Pins

Whisky à Gogo, La Pinède, Av Leonetti, t 04 93 61 26 40. *Closed Nov.*

Le Village Voom Voom, 1 Bd de la Pinède, t 04 92 93 90 00. Haunt of older shakers and movers.

Eden Casino, Bd Baudoin, t 04 92 93 71 71.

Le Duc, 142 Bd Wilson, t 04 93 67 78 87.

Xtrême Café, 129 Rue Aubernon, t 04 93 34 03 90. Young, trendy place with cocktails and an Internet café.

Café Cosy, 3 Rue Migrainier, t 04 93 34 81 55. A charming place to sip wine away from the hubbub.

annoyance that Dor had intended all along to make his efforts into the **Musée Picasso** (t 04 92 90 54 20; *open summer Tues, Thurs, Sat and Sun 10–6, Wed and Fri 10–8; winter 10–12 and 2–6; closed Mon and hols; adm*). Because of the post-war lack of canvases and oil paint, Picasso had to find new materials; he began by painting directly on to the château walls and then purloined some 19th-century portraits which had been stashed in an old cupboard and forgotten, and painted over the top of them. Then he discovered the large fibro-cement boards being used for the construction of the prefabricated houses which were being hurriedly thrown up after the war, and painted over these with boat paint using broad house-painters' brushes. You can't help but get the feeling that he was exuberantly happy, inspired by the end of the war, his love of the time (Françoise Gilot) and the mythological roots of the Mediterranean, expressed in *La Joie de vivre*, *Ulysse et ses sirènes* and 220 other paintings, drawings and ceramics. In the same year that Picasso began using the château as a studio, he also visited the local ceramic-producing village of Vallauris (*see* pp.149–50) and, with his usual enthusiastic abandon, began throwing himself into the creation of whimsical clay sculptures, many of which are also exhibited here, including some of the *Tanagra*, an ebullient series of ceramic bottles metamorphosed into curvaceous women.

The museum is a deeply civilized space, with room for the imagination, without much effort, to dispense with the crowds and see how Antibes might have been not that long ago. Outside, the garden is crammed with sculptures by prominent local artists, from skinny bronze and stone statues by Germaine Richier, balanced high in silhouette along the fortified wall, to Arman's *A Ma Jolie*, an alarming eruption of bronze guitars. Miró submerged his enormous *Sea Goddess* in a nearby sea cave, where she languished for 15 years before moving into infinitely more comfortable surroundings here. Among the other artists represented, note the eight striking works on the top floor that Nicolas de Staël painted in Antibes shortly before he committed suicide (or merely fell out of the upstairs window) in 1955. Below, you may see a speedboat cross the sea like a slow rip in a blue canvas.

Just across the street is the church of the **Immaculate Conception**, where a leaflet in your chosen language entreats you to 'Listen...listen to the silent echo of prayers down the ages...', but you'll have to listen hard for silence over the Almighty Muzak. Built over a Greek temple, it's a hotchpotch of art and idols, gawpers, hawkers and rows of burning candles dedicated to St Sebastian, St Roch and Ste Réparate.

Further south, at the end of Promenade Amiral de Grasse, the Vauban-built Bastion St-André houses the **Musée d'Archéologie** (*t 04 92 90 54 35; open June–Sept Tues–Sun 10–6, Wed and Fri 10–8; Oct–May Tues–Sun 10–12 and 2–6; tour Fri 3pm; closed Mon; adm*), where Greek and Etruscan amphorae, monies and jewels dredged up from the sea and soil trace the history of Antibes. More Greek connections are around the corner – at No.8 Rue Bas-Castellet, Nikos Kazantzakis penned *Zorba the Greek*.

Cap d'Antibes and Around

Further south along the peninsula (follow the scenic coastal D2559) the delightful, free, sandy (and therefore packed) beach of **La Salis** marks the start of Cap d'Antibes, scented with roses, jasmine and the smell of money – there's more concentrated here than almost anywhere else in France. Jules Verne was among the first to retreat here, where he found the inspiration for *Twenty Thousand Leagues under the Sea*; nowadays, to maintain the kind of solitude and high-tech luxury enjoyed by Captain Nemo aboard the *Nautilus*, the owners of the Cap's villas need James Bond security systems and slavering Dobermanns. At No.62 Boulevard du Cap is the lovely **Parc Gustave Thuret**, with a villa which can't be visited, but a free garden (*t 04 93 67 88 00; open daily 8–5.30*), laid out in 1866 as an acclimatization station, where the first eucalyptus was transplanted to Europe (the park now contains over 100 varieties). The botanist Gustave Thuret brought roses, along with his other exotic blooms, to Antibes at the end of the 19th century; the locals scoffed at this '*fada de Parisien*' but, a century later, the garden boasts the creation of a third of the world's rose varieties.

The **Plateau de la Garoupe** is the highest point of the headland, with a lighthouse, a grand view stretching from Bordighera to St-Tropez and the ancient seamen's **Chapelle de la Garoupe**. Its two naves, one 13th-century and one 16th-century, hold a fascinating collection of *ex votos*, the oldest one commemorating a surprise attack on Antibes by Saracen pirates. In the twin chapels are two humble wooden statues: a black virgin, Notre Dame de la Garde, and Our Lady of the Safe Haven.

Back on the coast, the private **Plages de la Garoupe** offer a pricey taste of *la dolce vita*. From behind the beach, the **Sentier Tirepoil** winds spectacularly up to the point at wave-lashed Cap Gros. At the tip of the peninsula is **Villa Eilenroc** (*Av de Beaumont, t 04 93 67 74 33; gardens open Tues and Wed 9–5; part of villa open Wed 9–12 and 1.30–5; closed July–Aug and Christmas–New Year*), which was designed by Charles Garnier (architect of the Paris opera house and the casino at Monte-Carlo) for a Dutch millionaire who spelled his wife's name (Cornélie) in reverse and used it to christen his lavish new seaside home. Jules Verne spent three years here, getting twenty thousand leagues away from it all, and its last owner, a rich and philanthropic American, donated the property to the municipality of Antibes.

Further west, a 12th-century tower holds the **Musée Napoléonien** (*Av Kennedy, t 04 93 61 45 32; open Nov–Sept Mon–Fri 9.30–12 and 2.15–6, Sat 9.30–12; closed Sun and Oct*), with model ships and items relating to Napoleon's connections with Antibes – he left Madame Mère and his sisters here during the siege of Toulon (they were so poor that the girls had to steal figs) and began 'The Hundred Days' at Golfe-Juan.

The Cape is practically synonymous with the **Hôtel du Cap Eden Roc**, originally built in 1870 as the Villa Soleil, a home for impoverished artists founded by newspaper magnate Hippolyte de Vilemessant and the author Adolphe d'Ennery, and one of the very first hotels on the coast to feature an outdoor swimming pool – which, for a princely sum, is still open to the right type of non-resident. After a flurry of popularity with the Russians and the English at the end of the 19th century, when it was the Grand Hôtel du Cap, it sank into a genteel retirement before being resuscitated by the indefatigable New York newspaper magnate James Gordon Bennett (*see* pp.46 and 122). It played a major role in the creation of the Riviera's summer season, when popular American socialites Gerald and Sara Murphy began to come down here from Paris in 1923, discovering the hitherto unheralded joys of sunbathing on the beach when Antoine Sella, the owner of the Grand Hôtel, kept it open in July and August in an attempt to recoup losses from a bad winter season. They had the place to themselves, along with Picasso's family and a Chinese couple. That same summer, top trendsetter Coco Chanel astonished everyone with her suntan, and a fad was born. In 1925, Sella revamped Eden Roc, which, with its eight unimaginably luxurious *cabanons* (chalets) on the beach, is still rated as the most beautiful place for a swim and a tan on the whole Riviera. The Murphys, famous for holding the very best parties, bought a house on the beach, where they created and lived the carefree but elegant sunny seaside existence that became the essential myth of the Riviera, sharing it with everyone who happened by, including Zelda and Scott Fitzgerald, the latter of whom based his characters Dick and Nicole Diver in *Tender is the Night* on the Murphys.

Juan-les-Pins

When a good idea is in the air, it's not uncommon for different people to pick up on it. In 1924, Edouard Baudoin, a Nice restaurateur, saw a film about Miami Beach and was inspired to recreate it on the Côte. He found his location at Juan-les-Pins among the silver sands and pines of the best natural beach on the Riviera, bought some land, and opened a restaurant and a little casino. As it had suddenly become desirable to bake brown on the beach, Baudoin's investment flourished, attracting the attention of the ever-acquisitive Frank Jay Gould, who bought Baudoin out, built roads and injected the essential money and publicity to help Juan-les-Pins really take off. By 1930 it was the most popular and scandal-ridden resort on the Riviera, where women first dared to bathe in skirtless suits. The presence of Edith Piaf and Sidney Bechet boosted its popularity in the 1950s. It's still going strong, not a beauty but a brash and sassy tart of a resort, with nightclubs, strings of minuscule private beaches and a magnificent jazz festival in the last two weeks of July. All the young come here from Antibes and further (the rich and posh go to Nice).

Golfe-Juan and the Route Napoléon

Next up the coast is **Golfe-Juan**, with its pines, sandy beach and marina; although one might think that there was nothing left that hasn't succumbed to redevelopment fervour, this resort is now undergoing extensive redevelopment of the redevelopment. It is famous as the very spot where Napoleon disembarked from Elba on 1 March 1815, proclaiming that 'the eagle with his national colours will fly from bell tower to bell tower all the way to the towers of Notre-Dame'. Determined to wash away the bitter taste of his abdication a year previously in Fontainebleau, Napoleon intended to overthrow the monarchy of Louis XVIII as rapidly and ruthlessly as possible. An obelisk and a column commemorate the landing, which, in fact, was slightly less than momentous: the locals quickly arrested a few of his men, a cold reception that, along with the substantial garrison at Marseille, decided the eagle to sneak along the back roads to Paris. In one of many Napoleonic coincidences, as Bonaparte landed he met the Prince of Monaco, who informed him that he was on his way to reclaim his tiny realm after being removed during the Revolution. 'Then, Monsieur, we are in the same business,' Napoleon told him, and each continued on his way, the Prince to his orange groves, Napoleon to Waterloo.

The path he took was repackaged by the French in the early 1930s to become the scenic, touristy **Route Napoléon**, which is marked with the eagle symbol and enough plaques and monuments to satisfy even Napoleon's stupendous ego. The route twists up from Golfe-Juan through Digne and Sisteron and culminates in Grenoble, where the eagle was finally welcomed on 7 March 1815 with cries of 'Vive l'Empereur'.

Vallauris

Two kilometres inland from Golfe-Juan, **Vallauris** has two things in common with Biot: it was given an injection of Genoese in the late 15th century, and it was famous for its pottery, in this case useful household wares. The original village was built in 1138 on land belonging to the Lérins Abbey (see p.193), but the wars, plagues and famines of the 14th century virtually wiped out the unfortunate populace. The monks had always encouraged pottery production, and the influx of Genoese at the end of the 15th century brought new enthusiasm and skill to the art. By the end of the 19th century, almost three-quarters of the town were potters, but half a century later, because of competition with aluminium, the industry was on its last legs.

Then in 1946 Picasso, who was working in his lofty damp studio at the Château Grimaldi (see pp.172–5), rented a small villa in town and met Georges and Suzanne Ramié, owners of the Poterie Madoura. Playing with the clay in their shop, Picasso discovered a new passion, and he spent the next few years working with the medium – although Suzanne, watching his unorthodox methods, remarked that 'an apprentice who worked as Picasso does would never find a job'. He gave the Ramiés the exclusive right to sell copies of his ceramics, and you can still buy them at **Madoura** (t 04 93 64 66 39), just off Rue du 19-Mars-1962. Thanks to Picasso, 200 potters now work in Vallauris, their *ateliers* lining Avenue Georges Clemenceau.

In 1951 the village asked Picasso if he would decorate a deconsecrated chapel next to the castle. The result is the famous plywood paintings of *La Guerre et la Paix*, said to have taken Picasso less time to do than if a house-painter had painted the wall. The work was as spontaneous as *Guernica* was planned, and every bit as sincere. Known as the **Musée National Picasso** (*Place de la Libération, t 04 93 64 16 05, www.musee-picasso-vallauris.fr; open Oct–May Wed–Mon 10–12.15 and 2–6; mid-June–Sept Wed–Mon 10–12.15 and 2–5; closed Tues and hols; adm*), the chapel is dimly lit; Picasso wanted visitors to discover the paintings gradually. On the left is the *War* panel, painted in numb shades of grey, black and green, with dark silhouetted figures hurling weapons. Skeletal, white-eyed horses drag a cart over blood-red earth; in it, a soldier brandishes a sword dripping with blood at the Guardian of Peace bearing a shield with a white dove. Opposite, on the *Peace* panel, painted almost entirely in serene blue and white, figures dance and play beneath a blooming tree and a huge vibrant sun. At the furthest end of the chapel is a simple mosaic of four different coloured figures holding aloft a globe marked with a dove, symbol of an ideal society untouched by bigotry.

The same ticket admits you to the **Musée Municipal** (*same details*) in the adjoining 16th-century castle, a former priory of the Lérins monks. Only the 12th-century **Chapelle Ste-Anne** survives from the castle's previous incarnation. It used to have many original pieces by Picasso until art thieves struck in 1989; now to be seen are the winners of the Biennales Internationales de la Céramique d'Art, and paintings and collages by Italian abstract master Alberto Magnelli (1888–1971). There is also a large collection of glowing pieces by the influential Massier family, who began the tradition of decorative ceramics more than a century before Picasso arrived on the scene and took all the glory. On Rue Sicard, there is more pottery and an exhibition of pottery techniques at the **Musée de la Poterie** (*t 04 93 64 66 51; open May–Sept daily 10–12 and 2–6; Oct–April Mon–Sat 2–6*), which forms part of a still-functioning artist's studio. A grumpy bronze man with a sheep glowers out of Place Paul Isnard: the sculpture was Picasso's gift to the town. Also here, beneath the walls of the Baroque church, is the bustling daily market, which sells the cut flowers and flower-scented perfumes which constitute the second string to Vallauris' economic bow.

In recent years Vallauris has suffered from a spate of thefts, often violent, from cars stuck in traffic, known locally as the 'Vallauris handbag grab'. Visitors are advised to roll up windows and close sun roofs when driving through the town.

Sophia-Antipolis

Meanwhile, as all this modern art appreciation and nightclubbing goes on around Antibes, 15,000 international business people are punching away on their new generation computers in France's Silicon Valley, the spooky new town complex of Sophia-Antipolis, off the D103 north of Vallauris, where cars are directed Scalextric-style around endless bends and roundabouts. Created in 1969 and funded in part by Nice's chamber of commerce, it is the first stage of the Route des Hautes Technologies and seems popular with executives: Air France's international reservations network is here, as well as Dow Corning, Toyota and others. The *commune* is divided into four sectors, like a spaceship, each dedicated to a different area of business: electronics, communications and computers form one sector; health and biotechnology form the second; teaching and research make up the third; and the fourth is devoted to environmental sciences. Each sector is provided with its own shops and services and almost 1,000 businesses from France and elsewhere have been attracted here. J.G. Ballard's novel *Super-Cannes* explores the psychologically and morally deadening effect of a loosely fictional artificially created business town just on this spot; how much resemblance his nightmare vision bears to reality is entirely up for debate.

Grasse

It was Catherine de Médicis (de' Medici) who introduced artichokes to the French and the scent trade to Grasse. Although it may seem obvious that a town set in the midst of France's natural floral hothouse should be a Mecca for perfume-making, Grasse's most important industry throughout the Middle Ages was tanning imported sheepskins from the mountains of Provence and buffalo hides from her Italian allies, Genoa and Tuscany. Part of the tanning process made use of the aromatic herbs that grew nearby, especially powdered myrtle, which gave the leather a greenish lustre.

Getting There

There are no trains, but there are frequent **buses** from Cannes and Nice to Grasse. The *gare routière*, t 04 93 36 37 37, is on the north side of town, at the Parking Notre-Dame-des-Fleurs. Leave your car here or in one of the other places just outside the centre: Grasse's steep streets are narrow for motorists.

Tourist Information

Grasse: Palais des Congrès, 22 Cours Honoré Cresp, t 04 93 36 66 66, f 04 93 36 86 36, *info@grasse-riviera.com*; also 3 Pl de la Foux, t 04 93 36 21 68, f 04 93 36 21 07, *tourisme. grasse@wanadoo.fr, www.grasse-riviera.com*. Open Oct–June Mon–Sat 9–12.30 and 2–6; July–Sept Mon–Sat 9–7, Sun 9–1 and 2–6.

Market Days

Grasse: Tues–Sun, Place aux Aires, general market; 1st and 3rd Fri of the month, Cours H. Cresp, antiques.

Where to Stay and Eat

Grasse ✉ 06130

★★★**Hôtel-Résidence des Parfums**, Rue Eugène Charabot, t 04 92 42 35 35, f 04 93 36 35 48, *www.odalys-vacances.com* (*expensive– moderate*). Pretty views, a pool, sauna and Jacuzzi; it also offers a 1hr 'Introduction to Perfume', lending you a 'nose' to help create your own perfume. Restaurant (*moderate*).

★★★**Auberge du Colombier**, 2085 Route Départmentale, Roquefort-les-Pins, t 04 92 60 33 00, f 04 93 77 07 03, *info@auberge-du-colombier.com, www.auberge-du-colombier. com* (*expensive–moderate*). Sixteen kilometres east of Grasse, in a delightful white *mas* with cheerfully decorated rooms, expansive gardens with a swimming pool and an extraordinary restaurant (*expensive*) – try the *ravioli* stuffed with wild mushrooms and scattered with roasted hazelnuts. *Hotel closed 6–25 Jan, restaurant closed Tues.*

★★**Charme Hôtel du Patti**, Place du Patti, t 04 93 36 01 00, f 04 93 36 36 40, *hotelpatti @libertysurf.fr, www.chez.com/hotelpatti* (*moderate*). Very comfortable modern rooms, all with air-conditioning and TV, and a restaurant (*moderate*), in the centre of medieval Grasse.

Grasse's culinary specialities are rather an acquired taste; typical examples are *sous fassoun* (cabbage stuffed with pig's liver, sausage, bacon, peas and rice and cooked with turnips, beef, carrots, etc.) and *tripes à la mode de Grasse*.

Bastide Saint-Antoine, 48 Rue Henri Dunant, t 04 93 70 94 94, *www.jacques-chibois.com* (*very expensive*). For a Tuscan feast in glorious al fresco surroundings, try chef Jacques Chibois' sumptuous creations.

Le Mas des Géraniums, Rte de Nice, Quartier San Peyre, Opio, t 04 93 77 23 23 (*expensive–moderate*). Authentic, aromatic country fare underneath bowers and on the lush garden terrace. *Closed Tues and Wed in mid-Nov–mid-Jan.*

Brasserie des Arcades, Place aux Aires, t 04 93 36 00 95 (*moderate–cheap*). Reasonably priced lunch underneath the arches, with Provençal dishes and fishes. *Closed Mon out of season.*

In Renaissance Italy, one of the most important status symbols an aristocrat could flaunt was fine, perfumed gloves. When Catherine de Médicis asked Grasse, Tuscany's old trading partner, to start supplying them, the Grassois left the buffalo hides behind to become *gantiers parfumeurs*. When gloves fell out of fashion after the Revolution, they became simply *parfumeurs*, and when Paris co-opted the business in the 19th century the townspeople concentrated on what has been their speciality ever since – distilling the essences that go into that final, costly, tiny bottle. And in that, this picturesque but unglamorous hill town leads the world, with approximately 30 *parfumeries*, even though most of the flower fields that surrounded Grasse only 40 years ago have now been planted with poxy, boxy villas.

Vieille Ville

Grasse's name comes from *grâce* – the state in which its original Jewish inhabitants found themselves once they converted to Christianity. In the Middle Ages it was an independent city-state on the Italian model, with close ties to the republics of Genoa and Pisa – evident in the austere Italian style of its architecture. During the 13th-century turmoil between the Guelphs and the Ghibellines, the town put itself under the protection of the Count of Provence. Today, a large percentage of the population hails from North Africa: the perfume magnates themselves live in Mougins and surrounding villages.

The one place where they often meet is at the morning food and flower market in arcaded **Place aux Aires** near the top of the town, where the handsome Hôtel Isnard (1781), with its wrought-iron balcony, looks as if it has escaped from New Orleans. From here, Rue des Moulinets and Rue Mougins-Roquefort lead to the Romanesque **Cathédrale Notre-Dame-du-Puy**, its spartan façade similar to churches around Genoa and matched by its spartan nave. The art is to the right: the *Crown of Thorns* and *Crucifixion* by Rubens at the age of 24, before he hit the big time; a rare religious subject by Fragonard, the *Washing of the Feet*; and, most sincere of all, a reredos by Ludovico Brea which depicts St Honorat having a chat with Pope Clement and St Lambert, the bishop of Vence between 1114 and 1154.

Across the Place du Petit-Puy, a plaque on the **Tour du Guet** (the former bishops' palace) commemorates the Grassois poet Bellaud de la Bellaudière, whose songs of wine and women, the *Obras et Rimos Provençalos* (1585), are the high point in Provençal literature between the troubadours and Mistral. But then, as now, it's a rare poet who can live off his verse: Bellaud supplemented his income by joining a band of brigands and sang his swansong on a scaffold.

Place du Cours and Four Museums

The Cannes road leads into Grasse's promenade, Place du Cours, with pretty views over the countryside. Close by, at 23 Boulevard Fragonard, is the **Musée Jean-Honoré Fragonard** (*t 04 93 36 01 61; open June–Sept daily 10–7; Oct–May Wed–Mon 10–1 and 2–5.30; closed Nov; adm*), in the 17th-century house of a cousin of Grasse's most famous citizen, Jean-Honoré Fragonard (1732–1806). Son of a *gantier parfumeur*, Fragonard expressed the inherent family sweetness in chocolate-box pastel portraits and mildly erotic rococo scenes of French royals trying their best to look like well-groomed poodles. Some of these are on display, along with copies of *Le Progrès de l'amour dans la cœur d'une jeune fille*, which even Fragonard's client, Mme du Barry, Louis XV's most beautiful mistress, rejected as too frivolous (the originals are in the Frick Collection in New York). Losing La Barry's favour was the beginning of the end for Fragonard; he lost most of his clients to the guillotine and in 1790 he washed up in Grasse feeling out of sorts, until one very hot day in 1806 he died from a cerebral haemorrhage induced by eating an ice-cream. Just north of the Cours at 2 Rue Mirabeau, the **Musée d'Art et d'Histoire de Provence** (*t 04 93 36 01 61; same hours as Musée Fragonard*) has its home in the 1770 Italianate mansion built by the frisky sister of Count Mirabeau of Aix, who was married to one of several degenerate marquises who pepper the history of Provence – this one, the Marquis de Cabris, is remembered in Grasse for having covered the walls of the city with obscene graffiti about the local women. Besides Gallo-Roman funerary objects, *santons* and furniture in all the Louis styles, there's Count Mirabeau's death mask, his sister's original bidets, an exceptional collection of faïence from Moustiers and Apt, and paintings by Granet.

At 8 Cours Honoré Cresp, the **Musée International de la Parfumerie** (*t 04 93 36 80 20; same hours as Musée Fragonard*) displays lots of precious little bottles dating from Roman times to the present, plus bergamot boxes of the 18th century and Marie-Antoinette's travel case, while around the corner at 11 Bd du Jeu-de-Ballon the **Musée de la Marine** (*t 04 93 40 11 11, www.musee-amiral-de-grasse.com; open June–Sept daily 10–7; Oct–May Mon–Sat 10–5; closed Nov; adm*) is devoted to the career of the intrepid Amiral de Grasse, hero of the American War of Independence.

Parfumeries

It's hard to miss these in Grasse, and if you've read Patrick Süskind's novel *Perfume* the free tours may seem a bit bland. The alchemical processes of extracting essences from freshly cut mimosa, jasmine, roses, bitter orange, etc. are explained – you learn that it takes 900,000 rosebuds to make a kilo of rose essence, which then goes to the *haute couture* perfume-bottlers and hype-merchants of Paris. Even more alarming are some of the other ingredients that arouse human hormones: the genital secretions of Ethiopian cats, whale vomit and Tibetan goat musk.

Tours in English are offered by: **Parfumerie Fragonard**, in the 18th-century converted tannery at 20 Bd Fragonard (*t 04 93 36 44 65, www.fragonard.com*), or at the spanking-new factory at Les 4 Chemins, on the Route de Cannes; **Molinard**, 60 Bd Victor Hugo (*t 04 93 36 01 62, www.molinard.com*); and **Galimard**, 73 Rte de Cannes (N85) (*t 04 93 09 20 00, www.galimard.com*). The visits are free and they don't seem to mind too much if you don't buy something at the end.

If you want to try your hand at creating your own perfumes, you can study under a 'nose' at the **Studio des Fragrances** (*t 04 93 09 20 00; two-hour course, €34*), or at the **Molinard Atelier** (*telephone same as parfumerie; 90-minute course, €40*). Or you can visit a flower plantation: Mr Biancalana (*t 04 93 60 12 76*) offers guided tours of his, which has been in his family for three generations and offers 'initiation in flower-picking' – jasmine in summer and roses in May and June (€5 *per person*).

Around Grasse: Dolmens and Musical Caves

The Route Napoléon (N85) (*see* pp.177–8), laid out in the 1930s to follow the little emperor's path to Paris, threads through miles of empty space on either side of medieval **St-Vallier-de-Thiey** (12km from Grasse), a popular gathering place for walkers. The ancient plane tree at the centre of the village square is circled by an old stone bench engraved with the words '*Napoléon s'est assis ici le 2 mars 1815*'. Things were busier here around 800 BC, when the people built elliptical walls with stones as high as 6ft. An alignment of 12 small **dolmens**, most of them buried under stone

Tourist Information

St-Vallier-de-Thiey: 10 Place du Tour, t/f 04 93 42 78 00, *tourisme@saintvallierdethiey.com, www.saintvallierdethiey.com. Open Mon–Sat 9–12 and 3–6, Sun 10–12; shorter hrs in winter.*

Market Days

St-Vallier-de-Thiey: Fri am and Sun, Oct–mid-May: Place St-Roch; mid-May–Sept at the Grand Pré.

Where to Stay and Eat

St-Vallier-de-Thiey ✉ 06460

★★Le Préjoly, Place Rougière, t 04 93 42 60 86, f 04 93 42 67 80, *prejoly@wanadoo.fr* (*inexpensive*). Seventeen reasonably priced rooms and an excellent restaurant (*moderate*) frequented by film stars up from the Cannes Film Festival. *Closed mid-Nov–Jan; restaurant closed Sun eve and Mon out of season.*

tumuli, stands between St-Vallier and St-Cézaire-sur-Siagne; a flat rock nearby is known as the *pierre druidique* (St-Vallier's tourist office has a map on the wall).

Just to the southwest, signposted on the D5, there's a subterranean lake in the **Grotte de Baume Obscure** (*t 04 93 42 61 63; open July–Aug daily 10–6; May–June and Sept Mon–Sat 10–5, Sun 10–6; Oct–April Tues–Sun 10–5; closed mid-Dec–mid-Feb*), with a high-tech sound and light show, plus underground pools and waterfalls. More caves can be found just off the D4 south of St-Vallier-de-Thiey: the distinctly less high-tech **Grottes des Audides** (*t 04 93 42 64 15, www.grottesdesaudides.free.fr; open July–Aug daily 10–6; mid-Feb–June and Sept–Oct Wed–Sun 2–5; Nov–mid Feb by appt only*), where you will have to rely on your own well-shod feet to take you underground. **Cabris**, 6km west of Grasse on the D4, a pretty *village perché* once favoured by Camus, Sartre and Antoine de Saint-Exupéry, is now a town of artisans and perfume executives. The D11 and D13 to the west lead to more caves: the red **Grottes de Saint-Cézaire** (*t 04 93 60 22 35, www.lesgrottesdesaintcezaire.fr; open July–Aug daily 10.30–6.30; June and Sept daily 10.30–12 and 2–6; April–May and Oct daily 2.30–5; Nov–Mar Sun only 2.30–5; adm*), where the iron-rich stalactites, when struck by the guide, make uncanny music. **St-Cézaire-sur-Siagne** itself is an unspoiled medieval town; its white 13th-century cemetery chapel, built on pure, sober lines, is one of the best examples of Provençal Romanesque on the coast.

Mougins

Cooking, that most ephemeral of arts, is the main reason most people make a pilgrimage to Mougins, a luxurious, fastidiously flawless village of *résidences secondaires*, with more gastronomy per square inch than any place in France, thanks to the magnetic presence of Roger Vergé (*see* 'Where to Stay and Eat', overleaf). But there are a few sights to whet your appetite before you surrender to the table: a **Musée de la Photographie** (*Porte Sarrazine, t 04 93 75 85 67; open July–Sept daily 10–8; Oct and Dec–June Wed–Sat 10–12 and 2–6, Sun and hols 2–6; closed Nov; adm*), with changing exhibitions showcasing both new and established photographers, a collection of photographs of Mougins at the turn of the last century, and a permanent collection which features the work of Jacques-Henri Lartigue, who lived in nearby Opio, among others. For the voyeuristic, there is a large number of

Tourist Information

Mougins: 15 Av Mallet, **t** 04 93 75 87 67, **f** 04 92 92 04 03, *tourisme@mougins-coteazur.org*, *www.mougins-coteazur.org*. Open June–Sept daily 10–8; Oct–May Mon–Sat 10–5.30.

Where to Stay and Eat

Mougins ✉ 06250

★★★★Le Moulin de Mougins, Av Notre-Dame-de-Vie, **t** 04 93 75 78 24, **f** 04 93 90 18 55, *info@moulin-mougins.com*, *www.moulin-mougins.com* (*very expensive*). In 1969 chef Roger Vergé bought a 16th-century olive mill near Notre-Dame-de-Vie and made it into this internationally famous restaurant, which also has three rooms and two apartments overlooking the sculpture gardens and wisteria-covered terraces. Of late, France's gourmet bibles have been sniffing that the mild-mannered celebrity chef has lost a bit of his touch – and little faults seem big when you shell out €150 for a meal (though there are menus from €40) But it's still a once-in-a-lifetime experience for most, in the most enchanting setting on the Côte. *Closed Dec–mid-Jan.*

★★★★Les Muscadins, 18 Bd Courteline, **t** 04 92 28 28 28, **f** 04 92 92 88 25, *muscadins@alcyons.fr*, *www.lesmuscadins.com* (*very expensive*). The *nouvelle cuisine* and chocolate desserts at this hôtel-restaurant have received excellent reviews, and the hotel has individually decorated sumptuous rooms of charm and character.

L'Amandier, Place des Patriotes, **t** 04 93 90 00 91 (*expensive*). If you can't get a table at

the Moulin de Mougins, Vergé has recently opened this new, simpler restaurant, located up a winding staircase in a 14th-century olive oil mill above his shop in central Mougins. Dishes of the day are chalked up on a huge blackboard, the ivy-covered terrace is utterly romantic and menus start at an excellent €28. In the **shop** below, **Les Boutiques du Moulin**, stock up on crystal glasses, kitchenware and a selection of the master's sauces and *compotes*. For those who still haven't had enough Vergé, he has also opened a **cookery school** above L'Amandier; contact **t** 04 93 75 35 70, **f** 04 93 90 18 55 for details.

Le Feu Follet, Place du Commandant Lamy, **t** 04 93 90 15 78, **f** 04 92 92 92 62, *battaglia@feu-follet.fr* (*moderate*). An affordable restaurant offering several excellent menus – try the *rognons de veau à la graine de moutarde*. *Closed Mon, and mid-Dec–mid-Jan.*

La Brasserie de la Méditerranée, Place du Cdt Lamy, **t** 04 93 90 03 47 (*moderate*). Serves grilled *gambas* with ginger and other seafood delights accompanied by heavenly home-made bread. *Closed Jan.*

Le Bistrot, Place du Cdt. Lamy, **t** 04 93 75 78 34 (*moderate*). For traditional dishes such as roast quail, beef stew and aubergine caviar, try this vaulted, wooden-beamed bistro. Don't miss the fig tart. *Closed Wed lunch, Thurs lunch and Sat lunch out of season; closed every lunch July–Aug.*

Le Rendez-vous de Mougins, Place du Cdt Lamy, **t** 04 93 75 87 47 (*moderate*). A local favourite, with aromatic dishes like beef with wild mushroom sauce and sea bass with truffles.

photographs depicting Picasso at work and at play – André Villars, who was personally responsible for the establishment of the museum, took many of them, and others are by famous names like Robert Doisneau, Jacques-Henri Lartigue and Raph Gatti. Further exhibitions are held in the old village **Lavoir** in the pretty Place de la Mairie.

Two kilometres southeast of Mougins, Picasso spent the last 12 years of his life in a villa next to the exquisite hilltop **Chapelle Notre-Dame-de-Vie** (*open Sun 9–10am*), a 12th-century priory founded by monks from St-Honorat and rebuilt in 1646. Until 1730, when the practice was banned, people would bring stillborn babies here to be brought back to life just long enough for them to be baptized and avoid limbo.

Appropriately located just off the *autoroute* to Cannes, at the Aire des Breguières, the de luxe **Musée de l'Automobiliste** (*Chemin Font-de-Currault, t 04 93 69 27 80; open April–Sept daily 10–7; Oct–Mar daily 10–6; adm*) is a modernistic cathedral to the car. It has everything from Alfa-Romeos to Zundapps, and a string of very classy Bugattis and Rolls-Royces; every vehicle (and there are almost 100 of them, the oldest dating back to 1838) is in working order.

Just north of Mougins, on the N85 towards Grasse, is the pretty village of **Mouans Sartoux**, which rose from the ashes of two Saracen-beleaguered communities. In the 16th century, feisty Suzanne de Villeneuve fought off the duplicitous duke of Savoy and chased him all the way to Cannes after he had razed her château to the ground despite an earlier promise. The restored 500-year-old château, owned by the town since 1989, has become the **Espace de l'Art Concret** (*t 04 93 75 71 50; open June–Sept daily 11–7; Oct–May daily 11–6; adm*), the brainchild of a local collector, Sybil Albers-Barrier, and her companion, Gottfried Honegger, the celebrated Concrete artist, who wanted to establish a 'museum imagined by artists'. The exhibits are rotated, rearranged and juxtaposed to inspire visitors to engage actively with the art rather than viewing it passively. Guides will occasionally prod visitors into a strangled reaction to the art which surrounds them, in keeping with the centre's 'didactic and political goals' – but most rather seem to enjoy the experience. Not surprisingly, the gallery is also an education and research centre. A few pieces are fixed, such as the four granite slabs of Ulrich Rückheim's *Africa Nero* in the courtyard and Honegger's carved sculptures *Division 1* and *Division 10* which stand in silhouette in the garden.

Cannes

In 1834 the 3,000 fisherfolk and farmers of Cannes were going about their business when Lord Brougham, retired lord chancellor, and his ailing daughter, stuck in the village because a cholera epidemic in France had closed the border with Savoy, checked into its one and only hotel. As they waited, Lord Brougham was so seduced by the climate and scenery that he built a villa, where he subsequently spent every winter. English milords and the Tsar's family played follow-my-leader and flocked down to build their own villas nearby. 'Menton's dowdy. Monte's brass. Nice is rowdy. Cannes is class!' was the byword of the 1920s. Less enthusiastic commentators mention the dust, the bad roads, the uncontrolled building and the turds bobbing in the sea. If nothing else, the French Riviera proper ends with a bang at Cannes.

As the spunky sister city of Beverly Hills, France's Hollywood and a major year-round convention city (Cannes was the first place on the Côte d'Azur to note that business travellers spend more than three times as much per head as tourists), Cannes offers a moveable feast of high fashion, showbizzy trendiness and glittering nightlife. Depending on your mood, and perhaps on the thickness of your wallet, you may find it appalling or amusing, or just plain dizzy. You can always catch the next boat to the offshore Iles de Lérins, some of the most serene antidotes to any city.

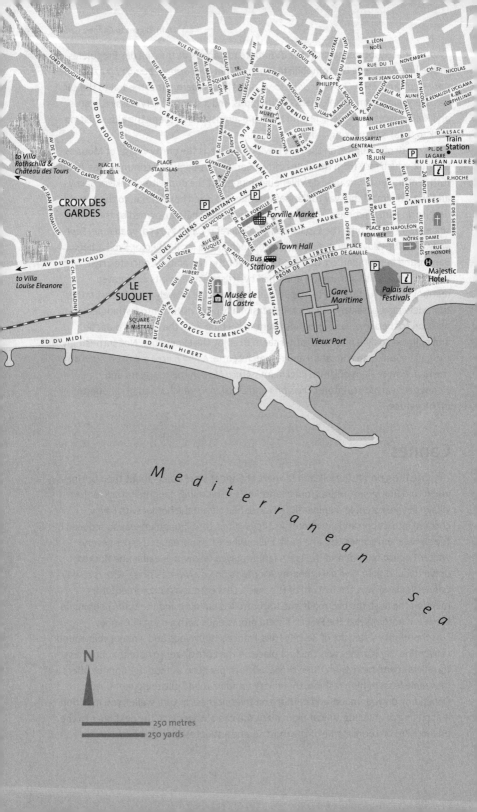

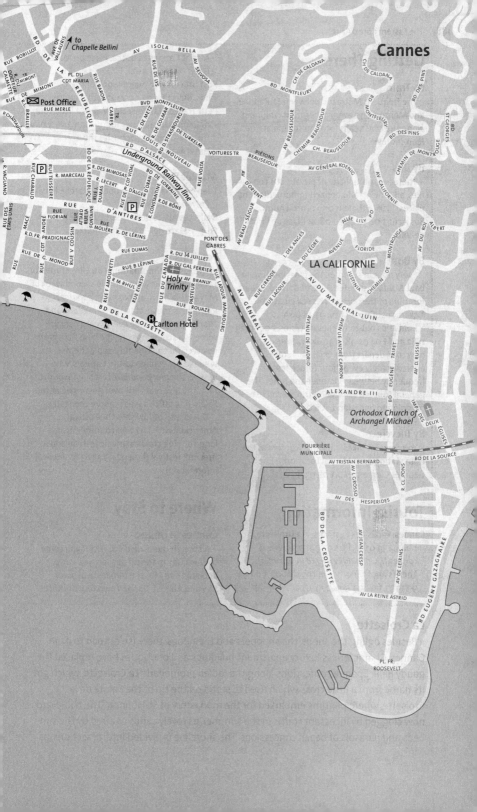

Getting There

By Train

The frequent Métrazur between St-Raphaël and Menton, and every other train whipping along the coast, calls into the station at Rue Jean-Jaurès.

By Bus

There is a multiplicity of private bus companies, all arriving and departing from different places; luckily, there is one central number, Bus Azur, t 04 93 45 20 08, at Place de l'Hôtel-de-Ville.

By Boat

Every hour in summer, the glass-bottomed boat *Nautilus*, at Jetée Albert Edouard, departs for tours of the port and its sea creatures. Tickets cost €11; call t 04 93 38 66 33.

Boat trips out to the Iles de Lérins, t 04 93 39 11 82 and t 04 92 98 71 30, *www.trans-cote-azur.com*, depart from Quai St-Pierre approximately every hour (much less frequently between October and June). The general tour is a whirlwind trip, so you're best off going to one island at a time.

By Bicycle

You can rent bikes, cars and scooters at the train station or at Mistral Location, 4 Rue Georges Clemenceau, t 04 93 99 25 25.

Tourist Information

Cannes: Palais des Festivals, 1 La Croisette, t 04 93 39 01 01, f 04 93 99 37 34, *www.cannes.fr. Open daily 9–7 (8 in summer).* There's another office in the station, t 04 93 99 19 77, f 04 93 39 40 19. *Open Mon–Sat 9–7.*

Also at Cannes La Bocca, Place du Marché. *Open Mon–Sat 9–7.*

Post office: 22 Bivouac Napoléon.

Taxis: daily t 04 92 99 27 27. 24hr service.

Petit Train de la Croisette: Makes a little tour of Cannes in summer 10am–11pm every hour from La Croisette, opposite the Hôtel Majestic.

Market Days

Tues–Sun: Marché de la Bocca, Marché Forville, Provençal markets.

Daily: Les Allées de la Liberté, flower market.

Fri 3–7: Place de l'Etang, flea market.

Festivals

The **Festival International du Film** erupts for 12 days beginning around the second week of May with a hurricane of hype, *paparazzi*, journalists, movie stars, gawking fans and characters who come every year There are some 350 screenings; most of the tickets are reserved for the cinema people themselves, while 10 per cent go to the Cannois, who bestow the *prix populaire* on their favourite film. The few seats left over go on sale at the Palais' box office a week before the festival.

The month of July sees the **Festival Américain**, with jazz and country music, a long-running **classical music festival** and a **firework festival** (t 04 92 99 33 83 for festival information).

Where to Stay

Cannes ✉ 06400

Although there are discounts if you come to Flash City in the off-season, you can't book too early for the film festival or for July and August. Cannes' two tourist offices

La Croisette

Besides ogling the shops, the shoppers and their dogs, there isn't much to do in Cannes. Characterless luxury apartment buildings and boutiques have replaced the gaudy Belle Epoque confections along the fabled promenade **La Croisette**, which got its name from a little cross which used to stand on the tip of the Pointe de la Croisette, where pilgrims embarked for the monastery of St-Honorat. The boulevard is now clogged by incessant traffic in the summer, its lovely sands covered by the sun beds and parasols of beach concessions. The shoreline is divided into 32 sections, as

offer a free reservation service, but they won't be much help at that time of year if you want a room that costs less than a king's ransom.

Luxury

★★★★★Carlton, 58 La Croisette, t 04 93 06 40 06, f 04 93 06 40 25, *cannes@interconti. com*, *www.cannes.interconti.com* (*luxury*). One of the landmarks of the Riviera, with its two black cupolas, said to be shaped like the breasts of the *grande horizontale* Belle Otero, the celebrated Andalucían flamenco dancer and courtesan of kings. It has been given a thorough renovation by its Japanese owners, and the 7th floor now boasts a pool, casino and beauty centre.

★★★★★Majestic Barrière, 10 La Croisette, t 04 92 98 77 00, f 04 93 38 97 90, *www. lucienbarriere.com* (*luxury*). Movie stars' favourite with its classic French décor, heated pool, private beach, etc. *Closed 15 Nov–28 Dec.*

★★★★★Martinez, 73 La Croisette, t 04 92 98 73 00, f 04 93 39 67 82, *martinez@concorde-hotels.com*, *www.hotel-martinez.com* (*luxury*). This hotel has kept its Roaring Twenties character, but now has all imaginable modern comforts, including tennis courts, a heated pool, two new luxury suites and, from the 7th floor, views over the city. *Discounts for stays of over five days.*

★★★Bleu Rivage, 61 La Croisette, t 04 93 94 24 25, f 04 93 43 74 92, *bleurivage@wanadoo. fr*, *www.frenchriviera-online.com/bleurivage* (*very expensive–expensive*). A renovated older hotel on the beach, where rooms overlook the sea or the garden.

★★★Hôtel Vendôme, 37 Bd d'Alsace, t 04 93 38 34 33, f 04 97 06 66 80, *hotel.vendome@ wanadoo.fr* (*expensive–moderate*). This pink 19th-century villa has recently been beautifully renovated and sits in a private garden in the heart of the town.

★★★Molière, 5 Rue Molière, t 04 93 38 16 16, f 04 93 68 29 57, *www.hotel-moliere.com* (*expensive–moderate*). Sitting in a garden, with bright rooms and terraces. *Closed mid-Nov–end Dec.*

If you aren't in Cannes on an MGM expense account, there are other alternatives.

★★Select, 16 Rue Hélène Vagliano, t 04 93 99 51 00, f 04 92 98 03 12, *hotel-select-06@ wanadoo.fr*, *www.hotel-select-cannes.com* (*moderate*). A quiet, comfortable, modern choice with air-conditioned rooms, all with private bathroom.

Chanteclair, 12 Rue Forville, t/f 04 93 39 68 88 (*moderate–inexpensive*). Good double rooms with showers. *Closed Nov–Dec.*

Auberge de Jeunesse, 35 Av de Vallauris, t/f 04 93 99 26 79. To the west, in Cannes La Bocca.

Chalit Auberge de Jeunesse, 27 Av Maréchal Gallieni, t 04 93 99 22 11, f 04 93 39 00 28, *le-chalit@wanadoo.fr. Closed Nov.*

Eating Out

La Palme d'Or, Hôtel Martinez (*see* above), t 04 92 98 74 14 (*very expensive*). The Alsatian chef, Christian Willer, and co-chef Christian Sinicropi prepare succulent dishes served in a fabulous Art Deco dining room. *Closed mid-Nov–mid-Dec, and Mon–Tues; open daily during film festival.*

Le Fouquet's, Hôtel Majestic (*see* above), t 04 92 98 77 05 (*expensive*). Chef Bruno Oger, named as one of France's top chefs, now presides over this sister restaurant to the acclaimed Paris original. **La Villa des Lys**,

memorably named as 'Waikiki', 'Le Zénith' and 'Long Beach' (which is all of a few metres long). There is one rare public beach in front of the fan-shaped **Palais des Festivals**, a charmless 1982 construction. **Hand-prints** of film celebrities line the *Allée des Etoiles* by the *Escalier d'Honneur*, where the limos pull up for the festival. Outside May, this monster disgorges conventioneers attending events such as the Festival of Hairdressing or Dentistry.

For all the present emphasis on glitter, tourist Cannes still remembers its English roots. Behind the Carlton Hotel, at 2–4 Rue Général Ferrié, the **Holy Trinity Church** was

t 02 92 98 77 41, remains at the hotel, and is also run by Oger, but in a smaller venue.

Lou Souléou, 16 Bd Jean Hibert, t 04 93 39 85 55 (*expensive–moderate*). For affordable seafood and views of its original habitat; try an authentic *bouillabaisse* and a pretty good *aïoli*. *Closed Mon and Wed eve, and Nov.*

Brasserie des Artistes, 5 Rue Rouguière, t 04 93 39 09 02 (*expensive–moderate*). Fresh food till late. *Closed Sun.*

Le Baoli, Port Canto, t 04 93 43 03 43 (*moderate*). Indonesian décor, fusion food and glitterati; witih a tree-shaded terrace. *Closed Nov–April.*

Caffé Roma, 1 Square Mérimée, t 04 93 38 05 04 (*moderate*). Decent Italian food served in a brasserie with terrace overlooking the Palais.

Hôtel Brasserie du Marché, 10 Rue Monseigneur Jeancard, t 04 93 48 13 00 (*cheap*). Retains the ambience of the old village and has tasty daily specials.

Café FNAC, 83 Rue d'Antibes, t 04 97 06 29 29 (*cheap*). For good coffee, sandwiches and home-made brownies.

Nightlife

Film

For stars on celluloid, sometimes in their original language (*version originale*, or *v.o.*):

Les Arcades, 77 Rue Félix Faure, t 04 93 39 00 98.

Olympia, 16 Rue Pompe, t 04 93 39 13 93.

Star, 98 Rue d'Antibes, t 04 93 68 81 07.

Casino

The casinos draw in some of the highest rollers on the Riviera, although the adjoining casino discos are fairly staid:

Casino Croisette, Palais des Festivals, t 04 92 98 78 00.

Palm Beach Casino Club, Palm Beach, t 04 97 06 36 90.

Bars and Clubs

To get into the most fashionable clubs (those with no signs on the door) you need to look as if you've just stepped off a 100ft yacht to get past the sour-faced bouncers.

Jimmy'z, at the Casino in the Palais des Festivals, t 04 92 98 78 78. A glitzy showcase billing itself '*La discothèque des stars*'; it's certainly for those with stars in their eyes – gamblers, their ladies and mainstream music. *Open Thurs, Fri, Sat 11.30pm–dawn. Open Sun for thé dansant.*

La Chunga, 24 Rue Latour-Maubourg, t 04 93 94 11 29. There's usually live music to go with the food (*meals expensive*). *Open 8.30pm–dawn. Closed Sun and Mon before Festival, and mid-Nov–end Dec.*

Le Whisky à Gogo, Lady Bird, 115 Av de Lérins, t 04 93 43 20 63. A well-heeled crowd grinding away to the top of the pops.

Cat Corner, 22 Rue Macé, t 04 93 39 31 31. Dance until dawn at the hottest place in town.

Broom's Bar, Hôtel Gray d'Albion. With a piano bar. It also has a disco on Sunday night –

Jane's Club, t 04 92 99 79 59.

Zanzi-Bar, 85 Rue Félix Faure, t 04 93 39 30 75. A gay bar of long standing. *Open 6pm–6am*.

Disco 7, 7 Rue Rouguière, t 04 93 39 10 36. Dancing and a transvestite show (€15 *cover charge*). *Open 11.30pm–6am.*

In summer, a number of **discos** erupt on the beach. They change each year. Either just get down there and check them out, look out for flyers or ask around at bars and cafés.

rebuilt in 1971 on the site of its 19th-century predecessor, preserving some Victorian odds and bobs: a mosaic, glass medallions of the arms of the Archbishop of Canterbury and the bishop of Gibraltar, and other Anglican paraphernalia. Built from ferro-concrete, the church's glories are its stained glass and 1970s style, enough to give points to your collars and make you reach for your platforms.

Follies and Fancies

East of La Croisette is **La Californie**, home to some of the most eccentric real estate on the Côte since the mid-19th century, when Eugène Triper, the French consul to

Birth of a Festival

In 1938, Philippe Erlanger, the Popular Front's minister of tourism, was given the task of finding a suitable venue for a festival to rival Mussolini's new Venice film festival: the French were not about to let the Fascists have all the starlets to themselves. Erlanger went down to the Côte d'Azur, where his Villefranche friends, especially Jean Cocteau, took a close interest in his mission. Erlanger had a weakness for Cannes, but it lacked hotels, and he was about to choose Biarritz instead when Cocteau intervened and insisted on Cannes: it would be more fun, he said.

The first festival, slated to start 1 August 1939, was cancelled owing to a party-pooper named Hitler, spoiling a huge cardboard model of Notre-Dame erected on the beach and forcing a liner full of movie stars sent over by MGM to sail home unrequited. The second festival, in 1946, drew some 50 journalists who hobnobbed and drank complimentary rosé wine. The jury gave every film a prize, which set the tone from the start: the competition bit was only an excuse for a week of carousing and hanky panky; the real festival would always be outside the screenings. Cannes' historians cite 1954 as the year when everything coalesced, when the essential ingredients of sex and scandal were added to the glamour of film: the décolletage of newcomer Sophia Loren made a big impression, grabbing attention and headlines away from Gina Lollobrigida. Another well-endowed starlet (English this time) named Simone Silva went on to the Iles de Lérins for a photo session with Robert Mitchum and removed her brassière. Two hours later she was told to leave Cannes and a few years later, no longer able to find work because of her precocious gesture, she committed suicide. Cannes should have made her an honorary citizen. Two years later, the new sensation was Brigitte Bardot, who coyly spun her skirts around to reveal her dainty *petites culottes*. The atmosphere was so ripe that even the straightest of arrows, Gary Cooper and Esther Williams, had flings during the festival.

These days would-be starlets strip down completely and bump and grind on the Croisette hoping to attract attention, any kind of attention, from the 6,000 journalists. The directors and stars, all carefully groomed in the spirit of Riviera-casual, give the same careful interviews all day. Although the big American studios have traditionally shunned the festival – what's the point, they said, when their own Oscars mean more at the box office than a Cannes Palme d'Or – the importance of the international entertainment market has brought a growing stream over from Hollywood. The wheeling and dealing that goes on can sometimes come from unexpected quarters. In 1993, a ship full of raw Russian sailors caused a sensation by anchoring within spitting distance of the Palais des Festivals with a vast contraband cargo of vodka and smoked salmon. The next day, most of the jurors slept through the screening of the films in competition. Nor was it the last time.

Other European film festivals in Berlin and Venice have of late given Cannes a run for its money, and critics have suggested that Cannes has had its day. After all, the average age of film-makers in the main competition is now 53 years old. But Cannes shouldn't be shrugged off just yet. In true Riviera style it rollicks on, courting controversy wherever possible – if only just for the publicity.

Moscow, and his aristocratic young Russian wife built the Villa Alexandra with great flamboyance in an oriental style. It has since been demolished, but there are plenty of other follies to gawp at – like the 'medieval' **Château Scott** at 151 Avenue Maréchal Juin, or the cottagey **Villa Rose-Lawn**, 42 Avenue Roi Albert, with its half-timbering.

There is also the neoclassical palace **Le Californie** at 27 Avenue Roi Albert, or the **Moorish villa** on Avenue Costabelle. Dating from the early part of the 20th century are the Art Deco **Villa les Ondes** on Bd Stalingrad, and the Villa Fiesole, now known as the **Villa Domergue** after its owners, artist Jean-Gabriel Domergue and his sculptress wife, Odette, who have bequeathed the villa to the town. Among these opulent piles is the **Chapelle Bellini**, once part of a lavish, Tuscan-style palace built at the end of the 19th century. The painter Bellini used it as a studio until his death in 1989, and his paintings are scattered amid the Baroque excess of the chapel interior.

Russian nobility mingled with the playboys, all outdoing each other in architectural eccentricity, in this swanky part of town. The onion-domed Orthodox church of the **Archangel Michael**, on Boulevard Alexandre III, was built to accommodate the substantial court of Tsarina Marie Alexandrovna. Members of the Imperial family wintered here before the Russian Revolution and were buried here after it. The interior is filled with extraordinary glowing icons and bannered messages from the Imperial family; the church choir is rumoured to set spines tingling.

There are more follies on the other side of Cannes in **La Croix des Gardes**, or the Quartier des Anglais; this is where Lord Brougham first built the Palladian-style **Villa Eléonore-Louise** (24 Av du Docteur Picaud). English friends followed and were seduced, among them Sir Thomas Woodfield, who built a Gothic castle, the **Château des Tours** (or the Villa Ste-Ursule), with pink gneiss at 6 Av Jean de Noailles. Woodfield's gardener, John Taylor, noted the increasing exchange of properties and set up Cannes' first real-estate agency. Among the other architectural landmarks is the very grand neoclassical **Villa Rothschild**, built by Baron Rothschild in 1881.

The Old Port and Le Suquet

The **Vieux Port**, with its bobbing fishing boats and plush luxury craft, is on the other side of the Palais des Festivals. Plane trees line the **Allées de la Liberté**, where the flower market and Saturday fleamarket take place. Two streets further back, narrow pedestrian **Rue Meynadier** is the best place to buy cheese (Ferme Savoyarde) and fresh pasta (Aux Bons Raviolis), near the sumptuous **Forville** covered market. Cannes' cramped old quarter, **Le Suquet**, rises up on the other side of the port, where the usual renovation and displacement of the not-so-rich is just beginning. At the city's highest point, the monks of St-Honorat built the square watchtower, the **Tour du Mont Chevalier**, in 1088, and their priory is now the **Musée de la Castre** (*t 04 93 38 55 26; open June–Aug Tues–Sun 10–1 and 3–7; Sept Tues–Sun 10–1 and 2–6; Oct–Mar Tues–Sun 10–1 and 2–5; April–May Tues–Sun 10–1 and 2–6; closed Mon; adm, free first Sun of month*), a little museum at a little price, with an archaeological and ethnographic collection donated by a generous Dutch baron in 1873, containing everything from Etruscan vases to pre-Columbian art and a 40-armed Buddha.

The Iles de Lérins

When Babylon begins to pall, you can take refuge on a delightful pair of green, wooded, traffic-free islets just off the coast. Known in antiquity as Lero and Lerina, they are now named after two saints who founded religious houses on them at the end of the 4th century: little **Ile Saint-Honorat** and the larger **Ile Sainte-Marguerite**. (Take water and a picnic, for there is only a smattering of expensive little shops and cafés on Sainte-Marguerite and just one restaurant on Saint-Honorat.)

Saint-Honorat, Isle of Snakes

According to legend, when St Honorat landed on the islet that bears his name in 375 he found it swarming with noxious snakes and prayed to be delivered of them. They immediately dropped dead, but the stench of the cadavers was so hideous that Honorat climbed a palm tree and prayed again, asking for the bodies to be washed away. God obliged again, and in memory the symbol of the island became two palm trees intertwined with a snake.

St Honorat shares with Jean Cassien of St-Victor in Marseille the distinction of introducing monasticism to France. The island became a beacon of light and learning in the dark ages; by the 7th century the monastery of St-Honorat had 4,000 monks, and 100 priories and lordships on the mainland (including Cannes, which belonged to the monastery until 1788). Its alumni numbered 20 saints, including St Patrick, who, before going to Ireland, trained here and picked up some tips on dealing with pesky snakes. The monastery was also a big boon to local sinners: a journey to St-Honorat could earn a pilgrim an indulgence equal to a journey to the Holy Land. Other visitors, especially Saracen pirates, were not as welcome. To protect themselves, the monks built a fortress, connected to the abbey by means of an underground tunnel. Although the original abbey is long gone, the evocative, crenellated **donjon** remains strong, lapped by the wavelets on three sides. There's a vaulted cloister and chapel, and a terrace with views that stretch to the Alps. In 1869, Cistercians from Sénanque purchased St-Honorat, rebuilt the **abbey** (which still offers accommodation for visitors) and have done all they can to preserve the islet's beauty and serenity, so close and yet so far from the sound and fury of Cannes. The monks who live there continue to cultivate part of the island, producing honey, wine and a liqueur called Lérina, all described in their website, *www.abbayedelerins.com*.

Sainte-Marguerite and the Man in the Iron Mask

Legend has it that Marguerite, sister of St Honorat, founded a convent for holy Christian women on this island, but it broke her heart that her austere brother would only come to visit her when a certain almond tree blossomed. Marguerite asked God to make him come more often and her prayer was answered when the almond tree miraculously began to bloom every month. Ste-Marguerite has nicer beaches than St-Honorat, especially on the south end of Chemin de la Chasse. At the beginning of 2003, the island's forest became a nature reserve.

On the north end stands the gloomy **Fort Royal** (*t 04 93 38 55 26; open April–Sept Tues–Sun 10.30–1.15 and 2.15–5.45; Oct–Mar Tues–Sun 10.30–1.15 and 2.15–4.45; closed Mon and hols; adm*), with a little **aquarium** and a **Musée de la Mer** which displays finds from submarine digs. The fort was built by Richelieu as a defence against the Spaniards (who got it anyway) and improved by Vauban in 1712. By then the fortress mainly served as a prison, especially for the mysterious Man in the Iron Mask, who was transferred here from Pigneroles in 1687 and ended up in the Bastille in 1698. Speculation about the man's identity continues at least to divert historians (who insist that the mask was actually leather): was he Louis XIV's twin, as Voltaire suggested, or, according to a more recent theory, the gossiping son-in-law of the doctor who performed the autopsy on Louis XIII and discovered that the king was incapable of producing children? Later prisoners included six Huguenot pastors who dared to return to France after Louis XIV's revocation of the Edict of Nantes; they were kept in solitary confinement until all but one of them went mad.

The Western Côte d'Azur

09

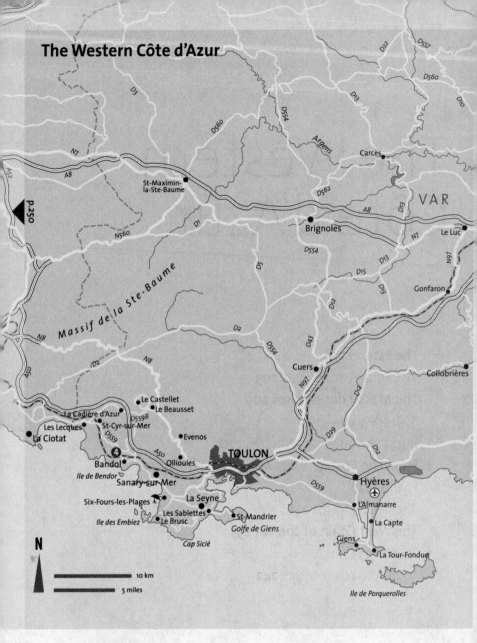

The Western Côte d'Azur

VAR

Highlights

1 The venerable Cité Episcopale in Fréjus
2 Razzle-dazzle St-Tropez and its beaches
3 Walking and diving in the national park of Port-Cros island
4 Wine and the *pastis* king's island, in Bandol

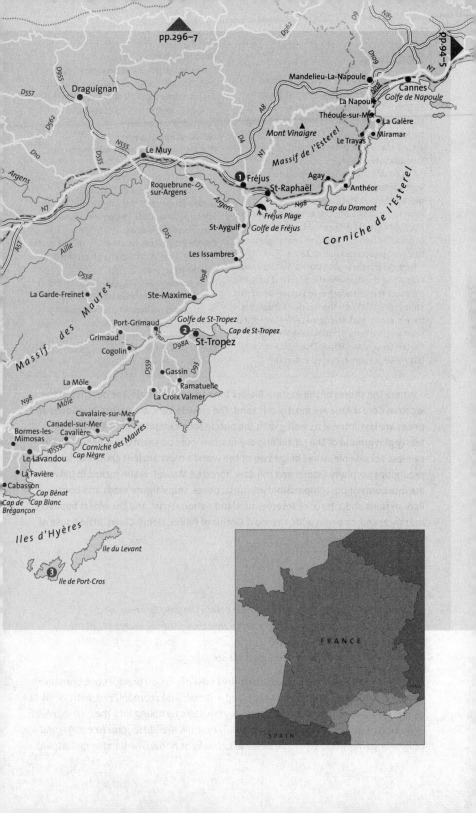

pp.296–7

pp.94–5

D9

N85

D562

D955

D557

Draguignan

D262

D10

Argens

N7

A57

Aille

D558

D25

D1

Roquebrune-
sur-Argens

Argens

N555

D555

Le Muy

A8

D4

N7

Massif de l'Esterel

Mont Vinaigre

Mandelieu-La-Napoule

La Napoule

Théoule-sur-Mer

Le Trayas

1 Fréjus

St-Raphaël

Agay

Anthéor

Fréjus Plage

Golfe de Fréjus

St-Aygulf

Ng8

Cap du Dramont

Cap de Napoule

Cannes

Golfe de Napoule

La Galère

Miramar

Corniche de l'Esterel

Les Issambres

Ng8

La Garde-Freinet

Massif des Maures

Ste-Maxime

Port-Grimaud

Golfe de St-Tropez

2 St-Tropez

Cap de St-Tropez

Grimaud

Cogolin

D98A

D559

La Môle

Gassin

Ramatuelle

D93

Môle

N98

La Croix Valmer

Cavalaire-sur-Mer

Canadel-sur-Mer

Cavalière

Bormes-les-
Mimosas

D559

Corniche des Maures

Cap Nègre

Le Lavandou

La Favière

Cabasson

Cap Bénat   Cap Blanc

Cap de
Brégançon

Iles d'Hyères

Ile du Levant

3 Ile de Port-Cros

FRANCE

SPAIN

Beaches

This region contains some of the most enticing beaches in France. From Cannes to St-Tropez the dramatic corniche road offers glimpses down to small sandy coves hiding between jagged rocks. This is, above all, a place to take your time, stopping where fancy dictates.

The beaches of St-Tropez are actually 5km south of the town – Plage de Tahiti is the most infamous, Plage de Pampelonne the least spoiled. True aficionados head south to Plage de l'Escalet and round Cap Lardier to Gigaro. The footpath east of Gigaro takes you to a well-patronized nudist beach.

From St-Trop to Toulon the road climbs and falls along the Corniche des Maures. Some of the most revered beaches in Europe lie off this stretch of coastline – the Iles de Porquerolles have national park status and offer unrivalled sand (catch a ferry from Hyères). West of Toulon, Sanary and Bandol have thin strips, but these get very crowded in summer.

Best Beaches

Esterel coast: dozens of tiny coves between St-Raphaël, Boulouris and Agay, marked with yellow signs along the corniche road.

St-Aygulf: long sand, lots of space, but crowded in summer.

Les Issambres: as above.

Port Grimaud: long beach backing on to Spoerry's *cité lacustre*.

St-Tropez: Plage de Tahiti, Plage de Pampelonne, Plage de l'Escalet.

Gigaro: long beach, a favourite with families.

St-Clair: just outside Le Lavandou; views across to the islands.

Cap de Brégançon: wilder coves, off the beaten track. Cabasson is the French president's summer retreat.

Ile de Porquerolles: Plage de Notre-Dame, or any of the northern coastal beaches.

Ile du Levant: Héliopolis, premier nudist beach.

Hyères: large town beach.

St-Cyr: 2km of fine sand with a gentle slope; perfect for small children.

Where the shores of the eastern Riviera tend to be all shingle, the beaches of the western Côte d'Azur are mostly soft sand. The crowds, cars, art, yachts, boutiques and prices are less intense as well – with the outrageous exception of St-Tropez, the pretty playground of the jet set and dry-martini louts on yachts. Just behind these careless seaside pleasures bulge two of the world's most ancient chunks of land, the prodigious porphyry Esterel and the dark, forested Maures, while tucked in between are museums of post-impressionism, music boxes, ships' figureheads and booze; Roman ruins and a tortoise reserve; an island national park and the oldest baptistry in France; and, to begin with, the most Gothic of follies, Henry Clews' little house of horrors in La Napoule.

The Esterel

The Esterel is supposed to receive its name from the fairy Esterelle, who intoxicates and deceives her ardent lovers and thus fittingly makes her home on the Coast of Illusion.

Douglas Goldring, *The South of France* (1952)

Between Cannes and St-Raphaël this fairy Coast of Illusion provides one of nature's strangest interludes: a wild *massif* of blood-red cliffs and promontories, with sandy or shingle beaches amid dishevelled porphyry boulders tumbling into the blue, blue sea – the kind of romantic landscape where holy hermits like St Honorat (*see* p.193) and unholy brigands like Gaspard de Besse felt equally at home. The handsome Gaspard,

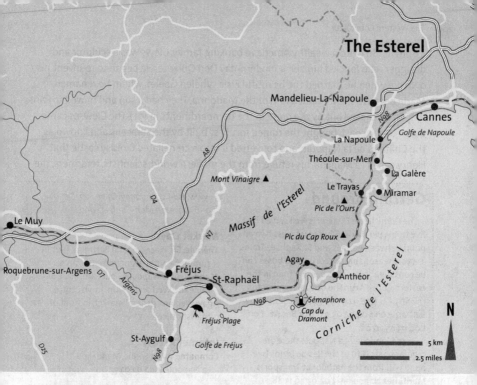

Mandelieu-La-Napoule

Cannes

Golfe de Napoule

La Napoule

Théoule-sur-Mer

La Galère

Le Trayas

Miramar

Mont Vinaigre ▲

Massif de l'Esterel

Pic de l'Ours ▲

Pic du Cap Roux ▲

Agay

Anthéor

Le Muy

Corniche de l'Esterel

Roquebrune-sur-Argens

Fréjus

St-Raphaël

Argens

Sémaphore

Cap du Dramont

Fréjus Plage

St-Aygulf

Golfe de Fréjus

N

5 km

2.5 miles

from a bourgeois family of Besse-sur-Issole, was himself the stuff of romance – a generous highwayman with courtly manners, a lover of good food and wine, a scholar who entertained the jury at his trial in Aix by reciting passages of Homer and Anacreon in Greek. When they hanged him anyway, many a woman wept bitter tears (others wondered where he hid all his booty – it has never been found). Unfortunately, the virgin cork forests that once hid Gaspard's band in the Esterel have been ravaged by fire – environmental tragedies with the side effect of clearing sites for property brigands and their grotesque cement-mixers, who race neck-and-neck with the forestry service's gallant attempts to reforest the arid mountain with drought- and disease-resilient pines and ilexes. Come in the spring, when wild flowers ignite this Fauvist volcanic fairyland; in summer, to lower the risk of accidental fires, the internal roads are often closed to traffic.

Mandelieu-La Napoule

Golf is what makes Mandelieu famous. There are nine- and 18-hole courses; the first was laid out a hundred years ago by the nephew of the Tsar, the latest by an American. The brochures speak of 'panoramas to stop you from breathing'. If you recover your breath, down below on the coast, Mandelieu's sister town, La Napoule, has the usual beaches and hotels and the nuttiest folly ever built by a foreigner on this shore, the **Fondation d'Art Henry Clews** (*t 04 93 49 95 05; open Feb–Oct daily 10–6, guided tours daily at 11.30, 2.30, 3.30 and 4.30; adm*), a pseudo-medieval fantasy castle beautifully set near the Pointe des Pendus (Hanged Men's Point), built by a pseudo-medieval artist, Henry Clews.

Born in 1863 into a wealthy American banking family, Clews was a sculptor and designer who fancied himself a modern-day Don Quixote. He began to re-invent his own life when he married the beautiful Elsie Whelen Goelet, whom he renamed Marie because she reminded him of the Madonna. They had a son and moved to Paris, only to be chased out by the noise of the bombardments in 1917. The Clewses came down to the coast, bought the ruined fort first built by the Saracens and known as the Château de la Napoule, and converted it into a crenellated fantasy castle that Henry called La Mancha, his refuge from the modern world, scientists, reformers, the

Getting Around

The Corniche de l'Esterel is well served by five trains per day and buses (at least two an hour) between Cannes and St-Raphaël. Trains are very reasonably priced, but the buses can be considerably more expensive than in the eastern Côte d'Azur. The central number for the SNCF is **t** 08 92 35 35 35; for buses, call SVA Beltrame on **t** 04 94 95 95 16 or Bus Azur on **t** 04 93 45 20 08.

From Mandelieu-La Napoule there are regular boats (€11) to the Iles de Lérins (*see* pp.193–4) from the harbour at **Transports Maritimes Napoulais**, **t** 04 93 49 15 88, *April–Oct*. For bike hire, try Location 2 Roues, Mandelieu-La Napoule, **t** 04 92 97 27 37.

Tourist Information

Mandelieu-La Napoule: Rue Jean Monnet, **t** 04 93 93 64 66, **f** 04 93 93 64 65. For hotel reservations: *centraleresa@ot-mandelieu.fr*, *www.ot-mandelieu.fr*. *Open Mon–Fri 9–12.30, 1.30–6*.
Bd Henry Clews, La Napoule, **t** 04 93 49 95 31, **f** 04 92 97 99 57. *Open April–June and Sept–mid-Oct Mon–Fri 10–12.30 and 1.30–6; July–Aug daily 10–7. Closed mid-Oct–Mar*.
Av de Cannes, Termes, **t** 04 92 97 99 27, **f** 04 92 97 09 18. *Open mid-Oct–Mar Mon–Sat 9.30–12.30 and 1.30–5.30; April–June and Sept–mid-Oct Tues–Sat 9.30–12.30 and 2–6; July–Aug daily 9.30–12 and 2–6*.
Théoule: 1 Corniche d'Or, **t** 04 93 49 28 28, **f** 04 93 49 00 04, *www.theoule-sur-mer.org*. *Open summer Mon–Sat 9–7, Sun 10–3; winter Mon–Sat 9–12 and 2.30–6.30*.
Agay: Place Giannetti, **t** 04 94 82 01 85, **f** 04 94 82 74 20, *agay.tourisme@wanadoo.fr*, *www.esd-fr.com/agay*. *Open Feb–Oct daily 9–6; Nov–Jan Mon–Sat 9–12 and 2–6*.

Market Days

Théoule: Fri, Place Général Bertrand; Tues in summer, Port de Figueirette-Miramar, .
Mandelieu-La Napoule: Thurs am, Place St Fainéant; Wed and Fri am, town centre.
Agay: Wed am, general market, in front of tourist office.

Internet Access

Computec, Av de Fréjus, Mandelieu-La Napoule, **t** 04 92 97 75 00.

Where to Stay and Eat

Mandelieu-La Napoule ✉ 06210
★★★★**Ermitage du Riou**, Av Henry Clews, **t** 04 93 49 95 56, **f** 04 92 97 69 05, *hotel@ermitage-du-riou.fr*, *www.ermitage-du-riou.fr* (*luxury–expensive*). A luxurious refuge built like a Provençal bastide, with a garden and pool overlooking the sea. Restaurant (*very expensive–expensive*).
★★★**Hostellerie du Golf**, 780 Av de la Mer, **t** 04 93 49 11 66, **f** 04 92 97 04 01, *hoteldu golf@aol.com* (*moderate*). With a pool, restaurant, and rooms with terraces.
★★**La Calanque**, Av Henry Clews, **t** 04 93 49 95 11, **f** 04 93 49 67 44 (*inexpensive*). Much more affordable, with a shady terrace, restaurant (*moderate*) and views of the sea and Clews' folly. *Closed Nov–Mar*.
L'Armorial, Bd Henry Clews, **t** 04 93 49 91 80 (*expensive–moderate*). In an elegant residence by the sea, this restaurant serves a *bouillabaisse* that must rank among the best to be found in the region, plus immaculately prepared dishes such as Roquefort terrine.

middle class, democrats and everything else (although everyone noticed he didn't extend his hatred to telephones and the other mod cons of the day). Over the door he carved his life's motto: 'Once Upon a Time'.

Once installed, the Clewses rarely left the fairytale world they created. Henry designed the costumes, not only for himself and Marie but also for the maids and the Senegalese butler. They filled the château and garden with peacocks, flamingos and other exotic birds, and loved to stage dramatic, elaborate dinner parties that to the bewildered guests seemed to come straight out of a Hollywood movie. The most

Save room for the chocolate charlotte and truffles. *Closed Wed out of season.*
Le Boucanier, Port la Napoule, t 04 93 49 80 51 (*moderate*). For dinner, try the *soupe de poissons* or *plateau de fruits de mer*. *Closed Thurs in winter, and mid-Nov–Dec.*

Théoule-sur-Mer ✉ 06590
★★★★**Miramar Beach Hôtel**, 47 Av de Miramar, t 04 93 75 05 05, f 04 93 75 44 83, *reservation@mbhotel.com, www.mbhriviera. com* (*luxury–very expensive*). A luxurious, Provençal-style 'thalasso-energy' centre, spilling down in ochre-coloured balustraded terraces to the water's edge. The grounds include pools, private beaches, beauty treatments and a gastronomic restaurant, **L'Etoile des Mers** (*very expensive–expensive*), which, under chef Laurent Modret, has been garnering a substantial reputation; the many dishes to linger over include lamb with caramelized onions and apricots.
Le Jardin de la Mer, 54 Av de Lérins, t 04 93 49 96 95 (*expensive–moderate*). Fish tanks flash with shoals of exotic fish; some are stocked with langoustines and lobsters heading for the pot. Among the specialities are *crème brûlée* with chestnut *confit*.

Le Trayas ✉ 83700
★★**Le Relais des Calanques**, Corniche de l'Esterel, t 04 94 44 14 06, f 04 94 44 10 93 (*expensive*). Right on the sea, this hotel has 14 rooms, a pool, two tiny private beaches and a good fish restaurant (*moderate*) on a terrace over the red sea rocks. *Closed Oct–April; restaurant closed Tues.*
Auberge de Jeunesse, 9 Av de La Véronèse, t 04 93 75 40 23, *www.fuaj.org* (*moderate*). Superb, but, as usual with youth hostels, as if challenging the hardiness of youth, hard to

reach – 2km uphill from the station (last bus from the train station 7.30pm); has superb views, however. In summer, book (card required). *Closed Jan–mid-Feb.*

Anthéor ✉ 83700
★★**Les Flots Bleus**, on the N98, t 04 94 44 80 21, f 04 94 44 83 71, *www.hotel-cote-azur.com* (*inexpensive*). All rooms have grandiose views of the sea and the Esterel, though the trains pass close by and it is just off the main road. Good value, however, and the seafood served on the tree-shaded terrace (*moderate*) is fresh and copious. *Closed Nov–Mar.*

Agay ✉ 83700
★★★**Sol e Mar**, Plage Le Dramont, t 04 94 95 25 60, f 04 94 83 83 61, *hotelsolemar@club-internet.fr* (*expensive*). Right on the sea, with two saltwater pools and an excellent restaurant (*moderate*). *Closed mid-Oct–Mar.*
★★★**France Soleil**, Bd de la Plage, t 04 94 82 01 93, f 04 94 82 73 95 (*moderate*). In Agay itself, a reliable choice on the beach. *Closed Nov–Easter.*

Inland
★★★★**Auberge des Adrets**, along the N7, just beyond Mt Vinaigre, t 04 94 82 11 82, f 04 94 82 11 80, *www.auberge-adrets.com* (*very expensive*). Once a lonely inn (dating back to 1653) and notorious haunt of bandits like Gaspard de Besse, this has become one of the most romantic hideaways on the Côte. The dining room (*expensive*) has low beamed ceilings and a huge fire, and the bedrooms are the latest in *chi-chi chic*, with Christian Dior furnishings. *Closed Nov; restaurant closed Sun pm and Mon except July–Aug.*

lasting feature of all is Henry's personal mythology, devoted to something he called Humormystics, amply illustrated in stone throughout the castle, cloister capitals and gardens: weird monsters and grotesques, human figures and animals, many in egg and phallic shapes with cryptic inscriptions and most carved in stone out of his private quarry in the Esterel with the help of 12 stonecutters. Here, too, is Clews' own self-designed tomb and epitaph ('Grand Knight of La Mancha Supreme Master Humormystic Castelan of Once Upon a Time Chevalier de Marie'), completed by Marie, who survived until 1959 and made sure all was preserved intact by founding the charitable La Napoule Arts Foundation, where American and French artists and writers can work immersed in Clews' phantasmagoria.

Corniche de l'Esterel

Laid out by the French Touring Club way back in 1903, the Corniche de l'Esterel (N98) is dotted with panoramic belvederes overlooking the extraordinary red, blue and green seascapes below. The largest beaches of sand or shingle are served by snack wagons in the summer and, in between, with a bit of climbing, are rocky coves and nooks you can have all to yourself.

Heading south from La Napoule, **Théoule-sur-Mer**, which claims to be only ten minutes from Cannes' Croisette, has small beaches and an 18th-century seaside soap factory converted into a castle. This isn't bad compared to **La Galère** (the next town south on the same road), infected in the 1970s by a private housing estate which looks as if it were modelled on cancer cells. This is a suburb of fashionable **Miramar**, where the best thing to do is avoid the strings of stuffy private beaches and walk out along **Pointe de l'Esquillon** for the view of the sheer cliffs of Cap Roux plunging into the sea. The nearby slopes and jagged shore, pierced with inlets and secret coves, belong to the villas and hotels of **Le Trayas**.

Beyond Le Trayas, a road at **Pointe de l'Observatoire** ascends to the **Grotte de la Ste-Baume**, where St Honorat resided as a hermit when four-star views were free of charge. Meanwhile the corniche road itself twists and turns towards **Anthéor,** which has a good little beach, and the Esterel's biggest resort, **Agay**, a laid-back village set under porphyry cliffs, around a perfect horseshoe bay rimmed with sand and pebble beaches. For all that, a corner of it has sold its soul to the developers, who have constructed a 'model Provençal village': a brash, synthetic concrete lump which has all the charm and authenticity of a TV dinner. In 1944 the American 36th Division disembarked just to the west at the **Plage du Dramont**, where you can pick up the path to the Sémaphore du Dramont (about an hour's walk) for panoramas over the **Gulf of Fréjus** and the two porphyry sea rocks (called the 'Lion de la Mer' and the 'Lion de la Terre') at its entrance. The 'medieval' tower on the minuscule island now called the Ile d'Or was in fact built during the Belle Epoque by an eccentric doctor, who liked to invite celebrities to his 'Kingdom of the Black Isle' and patronize them from his throne. The island and the mad doctor became the inspiration for Hergé's book *Tintin and the Black Isle*. The area also seems to have made an impression in Neolithic times: there's a menhir and other, rather mysterious engraved stones on the ancient road from Dramont to Agay.

The Esterel: Inland Routes

From Cannes, the N7 follows the path of the Roman Via Aurelia, passing through the bulk of the Esterel's surviving cork forest. This is ravishing scenery, ravished by the world that wants to see it. It is possible to see it underneath all its tourists, at least at dawn, in sunny near-silence, when only a few sleepy campers are stirring. The road winds past the old Auberge des Adrets, a 17th-century inn and notorious haunt of bandits like Gaspard de Besse, now the plushest of four-star hideouts (*see* 'Where to Stay', p.201). The high point of the trip, both literally and figuratively, is **Mont Vinaigre**, rising to 1,968ft; from the road a path leads to its summit (about 30 minutes) and a fantastic viewing platform in an old watchtower. Oleander lines the tumbling gorge of the **Ravin de Perthus** further inland, and you can wiggle left off the N7 from Mandelieu at Pont St-Jean and climb up to the Col de la Cadière and the Col Notre-Dame for more vertiginous views over the red rocks and out to sea. Other hairpinning roads begin in Agay and lead to within walking distance of the Esterel's most dramatic features: the hellish **Ravin du Mal-Infernet**, and a scattering of panoramic peaks – the **Pic de l'Ours** and **Pic du Cap Roux** have afforded vision-inspiring views since the 6th century, when the area was littered with hermits. From here the Esterel is at her most stunning, and the Coast of Illusion a flaming vision of colour and light.

St-Raphaël and Fréjus

Between the Esterel and the Massif des Maures, in the fertile little plain of the Argens river, St-Raphaël and Fréjus are the big noises on the coast between Cannes and Hyères. After the fireworks of the Esterel, St-Raphaël has – guess what? – more beaches, holiday flats and yachts, and is swollen so big as to merge with its venerable neighbour Fréjus (Forum Julii), a market town and naval port on the Via Aurelia founded by Julius Caesar himself to rival Greek Marseille. Octavian made it his chief arsenal, to build the ships that licked Cleopatra and Mark Antony at Actium. Even today, Fréjus is a garrison town, with France's largest naval air base.

St-Raphaël

Once the fiefdom of the ambitious François Léotard, leader of the centre-right UDF party, and now run like a tight ship by Mayor Georges Ginesta, St-Raphaël has money, if not much heart. Its once glittering turn-of-the-20th-century follies and medieval centre were bombed to smithereens in the war, sparing only the Victorian-Byzantine church of **Notre-Dame-de-Lépante** in Bd Felix-Martin (with a popular altar to St Antoine, patron saint of lost objects, surrounded with grateful plaques for services rendered) and the **Eglise des Templiers** or St-Pierre (1150), with its Templar watch-tower, in Rue des Templiers (just north of the station). This is the third church to occupy the site, re-using the same old Roman stones – one in the choir vault is carved with something you won't often see in church: a flying phallus, an ancient charm for averting evil (Pompeii has lots of them). In the 17th century, the chapel was fortified and rebuilt along with the crenellated seigneurial mansion next door. If the church is

Getting There and Around

By Train

St-Raphaël is the terminus of the Métrazur trains that run along the coast to Menton. Other trains between Nice and Marseille call at both St-Raphaël and Fréjus stations, making it easy to hop between the two towns; St-Raphaël also has direct connections to Aix, Avignon, Nîmes, Montpellier and Carcassonne, and it's 4hrs 30mins on the TGV from Paris.

By Bus

Both towns have buses for Nice airport and Marseille (Cars Phocéens, t 04 91 50 57 68, and Beltrane, t 04 94 95 95 16), pricier ones for St-Tropez and Toulon (SODETRAV, t 04 94 95 24 82), and buses inland for Bagnols, Fayence and Les Adrets (Gagnard, t 04 94 95 24 78).

There is an information point at the bus station in St-Raphaël, but it is better to get timetables from the tourist information office opposite the train station.

By Boat

Les Bateaux de St-Raphaël, t 04 94 95 17 46, www.tmr-saintraphael.com. Depart regularly from the Vieux Port, Centre Ville, to St-Tropez and Port Grimaud, and make day excursions to the Iles de Lérins and Ile de Port Cros (April–Oct), as well as jaunts around the Golfe de Fréjus and its *calanques* (creeks); be sure to reserve in July–Aug.

Taxis

Call t 04 94 83 24 24.

Bike Hire

Cycles Thierry, St-Raphaël, t 04 94 95 48 46. Also does watersport rentals.
A Tout Cycles, St-Raphaël, t 04 94 95 56 91.
Action 2 Roues, Fréjus, t 04 94 44 48 34.
Cycles Patrick Béraud, Fréjus, t 04 94 51 20 20.
Holiday Bikes, Fréjus, t 04 94 52 30 65.

Tourist Information

St-Raphaël: Rue Waldeck Rousseau (opposite the train station), t 04 94 19 52 52, f 04 94 83 85 40, www.saint-raphael.com. Open July–Aug daily 9–7; rest of year Mon–Sat 9–12.30 and 2–6.30. There is also a hotel reservation service across the road at the station: t 04 94 19 10 60, f 04 94 19 10 67, reservation@saint-raphael.com.

Fréjus: 325 Rue Jean Jaurès, t 04 94 51 83 83, f 04 94 51 00 26, www.ville-frejus.fr. Open summer Mon–Sat 10–12.30 and 2.30–6.30, Sun and public hols during school hols 10–12 and 3–6, winter Mon–Sat 9–12, 2–6, Sun and public hols during school hols 10–12 and 3–6.

Fréjus-Plage: Bd de la Libération, t 04 94 51 48 42. Open June–Sept Mon–Sat 10–12.30 and 3–6.30; Sun and hols 10–12 and and 3–6.

Market Days

St-Raphaël: daily, general fruit, vegetable and other fresh local produce market in Place

closed, pick up the key at the adjacent **Musée de Préhistoire et d'Archéologie Sous-marine** (t 04 94 19 25 75; open June–Sept Tues–Sat 10–12 and 3–6.30; Oct–May Tues–Sat 10–12 and 2–5.30; adm). For centuries there were rumours of a sunken city off St-Raphaël, apparently confirmed by the bricks that divers kept bringing to shore. Jacques Cousteau went down to see and found, not Atlantis, but a Roman shipwreck full of building materials. Some are displayed here, along with a fine collection of amphorae. There is also a reconstruction of a Roman galley and a room devoted to the strange menhirs and dolmens of the eastern Var region. This is much the prettiest part of town, with a little maze of winding streets hemmed in by peeling houses, and a great place to pick up some very colloquial French at the rowdy food market.

The seafront is popular with ageing *flâneurs* (loafers) and yachting types strolling along the palm- and plane-tree-edged boulevard in the footsteps of Alexandre

Victor Hugo and Place de la République; daily, fish market in the Vieux Port; Tues, flea market in the Place Coullet.

Fréjus: Wed and Sat am, fresh local produce market in front of the city hall; Sat am, and 2nd Sun in June and Sept, flea market.

Internet Access

Cyberbureau, 123 Rue Waldeck Rousseau, St-Raphaël, t 04 94 95 29 36. *Closed Sat.*

Where to Stay and Eat

St-Raphaël ✉ 83700

The town of the archangel is rich in pricey campsites and grotesque holiday villages, but a few hotels stand out. The best choices are outside the centre.

***Golf de Valescure, Av Paul L'Hermite, t 04 94 52 85 00, f 04 94 82 41 88, *www. valescure.com* (*expensive*). This has been in the same family for five generations, with tennis and a pool when you're not on the links (*golf packages*).

***Le San Pedro, Av du Colonel Brooke, t 04 94 19 90 20, f 04 94 19 90 21, *www. hotel-sanpedro.com* (*expensive*). Good option in Valescure, which was the old artists' quarter before the First World War. *Restaurant* (*expensive*) *closed Tues, plus Wed lunch in winter.*

**Les Pyramides, 77 Av P. Doumer, t 04 98 11 10 10, f 04 98 11 10 20, *www.saint.raphael. com/pyramides* (*inexpensive*). This has a little garden. *Closed mid-Nov–mid-Mar.*

Centre International Le Manoir, Chemin de l'Escale, near the Boulouris station, t 04 94 95 20 58, f 04 94 83 85 06, *www.cei-manoir.com* (*inexpensive*). A youth hostel that is more like a holiday village; by the beach (*ages 18–35 only*). *Closed mid-Nov–mid-Mar.*

L'Arbousier, 6 Av de Valescure, t 04 94 95 25 00 (*expensive*). Combines charm and excellent, aromatic gourmet food for half the price you'd pay elsewhere. *Closed Sun eve, Mon and Wed eve out of season.*

Pastorel, 54 Rue de la Liberté, t 04 94 95 02 36 (*moderate*). Try the Friday special €26 *aïoli* menu at Pastorel, an excellent address since 1922, with a pleasant, no-nonsense proprietress and an attractive garden terrace. Madame Pastorel's grandson heads the team in the kitchens. *Closed end of Dec–end of Jan, plus Sun eve, Mon and Tues; closed all lunchtimes and Mon in July–Aug.*

Bleu Marine, Port Santa Lucia, t 04 94 95 31 31 (*moderate*). An excellent lunchtime menu, including wine, with dishes such as a light cod fillet with shellfish.

Les Terrasses de L'Orangerie, Promenade René Coty, t 04 94 83 10 50 (*moderate*). A Belle Epoque brasserie with sea views. *Closed Tues eve, Sun eve and Wed; also closed Jan.*

La Sarriette, 45 Rue de la République, t 04 94 19 28 13 (*moderate*). The house speciality is a regal *pied de cochon*, plus plenty of excellent alternatives at this humble, friendly little place. *Closed Sun eve and Mon.*

L'Aristocloche, 15 Bd St-Sébastien, t 04 94 95 28 36 (*moderate–cheap*). Friendly and

Dumas, Hector Berlioz and F. Scott Fitzgerald (who wrote *Tender is the Night* here). There are brief echoes of the golden days of the Belle Epoque in the handful of regal villas which escaped the bombs, but nowadays St-Raph, as everyone calls it, has hung up its smoking jacket and settled into comfortable middle age, with nondescript apartment buildings overlooking carefully kept lawns and a seafront which looks like a theme park for the over 50s. There is a new **cultural centre**, however (*Place Gabriel Péri, t 04 98 11 89 00; open Tues–Sat 8.30–7*), which hosts exhibitions and concerts.

At the eastern edge of town, heading up to the outlying *commune* of Boulouris, is the monstrous new marina, **Port Santa Lucia**, with a handful of neon-lit bars and restaurants. Behind it, the 8km **Sentier du Littoral** starts to wind its way around the coast, over rough steps cut into the red rock and past tiny pockmarked coves.

old-fashioned; there is home-made bread to go with the *estouffade provençale de bœuf* and *nougat glacé à la lavande*. Local products are for sale outside the restaurant on market days. *Closed Sun and Mon.*

Piccola Sicilia, 108 Rue de la Garonne, t 04 94 83 11 32 (*cheap*). Enormous platefuls of Sicilian home cooking. Make time for a much needed siesta afterwards. *Closed Mon eve in summer; all day Mon in winter.*

Fréjus ✉ 83600

★★★**L'Aréna**, 139 Rue du Gal. de Gaulle, t 04 94 17 09 40, f 04 94 52 01 52, *www.arena-hotel.com* (*expensive*). Colourful, air-conditioned rooms, a pool and good food (*expensive*) in old Fréjus. *Closed mid-Dec–mid-Jan; restaurant closed Mon eve and Sun eve, and Nov.*

Bellevue, by the cathedral in Place Paul Vernet, t 04 94 17 21 58, f 04 94 51 42 46 (*inexpensive*). The best of the cheapies, with 12 rooms.

Auberge de Jeunesse, t 04 94 53 18 75, f 04 94 53 25 86, *www.fuaj.org* (*inexpensive*). This is 2km from Fréjus' historic centre, in a large park east on the N7; take the shuttle bus from the station at St-Raphaël (platform 7). It also has a small campsite. *Closed mid-Nov–Feb.*

Le Mérou Ardent, 157 Bd de la Libération, t 04 94 17 30 58 (*moderate*). A terrace overlooking the beach, a delicious monkfish with prawns, and a rich *fondant au chocolat*. *Closed Wed eve and Thurs, but check.*

Le Bateau, 1-2 Quai Octave, t 04 94 17 00 00 (*moderate*). A large and modern brasserie, but the service is impeccable and the food remarkably good – try the *choucroute royale* or the salmon.

Les Potiers, 135 Rue des Potiers, t 04 94 51 33 74 (*moderate*). Sparky *nouvelle cuisine* restaurant on a quiet back street in the old town. *Closed Tues, Wed lunch, and 3 wks Dec.*

Le Cadet Rousselle, 25 Place Agricola, t 04 94 53 36 92 (*cheap*). Eat a filling meal for less money at this popular *crêperie/saladerie*, tucked inside the Place Agricola near the cinema. *Closed mid-Dec–mid-Jan, Mon, and Thurs lunch.*

Entertainment and Nightlife

St-Raphaël

Casino de St-Raphaël, t 04 98 111 777. Gambling and dancing.

Le Seven, 171 Quai Albert Ier, t 04 94 83 93 07. *Closed Mon.*

Coco-Club, Port Santa Lucia, t 04 94 95 95 56. Live music and piano bar.

Le Lido, t 08 36 68 69 28. Cinema with an annual arts festival in September.

Loch Ness, Av de Valescure, t 04 94 95 99 49. Despite the name, a lively Irish pub.

Fréjus-Plage

Maison de la Bière, 461 Bd de la Libération, Fréjus-Plage, t 04 94 51 21 86. Over one hundred beers.

Fréjus

The Roman Town

Founded in 49 BC, Forum Julii (Julius' Market) was the first Roman town of Gaul, but not the most successful; the site was malarial and hard to defend, and eventually the Argens river silted up, creating the vast sandy beach of **Fréjus-Plage** but leaving the Roman harbour, once famous for its size, high and dry a mile from the sea. The port, now smelling rather pungent even for hardy 18th-century noses, was filled in in 1774. A path tracing the ruined quay begins at **Butte St-Antoine**, south of central Fréjus, but it's hard to picture 100 Roman galleys anchored in the weeds. Its one monument, the Lanterne d'Auguste, isn't even Roman, but a medieval harbourmaster's lodge built on a Roman base. Other fragments of Forum Julii are a long hike across the modern town – Fréjus is one place where those ubiquitous tourist trains come in handy.

The best preserved is the ungainly greenish **Amphithéâtre Romain**, Rue Henri Vadon (*open Nov–Mar Mon–Fri 10–12 and 1–5.30, Sat 9.30–12.30 and 1.30–5.30, Sun 8–5; April–Oct Mon–Sat 10–1 and 2.30–6.30, Sun 8–7*), flat on its back like a beached whale with the rib arches of its vomitoria exposed to the sky. Arches from a 40km aqueduct still leapfrog by the road to Cannes. North, on Av du Théâtre Romain, the vaults of the **Théâtre Romain** (*open as amphithéâtre; adm, free Sun*) survive, although the seating has had to be replaced (the coastal road once ran right through its middle). Rock concerts and bullfights now fill the bill.

La Cité Episcopale: the Oldest Baptistry in France

On a map marked with the walls that once contained Forum Julii, modern Fréjus looks like the last lamb-chop on a platter. The Saracens had much of the rest of it in the 10th century, coming back seven times to pillage and destroy the bits they missed. When the coast was clear in the 12th century, the Fréjussiens rebuilt their Cathédrale St-Léonce in Place Formigé, and in the 16th century gave it a superb pair of Renaissance doors carved with sacred scenes, a violent Saracen massacre and portraits of aristocratic ladies and gents, including King François Ier. Inside, over the sacristy door, there's a *Retable de Ste-Marguerite* (*c.* 1450) by Jacques Durandi, of the School of Nice. St Marguerite of Antioch is the patron saint of women in childbirth, and her crown of pearls symbolizes her purity and humility.

The cathedral was the centre of a mini **Cité Episcopale,** incorporating a crenellated defence tower, a chapterhouse and a bishop's palace (*t 04 94 51 26 30, www.monum. fr; open mid-May–mid-Aug daily 9–6.30; mid-Aug–mid-May Tues–Sun 9–12 and 2–5; adm*), all built with the characteristic warm red stone of the Esterel mountain range. The tour includes the baptistry, the one bit of Fréjus the Saracens missed: late 4th century, octagonal (like all early baptistries it was modelled after the original, built in the 320s by Constantine in Rome) and defined by eight black granite columns with white capitals lifted from the Roman forum. Only adults were baptized in the early days. The pagans would enter the narrow door and have their feet washed at the terracotta basin; the bishop would then baptize them in the pool in the centre, and as new Christians they would exit through the larger door to attend Mass. Fairest of all is the 12th-century **cloister**, with slim marble columns and a 14th-century ceiling coffered into 1,200 little vignettes, of which a third still have curious paintings that comprise a whole catalogue of monkish fancies: grotesques, mermaids, animals, portraits and debaucheries. Upstairs, the **Archaeology Museum** (*t 04 94 52 15 78; open Nov–Mar Mon–Sat 10–12 and 1.30–5.30; April–Oct Mon–Sat 10–1 and 2.30–6.30*) has a collection of finds from Forum Julii, among them a perfectly preserved mosaic, a fine head of Jupiter and a copy of the two-faced bust of Hermes discovered in 1970.

Just off Place Formigé, at 53 Rue Sieyès, are two **Atlantes**, all that remains of the house of the Abbé Sieyès (1748–1836), pamphleteer of the Revolution, deputy at the Convention and mastermind of the 18th Brumaire coup that brought Napoleon to power. Later exiled as a regicide, the abbot returned to Paris in 1830, and when asked to sum up his career in politics he gave the famous laconic reply: 'I survived.'

Around Fréjus

Just outside Fréjus stand a scattering of remarkable monuments recalling the rotten days of the First World War, when states supplemented their manpower by importing men from the colonies to fight wars that weren't theirs. In 1917 the Vietnamese built the colourful **Pagode Hong Hien** as a memorial to their 5,000 dead, 2km from the centre on the N7 (*t 04 94 53 25 29; open daily 9–12 and 2–7; adm*), surrounded by protective dragons and white elephants. Almost next door, an imposing necropolis dedicated to the soldiers of the Indonesian wars is slotted into the flanks of the hill, and contains the remains of more than 24,000 soldiers and civilians involved in the terrible collapse of France's former colonial empire.

The Sudanese sharpshooters at the local marine base built the **Mosquée Missiri** (a concrete reproduction of the Missiri Mosque at Djenne, Mali) on Rte de Bagnols-en-Forêt, 5km from Fréjus by way of the N7 and D4 towards Fayence, which, although on a corner of military land, has been sadly abandoned to graffiti. Further along the D4, the **Musée des Troupes de Marine** (*t 04 94 40 81 75; open mid-June–mid-Sept Sun, Mon and Wed–Fri 10–12 and 3–7; winter 2–5; closed Tues and Sat*) covers the history of the marines from 1622 to the present. Another mile further on, at Le Capitou, you can drive and walk through the **Parc Zoologique** (*t 04 98 11 37 37; open June–Aug daily 10–6; Mar–May and Sept–Oct 10–5; Nov–Feb 10.30–4.30*), where parrots and yaks don't look too out of place under the parasol pines.

Just off the N7, in the **Tour de la Mare** district of Fréjus, is Notre-Dame de Jérusalem, the **Chapelle Cocteau** (*Av Nicolaï, La Tour de la Mare, t 04 94 53 27 06; open April–Oct Mon–Fri 2.30–6.30, Sat 10–1 and 2–6.30; Nov–Mar Mon–Fri 1.30–5.30, Sat 9.30–12.30 and 1.30–5.30; adm*), an octagonal chapel of soft grey stone surrounded by cypress, pine and olive trees and grazing donkeys, originally designed by Jean Cocteau in the 1960s. The chapel was to form part of a larger project to build an artists' residence, but, only months after the cornerstone was laid, Cocteau died, and the bold scope of the original idea shrank when faced with municipal apathy and lack of funds. Finally, in 1988, the city contacted Cocteau's partner and heir, Edouard Dermit, also an artist; after examining Cocteau's original plans and models, he finally painted the chapel himself. Inside is an anarchic flurry of colour and form; limbs radiate from the glass window in the dome (symbolizing the *Resurrection of the Dead*) and colours bounce off the walls from the brilliant stained-glass windows. The frescoes are gentler pastel affairs: among the guests at the *Last Supper* are Cocteau himself, his close friend Francine Weismuller and the handsome face of Cocteau's friend and lover Jean Marais, who appears elsewhere as a blue-winged angel. Scattered throughout the chapel is the sturdy form of the cross of Jerusalem, which also tops the terracotta roof tiles; Cocteau dedicated the chapel to the Jerusalem Order of the Knights of the Holy Sepulchre, who supposedly guarded Christ's tomb. A millstone from an old olive mill, representing the great stone which was rolled away from the tomb, does service as an altar, with a cross and candlesticks also in the form of the Jerusalem Cross. Services are held here on the weekend closest to 15 September, when the holiday of the Tour de la Mare is celebrated.

Ten kilometres up the Argens river from St-Aygulf (Fréjus' resort suburb to the west), the picturesque 16th-century village of **Roquebrune-sur-Argens** offers a break from coastal craziness with a wine and orchid centre that boasts the largest mulberry tree in France. Then there's a comforting maze of higgledy-piggledy streets (markets take place on Tuesdays at the Place Ollier and on Fridays at the Place Alfred Perrin), and the curious 16th-century church of Sts Peter and Paul, which originally had a Gothic twist but was given an awkward facelift in the 18th century. More prehistoric and Roman artefacts are at the **Musée du Patrimoine Roquebrunois** in the Chapelle St-Jacques (*Rue de l'Hospice, t 04 94 45 34 28; open June–Sept Tues–Sat 10–12 and 2–6; Oct–May Thurs and Sat 10–12 and 2–6; adm*). Along the road to Le Muy, the Rochers de Roquebrune form a peculiar red baby massif that toddled away from the Esterel.

The Massif des Maures

Between Fréjus and Hyères, the coast bulges out and up again to form the steep rolling hills and arcadian natural amphitheatres of the ancient Massif des Maures. Although it lacks the high drama of the Esterel, this mountain range (2,300ft at its highest point) is just as much a geological oddball, its granite, gneiss and schist completely unrelated to the limestone that dominates the rest of Provence. The name Maures is derived from *maouro*, Provençal for black, describing its dark, deep forests of umbrella and Aleppo pines, chestnuts and cork. For centuries the latter two trees provided the main source of income of the few inland villages.

Until the 19th century this was the most dangerous coast in France. The Saracens made it their chief stronghold in the area in 846, building forts (*fraxinets*) on each hill

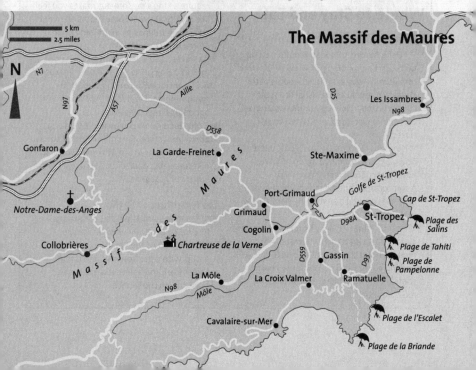

to watch for ships to plunder, and to defend themselves from the Franks. They were finally forced out in the campaign of 972, led by William of Provence, who was greatly assisted by a knight from Genoa named Grimaldi, the first of that family to make waves. But although the pirates had to abandon their *fraxinets*, they hardly abandoned the coast, and maintained a reign of terror that continued until 1830, when the French captured Algiers. A hundred years later, the fashion for seaside bathing spread west from the Riviera, giving every crowded beach a holiday town to call its own.

Ste-Maxime and Port Grimaud

In the seaside conurbation spread between Fréjus and St-Tropez, the only place that may tempt a detour is Ste-Maxime, a modern resort town with a shady, older nucleus by the port and a beach of golden sand facing St-Tropez. It willingly takes the overflow of fashionable and bankable holidaymakers from the latter, and is an attractive proposition as it's easy to commute by frequent boat to the capital of see-and-be-seen (St-Tropez may not look far away, but it's a 2hr traffic jam in high season).

Tourist Information

Ste-Maxime: 1 Promenade Simon Lorière , **t** 04 94 55 75 55, **f** 04 94 55 75 56. *Open Sept Mon–Sat 9–12 and 2–7; Oct–Mar Mon–Sat 9–12 and 2–6; April–May Mon–Sat 9–12.30, 2–6.30; June Mon–Sat 9–12.30 and 2–7, Sun 10–12 and 4–7; July–Aug Mon–Sat 9–8, Sun 10–12 and 4–7.*

Where to Stay and Eat

Ste-Maxime ✉ 83120

★★★★**Belle Aurore**, 5 Bd Jean Moulin, **t** 04 94 96 02 45, **f** 04 94 96 63 87, *www.belleaurore. com* (*luxury–very expensive*). Rooms with character as well as the usual four-star comforts and a fine restaurant (*expensive*). *Closed mid-Oct–April; restaurant closed Wed.*

★★★**Hôtel Jas Neuf**, 112 Av du Débarquement **t** 04 94 55 07 30, **f** 04 94 49 09 71, *www. hotel-jasneuf.com* (*very expensive*). A comfortable huddle of Provençal-style buildings around a swimming pool. *Closed mid-Oct–mid-Mar.*

★★★**Le Petit Prince**, 11 Av St-Exupéry, **t** 04 94 96 44 47, **f** 04 94 49 03 38 (*moderate*). A small, modern hotel 50m from the beach, with a parking garage and no-nonsense charm; some rooms have been refurbished and most have balconies.

★★★**Domaine du Calidianus**, Bd Jean Moulin, **t** 04 94 96 23 21, **f** 04 94 49 12 10 (*expensive*). Glam and newly refurbished hotel, with all mod cons and a decent restaurant (*moderate*). *Closed Jan and Feb; restaurant closed mid-Sept–mid-June.*

★★**Mas des Brugassières**, Pont-de-la-Tour, **t** 04 94 55 50 55, **f** 04 94 55 50 51, *www. mas-des-brugassieres.com* (*moderate*). A comfortable farmhouse, which doesn't require a king's ransom but makes you feel like royalty anyway. Some rooms open out onto the gardens and swimming pool. *Closed mid-Oct–mid-Mar.*

★★**Le Revest**, 48 Bd Jean Jaurès, **t** 04 94 96 19 60, **f** 04 94 96 32 19 (*moderate–inexpensive*). Central, with parking, a rooftop swimming pool and food (*half-board optional*). *Closed Nov–Mar.*

Le Lotus Bleu, 30 Av Gal Leclerc, **t** 04 94 49 28 00 (*moderate*). One of the best of the 80-odd restaurants in Ste-Maxime. *Closed lunch mid-June– mid-Sept. Closed Wed and Thurs lunch out of season.*

Les Issambres ✉ 83380

★★★★**La Villa Saint Elme**, **t** 04 94 49 52 52, **f** 04 94 49 63 18, *www.saintelme.com* (*luxury*). Part of the Small Luxury Hotel group, with a gastronomic restaurant (*expensive*), and a new, less expensive brasserie on the terrace.

If you do stay, there's the **Musée des Traditions** (*t 04 94 96 70 30; open Wed–Sun 10–12 and 3–6 (July–Aug till 7), Mon 3–6; closed Sat and Tues; adm*), opposite the port in the 16th-century square tower (Tour Carrée des Dames), built by the monks of the Iles de Lérins, who also named the town after one of their alumni. The remarkable **Musée du Phonographe et de la Musique Mécanique** is in the unlikely setting of the wooded Parc de St-Donat, 10km north towards Le Muy on the D25 (*t 04 94 96 50 52; open Easter–Sept 10–12 and 3–6; closed Mon and Tues; adm*). About half of the music boxes, barrel organs, automata and player pianos still work, as well as some of the rare prizes: one of Edison's original phonographs of 1878, an accordion-like 'Melophone' of 1780, a 1903 dictaphone and an audiovisual '*pathégraphe*' to teach foreign languages, built in 1913. For Côte d'Azur-style R and R, the beaches to the west of town are the nicest: **La Nartelle** is the most popular. The **Plage des Eléphants** appears in the children's book *Voyage de Babar*, written by Jean de Brunhoff (1899–1937), who lived in Ste-Maxime.

From Ste-Maxime, the road passes through **Port Grimaud**, a marina designed in 1968 by Alsatian architect and entrepreneur François Spoerry, inspired by the lagoon complexes around St Petersburg, Florida, where wealthy homeowners, like Venetians, can park their boats by the front door. The tourist office now likes to call it 'Venise Provençale'. The traditionally styled, colourful houses themselves are a preview of the real McCoys in St-Tropez; the pseudo-Romanesque fortified church of **St-François**, sitting on its own islet, has aggressive and annoying stained-glass windows designed by the late Hungarian Op artist Victor Vasarely (1908–97).

St-Tropez

It made the headlines in France when St-Tropez's mayor forced the discos to close at 2am and declared the beaches off limits to dogs, inciting the fury of 'Most Famous Resident' Brigitte Bardot, that crusading Joan of Arc of animal rights who married a National Front politician and in a recent autobiography referred to her son as a 'tumour'. But then again, BB has always been a bit ahead of the rest of us, ever since she came down here to star in Roger Vadim's *Et Dieu...créa la femme* in 1956 and incidentally made this lovely fishing village into the national showcase of free-spirited fun, sun and sex, all boxed in the glitter litter of fashion and wealth. Everyone who wants to be associated with these desirable things tries to squeeze into St-Tropez in the summer, booking one of the few hotel rooms nearly a year in advance, or just coming down for the day for a gawk at the yachts.

Significantly, BB has moved on, miffed at the *commune*'s tolerance for immigrants and its lack of sufficient enthusiasm for animal rights. No one seems to miss her much; in fact, the locals wish other folks would follow suit. St-Tropez, it appears, is a victim of its own success. The French call it 'St-Trop', pronouncing the 'p', so it's not 'St-Too Much' – but in the summer it really is too much: too many people (100,000 on an average day) clogging the roads, lanes and beaches; too much rubbish; too many artists hawking paintings around the port; too many crowded cafés and restaurants

200 metres
200 yards

N

Tour du Portalet
R. SAINT ESPRIT
RUE PORTALET
QUAI F. MISTRAL
MOLE JEAN REVEILLE
QUAI D'ESTIENNE D'ORVES
PLACE GAREZZIO
Tour Suffren
RUE DE CEPOUN SANMARTIN
RUE SIBILLE
QUAI JEAN JAURES
Vieux Port
PLACE AUX HERBES
Nouveau Port
QUAI DE L'EPI
QUAI H. BOUCHARD
QUAI SUFFREN
PAS DU PORT
Statue de Bailli de Suffren
Musée de L'Annonciade
QUAI G. PERI
PLACE GRAMMONT
RUE GEORGES CLEMENCEAU
RUE DE L'ANNONCIADE
Maison des Papillons
AV. DU 11 NOVEMBRE 1918
RUE HENRI SEILLON
RUE ALLARD
RUE DES CHARRONS
RUE ETIENNE BERNY
TRAV. DE MERMOT
RUE DE LA POSTE
RUE DR. BOUTIN
RUE GRENOUILLERE
RUE DES TISSERANDS
AV. DU 8 MAI 1945
RUE DE MARBRIER
TRAV. DE LA GENDARMERIE
RUE DE LA CROIX DE FER
RUE J. AICARD
RUE JOSEPH QUARANTA
PLACE CROIX DE FER
RUE DE FER
TRAV. TONNELIER
SQUARE J. MOULIN
PLACE BLANQUI
BD LOUIS BLANC
AV DU GENERAL DE GAULLE
AV. GENERAL LECLERC
AV. PAUL ROUSSEL

charging unholy prices. Recently, the local newspaper, *Le Bavar*, began a campaign to limit access into the town, erecting a barrier and limiting entry by car only to people who are staying at least one night. Other proposals are to freeze the building of new rental accommodation, to decrease the number of places at campsites and to triple the size of the local police to enforce local will. The next elections promise to bring all this to a head, although, curiously enough, the rest of the Var seems to have little sympathy for the Tropéziens' plight.

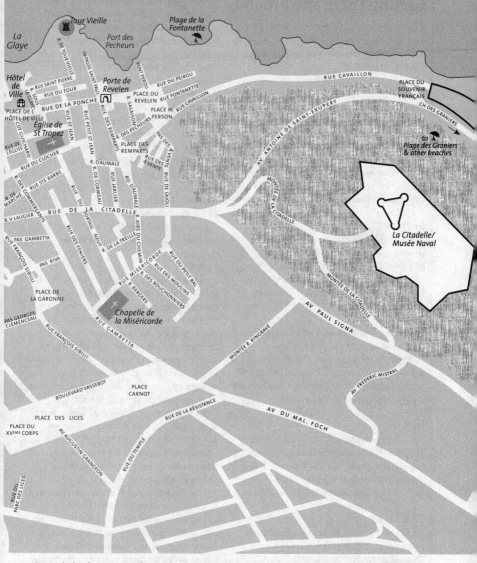

Outside high season, it's much easier to understand what started all the commotion in the first place – St-Tropez is a dishy little place, full of colour and character. Only beware that in winter it's the only town on the Côte d'Azur that faces north, and can be extremely blustery.

History: Proto-National-Front Ligurians and Celebrity Cosmetics

One of the strangest but most prophetic legends along the coast has it that St-Tropez's first incarnation, the Greek colony Athenopolis, was founded by Praxiteles'

Getting There and Around

On its peninsula, St-Tropez is a dead end; the one road leading into it (D98A), and the lanes leading off to the beaches are packed solid from June to August.

By Air

Nice airport is about 90km away; Toulon–Hyères airport is about 50km. If you planned to flit in on your chopper, think again: St-Tropez's airport has closed. However, this has caused enough consternation in the right places for a new project: a summer-only floating heliport, 4km offshore, with a fleet of speedboats to race passengers to the shore.

By Train

There is no train station in St-Tropez. The nearest TGV stop is at Les Arcs (t 04 94 99 60 00), from where shuttle buses take travellers into St-Tropez twice a day. Call SODETRAV on t 04 94 97 88 51 for timetable information.

By Bus

Besides the St-Raphaël–Hyères coastal bus (t 04 94 97 88 51, or the gare routière in St-Tropez, t 04 94 54 62 36), there's a bus in season linking Toulon to St-Tropez (t 04 94 18 93 40). Note that there's no place to leave your luggage if you want to stop en route.

By Boat

You may be better off catching a boat from St-Raphaël (gare maritime, t 04 94 95 17 46) or Ste-Maxime (MMG t 04 94 96 51 00). There are boat-taxis which also offer tours of the Gulf: call Taxi Bateau Vasse, t 04 94 54 40 61.

Other Transport

The ghastly traffic makes bike and moped hire an attractive alternative: try M.A.S, 3 Rue Quaranta, near St-Tropez's Place Carnot, t 04 94 97 00 60 (closed mid-Oct–Mar).

Tourist Information

St-Tropez: Maison du Tourisme du Golfe de St-Tropez/Pays des Maures, t 04 94 55 22 00, f 04 94 55 22 01, www.golfe-infos.com, at the N98/D559 junction just before the traffic gridlock, is a tourist's godsend. With fountains and sculptured pools, this is the Var tourist board's pièce de résistance. The helpful staff will call ahead to St-Tropez to book hotels, advise on restaurants and book excursions (both coastal and inland) and wine tours. If you accidentally whizz past, head into St-Tropez and the office at Quai Jean Jaurès, t 04 94 97 45 21, f 04 94 97 82 66. Open summer Mon–Fri 9–7.30, Sat 9.30–6.30, Sun 10–6; spring and autumn Mon–Fri 9–7, Sat 9.30–6; winter Mon–Fri 9–6.30, Sat 9.30–5.30.

Market Days

St-Tropez: Tues and Sun am, Place des Lices, , general market; mornings except Mon in winter, Place aux Herbes, fish market.

Festivals

Not to be missed if you're anywhere in the vicinity, the **Bravade des Espagnols** (15 June) sees St-Tropez's finest lads and lasses in 18th-century uniforms and Provençal costumes for a morning procession of the relics of St Torpes. At every square the band stops playing as the 'soldiers' fire an earsplitting fusillade from their blunderbusses straight into the stone pavement, while clouds of acrid smoke choke bystanders.

St Torpes himself is honoured with an even more important two-day shooting-spree bravade in the middle of May.

Besides the bravades, the most exciting annual event in St-Tropez is **Les Voiles de St-Tropez**, the last French yacht race, 'pour fêter la fin de la saison et de l'été' (first week of October). The oldest and most beautiful yachts in the world take on the autumn billows. There are two crowds: them and us (sailors and lubbers). Lubbers can follow the course by sea in special boats, or by helicopter.

Local Wine

For wine, there are several domaines which are open to the public for tours and tastings: **Cave de Saint-Tropez**, Av Paul Roussel, t 04 94 97 01 60.

Château Minuty Maton-Farnet, Route de Ramatuelle-Gassin, t 04 94 56 12 09, *www.nova.fr/minuty*. Offers tastings and tours of the *caves*. *Open summer Mon–Fri 9–12.30 and 2–6.30, Sat and Sun 10–12 and 3–6.30; closed weekends in winter*.

Domaine du Bourrian: 2496 Chemin du Gourrian-Gassin, t 04 94 56 16 28. A big operation, with Côtes de Provence and Pays de Maures wines. *Closed Sun in winter*.

Maîtres Vignerons de Saint-Tropez: Carrefour de la Foux-Gassin, t 04 94 56 32 04. A shop with a varied selection of what is available in the Maures; it also sells regional produce.

Shopping

Although many of the once trendsetting boutiques are now owned by design chains, a few exclusive shops remain for die-hard fans.

Autour des Oliviers, 2 Place des Oliviers. Provençal specialities, especially olive oil.

Galeries Tropéziennes, 55 Rue Gambetta. For fabrics, espadrilles, garden furniture and everything else.

Gas Bijoux, Rue Garonne. Specializing in costume jewellery made of coral and turquoise.

La Pause Douceur, 11 Rue Allard. De luxe chocs.

Rondini, 16 Rue G. Clemenceau. For the famous *sandales tropéziennes*, invented in 1927 on the gladiator model. If they don't have your size they may be able to make them.

Rues Allard and Sibilli: All the top-notch designers, from Lacroix and Versace to Donna Karan and Calvin Klein.

Sugar: Rue Victor Laugier. Upmarket cotton tops, shorts and sandals.

Where to Stay

St-Tropez ✉ 83990

If you haven't already booked a hotel long before, forget about arriving in St-Tropez on the off chance between July and September.

There are acres of campsites in the area, although in the summer they are about as relaxing as refugee camps; the tourist offices keep tabs on which have a few inches to spare. As for prices, expect them to be about 20 per cent higher per category than anywhere else on the coast. And if you come in the off season, beware that most hotels close in the winter.

Luxury

★★★★Le Byblos, Av Paul Signac, t 04 94 56 68 00, f 04 94 56 68 01, *www.byblos.com*. Built by a Lebanese millionaire and designed like a *village perché*, with rambling corridors, patios and opulent rooms. In the middle there's a magnificent pool, and the nightclub is one of most desirable to be seen in. There is now a *nouvelle cuisine* restaurant, **Spoon**, t 04 94 56 68 20 (*very expensive*). *Closed mid-Oct–Easter*.

★★★★Résidence La Pinède, Plage de la Bouillabaisse, t 04 94 55 91 00, f 04 94 97 73 64, *www.residencepinede.com*. The *luxe, charme et volupté* of this Relais & Châteaux place has given it the current edge. Dining *à la carte* in its gourmet restaurant comes at an appropriate price. *Closed Oct–Easter*.

★★★★La Bastide de Saint-Tropez, Rte des Carles, t 04 94 55 82 55, f 04 94 97 21 71, *www.bastidesaint-tropez.com*. Similarly swish, but perched on a hill, this has an even better, Michelin-starred restaurant, **L'Olivier** (*very expensive*). Served in a garden of oleander, figs and parasol pines, the food is flamboyant, generous and exceptionally delicious. *Closed Jan–mid-Feb*.

★★★★Le Yaca, 1 Bd d'Aumale, t 04 94 55 81 00, f 04 94 97 58 50, *www.hotel-le-yaca.fr*. Once home to Colette, and before her to Paul Signac. A rambling, but very chic, fusion of three small cottages; most of the rooms look on to a courtyard bursting with flowers. *Closed Oct–Easter; restaurant closed Mon*.

★★★★La Ponche, 3 Rue des Remparts, t 04 94 97 02 53, f 04 94 97 78 61, *www.laponche. com*. Picasso's old watering hole, in the old town – a charming, romantic nook to entice your special darling. The rooms overlooking the street can be noisy, but there is double glazing and air-conditioning. *Closed Nov–mid-Feb*.

Very Expensive–Expensive

★★★Le Sube Continental, 15 Quai Suffren, t 04 94 97 30 04, f 04 94 54 89 08. The oldest hotel in town and a historic monument to boot, with views over the port. *Closed Jan–mid-Feb.*

Expensive
★★★**Lou Troupelen**, Chemin des Vendanges, **t** 04 94 97 44 88, **f** 04 94 97 41 76, *www.nova. fr/lou-troupelen*. Quiet rooms in an old farmhouse. *Closed mid-Oct–Easter.*

Moderate
★★**Les Lauriers**, Rue du Temple, **t** 04 94 97 04 88, **f** 04 94 97 21 87. Modern, pleasant rooms with air-conditioning, in a garden setting. *Closed Jan.*

Eating Out

While in St-Trop, you may want to try a *tropézienne*. This local speciality is a sponge cake sliced horizontally and filled with raspberry or strawberry jam, and topped with whipped cream.

Very Expensive
Leï Mouscardins, Tour du Portalet, **t** 04 94 97 29 00. For pure atmosphere and the best creative food in town, book a table overlooking the harbour at Leï Mouscardins; it may be one of the high points of your holiday. *Closed Dec–Jan, and Tues and Wed, except summer. Also closed lunch during June–Sept.*

Expensive
Le Club 55, Plage de Pampelonne, **t** 04 94 55 55 55. One of the oldest and best-known beach restaurants.
La Voile Rouge, Plage de Ramatuelle, **t** 04 94 79 84 34. The current fashionable favourite.
La Ramade, Rue du Temple, **t** 04 94 97 00 15. Fish specialities, served in a garden terrace. *Closed Jan–mid-Feb, and Mon except July–Sept.*

Moderate
Tahiti Plage, Le Pinet, **t** 04 94 97 18 02. Also very fashionable. *Closed Oct–Easter.*
Moorea, Rte de Tahiti, **t** 04 94 97 18 17. More down-to-earth. *Closed Nov–Easter.*

Chez Maggi, 5 Rue Sibille, **t** 04 94 97 16 12. A busy, fashionable, gay bar/restaurant serving up good Franco-Italian cuisine, such as delicious *petits farcis provençaux*, to a youthful clientele in a small room adjoining the raucous bar area. *Closed mid-Oct–Feb*
Plage des Jumeaux, **t** 0494 55 21 80. If you want to eat right on the beach, head here for lunch.
Bar du Soleil, Rte de Tahiti, **t** 04 94 97 81 24. Another more modest beach joint.
L'Echalote, 35 Rue du Général Allard, **t** 04 94 54 83 26. Here you can beef up on your black puddings and all things meaty. *Closed mid-Nov–Dec and Thurs lunch.*
Café des Arts, Place des Lices, **t** 04 94 97 02 25. A quiet alternative on this popular square, with seafood specialities. *Closed mid-Oct–mid-April.*

Entertainment and Nightlife

The bars in Place des Lices provide an entertaining sideshow in which to pass the early part of the evening.
Sénéquier, by the port, **t** 04 94 97 09 00. A St-Trop institution. *Closed Nov.*
La Bodega du Papagayo, Quai de l'Epi, **t** 04 94 97 76 70. An attractive bar haunted by a younger clientele. Has an equally attractive restaurant (*moderate*). *Restaurant closed Wed in season.*

Dancing and much besides goes on until dawn at St-Trop's clubs. Don't take it personally if you have trouble getting in; St-Tropez's bouncers have a formidable reputation to uphold.
VIP Room, by the new port, **t** 04 94 97 14 70. *Closed Oct–Easter.*
Les Caves du Roy, Hôtel Le Byblos (*see* p.215), **t** 04 94 97 16 02. Full of stars.
Cabane Baiy-Bou, west edge of Pampelonne beach, **t** 04 94 79 84 13. Fantastic Thai food, open late in the summer.
Le Pigeonnier, Rue de la Ponche, **t** 04 94 97 84 26. One of the best-known gay clubs, *open till 4am.*

famous model Phryne, who had a face like a toad but the body of a goddess. Put on trial in Athens for unseemly behaviour, she lifted up her skirt, astonishing the jury with her charms, and was acquitted on condition that she leave Athens. She ended up out here in the Wild West of antiquity, married to a Ligurian chieftain. Together they founded Athenopolis, but the story has a sad end: Phryne was sacrificed to the Ligurian gods with the request that they should please keep foreigners away in the future.

In AD 68, Torpes, a Christian officer of Nero, was beheaded in Pisa. As anyone who has studied the *Lives of the Saints* knows, the Romans had no lack of ingenuity in dealing with martyrs; in this case, they buried Torpes' head in Pisa and put his body in a boat with a dog and a cock, who were slowly to devour it. But the animals had no appetite and their boat floated safely to Athenopolis (the Roman Heraclea Cacabria) which eventually adopted St Torpes' name. The saintly trunk was hidden and lost during the Saracen attacks, one of which destroyed St-Tropez in 739.

St-Tropez was repopulated in 1470 with settlers imported from Genoa. Good King René of Provence exempted them from taxes in return for defending the coast, and until the 17th century the Tropéziens enjoyed a special autonomous status under their Capitaines de Ville. Their most glorious moment came on 15 June 1637, when they courageously beat off an attack by 22 Spanish galleons, an event annually celebrated in the Bravade des Espagnols. Later invaders were more successful. The first famous visitor from the outside world, Guy de Maupassant, drifted into the port in 1880s and in his pre-syphilitic madness gave the villagers a preview of the 1960s. In 1892 the post-Impressionist painter Paul Signac was forced by the weather to anchor his yacht at St-Tropez; enchanted, he bought a villa called La Hune and invited his friends down to paint. St-Tropez was a revelation to many: Matisse, who had previously worked in a rather dark style, came down in 1904 and produced his key, incandescent picture of nudes on a St-Tropez beach, *Luxe, calme et volupté*, and joined the Fauvist revolution begun by Signac's friends Derain, Vlaminck, Van Dongen and Dufy; today their hot-coloured canvases illuminate the town's local museum.

Writers, most famously Colette, joined the artists' 'Montparnasse on the Mediterranean' in the 1920s, but, even then, thoughts of making a franc out of fashion and beauty were in the air; Colette herself had a shop in the port selling Colette-brand cosmetics in the 1930s. The third wave of even more conspicuous invaders – Parisian existentialists and glitterati – began in earnest in the 1950s, when Françoise 'Bonjour Tristesse' Sagan and Bardot made it the pinnacle of chic. Back then, Sartre could sit in the Café Sénéquier and write *Les Chemins de la Liberté* in peace, but these days he'd be hard put to it even to think, with all the showbiz comets who come to be seen and the paparazzi who dutifully come to snap them when they appear. Joan Collins has a house here, so has George Michael, and Elton John's manager paid £7m in 1995 to join the set. Guest appearances have been made by Prince Albert of Monaco, Clint Eastwood, Naomi Campbell, Robert De Niro, Jack Nicholson, Rupert Everett and even a cavorting once-royal British duchess (for an oral pedicure).

Musée de l'Annonciade

Quai de l'Epi, t 04 94 97 04 01; open June–Sept 10–12 and 3–7;
Oct–May 10–12 and 2–6; closed Tues, holidays and Nov; adm.

If everything about St-Tropez in the summer fills you with dismay, let this be your reason to visit. Housed in a 17th-century chapel next to the port, the museum concentrates on works by painters in Paul Signac's St-Tropez circle, Postimpressionists and Fauves who began where Van Gogh and Gauguin left off and blazed the trail for Cubism – and blaze their works do, saturated with colour that takes on a life of its own with Vlaminck (*Le Pont de Chatou*) and Derain (*Westminster Palace* and *Waterloo Bridge*). Seurat's small but fascinating *Canal des Gravelines* (1890), the oldest painting of the collection, gives an idea of his mathematical, optical treatment of Impressionism, a style from which his disciple, Signac, moved away while in St-Tropez.

The collection started out in a one-room gallery in the town hall, known by its Provençal name, the Museon Tropolen, but soon outgrew its cramped quarters and was moved to the disused chapel by the port. It had belonged to the Pénitents Blancs, who took care of fishermen maimed in fishing accidents, but was taken over during the anti-clerical fervour of the Revolution and used first for storing sails, then for building boats, and finally to house orphans, before sinking into disuse. After the Second World War the chapel was gutted and restored, uncovering lovely original features like the nave and choir.

Other highlights include Braque's *Paysage de l'Estaque*, painted in homage to Cézanne; Matisse's *La Gitane* (1906); Vuillard's *Deux Femmes sous la lampe*; Bonnard's *Nue devant la cheminée* and *La Route rose*; and key works by Van Dongen, Friesz, Dufy, Marquet and Cross. Upstairs, loafers lounge in leather armchairs among Aristide Maillol's graceful sculptures and gaze out through windows framing sky and sea far above the crowds and bustle.

From the Port to the Citadelle

Just outside the museum, the port is edged with the colourful pastel houses that inspired the Fauves, a scene that regains much of its original charm if you can get up before the trippers and the scores of hack painters who block the quay. It was demolished during the war and, by the time it was rebuilt, the bohemian élite from Paris had already chosen the town as their summer quarters, with the result that new shops and restaurants took the place of the old boathouses and storing sheds. The view is especially good from the **Môle Jean Réveille**, the narrow pier which encloses the yacht-filled port and looks out, so they say, across the bay to Sardinia and back towards the Alps on very clear days. In the street above, the 19th-century church of **St-Torpes** contains a gilt bust of St Torpes and a sculpture of his little boat, carried in the *bravades*.

Seek out Place de l'Ormeau, Rue de la Ponche and Place aux Herbes, poetic corners of old St-Tropez that have refused to shift into top gear. The rambling little **Quartier de la Ponche**, with several coolly chic restaurants and bars, folds itself around the shore and the tower of the now defunct **Château de Suffren**. Suffren was an

18th-century admiral who spent two years battling in the East Indies and could never reconcile himself to the boredom of his life afterwards; his statue overlooks the port. The narrow Rue de la Ponche leads out to a point surmounted by the **Tour Vieille**, usually crawling with unfeasibly acrobatic children, with a little beach which is very nice for a quick dip.

You can look down on shiny roof tiles from the 16th- to 18th-century *citadelle* at the top of town (or visit its little **Musée Naval**, *t 04 94 97 59 43; open May–Sept 11–5.30; Oct–April 10–12.30 and 1.30–5.30, guided tours 2pm; closed Tues and Nov; adm*). Another essential ingredient of St-Tropez is the charming Place Carnot, better known by its old name of **Place des Lices**, an archetypal slice of Provence with its plane trees, its Tuesday and Saturday markets, its cafés and eternal games of *pétanque*.

Beaches and St-Tropez's Peninsula

Although the beaches begin even before you enter St-Tropez, those famous sandy strands where girls first dared to bathe topless (circumventing local indecency laws by placing Coke bottle tops over their nipples) skirt the outer rim of the peninsula. In the summer, minibuses link them with Place Carnot, a good idea as beach parking is as expensive as the beaches themselves. (Note that St-Tropez lost its Blue Flag status in 2001, although most of the crowd here don't bother with swimming.)

Plage des Graniers is within easy walking distance, but it's the most crowded. A path from here skirts Cap de St-Tropez and, in 12km, passes **Plage des Salins** (4km direct from St-Tropez) and the gay beach **Neptune**, and ends up at the notoriously decadent **Plage de Tahiti**, the movie stars' favourite. Tahiti occupies the north end of

Where to Stay and Eat

Ramatuelle ⊠ 83350

★★★★Château Hôtel de la Messardière, Rte de Tahiti, t 04 94 56 76 00, f 04 94 56 76 01, www.messardiere.com (luxury). For sheer self-indulgence you can't beat this: a late 19th-century folly on a height overlooking the sea, ultra-comfortable, with a superb panoramic restaurant (very expensive–expensive) and exquisite, exotic dishes. Restaurant open eves only. Closed mid-Oct–mid-Mar.

★★★Hostellerie Le Baou, Av Gustave Etienne, t 04 98 12 94 20, f 04 98 12 94 21, www. chateauxhotels.com (luxury–very expensive). Though it has become part of a luxury chain with modern rooms, the views are enchanting, and it also has a heated pool and a restaurant serving delicious sunny Provençal treats. Closed mid-Oct–mid-April.

★★★La Figuière, Rte de Tahiti, t 04 94 97 18 21, f 04 94 97 68 48 (expensive). An old farm-house in a vineyard, with tennis, a pool and restaurant. Closed Oct–mid-April.

★★★La Ferme d'Augustin, Route de Tahiti, t 04 94 55 97 00, f 04 94 97 40 30, vallet. ferme.augustin@wanadoo.fr, www.ferme augustin.com (expensive). Set in a garden, a stone's throw from the sea. Closed mid-Oct–mid-Mar.

Gassin ⊠ 83580

★★Bello Visto, Place deï Barri, t 04 94 56 17 30, f 04 94 43 45 36, www.bello-visto.com (moderate). Simple and charming rooms next to Gassin's magnificent belvedere; book early for a chance of staying in one. The restaurant has a pleasant terrace. Closed Nov–Mar; restaurant closed Tues.

Auberge La Verdoyante, 866 Rte de Coste-Brigade, t 04 94 56 16 23 (moderate). On the outskirts of Gassin, this seems lost in the countryside, an old Provençal manor serving traditional old Provençal dishes. Reservations advised; closed Wed and mid-Oct–Mar.

the 5km **Plage de Pampelonne**, lined with cafés, restaurants and luxury concessions where any swimming costumes at all are optional.

On the other side of Cap Camarat, **Plage de l'Escalet** is hard to reach, but much less crowded and free (take the narrow road down from the D93). From L'Escalet you can pick up the coastal path and walk in an hour and a half to the best and most tranquil beach of all, **Plage de la Briande**.

The centre of the peninsula, swathed with Côtes de Provence vineyards, is dominated by two villages of sinuous vaulted lanes and medieval houses: **Gassin**, up a dizzy series of hairpin turns, and below it the larger **Ramatuelle**. Both were Saracen *fraxinets*, and both have caught serious cases of artsy fashion flu from St-Trop, but they still make refreshing escapes from the anarchy down below. In Ramatuelle's cemetery you can see the romantic tomb of actor Gérard Philippe (*Le Diable au corps* and *Fanfan la Tulipe*), who was only 37 when he died in 1959.

Into the Massif des Maures

Beckoning just a short drive from the coastal pandemonium are the quiet chestnut woodlands of the Massif des Maures, or at least what's left of them after a quarter of the forest burned to the ground in 1990; note that some of the few roads that penetrate the mountain may be closed in dry summers. The main walking path through the hills, the GR9, begins at Port Grimaud and passes through La Garde-Freinet on its way west to Notre-Dame-des-Anges; if you're going by road, the most rewarding route is the D14, beginning at Grimaud.

Cogolin and Grimaud

Perhaps by now you've noticed signs advertising pipes from **Cogolin**, not an especially pretty town but a busy one. For once the craftsmen are not just loose ends from Paris selling artsy gimcracks to tourists; for over two centuries the famous pipes of Cogolin have been carved from the thick roots of the briars (*erica arbores*) that grow up to 20ft high in the Maures. Visit **Courrieu Pipes** (*58 Av G.-Clemenceau, t 04 94 54 63 82, www.courrieupipes.fr; open daily 9–12 and 2–6*). A second craft was started up in the 1920s by Armenian immigrants, who introduced their ancestral art of hand-knotted wool rugs, the origin of a local industry that now sells its *tapis de Cogolin* to the best addresses in Paris and the Arab emirates. Another important industry harvests an ancient swamp to make top-quality reeds for saxophones. And Provence's only bamboo forest provides the raw material for Cogolin's furniture.

Cogolin's church of **St-Sauveur** has some pretty Renaissance art inside, in particular a Florentine wood *triptyque* (1540), but the pilgrims who come to Cogolin are more likely to be French film buffs: the granddaughter of Pagnol's favourite character actor has opened the **Musée Raimu** in his memory, in the basement of the local cinema (*18 Av Georges-Clemenceau, t 04 94 54 18 00, www.musee-raimu; open summer daily 10–12 and 4–7; winter Mon and Wed–Sat 10–12 and 3–6; Sun 3–6; closed Tues; adm*), packed full of posters and re-creations of favourite scenes (like the card game in

Getting Around

Grimaud and Cogolin are stops on the St-Raphaël–St-Tropez **bus** routes.

Other villages are much harder to reach by public transport: two buses a day go from Le Lavandou to La Garde-Freinet, and there's but one linking La Garde-Freinet and Grimaud to Toulon. There is a nearby **helipad** for Grimaud, however, t 04 94 43 39 30, *www. helicopter-saint-tropez.com.*

Tourist Information

Cogolin: Place de la République, t 04 94 55 01 10, f 04 94 55 01 11, *www.cogolin-provence.com. Open mid-June–mid-Sept Mon–Sat 9–1 and 2–7; mid-Sept–mid-June Mon–Fri 9–12.30 and 2–6.30, Sat 9.30–12.30.* Has a list of *chambres d'hôtes* and *gîtes*.

Grimaud: 1 Bd des Aliziers, t 04 94 55 43 83, f 04 94 55 72 20, *bureau.du.tourisme. grimaud@wanadoo.fr, www.grimaud-provence.com. Open Oct–Mar daily 9–12.30, and 2.15–5.30; April–June daily 9–12.30 and 2.30–6.15; July–Aug daily 9–12.30 and 3–7.*

La Garde-Freinet: 1 Place Neuve, t 04 94 43 67 41, f 04 94 43 08 69, *ot_lgf@ club-internet.fr, www.lagardefreinet-tourisme.com. Open July–Aug Mon–Sat 10–12.30 and 3–6.30, Sun 9.30–12; Nov–Feb Mon–Sat 10–12.30 and 2–5.30; Sept–Oct and Mar–June Mon–Sat 10–12.30 and 2.30–6.*

Collobrières: Bd Caminat, t 04 94 48 08 00, f 04 94 48 04 10, *ot@collotour.com, www. collotour.com. Open July–Aug Mon 2–6, Tues–Sat 10–12.30 and 3–6.30; Sept–June Tues–Sat 10–12 and 2–6.*

Market Days

Cogolin: Wed am, Place Victor Hugo; Sat am, Place de la République.

Grimaud: Thurs, Place Vieille; Ascension Thurs, wool market.

La Garde-Freinet: Wed and Sun am, Place Neuve.

Collobrières: Thurs am in summer, larger on Sun am; Place de la Mer, chestnut market, last three Suns of October; annual fair 1 Nov.

Gonfaron: Thurs am, Provençal market.

Where to Stay and Eat

Grimaud ✉ 83310

Le Verger, Route de Collobrières, t 04 94 55 57 80, f 04 94 43 33 92 (*expensive*). A Provençal building a kilometre west of Grimaud. French windows lead out into the quiet gardens and dinner is served by the pool. *Closed Nov–Easter.*

★★★La Boulangerie, Rte de Collobrières, t 04 94 43 23 16, f 04 94 43 38 27 (*expensive*). For more great views and silence. Swimming pool and tennis. *Closed mid-Oct–Easter.*

★★★Hostellerie du Coteau Fleuri, Place des Pénitents, t 04 94 43 20 17, f 04 94 43 33 42, *www.coteaufleuri.fr* (*moderate*). A comfortable stone inn, almost hidden by flowers and ivy, built in the 1930s on the quiet western outskirts of town, with grand views over the vineyards and the Maures; its restaurant (*expensive*) serves reliably good Provençal dishes. *Closed mid-Nov–mid-Dec; restaurant closed Tues exc in July–Aug, and closed lunch in July–Aug.*

Les Santons, Rte Nationale, t 04 94 43 21 02 (*expensive*). Indulge in a gourmet spread of lobster salad, seafood or thyme-scented *selle d'agneau* in dining rooms full of *santons*. *Closed Nov–Mar.*

Café de la France, Place Neuve, t 04 94 43 20 05 (*moderate*). Pennywise, the best bet for food, in an old stone house with a summer terrace. *Closed Nov–Feb and Sun eve in Mar.*

La Garde-Freinet ✉ 83680

La Sarrazine, Route Nationale, t/f 04 94 55 59 60 (*expensive*). With very filling menus, and specializing in *gâteau d'agneau.*

Collobrières ✉ 83610

Notre-Dame, 15 Av de la Libération, t 04 94 48 07 13, f 04 94 48 05 95 (*inexpensive*). Adequate rooms, a garden and a restaurant (*moderate*). *Closed mid-Dec–Jan and Tues.*

Hôtel Restaurant des Maures, 19 Bd Lazare Carnot, t 04 94 48 07 10 (*inexpensive*). Has a decent restaurant.

La Petite Fontaine, Place de la République, t 04 94 48 00 12 (*moderate*). Dine on polenta, rabbit in garlic, mushrooms and the local wine. Book. *Closed 15–30 Sept and school hols; restaurant closed Mon and Sun eve.*

César). Raimu made more than 50 films between 1912 and 1946, among them the Pagnol adaptations *Marius, César, Fanny,* and *La Femme du boulanger.* The letters and photographs are given a personal touch with the commentary of Isabelle Nohain, Raimu's granddaughter, who recounts her memories of this notoriously difficult but well-loved comedian, whom Orson Welles called the 'greatest actor in the world'.

Unlike Cogolin, **Grimaud** is all aesthetics and boutiques. A former Saracen and Templar stronghold, it can hold its own among the most perfect *villages perchés* on the coast, crowned by the ruined castle of the Grimaldis, after whom the village is named. From its rubble you can look down on the old windmill which has recently been restored and is now in working order. The Romanesque church of **St-Michel** is in surprisingly good nick; from here, Rue des Templiers (formerly Rue des Juifs), lined with arcades from 1555, passes the **House of the Templars.** This is one of the few surviving structures in Provence built by that religious and military order of knights founded in Jerusalem during the First Crusade in 1118. Before their wealth, influence and secret rites incited the deadly envy of King Philip the Fair of France and Pope Clement V, the Templars acquired extensive properties in exchange for their military services. They often built their castles and churches in Jewish or Saracen quarters, both to learn from their ancient wisdom and to protect them from the Christians – hence the damning charge of heresy raised against them by pope and king, who conspired together to dissolve the order in 1307. At the top of the village is the dark and dank **Chapelle des Pénitents,** with damp stone walls, an incongruous, brilliantly gilded altar and a gruesome statue of martyred saint Theodori, gazing out with an expression of mild reproach despite the seven knives sticking out of her chest.

La Garde-Freinet

When Charles Martel defeated the Moorish invaders at Poitiers in 732 and pushed them back to Spain, a few managed to give the Franks the slip and escape into Provence, where they generally made a nuisance of themselves (but are also credited with introducing the tambourine, medicine and flat roof tiles). Their strongholds, or *fraxinets,* gave their name to La Garde-Freinet, a large village full of medieval charm and British ex-pats. A path, past chestnuts said to be 1,000 years old, ascends to the site of the **Saracen fortress** (the standing walls are from the 15th century); from here lookouts would signal the approach of fat merchant ships down to the pirates' cove of St-Tropez.

One of the arts brought to Provence by the Saracens was working in cork, which involves stripping the tree of its outer layer of bark during certain years when the tree can survive the loss; the bark is then boiled, cut into strips, boiled again and set to dry and season for six months before being carved into bottle stoppers. This was the chief industry in the 19th century, and in 1851 the cork workers of La Garde-Freinet, men and women, formed a co-operative that stood up to the bosses, beginning an experiment in socialism in the same dark year as Louis Napoléon declared himself emperor; you don't have to be an historian to guess what happened. Things are quieter now in La Garde-Freinet. There is a small exhibition on the bottle stopper above the tourist office (*open Tues–Sat 10–12.30 and 3–6*). The only other thing to do in La Garde-Freinet, according to the tourist office, is walk (at least they provide very helpful pamphlets).

Collobrières and Around

Six kilometres off the D14 from Grimaud stands the moody, ruined **Chartreuse de la Verne** (*t 04 94 43 45 41; http://la.verne.free.fr; open summer Wed–Mon 11–6; winter Wed–Mon 11–5; closed Tues, religious hols and Jan; adm*), founded in 1170 in one of the most romantically desolate corners of France. Rebuilt several times before it was abandoned and burned in the Revolution, the vast and impressive Carthusian complex (great and small cloisters, guest house, church and porch) is mostly of interest for its use of local stone – a combination of reddish schist and hard greenish serpentine. Since 1983, restoration work has been carried out by the Brothers of Bethlehem. The back gate of the larger cloister leads up to the remnants of an old windmill and another lovely view across the chestnut trees and oaks.

Near the crossroads for the Chartreuse, a minor road leads to the *garde forestière* Ferme Lambert, where you can ask permission to see the two largest **menhirs** in Provence (11ft and 10ft high) and the largest chestnut tree, the **Châtaignier de Madame** (33ft in circumference).

The air is sweet in the biggest settlement of the western Maures, **Collobrières**, an attractive old village full of quirky fountains (the oddest is of a small boy carrying a large fish in the village square) and scented with chestnuts being ground into paste and purée or undergoing their apotheosis into delectable *marrons glacés*. In late October there is a chestnut festival for true devotees – and parades of cows to be judged and admired at the **Fête de la Transhumance** in spring. The village's name comes from *couleuvre* (grass snake), owing to the snake-like patterns in the prevalent serpentine stone. But the thick forests all around are known for other natural delights: boar and deer (and their hunters), not to mention a fabulous array of mushrooms.

Due north of Collobrières, narrow roads squiggle up through the forests to **Notre-Dame-des-Anges**, a sanctuary constructed on an ancient pagan site which has drawn pilgrims since long, long before the vogue for Our Lady took off. It sits on top of the highest point in the Var (2,500ft), with brave views over the Maures.

Further squiggles north will bring you to **Gonfaron** where, according to legend, donkeys fly. At the time of the annual village procession of St Quinis (whose chapel perches above the village on an isolated hill), the local people used to clean their porches in his honour; in the 17th century, one recalcitrant shopkeeper refused and challenged that he would only toe the line when the statue flew over his refuse heap. Moments later he found himself and his donkey at the top of a nearby hill before both were hurled into a ravine. There's a **donkey sanctuary** (*hameau des ânes*) out on Route des Mayons (*call t 04 94 78 32 10 for information*), where most of the inmates manage to stay on the ground and obligingly pull tourists around on traps, and a local museum, the **Eco-musée du Liège** (*t 04 94 78 25 65; open Mon and Wed–Sat 9–12 and 2–5, Sun 9–12; adm*), dedicated to the art of cork production, where the craftsmen scoff at the introduction of plastic wine corks which has put many a Portuguese family out of work recently. The villagers also boast that both Julius Caesar and Louis XIV demanded to taste the local wine; you can try it yourself at a tour of a local wine production centre run by the proudly named **Maîtres Vignerons de Gonfaron** (*t 04 94 78 30 02*).

Just east (off the N97 or the A8 and near the donkey sanctuary), the **Village des Tortues** (*t 04 94 78 26 41, www.tortues.com; open Mar–Nov daily 9–7; closed Dec–Feb, when a notice on the gates explains that 'the tortoises are sleeping'; adm*) is devoted to saving France's last native land tortoise, the yellow and black Hermann's tortoise of the Maures. Some 1,200 tortoises live at this non-profit-making centre until they reach the age of three, when they are released into the Maures, where the lucky ones will live to be 80. Occasionally, the dafter ones amble ponderously across the motorway, bringing breakneck drivers to a screeching halt. The best months to visit the centre are April and May when the tortoises mate, June when they lay their eggs and September when the eggs hatch.

From the Corniche des Maures to Hyères

Apart from fashionable pockets like Bandol and Cassis, the Corniche des Maures is the last glamorous hurrah of the Côte d'Azur, where celebrities and other big money types have villas among the pines and flowers by the silver sand. No railways come between the towns and the sea, and the main road in season is a slow purgatory of fed-up motorists and bus passengers.

Baie de Cavalaire

The bay on the underside of the St-Tropez peninsula, with its clear coves and large beaches of silken sand, has been given lock, stock and barrel to the property promoters. **La Croix-Valmer** is all new, although the story of its name dates back to Emperor Constantine who, as mere co-emperor of Gaul, was on his way to Rome when he saw a cross lit against the sky here, telling of his future destiny as the victor at the Milvian bridge in Rome – where he would see another cross – and his role as the first Christian emperor. The longest beach in the bay is at **Cavalaire-sur-Mer** which, like La Croix-Valmer, is more popular with families than movie stars.

Between Cavalaire-sur-Mer and Le Rayou Canadel, the **Domaine du Rayol** (*Av des Belges, t 04 98 04 44 00, www.domainedurayol.org; open 25 Jan–Mar Tues–Sun 9.30–12.30 and 2–5.30; April–Sept Tues–Sun 9.30–12.30 and 2,30–6.30; Oct–21 Nov Tues–Sun 9.30–12.30 and 2–5.30; closed 22 Nov–24 Jan; adm*) is well worth a stop for its Mediterranean gardens with global flora: South African, New Zealand, Mexican and Californian species thrive and abound among avenues and steps, a chance to glut your eyes on greenery after the Côte de Cement.

For a quiet detour inland, take the narrow D27 from Canadel-sur-Mer, west of Cavalaire, to **La Môle**, a tiny village with a two-towered château, where Antoine de Saint-Exupéry (pilot, and author of *The Little Prince*) spent much of his youth. Behind the 18th-century village is the site of its ancient counterpart, tucked under the massive basalt Rocher de Sainte-Magdeleine, with the still discernible ruins of the 11th-century church.

Bormes-les-Mimosas and Le Lavandou

Persevering west past Cap Nègre and the exclusive villages of **Pramousquier** and **Cavalière** you find the big boys on the Corniche-des-Maures, the fishing port and resort of Le Lavandou and **Bormes-les-Mimosas**, a cute hyper-restored medieval enclave that added the mimosas to tart up its name in 1968, although the honour of first planting and commercializing these little yellow Mexican ball blooms goes to Cannes, where in 1880 a gardener carelessly tossed a branch someone had given him into a pile of manure and *voilà*, the next morning he had the lovely flowers that are now the totem of the Côte d'Azur.

At the summit of the village is the **Château de Pos**, now a private residence and displaying the last word in restoration techniques; far nicer is the footpath which leads up to the delightful, austere **Chapelle Notre-Dame-de-Constance**, built at the insistence of Constance de Provence in the 13th century. The 18th-century church of **St-Trophyme** is packed out in summer with rubber-neckers trying to get a glimpse of the President of France, whose summer residence is out on Cap de Brégançon, and the **Chapelle St-François** is full of *pétanque*-players praying for good fortune in the World Pétanque Championships, which take place annually in September in the

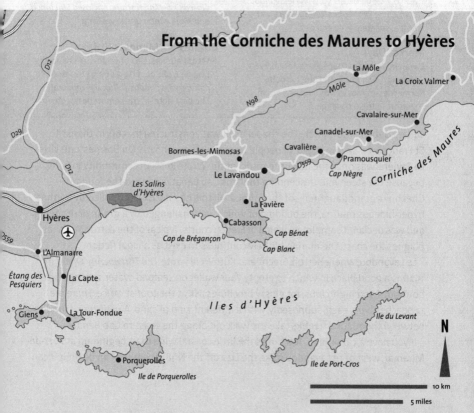

From the Corniche des Maures to Hyères

La Môle
La Croix Valmer
Môle
N98
Cavalaire-sur-Mer
Canadel-sur-Mer
Cavalière
Bormes-les-Mimosas
Pramousquier
D559
Le Lavandou
Cap Nègre
Corniche des Maures
Les Salins d'Hyères
La Favière
Hyères
Cabasson
Cap Bénat
Cap de Brégançon
Cap Blanc
L'Almanarre
Étang des Pesquiers
La Capte
Iles d'Hyères
Ile du Levant
Giens
La Tour-Fondue
N
Porquerolles
Ile de Port-Cros
Ile de Porquerolles
D12
D29
D12
D559

10 km
5 miles

Getting Around

Besides slow and expensive **buses**, there are summer **boat** connections from Cavalaire-sur-Mer and year-round services from Le Lavandou to the Iles d'Or. Call the Vedettes Iles d'Or, **t** 04 94 64 18 17. To explore the hinterland, you can rent bicycles or scooters at **Holiday Bikes**, Rue du Port, **t** 04 94 15 19 99. Parking is at a premium in both Cavalaire-sur-Mer and Bormes-les-Mimosas.

Tourist Information

Cavalaire-sur-Mer: Maison de la Mer, **t** 04 94 01 92 10, **f** 04 94 05 49 89, *www.golfe-infos. com/cavalaire*.

Bormes-les-Mimosas: Place Gambetta, **t** 04 94 01 38 38, **f** 04 94 01 38 39, *www.bormesles mimosas.com. Open Oct–Mar Mon–Sat 9–12.30 and 2–6; April–Sept daily 9–12.30 and 3–6.30.*

Le Lavandou: Quai Gabriel Péri, **t** 04 94 00 40 50, **f** 04 94 00 40 59, *www.lelavandou. com. Open Oct–April Mon–Sat 9–12 and 3–6; May–Sept daily 9–12 and 3–7.*

Market Days

Cavalaire: Wed am, Place Jean Moulin.Every morning, fish market, at the harbour.
Bormes-les-Mimosas: Wed am, Sat am in season, in the old village.

Pin-de-Bormes: Tues am.
Le Lavandou: All year am only. June–Sept, Plage de Cavalaire.

Where to Stay and Eat

Cavalaire-sur-Mer ✉ **83240**
★★★Hôtel La Calanque, Rue de la Calanque, **t** 04 94 01 95 00, **f** 04 94 64 66 20, *www. hotel-la-calanque.com* (*luxury–very expensive*). Modern, and 20ft above the sea on the cliff edge, with smart, balconied rooms, a swimming pool, jacuzzi, tennis courts and a pretty seafood restaurant on a shady terrace. *Closed Jan–mid-Mar, and Mon out of season.*
★★Hôtel Raymond, Av des Alliés, **t** 04 94 01 95 95, **f** 04 94 01 95 96, *www.hotel-raymond. com* (*expensive–moderate*). An earthy Logis de France establishment with a dollop of old-fashioned charm. It has a little pool and a children's play area, and a decent restaurant, **Le Mistral**, specializing in *bouillabaisse. Closed Oct–Mar; restaurant closed Sun lunch and Mon; winter open eves only.*

Bormes-les-Mimosas ✉ **83230**
★★★Les Palmiers, 240 Chemin du Petit Fort, **t** 04 94 64 81 94, **f** 04 94 64 93 61, *les. palmiers@wanadoo.fr* (*luxury–moderate*). The best hotel in the *commune* is a steep

square outside the church. The chapel itself was constructed in 1560, in thanks to St François for saving the local people from the plague in 1481. On Bormes' outskirts, **La Favière**, was once the favourite resort of the White Russian community in Paris, because the steep hills descending towards Cap Bénat reminded the founder – Chekhov's granddaughter – of the Crimea. All this has since been spoiled by Bormes' hyper-hideous marina, the building of which was challenged by a group of residents and was declared completely illegal in French courts. Typical of the corruption that plagues the coast, the marina blithely continues to exist as a legal fiction.

Le Lavandou, where Bertolt Brecht and Kurt Weill wrote *The Threepenny Opera* in 1928, is a good place in which to empty your wallet on seafood, water sports, boutiques and nightclubs; for glossy brochures ask at the tourist office. There are 12 beaches here, each, supposedly, with a different kind of sand. A *petit train* trundles between them. For a freebie, take the walk out along the coast to Cap Bénat.

If you have a car or bike, don't miss the little coastal wine road, beginning at **Port-de-Miramar**, west of Le Lavandou (take the D42 off the N98); it passes Cap de Brégançon

drive south along the D41 to Cabasson, and is only a few minutes from the sea; its restaurant serves solid classic food, which is a good thing as half-board is obligatory in the summer. *Closed mid-Nov–Jan.*

***Grand Hôtel**, 167 Rte de Baguier, **t** 04 94 71 23 72, **f** 04 94 71 51 20, *www.augrandhotel. com (moderate–inexpensive).* Splendid sea views and characterful yet modern rooms. Very good value. *Closed Nov–mid-Feb.*

Lou Portaou, 1 Rue Cubert-des-Poètes, **t** 04 94 64 86 37, **t** 04 94 64 81 43 *(expensive).* In a 12th-century guardhouse, serving excellent seasonal regional dishes. Book early in summer. *Closed Tues out of season and mid-Nov–20 Dec; closed lunch June–Sept.*

La Tonnelle, 23 Place Gambetta, **t** 04 94 71 34 84 *(moderate).* Tables are set under a gallery of vines and the food is made entirely from local ingredients with the finesse of a master and perfectionist. The prices are very reasonable by Côte standards. *Closed lunch July–Aug, Wed and Thurs in Oct–April, and Wed and Thurs lunch in May–June and Sept.*

Le Lavandou ✉ 83980

****Les Roches**, 1 Av des Trois-Dauphins, Aiguebelle-Plage, **t** 04 94 71 05 07, **f** 04 94 71 08 40, *www.hotelprestige-provence.com (luxury).* Set magnificently over the *calanques* 4km east of Le Lavandou, Les Roches has modern rooms furnished with Internet access, as well as a private beach, a pool and tenniscourts. The hotel and restaurant have recently been bought and renovated by a luxury hotel chain, with corresponding drop in friendliness. *Closed Jan–Feb.*

***Auberge de la Calanque**, 62 Av du Général de Gaulle, **t** 04 94 71 05 96, **f** 04 94 71 20 12, *lacalanque@wanadoo.fr (very expensive–expensive).* Large airy rooms with wonderful views, very affable staff and a decent restaurant *(expensive–moderate). Half board obligatory in summer. Closed Nov–Mar; restaurant closed Wed lunch and Thurs lunch in summer.*

***Belle Vue**, Chemin du Four-des-Maures, St-Clair, **t** 04 94 00 45 00, **f** 04 94 00 45 25, *hotelbellevue@wanadoo.fr, www.lelavandou. com/bellevue (expensive–moderate).* Charming and as good as its name, with views over the coast. *Closed Nov–Mar.*

****L'Escapade**, 1 Chemin du Vannier, **t** 04 94 71 11 52, **f** 04 94 71 22 14, *hotelescapade@ wanadoo.fr (inexpensive).* A small but very cosy hotel in a quiet lane, with air-conditioning and TV. *Half-board obligatory in summer.*

Tamaris, Plage St-Clair, **t** 04 94 71 79 19 *(expensive).* Fresh grilled fish, *bouillabaisse* and *langoustes* that will warm the cockles of your heart. *Closed Nov–Mar.*

and its fortified château (the official summer retreat of the President of France), and leads southeast to the delicious beach at **Cabasson** *(free, but you must pay for parking),* with a campsite and hotel.

Hyères

Known as Olbia by the Greeks from Marseille, who founded it in 350 BC, as Pomponiana by the Romans and as Castrum Arearum ('town of threshing floors') during the Middle Ages, Hyères claims to be the original resort of the Côte d'Azur, with a pedigree that goes back to Charles IX and Catherine de Médicis, who wintered here in 1564. It knew its greatest fame in the early 19th century, when people like Empress Josephine, Pauline Borghese, Victor Hugo, Tolstoy and Robert Louis Stevenson built villas here and invited one another to teas and soirées, before it faded genteelly from fashion in the 1880s. For despite its mild climate and lush gardens, Hyères was, unforgivably, three miles from the newly popular seaside. But the town had more

Getting There and Around

By Air

Hyères-Toulon Airport is served by Air France from Paris (for national information, call **t** 0802 802 802) and sometimes by various budget airlines from London.

By Train

Hyères is a dead end, linked to Toulon but nowhere else; the station is 1.5km south of town, but there are frequent buses into the town centre.

By Bus

Buses can be tricky. Call first. SODETRAV, 47 Av Alphonse Denis, **t** 04 94 12 55 12, serves routes west to Toulon and east to Le Lavandou. City buses (from the *gare routière* in the town centre) link Hyères to Hyères-Plage and the Giens peninsula.

By Boat

Boats for all three of Hyères' islands – Porquerolles, Port-Cros and Le Levant – depart at least twice a day, year-round, from **Port Saint-Pierre** in Hyères (**t** 04 94 12 54 40) and **Le Lavandou** (**t** 04 94 71 01 02), with additional sailings in the summer. There are more frequent connections from **La Tour-Fondue**, at the tip of the Giens peninsula, to Porquerolles (**t** 04 94 58 21 81), and in summer boats also sail from Toulon to Porquerolles.

Note that inter-island connections are more rare; check the schedules before setting out.

By Bicycle

Bicycles can be hired from **Holiday Bikes**, Centre Commercial Nautique, **t** 04 94 38 79 45.

Tourist Information

Hyères: 3 Av Ambroise Thomas, **t** 04 94 01 84 50, **f** 04 94 01 84 51, *info@ot-hyeres.fr*, *www.ot-hyeres.fr*. *Open winter Mon–Fri 9–6, Sat 10–4; summer Mon–Sat 8.30–7.30, Sun 9–1 and 3–7.*

Porquerolles: on the port, **t** 04 94 58 33 76, **f** 04 94 58 36 39, *www.porquerolles.com*. *Open April–Sept 9–5.30; Oct–Mar 9–12.30.*

Market Days

Tues and Sat: Place de la République and Av Gambetta, farmers' market.
Tues, Thurs and Sat: Place de la Vicomtesse de Noailles, organic produce.
Sat: Av Gambetta, large market.
Sun am: La Capte, flea market.

Local Wine

The local wine to look out for is **Côte des Iles**, which is exquisite but rare. Try some at: **Domaine de la Courtade**, at La Courtade, **t** 04 94 58 31 44, *www.la-courtade.com* (*open for visits by appointment only*).

Where to Stay and Eat

Hyères Town ✉ 83400

★★Hôtel du Soleil, 2 Rue des Remparts, **t** 04 94 65 16 26, **f** 04 94 35 46 00, *www.hotel-du-soleil.fr* (*moderate*). A pleasant, quiet choice near Parc St-Bernard. It's very difficult to drive through this part of town, so park and walk.

★★Les Orangers, 64 Av des Iles d'Or, **t** 04 94 00 55 11, **f** 04 94 35 25 90, *orangers@var-provence.com*, *www.var-provence.com* (*inexpensive*). A sturdy Provençal-style building near the restaurants and brasseries just to the east of the Rue Gambetta, and one of the prettiest and most comfortable hotels in town.

★Reine Jane, Ayguade, between Bormes-les-Mimosas and Hyères, **t** 04 94 66 32 64, **f** 04 94 66 34 66, *reine.jane@wanadoo.fr*, *www.perso.wanadoo.fr/hotel.reine.jane* (*inexpensive*). Good rooms and food

than one egg in its basket, and has since made the most of its salt pans on the peninsula, exploited since ancient times, and its nurseries of date palms (developed from a Californian species adaptable to sand and salinity), most of which are exported to Saudi Arabia and the Arab emirates. Now 'Hyères-les-Palmiers', if you please, it has recently won a national award for its parks and gardens.

(*moderate*) at bargain prices. *Closed first two weeks in Jan; restaurant closed Wed.*

La Colombe, Impasse Vieille, Bayorre, t 04 94 35 35 16 (*moderate*). For a more elaborate dinner, try the delicious *turbot au beurre d'herbe tendre.* Service on the patio in summer. *Closed Sat lunch, Sun eve and Mon lunch.*

Le Bistrot de Marius, 1 Place Massillon, t 04 94 35 88 38 (*moderate*). A tiny stone establishment with big platefuls of Provençal favourites, a very jolly host and tables out on the main square in summer. *Closed mid-Nov–mid-Dec and Jan.*

Les Jardins de Bacchus, 32 Av Gambetta, t 04 94 65 77 63 (*moderate*). Pulls out all the stops with its rich, flavoursome Provençal dishes and quietly elegant surroundings. *Closed Sun eve and Mon in winter; Sun lunch and Mon in summer and 1 wk Jan.*

Ile de Porquerolles ✉ 83400

There are seven hotels on the island, all priced above the odds and all booked months in advance in the summer. The best are:

****Mas du Langoustier, t 04 94 58 30 09, f 04 94 58 36 02, *langoustier@compuserve.com*, *www.langoustier.com* (*luxury–very expensive*). A romantic old inn between the woods and a long sandy beach, with lovely rooms and a superb restaurant (*expensive*), where the chef imaginatively combines the best ingredients of Provence. The wine list includes Porquerolles' famous rosé. *Closed mid-Oct–April.*

**Sainte-Anne, t 04 98 04 63 00, f 04 94 58 32 26, *steanne.porquerolles@wanadoo.fr* (*expensive*). A bit dilapidated, but stays open longer than the rest; half board is compulsory in season, but the food is good. *Closed mid-Dec–Feb.*

**Auberge des Glycines, 22 Place d'Armes, t 04 94 58 30 36, f 04 94 58 35 22, *www.aubergedesglycines.net* (*expensive–moderate*). A small and charming inn,

with rooms decorated in Provençal fabrics and set around a tranquil courtyard.

**Relais de la Poste, Place d'Armes, t 04 98 04 62 62, f 04 94 58 33 57, *relaisposte@aol.com*, *www.lerelaisdelaposte.com* (*moderate*). This was the island's first hotel and has pleasant Provençal-style rooms with loggias and a simple *crêperie. Closed Oct–Mar.*

Il Pescatore, t 04 94 58 30 61 (*moderate*). For all things fish: not just the predictable *bouillabaisse*, but *carpaccio* and *sashimi.* Eat on the restful terrace overlooking the boats bobbing in the port. *Closed Nov–Feb.*

Port-Cros ✉ 83400

There is only one choice on paradise, and it needs to be booked long in advance.

***Le Manoir d'Hélène, t 04 94 05 90 52, f 04 94 05 90 89 (*luxury–expensive*). An 18th-century mansion set among the eucalyptus groves, with an outdoor pool and a fine little restaurant (*expensive*). *Closed Oct–Mar.*

Ile du Levant ✉ 83400

La Brise Marine, Corniche des Arbousiers, t 04 94 05 91 15, f 04 94 05 93 21, *info@labrisemarine.fr*, *www.labrisemarine.fr* (*moderate*). At the summit of the islet, with pretty rooms situated around a patio with a swimming pool. *Closed mid-Sept–April.*

Entertainment and Nightlife

With bar life in Toulon restricted to seedy sailors' bars and nefarious goings-on in the old town, most Toulonnais head to Hyères for a night out, crowding the many bars and clubs.

For a bop, try the newly reopened **Casino des Palmiers**, t 04 94 12 80 80, in the centre of Hyères-les-Palmiers.

'*Mit Palmen und mit Ice-cream, ganz gewöhnlich, ganz gewöhnlich…*' (With palms and ice-cream, quite usual, quite usual…) So Bertolt Brecht, and so Hyères. There isn't much to do but take a brief wander into the Vieille Ville, beyond **Place Massillon**. Here stands the **Tour des Templiers**, a remnant from a Templar's lodge, and, on top of a monumental stair, the collegiate church of **St-Paul** (1599) (*t 04 94 65 83 30; open*

April–Sept Wed–Mon 10–12 and 4–7; Oct–Mar Wed–Mon 10–12 and 2–5.30; closed Tues), with 400 *ex votos* dating back to the 17th century. Inside also is a set of *santons* too large to move. The Renaissance house next to St-Paul doubles as a city gate, through which you can walk up to **Parc St-Bernard**, with Mediterranean plants and flowers.

At the upper part of the park, the so-called Château St-Bernard, or **Villa Noailles** (*open summer Wed–Sun 10–12 and 4–7; winter Wed–Sun 10–12 and 2–5; closed Mon and Tues*), was designed as a *château cubiste* by Robert Mallet-Stevens in 1924 for art patron Vicomte Charles de Noailles, the financier of the first film by Cocteau, *Blood of the Poet* (1930), and of Salvador Dalí and Luis Buñuel's *L'Âge d'or* – which nearly got Noailles excommunicated, not to mention thrown out of the Jockey Club. Austere cement on the outside, furnished with pieces commissioned from Eileen Gray and designers from the Bauhaus, this vast villa, with 15 guest rooms and a covered pool, was a busy hive of creativity between the wars – it even stars in Man Ray's murky 1929 film *Le Mystère du Château de Dé*. You can visit the house during exhibitions, or the exotic garden, the **Parc St-Bernard**, any day for free. The garden has recently been linked to that of Edith Wharton, author of *The Age of Innocence*, who lived on the same slope in a former convent of St Claire. The **Parc Sainte-Claire** is spread over 28 terraces (*open summer daily 8–7; winter daily 9–5*) and encompasses the little house, **La Solitude**, where Robert Louis Stevenson stayed and wrote *A Child's Garden of Verses*. Further up the hill are the hollow walls and towers of the **Vieux Château**, with an overview of Hyères' peninsula and jumble of hills.

In 1254, when Louis IX returned to France from the Crusades, he disembarked at Hyères and went to pray in the 13th-century Franciscan church in Place de la République, now named **Saint-Louis** in his honour. Below, in Place Th. Lefebvre, the heart of 19th-century Hyères, a **Musée Municipal** (*t 04 94 00 78 42; open 10–12 and 2.30–5.0; closed Tues, Sat and Sun*) houses the fragmentary remains of Hyères' Greek and Roman seaside predecessors, as well as two engraved menhirs and a Celto-Iberian figure holding two heads, similar to the statues at Roquepertuse in Aix. Further south, on Avenue Gambetta, you can relax in the **Jardin Olbius-Riquier** among the palms, rare tropical and semi-tropical trees and cacti. There is a lake and a small **zoo** (*open 9–6*) for the kids, with birds, ponies, etc. Two neo-Moorish villas from the 1880s remain in this part of town: the **Villa Tunisienne** in Avenue Beauregard and the **Villa Mauresque** in Avenue Jean Natte.

The Giens Peninsula

Over the centuries, the island that was Giens has been anchored to the mainland by two sand bars whose arms embrace a salt marsh, the **Etang des Pesquiers**. Although the link has historically been dodgy – Giens became an island again in the storms of 1811 – it hasn't stopped people from building villas and hotels, especially on the isthmus at **La Capte**.

The barren west arm, dotted by shimmering white piles of salt, is traversed by the narrow *route du sel* beginning at **Plage de l'Almanarre**. In 1843 the archaeologist king, Frederick VII of Denmark, excavated the ruins of the Greco-Roman town at **Almanarre**. Most of it has been reclaimed by the sand, but the remaining sites are open (*t 04 94*

57 98 28; open April–Sept Sat 10–12 and 2–5, Sun 10–12 and 2–5; closed Oct–Mar). There are Merovingian tombs in the 12th-century Chapelle St-Pierre.

The 'salt road' ends in **Giens**, a quiet little hamlet under a ruined castle that was the last home of the 1961 Nobel-Prize-winning poet St-John Perse, who is buried in the cemetery; further up are views from the ruined castle. To the south, **La Tour-Fondue** is the principal port for Porquerolles, although the often violent seas around the peninsula have caused scores of shipwrecks. In 1967 an intact cargo ship dating from the time of the Roman republic was found in the Golfe de Giens, with sealed amphorae containing a clear liquid with reddish mud on the bottom – the ultimate fate of red wine aged too long.

The Iles d'Hyères

Known as the Stroechades, or 'chaplet', by the ancient Greeks, and in the Renaissance as the Iles d'Or owing to the shiny yellow colour of their rock, Hyères' three islands are voluptuous little greenhouses that have seen more than their share of trouble. In the Middle Ages they belonged to the monastery of St-Honorat, and attracted pirates like moths to a flame; in 1160, after the Saracens carried off the entire population, the monks gave up and just let the pirates have the islands.

The expansion of the Ottoman Empire throughout the Mediterranean in the 16th century made the kings of France sit up and notice the Saracens, and in 1515 an attempt was made to preach a crusade against the Hyères pirates, but the crusading spirit was long past. François Ier had a golden opportunity to install the then home-less Knights of St John on Porquerolles, but the two parties couldn't agree on terms and the Knights settled for Malta, which then belonged to Spain, paying their famous rent of one golden falcon. François had to build his own forts and send settlers to man them against Charles V and other sea predators, but again the pirates carried everyone off.

Henri II, son of François, thought he had a good idea in populating the islands with criminals and malcontents. By this time, however, France had found the solution to her pirate problem: becoming allies with them and the Turks. On one memorable occasion in 1558, the French navy had a big party on Porquerolles to help the noto-rious Barbarossa and his cut-throats celebrate the end of Ramadan. Then the new inhabitants of the islands spoiled Henri's plans by following their instincts and becoming pirates themselves, capturing numerous French ships and once even pillaging the naval base in Toulon. It took another century to eradicate them.

Later rulers rebuilt the island's forts. In the late 19th century they were variously used to quarantine veterans of the colonial wars and as sanctuaries for homeless children: Le Levant and Porquerolles became Dickensian orphanages and juvenile penal colonies. In both cases the young inmates rebelled, and many were killed. Industrialists opened sulphur plants on the islands that no other place in France would have tolerated, and the navy bought Le Levant in 1892 and blew it to pieces as a firing range. In the 1890s fires burned most of the forests on Porquerolles and

Port-Cros. Fortunately, in this century, the French government has moved to protect the islands; strict laws protect them from the risks of fire and developers.

Porquerolles

Largest of the three, Porquerolles stretches 7km by 3km and has the largest permanent population, which in the summer explodes to 10,000. Its main village, also called Porquerolles, was founded in 1820 as a retirement village for Napoleon's finest soldiers and invalids. It still has a colonial air, especially around the central pine-planted **Place d'Armes**, the address of most of Porquerolles' restaurants, bars, hotels and bicycle hire shops. Even the village church was built on the orders of the Ministry of War, and has military symbols on the altar. Although the cliffs to the south are steep and dangerous for swimming, there are gentle beaches on either side of the village, especially the white-sand **Plage Notre-Dame** to the east and **Plage d'Argent** to the west. The previous owner of the island (an eccentric Belgian, who discovered Mexico's largest silver lode) took a special interest in acclimatizing flora, such as the *bellombra*, a Mexican tree with huge roots and elephant-skin-like bark, but today green thumbs concentrate on vines.

Between Porquerolles and Giens the now deserted little islet of **Grand Ribaud** was used in the early 1900s for 'spiritualist experiments' and other research by one Dr Richet, who also imported kangaroos. The kangaroos liked the islet, we are told, but banged themselves to untimely deaths by jumping too exuberantly on the sharp rocks.

Port-Cros

Although barely measuring a square mile, Port-Cros, rising to 640ft, is the most mountainous of the three islands. Since 1963 it has been a national park, preserving not only its forests of pines and ilexes, recovered from a devastating fire in 1892, but nearly a hundred species of birds; brochures will help you identify them as you walk along the mandatory trails. There is a selection of trails: the *sentier botanique* is for visitors pressed for time, while at the other end of the scale there's a 10km *circuit historique* for the lucky ones who have a packed lunch and all day. Two curiosities of the island are its abundant native catnip and its *euphorbe arborescente*, which loses all its leaves in the summer and grows new ones in the autumn. Like the national park in the Florida Keys, Port-Cros also protects its surrounding waters, rich in colourful fish and plant life. There's even a 1,000ft 'path' which divers can follow from Plage de la Palud to Rascas islet, clutching a plastic guide sheet that identifies the underwater flora. Of late, some of the more fragile plants around the island have suffered as a result of Port-Cros' extraordinary popularity – from the emissions and anchors of the thousands of pleasure craft that call here each year.

Ile du Levant

The French navy still hogs almost all this flowering island, but they no longer use it for target practice. Nowadays, they test aircraft engines and rockets, which are marginally quieter. The island's remaining public quarter is occupied by **Héliopolis**,

France's first nudist colony (1931). Anyone who's been to St-Tropez and other fashionable Côte beaches will find the idea of a specially reserved nudist area quaint by now, but Héliopolis still has its determined Adams and Eves, especially because it's so warm: 60 members of the colony stick it out here all year.

The West Coast of the Var

Toulon

If Provençal traditionalists (and they are landlubbers all) look upon the cosmopolitan Côte d'Azur as an alien presence, they feel equally ill at ease in the south's two great ports, Toulon and Marseille: to the Provençals they are dangerous, salty cities, populated by untrustworthy strangers and prostitutes. But while Marseille is essentially a city of merchants and trade, Toulon has always been the creature of the French navy. Whatever piquant charms it once had were bombed into oblivion in the Second World War and are only now slowly being restored.

History

For some reason the deepest, most majestic natural harbour in the Mediterranean tempted neither the Greeks nor the Romans. Instead Toulon (originally Telo Martius) was from Phoenician times a centre for dyeing cloth, thanks to its abundant murex shells (the source of royal purple) and the dried red corpses (*kermès*) of the *coccus illicis*, an insect that lived in the surrounding forests of oaks. Toulon's destiny began to change when Provence was annexed to France in 1481. The first towers and walls went up under Louis XII in 1514; Henri IV created the arsenal, but it was Louis XIV who changed Toulon forever, making it the chief port of France's Mediterranean fleet, greatly expanding the arsenal and assigning Vauban the task of protecting it with his star-shaped forts, built by forced labour. It was during this period that Toulon became the most popular tourist destination in Provence, when well-heeled visitors came to see, not the new navy installations, but the miserable galley slaves – Turkish prisoners, African slaves, criminals and, later, Protestants – chained four to an oar, where they worked, ate and slept in appalling conditions. The 17th century was such a rotten time that there were even volunteers for the galleys, distinguished by their moustaches and less likely to feel the cat o' nine tails.

Toulon's history is marked by three disasters. In 1720 nature's neutron bomb, the plague, killed 15,000 out of 26,000 inhabitants. The second disaster began after the execution of Louis XVI, when Toulon's royalists had confided the city to the English and their Spanish and Sardinian allies. In 1793 a ragamuffin Revolutionary army of volunteers and ruffians under the painter Carteaux, fresh from massacring 6,000 people in Lyon, arrived at the gate of Toulon and began an ineffectual siege of two months. A young Napoleon Bonaparte came on the scene and convinced the commissioners to put him in charge of the artillery. Bonaparte turned his guns to the west side of the harbour, on the English redoubt of Mulgrave, so well fortified that it was

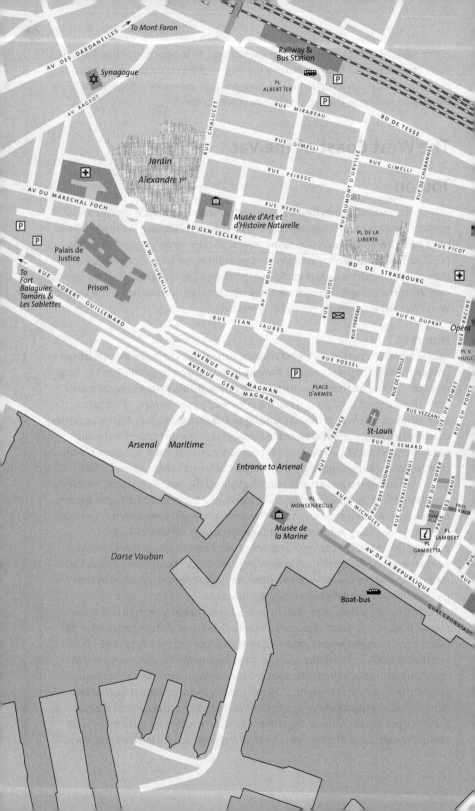

Central Toulon

Cemetery

RUE GIMELLI

BD DE TESSE

RUE D'ANTRECHAUS

RUE VICTOR CLAPPIER

RUE TRUGUET

RUE PICOT

BD DE STRASBOURG

RUE CORNEILLE

RUE MOLIÈRE

RUE RAIMU

Fontaine des 3 Dauphins

RUE FR. FABIE

RUE DE LORGUES

POL

RUE P. LANDRIN

RUE HOCHE

PL PUGET

RUE PYAT

RUE BAUDIN

PL ST-VINCENT

Halles

RUE D'ASTOUR

RUE J. ALCARD

RUE MAIRAUD

RUE ST-BERNARD

RUE DES REMPARTS

AV GEORGES CLEMENCEAU

AV CDT MARCHAND

BD RAYNOUARD

BD DE LA DÉMOCRATIE

AV PHILIPPE LEBON

AV MARCEL CASTIE

AV COL FABIEN

AV COL FABIEN

Jardin du Champ de Mars

Square Kennedy

COURS LAFAYETTE

RUE V. COURDOUAN

ALL DE LA LÉGION ÉTRANGÈRE

RUE ZOLA

RUE BASTIDE

PL DE LA CATHÉDRALE

Cathédrale Ste-Marie

Musée du Vieux Toulon

RUE GARIBALDI

A. DAUMAS

RUE ST-ANDRIEUX

PL DE LA POISSONERIE

H. SEILLON

Hôtel de Ville

St-François-de-Paule

COURS LAFAYETTE

PL DU MURIER

RUE POMME DE PIN

AV DE LA RÉPUBLIQUE

RUE DU MURIER

AV DE LACAGNE

QUAI DE LA SINSE

Darse Vieille

Customs

To Tour Royale

ROND-POINT BONAPARTE

Stade Mayol

AV F. ROOSEVELT

RUE H. PERTUS

PLACE POMPIDOU

AV F. ROOSEVELT

St-Pié X

Pedestrian Street

200 metres
200 yards

N

Getting There and Around

Toulon is the major local transport hub.

By Air

Toulon's airport (t 04 94 00 83 83) is out near Hyères (for information, call t 08 25 01 83 87; for domestic flight reservations, call the airlines. Budget airlines from London sometimes fly the route.

By Train

The train station is on the northern side of Toulon in Place Albert Ier, with four daily TGVs to Nice and Marseille, four direct to Paris (taking just over 4hrs), and frequent connections up and down the coast and to Hyères. SNCF: t 08 92 35 35 35.

By Bus

For St-Tropez and the coast between Hyères and St-Raphaël, catch an expensive SODETRAV bus from the *gare routière* (which is right next to the train station), t 04 94 12 55 12. Buses run by Ouest Littoral Cars (which leave from Av Vauban, running south from the station), t 04 94 74 01 35, will take you to Bandol, La Seyne, Six-Fours and Sanary.

From Quai Cronstadt, pleasant and very reasonably priced sea-buses go to La Seyne, Les Sablettes and St-Mandrier.

City bus and sea-bus info can be obtained from RMTT on t 04 94 03 87 03.

By Boat

From May to August there are daily sailings (weekly in September) to Corsica and frequent sailings to Sardinia (SNCM, Av de l'Infanterie-de-Marine, t 0825 801 701; Corsica Ferries, t 0825 095 095).

Companies departing from Quai Cronstadt offer tours of Toulon's anchorages and battleships, the Grande Rade and Petite Rade, and the surrounding coasts and islands:

Trans-med 2000, t 04 94 92 96 82. Tours to the Ile de Porquerolles, July–Aug.

Les Bateliers de la Rade, t 04 94 46 24 65. Also has crossings to all three Iles d'Hyères, June–Aug.

Transport Maritime Toulonnais, t 04 94 23 25 36.

Catamaran Alain II, t 04 94 46 29 89.

SNRTM, t 04 94 62 41 14. Tours of the *rades*. For sea-buses, *see* above.

Bicycle and Scooter Hire

Espace Vélo/Cycles Cutaia, 395 Av Franklin Roosevelt, **t** 04 94 42 61 90.

Motard Service, 282 Bd Léon Bourgeois, **t** 04 94 03 94 04. Motorcycles and scooters.

Tourist Information

Toulon: Place Raimu, **t** 04 94 18 53 00, **f** 04 94 18 53 09, *www. toulontourisme.com*. Open June–Sept Mon–Sat 9–6, Sun 10–12; Oct–May Mon–Sat 9.30–5.30, Sun 10–12. The tourist office can also help finding *chambres d'hôtes*.

Post office: The main post office is at Rue Ferréro (behind the Galeries Lafayette), **t** 04 94 18 51 00. There's another at Place de la Poissonnerie (behind the City Hall).

Internet: Cap Games, 7 Rue Corneille, **t** 04 94 93 92 52.

Market Days

Toulon: On Cours Lafayette every morning except Monday – don't miss it; big flea

---

nicknamed 'Little Gibraltar' (now Fort Caire), and had captured it by 19 December. In spite of the opposition of the English commander Samuel Hood, the allies decided to abandon Toulon to its fate. The thousands who couldn't escape were mercilessly slaughtered by the Jacobins. The hitherto unknown Bonaparte, promoted to brigadier-general, became the darling of the Convention. Although the Revolutionaries hailed the galley slaves as 'the only decent men of the infamous city', convicts (like Jean Valjean in *Les Misérables*) continued to be sentenced to the *bagnes* (penal camps) in Toulon until the 1850s. Chained in pairs, with rats for pets, the cons envied the lucky few who made a fortune as executioners: 20 *livres* for breaking a

markets on the eastern (industrial zone) outskirts of the city on Sunday morning.

Festivals

The **Fête de la Musique** takes place through June and July, with concerts in town and surrounding areas. July also sees the **Festival de Jazz**, t 04 94 09 71 00.

Rhythm' Estival, in early August, is a world music festival (**t** 04 94 09 71 00).

Sports

Toulon's **rugby** team is one of the best in France and passions can run high; for tickets at the home pitch, Stade Mayol, call **t** 04 94 41 08 10.

Where to Stay

Toulon ✉ 83000

Prices are about one-third less than on the fashionable Côte, and fall even lower in the low season.

***La Corniche, 17 Littoral F. Mistral, Le Mourillon, t 04 94 41 35 12, f 04 94 41 24 58, *www.cornichehotel.com* (*expensive–moderate*). Part of the Best Western chain, this cleverly designed modern Provençal hotel is near the beach. There is a restaurant built around the massive trunks of three maritime pines, serving refined seafood and meat dishes. *Restaurant closed Sat lunch and Sun eve.*

Résidence du Cap Brun, 192 Chemin de l'Aviateur-Gayraud, off Corniche Général de Gaulle, t 04 94 41 29 46, f 04 94 63 16 16, *www.gaudefroy-receptions.com* (*moderate*).

A magical old white villa set on a cliff top beyond the beaches of Mourillon. Surrounded by pine and plane trees and a world away from the urban hubbub of Toulon, it has a small swimming pool and a steep stone path down to the shore. *No restaurant. Closed Nov–Mar.*

**Grand Hôtel du Dauphiné, 10 Rue Berthelot, t 04 94 92 20 28, f 04 94 62 16 69, *www. grandhoteldauphine.com* (*inexpensive*). In the pedestrian zone, not far from the opera, this is a comfortable, friendly older hotel, air-conditioned, with discounted parking.

*Le Jaurès, 11 Rue Jean Jaurès, t 04 94 92 83 04, f 04 94 62 16 74, *www.hoteljaures.fr* (*inexpensive*). The top bargain choice; the rooms all have baths.

*Molière, 12 Rue Molière, t 04 94 92 78 35, f 04 94 62 85 82 (*inexpensive*). Another good bargain place. *Closed Jan.*

Eating Out

Le Lingousto, Rte de Pierrefeu, Cuers, t 04 94 28 69 10 (*expensive*). Toulonnais in search of a special meal drive 20km northeast to Cuers to eat at Le Lingousto, located in an old *bastide*, where the freshest of fresh local ingredients are transformed into imaginative works of art – langoustines with pasta, omelettes with *oursins* (sea urchins), cheeses that have 'worked' to perfection and divine desserts. *Closed Sun eve and Mon, and Jan.*

Le Jardin du Sommelier, 20 Allées Amiral Courbet, t 04 94 62 03 27 (*expensive*). Gastronomic Provençal cuisine with wines to match in a small, intimate dining room, perfect for '*un tête-à-tête en amoureux*'. *Closed Sat lunch and Sun.*

---

nobleman (crushing all his bones, but not shedding a drop of his noble blood), 15 for a hanging or burning alive, down to two for cutting off a nose. They were forced to wear chains weighing 7kg day and night and to wear coloured hats: red for those who were under a short-term sentence, green for those condemned for life and brown for deserters. In 1860 the convicts were packed off out of sight to Devil's Island in French Guyana and in 1874 the penal colonies of Toulon shut up shop for good.

The city's most recent sufferings began in 1942, when the Germans took the city by surprise and the Vichy Amiral Laborde blocked up the harbour by scuttling the entire Mediterranean fleet to keep it from falling into the hands of the enemy.

Les Pins Penchés, 3182 Av de la Résistance, t 04 94 27 98 98, *www.restaurant-pins-penches.com* (*expensive*). A new gourmet restaurant with plenty of accolades and acres of gardens. *Closed Sun eve, Mon all day and Tues lunch in winter*.

Le Cellier, 52 Rue Jean Jaurès, t 04 94 92 64 35 (*expensive–moderate*). Jovial and friendly, with good menus. *Closed Sun*.

Le Lido, Littoral Frédéric Mistral, t 04 94 03 38 18, *www.lelidodetoulon.com* (*moderate*). A restaurant with nice nautical décor and a window on to the kitchen where you can watch your fresh fish being prepared. *Closed Sun eve and Mon in winter*.

La Chamade, 25 Rue Denfert-Rochereau, t 04 94 92 28 58 (*moderate*). Another local favourite which offers a serious fixed three-course menu prepared by chef Francis Bonneau. *Closed Sun and first 3 wks Aug*

Le Village, 10 Rue Dumont-d'Urville, t 04 94 22 03 03 (*moderate*). Southwest and Provençal cuisine, with live jazz and theatre. *Closed Sat lunch, Sun and Aug*.

Les Enfants Gâtés, 7 Rue Corneille, t 04 94 09 14 67 (*moderate–cheap*). Traditional Provençal cuisine in a trendy setting in the centre of town. *Closed Sun in winter, weekends in summer*.

Entertainment and Nightlife

Pick up a paper or copy of the monthly *Fiesta* to tell you what's really going on. Toulon has some good theatre, dance and jazz, but it's not very easy to find out what.

Northwest of Toulon (in Ollioules), a 17th-century tower was converted in 1966 into a handsome theatre, to host cultural events. The mayor infamously stamped down on its artistic freedom in the mid-1990s, but it has recently reopened as the **Châteauvallon Theatre**, with a varied and experimental programme of performing arts. It hosts the Festival de la Danse et de l'Image.

Music

Opéra, Place Victor Hugo, t 04 94 92 70 78. For opera, ballet and inane comedies in winter.

Zénith-Oméga concert hall, Place des Lices, t 04 94 22 66 77. Rapidly becoming the number one rock venue in the south of France – hosting the likes of Elton John and Lenny Kravitz.

Bar à Thym, 32 Bd Cunéo, t 04 94 41 90 11. Live rock and DJs on a more relaxed scale.

Cinemas

Pathé Liberté, 4 Place de la Liberté, t 08 92 69 66 96. Six screens and comfortable seats.

Pathé Grand Ciel, opposite the university at La Garde, t 08 92 69 66 96. Twelve screens and films in their original language (*v.o.*).

Le Royal, Rue Bertholet, t 08 92 68 03 89. Films in their original language.

Bars and Clubs

There is no lack of **bars**, especially around Rue Pierre Sémard, but in general they're not places where you'll feel comfortable alone. Toulon society prefers the bars along Littoral Frédéric Mistral on Mourillon beach, or drives to Hyères or Le Lavandou.

Boy's Paradise, 1 Bd Pierre Toesca, t 04 94 09 35 90. One of the Riviera's most famous gay nightclubs.

On 15 August 1944, after flattening the picturesque old port with aerial bombing raids, the Allies landed and the French army, under Général De Lattre de Tassigny, recaptured Toulon, but not before the entrenched Germans blew up the citadel, the harbour and the dockyards. Toulon was rebuilt quickly, although without a great sense of design or beauty. The end of the 20th century was not kind to Toulon. The shipbuilding yards in La Seyne closed down, putting thousands out of work, and the ugly forces of reaction succeeded in electing France's first National Front deputy, followed by the election of a National Front mayor whose xenophobic, anti-cultural antics were a national affront until his defeat in the last few years by one of Jacques

Chirac's allies, Hubert Falco. Now, with the opening of several restaurants and new museums, Toulon is beginning to rise from its own ashes.

Central Toulon

From the train station, Av Vauban descends to Av du Maréchal Leclerc; on the right at No.113 is the grandly gloomy municipal museum and library: inside are the **Musée d'Histoire Naturelle** (*t 04 94 36 81 10; open Mon–Fri 9.30–12 and 2–6, Sat and Sun 1–8*) and the **Musée d'Art** (*t 04 94 36 81 01; open daily 1–6.30; closed hols*). The natural history museum has all kinds of stuffed birds and beasts – from stately 'Clem', a lioness who was once a popular attraction at Toulon zoo, now come down in the world and playing to a much diminished audience, to a tiny, ratty *Musareigne etruseque*, the smallest mammal in the world, hiding behind a magnifying glass. The art museum contains an above-average collection of paintings and sculptures, including a Fragonard and some sculptures by Vernet and Pierre Puget. There's also an especially strong contemporary collection upstairs with Bacon, Arman, Yves Klein and Christo, among others, but you will be lucky if you see it all together; the museum usually focuses on local artists and lends out the heavyweights of its collection.

Next door is the quiet, spacious **Jardin Alexandre I**^{er}, with lovely magnolias and cedar trees. In the centre is an indomitable bust of Puget and a monument to the soldiers of the First World War. The Toulonnais do pretty well for local free museums: across the road, heading towards the centre of the town, the **Hôtel des Arts** (*236 Av du Maréchal Leclerc, t 04 94 91 69 18; open Tues–Sun 11–6*), is a lofty, elegant building devoted to modern art which, again, usually puts the spotlight on the work of local artists.

Avenue J. Moulin continues down to the large bleak square of **Place d'Armes**, decorated with ordnance from the adjacent arsenal, one of the biggest single employers in southeast France with some 10,000 workers. Alongside the arsenal in Place Monsenergue are miniature versions of the ships that it once made, displayed in the **Musée de la Marine** (*t 04 94 02 02 01; open Wed–Mon 10–12 and 2–6; closed Tues; adm*). France's great Baroque sculptor and architect Puget started out in Toulon carving and painting figureheads for the ships, and the museum has works by his followers. The grand Baroque entrance to the building itself is the original Louis XIV arsenal gate of 1738.

The best surviving works of Puget in Toulon are the two **Atlantes** (1657) on Quai Cronstadt, *Force* and *Fatigue*, whose woe and exhaustion may well have been modelled on the galley slaves. (You can see early copies of them in the Musée d'Art, *see* above.) They once supported the balcony of the old Hôtel de Ville, and were packed off to safety just before the bombings in the last war. Off the Quai, Rue d'Alger, now a popular evening promenade, used to be the most notorious street in Toulon's **Vieille Ville**, or '*le petit Chicago*', the pungent pocket of the pre-war town. Some of the narrow streets off here – known locally as 'the gut' – are still distinctly unsavoury after dark. However, blocked off from the sea by rows of ugly new buildings, the shifty bars and shabby flats are giving way to fashionable cafés and boutiques. Adding further swish to the neighbourhood is the **Maison de la Photographie** (*Rue Nicholas Laugier,*

Place du Globe, **t** *04 94 93 07 59; open Tues–Sat 10–12.30 and 1.30–6*), which showcases local talents alongside legends such as Robert Doisneau and Bernard Faucon.

Further east, at 69 Cours Lafayette there's the dingy **Musée du Vieux-Toulon** (**t** *04 94 62 11 07; open 2–5.45; closed Sun and hols*), with sketches by Puget, historical odds and ends, Provençal costumes and a 19th-century model of the town. Around the corner is the cathedral of **Ste-Marie**, 17th-century on the outside and Romanesque-Gothic within, although its features are barely discernible in the gloomiest interior in the south of France; during the Revolution an attempt to convert it into a stable failed when the horses threw their riders rather than enter it. Cours Lafayette itself used to be known as '*le pavé d'amour*', a favourite trysting spot, but young lovers today would have a hard time fighting their way through the babel of the colourful daily market that now runs its length. Come early in the morning to take it in, along with the fish market in Place de la Poissonnerie.

In attractive, café-lined Place Puget, at the top of the adjacent pedestrian quarter, is Toulon's prettiest fountain, the **Fontaine des Trois Dauphins**, sculpted by two young Toulonnais in the 18th century and now almost hidden by foliage. North of the three dolphins is Toulon's main street, Boulevard de Strasbourg, site of the **Opéra** (*see* 'Entertainment and Nightlife', p.238), the biggest opera-house in Provence, noted for its acoustics, with an interior inspired by Charles Garnier. In Place Victor Hugo, in front of the Opéra, there is a wistful statue of the actor Jules Muraire, affectionately known as 'Raimu' (*see* pp.220–22), who was born at 6 Rue Anatole France, off the Place des Armes, in 1883. A bronze reconstruction of a famous scene from the hugely popular film, *César*, based on a Pagnol novel, sits outside the tourist ofice.

Mont Faron

Toulon looks better seen from a distance. Bus 40 will take you to Bd Amiral Vence in **Super-Toulon** (bus stop *Téléphérique*), site of the terminus of the little blue **funicular** (**t** *04 94 92 68 25; open Tues–Sun 9.30–12 and 2–5.30; closed Mon; not advisable in high winds; adm*) that runs to the top of 1,755ft Mont Faron (which means 'lighthouse mountain' in Provençal). There's a narrow hairpin road circuit as well, beginning in Av Emile Fabre. Besides a tremendous view over the city and its harbours, there's the **Musée Mémorial du Débarquement** (**t** *04 94 88 08 09; open Tues–Sun 9.45–11.45 and 1.45–4.30; closed Mon; adm*), devoted to the August 1944 Allied landing in Provence, with models, uniforms and breathless 1944 newsreels. It shares the summit with a **zoo** (**t** *04 94 88 07 89; open daily 2–5.30; closed mornings in winter on rainy days; adm; combined tickets for the funicular and the zoo are available*), which specializes in breeding wildcats, including jaguars, tigers and lions. In 1997 a 'discovery path' was created among the wooded parks of the peak, with well-marked walking trails and picnic spots (the tourist office has a booklet with a map) where you can escape the city stickiness in summer.

Around the Harbour

The first stop should be the new **Musée des Arts Asiatiques** in Villa Jules Verne (*106 Bd Eugène Pelletan,* **t** *04 98 00 41 00; open May–mid-Oct Tues–Sun 1–7; mid-Oct–April*

Tues–Sun 12.30–6; closed Mon), which includes 18th- and 19th-century pieces from Southeast Asia and Tibet (many from the collection of Baron de Rothschild). Bus nos.3 and 13 from in front of the station or on Av du Maréchal Leclerc will take you to the **Plage du Mourillon**, Toulon's largest beach and site of the city's oldest fort, Louis XII's 1514 Grosse Tour or Tour Royale, which once guarded the eastern approaches to Toulon with its rounded walls, 16–24ft thick. In later years the lower part, excavated out of the rock, was used as a prison; it now contains an annexe of the **Musée de la Marine** (*t 04 94 02 02 01; open Mon–Sat 10–6.30; closed Sun; adm*), with more figureheads in a baleful setting. Two beautiful coastal paths – the Sentier des Douaniers and the gentler Promenade Henri Fabre – leave from the Plage du Mourillon (both were damaged by severe storms in September and December 1999). They offer glimpses of tiny, hidden rocky coves shaded by umbrella pines and are about as near as you will get to an empty beach.

The west shore of the Petite Rade is Toulon's business end: although the yards of **La Seyne** are now closed, there is a dense mass of factories and industry. To the south, at L'Aiguillette, stood 'Little Gibraltar' near **Fort Balaguier**, another English stronghold that fell to Bonaparte; this now contains the **Musée Naval Municipal du Fort Balaguier** of Napoleana (*t 04 94 94 84 72; open winter Tues–Sun 10–12 and 2–6; summer Tues–Sun 10–12 and 3–7; closed Mon; adm*).

Further south is the residential suburb of **Tamaris**, once the home of officers and their families, where George Sand wrote her novel *Tamaris* in 1861. In the 1880s the mayor of nearby Sanary purchased much of Tamaris in the hope of turning it into a resort. This mayor had a more exciting career than most: born Michel Marius in Sanary in 1819, he was employed by the Ottoman Empire as a builder of lighthouses, a job he performed so well that the Sultan made him a pasha before sending him home in 1860 with a fat pension. Inspired by what he had seen in Turkey, Michel Pasha commissioned a number of fantasy neo-Moorish buildings in the area. In 1890 he decided to create a palace for his wife, inspired by Florentine villas. It has a lavishly garlanded façade, Italian balustrades and an unhappy ending: three years after work had begun, Michel Pasha's wife was knifed by a madman and, as a consequence, he dropped the project and the house remained unfinished and abandoned for a century. Now the **Villa Tamaris Pacha** (*t 04 94 06 84 00; open Tues–Sat 2–6.30*) is an elegant art gallery. The resort was a flop, but a fad for neo-Moorish confections swept across the Riviera at the turn of the century.

Beyond the fine sands of **Les Sablettes** beach, the hilly St-Mandrier peninsula closes off the west end of the Grande Rade, which was an island until the mid-17th century. The quiet and unassuming fishing village and marina of **St-Mandrier-sur-Mer** is easily accessible by sea bus (28M) from Quai Cronstadt in Toulon and has a little sandy beach by the port and a wonderful, wild (if pebbly) beach, **Plage de la Cadoulière**, on the opposite side of the isthmus, popular with windsurfers and without a beach concession in sight.

Coastal paths (*sentiers littoraux*), which are marked with yellow painted signs, leave from here to the equally unravaged **Plage de Cavalas** and the more sophisticated **Plage de St-Asile**, a favourite with families. In the woods on the hills above the fishing village is a Franco-Italian cemetery with wide views over the *rades* – and the flat grey forms of the frigates and aircraft carriers of the navy fleet. The tip of the peninsula belongs to the French navy and is out of bounds.

Toulon to Les Lecques

West of Toulon, the coast tosses out the curious peninsula of Cap Sicié, with the old town of Six-Fours, before ending in a string of small towns with sandy beaches, including Sanary, fashionable Bandol (one of the coast's great wine towns) and Les Lecques. Offshore, you can be entertained on Paul Ricard's two little islets, or amuse yourself inland exploring the hills, woods, vineyards and gorges around Ollioules, La Cadière-d'Azur and Le Castellet.

Around Cap Sicié: Six-Fours

Cap Sicié, like a clenched fist punching the sea, takes the brunt of the wind and rough swells from the west. If you can, avoid the depressing main roads and urban sprawl that cut across the peninsula from Les Sablettes to Sanary, and take the **Corniche Varoise**, a minor road that circles the cliffs of the Cap (not recommended on windy days, however). The cliffs tower up to 1,100ft over the sea at **Notre-Dame-du-Mai**, named after a sanctuary much esteemed by sailors, who always approached it barefoot.

On the west side of the peninsula, the little port of **Le Brusc**, set amid cliffs and pines, has two or three departures every hour for the **Ile des Embiez**, owned by Paul Ricard, the *pastis* baron. Ricard has left the seaward side of the island alone, but facing the mainland he is developing what he calls 'the leisure centre of the future', a vast marina and the **Fondation Océanographique Ricard** (*t 04 94 34 02 49; open July–Aug daily 10–12.30 and 1.30–5.30; Sept–June Wed and Sat 2–5.30, Mon, Tues, Thurs, Fri and Sun 10–12.30 and 1.30–5.30; adm*), with 100 Mediterranean species.

The rough winds and waves off Cap Sicié's west coast offer an exciting challenge to surfers and windsurfers, who get their kicks at **Brutal Beach** and **Plage de Bonnegrâce**, part of the *commune* of **Six-Fours-les-Plages** (from the Latin *sex furni*, six ovens). The village once stood on the isolated mountain nearby, but was destroyed in the 19th century to build the **fort** (no entry, but you can drive up to the barbed wire outside for the view). Two churches were spared: a 10th-century **oratory** on the road to Le Brusc, commemorating a victory over Saracen pirates, and the 12th-century Collegiate church of **St-Pierre-aux-Liens** (*t 04 94 34 24 75; open Oct–May Mon–Sat 2–6, Sun 10–12 and 2–6; June–Sept Mon–Sat 3–7, Sun 9–12 and 3–7*), built in pure Provençal Romanesque over a 5th-century baptistry; Palaeo-Christian coins and gems found here are displayed in a case. The church has a number of medieval works of art, including a polyptych of Provence's favourite saints by Jean de Troyes (1520). The niche behind the altar, built to hold the Eucharist, was until 1914 (when the practice was banned) used by the faithful to deposit scraps of cloth taken from the clothes of dead relatives when they came to pray for their souls.

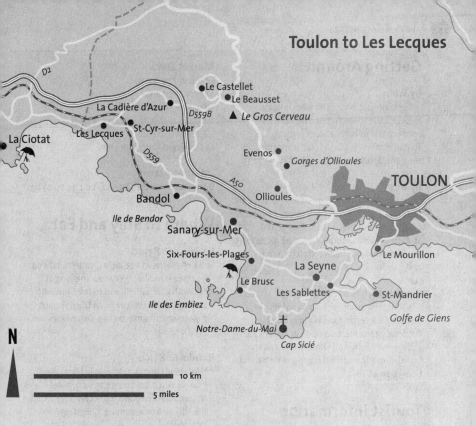

D2

Le Castellet
Le Beausset
La Cadière d'Azur
D559B
▲ *Le Gros Cerveau*
St-Cyr-sur-Mer
Les Lecques
La Ciotat
D559
Evenos
Gorges d'Ollioules
TOULON
A50
Ollioules
Bandol
Ile de Bendor
Sanary-sur-Mer
Le Mourillon
Six-Fours-les-Plages
La Seyne
Le Brusc
Les Sablettes
St-Mandrier
Ile des Embiez
Notre-Dame-du-Mai
Golfe de Giens
Cap Sicié

N

10 km

5 miles

North of here off the D63 is the stone-built **Chapelle Notre-Dame-de-Pépiole** (*usually open 3–6, and for services Sun 9.30–11*), with three little barrel-vaulted naves modelled after the earliest Syrian churches. It dates back to at least the 8th century, the date of fragments of Islamic ceramics found inside, and may even be Carolingian.

Sanary-sur-Mer, Ollioules and the Big Brain

Provençal for St-Nazaire, **Sanary** is a little resort of pink and white houses and a sandy beach, once picked out by the Kislings and Aldous Huxley as a good place to live, far from the Babylon further east. After 1933, Huxley was joined by the cream of anti-Nazi German intelligentsia, led by Thomas and Heinrich Mann and Bertolt Brecht. But Sanary was not far enough away, and under the Vichy régime many Germans were rounded up and imprisoned in an internment camp near Aix. On Sanary's promontory, the chapel **Notre-Dame-de-Pitié** has a delightful collection of naïve *ex votos*.

Ollioules' name comes from olives, although these days it's better known for its wholesale Mediterranean flower market. The town itself has the typical Provençal charms – arcaded lanes, a medieval castle and a Romanesque church – and numerous artisans who make barrels, birdcages, nougat, olive woodwork, goat's cheese and the like, a welcome respite from the lavender sachets and *santons*. Three signposted walks head out of town into the hills and up to the Gorges d'Ollioules.

Getting Around

By Train

The train station for Ollioules is halfway between the town and Sanary, with bus connections to both. Bandol is on the Toulon–Marseille TGV. For train information, the general SNCF number is t 08 92 35 35 35.

By Bus

Six-Fours and Sanary are easiest reached by bus from Toulon. SODETRAV buses, t 04 94 18 93 40, run from Toulon to St-Tropez and St-Raphaël, and Littorals Cars, t 04 94 74 01 35, leave Toulon from Rue Vauban for Sanary and Bandol.

Bike and Surfboard Hire

In Bandol you can hire a bike to explore the beautiful hinterlands at **Holiday Bikes**, 127 Route de Marseille, t 04 94 32 21 89. Or catch some waves by hiring windsurfers and surf boards from the **Société Nautique de Bandol**, t 04 94 29 42 26.

Tourist Information

Ollioules: 116 Rue Philippe de Hauteclocque, t 04 94 63 11 74, f 04 94 63 33 72, *office-tourisme@ollioules.com, www.ollioules.com. Open summer Mon–Sat 9–12 and 4–8; winter Mon–Fri 9–12 and 3–6, Sat 9–12.*
Bandol: Allée Vivien, t 04 94 29 41 35, f 04 94 32 50 39, *otbandol@bandol.fr, www.bandol.fr. Open winter Mon–Fri 9–12 and 2–6, Sat 9–12; summer daily 9–7.*

Market Days

Le Brusc: Thurs am.
Sanary: Wed am.
Ollioules: Thurs and Sat.
Bandol: Daily, with a bigger market on Tues am.
La Cadière-d'Azur: Thurs am.

Internet Access

Boss, Rue des Ecoles, Bandol, t 04 94 29 03 03.

Where to Stay and Eat

Le Brusc ✉ 83140

Le Saint-Pierre, 47 Rue de la Citadelle, t 04 94 34 02 52 (*moderate*). Marcel, 'the king of *bouillabaisse*' will fill you to the brim with the well-priced offerings on the delicious menu, which is mostly fish. *Closed Tues eve, Wed and Jan.*

Bandol ✉ 83150

★★Hôtel Bel Ombra, 31 Rue de la Fontaine, t 04 94 29 40 90, f 04 94 25 01 11, *hotel.bel.ombra@wanadoo.fr* (*inexpensive*). Quiet, friendly and unassuming. *Closed mid-Oct–Mar.*
★★L'Oasis, 15 Rue des Ecoles, t 04 94 29 41 69, f 04 94 29 44 80, *www.oasisbandol.com* (*inexpensive*). West of the port, with a cool, shady garden and just a short walk from the beach. However, rooms can be stuffy and the street is noisy in high season. Restaurant (*moderate*); *half- or full board compulsory mid-June–mid-Sept. Closed Dec; restaurant closed Sun eve.*

A kilometre north of town, just past the romantic ruins of an 18th-century oratory, the Celto-Ligurian Iron Age *oppidum* of **La Courtine** is built on a basalt rock and covered with wild roses planted by two frustrated amateur archaeologists when they got tired of excavating. You can still make out the dry-stone walls and wells. Over 300 Greek coins engraved with the features of Hercules and Hecate were discovered here, donated to a sanctuary destroyed by Romans in 123 BC.

Evenos is an extraordinary *village perché* just to the north off the N8; a granite-grey huddle of houses patched with the remains of the 16th-century château which glowers byronically at the summit of the village. A footpath leads around the castle ruins and offers glimpses of the the dramatic scenery, especially the fantastical yellow-tinted **Gorges d'Ollioules**, a natural Gothic landscape much admired by Victor

L'Auberge du Port, 9 Allée J. Moulin, **t** 04 94 29 42 63, *www.ile-rousse.com* (*expensive–moderate*). Bandol's gourmet rendezvous, specializing in seafood; you can go the whole hog on a *menu dégustation*, or pick from the extensive menu of local fish specialities.

Le Jérôme, on the waterfront, near the tourist office, **t** 04 94 32 55 85 (*moderate*). A restaurant and pizzeria serving huge portions at attractive prices with cheerful, genuine service.

Ile de Bendor ✉ 83150

★★★Delos, **t** 04 94 29 11 60, **f** 04 94 32 41 44 (*expensive*). Big, comfortable rooms decorated in extravagant bad taste – but the views of the sea and the watersports make up for it. *Closed Jan–Feb.*

★★★Hôtel Soukana, **t** 04 94 25 06 06, **f** 04 94 25 04 89 (*expensive*). This has lots of activities and an occasionally raucous but cheerful clientele, plus a restaurant (*moderate*). *Closed Nov–mid-June.*

La Cadière-d'Azur ✉ 83740

★★★Hostellerie Bérard, Av Gabriel Péri, **t** 04 94 90 11 43, **f** 04 94 90 01 94, *berard@hotel-berard.com, www.hotel-berard.com* (*expensive*). The one hotel in the village is a charming and luxurious place to stay: a 16th-century convent building with a shady terrace, a heated swimming pool, gardens and a good restaurant with splendid views, serving delicately perfumed dishes. You may want to avoid it in July, August and November, when all the bus tours arrive

for **cookery courses** with the master chef – or you may want to arrange to join them. *Closed mid-Jan–mid-Feb; restaurant closed Mon lunch and Sat lunch.*

Le Castellet ✉ 83330

★★★Le Castel Lumière, **t** 04 94 32 62 20, **f** 04 94 32 70 33, *www.lecastellumiere.com* (*moderate*). Next to the medieval gate in the village, Le Castel Lumière has six rooms and an excellent restaurant (*expensive*), partially funished with antiques, with panoramic views. The staff can be a little sniffy. *Closed Sun eve, Mon in summer and Jan.*

★★★Castel Sainte-Anne, 81, Chemin de la Chapelle, 2km northwest on the D26, **t** 04 94 32 60 08, **f** 04 94 32 68 16, *castelsaintanne@hotmail.com* (*inexpensive*). A cosy niche that won't break the bank, with a terrace, garden and pool.

Les Lecques ✉ 83270

★★★Grand Hôtel des Lecques, 24 Av du Port, **t** 04 94 26 23 01, **f** 04 94 26 10 22, *www.lecques-hotel.com* (*expensive–moderate*). A white villa with a gastronomic restaurant set in lovely gardens just a stone's throw from the beach. The staff can be snooty. *Half-board only in season. Closed Nov–mid-Mar.*

★★Le Chanteplage, Place de l'Appel-du-18-Juin, **t** 04 94 26 16 55, **f** 04 94 26 25 71 (*moderate*). Right on the seafront, with great views of the coastline and a genial host. *Closed mid-Nov–Feb.*

Hugo. The strange strains of the *tambourin provençal* and the Provençal flute might well be heard from the local bar, hotel and restaurant, a tiny establishment called La Voute which clings to the cliffside amid a flurry of chickens and ducks. The owner and his family are staunch upholders of Provençal traditions and language and, if you are lucky, Patrick, the charismatic local *musicien félibre*, will be there enjoying a drink, playing his drum and whistle and regaling his friends with stories.

The D220 from Ollioules leads on to the wooded mountain ridge of **Le Gros Cerveau**, or 'Big Brain', a curious name of uncertain derivation and site of another *oppidum*. It, too, has strange rock formations and is pitted with caves, where 'witches' hid in the time of Louis XIII – in 1616 three were sentenced to be strangled, hanged, and then burned for good measure.

Bandol

Travellers will find Bandol, sheltered from the mistral, either a preview or a *déjà vu* of the typical Côte d'Azur town: pretty houses and lanes festooned with flowers, palm trees, boutiques, a casino, the morning market in Place de la Liberté, and an over-saturation of villas on the outskirts.

But Bandol has something most of the Riviera hotspots lack – its own excellent wine and a little island, **Ile de Bendor**. A barren 6-hectare rock when Paul Ricard bought it with his *pastis* fortune in 1950, it is now an adult playground, a masterpiece of architectural dissonance from the 1950s and '60s – Ricard himself hopes that it will some day fall in ruins and become 'a 20th-century Delos'. There's a diving and wind-surfing school, a nautical club, an art school and gallery, a business centre, hotels and the **Exposition Universelle des Vins et Spiritueux** (*t 04 94 29 44 34; open Easter–Sept Thurs, Fri and Sun–Tues 10.30–12.30 and 3–7, Sat 3–7; closed Wed*). The building is deco-rated with frescoes by art students and the displays of 8,000 bottles and glasses from around the world will whet your thirst for some Bandol AOC.

Apart from wine, Bandol offers its visitors pink flamingos, toucans, cockatoos and disgusting Vietnamese pigs in a lovely garden of tropical flora, the **Jardin Exotique et Zoo de Sanary-Bandol**, Route du Beausset, 3km east on the D559 (*t 04 94 29 40 38, www.zoosanary.com; open summer daily 8–12 and 2–7; winter 8–12 and 2–6; adm*). It's near the Moulin de St-Côme, where you can tour the most important olive press in the Var (or, in December and January, watch it at work) and buy a bottle of oil to take home.

North of Bandol are a pair of medieval wine-producing *villages perchés*, both restored, both lovely nonetheless, and neither as virgin as their olive oil. **La Cadière-d'Azur**, definitely a lesser perched village in terms of height, sits on a hill with cliffs sliced sheer on the north side, enjoying views out to the Massif de Ste-Baume and the noisy *autoroute*. Noisiest of all is a local mynah bird who has trained himself to mimic car alarms. **Le Castellet** is perched more precariously over its sea of vines. Much refur-bished, it looks like a film set, and indeed has often been used as such (Marcel Pagnol got here first, for his *Femme du boulanger*); its 12th-century church is attractively austere, although the same cannot be said of the streets full of arty shops.

East of here (follow the D26 towards the N8), the 16th-century agricultural village of **Le Beausset** sits on a plain 2.5km from the 12th-century **Chapelle Notre-Dame-du-Beausset-Vieux** (*t 04 94 98 61 53; open Mon, Thurs and Fri 2–5.30, Tues, Wed and Sun 9.30–5.30, Sat 9–5.30*), with a basalt altar that once served as a millstone in an olive press, and *santons* from the 16th century.

Les Lecques and St-Cyr-sur-Mer

West of Bandol, Les Lecques is an unassuming family resort with a long fine sand beach, set in front of the old Bandol AOC town of **St-Cyr-sur-Mer**, which has some-thing in common with New York – a Statue of Liberty, a scale model of Bartholdi's *grande dame* in Place Portalis, just cleaned up and looking splendid. It's a bustling little place, with a popular market and a formal rose garden, created after France won

Bandol Wine

When a courtier asked Louis XV the secret of his eternal youth, the king replied, 'The wines of Rouve (in Bandol), which give me their vigour and spirit.' They had to have a certain vigour to survive the journey to Versailles, sloshing about in barrels in slow boats from the Mediterranean to the Atlantic and up the Seine. Today Bandol still flexes its charming muscle; averaging €6–9 a bottle, it gets top marks in Provence for value for money.

The arid, wine-coloured *restanques* (terraces) cut into the mountain flanks in the eight *communes* around Bandol have produced wines since 600 BC. Dominated by small, dense mourvèdre grapes (which account for at least 50 per cent of the blend) mixed with cinsault and grenache, the reds are sombre of tone and require patience to reach their peak. Top vintages from **Domaine Tempier** and **Château de Pibarnon** are widely acknowledged as some of the best reds in the world. Bandol also comes in pale salmon-hued rosés, known for their delightful perfume, and dense whites that are to the taste what wild roses are to the nose, and make the ideal accompaniment to grilled fish – 1997 and 1998 were great years.

Some Bandols have extraordinary pedigrees: **Château des Salettes**, at La Cadière-d'Azur (t 04 94 90 06 06, f 04 94 90 04 29), has been in the same family since 1602. The **Domaine Tempier**, up in Le Plan-de-Castellet, t 04 94 98 70 21, f 02 04 94 90 21 65, is widely recognized to produce some of the finest wines in the area.

Other estates to visit are the organic **Domaine de la Tour du Bon**, at Le-Brulat-du-Castellet, t 04 94 32 61 62, f 04 94 32 71 69 (by appointment only), the rising superstar estate, and **Domaine Ray-Jane**, at Le-Plan-du-Castellet, t 04 94 98 64 08, f 04 94 98 68 72, where, besides wine, visitors can examine France's largest collection of cooper's tools. The Comte de Saint-Victor's estate of **Château de Pibarnon**, at La Cadière-d'Azur, t 04 94 90 12 73, f 04 94 90 12 98, is sculpted into rugged limestone flanks geologically millions of years older than their neighbours, which give its spicy reds, charming rosés and fruity whites a personality all their own.

Domaine de la Laidière, at Sainte-Anne d'Evenos, t 04 94 90 37 07, f 04 94 90 38 05, *www.laidiere.com*, is one of the most quality-conscious estates of the area, producing red, white and rosé, with the red wine the finest.

Next to the tourist office, the **Maison des Vins de Bandol** sells most of the labels and has a list of estates open for visits, t 04 94 29 45 03.

See www.vins-de-bandol.com.

the football World Cup in 1998. In the middle of it is a life-size poster of local hero Franc LeBœuf, who comes from the town, arms spread in victory. It also offers the cool, wet delights of **Aqualand** (*t 04 94 32 08 32; open June–Sept*).

Les Lecques itself is one of several places that claim to be ancient Tauroentum, a colony of Greek Marseille where Caesar defeated Pompey in a famous naval battle and gained control of Marseille. But most of the finds in Les Lecques so far have been Roman, as displayed in the **Musée de Tauroentum** on the road to La Madrague (*t 04 94 26 30 46, www.saintcyrsurmer.fr/culture/tauroentum/musee.htm; open*

June–Sept Wed–Mon 3–7; closed Tues; other times Sat, Sun and hols only 2–5; adm). The museum protects the remains of two Roman villas built around the year AD 1, with mosaics and bits of fresco, vases and jewellery, and, outside, an unusual two-storey tomb of a child. Ancient Tauroentum itself is supposed to be somewhere just offshore, lost under the sea. You can look for traces of it along a lonely coastal path (marked with yellow signs) that begins near the museum and continues to Bandol; along the way are little *calanques* for quiet swims.

Metropolitan Provence

10

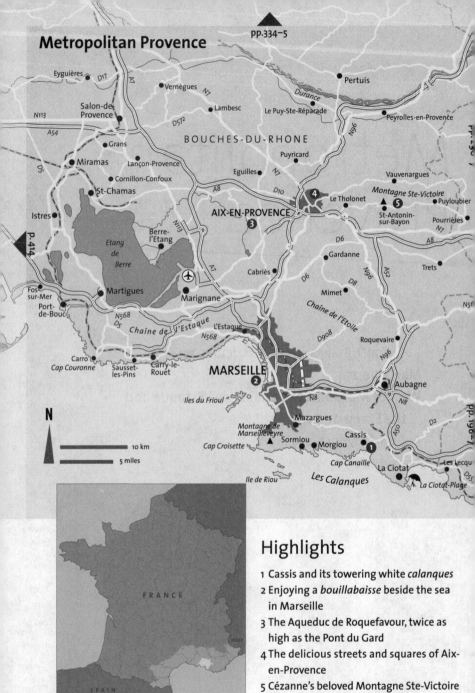

Metropolitan Provence

pp.334–5

Eyguières
D17
Vernègues
N7
Pertuis
Durance
Salon-de-Provence
Lambesc
Le Puy-Ste-Réparade
Peyrolles-en-Provence
N113
A54
N96
Grans
BOUCHES-DU-RHONE
D572
Miramas
Lançon-Provence
Puyricard
Vauvenargues
Cornillon-Confoux
Eguilles
N7
St-Chamas
D10
Montagne Ste-Victoire
Puyloubier
Istres
AIX-EN-PROVENCE
Le Tholonet
St-Antonin-sur-Bayon
Pourrières
Berre-l'Etang
N7
Etang de Berre
D6
A8
Trets
Gardanne
Cabriès
A52
D6
D8
Mimet
Martigues
Marignane
Chaîne de l'Etoile
Fos-sur-Mer
N56
Port-de-Bouc
N568
Chaîne de l'Estaque
L'Estaque
D908
Roquevaire
D5
N568
N96
Carro
Aubagne
Cap Couronne
Sausset-les-Pins
Carry-le-Rouet
MARSEILLE
N8
N8
Iles du Frioul
D2
Mazargues
Montagne de Marseilleveyre
Sormiou
Cassis
Cap Croisette
Morgiou
Cap Canaille
La Ciotat
Les Lecqu
Ile de Riou
Les Calanques
La Ciotat-Plage
D55

p. 414

pp. 196-7

N

10 km

5 miles

FRANCE

ITALY

SPAIN

Highlights

1 Cassis and its towering white *calanques*

2 Enjoying a *bouillabaisse* beside the sea in Marseille

3 The Aqueduc de Roquefavour, twice as high as the Pont du Gard

4 The delicious streets and squares of Aix-en-Provence

5 Cézanne's beloved Montagne Ste-Victoire

Best Beaches

The sandy beach at **Cassis**, p.254, is pretty, with a dramatic backdrop of cliffs, but it gets crowded in summer.

Marseille has an artificial town beach, the Plage du David, which is lively at all times of the year, with soccer, kite-flying, skate-boarding and windsurfing.

For more adventurous sand you need head into the *calanques*, pp.254 and 272–3, where you can walk the clifftop path and descend at will; boats run from Cassis and Marseille.

To the west of Marseille, the Côte Bleue, the playground of the Marseillais, gets crowded during weekends in summer. The beaches are mediocre; **Sausset-les-Pins**, p.275, has sand and caravans; the best is at **Carro**, the furthest from Marseille, hence the quietest.

For real sand you need to continue west, to the **Camargue** (*see* pp.438–50).

Although this is the business end of Provence, the most densely populated, hurly-burly, industrial and everything-else-you've-come-to-get-away-from part of Provence, the region holds several trump cards: elegant and lively Aix-en-Provence, with its incredible markets and its landscape synonymous with the paintings of Cézanne; a tumultuous coastline ripped into the bones of the earth between La Ciotat and Marseille; and Marseille itself, every bit as good as its magnificent setting, as bad as any big port city, and as ugly as the fish in its heavenly *bouillabaisse*. Another plus is the state-funded museums in the *département* of the Bouches du Rhône. There are some good ones, and only Paris has more than Marseille.

La Ciotat, Cassis and the *Calanques*

Before settling down and creating the broad, smooth bay that permits the existence of Marseille, the Provençal coast bucks and rears with the fury of wild horses. La Ciotat, located halfway between Toulon and Marseille, is a hard-nosed and gritty shipbuilding town, while chic, well-heeled Cassis is endowed with a dramatic setting, a bijou harbour and delicate wine.

La Ciotat: the World's First Film Set

A safe anchorage with fresh water and beaches, protected from the winds by an eroded rock formation known as the Bec de l'Aigle ('eagle's beak'), La Ciotat has seen ancient Greeks, pirates, fishermen and, since the time of François Ier, shipbuilders – though instead of galleys to battle the Holy Roman Empire, the yards now produce vessels to transport liquefied gas. La Ciotat has also given the world two momentous pastimes. First came motion pictures, which were pioneered here in 1895 when Auguste and Louis Lumière filmed a train pulling into La Ciotat station (*L'Entrée d'un train en gare de La Ciotat*), a clip that made the first film spectators jump out of their seats as the locomotive seemed to bear down upon them; the **Eden Théâtre**, where it was shown on 28 December 1895, is presently closed, but the town is raising funds for its restoration. The second is *pétanque*, that most Provençal of sports, which came

Getting Around

La Ciotat is a main stop for **trains** (t 08 36 35 35 35) between Marseille and Toulon; regular buses (t 04 42 08 90 90) cover the 3km from the station to the Vieux Port.

Cassis has less frequent services and its train station is just as far from the centre; if you're coming from Marseille, take one of the frequent coaches, which drop you off at bd Anatole France, near the tourist office.

Boats leave from Cassis throughout the day for the *calanques* (t 04 42 01 90 83).

Bike Hire

Lleba Cycles, 3 bis Av Frédéric Mistral, La Ciotat, t 04 42 83 60 30.

Carnax Bikes, Av Foche, Cassis, t 06 03 78 57 85.

Tourist Information

La Ciotat: Bd Anatole France, t 04 42 08 61 32, *www.laciotatourisme.com. Open June–Sept Mon–Sat 9–8, Sun 10–1; Oct–May Mon–Sat 9–12 and 2–6.*

Cassis: Oustau Calendal, Quai des Moulins, t 08 92 25 98 92, *www.cassis.fr. Open July and Aug Mon–Fri 9–7, Sat, Sun and hols 9.30–12.30 and 3–6; June and Sept Mon–Fri 9–12.30 and 2–6.30, Sat and Sun 10–12; Mar–May and Oct Mon–Fri 9.30–12.30 and 2–6, Sat 10–12 and 2–5, Sun and hols 10–12; Nov–Feb Mon–Fri 9.30–12.30, Sat 10–12 and 2–5, Sun 10–12.*

Market Days

La Ciotat: Tues and Sun am, plus July and Aug 8pm–midnight on the Vieux Port.
Cassis: Wed and Fri am.

Festivals

La Ciotat: **Screenwriter's Festival**: April.
Cassis: **Fishermen's Festival**: last weekend June.

Where to Stay and Eat

La Ciotat ✉ 13600

Quai Stalingrad, near the shipyards, has the best choice of restaurants with cheap menus, most featuring seafood.

★★★Miramar, 3 Bd Beaurivage, t 04 42 83 33 79, *www.miramarlaciotat.com* (*expensive– moderate*). A classy hotel amid pine groves by the beach. Its restaurant, **L'Orchidée**,

into being here in 1907, when one old-timer's legs became paralysed and he could no longer take the regulation steps before a throw, as laid down in the laws of *boules*. The rules were changed for him and, as everyone enjoyed working up less of a sweat, they stuck.

Most visitors to La Ciotat keep to the beaches and marina around **La Ciotat-Plage** (where you'll find a monument to the Lumière brothers), but it's really the business side of things, around the **Vieux Port**, that affords the best loafing opportunities; in the evening the shipyard cranes come to resemble luminous mutant insects. The **Musée Ciotaden** (*Quai Ganteaume, t 04 42 71 40 99; open mid-June–mid-Sept Wed–Mon 4–7; mid-Sept–mid-June Wed–Mon 3–6*) is dedicated to the history of La Ciotat and its shipyards.

Beyond the latter, amid the wind-sculpted rocks and dishevelled Mediterranean flora of the Bec de l'Aigle, is the clifftop **Parc du Mugel** (bus 3 from the Vieux Port). Avenue de Figuerolles continues from here to the red pudding-stone walls and pebble beach of the **Calanque de Figuerolles**, with its hunchback monkish rock formation, once painted by Georges Braque.

Floating offshore, the wee **Ile Verte** can be reached by boat from Quai Ganteaume; it has a restaurant and views back to the mainland that explain how the 'eagle's beak' got its name.

t 04 42 83 09 54, is the best in town. *Restaurant closed Sat lunch, Sun eve, Mon.*

La Rotonde, 44 Bd de la République, t 04 42 08 67 50, *www.hotellarotonde-laciotat.com* (*moderate*). The best bet near the Vieux Port.

*Beaurivage, 1 Bd Beaurivage, t 04 42 98 04 34 (*moderate*). A good budget choice. *Closed Oct–Feb.*

République Indépendante de Figuerolles, Calanque de Figuerolles, t 04 42 08 41 71 (*inexpensive*). A grandly named *chambre d'hôte* on the beach, with a very good restaurant (*moderate*) that becomes Russian between December and May. *Closed Nov–mid-Dec.*

Cassis ✉ 13260

****Les Roches Blanches**, 9 Av des Calanques, t 04 42 01 09 30, *www.roches-blanches-cassis.com* (*expensive*). The most spectacular hotel in the area, perched on the promontory overlooking Cassis bay. Rooms are a tad small but very comfortable; there's a private beach and sun terraces.

***Les Jardins de Cassis**, Rue Auguste Favier, t 04 42 01 84 85, *www.hotel-lesjardinsde-cassis. com* (*expensive–inexpensive*). A Provençal-style oasis set amidst lemon groves and bougainvillaea, with a pool and restaurant. *Closed Nov–Mar.*

***Le Royal Cottage**, 6 Av du 11-Novembre, t 04 42 01 33 34, *www.royal-cottage.com* (*expensive*). A hotel just above the port, in a quiet park, with a pool, air-conditioning and well-equipped rooms, but no restaurant. *Closed Christmas–New Year.*

Le Grand Jardin, 2 Rue Pierre Eydin, t 04 42 01 70 10 (*inexpensive*). A hotel offering modern rooms, with a terrace, in the centre of town.

Le Laurence, 8 Rue de l'Arène, t 04 42 01 88 78 (*inexpensive*). A reasonably priced option with views up to the château. *Closed Nov–Jan.*

Chez César, 21 Quai des Baux, t 04 42 01 75 47 (*moderate*). Fresh seafood served up amidst Marcel Pagnol décor. The rosy-pink local sea urchins (*oursins*) feature prominently when in season. *Closed Tues eve and Wed.*

Nino, 1 Quai Barthélémy, t 04 42 01 74 32 (*moderate*). A restaurant offering tasty fish soup, grilled prawns and more on a summery seaside terrace. *Closed Sun eve and Mon.*

Route des Crêtes

If you sneer at vertigo and laugh in the face of hairpin turns, ignore the main road between La Ciotat and Cassis, and instead twist and turn along the 17km **Corniche des Crêtes**. Alternatively, a footpath cuts through the road loops, taking about four hours. You will be rewarded with plunging views from France's highest cliffs: the **Falaises du Soubeyran**, or Grande Tête ('big head', 1,309ft), and craggy **Cap Canaille**. From Pas de la Colle, the road and path descend to the ancient Gallo-Roman Portus Carcisis, now known as Cassis.

Cassis and the *Calanques*

The old coral-fishing village of Cassis, with its fish-hook port, white cliffs, beaches and quaint houses spilling down steep alleyways, was a natural favourite of the Fauve painters. Since their day, the village has made the inevitable progression from fishing to artsy to chic, and is now beyond the purse of most fishermen and artists. The swanky, modern **Casino Municipal** does a roaring trade thanks to its proximity to the gambling-mad Marseillais, and in summer so many tourists descend on the little port that it's often elbow-room only here and on the pebbly **Plage de Bestouan**. When they're not counting wads of banknotes, the Cassidans bestir themselves to make one of the most delicious, fragrant white wines of Provence (*see* overleaf).

Wine: Cassis AOC

In Cassis, they say their white wine obtained its divine quality when God came down the road from heaven and shed a tear at the plight of a family trying to scratch a living from the rocky amphitheatre overlooking the village. The divine tear fell on a vine and *voilà*, it gave birth to a dry wine of a pale green tint, with a bouquet of heather and rosemary.

The Cassis district is minute but was one of the first to be granted AOC status (1936). Ugni blanc, marsanne, clairette and bourboulenc are the dominant grapes of this pale cocktail, popularized abroad by the late James Beard and considered by the Marseillais to be the only liquid worthy of washing down *bouillabaisse*, grilled red mullet and lobster. Try some in the vast, ancient cellars of **Clos Sainte-Magdeleine**, **t** 04 42 01 70 28, and **Château de Fontcreuse**, Route de La Ciotat, **t** 04 42 01 71 09, the district's only real château, which between the wars was the property of a retired English colonel who improved the stock and carved out new vineyards in the steep limestone hills.

Until 1990, Cassis had yet another profitable trade: exporting crystal-white stone, hewn from the sheer limestone cliffs that stand like a great jagged sea wall between Cassis and Marseille. Here and there the cliffs are pierced by startling tongues of lapis lazuli hue – mini-fjords known as *calanques*. The nearest, **Port-Miou**, is accessible by car or foot (a 30min walk): its hard, white stone was cut for the Suez Canal. Another 1.5km hike will take you to **Port-Pin**, with a pretty beach, and from there it's another hour to **En-Vau**, the most beautiful of them all, with a small skinny-dippers' beach tucked under the sheer cliffs, where daring human flies dangle from threads (you can also reach En-Vau with less toil from a car park on the Col de la Gardiole). Serious walkers can continue along the GR98 all the way to Marseille.

Note that since being ravaged by forest fires in 1990 the paths to the *calanques* have been **off limits** from mid-June to the second Saturday in September, when the only way to visit is by motor boat from Cassis port; excursions depart frequently through the day. If they let you disembark in the *calanques*, you must stick to the shore.

Marseille

Marseille isn't a city; it's a shock.
Marseille tourist office

Amid Provence's carefully nurtured image of lavender fields, rosé wine and *pétanque*, Marseille , France's second city and the world's eighth largest port, is the great anomaly. Like New York, it's been the gateway to a new world for hundreds of thousands of immigrants. Many have gone no further, creating in Marseille perhaps the most varied mix of cultures and religions in Europe, 'the meeting place of the entire world', as Alexandre Dumas called it. It is traditionally the great anti-Paris, ever defiant of central authority and bigwigs in any form, be they Julius Caesar, Louis XIV, Napoleon, Hitler or De Gaulle.

Central Marseille

Getting There and Around

By Air

Marseille's airport, *www.marseille.aeroport. fr*, is northwest of the city at Marignane; call **t** 04 42 14 14 14 for flight information. Air France, BA and easyJet have regular flights to Marseille from London; *see* **Travel**.

A bus every 20mins (**t** 04 91 50 59 34) connects the airport with the train station, Gare St-Charles, taking 25mins.

By Train

Gare St-Charles (1er), **t** 0801 813 813, the main train station with its great ironwork vault designed by Gustave Eiffel, has rail links with nearly every town in the south. The TGV to Paris takes 3hrs.

By Boat

For ferries to Algeria (politics permitting), Corsica, Sardinia and Tunisia, contact **SNCM**, 61 Bd des Dames (1er), **t** 0891 701 801, *www.sncm.fr*.

On a smaller scale, there's a pedestrian-only 'ferryboat' across the Vieux Port, immortalized by Marcel Pagnol.

By Métro and Bus

Marseille has an efficient bus network and two métro lines; the métro is safe, quick and highly efficient, but the buses can be pretty hard work. Pick up the useful *plan du réseau* at the tourist office or at the RTM (Réseau de Transport Marseillais) information desk close to the Bourse, 6–8 Rue des Fabres (1er), **t** 04 91 91 92 10.

Tickets are valid for an hour, or you can buy a day pass; both are transferable between bus and métro. Night buses (Fluobus) run from La Canebière across town.

The *gare routière*, **t** 04 91 08 16 40, *www. lepilote.com*, located at 3 Place Victor Hugo, has connections to Aix-en-Provence, Cassis, Nice, Arles, Avignon, Toulon and Cannes.

RTM also runs a daily bilingual tour bus, *Le Grand Tour*, with 3hr guided tours of historic Marseille. It leaves at 2pm from the Vieux Port directly in front of the boats for the islands, and allows you half an hour to wander around Notre-Dame-de-la-Garde.

By Taxi

Marseille's taxi drivers seem to be maniacs to a man. If you need one, call **t** 04 91 02 20 20, and make sure the meter is switched on at the start of your journey.

Car Hire

Car hire firms in Gare St-Charles include **Avis**, **t** 0820 61 16 36, *www.avis.fr*. **Hertz** is at 16 Bd Charles Nédelec (1er), **t** 04 91 14 04 24, *www.hertz.fr*, and **Thrifty** at Place des Marseillaises (1er), **t** 04 91 95 00 00, *www. thrifty.co.uk*.

Driving in central Marseille is not for the faint-hearted, and if you park in the street, only leave things inside the car that you don't want any more.

Tourist Information

Marseille: 4 La Canebière (1er), by the Vieux Port, **t** 04 91 13 89 00, *www.marseille-tourisme.com*. Open July–Sept Mon–Sat 9–7.30, Sun 10–6; Oct–June Mon–Sat 9–7, Sun 10–5. There's also an office in the train station, **t** 04 91 50 59 18.

Check at the La Canebière office for tours of the Opéra Municipal and the Vieux Port forts, and for '*Taxi Tourisme*' – 4 set-price taxi tours of the city, with an English cassette guide.

Post office: The central post office is at 1 Place de l'Hôtel-des-Postes (1er), **t** 04 91 15 47 00.
Emergencies: The hospital is at 264 Rue St-Pierre (5e), **t** 04 91 49 91 91.

Special **information centres** exist for young people, at the very helpful CRIJPA, 96 La Canebière (1er), **t** 04 91 24 33 50; for **disabled visitors**, at the Service Municipal des Handicapés et Inadaptés, at the Mairie, 128 Av du Prado (8e), **t** 04 91 81 58 80; and for **crime victims**, at AVAD, 7 Rue de la République (2e), **t** 04 96 11 68 80.

Market Days
Daily: Place A. et F. Carli (1er, Ⓜ Noailles), old book, postcard and record market.
Every other Sun am: Cours Julien (6e; Ⓜ Notre-Dame-du-Mont), flea market.

Festivals

There are a number of festivals and street parties in Marseille at any given time in the summer, from the lively, eclectic neighbourhood parties of the **Fête du Panier** in late June to the **International Documentary Film Festival** in early July.

If you're around in July it's hard to miss the celebrations for the city's largest party the, **Festival de Marseille** (for tickets call **t** 04 91 99 02 50 or see *www.festivaldemarseille.com*).

Internet Access

Génération Cyber Café, 11 Rue Ferrari (5e), **t** 04 91 47 34 37.

Cyber Café, 1 Quai de Rive Neuve (1er), **t** 04 91 33 74 98.

Shopping

Rue St-Ferréol, home of the Galeries Lafayette and Virgin Megastore, is the centre of the city's shopping district; parallel Rue Paradis has the upmarket boutiques, and Rue de Rome is a good place to look for fake leopardskin.

Marseille holds its market of clay Christmas crib figures, the Foire aux Santons, from end Nov to Jan; at other times, you can see generations of and even buy *santons* at **Marcel Carbonel** (**t** 04 91 54 26 58, *www.santons-marcel carbonel. com*) in the old port at 47 Rue Neuve Ste-Catherine (7e), and even see them being made.

Sports and Activities

The **Olympique de Marseille** (OM; Stade Vélodrome Municipal, Bd Michelet, 8e, **t** 04 91 76 56 09) is France's most enthusiastically supported football squad and tickets for matches often sell out.

Windsurf boards can be hired at Pacific Palissades, Port de la Pointe Rouge (8e), **t** 04 91 73 54 37, or neighbouring Sideral Times Club, **t** 04 91 25 00 90.

Skatepark, Plage Vieille-Chapelle (8^e; no.47 bus), is known as one of the best in the world, and has a strong family atmosphere.

Where to Stay

Marseille ✉ 13000

Marseille's top-notch hotels are the bastion of expense-account businessmen and -women, while its downmarket numbers attract working girls of a different kind. Be sure to book ahead if you're coming in mid-Sept, when Marseille holds its fair and there are no hotel rooms for love or money.

Luxury

****Le Petit Nice Passédat, Anse de Maldormé (7e), off Corniche J.F. Kennedy, **t** 04 91 59 25 92, *www.petitnice-passedat.com*. Marseille's most refined, exclusive hotel, a former villa overlooking the Anse de Maldormé, with a fine restaurant, **Le Passédat** (*see* p.259). *Restaurant closed Sun and Mon.*

Very Expensive

****Mercure Marseille Beauvau Vieux Port, 4 Rue Beauvau (1er), **t** 04 91 54 91 00, *www.accorhotels.com*. A wood-panelled and comfortable hotel overlooking the Vieux Port, with quiet, air-conditioned rooms but no restaurant. Chopin and George Sand canoodled here.

Expensive

***New Hôtel Bompard, 2 Rue des Flots-Bleus (7^e), **t** 04 91 99 22 22, *www.new-hotel.com*. A modern hotel that seems remote from the city, situated above the Corniche J.F. Kennedy (take bus 61 from Ⓜ Joliette or St-Victor) in its own peaceful grounds, with rooms overlooking a garden. There are also *'mas'* suites with kitchenettes.

Moderate

***Le Corbusier, 280 Bd Michelet (8e), **t** 04 91 16 78 00, *www.hotelcorbusier.com*. A hotel-restaurant incorporated into the *unité d'habitation* designed by Le Corbusier (*see* pp.270–71), providing a treat for students of architecture. The 22 rooms get booked up well in advance.

Le Richelieu, 52 Corniche J.F. Kennedy (7e), **t 04 91 31 01 92, *www.lerichelieu-marseille. com*. Good-value, nicely decorated rooms. The breakfast terrace overlooks the sea.

★★Péron, 119 Corniche J.F. Kennedy (7e), **t** 04 91 31 01 41, *www.hotel-peron.com*. An old-fashioned, family-run hotel with bright and colourful rooms.

Inexpensive

★★Azur, 24 Cours Franklin Roosevelt (1er), Ⓜ Canebière-Réformés, **t** 04 91 42 74 38, *www.azur-hotel.fr*. Average rooms with frills such as colour TV and garden views.

★★Moderne, 11 Bd de la Libération (1er), **t** 04 91 62 28 66. Nice enough rooms with en suite showers and TV.

★★Montgrand, 50 Rue Montgrand (6e), **t** 04 91 00 35 20, *www.hotel-montgrand-marseille. com*. A palatable budget choice.

Auberge de Jeunesse de Bois-Luzy, Allée des Primevères (12e), **t** 04 91 49 06 18, *www.fuaj. org*. The better of Marseille's two hostels, in a 19th-century château overlooking the city (take bus 6 or 8 from La Canebière, or bus K after dark; direction La Rose).

Eating Out

The Marseillais claim an ancient Greek – even divine – origin for their ballyhooed **bouillabaisse**: Aphrodite invented it to beguile her husband Hephaestos to sleep so that she could dally with her lover Ares (seafood and saffron being a legendary soporific). Good chefs prepare it just as seriously, and display like a doctor's diploma their *Charte de la Bouillabaisse* guaranteeing that their formula more or less subscribes to tradition: the saffron and garlic-flavoured soup cooked on a low boil (hence its name) is based on *rascasse* (scorpion fish, the ugliest fish in the Med and always cooked with its leering head attached), which lives under the cliffs and has a bland taste that enhances the flavour of the other fish, especially *fielas* (conger eel), *grondin* (gurnard) and *saint-pierre* (John Dory).

On menus you'll usually find three degrees of *bouillabaisse*: simple or *du pêcheur*, made from the day's catch with a few shellfish thrown in; *royale*, with half a lobster included; and, most expensive of all, *royale marseillaise*, the real McCoy, with all the right fish. When it's served, the fish is traditionally cut up

before you and presented on a side dish of *aïoli* or *rouille*, a paste of Spanish peppers.

General Restaurants

Restaurant Michel, 6 Rue des Catalans (7e), **t** 04 91 52 30 63 (*very expensive*). A posh joint with the best, swankiest *bouillabaisse*, the haunt of politicians and showbiz people. *Closed mid–end Feb*.

Miramar, 12 Quai du Port (2e), **t** 04 91 91 10 40 (*very expensive*). A restaurant where you can count on eating some reliable traditional fare. *Closed Sun and Mon*.

Les Mets de Provence Chez Maurice Brun, 2nd floor, 18 Quai de Rive-Neuve (7e), **t** 04 91 33 35 38 (*expensive*). A 50-year-old restaurant proving that there's more than *bouillabaisse* on the Marseille culinary scene. The genuine Provençal spreads include a grand 3-course lunch menu that starts with 8 *hors-d'œuvre* and includes wine. *Closed Sat lunch, Sun, and Mon lunch*.

Une Table au Sud, 2 Quai du Port (2e), **t** 04 91 90 63 53 (*expensive*). Acclaimed cuisine from a young chef who was taught by the legendary Alain Ducasse. *Closed Sun, Mon, 1st wk Jan and 3 wks Aug*.

Le Marseillois, Quai du Port (2e), **t** 04 91 90 72 52 (*expensive–moderate*). A restaurant set on a sailing boat moored stern-on, with local fare and plenty of atmosphere. *Closed Sun and Mon*.

Les Arcenaulx, 25 Cours Honoré d'Estienne d'Orves (1er), **t** 04 91 59 80 30, *www.les-arcenaulx.com* (*moderate*). A restaurant situated in a busy square next to a bookshop, offering fresh market fare. *Closed Sun*.

Oscar, 24 Quai du Port (2e), **t** 04 91 90 26 86 (*moderate*). An extremely popular establishment where you can get a tasty *bouillabaisse*. *Closed Sat and Sun*.

International and Late-night Eating

Marseille's unique ethnic mix, which includes Corsicans, Armenians, Jews, Greeks, Turks, Italians, Spaniards and Algerians, means it has an unrivalled selection of inexpensive cuisines from around the world.

Au Roi du Couscous, 63 Rue de la République (2e), **t** 04 91 91 45 46 *(moderate)*. The best couscous in town. *Closed Mon*.

Shabu Shabu, 30 Rue de la Paix (1er),
t 04 91 54 15 00 (*moderate*). Good Japanese
cuisine. *Closed Sun, Mon lunch.*

Le Mas Lulli, 4 Rue Lulli (1er), by the Opéra,
t 04 91 33 25 90 (*moderate*). A place where
night owls can assuage their hunger pangs
with good pasta dishes and grills. *Open daily
until 6am; closed Aug and 1st week Sept.*

La Gentiane, 9 Rue des Trois-Rois (6e),
t 04 91 42 88 80 (*moderate*). A good place for
vegetarians. *Closed Sun and Mon.*

Country Life, 14 Rue Venture (1er), t 04 96 11 28 00
(*cheap*). A handy vegetarian option.
Open lunchtimes, Mon–Fri only.

Along the Beaches and the *Calanques*

Le Passédat, Le Petit Nice Passédat hotel
(*see* p.257), t 04 91 59 25 92 (*very expensive*).
Ravishing food served in an exotic garden.
Closed Sun and Mon.

L'Epuisette, Vallon des Auffes (7e), t 04 91 52
17 82, *www.l-epuisette.com* (*very expensive–
expensive*). A seafood institution. *Closed
Sun and Mon.*

Chez Fonfon, Vallon des Auffes (7e), t 04 91 52
14 38 (*expensive*). Provençal specialities in a
peaceful spot on the fishing port overlooking
the Château d'If and Frioul islands. *Closed
Sun, and Mon lunch.*

La Grotte, 1 Rue Pebrons, Calanque de
Callelongue (8e), t 04 91 73 17 79 (*expensive–
moderate*). A pizza favourite by the sea.

Pizzeria Jeannot, Vallon des Auffes, t 04 91 52
11 28 (*moderate*). Fancy pizza. *Closed Sun eve
and Mon in winter, Mon only in summer.*

Entertainment and Nightlife

Marseille may be going on 3,000 years old,
but the old girl's still kicking – sometimes in the
wrong places, especially after 10pm in
the streets between the station and the Port.
But you don't have to be a brawny sailor to
have a good time: Marseille has lively after-dark
pockets, especially round Place Thiars, Cours
Honoré Estienne d'Orves and Cours Julien.

Find out what's on in *Taktik*, free at the
tourist office, or in *La Marseillaise*, *Le Provençal*
or the Wednesday edition of *Le Méridional*.

Theatre

Marseille has a vibrant theatre scene.

Théâtre National de la Criée, 32 Quai de Rive-
Neuve (7e), t 04 91 54 70 54. The theatre
where director Marcel Maréchal has put on
performances to wide acclaim since 1981.

Théâtre Les Bernardines, 17 Bd Garibaldi (1er),
t 04 91 24 30 40. A theatre hosting a mix of
experimental dance and theatre.

Théâtre du Merlan, Av Raimu (14e), t 04 91 11
19 21. Avant-garde theatre.

Cinemas

César, 4 Place Castellane (6e), t 04 91 37 12 80.
A cinema showing first-run films in their
original language (*v.o.*).

Cinéma Alhambra, 2 Rue du Cinéma (16e),
t 04 91 03 84 66. Old movies and art films
shown in *v.o.*

Les Variétés, 37 Rue Vincent Scotto, off
La Canebière (1er), t 04 96 11 61 61. A swish
place with first-run films in *v.o.*

Classical Music

The city has always had a special affinity
with music; Berlioz claimed it understood
Beethoven five years before Paris did.

Opéra Municipal, Place Reyer (1er), t 04 91 54
94 15. Italian opera and occasional ballets
by the Ballet National de Marseille.

Ballet National de Marseille, 20 Bd Gabès (8e),
t 04 91 32 72 72, *www.ballet-de-marseille.com*.
The city's ballet company.

Abbaye St-Victor, 3 Rue de l'Abbaye (7e),
t 04 96 11 22 60. A chamber music festival
venue (Oct and Dec).

Iles du Frioul. A music festival venue in July.

Bars and Clubs

Nightlife in Marseille is concentrated in
several zones. Place Jean Jaurès/Cours Julien
and around is perhaps the trendiest place.
There are also bars and Latin clubs aplenty
along the seafront at Plage de Borély (8e), and
a number of new places at Escale Borély.

Chocolat Théâtre, 59 Cours Julien (6e), t 04 91
42 19 29. Music, pastries and *plats du jour*
(*moderate*). *Closed Sun, and Mon eve.*

Espace Julien, 39 Cours Julien (6e), t 04 91 24
34 14, *www.espace-julien.com*. Jazz, rock and
reggae, plus a café with live music.

Unfortunately, Marseille has also shared some of New York's less savoury traits: racism, smuggling of all sorts, its lingering *French Connection* reputation earned by the petty crooks and hardened gangsters of the French mafia or *milieu* (one of whom, according to a recent theory, was the man on the famous grassy knoll who shot JFK). Unemployment is disproportionately high (up to 30 per cent in some *arrondissements*), and xenophobia thrives. Recent presidential elections saw Marseille vote 25 per cent for National Front leader Jean-Marie Le Pen, yet the city was also the scene of the most seething anti-Le Pen demonstrations.

'These Marseillais make Marseilles hymns, and Marseilles vests, and Marseilles soap for all the world; but they never sing their hymns, or wear their vests, or wash with their soap themselves,' wrote Mark Twain. So what *do* they do? Marseille, in spite of character to spare, is a great unknown, a metropolis of 111 villages that in its 2,600 years has contributed precious little to civilisation; it is the eternal capital of great expectations, 'a city that's been waiting for Godot', according to an editor in one of Marseille's young publishing houses.

But one senses that its long bottled-up juices are about to be uncorked. Today's Marseille has a jaunty new look, through a renewed sense of local pride as well as through the state funds for restoration that came with its recently declared status as a *ville d'art*. But it's not all about looks; people are also waking up to the fact that this very old city is the last place on the French Med with an real edge or swagger – you can feel it in the colourful, vibrant spontaneity in the streets and cafés, in the rhythms of the drum pounding at an OM game, and during carnival, when a home-made explosion of energy and fun flow like hot lava down La Canebière. Luc Besson's film *Taxi* was an unexpected international hit that led to a sequel, and local group IAM continue to control the French hip-hop sence with their distinctive sound.

Yet as Marseille becomes hip and savvy, it also very much wants to remain distinctly Marseille, and residents are taking an increasingly jaundiced view of the new TGV trains that link the city to its old rival Paris in three short hours. The *envahisseurs* have already purchased their first holiday flats...

History

The story goes that in 600 BC Greek colonists from the Ionian city of Phocaea, having obtained the approval of the gods, loaded their ship with olive saplings and sailed towards Gaul. They found a perfect bay, and their handsome leader, Protis, went to the local king to obtain permission to found a city. It just so happened that that very day the king was hosting a banquet for the young men of his land, after which, according to tradition, his daughter Gyptis would select her husband. Protis was invited to join and, thanks to his great beauty, was chosen by the princess. For his new wife's dowry, Protis asked for the land the Greeks coveted near the mouth of the Rhône, including the Lacydon (the Vieux Port). He named the new city Massalia.

Massalia boomed from the start. By 530 BC it had its own treasury at Delphi, and its own colonies, from Málaga to Nice; it traded for tin with Cornwall; and its great astronomer, Pytheas, explored the Baltic and in 350 BC became the first scientist to calculate latitudes accurately. As a commercial rival of Carthage, the city allied itself with Rome in the Punic Wars, and profited from the latter's conquests in Spain and Gaul. By the 2nd century BC, Massalia had a population of 50,000 and was ruled by a merchant oligarchy whose political astuteness was admired by Aristotle and Cicero. This astuteness failed them when they sided with Pompey, calling down the vengeance of Caesar, who conquered their city after a long siege and seized all of Massalia's colonies with the exception of Nice and Hyères. Yet even after the 2nd century AD, when Massalia adopted Roman law, it remained a city apart, the westernmost enclave of Hellenism, with famous schools of Greek rhetoric and medicine.

As the Pax Romana crumbled, Marseille nearly went out of business, taking hard knocks from Goths, Franks, Saracens and then the Franks again in the 8th century under Charles Martel. Plagued by pirates, business stayed bad until the 11th century, when the Crusaders showed up looking for transport to the Holy Land. This was the get-rich-quick opportunity of the Middle Ages, and though Genoa and Venice grabbed the biggest trading concessions in the Levant, Marseille too grew fat on the proceeds. Briefly a republic, the city soon saw its real power passed to a merchant oligarchy; from 1178 to 1192 the big boss was the cultivated En Barral, patron of two of Provence's greatest troubadours, the mad Peire Vidal (see p.42) and Folquet of Marseille.

Trumped by Kings: Charles d'Anjou to Louis XIV

When Charles d'Anjou acquired Provence in 1252, he confiscated Marseille's entire fleet to make good his claim on Sicily. Thanks to the monumental arrogance of the Angevins, the ships were annihilated in the revolt of the Sicilian Vespers (1282). With its legitimate commerce undermined by its own rulers, Marseille became a den for pirates and went into such a decline that it became an easy target for the Angevins' rival, Alfonso V of Aragon, who destroyed as much of it as he could in 1423.

Coming under French rule in 1481 meant, for Marseille, tumbling headlong into the power-grasping scrum known as the Wars of Italy (1494–1559). The city's galleys went to war again, this time for François Ier, earning the fury of Emperor Charles V, who sent his henchman, the rebel Constable of Bourbon, to besiege the city. Marseille resisted heroically and François Ier showed his gratitude by giving the city the freedom to trade at will in the eastern Mediterranean. Once again the money rolled in, to be pumped into new industries, especially soap and sugar.

Marseille's longing to be left alone to mind its own affairs put it squarely at odds with Louis XIV; for 40 years the city thumbed its nose at His Solar Majesty while scrambling to retain its autonomy. By 1660, the king had had enough: he opened up a great breach in Marseille's walls and humiliated the city by turning its own cannons back on itself. The central authority that Louis forced on Marseille was dangerously lax when it came to issues crucial to the running of a good port – such as quarantine. The result, in 1720, was a devastating plague that spread throughout Provence.

Tunes, Booms and Busts

Marseille buried its dead and went right back to business. New markets in the Middle East, North Africa and America made it Europe's greatest port in the 18th century. Its industries (soap, woollens, porcelain, tarot cards) blossomed – then withered away in the Revolution, which for 10 years bitterly divided workers and the oligarchy. The former did their share in upholding the Revolution; as 500 volunteers set off for Paris in July 1792, someone suggested singing the new battle song of the Army of the Rhine, composed by Claude-Joseph Rouget de l'Isle. It caught on, and as the Marseillais marched along they improved the rhythm and harmonies. By the time they reached Paris, the 'song of the Marseillais' was perfected and became the hit tune of the Revolution, and subsequently the most rousing and bloodcurdling of national anthems.

However, as the Revolution devolved into the Terror, Marseille was found so wanting in proper politics that it was known in Paris as the 'ville sans nom'. Any building that had sheltered an anti-Revolutionary was demolished, including the famous monastery of St Victor. The misery continued under Napoleon, who was added to the list of Marseille's bogeymen when he provoked the continental blockade by the British and ruined trade. Recovery came with the Second Empire, the conquest of Algeria in 1830 and the construction of the Suez Canal. Soon Marseille was more prosperous than ever, and more populous, with some 60,000 new immigrants every decade between 1850 and 1930 – Greeks and Armenians fleeing the Turks, Italians fleeing Fascism and, later, Spaniards fleeing Franco.

After becoming one of the first French cities to vote socialist (in 1890), Marseille's reputation took a nosedive. Corruption, rigged elections and an open link between the Hôtel de Ville and the bosses of the *milieu* were so rampant that in 1938 Paris dissolved the municipal government and ran the city at a distance. Yet the 1930s also saw the film release of Marcel Pagnol's classic Marseillais trilogy *Marius*, *Fanny* and *César*, which helped create throughout France an insatiable appetite for *opérette marseillaise*; even Joséphine Baker sang the tunes of Marseille's great songwriter Vincent Scotto.

In 1953 Marseille elected a socialist mayor – Gaston Deferre, the antagonist of De Gaulle, who reigned until his death in 1986. Deferre oversaw rapid and difficult changes: a sharp decline in trade when France lost its colonies, and a population that exploded from 660,000 in 1955 to 960,000 in 1975. To accommodate the new arrivals (mostly North Africans and French refugees from Algeria), the city infested itself with the shoddy high-rise housing that scars it to this day. Unemployment rose as the traditional soap and fat industries plummeted, while new projects, such as the steel mills and port at Fos-sur-Mer, failed to provide as many jobs as expected, fuelling the racial tensions and organized crime that still give the city its rough reputation. This image has softened, but there are still muzzled rottweilers at every métro station.

Even when the city, or at least its revered soccer team, L'Olympique de Marseille, won the European championship in 1993, the team got itself banned from the 1994 European competition for match fixing and bribery. The team's flamboyant then-owner, maverick politician, businessman and Euro-deputy Bernard Tapie, served eight months in Marseille's most notorious jail for the offences. The scandal continues, with a recent audit revealing more than 85 per cent of the club's revenue going to players' salaries alone.

Orientation

Marseille, with 11 neighbourhoods and 16 *arrondissements*, is one of Europe's largest cities, sprawling over twice as many acres as Paris. The northernmost neighbourhoods are the poorest, the first addresses of many new immigrants; the Panier (*see* pp.264–7) and neighbourhoods around the station constitute the North African quarters, lively during the day although uncomfortable to wander in after dark on a poorly lit road. The southern neighbourhoods, with their parks and access to the beaches, are distinctly more monied and sanitized. A circle of hills divides the city from the mainland, physically and psychologically.

The Vieux Port, the heart of the city since its founding, is now used only for pleasure craft and boats out to the islets of Frioul and the Château d'If, while commercial port activities are concentrated to the north in the Rade de Marseille. To the south of the Vieux Port, the golden Virgin of Notre-Dame de la Garde towers high over her beloved city, while to the west the Parc du Pharo marks the beginning of a corniche road along the coast to Cap Croisette, lined with coves, beaches and restaurants, with a mountain, Marseilleveyre, that you can climb at the end for a view of all of the above.

Less well known than all the scandals is Marseille's reorientation, for the first time in its history, away from the Mediterranean and towards Europe. There's a new TGV rail link with Paris, and a canal will link the Rhône with the Rhine by 2010. Marseille is now the most important research centre in France after Paris, home of a major science university, inventor of a new, fifth-generation computer language, and site of COMEX, the world's leading developer of underwater technologies.

The Vieux Port

Marseille the urban mangrove entwines its aquatic roots around the neat, rectangular Vieux Port, inhabited for the past 2,600 years. It's now a huge marina with more than 10,000 berths; its cafés have fine sunset views, though in the morning the action and smells centre around the Quai des Belges and its boatside **fish market**, where the key ingredients of *bouillabaisse* are touted in a racy *patois* as thick as the soup itself. From the Quai des Belges, *vedettes* sail to the Château d'If and Iles de Frioul (*see* p.273), past the two bristling fortresses that still defend the harbour: to the north **St-Jean**, first built in the 12th century by the Knights of St John, and to the south **St-Nicolas**, built by Louis XIV to keep a close eye on Marseille rather than the sea.

A bronze marker in the Quai des Belges pinpoints the spot where the Greeks first set foot in Gaul. Yet Marseille concealed its age until the 20th century, when excavations for the glitzy new shopping mall, the Centre Bourse, revealed the eastern ramparts and gate of Massalia, dating back to the 3rd century BC, now enclosed in the **Jardin des Vestiges**. On the ground floor of the Centre Bourse, the **Musée d'Histoire de Marseille** (*t* 04 91 90 42 22; open Mon–Sat 12–7; adm) displays models, everyday items, mosaics and a 3rd-century BC wreck of a Roman ship, discovered in 1974. Built from 15 different kinds of pine, it had become so fragile that it had to be freeze-dried, like instant coffee, to prevent further deterioration and aid preservation.

Elaborate antique models of later ships that sailed into the Vieux Port and items related to Marseille's trading history are the main focus of the **Musée de la Marine et de l'Economie de Marseille** (*t 04 91 39 33 33; open Wed–Sun 10–6; closed Tues; adm*). It's housed in the 1860 **Palais de la Bourse**, France's oldest stock exchange, built during the reign of Napoléon III to obliterate an unrepentant democratic quarter that spilled much blood in the Revolution of 1848. But this corner, stock exchange or not, remained a vortex for violence: a plaque on the Canebière side of the Bourse recalls that King Alexander of Yugoslavia was assassinated here in 1934.

Just up La Canebière from here, at No.11, the **Musée de la Mode** (*t 04 91 17 06 00; open summer Tues–Sun 10–5; winter Tues–Sun 11–6; closed Mon; adm*) has a wardrobe full of Chanel clothes and other pieces from the 1930s to the present, but they're not always on display. The emphasis is on changing exhibitions.

Le Panier

On sunny afternoons the Marseillais laze like contented cats in the cafés lining the north end of the Vieux Port – a custom probably as old as the city itself. Behind them is the oldest part of the city, known rather oddly as Le Panier ('the basket') after a popular 17th-century cabaret, although its weave of winding narrow streets and stairs dates from the time of the ancient Greeks. When the well-to-do moved out in the 18th century, Le Panier was given over to fishermen and a romanticized underworld; guides were published to its 'private' hotels and the hourly rates of their residents.

Before the war Le Panier was a lively Corsican and Italian neighbourhood, and later its warren of secret ways absorbed hundreds of Jews and other refugees from the Nazis, hoping to escape to America (*see* box, opposite). In January 1943, Hitler cottoned on to the leaks in Marseille and, in collusion with local property speculators, gave the order to dynamite everything between the Vieux Port and halfway up the hill, to the Grand'Rue/Rue Caisserie. Given just one day to evacuate, the 20,000 departing residents were screened by French police and the Gestapo, who selected 3,500 for the concentration camps and sent them out of the city in a long line of tram cars. A monument in the quarter commemorates the destruction and deportees who never returned.

Santons

Christmas crèches with figures of the Nativity go back a long way in Provence. According to tradition, St Francis set up the first crèche in the 13th century, but some say it may have been his mother (from Tarascon or Beaucaire) who showed him how. At any rate, every church in Provence had a crèche at Christmas, and when the Revolution closed the churches in 1789, the people sorely missed their nativity scenes. It was then that Jean-Louis Lagnel (1764–1822) of Marseille invented *santons* (little saints) – handpainted clay figures in traditional Provençal dress doing traditional Provençal things, that people could afford and take into their homes. They were an instant success, and in 1806 the first *santon* fair was set up along the Canebière. It's still going strong, from the end of November to Epiphany.

One Good Man

In the early 1940s, in spite of open visa quotas, the US Department of State with its prejudiced, bury-its-head-in-the-sand bureaucracy maintained a policy of turning back ships of refugees from Hitler. Consulates in Europe were advised, as one memo put it, 'to resort to various administrative devices which would postpone and postpone and postpone the granting of the visas'. In one particularly shameful episode, the US Vice Consul in Lyon denied visas to Jewish children because their parents might be arrested, leaving their children to become public charges in the USA.

The one hero in the story was Varian Fry. Two months after the Nazis occupied Marseille, 32-year-old Fry, editor of a New York foreign policy review, arrived in the city as the representative of a privately funded group called the Emergency Rescue Committee. Although he had no previous experience in the field, and in spite of the considerable risks from the Gestapo and Vichy and the opposition of his own government, Fry quickly made himself an expert in obtaining false papers, forging documents and organizing safe transport out of Marseille: among the 1,500 people he saved were Marcel Duchamp, Marc Chagall, Hannah Arendt, André Breton and Max Ernst. Fry worked for 13 months before he was expelled from Marseille. On his return to the United States, he published an article on the systematic persecution of the Jews and the concentration camps, which made later pleas of official ignorance ring less than true.

Just before Varian Fry died in 1967, the French government awarded him the Legion of Honour. And in October 2000 a square next to the American consulate (on Boulevard Paul Peytral) was named in his honour, Place Varian Fry. Presiding over the dedication ceremony was the US ambassador to France, Felix Rohatyn, who as a child was spirited out of occupied Marseille, in all likelihood by the good offices of Fry.

Two buildings were protected from the dynamite: the 17th-century **Hôtel de Ville** (*conferences and guided tours only; enquire at tourist office*) on the quay and, behind it, in Rue de la Prison, the **Maison Diamantée**, Marseille's 16th-century Mannerist masterpiece, named after the pyramidical points of its façade. It holds the **Musée du Vieux Marseille** (*temporary exhibitions only; enquire at tourist office*), a delightful attic where the city stashes its odds and ends, including Provençal furniture; 18th-century Neapolitan Christmas crib figures and *santons* (*see* box, left) playing cards and tarot cards, long an important local industry; and poignant photos of Le Panier before it was blown to smithereens. Some of the cheap housing thrown up after the war in Place du Mazeau has been demolished in turn to make way for a museum dedicated to the flamboyant sculptor and native Marseillais César.

The dynamite that blew up lower Le Panier was responsible for revealing the contents of the **Musée des Docks Romains** (*2 Place Vivaux, t 04 91 91 24 62; open June–Sept Tues–Sun 11–6; Oct–May Tues–Sun 10–5; adm*), built over a stretch of the vast 1st-century AD Roman quay, where wine and grains were stored in *dolia*, or massive jars. Exhibits describe seafaring in the ancient Mediterranean.

One last survivor of the pre-war Le Panier is the oldest house in Marseille, the **Hôtel de Cabre** (1535), a Gothic–Renaissance confection on Grand'Rue. The city's oldest café, the 1903 **Café Parisien**, with colourful mosaics intact, is just up from here on Place Sadi Carnot.

The Panier retains its original crusty character atop the well-worn steps of **Montée des Accoules** and around **Place de Lenche**, which was once the marketplace or *agora* of the Greeks: lanky cats prowl around, laundry flaps, cement mixers grind away, people sit on the pavement in kitchen chairs – it still feels more Greek than French, although that may soon change. A five-year programme to rehabilitate 1,700 of the Panier's 3,000 homes and flats has begun in earnest, with the ground floors set aside for shops of 'touristic interest' (although there is no evidence of *santon* and lavender oil shops yet).

Signs point the way through the maze to the top of Rue du Petit Puits and the elegant **Vieille-Charité**, designed by Pierre Puget, a student of Bernini, court architect to Louis XIV and native of Le Panier. Built by the city fathers between 1671 and 1745 to take in homeless migrants from the countryside, this is one of the world's most palatial workhouses, with three storeys of arcaded ambulatories in pale pink stone, overlooking a court with a sumptuous elliptical chapel crowned by an oval dome – a curvaceous Baroque work forced into a strait-laced neo-Corinthian façade in 1863. Although the complex became a barracks after the Revolution, it returned to its original purpose in 1860, housing families displaced first by the construction of the Bourse and later by the Nazis' destruction of Le Panier. By 1962, the Charité was in so precarious a state that everyone was evacuated, and Le Corbusier, happening through, warned the city it was in danger of losing a masterpiece. A long restoration ensued and in 1985 it reopened – a shelter no longer for the homeless but for culture.

The middle gallery of the Charité houses the excellent **Musée d'Archéologie Méditerranéenne** (*t 04 91 14 58 80; open Tues–Sun 10–5; adm*), featuring a collection of ancient Mediterranean artefacts. The remarkable collection of Egyptian art (the second-best in France after the Louvre) has a range of fine art and sculpture plus bric-a-brac and cat, ibis and crocodile mummies; there are also beautiful works from ancient Cyprus, Susa, Mesopotamia, Greece (including a good section of vases), and pre-Roman and Roman Italy. Another section is devoted to the reconstructed sanctuary of Roquepertuse from Velaux, near Aix. Built by a head-hunting Celto-Ligurian tribe called the Salians, the sanctuary has pillars pierced with holes to hold skulls, a lintel incised with the outline of four horse heads (these symbolically transported the dead soul), and Buddha-like figures sitting in the lotus position. Similar temples found in Entremont (*see* pp.293–4) and Mouriès suggest a common religion, perhaps a chthonic cult in which warriors went to commune with the spirits of their dead heroes.

The Charité also houses the **Musée d'Arts Africain, Océanien et Amérindien** (*t 04 91 14 58 38; open Tues–Sun summer 11–6, winter 10–5; adm*), with a fascinating collection of ritual artefacts, especially those dealing with more recent cultures obsessed with human heads and skulls, as in the Amazon and Vanuatu (don't miss the Aztec skull with the tiniest turquoise tiles imaginable). On the ground floor is a café, a cinema, and a bookshop with a good selection of world music and French-language art books.

Just to the west, looming over the tankers and cargo ships drowsing in Marseille's outer harbour basin, are the two 'majors'. The striped neo-Byzantine, empty and unloved **Cathédrale de la Major** (*open Tues–Sat 9–6, Sun and Mon 9–12 and 2.30–6.30*) was built in 1853 with the new money coming in from the conquest of Algeria – enough to make it the largest church built in France since the Middle Ages. Now utterly isolated by lanes of frantic traffic, the pile is held up by 444 marble columns; predictably, somehow, the monster is not only ugly but dangerous, and has to be encased in nets in order to keep the rare visitor from being brained by bits of falling stone. An EU-financed project is trying to remedy traffic problems by building a tunnel underneath the area, which may go some way to restoring the area's former tranquillity.

The cathedral's Romanesque predecessor, the **Ancienne-Major**, is in no better nick, having already had its transept brutally amputated for the new cathedral (note the poor angel, gesturing sadly without a hand); it's now fenced off and propped up with wooden planks. If you get a chance to go inside, don't miss the Ancienne-Major's crossing, a fantasy in brick that sets an octagonal dome on four stepped conical squinches, a typically Provençal conceit. One chapel has a *Descent from the Cross* (early 16th-century) by Nicolas della Robbia; the altar of saints Lazarus, Martha and Mary Magdalene in Carrara marble (1475–81) is by Francesco Laurana and was considered by Anthony Blunt 'the earliest purely Italian work on French soil'. What you never get to see is the Ancienne-Major's old curiosity shop of relics: part of Jesus' cradle and one of his tears, St Peter's tooth and, best of all, the fishbones left over from the feast at the Sermon on the Mount.

South of the Vieux Port: Quai de Rive Neuve and Abbye St-Victor

In the last decade, this part of the Old Port has made a comeback: during lunchtimes and on summer evenings half of Marseille seems to descend on its bars, restaurants, theatres and clubs on the quay, Rue Saint-Saëns and Place Thiars. The oldest cultural institution here is the **Opéra**, two blocks south of the port in Place Reyer, built in 1924 and graced with Art Deco Greek gods and a pure Art Deco interior (contact the tourist office about tours).

Two streets back, at 19 Rue Grignan, is a *hôtel particulier* housing the **Musée Cantini** (*t 04 91 54 77 75; open June–mid-Sept Tues–Sun 11–6; mid-Sept–May Tues–Sun 10–5; adm*) with its modern art and frequent special exhibitions, which have included Francis Picabia, Max Ernst, André Masson, Francis Bacon, Balthus, César, Arman and Ben. Permanent displays at the museum include Paul Signac's shimmering *Port de Marseille*, and the first Cubist views of L'Estaque that Raoul Dufy painted with Georges Braque in 1908; the greater part of its post-1960 works have been moved into the Musée d'Art Contemporain (*see* p.272).

On **Quai de Rive Neuve** you'll find ship's chandlers' shops, restaurants and the national theatre, **La Criée**, installed in a former fish auction house (*see* p.259). For better or worse, its presence has tamed the once salty Rive Neuve bars, including the **Bar de la Marine**, which is no longer recognizable as the set for the famous card-playing scene in Marcel Pagnol's *Marius*. Further along the *quai*, steps lead up to battlemented walls and towers good enough for a Hollywood castle, defending one of the oldest Christian shrines in Provence, the **Abbaye St-Victor** (*open daily 9–7*). St-Victor was founded in AD 416 by St Jean Cassien, formerly an anchorite in the Egyptian Thebaid. One account has it that he brought with him from Egypt the mummy of St Victor, though the more popular version says Victor was a Roman legionnaire who converted to Christianity and slew at least one sea serpent (see the relief over the door) before being ground to a pulp between a pair of millstones. In art he sometimes looks like Don Quixote, with a windmill.

St-Victor may be Marseille's oldest church, but it's no fuddy-duddy: like Broadway, it has an electronic sign at the entrance reeling off news, and the side aisles are equipped with TV screens so all the parishioners can view mass at the high altar – doings Jean Cassien never imagined 1,600 years ago when he excavated the first chapels in the flank of an ancient stone quarry near a Hellenistic necropolis, which he expanded for Christian use as a *martyrium* (a rock-cut burial niche surrounding the tomb of a martyr). In the 11th century, when the monks of St-Victor adopted the Rule of St Benedict, they added the church on top, turning the old chapels into a labyrinthine **crypt** (*open daily 8.30–6.30; adm*). Although now well lit, this curious termitarium, with ceilings 6–60ft in height, is suffused with ancient mystery – some of the beautifully sculpted sarcophagi date from the 3rd century AD and were found to contain seven or eight dead monks crowded like sardines, providing proof of the popularity of an abbey that founded 300 monastic houses in Provence and Sardinia. Then there's the 5th-century sarcophagus of St Jean Cassien, showing the saint preaching among the columns, and the cave-like 5th-century chapel, carved with a pair of weird old faces and stained green with moss, traditionally enshrining one of Marseille's three Black Virgins (supposedly Christian adaptations of Artemis, the patroness of Massalia). A primordial Candlemas rite begins here every 2 February: the archbishop comes to bless green candles before the Virgin, who gets to go out in a procession that ends at the abbey's bakery, where small loaves (*navettes*) are baked in the shape of boats – a similar custom, in the temples of Isis, once heralded the start of the navigation season. The faithful then take the green candles home to light at wakes as a symbol of rebirth.

Notre-Dame-de-la-Garde

Just northwest of St-Victor is Louis XIV's **Fort St-Nicolas**, and beyond that is the **Château du Pharo** (bus 83 from the Vieux Port), built by Napoléon III as a gift for his wife, the Empress Eugénie, who never got around to seeing it. The gardens, with striking views over the port, were until recently used for concerts and summer theatre, though now host only conventions and weddings. You can still walk around the grounds, and beyond are the *calanques* (*see* pp.272–3). The prize 360° view, though, is from Marseille's watchtower hill, an isolated limestone outcrop towering 530ft above the city, crowned by **Notre-Dame-de-la-Garde** (*open daily summer 7am–7.30pm; winter 7–5.30*), a neo-Byzantine/Romanesque pile with an unfortunate resemblance to a locomotive. It's a killer walk, and even fairly hair-raising to drive – let bus 60 do the work from Place aux Huiles on Quai de Rive-Neuve). The landmark supports France's largest golden mega-Madonna, 33ft high and shining like a beacon out to sea. In 1214 a monk of St-Victor built the first chapel here and over the decades it gained a reputation for the miracles performed by a statue of the Virgin, Marseille's 'Bonne Mère'. The chapel's florid Second Empire architecture attracted some real bombs when the Nazis made it their headquarters and last stand, and you can still see some of the dents. But besides the view, the main attraction is the basilica's great collection of ex votos, painted by fishermen and sailors.

La Canebière

Before La Canebière itself was laid out in Louis XIV's expansion scheme of 1666, this area was the ropemakers' quarter. The hemp they used has given its name to Marseille's most famous boulevard – chanvre in French, but in Provençal more like the Latin cannabis. It's a not entirely inappropriate allusion, for this was the high street of French dolce far niente, an essential ingredient of music-hall Marseille, which could swagger and boast that 'the Champs-Elysées is the Canebière of Paris'. In its day, the thoroughfare sported grand cafés, fancy shops and hotels where travellers of yore had their first thrills before sailing off to exotic lands, but these days La Canebière – or 'Can o' beer' as English sailors know it – has suffered the same fate as the Champs-Elysées: banks, airline offices and heavy traffic. Trees would do it some good.

Some of La Canebière's old pizzazz lingers in the lively streets to the south around 'Marseille's stomach', the **Marché des Capucins**, a grazer's heaven, where the air is filled with tempting, exotic smells and most of the shops are North African. Here, too, is Noailles station, the last resting place for the city's retired omnibuses and tramways, the **Galerie des Transports** (t 04 91 54 15 15; open Oct–May Tues–Sat 10–5; June–Sept Tues–Sat 11–6); Marseille's last working tram still has its terminus here. Behind this hurly-burly stretches the **Cours Julien**, a favourite promenade and pétanque court, lined with antiques shops, galleries and trendy restaurants, which gets distinctly more rough and ready toward Place Notre-Dame-du-Mont, with its spectacular displays of graffiti. Funky cafés and galleries are also to be found on the nearby Rue des Trois Rois.

North, and perpendicular to La Canebière, extends another tarnished grand boulevard, **Cours Belsunce**. Until 1964, No.54 was the site of the famous neo-Moorish/Art Nouveau music hall where Maurice Chevalier and Fernandel once starred, and where Tino Rossi and Yves Montand had their stage debuts. Now the cours leads only to the **Porte d'Aix**, a fuzzy-minded Roman triumphal arch, vintage 1823, erected to Louis XVI or Liberty or both, and adorned with statues of virtues such as Resignation and Prudence, whose heads (much like Louis XVI's) suddenly fell off in 1937 and rolled down the street. This quarter, like Le Panier, is now mostly North African: Marseille's mosque is just on the other side of the arch.

Palais Longchamp and Environs

In 1834 Marseille suffered a drought so severe that it dug a canal to bring in water from the Durance. This 80km feat of aquatic engineering ends with a heroic splash at the **Palais Longchamp**, a delightfully overblown nymphaeum and cascade, populated with stone felines, bulls and a buxom allegory of the Durance, and currently undergoing an almost €6 million restoration programme (Ⓜ Cinq-Avenues-Longchamp; bus 80 from La Canebière). Behind the palace stretch the public gardens, an observatory (one of four in this city, which has been the home of many famous astronomers) and a little zoo; in the right wing of the palace itself, some of the creatures from it are embalmed in the **Muséum d'Histoire Naturelle**, sharing space with their fossilized ancestors (*t 04 91 14 59 50; open summer Tues–Sun 11–6, winter Tues–Sun 10–5; adm*).

The left wing of the Palais Longchamp houses the **Musée des Beaux-Arts** (*t 04 91 14 59 30; open Tues–Sun summer 11–6, winter 10–5; adm*). Formed around art that was 'conquered' by Napoleon's army, it is home to some second-rate canvases by Italian masters such as Perugino, and some stagey burlesques such as Rubens' violent *Boar Hunt* (in which ladies daintily watch the spurting blood) or Louis Finson's *Samson and Delilah* (1600), with a nasty Delilah tugging the ear of a very dirty-footed Samson. The mood changes with Michel Serre's scrupulously dire *Scenes of the Marseille Plague of 1720*, where a large percentage of the plague's 40,000 victims are shown dropping like flies while healthy rich men in suits prance by on horseback, looking politely sympathetic. These same gentlemen never dismounted to assist Marseille's native artists, either – even an establishment figure such as Baroque sculptor, architect and painter Pierre Puget (1671–1745), who has a room devoted to him. Then there's Françoise Duparc (1726–76), a follower of Chardin , who worked in England for most of her life ; and the satirist Honoré Daumier (1808–97), who went to prison for his biting caricatures of Louis-Philippe's toadies, here represented by *Spitting Image*-style satirical busts modelled after his drawings. Here, too, is Van Gogh's roving, bohemian precursor Adolphe Monticelli (1824–86), who sold his paint-encrusted canvases of fragmented colour for a day's food and drink in the cafés along La Canebière. Also of note are paintings by Provençal pre-Impressionists, especially 18th-century scenes of Marseille's port by Joseph Vernet and sun-drenched landscapes by Paul Guigou.

Just across Boulevard Longchamp at No.140, the **Musée Grobet-Labadié** (*t 04 91 62 21 82; open summer Tues–Sun 11–6,winter Tues–Sun 10–5; adm*) contains a private collection as interesting for its eclecticism as for any individual painting, table, plate, instrument, tapestry or iron lock.

Heading South: Le Corbusier and Mazargues

The building that achieves speed will achieve success.

Le Corbusier

To pay your respects to Modular Man, you need to take bus 21 from the Bourse down wide Avenue du Prado and Boulevard Michelet (a perfect spot for rollerblading, if you happen to have brought your skates) and past the swish Vélodrome football stadium to the *Corbusier* stop.

In 1945, during the height of Marseille's housing crisis, the French government commissioned Le Corbusier to build an experimental *unité d'habitation*, derived from his 1935 theory of '*La Cité Radieuse*'. Le Corbusier thought the solution to urban *anomie* and transport and housing problems was to put living space, schools, shops and recreational facilities all under one roof, in a building designed according to the human proportions of Leonardo da Vinci's Renaissance man-in-a-circle, reborn as Le Corbusier's wiggly Modular Man symbol. You can see the Man in relief on the concrete *pilotis*, or stilts – the most revolutionary aspect of the building. Le Corbusier, who anticipated the future importance of cars, intended that the ground level should be for parking.

For a city like Marseille, where people enjoy getting out and about at ground level, the building was a ghastly aberration, and was nicknamed the *casa de fada*, or 'house of the mentally deranged'. Plans for other *unités* were stifled and in 1952 the state sold the flats off as co-ops. But architects were entranced, and for the next 30 years thousands of buildings in every city in the world went up on *pilotis*, before everyone realized that the Marseillais were right all along: it is madness to deprive a building of its most important asset, a ground floor. The *unité*'s genuinely good points, unfortunately, had few imitators – each of its 337 flats is built on two levels and designed for maximum privacy; each has fine views over the mountains or sea. Of the original extras, only the school, the top-floor gym and the communal hotel for residents' guests (*now open to all; see* p.257) have survived. The hotel also offers tours by appointment.

Bus 21 continues towards **Mazargues**, a once-fashionable *banlieue* under the Montagne de Marseilleveyre, famous in the 19th century for its climate. When its residents died, at a ripe old age, they often chose to be remembered in the local cemetery by a mini-monument to their life's work – there are stone hedge-clippers, fishing boats, hoes and, on the tomb of an omnibus driver, a tramway.

Marseille's Corniche and Parc Borély

Why go to the Riviera when Marseille has one of its very own? From the Vieux Port, you can catch bus 83 past the Parc du Pharo to **Corniche J.F. Kennedy**, a dramatic road overlooking a dramatic coast that must have reminded the ancient Greek colonists of home – now improved with artificial beaches, bars, restaurants, villas and nightclubs.

Amazingly, until the road was built in the 1850s, the first cove, the picture-postcard **Anse des Catalans**, was so isolated that the Catalan fisherfolk who lived there as squatters in the ruins of the old Lazaretto (quarantine station) could hardly speak French. This now has the most popular (and the only real) sandy beach. From the bus stop *Vallon des Auffes* you can walk down to the fishing village of **Anse des Auffes** ('of the ropemakers'), isolated from the corniche until after the Second World War and still determinedly intact.

Other typical quarters with still more piquant names lie further on: **Anse de Maldormé** and **Anse de la Fausse Monnaie**. As soon as the corniche was built, the wealthy families of Marseille planted grand villas along it: the Château Talabot is one of the most spectacular. The corniche then descends to the artificial **Plage Gaston Deferre**, where a copy of Michelangelo's *David* holds court at the corner of Avenue du Prado, looking even more smugly ridiculous than he does in Florence. Beyond the big fellow opens the cool green expanse of **Parc Borély**, which is great for cycling or rollerblading, and has a café/restaurant, golf course and running track, as well as a **botanical garden** (*t 04 91 55 24 96; open summer Mon–Fri 1–4.45, Sat, Sun and hols 3–6.45; winter daily 2–5*), duck ponds and the **Château Borély**, an 18th-century palace built according to the strictest classical proportions for a wealthy merchant and unique for its surviving interior decoration. Behind it, Avenue de Hambourg leads into Sainte-Anne, another former village, where César's Giant Thumb emerges at the Boulevard de Haïfa, signalling the vast **Musée d'Art Contemporain** at No.69 (*t 04 91 25 01 07; open summer Tues–Sun 11–6, winter Tues–Sun 10–5; adm*), with a large collection of post Second World War art (New Realists, Arte Povera, 'individual mythologies' and more).

The *Calanques* and Grotte Cosquer

To continue east along the coast from Parc Borély, you'll need to change to bus 19, which passes by another beach and the **Musée de la Faïence**, in the 19th-century Château Pastré (*157 Avenue de Montredon, t 04 91 72 43 47; open summer Tues–Sun 11–6, winter Tues–Sun 10–5; adm*), with an exceptional collection of faïence from Neolithic times to the present, particularly the famous ware made in Marseille and Moustiers from the 17th century on.

Bus 19 poops out just after Calanque du Mont Rose, Marseille's nudist beach. Bus 20 from here continues to Cap Croisette, a miniature end-of-the-world at the base of the Montagne de Marseilleveyre – which forms a backdrop to the fishing hamlet in the Calanque des Goudes – and the pebble beach at Calanque de Samena, facing the islets of Maître and Tiboulen. The road gives out at the narrow Calanque de Callelongue, where the GR98 coastal path to Cassis begins (*see p.253*). Another path from here leads in two hours to the summit of Marseilleveyre (1,417ft), with grand views over Marseille, its industrial *rade* and the islands.

In 1991 the next *calanque*, the beautiful, chalky, jagged **Calanque de Sormiou**, made national headlines when a local diver called Henri Cosquer discovered a hollow 130ft under the sea that hid the entrance to a tunnel. Cosquer swam up the tunnel and after 220 yards found himself in a subterranean cave above sea level, to his astonishment covered with paintings of running bison, horses, deer and the ancestors of the modern penguin. Along with the art, Cosquer found a number of 'negative' handprints, which were made by blowing colour around a hand in order to create its outline on the wall. Similar 'artists' signatures' mark the famous painted caves in the Dordogne.

Although first dismissed as a forgery, mainly because no similar works have ever been found in Provence, the **Grotte Cosquer** is now recognized by prehistorians as a contemporary of Lascaux (*c. 27,000 BC*). At the time, when much of the northern hemisphere's water was concentrated in Ice Age glaciers, the level of the Med was much lower, so that the entrance to the cave was on dry land. The climate of Provence was also considerably colder – hence the bison and penguins. To protect the art, the cave has been walled up, but reproductions are on display via the Internet at *www.culture.gouv.fr*.

Sormiou and the more distant *calanques* are most painlessly reached from Marseille by boats from the Quai des Belges (*t 04 91 55 50 09, www.answeb.net/gacm; mid-June–Sept*). Or take bus 21 from La Canebière to the end of the line (Luminy) and walk 40 minutes to **Calanque de Morgiou**, dotted with seaside *cabanons*, or to the wilder **Calanque de Sugiton**.

The Château d'If and Iles du Frioul

'*If*' in French means yew, a tree associated with death; it's an appropriately sinister name for this gloomy precursor of Alcatraz, the **Château d'If** (*t 04 91 59 02 30; open except in rough seas Oct–Mar daily 9–5.30, April–Sept 9–6.30; boats from Quai des Belges, t 04 91 55 50 09; departures hourly 9–5*), built by François Ier in 1524, to defend Marseille from Emperor Charles V. Even while Alexandre Dumas was still alive, visitors came to see the cell of the Count of Monte-Cristo, and a cell, complete with escape hole, was obligingly made to show to visitors. Real-life inmates included Mirabeau, imprisoned by his father-in-law for running up debts in Aix-en-Provence (*see* p.285); a Monsieur de Niozelles, condemned to six years in solitary confinement for not taking his hat off in front of Louis XIV; and, after the revocation of the Edict of Nantes, thousands of Protestants, who either died here or went on to die as galley slaves elsewhere.

The two other islands in the archipelago, **Pomègues** and **Ratonneau**, are white as bones and nearly as dry, tortured into crags and lumps by the mistral. Boats run as for the Ile d'If, with an early boat at 6.45 for Pomègues and Ratonneau only. They were originally hunting and fishing reserves and witnessed, in 1516, one of the first rhinos in Europe, who rambled here en route to Pope Leo X's menagerie in Rome. Later used as quarantine islands, they are now linked by a causeway at Port du Frioul, a marina designed by Le Corbusier's pupil, José Luis Sert. Scores of swimming coves can be easily reached by foot, along paths lined with aromatic herbs and plants especially adapted to the extremely dry climate. A 20-minute path leads to the **Hôpital Caroline**, built in the 1820s on Ratonneau, where the winds blow the strongest – on the theory that they would help 'purify' infectious diseases. Now used as the venue for a summer festival, the hospital has excellent views of Marseille – as Marseille was meant to be seen, from the sea – that must have been heartbreaking to the imprisoned patients.

West of Marseille: The Chaîne de l'Estaque and the Etang de Berre

Whatever personality of its own this region once had has been thoroughly chewed and swallowed by the metropolis next door. Once sheltering attractive, out-of-the-way retreats, the Estaque coast and the broad lagoon of Berre behind it have totally succumbed to creeping suburbia in the last three decades; isolated corners that once knew only hamlets of poor fishermen now suffer some of the biggest industrial complexes in France. Still, the 'Côte Bleue', as the tourist offices call the Estaque coast, is a very attractive piece of coastline. Especially in the east,

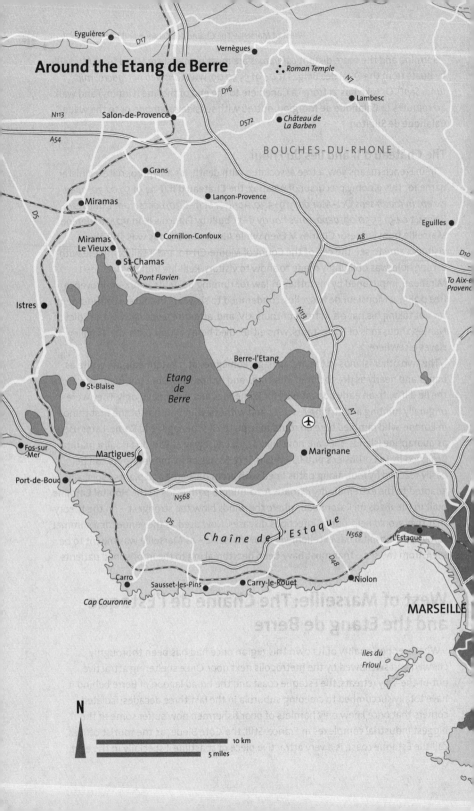

Around the Etang de Berre

Eyguières

D17

Vernègues

∴ *Roman Temple*

N7

Lambesc

D16

Salon-de-Provence

D572

Château de La Barben

N113

A54

B O U C H E S - D U - R H O N E

Grans

Lançon-Provence

Eguilles

Miramas

A8

Miramas Le Vieux

Cornillon-Confoux

D10

St-Chamas

Pont Flavien

To Aix-en-Provence

D5

Istres

N113

Etang de Berre

Berre-l'Etang

A7

St-Blaise

Fos-sur-Mer

Marignane

Martigues

Port-de-Bouc

N568

D5

Chaîne de l'Estaque

N568

L'Estaque

Carro

D48

Niolon

Sausset-les-Pins

Carry-le-Rouet

Cap Couronne

MARSEILLE

Iles du Frioul

N

10 km

5 miles

the mountains plunge straight into the sea, with sheltered *calanques* between them; there is no road along the coast until Carry-le-Rouet.

L'Estaque to Sausset-les-Pins

Leaving Marseille on the N568, you will pass the industrial suburb, docks and marinas of L'Estaque (take bus 35 from the Vieux Port). This was a favourite subject of Paul Cézanne, who came to this spot off and on for 15 years to paint, and whose vision of a new, classical Provence transformed the town's smokestacks into Doric columns. He was followed by Georges Braque, Raoul Dufy, Albert Marquet and other artists; the Marseille tourist office has a brochure pinpointing the spots where they set up their easels, but you'll be disappointed if you come expecting to recognize too many of the scenes.

The road then crosses over the Souterrain du Rove, which holds the distinction of being the longest ship tunnel in the world. A partial collapse closed it in the 1960s, and no one has found it worth repairing since. Tortuous side roads from the N568 will take you down to two pleasant enclaves harbouring old fishing villages, Niolon and Méjean.

The reputation of **Carry-le-Rouet**, which is the biggest town on this stretch of the coast, is based on horse-faced actor Fernandel and on sea urchins; it celebrates the latter with a festival each February. The beach is often oversubscribed; Carry is fast being surrounded by the weekend villas of the Marseillais.

Sausset-les-Pins, the next town along the coast, suffers much the same problem; however, if you press on further, there are a number of popular, if also often crowded, beaches around **Carro** and especially at **Cap Couronne**, which is a favourite among the Marseillais.

Marignane and Martigues

On the lagoon side of the Chaîne de l'Estaque, facing inland across the Etang de Berre, the distinguished old city of **Marignane** has been completely engulfed by Marseille's sprawl and airport. In the centre of the old town, you can pay a visit to its 14th-century château (now the *mairie*), an eccentric work with mythological frescoes.

From here, making a clockwise tour around the Etang de Berre, the next stop is **Martigues**, a sweet little city full of salt air and sailboats, not a compelling place to visit but probably a wonderful place to live. If Carry-le-Rouet serves up sea urchins to visitors in February, Martigues can answer with its own speciality – fresh sardines – during its Sardine Festival in July and August.

Martigues sits astride the Canal de Caronte, which links the lagoon and the sea, lending it a slight but much-trumpeted resemblance to Venice. According to legend, the city was founded by and named after the Roman general Marius; the oldest part of town is the Ile Brescon, at the head of the channel, with the Baroque church of the Madeleine and a number of 17th- and 18th-century buildings. One of its prettiest corners is a quay called the **Miroir des Oiseaux**, the 'mirror of birds'. On the mainland, the **Musée Ziem** (*Bd du 14 Juillet, t 04 42 41 39 60; open July and Aug Wed–Mon 10.30–12 and 2.30–6.30; Sept–June Thurs–Sun 2.30–6.30, Wed 10–12 and 2.30–6.30;*

Tourist Information

Carry-le-Rouet: Av Aristide Briand, **t** 04 42 13 20 36, *www.carry-le-rouet.com*. *Open July and Aug Mon–Sat 9–12 and 3–6, Sun 10–12; Sept–June Tues–Sat 10–12 and 2–5.*

Martigues: Rond-Point de l'Hôtel de Ville, **t** 04 42 42 31 10, *www.martigues-tourisme. com*. *Open summer Mon–Sat 9–7, Sun and hols 9.30–1; winter Mon–Fri 9–6.30, Sat 9–12.30 and 2.30–6, Sun 9.30–1.* Provides detailed descriptions of walking and driving tours of the area.

Salon-de-Provence: 56 Cours Gimon, **t** 04 90 56 27 60, *www.salon-de-provence.org*, *www. visitprovence.com*. *Open July and Aug Mon–Sat 9.30–6, Sun 10–12; Sept–June Mon–Sat 9.30–12.30 and 2–6.*

Market Days

Carry-le-Rouet: Tues and Fri.
Martigues: Thurs, and Sun am.
Salon-de-Provence: Wed and Sun am.

Where to Stay and Eat

Carry-le-Rouet ✉ 13620
Most people here have villas or are on day-trips from the city, so accommodation is scarce and functional.

La Tuilière, 34 Av Draïo-de-la-Mar, **t 04 42 44 79 79, *latuiliere@libertysurf.fr* (*moderate*). Modern, comfortable rooms, some with sea views, with a pool and air-conditioning.

L'Escale, 3 Bd des Moulins, **t** 04 42 45 00 47 (*expensive*). A monthly changing gourmet menu served on attractive seaside terraces. *Closed Sun eve, Mon and Oct–Mar.*

Le Calypso, Quai Vayssière, **t** 04 42 45 10 64, (*moderate*). A seafood restaurant behind the port, with great sea views. *Closed Nov–Feb, and Sun eve and Mon in summer.*

Martigues ✉ 13500
L'Eden, Bd Emile Zola, **t 04 42 07 36 37, *www. hoteleden.fr* (*inexpensive*). A reasonable option on the outskirts, with great sea views.

adm) has paintings left to Martigues by landscape artist Felix Ziem, and works by Provençal painters Guigou, Monticelli and Loubon, as well as archaeology exhibits.

Fos-sur-Mer

The French, many of whom are fascinated with technology, actually come to visit this gigantic industrial complex. Fos has an **information centre** on Avenue Jean Jaurès (**t** *04 42 47 71 96*), and there are guided tours. You too might consider a drive through – in its way, Fos is the most astounding, unsettling sight in Provence. Before 1965, when France's Mephisthophelean economic planners commandeered it to replace the overcrowded port of Marseille, this corner of the Camargue was pristine marshland. Today it is the biggest oil port, and the biggest industrial complex, on the entire Mediterranean. In area it is considerably larger than Marseille.

To a degree, it makes sense to concentrate unpleasant industry all in one place. But when you're driving past the 19km of chemical plants, steel mills and power lines rising out of the void like a mirage, your senses rebel. Economically, the 'ZIP' (*zone industrielle-portuaire*) is a failure; as planning, it is stupidly primitive, ecologically disastrous and demeaning to the people who live and work in it: the perfect marriage of corporate gigantism and bureaucratic simple-mindedness.

West and North of the Etang de Berre

Along the western shore of the Etang de Berre there is more of the same, engulfing a number of ancient villages, such as **St-Blaise**, which contains a Romanesque church and a wealth of ruins that are currently being excavated,

★★Le Cigalon, 35 Bd 14- Juillet, t 04 42 80 49 16 (*inexpensive*). A central hotel with modern rooms, air-conditioning and a restaurant (*moderate*). *Restaurant closed Mon lunch, Wed, and Sun eve.*

Miroir aux Oiseaux, 4 Rue Marcel Galdy, t 04 42 80 50 45 (*moderate*). Traditional gourmet food on a terrace overlooking the attractive quay. *Closed Sun eve, Mon, and Sat lunch.*

Salon-de-Provence ✉ 13300

★★★★Le Mas du Soleil, 38 Chemin Saint-Côme, t 04 90 56 06 53, www.lemasdusoleil.com (*luxury*). Elegant, air-conditioned rooms, a pool and terrace, and a traditional restaurant serving beautifully presented food.

★★★★Abbaye Ste-Croix, Val-de-Cuech (D16), t 04 90 56 24 55, www.relaischateaux.com/ site/us/re_saintecroix.html (*luxury– expensive*). A Relais & Châteaux place 5km out of town, with lovely rooms overlooking a medieval cloister. There's a pool, horse-riding and a posh restaurant. *Closed Nov–mid-Mar.*

★★Domaine de Roquerousse, on Route d'Avignon 4km from town, t 04 90 59 50 11, www.roquerousse.com (*moderate–inexpensive*). Pretty rooms and a restaurant (*moderate*) in the individual buildings of a 19th-century *mas*, in a park, with a pool and tennis courts.

★★Vendôme, 34 Rue Maréchal Joffre, t 04 90 56 01 96, www.hotelvendome.com (*inexpensive*). A bright, pretty and old-fashioned hotel with spacious rooms and a courtyard.

La Salle à Manger, 6 Rue Maréchal Joffre, t 04 90 56 28 01 (*moderate*). A restaurant in an exuberantly floral 19th-century mansion, offering a choice of delicious if extravagant dishes (ostrich *carpaccio*, for instance, and 40 puddings) to match the décor. *Closed Sun eve and Mon.*

La Brocherie des Cordeliers, 20 Rue d'Hozier, t 04 90 56 53 42 (*moderate*). The 13th-century chapel that once hosted Nostradamus' mortal remains, offering local cuisine. *Closed Sun and Sat lunch.*

including a rare stretch of Greek wall. Of the two large towns here, **Istres** has a Provençal-Romanesque fortified church, Notre-Dame-de-Beauvoir, and a Musée Archéologique (*t 04 42 55 50 08; open Oct–May daily 2–6; June–Sept 2–7; adm*), filled with mostly Roman-era finds that were discovered by divers in the Golfe de Fos. **Miramas** is more attractive, with the ruins of its medieval predecessor nearby at Miramas le Vieux. There's also a railway museum (*t 06 85 13 38 47*).

St-Chamas, southeast, has an impressive Baroque church. The Via Domitia passed this way, and over a small stream south of the village stands one of the finest and best-preserved Roman bridges anywhere, the **Pont Flavien**. Built in the 1st century AD, the single-arched span features a pair of very elegant triumphal arches at the approaches, decorated with Corinthian capitals, floral reliefs and stone lions. But life went on here even earlier than that, and there are troglodyte dwellings to prove it.

North of the Etang, towards Salon-de-Provence, lie three attractive villages: **Cornillon-Confoux**, on a steep hill with a wide view, **Grans** and **Lançon-Provence**; the latter is home of some of the most exquisite AOC Coteaux d'Aix-en-Provence wines (*see p.293*).

Salon-de-Provence

The home of Nostradamus should be a more interesting place. Aix-en-Provence's disagreeable little sister, Salon is quite well off from processing olive oil, making soap and being home to the French airforce training school. The town seems aptly named: it's a little bourgeois parlour, smug and stuffy and neat as a pin. Its spirit is captured perfectly in the antiseptic, gentrified Vieille Ville, ruined by a hideous and insensitive restoration programme in the last few years. Even the antiseptic has its surprises, however: surely the snazziest tiled loos in France (underneath Place du Général de Gaulle), and the Ecole des Bergers, France's national school for shepherds.

The old quarter, surrounded by a ring of boulevards, is entered by the 18th-century **Porte de l'Horloge**, with its ironwork clock tower. In the centre, at the highest point of Salon, is the **Château de l'Empéri**, parts of which go back to the 10th century. Long a possession of the archbishops of Arles, it now houses the **Musée National de l'Empéri** (*t 04 90 56 22 36; open July and Aug daily 10–6; rest of year Wed–Mon 10–12 and 2.30–6; adm*), which contains a substantial hoard of weapons, bric-a-brac and epauletted mannequins on horseback, covering the history of France's army from Louis XIV to 1918, with an emphasis on Napoleon.

The slightly kitsch **Musée Grévin de la Provence** (*t 04 90 56 36 30; open July and Aug Mon–Fri 10–6, Sat and Sun 2–6; Sept–June Mon–Fri 10–12 and 2–6, Sat and Sun 2–6; adm*), run by the Parisian waxwork family Grévin, illustrates the history of Provence by means of 54 waxwork figures, from Marius' battle with the Barbarians, through a lifeless Napoleon, to Pagnol's 'Manon des Sources'.

East of Salon along the D572, the **Château de la Barben** once belonged to Napoleon's favourite sister, Pauline Borghese, and now has a little zoo in the grounds for kids.

Nostradamus

Salon's most famous citizen was born in St-Rémy-de-Provence in 1503, to a family of converted Jews. Trained as a doctor in Montpellier, young Michel de Nostredame made a name for himself by successfully treating plague victims in Lyon and Aix-en-Provence. In 1547 he married a girl from Salon-de-Provence and settled down there, practising medicine and pursuing a score of other interests besides – studying astrology, publishing almanacs and inventing new recipes for cosmetics and hair dyes. The first of his *Centuries*, ambiguous quatrains written in the future tense, were published in 1555, achieving celebrity for their author almost immediately.

Nostradamus himself said that his works came from 'natural instinct and poetic passion'; in form they are similar to some other poetry of the day, such as the *Visions* of Du Bellay. It may be that he had never intended to become an occult superstar – but when the peasants start bringing you two-headed sheep asking for an explanation, and when the Queen Regent of France sends an invitation to court, what's a man to do? Nostradamus went to Paris, and later Charles IX and Catherine de Médicis came to visit him in Salon. The Salonnais didn't appreciate such notoriety; if not for Nostradamus's royal favour, they might well have put him to the torch.

Now they've made up, and you can visit the **Maison de Nostradamus**, just inside the Porte de l'Horloge (*11 Rue de Nostradamus, t 04 90 56 64 31; open Sept–June Mon–Fri 9–12 and 2–6, Sat and Sun 2–6; July and Aug Mon–Fri 10–6, Sat and Sun 2–6; adm*). On his death in 1566, Nostradamus was, oddly, buried inside the wall of the Cordeliers' church; tales spread that he was still alive in there, writing his final book of prophecies. After his tomb was desecrated in the Revolution, he was moved to the Dominican church of St-Laurent, on Rue du Maréchal Joffre, where he remains.

North of Salon on the D17, **Eyguières** is an archetypal Provençal village, with some Celtic–Greek tombs above the ruins of a medieval castle; their contents may be seen in the **Centre d'Etudes Archéologiques** (*t 04 90 59 82 44; open Sat am or by appointment; donation appreciated*). Also note the 10th-century Chapelle St-Vérédème.

Vernègues, in a forgotten corner of Provence (take the D16 northeast of Salon), has a ruined castle and, just southeast, the ruins of a 1st-century BC Roman temple.

Aix-en-Provence

Elegant and honey-hued, the old capital of Provence is splashed by a score of fountains – a charming reminder that its very name comes from its waters, *Aquae Sextiae*. It's sweet water, mind you, with none of the saltiness and excesses of Marseille. For if chaotic Marseille is the great anti-Paris, Aix-en-Provence is the stalwart anti-Marseille – bourgeois, cultured, aristocratic, urbane, slow-paced and convivial. Since 1948, it has hosted France's most élite festival of music and opera, while its 600-year-old university not only teaches the arts and humanities to the French but instructs foreign students in the fine arts of French civilization (the more 'practical' science departments are in Marseille). If a fifth of Aix's 150,000 souls are students, another large percentage are doctors, lawyers and professors, financial and underworld nabobs who commute to Marseille. But as cultured as it is, Aix can never quite live down having mocked and laughed at Paul Cézanne, the one real genius it ever produced.

History

The first version of Aix, the *oppidum* of Entremont, was the capital of the Salyens, a Celto-Ligurian tribe who liked to decapitate their enemies and tie their heads to the tails of their horses. By 123 BC they had pulled this trick once too often on the Greeks of Massalia, who called in their Roman allies to teach them a lesson. Under Sextius Calvinus, the Romans did just that, and founded a camp by a nearby thermal spring that they named Aquae Sextiae Salluviorum.

Just 20 years later, in 102 BC, these Latin frontiersmen woke up one day to find 200,000 ferocious Teutones with covered wagons at their door, en route to Italy – looking not for a place to camp but for *Lebensraum*. The strategies of the great Roman general Marius caught them unawares, and, in the battle that raged around Aix, so many Teutones were killed or committed suicide that for decades Aix enjoyed bumper crops thanks to soil enriched with corpses. The mountain where Marius' final triumph took place was renamed Montagne Ste-Victoire.

Although by the next century Aquae Sextiae was a bustling town on the Aurelian Way, invaders in the Dark Ages destroyed it so thoroughly that little survived. Only in the 11th century did Aix begin to revive: the Bourg St-Sauveur grew up around the cathedral with such vigour that in the early 13th century the counts of Provence chose it as their capital. In 1409, Louis II d'Anjou endowed the university, and in the

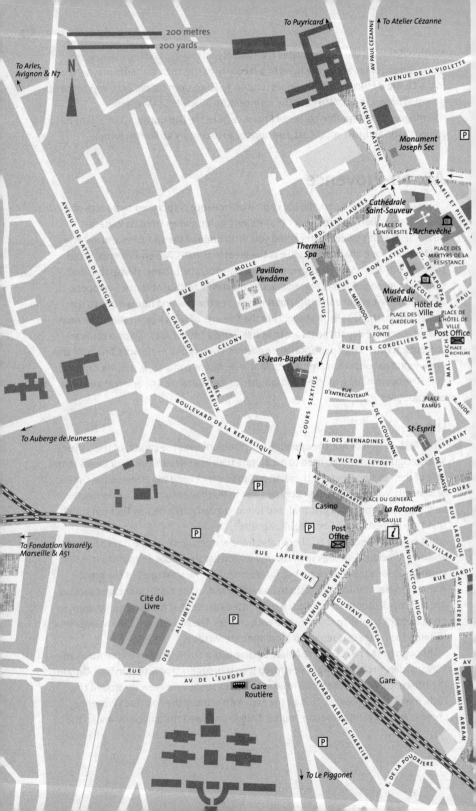

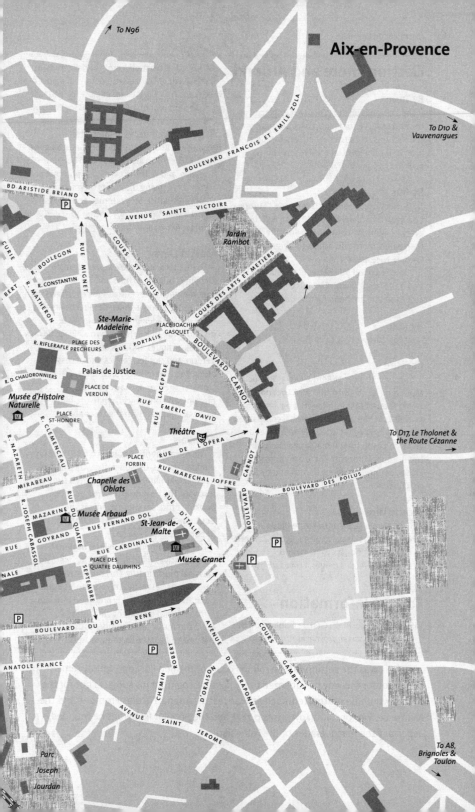

Getting There and Around

By Train

The station is on Rue Gustave Desplaces, at the end of Av Victor Hugo; there are hourly connections to Marseille, and less frequent links to Toulon (central train reservations, **t** 08 36 35 35 35).

By Bus

The hectic *gare routière* is on Av de l'Europe, **t** 04 42 91 26 80, *www.lepilote.com*, with buses every 20–30mins to Marseille and direct to Marseille airport, and others to Avignon, Cannes, Nice and Arles.

There is a good bus network around town, **t** 04 42 26 37 38, *www.aixenbus.com*. Tickets cost €1.10 and are good for one hour.

By Taxi

Av de l'Europe, **t** 04 42 27 71 11.

Car Hire

You can hire a car at **Rent a Car**, 35 Rue de la Molle, **t** 04 42 38 58 29, and **ADA Location**, Av Henry Mouret (A51 into town), **t** 04 42 52 36 36, as well as at the big multinational companies.

Parking isn't easy, especially on market days, and don't even try the main road through town, Cours Mirabeau. There are car parks in Place des Cardeurs, Place Carnot and by the coach station.

Bicycle Hire

Bikes are available at **La Route Bleue**, 5 Place Narvik, **t** 04 42 27 92 34, **Cycles Zammit**, 27 Rue Mignet, **t** 04 42 23 19 53, and **La Rotonde**, 2 Av des Belges, **t** 04 42 26 78 92.

Tourist Information

Aix-en-Provence: Pl. du Gén de Gaulle, **t** 04 42 16 11 61, *www.aixenprovencetourism.com*.

One of the most pleasant tourist offices in the south of France, with details of a host of circuits to navigate and explore: by yourself with a map, or in guided groups; on foot, by bus or car; in town or around the country-side; and whether your interest is in painting, architecture, history or just a good walk. The office also has a hotel booking service, and sells the carte Visa pour Aix et le Pays d'Aix, giving discounts on museums, concerts, dance programmes and bus trans-port. *Open Mon–Sat 8.30-7, Sun 10–1 and 2–6; longer hours in summer.*

Market Days

There's local produce every morning in Place Richelme, but Tues, Thurs and Sat are the days to come, when the centre of Aix overflows with good things: food in Place des Prêcheurs and Place de la Madeleine, flowers in Place de l'Hôtel-de-Ville (also known as Place de la Mairie), antiques and *brocante* in Place de Verdun, and clothes, fabrics and accessories along Rue Riflerafle; on Saturday nights in summer the stands stay open late, all bustling and brightly lit, while the birds squawk indignantly in the trees above.

Festivals

The Aix authorities publish a free monthly guide to events, *Le Mois à Aix*, which comes in especially handy during the city's summer festivals. The headquarters and general booking office for these events is the **Boutique du Festival**, 11 Rue Gaston de Saporta, **t** 04 42 17 34 34.

The most famous is the **International Opera Festival**, featuring celebrity opera and classical music in July. This highbrow (and *very* expensive) festival now features equally outstanding theatre. It is preceded by a less formal **Music Festival** that includes jazz, big-band music and chamber music, during the 2nd and 3rd weeks of June. At the end of

1450s Aix was the setting for the refined court of the Bon Roi René, fondly remembered not for the way he squeezed every possible *sou* from his subjects but for the artists whom he patronized, such as Francesco Laurana, Nicolas Froment and the Maître de l'Annonciation d'Aix (*see* p.287), and the popular festivities he founded, especially the masquerades of the Fête-Dieu.

July and into Aug the **International Dance Festival** (*www.danse-a-aix.com*) hosts performances ranging from classical ballet to jazz and contemporary dance.

Internet Access

Virtualis, 40 Rue des Cordeliers, t 04 42 26 02 30.
Game's Friends, 46 Rue Puits Neuf,
  t 04 42 63 21 78.

Shopping

The traditional souvenirs of Aix are its marzipan and glazed melon sweets in the shape of boats, *calissons*, which have been made here since 1473. You can buy them at **Béchard**, 12 Cours Mirabeau, t 04 42 26 06 78, and **Confiserie Brémond**, 16 Rue d'Italie, t 04 42 38 01 70. The better grocers sell the prize-winning *huile d'olive du pays d'Aix*: Aix calls itself 'the capital of the olive tree since the 18th century'. You can buy local, world-renowned **pottery** at Terre du Soleil, 6 bis Rue Aude, t 04 42 93 04 54.

Where to Stay

Aix-en-Provence ✉ 13100

If you come in the summer during the festivals, you can't book early enough; Aix's less pricey hotels fill up especially fast (if you have a car, check where to stay around Aix as well, *see* p.292).

Luxury

★★★★Villa Gallici, Av de la Violette, t 04 42 23 29 23, *www.gallici.com* (*luxury*). A member of the Relais & Châteaux group just north of the centre, with all the warm atmosphere of an old Provençal *bastide*, charming rooms, a garden, restaurant (*very expensive*), pool, and parking. *Closed Jan.*

★★★★Le Pigonnet, 5 Av du Pigonnet, t 04 42 59 02 90, *www.hotelpigonnet.com* (*luxury*). A romantic old *bastide* on the southern outskirts of the city, with rose arbours, a swimming pool, lovely rooms furnished with antiques, an excellent restaurant (*expensive*) and splendid views out over the Aix countryside. *Restaurant closed Sat, and Sun lunch.*

Very Expensive–Expensive

★★★Hôtel des Augustins, 3 Rue de la Masse, off Cours Mirabeau, t 04 42 27 28 59, *www.hotel-augustins.com* (*very expensive–expensive*). A 12th-century convent converted into a hotel, with elegant rooms.

★★★Mercure Paul Cézanne, 40 Av Victor Hugo, t 04 42 91 11 11, *www.hotelaix.com* (*very expensive–expensive*). An exceptional little hotel located just two blocks from the train station, furnished with antiques and serving delicious breakfasts. There's air-conditioning and Internet access.

★★★Grand Hôtel Nègre-Coste, 33 Cours Mirabeau, t 04 42 27 74 22, *www.hotelnegrecoste.com* (*expensive–moderate*). A renovated, elegant 18th-century hotel that still hoists guests in its original elevator. There's no restaurant.

Moderate

★★★Le Manoir, 8 Rue d'Entrecasteaux, t 04 42 26 27 20, *www.hotelmanoir.com* (*moderate*). A quiet hotel built around a 14th-century cloister, with a garden and a private car park. *Closed Christmas–end Jan.*

★★Artea, 4 Bd de la République, t 04 42 27 36 00, *www.hotel-artea-aix-en-provence.com* (*moderate*). The former home of composer Darius Milhaud (who grew up in the city), now a comfortable hotel with air-conditioned rooms with satellite TV and en suite baths (but no mementoes of Milhaud). Discounts

---

When René died at Aix in 1486, France absorbed his realm but maintained Aix's status as the capital of Provence, seat of the provincial Estates, the governor and the king-appointed *Parlement* – the latter institution so unpopular that it was counted as one of the three 'plagues' of Provence, along with the mistral and the Durance. In the 17th and 18th centuries, this unloved élite built themselves more than 160 refined

may be available out of season; check with staff when booking.

★★Le Prieuré, Route de Sisteron, 2km north of centre, **t** 04 42 21 05 23 (*moderate–inexpensive*). A hotel situated in a charming 17th-century building overlooking a garden designed by Andre Le Nôtre of Versailles fame. There's no restaurant.

Inexpensive

★Hôtel Paul, 10 Av Pasteur, **t** 04 42 23 23 89, *www.aix-en-provence.com/hotelpaul* (*inexpensive*). An old-fashioned hotel near the cathedral, with a garden.

Hôtel des Arts, 69 Bd Carnot, **t** 04 42 38 11 77 (*inexpensive*). Basic, clean and good value.

Auberge de Jeunesse, 3 Av Marcel Pagnol, Jas-de-Bouffan (bus nos.4 or 6), **t** 04 42 20 15 99 (*inexpensive*). A clean and tidy but rather unfriendly hostel far from the centre.

Eating Out

Le Clos de la Violette, 10 Rue de la Violette, **t** 04 42 23 30 71 (*very expensive*). A lovely restaurant long considered the best in Aix, serving Provençal *haute cuisine*, including truffles in season. *Closed Sun, Mon lunch and Wed lunch.*

Café Bastide du Cours, 43–7 Cours Mirabeau, **t** 04 42 26 55 41, *www.cafebastideducours. com* (*expensive–moderate*). A constantly busy restaurant that's been in business since 1806, serving food and every imaginable kind of beverage throughout the day. There are also some plush *chambres d'hôte* (*luxury–very expensive*).

La Vieille Auberge, 63 Rue Espariat, **t** 04 42 27 17 41 (*expensive–moderate*). A cosy, popular place serving tasty Provençal and gourmet dishes created by an award-winning chef. *Closed Mon and Jan.*

Le Bistro Latin, 18 Rue de la Couronne, **t** 04 42 38 22 88 (*moderate*). Imaginative variations

on local themes, such as lentil and sausage terrine, at refreshingly reasonable prices. *Closed Sat lunch, Sun lunch and Mon lunch.*

Laurane et Sa Maison, 16 Rue Victor Leydet, **t** 04 42 93 02 03 (*moderate*). Provençal cuisine at its best, in a cosy atmosphere. Popular with locals. *Closed Sun and Mon.*

Chez Maxime, 12 Place Ramus, **t** 04 42 26 28 51 (*moderate*). Delicious meat or fish dishes, accompanied by a list of 500 wines, served on a shady terrace or by a cosy fireplace. *Closed Sun, and Mon lunch.*

Le Petit Verdot, 7 Rue d'Entrecasteaux, **t** 04 42 27 30 12 (*moderate*). An authentic bistro with red wines by the glass accompanied by ancient jazz records and simple dishes or *charcuterie*. *Eves only, closed Sun.*

Trattoria Chez Antoine, 3 Rue Clemenceau, **t** 04 42 38 27 10 (*moderate–cheap*). Fresh pasta and other Italian and Provençal dishes served in an intimate, laid-back atmosphere.

Entertainment and Nightlife

Mazarin, 6 Rue Laroque and **Renoir**, 24 Cours Mirabeau, **t** 0892 687 270. Cinemas showing films in their original language (*v.o.*).

Pasino, just off La Rotonde, **t** 04 42 59 69 00. Aix's casino. *Open 10am–dawn.*

Bars and Clubs

Hot Brass, west of centre on Chemin de la Plaine des Verguetiers, **t** 04 42 21 05 57. One of the many jazz clubs kept in business by the large student population.

L'IPN, basement, 23 Cours Sextius. One of Aix's few rock clubs.

Club 88, La Petite Calade, north of town near N7, **t** 04 42 23 26 88. A bustling club 8km from the centre.

Scat Club de Jazz, Rue de la Verrerie, **t** 04 42 23 00 23. Live jazz at weekends.

hôtels particuliers in golden stone, inspired by northern Italian Baroque architecture, bequeathing Aix a rich, harmonious urban fabric. Even the real plague of cholera in 1720 contributed to the city's embellishment when it contaminated the water supply; once new sources had been piped in, the city built its fountains to receive them.

In 1789 the tumultuous Count Mirabeau became a popular hero in Aix when he eloquently championed the people and condemned Provence's *Parlement* as unrepresentative; in 1800 the whole regional government was unceremoniously packed off to Marseille. Aix, the 'Athens of the Midi', has found enough to keep it busy without it, tending its university, making its sweets, hosting music festivals and, as of 1997, inaugurating a new thermal spa for the spring that gave the city its name.

Cours Mirabeau

Canopied by its soaring plane trees, decked with fountains and flanked by cafés, banks, *pâtisseries* and *hôtels particuliers* from the 17th and 18th centuries, **Cours Mirabeau** is the centre stage for Aixois society. Dubbed 'the most satisfying street in France' and laid out in 1649 to replace the south walls, it begins in Place du Général de Gaulle, which takes the old roads from Marseille and Avignon and spins them around the pompous Second Empire fountain **La Rotonde**. Other fountains punctuate the cours itself: the lumpy, mossy **Fontaine d'Eau Chaude**, oozing up its much-esteemed 34°C water and, at the far end, the **Fontaine du Roi René**, with a fairytale statue of the good monarch holding up a bunch of the muscat grapes he introduced to Provence (along with the turkey and silkworm, discreetly omitted by the sculptor).

Of the fine *hôtels particuliers* on the Cours, No.12 is where Count Mirabeau wed the aristocratic Emilie de Covet-Marignane in 1772, after playing a dastardly trick on her. When the young lady refused his marriage proposal, he sneaked into her house and appeared in the morning on her balcony, clad only in his nightshirt and socks, publicly compromising her virtue. In revenge, his new father-in-law refused the couple any money, and when Mirabeau ran up huge debts, signed the order to have him locked up in the Château d'If. Mirabeau returned to Aix to plead in the subsequent divorce case, but despite his unparalleled eloquence he lost the appeal. Thus rebuked by his noble peers, he returned to Aix in 1789 as a member of the Third Estate and proceeded to attack their privileges – a trial run for his role in igniting the Revolution in Paris.

Artist Paul Cézanne grew up at 55 Cours Mirabeau, the son of a hatter who later turned banker (on the façade you can still make out the sign of the *chapelier*). Nearby, at No.53, the elegant mirrored café **Les Deux Garçons** ('Les Deux G') has been Aix's smartest place to see and be seen since the Second World War, with a reputation and prices similar to those of Paris' café–citadels of artsy existentialist mumbo-jumbo; until recently, North Africans were not admitted to enjoy its rarefied air. It looks across towards the weighty façade of the 1647 **Hôtel Maurel de Pontevès** (No.38), the building that inspired Aix's secular Baroque, still supported after all these years by two musclebound stone giants, 'the only ones who do any work at all on the cours', as the saying went in the days of Aix's parliament.

South of Cours Mirabeau, the straight lanes of the **Quartier Mazarin**, lined with *hôtels particuliers* and antiques shops, were laid out according to the rules of Renaissance urban design by the archbishop brother of the famous cardinal.

At 2a Rue du Quatre-Septembre, the **Musée Paul Arbaud** (*t 04 42 38 38 95; open Mon–Sat 2–5; closed Jan; adm*) is the city's overflow tank for odds and ends, especially Provençal ceramics and a few hundred portraits of Mirabeau's over-large pockmarked head.

Musée Granet

Place St-Jean-de-Malte, t 04 42 38 14 70; closed for renovation until 2006.

Walk two streets south of the Musée Arbaud and then turn left at the Fontaine des Quatre Dauphins ('fountain of the Four Dolphins'), unusually equipped with teeth and scales, to reach the much more substantial archaeology and art collections of the Musée Granet, which is housed in the priory of the Knights of Malta (1675), next to the church of St-Jean-de-Malte, where the counts of Provence lie buried.

The museum's basement and ground floor are devoted to archaeology, especially everyday items and sculptures dating from the Celto-Ligurian *oppidum* of Entremont. Appropriately enough for residents of the land that would invent the guillotine, the overall theme is cult decapitation. The remains of 15 embalmed heads were discovered in the sanctuary, and the sculptures on display here, like death masks, may have been carved to replace real heads that mouldered away; according to Tertullian, the Celts would spend nights with their dead ancestors, seeking oracular advice. The heads, either singularly or in bunches, were once held as trophies by at least five statues of warriors: one has the same face as the famous gold mask of Agamemnon from Mycenae; another head resembles not so much that of a dead man as a resurrected youth. There are also finds from Roman Aquae Sextiae (note the fine sarcophagus depicting Leda and the swan, discovered in the cathedral), a superb statue of a Persian warrior (200 BC) of the Pergamon school, and Egyptian steles and cats.

Celtic head cults seem benign next to *Jupiter and Thetis* (1811), arguably Ingres' most objectionable canvas, holding court upstairs in a whole room of neoclassical mythologies inspired by Jacques-Louis David. The real culprit behind this smirking art is Napoleon, whose totalitarian approach to statecraft opened a Pandora's box of kitsch: art like this is born when cloying sentiment and a cynical manipulation of the classical past are used to serve political ends. The expression on Jupiter's sublimely stupid face not only sums up a whole era, but looks ahead to the even more cynical kitsch-mongers of the 20th century, who make Napoleon look like Little Red Riding Hood.

There are other, more palatable works by Ingres, including the *Portrait of François Granet* (1775–1849), the artist from Aix after whom the museum is named, painted while the two sojourned at Rome's Villa Medici. Granet himself was capable of neoclassical folderol and received more than his share of commissions from the clergy, but he also painted Provençal landscapes in the same vein as Guigou, Loubon and Monticelli, who are also present.

There are 17th-century portraits of Aixois nobility, made fluffy and likeable by Largillière and Rigaud; Dutch and Flemish masters (Teniers, Brit, Neefs, Rubens, Robert Campin, and a sumptuous anonymous 15th-century triptych of the *Adoration of the Magi*); and the Italians (Alvise Vivarini, Previtali, Guercino, Preti, the mysterious, grave 15th-century Maître de l'Annonciation d'Aix, and from Carlo Portelli a bizarre 16th-century Counter-Reformation blast, the *Allegory of the Church Suffering, Militant, and Triumphant*).

But what of Paul Cézanne, who took his earliest drawing classes in this very building? For many years he was represented by three measly watercolours (no one in Aix would buy his works), until 1984, when the French government finally rectified the omission by depositing eight small canvases here that touch on the major themes of his work.

Vieil Aix

North of Cours Mirabeau, the narrow lanes and squares of Vieil Aix concentrate not only some of Provence's finest architecture, but the region's most delightful shopping, especially on market days (*see* p.282). Enter the casbah by way of Rue Espariat from Place du Général de Gaulle, and you'll come to a cast-iron Baroque campanile and the church of **St-Esprit**, where a 16th-century retable has portraits of 12 members of the first Provençal *Parlement* cast in the roles of the Apostles. Further up, just beyond Aix's most elegant little square, the cobbled, fountained **Place d'Albertas**, you can pop into the lavish, Puget-inspired Hôtel Boyer d'Eguilles of 1675, now the **Muséum d'Histoire Naturelle** (*6 Rue Espariat, t 04 42 27 91 27, www. museum-paca.org; open daily 10–12 and 1–5; adm*) – well worth it for its impressive 17th-century interior, its grand staircase and its clutch of petrified dinosaur eggs.

Rue Espariat ends at Place St-Honoré, just south of the neoclassical **Palais de Justice**, a dull building of the 1760s that hardly merited the demolition of a well-preserved Roman mausoleum and the medieval palace of the counts of Provence.

Aix's flea and food markets take place in the adjacent Place de Verdun and **Place des Prêcheurs**, laid out in 1450 by King René for popular entertainments and executions of all sorts, including, in 1772, the burning in effigy of the Marquis de Sade and his valet after they were caught sodomizing prostitutes in Marseille. Here, the former Dominican church of **Ste-Marie-Madeleine** has a pleasant Second Empire façade, paintings by Rubens and Van Loo, and a gentle 13th-century polychrome statue of Notre-Dame-de-Grâce standing on a moon. However, the show-stopper is the central panel of the *Triptych of the Annunciation*, a luminous work of 1445 painted for a local draper – the two lateral panels are in Rotterdam and Brussels. Commonly attributed to Barthélémy d'Eyck, illuminator of King René's courtly allegories in the *Livre du Cœur d'Amour Epris* (now in Vienna's National Library), the central panel has provoked endless controversy over its singular, possibly heretical iconography: the angel Gabriel, winged with owl feathers (a bird of evil omen), kneels in the porch of a Gothic church, decorated with a bat and a dragon. From on high, an unconventionally gesturing God the Father sends in a golden stream of breath a foetus bearing a cross, just missing a monkey's head; a vase of flowers holds poisonous belladonna.

The more orthodox blooms of Aix's flower market lend an intoxicating perfume to Place de l'Hôtel de Ville (Place de la Mairie) in the very heart of Vieil Aix, a lovely square framed by the stately, perfectly proportioned **Hôtel de Ville** (1671), decorated with stone flowers and fruits and intricate iron grilles, and the flamboyant **Tour de l'Horloge** (1510), with clocks telling the hour and the phase of the moon, and wooden statues that change with the season. Note, too, the former grain market in the same square (now the post office), crowned by a handsome allegory of a river and city, the latter dangling a dainty foot over the cornice.

From here, Rue Gaston de Saporta is home to the **Musée du Vieil Aix** (*No.17, t 04 42 21 43 55; open April–Oct Tues–Sat 10–12 and 2.30–6; Nov–Mar Tues–Sat 10–12 and 2–5; adm*), housed in another grand 17th-century *hôtel particulier* with another magnificent staircase. It stores some quaint paintings on velvet, a bevy of *santons* in a 'talking Christmas Crib' and marionettes made in the 19th century to represent the biblical, pagan and local personages who figured in King René's Fête-Dieu processions, beginning with a figure representing Moses and someone tossing a cat up and down, and ending with Death swinging his scythe.

Cathédrale Saint-Sauveur, Musée des Tapisseries and Monument Joseph Sec

Rue Gaston de Saporta continues north to Place de l'Université, which was once part of the forum of Roman Aix, and the **Cathédrale Saint-Sauveur**, a dignified patchwork of periods and styles crowned by an octagonal bell-tower. The flamboyant Gothic west portal of 1340, decorated with scenes of the Transfiguration and the Apostles said to be by King René, was mutilated in the Revolution and partially restored in the 1830s; only the lovely Virgin on the central pillar was spared, when someone popped a red cap of Liberty on her head and made Mary a Marianne. Fortunately, the Revolutionaries forgot to axe the doors; under their protective covers they have some beautiful high reliefs of prophets and sibyls by Jean Guiramand of Toulon, sculpted 1508–10.

The interior has naves for every taste: from right to left you'll fine Romanesque, Gothic and Baroque. Tucked away by the door inside the Romanesque nave, the octagonal **baptistry** dates from c. 375, when Aix was made a bishopric. The font is encircled by columns recycled from the temple of Apollo that once stood on this site in the forum.

The cathedral's most famous treasure, Nicolas Froment's *Triptyque du Buisson Ardent* (1476), is under restoration, and a copy is on view in the foyer. On the lateral panels are portraits of a well-fed King René, who commissioned the work, and his second wife, while the central scene depicts the vision of a monk of St-Victor of Marseille, who saw the Virgin and Child appear amidst the miraculous burning bush vouchsafed to Moses. The flaming green bush symbolizes her virginity (it burns without being consumed); the mirror held by the Child symbolizes his incarnation. The meticulously detailed castles in the background seem to have been inspired by those of Tarascon and Beaucaire.

On the same wall, from the same period, another triptych has scenes from the Passion with saints Maximin and Mitre. Mitre, a 4th-century Greek slave serving a cruel master in Aix, was accused of sorcery and had his head chopped off by Roman soldiers. His trunk then picked up the head (which was already adorned with a halo) and carried it into the cathedral. The sight scared the children but made the Romans, who had a modern sense of humour, laugh until they cried, at least according to the 15th-century *Martyrdom of St Mitre*, which may be on display in the chapel tucked behind the high altar, where the saint's 5th-century sarcophagus once emitted an ooze collected by the faithful to heal eye diseases. The high altar itself is decorated with tapestries on the lives of Christ and the Virgin made in Brussels in 1510. These originally hung in Canterbury Cathedral but were sold off by the Commonwealth and purchased by a cathedral canon in Paris for next to nothing in 1656.

In the Baroque aisle is the striking **Altar des Aygosi** (1470), formerly attributed to Francesco Laurana but now to Audinet Stephani, an itinerant sculptor from Cambrai. On top, the Crucifixion is surrounded by symbols: the sun and moon on either side represent universality; the skull of Adam set at the base of the cross is purified by the blood from Christ's wounds, while, above, the pelican feeds her nestlings with her own blood, according to a popular medieval misconception. Below stand saints Anne, Marcel and Marguerite, the latter emerging from the shoulders of an embarrassed-looking dragon who swallowed her whole. The guardian will on request also unlock the airy, twin-columned, 12th-century **cloister**, with capitals daintily carved, though in an awful state of repair.

To the right and back of the cathedral, the grand 17th–18th-century residence of Aix's archbishops, the **Archevêché**, is the setting for the festival's operas. It also houses the **Musée des Tapisseries** (*t 04 42 23 09 91; open Wed–Mon 10–12.30 and 1.30–5; adm*), containing three sets of light-hearted Beauvais tapestries that were hidden under the roof during the Revolution and rediscovered only in the 1840s. The set known as the *Grotesques* (1689) features arabesques, animals, dancers and musicians; there are nine rococo scenes from the story of *Don Quixote* (1740s), and four on the subject of *Jeux Russiens* (1769–93), inspired by the rustic frolics that the court of Louis XVI got up to in the backwoods of Versailles.

Just north of the cathedral on Avenue Pasteur stands the 1792 **Monument Joseph Sec**, an eccentric discourse on the Revolution that spoiled those pampered bucolic daydreams. Sec, the builder, was a Jacobin who made his fortune floating timber down the Durance, and no one has ever satisfactorily explained the meaning behind the reliefs and statues of biblical characters, allegories and masonic symbols he chose for his monument 'dedicated to the municipality of a law-abiding town'. This obsession with law is continued in the inscriptions ('Risen from cruel slavery/ I have no master but myself/But of my freedom I desire no other use/than to obey the law') and presence of Moses (with horns) on top. Behind the monument are seven more statues in *exedrae*, including one of a woman driving a stake into a man's head, which must bemuse the Aixois who come to get their jabs in the adjacent vaccination centre.

Cézanne, the Pavillon de Vendôme and Cité du Livre

Paul Cézanne spent an idyllic childhood roaming Aix's countryside with his best friend, Emile Zola, and as an adult painted those same landscapes in a way that landscapes had never been painted before. The **Atelier Cézanne** (*9 Avenue Paul Cézanne, t 04 42 21 06 53, www.atelier-cezanne.com; open Oct–Mar daily 10–12 and 2–5; April–June and Sept daily 10–12 and 2–6; July and Aug daily 10–6; adm*), the studio that he built in 1897, located half a kilometre north of the cathedral, has been rather grudgingly maintained as it was when the master died in 1906, with a few drawings, unfinished canvases, his smock, palette, pipe and some of the bottles and skulls used in his still-lifes. For a better understanding of Cézanne and his art, pick up the free *Circuit Cézanne* from the tourist office, which points out the places where Cézanne liked to plant his easel around Aix.

Cézanne's family home at Jas-de-Bouffan is now dominated by the irritating black and white cubic forms of the **Fondation Vasarély** (*t* 04 42 20 01 09; *open summer daily 11–7; winter Mon–Sat 10–1 and 2–6; adm*), inaugurated in 1976 by the late op/geometric/kinetic artist at the height of his fame. The foundation is unpersuasively dedicated to promoting 'more human' urban development.

Along the boulevards to the west of Vieil Aix, in what was open country in 1665, a local cardinal built himself a lavish summer folly and park, the **Pavillon de Vendôme** (*32 Rue Célony, t* 04 42 21 05 78; *open Wed–Sun 10–12.30 and 1.30–4.45; adm*). The building's delightful exterior includes a pair of atlantes who, judging by their pained expressions, have just been staring into one of Vasarély's more fiendish optical illusions. Part of the interior décor is intact, complete with 17th- and 18th-century patrician furnishings and paintings.

Near the bus station at 8 Rue des Allumettes, the modern **Cité du Livre** collects several cultural entities under one roof, including the **Bibliothèque Méjanes** (*t* 04 42 91 98 85, www.citedulivre-aix.com; *open Tues–Sat 2–6*), with a rich collection of incunabula and illuminated manuscripts, some of which are usually on display; you can also sit in a booth and take in a wide selection of celebrated operas and concerts filmed from 1950 to the present day; and the **Fondation St-John Perse** (*t* 04 42 25 98 85, www.up.univer-mrs.fr/~wperse; *open Tues–Sat 2–6*), a museum and study centre bequeathed to Aix by the French poet who won the Nobel Prize in 1960.

Aix-urbia

East around the Montagne Ste-Victoire

The rolling countryside around Aix-en-Provence is the quintessence of Provence for those who love Cézanne: the ochre soil, the dusty green cypresses – as still and classical as Van Gogh's are possessed and writhing – the simple geometry of the old *bastides* and villages and the pyramidal prow of the bluish-limestone Montagne Sainte-Victoire. These landscapes are so inextricably a part of Cézanne's art that one can only wonder who created what. What if this grouchy, lonely genius had been born in Birmingham or New Jersey?

Along the south flank of the Montagne Ste-Victoire runs the **Route Cézanne** (D17), beginning at the wooded park and Italianate château of **Le Tholonet** (3km from Aix). Here Cézanne often painted the view towards the mountain which haunts at least 60 of his canvases ('I am trying to get it right,' he explained). The château belongs to the local canal authority, while the park is used as a venue for Aix's music festival (take the bus from La Rotonde).

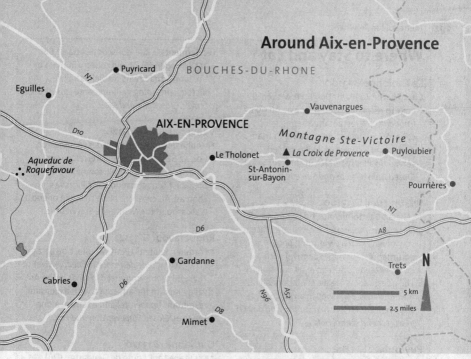

BOUCHES-DU-RHONE

Puyricard

Eguilles

N7

AIX-EN-PROVENCE

D10

Vauvenargues

Montagne Ste-Victoire

▲ *La Croix de Provence*   Puyloubier

Le Tholonet

St-Antonin-
sur-Bayon

*Aqueduc de
Roquefavour*

Pourrières

N7

D6

A8

Gardanne

Trets

N

Cabries

D6

5 km

N96

A52

2.5 miles

Mimet

D8

The entire 60km route around Montagne Ste-Victoire is striking and unspoiled; the mountain's wild shoulders are covered with maquis and holm oaks, growing back after a devastating fire in 1989, or tamed with vineyards. The short detour up to **Beaurecueil** is repaid with lovely views, while further east **St-Antonin-sur-Bayon** is home to the **Maison de Sainte-Victoire** (*t 04 42 66 84 40*), an information centre on the mountain; the GR9 (*see* p.76) begins nearby.

The ascent of **Montagne Ste-Victoire** takes about two hours (bring some sturdy shoes, a hat and a bottle of water); there's a 17th-century stone *refuge* with water and a fireplace if you want to spend the night. Crowning the precipitous west face, the 55ft **Croix de Provence** (which Cézanne never painted) has been here, in one form or another, since the 16th century. Legend has it that Marius stood on the spot, watching his troops annihilate the Teutones, then, at the urging of his sibyl Marthe, had 300 defeated chieftains brought up and tossed into the **Garagai**, Ste-Victoire's mighty chasm.

One legend claims that the floor of the Garagai is occupied by an enchanted lake and meadows, the abode of the legendary Golden Goat of Provence; shepherds, they say, would lower their sick sheep and cows down on ropes so that they could graze on the therapeutic grass. Other stories claimed that the chasm was the entrance to hell, or linked to the fountain of Vaucluse (*see* p.357) – in fact, fluoride that was released here surfaced there three months later. In the 17th century, curiosity reached such a pitch that the *Parlement* in Aix offered a condemned man his freedom if he would agree to be lowered into the Garagai and tell what he found. Carefully trussed, the man went down, but was strangled in the ropes before he reached the bottom.

Where to Stay and Eat

Le Tholonet ✉ 13100

Chez Thomé, La Plantation (in town centre next to *pétanque* courts), **t** 04 42 66 90 43 (*moderate*). A restaurant offering good country fare, including some vegetarian dishes and a choice of divine desserts, served on a leafy terrace in summer. *Closed Mon all year and Sun eve in winter.*

Beaurecueil ✉ 13100

★★★Relais Sainte-Victoire, t 04 42 66 94 98, (*expensive–moderate*). A ravishing place to stay or eat, with a swimming pool, a gourmet restaurant (*expensive*) with a lovely veranda, and, above all, tranquillity. The guest rooms are air-conditioned and have terraces. Book well in advance. *Closed Sun eve, Mon, Fri lunch in summer, all day Fri in winter and school hols.*

Puyloubier ✉ 13114

Relais de Saint-Ser, on D17 between Puyloubier and St-Antonin-sur-Bayon, **t** 04 42 66 37 26, (*inexpensive; restaurant moderate*). A small place for guests who want to get away from it all, though it's occasionally besieged by conference groups. *Closed Jan; restaurant closed Sun eve all year, lunch only Oct–May.*

Les Sarments, 4 Rue-qui-Monte, **t** 04 42 66 31 58 (*moderate*). An old country inn, run by the family that owns the Relais Sainte-Victoire, providing well-prepared *cuisine du terroir. Closed Jan and Mon.*

Vauvenargues ✉ 13126

★Moulin de Provence, 33 Av des Maquisards, **t** 04 42 66 02 22 (*inexpensive; restaurant moderate*). Twelve simple rooms and a breakfast terrace overlooking Picasso's château. An excellent place to begin or end a walk around the Montagne Ste-Victoire.

Roquefavour ✉ 13122

★★Arquier, Route du Petit-Moulin, **t** 04 42 24 20 45, *www.logis-de-france.fr* (*inexpensive*). Peaceful rooms immersed in trees in the Arc valley, next to the aqueduct, with a pleasant restaurant (*moderate*) and a terrace along the river. *Closed Sun eve, Mon and Feb.*

Gardanne ✉ 13320

★★★L'Etape Lani, Route de Gendarme (D6), **t** 04 42 22 61 90, *www.lani.fr* (*inexpensive*). A hotel with comfortable, well-equipped rooms and a restaurant (*expensive–moderate*) where you can enjoy delicate seasonal dishes. *Closed Sat lunch, Sun eve, Mon and first 3 wks Aug.*

Further to the east, the D17 passes through **Puyloubier**, which is a pleasant wine village. So too is **Pourrières**, in spite of being named after *campi putridi*, the fields of putrefaction, where the unburied corpses of the Teutones rotted after Marius' victory (*see* p.279); local farmers made vine trellises from their bones. A trophy was erected to Marius here, showing the victorious general being carried shoulder-high on his shield by his soldiers. When it eroded away, parts of it were salvaged and reconstructed as a fountain.

From Pourrières, the mountain circuit winds through the pines (D23), and when it reaches Le Puits de Rians veers back west towards Aix-en-Provence through the forested Vallée de l'Infernet (D10).

Northerly approaches to the summit of Ste-Victoire begin at Cabassols or **Vauvenargues**. The 14th-century Château de Vauvenargues, strikingly set apart from the village, was the home of Luc de Clapiers (1715–47), author of the *Introduction à la connaissance de l'esprit humain*, in which he wrote that 'the highest perfection of the human soul is to make it capable of pleasure'. In 1958 the château was purchased by Picasso, who probably would have agreed with him; Picasso's grave is in the grounds but is off limits along with the rest of the château ('No admittance! Don't insist! The museum is in Paris!'). The idyllic D11 (parallel to the GR9) descends north of Vauvenargues for 13km to Jouques, sheltered in a cool, green valley.

Puyricard and the Arc Valley

Four kilometres to the north of Aix-en-Provence, overlooking the modern city, is the plateau where the city's story began, the Celto–Ligurian *oppidum* of **Entremont**. For a place that lasted less than a century – it was founded in the 2nd century BC and destroyed by the Romans in 122 BC – it was a highly impressive achievement, its clusters of stone houses once sheltering some 5,000 souls. You can trace the

---

Wine: Coteaux d'Aix-en-Provence and La Palette

This relatively recent AOC district has begun to make a name for its red, rosé and white wines. Coteaux d'Aix-en-Provence originates in 50 *communes* in the highlands stretching from the Durance to Marignane, west to Salon-de-Provence and east to the flanks of Montagne Ste-Victoire, and consists of the region's traditional syrah, grenache, cinsault, mourvèdre and carignan grapes, enhanced in the past 20 years with the addition of Cabernet Sauvignon, a stock that has improved the wine's ageing ability. Coteaux d'Aix's sunny whites are made from sauvignon, grenache blanc and ugni – but never from René's sweet muscat grapes, although these now grow merrily in Roussillon.

Many growers welcome visitors, such as Puyricard's **Château du Seuil**, t 04 42 92 15 99, a handsomely restored 13th-century *bastide*, where reds and whites from the late 1990s are an excellent buy.

Or head further north, 20km from Aix, to Le Puy Ste-Réparade and the lush estate of **Château de Fonscolombe**, on the banks of the Durance, t 04 42 61 70 00, where James de Roany produces classic, fragrant red, rosé and white wines.

Further afield, another estate that welcomes visitors also supplies some of France's best restaurants: Jean Bonnet's 120-hectare **Château de Calissanne**, overlooking the Etang de Berre on the site of an ancient Celtic *oppidum* (on the D10, close to Lançon-Provence), t 04 90 42 63 03. On the south bank of the lagoon, one of the sunniest corners of France, **Château St-Jean**, at Port-de-Bouc near Fos-sur-Mer, t 04 42 21 01 02, produces prize-winning rosés (dominated by Counoise, an old-fashioned stock, mixed with Grenache and Carignan) and reds full of old-fashioned finesse.

La Palette is a venerable, microscopic AOC region on a north-facing limestone scree east of Aix, on the left bank of the Arc; although fairly sheltered from the mistral, it has cooler summer and winter temperatures than its environs. La Palette's red, white and rosé nectar has been served at the royal fêtes of such diverse monarchs as King René and Edward VII, but only two estates still produce this rare fine wine of the south, aged in small casks: the celebrated 150-year-old **Château Simone**, at Meyreuil, off the pretty D58H, t 04 42 66 92 58, where dark, violet-scented reds are kept for three years in caves carved out by 16th-century Carmelites; and **Château Crémade**, t 04 42 66 76 80, a 17th-century *bastide* in Le Tholonet, which bottles magnificent, well-structured red wines and a fruity *blanc de blancs*.

foundations of the large public building that produced the sculptures that now reside in the Musée Granet in Aix (*bus 20 from Aix tourist office every half-hour; open Wed–Mon 9–12 and 2–6*).

The same bus continues north to **Puyricard**, and the **Chocolaterie Puyricard** (*420 Route du Puy-Ste-Réparade*, **t** 04 42 96 11 21), where some of the most delectable (and expensive) fresh chocolates you'll ever taste are made in the traditional pre-Willy Wonka manner, 4km away in the factory; try the *clous de Cézanne*.

To the west of Aix, the D64 continues for 10km from the Fondation Vasarély to the three-tiered **Aqueduc de Roquefavour** (1847), twice as high as the Pont du Gard and built across the steep valley of the river Arc to bring the waters of the Durance to Marseille. The wooded setting is delightful – the Arc is the river where Cézanne painted his famous proto-Cubist scenes of bathers.

The edge of the Arc valley is dotted with old farms and *villages perchés*: **Eguilles**, north on the D543, with fine views from its William Morris-style medieval château (now the *mairie*); and south, off the busy Aix–Marseille routes, lofty **Cabriès** and **Mimet**. **Gardanne**, an old village often painted by Cézanne, has remained unchanged, though it is now defended by an ugly ring of industry and highways.

The Provençal Alps

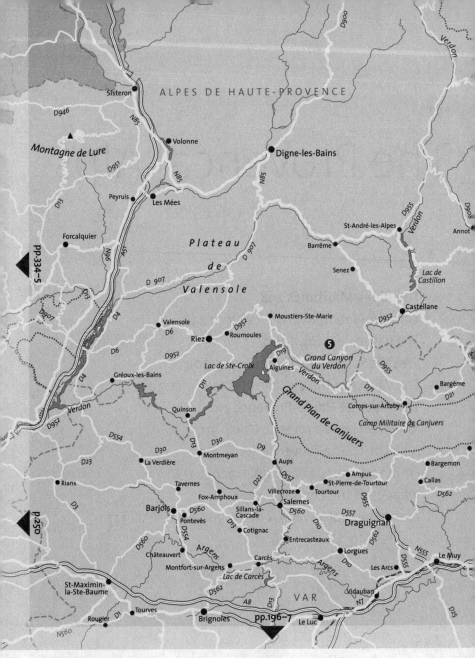

Highlights

1 Alpine heights and wild flowers in the Parc National du Mercantour
2 The enigmatic prehistoric engravings of the Vallée des Merveilles
3 Notre-Dame-des-Fontaines, the 'Sistine Chapel' of the Alpes-Maritimes
4 The mountain-climbing Train des Pignes from Nice to Digne-les-Bains via Entrevaux
5 The Grand Canyon du Verdon, France's answer to Arizona's natural wonder

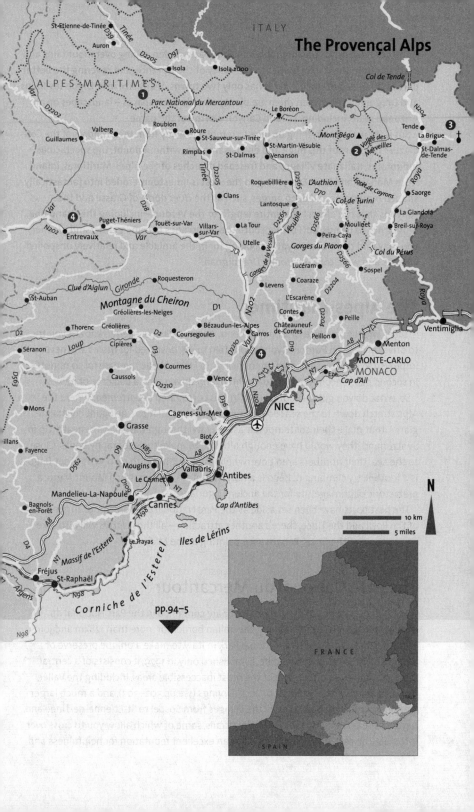

The Provençal Alps

ITALY

St-Étienne-de-Tinée
Auron
Isola
Isola 2000
Col de Tende

ALPES MARITIMES ①
Parc National du Mercantour
Le Boréon
Tende
La Brigue ③
St-Dalmas-de-Tende

Guillaumes
Valberg
Roubion
Roure
St-Sauveur-sur-Tinée
Mont Bégo ▲
Vallée des Merveilles ②
Saorge
La Giandola
Breil-sur-Roya

Rimplas
St-Martin-Vésubie
St-Dalmas
Venanson
Facel de Cayrons
L'Authion ▲
Col de Turini

Roquebillière
Clans
Lantosque
Moulinet
Peïra-Cava

Entrevaux ④
Puget-Théniers
Touët-sur-Var
Villars-sur-Var
La Tour
Utelle
Gorges du Piaon
Col du Pérus
Ventimiglia

Clue d'Aiglun
Gironde
Roquesteron
Levens
Lucéram
Coaraze
Sospel

Montagne du Cheiron
Gréolières-les-Neiges
Bézaudun-les-Alpes
Carros
L'Escarène
Contes
Peille

Thorenc
Gréolières
Coursegoules
Châteauneuf-de-Contes
Peillon
Peïllon

Séranon
Cipières
Courmes
Vence
Éze
MONTE-CARLO
MONACO
Menton

Caussols
Mons
Loup
Cagnes-sur-Mer
Cap d'Ail

Fayence
Grasse
Biot
NICE

Mougins
Le Cannet
Vallauris
Antibes

Mandelieu-La-Napoule
Bagnols-en-Forêt
Cannes
Cap d'Antibes
Iles de Lérins

N

10 km
5 miles

Le Trayas
Massif de l'Esterel
Corniche de l'Esterel

Fréjus
St-Raphaël
Argens

pp.94–5 ▼

FRANCE

ITALY

SPAIN

The Côte d'Azur has an admirably spacious back garden, rolling over mountains and plateaux from the Italian border to the valley of the Durance, and covering the better part of three *départements*. Yet it has only two towns of any size in it: Digne-les-Bains and Draguignan. Between them are plenty of wide open spaces – landscapes on an Arizonan scale, including a Grand Canyon worthy of the name.

But is there really anything up here to tempt you away from the fleshpots of the Côte d'Azur? The stars of this huge and diverse area are, without doubt, the spectacular mountains, Italianate villages and frescoed churches of the Alpes-Maritimes, inland from Monaco and Nice. Everything to the west is limestone, eroded into fantastically shaped mountains and deep gorges, such as the *clues* north of Grasse and the canyons that run almost the entire length of the Verdon – including the Grand one, a sight not to be missed. Further south the landscapes become gentler and greener; you may find the Provence you're looking for in the amiable and relatively unspoiled villages and wine country around Draguignan.

The Alpes-Maritimes

'*Lacet*' means shoelace, or a hairpin bend. It's a word you'll need to know if you try to drive up here, on Europe's worst mountain roads, designed for mules and never improved. When you see a sign announcing '20 *lacets* ahead', prepare for 10 minutes in second gear, encounters with demented lorry drivers, and a bad case of nerves.

So, what do you get for your trouble in this corrugated *département* where the Alps stretch down to the sea? For starters, these are real Alps – arrogant crystalline giants, that make their contempt felt as we crawl through the valleys beneath. Up in Switzerland, they would have enough altitude to make the geography books. Close to the sea, their numbers aren't overwhelming – but if you think 9,197ft Mont Bégo is a foothill, try climbing it. Bégo is a holy mountain, an Ararat or a Mount Meru, a prehistoric pilgrimage site for the ancient Ligurians.

The best parts have been set aside as the Parc National du Mercantour. In the valleys of the Roya and the Tinée, there's another attraction – all those *lacets* will also take you to some of the finest Renaissance painting in the Midi.

The Parc National du Mercantour

The highest regions of this *département* are contained in the Parc National du Mercantour, which stretches along the Italian border for more than 128km and joins with the adjacent Argentera National Park in Italy to make a unique preserve of alpine and Mediterranean wildlife. Established only in 1979, it consists of a central 'protected zone', a narrow strip of the most inaccessible areas, including the Vallée des Merveilles with its prehistoric rock carvings (*see* pp.302–303), and a much larger 'peripheral zone' that includes all the villages from Sospel to St-Etienne-de-Tinée and beyond. There are many excellent hiking trails, some of which allow you to cross over into Italy. The park rangers, all local, have an excellent reputation for helpfulness and

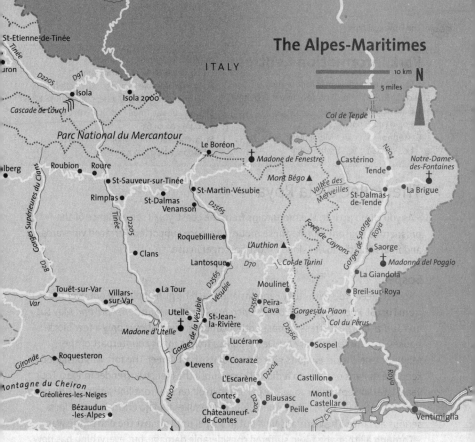

The Alpes-Maritimes

knowledge. They enforce some strict rules in the protected zone: no tents, dogs or fires, no motor vehicles (though all-terrain vehicles have recently been allowed on trails only, as an experiment), and no collecting of flowers, insects or anything else.

The most spectacular alpine fauna, and the sort you're most likely to see, are the birds of prey: golden eagles, falcons and vultures. A recent addition, reintroduced from the Balkans after becoming extinct here, is the mighty *gypaète barbu* (lammergeyer), a 'bearded' vulture with a bizarre face, orange-red feathers, black wings and a reputation for carrying off lambs and children. On the ground, there's the ubiquitous stoat or ermine, popping out of the snow in his white winter coat and looking entirely too cute to be made into royal coat linings. There's also his bulkier cousin, the marmot, and plenty of boars, foxes, *mouflons* (wild mountain sheep), chamois and, in the more inaccessible places, *bouquetins* (ibex). All of these have been rapidly increasing in number since the establishment of the park.

As for wildflowers, the symbol of the park is the spiky *saxifrage multiflora*, one of 25 species found nowhere but here. Edelweiss exists in the park, but is as elusive as anywhere else. Beyond these exotic blooms, there is a tremendous wealth of plant life. Blue gentians and anemones are everywhere, as well as hundreds of other species, in microclimates that range from Mediterranean to alpine. Half the flowers found in France are represented here.

Park Information Centres

See also *www.parc-mercantour.com*.
Nice, 23 Rue d'Italie, ✉ 06000. **Tende** ✉ 06430:
Gare de St-Dalmas,
t 04 93 04 67 00.
Castérino (Vallée des Merveilles) ✉ 06430:
t 04 93 04 87 79. *Summer only.*

Minière: Maison de la Minière,
t 04 93 04 68 66. *Summer only.*
St-Martin-Vésubie ✉ 06450: Rue Kellermann
Sérurier, Place de la Mairie, **t** 04 93 16 78 88.
St-Sauveur-sur-Tinée ✉ 06420: on D2205,
t 04 93 02 01 63.
St-Etienne-de-Tinée ✉ 06660: Quartier de
l'Ardon, **t** 04 93 02 42 27.

The Vallée de la Roya

As you climb up into the mountains from the coast, you'll see evidence of the prosperous peasant culture these mountains once supported. Terraced vineyards and fields line the lower slopes, most no longer in use.

Sospel

Sospel greets you with rusty cannons and machine guns, pointing out over the road from **Fort St-Roch** (*t 04 93 04 00 70; open July–Sept Tues–Sun 2–6; April and May Sat and Sun 2–6*). The fortress, almost entirely underground, shows only a few block-houses, in a sort of military Art Deco; it dates from a 1930s counterpart of the Maginot Line. Inside, exhibits give details of its short career. The fort was designed to keep the Italians out, which it did with ease until the French surrender in 1940. Four years later, in September 1944, Sospel found itself on the front line again – the vexing *sitzkrieg* of the Provençal mountains, where the Allies had no effort to spare for a serious advance. The Germans held out in Sospel until almost the end of the war.

Through all that, the town suffered considerable damage, but everything has now been entirely, and lovingly, restored, including Sospel's landmark, the **Pont Vieux**, the base of which dates back to the 10th century. The tiny tower in the middle of the bridge was the toll on the salt road; in the Middle Ages, salt from the flats of Toulon and Hyères was taken by boat to Nice, and from there by convoys of mules to Piedmont and Lombardy. Now the toll bridge houses the tourist information office.

The **Cathédrale St-Michel**, set in a handsome arcaded square, retains its original 12th-century bell-tower, but the rest has been Baroqued with charming tastelessness inside and out, including a wonderful circus-tent baldachin over the altar, dripping with gilt and tassels. A chapel to the left discreetly hides a fine *Annunciation* by Ludovico Brea, as well as another retable of the Virgin in a Gothic frame, possibly also by Brea or one of his followers. Don't miss a wander around the narrow winding streets of the rest of the old town, and another arcaded square, **Place St-Nicolas**, with a 15th-century fountain, on the other side of the bridge.

Breil-sur-Roya and Saorge

To the north, the D2204 is the best route into the Vallée de la Roya, with only a few dozen *lacets* and one mountain pass; the other route, following the D93 and the N204, is slightly shorter, but it passes two border crossings in and out of Italy.

Breil-sur-Roya, the first town in the French part of the valley, has two peculiar attractions: the unidentifiable black pseudo-turkeys who live in the river Roya under the bridge, and the 18th-century church of Sancta-Maria-in-Albis, which has some large cracks in its ill-formed walls that seem ready to bring the place down around the ears of the faithful. Inside there is another retable attributed to Brea, though it's not a very good one.

Further to the north, the village of **La Giandola** sits among the olive groves that once were the Vallée de la Roya's only resource, and beyond that you'll come to the **Gorges de Saorge**.

After the gorges, the village of **Saorge** is a truly magnificent sight with its neat and tidy rows of Italian slate-roofed, green-shuttered houses that are perched on a height like some remote Byzantine monastery and punctuated by church steeples with cupolas made of coloured tiles. Saorge guards the Roya valley, and the Piedmontese made it a key border stronghold. You won't see more than the ruins of their fort today, however – it was destroyed after a young commander named Bonaparte took it during the wars of the Revolution. The town suffered further during the Second World War, when its inhabitants were evacuated and forced to spend the duration in Antibes.

Getting Around

Of all the hinterlands of Provence, this is the region most difficult to navigate by car, and the most convenient for public transport.

By Train

One of the best ways to see the Vallée de la Roya is from that alpine rarity – a train. The railway line from Nice that runs to Cuneo in Italy offers spectacular scenery and serves L'Escarène, Sospel, Breil-sur-Roya, St-Dalmas-de-Tende and Tende (5 daily). One train a day goes on to Turin. Don't miss the historic train cars parked at Sospel station, including an old Orient-Express.

By Bus

Sospel has daily buses to and from Menton, which take 20 minutes. There are regular bus services from Nice to L'Escarène, Contes and Lucéram, and a range of buses from Sospel into the smaller valleys (t 04 93 04 01 24 or t 04 93 04 01 40).

Tourist Information

Sospel: on Pont Vieux, t 04 93 04 15 80, www.royabevera.com. Open May–Oct daily

9–12.30 and 2.30–6.30; Nov–April daily 9.30–12.30 and 2.30–5.30.
Breil-sur-Roya: Mairie, 17 Place Biancheri, t 04 93 04 99 76. Open summer 8.30–12.30 and 1–6; winter Mon–Sat 9–12 and 2–5.30.
Tende: Av du 16 Sept 1947, t 04 93 04 73 71, www.tendemerveilles.com. Open June–Sept daily 9–12.30 and 2–6; Oct–May Mon–Sat 9–12.30 and 2–5.30.

Market Days

Sospel: Thurs, farmers' market.
Breil: Tues, farmers' market.
Tende: Wed; plus Tues, Sat and Sun am, farmers' market.

Where to Stay and Eat

Sospel ✉ 06380

**L'Auberge Provençale, Route du Col de Castillon, about 2km from town, t 04 93 04 00 31, www.aubergeprovencale.fr (moderate). An inn with a terrasse with a magnificent view over Sospel. Closed Thurs mid-Nov–mid-Dec.
Domaine du Paraïs, off D2566 towards Moulinet at La Vesta, t 04 93 04 15 78 (moderate–inexpensive). A chambre d'hôte

Saorge is just as attractive from close up, an ancient border village with customs and a dialect all its own, a little bit Occitan and a little bit Ligurian Italian; instead of *rue* or *via* on the street signs, you'll see *caréra* or *chu* or *ciassa*. The streets – stairways more often than not – climb and dive and duck under arches.

The sights themselves require a kilometre's hike to the outskirts. There you'll find an 18th-century Franciscan monastery, in elegant Piedmontese Baroque, and beyond that the 11th-century chapel of the **Madonna del Poggio**, with some Renaissance frescoes, including a Marriage of the Virgin.

To the west of Saorge, you can penetrate into the southernmost corner of the Mercantour National Park, up the narrow D40 into the **Forêt de Cayrons** (or Caïros).

Vallée des Merveilles

Before going any further, make sure you understand that the Roya is a cul-de-sac; there's no way out except by retracing your steps or continuing through the Tende tunnel to Cuneo, Italy. After Saorge, the mountains close in immediately, with the **Gorges de Bergue et de Paganin**; these end at the village of **St-Dalmas-de-Tende**, once the border post between France and Italy and now the gateway to the **Vallée des Merveilles**.

---

located outside Sospel (unfortunately you'll really need a car to get here), set in a villa that was taken over by officers during the Second World War and which has now been proudly restored by its owners. *Book ahead*.

★★Hôtel des Etrangers, 7 Av de Verdun, t 04 93 04 00 09, www.sospel.net (*inexpensive*). A hotel offering 35 simple rooms, 12 with balconies, plus a swimming pool. *Closed Nov–Feb*.

L'Escargot d'Or, 3 Bd de Verdun, t 04 93 04 00 43 (*moderate*). The best place in town to eat, specializing in meat fondues. Ring ahead to reserve, and to check that they're open out of season.

Breil-sur-Roya ☒ 06540

★★Castel du Roy, Route de Tende, t 04 93 04 43 66, www.hotelmenton.com/hotel-castel-du-roy (*moderate–inexpensive*). A modern, comfortable option spread out among a number of different buildings close to the river, with a swimming pool and a highly rated restaurant. *Closed Nov–Mar*.

★★Le Roya, village square, t 04 93 04 48 10, (*inexpensive*). A functional choice.

Saorge ☒ 06540

Le Bellevue, 5 Rue Louis Périssol, t 04 93 04 51 37 (*moderate*). The only hotel in the village, with good views and a restaurant. *Closed Tues eve and Wed*.

Lou Pountin, Rue Revelli, t 04 93 04 54 90 (*cheap*). Excellent pizzas. *Closed Wed*.

La Brigue ☒ 06430

★★Le Mirval, Rue Vincent Ferrier, at west end of village, t 04 93 04 63 71, www.lemirval.com (*inexpensive*). The best of the three hotels here; some rooms have good views and the management can arrange trips (*expensive*) into the Vallée des Merveilles. *Closed Nov–Mar*.

Castérino ☒ 06430

If you're doing the Merveilles on your own, it's most convenient to start from Castérino, a hamlet at the end of the D91.

★Les Melèzes, t 04 93 04 95 95 (*moderate–inexpensive*). Small but comfortable rooms and a good restaurant (*moderate*). *Restaurant closed Tues eve and Wed out of season*.

Santa Maria Maddalena, t 04 93 04 65 93, (*inexpensive*). A *gîte d'étape* with a restaurant; half board is obligatory in season. *Closed mid-Nov–Dec and April*.

From about 1800 BC onwards, the Ligurian natives of these mountains began scratching pictures and symbols on the rocks here. They kept at it for 800 years, until more than 100,000 inscriptions decorated the valley: human figures, religious symbols (plenty of bulls, horns and serpents), weapons and tools. Most defy any conclusive interpretation – they are circles, spirals and ladders or chequerboard patterns of the kind found all over the Med (the Val Camonica in north Italy has even more carvings, from the same era). Why they were made is an open question; one very appealing hypothesis is that this valley, beneath Mont Bégo, was a holy place and a pilgrimage site, and that the carvings can be taken as *ex votos* made by the pilgrims.

The presence of these symbols has brought the valley some notoriety – superstition gave the surroundings place names like Cime du Diable (Devil's Peak) and Valmasque (*masco*, mask, was an old local word for sorcerer). The first person to study the site systematically was an Englishman, Clarence Bicknell, in the early part of the 20th century. As the prime attraction of the Parc National du Mercantour, the valley gets its fair share of visitors these days. Besides the carvings, the landscape itself is worth the hike, including a score of mountain lakes, mostly above the treeline, all in the shadow of rugged, uncanny **Mont Bégo**, highest of the peaks around the Roya; the mountain's name, as far as anyone can tell, comes from an Etruscan god of storms.

Don't just wander up here like some fool tourist, looking for Neolithic etchings. Plan the trip out beforehand, with advice from the park information offices. They will probably recommend a guided tour; the symbols are plentiful, but nonetheless inconspicuous and hard to find. Outside the summer months, many will be covered in snow. To tour the valley is *at least* a 20km round-trip trek from the *refuge* at Les Mesches, at the end of the road west from St-Dalmas. There are hotels in nearby **Castérino** (*see* opposite) and *refuges* within the park if you want to stay over; make arrangements at the park office. Four-by-fours can also take you around (expensively) from St-Dalmas.

La Brigue and Notre-Dame-des-Fontaines

Vittorio Emanuele II, the last king of Piedmont–Sardinia and the first of unified Italy, may have been utterly useless at his job, but as a hunter few crowned heads could match him. When he arranged to give away the county of Nice in 1860, he stipulated only that the Upper Roya, above St-Dalmas-de-Tende, be left for him as a hunting reserve (to add to a few others he had, strung out across Italy, including the famous Isle of Montecristo). The few inhabitants had already voted (under French supervision) on union with France; suspiciously, 73 per cent of the electorate abstained. So this had to wait until 1947, when another plebiscite was held and the valley became France's latest territorial acquisition.

Tende, a dour, slate-roofed *bourg*, is the only town. No longer a dead end since the road tunnel through to Italy was built, it has become a busy place by local standards. It has the ruined castle of the Lascaris, long-time feudal lords of the Roya, and a late Gothic church, Ste-Marie-des-Bois, with a pretty sculpted Renaissance portal, and painted façade and ceiling. Don't miss its cemetery, built on steps for lack of space. On Avenue du 16 Septembre 1847, the **Musée des Merveilles** (*t 04 93 04 32 50,* *www.museemerveilles.com; open Wed–Mon May–mid-Oct 10–6.30, mid-Oct–April 10–5; adm*) has copies and photos of the rock engravings, as well as ethnographic exhibits on life in the valley from prehistoric times up to the 18th century.

East of St-Dalmas-de-Tende, the D143 takes you into La Brigue, a minute region (partly in Italy) that grows apples and pears and raises trout. **La Brigue**, the tiny capital, has some fine paintings in its church of St-Martin, another late Gothic work of the 15th century: three altarpieces by Ludovico Brea and his followers, along with Italian paintings from the 17th and 18th centuries. The people who live here seem to have an elevated opinion of tourists, since the only ones who pass through have come a long way to see their paintings and, more importantly, those by Giovanni Canavesio at **Notre-Dame-des-Fontaines**, 4km from the village of La Brigue. The name comes from seven intermittent local springs, miniature versions of the Fontaine-de-Vaucluse (*see* p.357), gushing out of the rock or stopping according to pressure and the water table; these can still be seen, though now they are on the Italian side of the border.

The Upper Roya may not have been much of an economic or strategic gain for France, but artistically it was a real prize – the country's total number of good Renaissance frescoes went up considerably. Giovanni Canavesio, from Piedmont, is not well known outside his own region, but he was a painter in the best north Italian Renaissance tradition, characterized by bright colours, exquisite, stylized draughtsmanship and an ability to put a genuine religious feeling into his frescoes that recalls Fra Angelico. His works in this rural chapel, done in the 1490s, include 26 large scenes of the Passion of Christ in the nave, and on one of the side walls a tremendous Last Judgement – a gentle reminder that God wasn't joking. All the tortures of the damned are portrayed in intricate detail, as the devils sweep them into the gaping Mouth of Hell. Around the choir, on the triumphal arch, he painted scenes from the life of Mary, from the *Birth of Mary* to the *Presentation at the Temple*.

The frescoes in the choir itself are by Giovanni Baleison. Done in the 1470s, in a more old-fashioned style that still shows the influence of Byzantium, these include the *Four Evangelists* on the vaulted ceiling, the four *Doctors of the Church* (Ambrose, Jerome, Gregory and Augustine) under the arch, and more scenes from the life of Mary, including an *Assumption*, the *Reproach of Thomas* and the *Visit to the Tomb*.

West of Sospel: The Paillon Valley

There is some painting here too, in the rugged mountains between Sospel and the valley of the Var. The Italian influence shows itself in another way – the road map looks like a plate of spaghetti, with more twists and bends than anywhere in the *département*. Lacking a mule, you'll need to return to Sospel to get out of the valley.

L'Escarène

The D2204 west will take you to L'Escarène, a lovely Italianate village that used to serve as a posting station between Turin and Nice. From the bridge you can see the houses overhanging the river, and you can visit the **Chapelle des Pénitents-Blancs**,

Getting Around

All the villages in the Paillon are served by at least two buses a day from Nice.

Tourist Information

Coaraze: Place Ste-Catherine, at village entrance, t 04 93 79 37 47.

Contes: Place Albert Ollivier, t 04 93 79 13 99, www.ville-contes.fr. Open Mon–Sat 2–5.

Lucéram: Place Adrian Barralis, t 04 93 79 46 50, www.luceram.com. Open Tues–Sun 9–12 and 2–6.

Market Days

Contes: Sat am.

Lucéram: Christmas market.

Where to Stay and Eat

Chic sophistication goes only as far as the foothills. In these mountains, so close to Nice and Monte Carlo, food and accommodation are surprisingly basic and humble.

Lucéram ✉ 06440

**Trois Vallées, Moulinet, t 04 93 91 57 21, troisvallees@wanadoo.fr (moderate). A handsome chalet in the woods at the top of Col de Turini, north of Lucéram, with 20 adequate rooms and a restaurant (moderate) offering roast boar and more, plus great views.

La Bocca Fina, 5 Place Adrian Barralis, t 04 93 79 51 54 (moderate). Traditional cooking, served on a terrace. Closed Wed eve.

Coaraze ✉ 06390

Coaraze, with its sundials and restored houses, seems to get more visitors than the other villages, perhaps because it has the most attractive mountain hideaway in the area.

Auberge du Soleil, 5 Chemin Camin de la Beguda, t 04 93 79 08 11 (moderate). An inn in a dreamy location at the top of the village, with a pool and a fine restaurant with a memorable view from its terrace. This end of the village is closed to traffic – call ahead if you need help with your baggage. Closed Nov–mid-Feb.

with its spectacular rococo stucco decoration. There are some peculiar landscapes to the south of the village: stone quarries on the road to Nice have carved out a huge, nearly perfect ziggurat; the road is sometimes closed in the mornings for blasting. In the hills above, around Blausasc, 19th-century deforestation has left a lunar wasteland of bare rock; the government is currently building water channels to keep the erosion from spreading.

Lucéram

North of L'Escarène, Lucéram is an old shoe of a village, well worn and a bit out at the toes. Full of arches and tunnels like Saorge, it contains some remains of walls and towers on the mountainside, which make for a steep but pleasant excursion if you want to circumnavigate them. The church of **Sainte-Marguerite** is second only to Notre-Dame-des-Fontaines as an artistic attraction. Amidst the gaudy Baroque stucco of the interior, the altarpieces of the Nice school seem uncomfortably out of place. The best, with an innocence and spirituality matched by few other saintly portraits, is the Retable de Ste-Marguerite over the main altar, which has been attributed to Ludovico Brea. Marguerite, a martyr of Antioch, is another popular Provençal dragon-slayer, one who is often confused with St Martha (see pp.406–407). Brea made her exceedingly lovely; the Tarasque-like demon at her feet obviously never stood a chance.

The other retables around the church include saints Peter and Paul (with the keys and sword), St Claude, St Lawrence (with his grid-iron, upon which he was barbecued) and St Bernard, all by unknown 15th-century artists; Giovanni Baleison contributed a good one of St Anthony of Padua (1480) in the Chapelle du Trésor. It keeps company with a **Trésor** of awful clutter: reliquaries, monstrances and statuettes, including a silver image containing relics of St Marguerite. Outside the church, **Chapelle St-Jean** was built by the Knights of St John – the Knights of Malta, who had a commandery here. Its beautiful exterior is painted to imitate precious marble (though the inside is full of electricity generators).

If you have the time, there are some worthwhile digressions into the mountains around Lucéram, beginning just outside the village with two more chapels with frescoes by Giovanni Baleison, similar to his work at Notre-Dame-des-Fontaines: **St-Grat** (on the road towards L'Escarène) and **Notre-Dame-de-Bon-Cœur** (on the road for Coaraze); the sacristan in Lucéram has the keys for both. East of Lucéram, a half-hour climb up into the hills, there is a wild spot with a huge circular prehistoric wall, the site of a fortified village from the time of the inscriptions in the Vallée des Merveilles – a logical place for such a settlement, with a fine view of holy Mont Bégo.

North of Lucéram, the D21 and D2566 take you past Peïra-Cava, a resort for the French military and their families, to the Forêt de Turini, centred around a 4,987ft mountain pass, the **Col de Turini**, at the tip of three river valleys. Up above the pass are several old forts, near the summit of L'Authion, an eyrie that commands almost all the Alpes-Maritimes. These were one of the Germans' last redoubts in the war; signs of the battle are still evident, especially around the **Fort des Mille Fourches**, damaged, incredibly, by bombardment from the sea in 1945.

The Devil's Tail and Other Tales

A long tour on the D2566/D15 west from Lucéram (7km for the crow, 19 for you) will take you with some difficulty to **Coaraze**, a village that is a magnet for stories. One is its name, *Caude Rase* in medieval times, or the 'cut tail' of the Devil. The villagers back then somehow trapped Old Nick, who had to give up his tail like a lizard to get away. Coaraze has also attracted its share of artists lately; one has given the village centre a lizard mosaic to commemorate the event. Other artists, including Jean Cocteau, have contributed a number of colourful ceramic sundials around the village.

Another legend deals with the abandoned village of **Roccasparvière**, a four-hour walk from Coaraze in the mountains. Queen Jeanne of Provence, the story goes, once took refuge from her enemies here. The plot differs in every version, but in most of them someone in the village kills Jeanne's twin sons and serves them up for dinner. '*Roc, méchant roc,*' Jeanne cursed. '*Un jour viendra où plus ne chantera ni poule ni coq.*' No chickens indeed are singing in Roccasparvière today, but spoilsport historians say it was because the village well dried up.

Another tortuous 10km south of here on the D15, **Contes** has its stories too. One fine day in 1508, the village was attacked by a horde of caterpillars. Apparently it was not the first time; the area has a colourful species the French call *chenilles processionnaires*, who enjoy a promenade in town every now and then. This time, the Contois had had enough; they called in the bishop of Nice, who brought inquisitors and exorcists, and made anathemas and proclamations until the caterpillars finally grew uncomfortable and went home. Such affairs were not uncommon, especially in old France. Animals, too, were considered subject to God's law; horses and dogs occasionally went on trial for their indiscretions when times were dull.

Contes has another altarpiece in the Brea manner in its church, and down by the river a well-preserved forge with a water-powered hammer, near the communal olive oil press. Here, and in many villages in the mountains, the oil presses are still in use. Across the river, and 9km up in the Ferion mountains, there is another abandoned village to explore, 2km outside **Châteauneuf-de-Contes** (*road open Sat, Sun and hols*).

The Valleys of the Vésubie and the Tinée

The extensive valley of the river Vésubie is almost completely isolated from the regions to the east; from Lucéram the only ways across are the D21/D2566/D70 through the Col de Turini, or the miserable D2566/D73 directly over the mountains. There's an equally tortuous route from Contes, the D815/D19.

Levens to Lantosque

The Vésubie flows into the Var near **Levens**, a big walled village high on a small plain, with a big church and a scattering of small private art galleries. Beneath it, the main road up the valley, the D2565, follows the scenic **Gorges de la Vésubie**. From St-Jean-la-Rivière, at the end of the gorge, a winding 15km detour leads to the sanctuary of the **Madone d'Utelle**, one of the most popular pilgrimage sites in Provence, with a chapel full of naïve *ex votos* to Notre-Dame-des-Miracles, many from sailors, and a spectacular view as far as the sea.

Lantosque, the next village up the valley from St-Jean, is a humble place that is regularly shaken by landslides and earthquakes. Lantosque was occupied by the Austrians in the Revolution. One of them must have been *un bon coq*, as the French say; it's a joke in the other villages that you can always find someone in Lantosque named Otto.

St-Martin-Vésubie

At the top of the valley, St-Martin is the only town for a great distance in any direction, and a base for tackling the upper part of the Mercantour. It's as unaffectedly cute as a town can be, and once it was a spa of some repute. In the delightful and shady town square is an old fountain where the mineral waters used to flow, with inscriptions testifying to their 'organoleptic properties'. The medieval centre is traversed by a lovely street (Rue du Docteur Cagnoli) with a mountain spring flowing down a narrow channel in the middle, as in a garden of the Alhambra. On this street you'll see an impressive Gothic mansion, the **Palais Gubernatis**, and the parish church, housing an altarpiece attributed to Brea and a polychrome wooden statue of the Virgin from the 14th century.

Getting Around

There are no trains in either the Vésubie or the Tinée valleys, and the coach service is sketchy.

St-Martin-Vésubie can be reached by **bus** from the *gare routière* in Nice (Cars TRAM, **t** 04 93 89 47 14); buses for St-Sauveur and St-Etienne in the Tinée also leave from here.

Roads in this area are as difficult as those to the east; service stations are few, so fill your tank whenever you get the opportunity.

Tourist Information

Levens: 3 Place de la République, **t** 04 93 79 71 00. *Open Mon–Fri 9–12 and 3–6.30, Sat 9–12 and 3–5.30; July and Aug also Sun 10–1.*
St-Martin-Vésubie: Place Félix Faure, **t** 04 93 03 21 28, *www.saintmartinvesubie.fr. Open July and Aug daily 9–12.30 and 3–7; Sept–June Mon–Sat 9–12 and 2.30–5.30, Sun 9–12.*

Market Days

Levens: Country show, first Sat in June.
St-Martin-Vésubie: Tues, Thurs, Sat and Sun in summer.

Where to Stay and Eat

In the mountains look out for locally made liqueurs, an alpine speciality: *myrtille* (bilberry), pear or something called *genépi Meunier*, made from an alpine herb that is closely related to absinthe.

Levens ✉ 06670

La Vigneraie, 82, Route de St-Blaise, on Nice road south of village, **t** 04 93 79 77 60 (*inexpensive*). A friendly *auberge* with comfortable rooms. Full board is a veritable bargain, and it would be madness not to take it at a hostelry that locals travel miles to visit for Sunday lunch in its restaurant (*moderate; book early*). *Closed mid-Oct–Jan.*

Lantosque ✉ 06450

★★★Hostellerie de l'Ancienne Gendarmerie, on riverbank, **t** 04 93 03 00 65, *www.*

hotel-lantosque.com (*moderate*). This hotel in a former police station occupies a pretty hillside site on the way up to the Parc du Mercantour, and has rooms looking on to the garden and a swimming pool. The restaurant (*expensive*) specializes in sea fish and *escargots*. *Closed Nov–Mar.*

St-Martin-Vésubie ✉ 06450

La Chaumière du Cavalet, Le Boréon, **t** 04 93 03 21 46, *www.lecavalet.com* (*moderate*). Simple accommodation in a lovely lakeside setting outside St-Martin, at the forest edge. The restaurant is excellent. *Closed Nov–Mar.*
★★La Bonne Auberge, Allée de Verdun, **t** 04 93 03 20 49 (*inexpensive*). A welcoming and pretty place with pleasant rooms and a cosy cellar restaurant (*moderate*). *Closed mid-Nov–mid-Feb.*
★Hôtel des Alpes, Place Félix Faure, **t** 04 93 03 21 06 (*inexpensive*). Adequate modern hotel across the square from La Bonne Auberge.
La Treille, Rue du Docteur Cagnoli, **t** 04 93 03 30 85 (*moderate*). The place to come for some of the best pizza this side of the border, baked in a proper pizza oven. Pasta and a few more ambitious dishes also crop up on the menu. *Closed Mon–Fri in winter.*
Le Bella Vista, 1 Place St-Jean, Venanson, **t** 04 93 03 25 11 (*inexpensive*). A simple place outside St-Martin, with its own restaurant (*moderate*). *Closed Mon.*

The Tinée Valley

Don't expect anything out of the ordinary in the sparsely populated, little-visited Tinée valley: simple country inns with restaurants are the rule.

Auberge St-Jean, Clans ✉ 06420, **t** 04 93 02 90 21 (*inexpensive*). A simple inn with just two rooms. *Closed Nov.*
Chalet du Val de Blore, Valdeblore ✉ 06420, on D2565 west of St-Dalmas, **t** 04 93 02 83 29 (*inexpensive*). A family hotel offering 35 extremely simple rooms in a modern chalet building, and a restaurant where you can enjoy Niçois home cooking. In summer there's a 7-night minimum stay. *Closed Nov.*

In the vicinity, **Venanson** is a beautiful village up in the mountains above St-Martin, with a small church full of frescoes by Giovanni Baleison. To the east, up into the Parc du Mercantour on the D94, the **Sanctuaire de la Madone de Fenestre** was an ancient holy site near the present Italian border; the name comes from a natural window in a nearby mountain peak. During the course of its long history the chapel has burned four times. In the Middle Ages the Templars held the site; they were massacred in the 14th century and their ghosts were often seen in the neighbourhood.

Hiking trails from here can take you on a very scenic route to the Vallée des Merveilles. Another road from St-Martin, the D89, leads northwest up a valley between the peaks of Mont Archas and Cime du Piagu to the resort village of **Le Boréon**; this is a lovely area, with many hiking trails, a waterfall (near the village) and some mountain lakes near the Italian border.

The Valley of the Tinée

There's nothing splashy or spectacular about the Tinée. People who love the Mercantour follow the slow D2205 along its length, from the N202 out of Nice up to the protected zone of the park. Skiers flock in winter to the modern resorts of Isola 2000 and Valberg. But outside their punctual visitations, there is a sort of pious hush in this valley, which is serenely beautiful even by alpine standards. In the lower part of the valley, the scenery is as much indoors as out; prosperity during the 15th and 16th centuries allowed the villages of the Lower Tinée to decorate their modest churches with fine Renaissance frescoes by artists of the Nice school.

The river flows into the Var with a climax at the **gorges**, across the mountains from Utelle. To the northeast, **La Tour** has frescoes from 1491 in its Chapelle des Pénitents-Blancs. The traditional subjects are represented: the Passion and a colourful Last Judgement, with Christ sitting on a rainbow and allegorical figures of the Seven Deadly Sins riding on fantastical animals, accompanying the damned to hell.

The next paintings are at **Clans**, in two chapels just outside the village. St-Antoine offers more Sins, from an unknown, late 15th-century hand; they accompany some 20 rather peculiar scenes from the *Life of St Anthony* – cooking eggs and exorcizing female demons. St-Michel has frescoes by an Italian named Andrea de Cella, *c.* 1515, including St Michael 'fishing for souls' – an odd conceit that goes back to the art of the Byzantine era. The parish church in the centre of the village has pictures too: surprisingly, a rare late medieval hunting scene.

Next up the valley, there is a pleasant detour on the D2565 through Valdeblore, the only reasonable road through to the Vésubie. It begins at **Rimplas**, and the nearby **Chapelle de la Madeleine**, a conspicuous landmark occupying a gorgeous site overlooking the valley, and continues through **St-Dalmas**, where there is a large and sophisticated Romanesque church, the Eglise de l'Invention de la Sainte-Croix, with fragments of its original frescoes.

Continuing up the Tinée, the next stop is **St-Sauveur-sur-Tinée**, throbbing metropolis of the valley, with its 496 souls. From here you can follow the Vionène valley west through the rugged and lovely villages of **Roure** and **Roubion**. The former, set amidst the biggest larch forest in Europe, has more painting: a Brea (attributed) altarpiece in the church of St-Laurent, and unusual frescoes of the lives of St Sebastian and St Bernard in the chapel outside the village. All these chapels outside villages, incidentally, are a regional peculiarity, set outside the gates as if to avert evil influences, and often dedicated to plague saints such as Sebastian. Roubion has a Sebastian chapel too, with another frescoed set of Deadly Sins.

Continuing in this direction, the next town is the modern ski resort of **Valberg**. There is alpine scenery in these parts, but little else; the best of it is in the long, lonely canyons stretching south off the D30/D28: the **Gorges Supérieures du Cians** and the **Gorges de Daluis**.

The uppermost part of the Tinée, following the D2205, runs through the northern half of the Parc du Mercantour, never more than a few kilometres from the Italian border. After St-Sauveur-sur-Tinée come the **Gorges de Valabres**, decorated with an EDF electric plant that somehow managed to sneak inside the park borders.

Isola, on the other side of the river, has some more appealing sights, both just off the D2205: a magnificently tall waterfall, the **Cascade de Louch**, and an impressive Romanesque bell-tower, the only survival from an abbey washed away by a flood 300 years ago. A good road takes you up to the Italian border and **Isola 2000**, a British-built, modern, concrete ski resort that does good business because of its proximity to the coast. Everywhere else to the north is at ski level, and almost all the villages have learned to adapt their lives and habits to the seasonal invasions of the ski-bunnies.

If you haven't yet had enough Renaissance frescoes, you may want to follow the Tinée to its source. In **Auron**, the 12th-century church of St-Erige has a sequence of paintings of that obscure Provençal saint, along with the Parisian St Denis, a stranger in these parts.

St-Etienne-de-Tinée has two painted rural chapels: St-Sébastien, with a cycle of works by Canavesio and Baleison, in very bad shape, and the chapel of the Couvent des Trinitaires, where the subject is, of all things, the great naval victory of the Venetians and Spaniards over the Turks at Lepanto in 1571.

The Alpes de Haute-Provence

Clearly we find ourselves in a place that is out of the ordinary.
You need a strong character, and a little bit of soul.

Jean Giono

There is something of the Wild West in this *département*, which comes complete with lofty plateaux and canyons; it even has a Grand Canyon of its own. Provence's wide open spaces are full of lavender fields and fresh air, and are a wonderful place to whitewater raft, hang-glide, horseride, climb or hike. The **Maison des Alpes de Haute-Provence** (*19 Rue Docteur Honnorat, ✉ 04005 Digne-les-Bains, t 04 92 31 57 29*), publishes some free and extremely useful practical guides to the region.

Alpes de Haute-Provence North

Villars-sur-Var to Entrevaux along the N202

The N202 is the east–west traffic chute, following the upper Var, and the only convenient way to get through the mountains north of Grasse. It isn't scenic, though the gravelly, impossibly blue Var makes a refreshing sight alongside; it may, however, be an antidote to claustrophobia after traversing too many gorges. The trip begins with a local novelty – wine – at **Villars-sur-Var**. The centre of the only, tiny AOC wine region in the mountains, Villars was almost abandoned before the awarding of the *dénomination* in the 1970s. Production has vastly increased since then, and you'll occasionally see this variety of Côtes-de-Provence in trendy restaurants on the coast

Getting Around

Buses are so rare they aren't worth the trouble, but it can be fun seeing this region by riding the scenic, recently modernized, narrow-gauge **rail line** from Nice to Digne, familiarly called the Train des Pignes. It follows the Var, and some trains stop at villages along the way: Villars-sur-Var, Puget-Théniers, Entrevaux and Annot. This is not the SNCF but a line called Chemin de Fer de Provence (in Digne, call **t** 04 92 31 01 58 for details; in Nice go to the Gare du Sud, 1 bis Rue Alfred Binet; or check *www.trainprovence.com*).

Tourist Information

Puget-Théniers: RN202, **t** 04 93 05 05 05, *www.provence-val-dazur.com*. *Open June–Sept daily 9–12 and 2–7; April–May and Oct 9–12 and 2–6; Nov–Mar Mon–Sat 9–12 and 2–5.*

Entrevaux: at Porte Royale du Pont-Levis, **t** 04 93 05 46 73, *www.entrevaux.com*. *Open Feb–April Mon–Fri 9–12 and 1–5.30; May and June daily 9–12 and 1–5.30; July and Aug daily 9–7; Sept–Nov 9–12 and 1.30–5.30.*

Market Days

Entrevaux: Fri am.

Where to Stay and Eat

Because it's the only good road across this region, the N202 has the best selection of places to stay and eat along its length, including a few that are rather better than the average *routier*.

Touët-sur-Var ✉ 06710

Restaurant des Chasseurs, **t** 04 93 05 71 11 (*moderate*). Appreciative locals come here to enjoy fish and game; try the ravioli and the rabbit stew. There are also a few rooms to stay in. *Closed Mon eve and Tues.*

Puget-Théniers ✉ 06260

Hôtel Alizé/Restaurant l'Amandier, Rue Alexandre Barety, **t 04 93 05 06 20, *hotel. alize@wanadoo.fr* (*inexpensive*). Fifteen rooms and a restaurant (*moderate*). *Restaurant closed Mon and Nov.*

Les Acacias, Le Planet, **t** 04 93 05 05 25 (*moderate*). A great place to dine, featuring duck, pigeon and rabbit prepared in some imaginative ways. *Closed Wed.*

Entrevaux ✉ 04320

Hostellerie Vauban, 4 Place Louis Moreau, **t 04 93 05 42 40 (*inexpensive*). The only hotel in Entrevaux, with a restaurant (*moderate*). *Closed Jan; restaurant closed Sun eve and Mon.*

Mme Gaydon, **t** 04 93 05 06 91 (*inexpensive*). *Chambres d'hôtes.*

L'Echauguette, Place Charles Panier, **t** 04 93 05 49 60 (*moderate*). A restaurant with outside tables and menus featuring seafood. Try the starter salad served with the local speciality, a beef sausage called *secca*.

Le Pont-Levis, Place Louis Moreau, **t** 04 93 05 40 12 (*moderate*). Good cuisine and a great view of the fort, village and valley. *Closed Fri.*

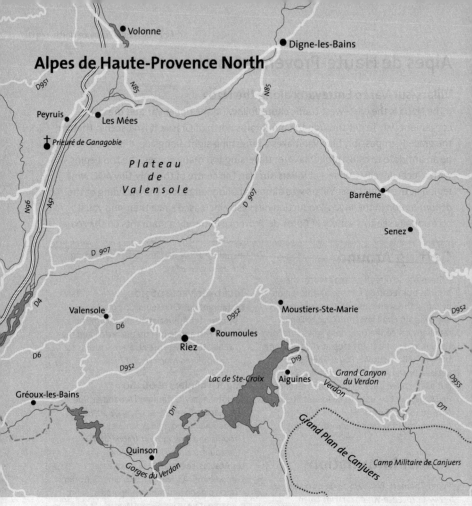

Volonne

Digne-les-Bains

D951

N85

N85

Peyruis

Les Mées

A51

† *Prieuré de Ganagobie*

P l a t e a u
d e
V a l e n s o l e

D 907

Barrême

N96

Senez

D 907

D4

D6

Valensole

D6

Moustiers-Ste-Marie

D952

D952

Roumoules

Riez

D19

Gréoux-les-Bains

Lac de Ste-Croix

Aiguines

Grand Canyon
du Verdon

Verdon

D955

D71

D6

D952

D11

Grand Plan de Canjuers

Quinson

Gorges du Verdon

Camp Militaire de Canjuers

– perhaps more for its curiosity value than for anything else. The village church has a few Renaissance pieces: a retable of St John the Baptist and an Italian fresco of the Annunciation, both anonymous works from the early 16th century.

Next comes a postcard shot: **Touët-sur-Var**, seemingly pasted up on the side of a cliff, with much of its medieval defences intact. **Puget-Théniers**, the biggest village on this stretch of the Var, is more open and welcoming, a shady oasis after the stark mountain landscapes, where you may stop for lunch and look at more pictures. There are two genuine jewels among a number of altarpieces in the parish church: Antoine Ronzen's *Notre-Dame-du-Secours* and Mathieu d'Anvers' *Passion*, both done about 1525. A monument by Aristide Maillol in the town square commemorates Puget's pride: a local boy named Auguste Blanqui, who became a journalist and one of the leaders of the Paris Commune in 1870, for which he paid by spending 36 years in prison.

Under the sweeping twist of its cliffs, **Entrevaux** is the strategic key to the valley. There has been a fort of some kind here since Roman times, and its present incarnation is particularly impressive – the work of Louis XIV's celebrated engineer Sébastien

Vauban, high above the village, complete with Second World War additions. At the time it was built, the French–Piedmontese border was only a few miles away (it is now the departmental boundary between Var and the Alpes-Maritimes). The entrance is a fortified bridge, rebuilt by Vauban on medieval foundations. Around the village, vestiges of its old garrison days can be seen: barracks and powder-houses, and an ancient drawbridge, still in working order, behind the 17th-century cathedral (*contact tourist office for opening hours and adm; guided tours available*).

There's a honeycomb of buildings and narrow alleys where people live; if you wander through the smelly damp alleys there are flowers high up in the windows, duvets thrown over the sills in the mornings. The serious part of the fort is a hard 15-minute climb if you're fit; take water, a sunhat, some historical imagination and some coins for the turnstile and you're on your own to explore the derelict tunnels and dungeons – once deliciously dangerous, now undergoing restoration to make them safe. The landscape below, with the little Train des Pignes (*see* p.311), is as unlikely as an alpine train set. Try to get up there before 9am, when the first of the coaches are beginning to fit themselves in below. (Check out the barking dog behind the hotel just across the road from the gate; it's a parrot.) Harley fans will enjoy Entrevaux's **Musée de la Moto** (*t 04 93 79 12 70; open June–Sept 10–12.30 and 2–6; closed Oct–May*), a collection of motorcycles from 1901 to 1967.

The Clues and the Esteron Valley

South of the Var is a grim and lonely region; you can see Nice and Cannes from the summit of the **Montagne du Cheiron** in its centre, but from here the Riviera beaches seem a world away. A *clue*, or more properly *cluse*, is a transverse valley, formed between the limestone folds of the mountains; here the name is given to the many narrow gorges that make life and communications in the area difficult. Local villages are humble and crumbling and few, and the roads across are winding and exasperating.

From Puget-Théniers, the D2211A/D17 takes you to **Roquesteron**, a fortified village divided into two parts (before 1860 one was Piedmontese, one French). West of the village, a bad road, the D10, leads off into the isolated **Clue d'Aiglun**, perhaps the most dramatic of the *clues*, with a big waterfall. On the other side of the mountains, the D2211A leads to **Briançonnet**, a spectral village with great views and bits of Roman inscriptions built into the old houses; beyond here is the **Clue de St-Auban**.

The more southerly route – which has a choice of roads running east–west, some of them conveniently reached from Vence or Nice – passes some lovely *villages perchés*: **Bézaudun-les-Alpes**, **Coursegoules**, **Gréolières** and **Cipières** (follow the D1/D8/D2 from Carros on the Var, to the north of Nice), all of which are starting to be colonized by people from the Riviera. Gréolières, under the Montagne du Cheiron, has an enormous ruined castle; from here you can follow the D603 into the **Gorges du Loup** towards Grasse, or take the D2/D802 on to the Cheiron and the new ski station of **Gréolières-les-Neiges**.

The Lac du Castillon and Mumbo Jumbo

After Entrevaux, the Var turns northwards, while the main road continues west, past the charming, modest mountain resort of **Annot** and the **Gorges du Galange**. Further west, the country becomes even stranger and lonelier; long monotonous stretches lull you to sleep until suddenly the road sinks into a wild gorge, or confronts a patch of striated mountains that look like gigantic *millefeuille* pastries tumbled over the landscape. Grey is the predominant colour, making a startling contrast with the opaque blue sheet of the **Lac de Castillon**, backed up behind the Barrage de Castillon, a mighty 292ft concrete dam begun in 1942 under the Vichy government, with a distinctly grim, wartime look about it. **St-André-les-Alpes**, on the north end of the lake, is France's hang-gliding capital.

And what is that warped theme park on the west shore? Why, that's **Mandarom Shambhasalem**, the centre of Aumism, a fruitcake of a cult that half-bakes bits of every religion into its mix. You can visit most afternoons (road up from Castellane): the cult statues of the world's religious élite are enough to make the average *santon* look like a Michelangelo.

Castellane

Castellane, which lies a few kilometres to the south of the lake, has become the capital of the Grand Canyon and the base for visiting what must be considered one of the greatest natural wonders in the whole of Europe. The town is centred round a pretty square full of plane trees (the grilles surrounding the trees are have been designed in the shapes of plane leaves) where local people come to challenge one another at a game or two of *boules* and to amiably hang out, taking the air and shooting the breeze. But its edges are inundated with up-to-the-minute sports shops supplying slick whizz-gimmickry for any sport you could or couldn't conceive of (such as bungee-jumping).

The village also contains a pretty *mairie* and a church, where the 597ft ascent up Castellane's landmark square rock begins: you can either pick up the key for the chapel on top from outside the *curé*'s house, or else collect it on your way up from the last person coming down. Castellane's snappy motto 'Napoleon stopped here. Why don't you?' comes from its spot on the **Route Napoléon**, the road that was taken by the emperor on his return from the island of Elba. These days it's a tourist trail starting from Napoleon's landing point at Golfe Juan and ending at his destination, Grenoble.

The Grand Canyon du Verdon

The most surprising thing about the **Grand Canyon du Verdon** is that it was not 'discovered' until 1905. That the most spectacular canyon on the continent could be

Tourist Information

Castellane: Rue Nationale, t 04 92 83 61 14, *www.castellane.org*. Open July–Aug Mon–Sat 9–12.30 and 2–7, Sun 10–12.30; April–June and Sept–Oct Mon–Sat 9–12 and 2–6; Nov–Mar Mon–Fri 9–12 and 2–6. Offers guided tours.

Market Days
Castellane: Wed and Sat.

Where to Stay and Eat

Castellane ☑ 04120
**Grand Canyon du Verdon, Falaise des Cavaliers, 14km east of village of Aiguines, t 04 94 76 91 31, *www.aiguines.com/cav1/htm* (*expensive–moderate*). A hotel with 15 rooms, 10 with balcony, and a glassed-in restaurant terrace (*moderate*) looking down 984ft on to the Canyon. *Closed Nov–April; restaurant closed Mon eve and Tues.*
***Nouvel Hôtel du Commerce, Place de l'Eglise, t 04 92 83 61 00, *www.hotel-fradet.*

com (*moderate–inexpensive*). A friendly and comfortable choice. The restaurant serves a range of Provençal cuisine on a terrace. *Closed mid-Oct–Feb; restaurant closed Tues, and Wed lunch.*
**Ma Petite Auberge, Bd de la République, t 04 92 83 62 06, *www.guideweb.com/ provence/hotel/ma-petite-auberge* (*moderate–inexpensive*). Fifteen plain rooms and a restaurant (*moderate*). *Closed Wed, Thurs out of season, Thurs lunch July and Aug, and Nov–mid-Feb.*
**Hôtel La Forge, Rue du Lieutenant Blondeau, t 04 92 83 62 61, *http://perso.wanadoo.fr/ forge* (*inexpensive*). A reasonably priced option with a terrace from which to view the village, and a restaurant (*cheap*). *Closed mid-Dec–Jan; restaurant closed Fri eve and Sat except July and Aug.*
Moulin de la Salou, Route des Gorges du Verdon, t 04 92 83 78 97 (*inexpensive*). A 17th-century mill converted into a hotel with a restaurant. Situated just outside the town, it offers beautiful views and is very family-friendly.

so overlooked speaks volumes about the French – their long-held aversion to nature, which they are now working so enthusiastically to correct, and the traditional disdain of Parisian authorities for the Midi. The locals always knew about it, of course; agriculturally useless and almost inaccessible, the 21km canyon had an evil reputation for centuries as a haunt of devils and 'wild men'. Even after a famous speleologist named Edouard-Alfred Martel brought it to the world's attention at the beginning of the century, many Frenchmen weren't impressed. In the 1950s the government decided to flood the whole thing for another dam (the tunnels they dug are still visible in many places at the bottom); when the plan was finally abandoned, it was for reasons of cost, not natural preservation.

The name 'Grand Canyon' was a modern idea; when the French became aware of its existence, comparisons with that grandaddy of all canyons in Arizona were inevitable. It does put on a grand show: sheer limestone cliffs as much as half a kilometre apart, snaking back and forth to follow the meandering course of the Verdon; in many places there are vast panoramas down the length of it. There are roads along both sides, though not for the entire distance. Most of the best views are from the so-called **Corniche Sublime** (D71) on the southern side; if you want to explore the bottom, ask about trails and the best way to approach them (it's a long trek) at the tourist information office in Castellane.

The lands south of the canyon are some of the most desolate in France; you will find them either romantic or tiresome depending on your mood. But either mood will be definitively broken when columns of tanks and missile-carriers come rattling up the road. The army has appropriated almost all of this area, the **Grand Plan de Canjuers**, for manoeuvres and target practice; you'll see their base camp on the D955 towards Draguignan.

Directly west of the canyon, a less spectacular section of the Verdon has indeed been dammed up, forming the enormous **Lac de Ste-Croix**. There is yet another dam further downstream, and the next 40km of the river valley are underwater too: the **Gorges du Verdon**, in parts as good as the Grand Canyon, but sacrificed forever to the beaverish Paris planners. It's wild country on both sides, and access is limited since the roads are few. Beyond the dam, on the way to Manosque and the Luberon, **Gréoux-les-Bains**, with its above-average number of launderettes and poodles, is a favourite with the rheumatic set, who regularly treat their aching bones to a jolt of sulphurous, radioactive water at the baths. It is a clinical, eerie, hairdresser-smelling place, with New Age oddities on sale as if by money-changers at the temple. This was a fashionable resort in the early 19th century, when Napoleon's tearaway sister Pauline Borghese dropped by, but that's about it. The village turns its back on the shabby castle, built in the 12th century by the Templars, which is occasionally used as a theatre and houses the tourist office.

Slightly further east on the banks of the Gorges du Verdon, **Quinson** has plenty of outdoor pursuits on offer, such as kayaking and hiking, as well as the Norman Foster-designed **Musée de Préhistoire des Gorges du Verdon** (*t 04 92 74 09 59; www.museeprehistoire.com; open July and Aug daily 10–8; April–June and Sept Wed–Mon 10–7; Oct–15 Dec and Feb–Mar Wed-Mon 10–6; closed 16 Dec–Jan; adm*), which claims to be the biggest of its kind in Europe. There are also reconstructed prehistoric huts nearby on the banks of the river.

Riez and Moustiers

The **Plateau de Valensole**, north of the Verdon and the Lac de Ste-Croix, is a hot, dry plain of olive and almond trees, and one of the big lavender-growing areas of Provence – come in July to see it in full bloom. **Riez**, in the middle, is an old centre for lavender-distilling, now adapted to tourism. Ruined medieval houses have been restored, and artists and potters have moved in. It's pretty but bustling, a good place to dawdle in. Riez was an important Celtic religious site, though it isn't clear exactly which deity it honoured. Testimonies to later piety can be seen at the western edge of town, thought to have been the centre of Roman-era Riez: four standing columns of a Roman temple of Apollo, and a 6th-century baptistry that is one of the few surviving monuments in France from the Merovingian era. Octagonal, like most early Christian baptistries, it has eight recycled Roman columns and capitals; all the rest was heavily restored during the 19th century. Inside it there is a small museum of archaeological finds, the **Musée Nature en Provence** (*open July–Sept Mon–Sat 9–1*

Tourist Information

Quinson: Chapelle de la Rue St-Esprit, Rue St-Esprit, **t** 04 92 74 01 12, *www.quinson.fr. Open July and Aug daily 9.30–12.30 and 2–5.30; Sept–June Mon–Sat 9.30–12.30 and 2–5.30.* Has detailed lists of park activities.

Riez: 4 Allée Louis Gardiol, **t** 04 92 77 99 09, *www.ville-riez.fr. Open July–Sept Mon–Sat 9–1 and 3–7; Oct–June Mon–Sat 8.30–12.30 and 1.30–4.30.*

Moustiers-Ste-Marie: Place de l'Eglise, **t** 04 92 74 67 84, *www.ville-moustiers-sainte-marie.fr. Open July and Aug 9.30–12.30 and 2–7.30; June and Sept 10–12.30 and 2–6.30; Mar and Oct 10–12.30 and 2–5.30; April and May 10–12.30 and 2–6; Nov 10–12 and 2–5; Dec–Feb 2–5.* For the **Parc Naturel du Verdon**, call **t** 04 92 74 63 95.

Market Days

Riez: Wed and Sat.
Moustiers: Fri.

Where to Stay and Eat

Quinson ✉ 04500
★★Relais Notre-Dame, **t** 04 92 74 40 01, *www.quinson.fr/relaisnotredame* (*inexpensive*). An inn with a garden and a swimming pool,
but most importantly offering a genuinely warm welcome and very good food (*moderate*). *Closed mid-Dec–Jan; restaurant closed Mon eve, plus Tues out of season.*

Moustiers-Ste-Marie ✉ 04360

★★★★La Bastide de Moustiers, just outside village at La Grisolière, **t** 04 92 70 47 47, *www.bastide-moustiers.com/Bastide* (*expensive*). Celebrity chef Alain Ducasse's 17th-century hotel, with 12 individually fashioned and comfortable rooms, a Jacuzzi, a swimming pool, a riding stable and more besides. The food is predominantly local, picked fresh from the kitchen garden, and innovative – herb and vegetable tart, then spit-roasted baron of lamb, followed by cherries baked in batter could be one memorable dinner. *Restaurant closed Wed and Thurs mid-Dec–Feb.*

★★Belvédère, **t** 04 92 74 66 04 (*inexpensive*). An affordable option up in the village, with its own restaurant (*cheap*). *Restaurant closed Mon out of season and Dec.*

Les Santons, Place de l'Eglise, **t** 04 92 74 66 48 (*expensive*). A restaurant with a gorgeous setting up at the top of the village; the standard of cooking matches the superlative views. *Book in advance. Closed Mon eve, Dec and Jan.*

and 3–7; Oct–June Mon–Sat 8.30–12.30 and 1.30–4.30; adm), which includes an altar with bull horns. Inside the medieval gates of the town are two pretty fountains that were recycled from Roman remains, and a number of modest palaces and chapels that recall the town's prosperity in the 16th to 18th centuries.

Fourteen kilometres west of Riez, introspective, overlooked **Valensole** is an ancient village built over the ruins of its Roman predecessor.

Some 15km to the east on the D952, **Moustiers-Ste-Marie** gets all the attention, spectacularly hanging on the west cliffs of the Grand Canyon du Verdon. Like Castellane on the other side, it is a popular base for visiting the canyon, and gets busy in summer. The town will be familiar to anyone who haunts the museums of the Midi, as Moustiers in the old days was Provence's famous centre for painted ceramics. The blue and yellow faïences, usually painted with country scenes or floral designs, were often works of art in their own right; first popular in the time of Louis XIV, they were made here as late as the 1870s.

Today, a large number of potters, some of them talented and some of them pretty awful, clutter the village streets, capitalizing on the perfect clay of the region (and on the tourists). You can compare their efforts with the originals at the **Musée de la Faïence,** a small collection situated on Place du Presbytère (*t 04 92 74 61 64; open April–Oct Wed–Mon 9–12 and 2–6, July and Aug to 7pm, school hols Mon and Wed–Fri 2–5; adm*).

In the middle of the village is the deep-set 12th-century **parish church**, with a kink in it. Moustiers' other distinction, as everyone in Provence knows, is the **Cadeno de Moustié**, a 783ft chain suspended between the tops of two peaks overlooking the village. A knight of the local Blacas family, while a prisoner of the Saracens during the Crusades, made a vow to put it up if he ever saw home again; the star in the middle comes from his coat of arms. The original (thought to be solid silver, but really plated) was stolen in the Wars of Religion and a replacement didn't appear until 1957. A climb up under the chain will take you to the **Chapelle Notre-Dame-de-Beauvoir**, where a notice piously requests that pilgrims do not write on the walls but inscribe their names on the heart of the Virgin instead.

Also Worthy of Your Attention...

Digne means 'worthy', and one suspects a degree of deliberate etymological mutation in the gradual name change from the local Gaulish tribe, the Bodiontici, whose capital this was, to Roman Dinia, and finally to Digne-les-Bains. The capital of *département* number 04 (Alpes de Haute-Provence), and the only city in a long stretch of mountains between Orange and Turin, over in Italy, Digne has a single thriving boulevard of cafés and touristic knick-knackery mixed with smart shoe shops, posh chocolates and more than one bookshop. It has recently rediscovered its role as a spa, and you will be given a glossy pamphlet in the tourist office consisting entirely of pictures of people smiling in the thermal baths. In the town's minuscule medieval centre you can see the crumbling, down-at-heel, 15th-century **Cathédrale de St-Jérome**; this and its surrounding brightly painted houses stand shoulder to shoulder with some daring grey municipal buildings.

Tourist Information

Digne-les-Bains : Rond-Point du 11 Novembre,
t 04 92 36 62 62, *www.ot-dignelesbains.fr*.
*Open July–Sept Mon–Sat 8.45–12.30 and
1.30–6.30, Sun 10–12 and 3–6; Oct–June
Mon–Sat 8.45–12 and 2–6.*

Market Days

Digne-les-Bains: Wed and Sat.

Festivals

Digne-les-Bains: Festival de Théâtre, end June.

Where to Stay and Eat

Digne-les-Bains ✉ **04000**
★★★★**Le Grand Paris**, 19 Bd Thiers, t 04 92 31
11 15, *www.hotel-grand-paris.com* (*expensive–
moderate*). A distinguished hotel set in a
restored 17th-century monastery, with an
excellent restaurant (*expensive*). *Closed
Dec–Feb.*
★★**Hôtel de Provence**, 17 Bd Thiers, t 04 92 31
32 19 (*inexpensive*). A centrally located
little hotel with comfortable rooms and
a good restaurant.

Out of town is something entirely unexpected: the **Fondation Alexandra David-Néel**
(*27 Avenue du Maréchal Juin, t 04 92 31 32 38, www.alexandra-david-neel.org; guided
tours daily July–Sept 10.30, 2, 3.30 and 5, rest of year 10.30, 2 and 4*), the former home of
a remarkable Frenchwoman who settled here in her 'Himalayas in miniature' after a
lifetime exploring in Tibet. Ms David-Néel called this house *Samten Dzong*, the 'castle
of meditation', and Tibetan Buddhist monks attended her when she died here in 1969
at the age of 101. The Dalai Lama has since come twice to visit. There are exhibits of
Tibetan art and culture, photographs and Tibetan crafts on sale. In summer, there are
up to 40 people crammed into this tiny museum, so be prepared to wait in the
garden. Staff will be happy to play the commentary in English if you ask.

At Place Paradis there is an old bunker in the hillside housing the **Musée de la
Seconde Guerre Mondiale** (*t 04 92 31 54 80; open Wed 2–5; July and Aug Mon–Thurs
2–6, Fri 2–5.30*), a museum about the last world war.

At St-Benoit, the **Musée Promenade** (*t 04 92 36 70 70; open Mon–Fri 9–12 and 2–5.30;
Nov–Mar Mon–Fri 9–12 and 2–4.30; adm*), which forms part of the Réserve Naturelle
Géologique de Haute-Provence, houses the largest geology collection in Europe,
including an impressive wall of ammonites.

Follow Boulevard Gassendi to the eastern edge of town, passing the peculiar
neoclassical **Grande Fontaine** (1829), and you will find Digne's former cathedral,
Notre-Dame-du-Bourg, a large Lombard-style Romanesque building of the 12th
century, complete with a bell tower of that date, a deep-set Romanesque arch below
a beautiful rose window, and fresco fragments.

Alpes de Haute-Provence South

If you get off the motorway, the route across the Var from Grasse to Aix-en-Provence
takes you through some charming villages, and some not so charming. Within an
hour it can show you lush green landscapes, as well as lonely steel-grey plateauxs
where only dolmens and army bases grow. The greener parts are wine-growing
country too, falling within the largest AOC region in France, Côtes-de-Provence.

From Fayence to Draguignan

This first leg of the journey is close enough to the coast to have become thoroughly colonized by the holiday-home set.

Fayence, a large village of moderate cuteness, has plenty of Englishmen and estate agents. Built on a steep hillside like Grasse, its road winds back and forth up to the centre, which is pleasant enough: there is a *mairie* perched on an arch over the main street, a forgotten 18th-century church and a view not to be missed from the Tour de l'Horloge at the very top of the village. Check the view you see against the ceramic panoramas painted and baked into tiles under your hands.

North of Fayence is some lovely, wild countryside; off the D37, **Roche Taillée** has a Roman aqueduct still in use, entirely carved out of the rock, along a steady descent of some 5km. Also from the D37, you'll see the towers of an impressive 17th-century castle, the **Château de Beauregard**, a private home.

Further north, **Mons** is a beautiful and strange village of narrow streets overhung with arches. The language of its inhabitants still conserves some Ligurian Italian words; the people of Mons were totally wiped out in the Black Death of 1348, and colonists from the area around Genoa and Ventimiglia were brought in to replace them. There are a large numbers of **dolmens** in the area; some are inaccessibly located on the base of the Canjuers army camp, the borders of which are only 2km away.

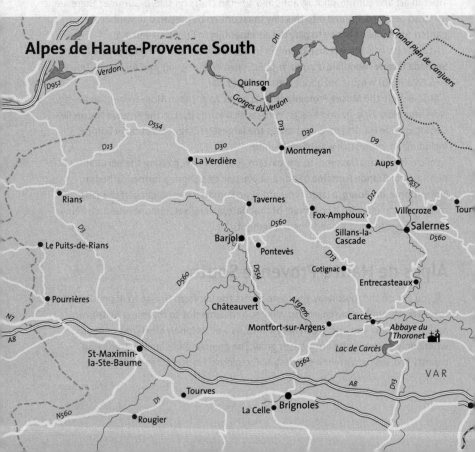

Alpes de Haute-Provence South

West of Fayence, the old farmhouses may now all be bijoux holiday homes, but the scenery is captivating; the main road, the D562 to Draguignan, is fine, but even better is the winding D19/D25, passing through three pretty villages. **Seillans**, with its cobbled streets leading up to the restored castle, has been occupied since the time of the Ligurians. It's one of the most beautiful villages in France and, like the others, it's got a plaque to prove it. The village lives on flowers, and was the last home of Surrealist Max Ernst; visit the little Orange Tree Gallery, Route de Bargemon (*open Thurs–Sat 2.30–6.30*) to see modern paintings and some Elisabeth Frink sculptures.

Bargemon, further west, is just as old; behind its medieval gates are several fountains and a 15th-century church with a Flamboyant-Gothic portal and heads sculpted by Pierre Puget. It leapt to fame recently when the ubiquitous Posh and Becks acquired a holiday home there. From here you can take a detour north through the thoroughly depressing Canjuers military zone to **Bargème**, the highest village in the Var (3,589ft), which is still encircled by its walls and ruined castle, although only a few people live there year-round to enjoy it.

Last before you reach Draguignan is **Callas**, which lies beneath a ruined castle. The D25 south of Callas, as far as Le Muy, is a beautiful drive through forests, with the **Gorges de Pennafort** and a waterfall along the way; it is also one of the best wine roads in the region, with a few places to stop and sample Côtes-de-Provence along the way (*see pp.330–31*).

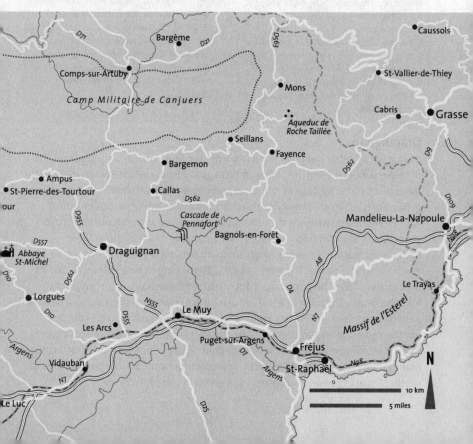

Getting Around

By Train

The main Provençal railway follows the motorway from Aix-en-Provence and Marseille to Cannes; for Draguignan you'll usually have to change at Les Arcs.

Draguignan and Brignoles are well served.

By Bus

Draguignan is also the hub for inter-village buses, though as always these are few and generally inconvenient.

There are several buses daily to Grasse, stopping off at Bargemon, Seillans and Fayence along the way, and several daily travelling in the other direction, to Tourtour and Aups, with at best one or two to the other villages.

By Car and Bicycle

Driving in this southern half of the Provençal mountains is much less trouble than it is in the areas to the north and east; roads are better and service facilities are more common.

You can take the A8 motorway straight across and miss everything, but the villages to the east and west of Draguignan offer some of the most delightful opportunities for casual touring in Provence; it's good bicycling country too.

There are two possible itineraries to consider:

From Fayence (west of Grasse on the D562) to Le Muy, through the lovely villages along the D19 and D25 (the latter is the wine route).

From Draguignan, west on the D557, dipping into the mountains on the D77 for Aups, then the D22 for Sillans-la-Cascade and Cotignac, and westwards again (D32) to Fox-Amphoux or (D560) Barjols.

Tourist Information

Fayence: Place Léon Roux, t 04 94 76 20 08, www.paysdefayence.com. Open 15 June–15 Sept Mon–Sat 9.15–12.15 and 2.30–6.30, Sun 9.30–12; 16 Sept–14 June Mon–Sat 9–12 and 2–6.

Seillans: Le Valat, t 04 94 76 85 91, www.seillans-var.com. Open July–Aug Tues–Fri 10–12.30 and 3–6.30, Mon and Sat 3–6.30, Sun 10–1; April–Sept Tues–Fri 10–12.30 and 3–6.30, Mon and Sat 3–6.30; Oct–Mar Tues–Fri 10–12.30 and 3–6, Sat 3–6. Guided tours are available all year (including some in English) Thurs am, plus Tues in July and Aug.

Draguignan: 2 Av Carnot, t 04 98 10 51 05, www.ville-draguignan.fr. Open July and Aug Mon–Sat 9–6, Sun 9–1; Sept–June Mon–Sat 9–6. Guided tours in summer daily at 10.30 and 4.30.

Draguignan

Draguignan gets a bad press, especially from the timid English: ugly, depraved, full of soldiers; *avoid it if you can*... We watched a young fellow on the Boulevard Maréchal Joffre being run in by a pair of municipal policemen – clean-shaven, brutishly intelligent, all dressed up military-style in black and silver like American cops. Beautiful women waltzed by, swinging their handbags and smiling at the unfortunate; flaccid shopkeepers squinted furtively through immaculately clean windows. There's no better free theatre in Provence. Tough, sharp-edged Draguignan is not French so much as French Colonial. The army owns it – it's the biggest base in France – and its dusty, palm-shaded boulevards (laid out in 1849 by Baron Haussmann, *préfet* of the Var, who treated the town to a trial run of his urban planning efforts in Paris) pass the national schools of artillery and military science. Draguignan's symbol is the *drac* – another Provençal dragon, chased out by an early bishop, though its fire-spitting image can still be seen everywhere. Draguignan could be Saigon or Algiers or Dakar, a cinematic fantasy in a wreath of *Gauloise* smoke, waiting for the Warner Bros cameras to capture Bogart, Lorre and Greenstreet conspiring in some tawdry nightclub.

Market Days

Fayence: Tues, Thurs and Sat.
Draguignan: Wed and Sat.

Festivals

Callas: Festival de la Musique Ancienne,
late July, **t** 04 94 76 61 07.

Where to Stay and Eat

Fayence ✉ 83440

***Moulin de la Camandoule**, Chemin de
Notre-Dame-des-Cyprès, **t** 04 94 76 00 84,
www.camandoule.com (*expensive–moderate*).
A lovely old olive-oil mill, restored by a
British couple and offering all the amenities,
including a garden, a pool and a restaurant
(*expensive*). Half-board obligatory Mar–Oct.
Restaurant closed Jan.

**Auberge de la Fontaine, Route de Fréjus,
t 04 94 76 07 59 (*inexpensive*). A basic,
family-run hotel and restaurant (*moderate*).

La Sousto, 4 Rue du Paty, **t** 04 94 76 02 16
(*inexpensive*). A small, good-value place
with charming rooms with kitchenettes,
overlooking the valley.

Le Castellaras, Route de Seillans, **t** 04 94 76
13 80 (*expensive*). Refined, sunny cuisine such
as courgette flowers stuffed with ratatouille,
plus a great wine list. *Closed Tues.*

Seillans ✉ 83440

***Les Deux Rocs**, Place Font-d'Amont,
t 04 94 76 87 32 (*moderate*). A highly
recommended hotel where you're assured
a warm English-speaking welcome. There are
14 rooms and near-perfect food, including
sublime desserts. It's a favourite among
Americans. *Closed Dec–Mar, Tues lunch out
of season.*

Bargemon ✉ 83620

Auberge des Arcades, Av Pasteur, **t 04 94 76
60 36 (*moderate*). A noisy and slightly run-
down but serviceable option with its own
restaurant (*expensive–moderate*). *Closed Jan;
restaurant closed Mon and Tues in winter.*

Draguignan ✉ 83300

**Les Etoiles de l'Ange, Av de Tuttlingen,
on D557 towards Lorgues, **t** 04 94 68 23 01,
ange.provence.hotel@wanadoo.fr
(*moderate*). The only really decent place in
the area, situated outside of the town
itself and offering clean and modern if
somewhat characterless rooms. The view
makes up for it. *Closed Nov–one week
before Easter.*

Le Galoubet, 23 Bd Jean Jaurès, **t** 04 94 68 08 50
(*moderate*). A restaurant serving good
seafood dishes. *Closed Mon and Sun eves
and last 2 wks Aug.*

Have your papers in order and try not to exceed the speed limits. Touring in
Provence you'll be bound to pass through here, and it's a pleasant stop, really. The
Saturday market is especially good, and there are a few things to see: the 17th-century
Tour de l'Horloge, Draguignan's architectural pride; and a small **Musée Municipal** at
no.9 Rue de la République (**t** *04 94 47 28 80; open Mon 2–6, Tues–Sat 9–12 and 2–6*)
with a picture gallery (including *Child Blowing a Soap Bubble*, by Rembrandt, a portrait
by Camille Claudel, faïences from Moustiers and porcelain from China).

The **Musée des Arts et Traditions Populaires** (*15 Rue Joseph Roumanille, **t** 04 94 47
05 72; open Tues–Sat 10–12 and 2–6, Sun 2–6; adm*) offers a complete and rather
didactic overview of everything that you'll never see in the real Provence any more
– anything from mules to silk culture, along with reconstructions of scenes of country
life, including kitchens, barns, festivals and, naturally, some antique *boules* and
tambourins. A pretty old merry-go-round with painted horses steals the show.

There's an **American war cemetery** and memorial on Boulevard John Kennedy, with
a bronze map tracing the route of the approximately 150,000 men of the 7th army
who disembarked in the south of France in the two weeks following D-Day.

Just outside town, on the D955 towards the Canyon du Verdon, is one of the biggest and most spectacular dolmens in Provence, the **Pierre de la Fée**; the table stone weighs 20 tonnes.

Villages of the Central Var

As you head west from Draguignan, you have two choices. If aesthetics are a bigger consideration than time, don't bother with the A8 motorway or the parallel road through Brignoles and St-Maximin-la-Ste-Baume; instead, take the D557 or D562 directly west for a leisurely tour through some of Provence's loveliest, most typical landscapes. Though this area gets its share of foreign and Parisian summer folk, it isn't quite chic – compared with similar but totally colonized places like the Luberon. But there's enough lavender and blowing cypresses, plenty of wine, and a dozen relentlessly charming villages that won't trouble you with any strenuous sightseeing.

From Lorgues to Aups

Lorgues is the first village, with an ensemble of 18th-century municipal decorations: a fountain, the huge, dignified church of St-Martin, and the inevitable avenue of plane trees – one of the longest and fairest in Provence. To the north, along the D10, you'll pass the **Abbaye St-Michel**, a recently refounded Russian Orthodox monastery; its handmade wooden chapel, a replica of a Russian church, may be visited.

Further north, there are a number of pretty villages around the valley of the Nartuby: **Ampus**, **Tourtour**, over-restored but up on a height with views down to the sea, and **Villecroze**, with its vaulted lanes. At the edge of the Grand Plan de Canjuers, Villecroze is built up against a tufa cliff; there is an unusual park at the base of it, with a small waterfall and a cave-house that was dug into the rock in the 16th century.

Aups was a Ligurian settlement and a Roman town; its name comes from the same ancient root as 'Alps'. It has a reputation for being different; a monument in the town square records Aups' finest hour, when the citizens put up a doomed republican resistance to Louis-Napoléon's coup of 1851. The village is known in the region for its Thursday truffle market, held through the winter months. The village church is oddly below surface level; the ground level around it was raised to avoid the frequent flooding of the old days. Aups, like the other villages, has not completely escaped Riviera modernism. The **Musée Simon Segal** (*Avenue Albert Ier*, *t 04 94 70 01 95; open mid-June–mid-Sept daily 10–12 and 4–7; adm*), founded by an eponymous Russian artist, contains his and other 20th-century works.

Salernes, south of Aups, has been known for more than 200 years as a manufacturer of tiles – the small, hexagonal terracotta floor-tiles called *tomettes* that are as much a trademark of Provence as lavender. They still make them, and, in a day when French factory-made tiles all come in insipid beige, they are at a premium. Lately Salernes' factories and individual artisans have been expanding into coloured ceramics and pottery; there are a few shops in the village and factory showrooms on the outskirts. Despite such a workmanlike background, the village itself is rather drab, with a medieval fountain and a simple 13th-century church in the centre.

Tourist Information

Salernes: Place Gabriel Péri, **t** 04 94 70 69 02, *www.ville-salernes.fr. Open July and Aug Mon–Sat 9–7, Sun 10–1 and 3–6; Sept–June Tues–Sat 9.30–12.30 and 2–6, Sun 11–12.30.*
Cotignac: 2 Rue Bonaventure, **t** 04 94 04 61 87. *Open summer Tues–Sat 9.45–12.45 and 3.30–6.30 (6 on Sat); winter Tues–Fri 9–1 and 3–6, Sat 9–1. Has detailed lists of chambres d'hôtes outside the village.*
Barjols: Bd Grisolle, **t** 04 94 77 20 01, *www.ville-barjols.fr. Open daily 9–12 and 2–6.*

Market Days

Aups: Wed and Sat; truffle market Thurs am in winter.
Barjols: Sat am.
Salernes: Wed am and Sun am.

Where to Stay and Eat

Lorgues ✉ 83510

Lorgues, 13km from Draguignan, is a pleasant place to stay if you happen to be passing through.

Chez Bruno, Route de Vidauban, Campagne Mariette, **t** 04 94 85 93 93, *(expensive)*. Three luxurious rooms and one suite at prices that extend into the ozone layer, in a very special old *mas* where the chef does wonderful things with truffles *(very expensive). Closed Sun eve and Mon.*

Tourtour ✉ 83690

Easily the poshest of the villages in this region, Tourtour can also boast the most luxurious accommodation.
****Bastide de Tourtour, Montée St-Denis, **t** 04 98 10 54 20, *www.verdon.net (expensive)*. A modern Relais & Châteaux complex with a swimming pool, a tennis court and all the other amenities, including a highly reputed restaurant offering a blend of Provençal cooking and classic French cuisine. *Restaurant closed lunch Mon–Fri except July and Aug.*
***Le Mas des Collines, Route de Villecroze, **t** 04 94 70 59 30 *(expensive–moderate)*. A charming little hotel offering tranquillity, air-conditioned rooms and a very pretty swimming pool overlooking the valley below Tourtour. *Restaurant closed Nov–Mar.*

Further west, **Sillans** has lately been calling itself Sillans-la-Cascade, to draw attention to the 118ft waterfall just south of the village (it dries up in summer). Beyond that, **Fox-Amphoux** is worth a visit just to hear the locals pronounce the name; this minuscule, well-restored village of stepped medieval alleys sits on a defensible height. There is a ruined castle and, on the trail to the hamlet of Amphoux, an odd cave-chapel, Notre-Dame-du-Secours, hung with *ex votos*, many from sailors.

Abbaye du Thoronet

South of Salernes, **Entrecasteaux** is dominated by a 17th-century castle, completely restored in the 1970s by a Scotsman named McGarvie-Munn; visitors are admitted, but there's nothing to see and the fee is exorbitant. Further south, the artificial **Lac de Carcès** has been a favourite with fishermen since the dam was built in the 1930s. To the east are the biggest bauxite mines in France, which are playing hell with one of the most impressive medieval abbeys in Provence.

The **Abbaye du Thoronet** (*t* 04 94 60 43 90; *open April–Sept daily 9–6, Sun 9–12 and 2–6; Oct–Mar Mon–Sat 10–1 and 2–5; adm*) was the first Cistercian foundation in Provence, built on land donated by count Raymond Bérenger of Toulouse in 1136; the present buildings were begun about 1160. Like most Cistercian houses, it was in utter decay by the 15th century; and, like so many other medieval monuments in the Midi, it owes its restoration to Prosper Mérimée, Romantic novelist (writer of *Carmen*,

***Auberge St-Pierre**, Route d'Ampus, St-Pierre de Tourtour, **t** 04 94 50 00 50 (*moderate*). An up-to-date working farm built around a hotel 3km east of town, with exceptional rooms in an 18th-century house and a fine restaurant offering authentic Provençal food. Swimming pool, gym, tennis courts, and archery and fishing facilities. Just beware of the hostess when she is tired. *Closed mid-Oct–Mar; restaurant closed Wed.*

Les Chênes Verts, 2km from town on Route de Villecroze, **t** 04 94 70 55 06 (*expensive*). A restaurant offering wonderful classical food featuring lobster, seafood, truffles and game in season. *Closed Tues, Wed and June.*

Salernes ✉ 83690

La Fontaine, Place du 8-Mai-1945, **t** 04 94 70 64 51 (*expensive–moderate*). A good place to sample a simple dish of *magret* or stewed rabbit, with outside tables for fine weather dining. *Closed Sun eve, Mon, plus Tues in winter, and Jan–mid-Feb.*

Sillans-la-Cascade ✉ 83690

Hôtel-Restaurant des Pins, on D32, **t** 04 94 04 63 26 (*inexpensive*). An extremely popular restaurant set in an old stone house, serving the likes of grilled meats with shrimps for starters and other good food (*moderate*). It also has a few rooms, but you'll need to make your reservation way in advance during the summer. *Closed mid-Jan–Feb, and Wed eve and Thurs out of season.*

Fox-Amphoux ✉ 83670

***Auberge du Vieux Fox**, Place de l'Eglise, **t** 04 94 80 71 69 (*moderate*). One of the most pleasant village inns in the whole of Provence, with a delightful restaurant.

Cotignac ✉ 83570

Maison Gonzagues, 9 Rue Léon Gérard, **t** 04 94 72 85 40, *www.maison-gonzagues-cotignac.com* (*expensive*). The only hotel in the town centre, set in a lovingly restored 18th-century *hôtel particulier* and run by a member of the local tourist office. Street parking is difficult here.

Les Trois Marchés, 11 Cours Gambetta, **t** 04 94 04 65 99 (*moderate*). A restaurant offering fresh, simple fare and attentive service in intimate surroundings. *Closed Jan and Feb.*

among other works) and state inspector of historic monuments under Napoléon III. He chanced upon it in 1873, when most of the roof was gone, the galleries were overgrown with bushes and the refectory was inhabited by cows.

It often seems as if the restoration is still under way; you may find Thoronet full of props, scaffolding and concrete piers, as its keepers experiment desperately to save it from being shaken to pieces by the bauxite lorries rumbling past on the D79. The mines themselves (nearby, but screened by trees) have caused some subsidence, and cracks are opening in the walls. Nevertheless, this purest and plainest of the Cistercian 'Three Sisters' of Provence (along with Silvacane, pp.345–6, and Sénanque, pp.356–7) is worth a detour. In keeping with the stern austerity of Bernard of Clairvaux, it displays sophisticated Romanesque architecture stripped to its bare essentials, with no worldly splendour to distract a monkish mind, only grace of form and proportion. The elegant stone bell-tower would have been forbidden in any other Cistercian house (to keep local barons from commandeering them for defence towers), but those in Provence got a special dispensation – thanks to the mistral, which would have blown a wooden one down with ease. There are no such compromises in the blank façade, but behind it is a marvellously elegant interior; note the slight point of the arches, a hint of the dawning Gothic – Thoronet was begun in the same year as France's first Gothic churches, in the north at St-Denis and Sens.

The **cloister**, with its heavy arcades, is equally good, enclosing a delightful stone fountain-house. There's a cellar to visit, too, to see how the monks fared, and a modern chapel where people pray and visitors gawp and take photographs over the sign clearly requesting that they do not.

If you like fine rosé wine, visit the nearby **Domaine de l'Abbaye** (*t* 04 94 73 87 36), where wine-grower Franc Petit makes some of the best. His secret? Hand-picking the grapes by moonlight, when temperatures are cooler and the grapes avoid the shock of coming in from the hot sun into the cool of the *pressoir*. The grapes supposedly keep more of their strength, and the wine is bottled in a distinctive sky-blue bottle to protect it from the light.

Cotignac and Barjols

Cotignac is one of the cutest of the cute, a Sunday supplement-quality Provençal village where everything is just right, and everyone knows it. Almost half the town's 2,000 permanent residents are British, so don't be surprised to hear English spoken. There are no sights, but one looming peculiarity: the tufa cliffs that hang dramatically over it. In former times these were hollowed out for wine cellars, stables or even habitations; today there are trails up to them for anyone who wants to explore. At the base of the cliffs there is a meadow where Cotignac holds its summer music festival.

Westwards on the D13/D560, the landscapes are delicious and drowsy; **Pontevès** will startle you awake again, with its castle with a remarkable setting atop a steep conical hill. Long the stronghold of the Pontevès family, feudal rulers of most of this region, the apparition loses some of its romantic charm after the climb up; there's nothing inside but a few houses, La Poste and a food shop.

Three kilometres further on, **Barjols** has little cuteness but much more character. This metropolis of 2,000 souls owes its existence to leather tanning, an important industry here for the last 300 years. There is still one shoe factory left, but Barjols is now little more than a market town, although it retains an urban and somewhat sombre air: elegant rectangular squares of the 18th century, and moss-covered fountains (there are 42 of them) and *lavoirs* similar to the ones in Aix – hence its nickname 'the Tivoli of Provence'.

To see Barjols at its best, come on 16–17 January, the feast of St Marcel (Marcellus, the 4th-century pope), whose gaudy relics, stolen in the Middle Ages from a Provençal monastery, can be seen in the 16th-century parish church. There'll be a bit of dancing and, equally unusual for Provence, the essentially pagan slaughter and roasting of an ox, accomplished to the sound of flutes and *tambourins*.

Along the Motorway: From Draguignan to Aix

With the Var's rocky coast, and the mountains behind it, the only easy route across the *département* is a narrow corridor through Brignoles and St-Maximin-la-Ste-Baume. The French have obligingly plonked a motorway across it, successor to the Via Aurelia and the St-Maximin pilgrims' route as the great high road of Provence.

Tourist Information

Brignoles: Hôtel de Clavier, Rue du Palais,
t 04 94 69 27 51, www.officedetourisme-
brignoles.com. Open Mon–Fri 9–12 and 2–6.
There's also an office at Carrefour de
l'Europe, t 04 94 72 04 21. Open Mon–Sat
9–12.30 and 2–7.30, Sun 10–12 and 2.30–6.30
(closed Sun in winter).
St-Maximin-la-Ste-Baume: Place de l'Hôtel de
Ville, t 04 94 59 84 59, www.stmaximin.
enprovence.com. Open daily July and Aug
Mon–Sat 9–12.30 and 2.30–6.30, Sun 10–12.30
and 2.30–6.30; Sept–June Mon–Sat 9–12.30
and 2–6, Sun 10–12.30 and 2–5.30.

Market Days

Brignoles: Sat.
St-Maximin-la-Ste-Baume: Wed.

Where to Stay and Eat

Les Arcs ✉ 83460

★★★**Le Logis du Guetteur**, Place du Château,
t 04 94 99 51 10, www.logisduguetteur.com
(*expensive*). An exceptional hotel–restaurant
in a lavishly restored castle dating in parts
from the 11th century, at the top of the old
town. There's a garden and a pool, and some
of the rooms have wonderful views. The
restaurant serves ambitious *haute cuisine*,
including stuffed sole and elaborate
desserts. *Closed mid-Jan–Feb.*

Brignoles ✉ 83170

★★**La Grillade au Feu de Bois**, on N7 in village
of Flassans-sur-Issole (✉ 83340), t 04 94 69
71 20 (*expensive–moderate*). A gracious and
friendly farm hotel with 16 rooms and a
restaurant serving admirable home cooking.
Relais des Templiers, Place Gabriel Péri, Mont-
fort-sur-Argens, 6km north of Brignoles,
t 04 94 59 55 06 (*moderate*). A peaceful place
for an intimate meal, with a handful of
tables and *table d'hôte*. A number of rooms
are also available. *Closed Mon and Nov.*
Saigon, Place St-Louis, t 04 94 59 14 51 (*moderate–cheap*). A good Vietnamese restaurant.

St-Maximin-la-Ste-Baume ✉ 83470

★★**Hôtel Le Plaisance**, 20 Place Malherbe,
t 04 94 78 16 74 (*moderate–inexpensive*).
The only decent place to stay if you are
compelled to spend the night here, with
pale orange shutters. *Closed Jan–Feb.*

Les Arcs and Le Luc

Picking up the D555 to the south of Draguignan, you'll pass through **Les Arcs**, a
village of stepped streets, pink stone and ivy. Next comes **Le Luc**, which is practically
strangled by the motorway but is a game town nevertheless, with another steep
medieval centre, a castle on top and a restored Romanesque church flanked by a
16th-century tower.

To entertain the hordes of coast-bound tourists there's a **Musée Régional du Timbre**,
housed in a 17th-century château on Place de la Convention (*t 04 94 47 96 16, www.
lemuseedutimbre.com; open Wed and Thurs 2.30–5.30, Fri–Sun 10–12 and 2.30–5.30;
closed Sept*), and another small museum in a 16th-century church, the **Musée
Historique du Centre Var** (*24 Rue Victor Hugo, t 04 94 60 70 12; open mid-May to
mid-Oct Mon–Sat 3–6*).

Brignoles

The biggest date in Brignoles' history, perhaps, is 25 September 1973, when several
thousand dead toads rained down from the sky – an event that does not seem to be
commemorated in any way. Little else has ever happened here. This gritty but
somehow likeable place earns its living mining bauxite. It has an attractive medieval
centre, and a museum to remember.

Musée du Pays Brignolais (Regional Museum)

Place du Palais des Comtes de Provence; **t** *04 94 69 45 18, www.musee brignolais.com; open April–Sept Mon–Sat 9–12 and 2.30–6, Sun 9–12 and 3–6; Oct–Mar Mon–Sat 10–12 and 2.30–5, Sun 10–12 and 3–5; adm.*

At the top of the old town, in a palace that was the summer residence of the counts of Provence, Brignoles' incredible curiosity shop has grown to fill the whole building since a local doctor began the collection in 1947. Over two floors packed with fossils, oil presses, cannon balls and roof tiles, you'll see things you never dreamed existed.

In the place of honour, near the entrance, is the original model of a great invention by Brignoles' own Joseph Lambot (1814–87): the steel-reinforced concrete canoe. Contemporary accounts on display suggest the thing floated, but the idea somehow never caught on. Lambot probably never collected a *sou* for his revolutionary new construction technique, since found to be better adapted to skyscrapers.

It's a hard act to follow, but just across the room is a provocative **sarcophagus**, dated *c.* AD 175–225, that is nothing less than the earliest Christian monument in France. Well sculpted and well preserved, the imagery is a remarkable testament to religious transition. The centre shows a familiar classical scene, a seated god receiving a soul into the underworld – but whether the god is Hades, Jesus or someone else remains a mystery. Also present are Jesus as the 'Good Shepherd', a figure that may be St Peter (fishing, figuratively, for souls), another that seems to be a deified Sun, and another early Christian symbol, an anchor. The sarcophagus is believed to be Greek, possibly made in Antioch or Smyrna; how it got here no one knows.

Nearby is a rare but badly worn Merovingian tombstone, and a part of the counts' palace, the chapel of **St-Louis-d'Anjou**, a Provençal bishop who may be better known in California – the town of San Luis Obispo is named after him. The chapel houses a hoard of gaudy church clutter, with Louis' chasuble and rows of wax saints under glass. After that, you may inspect a reconstructed Provençal farm kitchen, and a reconstructed mine tunnel. Other prizes await on the second floor: a plywood model of Milan cathedral by a local madman, a stuffed weasel and large collections of owls and moths. Local painters are exhaustively represented: some of the finest works are 19th-century *ex votos* in the French tradition, with the Virgin Mary blessing people falling off wagons and out of windows. Even after all this, Gaston Huffman's *Allegory of Voluptuous Folly* takes the cake – a medieval conceit in a modern style, with a delicious lady in a little boat enjoying the caresses of a cigar-smoking pig. Rue des Lanciers, the spine of old Brignoles, begins opposite the museum's front door, passing the 13th-century **Maison des Lanciers**, where the counts' guards stayed when visiting.

West of Brignoles, there are two sights of some interest off the main road, both of which you'll need to talk your way in to: first the half-ruined **Abbaye de la Celle**, an ancient foundation (started in the 6th century) that made a reputation for itself due to the open licentiousness of its nuns, and which was dissolved in 1770; the buildings are now part of a farm. Second, also on a farm, off the D205 6km east of Tourves, is the **Chapelle de la Gayole**, an early Romanesque cemetery chapel in the shape of a Greek cross (built in 1029, though parts of it go back to the 700s).

Wine: Côtes-de-Provence – La Vie en Rose

Half of all French rosés originate in the Republic's largest AOC region, the 18,000-hectare Côtes-de-Provence. The growing area stretches from St-Raphaël to Hyères, with separate patches around La Ciotat and Villars-sur-Var, and a wide swathe south and west of Aix-en-Provence. Based on grenache, mourvèdre, cinsault, tibouren, cabernet and syrah grapes, Côtes-de-Provence rosé is a dry, fruity, and elegant summer wine that doesn't have to worry about travelling well: more than enough eager oenophiles travel to it every holiday season. Unfortunately its price has travelled too, and there are no prizes for guessing which way. It is, however, possible to find good inexpensive alternatives, since some estates produce a *vin de pays*. This is often as good as wines with full *appellation contrôlée* status.

An excellent example is **Château d'Astros**, at Vidauban, t 04 94 99 73 00, which produces a wonderful range of Vin de Pays des Maures: red, white and rosé. The property is run by M. Galliano. A visit to this grand rambling house and estate in the forest is great fun. One can also buy it draught – either supply your own containers or buy one from the owner.

Côtes-de-Provence reds (20 per cent of the production) are much finer today than the rough plonk Caesar issued to his legions, most notably the special *cuvées* put out by the better estates. The whites, of clairette and ugni blanc grapes, are scarcer still, and account for only five per cent of the AOC label. With 57 cooperatives and 350 private cellars, Côtes-de-Provence is easily sampled, especially along the signposted 400km Route des Vins, which you can pick up at Le Luc or Le Muy from the A8 or N7, or at Fréjus, Les Arcs and Puget-sur-Argens.

St-Maximin-la-Ste-Baume

St-Maximin has always divided the views of its visitors. 'Considerable charm,' gushes one guidebook; 'another pretty Provençal village,' suggests another. Prosper Mérimée, back in 1834, had another view: 'St-Maximin is a miserable hole between Aix and Draguignan.' You can decide for yourself.

But once upon a time, the Miserable Hole was a goal for the pious from all over France. According to legend, the site was the burial place of the Magdalen and her companions St Maximin, the martyred first bishop of Aix, and St Sidonius. Their bodies, supposedly hidden from Saracen raiders in a crypt, had disappeared and were conveniently 'rediscovered' in 1279 by the efforts of Charles II of Anjou, count of Provence. Inconveniently, the body of the Magdalen was already on display at the famous church of Vézelay, in Burgundy. Nevertheless, an ambitious basilica and abbey complex was begun, and eventually the pope was convinced or bribed into declaring St Maximin's relics the real McCoy. The pilgrim trade made St-Maximin into a town; among the visitors were several kings of France, the last being Louis XIV.

There were wild times during the Revolution; St-Maximin renamed itself 'Marathon', and was briefly under the command of Lucien Bonaparte, who was calling himself 'Brutus'. This most devoutly revolutionary of Bonapartes saved the basilica from a sacking. As the local legend tells it, an official from Paris came down to oversee its

Two of the best-known producers are at Trets, on the D56 southwest of St-Maximin-la-Ste-Baume: **Château Ferry-Lacombe**, t 04 42 29 40 04, where the vines are planted on ancient Roman terraces (along with the pink stuff, you can find the excellent Cuvée Lou Cascaï); and the **Château Grand'Boise**, t 04 42 29 22 95, where the subtle red Cuvée Mazarine and a flowery blanc de blancs are grown amid a large forest.

Near Le Luc, Hervé Goudard's **Domaine de St-Baillon**, on the N7 at Flassans-sur-Issole, t 04 94 69 74 60, mixes syrah and cabernet sauvignon to produce its truffle-scented Cuvée du Roudaï. Just under the cliffs of Montagne Ste-Victoire, **Domaine Richeaume**, at Puyloubier, t 04 42 66 31 27, in Provence's most modern and efficient *cave*, run by Sylvain Hoesch and producing along with rosés an interesting selection of red wines, one of pure syrah and another of pure cabernet sauvignon. At La Londe-les-Maures east of Hyères, **Domaines Ott**, Clos Mireille, Route de Brégançon, t 04 94 01 53 50, *www.domaines-ott.com*, offers one of the *appellation*'s top white wines, of ugni and semillon grapes aged in wooden barrels. The estate's top rosé, '*cœur de grains*', is one of the most sought-after wines in the region... and has a price to match.

A much higher percentage of red wine is produced in the cooler, drier Coteaux Varois, a region of 28 *communes* around Brignoles in the central Var, beginning a few miles north of the Bandol district east of La Ciotat and extending north as far as Tavernes. This old *vin de pays* has been elevated to the ranks of VDQS; all the vintners along the N7 and the other roads outside Brignoles hang out signs to lure you in.

You can try a good (and organic) Coteaux Varois at the **Domaine de Bos Deffens**, on the Cotignac road just east of Barjols. Or sample Coteaux Varois at **Château Thuerry**, set in a wooded landscape at Villecroze, t 04 94 70 63 02.

liquidation, but Brutus had him greeted with the 'Marseillaise', played all stops out on the church's great organ.

Basilica Ste-Marie-Madeleine

After its ramshackle, unfinished façade, on a desolate square decorated only by a faded Dubonnet sign, this basilica's interior seems like an apparition: it's the only significant Gothic building in Provence. Despite the prevailing gloom and the hosts of awful, neglected 18th- and 19th-century chapels and altars, it's worth a visit for the tall arches of the nave and the lovely apse, with its stained glass, which leave an impression of dignity and grace.

The original decoration is spare: coats of arms and effigies of Charles of Anjou and Queen Jeanne on some of its capitals. Among the later additions, the most impressive is the enormous, aforementioned **organ** with almost 3,000 pipes, all the work of one man, a Dominican monk named Isnard (1773). Another Dominican, Vincent Funel, was responsible for the lovely choir screen (1691).

To the left of the high altar, don't miss the retable of the *Passion of Christ* (1520) by an obscure Renaissance Fleming named Ronzen, with 22 panels of the familiar scenes with some surprising backgrounds: the papal palace in Avignon, the Colosseum and Venice's Piazzetta San Marco. Stairs lead down to the **crypt**, a funeral vault from the 4th or 5th century AD, where the holy sarcophagi lie with a host of eerie reliquaries.

The Couvent Royal

The monastery attached to Ste-Marie-Madeleine was a 'royal' convent because the kings of France were its titular priors. After losing it in the Revolution, the Dominican Order bought back the monastery and church in 1859. Apparently St-Maximin proved too depressing even for Dominicans; they bolted for Toulouse in 1957, leaving the vast complex in a terrible state. Restorations have been going on fitfully since the 1960s. The buildings include the imposing **hospice** from the 1750s (now the town hall), to the left of the basilica's façade; the rest, behind it, now houses an institute for cultural exchanges. The best part is the **cloister**, with some Lebanon cedars and a charming subtropical garden in the centre. One of the arcades is a Gothic original of 1295.

The Massif de la Ste-Baume

If you're heading towards Marseille or the coast from here, you might consider a detour into this small but remarkable patch of mountains. Rising as high as 3,199ft, and offering views over the sea and as far north as Mont Ventoux, the massif shelters a small forested plateau called the **Plan d'Aups**. This is a northern-style forest, including maple, beech and sycamore, as well as scores of species of wildflowers and other plants not often seen around the Mediterranean. They have remained in their primeval state because the massif is holy ground, the site of the **cave** (*Sainte-Baume*, or holy grotto) where, according to legend, the Magdalen spent the last years of her life as a hermit. The cave, furnished as a chapel, formed part of the pilgrimage to St-Maximin from the Middle Ages on, and can be seen today along the D80. Some monastic communities grew up around the site, and you can visit the 13th-century Cistercian **Abbaye de St-Pons**, near the loveliest part of the forests (the Parc de St-Pons). The St-Maximin tourist office has details of guided tours.

Northern Provence:
The Vaucluse

12

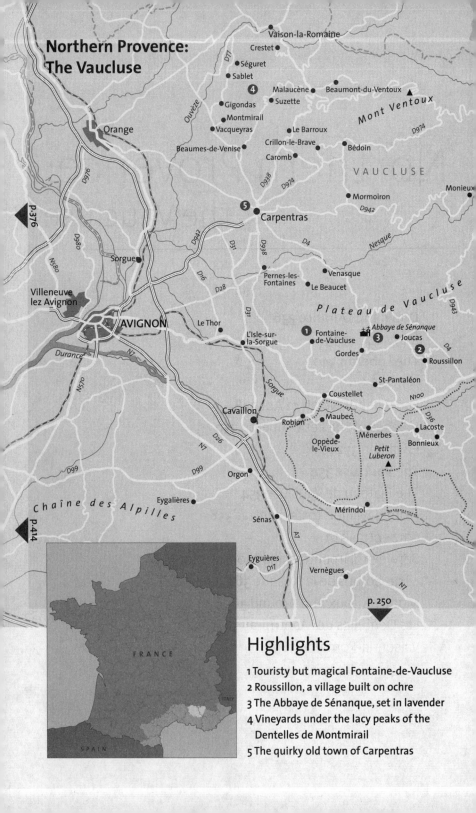

Northern Provence: The Vaucluse

Highlights

1 Touristy but magical Fontaine-de-Vaucluse
2 Roussillon, a village built on ochre
3 The Abbaye de Sénanque, set in lavender
4 Vineyards under the lacy peaks of the Dentelles de Montmirail
5 The quirky old town of Carpentras

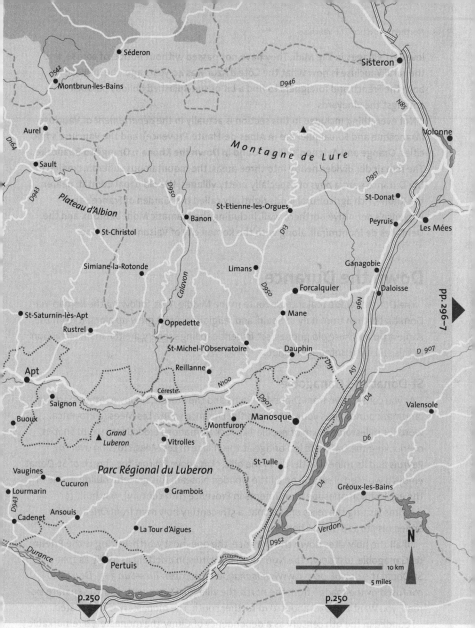

pp. 296-7

p.250

p.250

10 km

5 miles

N

The 'Three Plagues of Provence', according to tradition, were the mistral, the Durance and the *Parlement* at Aix. The *Parlement* is ancient history, but the other two still serve to define the troublesome boundaries of this region: the long curve of the wicked, boat-sinking, valley-flooding Durance river to the south, and a line of long, ridge-like mountains, Mont Ventoux and the Montagne de Lure, to the north – folk wisdom has always credited these northern boundary-stones of Provence as the source of the terrible mistral. But the lands between these natural prodigies are the eye of the hurricane, with some of the most civilized countryside and loveliest villages in the Midi. They have not passed without notice, of course, and the rural Vaucluse is now what the Côte d'Azur was 40 years ago: the in-place for both the French and foreigners to find a bit of sun-splashed holiday paradise amongst the vineyards.

Not everything included in this section is actually in the *département* of Vaucluse (Manosque and Forcalquier are in Alpes-de-Haute-Provence); and the Vaucluse's two cities, Orange and Avignon, will be found in **Down the Rhône 1: Orange to Beaucaire**. The remainder divides neatly into three areas: the mountainous Luberon, cradled in the Durance's arc, a *pays* of especially pretty villages; the old papal Comtat, nearer the Rhône, rich agricultural lands rightfully called the 'Garden of France'; and Provence's definitive northern wall, including the dramatic Mont Ventoux and the Dentelles de Montmirail, along with the Roman city of Vaison-la-Romaine.

Down the Durance

The Durance was a major trade route in the Middle Ages, following the Roman Via Domitia that ran from Italy to Spain, and religious centres grew up along it from the earliest times. These old priories, set in gentle rolling scenery, are the main attraction in this still fairly untouristy region.

St-Donat and Ganagobie

As you come down from Digne-les-Bains and the Provençal Alps, a rather startling landmark punctuates your entry into the Durance valley: **Les Mées** (a Provençal word for milestones), 2km of needle-like rock formations eroded into weird shapes, overlooking the D4. There is a bridge at the village of Les Mées, crossing over to **Peyruis** and its ruined castle. Up in the hills, 5km above Peyruis, the church of **St-Donat** enjoys a wonderful setting on a little wooded plateau. This graceful building, one of the earliest Romanesque monuments in Provence (11th century), was built for pilgrims visiting the relics of St Donat, a 5th-century holy man from Orléans who ended his life as a hermit here.

Of all the holy sites down the Durance, the one most worth visiting is the **Prieuré de Ganagobie**, just down the N96 south of Peyruis, in a setting as lovely as that of St-Donat (*t 04 92 68 00 04, www.ndganagobie.com; open Tues–Sun 3–5*). Don't be confused by the roads – from the north, the village of Ganagobie is up a separate side road; you want the D30, about 3km further south. The monastery is signposted.

Founded in the 9th century as a dependency of Cluny, the monastery's remarkable church was built some 200 years later. Its portal, though rebuilt in the 17th century, still has its original tympanum relief: a Christ in Majesty with the four Evangelists, one of the finest such works in Provence. Inside is another rare decoration: **mosaics** with geometric designs and peculiarly styled animals in red, black and white. Discovered and restored in the 1960s, they were part of the church's original pavement. Ganagobie used to have the relics of a certain St Transit; he is not found in any hagiography, and it seems that in the Middle Ages the habit of carrying holy relics

Getting Around

The valley of the Durance is the main corridor for public transport. A **railway** line passes Manosque and continues along the bottom edge of the Luberon, serving Pertuis on its way to Aix-en-Provence and Marseille.

Manosque is also the hub for **buses**, with several daily to Aix-en-Provence and Marseille, and also one or two a day to Forcalquier and Digne-les-Bains, stopping in Les Mées.

Tourist Information

Forcalquier: 13 Place du Bourguet, **t** 04 92 75 10 02, www.forcalquier.com. Open mid-June– mid-Sept Mon–Sat 9–12.30 and 2–7, Sun 10–1; mid-Sept–mid-June Mon–Sat 9–12 and 2–6.
Manosque: Place Dr Joubert, **t** 04 92 72 16 00, www.manosque-tourisme.com. Open mid-June–mid-Sept Mon–Sat 9–12.15 and 1.30–6.30, Sun 10–12; mid-Sept–mid-June Mon–Sat 9–12.15 and 1.15–6.

Market Days

Banon: Tues am.
Manosque: Sat am.

Internet Access

Infocopie, 92 Av du Majoral Arnaud, Monasque, **t** 04 92 72 75 34.

Where to Stay and Eat

Dabisse-Les Mées ✉ 04190

Le Vieux Colombier, on D4, **t** 04 92 34 32 32, (expensive–moderate). A pleasant old farmhouse with a dovecote, specializing in succulent pigeon but also offering some superb cheeses and a wonderful selection of desserts. Closed Wed, Sun eve.

Forcalquier ✉ 04300

★★Auberge Charembeau, Route de Niozelles, 2.5km east of town, **t** 04 92 70 91 70, www.

charembeau.com (moderate). A hotel situated in a Revolutionary-era farmhouse outside of town, with a swimming pool. There's no restaurant, but some of the rooms have kitchenettes; some are inexpensive, some expensive. Closed mid-Nov–mid-Feb.

★★Le Colombier, Mas Les Dragons, 3km south of town, **t** 04 92 75 03 71, http://pageperso.aol.fr/lecolombier (moderate–inexpensive). A sensitively restored mas with a shady garden and a swimming pool, located out in the pretty countryside surrounding Forcalquier. Half-board is obligatory in summer. Closed Feb.

★★Grand Hôtel, 10 Bd Latourette, **t** 04 92 75 00 35 (inexpensive). A perfectly acceptable option for its price range, with the attraction of a garden out the back.

Manosque ✉ 04100

★★François Ier, 18 Rue Guilhempierre, **t** 04 92 72 07 99, www.hotelfrancois1.com (inexpensive). A central, quiet, if a little old-fashioned small hotel.

★★Le Provence, Route de la Durance, **t** 04 92 87 75 72 (inexpensive). A modern hotel on the outskirts, with air-conditioned rooms.

Le Petit Pascal, 17 Promenade Aubert-Millot, near Porte Saunerie, **t** 04 92 87 62 01 (cheap). A one-woman operation in a hole-in-the-wall with no sign, offering delicious home cooking; worth looking out for. Open lunch only.

Valensole ✉ 04210

★★★★Hostellerie de la Fuste, across Durance on D4, near Manosque, **t** 04 92 72 05 95, www.lafuste.com (expensive). This is the only luxury hotel-restaurant in this area. The rooms, situated in a restored bastide with a swimming pool, are fine, but the real attraction is the elegant, highly rated restaurant. Usually closed Nov; restaurant closed Sun eve and Mon in winter.

in procession on a holiday (a transit) led to the invention of a new saint. Such things happened all the time in the Midi. (And there must have been some Provençaux colonists involved in a similar occurrence very much later, in New Orleans, where the faithful in one parish still beseech favours at the altar of St Expédite: a statue of a female saint had arrived during the building of the church; no one knew who she was – but then they found her name on the packing crate.)

The lovely area around the priory is a great place for a picnic, or some unambitious hiking along the old trails, with a few *bories* (*see* pp.354–5), medieval quarries and views over the valley.

Forcalquier, Mane and Around

Nowadays on the drowsy side, and a bit too large and musty to attract the holiday-home-restoring crowd, **Forcalquier** only bestirs itself on Mondays for its market. Yet in the 11th and 12th centuries, it was a miniature capital of a small-fry mountain state whose counts often made life difficult for the counts of Provence. Alphonse II managed to get it in 1209, by marriage, and later Provençal rulers such as Raymond Bérenger V made Forcalquier a favoured residence during the 14th century. They left few traces: an obelisk in front of the stern Gothic cathedral commemorates Marguerite de Provence-Forcalquier, wife of Saint Louis; there's a Gothic fountain with the warrior angel and monkey faces in Place St-Michel; and also Europe's only listed **cemetery** (*open daily 9–5*), its ancient yew hedges trimmed to form the arcades of a cloister. A tower and other scanty remains of Forcalquier's citadel overlook the town, next to an octagonal chapel, crowned with a statue of the Virgin, honouring Pope Urban II, who came here to raise men and money for the First Crusade.

The well-restored 13th-century **Couvent des Cordeliers** (*guided tours mid-June–mid-Sept 11, 2.30 and 4.30; check with tourist office rest of year; closed Dec and Jan; adm*), parts of which were originally the counts' palace, was given to the Franciscans by Raymond Bérenger V; it has medieval art, a Franciscan cloister garden and frequent exhibitions in summer. The **Musée Municipal** in the Hôtel de Ville, Place du Bourguet (*t 04 92 75 00 14; open mid-June–mid-Sept Mon–Sat 10–12; rest of year Thurs 3, or by appointment; adm*) has a small collection of antiquities, old furniture, ceramics from Moustiers and Apt, and items from daily life.

The lands around Forcalquier are some of the most beautiful in this part of Provence, full of oak forests and sheep meadows, rustic, peaceful and not yet as touristy as the Luberon to the south. Six kilometres west, in **Mane**, the 12th-century Benedictine **Prieuré (Musée) de Salagon** (*t 04 92 75 70 50; open May–Sept daily 10–12 and 2–7; Oct–Dec and Feb–April Sat and Sun 2–6; closed Jan; guided tours April–Oct Sun 3.30; June, July and Aug daily 4pm; adm*) was built on the site of a Gallo–Roman farm and 5th-century Christian cemetery. Beautifully restored by the Conseil Général, the priory has medieval and medicinal gardens and houses the frequent exhibitions of the Alpes de Lumières, an organization dedicated to preserving and documenting local culture and customs. Mane's 18th-century **Château de Sauvan** (*t 04 92 75 05 64; guided tours 3.30 July and Aug Sun–Fri, rest of the year Thurs, Sun and hols; adm*), owned by a friend of Marie Antoinette, is a fine example of French classicism, with period furnishings.

Twelve kilometres south of Forcalquier lies the **Observatoire de Haute-Provence**, near St-Michel-l'Observatoire (*t 04 92 70 64 00; open Wed, April–Sept 2–4, Oct–Mar at*

3pm; adm). Scientists were attracted to the area by a study in the 1930s that found that the *pays de Forcalquier* had the cleanest, clearest air and the least fog of anywhere in France. There are guided tours, sadly only during the day, with films and a look at photos and the telescope.

This is also a region of *villages perchés*: **Dauphin**, just to the south, and **Oppedette**, to the west, overlooking the scenic canyon of the Calavon river. To the north, **Limans**, under brooding the bald Montagne de Lure, is famous for its luxurious 16th-century *pigeonniers*, while **Banon** to the northwest is synonymous with Provence's most famous sheep's cheese, and holds a goat's cheese fair each May. Most impressive of all, perhaps, is **Simiane-la-Rotonde**, set high on a small plateau. The *rotonde* is a peculiarly shaped 12th-century **donjon** dominating the village (*t 04 92 75 91 40; open April–mid-June and last 2 weeks Sept Wed–Mon 3–5.30; mid-June–mid-Sept Mon–Sat 10–12 and 3–7, Sun 3–7; Oct–Mar by reservation for groups only; adm*), with Romanesque carvings around what may have been a chapel – all that's left of a feudal castle. Simiane is by far the most chic of the villages in this area, with plenty of restored second homes; it's a charming place nevertheless, with a late Gothic church and an old covered market supported on stone pillars.

Manosque

By far the biggest town in this part of the Durance valley (with a population of 20,000), Manosque is unavoidable. Nicknamed '*Manosque la Pudique*' (the modest or shamefaced) by François I er after a beautiful girl from the village who disfigured herself rather than surrender to his unwanted advances, it was for centuries a drowsy place, with no other distinction than being the home town and lifetime abode of writer Jean Giono (1895–1970). Today, acres of concrete suburban sprawl press against the hill-top medieval centre, and the traffic can be as ferocious as Marseille's. The culprit is Cadarache, France's national nuclear research centre, a huge complex to the south across the Durance, which was set up in 1959; most of its workers live around Manosque.

Manosque's tidy, teardrop-shaped centre, an oasis amidst the sprawling disorder, is entered through two 14th-century gates, the **Porte Saunerie** and the **Porte Soubeyran**, designed more for decoration than defence. Inside are two unremarkable churches on quietly lovely squares: **St-Sauveur**, made in bits and pieces from the 13th–18th centuries, but attractive nevertheless, and **Notre-Dame-de-Romigier**, with a Renaissance façade; the altar is an early Christian sarcophagus with reliefs of the Apostles.

Manosque has a pair of newer attractions just outside the historic centre. A 19th-century *hôtel particulier* holds the **Centre Jean Giono**, just outside Porte Saunerie (*1 Boulevard Elemir Bourges; open Tues–Sat 2–6; adm*), dedicated to Manosque's literary lion, with an exhibition on his life and works, a library, and a *vidéothèque* with interviews and the films made from Giono's writings. A few doors down, the **Fondation Carzou** (*open Fri–Sun 10–12 and 2.30–6.30*), in the neoclassical church at the Couvent de la Présentation, has frescoes by contemporary Armenian painter Jean Carzou based on the Apocalypse and New Jerusalem.

The Luberon

As is the case with many a fair maiden, the Luberon's charms are proving to be her undoing. This is Peter Mayle country, the stage-set for his surprise bestseller *A Year in Provence*. Yes, this is that magical place where the natives are endlessly warm and human, the vineyards ever-so-lovely in autumn, and the lunch in the little bistro worth writing about for pages and pages. All true, in fact – but now everybody knows it, and the trickle of outsiders who began settling here in the 1950s, permanently or in holiday homes, has become a flood, to the extent that the French have even given up and dropped their accent – the Lubéron has become the Luberon, with a much-disputed change of pronunciation to go with it.

How you experience the Luberon also depends on what time of year you come. Most of the year it's quiet as a grave; in summer it can seem like St-Tropez-under-the-Poplars, with crowds of Brits, Americans and Parisians milling about. It's hard to imagine why anyone would want to come in August; if you insist, book a hotel months in advance.

The Regional Park

Like many parts of rural Provence, the Luberon presents a puzzling contrast. How did these villages become such civilized places, set amidst a landscape (and a population) that is more than a little rough around the edges? The real Luberon is a land of hunters

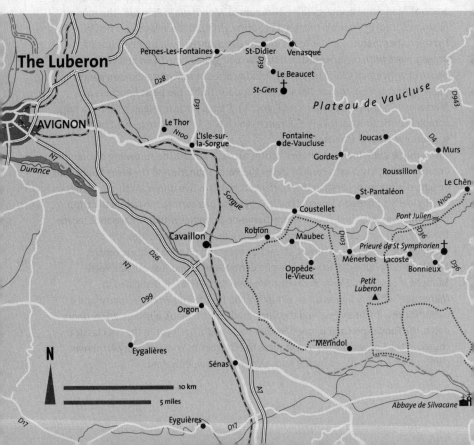

stalking wild boar over Appalachian-like ridges, and weatherbeaten farmers in ancient Renaults full of rabbit cages and power tools. There are equally scenic and rustic areas of Provence that merit being frozen into a nature preserve, but the Luberon was most in danger of being destroyed by a rash of outsiders and unplanned holiday villas.

The **Parc Régional du Luberon,** now ranked as a Biosphere Reserve by UNESCO, was founded in 1977, in a co-operative arrangement between the towns and villages that covers most of the territory between Manosque and Cavaillon, though quite a few places (often where the mayor is an estate agent or a notary) have decided not to participate at all. The Luberon is not an exceptional nature area like the Mercantour National Park (*see* pp.298–300). Still, the park protects rare species such as Bonelli's eagle, which is nearing extinction. It also keeps the Luberon from being overwhelmed by new buildings.

The Pays d'Aigues

The southern end of the Regional Park, the Pays d'Aigues, is the sleepier corner of the Luberon, a rolling stretch of good farmland sheltered by the Grand Luberon mountain to the north. **Pertuis,** a busy crossroads town along the D973, is the modest capital of the *pays*, with a bit of an aristocratic air; it earned the *fleur de lis* on its arms for its loyalty to the French crown during the Wars of Religion. Prosperity in the 17th century has left it a number of fine buildings in the historic town centre.

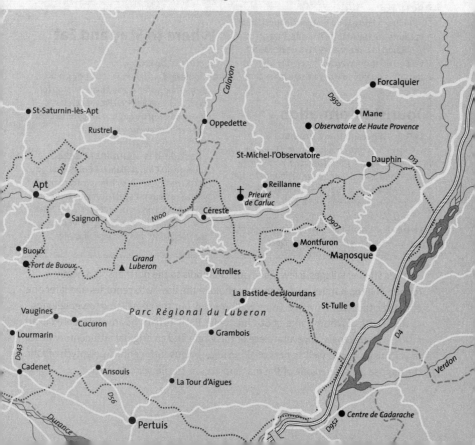

Getting Around

Public transport is woefully inconvenient in the Luberon. It is possible to get around the villages, but just barely. Try to avoid the *villages perchés* in July and Aug, when tour buses cause traffic jams.

By Train

Apt is on an SNCF branch line, with a few trains daily to Cavaillon and Avignon.

By Bus

Buses (t 04 90 74 20 21) from Apt leave from Place de la Bouquerie by the river; there are one or two daily to Roussillon, Avignon and Aix-en-Provence, stopping at Bonnieux, Lourmarin, Cadenet and Pertuis; and one to Digne-les-Bains, stopping at Céreste. From Cavaillon there are buses to L'Isle-sur-la-Sorgue, Pernes-les-Fontaines and Carpentras (several daily), to Apt and Avignon, and occasionally to Bonnieux and other western Luberon villages.

By Horse

Finding a horse is no problem in most areas; in **Lauris**, try the Mas de Rocaute, t 04 90 08 29 58, and in **Cairanne** try L'Ecurie de Muzet, t 04 90 46 12 99, which offers 2-day tours of the Côtes du Rhône vineyards on horseback.

Tourist Information

La Tour d'Aigues: In the château, t 04 90 07 50 29, *www.provenceguide.com. Open July and Aug Mon 2.30–6, Tues 10–1, Wed–Sun 10–1 and 2.30–6; April–June, Sept and Oct Sun and Mon 2.30–6, Tues 10–1, Wed–Sat 10–1 and 2.30–6; Nov–Mar Sun and Mon 2–5, Tues 10–12, Wed–Sat 10–12 and 2–5.*

Pertuis: Le Donjon, Place Mirabeau, t 04 90 79 15 56, *www.vivreleluberon.com. Open*

Sept–June Mon 10–12 and 2–6, Tues–Fri 9–12 and 2–6, Sat 9.30–12 and 2.30–6; July and Aug Mon 10–12.30 and 2–7, Tues–Fri 9–12.30 and 2–7, Sat 9.30–12.30 and 2.30–7.

Lourmarin: Av Philippe de Girard, t 04 90 68 10 77, *www.lourmarin.com. Open Mon–Sat 9.30–12.30 and 3–6, Sun 9.30–12.*

Cadenet: 11 Place du Tambour-d'Arcole, t 04 90 68 38 21, *www.provenceguide.com. Open Mon–Sat 9.30–12.30 and 2–6. Includes a shop selling items by Cadenet's basket-weavers, the village's old craft speciality.*

Regional Park Information: Maison du Parc du Luberon, 60 Place Jean Jaurès, Apt, t 04 90 04 42 00. An information centre with exhibitions and a shop, as well as information on bike routes.

Market Days

Pertuis: Fri.
La Tour d'Aigues: Tues.
Cucuron: Tues.
Lourmarin: Fri.
Cadenet: Mon.

Where to Stay and Eat

Pertuis ✉ **84120**

Le Boulevard, 50 Bd J.B. Pecout, t 04 90 09 69 31 (*moderate*). A good place to stop for tasty and kindly priced Provençal classics, if you're passing through at lunchtime. *Closed Sun eve, Tues eve and Wed.*

La Bastide-des-Jourdans ✉ **84240**

*****Auberge du Cheval Blanc**, Le Cours, t 04 90 77 81 08 (*moderate*). A picture-postcard hotel with a restaurant specializing in game and trout, served on an outdoor terrace. *Closed Feb; restaurant closed Thurs, Fri lunch in summer, Thurs and Fri lunch in winter.*

Of the smaller villages, a few stand out: **Grambois** to the northeast is a neatly rounded hilltop hamlet, a Saracen stronghold in the 8th–10th centuries and later one of the 12 citadels of Provence. Some walls remain, but the crenellated tower belongs to the church of Notre-Dame-et-St-Christophe. Both its patrons are represented in art inside: a good Renaissance altarpiece of the Virgin and an original 14th-century fresco of St Christopher, as well as, best of all, an anonymous 16th-century polyptych of John the Baptist, considered one of the masterpieces of the Provençal school.

La Tour d'Aigues ✉ 84240

★★Les Fenouillets, Bd St-Roch, t 04 90 07 48 22, *www.lesfenouillets.com* (*inexpensive*). A budget option with simple rooms but a swimming pool nearby, and a restaurant with outdoor tables that's the town's best bet for lunch.

Lourmarin ✉ 84160

Lourmarin, small as it is, has become *the* chic destination in the southern Luberon and has some of the best restaurants in the region.

★★★★Moulin de Lourmarin, Rue du Temple, t 04 90 68 06 69, *www.moulindelourmarin. com* (*luxury–expensive*). A classy one-time olive mill on the western perimeter of the village, with views over the château and nearby hills. Provençal meets Art Nouveau in the tasteful decoration, and the restaurant serves attractive and delicious Provençal dishes. Cookery courses are also available. *Book well in advance. Closed mid-Jan–Feb.*

★★★Hôtel de Guilles, Route de Vaugines, t 04 90 68 30 55,*www.guilles.com* (*expensive–moderate*). A restored farmhouse just east of the village, part of the Relais du Silence, with all the amenities, including a tennis court, a pool and gardens. *Closed Dec–mid-Mar; restaurant eve only.*

★★Hostellerie le Paradou, Route d'Apt (D943), t 04 90 68 04 05, *www.leparadou-lourmarin. com* (*moderate–inexpensive*). A hotel in a dreamy setting north of Lourmarin at the entrance to the Combe de Lourmarin (*see p.351*), with pleasant rooms and a restaurant (*moderate*). Half-board obligatory in season.

Villa St-Louis, 35 Rue Henri de Savournin, t 04 90 68 39 18, *www.style-luberon.com/ heberg_stlouis.htm* (*moderate–inexpensive*). A charming *chambre d'hôte* in a 19th-century house on the edge of the village, with a very affable proprietress.

La Fenière, Route de Cadenet, t 04 90 09 88 42 (*expensive*). A restaurant offering old Provençal favourites cooked in an expert and innovative way. The menu includes such dishes as batter-fried courgette flowers and a hearty *daube. Closed Sun eve, Mon and Tues lunch.*

Le Bistrot, Av Raoul Dautry, t 04 90 68 29 74 (*moderate*). A restaurant overlooking the château and offering a wide choice of Provençal and Lyonnais cuisine, together with some vegetarian dishes. *Closed Mon lunch and Thurs July and Aug.*

Michel-Ange, Place de la Fontaine, t 04 90 68 02 03 (*moderate*). A restaurant offering a good selection of reasonably priced vegetarian, fish and organic dishes. *Closed Tues Oct–Easter, and Wed except July and Aug.*

La Récréation, 15 Rue Philippe de Girard, t 04 90 68 23 73 (*moderate*). A good bet, with a terrace facing the château and a menu of fresh organic Provençal fare, including some good lamb dishes with garlic. *Closed Wed.*

Cadenet ✉ 84160

Cadenet is less expensive and less touristy than Lourmarin, and is a good alternative as a place to stay

★★Mas du Colombier, Route de Pertuis, t 04 90 68 29 00, *http://mas-du-colombier.com* (*moderate–inexpensive*). A pleasant enough place with a swimming pool, set in an old vineyard. *Closed mid-Nov–Jan.*

Stefáni, 35 Av Gambetta, t 04 90 68 07 14 (*cheap*). A restaurant serving a range of delicious dishes on its panoramic terrace. *Closed Tues eve and Wed.*

Ansouis, to the north of Pertuis on the D56, is a *village perché* built around the sumptuously furnished Château de Sabran (*t 04 90 09 82 70; open Feb and Mar Wed–Mon 2.30–6; April–Oct daily 2.30–6; Nov–Jan Sat and Sun 2.30–6; adm*), first mentioned in print in 961 and still in the hands of the original family. A Henry IV monumental stair leads to Flemish tapestries, Italian Renaissance furniture, portraits and later Bourbon bric-a-brac. The atmosphere is wonderfully snooty. The **Musée Extraordinaire Georges Mazoyer** (*t 04 90 09 82 64; open daily summer 2–7, winter 2–6;*

adm) has some of this and some of that – sculptures, stained glass and other work by its namesake, plus fossils and displays on underwater life.

For an airier, more pleasant castle without the bric-a-brac, try **La Tour d'Aigues**, just to the east. The château here, in fact, doesn't even have a roof. The Baron of Cental was still making repairs to damage caused by a fire in 1782 when the Revolution came and the local peasantry torched the place for good. What's left is a thoroughly elegant Renaissance shell, begun in 1555 by an Italian architect, Ercole Nigra, imitating the styles then fashionable in Paris. The entrance, a huge triumphal arch carved with trophies, was inspired by the Roman arch at Orange (*see* p.380). One of the château's side towers has been rebuilt, and the Conseil de Vaucluse, which now owns it, plans to restore the rest a little at a time as funds are available. There is a small **museum** in the cellar (*t 04 90 07 50 33; www.chateau-latourdaigues.com; open July and Aug daily 10–1 and 2.30–6.30; Sept–Oct Wed–Sat 10–1 and 2.30–6, Sun and Mon 2.30–6, Tues 10–1; Nov–Jan Wed–Sat 10–12 and 2–5, Sun and Mon 2–5, Tues 10–12; April–June Wed–Sat 10–1 and 2.30–6, Sun–Tues 2.30–6; closed Feb and Mar; adm*), exhibiting both pottery and displays on the history of Aigues. La Tour also has an unusual Romanesque church, **Notre-Dame de Romegas**, with an apse at either end – originally built facing the east, it was turned around in the 17th century when some clerical stickler for the rules had a second apse built.

Heading west, and still on the south flank of the Grand Luberon, **Cucuron** was found perfect enough to be used as the set for *Le Hussard sur le toit* (*The Horseman on the Roof*), the film adaptation of a novel by Jean Giono; the view of the same roofs is especially pretty from the Donjon St-Michel. Cucuron's market takes place on the banks of its little lake, surrounded by ancient plane trees. The town also holds a renamed May tree celebration in late May, in which the highest poplar tree is cut down and paraded through the streets to the local church, where it remains until August. The D56 leads on to **Vaugines**, a lovely little place (the setting for many scenes in *Manon des Sources* and *Jean de Florette*) and Lourmarin.

Lourmarin and Cadenet

Further west, into the heart of the Luberon, **Lourmarin** was the last home of Albert Camus. This is an unusual village, densely packed almost to the point of claustrophobia; many of its houses have tiny courtyards facing the street. It's too cute for its own good – few villages, even in the Luberon, are so beset by tourists. Its landmark is a grand bell-tower, so everyone always knows what time it is, and its main attraction is another 16th-century **château** (*t 04 90 68 15 23; open for guided tours May, June and Sept 10, 11, 2.30, 3.30, 4.30 and 5.30; July and Aug every 30mins 10–11.30 and 3–6; Oct–Dec and Feb–April 11, 2.30, 3.30 and 4.30; Jan open Sat and Sun afternoons or by appointment; adm*). This was the residence of the counts of Agoult for three centuries; its last countess was the mother of Franz Liszt's three children, one of whom, Cosima, married Richard Wagner. Well restored, the 'Villa Médicis de Provence', as it's called, is now the property of the Académie of Aix, who use it for cultural programmes, concerts and exhibitions. The rooms have rare furnishings (don't miss the Aztec fireplace) and art, including the lovely *Lute Player* by the school of Leonardo da Vinci and a collection of engravings by Piranesi. If you are looking for the existentialist, Albert Camus can be found buried on the left-hand side of the pretty cemetery.

Cadenet, a big village overlooking the rocky bed of the Durance, is only 5km away, but the difference is like that between day and night. An ancient place, Cadenet began as a pre-Celtic *oppidum*; even older are some of the cave dwellings that can be seen in the cliffs behind the village (others were refuges for persecuted Waldensian Protestants in the 16th century; *see* below). It's also a very attractive village. On the **Place du Tambour d'Arcole**, one of the focal points of the Monday market, is a bronze statue of Cadenet's favourite son, André Estienne, a 15-year-old drummer boy who once managed a difficult river crossing for Napoleon's troops – wading right in and beating the charge under direct Austrian fire. The embarrassed soldiers could only follow. Have a peek inside the parish church, **St-Etienne**, on the northern edge of town. The baptismal font has well-preserved reliefs of a Bacchic orgy; scholars call it 3rd-century but disagree over whether it was originally a sarcophagus or a bathtub. The new **Musée de la Vannerie** (*t 04 90 68 24 44; open all day Mon and Thurs–Sat, Wed pm and Sun pm, call for hours; closed Tues; adm*) is dedicated to Cadenet's age-old occupation, wickerwork and basketry.

West of Cadenet, **Mérindol** isn't much to look at, but it's worth a mention as a symbol of a very dark page of the Luberon's history. When plagues and war depopulated the region in the 14th century, immigrants from the Alps and from Italy came to work the land. Many were peaceful, hard-working Waldensian dissenters; when the Reformation began, the authorities would no longer tolerate them. In 1540, the *Parlement* of Aix oversaw the burning of 19 Waldensian villages in the Luberon, including Mérindol and Lourmarin. More than 3,000 innocents were butchered, and hundreds more were sent off to the king's galleys. There is a **Waldensian museum**, La Muse, in the village, which contains extensive archives (*t 04 90 72 91 64; call for opening hours*). The ruins of Mérindol's castle house a Waldensian memorial; also note the curious onion-domed tower, called a 'Saracen bulb' in French.

The Abbaye de Silvacane

t 04 42 50 41 69; open July–Sept daily 10–6; Oct–June Wed–Mon 10–1 and 2–5; adm.

Life as a medieval Cistercian was no picnic. Besides the strict discipline and a curious prejudice against heating, there was always the chance the Order might send you to somewhere in the middle of a swamp. They built this, the first of the 'Three Sisters of Provence', in just such a location – the 'forest of rushes' (*silva cana*), south of the Durance, 7km from Cadenet – because they meant to reclaim it. It took a century or two, but they did the job, as you can see today from the fertile farmlands around Silvacane. A Benedictine community had already been established here when the Cistercians arrived in 1147. Work began on the present buildings soon after, partially financed by the barons of Les Baux, and Silvacane became quite prosperous. However, bad frosts in the 14th century killed off all the olives and vines, starting

Silvacane on its long decline. When the government bought the complex to restore it in 1949, it was being used as a barn.

The church is as chastely fair as its younger sisters at Sénanque (*see* pp.356–7) and Thoronet (*see* pp.325–6), and perhaps more austere and uncompromising still: even the apse is a plain rectangle. There is hardly any sculptural decoration (though there are scores of masons' marks on the columns and vaulting). The adjacent **cloister** now contains a herb garden and a lovely broken fountain. Note the capitals on the arcades, carved, oddly, with maple leaves.

Northern Luberon: Along the N100 to Apt

Starting at Forcalquier, this route follows the northern slopes of the mountains, which generally constitutes much more scenic country than the other side, with pretty villages such as **Reillanne**, which was nearly deserted 100 years ago but is now making a comeback, and **Céreste**, a village that grew up as a stopping point on the Via Domitia, with a Roman bridge as a landmark.

Between the two, you can make an excursion to the **Prieuré de Carluc** (*call t 04 42 54 22 70 to arrange guided tours July and Aug 3.30–7; adm*), with a 12th-century Romanesque chapel and unique ruins of the original early Christian priory, partly carved out of a rocky outcrop. Like Notre-Dame-du-Groseau on Mont Ventoux (*see* p.366), this was an ancient religious site built around a sacred spring; the ruins around the rock include a Gallo-Roman cemetery.

The narrow roads south of the N100 are some of the most beautiful in the Luberon, passing through **Vitrolles** or **Montfuron**, with its lofty ruined castle, on their way to the Pays d'Aigues. There are also several hiking trails, from Vitrolles or from **Saignon**, 5km southeast of Apt, leading up to the summit of the Grand Luberon, the **Mourre Nègre**, with views that take in all of the Vaucluse and beyond. Saignon itself is a beautiful *village perché* between two crags, boasting a well-preserved 12th-century church of Sainte-Marie, with a curious lobed façade and a reliquary of the True Cross inside. You can also tour the **Potager d'un Curieux** (*t 04 90 74 44 68; open July and Aug Mon–Fri for guided tours by appt; Sept and Oct by appt only*), a beautiful collection of forgotten plants, flowers and herbs.

Apt

The capital of the Luberon (pop. 15,000 and growing) also claims to be the 'World Capital of Candied Fruits', with one big factory and plenty of smaller concerns that make these and every other sort of sweet. And there is a certain stickiness about Apt itself; everyone in the Luberon comes here for the huge, animated Saturday market, but no one has ever admitted to liking the place, at least not in print. Roman Colonia Apta Julia, a colony refounded over a Celtic village, was the capital of the area even then. Despite languishing for a few dark centuries before being rebuilt in the 12th century, the streets still bear traces of a rectangular Roman plan, bent into kinks and curves through the ages.

The Cathedral and More Dubious Provençal Saints

We can guess that the **Rue des Marchands**, the main shopping street of Apt, roughly follows the course of its Roman predecessor. It leads to the **Tour de l'Horloge** (1567), the bell-tower of Apt's old **Cathédrale Ste-Anne**. Begun in the late 12th century and tinkered with incessantly until the 18th, it has an ungainly exterior concealing a wealth of curiosities within. There is some fine 14th-century stained glass in the apse, an early Christian sarcophagus and an odd golden painting of John the Baptist in two chapels on the north side, plus an interesting *trésor* with books of hours, reliquaries and a number of Islamic ivories. Another trophy that made its way here from the east is a linen banner, which was brought back from the Crusades by a lord of Simiane; because its origin was forgotten, it came to be revered in Apt as the veil of St Anne.

Few regions of Europe had such a longing for relics as Provence in the Dark Ages. Other peoples, the Germans and Venetians, had a kleptomanic urge to steal holy bones when no one was looking; the Provençaux, showing less initiative but greater imagination, simply invented them. We met St Transit at Ganagobie (*see* pp.336–7), and the crypt here has two more. According to legend, the bones of St Anne, the mother of Mary, were miraculously discovered in this crypt in the 8th century, occasioning the building of the first cathedral. In those days, any early Christian

Tourist Information

Apt: 20 Av Philippe de Girard, t 04 90 74 03 18, *www.ot-apt.fr. Open May–Sept Mon–Sat 9–7, Sun 9.30–12.30; Oct–April Mon–Sat 9–12 and 2–6.*

Market Days

Apt: Sat general market and Tues farmers' market (May–Oct), Cours Lauze de Perret.

Where to Stay and Eat

Apt ✉ 84400

As rooms in the smaller villages are hard to come by, you'll probably end up staying in Apt. The tourist office has lists of *chambres d'hôtes*, *auberges* and campsites.

- ***Auberge du Luberon**, 18 Place du Faubourg du Ballet, t 04 90 74 12 50, *www.auberge-luberon-peuzin.com* (*moderate–inexpensive*). Pleasant rooms and a restaurant where the speciality is rabbit with figs, and dishes with *confit d'Apt. Closed Sun eve, Mon lunch and Nov–mid-Dec.*
- **Le Palais**, 24 Rue du Ar A. Gros, t 04 90 04 89 32 (*inexpensive*). A simple, comfortable budget hotel. *Closed Nov–Feb.*

La Platane, 8 Rue Jules Ferry, t 04 90 04 74 36 (*moderate*). Fresh dishes made using organic market produce. *Closed Sun.*

Around Apt

- ****Relais de Roquefure**, Le Chêne, 4km west of town on N100, t 04 90 04 88 88, *www.relaisderoquefure.com* (*moderate*). An old stone-built inn with a swimming pool and restaurant. *Closed Jan–mid-Feb and Tues.*

Auberge du Presbytère, Place de la Fontaine, Saignon, t 04 90 74 11 50, *www.auberge-presbytere.com* (*moderate*). Two 10th- and 11th-century buildings in the town centre, with a magnificent view over the Luberon, charming, homey rooms and a fine intimate restaurant. Worth the detour. Make sure to book ahead. *Closed mid-Nov–mid-Feb; restaurant closed Wed and Thurs lunch in summer.*

Bernard Mathys, Le Chêne, 4km west of town on N100, t 04 90 04 84 64 (*very expensive–expensive*). A lovely restaurant set in an 18th-century house, offering delightful meals with all the trimmings (the vegetables are especially good). *Dinner only; closed Tues and Wed, and mid-Jan–mid-Feb.*

burial dug up was likely to be elevated to saint status; beyond that, scholars guess the Anne invented for the occasion was less the biblical figure than a dim memory of the primeval pan-European mother goddess, who was known as Ana, or Dana, to the Celts, the Romans (Anna Perenna), and nearly everyone else. Next to her are the bones of 'St Auspice', claimed to be Apt's first bishop but really the sacred auspices of pagan times (divination from bird flight or from the organs of sacrificed animals) – another verbal confusion like St Transit.

Fruits and Fossils

Apt also has a good **Musée d'Archéologie et d'Histoire** (*27 Rue de l'Amphithéâtre, t 04 90 74 00 34; open June–Sept Mon and Wed–Sat 2–5; Oct–May Mon and Wed–Fri 2–5, Sat 10–12 and 2–5; closed Tues and Sun; adm*), with archaeological finds going back to the Palaeolithic period, late Roman sarcophagi, recent Roman and medieval finds from the centre of Apt, painted *ex votos* and a display of Apt's once-flourishing craft of faïence, which had its heyday in the 18th century.

The town's other attraction is the **Maison du Parc du Luberon** (*see p.342 for contact information; open Mon–Sat 9–12 and 1.30–6, to 7pm in summer*), the headquarters and information centre of the Regional Park in a restored 17th-century building; it has exhibits on the region's natural life, including a push-button Palaeontology Museum for the children, an interesting gift shop, and all the information you'll ever need on the wild areas of the Luberon.

Finally, you can take a tour of the **Aptunion Factory**, west on the N100 (*t 04 90 76 31 31, www.kerryaptunion.com; shop open Mon–Sat 9–12 and 2–6; factory visits by appt*), where they make most of those crystallized fruits, by sucking the water out of the fruit and replacing it with a sugar solution – a bit like embalming.

Red Villages North of Apt

Technically, this isn't part of the Luberon, though it is within the boundaries of the Regional Park. Above Apt, on the southern slopes of the Plateau de Vaucluse, the geology changes abruptly. The plateau is mostly limestone, which erodes away to make caves and water tricks such as the Fontaine-de-Vaucluse (*see p.357*). This part has sandy deposits full of iron oxides – ochre, the material used in prehistoric times as skin-paint, and later to colour everything from soap to rugs. Centuries of mining have left some bizarre landscapes – cliffs and pits and peaks in what locals claim are '17 shades of red', as well as yellow and cream and occasionally other hues.

Rustrel to Roussillon

Rustrel, northeast of Apt on the D22, was one of the mining towns until 1890. The huge, ruddy mess they left is called the **Colorado**; there are hazily marked routes around it for tourists, although you may have to pay for a proper map. From here, the D179 west takes you to **St-Saturnin-lès-Apt** (St Saturnin is probably the Roman god Saturn). Inside a modern ring of bungalows, this old village had little to do with

Tourist Information

Roussillon: Place de la Poste, t 04 90 05 60 25, *www.ot-pays-roussillonais.org. Open July and Aug Tues–Fri 9–12 and 1.30–6.30, Mon and Sat 10–12 and 2–5.30, Sun 2–6; Sept–June Mon–Sat 10–12 and 2–5.30.*

Market Days

Roussillon:Thurs, Place du Pasquier.

Where to Stay and Eat

St-Saturnin-lès-Apt ✉ 84490

St-Saturnin-lès-Apt is a friendly village, and though it's bit out of the way it is a good, reasonably priced choice for a base.

*Hôtel Les Voyageurs, Place Gambetta, t 04 90 75 42 08, *voyageurs@provence-luberon.net* (*inexpensive*). A delightfully old-fashioned Logis de France with a restaurant (*moderate*). *Closed end Jan–end Feb; restaurant closed Wed and Thurs lunch, Sun eve in winter.*

Le Saint-Hubert, Place de la Fraternité, t 04 90 75 42 02 (*inexpensive*). A hotel with 8 rooms and a restaurant with a pretty terrace. Note the 'wallpaper' in the bar. *Closed Jan; restaurant closed Mon.*

Roussillon ✉ 84220

***Mas de Garrigon, Route de St-Saturnin-d'Apt, t 04 90 05 63 22, *www.masdegarrigon-provence.com/provence.htm* (*expensive*). A well-restored farmhouse with all the amenities that you could hope for, including lovely rooms named after writers and a gourmet restaurant (both overpriced).

Half-board is obligatory in summer. *Restaurant closed mid-Oct–mid-May.*

**Rêves d'Ocres, Route de Gordes, t 04 90 05 60 50 (*moderate*). A pleasant, cheaper option, with convenient parking. *Closed Nov–Jan.*

Le Val des Fées, Rue R. Casteau, t 04 90 05 64 99 (*moderate*). A reasonably priced restaurant with lovely views over the ochre from its terrace. *Closed Wed exc July and Aug, and Nov and Jan.*

Joucas ✉ 84220

****Hostellerie Le Phébus, Route de Murs, t 04 90 05 78 83, *www.lephebus.com* (*luxury–expensive*). A hotel done in exquisite taste, with views over Roussillon's red hills, and a garden, pool, tennis court and excellent restaurant, with Provençal dishes made with the freshest herbs. Half board is obligatory in summer. *Closed mid-Oct–mid-Mar.*

****Le Mas des Herbes Blanches, t 04 90 05 79 79, *www.relaischateaux.com* (*luxury–expensive*). A sumptuous Relais & Châteaux spread in an old *mas*, with a beautiful setting and a restaurant (*expensive–very expensive*). *Closed Jan and Feb.*

**La Bergerie, Route de Murs, t 04 90 05 78 73 (*expensive–moderate*). An average, overpriced country hotel with 20 rooms, a pool and a restaurant (*moderate*). Half board obligatory in summer. *Closed Nov–Mar.*

Le Mas du Loriot, Murs, t 04 90 72 62 62, *www.masduloriot.com* (*expensive–moderate*). An intimate, friendly and refined option in a new Provençal *mas*, with 8 rooms and a pool, and a restaurant (*moderate*) open 4 nights a week. *Closed mid-Nov–mid-Mar.*

mining, but it has always grown nice red cherries; there are plenty of ruins, including a castle and bits of three different sets of walls (13th–16th centuries), a windmill for a landmark, and a simple Romanesque chapel from the 1050s. And you don't get the hordes of tour buses as in nearby Gordes or **Roussillon**. To the southwest, the latter occupies a spectacular hill-top site, and well it should – centuries of mining have removed nearly everything for miles around. The Association Terre d'Ocres, an organization that wants to get the business going again, has an information centre in the village and can direct you on a walk through the old quarries, known locally as the Sables de Roussillon. Further information on the ochre is available at the Conservatoire des Ocres et des Pigments Appliqués (**t** *04 90 05 66 69, www.okhra.com*).

Samuel Beckett spent the war years exiled in Roussillon; the rural peace and quiet gave him a nervous breakdown. His house is being restored as the Maison Samuel Beckett, with an adjoining cultural centre. Roussillon was also 'Peyrane' in Laurence Wylie's *Village in the Vaucluse;* the one place readers will recognize from the 1950s is Bar Castrum, with its old poster of the film *Marius* on the wall.

South of Roussillon and the N100 is a well-preserved Roman bridge, the **Pont Julien**. The little stone village of **Joucas**, just north of Roussillon, is quiet and uncommercial, although its surrounding hotels have taken up catering for upper-class tourists. North of here, at **Murs**, you can pick up the scenic D4 across the Plateau de Vaucluse and its gorges to **Venasque**.

Villages of the Petit Luberon

West of Apt, and south of the N100, is a string of truly beautiful villages that have become the high-rent district of the Luberon, one of the poshest rural areas in France. Don't come here looking for that little place in the country to fix up; it's all been done, as long as 40 years ago. The first to arrive were the Parisians, including many artists, intellectuals and eccentrics, giving the place a reputation as 'St-Germain-in-the-Luberon'. Since the 1960s, a wave of outsiders looking for Provençal paradise, including many Americans, have transformed the place. None of this is readily apparent, apart from the infestations of swanky villas on many hillsides outside the Regional Park boundaries. The villagers, a bit richer now, take it in their stride and carry on as they always have – separate worlds, existing side by side.

The biggest and busiest of the villages, **Bonnieux** is also one of the loveliest, a belvedere overlooking the whole of the Petit Luberon. The ungainly modern church at the bottom of the village contains four colourful 16th-century wood paintings of the Passion of Christ; the other attraction, so to speak, is the **Musée de la Boulangerie**

Wine: Côtes-du-Luberon

Between the mountains of the lower Durance and the Calavon valley around Apt are the vineyards that produce AOC Côtes-du-Luberon – mostly young ruby wines made from grenache, syrah, cinsault, mourvèdre and carignan; the whites come from Bourboulenc and Clairette. One high-profile producer is the extraordinary hi-tech cellar at the **Château Val-Joanis**, in Pertuis, **t** 04 90 79 20 77, where the red, with a high percentage of syrah, is good quality and a good buy.

On the more traditional side, **Château de l'Isolette**, on the main road between Bonnieux and Apt, **t** 04 90 74 56 79, is run by the Pinatels, a family that has been making wine since the 16th century. Over the past decade the estate has won scores of medals, especially for its red wines aged in oak barrels, such as the Grande Sélection; they also do a fine blanc de blancs and rosé. In Bonnieux itself, look for **Château La Canorgue**, Route du Pont Julien, **t** 04 90 75 81 01, a beautiful 16th-century château whose wines, made from organically grown grapes, consistently win medals in international competitions.

Tourist Information

Bonnieux: 7 Place Carnot, **t** 04 90 75 91 90, *www.provenceguide.com. Open April–Oct Mon 2–6, Tues–Sat 9.30–12.30 and 2–6.*

Market Days

Bonnieux: Fri am.
Lacoste: Tues am.
Oppède-le-Vieux: Sat am.

Where to Stay and Eat

Bonnieux ✉ 84480

***Hostellerie du Prieuré**, Rue Jean Baptiste Aurard, **t** 04 90 75 80 78 (*expensive–moderate*). An 18th-century priory in the village centre; the rooms have a view and there's a garden and gourmet restaurant. *Closed Nov–Feb.*

****Hôtel Le César**, Place de la Liberté, **t** 04 90 75 96 35, *www.hotel-cesar.com* (*moderate*). An 18th-century hotel in the centre. Ask for rooms at the back to avoid the noise of the street. There are some *inexpensive* rooms with shared bathrooms. *Closed mid-Nov–mid-Mar; restaurant closed Thurs.*

Le Fournil, 5 Place Carnot, **t** 04 90 75 83 62 (*moderate*). A restaurant carved out of the cliff, serving light fare. *Closed Mon, Jan and Feb.*

Le Pistou, 6 Place du 4 Septembre, **t** 04 90 75 88 01 (*moderate*). An imaginative menu based on fresh local produce.

La Flambée, 2 Place du 4 Septembre, **t** 04 90 75 82 20 (*inexpensive*). A reasonable pizzeria.

Buoux ✉ 84480

Auberge des Seguins, Les Seguins (off D113), **t** 04 90 74 16 37 (*moderate*). An isolated hotel above Buoux, near the fort, for those who really want to get away from it all and enjoy simple rooms and home cooking in a memorable setting with a pool. Half-board is obligatory. *Closed Jan.*

Ménerbes ✉ 84560

***Le Roy Soleil**, D103, **t** 04 90 72 25 61, *http://roy-soleil.com* (*luxury–expensive*). A hotel in a 17th-century building in an olive grove overlooking Ménerbes, with a pool and an excellent restaurant. *Closed Dec–mid-Mar.*

Oppède-le-Vieux ✉ 84580

****Le Mas des Capelans**, N100, **t** 04 90 76 99 04, *www.masdescapelans-luberon.com* (*expensive–moderate*). A pleasant country hotel in a former stable, with a pool, a terrace and a playground. *Closed Nov–mid-Feb.*

L'Oppidum, Place de la Croix, **t** 04 90 76 84 15 (*moderate*). Good-value local produce served up amidst local works of art beneath ruined medieval walls. *Closed lunchtimes.*

(*Rue de la République*, **t** *04 90 75 88 34; open April–June and Oct Sat and Sun 10–12 and 3–6.30; July and Aug Wed–Sun 10–12 and 3–6.30; adm*), which as the name suggests will tell you everything you wanted to know about Provençal bread.

There are some wonderfully scenic excursions from here. The D36/D943 south to Lourmarin is the only good road across the spine of the Luberon; it passes through a long and beautiful gorge called the **Combe de Lourmarin**. East of Bonnieux off the D943, a side road, the D113, takes you up into the mountains, passing the slender, elegant Romanesque bell-tower of the **Prieuré de St-Symphorien**, and up to the hamlet and cliffs of **Buoux**, which has of late become something of a climber's mecca; above it, the ruined medieval **Fort de Buoux** offers tremendous views over the heart of the Luberon. Nearby is the beginning of a **nature trail** marked out by the Regional Park, with placards on the Luberon's flora and fauna all along the way.

Lacoste, located to the west of Bonnieux on the D109, is a trendy *village perché*, home to an American school run by the Cleveland Institute of Art. Overlooking the village is a gloomy ruined castle, the one-time home of no less a personage than the Marquis de Sade (d. 1814). The French are a bit embarrassed by the author of *Les 120*

Journées de Sodome, but he certainly wasn't insane, and he is a literary figure of some note, taking to extremes the urge for self-expression that came with the dawn of the Romantic movement. He did have his little weaknesses, which kept him in and out of the calaboose for decades, on charges such as pushing 'aphrodisiac bonbons' on servant girls, and worse. The scion of a respectable old Provençal family, he spent a lot of time here when Paris grew too hot for him. Oddly enough, the Marquis seems to have been a descendant of Petrarch's Laura – Laura de Sade (*see* Avignon, pp.386, 392 and 399–400). The thought of it obsessed him all his life, and he saw her in visions in the castle here. The castle, which was burned in the Revolution, is now fully restored. It has recently been bought by Pierre Cardin and is open to the public for concerts and theatre events.

Continuing along the D109, you come to **Ménerbes**, a honey-coloured, artsy and cuter-than-cute town. As the former home of professional expat Peter Mayle, it now attracts legions of fans of *A Year in Provence*, who come here by the busload to pay homage and buy a postcard; there's really not a good deal else to do here. Ménerbes is so narrow that from certain angles it resembles a ship, cruising out of the Luberon toward Avignon; at the top is a small square, measuring about 18ft across, with balconies on either side.

The D188 from here takes you amongst waves of vines, to, fittingly, the world's first and only corkscrew museum, the **Musée du Tire-Bouchon**, at Domaine de la Citadelle (*t 04 90 72 41 58; open Mon–Sat April–Oct 10–12 and 2–7, Nov–Mar 10–12 and 2–5; adm*) just to the west of Ménerbes. The museum houses a collection of weird and wonderful bottle poppers, from 17th-century attempts to a bejewelled Cartier de luxe model and an extensive display of pornographic corkscrews.

From here the D188 continues through grand scenery almost to the top of the Petit Luberon, and **Oppède-le-Vieux**, with its even gloomier ruined castle, the home of the bloodthirsty Baron d'Oppède, leader of the genocide against the Waldensians in the 1540s (*see* p.16). The road west of Oppède, by way of Maubec and Robion towards Cavaillon, is equally pretty; **Maubec**, with its Baroque church, may be the Luberon village of your dreams.

Cavaillon

Lacking anything more compelling, Cavaillon has become famous for its melons. As one of the biggest agricultural market towns in all of France, it ships a million tonnes or so of these and all the other rich produce of the surrounding plains to Paris every year. Back in the 19th century, Alexandre Dumas loved Cavaillon's melons so much that he agreed to supply the local libraries with his books in exchange for a dozen of them a year.

Cavaillon is built under a steep hill overlooking the Durance, the **Colline St-Jacques**, where a Neolithic settlement has been uncovered next to a medieval chapel; it is a short climb up from central Place du Clos, with views on top stretching from Mont Ventoux to the Alpilles. Roman-era Cavaillon has left behind only a 1st-century AD

Tourist Information

Cavaillon: Pl François Tourel, **t** 04 90 71 32 01, *www.cavaillon-luberon.com. Open mid-Mar– mid-Oct Mon–Sat 9–12.30 and 2–6.30; mid- Oct–mid-Mar Mon–Fri 9–12 and 2–6, Sat 9–12.*

Market Days

Cavaillon:Mon; it competes with Apt's as the most important in the Vaucluse.

Festivals

Melon Festival, early July.

Where to Stay

Cavaillon ✉ 84300

If you need a change from French food, there are Indian, Tex-Mex, Vietnamese and other restaurants along Bd Gambetta.

Hôtel du Parc, 183 Place François Tourel, **t 04 90 71 57 78,*www.hotelduparccavaillon. com (moderate–inexpensive).* An old hotel that makes a pleasant place to stay, with a homely feel and private parking.

Toppin, 70 Cours Gambetta, **t 04 90 71 30 42, *hotel.toppin.gesnot@wanadoo.fr (inexpensive).* A venerable and well-kept

option with private parking facilities. *Closed Christmas and New Year.*

Eating Out

Le Pantagruel, 5 Place Philippe de Cabassole, **t** 04 90 76 11 98 *(expensive–moderate).* A *restaurant gastronomique* under big stone arches opposite the market, using organic produce. *Closed Mon lunch and Sun.*

Fin de Siècle, 46 Place du Clos, **t** 04 90 71 12 27 *(expensive–moderate).* Famed for its old- fashioned décor; try stuffed chicken breast or salmon cakes. The café next door is a listed monument. *Closed Aug–Dec, Tues, Wed.*

Côté Jardin, 49 Rue Lamartine, **t** 04 90 71 33 58 *(moderate).* A popular local restaurant with traditional dishes made from fresh market produce. *Book. Closed Sun and Mon eve.*

Le Prévôt, 353 Av de Verdun, **t** 04 90 71 32 43, *(moderate).* A restaurant offering organic Provençal cuisine, and themed menus during the town's food festivals. Booking is required. *Closed Sun eve and Mon.*

L'Oustau, 21 Av Pierre Semard, opposite station, **t** 04 90 76 04 58 *(cheap).* Generous dishes, including a huge seafood salad. *Closed Tues eve and Sun.*

---

arch, at the foot of the hill. Unlike the arches of Carpentras and Orange, this one probably doesn't mark any particular triumph; it is four-sided, a *quadroporticus*, and, like the only similar construction, the Arch of Janus in Rome, it probably was a simple decoration for – appropriately enough – a marketplace. Its decorative reliefs, mostly fruits and flowers, are now too eroded to be seen very clearly.

Cavaillon's other attractions include a small **archaeological museum**, in the chapel of the Musée de l'Hôtel-Dieu off Cours Gambetta (**t** *04 90 76 00 34; open June–mid-Sept Mon and Wed–Sat 9.30–12.30 and 2.30–6.30; mid-Sept–mid-April Mon and Wed–Fri 10–12 and 2–6.30; adm*); the odd-shaped, rather forbidding Romanesque cathedral of **Notre-Dame-et-St-Véran**, with a tatterdemalion 17th-century interior and a pretty cloister; and an ornate 18th-century **synagogue**, similar to the one in Carpentras, with a small museum, on Rue Hébraïque (*same hours and tel no. as museum*). Before the Revolution, Cavaillon had the biggest Jewish population in the papal enclave; among them were the ancestors of the composer Darius Milhaud. Segregated in a tiny ghetto around the synagogue, the community prospered despite occasional gusts of papal persecution; after the Revolution most of Cavaillon's Jews moved to the larger cities of Provence, and there is none living in the town today. The museum offers guided tours of the synagogue and the old Jewish community, as well as of the old towns and countryside.

The Vaucluse

The Plateau de Vaucluse

The Plateau de Vaucluse is the high ground that runs between the Luberon and Mont Ventoux to the north. Beware that both Gordes and Fontaine-de-Vaucluse can get crowded out by the heaving coachloads in the summer.

Gordes

The first thing you'll notice about this striking *village perché* is that it has a rock problem. They have it under control; the vast surplus has been put to use in houses and sheds, and also for the hundreds of thick stone walls that make Gordes seem more like a southern Italian village than one in Provence. The stones made agriculture a bad bet here, so the Gordiens planted olives instead, and became famous for them – at least until the terrible frost of 1976 killed off most of the trees. But without ever asking for it, Gordes has found something easier and more profitable: art tourism, with exhibitions and concerts in the summer.

Gordes was a Résistance stronghold in the war and suffered for it, with wholesale massacres of citizens and the destruction of much of the village; after the war it was awarded the Croix de Guerre. The damage the Nazis did has been repaired; the village centre, all steep, cobbled streets and arches, is extremely attractive. At the centre, you may see flocks of well-scrubbed art students lounging on the steps of the imposing château built by the lords of Simiane in the 1520s. They are making their pilgrimage to an avant-garde that no longer exists. Even the rearguard – a 'didactic museum' of the works of the late Hungarian op art/poster artist Vasarély – has ducked out of Gordes, apparently for good, victim of an unseemly quarrel over money between Vasarély's heirs and the management. If you're disappointed, the **Galerie Pascal Lainé** (*t 04 90 72 00 90*) in Place du Château has an exhibition of his works.

To see what real art's all about, walk over to Gordes' parish church of **St-Fermin**, with its memorable 18th-century interior of purple, pink and gilded jiggumabobs, a lodge brother's fantasy seraglio. A statue of the Magdalen on the right looks down on it with a jaundiced eye. The **château** itself (*t 04 90 72 02 75; open 10–12 and 2–6; adm*) has a superb Renaissance fireplace, the second largest in France, and a hotchpotch of art in the Musée Pol Mara up on the second and third floors.

Around Gordes: Les Bories and Another Bore

Across the Midi they are called *bories*, or *garriotes*, or *capitelles*, or a dozen other local names. In Provence, there are some 3,000 of them, but the largest collection in one place is the **Village des Bories**, south of Gordes off the D2 (*t 04 90 72 03 48; open daily 9–sunset; adm*). A *borie* is a small dry-stone hut, usually with a well-made corbelled dome or vault for a ceiling. Because of their resemblance to Neolithic works (such as the *nuraghi* of Sardinia), they have always intrigued scholars. Recently it has been established, however, that though the method of building goes way back, none of the *bories* you see today is older than the 1600s. Elsewhere they are usually shepherds'

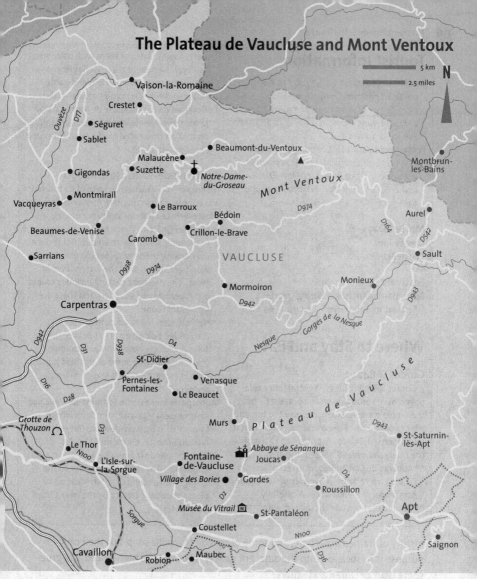

The Plateau de Vaucluse and Mont Ventoux

5 km
2.5 miles

N

Vaison-la-Romaine

Crestet

Séguret

Sablet

Malaucène
Suzette
Notre-Dame-du-Groseau

Beaumont-du-Ventoux

Montbrun-les-Bains

Gigondas

Mont Ventoux

D974

Aurel

Vacqueyras
Montmirail

Le Barroux
Bédoin
Crillon-le-Brave

Beaumes-de-Venise
Caromb

VAUCLUSE

Sault

Sarrians

Mormoiron

Monieux

Carpentras

D942

Gorges de la Nesque

D943

Nesque

D938
D974

St-Didier

D4

Venasque

Pernes-les-Fontaines
Le Beaucet

Plateau de Vaucluse

D943

St-Saturnin-lès-Apt

Grotte de Thouzon

Murs

Le Thor

Abbaye de Sénanque

L'Isle-sur-la-Sorgue

Fontaine-de-Vaucluse
Joucas

Village des Bories
Gordes

Roussillon

Apt

Musée du Vitrail
St-Pantaléon

Coustellet

Saignon

Sorgue

N100

Cavaillon

Robion
Maubec

huts, but these are believed to have been a refuge for the villagers in times of plague. This group of 12 *bories* has been restored as a rural museum. You'll see other *bories* all around Gordes; some have been restored as holiday homes, and one has even become an expensive restaurant. Determined *borie*-hunters should also tour the large concentrations in the countryside around Bonnieux, Apt, Buoux, St-Saturnin-lès-Apt and Saumane-de-Vaucluse, north of Fontaine-de-Vaucluse.

South of Gordes, there is a beautiful, simple Romanesque church in the hamlet of **St-Pantaléon**. To the west of that, watch out for the well-publicized **Musée du Vitrail** (stained glass) and **Musée du Moulin des Bouillons** (*both t 04 90 72 22 11; open April–Oct Wed–Mon 10–12 and 2–5; adm*), where another little Vasarély has set up shop near the oldest intact olive oil press in France. There are indeed exhibits on the

Tourist Information

Gordes: Le Château, t 04 90 72 02 75, *www.gordesvillage.com. Open July and Aug Mon–Sat 9–12.30 and 2–6, Sun 10–12.30 and 2–6; Sept–June Mon–Sat 9.30–12.30 and 2–6, Sun 10–12.30 and 2–6.*

Fontaine-de-Vaucluse: Chemin de la Fontaine, t 04 90 20 32 22, *officetourisme.vaucluse@wanadoo.fr. Open June–Sept Mon–Fri 10–1 and 2–6; Oct–May Mon–Fri 9.30–12.30 and 1.30–5.30.*

Market Days

Gordes: Tues.
Coustellet: Sun am.

Festivals

Roussillon: International String Quartet Festival, mid-June–Sept, t 04 90 75 89 60.

Where to Stay and Eat

Gordes ✉ 84220

Gordes is big business – several fancy villa-hotels have sprung up on the outskirts – but the whole scene is expensive, over the top and a bit exploitative of the credulous, who want it and deserve it. The tourist office has a list of the many *chambres d'hôtes* in the area.

**Auberge de Carcarille, southwest of town on D2, t 04 90 72 02 63, *www.auberge-carcarille.com* (*expensive–moderate*). A carefully restored *mas* outside the village, with pretty rooms, some of them with balconies, a swimming pool, and a reasonable restaurant specializing in fish and game. *Closed mid-Nov–Dec except 27 Dec–31 Dec.*

Le Bouquet de Basilic, Route de Murs, t 04 90 72 06 98 (*moderate–cheap*). Fresh, organic, vegetarian-orientated food. *Closed Thurs and Christmas–mid-Jan.*

Fontaine-de-Vaucluse ✉ 84800

Fontaine-de-Vaucluse, in spite of its touristic vocation, is a pleasant place to stay or dine.

Hostellerie Le Château, in former *mairie*, Quartier Château Vieux, t 04 90 20 31 54, (*moderate*). A hotel with an outdoor terrace overlooking the Sorgue (behind glass, so you won't get splashed by the waterwheel in front). The excellent cooking includes *rouget à la tapenade* (red snapper), and there are 5 pleasant rooms.

**Le Parc, near river and centre at Les Bourgades, t 04 90 20 31 57 (*inexpensive*). A simple, pretty hotel with a restaurant (*moderate*) serving some of the best Italian food in Provence. *Closed Nov–mid-Feb; restaurant closed Wed.*

Auberge de Jeunesse de Fontaine-de-Vaucluse, Chemin de la Vignasse, 1 km from village, t 04 90 20 31 65, *www.fuaj.org* (*inexpensive*). A tranquil hostel. *Closed mid-Nov–Feb.*

Philip, Chemin de la Fontaine, t 04 90 20 31 81 (*moderate*). The closest restaurant to the spring, with a menu of mostly fish, and a pleasant outside terrace by the river. *Closed Nov–Easter.*

history of stained glass here, and some others on Marseille soap, but their only purpose is to suck you into the adjacent gallery to look at the high-priced and gruesome work of Duran and others.

Further south still, at **Coustellet**, the **Musée de la Lavande** (*t 04 90 76 91 23; www.museedelalavande.com; open daily summer 10–12 and 2–6, winter 10–12 and 2–5; closed Jan; adm*) reveals all you have ever wanted to know about lavender.

Abbaye de Sénanque

The loveliest of the Cistercian 'Three Sisters' lies 4km north of Gordes on the D177. The church may be almost a double of the one at Thoronet (*see* pp.325–6), but built in the warm golden stone of the Vaucluse and set among lavender fields and oak groves, it makes quite an impression. The Benedictine monks of Ile St-Honorat, who hold the title, returned in 1988; they cultivate honey and lavender in the grounds.

The **church** (*t 04 90 72 05 72; www.senanque.fr; open Feb–Oct Mon–Sat 10–12 and 2–6, Sun 2–6; Nov–Jan Mon–Fri 2–5, Sat and Sun 2–6; adm*), begun about 1160, shows the same early Cistercian seriousness as Thoronet and Silvacane (*see* pp.345–6), and has been changed little over the centuries; even the original altar is present. Most of the monastic buildings have also survived, including a lovely **cloister**, the *chauffoir*, the only heated room, where the monks transcribed books, and a refectory with displays giving a fascinating introduction to Sénanque and the Cistercians.

Fontaine-de-Vaucluse

More than a century ago, explorers found the source of the Nile. They're still looking for the source of the little Vaucluse river called the Sorgue. It's underground; the best spelunkers in France have been combing the region's caves for decades without success, and in 1983 a tiny, specially made submarine probe (the *Sorguonaute*) sent back data from some 820ft below the surface of the **Fontaine-de-Vaucluse**, where the Sorgue makes its daylight debut through a dramatic hole in a cliff in the beautiful valley the Romans called Vallis Clausa – the origin of Vaucluse. A second probe, *Sorguonaute II*, was sent down in 1984, and imploded soon after immersion; finally, in 1985, a device usually used in oil exploration – the *Modexa 350* – plunged to a bed 1,024ft below, though the passages that carry the stream into this remain unexplored.

Medieval legends record St Véran, patron of Cavaillon, dispatching a dragon near the source – a sure sign this was an ancient holy place, given the close connection between underground water and mythological serpents everywhere in Europe. The more prosaic Romans channelled the water into an aqueduct, remains of which can still be seen along the D24 towards Cavaillon. In later times, among those attracted by Provence's greatest natural wonder was Petrarch, who beginning in 1327 spent many seasons in a villa by the river bank writing his *De Vita Solitaria*, until 1353, when a band of brigands sacked the village and frightened him back to Italy.

The Fontaine is still an exquisite place, but the 540 or so residents of the town of Fontaine-de-Vaucluse have not been able to keep the place from being transformed into one of Provence's more garish tourist traps. To reach it, from the car park next to the church you'll have to walk a noisy 2km gauntlet of commerciality, with everything from *frites* stands to a museum of authentic Provençal *santons* and a museum of medieval torture instruments. Incredibly, many of the attractions are worthwhile. There is **Norbert Casteret's Musée de Spéléologie (Ecomusée du Gouffre)** (*t 04 90 20 34 13; open Wed and Sun 10–12 and 2–5; adm*), a 'subterranean world' of underground rarities and informative exhibits overseen by France's best-known cave explorer, and **Vallis Clausa** (*t 04 90 20 34 14; open daily 9–12.30 and 2–6.30*), an art gallery containing a paper mill powered by old wooden wheels in the river that continues to make paper the 15th-century way for art books and stationery.

Most surprising of all, in a sharp modern building, is the **Musée d'Histoire 1939–1945** (*t 04 90 20 24 00; open Wed–Mon 10–12 and 2–6, July and Aug 9–7; Mar, Nov and Dec Sat and Sun 10–12 and 2–6; adm*), a government-sponsored institution that opened in 1990 and recaptures the wartime years vividly with two floors of explanatory displays, vignettes of daily life under the Nazis, newsreels and magazines, weapons and other relics. As at Gordes, Résistance life around Fontaine-de-Vaucluse was no joke; among the exhibits is a tribute to Fontaine's mayor, Robert Garcin, whose aid to the *maquis* earned him a one-way ticket to Buchenwald in 1944.

Finally, there is the spring itself, which is well worth the trouble even if you come off-season. In spring, and occasionally in winter, it pours out at a rate of as much as 200 cubic metres per second, forming a small, intensely green lake under the cliff. From late spring until autumn it is greatly diminished, and often stops overflowing altogether (the water appears slightly further down the cliff); its unpredictability is as much a mystery as its source. It is a beautiful spot; if you're ambitious, it is also the beginning of two excellent hiking trails (the GR6 and GR97) leading up into some of the most scenic parts of the Plateau de Vaucluse. More easily, you can climb up to the ruined 13th-century **château**, once owned by Petrarch's friend Philippe de Cabassole.

Before you leave, have a look at the village church, **Ste-Marie-et-St-Véran**. Begun in 1134, this lovely Romanesque building incorporates Roman and Carolingian fragments, including some bits of floral arabesques and the columns and capitals around the altar. The cornice outside is decorated with winsome rows of human and animal faces. Inside, there is the 6th-century Merovingian tomb of St Véran, and a good painted altarpiece of the Crucifixion, donated in 1654 by the village's *confrérie* of paper-makers. Also on the way out, peek in at the **Musée Pétrarque** (*t 04 90 20 37 20; open April–mid-Oct Wed–Mon 10–12 and 2–6; end Oct 10–12 and 2–5; closed Nov–Mar; adm*), a subdued look at the life and times of the poet during his stay in the town. Note the column, erected in 1804 by the Athenaeum Valclusianum to celebrate the 500th anniversary of his birth.

From Cavaillon to Carpentras

Until the Revolution, the western Vaucluse plains stretching from Cavaillon north to Vaison-la-Romaine were known as the Comtat Venaissin, a county that was a part of the papal dominions in France, though legally separate from Avignon. Saint Louis had stolen the territory from the counts of Toulouse in 1229, as part of the French Crown's share of the booty after the Albigensian crusade, and Philip III passed it along to the popes in 1274 to settle an old dispute. It was a worthy prize – medieval irrigation schemes had already made the rich lands of the Comtat the 'Garden of France', an honorific it still holds today as the most productive agricultural region in the country. Besides Cavaillon's famous melons, this small area has five per cent of all France's vineyards, including its best table grapes, and still finds room to grow tonnes of cherries, asparagus, apples and more. All this intensive agriculture doesn't do the scenery any harm, and passing through it you'll find some fat, contented villages that make the trip worthwhile.

L'Isle-sur-la-Sorgue and Le Thor

The Sorgue, that singular river that jumps out of the ground at Fontaine-de-Vaucluse and makes fly fishermen happy all the way to the suburbs of Avignon (it's one of

France's best trout streams), has one more trick to play before it reaches the Rhône. At L'Isle-sur-la-Sorgue, it briefly splits into two channels to make this Provençal Venice, a charming town of more than 17,000 souls – an island indeed. In the Middle Ages, as a scrappy semi-independent *commune*, L'Isle-sur-la-Sorgue dug two more channels and put the water to work running mills and textile factories; when trouble came, as during the Wars of Religion, the town knew how to keep out invaders by flooding the surrounding plains and making itself even more of an island.

Today, L'Isle-sur-la-Sorgue still makes fabrics and carpets, but it is best known as the antiques centre of Provence, with a number of permanent shops on the southern edge of town, around Avenue des Quatre-Otages, and a big 'antiques village' by the train station, open on Sundays (*some booths also open Sat and Mon*). Circumnavigating the town is a pleasant diversion; you pass a number of old canals and wooden mills, some still in use, and houses with little front terraces built over the

Tourist Information

L'Isle-sur-la-Sorgue: Place de la Liberté, t 04 90 38 04 78, *www.ot-islesurlasorgue.fr*. *Open Mon–Sat 8–12.30 and 2.30–6, Sun 9–12.30*.
Le Thor: Place du 8-Mai-et-11-Novembre, t 04 90 33 92 31, *www.oti-delasorgue.fr*. *Open Jan–Oct and Dec Tues–Fri 10–12 and 2–6, Sat 10–12, Mon 2–6; closed Sun and Nov.*.
Pernes-les-Fontaines: Place Gabriel Moutte, t 04 90 61 31 04, *www.ville-pernes-les-fontaines. fr*. *Open July and Aug Mon–Sat 9–12 and 2–7, Sun 9–12; April–June and Sept Mon–Sat 9–12 and 2–6; Oct–Mar 9–12 and 2–5*.

Market Days

L'Isle-sur-la-Sorgue: Thurs and Sun; antiques market Sun.
Le Thor: Sat and Wed am.
Pernes-les-Fontaines: Sat am.

Where to Stay and Eat

L'Isle-sur-la-Sorgue ✉ 84800

L'Isle-sur-la-Sorgue can be a delightful place for a stay when not ravaged by tour buses.
***Mas de Cure Bourse, 120 Chemin Serre, Route de Caumont, Velorgues, 2km south of town on D938, t 04 90 38 16 58 (*expensive–moderate*). A restored 18th-century inn, with a swimming pool, extensive gardens, 13 rooms and a restaurant where the *poêlé de faisan mariné '1000 choux'* (marinated pheasant) is a treat. *Restaurant closed first 3 weeks in Nov and 2 weeks in Jan, and Mon and Tues lunch*.

**La Gueulardière, 1 Av Jean Charmasson, t 04 90 38 10 52 (*inexpensive*). Cosy rooms and a garden terrace for dining (*moderate*); specialities include *gâteau d'aubergines aux foies de volaille* (aubergine cake with duck, chicken and goose liver). *Closed 1 month in winter (call ahead); restaurant closed Tues lunch and Wed in winter*.
Le Vivier de la Sorgue, Cours Fernande Peyre, Rte de Carpentras, t 04 90 38 52 80 (*moderate*). Tasty fish dishes served on a lovely terrace over the river. *Closed Sun and Mon*.
Le Carré d'Herbes, 13 Av des Quatre-Otages, t 04 90 38 62 95 (*moderate*). Provençal specialities with an exotic touch. *Closed Tues eve and Wed*.

Pernes-les-Fontaines ✉ 84210

***L'Hermitage, Route de Carpentras, t 04 90 66 51 41, *http://hotel-lhermitage.com* (*moderate*). A quiet hotel with a pool.
**Prato Plage, Route de Carpentras, t 04 90 61 31 75 (*inexpensive*). A 20-room hotel with a restaurant (*cheap*).
Le Palépoli, Route de Carpentras, t 04 90 61 34 00 (*moderate*). Some of the best Italian food in Provence; try the *spaghetti alle vongole*, carpaccio and tiramisu. *Closed Sat lunch*.

Venasque ✉ 84210

Auberge de la Fontaine, Place de la Fontaine, t 04 90 66 02 96, *www.auberge-lafontaine. com* (*expensive*). Five luxury suites and the best food in the village (*expensive–moderate*). Cookery lessons are available. *Closed mid-Nov–mid-Dec; restaurant closed Wed*.

rushing water. There are two mills along Rue Jean Théophile, a street that will also take you to the 18th-century **Hôtel-Dieu** (hospital), with a sumptuous chapel and a perfectly preserved pharmacy of that era that can be visited (*ask at tourist office*), an ensemble of Moustiers faïence and ornate carved wood.

There are frequent art exhibitions in an 18th-century palace, the **Musée Donadei Campredon** (*20 Rue Dr Tallet, t 04 90 38 17 41; adm*), and right in the centre is the town's beached whale of a church, 17th-century **Notre-Dame-des-Anges** (*open Tues–Sat 10–12 and 3–6*), sprawling across Place de l'Eglise. Even in a region full of marvellously awful churches, this one is a jewel – a mouldering imitation of Roman Baroque outside and gilt everything within. Opposite the façade, note the old firm of Fauques-Beyret, the prettiest drapery shop in Provence, with a fine Art Nouveau front; inside and out, nothing seems to have changed since about 1900.

To the west of L'Isle-sur-la-Sorgue, the N100 leads to **Le Thor**, which boasts one of the best Romanesque churches in the whole of Provence, carrying the intriguing name of **Notre-Dame-du-Lac**. Begun about 1200, it is a work of transition that bears witness to the giving way of the Provençal-Romanesque to Gothic influences, as can be seen in the pointed vaulting of the nave. The sculptural decoration is spare but elegant, emphasizing the perfect symmetry of one of the last great medieval buildings in this region.

Some 3km north of Le Thor on the D16 are the **Grottes de Thouzon** (*t 04 90 33 93 65; www.grottes-de-thouzon.com; open April–June, Sept and Oct daily 10–12 and 2–6; July and Aug daily 9.30–7; Nov–Mar Sun and bank hols 2–6; by guided tour only, in French; adm*). Of all the caves in Provence, this may be the one most worth seeing – weird and colourful, with rare needle-slender stalactites hanging down as much as 10ft.

Pernes-les-Fontaines

L'Isle-sur-la-Sorgue's tiny neighbour to the north, Pernes-les-Fontaines, has only a single drowsy stream passing through it, the Nesque. In the 18th century, perhaps out of jealousy, the Pernois took it into their heads to build decorative fountains instead. They got a bit carried away and now there are 50 of them, or one for every 190 inhabitants. The fountains contribute a lot to making Pernes one of the most delightful towns in the Vaucluse. It is an introspective place, still turning its back on the world, sheltering inside a circuit of walls that was demolished 100 years ago, to be replaced by a ring of boulevards. Pernes is for walking; the Pernois have used the centuries to make their town an integrated work of art, looking exactly the way they want it to look, and there's a surprise around every corner.

Starting from the centre, the old **bridge** over the Nesque is embellished at both ends, with the 16th-century Porte de Notre-Dame, the Cormorant fountain and the small chapel of Notre-Dame-des-Grâces, from the same era. Behind it, the 12th-century church of **Notre-Dame-de-Nazareth** includes some Gothic chapels and reliefs of Old Testament scenes. The relative simplicity of its interior, in contrast with so many other Provençal churches, is a reminder of Pernes' earnest Catholicism through the centuries (one of its current economic mainstays, incidentally, is making the communion hosts for all the churches of France). Note the **Tour de l'Horloge**, once the keep of the castle of the counts of Toulouse, now crowned with a pussycat weather vane (*you can climb up daily Mar–Sept 9–6.30, Oct–Feb 10–5*). Ask at the tourist office for a guide to take you around to the **Tour Ferrande**, on Rue Gambetta. This unassuming medieval tower, next to a fountain with carved grotesques, contains some of the oldest frescoes in France (*c*. 1275), with vigorous, primitive scriptural scenes, Charles of Anjou in Sicily, St Sebastian and St Christopher, and one Count William of Orange battling against a giant.

East of Pernes-les-Fontaines is a very odd place, **Le Beaucet** (on the D39 south of St-Didier), where the people used to live in cave-houses, some of which can still be seen, along with a ruined castle. Above it, in the mountains, a spring similar to Fontaine-de-Vaucluse has given rise to one of the biggest pilgrimage sites in Provence, a well-decorated chapel dedicated to the 12th-century **St-Gens**, who was a rain-maker and a tamer of wolves.

Venasque, further east, was the old capital of the Comtat Venaissin, and gave the county its name. Though a pretty village, and lately fashionable, nothing is left of its former distinction but the usual ruined fortifications and a venerable baptistry (really a 6th-century Merovingian funeral chapel reworked in the 12th century).

The D4, connecting Carpentras and Apt, was the main road of the Vaucluse in medieval times; it is still a lovely route, passing southeast from Venasque through the **Forêt de Venasque** and some rocky gorges on the edge of the Plateau de Vaucluse.

Carpentras

The average French town of 30,000 or so, unless it has some great historical importance or major monument, is likely to be a rather anonymous place. Carpentras isn't. Perhaps because of its long isolation from the rest of France, under papal rule but really run by its own bishops, Carpentras has character and a subtle but distinct sense of place. Despite recent attempts at urban renewal in the old town, it is still a bit unkempt and is an interesting place to visit. There are some cockeyed monuments, and some surprises. The rest of Provence pays Carpentras little mind; ask anyone, and they'll probably remember only that the town is famous for caramels, mint-flavoured ones called *berlingots*.

As in many other French towns, you'll have to cross a sort of motorway to get to the centre: a ring road of boulevards was created when the town walls were knocked down in the 19th century (it's one way and very fast – miss a turn and you have to go round again).

One part of the fortifications remains, the towering 14th-century **Porte d'Orange**, built in the 1360s under Pope Innocent IV. When you get in, you'll find an amiable and lively town, especially when the gorgeous produce of the Comtat farmers rolls in for the Friday market. The stands fill half the town, but the centre is Rue des Halles, with the **Passage Boyer**, an imposing glass-roofed arcade built by Carpentras' unemployed in the national public works programme begun after the 1848 revolution.

Getting There and Around

Carpentras is the node for what little there is of **coach** transport in the northern Vaucluse, with good connections to Avignon (some by way of Pernes-les-Fontaines and L'Isle-sur-la-Sorgue) and Orange, one every day to Marseille, and one or two a day to Vaison-la-Romaine and some of the villages of the Dentelles de Montmirail, including Beaumes-de-Venise and Gigondas. Almost all buses stop at Place Aristide Briand on the ring boulevard. There are also several daily SNCF **trains** to Orange and Avignon.

Tourist Information

Carpentras: 1 Place Aristide Briand, **t** 04 90 63 00 78, *www.tourisme.fr/carpentras. Open July and Aug Mon–Sat 9–1 and 2–7, Sun 9.30–1; Sept–June Mon–Sat 9.30–12.30 and 2–6.*

Market Days

Carpentras: Fri am (including truffles during the season, Nov–Mar).

Where to Stay and Eat

Carpentras ✉ 84200

Carpentras is left out of the annual tourist visitations, and accommodation here is limited.

★★Le Fiacre, 153 Rue Vigne, **t** 04 90 60 49 73, *www.hotel-du-fiacre.com (moderate).* An elegant old hotel in an 18th-century building. The room on the top floor offers a clear view of Mont Ventoux. Some rooms are *expensive,* some *inexpensive.*

★Hôtel du Théâtre, 7 Av Albin Durand, **t** 04 90 63 02 90 *(inexpensive).* The budget choice, situated on the ring boulevard. *Closed Christmas and New Year.*

Le Vert Galant, Rue de Clapies, **t** 04 90 67 15 50 *(expensive–moderate).* Innovative regional cuisine. *Closed Sat and Mon lunch, Sun eve.*

Le Marijo, 73 Rue Raspail, **t** 04 90 60 42 65 *(moderate).* Traditional Provençal food. *Closed Jan, Sun in winter, and Sun lunch and Tues lunch in summer.*

Chez Serge, 9 Rue Cottier, **t** 04 90 63 21 24 *(moderate).* A stylish restaurant in the centre, with a rooftop terrace. Wood-fired pizzas are the speciality. *Closed Sun.*

Cathédrale St-Siffrein

Open Tues–Sat 10–12 and 2–6.

Undoubtedly, this is one of the most absurd cathedrals in Christendom. It's had so many architects, in so many periods, and no one has ever been able to get it finished and get it right. Worst of all is the mongrel façade – Baroque on the bottom, a bit of Gothic and who knows what else above – like a likeable mutt who follows you home and you end up keeping. Begun in the 15th century, it saw remodellings and restorations in fits and starts until 1902. Some of the original intentions can be seen in the fine Flamboyant-Gothic portal on the southern side, called the **Porte Juive** because Jewish converts were taken through it, in suitably humiliating ceremonies, to be baptized. Just above the centre of the arch is Carpentras' famous curio, the small sculpted *Boule aux Rats* – a globe covered with rats. The usual explanation is that this has something to do with the Jews, or heretics. But bigotry was never really fashionable among 15th-century artists, and more likely this is a joke on an old fanciful etymology of the town's name: *carpet ras,* or 'the rat nibbles'.

The interior, richly decorated in dubious taste, includes some stained glass of the 16th century (much restored) and an early 15th-century golden triptych (left of the high altar) by the school of Enguerrand Quarton – an island of calm among so much busyness. The sacred treasures are in a chapel on the left: the relics of St Siffrein, one of the most obscure of all saints, not even mentioned in any early hagiographies; and the *Saint-Mors*, the 'holy bridle bit', said to have been made by St Helen out of two nails of the Cross as a present for her son, the Emperor Constantine.

Next to the cathedral, the **Palais de Justice** (1640) is the former archbishops' palace, occupying the site of an earlier palace, which, for the brief periods that popes such as Innocent IV chose to stay in Carpentras, was the centre of the Christian world. The present building, modelled after the Palazzo Farnese in Rome, contains interesting frescoes from the 17th and 18th centuries, including mythological scenes, and also views of Comtat villages and towns (ask the concierge to show you around).

The Triumphal Arch and the Secret Cathedral

Everyone knows that if you walk around a church widdershins (against the sun or counterclockwise), you'll end up in fairyland, like Childe Harolde. Try it in Carpentras, and you'll find some strange business. The 28ft Roman **triumphal arch**, which is tucked away in a corner between the cathedral and the Palais de Justice, was built about the same time as that of Orange, in the early 1st century AD. Anyone who hasn't seen Orange's would hardly guess this one was Roman. Of all the ancient Provençal monuments, this shows the bizarre Celtic quality of Gallo-Roman art at its most stylized extreme, with its reliefs of enchained captives and trophies. In the 14th century, the arch was incorporated into the now-lost episcopal palace. By 1640, when it was cleared, it was serving an inglorious role separating the archbishop's kitchens from his prisons. Originally, it must have connected the palace with the earlier Romanesque cathedral.

Now, look at the clumsily built exterior wall of the present cathedral, opposite. There are two large gaps, through which you can have a peek at something that few books mention, and that even the Carpentrassiens seem to have forgotten: the **crossing and cupola** of the 12th-century cathedral, used in the rebuilt church to support a bell-tower (later demolished) and neglected for centuries. In its time this must have been one of the greatest buildings of Provence, done in an ambitious, classicizing style – perhaps too ambitious, as its partial collapse in 1399 necessitated the rebuilding. The sculpted decoration, vine and acanthus-leaf patterns, along with winged creatures and scriptural scenes, is excellent work; some of it has moved to the town museum.

The Synagogue and Museums

Behind the cathedral and palace, two streets north up Rue Barret, is the broad Place de l'Hôtel-de-Ville, marking the site of Carpentras' Jewish ghetto. Before the Revolution, more than 2,000 Jews were forced to live here in unspeakable conditions, walled in and obliged to pay a fee any time they wanted to leave. A small population remains, one that is only just recovering from the trauma of some brutish desecration by four neo-Nazis in the local Jewish cemetery in 1990. The crime stirred up passions, rumours and bitterness on a national scale until March 1997, when some local skinheads finally confessed, and apologized in court. All that remains of the old ghetto is the **synagogue** at the end of the square (*t 04 90 63 39 97; open Mon–Thurs 10–12 and 3–5, Fri and hols 10–12 and 3–4*). Constructed in 1741, it has a glorious decorated interior in the best 18th-century secular taste.

Other attractions in town include the **Hôtel-Dieu** on Place Aristide Briand (*t 04 90 63 00 78; open Mon, Wed and Thurs 9–11.30*), an 18th-century hospital with a well-preserved pharmacy and an attractive chapel containing the tomb of Carpentras' famous bishop and civic benefactor, Monseigneur d'Inguimbert (1735–73). This hospital is his monument, along with the important library he left to the town and the beginning of the collections in the **Musée Comtadin-Duplessis** on the ring road (*Bd Albin Durand, t 04 90 63 04 92; open Wed–Mon April–Sept 10–12 and 2–7, Oct–Mar 10–12 and 2–4; adm*). Here are displayed artefacts and clutter from Carpentras' history, old views of the town, and 16th- and 17th-century paintings, many by local artists.

Between Carpentras and Mont Ventoux: The Gorges de la Nesque

Heading north for Mont Ventoux and Vaison-la-Romaine, you might consider a slight detour to the east, along the D974. Towards the village of **Bédoin**, a small resort below Mont Ventoux famous for its enormous forest, you will pass Carpentras' **aqueduct** – not Roman but a 17th-century work, impressive nevertheless. **Crillon-le-Brave**, just west, was the birthplace of Henri IV's companion-at-arms and has a belvedere with splendid views on to Mont Ventoux. **Caromb**, west of the D974 on the D55, is an attractive village that has kept parts of its medieval fortifications, as well as a surprisingly grand church, Notre-Dame-et-St-Maurice, with a wealth of Renaissance decoration inside.

From here the skyline is dominated by **Le Barroux**, a dramatically perched village built around a 13th-century **château** (*t 04 90 62 35 21; open Sat and Sun April and May 10–7; daily June 2.30–7, July–Sept 10–7, Oct 2–6; adm*) that belonged to the Seigneurs of Baux. Follow the signs in the village up to the lofty Benedictine monastery of Ste-Madeleine, set in a geometrical lavender garden, a fine example of Provençal Romanesque – built in the late 1970s. Come at 9.30am (10 on Sundays) to hear the 50 monks sing Gregorian chant for an uncanny journey straight back to the days when Romanesque was spanking new.

Where to Stay and Eat

Le Barroux ✉ 84330

★★★Hostellerie François Joseph, Chemin des Rabassières, t 04 90 62 52 78, www.hotel-françois-joseph.com (*expensive– moderate*). A hotel situated below the monastery, surrounded by flowerbeds and acres of woods and so quiet that guests awaken to birdsong. There's a swimming pool, a small spa and a restaurant, and the bright rooms are well equipped with TVs and mini-bars; many have kitchenettes too. Bikes are available for hire. *Closed one week at Easter.*

Le Four à Chaux, Route de Malaucène, by crossroads for Caromb, t 04 90 62 40 10 (*moderate*). Refined, traditional dishes. *Closed Mon and Tues, open Tues July and Aug.*

Crillon-le-Brave ✉ 84410

★★★★Hostellerie de Crillon-le-Brave, Place de l'Eglise, t 04 90 65 61 61, www.crillonlebrave.com (*luxury–expensive*). A sumptuous hotel in an old manor house, run by a Canadian infatuated with Provence. The views of Mont Ventoux are complemented by the hotel's guide to walks in the area. *Closed Jan–mid-Mar; restaurant closed lunch Mon–Fri.*

Or take a tour through the centre of the Plateau de Vaucluse, on the D942 almost as far as Sault, then return on the D1. Few ever take it, though those who don't miss the most spectacular scenery the Vaucluse has to offer: the dry, rugged **Gorges de la Nesque**, leading to Sault and the Plateau d'Albion (*see* p.366). **Monieux**, at the eastern end of the Gorges, is a strange and isolated village that seems to have grown out of the rocky cliffs. There are caves and underground streams in the neighbourhood; experiments with dyeing the water have suggested that one of the sources of the Fontaine-de-Vaucluse may be here.

Mont Ventoux and Around

You can pick it out from almost anywhere on the plains around Carpentras, a commanding presence on the northern horizon. Mont Ventoux, a bald, massive humpbacked massif more than 18km across, is the northern boundary stone of Provence, and it has always loomed large in the Provençal consciousness. For the Celts, as for the peoples who came before them, it was a holy place, the Home of the Winds; excavations at its summit in the early 20th century brought to light hundreds of small terracotta trumpets, a sort of *ex voto* that has never been completely explained. Winds, in Provence, inevitably suggest the mistral, and as the source of that chilling blast Mont Ventoux has always had a somewhat evil reputation among the people; medieval Christians sought to exorcize it, perhaps, with the string of simple chapels that mark its slopes.

Mountain climbers will find a special interest in Mont Ventoux, if only because the sport was invented here. Petrarch, that admirably modern soul, went up with his brother in 1336 – this, according to historian Jacob Burckhardt, was the first recorded instance of anyone doing such an odd thing simply for pleasure. The experience had an unexpected effect on the poet. Reading a passage from his *Confessions of St Augustine* at the summit, he was seized with a vision of the folly of his past life and resolved to return to Italy: '...and men go forth, and admire lofty mountains and broad seas, and roaring torrents, and the course of the stars, and forget their own selves in doing so.' For us the trip will be easier, if perhaps less profound; Edouard Daladier, the Carpentrassien who became French prime minister in the 1930s, had a road built to the top (the D974).

Malaucène and the Fountain of Groseau

The base for visiting the mountain is **Malaucène**, an open, friendly village on the road from Carpentras to Vaison-la-Romaine. Piled under a little conical nib of a hill, its landmark is the enormous church-cum-fortress of St-Michel-et-St-Pierre, built in 1309 by Pope Clement V. From here, the D153 was the ancient route around Mont Ventoux, passing a pair of medieval chapels and a ruined defence tower around the village of **Beaumont-du-Ventoux.** Nowadays, the ancient route peters out into a hiking trail, the GR4.

Wine: Côtes-du-Ventoux

The vineyards of this little-known AOC region are situated on the lower slopes of Mont Ventoux. The area is known principally for its reds, which are similar in style to the Côtes-du-Rhone AOC. The best estates, such as the **Domaine des Anges**, make wines with a high proportion of Syrah in the blend, giving them depth and structure.

A 15th-century glassworks, **Domaine de la Verrière**, at Goult, t 04 90 72 20 88, has been transformed into another of the area's best sources of wine. M. Maubert produces a wine of unusual concentration, full of broad, spicy flavours that complement the local dishes perfectly. The Perrin brothers, famous for producing one of the finest and most sought-after Châteauneuf-du-Pape wines at Château de Beaucastel, also make a very fine Côtes-du-Ventoux at their purpose-built winery on the outskirts of Orange, **La Vieille Ferme, t** 04 90 34 25 64.

The D974, into the heart of the massif, passes a pre-Celtic site dedicated not to wind, but water. **Notre-Dame-du-Groseau**, an unusual 11th-century octagonal chapel, marks the spot today. Originally, this was part of a large monastery, now completely disappeared. Pope Clement V used it as his summer home, and his escutcheon can be seen painted inside (the *curé* at Malaucène has the key). But this was also a holy spot in remotest antiquity; the iron cross outside the chapel is planted on a stone believed to have been a Celtic altar. *Groseau* comes from *Groselos*, a Celtic god of springs; the object of veneration is a short distance up the road, the **Source du Groseau**, pouring out of a cliff face. The Romans, as at Fontaine-de-Vaucluse, channelled the spring into an aqueduct, here for the city of Vaison-la-Romaine; fragments of this can still be seen.

Further up the mountain, the almost permanent winds make themselves known and vegetation becomes more scarce (despite big reforestation programmes). The D974's big day comes, almost every summer, when the Tour de France puffs over it, in probably the most tortuous part of the race; it was here that the English World Champion Tommy Simpson collapsed and died in 1967, and there is a memorial to him 1km from the summit. The top of Ventoux (6,200ft) is a gravelly wasteland, embellished with communications towers and a meteorological observatory. Coming down the eastern side of the mountain takes you into one of the least-visited backwaters of Provence, a land of shepherds, boar and *cèpes*.

There are a few attractive villages: **Sault**, a UNESCO World Heritage site on its outcrop, surrounded by bucolic landscapes, forests and lavender fields, with a quirky **Musée Municipal (t** 04 90 64 02 30; *open July and Aug Mon–Sat 3–6; call for other dates or group visits*) of fossils, village curios and archaeology (even a mummy); and, further north, two medieval *villages perchés*, **Aurel** and **Montbrun-les-Bains**. To the south of Sault, the lonely **Plateau d'Albion** takes its name (like the English Albion, the Alps and the Provençal village of Aups) from an ancient Indo-European root meaning 'white' – from the odd limestone mountains around it, that seem to be covered in snow. The landscape can be a bit eerie – even more so when you consider

Tourist Information

Malaucène: Place de la Mairie, t 04 90 65 22 59.
*Open summer only, Mon–Sat 9.30–12.15 and
3–6, Sun 9.30–12.30.*
Sault: Av de la Promenade, t 04 90 64 01 21,
*www.saultenprovence.com. Open July and
Aug Mon–Sat 8.30–1 and 2–7, Sun 9–1;
April–June and Sept Mon–Sat 9–12 and 2–6,
Sun 9.30–12.30; Jan–Mar Mon–Sat 9–12 and
2–6; Oct–Dec Mon–Sat 9–12 and 2–5.*

Market Days

Malaucène: Wed.
Sault: Wed.

Where to Stay and Eat

Malaucène ✉ 84340

Malaucène makes a good base for visiting
Mont Ventoux and the Dentelles de Montmirail.
Hostellerie La Chevalerie, Place de l'Eglise,
Les Remparts, t 04 90 65 11 19 (*moderate*).
A peaceful and comfortable option by
St-Michel-et-St-Pierre. The restaurant has a
charming terrace. *Closed Wed and Tues eve
out of season.*
**L'Origan, Cour des Isnards, t 04 90 65 27 08
(*inexpensive*). A clean, shipshape hotel in the
centre, with a restaurant (*moderate*) serving
dishes such as guinea fowl with morels.
Closed Mon and Nov–mid-Mar.

La Maison, Hameau de Piolon, outside
Beaumont-du-Ventoux, t 04 90 65 15 50,
(*moderate–inexpensive*). The best cooking in
the area. There's only one menu but it has a
wide selection of dishes, many with a touch
of the southwest; try the *pintadeau en
croûte* (guinea hen in pastry). *Closed Mon
and Tues and Nov–Mar; July and Aug eves
and Sun lunch only.*

Sault and Aurel ✉ 84390

***Hostellerie du Val de Sault, Route St-Trinit,
Sault, t 04 90 64 01 41, *http://valdesault.com*
(*expensive*). A handsome hotel 2,494ft up
and facing Mont Ventoux, with 11 rooms and
5 suites surrounded by trees and gardens;
equipped with a pool, a gym, a *terrain de
pétanque*, a lavender spa and a good restaurant (*expensive–moderate*) specializing in
truffles in season. Half-board in summer.
Closed Nov–Mar and Mon–Fri lunch in winter.
***Domaine des Tilleuls, Route du Mont
Ventoux, t 04 90 65 22 31, *www.domaine
destilleuls.com* (*moderate*). A new hotel with
spacious, sparsely decorated rooms and a
large garden with a swimming pool.
Private parking is available. Great option
for families.
*Relais du Mont Ventoux, Aurel, t 04 90 64
00 62 (*inexpensive*). A reasonably priced inn
with plain, comfortable rooms and a restaurant (*moderate*) with no surprises but some
good vegetarian choices. *Closed Nov–Feb.*

that much of this territory, around the village of St-Christol, has been taken over for a
complex of bases where France keeps most of its nuclear missiles.

Les Dentelles de Montmirail

Montmirail's 'lace' is a small crown of dolomitic limestone mountains opposite
Mont Ventoux on the other side of Malaucène. Eroded by the wind into a lace-like
fantasy of thick columns and spikes, the peaks form an ever-changing pattern as you
circle around them. This is superb walking country, and superb wine country.

Wine and Antiques

The ideal overview of Les Dentelles is along the D90 from Malaucène to Beaumes-
de-Venise, passing by way of **Suzette**, a cluster of sun-bleached stone houses and a
bar-pizzeria enjoying a dream-like vision of the mountains at their most fantastical.

Tourist Information

Beaumes-de-Venise: Maison des Dentelles, Place du Marché, t 04 90 62 94 39, *www.provenceweb.fr. Open Mon–Sat 9–12 and 2–6.* There's also an office on Cours Jean Jaurès. *Open same hours.*

Gigondas: Rue du Portail, t 04 90 65 85 46, *www.begond.fr/village/gigondas.html. Open Jan–Mar, Nov and Dec Mon–Sat 10–12 and 2–5; April–June, Sept and Oct daily 10–12.30 and 2.30–6; July and Aug Mon–Sat 10–12.30 and 2.30–6.30, Sun 10–1.*

Market Days

Beaumes-de-Venise: Tues.

Where to Stay and Eat

Beaumes-de-Venise ✉ 84190

Auberge St-Roch, Av Jules Ferry, t 04 90 65 08 21 (*moderate*). A quiet, old-fashioned inn with a modest restaurant serving seafood and local dishes. *Closed Dec; restaurant closed Tues–Thurs in winter.*

Vacqueyras ✉ 84190

★★★Hôtel Montmirail, Châteaux des Eaux, t 04 90 65 84 01, *www.hotelmontmirail.com* (*moderate*). A secluded hotel, once part of the spa (*see* opposite), with a pool, garden and restaurant. *Closed mid-Oct–mid-Mar.*

★★Le Pradet, Route de Vaison, t 04 90 65 81 00, (*moderate*). A quiet new complex on the edge of the village.

★Hôtel-Restaurant Les Dentelles, t 04 90 65 86 21 (*inexpensive*). Seven comfortable modern rooms and so-so food.

Gigondas ✉ 84190

★★Les Florets, Route des Dentelles, 2km from town, t 04 90 65 85 01, *www.hotel-lesflorets.com* (*expensive–moderate*). Simple, rustic

rooms and a pleasant restaurant, offering plenty of peace and quiet in the middle of a vineyard. Half-board obligatory in summer. *Closed Jan–mid-Mar. Restaurant closed Wed, and Mon eve and Tues in winter.*

L'Oustalet, Place du Portail, t 04 90 65 85 30, (*expensive*). A good restaurant set in a neoclassical building; the beef in wine comes recommended. *Closed Sun and Mon exc Sun lunch in Jan.*

Violès ✉ 84150

Le Mas de Bouvau, Route de Cairanne, t 04 90 70 94 08 (*inexpensive*). A charming family-run hotel-restaurant among the vines, serving specialities from southeast France such as duck *confit, magret, foie gras,* pigeon and rabbit (*moderate*). *Closed Sun eve, Mon and mid-Dec–Jan.*

La Farigoule, Le Plan de Dieu, t 04 90 70 91 78 (*inexpensive*). A pleasant old farmhouse offering bed and breakfast and bike hire. *Closed Nov–Mar.*

Séguret ✉ 84110

★★★Domaine de Cabasse, on D23 towards Sablet, t 04 90 46 91 12, *www.domaine-de-cabasse.fr* (*expensive*). A hotel forming part of a Côtes-du-Rhône estate, with 14 comfortable rooms with terraces, a swimming pool and an excellent restaurant where you can enjoy truffle-based dishes during the season and an array of other rather extravagant dishes year-round. *Closed Nov–Mar.*

La Table du Comtat, t 04 90 46 91 49 (*expensive*). A good restaurant in the heart of the village, well known for its refined cuisine, which includes *julienne de truffe en coque d'œuf. Closed Oct–June, Tues eve and Wed.*

Le Mesclun, Rue des Poternes, t 04 90 46 93 43 (*moderate*). Simple local fare. *Closed Mon and Sun eve.*

If you're in no hurry, steep semi-paved roads from Suzette plunge into the heart of the mountains for more of the same, towards Séguret to the west, or north to **Crestet**, a half-restored *village perché* with a castle, more fabulous views and an art centre.

The D90 takes you into Côtes-du-Rhône country (*see* p.370), beginning with **Beaumes-de-Venise,** the metropolis of Les Dentelles, where worthies sit on the wall sunning themselves like fat cats. There's a ruined castle and a small archaeological museum. Don't expect any canals: 'Beaumes' comes from the Provençal word for cave, and the Venise from a corruption of Comtat Venaissin – the papal county.

North along the D7, the Romanesque chapel of **Notre-Dame-d'Aubune** overlooks the Comtat plain, its lofty bell-tower decorated with classical pilasters. A track leads up the *Côte Balméenne*, where terraces were settled by the Celto-Ligurians, Greeks, Romans and Saracens. Since the archaeologists had their way with it in the 1980s, the terraces have been replanted with olive, almond and fruit trees.

Vacqueyras, a dusty little crossroads devoted entirely to wine, has a by-road (the D233) up to Montmirail, a spa once famous for its purgative waters. It was sold off after the Second World War: a Greek shipping tycoon now owns the grand Victorian villa, while the rest of the spa is now a hotel (*see* opposite). A few kilometres north of Vacqueyras, **Gigondas**, like so many wine villages in the south, is much smaller than its fame: small and sweet, it overlooks the immaculate vineyards and is full of shops allowing you to *déguster* the eponymous red nectar. The château on top of the village has been turned into a modest outdoor sculpture garden.

The tourist offices sell maps of the paths through Les Dentelles: the GR4 passes nearby, and steep white roads lead back to Beaumes-de-Venise or to the Col du Cayron and **Lafare** for more lovely Dentelles scenery.

Sablet, north of Gigondas, is another pretty, hard-working wine village packed on a hill, with old covered lanes to explore. Most of the passing tourists home in on **Séguret**, built on a terrace over the vine-striped Ouvèze plain. It bears the burden of being 'One of the Most Beautiful Villages in France' with a fair amount of grace: there's no room for cars, and none for more than a handful of artists and *santonniers*. Note the funny weathered faces on the 14th-century Fontaine des Mascarons. Séguret is a good base for hiking; there are two trails (GR4 and GR7) and one village track that passes through a gap in the Dentelles to the eastern side. The back road to Vaison-la-Romaine is steep but beautiful.

Vaison-la-Romaine

Vaison, in all its 2,400 years, has never been able to make up its mind which side of the river Ouvèze it wanted to be on. Locals have always been wary of the river's mighty potential for destruction, and the town's peregrinations from bank to bank have left behind a host of monuments, including extensive Roman ruins. Such circumspection was proved justified in 1992 when, on the night of 22 September, the Ouvèze burst its banks and swept away houses, caravans, bridges and roads, drowning 30 people in one of the worst French floods of the century. The town's riverside is still being rebuilt, and the scars of the tragedy are yet to heal.

Yet, as the tourist office proclaims, the best way to support Vaison is to visit. The Roman ruins were untouched, and life goes on: Vaison is a pleasant and beautiful place, and despite the summer crowds, if you're interested in the Romans or the Middle Ages it's a mandatory stop. The Vaison festival draws large crowds in July and August, when theatre groups, choirs and musicians from around the world perform.

Wine: Côtes-du-Rhône Sud

Wines called Côtes-du-Rhône originate in 263 *communes* within the 200km between Vienne and Avignon. Because of the diversity of growing conditions in such a vast area, from hot rocky plains to steep green slopes, the district is a crazy-quilt of local varieties. You may find any mix of 13 varieties of grapes in a bottle of southern Côtes-du-Rhône, but the dominant forces are grenache, which gives it tannin and its famous sturdy quality, cinsault, which counterbalances with its delicacy and finesse, and syrah, which contributes fragrance and ability to age.

The star of the Dentelles is Gigondas, its very name derived from 'joy', or Jocunditas, a holiday camp for Roman soldiers. Part of their delight, according to Pliny, was in the wine, one of the most subtle, noble, dark and fragrant of all Côtes-du-Rhônes, the perfect match for pheasant, partridge, wild rabbit or truffles. If you are looking for red wines to keep, consider the Signature and Pavillon de Beaumirail labels, aged in oak barrels at the **Cave des Vignerons de Gigondas**, t 04 90 65 86 27, responsible for 20 per cent of the total Gigondas production.

As usual, for the finest wines one has to go to the individual estates, where the best wine-makers can concentrate on producing small quantities of wine from the very best vineyard sites. Jean-Marc Autran, the young superstar of Gigondas, makes elegant Gigondas and rich Sablet at the **Domaine de Piaugier**, Sablet, t 04 90 46 96 49. The **Domaine Les Pallières**, in Gigondas, t 04 90 65 85 07, is currently run by the Brunier family. The **Domaine Les Goubert**, t 04 90 65 86 38, also in Gigondas, offers the dense Cuvée Florence and, more unusual for the Dentelles, a Sablet Blanc – a fine white wine from ancient clairette vines.

Vacqueyras, the minute region just to the south of Gigondas, produces sober and full-bodied wines; some of the finest used to be made by a Provençal-speaking Pole named Jocelyn Chudzikiewicz at the **Domaine des Amouriers**, Les Garrigues, Sarrians, t 04 90 65 83 22. Chudzikiewicz died tragically aged 46 in 1997 in a motorbike accident; the estate is run on behalf of his heirs by Patrick Gras. Try the **Château de Montmirail**, in Vacqueyras, t 04 90 65 85 12, a long-established family vineyard that also does a delightfully mellow Gigondas.

The small *appellation* of Beaumes-de-Venise produces good reds, but is rightly famous for its rich sweet white wine made from the muscat grape. The wine is made by partially fermenting very ripe grapes and arresting the fermentation by the addition of alcohol, which kills off the yeasts, leaving much of the sugar and giving the wine an extra potency. The locals find the rather eccentric British habit of treating it as a dessert wine highly amusing: they drink it as an apéritif. The local co-operative makes a very good example.

The two leading estates are **Domaine de Durban**, which is owned by M. Leydier, t 04 90 62 94 26, and the Perrin brothers of **La Vieille Ferme**, t 04 90 34 25 64, on the outskirts of Orange. The Côtes du Rhône region experienced a very difficult 2002 vintage following the floods that devastated the area. Fortunately, 1998–2001 produced a string of good-to-great vintages, so there is no shortage of good wine from this area on the market.

History

Vaison-la-Romaine began on the heights south of the Ouvèze as a Celtic *oppidum*. During the late 2nd century BC, the Romans took control of it and refounded it as Vasio Vocontiorum, a typical colony on the gentler slopes to the north of the river. For an out-of-the-way site, Vasio prospered spectacularly for the following five centuries, an *urbs opulentissima* with a large number of wealthy villas and as many inhabitants as it has today.

Vaison survived the age of invasions better than many of its neighbours; church councils were held here in the 6th century, a time when the city could afford to begin its imposing cathedral. In the coming centuries, bishops ruled in Vaison as the city slowly declined. In perhaps the 8th century, the counts of Toulouse acquired the site of the old Celtic *oppidum* and built a castle on it. While they carried on a chronic quarrel with the bishops, most of the people were abandoning the Roman town for the freedom and safety of the heights, the beginnings of what is now the Haute-Ville. In the 14th century, Vaison fell into the hands of the Pope, along with the rest of the Comtat Venaissin, and did not become part of France until the Revolution.

In the 19th century, on the move once more, the Vaisonnais were abandoning the Haute-Ville for the riverbank. In 1840 the first excavations were undertaken in the Roman city. Yet Vaison had to wait for a local abbot, Chanoine Sautel, to do the job seriously. He dug from 1907 until 1955, financed mostly by a local businessman.

Tourist Information

Vaison-la-Romaine: Place du Chanoine Sautel, **t** 04 90 36 02 11, *www.vaison-la-romaine.com*. Open mid-July–mid-Aug daily 9–1 and 2–6.45; mid-Aug–mid-Oct and mid-April–mid-July Mon–Sat 9–12 and 2–5.45, Sun 9–12; mid-Oct–mid-April Mon–Sat 9–12 and 2–5.45.

Market Days

Vaison-la-Romaine: Tues, in the lower town; farmers' market Tues, Thurs, Sat in summer.

Where to Stay and Eat

Vaison-la-Romaine ✉ 84110

Vaison has plenty of accommodation to go around, and in the crowded summer months you might end up here even if you would have preferred to be in one of the villages of Les Dentelles.

La Bastide de Vaison, Quartier les Auries, west of town on D977, **t 04 90 36 03 15, *www.hotel-labastide.fr.st* (*moderate–inexpensive*). A modernized farmhouse with a pool. *Closed mid-Nov–Mar, and Sun out of season.*

***Le Beffroi, Rue de l'Evêché, Cité Médiévale, **t** 04 90 36 04 71, *www.le-beffroi.com* (*expensive–moderate*). A hotel situated in a picturesque 16th-century house, representing a real bargain for its category. *Closed mid-Jan–mid-Mar.*

La Fête en Provence, Place du Vieux-Marché, **t** 04 90 36 36 43, *www.la-fete-en-provence.com* (*expensive–moderate*). A nicely secluded hotel with a restaurant that serves its own *foie gras de canard*. *Closed mid-Nov–mid-Mar.*

Le Brin d'Olivier, 4 Rue du Ventoux, **t** 04 90 28 74 79 (*moderate*). An intimate, romantic hotel that was opened by a young couple in 1995, with just 3 rooms and a pretty inner courtyard. The restaurant (*expensive–moderate*) offers fresh and imaginative Provençal cuisine in which fresh herbs hold pride of place. *Closed Wed and Thurs, and Sat lunch out of season.*

Le Burrhus, 1 Place Montfort, **t 04 90 36 00 11, *www.burrhus.com* (*moderate–inexpensive*). A gorgeous hotel with minimalist but comfortable rooms with Art Deco touches and air-con, and a shady terrace. It also hosts exhibitions. *Closed mid-Dec–mid-Jan.*

The Ruins

Open Mar–May daily 10–12.30 and 2–6; Feb and Oct 10–12.30 and 2–5.30;
June–Sept daily 9.30–6.15; Nov–Feb Wed–Mon 10–12 and 2–4.30;
Site Puymin open July and Aug 9.30–6.45; same adm for both, also
includes cathedral cloister.

The canon uncovered almost 11 hectares of Roman Vaison's foundations, while the modern town grew up around the digs. There are two separate areas, the **Quartier de la Villasse** and the **Site Puymin**; their entrances are on either side of the central Place du Chanoine Sautel, by the tourist information pavilion.

Vaison's ruins are an argument for leaving the archaeologists alone; with everything sanitized and tidy, interspersed with gardens and playgrounds, there is the unmistakable air of an archaeological theme park. The Villasse is the smaller of the two areas; from the entrance, a Roman street takes you past the city's **baths** (the best parts are still hidden under Vaison's post office) and the **Maison au Buste d'Argent**, a truly posh villa with two *atria* and some mosaic floors. It has its own baths, as does the adjacent **Maison au Dauphin**; beyond this is a short stretch of a **colonnaded street**, a status embellishment in the most prosperous Roman towns.

The Puymin quarter has more of the same: another villa, the **Maison des Messii**, is near the entrance. Beyond that, however, is an *insula*, or block of flats for the common folk, as well as a large, partially excavated quadrangle called the **Portique de Pompée**, an enclosed public garden with statuary that was probably attached to a temple. On the opposite side of the *insula* is a largely ruined *nymphaeum*, or monumental fountain. From here you can walk uphill to the **theatre**, restored and used for concerts in the summer, and the **museum**, displaying the best finds from the excavations. You'll learn more about Roman Vaison here than from the bare foundations around it; there is a model of one of the villas as it may have looked. All the items a Roman museum ought to have are present: restored mosaics and fragments of wall paintings, some lead pipes, inscriptions, hairpins and bracelets, and of course statuary: municipal notables of Vaison, a wonderful monster *acroterion* (roof ornament) from a mausoleum, and a few marble gods and emperors – including a startling family portrait with the emperor Hadrian completely naked and evidently proud of it, next to his demurely clothed empress Sabina, smiling wanly.

The Cathedral of Notre-Dame-de-Nazareth

The French, with their incurable adoration of anything Roman, neglect Vaison's real attraction, one of the most fascinating medieval monuments of the Midi. A treasure house of oddities, it is a reminder that there is more to the art and religion of the Middle Ages than meets the eye, and much of significance that is lost to us forever. It stands half a kilometre west of the ruins, on Avenue Jules Ferry.

The church was begun in the 6th century. Its **apse** is the oldest part; looking at it from the outside, you'll see where excavations have uncovered the dressed Roman stones and drums of columns that were recycled to serve as a foundation. The rest of the structure dates from a rebuilding that began in the 12th century, including some handsome sculptural decoration around the portals, cornices and bell-tower. The first clues to the mystery of this church can be seen near the top of the façade: a rectangular **maze**, and a triangular figure that may be a mystic representation of the Sun. Even with this, the exterior is subdued, and the muscular perfection of the columns and vaults inside comes as a surprise.

The 12th-century nave is Romanesque at its best, but still the eye is drawn down it to the magnificent, arcaded interior of the apse. There is nothing like this apse in France; it is a place to muse on time and fate – the last surviving work of Roman Provence, the wistful farewell of a civilization that can be heard across the centuries. Almost incredibly, the 6th-century marble **altar** is still present, carved in a beautiful wave-like pattern. Also here are the original bishop's throne, and benches set around the semicircle of the apse where the monks would sit: the earliest form of a choir, as in the churches of Ravenna.

In the medieval nave, some of the decoration is as provocative as that on the façade. At the rear, near a column that survives from the original basilica, you'll notice the figure of an unidentifiable 'hairy person', extending a hand in a gesture of benediction. Elaborate masons' marks are everywhere. Odd figures of the Evangelists embellish the squinches of the fine octagonal cupola; behind one of them, high up, on the second column on the right side of the nave, is what appears to be a little devil. You'll meet his big brother in the cloister.

Look around as you enter the cloister. Grinning over the ticket-booth to the cloister is Vaison's most famous citizen – Old Nick himself, with horns and goatee, carved into the stone as large as life. This is not a personage one usually sees portrayed in cathedral cloisters, and no one has ever come up with an explanation for his presence here – one unlikely guess is that it's really Jesus, superimposed over a crescent moon. This is a small but graceful cloister from the 12th century, with finely carved capitals and architectural fragments displayed around the walls.

And if you think the Devil and all the other curiosities were simply fanciful decoration, look up from the cloister at the Latin verse inscription, running the entire length of the church's southern cornice:

I exhort you, brothers, to triumph over the party of Aquilon [the north],
faithfully maintaining the rule of the cloister, for thus will you arrive at
the south, in order that the divine triple fire shall not neglect to illuminate
the quadrangular abode in such a way as to bring to life the arched
stones, to the number of two times six. Peace to this house.

The medieval Latin is in parts obscure enough for other interpretations to be possible, but these tend to be even stranger. The 12 stones seem to be pillars of the cloister, the 'quadrangular abode'. The rest is lost in arcane, erudite medieval mysticism, wrapped up with the architecture and unique embellishments, and undoubtedly with a monastic community that was up to something not entirely orthodox. Like most medieval secrets, this one will never be completely understood.

Chapelle St-Quenin

A bit of a climb to the north, on Avenue de St-Quenin, you can continue in this same vein of medieval peculiarity. St-Quenin, a chapel dedicated to a 6th-century bishop who became Vaison's patron saint, fooled people for centuries into thinking it a Roman building. Its apse, unique in France, is triangular instead of the usual semicircle, and crowned with a cornice that includes fragments from Roman buildings as well as primitive reliefs that may date from Merovingian times. It is difficult to ascribe any special significance to this odd form. Probably constructed in the 11th or 12th centuries, it may be simply an architectural experiment, typical of the creative freedom of the early Romanesque. On the front of the chapel is a Merovingian-era relief of two vine shoots emerging from a vase – a piece of early Christian symbolism that has become the symbol of Vaison.

The Haute-Ville

From Roman and modern Vaison, the medieval version of the town is a splendid sight atop its cliff, a honey-coloured skyline of stone houses under the castle of the counts of Toulouse. Almost abandoned at the turn of the last century, the Haute-Ville is becoming quite chic now, with restorations everywhere and more than a few artists' studios. You reach it by crossing the Ouvèze on a **Roman bridge**, still in good nick after 18 centuries of service (although it had to be repaired after the last floods; note the plaque, in Latin), then climb up to the gate of the 14th-century fortifications, next to the **Tour Beffroi**, the clock tower that is the most prominent sight of the Haute-Ville's silhouette. The cobbled streets and the shady **Place du Vieux-Marché**, with its fountain, are lovely; trails lead higher up to the 12th–14th-century **castle**, half ruined but offering a view.

Down the Rhône 1:
Orange to Beaucaire

13

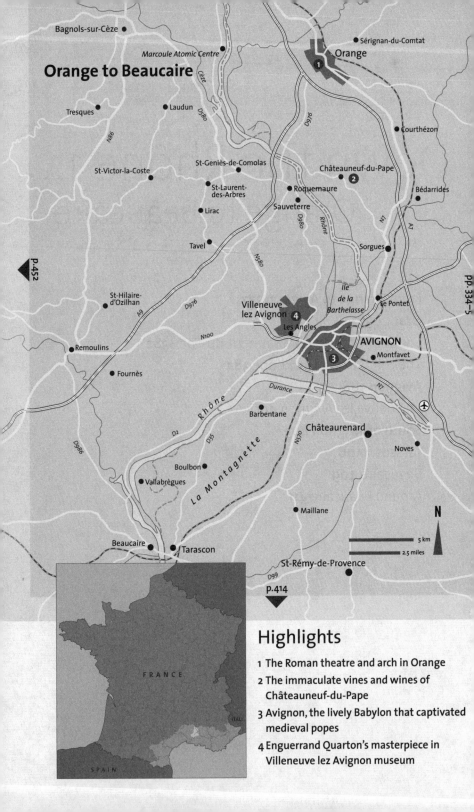

Orange to Beaucaire

Bagnols-sur-Cèze

Marcoule Atomic Centre

Orange

Sérignan-du-Comtat

Courthézon

Tresques

Laudun

St-Geniès-de-Comolas

Châteauneuf-du-Pape

Bédarrides

St-Victor-la-Coste

St-Laurent-des-Arbres

Roquemaure

Sauveterre

Lirac

Sorgues

Tavel

St-Hilaire-d'Ozilhan

Villeneuve lez Avignon

Ile de la Barthelasse

Le Pontet

Les Angles

AVIGNON

Remoulins

Montfavet

Fournès

Rhône

Durance

Barbentane

Châteaurenard

Noves

La Montagnette

Boulbon

Vallabrègues

Maillane

Beaucaire

Tarascon

St-Rémy-de-Provence

N

5 km

2.5 miles

p.414

FRANCE

SPAIN

ITALY

Highlights

1 The Roman theatre and arch in Orange

2 The immaculate vines and wines of Châteauneuf-du-Pape

3 Avignon, the lively Babylon that captivated medieval popes

4 Enguerrand Quarton's masterpiece in Villeneuve lez Avignon museum

p.452

pp.334-5

Despite Frédéric Mistral's best efforts in the epic 1896 *Poème du Rhône*, this is not a lyrical river, neither fair of face nor full of grace. Its nickname *malabar*, the strongman, describes it well: deep and swift-flowing with muscular currents, banks like bulging biceps, and secret depths hosting legendary man-eating monsters such as the Tarasque and Drac. For the Rhône is a Saturday's child and has to work for a living: after serving the industries and nuclear plants to the north, it does it all again in Provence, at France's biggest centre for the processing of nuclear waste, Marcoule, at the hydroelectric plant and satanic mills of Avignon's industrial quarter, and at the paper mills near Tarascon.

Historically, most of the Rhône's traffic has come south with the current, ferrying the blond barbarians, the eaters of *frites* and drinkers of beer, down to the sultry Mediterranean. The river also divided the spoils: Provence, situated on the east bank, owed allegiance to the emperor and pope; Languedoc, on the west, belonged to the kingdom of France after the Albigensian Crusade. Rhône boatmen called the banks, not port and starboard, but Empire and Kingdom. On the empire's side are Orange, with its famous Roman theatre; Châteauneuf-du-Pape and Avignon, where 14th-century popes spent what Petrarch called their 'Babylonian exile'; and Tarascon, favoured home of Provence's Bon Roi ('Good King') René.

From Orange to Avignon

Orange

There seems to have been a settlement of some kind around the hill of St-Eutrope in prehistoric times, and the city's chronicles date from 35 BC, giving it enough time for all imaginable Oranges to have come and gone.

The present incarnation must be one of the sadder ones – this is a miasmic provincial town with a few cosy corners among the prevailing drabness. Fate, or the lack of a bypass road, has made its streets a kind of Le Mans for heavy lorries, fouling the air, menacing pedestrians and coating the old houses with a sooty film. Nevertheless, there are two ancient monuments unmatched in France, and some surprises besides. You'll probably like it best on a Sunday, when the law bans trucks from the road.

History

Rome took good care of its soldiers; keeping its word by them was one secret of the Empire's success. Nine years after Julius Caesar's death, many veterans of the Second Gallic Legion were ready for their promised retirement. The pattern was already set. Rome would establish a colony for them in the lands that they had conquered, often replacing a native village they had destroyed; the veterans farmed their allocated lands, and could look forward to real wealth in their declining years as the colony grew into a town. The colony that became Orange was called Colonia Julia Secundanorum Arausio. Exceedingly prosperous throughout Roman times, it survived the Visigothic conquest in 412; it was the site of two Church councils in the following decades. The chronicles are largely blank from then until the mid-12th century, when the city's feudal lord was Raimbaut d'Orange, troubadour and patron of troubadours. Even then, history was on the back burner; the city and its hinterlands were often put in hock to pay Raimbaut's debts, while he presided over the most brilliant of Provençal courts. He died in 1173, at the age of only 29, and Orange passed to the counts of Baux.

In the 14th century it was a thriving place, with a municipal charter and even a university. In 1530 the city became the property of the German house of Nassau, just in time for the Reformation and the most unusual page of the city's history, an odd chance that would let Orange lend its colour to the Dutch, the Northern Irish, the Orange Free State and Orange, New Jersey. The Nassaus declared for Protestantism, and Orange rapidly became the dissenters' chief stronghold in Provence, a home for thousands of refugees and a thorn in the side of arch-Catholic Avignon, just to the south. Soon after, William of Nassau – William of Orange – became the first *stadhouder* of the United Provinces and led the fight for Dutch independence. Orange held fast through all the troubles of the Wars of Religion, and came out of it a Dutch possession, giving its name to the Netherlands' present-day royal family.

Maurice of Nassau, in the early 17th century, did Orange a bad turn by destroying most of its ancient ruins, using their stone for the new wall he was building against the French. It didn't keep them out for long. In 1672, during one of his wars against the Dutch, Louis XIV seized the city and demolished its wall and castle.

Getting There and Around

The **train** station (**t** 04 90 11 88 03) on Avenue Frédéric Mistral has direct links with Paris, Avignon, Arles, Marseille, Nice and Cannes.

Buses depart from Cours Portoules, **t** 04 90 34 15 59, several times a day for Carpentras, Vaison-la-Romaine, Avignon and Séguret.

Bike Hire

Cycles Dupont, 23 Av Frédéric Mistral, **t** 04 90 34 15 60.

Picca, 544 Av de Verdun, **t** 04 90 51 69 53.

Tourist Information

Orange: 5 Cours Aristide Briand, **t** 04 90 34 70 88, *www.provence-orange.com. Open April–June and Sept Mon–Sat 9.30–7; July and Aug Mon–Sat 9.30–7, Sun 10–4; Oct–Mar Mon–Sat 10–1 and 2–5.* There's another office opposite the Théâtre Antique. *Open April–June and Sept Mon–Sat 10–12.30 and 2.30–6.*

Market Days

Orange: Thurs am, Cours Aristide Briand. In summer, Sat am, Place de la République.

Where to Stay and Eat

Orange ✉ **84100**

***Arène**, Place de Langes, **t** 04 90 11 40 40, (*moderate*). A pleasant option on a quiet square. *Closed Nov.*

Le Glacier, 46 Cours Aristide Briand, **t** 04 90 34 02 01, *www.avignon-et-provence. com/hotelglacier* (*moderate–inexpensive*). A typical *logis* establishment, with friendly hosts and private parking. Some rooms have air-conditioning. *Closed end Dec.*

St-Jean, 7 Cours Pourtoules, **t** 04 90 51 15 16, *www.hotelsaint-jean.com* (*moderate–inexpensive*). A charmingly restored 17th-century *hostellerie* with private parking, just steps from the Roman amphitheatre. *Closed Jan.*

St-Florent, 4 Rue du Mazeau, **t** 04 90 34 18 53, *www.hotelsaintflorent.free.fr* (*inexpensive*). A decent budget choice; all rooms have bath and TV. *Closed Jan and Feb.*

Le Yaca, 24 Place Sylvain, **t** 04 90 34 70 03 (*cheap*). A pretty restaurant with a range of appetizing Mediterranean menus. *Closed Tues eve, Wed and Nov.*

French rule, particularly after the revocation of the Edict of Nantes in 1685 (*see* p.16), was a disaster; Orange, like many other towns in the south, lost many of its best citizens. The city has never really recovered, but it earns a fair living today from industry, and from the army and airforce bases that make it one of the most important military centres in France. Having twice elected a National Front mayor didn't help it either. Although the ultra-right Mayor Bompard claims to have spruced up the town (for which he is known as the 'flowerpot mayor'), he has also cut off all funds to cultural associations for ethnic minorities and banned a selection of left-wing literature from the public library.

Théâtre Antique

t 04 90 51 17 60, www.theatre-antique.com; open daily April, May and Sept 9–7, June–Aug 9–8, Mar and Oct 9–6, Jan, Feb, Nov and Dec 9–5; free audio guides; tours t 04 90 11 02 31; adm; ticket valid for Musée Municipal, p.380.

The architects might be distressed to hear it, but these days the most impressive part of this huge structure is its back wall. 'The best wall in my kingdom,' Louis XIV is said to have called it. If the old prints in the municipal museum are accurate, this rugged, elegant, sandstone cliff facing place des Frères Mounet was originally adorned with low, temple-like façades. In its present state, it resembles a typical Florentine Renaissance palace, minus the windows. The classically minded architects of the 15th century all travelled in Provence, and perhaps this stately relic of Rome at its best had a hidden influence that would have made its architects proud.

Built in the early 1st century AD, the theatre is a testimony to the culture and wealth of Arausio. Like the Colosseum in Rome, it even had a massive awning (*velum*), a contraption of canvas and beams that could be raised to cover most of the 9,000 spectators. All over the Mediterranean, theatres fell into disuse as part of the cultural degradation of the late Empire. This one was probably already abandoned when it burned down in the 4th or 5th century. In the Middle Ages, other buildings grew up over the ruins; old prints show the semicircular tiers of seats (*cavea*) half-filled in and covered with ramshackle houses.

The site is typical for a Roman theatre, backed into the hill of St-Eutrope, where the banks of seats could be built on the slope. These have been almost completely restored. Since 1869, Orange has used the theatre for a summer festival called *Les Chorégies*. Mistral and the Félibres (*see* pp.38–9) were active in its early years, when Greek and Roman plays were often on the bill; today contemporary drama and opera are more common.

Unlike Greek theatres, which always opened to a grand view behind the stage, those of the Romans featured large stage buildings, serious architectural compositions of columns, arches and sculptured friezes. This is what the great exterior wall is supporting; Orange's stage building (which is 115ft high) is one of two complete specimens that remain to us (the other is at Aspendos in southwestern Turkey), although the fragments of its decoration are mostly in the municipal museum across the street. A statue of Augustus remains, in the centre, over an inscription honouring the people of Arausio and welcoming them to the show. Outside the theatre, the foundations of a temple have been excavated, along with a semicircular ruin that may have been a nymphaeum or a gymnasium.

Musée Municipal

t 04 90 51 17 60; same hours as Théâtre Antique, see p.379; ticket also valid for Théâtre Antique.

Make sure you save some time for this bulging curiosity shop, situated directly opposite the theatre on Place des Frères Mounet; it is one of the most fascinating town museums in Provence. As expected, the main rooms are given over to Roman art, including an exceptional frieze of satyrs and Amazons from the theatre. The *plan cadastral* (land survey) is unique: a stone tablet engraved with property records for the broad Roman grid of farmland between Orange and Montélimar. The first pieces of it were discovered in 1856, though no one guessed what they were until the rest turned up, between 1927 and 1954; since then they have been a great aid to scholars in filling in some of the everyday details of Roman life and law.

Climbing the stairs into the upper levels of the museum, you'll pass rooms of Dutch portraits and relics of Nassau rule, and a collection of works by the Welsh Impressionist Frank Brangwyn (who was, in fact, born in Bruges): heroic compositions among wharves and factories, along with some lovely country scenes. The most unexpected exhibit is the **Salle des Wetter**, a remarkable relic of the Industrial Revolution in France. The Wetters were a family of mid 18th-century industrialists who produced *indiennes*, printed cotton cloth much in demand at the time. They commissioned an artist named G. M. Rossett to paint a record of their business; this he did (1764) in incredible detail, on five huge, colourful, naïve canvases showing every aspect of the making of *indiennes*, from the stevedores unloading the cotton on the docks to the shy, serious factory girls in the great hall – the Wetters were among the first in France to stumble on the factory system, and employed more than 500 people.

Old Orange and the Triumphal Arch

Touring old Orange does not handsomely reward the visitor. You can walk up the hill of **St-Eutrope** for a view over the town and a look at the foundations of the castle destroyed by the French; in the city centre, there is only an utterly pathetic cathedral, begun in 529 over a temple of Diana and rebuilt to death between 1561 and 1809. One thing Orange does have is original street names – sometimes unintentionally hilarious ones, such as Impasse du Parlement.

Rue Victor Hugo, roughly following the route of the ancient Roman main street, leads to Orange's other Roman attraction. The **Arc de Triomphe**, which was built around AD 20, celebrates the conquests of the Second Gallic Legion with outlandish, almost abstract scenes of battling Romans and Celts. This is the epitome of the Provençal-Roman style: excellent, careful reliefs, especially in the upper frieze, portraying a naval battle, though with a touch of Celto-Ligurian strangeness in the details. Odd oval shields are a prominent feature, decorated with heraldic devices and thunderbolts. Seemingly random symbols at the upper left – a whip, a pitcher, something that looks like a bishop's crozier, and others – are in fact symbols of animal sacrifice and marine attributes (the 'crozier' is the prow of a ship). On the sides of the arch are heaps of arms – 'triumphs' – that were to influence the militaristic art fostered by rulers such as Emperor Charles V in the Renaissance. Little more than half a century before this arch was built, Orange was still Rome's wild frontier, and art such as this evokes it vividly. Note the standards the legionaries are carrying: not the Roman eagle, but a boar.

When frontier days returned to Orange, in the Middle Ages, the arch was expanded into a castle by Raymond of Baux – an act typical of that haughty family. It is said that Raymond arranged it so that the battle reliefs would be a wall of his dining hall; we have his arrogance to thank for their relatively good state of preservation. To sample some of the area's more recently created marvels, try the **Palais du Vin**, on RN7 (**t** 04 90 11 50 00, www.lepalaisduvin.com; open Mon–Sat 10–12.30 and 2–7, Sun 9–1), which offers a *vinothèque* (wine library), tastings and a restaurant.

Around Orange: Sérignan-du-Comtat and the 'Virgil of Insects'

Eight kilometres northeast of Orange on the D976, you can pay your respects to the great entomologist, botanist, scientist and poet Jean-Henri Fabre (1823–1915). Born into poverty, the largely self-taught Fabre qualified as a *lycée* teacher of sciences in Avignon, only to be fired in 1870 for explicitly describing the sex life of flowers to a night class of spinsters. Left without means, he borrowed money from his friend John Stuart Mill and settled in Orange for nine years, cranking out books on popular science on the average of one every four months – he was to produce more than 100 in total. He made enough in royalties to pay back his debts and in 1879 to buy an abandoned property in Sérignan that he called **L'Harmas**, the 'fallow land' (**t** 04 90 70 15 61; *closed until 2006*). Fabre walled in the garden and planted 1,000 species of flowers and herbs, letting them run wild to create the perfect environment for his true passion: observing insects. Over the years he wrote 10 volumes of *Souvenirs entomologiques*, works of such beauty that he was twice nominated for the Nobel Prize for Literature. The Japanese, in particular, are huge fans; reissues of Fabre's books in Japan in 1991 sold more than a million copies.

L'Harmas was bought by the state in 1922 (it's part of the Musée National d'Histoire Naturelle, based in Paris), and has been left as it was during Fabre's life: you can see his curious apparatus for observing insects, his collections of fossils, shells, rocks, insects, plants, eggs, coins and bones (including some human bones, chewed on by cannibals – *not* found locally, mind), letters from Darwin, and his harmonium, which he would play to accompany the lullabies and songs he wrote in Provençal. Most extraordinary of all is the display of a selection of his 700 watercolours of the fungi of the Vaucluse, so real that you can hardly believe they are only two-dimensional.

The village has erected a statue to Fabre, magnifying glass in hand, in front of the convex Baroque façade of the parish church, and you can visit his grave in the village cemetery, with its Latin inscriptions, one from Seneca: 'Those who we believe lost have been sent in advance.'

South of Orange: Châteauneuf-du-Pape

Je veux vous chanter, mes amis/Ce vieux Châteauneuf que j'ai mis
Pour vous seuls en bouteille/ Il va faire merveille!

Quand de ce vin nous serons gris /Vénus applaudira nos ris:
Je prends à témoin Lise/La chose est bien permise!

(My friends, I want to sing you/Of this old Châteauneuf that I've bottled just for you/
It will work miracles!/For when this wine makes us tipsy/Venus will crown our mirth/
I take Lise as my witness/No one will mind if I do!)

Pope John XXII's drinking song

Wine: Châteauneuf-du-Pape

An inspiration to both popes and lovers, Châteauneuf-du-Pape's reputation has remained strong through the ages; to safeguard it, in 1923 its growers agreed to the guarantees and controls that formed the basis for France's modern *Appellation d'Origine Contrôlée* (AOC) laws.

Several factors combine to give the wine its unique character: the alluvial red clay and the pebbly soil, brought down by a Rhône glacier in the last ice age; the mistral, which chases away the clouds and haze, allowing the sun to hit the grapes like an X-ray gun; and the wide palette of 13 varieties of grape that each winemaker can choose from: Grenache, Syrah, Cinsault, Mourvedre, Terret Noir, Vaccarese, Counoise and Muscardin for the reds (Grenache can also be white); and Clairette, Bourboulenc, Roussane, Picpoul and Picardan for the whites (Clairette and Picpoul can be red and white), 30 years ago dismissed as mere novelties and today celebrated as some of Provence's top wines – pale blond, with greenish highlights and a fresh, floral bouquet.

Because of the complex blends that give Châteauneuf its voluptuous qualities, the grapes are sorted by hand – uniquely among southern wines. The end result must have the highest alcoholic minimum of any great French wine (12.5%), a level achieved by spacing the vines a good 6–7ft apart to soak up the maximum amount of sun, and from the heat-absorbing pebbles underneath the vines that keep the grapes toasty after dark. Light, soft and fast to mature, a Châteauneuf-du-Pape red can be enjoyed much earlier than its Rhône rivals (often in three years) but only gets better the longer you can bear to wait.

In its home town, the wine is not exactly hard to find; even in the cellars it's not cheap, though, because a good deal of the *cuvées* dating from the late 1980s and early 1990s are superb, if somewhat difficult to get hold of. Contact the tourist office for a copy of a map of the vineyards: perhaps the best-known among the array of excellent wineries that welcome visitors are the **Château La Nerthe, t** 04 90 83 70 11, with its fascinating ancient cellars, and the vaulted cellars of **Château de la Gardine, t** 04 90 83 73 20.

You'll begin to understand why Châteauneuf's wines are so expensive when you pass through the vineyards between Orange and Avignon. Blink, and you'll miss them. This pocket-sized wine region, tucked between the outskirts of Avignon and Orange, has become one of the most prosperous corners of France; every available square inch is covered with vines of a rare beauty, so immaculately precise and luxuriant that they resemble bonsai trees. Such good fortune is not without its disadvantages, however.

Châteauneuf-du-Pape, the very attractive village that gives the wine its name, has not resisted the temptation to become the Midi's foremost oenological tourist trap; along the main street there are few grocers or boutiques but plenty of wine shops, and in places it is hard to see the buildings for the signs advertising other shops or the winemakers' estates in the hinterlands.

In Bédarrides, the vineyards of **Domaine du Vieux Télégraphe**, 3 Route de Châteauneuf, **t** 04 90 33 00 31, occupy a rugged promontory topped by a tower once used for optic telegraphic experiments; the 1993 and 95 reds and whites are excellent buys.

The three finest estates are in a class of their own and have such highly individual styles as to be unmistakable even when they're tasted blind. **Le Clos des Papes**, **t** 04 90 83 70 13, is run by the highly intelligent and innovative Paul Vincent Avril. Avril is alone in employing humidifiers in his cellar to alleviate the drying effects of the mistral wind in particular and the heat in general. As a consequence, his wines have the best-defined fruit of the region and are the most elegant. With age, Avril's Châteauneuf-du-Pape can taste like expensive claret.

The wines of **Château de Beaucastel**, in Courthézon, **t** 04 90 70 41 00, have been consistently among the top wines of the *appellation* – in particular, the superb 1994 red, and a very classy 1991 white.

The most extraordinary source of Châteauneuf-du-Pape and possibly one of the country's most interesting wines is made by Emmanuel Raynaud at **Château Rayas**. His wines are a must for all keen wine lovers: they are the product of a bygone era – wines of incredible concentration and depth with the capacity to age for 20 years or more. Wines such as these are increasingly rare in an age when technology, which has helped to ensure that most wine is well made, also means that too many are sound but mediocre.

Recent vintages fared as follows: 2003 was exceptional, after a long, hot, sunny summer; 2002 was a virtual write-off because of violent storms and huge rainfall, and 2001 was mixed, with some excellent wines available from respected sources (try before you buy) and others lacking acidity or being over-alcoholic.

Going further back, 2000 is a top-class vintage with plenty of fruit, ripe tannins and and overall roundness that makes it easy to drink but also capable of ageing, and 1999 and 1998 were both outstanding vintages. Most 1998 and 1999 wines make very good drinking now, but the top estates and *appellations* have produced wines that can be kept many years. The top Châteauneuf-du-Papes from these two vintages are simply wonderful wines.

Tourist Information

Châteauneuf-du-Pape: Place du Portail, t 04 90 83 71 08, http://perso.wanadoo.fr/ot-chato9-pape. Open July and Aug Mon–Sat 9.30–9, Sun 10–1.30 and 2–6; April–Oct Mon–Sat 9.30–12.30 and 2–6; Nov–Mar Mon, Tues and Thurs–Sat 9.30–12.30 and 2–6.

Market Day

Châteauneuf-du-Pape: Fri am, Av des Bosquets.

Festivals

June and July: Floraisons musicales.
Aug: Fête Médiévale de la Véraison, a local town festival.

Where to Stay and Eat

Châteauneuf-du-Pape ✉ **84230**
****Château des Fines Roches, 2km south of town on D17, t 04 90 83 70 23 (expensive). An imposing and elegant but entirely fake château (19th-century vintage) with gardens, set among the vineyards. The kitchen shines when it comes to seafood dishes and desserts.

***La Sommellerie, on D17 towards Roquemaure, t 04 90 83 50 00, www.hotel-la-sommellerie.com (expensive). A restored 18th-century sheepfold with 12 peaceful rooms and 2 suites overlooking the swimming pool or the vines. The restaurant, presided over by Pierre Paumel, maître cuisinier de France, serves delicately perfumed Provençal dishes. Don't miss his reproductions of Van Gogh's paintings in spun sugar. M. Paumel also runs gourmet workshops. Closed Mon lunch in winter.

La Mère Germaine, 3 Rue du Commandant Lemaître, t 04 90 83 54 37, www.lameregermaine. com (inexpensive). A sweet old hotel-restaurant with a gourmet restaurant (expensive) serving tantalizing dishes such as agneau aïoli and galet de Châteauneuf-du-Pape The adjacent brasserie offers a moderate plat du jour and dessert. Closed Tues eve in winter and Wed and Feb.

Legend has it that one of the first things that Clement V did upon leaving Rome was inspect his vineyards to the north of Avignon. In 1316 his successor John XXII, who was a celebrated imbiber, went one better by building a castle here, which the Avignon popes used as a summer residence – a 14th-century version of Lazio's Castel Gandolfo. Sacked by the Protestants in the Wars of Religion, it was finally blown up by the retreating Germans in 1944; two crenellated walls are all that remain of it. Even if you don't like ruins or crowds, brave the hordes to have a look at the huge plain below you, and the Rhône muscling away on its route south to Avignon; wait till dusk if you can, for a magnificent sunset.

Down on the plain, on the Route d'Avignon, you can taste chocolate if you're bored with wine, at the **Chocolaterie Bernard Castelain** (t 04 90 83 58 90).

The Left Bank of the Rhône

Once you cross the Rhône into the Gard region, the land takes on a more arid and austere profile, its knobby limestone hills and cliffs softened by crowns of silver olives and the green pinstripes of vines, especially in the river-bend north of Villeneuve lez Avignon along the D976. The landmark here is **Roquemaure**, where Pope Clement V died his peculiar death (see p.39) in its now-ruined castle, although it's not his ghost who haunts it, but that of a lovely but leprous queen who was quarantined in the tower. After she died, Rhône boatmen would see her on summer nights, flitting along the bank, dressed in white and sparkling with jewels. Roquemaure's church of St-Jean-Baptiste, opened by Clement V in 1329, has sheltered since 1868 the relics of a certain St Valentine, whom it celebrates with a Festival of Lovers, involving locals in 19th-century costume (Terni, in Umbria, which enshrines the relics of its first bishop San Valentino in a basilica and celebrates his feast day on 14 February, would be surprised to learn this). The church also houses a superb organ of 1680, built for the Cordeliers in Avignon and transferred here in 1800, which still has all of its original pipes.

The D976 continues west past the charming little village of **Tavel**, a place that is just as haunted – in this instance by wine fiends come to slake their thirst on the pale ruby blood of the earth. **Lirac**, situated 2km to the north, is even smaller; a pretty kilometre's walk westwards from the village leads to the **Sainte-Baume**, a cave holy since time immemorial, and in which a statue of the Virgin was discovered in 1647; a hermitage was built on the outside of the cave-chapel.

To the north, little **St-Laurent-des-Arbres** used to be owned by the medieval bishops of Avignon, and has a fortified Romanesque church that was built in 1150, a tower and a castle keep.

Wine: Tavel and Lirac

The sun-soaked, pebbly limestone hills on the left bank of the Rhône are as celebrated for their rosés as Châteauneuf-du-Pape is for its reds and whites. Tavel, which has the longest pedigree, has been beloved of kings since the 13th century, when Philippe le Bel declared: 'It isn't good wine unless it's Tavel.' By the 1930s, the vine stocks – grenache, cinsault, bourboulenc, carignan and red clairette – were so old that Tavel nearly went the way of the dodo. Since revived to the tune of 825 healthy hectares, it has once again been crowned by the French as king of the rosés, the universal, harmonious summer wine that goes with everything from red meat to seafood. Be warned, however, that Tavel may be a little strong to less acclimatized, non-French constitutions.

Some growers add syrah and mourvèdre to give their Tavels extra body and colour, including the two best-known producers in the village, whom you can visit by ringing ahead: the de Bez family at the **Château d'Aquéria, t** 04 66 50 04 56, and the prize-winning **Domaine de la Mordorée, t** 04 66 50 00 75, where the talented Christophe Delorme also bottles a potent red Côtes-du-Rhône, Lirac and Châteauneuf-du-Pape.

The Lirac district begins 3km to the north of Tavel and encompasses four *communes* – Roquemaure, Lirac, St-Laurent-des-Arbres and St-Geniès-de-Comolas. Its pebbly hills are similar to those of Tavel, and the *appellation* differs in the addition of two grape varieties – white ugni and maccabeo – and the fact that everything doesn't come up rosé: Lirac is making a name for its fruity whites, with a fragrance reminiscent of the wildflowers of the nearby *garrigue*, and for its well-structured reds. Both 1998 and 1999 were fine years and can be sampled weekdays by appointment at **Domaine Duseigneur**, St-Laurent-des-Arbres, **t** 04 66 50 02 57, and at **Château St-Roch**, Roquemaure, **t** 04 66 82 82 59.

Where to Stay and Eat

Roquemaure ✉ 30150

***Château de Varenne, Sauveterre, 4km from town, **t** 04 66 82 59 45, *www.chateaudevarenne.com* (*expensive*). An 18th-century building set in a beautiful park with a pool. The restaurant serves seasonal specialities and a good range of seafood, and staff are helpful when it comes to suggesting wines. *Closed Wed out of season plus 2 wks Nov and 2 wks Feb.*

***Château de Cubières, Route d'Avignon, **t** 04 66 82 64 28 (*moderate*). Large gardens, a swimming pool and old-fashioned rooms combine to make for a restful stay in this 18th-century hotel; the annexe has modern, but equally stylish, rooms. The restaurant, **Le Lys d'Or** (*moderate*), serves French classics, *Closed Sun eve, Mon, Feb and Oct.*

Clément V, Rue Pierre Sémard (Route de Nîmes), **t 04 66 82 67 58, *http://hotel.clementv.free.fr* (*inexpensive*). An excellent, moderately priced hotel complete with a swimming pool. *Closed mid-Oct–mid-Mar.*

Tavel ✉ 30126

***Auberge de Tavel, Voie Romaine, **t** 04 66 50 03 41, *www.auberge-de-tavel.com* (*expensive*). Charming, quiet, well-equipped rooms and a good restaurant. *Closed Tues, Wed and Dec–Feb.*

La Louisia, north of town near St-Laurent-des-Arbres, at crossroads on N580, **t** 04 66 50 20 60 (*moderate*). A good place to try *gâteau de rascasse à l'américaine* (scorpion fish). The restaurant next door, **L'Escale**, is run by the same person and serves *bouillabaisse. Closed Sun eve and Mon.*

Avignon

Avignon has known more passions and art and power than any town in Provence, its mixture of excitement whipped to a frenzy by the mistral. But even the master of winds has never caused as much trouble as the papal court, a vortex of mischief that ruled Avignon for centuries, trailing violence, corruption and debauchery in its wake. 'In Paris one quarrels, in Avignon one kills,' wrote Hugo. In Avignon, Petrarch's platonic, courtly love for Laura was an aberration. 'Blood is hot there,' wrote an anonymous author in the 17th century, 'and the most serious occupation in the land is the search for pleasure... even most of the husbands are accommodating in love, and allow their wives the same freedoms they enjoy themselves.'

Avignon still has a twinkle in its eye; it is alive and ebullient, and has been one of France's most innovative cities ever since the Italian Renaissance filtered through here to the rest of Europe. As the cultural and publishing centre of the south, it rocked the cradle of the Félibrige, the Provençal literary movement (*see* pp.38–9), and since the Second World War it has been the stage for Europe's most exciting theatre festival. Charming it is not, yet, as an old Provençal proverb puts it: *Quau se lèvo d'Avignoun, se lèvo de la resoun* – 'He who takes leave of Avignon takes leave of his senses.'

History

Rome, AD 1303. Anarchy reigns, with popular riots, regular visits from foreign armies, and clans waging medieval gang warfare in the streets, transforming the tombs of the Caesars into urban fortresses. The papacy, although in the thick of it all, usually kept the papal person himself in places such as Viterbo and Anagni for safety's sake – just as it had the arrogant intriguer Boniface VIII, who was now fresh in his grave.

Getting There and Around

By Air

Avignon's airport (*www.avignon.aeroport.fr*) 8km southeast of town at Caumont, has Air France (**t** 04 90 81 51 51, **t** 0820 820820) flights from many French and European destinations. Avignon is 20mins by car from Nîmes airport, linked to London Stansted by Ryanair.

By Train

The train station is outside the porte de la République, central bookings **t** 08 36 35 35 35. Avignon is on the Paris–Marseille TGV line, and has frequent links to Arles, Montpellier, Nîmes, Orange, Toulon and Carcassonne.

There are direct trains from London to Avignon on Eurostar July–Sept, taking 6½hrs. **t** 08705 186 186, *www.eurostar.com*.

By Bus

The *gare routière* is also outside the Porte de la République, next to the train station (Avenue Monclar, **t** 04 90 82 07 35). There are plenty of daily buses to Carpentras, Cavaillon, St-Rémy-de-Provence and Orange, Arles, Nîmes, one early-morning run to Nice, Aix-en-Provence and Cannes (plus 5 to Aix), Marseille and Salon-de-Provence, Fontaine-de-Vaucluse, and some services to the Pont du Gard, Uzès, Châteaurenard, Châteauneuf-du-Pape and Tarascon.

For Villeneuve lez Avignon, take city bus 11 from the post office (buy tickets on board).

By Boat

Travellers of yore approached Avignon by boat – a thrill still possible with a **lunch or dinner cruise** with **Les Grands Bateaux de Provence**, based at Allées de l'Oulle, **t** 04 90 85 62 25, *www.avignon-et-provence.com/mireio*; the food is delicious and an afternoon's exploration of Arles is included. From mid-June–mid-Sept, the same firm runs regular **Bateau-Bus** trips between Avignon and Villeneuve lez Avignon. The tourist office has information on other cruise boats. You can also spend a week on the Rhône and Saône on the *Princesse de Provence* (*Mar–Nov*); contact Peter Deilmann, **t** (020) 7436 2931, *www.peter-deilmann-river-cruises.co.uk*.

There is also a free shuttle from the foot of Pont St-Bénezet to the Ile de la Barthelasse, (*daily July and Aug 10–8; Sept 2–6*).

Car aHire

Veo, 51 Av Pierre Sémard, **t** 04 90 87 53 43, **Sixt**, 3 Bd Saint Ruf, **t** 04 90 86 06 61.

There are **free car parks** outside the city walls; Parking de l'Ile Piot has a free shuttle to the town centre.

Bike Hire

Holiday Bikes, 20 Bd St-Roch, **t** 04 32 76 25 88. **Provence Bike**, 52 Bd St-Roch, **t** 04 90 27 92 61. **CM84**, 80 Rue Guillaume Puy, **t** 04 90 86 32 49.

Tourist Information

Avignon: 41 Cours Jean Jaurès, **t** 04 32 74 32 74, *www.avignon-tourisme.com*. *Open April–Oct Mon–Sat 9–6; July Mon–Sat 9–7, Sun 10–5; Nov–Mar Mon–Fri 9–6, Sat 9–5, Sun 10–12.* A helpful office offering guided city tours April–Oct Tues, Thurs, and Sat am.

Post office: Cours Président Kennedy, just inside the Porte de la République, near the train station.

Market Days

Tues–Sun am: covered market, Les Halles, Place Pie.
Sat and Sun: food market in Place Crillon and at Marché des Remparts, Av du 7e Génie;
Sat am: flower market, Place des Carmes.
Sun am: flea market, Place des Carmes.
Sat and Sun am: travelling market at Rempart St-Michel.

Festivals

In 1947 Jean Vilar with his Théâtre National Populaire founded the **Avignon Festival**, with the aim of bringing theatre to the masses. It is now rated among the top international theatre festivals in Europe, and in July and August Avignon overflows with performances by the Théâtre National and others, the cinemas host films from all over the world, and there are concerts in churches.

The **Maison Jean Vilar** (8 Rue de Mons, **t** 04 90 86 59 64, *www.maisonjeanvilar.org*) is the nerve centre and hosts exhibitions, films and lectures the rest of the year (*open Tues–Sat 9–12, 1.30–5.30; 10.30–6.30 during festival; closed Aug*). For festival bookings, contact the **Bureau du Festival d'Avignon**, Espace Saint-Louis, 20 Rue Portail Boquier, 84000 Avignon, t 04 90 27 66 50, *www.festival-avignon.com*.

During the festival, Avignon's squares and streets overflow with fringe (or 'Off') performers. To receive the Off programme, contact Avignon–Public-Off, BP5-75521 Paris Cedex 11, t 01 48 05 01 19, *www.avignon-off.org*.

Otherwise, there seems to be some sort of festivity every month, whether it's the **New Wine Festival** (Nov), **Passion for Horses** (*Cheval Passion*, Jan), contemporary dance (Feb), a **Triathlon** (June) or **fireworks** on 14 July. The monthly broadsheet *Rendez-Vous*, from the tourist office, has exhaustive listings of what's going on.

Shopping

Chic designer shops are found along Rue Saint-Agricol and Rue Joseph Vernet. *Pâtisseries* in this area sell Avignon's gourmand speciality, *papalines*, made of fine chocolate and a liqueur, *d'Origan du Comtat*, distilled from 60 herbs picked from the slopes of Mont Ventoux and said to be a sure cure for cholera. You will find all the regional specialities: *fruits confits d'Apt*, *berlingots de Carpentras*, *melon de Cavaillon*, *nougat de Sault*, *truffe de Carpentras et du Tricastin*, garlic, olives, honey, *pastis*, goat's cheese, *fougasse* (a kind of French focaccia) and *herbes de Provence*.

There are also essential oils, *santons*, bold Provençal fabrics, local pottery and soaps. Behind the Hôtel de Ville, in Place de l'Horloge, the **Maison des Pays de Vaucluse**, t 04 90 80 80 00, has a large display of regional products and crafts.

Where to Stay

Avignon ✉ 84000

Avignon gets packed in July and August and many places raise their rates. There are other choices across the river in Villeneuve lez Avignon (*see* p.401), and a huge number of chain hotels around the suburbs.

The area also has a large number of *gîtes* and rooms in private homes, some on the idyllic Ile de la Barthelasse. For one of these, contact the **CDT Vaucluse**, 21 Rue Collège de la Croix, t 04 90 80 47 00.

★★★★**Hôtel d'Europe**, 12 Place Crillon, t 04 90 14 76 76, *www.heurope.com* (*luxury–expensive*). The oldest hotel in town, built in the 16th century and converted to an inn in the late 18th century. Classically formal, it has Louis XV furnishings. Napoleon stayed here, as did the eloping Robert Browning and Elizabeth Barrett. *Restaurant closed Sun and Mon lunch.*

★★★★**Clarion Cloître Saint-Louis**, 20 Rue Portail Boquier, t 04 90 27 55 55, *www.cloitre-saint-louis.com* (*very expensive–expensive*). A beautiful cloister built in 1589 as part of a Jesuit school of theology, now an island of tranquillity. Rooms have been modernized as befitting its recent chain hotel status; meals are served under the portico or by the rooftop swimming pool.

★★**Hôtel du Palais des Papes**, 3 Place du Palais, t 04 90 86 04 13, *www.hotel-avignon.com* (*expensive–moderate*). The hotel with the best views of the palace.

★★★★**La Ferme Jamet**, Ile de la Barthelasse, t 04 90 86 88 35, *www.avignon-et-provence.com/ferme-jamet* (*expensive–moderate*). A 16th-century farmhouse with rooms ranging in style from traditional Provençal to a Gypsy caravan, set around a tennis court and a swimming pool. *Closed Nov–Easter.*

★★**Hôtel d'Angleterre**, 29 Bd Raspail, t 04 90 86 34 31, *www.hoteldangleterre.fr* (*moderate–inexpensive*). A friendly, simple place. *Closed end Dec–late Jan.*

★**Splendid**, 17 Rue Agricol Perdiguier, t 04 90 86 14 46, *www.avignon-splendid-hotel.com* (*moderate–inexpensive*). A good-value option offering bright and comfortable rooms. *Closed last 2 weeks Nov.*

★★**Saint-Roch**, 9 Rue Paul Mérindol, t 04 90 16 50 00 (*inexpensive*). A quiet hotel with a delightful garden, just outside the walls of Porte St-Roch.

★**Mignon**, 12 Rue Joseph Vernet, t 04 90 82 17 30, *www.hotel-mignon.com* (*inexpensive*).

A bright and charming hotel with small modern rooms. *Closed Dec.*

Ile de la Barthelasse has four **campsites**, one of which, **La Bagatelle**, t 04 90 86 30 39, (*inexpensive*), offers dormitory rooms during the summer months.

Around Avignon

There are 3 exceptional hotel-restaurants within easy driving distance of Avignon.

★★★★**Hostellerie Les Frênes**, 645 Av des Vertes Rives, 84140 Montfavet (5km east of town on N107), t 04 90 31 17 93, *www.lesfrenes. com* (*luxury*). A Relais & Châteaux member with buildings set around a beautiful garden and swimming pool; antiques furnish the rooms. The food (*expensive*) is as marvellous as the setting. *Closed Nov–Mar.*

★★★★**Auberge de Cassagne**, 84130 Le Pontet (5km north of town on N7), t 04 90 31 04 18, *www.hotelprestige-provence.com* (*luxury–expensive*). A plush option with a pool, tennis courts, a sauna and a gym, and access to a golf course. The food and the wine cellar are faultless (*very expensive–expensive*). *Closed Jan.*

★★★**Hostellerie l'Ermitage Meissonnier**, 30 Av de Verdun, 30133 Les Angles (4km west of town on D900), t 04 90 25 41 68, *www. avignon-et-provence.com/meissonnier* (*moderate–inexpensive*). Sixteen rooms, a glorious restaurant (*expensive*) and cookery courses. *Closed first 2 wks Mar; restaurant closed Sun eve and Mon.*

Eating Out

Christian Etienne, 10 Rue de Mons, t 04 90 86 16 50 (*very expensive–expensive*). A very chi-chi but nonetheless popular choice for gourmet Provençal cuisine. *Closed Sun and Mon exc July.*

Hiély-Lucullus, 5 Rue de la République, t 04 90 86 17 07 (*expensive*). Avignon's gourmet bastion for the past 60 years, a resolutely old-fashioned place with a first-floor dining room. The kitchen never disappoints, with dishes such as *tourte* of quail and *foie gras*, and the legendary *cassoulet de moules aux épinards* (mussel stew with spinach). *Closed Tues, Wed, 1 wk Feb and 2 wks Nov.*

Le Petit Bedon, 70 Rue Joseph Vernet, t 04 90 82 33 98 (*expensive–moderate*). An Avignon institution offering well-prepared dishes seldom found elsewhere, such as *lotte au Gigondas*, angler-fish cooked in wine. *Closed Sun and Mon, 2nd and 3rd wks Aug, most of Jan.*

La Fourchette, 17 Rue Racine, t 04 90 85 20 93 (*moderate*). Hiély-Lucullus' less expensive sister restaurant, serving equally good cuisine at prices that won't bust your wallet. *Closed Sat, Sun, 3 wks Aug and last 2 wks Jan.*

Au Bain Marie, 5 Rue Pétramale, t 04 90 85 21 37 (*moderate*). A popular place serving a range of traditional French fare. *Closed Sat lunch, Sun and Mon lunch.*

Entrée des Artistes, 1 Place des Carmes, t 04 90 82 46 90 (*moderate*). A restaurant located in a quiet square, with a menu brimming with traditional Provençal cooking, including *pied de veau*. *Closed Sat and Sun and Aug.*

Woolloomoolloo, 16 bis Rue des Teinturiers, t 04 90 85 28 44 (*cheap*). A popular place with 'world cuisine' and live music. *Closed Mon in winter.*

Entertainment and Nightlife

Outside the Festival

Théâtre du Chêne Noir, 8 bis Rue Sainte-Catherine, t 04 90 86 58 11. One of Provence's most talented theatre companies.

Théâtre des Carmes, 6 Place des Carmes, t 04 90 82 20 47. Avignon's oldest permanent company, performing in the restored Gothic cloister of the Eglise des Carmes.

AJMI, 4 Rue Escalier Sainte-Anne, t 04 90 86 08 61. A jazz club with live music on Thurs.

Bars and Clubs

Pub Z, 58 Rue Bonneterie, t 04 90 85 42 84. A black-and-white striped bar with DJs.

Le Red Zone, 25 Rue Carnot, t 04 90 27 02 44, *www.redzonebar.com*. Bar with music.

Avignon

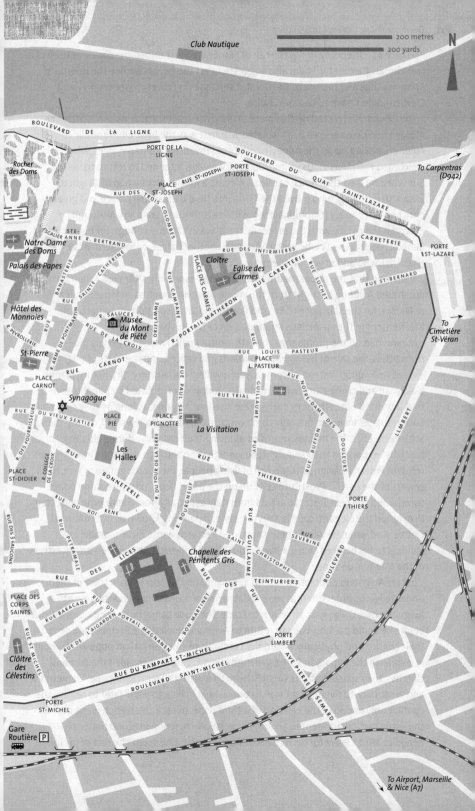

Boniface's arch-enemy, Philip the Fair of France, had just bribed the conclave to elect a Frenchman, Clement V. Philip also suggested that the new pope flee the inferno of Rome for the safer havens of the Comtat Venaissin in Provence (*see* p.358) – and Clement didn't have to be asked twice.

The Church had picked up this piece of Provence real estate as its spoils after the Albigensian Crusade (*see* p.14). Isolated within it was the little city-republic of Avignon, belonging to the Angevin counts of Provence – old papal allies, who welcomed their illustrious visitor. Clement V always intended to return to Rome, but when he died the French cardinals elected a former archbishop of Avignon, John XXII (1316–34), who moved the Curia into his old episcopal palace and greatly enriched the papacy (through alchemy, it was rumoured: *see* p.39). Although he enlarged the palace with the proceeds, it still wasn't roomy enough for his successor, Benedict XII (1334–42), who replaced it with another palace, or for Clement VI (1342–52), who added yet another.

It seemed that the popes meant to stay forever, especially after 1348, when Clement purchased Avignon outright from the young Angevin countess of Provence, Jeanne Ire of Naples, for the sale price of 80,000 florins and an absolution for her possible involvement in the suspicious strangulation of her husband.

Meanwhile, all the profits that the 14th-century papal machine generated – from tithes, the sale of indulgences, pardons and offices, and the visits of pilgrims – went to Avignon instead of Rome. Overcrowding, debauchery, dirt, luxury, plague, blackmail and crime came with the deal – troubles exacerbated by papal tolerance that admitted outcasts from everywhere else into Avignon, as long as they could pay. Such refugees included not only common criminals but also Jews and, during the Schism, heretics. The Italians, mortified at losing their cash cow during this 'Babylonian captivity', expressed their self-righteous indignation through the long-time Avignon resident Petrarch: 'Avignon is the hell of living people, the thoroughfare of vice, the sewers of the earth... Prostitutes swarm on the papal beds.' Yet these same popes summoned the best Trecento artists from Italy, especially from Siena, who perfected in Avignon the elegant, courtly, fairytale style of painting known as International Gothic. And when he wasn't being outraged, Petrarch wrote incomparable love sonnets to his beloved Laura, a mysterious figure believed to have been an ancestress of the Marquis de Sade.

In 1377 Avignon's population rose to approximately 30,000 souls, a third of them under religious orders. In that year, St Catherine of Siena convinced the seventh Avignon pope, Gregory XI, to return to Rome. The pope came, he saw, he sickened, but before he could pack his bags to return to Avignon, he died. The Roman mob seized their chance and physically forced the cardinals to elect an Italian pope who would re-establish the papacy in Rome. When the French cardinals escaped the Romans' clutches, they sparked off the Great Schism by electing a French antipope, Clement VII, and went back to Avignon. A Church council held in Pisa 30 years later to resolve the conflict only ended in the election of a third pope. In 1403 the French went over to the Rome faction and sent in an army to persuade Avignon's second antipope, Benedict XIII, to leave for his native Catalunya – where he spent the rest of his life bitterly raining anathemas and excommunications on all and sundry. When the Church finally decided on one pope, Avignon and the Comtat Venaissin settled in for three and a half centuries of relaxed rule by cardinal legates, under whom the debauchery and violence continued, although on a more modest level. The party really came to an end when the Comtat Venaissin was incorporated into France during the Revolution in a blood rite of atrocities and the destruction of centuries of art and architecture.

But even as part of France, Avignon has maintained its lively international character. Publishers who first set up shop with the popes stayed on under the cardinal legates, beyond the bounds of French censorship (there were 20 in town before the Revolution); in the 1850s they took on a new life publishing the works of the Félibrige. In 1946 actor Jean Vilar founded the Avignon Festival of Theatre and Film, the liveliest and most popular event in the Provençal calendar. The city was also European City of Culture in 2000, and some of its monuments have been listed as UNESCO World Heritage sites. The TGV has made Paris less than 3 hours away, and a summer Eurostar route direct from London brings even more of Europe to its door.

The Famous Half-Bridge

From the north, Avignon is a brave two-tiered sight: in front rise the sheer cliffs of the **Rocher des Doms**, which has been inhabited since Neolithic times, and behind it the sheer artificial cliffs of the Palais des Papes, the same colour as the rock and almost as haphazard a pile. The ensemble includes the **walls** that the popes wrapped around Avignon: bijou, toothsome garden walls ever since Viollet-le-Duc recrenellated them and filled in the moat in 1860. From the walls, four arches of a bridge leapfrog into the Rhône, sidle up to a waterbound, two-storey Romanesque chapel (the lower half of which is dedicated to St Nicolas, the patron of Rhône boatmen) and then stop abruptly mid-river, long before reaching Villeneuve lez Avignon on the distant bank. This is the famous **Pont St-Bénezet**, otherwise known simply as the Pont d'Avignon, begun in 1185 (*t 04 90 27 51 16, www.palais-des-papes.com; open daily, Nov–14 Mar 9.30–5.45; 15 Mar–Oct 9–7; Aug and Sept 9–8; during festival 9–9; adm*). It was built during a time when all bridges were the work of either devils or saints; in this case a shepherd boy named Bénezet, obeying the mandates of heaven, single-handedly laid the huge foundation stones. Originally 22 arches and three-quarters of a kilometre long, the bridge enriched Avignon with its tolls: its presence was a major factor in the popes' decision to live here. In 1660 the Avignonnais got tired of the constant repairs it demanded, however, and abandoned it to the monsters of the Rhône. Now only the four arches remain.

And did they ever '*danse, tout en rond*' on their bridge, as the nursery song would have it? No, they didn't, the historians say, although they may well have danced *under* it on the mid-river **Ile de la Barthelasse**, formerly a hunting reserve and the headquarters for many of Avignon's prostitutes and thieves. It was here that in later years the Avignonnais came for Sunday picnics. The Félibres (*see* pp.38–9) liked to bring pretty 'Félibresses' here to recite poetry. In summer people still come to cool off in its Olympic-size pool.

The Palais des Papes

*t 04 90 27 50 74, www.palais-des-papes.com; open Nov–14 Mar daily
9.30–5.45; 15 Mar–July and Oct daily 9–7; Aug and Sept daily 9–8; during
festival 9–9; adm. Last ticket 1hr before closing. Optional English audioguide.*

For a curious sensation, park directly under the popes' palace and take the lift up to
the traffic-free **Place du Palais**. Once crowded with houses, it was cleared by antipope
Benedict XIII to emphasize the message of the palace's vertical, impregnable walls:
'You would think it was an Asiatic tyrant's citadel rather than the abode of the vicar of
the God of peace,' wrote Mérimée. But the life of a 14th-century pope justified paranoia.
What is less obvious is that the life of a 14th-century pope and his cardinals, courtiers,
mistresses and toadies was also extremely luxurious. The palace was spared in the
Revolution only to end up serving as a prison and a barracks, and until 1920 its bored
residents amused themselves by chipping off frescoes to sell to tourists, so that on
most of the walls the only remaining decoration is an extraordinary variety of
masons' marks. The entrance is up the steps, in the centre of Clement VI's façade.

Old Palace: Ground Floor

After crossing the **Cour d'Honneur**, the great courtyard dividing Benedict XII's stern
Cistercian Palais Vieux (1334–42) from Clement VI's flamboyant Palais Neuf (1342–52),
you start the tour in the **Jesus Hall**, so called for its decorative monograms of Christ.
Once used to house the pope's treasure and account books, it now contains a hoard of
maps, views of old Avignon and curios, such as a pair of 17th-century bell-ringing
figures (*jacquemarts*). The most valuable loot was stored behind walls 10ft thick in
the windowless bowels of the **Angels' Tower**, its ceiling supported by a single stone
pillar resembling an enormous palm tree.

Next is the **Consistory**, where the cardinals met and received ambassadors; as its
lavish frescoes and ceiling burned in 1413, it now displays 19th-century pictures of
Avignon's popes and Simone Martini's *Virgin of Humility* fresco, detached from the
cathedral porch in 1960. Under the fresco, the restorers found Martini's *sinopia*, or
initial line sketch, etched in the stone. As an artist could only paint a small patch of
fresh, wet plaster a day, such *sinopie* were essential to maintain the composition,
and these, as is often the case in Italy, give a clearer idea of the painter's intent than
the damaged fresco itself. There are traces of *sinopie in situ* in the **Chapelle St-Jean**,
dedicated to both Johns, the Baptist and the Evangelist. Matteo Giovannetti of
Viterbo, a trecento charmer who left the bulk of his work in Avignon, did the frescoes
for Clement VI: saints floating overhead in starry blue landscapes (recall that at the
time ultramarine blue paint was even more expensive than gold). On one wall, John's
head is served to Herod at table, as if in a restaurant.

Old Palace: First Floor

The tour continues to the first floor and the banqueting hall, or **Grand Tinel**, hung
with 18th-century Gobelin tapestries. Although big enough for a football pitch, the
Grand Tinel was too small to hold all the cardinal-electors who would gather in a
conclave 10 days after a pope's death. Masons were brought in to accommodate

them: the arches at the far end were knocked down to give the cardinals more room to manoeuvre (in both senses of the word), while the doors and windows were bricked up to keep them from bringing in more food and endlessly prolonging the conclave. The trick always worked, for the appetites of the 14th-century Curia were Pantagruelian – the adjacent **Upper Kitchen** boasts a pyramidal chimney that could easily handle a roast elephant, or the menu of Clement VI's coronation feast: a total of 1,023 sheep, 118 cows, 101 calves, 914 kids, 60 pigs, 10,471 hens, 1,446 geese and 300 pike, topped off by 46,856 cheeses and 50,000 tarts, all consumed by just 3,000 guests – some 16 tarts per person, with a few thousand left over for the pope's midnight snack. Off the Grand Tinel, more delightful frescoes by Matteo Giovannetti decorate the **Chapelle St-Martial**, celebrating the French saint who came from the same Limousin village as Benedict XII.

New Palace

The tour continues from the Grand Tinel to the **Pope's Antechamber**, where he would hold private audiences, and then on to the **Pope's Bedroom** in the Tower of Angels, a room covered with murals of spiralling foliage, birds and birdcages. It leads directly into the New Palace and the most delightful room in the entire palace, the **Chambre du Cerf**, Clement VI's study, where he would come 'to seek the freedom of forgetting he was pope'. In 1343 he had Matteo Giovannetti (probably) lead a group of French painters in depicting outdoor scenes of hunting, fishing and peach-picking that not only quickened the papal gastric juices, but expressed what was then a revolutionary new interest in the natural world, where flowers and foliage were drawn from observation rather than copying a 'source'. The arrows direct you next to the **Sacristy**, crowded with statues of kings, queens and bishops escaped from Gargantua's chessboard, followed by Clement VI's **Great Chapel**, longer even than the Grand Tinel and just as empty, though the altar has been reconstructed. The **Robing Room** off the chapel contains casts of the Avignon popes' tombs. Revolutionaries bashed most of the figures that once adorned the elaborate **Chapel Gate**; through the bay window in front of this, the pope would bless and give indulgences to pilgrims. A grand stair leads down to the flamboyant **Great Audience Hall**, where Matteo Giovannetti's *Prophets* remains intact, along with outline sketches of a Crucifixion that would certainly have been splendid if it had ever been completed.

Around the Palace: Notre-Dame-des-Doms

Before spray paint, the posterity-minded had to record their passing with family emblems. None did it better than the family of the Borghese pope, Paul V; his nephew, legate in Avignon, produced the striking 1619 **Hôtel des Monnaies**, or mint, just across from the Palais des Papes, where reliefs of the Borghese dragon and eagle prance in garlands of fruit salad. To the left of the palace is Avignon's cathedral, **Notre-Dame-des-Doms**, built in 1150, its landmark square bell tower ridiculously dwarfed by a massive gilt statue of the Virgin added in 1859 – an unsuccessful attempt to make the church stand out next to the overwhelming papal pile. The interior has been fuzzily Baroqued like a soft-centre chocolate, but it's worth focusing on the good bits: the dome at the crossing, with an octagonal drum pierced by light, the masterpiece of this typically Provençal conceit; the 11th- or 12th-century marble bishop's chair in the choir; and in a chapel next to the sacristy, now the **Trésor** (*adm*), the flamboyant Tomb of John XXII (d. 1334) by English sculptor Hugh Wilfred, mutilated in the Revolution and restored in the 19th century with a spare effigy of a bishop on top to replace the smashed pope.

Next to the cathedral, ramps lead up to the oasis of the **Rocher des Doms**, which is now a garden enjoying panoramic views from the Rhône below to Mont Ventoux rising to the northeast. Peacocks squawk and preen in trees so crippled by the mistral they need crutches; you can tell the hour with your own shadow on a sundial called the *cadran solaire annalemmatique*, and admire a statue dedicated to an Armenian refugee named Jean Althen who 'introduced the cultivation of madder to the Midi' (don't laugh; used for producing dyes, madder was once the south's most important cash crop).

Musée du Petit Palais

t 04 90 86 44 58; open June–Sept Wed–Mon 10–1 and 2–6; Oct–May Wed–Mon 9.30–1 and 2–6.30; adm.

Overlooking the Rhône at the end of the Place des Papes stands the **Petit Palais**, built in 1318 and modified in 1474 to suit the tastes of Cardinal Legate Giuliano della Rovere – one day to become Michelangelo's patron and nemesis as Pope Julius II. In 1958 the Petit Palais became a museum to hold all the medieval works remaining in Avignon.

Although the scale of the Petit Palais can be daunting, it contains rare treats from the dawn of the Renaissance by artists hailing for the most part from Siena or Florence. But Avignon gets its say as well: the sculptures and pretty courtly frescoes from the 12th to the 14th centuries in the first two rooms demonstrate the city's role in creating and diffusing the late International Gothic style. The third room contains some fascinating fragments of the 35ft, eight-storey **tomb of Cardinal Jean de Lagrange** (1389), which stood in Avignon's temple of St-Martial before the Revolution. One bit that survived was the *transi*, or relief, of the decomposing corpse that occupied the lowest level of the tomb and was carved with morbid anatomical exactitude. Such *memento mori*, always used to contrast the handsome effigy of the deceased while alive, would soon become popular in northern France. The mouldering Cardinal Lagrange is one of the earliest examples, and may even be the prototype of the genre.

The next six rooms glow with the gold backgrounds (the better to show up in dim churches) of 14th- and early 15th-century Italian painting. Nearly all depict the Virgin and Child, a reflection of the cult of Mariolatry and chivalric ideals of womanhood that began where the troubadours left off. Although the subject matter is repetitive, it makes it easy to trace the medieval revolution in art and seeing, back in the good old days when art was content merely to imitate nature and not try to outdo her. The iconic, Byzantine flatness of the earliest paintings (especially Paolo Veneziano's *Virgin* of 1340, which has, remarkably, never been restored in its 660 years) begins to give way to a more natural depiction of space, composition and human form after the innovations of Giotto in Italy (especially Taddeo Gaddi, Pseudo Jacopino di Francesco, Lorenzo Monaco and Gherardo Starnina). Meanwhile, Sienese artists, following the lead of the great Duccio di Buoninsegna, took up a more elegant, stylized line and richer colours (Simone Martini and many works by Taddeo di Bartolo).

The taste of Avignon's popes for Sienese art made the latter the strongest influence in the International Gothic style forged at the papal court (Room 8), a style that the Sienese kept at long after the Florentines had moved on to new things – see Giovanni di Paolo's *Nativity* (1470), or Pietro di Domenico da Montepulciano's kinky *Vierge de Miséricorde* (1420), a delicate portrayal of a congregation sheltered under the Virgin's mantle while a band of flagellants whip themselves. Bridal chests (*cassoni*) were often used to illustrate cautionary tales for women: in Room 9 see Domenico de Michelino's *cassone* panels of 1450 on the story of *Suzanna and the Elders*.

Renaissance Gems, Sacred and Profane

Beyond the *salon de repos* hangs the museum's best-known work, Botticelli's *Virgin and Child*, a tender, lyrical painting from his youth, inspired by his (and Leonardo da Vinci's) master, Verrocchio. The next few rooms offer nothing as striking until Room 15 and its four delightful narrative panels from bridal chests (*c.* 1510) by the Maestro dei Cassoni Campana. This unknown master's meticulous miniaturist style is as rare as the subject of his cautionary tale, *The Minotaur*, beginning with Queen Pasiphae of Crete's love for a white bull, resulting in the birth of the Minotaur. The third panel shows Ariadne and her ball of twine and Theseus slaying the Minotaur in an exquisite circular labyrinth.

The sacred equivalent of the *cassoni* is in Room 16b: the *Sacra Conversazione* by Venetian Vittore Carpaccio, lyrical master of charm, colour and incidental detail. Such 'sacred conversations' portray the Virgin and saints meditating together on matters sublime, to the accompaniment of angelic music. To this, Carpaccio has added a landscape dominated by a natural rock bridge, where episodes from the lives of saints Jerome, Augustine and Paul the Hermit take place.

Lastly, Rooms 17–19 are devoted to works by French artists in Avignon, who after 1440 formed one of the most important schools of French Renaissance art. Influenced by the realism of Flemish oil painting (introduced to Avignon by Benedict XIII) and the almost abstract, decorative lines of the Italians, it concentrates on strong, simple images, as in the altarpiece *Virgin and Child between Two Saints* (1450), by the school's greatest master, Enguerrand Quarton, with a pair of luminous shutters with saints Michael and Catherine on the reverse by Josse Lieferinxe. Or take two works by an accomplished but unknown hand: the striking *Jacob's Dream* and the lyrical *Adoration of the Child* (*c.* 1500), where the well-dressed donor seems to have stumbled unexpectedly on to the divine mystery.

Place de l'Horloge and Quartier des Fusteries

Just below the Place du Palais, an antique carousel spins gaily in the lively centre of old Avignon, **Place de l'Horloge**, site of the old Roman forum, now full of buskers and holiday layabouts. The timepiece of its name is in the 1363 tower of the Hôtel de Ville; this originally belonged to a Benedictine monastery on the site, but was secularized with a clock and two *jacquemarts* who sound the hours. They aren't the only archaic figures here: many first-time visitors do a doubletake when they notice the windows on the east side of the square, filled with *trompe-l'œil* paintings of historic personages who all are linked in some way to the city.

Behind the Hôtel de Ville lies the **Quartier des Fusteries**, named after the wood merchants and carpenters who had their workshops here in the Middle Ages. These were replaced in the 18th century with *hôtels particuliers*: in one, the **Maison aux Ballons** (with little iron balloons on the window sills) at 18 Rue St-Etienne, Joseph de Montgolfier discovered the principle of balloon flight in 1782, when he noticed how his shirt, drying by the fire, puffed up and floated in the hot air. From the Quartier des Fusteries, the steep picturesque lanes of the **Quartier de la Balance** wind back up to the Place du Palais.

Off Place de l'Horloge and Rue St-Agricol, Rue du Collège-du-Roure leads to the fine mid 15th-century **Palais du Roure**, marked by a flamboyant gate topped with intertwining mulberry branches in memory of the Taverne de Mûrier that it replaced. Equally flamboyant was the 19th-century descendant of the Florentine family who built it, the Félibre poet Marquis Baroncelli-Javon, who preferred to spend his time as a cowboy in the Camargue and lent this town house to Mistral as a headquarters for his Provençal-language journal *Aïoli*. It now houses a study centre and exhibits on the language (*t 04 90 80 80 88; open to students only Mon–Fri 9–12 and 2–5.30; closed Aug; free guided tours Tues at 3pm, and by appt*).

Rue St-Agricol is named after the restored Gothic church of **St-Agricol** (1326); its treasure is the *Doni Retable*, a rare Provençal work from the Renaissance. At No.19 is the **Librairie Roumanille**, founded in 1855 by the Avignon poet Joseph Roumanille, father of the Félibrige (*see* pp.38–9). The bookshop published the movement's first masterpiece, Mistral's epic *Mireio* (1859), and continues to put out books in Provençal, while Avignon's literati chum around in the shop's atmospheric 19th-century *salon*.

Museums: Vouland, Calvet, Requien, Lapidaire and Mont de Piété

At the end of Rue St-Agricol curves Rue Joseph Vernet, lined with 18th-century *hôtels particuliers*, antiques shops, and pricey restaurants and cafés. The kind of overly ornate spindly furniture, porcelains and knick-knacks that originally embellished these mansions is on display nearby at No.17 Rue Victor Hugo, in the **Musée Louis Vouland** (*t 04 90 86 03 79, www.vouland.com; open May–Oct Tues–Sat 10–12 and 2–6, Sun 2–6; Nov–April Tues–Sat 2–6; adm*).

More exciting are the contents of the handsome Hôtel de Villeneuve-Martignan, at 65 Rue Joseph Vernet, first opened to the public as a 'cabinet of curiosities' in the late 18th century by collector Esprit Calvet. Now the **Musée Calvet** (*t 04 90 86 33 84; open Wed–Mon 10–1 and 2–6; adm*), it offers something for every taste: 6,000 pieces of wrought iron, Greek sculpture, 18th-century seascapes by Avignon native Claude-Joseph Vernet and paintings of ruins by Hubert Robert and Panini, mummies, a portrait of Diane de Baroncelli (grandmother of the Marquis de Sade), a bust of a boy by Renaissance sculptor Desiderio da Settignano, tapestries, prehistoric statue-steles, dizzy kitsch paintings of nude men (David's *Mort de Bara* and Horace Vernet's *Mazeppa and the Wolves*), as well as an excellent collection of 19th- and 20th-century paintings by Corot, Guigou, Soutine, Daumier, Dufy, Morisot, Utrillo, Seurat, Toulouse-Lautrec, Vlaminck and Rouault. For all that, the best part of this museum may be the building itself, a light and airy palace from the Age of Enlightenment that complements perfectly the soft, romanticized landscapes and portraits on the walls.

Adjacent to the Calvet museum, the **Musée Requien** (*t 04 90 82 43 51; open Tues–Sat 9–12 and 2–6*) is Avignon's fuddy-duddy natural history collection, where a massive beaver found in the Sorgue steals the show. Lastly, at 27 Rue de la République, in the chilly 17th-century chapel of a Jesuit college, are the stone sculptures of the **Musée Lapidaire** (*t 04 90 86 33 84; open Wed–Mon 10–1 and 2–6; adm*). It's worth popping in for the 2nd-century BC (or Merovingian) man-eating *Tarasque de Noves*, each hand gripping the head of a Gaul, while an arm dangles from its greedy jaws; for the statues of Gallic warriors, looking much nattier in their mail than Astérix; or for the unlabelled masks in petal-like hoods. There is good Renaissance sculpture as well, but the best is in the nearby church of **St-Didier** (1359), just to the north in Place St-Didier: Francesco Laurana's polychrome reredos of Christ bearing the Cross, called *Notre-Dame du Spasme* for the spasm of pain on Mary's face; it was one of the first Renaissance sculptures to reach France, executed for the Bon Roi René in 1478. Opposite, in the first chapel on the left, are some *c.*1360 Florentine frescoes, uncovered in 1952.

More 14th-century frescoes have been restored opposite the church in the **Livrée de Ceccano**, now the town library. Nearby, at 5 Rue Laboureur, the treasures of a serious art collector named Jean Angladon-Dubrujeaud have been opened to the public as the **Fondation Angladon-Dubrujeaud** (*t 04 90 82 29 03, www.angladon.com; open 10 Nov–12 April Wed–Sun 1–6; 13 April–9 Nov daily 1–6; other times by appt; adm*). These include Renaissance and Art Deco furniture, bronzes and African art, but the main reason for coming is a fine assortment of modern painting never before seen: works by Modigliani, Picasso, Manet, Degas and Cézanne, as well as the only Van Gogh on display in Provence, called *Les Wagons de chemin de fer*.

Situated in the 18th-century Hôtel de Caumont at 5 Rue Violette off the southern end of Rue Joseph Vernet, the **Lambert Collection** (*t 04 90 16 56 20, www.collection lambert.com; open July daily 11–7; Aug–June Tues–Sun 11–6*) features modern art by the likes of Basquiat, and has a café and bookshop attached.

Back past the Hôtel des Monnaies towards the Place des Carmes, the **Musée du Mont de Piété** (*6 Rue Saluces, t 04 90 86 53 12; open Tues–Fri 8.30–12 and 1.30–5, Mon 10–12 and 1.30–5*), the oldest pawnbroker's in France, houses the town archives and some silk desiccators that were used to work out the dry weight of Avignon's former chief commodity.

The Eastern Quarters

From Place St-Didier, Rue du Roi René is lined with chiselled palaces, one built on the site of the church of **Ste-Claire** (No.22), where Petrarch first saw his Laura on Good

Friday 1327. ('It was the day when the sun darkened, as God Himself vanished into death, when I was taken,' he wrote.) Laura died, probably of the plague, in 1348, and was buried nearby in the Franciscan **Couvent des Cordeliers**, by the corner of Rue des Lices and Rue des Teinturiers; only the Gothic bell tower survived the fury of the Revolution. In 1533 a humanist from Lyon claimed to have found Laura's tomb in the church, and such was Petrarch's reputation that François Ier made a special trip to Avignon to see it.

Rue des Teinturiers, the most picturesque street in Avignon, was named after the dyers and textile-makers who powered their machines on waterwheels in the Sorgue, two of which survive. Shaded by ancient plane trees, crossed by little bridges, it is a pleasant place to dawdle over a beer or dinner; it's hard to believe this Sorgue is the same stream that comes bursting like a bomb out of that other Petrarchan shrine, the Fontaine-de-Vaucluse (*see* p.358). Rue des Teinturiers turns into Rue Bonneterie on its way to Avignon's shopping district and Place Pie, home of the ugly-duckling new **market** (Les Halles), although the produce inside is fit for a swan.

Another evocative street, Rue du Vieux-Sextier, once the site of the Jewish ghetto, is the address of Avignon's 19th-century **synagogue**, while just beyond Place Carnot, **St-Pierre**'s flamboyant façade boasts a set of beautifully carved walnut doors (1551). Facing St-Pierre, Avignon's cosiest museum, **Musée Théodore Aubanel** (*t 04 90 86 35 02; morning visits by appt; adm*), is a private institution dedicated to printing in Avignon, and to the romantic poet and Félibre Théodore Aubanel, whose family still owns one of Avignon's oldest publishing houses. From Place St-Pierre, Rue Carnot continues to another charming square, the Place des Carmes, which is dominated by the 14th-century **Eglise des Carmes** (church of the White Friars), Avignon's biggest church, with a pretty cloister that has been refurbished as a Festival venue.

Visitors in the last century would continue from here along Rue Carreterie, out of the city gate and down the Lyon road to the **Cimetière St-Véran**, a romantic, shady park where John Stuart Mill and his wife Harriet are buried. Harriet died at the Hôtel d'Europe in 1858 – a loss so devastating for the philosopher of utilitarianism that he lived in a house by the cemetery until he himself died in 1873. Another celebrated tomb belongs to Maurille de Sombreuil, who became a heroine during the Revolution when, to save the life of her father, the governor of the Invalides, she drank a goblet of human blood. Contemporaries noted that she drank white wine after that.

Villeneuve lez Avignon

In 586, on Puy Andaon, the rock that dominates Villeneuve lez Avignon, a Visigoth princess-hermit named Casarie died in the odour of sanctity (holiness smells like crushed violets, apparently). In the 10th century, Benedictines built the abbey of St-André to shelter her bones and lodge pilgrims on the route to Compostela. St-André grew to become one of the mightiest monasteries in the south of France, and in 1226, when Louis VIII besieged pro-Albigensian Avignon, the abbot offered the king co-sovereignty of the abbey in exchange for royal privileges. And so what was once an

Getting There

Bus 11 runs every 30mins from the train station or Porte de l'Oulle in Avignon to Villeneuve lez Avignon.

Tourist Information

Villeneuve lez Avignon: 1 Place Charles David, **t** 04 90 25 61 33, *www.villeneuvelesavignon. fr/tourisme. Open July Mon–Fri 10–7, Sat and Sun 10–1 and 2.30–7; Aug daily 9–12.30 and 2–6; Sept–June Mon–Sat 9–12.30 and 2–6.* In summer there is also a branch office in the main Avignon tourist office (*see* p.387). **Note** that everything except the Chartreuse is **closed** throughout Feb and on Mon mid-Sept–mid-June.

Market Days

Villeneuve lez Avignon: Thurs, Place Charles David; Sat am, Place Jean Jaurès. On Sat am there's also a flea market.

Where to Stay

Villeneuve lez Avignon ✉ 30400

Villeneuve makes an attractive alternative to Avignon, and has some fine places to stay.

****Le Prieuré, 7 Place du Chapitre, **t** 04 90 15 90 15, *www.leprieure.fr* (*luxury–very expensive*). An exquisite and centrally located hotel that gives you the option of sleeping in a 14th-century *livrée*, where the rooms are furnished with antiques, or in the more comfortable annexe by the large swimming pool. Further attractions are its gardens, tennis court and splendid restaurant. *Closed Nov–mid-Mar.*

****Hostellerie La Magnaneraie, 37 Rue Camp-de-Bataille, **t** 04 90 25 11 11, *www. hostellerie-la-magnaneraie.com* (*luxury–expensive*). A Best Western hotel with old-fashioned rooms in a former silkworm nursery, and a modern annexe, plus a swimming pool, gardens and Le Prieuré's rival for the best restaurant in town. *Closed Jan.*

Aux Ecuries des Chartreux, 66 Rue de la République, **t** 04 90 25 79 93, *www ecuries-des-chartreux.com* (*moderate*). A delightful, nicely decorated 17th-century B&B with studios next to the Chartreuse.

Les Cèdres, 39 Av Pasteur, **t 04 90 25 43 92, *www.logis-de-france.fr* (*moderate*). A 17th-century building with a swimming pool, restaurant (*moderate*) and bungalows. *Closed Nov–Mar.*

L'Atelier, 5 Rue de la Foire, **t 04 90 25 01 84, *www.hoteldelatelier.com* (*moderate–inexpensive*). A charming and beautifully restored 16th-century building with stylishly furnished rooms and a walled garden, in the centre of town. *Closed Nov–mid-Dec.*

UCJG Centre YMCA, 7 bis Chemin de la Justice, **t** 04 90 25 46 20, *www.ymca-avignon.com* (*inexpensive*). A hostel with superb views of the Rhône and a pool.

Eating Out

Aubertin, 1 Rue de l'Hôpital, **t** 04 90 25 94 84 (*expensive*). An intimate, popular *restaurant gastronomique* under the porticoes. Book ahead. *Closed Sun, and Mon, and last 2 weeks Aug.*

La Maison, 1 Rue Montée-du-Fort, **t** 04 90 25 20 81 (*moderate*). An friendly old favourite with traditional Provençal food. *Closed Wed eve and Aug.*

abbey town became a frontier-fortress of the king of France, a new town (*ville neuve*), heavily fortified in case the pope over the river should start feeling frisky.

But Villeneuve was soon invaded in another way; wanton, squalid Avignon didn't suit all tastes, and the pope gave permission to his cardinals who preferred it not-so-hot to retreat across the Rhône into princely *livrées cardinalices* (palaces 'freed' from their original owners by the Curia). Though a dormitory suburb these days, Villeneuve still maintains a separate peace, with well-fed cats snoozing in the sun, leisurely afternoons at the *pétanque* court and some amazing works of art.

Around Town

In 1307, when Philip the Fair ratified the deal that made Villeneuve royal property, he ordered that a citadel be built on the approach to Pont St-Bénezet, named after guess who. As times grew more perilous, this bright white **Tour Philippe-le-Bel** (*t 04 32 70 08 57; open April–Sept Tues–Sun 10–12.30 and 2–6.30; Oct, Nov and Mar Tues–Sun 10–12 and 2–5; closed Dec–Feb*) was made higher to keep out the riff-raff, and from its terrace, reached by a superb winding stair, it offers splendid views of Avignon, Mont Ventoux and, on a clear day, the Alpilles.

From here, Montée de la Tour leads up to the 14th-century **Collégiale Notre-Dame** (*t 06 70 01 22 74; open Oct–Jan and Mar Tues–Sun 10–12 and 2–5, April–Sept 10–12.30 and 2–6.30; closed Feb*) once the chapel of a *livrée* and now Villeneuve's parish church. From Villeneuve's Chartreuse (charterhouse) it has inherited an elaborate marble altar of 1745, and it contains a copy of Enguerrand Quarton's famous *Pietà de Villeneuve lez Avignon* (the original is in the Louvre). The church's most famous work, a beaming, swivel-hipped, polychrome ivory statue of the Virgin, carved in Paris out of an elephant's tusk *c.*1320, has been removed to safer quarters in the nearby **Musée Pierre-de-Luxembourg** (*t 04 90 27 49 66; same hours as Tour Philippe-le-Bel; adm*), which is housed in yet another *livrée*.

The museum's other prize is the masterpiece of the Avignon school: Enguerrand Quarton's 1454 *Couronnement de la Vierge*, one of the greatest works of 15th-century French painting, commissioned for the Chartreuse (*see* below). Unusually, it portrays God the Father and God the Son as twins, clothed in sumptuous crimson and gold, like the Virgin herself, whose fine sculptural features were perhaps inspired by the ivory Virgin. Around these central figures the painting evokes the spiritual route travelled by the Carthusians through vigilant prayer, to purify the world and reconcile it to God. St Bruno, founder of the Order, saints, kings and commoners are present, hierarchically arranged, while the landscape encompasses heaven, hell, Rome and Jerusalem, and local touches such as the Montagne Sainte-Victoire (*see* p.290) and the cliffs of L'Estaque (*see* p.275).

Other notable works in the museum include a curious 14th-century double-faced Virgin, the 'Eve' face evoking original sin and the 'Mary' face human redemption; Simon de Châlon's 1552 *Entombment*; and, amid the uninspired 17th-century fluff, Philippe de Champaigne's *Visitation*.

La Chartreuse and Fort St-André

From the museum, take Rue de la République up as far as No.53, the **Livrée de la Thurroye**, the best-preserved in Villeneuve; a cardinal would maintain a household of 100 or so people here. Further up the street and up the scale rises what used to be the largest and wealthiest charterhouse in France, the **Chartreuse du Val de Bénédiction** (*t 04 90 15 24 24; www.chartreuse.org; open daily April–Sept 9–6.30, Oct–Mar 9.30–5.30; adm*). This began life as the *livrée* of Etienne Aubert who, upon his election to the papacy in 1352 as Innocent VI, deeded his palace to the Carthusians for a monastery. For 450 years it was expanded and rebuilt, acquired immense estates on either side of the Rhône from kings and popes, accumulated a precious library, two more cloisters and various works of art, and in general lived high on the hog by the usual Carthusian standards. In 1792, the Revolution forced the monks out, and the Chartreuse was sold in 17 lots; squatters took over the cells and outsiders feared to enter the cloisters after dark. Now repurchased and beautifully restored, the buildings house the CNES (Centre National des Ecritures du Spectacle), where playwrights and others are given grants to work in peace and quiet in some of the former cells; it hosts seminars, exhibitions and performances, especially during the Avignon Festival.

Still, the sensation that lingers in the charterhouse is one of vast silences and austerity, the hallmark of an order where conversation was limited (at least at the outset) to one hour a week; monks who disobeyed the rule of prayer, work and silence ended up in one of the seven prison cells that are set around the laundry in the Great Cloister, each with a cleverly arranged window on the prison chapel altar. Explanations (in English) throughout offer an in-depth view of Carthusian life: one cell has been furnished as it originally was. Pierre Boulez discovered that the dining hall, or *tinel*, has some of the finest acoustics in the whole of France, designed so that everyone could hear the monk who read aloud during mealtimes. In the Tinel's chapel are some ruined 14th-century frescoes by Matteo Giovannetti and his school: originally their work covered the walls of the huge **church**, now bare except for their masons' marks and minus its apse, which collapsed. The star attraction here is **Innocent VI's tomb**, which boasts an alabaster effigy under a fine Gothic baldachin. Innocent was solemnly reburied here in 1960: a century ago the tomb was being used as a rabbit hutch. Popes who took the name Innocent have tended to suffer similar posthumous indignities: the great Innocent III was found stark naked in Perugia cathedral, a victim of poisoned slippers, while the corpse of Innocent X – the last of the series – was dumped in a toolshed in St Peter's.

Gazing down into the charterhouse from the summit of Puy Andaon are the formidable bleached walls of **Fort St-André** (*t 04 90 25 45 35; open daily April–Sept 10–1 and 2–6; Oct–Mar 10–1 and 2–5*), built by the French kings around the old abbey in the 1360s, not only to stare down the pope over the river but to defend French turf during the heyday of the *Grandes Compagnies* (bands of unemployed mercenaries who pillaged the countryside and held towns to ransom). The two round towers afford a famous vantage point over Avignon; the southwestern tower is called the Tour des Masques (or Tour des Sorcières, or Tour des Fées); no one remembers why. Jumbly ruins are all that remain of the once splendid **Abbaye St-André** (*f 04 90 25 55 95; open April–Sept Tues–Sat 10–12.30 and 2–6, Oct–Mar Tues–Sat 10–12.30 and 2–5*) amid beautiful Italian gardens – sumptuous in springtime – restored and presided over by Roseline Bacou, a former curator at the Louvre.

South of Avignon

La Montagnette

Just south of Avignon and its confluence with the Durance, the Rhône curves to accommodate La Montagnette, a micro-region that is still something of a best-kept secret, near the tourist fleshpots of Provence and yet distant in spirit, self-contained and serene. La Montagnette itself is a striking, 10km-long outcrop of white stone, isolated from its sisters in the Alpilles and surrounded by orchards, a bijou landscape that **Barbentane** fits into like an old shoe. This friendly old town, which so loved its *farandole* that a man who could not dance it was not considered a fit husband, is still defended by the 14th-century **Tour Angelica**, its medieval gates and, near the church, the arcaded Renaissance **Maison des Chevaliers**. Outside the walls, the **château** (**t** 04 90 95 51 07; *open Easter–Oct Tues–Sun 10–12 and 2–6; also Wed July–Sept; mid-Feb–Easter Sun 10–12 and 2–6; adm*) was built in 1674, not for defence but for pleasure, by the Marquis de Barbentane, the king's ambassador to Tuscany. It would not look out of place in the Ile de France: the furnishings are Louis XV and Louis XVI, but the builder's Italian tastes permeate the other decoration. The enormous plane trees in the garden were brought over from Turkey by an earlier marquis in the 1670s.

On the D35 south of Barbentane, **Boulbon** was known as Bourbon until 1792, when the guillotine cut into the name's popularity. Still defended by its fairytale 10th-century walls built dramatically into and onto the rocky escarpment overlooking the Rhône, Boulbon is known for its unique 1 June *Cérémonie du St-Vinage*, in honour of its patron saint Marcellin: the men of the village each bring a full bottle of wine to the saint's Romanesque chapel and hear the Gospel in Provençal, after which the wine is blessed and God is toasted with a mighty swig. The bottle is then corked and for the rest of the year the blessed wine is used as a remedy for illnesses.

Tourist Information

Barbentane: 4 Le Cours, **t** 04 90 90 85 86, *www.barbentane.fr*. Open July–Sept Mon–Sat 9–1 and 2–6.30, Sun 10–12; April–June Mon 2–5, Tues–Sat 9–12 and 2–5, Sat 9–12; Oct–Mar Mon–Fri 2–5, Wed and Sat 9–12.

Market Days
Barbentane: Fri am.

Where to Stay and Eat

Barbentane ✉ 13570
★★Hôtel Castel Mouisson, at foot of La Montagnette in Quartier Castel Mouisson, **t** 04 90 95 51 17, *www.hotel-castelmouisson.com* (*moderate–inexpensive*). A typical Provençal hotel, with a swimming pool and tennis court, and bike hire. *Closed mid-Oct–mid-Mar.*

Le Saint-Jean, 1 Le Cours, **t** 04 90 95 50 44, *www.francemarket.com/hotel_saint_jean* (*inexpensive*). Decent rooms in the centre and a restaurant with average fare (*moderate*). *Restaurant closed Sun eve and Mon.*

Hostellerie de Frigolet, Abbaye St-Michel-de-Frigolet (*see* p.404), **t** 04 90 90 52 70, *www.frigolet.com* (*inexpensive*). A hostel run by the Prémontré monks, with 36 rooms and a restaurant, offering guaranteed quiet retreats for a day or two, or even a month.

Châteaurenard ✉ 13160
★★Les Glycines, 14 Av Victor Hugo, **t** 04 90 94 10 66 (*inexpensive*). A simple base with an average restaurant (*moderate*). *Restaurant closed Mon.*

Noves ✉ 13550
★★★★Auberge de Noves, 2km northwest of town on D28, **t** 04 90 24 28 28, *www.aubergedenoves.com* (*luxury–expensive*). A Relais & Châteaux *bastide* converted into one of the most prestigious Provençal hotels with heli-pad and lobster pools in a 15-hectare forest. The air-conditioned rooms have every comfort, and there are tennis courts and a pool in the grounds, and riding and golf nearby. The restaurant is a gastro-temple. *Closed Nov and Dec. Restaurant closed Mon and Tues lunch out of season.*

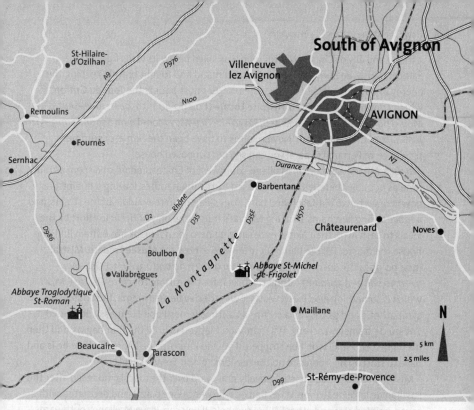

Leaving Barbentane on the D35E will bring you to the **Abbaye St-Michel-de-Frigolet**, founded around 1000 (*t 04 90 95 70 07, www.frigolet.com; guided tours by a monk Sept–Easter, Sun 4.10pm; all year by appointment for groups of 10 or more*). The word *frigolet* comes from the Provençal *férigoulo*, or thyme; this invigorating herb scents the air of La Montagnette. The monks of Montmajour (*see p.424*), enervated by the swamps, would come up here for a cure – some of it in the form of a liqueur called *Elixir du Révérend Père Gaucher*, still distilled and on sale here. It may also have an effect on sterility: in 1632, Anne of Austria, barren after 20 years of marriage, prayed in the Romanesque chapel of the Conception Immaculée for a son, and soon after gave the world Louis XIV. In gratitude, she sent the gilt *boiseries* framing 14 turgid Mignards. Another celebrity to pass through was young Frédéric Mistral, for whom the stories and customs of these hills were to become a powerful source of inspiration.

The Petite Crau

East of Barbentane and La Montagnette, **Châteaurenard** is one of Provence's main wholesale fruit and vegetable markets, a big bustling place under its plane trees. It lords over the rich verdant plain of the **Petite Crau**, a large marshland drained by the Romans, planted with market gardens and orchards of cherries and apricots, and protected from the huffing and puffing of the mistral by hedgerows and poplars – nothing at all like the rocky waste of the 'big' Crau. Two proud towers on Châteaurenard's hill are all that remain of the castle that first belonged to Reinardus, a friend and ally of Charles Martel, who was killed below its walls fighting the Saracens; his wife Emma took over the command and fought bravely, keeping the enemy at bay, then died of a broken heart. Her ghost haunts the **Tour du Griffon**, which contains the **Musée d'Histoire Locale** (*t 04 90 90 11 59; open June–Sept Mon–Thurs and Sun 10–12 and 2–6, Sat 10–12; Oct–May Mon–Thurs, Sat and Sun 3–5*). Just east of Châteaurenard, **Noves** claims to have been the home, or summer residence, of Petrarch's Laura: you can see her supposed house.

In 1830, Mistral was born in **Maillane**, southwest of Châteaurenard, and spent as much time as possible there. It's been bypassed by the main routes, leaving a quaint, dusty nowhere with two old-fashioned bars, dogs sleeping in the middle of the streets, and a *tabac* selling keychains sporting Mistral's mug – the only noticeable effort by the locals to cash in on their Nobel Prize slinging hero (he *does* look like Buffalo Bill). The house the master Félibre had built after 1876 is now the **Musée Frédéric Mistral** (*t 04 90 95 74 06; open April–Sept Tues–Sun 9.30–11.30 and 2.30–6.30, Oct–Mar 10–11.30 and 2–4.30; adm*) – don't mistake it for the rotting concrete Centre F. Mistral, which is something else. Preserved as it was the day he died in 1914, the house is 'as sympathetic and as cosy as a coffin,' as author James Pope-Hennessy described it. The guide, a sinewy cockerel of a man, won't let you in until the tour begins, and then his high-speed spiel won't be stopped. If you do interrupt, he'll forget where he is and have to start again. There are no concessions to non-French speakers.

Mistral's tomb, in the ghastly, gravelly graveyard over the road, is modelled after the Pavillon de la Reine Jeanne at Les Baux-de-Provence (*see* p.423), and decorated with a seven-pointed star and other Félibre symbols. If you can, leave Maillane southwards by the D27, and travel over beautiful fields and streams.

Tarascon

Few towns in Provence are as determinedly unglamorous as Tarascon. Most of the houses are not only unrestored but cry out for a lick of paint, and garages outnumber craft shops. Meanwhile, the rival fairytale castles of Tarascon and Beaucaire muse at each other across the Rhône like the embodiments of a bicommunal Walter Mitty daydream, reminders of heroism, romance, international markets, man-eating monsters and Alphonse Daudet's buffoonish anti-hero Tartarin, who never told a lie but, under the hot sun, was prone to imagine things. Provençal nationalists accuse Daudet (a native of Nîmes) of creating a stereotype that only heightened Paris' already smug attitude towards the Midi, to which Daudet replied that 'All Frenchmen have in them a touch of Tarascon.'

Tarascon and St Martha

All centuries have quirks that seem quaint to later generations: tulip-bulb speculation in the 18th, ladies' bustles in the 19th, muzak in the 20th. In the 11th and 12th centuries it was a mania for the body parts of saints – a fad so passionate that a sure candidate for the inner circle, such as St Francis, had bodyguards in his dying days to stop rival towns kidnapping him. If it had no fresh relics, every town with a saintly legend linked to it began digging for bones; and in Tarascon, *voilà*, in 1187 they just happened to stumble across the relics of St Martha. The 9th-century legend told how she found Tarascon bedevilled by the Tarasque, a man-eating amphibian whose ancestors are portrayed in Celtic sculpture chomping on human heads. Martha neatly tidied away the monster by showing it a cross, lassoing it with her girdle, then ordering it to the bottom of the Rhône, never to return. The new-found relics attracted so many pilgrims that the 12th-century **Collégiale Ste-Marthe** was enlarged in the 13th and 16th centuries into a curious Romanesque-Gothic hybrid. The church was bombed in the Second World War, but worse mischief had been done earlier in the Revolution, when the great south portal of 1197 was shorn of its sculptures. Nowadays, the chapels of the attractive five-aisled Gothic nave are filled with the lukewarm efforts of Mignard and Parrocel, masters of the Baroque fruitcake style, while in the crypt (part of the original church) there's a king-sized statue of Martha from 1400, and the slightly later *Effigy of Jean de Cossa*, seneschal of Provence, which is attributed to Francesco Laurana.

Getting There and Around

By Train

Nearly every east–west train between towns in Provence and Languedoc stops in Tarascon.

By Bus

Lignes du Gard buses run regularly between Tarascon, Nîmes and Avignon (t 04 66 29 27 29); CTM, from Tarascon station, go to Arles and Avignon (t 04 90 93 74 90).

Tourist Information

Tarascon: 59 Rue des Halles, t 04 90 91 03 52, *www.tarascon.org*. Open July and Aug Mon–Sat 9–7, Sun 9.30–12.30; Sept–June Mon–Sat 9–12 and 2–6.

Market Day

Tarascon: Tues am, Place de Verdun.

Festivals

The **Fête de la Tarasque** lasts for 5 days around St John's Day (24 June), and includes a procession headed by a reconstruction of the Tarasque, bonfires, costumes, bullfights, opera (the *Mireio*), dances, cavalcades and – yes – someone dressed as Tartarin.

On 5 Jan, there's the arrival of the **Three Kings** procession.

Where to Stay and Eat

Tarascon ✉ 13150

★★★Hôtel Mazets des Roches, Route de Fontvieille (D33), t 04 90 91 34 89, *www.guideweb.com/provencehotel/ mazets-des-roches* (*expensive–moderate*). A quiet, comfortable place with modern, air-conditioned rooms in a large park of tall pines, with a restaurant, pool, tennis courts and bike rental. Half-board obligatory in summer. *Closed Nov–Easter; restaurant closed Thurs and Sat lunch except July and Aug.*

★★★Hôtel de Provence, 7 Bd Victor Hugo, t 04 90 91 06 43, *www.alpilles.fr/provence tarascon* (*moderate–inexpensive*). A *hôtel particulier* in the centre, with large rooms.

★★Le Terminus, Place du Colonel Berrurier, t 04 90 91 18 95 (*inexpensive*). A basic option with a buffet restaurant offering 16 starters and 10 main dishes. *Closed mid-Feb–mid-Mar and Wed and Sat lunch.*

Auberge de la Jeunesse, 31 Bd Gambetta, t 04 90 91 04 08, *www.fuaj.org* (*cheap*). A hostel offering inexpensive food and bike hire. *Closed mid-Dec–Feb.*

Bistrot des Anges 3 Place du Marché, t 04 90 91 05 11 (*moderate–cheap*). A great place for lunch or snacks, with well-priced salads and tarts, in a nicely decorated building in a lively part of town. Dinner available weekends. *Open 9–6, and eves Fri and Sat.*

Château de Tarascon

t 04 90 91 01 93; open April–Aug Tues–Sun 9–7; Sept–Mar Tues–Sun 10.30–5; adm.

Rooted in a limestone rock over the Rhône, Tarascon's château gleams like white satin between the sun and the water. It's a storybook feudal castle with crenellations and a moat, named after the one character in Tarascon's history who was actually rounded out in flesh and blood. The Bon Roi René earned the 'Good' in his name for his good appetite and fondness for the good things of life, as well as for having the good sense not to let troubles or sorrows, of which he had many, get under his skin. He spent the last decade of his life (1471–80) surrounded by poets and artists in Tarascon, in this castle begun in 1401 by his father, Louis II of Anjou. After René's death and Provence's annexation to France, it underwent the usual conversion into a prison.

While the exterior is all business, the interior was designed with the good taste of René in mind – it's flamboyant and elegant, and now eloquently empty except for ten 17th-century tapestries on the Life of Scipio and a collection of 18th-century pharmaceutical pots. In the courtyard there are busts of the king and his second wife, Jeanne de Laval; here and there, sculptural titbits and faded ceiling panels offer clues to the original decoration. Graffiti by British sailors imprisoned here between 1754 and 1778 recall the castle's later use. Taking in the precipitous views from the top, you can see why no one ever tried to sneak up on it; or why, during the Revolution, Tarascon never needed to invest in a guillotine.

Elsewhere around Town

Perhaps because they haven't been prettified to death as in some Provençal towns, the streets of Tarascon, lined with rose, lemon and ochre houses with geraniums in the windows and laundry flapping in the breeze, make it a delightful place to wander around. The main **Rue des Halles** is still covered by medieval arcades. Halfway up it from the tourist office you'll find the Franciscan **Cloître des Cordeliers** (1450s), now open only for special exhibitions (*t 04 90 91 38 71*). At the top of Rue des Halles stands the handsome **Hôtel de Ville** (1648) – compare it with Beaucaire's, built 35 years later; the ceilings and original consuls' stalls are still intact. Near here, at 39 Rue Proudhon, the **Musée Souleiado** (*t 04 90 91 50 11; open May–Sept daily 10–6; Oct–April Tues–Sat 10–5*) is run by Souleiado (Provençal for 'sunray piercing through clouds'), France's leading manufacturer of block-printed textiles. Founded here in 1938 by Charles Deméry in the hopes of reviving a 200-year-old Tarascon industry, the museum holds 40,000 18th-century fruitwood blocks – still the basis for all the company's patterns. Brought back to fashion in the 1950s on such diverse backs as Bardot's and Picasso's, Souleiado's colour-drenched prints can be purchased in the nearby shop, or in the many boutiques in the south of France.

Lastly, there's the so-called **Maison de Tartarin** at 55 bis Boulevard Itam (*t 04 90 91 05 08; open April–Sept Mon–Sat 10–12 and 2–7; Oct–Mar Mon–Sat 10–12 and 1.30–5; adm*). The modern Tarasconnais say they have forgiven Daudet for making them ridiculous, for in the age of Tourist Man he has also made them famous. Daudet claimed that the character of Tartarin was derived from his cousin, a big-game hunter whom he accompanied on a lion hunt in Algeria, but there's another version: in the original story, published as a newspaper serial, Tartarin was named Barbarin after an old Tarasconnais family, the head of which had rejected the author's suit for the hand of his daughter. The family threatened to sue if Daudet used their name in his novel, so he changed it to the fictional Tartarin, then got his own back by making the whole town the butt of his jokes. In the house are mementoes from the three Tartarin novels, and photos from the plays and films. The garden has been planted to fit the book's exotic flora and baobab tree, where Tartarin held court with his tall tales.

Also on display is the famous **Tarasque**, a moustachioed armadillo covered with red spikes. Scholars argue whether the monster is named after the town or vice versa; when King René founded the *Jeux et courses de la Tarasque* in 1474, it was given a thick carapace to hide the men that made it walk, while fireworks blasted out of its nostrils and the people sang '*Lagadigadèu, la Tarasco, Lagadigadèu!*', or 'Let her pass, the Tarasque, let her dance.'

Beaucaire

Beaucaire can match Tarascon's stories tit for tat. It, too, was plagued by a river monster, called the **Drac** – a dragon in some versions, or a handsome young man – who liked to stroll invisibly through Beaucaire, before luring his victims into the Rhône by holding a bright jewel just below the surface. When the Drac became a father, he kidnapped a washerwoman to nurse his baby for seven years, during which time the woman learned how to see him when he was invisible. Years later, during one of his prowls through Beaucaire, she saw him and greeted him loudly. He was so mortified that he was never seen again, although like the Tarasque he makes an annual reappearance by proxy, on the first weekend in June. Beaucaire was also the setting of one of the most charming medieval romances: of **Aucassin**, son of the count of Beaucaire, and his 'sweet sister friend' Nicolette, daughter of the king of Carthage, whom Aucassin loved so dizzily that he fell off his horse and dislocated his shoulder, among other adventures.

But in those days Beaucaire was on everyone's lips. It was here, in 1208, that a local squire assassinated Pope Innocent III's legate, who had come to demand stricter measures against the Cathars. It gave Innocent the excuse he needed to launch the Albigensian Crusade against Beaucaire's overlords in Toulouse, and all their lands in Languedoc. In 1216, when the war was in full swing, Raymond VII, the son of the count of Toulouse, recaptured the town from its French occupiers, who took refuge in the castle. As soon as word reached Simon de Montfort, he set off in person to succour his stranded men and to teach Beaucaire a lesson, besieging the town walls, while his troops took up the fight from inside the castle, so that Beaucaire was sandwiched in a double attack. The siege lasted 13 weeks before the troops in the castle ran out of food and surrendered and Simon de Montfort had to admit to one of his very few defeats. In gratitude, Raymond VI granted Beaucaire the right to hold a duty-free fair. But five years later the town was gobbled up by France along with the rest of Languedoc.

Tourist Information

Beaucaire: 24 Cours Gambetta, **t** 04 66 59 26 57, *www.ot-beaucaire.fr*. Open Easter–Sept Mon–Fri 8.45–12.15 and 2–6, Sat 9.30–12.30 and 3–6; July also Sun 9.30–12.30; Oct–Easter Mon–Fri 8.45–12.15 and 2–6. Guided tours in English. Can also provide lists of *chambres d'hôtes*.

Market Days

Beaucaire: Thurs am and Sun am, Place de la Mairie and Cours Gambetta; Fri eves in July and Aug there's a market along the canal, with local produce, crafts and entertainment.

Where to Stay and Eat

For a real escape from the hustle and bustle, why not hire a **houseboat** and make the leisurely loop down the Rhône–Sète canal to the Camargue, west to Aigues-Mortes and up the Languedoc canal past St-Gilles to Beaucaire? Try **Connoisseur Holidays Afloat** (*see* p.75).

Beaucaire ✉ 30300

★★★Robinson, 2km north of town on Route de Remoulins (D986), **t** 04 66 59 21 32, *www.hotel.robinson.fr* (*moderate*). Thirty rooms set in acres of countryside, with a swimming pool, tennis court, playground and restaurant (*moderate*). Closed Feb.

★★★Les Doctrinaires, 6 Quai du Général de Gaulle, **t** 04 66 59 23 70, *www.hoteldoctrinaires.com* (*moderate–inexpensive*). A rather old-fashioned hostelry set in the former home of the Doctrinaire fathers of Avignon before the Revolution. The restaurant (*expensive–moderate*), which is set in the hotel's pretty courtyard, is a very pleasant place in which to have a meal. Closed Sat lunch, and mid-Dec–mid-Jan.

In 1464, Louis XI restored its freedoms and fair franchise; before long its Foire de la Ste-Madeleine became one of the biggest in western Europe. For 10 days in July, merchants from all over the Mediterranean, Germany and England would wheel and deal in the *pré*, a vast meadow on the banks of the Rhône; by the 18th century, when the fair was at its height, Beaucaire (with a population of 8,000) attracted some 300,000 traders, as well as acrobats, thieves and sweethearts, who came to buy each other rings of spun glass as a symbol of love's fragile beauty. So much money changed hands that Beaucaire earned as much in a week as Marseille did in a year. The loss of Beaucaire's duty-free privileges just after Napoleon lost at Waterloo put an end to the fair, and since then Beaucaire has had to make do with traffic on the Rhône and Rhône–Sète Canal, its quarries and its wine, ranging from good plonk to the more illustrious AOC Costière du Gard. But in the spring you can try one last legacy of the great fair in Beaucaire: the *pastissoun*, a patty filled with preserved fruits, introduced by merchants from the Levant. Nowadays Beaucaire is slightly down on its luck – roadworks occupy the main streets and driving and walking are not a pleasure.

The Château and Historic Centre

Louis XI's restoration of Beaucaire's rights paid off for a later Louis (XIII); in 1632, when the château was besieged by the troops of the king's rebellious brother, Gaston d'Orléans, the loyal citizens forced them out. To prevent further mishaps, Richelieu ordered Beaucaire's castle razed to the ground. But after the south wall had been demolished, the shell was left to fall into ruins romantic enough for an illustration to *Aucassin et Nicolette*. It's a fitting background to **Les Aigles de Beaucaire** (**t** 04 66 59 26 72, *www.aigles-de-beaucaire.com*; open mid–end Mar, Sept, Oct Thurs–Tues

2.30–4.30; April, May and June 2–5; July and Aug 3–6; closed Nov–mid-Mar; adm),
displays of the falconer's art in Roman costume. There are sweeping views of the
Rhône and the old fairgrounds, the Champ de Foire, from the 80ft **Tour Polygonale**.

In the castle gardens below, the **Musée Municipal Auguste Jacquet** (t 04 66 59 47 61;
open April–Oct Wed–Mon 10–12 and 2.15–6.45; Nov–Mar Wed–Mon 10.15–12 and 2–5.15;
adm) has finds from Roman Beaucaire (then clumsily called Ugernum), including a
fine statue of Jupiter on his throne, and another of the lusty Priapus found in a villa.
There's a geological collection, popular arts, and advertising posters and mementoes
from the fair, when thousands of brightly coloured cloths swung over the streets,
each bearing a merchant's name, his home address and his address in Beaucaire; it
was the only way in the vast, polyglot throng to find anyone.

From the château, arrows point the way to the venerable **Place de la République**,
shaded by giant plane trees, and the grand, elegant Baroque church of **Notre-Dame-
des-Pommiers** (1744), which perhaps more than anything proves how many annual
visitors this town once expected. It replaced a much smaller Romanesque church but
conserves, on its exterior transept wall (facing Rue Charlier), a superb 12th-century
frieze depicting Passion scenes in the same strong, lively relief as at St-Gilles (see
pp.445–7). The stately French classical **Hôtel de Ville** (1683) situated in Place Georges
Clemenceau was designed by Jacques Cubizol and bestowed on Beaucaire by
Louis XIV, who wanted to provide it with a monument worthy of its importance:
note Louis' sun symbols on the façade, the town's coat of arms set in the Collar of
St Michael (the French equivalent of the Order of the Garter – Beaucaire was the only
town in France awarded the honour), and Beaucaire's motto: 'Renowned for its Fair,
Illustrious for its Fidelity'.

If it's a holiday, there's likely to be some dramatic bull follies in the **Arènes**: 100 bulls
are brought in for the Estivales, a week-long re-creation of the medieval market and
other celebrations in late July. Beaucaire's razeteurs have a reputation as the most
daring of them all; statues of Clairon and Goya, the bulls that gave them the best
sport, greet visitors respectively by the Rhône bridge and in Place Jean Jaurès.

Around Beaucaire

The outskirts of Beaucaire are home to two attractions. **Le Vieux Mas**, 8km south on
the road to Fourques (t 04 66 59 60 13; open April–Oct daily 10–7; Nov–Mar Wed, Sat
and Sun 10–12.30 and 1.30–6; adm), is a living evocation of a Provençal farmhouse at
the turn of the 19th century, with a working blacksmith and other artisans, plus farm
animals and regional products. The **Mas Gallo Romain des Tourelles**, 4km southwest
at 4294 Route de Bellegarde (t 04 66 59 19 72; www.tourelles.com; open April–Oct daily
2–6; July and Aug Mon–Sat 10–12 and 2–7, Sun 2–7; Nov–Easter by appointment only), is
more original: since 1983 archaeologists have been working on the 210-acre vineyard
of Château des Tourelles (owned by the Durands for 250 years), excavating a huge 1st-
century AD agricultural estate that produced olives, wheat and wine, complete with a
pottery factory capable of producing 4,000 amphorae a day. The current Durand in

charge, Hervé, became so fascinated with the digs that, together with the Centre National de la Recherche Scientifique, he has recreated a Gallo-Roman winery – during the harvest you can watch the grapes as they are gathered and pressed in the old Roman way and later see the wine bottled, or rather amphora-ed, in jars ranging in size from 5 to 1,000 litres, wrapped in straw to keep them from breaking in transit. You can taste and buy the result, although there's no way of knowing how close it comes to the stuff quaffed by Nero and company – the Romans added lime, egg whites, plaster, clay, mushroom ashes and pig blood to 'improve' their wines, and Durand does not.

Beaucaire's Roman incarnation made its living transferring goods (including its wine) along the Roman 'superhighway', the **Via Domitia** that linked Rome to Spain. An 8km stretch of this has come through in remarkably good nick, especially in a place known as **Les Bornes Milliaires** (take the D999 1km northwest past the train tracks, turn left and continue for 800m, following the Enclos d'Argent lane). Nowhere else along the route have the milestones survived so well: these three, on the 13th mile between Nîmes and Ugernum, were erected by Augustus, Tiberius and Antoninus Pius.

In the same area, the unique and vaguely spooky **Abbaye Troglodytique Saint-Roman**, 4km up the D999 (*t 04 66 59 52 26; open daily April–June and Sept 10–6; July and Aug 10–6.30; Oct–Mar Sat and Sun 2–5; adm*), was founded in a cave during the perilous 5th century and laboriously carved out of the living rock. It was mentioned in the chronicles in 1363, when Pope Urban V made it a *studium*, a school open even to the poorest children, but by 1537 it had lost its importance and was engulfed in the construction of a fortress. When the fortress in turn lost its importance in the 19th century and was destroyed, the abbey was rediscovered: you can see the chapel, with its remarkable abbot's chair; the subterranean cells; the water cisterns and wine press; and 150 rock-cut tombs in the necropolis on the upper terrace, from where the dead monks had better views than the live ones down below.

Northeast of Beaucaire, **Vallabrègues**, 'the most Provençal town of Languedoc', was cut off from the rest of the Gard when the Rhône changed its bed. Surrounded by clumps of osier, it makes its living from wicker and basketry: learn all about it in the **Musée de la Vannerie et de l'Artisanat** (*Rue Carnot, t 04 66 59 26 04; open Easter–Oct Wed–Sun 3–7; adm*).

Down the Rhône 2:
The Alpilles, Crau and Camargue

14

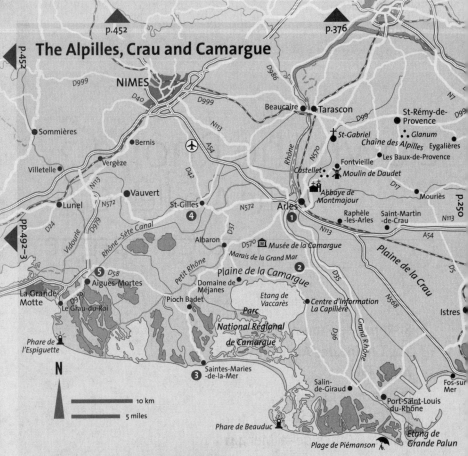

The Alpilles, Crau and Camargue

NIMES

Beaucaire · Tarascon

St-Rémy-de-Provence

† St-Gabriel · Glanum

Chaîne des Alpilles · Eygalières

Fontvieille · Les Baux-de-Provence

Castellet · Moulin de Daudet

Mouriès

Abbaye de Montmajour

Arles ①

Raphèle-les-Arles · Saint-Martin-de-Crau

Sommières

Bernis

Vergèze

Villetelle

Vauvert

St-Gilles ④

Lunel

Albaron

Musée de la Camargue

Marais de la Grand Mar

Plaine de la Camargue ②

Plaine de la Crau

Istres

Aigues-Mortes ⑤

La Grande Motte

Le Grau-du-Roi

Domaine de Méjanes

Pioch Badet

Etang de Vaccarès

Centre d'Information La Capilière

Parc National Régional de Camargue

Phare de l'Espiguette

N

10 km

5 miles

Saintes-Maries-de-la-Mer ③

Salin-de-Giraud

Port-Saint-Louis-du-Rhône

Fos-sur-Mer

Phare de Beauduc

Plage de Piémanson

Etang de Grande Palun

FRANCE

ITALY

SPAIN

Highlights

1 Ancient Roman and Dark Age Arles

2 The wildlife of the Camargue

3 The great Gypsy pilgrimage church of Saintes-Maries-de-la-Mer

4 The Romanesque sculpture at St-Gilles

5 Saint Louis' walled city of Aigues-Mortes

The Rhône that flows so majestically from the Swiss Alps down half of France comes to a rather messy end in the Camargue, dithering indecisively through a delta of swamps, salt pans and sand dunes. And yet if all the chapters of this book had to compete in a talent show, this would be the one to beat. It has wild bulls, horses and pink flamingos; it has the cowboys, Gypsies and the fancy dress of the Arlésiennes; it has Roman ruins, the best Romanesque art and the most romantic stories, worthy of Sir Walter Scott; it has the sharpest mountains, a plain so uncanny that it took a myth to explain it and the mistral-whipped landscapes painted by Van Gogh; and it has the biggest bullring, France's only AOC hay (from Arles) and all the aluminium ore you could ask for.

St-Rémy-de-Provence

Enclosed by a garland of boulevards lined with plane trees, St-Rémy's tranquillity has attracted its share of the famous. Nostradamus was born here, Gertrude Stein spent years here, Charles Gounod stayed here while writing his opera based on Mistral's *Mireille*, and Princess Caroline of Monaco drops in for discreet visits (St-Rémy used to belong to the family). Vincent Van Gogh spent his tragic last year in St-Rémy's asylum, which was commandeered to hold interned Germans in the First World War – the one who got Van Gogh's room was Albert Schweitzer.

Nowadays, St-Rémy is home to a good many artists, and there are always exhibitions going on. The newest attraction is the bizarre-looking organ in the church of **St-Martin** on Boulevard Marceau. Built in 1983, it is said to be one of the finest in the world; the Organ Festival in August pulls out all the stops, as do the Saturday afternoon concerts in summer (*July–Sept 3pm*).

Older attractions are two fine Renaissance palaces, both around Place Flavier, behind the church one street to the north. The **Hôtel Mistral de Mondragon** (1550) contains the **Musée des Alpilles** (*t 04 90 92 68 24; open July and Aug 10–12 and 2–7; April–June and Sept–Oct 10-12 and 2–6; Nov and Dec 10–12 and 2–5; closed Jan and Feb*), of local folk life and arts, with a special section on Nostradamus; the **Hôtel de Sade** has a small but interesting **Musée Archéologique** (*t 04 90 92 64 04; closed 2005, then open May–Aug 11–6; Sept–April 11–5; adm; guided tours in French every hour; combined ticket with Glanum and Musée des Alpilles available*). St-Rémy is the medieval successor to the abandoned Roman town of Glanum (*see* p.418); finds on display here include architectural fragments, statues and reliefs of deities from Hermes to the Phrygian god Attis, and Roman glass and jewellery.

The Grimaldi representative in St-Rémy lived in the beautiful 18th-century **Hôtel Estrine**, in Rue Estrine, now the **Centre d'Art Présence Vincent Van Gogh** (*t 04 90 92 34 72; open April–Dec Tues–Sun 10.30–12.30 and 2.30–6.30; adm*), where you'll find a permanent exhibition of photos and documents, plus a film on Van Gogh's life, as well as changing exhibitions of classic and contemporary art.

Other places to visit in the centre include the **Musée des Arômes** at 34 Bd Mirabeau (*www.florame.com*), with a display of scents, classic bottles and other items dating

Getting Around

By Bus

Although there are no trains, St-Rémy is surrounded by several big towns, so the bus service is a bit better than in other places. All buses leave from Pl de la République. There's at least one a day to Tarascon, more to Avignon. You can walk to Les Antiques (*see* below) and Glanum, but buses from St-Rémy to Les Baux-de-Provence only run July–Aug. The latter is better connected to Arles, with 4–5 buses a day, stopping at Fontvieille.

By Bicycle

The Alpilles are not too steep for cycling in most places; try **Karimoto**, Av de Fauconnet, t 04 90 92 54 00, *www.holiday-bikes.com*. You might enjoy a tour around the southern slopes of the Alpilles, looking for the spots where Van Gogh painted many of his landscapes (*inaccessible July–Sept*).

Tourist Information

St-Rémy-de-Provence: Place Jean Jaurès, on way to Les Antiques, t 04 90 92 05 22, *www.saintremy-de-provence.com*. Open Oct–Easter Mon–Sat 9–12 and 2–6; Easter–Sept Mon–Sat 9–12.30 and 2–7, Sun 10–12 and 3–6. Offers guided tours of Van Gogh's landscapes and the old town.

Market Days

St-Rémy-de-Provence: Wed am.

Where to Stay and Eat

St-Rémy-de-Provence ✉ 13210

St-Rémy gets heaps of tourists and has a wide choice of places to stay; it makes a convenient base for visiting the Alpilles and the Camargue.

****Hostellerie du Vallon de Valrugues**, chemin Canto Cigalo, t 04 90 92 04 40, *www.valrugues-cassagne.com* (*luxury– very expensive*). A hotel waiting to spoil you with lovely Provençal-style rooms, a pool, a sauna and Jacuzzi, a putting green and delicious meals in the palatial restaurant.

****Hôtel Les Ateliers de l'Image**, 36 Bd Victor Hugo, t 04 90 92 51 50, *www.hotelphoto.com* (*luxury–very expensive*). A photography gallery and workshop-cum-hotel, this place

back 3,000 years; and the 12th-century **Chapelle Notre-Dame-de-Pitié Donation Mario Prassinos**, near the tourist office on Avenue Durand Maillane (*t 04 90 92 35 13; open July–Aug daily 11–1 and 3–7; Mar–June and Sept–Dec daily 2–6; closed Jan and Feb*), containing 11 Peintures du Supplice painted for the chapel by Greek painter Mario Prassinos, long-time resident of nearby Eygalières, as well as a video on the artist and displays of some of the 105 works he donated to the government in 1985.

Les Antiques and Van Gogh's Asylum

The Romans had a habit of building monuments and impressive mausoleums on the outskirts of their towns, along the main roads. Just a 15-minute walk from the centre of St-Rémy-de-Provence, to the south on the D5, stand two of the most remarkable Roman relics in France. They were here long before the D5, of course; originally they decorated the end of the Roman road from Arles to Glanum, the ruins of which lie just across the D5. The **Triumphal Arch**, probably built in the reign of Augustus, was one of the first to be erected in Provence. Its elegant form and marble columns show the Greek sensibility of the artists – they are very far different from the strange Celtic-influenced arches of Orange and Carpentras. In the Middle Ages it inspired the creators of St-Trophime in Arles (*see* p.433). Evidently, someone long ago carted off the top for building stone; the slanted tile roof is an 18th-century addition to protect what was actually left.

oozes contemporary style in its 24 rooms and 8 suites (one with a treehouse). There's a swimming pool and a French–Japanese restaurant, **Chez l'Ami**, with a terrace with views on to the landscaped garden and beyond to the Alpilles. *Closed Jan–10 Feb.*

****Château des Alpilles**, D31, t 04 90 92 03 33, *www.chateaualpilles.com* (*very expensive*). A real haven outside the busy one-way rush of traffic around the centre, yet just a few steps outside town, in a park full of trees (some of them rare), with a tennis court and a swimming pool. It's all mirrors, period furniture (19th-century) and creature comforts. The restaurant is reserved for hotel guests. *Closed mid-Nov–mid-Feb; restaurant closed Wed.*

***Castellet des Alpilles**, 6 Place Mireille, t 04 90 92 07 21, *www.castelet-alpilles.com* (*moderate*). An old country mansion with pretty rooms and a lovely terrace under a century-old cedar. *Closed Nov–early Mar.*

Villa Glanum, 46 Av Vincent Van Gogh, t 04 90 92 03 59, *www.alpilles.com/villa.htm* (*moderate*). A place near the ruins, with surprising amenities for its price range: a pool and garden. *Closed Nov–mid-Mar.*

Hôtel du Cheval Blanc, 6 Av Fauconnet, t 04 90 92 09 28, *www.hotelcheval-blanc. com* (*inexpensive*). A centrally located and therefore noisy hotel, but a good spot if you want to look out on to the *place* when you wake. The owners are cheerful and helpful, and there's a private garage. *Closed Nov–Feb.*

La Maison Jaune, 15 Rue Carnot, t 04 90 92 56 14 (*expensive*). For dining in the centre of town, you won't do better than the panoramic terrace here, especially if you plump for the menu of Provençal specialities. *Closed winter Sun eve and Mon, summer Mon lunch and Tues lunch, plus Jan and Feb.*

L'Assiette de Marie, 1 Rue Jaume Roux, t 04 90 92 32 14 (*moderate*). An excellent place for vegetarians; try the home-made pasta. There's a good wine list. *Closed Thurs, lunch Mon–Fri in winter, and Jan.*

Le Bistrot des Alpilles, 15 Bd Mirabeau, t 04 90 92 09 17 (*moderate*). Fresh pasta, great desserts and a pleasant terrace. *Closed Sun.*

Charmeroy, 26 Bd Mirabeau, t 04 32 60 01 23 (*moderate*). A *salon de thé* serving genuine madeleines, Provençal-flavoured ice cream and a wide variety of teas. *Open Tues–Sun 10.30–12.30 and 3–7.*

Next to it, the so-called **Mausoleum** was really a memorial to Caesar and Augustus, erected by their descendants in the early 1st century AD. There is nothing else quite like this anywhere, and it is one of the best-preserved Roman monuments. The form is certainly original: it is a narrow four-faced arch on a solid plinth, surmounted by a cylinder of columns and a pointed roof, 56ft above the ground; inside are statues of Caesar and Augustus. The **reliefs** on the base are excellent: mythological scenes including a battle with Amazons, a battle of Greeks and Trojans and a boar hunt. At the top of the arch, you can make out a pair of winged spirits holding a civic crown of laurel – Augustus' symbol for his new political order.

Just across the road from Les Antiques, a shady path leads to the monastery of **St-Paul-de-Mausole** (*t 04 90 92 77 00; open April–Oct daily 9.15–7; Nov–Mar daily 10.15–4.45; adm*), in a beautiful setting with gardens all around. Founded in the 10th century, the complex includes a simple Romanesque church and a cloister. In 1810 the monastery buildings were purchased for use as a private hospital. This is the place Vincent Van Gogh chose as a refuge from the troubles of life in the outside world, in May 1890, not long after he chopped off the ear. He spent a year here, the most intense and original period of his career, painting as if possessed – 150 canvases and more than 100 drawings, including many of his most famous works, such as the *Nuit étoilée à Saint-Rémy* (*Starry Night*). The blueish mountains in the background of his work are the Alpilles. Appropriately enough, the patients and staff of the hospital have taken a keen interest in art therapy: you can see the results on the walls of the lovely cloister, as well as some interesting carved capitals.

Van Gogh painted the impressive Greco-Roman quarries just down the road, writing that they resembled a Japanese drawing. In the midst of the quarries, excavated out of the rock, the **Mas de la Pyramide** (*t 04 90 92 00 81; open daily 9–12 and 2–5, until 7 in summer; adm*) is one of the oldest farmhouses in the region – it dates at least from the 8th century. It contains typical Provençal furnishings and a collection of 19th-century farm tools.

Glanum

t 04 90 92 23 79; open April–Aug daily 9–7; Sept–Dec Tues 10.30–5; adm.

Glanum began as a Celtic settlement – a proper town, really, under a heavy cultural influence from the Greeks at nearby Marseille. The Romans under Marius snatched it around 100 BC, but not until the great prosperity of the Augustan Empire did the city begin to bloom. Almost all of the ruins visible today (as well as Les Antiques) date from this period. In a prelude to the fall of the Empire, the Franks and Alemanni ranged throughout Gaul in the 250s and 260s. In one of their last hurrahs before the recovering Roman legions drove them out, they sacked Glanum in 270. After that, the townspeople relocated to a healthier and safer site, today's St-Rémy; silt washed down from the Alpilles gradually covered the city and it passed out of memory until the 19th century, when some accidental finds alerted archaeologists to its presence. Excavations began in 1921, and have since uncovered a fascinating cross-section of Glanum, including its forum. More than Vaison-la-Romaine (*see* pp.369–74) or anywhere else in France, this is the place to really feel at home in the Roman world. But you'll have to work for it; only the foundations remain, and recreating Glanum will require a bit of imagination (see the museum in the Hôtel de Sade first).

From the entrance, to the left are the **Maison des Antes** and the **Maison d'Atys**, two typical wealthy homes built around peristyle courtyards. The latter had apparently been transformed into a sanctuary of Cybele and Attis; this cult was one of the most popular of the mystery religions imported from the east in Imperial times. Across the street are remains of a fountain and the *thermae* (baths), with mosaics, a *palaestra* (exercise yard) and a *piscina* (pool). Next door is a building with an exedra that was probably a temple; altars to Silenus were found inside. In this part of the street the sewers have been uncovered. The forum wasn't very impressive, by the standards of most Roman towns, and it is hard to make anything out today from the confusion of buildings from various ages that have been excavated. Beyond it, to the right, are foundations of temples; to the left are bases of another fountain and a monument. The street closes at a gate from Hellenistic times that was retained as the city expanded outside the original walls. Also retained was the *nymphaeum* beyond it, to the left; these decorated fountains were a common feature of Greek cities, built to allow travellers to refresh and clean up before entering the town.

The Chaîne des Alpilles

The ruins were nice, but there is an even greater treat ahead. The five twisting kilometres of the D5 that take you from Les Antiques into the heart of the Alpilles are, in fact, one of the greatest sensual experiences that Provence can offer. Vincent Van Gogh and cypresses, lushness and flowers are left behind; in a matter of minutes the road has brought you to another world. This world, incredibly, is at most 16km across, and a stone's throw away from the swamps of the Camargue and the sea. It is made up of thin, cool breezes and brilliant light; its colours are white and deep green, almost exclusively – in an astringent landscape of limestone crags and patches of scrubby *maquis*.

Les Baux-de-Provence

A l'asard, Bauthezar!
('Kill 'em at random, Balthazar!')
           Battle cry of the Seigneurs des Baux

From as early as 3000 BC, this exotic massif attracted its fair share of residents. The Alpille mountains are full of caves, many of which were once inhabited. The Ligurians took advantage of its natural defences to found an important *oppidum* at Les Baux, a steep barren plateau located in the centre of the massif, 11km from St-Rémy-de-Provence. In the Middle Ages, this made the perfect setting for the most feared and celebrated of Provence's noble clans. The Seigneurs des Baux are first heard of in the 10th century. 'A race of eaglets, vassals never,' as their slogan went, they never acknowledged the authority of the French king, the emperors, or anyone else, and their impregnable crag in the Alpilles allowed them to get away with it. They claimed to be descended from Balthazar, one of the magi at Bethlehem, and put the Christmas star on their feudal escutcheon.

The symbol was never a harbinger of glad tidings to their neighbours, however, for over the course of the following two centuries the lords of Baux waged incessant warfare on all comers, and occasionally on each other, gradually becoming a real power in Provence. They did it with flair, however, and the chronicles are full of good stories about them: one *seigneur* once besieged the castle of his pregnant niece and sent sappers to undermine her bedchamber. And they met memorable ends: one was stabbed to death by his wife, another flayed alive when he fell into the hands of his enemies.

All the while, the family headquarters at Les Baux maintained a polished court where troubadours were always welcome. It ended with a bang in 1372, when an even nastier fellow took over: Raymond de Turenne, a distant relation who was also a nephew of Pope Gregory IX. Taking advantage of confused times in the reign of Queen Jeanne, this ambitious and bloodthirsty intriguer found enough support, and enough foreign mercenaries, to bring full-scale civil war to Provence, bringing it the same kind of misery to which the rest of France had become accustomed in the Hundred Years' War.

When the last heir of Les Baux died in 1426, the possessions of the house were incorporated into the county of Provence. That isn't quite the end of the story; in the 16th century Les Baux began to thrive once more, first under Anne of Montmorency, who rebuilt the *seigneurs'* castle in the best Renaissance taste, and later under the Manvilles, who inherited it and made it a Protestant stronghold in the Wars of Religion. Cardinal Richelieu finally put this eternal trouble-spot to rest in 1632, demolishing the castle and sending the owners the bill for the job. Until the Revolution, the remains of Les Baux were, like St-Rémy, in the hands of the Grimaldis of Monaco.

After the demolition, the village that surrounded the castle of Les Baux almost disappeared; Prosper Mérimée, in the 1830s, reported only a few beggars living among its ruins. But Provençal writers kept the place from being forgotten – men such as Mistral (born at Maillane, near St-Rémy; *see* p.406, and Alphonse Daudet, whose famous windmill is just over the Alpilles (*see* p.424). In the last 50 years, Les Baux has become the second-biggest tourist attraction in France after the Mont St-Michel. The village below the castle has been rebuilt and repopulated in the worst way, and whatever spark of glamour survives in this tremendous ruin, you'll have to run the gauntlet of shops peddling trinkets, scowling dolls, herbs, *santons* and soaps to reach it.

The first sight to greet you as you trudge up from the car park is an elegant carved Renaissance fireplace, open to the sky and standing right next to a souvenir shop. Walk a bit further, bearing right, and you will come to the **Musée des Santons** on

Tourist Information

Les Baux-de-Provence: Maison du Roy, t 04 90 54 34 39, *www.lesbauxdeprovence.com*. *Open April–Sept Mon–Fri 9–7, Sat and Sun 10–7; Oct–Mar Mon–Fri 9–1 and 2–6, Sat and Sun 10–1 and 2–6*. Has a list of B&Bs.

Fontvieille: 5 Rue M. Honorat, t 04 90 54 67 49, *www.fontvieille-provence.com*. *Open mid-Sept–mid-June Mon–Sat 9–12 and 2–6; mid–June–mid-Sept Mon–Sat 9–12 and 2–6, Sun 9–12.15 and 2–6.30*.

Market Days

Fontvieille: Mon and Fri.

Where to Stay and Eat

Les Baux-de-Provence ✉ 13520

Les Baux, with its tourist hordes, isn't the most desirable place to stop over, and you'll have to pay a lot for the privilege.

★★★★**Oustau de Baumanière**, Route d'Arles, t 04 90 54 33 07, *www.oustaudebaumaniere. com* (*luxury*). A restored Relais & Châteaux affiliated farmhouse in magical setting in the Val d'Enfer, with all the amenities that you could hope for, including a highly rated restaurant (two Michelin stars; *very expensive*) affording spectacular views from its terrace, fabulous desserts and a formidable wine list boasting more than 100,000 bottles of Provençal treasures. *Closed Jan and Feb; restaurant closed Wed and Thurs lunch in winter*.

★★★★**La Cabro d'Or**, on D27, t 04 90 54 33 21, *www.lacabrodor.com* (*luxury–expensive*). A charming Relais & Châteaux hotel offering similar facilities to the Oustau de Baumanière, including a gourmet restaurant. *Closed Mon in winter and Tues lunch*.

★★★**Mas de L'Oulivié**, on D78F towards Fontvieille, t 04 90 54 35 78, *www.masde loulivie.com* (*expensive*). A modern hotel built in the traditional Provençal style among the olive groves and lavender fields. Lunch is served around a landscaped pool. An elegant, comfortable option with attentive service. *Closed Oct–mid-Mar*.

★★★**Le Mas d'Aigret**, on D27 (south of Les Baux), t 04 90 54 20 00, *www.masdaigret.com* (*expensive–moderate*). A hotel with great

Place Louis Jou, which you could easily give a miss. Further up the street, past the ramparts, is the **Porte d'Eyguières**, which until the 18th century was the only entrance to the city.

Up Rue de la Calade you come to Place de l'Eglise, where the 16th-century Hôtel des Porcelet has become the **Musée Yves Brayer** (*t 04 90 54 36 99; www.yvesbrayer.com; open daily April–Sept 10–12.30 and 2–6.30, Oct–mid-Jan and mid-Feb–Mar 10–12.30 and 2–5.30; adm*). Brayer (1907–90), a respected figurative painter, left his major works here – pictures of Spain and Italy as well as Provence. You can get a preview of his work in the 17th-century **Chapelle des Pénitents Blancs** opposite the museum, where he frescoed scenes of a shepherds' Christmas (*same hours as museum*).

St-Vincent, located in the same square, dates from the 12th and 16th centuries. This is probably the coolest and least crowded place in Les Baux; there's a Cistercian nave, and some stained glass by Max Ingrand (1955), donated by Prince Rainier of Monaco. The domed turret with gargoyles on the south side is a *Lanterne des Morts*, a rare medieval survival: whenever anyone died in Les Baux, it would be announced by a flame.

Also in the village are the Hôtel Jean de Brion and the Hôtel de Manville, on the Grand-Rue. The first houses the **Fondation Louis Jou** (*t 04 90 54 34 17; open for groups of at least 30 by appointment; adm*), containing Jou's engravings, as well as pre-20th-century ones, engravings by Dürer, Rembrandt and Goya, and early books. The second

---

views from some rooms, others opening on to the gardens, and still others (*chambres troglodytes*) hewn from the rock face. There is a swimming pool, and attention is paid to every detail. *Half-board obligatory mid-July–mid-Aug. Closed Nov–Mar.*

**Hostellerie de la Reine Jeanne, Grand' Rue, t 04 90 54 32 06, *www.la-reinejeanne.com* (*inexpensive*). A basic, relatively cheap option in the village itself, with a bird's-eye view and a restaurant (*moderate*). *Closed Nov–mid-Dec.*

Fontvieille ✉ 13990

****Auberge La Régalido, Rue Frédéric Mistral, t 04 90 54 60 22, *www.avignon-et-provence.com/regalido* (*luxury–expensive*). A luxurious Relais & Châteaux hotel in a restored mill, with lovely gardens and a restaurant that is a little temple of *haute cuisine* (with prices to match), serving *agneau des Alpilles* and a special menu dedicated to olives. *Closed Jan–Feb; restaurant closed Mon, and Tues lunch.*

***La Peiriero, 36 Av des Baux (just north of town) t 04 90 54 76 10, *www.hotel-peiriero.*

com (*expensive–moderate*). A family-friendly hotel with a large garden, a pool and table tennis. There are family rooms sleeping 4, and an inventive kid's menu. *Closed Nov–Mar.*

***Val Majour, Avenue d'Arles, t 04 90 54 62 33, *www.valmajour.com* (*moderate*). A hotel with well-furnished, quiet rooms, plus a swimming pool, a tennis court and Internet access for guests.

**Hôtel de la Tour, 3 Rue des Plumelets, t 04 90 54 72 21 (*moderate–inexpensive*). Budget *Logis de France* rooms in bungalows around a pool. *Closed Nov–mid-Mar.*

La Cuisine au Planet, 144 Grand-Rue, t 04 90 54 63 97 (*expensive*). A restaurant where you can tuck into excellent Provençal *haute cuisine*.

Le Homard, Route du Nord, t 04 90 54 75 34 (*moderate*). Appetizing home cooking; there's no lobster, despite the name, but *terrine de poisson, filet de rascasse* (scorpion fish) and *cassoulet* feature on the menus. You can accompany them with local Coteaux des Baux-en-Provence wines (*see p.422*). Make sure to reserve a table in advance. *Closed mid-Nov–20 Dec.*

Wine: Coteaux des Baux-en-Provence

The AOC wine of the Alpilles is rosé, like most of Provence's vintages, but in recent years the reds of Les Baux have made a quantum jump in terms of quality and attracted the most attention. This relatively new *appellation* comes under the heading of Coteaux d'Aix-en-Provence, and a majority of its growers are good environmentalists dedicated to growing grapes that are free from artificial fertilizers, pesticides and herbicides; the grapes that grow into it include grenache, cabernet sauvignon, syrah, cinsault, carignan and counoise.

A good source is the charming **Domaine de La Vallongue**, in Eygalières, t 04 90 95 91 70, which uses traditional methods to create organic wines: fresh, fruity, fragrant rosés and intense reds, hinting at vanilla and spice; they had a succession of good vintages in the late 1990s. **Domaine Hauvette**, in St-Rémy, t 04 90 92 03 90, is a tiny estate but one of the very few vineyards in the region that is both owned and run by a woman, Dominique Hauvette, whose wines (which are also organic) have a warm, velvety quality.

In Les Baux itself, at the foot of the cliffs, visitors can take a didactic nature walk through the vines of **Mas Ste-Berthe**, t 04 90 54 39 01, and learn all about the grapes, some of which (ugni blanc, sauvignon and grenache blanc) go into the white wine.

is the Hôtel de Ville. Both these and the Hôtel des Porcelet date from the architectural development of the 16th century, before the castle was destroyed.

Next comes the **citadel** (*t 04 90 54 55 56; open daily summer 9–9; spring 9–7.30; autumn 9–6.30; winter 9–5; adm*), and a museum to keep tramping tourists from the thing itself. The **Musée d'Histoire des Baux** is perfectly pleasant, with illustrations and archaeological finds as well as models in glass cases, to give you an overview, or to save you the walk over the site outside if the mistral is blowing.

When you see Les Baux itself, the ambience changes abruptly – it is a rocky chaos surreally decorated with fragments of once-imposing buildings. The path leads through this 'Ville Morte' (on the left are remains of the hospital and the Chapelle Saint-Blaise, where you can watch a slide show on the olive tree) to the tip of the plateau, where there is a monument to Provençal poet Charlon Rieu, and a grand view over the Alpilles.

Turning back, the path then climbs up to the **château** itself, which has bits of towers and walls everywhere, including the apse of a Gothic chapel that was carved out of the rock, and the long eastern wall that managed to survive Richelieu's explosives, dotted with a number of finely carved windows. What resembles a monolithic honeycomb is really a 13th-century pigeonry. Medieval siege engines have been reconstructed to add something of the spirit of the gangsters who built the place. The only intact part is the **donjon**. It's a rather treacherous climb to the top for a bird's-eye view over the site. Locals say the best time to see it is with a blanket, under a starry night.

An Infernal Valley and a Blonde Sorceress

South of Les Baux, on the western side, the **Pavillon de la Reine Jeanne** has nothing to do with the famous queen, but is a pretty Renaissance garden folly of 1581. The road that passes it will take you in another 3km to the **Val d'Enfer**, the wildest corner of the Alpilles, a weird landscape of eroded limestone, caves and quarries. One thing the Alpilles has a lot of is aluminium ore – bauxite – which was a useless mineral until the process for smelting it was discovered in the 19th century. Now there are bauxite mines all over southern Provence; those to be seen here are exhausted, but Jean Cocteau took advantage of the landscape to shoot part of his last film, *Testament d'Orphée*. Today the quarries host one of Les Baux's big attractions, the **Cathédrale d'Images** (*t 04 90 54 38 65; www.cathedrale-images.com; open mid-Feb–Mar and Oct–Dec 10–6; April–Sept 10–7; closed Jan–mid-Feb; last entry 5.15; adm*), a slick show where 30 projectors bounce giant pictures over the walls; the theme of the show changes annually.

Off the D27A, near the crossroads for Les Baux, the **Col de la Vayède** holds scanty remains of the pre-Roman *oppidum*; the lines of the walls can be traced in some places, and there are bits of wall and no fewer than three necropoli, with small niches carved into the rock to hold the ashes of the deceased. On the side of the hill facing the D27A, you can climb up a dirt path to see the mysterious relief called the **Trémaïé**. Neatly carved on a smoothed rockface are three figures and an effaced Latin inscription. It seems to be a Roman funeral monument, but local legend has it that the figures represent Marius, his wife and a blonde Celtic sorceress named Marthe who helped Marius in his campaigns against the Teutones. Another relief, less well preserved, can be seen a few hundred metres to the south. Finally, for hikers, there is the **GR6 trail**, which traverses the best parts of the Alpilles from east to west. It passes right through Les Baux.

St-Gabriel and Fontvieille

The eastern half of the Alpilles is the more scenic, and, if you're heading in that direction, lonely roads such as the D78 and D24 make worthwhile detours that won't take you more than a few kilometres out of the way; **Eygalières**, on the D24B, is a lovely village with a ruined castle.

Along the western fringes of the Alpilles, on the D33, you will pass the canal port of Ernaginum, later called St-Gabriel, which flourished from Roman times until the Middle Ages. You won't see anything; the drying-up of the old canal doomed the city to a slow death, and Ernaginum has disappeared more completely than any ancient city of Provence, leaving only the impressive 12th-century church of **St-Gabriel** standing alone in open fields. There is little to see inside and it's never open anyhow; the real interest is one of the finest Romanesque façades in the Midi. Very consciously imitating Roman architecture, it shows a stately portal with a triangular pediment, flanked by Corinthian columns. There are excellent sculpted reliefs on and above the tympanum: an *Annunciation*, *Daniel in the Lions' Den* and *Adam and Eve*, apparently just realizing they have no clothes on. Above it, a small Italianate rose window is surrounded by figures of the four Evangelists.

From here, the only village on the way to Arles is **Fontvieille**, best known for the **Moulin de Daudet**, south on the D33, a rare survivor among the hundreds of windmills that once embellished every hilltop of southern Provence. Alphonse Daudet never really lived here, but his *Lettres de mon moulin*, a collection of sentimental tales of the dying life of rural Provence in the late 19th century, is still popular across France today. The windmill has become a museum to Daudet, with photographs and documents. It has a huge car park where coaches like fridges on wheels disgorge cooled tourists, and local driving instructors take their pupils to practise.

Two kilometres further south, there are sections of two Roman **aqueducts** that served Arles, along with vestiges of a **Roman mill**, unique in Europe. This huge installation was a serious precursor to the Industrial Revolution, using the flow of the water to power 16 separate mills along a stretch of canal over a kilometre long; nothing like it has been found anywhere else. There's no tourist tack, not even a railing. Give Daudet a miss and visit this instead.

The Hypogeum of Castellet

On the D17, at the crossroads with the D82, you will find a very ruined castle that once belonged to the counts of Provence. The surrounding area, a low, flat-topped hill called Castellet, contains one of the most unusual and least-known Neolithic monuments in France. The **Hypogeum** consists of four covered avenues, carefully carved out of the rock or earth, under tumuli that have long since disappeared. They were made as collective tombs about 3500 BC or later by the Ligurians or their predecessors, and probably also served as a kind of temple. Many have carvings, cup-marks and sun-symbols, inside or near their openings. The sites are not marked, and you may have to scramble and scout to find their narrow, trapezoïdal entrances in the undergrowth. All are within 400 metres of the D17, three south of the road and one to the north.

From Castellet you'll see another hill, the **Montagne de Cordes**, located about half a kilometre to the south. Like Castellet, this was an island in Neolithic times. Nearby Montmajour (*see* below) was a third. The Cordes is private property and you'll need permission from the owner (in the farmhouse on the slopes) to see another remarkable tomb-temple, the **Grotte des Fées**, also known as the '*Epée de Roland*'; the tapering 230ft tunnel has two small side chambers that give it the shape of a sword.

Abbaye de Montmajour

Route de Fontvieille, t 04 90 54 64 17; open April–Sept daily 9–7; Oct–Mar Wed–Mon 10–5.

Just before Arles, the D17 passes one of the most important monasteries of medieval Provence. Founded in the 10th century, on what was at that time almost an island amidst the swamps, this Benedictine abbey was devoted to reclaiming the land – a monumental labour that would take centuries to complete. By the 14th century the monastery had grown exceedingly wealthy – a real prize for the Avignon popes, who gained control of it and farmed it out, along with its revenues, to friends and relations. Under such absentee abbots, it languished thereafter, and its great church was never completed. An attempt to reform it in 1639 included importing new monks; the old crew refused to go and sacked the abbey before they were chased out by royal troops.

Montmajour became a national property not in the Revolution, but five years earlier. The 1786 'Affair of the Diamond Necklace' was a famous swindle that involved both Marie-Antoinette and the great charlatan Cagliostro. One of the principal players was Montmajour's abbot, the Cardinal de Rohan; he got caught, and all his property, including the abbey, was confiscated. The abbey did service as a farmhouse, and its church as a barn, before restorations began in 1907. Consequently, there isn't a great deal to see.

At the church entrance you'll notice the **piers**, built into the adjacent wall of the cloister, that would have supported the nave had it been completed. The interior is austere and empty, but gives a good idea of the state of Provençal architecture *c.*1200, in transition from Romanesque to Gothic. The most interesting part is the **lower church**, a crypt with an unusual plan, including a long, narrow nave and a circular enclosure under the high altar, with radiating chapels behind it; its purpose remains obscure.

The **cloister** has some fanciful sculptural decoration; see if you can find the camel. Around the back of the church, you'll see a number of tombs cut out of the rock; these are a mystery, too, and may predate the abbey. The mighty 85ft **donjon** was built in the 1360s for defence, in that terrible age when the lords of Les Baux and a dozen other hoodlums were tearing up the neighbourhood; next to it, the tiny chapel of **St-Pierre** (usually closed) was the original abbey church, built on the spot where St Trophime (Trophimus) of Arles (*see* below) had his hermitage.

Ste-Croix

A few hundred metres behind the apse of the church, in the middle of a farm, stands what was the abbey's funeral chapel, **Ste-Croix**. Don't miss it, though you have to walk through the farmyard muck (it's visible from the road, near a barn). There are few buildings that demonstrate so convincingly the architectural sophistication of the Romanesque as this small work of the late 11th century, a central-plan chapel with apses along three sides and an elegant lantern on top. Some complex geometry and a mastery of proportions went into this simple but perfect form, based on the Golden Section. Too much decoration would be superfluous; there is only a discreet carved floral frieze along the cornice, along with some Moorish-style interlocking arches.

Arles

Like Nîmes, Arles has enough intact antiquities to call itself the 'Rome of France'; unlike Nîmes, it lingered in the post-Roman limelight for another thousand years, producing enough saints for every month on the calendar – Trophimus, Hilarius, Césaire and Genès are some of the more famous. Pilgrims flocked here for a whiff of

Getting Around

By Train

The train station on Av Paulin Talabot has frequent connections to Paris, Marseille, Montpellier, Nîmes, Aix-en-Provence, and towns in Spain.

There are also frequent train services to Avignon and Tarascon, and a less frequent service to Orange.

By Bus

The *gare routière* is just across the street from the train station, t 0800 19 93 13. There are several daily buses to Albaron and Saintes-Maries-de-la-Mer in the Camargue, as well as daily buses to Tarascon, Salon-de-Provence, Aix, Marseille, Avignon, Nîmes and St-Gilles, among other destinations; in July and Aug there are services to Aigues-Mortes.

(Before you hurry into Arles from here, step over the road for a minute to the bank of the Rhône and admire the city on the bend of the river – an unlikely spot for an unparalleled view.)

By Taxi

For a taxi day or night, call t 04 90 96 90 03 (Jardin d'Eté, Bd des Lices).

Car Hire

Europcar, t 04 90 93 23 24, and **Hertz, t** 04 90 96 75 23, can both be found on Av Victor Hugo.

Bike Hire

Hire a bike at the train station, at **Dall'Oppio Hugues**, Rue Portagnel, t 04 90 96 46 83 (*Mar–Oct*).

Tourist Information

Arles: Bd des Lices, next to Jules César hotel, t 04 90 18 41 20, *www.arles.org*. Open *April–Sept daily 9–6.45; Oct–Nov Mon–Sat 9–5.45, Sun 10.30–2.15; Dec–Mar 9–4.45, Sun 10.30–2.15*. There's another office in the train station, t 04 90 49 36 90; *open Mon–Sat 9–1*. If you intend to see more than two of Arles' monuments and museums, buy the €13.50 **global ticket** to save money (you can also pick one up at any of the museums). The office also sells tickets for various city tours in English.

Post office: 5 Bd des Lices, t 04 90 18 41 00.

Market Days

Sat: Bd des Lices and Bd Georges Clemenceau.
Wed: Bd Emile Combes.
First Wed of month: *foire à la brocante*, Bd des Lices.

Festivals and Annual Events

Arles does its best to keep visitors entertained. The free broadsheet *Farandole* gives details of everything from theatre, concerts, fairs and exhibitions to local basketball results.

their odour of sanctity, and asked on their deathbeds to be buried in the holy ground of the Alyscamps (*see* p.436). Nowadays, Arles is the largest *commune* in France; it's ten times larger than Paris, embracing 750 square kilometres of the Camargue and Crau plains; it has given the world the rhythms of the Gypsy Kings and the pungent joys of *saucisson d'Arles*, France's finest donkey-meat sausage.

Henry James wrote: 'As a city Arles quite misses its effect in every way: and if it is a charming place, as I think it is, I can hardly tell the reason why.' Modern Arles *is* charming, in spite of a scruffiness that seems more intentional than natural. For all the tourists, no town could seem less touristy; a paper mill across the Rhône wafts its stink over the down-at-heel old quarters, while grass grows between the pavement cracks around the Roman ruins and medieval palaces. Unhappily, Jeanne Calment, born here in 1876, who met Van Gogh as a young girl and was for a long while the oldest person in the world, died in 1997. The city's pride in her longevity continues though, and the way to her grave is clearly marked in the cemetery at Trinquetaille.

Easter is celebrated by a **Feria Pascale**, with four days of bullfights, most of them Spanish *corridas* (for ticket reservations for Arènes events, call **t** 04 90 96 03 70. On 24 June, the **Fête de St Jean**, there are typical Arlésien dances in costume around bonfires, and the distribution of blessed bread.

July is the busiest month, with a festival of music, dance and drama, the **Cocarde d'Or** bullfights, and the **Rencontres Internationales de la Photographie**, with shows and workshops, held in the Théâtre Antique. At the end of Aug there's the **Festival du Film Peplum**. The last bullfights of the year, held on the second Sun in Sept, coincide with the **Prémices du Riz**, or rice harvest.

Shopping

L'Arlésienne, 12 Rue du Président Wilson, **t** 04 90 93 28 05. Traditional clothes for women.

Arlys, 35 Place Voltaire, **t** 04 90 96 45 89. Provençal fabrics and *santons*.

Cabane Soleil, 15 Rue du Quatre-Septembre, **t** 04 90 96 07 34. Enchanting locally made puppets, as well as other modern curiosities in metal and wood.

Camille, 15 Bd Georges Clemenceau, **t** 04 90 96 04 94. Authentic *gardian* costumes.

Puyricard, 5 Rue de la République, **t** 04 90 93 46 91. The place to buy *calissons d'Aix*, or to come just to see the crystallized fruits,

marzipan models, chocolates and other bright goodies stacked like small sugared mountains.

Les Olivades, 2 Rue Jean Jaurès, **t** 04 90 96 22 17. Colourful Provençal fabrics.

Sia Decoration, Rue de la République, **t** 04 90 96 04 76. Good for souvenirs.

Any good butcher you come across in town will sell you spicy donkey-filled *saucissons d'Arles*.

Where to Stay

Arles ✉ 13200

Arles charges less for better accommodation than you'll get in cities such as Avignon or Aix-en-Provence.

If you arrive without a reservation, the tourist office provides a room-finding service for a small fee.

Luxury

****Jules César ('Chez Jules'), Bd des Lices, **t** 04 90 52 52 52, *www.hotel-julescesar.fr*. The luxurious grand-daddy of hotels in Arles, now part of the Relais & Châteaux chain, in a former Dominican monastery with a Caesar-ish temple porch tacked on. Rooms are vast, air-conditioned and furnished with Provençal pieces; the pool is heated and the gardens are beautiful. *See* p.430 for its restaurant, **Lou Marquès**. *Closed Nov–23 Dec*.

History

In 1975 the remains of a Celto-Ligurian settlement were uncovered close to the Boulevard des Lices. It's hard to imagine what its builders thought in the 6th century BC, when Greek traders from Marseille arrived and began to haggle over prices. We know at least that the Greeks were pleased, and over the years they established the site as their principal 'counter' for dealings with the Ligurians, calling it Arelate (meaning 'near sleeping waters' or, less poetically, 'bog town').

Business picked up considerably after Marius' legionaries transformed Arelate into a seaport by digging a canal to Fos (104 BC). In 49 BC the populace, tired of getting bum deals from the wily Greeks, readily gave Caesar the boats he needed to punish and conquer Marseille for siding with Pompey. In return, Arles was rewarded the spoils and received a population boost with a colony of veterans from the Sixth Legion. Most important of all, it got all the business that had previously gone through Greek

Very Expensive

****Nord Pinus**, Place du Forum, **t** 04 90 93 44 44, *www.nord-pinus.com*. The former favourite of the Félibres, poets and literati such as Stendhal, Mérimée and Henry James, now the haunt of top matadors and wealthy aficionados. The public spaces are full of heavy, dark furniture and bullfighting posters, rooms are spacious and beautifully decorated. Look out for the columns from a Roman temple in the façade. No restaurant. *Closed mid-Jan–mid-Feb.*

Expensive

***Hôtel d'Arlatan**, 26 Rue Sauvage, **t** 04 90 93 56 66, *www.hotel-arlatan.fr*. Near lively Place du Forum, this 12th–18th-century home of the comtes d'Arlatan has been run by the same welcoming family for five genera-tions. Wait for the lift standing on glass over Roman excavations; the house was built over part of the Constantine basilica, and in 1988 a Roman drain and a statue plinth from the 1st century BC were uncovered. The smaller rooms (24 and 38, with shared bath-room; *moderate*) have a view of the courtyard with its fountain. *Closed Jan.*

Moderate

***Auberge du Mas de la Fenière**, Allée des Prairies, Raphèle-les-Arles ✉ 13280, 5km east of Arles on N453, **t** 04 90 98 47 44, *www.lafeniere.com*. An attractive, ivy-covered inn on the edge of the Crau, with pleasant rooms, some with air-conditioning, and a restaurant (*expensive*) with an outdoor terrace, offering Camarguaise beef, duck with olives, salmon roulades and the like. *Closed Jan; restaurant closed Mon out of season.*

***Hôtel du Forum**, 10 Place du Forum, **t** 04 90 93 48 95, *www.hotelduforum.com*. A recently renovated hotel with a pool. *Closed Nov–Feb.*

Saint-Trophime, 16 Rue de la Calade, **t** 04 90 96 88 38, *www.hotel-saint-trophime.com*. A reasonable option situated in an old house with a central courtyard. *Closed mid-Jan–mid-Feb.*

Le Calendal, 5 Rue Porte-de-Laure (just in front of Arènes), **t** 04 90 96 11 89, *www.lecalendal.com*. A good hotel for families, with a buffet restaurant. Rooms overlook a garden with palms. *Closed Jan.*

Hôtel de l'Amphithéâtre, 5–7 Rue Diderot, **t** 04 90 96 10 30, *www.hotelamphitheatre.fr* (*moderate–inexpensive*). A stylish, good-value hotel behind the amphitheatre.

Ecole de Cuisine Provençale, 11 Rue Portagnel, **t** 04 90 49 69 20, *www.cuisineprovencale.com*. Cooking workshops run by Erick Vedel, the high priest of Provençal cuisine, plus three B&B rooms (*low moderate*).

Inexpensive

There is a wide choice of accommodation in the inexpensive bracket on the streets leading towards the train station.

Marseille. A bridge of boats was constructed over the Rhône, and the Colonia Julia Paterna Arelate Sextanorum became known far and wide for its powerful maritime corporations, called *utriculares* from their rafts that floated on inflated bladders.

Fortuitously situated at the crossroads of Rome's trading route between Italy and Spain and the Rhône, Arles increased rapidly in size, with each new century adding more splendid monuments – a theatre, several temples, a circus, an amphitheatre, at least two triumphal arches, and a basilica. Constantine had himself a grand palace built, together with baths that were as big as Caracalla's in Rome. In AD 395, Emperor Honorius made it the capital of the 'Three Gauls' – France, Britain and Spain – and as late as 418 it was recorded that 'Arles is so fortunately placed, its commerce is so active and merchants come in such numbers that all the products of the universe are channelled there: the riches of the Orient, perfumes of Arabia, delicacies of Assyria...'

★★Hôtel Le Cloître, 16 Rue du Cloître, **t** 04 90 96 29 50. A friendly and well-priced if somewhat austerely decorated hotel in the town centre, once part of a 12th-century cloister. *Closed Nov–mid-Mar.*

★★Hôtel du Musée, 11 Rue du Grand-Prieuré, **t** 04 90 93 88 88, *www.hoteldumusee.com.fr*. An attractively converted 17th-century residence located opposite the Musée Réattu. Quiet, subtly chic and friendly. *Closed Jan.*

★Hôtel de France et de la Gare, 2 Place Lamartine, **t** 04 90 96 01 24. A good budget option.

★Terminus et Van Gogh, 5 Place Lamartine, **t** 04 90 96 12 32. A bright and welcoming choice representing good value for this price range.

Auberge de Jeunesse, 20 Av Maréchal Foch, **t** 04 90 96 18 25, *www.fuaj.org*. A youth hostel reached by bus from Place Lamartine. *Closed 15 Dec–5 Feb.*

Eating Out

Lou Marquès, Jules César hotel (*see* p.328), **t** 04 90 52 52 523 (*expensive*). Arles' elegant citadel of traditional *haute cuisine*, offering dishes such as *carré d'agneau* with artichokes, and boasting an excellent wine cellar. *Closed Mon and Sat lunch, Nov and Dec.*

Le Jardin de Manon, 14 Av des Alyscamps, **t** 04 90 93 38 68 (*moderate*). A good place for lunch after a walk through

Les Alyscamps, serving *cuisine provençale* on a pretty back terrace. *Closed Wed and 2 wks Feb.*

La Charcuterie, 51 Rue des Arènes, **t** 04 90 96 56 96 (*moderate*). A popular restaurant serving traditional Lyonnais cuisine. *Closed Sun and Mon, and Aug.*

Entertainment and Nightlife

The most sociable bars in the city can be found in Place du Forum; for a spot of lazy watching-the-world-go-by, go for a chair in Place Voltaire or Bd des Lices.

Le Méjan/Actes Sud, 23 Place Nina Berberova, **t** 08 92 68 47 07. The liveliest place in Arles after dark, a complex that includes a book and record shop, an art gallery, a concert venue, 3 cinemas showing films in their original language (*v.o.*), a hammam, and a bar and restaurant where you can enjoy good couscous.

Cargo de Nuit, 9 Av Sadi Carnot, **t** 04 90 45 55 99. A bar offering live music and a philosophy night (*open till 5am Thurs–Sat*).

Le Femina, 14 Bd Emile Zola, **t** 04 90 96 10 10. A recommended bar and arthouse cinema.

Le Krystal, Chemin du Krystal, Moulès, **t** 04 90 98 32 40, *www.lekrystal.com*. An out-of-town nightclub.

Arles was one of the last cities to fall to the Visigoths, only to become their capital in 476. The Franks inherited it in 536, and Saracen raids were frequent. But on the whole the Dark Ages were not so dark in Arles; from 879 to 1036 it served as the capital of Provence-Burgundy (the so-called 'Kingdom of Arles'), a vast territory that stretched all the way to Lorraine. Most importantly, Arles was a centre of power for Christianity. Several major Church councils convened here, including one back in 314 that condemned the heresy of Donatism (the quite reasonable belief that sacraments administered by bad priests had no value). Arles' cathedral of St-Trophime became the most important church in Provence; in 597 its bishop, St Virgil, consecrated St Augustine as first Bishop of Canterbury, and as late as 1178, Emperor Frederick Barbarossa was crowned King of Arles at its altar.

After a busy career during the 11th and 12th centuries as a Crusader port and a pilgrimage destination, the city's special history ended in 1239 when Raymond

Bérenger, count of Provence, evicted Arles' imperial viceroy. As the city declined even the sea abandoned it, leaving the former port stranded between marshes and the rocky plain of the Crau, compressed in a time capsule of Roman monuments and ancient customs.

With the improved communications of the 19th century, Arles slowly resurfaced. The Roman amphitheatre was restored. The city's women, celebrated for their beautiful Attic features, inspired Daudet's story *L'Arlésienne* (1866) and Bizet's opera (1872). Its furniture-makers invented what has become the traditional south Provençal style, more elegantly rococo than the heavy pieces of northern Provence. The Félibres made much of the city for the striking costumes the women continued to wear, for its bullfights and for its *farandole*, a dance in 6/8 time dating back at least to the Middle Ages and perhaps to the ancient Greeks.

The Arles of Van Gogh

Vincent Van Gogh was a fervent admirer of Daudet, and it may well have been his stories that first brought him to Arles in February 1888. To his surprise, the city was blanketed with snow – a very rare occurrence and, in a way, an omen. When the snow melted it revealed an Arles made mean and ugly by new embankments along the Rhône, cutting the city off from its lifeblood (previously the flooding of the river had fertilized the countryside like the Nile in Egypt). At the same time, a new railway line was being installed by workers brought in from Belgium and housed in cheap buildings. Arles had never looked shabbier. But Van Gogh stayed, found a room to rent in a poor neighbourhood by the station, and painted the shabby Arles around him – the *Café de nuit* with its hallucinogenic lightbulb, *La Maison jaune* and *Le Pont de Langlois* (part of a ghastly irrigation project) – with colours so intense in their chromatic contrasts they seem to come from somewhere over the rainbow.

Van Gogh's dream was to found an art colony in Arles, similar to the one in Pont Aven in Brittany. He begged his overbearing friend Gauguin to join him, but when Gauguin finally arrived in October he found little to like in Arles, dashing Van Gogh's hopes. The tension between the two reached such a pitch in December that the overwrought Van Gogh went over the edge and confronted Gauguin with a razor. Gauguin stared him down and Van Gogh, despising himself, went back to his room, cut off his own ear and gave it to a prostitute. Arles was scandalized, and breathed a sigh of relief when Van Gogh committed himself to the local hospital, the Hôtel Dieu.

In May 1889 he left for the hospital in St-Rémy (*see* p.417). Van Gogh's output in Arles was prodigious (from February 1888 to May 1889 he painted 300 canvases), but not a single painting remains in the city. His admirers, looking for the places he painted, have just as little to see: the famous bridge, yellow house and café were destroyed in the Second World War or after; only the clock in Café de l'Alcazar in Place Lamartine remains as Van Gogh painted it (in *Café de nuit*), along with some of the plane trees around the Alyscamps. To make up for its belated appreciation of the mad, lonely genius who sojourned here, Arles has converted the Hôtel Dieu into a multimedia gallery, the **Espace Van Gogh** (*Rue Molière, t 04 90 52 05 50; call for opening times*), which displays work by other artists and also contains the town's library; it's worth a look inside at the lovely, colourful courtyard, restored to look as it did when Van Gogh painted it. Here, as elsewhere around Arles, the town has put up reproductions of his works. The **Fondation Vincent Van Gogh** (*24 bis Rond-Point des Arènes; t 04 90 49 94 04; www.fondationvangogh-arles.org; open April–Oct daily 10.30–8, Nov–Mar Tues–Sun 11–5*) exhibits work inspired by Van Gogh.

The Arènes and Théâtre Antique

Despite the pictures in children's history books, Rome was ruined not so much by tribes of horrid Vandals, but by the latter-day Romans themselves, who regarded the baths, theatres and temples they inherited as their private stone quarries. The same holds true of Arles' great monuments, except for the amphitheatre, **Les Arènes** (*t 04 90 96 03 70; open Nov–Feb daily 10–4.30; Mar–April and Oct 9–5.30; May–Sept 9–6.30*), all of 10ft wider than its rival in Nîmes. As enormous as it is, the amphitheatre originally stood another arcade higher and was clad in marble; as with most public buildings in the Roman Empire, no expense was spared on its comforts. A huge awning operated by sailors protected the audience from the sun and rain, and fountains scented with lavender and burning saffron helped cover up the stink of blood spilled by the gladiators and wild animals below. This temple of death survived in good repair because it came in handy. Its walls were tricked out with towers by Saracen occupiers and used as a fortress (like the theatres of Rome), and from the Middle Ages on it sheltered a poor, crime-ridden neighbourhood with two churches and 200 houses, built from stones prised off the amphitheatre's third storey. These were cleared away in 1825, leaving the amphitheatre free for bullfights and still able to pack in 12,000 spectators. The first was held in 1830, to celebrate the capture of Algiers.

A different fate was in store for the **Théâtre Antique** (*same hours as Arènes*), just south of the Arènes: in the 5th century, in a fury usually reserved for pagan temples, Christian fanatics pulled it apart stone by stone. A shame, because the fragments of fine sculpture they left in the rubble suggest that the theatre, once capable of seating 12,000, was much more lavish than the one in Orange. Of the stage, only two tall Corinthian columns survived; they were nicknamed 'the two widows', after being pressed into service as gibbets in the 17th and 18th centuries. The most famous statue of Roman Provence, the *Venus of Arles*, lay buried at their feet until she was dug up in 1651 and presented to Louis XIV to adorn the gardens of Versailles. Tiers of seats have been rebuilt for modern performances and costume pageants.

South of the theatre runs the **Boulevard des Lices** ('of the lists'), where large cafés under the plane trees provide ringside seats for the rollicking markets (*see* p.427). Since the 17th century, the boulevard, where visitors such as Van Gogh would go on Sunday to see the women dressed in their best costumes, has been the favourite promenade of Arlésiens. On either side of the street are the **Jardin d'Eté** (with a bust of Van Gogh) and **Jardin d'Hiver** (where the 5th-century BC *oppidum* was uncovered).

Place de la République: St-Trophime

From Boulevard des Lices, Rue Jean Jaurès (the Roman *cardo*) leads to the harmonious **Place de la République**, an attractive square on the Roman model, with a fountain built around a granite **obelisk** that once stood in the *spina* (or barrier) of the circus. Overlooking this pagan sun needle is one of the glories of Provençal Romanesque, the cathedral of **St-Trophime**. The original church, constructed by St Hilaire in the 5th century and dedicated to St Stephen, was rebuilt at the end of the 11th century, with the great **portal** added in the next – it is one of the best-preserved ensembles of Romanesque sculpture in the Midi. Inspired by the triumphal arches of Glanum and Orange, its reliefs describe the Last Judgement, mixing the versions of the Apocalypse and Gospel of Matthew. As angels blast away on their trumpets, the triumphant Christ sits in majesty in the tympanum, accompanied by the symbols of the four Evangelists, the 12 Apostles, and a gospel choir of 18 pairs of angels. On the left side, St Michael weighs each soul, separating the good from the evil for their just deserts in the afterlife – the fortunate in their long robes are delivered into the bosoms of Abraham, Isaac and Jacob, while the damned, naked and bound like a chain gang, are led off in a conga-line to hell: as in all great Romanesque art, the figures on this portal seem to dance to an inner, cosmic rhythm.

The large saints set back in the columned recesses below are, from left to right: Bartholomew, James the Minor, Trophime as bishop, John the Evangelist, Peter (over the man-eating lions), Paul, Andrew, Stephen (being stoned), James the Major and Philip. Van Gogh found it admirable but 'so cruel, so monstrous, like a Chinese nightmare, that even this beautiful example of so good a style seems to me to belong to another world and I am glad not to belong to it...'

After the sumptuous portal, the spartan nudity of the long, narrow nave is as striking as its unusual height. Aubusson tapestries dating from the 17th century hang across the top, and there are several palaeo-Christian sarcophagi along the sides. The best decoration here, however, is by a Dutchman by the name of Finsonius, who came down to Arles in 1610. Like Van Gogh, he stayed, mesmerized by the light and the colour, and he similarly met a bad end, drowning in the icy Rhône in 1642. St-Trophime contains three of his paintings: in the crossing, a beautiful *Annunciation* dating from 1610, the *Stoning of St Stephen* over the triumphal arch in the nave and, on the right, a singular *Adoration of the Magi*, with nightmare architecture and animals in attendance.

The Cloister

t 04 90 49 33 53; open same hours as Arènes (see above); come around midday to see the sculptures at their best.

Around the corner in Rue du Cloître is the entrance to St-Trophime's cloister. No other cloister in Provence is as richly and harmoniously sculpted as this one, which was carved in the 12th and 14th centuries by the masters of St-Gilles. Because Arles was as anti-Revolutionary as a town could be, this masterpiece was spared the wanton vandalism that destroyed so much elsewhere.

The north gallery is the oldest, supported by two monumental pillars adorned with statues; *St Peter* and *St Trophime* on the northwest are masterpieces of the classically influenced Arles school – even the foliage in the borders has a certain Corinthian air. The capitals in the Romanesque north and east galleries are carved with scenes from the New Testament, their figures moving to the same wonderful rhythms as those on the portal. The capitals of the more severe Gothic gallery to the south are elaborately carved with the life of St Trophime, while on the west the capitals closely resemble the south gallery of Montmajour's cloister (*see* p.425): note the Magdalene kissing Christ's feet and St Martha with the Tarasque.

Hôtel de Ville and the Cryptoportiques

Sharing Place de la République with the cathedral of St-Trophime is Arles' palatial **Hôtel de Ville**, built in 1675 after plans by Hardouin-Mansart, architect of the Hall of Mirrors at Versailles; here, his virtuoso signature is in the remarkable flat vaulting of the vestibule. Facing the inner courtyard are remnants of older civic buildings: sections of the 12th–15th-century palace of the *podestats* (or prefects of the Holy Roman Emperor), and the town hall of 1500, with a Roman tympanum and bell-tower modelled after the mausoleum of Glanum.

Just around the corner on Rue Balze is the cryptoporticus of the forum, the **Cryptoportiques** (*open Nov–Feb daily 10–11.30 and 2–6.30; Mar–April and Oct 9–11.30 and 2–5.30; May–Sept 9–6.30; adm*), entered through a long-unused Jesuit church, with an unusual wooden vaulted ceiling and a huge wooden Baroque retable that covers the entire apse. With the ramparts, this cryptoporticus was the first large construction of the Roman colony. Forming three sides of a rectangle measuring 289 by 192ft, these subterreanean barrel-vaulted double galleries of the 1st century BC were built as foundations for the monumental forum above. You can see a model of the forum's original appearance in the Musée de l'Arles Antique (*see* p.436); like the Imperial Fora in Rome, this one was built all at once, as a unified architectural grouping, consisting of a rectangle of colonnades for public business and a temple in the centre. No one knows for sure what other purpose a cryptoporticus may have served – for storage, or perhaps, as on Rome's Palatine Hill, for cool promenades. During the last war the galleries came in handy as an air-raid shelter.

The Museon Arlaten

29 Rue de la République, t 04 90 93 58 11; open April and May Tues–Sun 9.30–12.30 and 2–6; June Tues–Sun 9.30–1 and 2–6.30; July–Aug daily 9.30–1 and 2–6.30; Sept daily 9.30–12.30 and 2–6; Mar Tues–Sun 9.30–12.30 and 2–5; adm.

The indefatigable Frédéric Mistral (*see* pp.38–9) began his collection of ethnographic items from Provence in 1896; in 1904, when he won the Nobel Prize, he used the money to purchase the 16th-century Hôtel de Castellane-Laval to house his Museon Arlaten. Mistral's aim was to record the details of Provençal life for future generations. The evolution of the traditional Arlésienne costume is thoroughly documented, including the adjustments made to match fashion changes in Paris. The wearing of it declined along with the use of the Provençal language, in spite of the poet's folklore parades (the 'Festivals of Virgins') and his pronouncements that the costume, 'in the shadowy transition of the centuries, lets us see a lightning flash of beauty!' Nowadays, the female museum attendants here are the last people to wear the traditional costume, as they sit crocheting by the windows and gossiping (not in Provençal, but French).

Most memorable and strange are the life-size dioramas: a Christmas dinner at a *mas*, with a table groaning with wax food; a reed-thatched *cabane des gardiens*; and a visit to a new mother and her infant. The curious gifts of salt, a match, an egg and bread brought by the visitors symbolize the hope that the baby may grow to be wise, straight, full and good. The gallery of rituals has a prickly Tarasque retired from the procession at Tarascon, and a lock of golden hair discovered in a medieval tomb at Les Baux-de-Provence. One room is dedicated to the Félibrige, and another to Mistral himself, with the great man's cradle under glass. In the courtyard, a section of the forum was uncovered, complete with an *exedra* cut with 10 niches for statues.

To the north of Museon Arlaten, the café-filled **Place du Forum** is the centre of modern life in Arles, watched over helplessly by a **statue of Frédéric Mistral**, moustachioed and goateed like his near-double, Buffalo Bill. Mistral himself attended its unveiling in 1909, thanking his admirers, but regretting that they made him look as if he were waiting for a train.

The Thermes de Constantin and Musée Réattu

From Place de la République, Rue de l'Hôtel de Ville leads north to the ruins of Constantine's palace, of which only part of the baths, or **Thermes de Constantin**, remain (**t** 04 90 49 36 36; same hours as Cryptoportiques, see p.434; adm). Across the street stood the priory of the Knights of Malta, built in the 14th century. The knights, who came from all over Europe, were divided into eight *langues* (tongues), and this was the local HQ of the *langue de Provence*; the façade with gargoyles facing the river gives the best idea of its original appearance. After the Revolution, an academic painter named Jacques Réattu purchased the priory and his daughter made it into the **Musée Réattu** (*Rue du Grand-Prieuré*, **t** 04 90 49 37 58; open Jan–Feb and Nov–Dec daily 1–5.30; Mar–April and Oct 10–12.30 and 2–5.30; May–Sept 10–12.30 and 2–7; adm). Besides Reattu's own contributions, there are works by Théodore Rousseau, followers of Lorrain and Salvator Rosa, and one painting so marvellously, indescribably awful that it deserves a museum to itself: Antoine Raspail's portrait of himself and his family.

In 1972 the museum was jolted awake with a donation of 57 drawings from Picasso, in gratitude for the many bullfights he enjoyed in Arles. Nearly all date from January 1971 and constitute a running dialogue the artist held with himself on some of his favourite subjects – harlequins, men, women, the artist and his model – and, more unusually, the Tarasque. Other Picassos in the museum include a beautiful portrait of his mother, Maria, from the 1920s, and a sculpture of a woman with a violin. There are more recent works by César (a compacted motorbike) and Pol Bury (the bizarre *Monument horizontal no.3*, with 12,000 steel balls demonically clicking away on a table).

The Alyscamps

A 10min walk from centre; follow Rue Emile Fassin, first street south of Bd des Lices, eastwards. Same hours as Cryptoportiques, see p.434; adm.

One of the most prestigious necropoli of the Middle Ages, the Alyscamps owed its fame to the legend of St Trophime, a cousin of the proto-martyr St Stephen who became a disciple of St Paul. Paul sent Trophime to convert Gaul, and medieval hagiographers later confused him with a 2nd- or 3rd-century bishop of Arles of the same name. The story has it that Trophime arrived in Arles in the year AD 46 and held secret meetings with his new converts in the lonesome Roman cemetery of Alyscamps (believed to be a corruption of *Elisii Campi*, or Elysian Fields), which according to Roman custom was built outside the city walls, along the Via Aurelia. Trophime eventually attracted quite a following, and before he died he gave a special blessing to the Alyscamps; Christ himself attended the ceremony and left behind a stone imprint of his knee.

Burial in such holy ground was so desirable that bodies sealed in barrels with their burial fee attached were floated down the Rhône to Arles. Some rascals in Beaucaire took to robbing the dead of their coins as they floated downstream, but they were found out when the barrels miraculously returned upstream to the scene of the crime. At its greatest extent, the necropolis stretched for more than 2km and contained 19 chapels and several thousand tombs, many of them packed five bodies deep. Dante mentions it in the *The Divine Comedy* (IX, 112), and it makes an appearance in numerous *chansons de geste*. Ariosto wrote how Charlemagne's peers, cut down at Roncesvalles, were flown here and buried by angels.

The Alyscamps' mystique began to decline in 1152, when the relics of St Trophime were transferred to the cathedral. Grave-robbers pillaged the tombs and the most beautiful sarcophagi were given away as presents to Renaissance potentates. Under Louis-Napoléon, the Alyscamps itself was dismembered by a railroad, a canal, factories and a housing estate, leaving only one romantic, melancholy lane lined with empty, mostly plain sarcophagi. Little holes of mysterious purpose are carved into the stone of many of them, similar to holes in other tombs from the megalithic era; they may have held tiny oil lamps. Of the 19 chapels, all that remains is a 15th-century chapel that now serves as the ticket booth, along with the restored Romanesque **St-Honorat** at the far end. Its two-storey octagonal tower still stands, rebuilt in the 12th century by the monks of St-Victor in Marseille; in the apse you can see three Carolingian sarcophagi.

Musée de l'Arles Antique

Presqu'Ile du Cirque Romain, Av de la 1ʳᵉ D. F.L, t 04 90 18 88 88; open Mar–Oct daily 9–7; Nov–Feb daily 10–5; adm.

Arles' newest museum is in an eerie wasteland slightly out of town, opposite the Palais des Congrès (follow Boulevard des Lices to its western end, and pass under the motorway); in front of the museum you'll see foundations of the curve of Arles' Roman circus. The shiny modern building houses the contents of several of Arles' old museums. Though the ancient works themselves are not especially noteworthy, the detailed explanations (in French) and especially the brilliant architectural models bring the Roman city back to life in a way that few museums anywhere can match. Here you'll see how the Roman sailors wired up the sailcloth awning to shade the amphitheatre; how the city centre – the forum and temples – looked to the man in the street; how the army engineers made the floating bridge over the Rhône, and much more.

Among the exhibits are the pagan statues and sarcophagi that graced the former Musée d'Art Païen. Nearly everything here was made in the Arles region, with the exception of the beautiful white marble Hippolytus and Phaedra sarcophagus (2nd- or 3rd-century AD), with its hunting scenes. Two exceptional mosaics brought in from nearby Roman villas show the rape of Europa and Orpheus enchanting the wild beasts; there's a graceful but damaged dancing girl, and a headless statue of Mithras, the god of the legionnaires, his torso decorated with signs of the zodiac entwined by a serpent. The large statue of Augustus was found in the theatre, as was the *Venus of Arles*, represented here by a copy made before Louis XIV had it 'restored'. Although a fairly chaste specimen as marble love goddesses go, she earned from Théodore Aubanel the most hamfistedly erotic of all Félibre poems:

> *Laisso ti pèd toumba la raubo qu'à tis ancò*
> *S'envertouio, mudant tout ço qu'as de plus bèu:*
> *Abandouno toun ventre i pountoun dóu soulèu!*
> *Coume l'èurre s'aganto à la rusco d'un aubre,*
> *Laisso din mi brassado estregne en plen toun maubre:*
> *Laisso ma bouco ardènto e mi det tremoulant*
> *Courre amouros pertout sus toun cadabre blanc!*

> (Throw to your feet the robe that around your hips
> hangs, hiding all that is most beautiful about you:
> Abandon your stomach to the kisses of the sun!
> As ivy entwines the bark of a tree,
> Let me in my embraces clasp all of your marble;
> Let my ardent mouth and burning fingers
> run lovingly over your body so white!)

Arles' mothers use this armless Venus for their own ends – they bring their children to see her and warn: 'The same thing will happen to you if you keep biting your nails!'

Also here are the contents of the former Musée d'Art Chrétien, the best collection of 4th-century Christian sarcophagi of any museum. Carved by Arlésien sculptors between the years 330 and 395, these remarkably preserved tombs make a fascinating documentary of the newly victorious faith; as their pagan ancestors carved scenes from mythology, so these early Christians spared no expense to decorate their last resting places on earth with scenes from the Old and New testaments. Nearly every figure of importance wears a Roman toga; on the Sarcophage de Trinquetaille, discovered in 1974, the three Magi sport Phrygian bonnets.

Plaine de la Crau

Hercules, after completing his Tenth Labour, the theft of the cattle of Geryon, passed through Provence with the booty on his way home to Greece. He had some trouble with the native Ligurians, who apparently tried to pinch the cows. One thing led to another, and before long the big fellow found himself involved in a single-handed battle with the entire nation. As they advanced across the marshy plain, Hercules, armed only with his club, got down on his knees in despair at having nothing to throw at them. Zeus took pity on him and sent down a shower of stones, with which the hero soon put the Ligurians to flight. This was an unaccountably important story in the mythology of the Greeks; they and the Romans put the Hercules of this battle in the sky; the northern constellation that we know as Hercules, they called *Engonasis*, the 'kneeler'.

The carpet of stones Zeus sent is still there for all to see, on the weird wasteland called the Crau, which stretches from Arles to the Etang de Berre, between the Camargue and the Alpilles. The ancients found it fascinating, and many Greek and Roman writers attempted to explain it; Aristotle, a hopeless bird-brain at anything involving natural science, said the stones were formed by volcanoes, and 'rolled down naturally' to the low plain. In fact, the rounded stones are alluvial deposits from the Durance, from long ago when the river followed this path into the Rhône delta.

The empty, wind-blown Crau is a major element of the Provençal mystique; Mistral, for example, dragged his poor Mireille across it before she met her sad end. Today it does its best to keep up a romantic appearance. More than 100,000 sheep make their winter home here, nibbling the tufts of grass between the stones before migrating in the old-fashioned way up to the Provençal Alps in May or June; the stone shepherd huts are still one of the few features of the Crau. The French, unfortunately, have been trying to make it disappear. Most of the northern part has been reclaimed for farmland. The rest is crisscrossed with railways, canals and roads, and decorated with army firing ranges and the gigantic Istres military airport; there's even a dynamite plant.

There are no good roads over the unspoiled parts of the Crau, and the only village, **St-Martin-de-Crau**, is a dismal spot, but you can still see something of the original effect along the N568 (for Fos-sur-Mer and Marseille) and the N113 (for Salon-de-Provence), both east of Arles.

The Camargue

To its handful of inhabitants, the Camargue was the *isclo*, the 'island' between the two branches of the Rhône. The river's course has taken many different forms over the millennia; the present one, with its two arms, has created a vast marshland – this is France's salt cellar, its greatest treasure-house of waterfowl and the home of some of its most exotic landscapes. The two branches, the Grand and Petit Rhônes, really build separate deltas, leaving the space in between a soupy battleground where land and

Getting Around

Arles is the main jumping-off point for the Camargue.

By Train and Bus

The only public transport to the centre of the Camargue begins at the *gare routière* in Arles (t 0800 19 94 13; *www.lepilote.com* for bus timetables): there are one or two **buses** a day each to Saintes-Maries-de-la-Mer (via Albaron) and Salin-de-Giraud. St-Gilles has regular bus connections to Nîmes (five a day), a few to Arles and one to Lunel. There are also one or two SNCF **trains** to St-Gilles from Arles.

On Foot and Horseback, and by Bicycle and Jeep

Remember that the Camargue is really quite small – it's never more than 40km from Arles to the coast. A serious hiker could see the whole thing in 3 days.

It is perfect country for cycling, and there are a few places in Saintes-Maries-de-la-Mer to rent some wheels. Horses are even more popular; there are many places to hire one.

Destination Camargue, t 04 90 96 94 44, organizes day and half-day trips into the Camargue by jeep, from Mar for individuals and all year for groups.

By Boat

Blue-Line (t 04 66 87 22 66) and several other firms in St-Gilles rent out boats for trips through the Petite Camargue. At Saintes-Maries-de-la-Mer and St-Gilles there are various excursion boats that cruise around the Camargue.

Where to Stay and Eat

Almost all accommodation in the area is in Saintes-Maries-de-la-Mer (*see* pp.442–3), but if you want to stay in the eastern or central parts of the Camargue, away from the tourists, there are some possibilities.

Albaron ✉ 13123

Le Flamant Rose, on D37, **t 04 90 97 10 18, (*inexpensive*). A simple *Logis de France* with a restaurant (*moderate*). *Restaurant closed Wed lunch in summer, Wed in winter, and Feb and Mar.*

Salin-de-Giraud ✉ 13129

Hidden amidst vast salt pans, Salin doesn't even dream of drawing tourists.

*La Camargue, Bd de la Camargue, **t** 04 42 86 88 52 (*moderate–inexpensive*). The only place to stay in town, simple and basic. *Closed mid-Oct–mid-Mar.*

Les Saladelles, 4 Av des Arènes, **t** 04 42 86 83 87 (*moderate*). A good, popular restaurant for family dining, with a wide choice of dishes, including spicy *bœuf à la gardian*, chops and fish.

sea slowly struggle for mastery. With its unique coastline and wild expanses, the Camargue provides a soothing antithesis to the more crowded areas of the region. It is also ideal for outdoor activities, including hiking, climbing, diving, surfing and horse-riding (*see* above, and p.442, for details).

History

Ancient writers recorded the people of the Camargue hunting boar in the swamp forests and actually raking fish out of the mud; besides remarking on its curiosities, however, the Greeks and Romans left the area entirely alone. During the early Middle Ages, on the other hand, at least four monastic colonies were founded on the edges of the Camargue, not only to reclaim land but to collect that most precious of medieval commodities, salt. In this inhospitable country, these colonies disappeared long ago; the most important was the abbey of Psalmody, which became quite a power in Provence. Today only scant ruins of it can be seen, on a farm still called

Psalmody, to the north of Aigues-Mortes in the region called the Petite Camargue, west of the Petit Rhône.

By the 17th century, the monks gave way to cowboys (*gardians*), who created large ranches to exploit the two totem animals of the Camargue: the native black longhorn cattle that thrive on salt grass and have always been the preferred stock for Provençal bullfights, and the beautiful white horse, believed to have been introduced by the Arabs back in the Dark Ages. A true cowboy culture grew up – a romantic image dear to the Provençaux, and especially to Provençal writers such as Mistral.

There are still a few score *gardians* in the Camargue today, keeping up the old traditions. Big changes have come to the swampland in the last century. For a while, the French threatened to dispose rationally of this land altogether, with dykes and drainage schemes turning large areas into salt pans and rice fields. Fortunately, however, a few nature societies secured the creation of a wildlife reserve around the heart of the Camargue in 1928, and the government made a regional park of the area in 1970.

Flora and Fauna

First and most spectacularly, there are the flamingos (*flamants roses*), a symbol of the Camargue, and understandably so: several thousand of them nest around the southern lagoons. Probably no place in the Mediterranean has a wider variety of aquatic birds: there are lots of ducks, grebes, cormorants, curlews and ibis. The little egret is a common sight, though they spend the winter in Africa, as does the avocet, which looks like an aquatic magpie. There are also many purple herons, conspicuously striped on the head and breast. Not all are water birds; you may see an eagle or a majestic red kite (*milan royal*).

Deforestation in favour of ranches destroyed most of the natural habitat for land animals, but there are still boars, beavers and blue frogs. Trees are rare, although there are some umbrella pines and some scrubby, pink-flowered tamarisks. Common plants include the purple-flowered *saladelle* and the *salicorne* (samphire), which grows in tough clumps.

Among the fauna, we nearly forgot the most important – the hard-drilling, inescapable Camargue mosquito; make it your prime consideration when you visit, and take appropriate precautions.

Musée Camarguais

t 04 90 97 10 82; open April–June and Sept daily 9.15–5.45; July and Aug daily 9.15–6.45; Oct–Mar Sun and Mon 10.15–4.45; adm.

It was an inspiration on the part of the regional park management, creating this museum in what not long ago was a working Camargue cattle and sheep ranch, the Mas du Pont de Rousty, 9km southwest of Arles on the D570. The buildings are well restored and documented, giving a feeling of what life was like on the *mas* a century ago. There are special exhibitions on the *gardians*, on the fickle Rhône (you learn that 400,000 years ago it flowed past Nîmes), on Mistral's *Mireio*, and other subjects.

Outside, there are marked nature trails leading into the surrounding swampy plain, the **Marais de la Grande Mar**.

About 4km beyond the museum on the D570, little **Albaron** was one of the first inhabited centres of the Camargue; a stout medieval tower survives, built to guard Arles from any attack or pirate raid up the Petit Rhône.

The Etang de Vaccarès

For lazy motor tourists, the way to see the best of the Camargue is to take the D37, a left turn 4km south of the museum. After another 4km, a side road leads to the **Domaine de Méjanes** (*t* 04 90 97 10 10), with horse-riding and canoes; on summer weekends the *gardians* put on shows of cowboy know-how, and occasional bullfights. Further on, the D37 skirts the edges of the **Etang de Vaccarès**, the biggest of the lagoons and centre of the Camargue wildlife reserve. In some places, you can see flocks of nesting flamingos all year round. A side road, the D36B, leads down to Salin-de-Giraud, passing the **Centre d'Information La Capelière** (*t* 04 90 97 00 97; *open April–Sept daily 9–1 and 2–6; Oct–Mar Wed–Mon 9–1 and 2–5*), with exhibits on flora and fauna and guided nature walks around the lagoon.

The scenery changes abruptly at **Salin-de-Giraud**, a 19th-century industrial village that was devoted to the largest saltworks in Europe – a staggering 110 square km network of pans, annually producing 800,000 tonnes of salt. There's another nature centre on the D36, **La Palissade** (*t* 04 42 86 81 28; *open daily 9–5*), with white horses, bulls, audiovisual displays, a small aquarium, walks, and information on the flamingo-filled Etang de Grande Palun. The *salins* are barred from the Mediterranean by one of the longest and emptiest beaches in France, the **Plage de Piémanson** at the mouth of the Grand Rhône; the current is a bit treacherous for swimming. To get away from it all, head west of Salin for the **Plage de Beauduc** (signposted), where you'll find a couple of places that grill the day's catch.

With good local maps, in summer determined swamp fans can hike the 40km or so to Saintes-Maries-de-la-Mer, through the most unspoiled parts of the Camargue; a sea wall, the **Digue de la Mer**, provides a crossing around the lagoons, and the only hazards are secluded beaches that have been taken over by bands of *naturistes*. You might even make it over to the Camargue's forest, **Bois des Rièges**, on a large island at the southern end of the Etang de Vaccarès. Though officially off limits, as part of the nature reserve it can sometimes be reached on foot in summer. Be careful, though: this is the home of the Camargue's Abominable Snowman, the *Bête de Vaccarès*, a mysterious part-human creature first sighted in the 15th century.

Saintes-Maries-de-la-Mer

Set among the low sand dunes, the lively town of Saintes-Maries-de-la-Mer has an open-armed approach to visitors that long predates any interest in the Camargue and its ecological balance. For this is one of Provence's holiest places, and if you come

Getting Around

By Bus

There are at least 2 buses daily from Arles (55mins). In July and Aug there are direct services to Aigues-Mortes and Montpellier and St-Gilles and Nîmes.

By Boat

The paddlesteamer *Tiki III*, **t** 04 90 97 81 68, plys the Petit Rhône (*mid-Mar–Sept*). The *Camargue*, **t** 04 90 97 84 72, also offers trips.

On Horseback

The tourist office has a list of stables, some offering tours for beginners; they include: **Promenade à Cheval Pont de Gau** on the Route d'Arles, **t** 04 90 97 89 45.

By Jeep and Bike

Safari Nature Camargue, **t** 04 90 9789 33. Among firms offering jeep tours.
Le Vélociste, 8 Place Mireille, **t** 04 90 97 83 26 (*open Sept–June*). Bike hire.

Tourist Information

Saintes-Maries-de-la-Mer: 5 Av Van Gogh, **t** 04 90 97 82 55, *www.saintesmaries.com*. *Open daily July and Aug 9–8; May, June and Sept 9–7; April and Oct 9–6; Dec–Feb 9–5.*

Market Days

Saintes-Maries-de-la-Mer: Mon and Fri am, Place du Gitan.

Festivals

The **Pèlerinage des Gitans** (Gypsy Pilgrimage) is held on 24–25 May. The Gypsies began making the pilgrimage in numbers in the mid-19th century. In 1935, thanks to the Marquis de Baroncelli, 24 May was set aside as St Sarah's day. Although the famous all-night candle vigil by her statue has been abolished by bureaucratic killjoys, her statue is still carried to the sea by a procession of Gypsies, *gardians* and costumed Arlésiennes, where in imitation of ancient rain-making ceremonies it is sprinkled with sea water while all are blessed by the bishop. Afterwards, the beaches and streets are alive with music and flamenco, *farandoles*, horse races and bullfights, attended by as many tourists as Gypsies.

The whole ceremony happens again, with considerably fewer Gypsies and tourists, on the Sun nearest 22 Oct for Mary Salome.

Where to Stay

Saintes-Maries-de-la-Mer ✉ 13460

Book ahead for summer or the pilgrimages.
★★★★**Mas de la Foulque**, Route du Petit-Rhône, 4km from town, **t** 04 90 97 81 02, *www.masdelafoulque.com* (*luxury–expensive*). A stunningly decorated 12-room hotel by a lagoon, with private terraces, a heated pool, a lake, its own boat for coastal trips, and a restaurant using local organic produce. *Closed 15 Nov–15 Mar.*
★★★★**Le Pont des Bannes**, 3km north on D570, **t** 04 90 97 81 09, *www.pontdesbannes.net*

out of season you may still sense the dream-like, insular remoteness that made it the stuff of legend.

The pious story behind it all was promoted to the hilt by the medieval Church: after Christ was crucified, his Jewish detractors took a boat without sails or oars and loaded it with three Marys – Mary Salome (mother of the apostles James and John), Mary Jacobe, the Virgin's sister, and Mary Magdalene – plus Martha and her resurrected brother Lazarus, St Maximin and St Sidonius. As this so-called Boat of Bethany drifted offshore, Sarah, the black Egyptian servant of Mary Salome and Mary Jacobe, wept so grievously that Mary Salome tossed her cloak on the water, so that Sarah was able to walk across on it and join them. The boat took them to the Camargue, to this spot, where the elderly Mary Salome, Mary Jacobe and Sarah built an oratory, while their younger companions went to spread the Gospel, live in caves and tame the Tarasque.

(*very expensive*). Rooms in *cabanes de gardian*, plus a pool, garden and stables.

★★★**Hôtel de Cacharel**, Route des Cacharels, 5km from town, t 04 90 97 95 44, *www.hotel-cacharel.com* (*expensive*). A ranch-style hotel with a laid-back approach (no TVs) and excellent-value family rooms. There's no restaurant, but snacks and wine are available midday–8pm. Horseriding costs from €20 per hour.

★★★**Mas Sainte-Hélène**, Chemin Bas-des-Launes, t 04 90 97 81 09, *www.pontdes bannes.com* (*very expensive*). The Pont des Bannes' annexe, spread out along an islet in the Etang des Launes, allowing you to get eye to eye with the pink flamingos that parade on its waterside terraces.

★★★★**Le Mangio Fango**, Route d'Arles (D70), t 04 90 97 80 56, *www.hotelmangiofango. com* (*expensive–moderate*). A hotel offering a marriage of old materials and modern comfort, filled with crafts and paintings. There's a heated pool, simple, airy rooms, and a good restaurant (*expensive*) with a patio where you can enjoy wonderful seafood and excellent Camargue bull stew. *Closed Jan–mid-Feb and 3 wks Dec; restaurant closed Mon in winter.*

★**Le Delta**, Place Mireille, t 04 90 97 81 12 (*inexpensive*). A good-value option with 5 rooms and food. *Closed Jan; restaurant closed Mon except in season..*

Auberge de Jeunesse, Pioch Badet. t 04 90 97 51 72 (*inexpensive*). A youth hostel accessible by bus from Arles and Saintes-Maries-de-la-Mer. *Closed Nov, Dec and Jan.*

Eating Out

This is the place to try *bœuf gardian*, bull stewed in red wine with lots of garlic; *bouriroun*, an omelette with elvers from the Vaccarès; *salade de téllines*, made of tiny shellfish with garlic mayonnaise; and *poutargue*, Camargue caviar made from red mullet eggs.

Le Brûleur de Loups, Av Léon Gambetta, t 04 90 97 83 31 (*expensive–moderate*). An elegant choice with a terrace overlooking the beach, serving delights from the sea. *Closed mid-Nov and Dec, Tues eve and Wed.*

Hostellerie du Pont de Gau, Route d'Arles (D70), 4km north of town, t 04 90 97 81 53 (*moderate*). Jolly Provençal décor and great *bouillabaisse. Closed Wed, and Jan–mid-Feb.*

Activities and Entertainment

Entertainment in Saintes-Maries-de-la-Mer in summer includes nightly *Courses Camargues* in the bullring; guitars and buskers in the streets; and miles of white sand beaches, including a *plage naturiste* 6km to the east.

At Pont de Gau, 4km north, there's a **Centre d'Information du Parc Naturel Régional de Camargue** (*t 04 90 97 86 32; open summer daily 10–6; winter Sat–Thurs 9.30–5*), and a **Parc Ornithologique** (*t 04 90 97 82 62; open April–Sept 9–sunset; Oct–Mar 10–sunset; adm*), with walks through the marshlands and aviaries, frequented by some 200 species of birds, including rare ones.

In 1448, during the reign of the Bon Roi René (who was always pinched for money), the supposed relics of the two Marys were discovered, greatly boosting the local pilgrim trade. Saintes-Maries became, as Mistral called it, the 'Mecca of Provence'.

A few facts blazed the trail for the legend's ready acceptance. In the 4th century, a Roman writer described a settlement on this site called *Oppidum priscum Ra*. This lent its name to the first Christian church, Notre-Dame-de-Ratis, built over the site of a spring of fresh water – where a Gallo-Roman temple had been dedicated to three sea goddesses. *Ratis* was taken to mean raft (*radeau*), hence the connection not only with the Boat of Bethany but to ancient Egypt, where in the *Book of the Dead* the deceased sails in a boat without oar or sail, but with the image of Ra. Even the name Marie had a familiar ring to Provence's early Christians; not only for its resemblance to the word for mother (*Matre*), but also to Marius, a local cult figure after his defeat of the Teutones, who was advised by the blonde sibyl Marthe (as pictured near Les Baux-de-Provence; *see* p.423). Today, Saintes-Maries-de-la-Mer is best known for the pilgrimage of Mary Jacobe on 24 and 25 May. This attracts Gypsies from all over the world, who have canonized her servant Sarah as their patron saint. The reason seems to owe something to yet another coincidence – the discovery of the relics coincided with a great convergence of Gypsies in Provence in the 1440s, some of whom wandered up from North Africa and Spain, while others crossed into Europe by way of Greece and the Balkans. The Gypsies, however, claim that Sarah was not Egyptian but one of their own, Sarah-la-Kâli ('the black', but also recalling Hindu goddess Kali), who met the Boat of Bethany here and was the first of their tribe to be converted to Christianity. The Church obliged by 'discovering' the bones of Sarah in 1496.

The Church

In 869, during the construction of a new church to replace the 6th-century oratory 'built' by the two Marys, the Saracens swooped down in a surprise raid and carried off the archbishop of Arles, who just happened to be down to inspect the work. The pirates demanded a high ransom in silver, swords and slaves for their hostage, and were dismayed when the bishop died on them – but not so put out as to risk losing the ransom. They tied the bishop's corpse in all its vestments to a throne and made off with the loot before the Christians realized the hostage was dead.

In the face of the threat of similar shenanigans, stones were shipped down from Arles at great expense to rebuild the church in 1130. The result is, along with St-Victor in Marseille, the most impressive fortified church in Provence: a crenellated ship with loopholes for windows in a small pond of white villas with orange roofs. Inside, along the gloomy nave, are wells that supplied the church-fortress in times of siege; pilgrims still bottle the water to ensure their protection by St Sarah. In the second chapel on the left, near the model of the Boat of Bethany that is carried in the procession to the sea, is the polished rock 'pillow' of the saints, discovered with their bones in 1448.

The capitals supporting the blind arches of the raised choir are finely sculpted in the style of St-Trophime in Arles (*see* p.433). Under the choir is the **crypt**, where the relics and statue of St Sarah in her seven robes are kept; the statue has been kissed so often that the black paint has come off in patches. Here, too, is a *taurobolium*, or relief of a bull-slaying from an ancient mithraeum, the bits scratched away long ago by women who used the dust to concoct fertility potions, along with photos and *ex votos* left by the Gypsies.

From April to mid-November, you can take a stroll below the **bell-tower** (*t* 04 90 97 87 60; *open daily 10–12.30 and 2–6.30*), offering views stretching across the Camargue, which takes on a magical glow at sunset. This roof walk circles the lavish **upper chapel** (*usually closed*), dedicated to St Michael, which in times of need served as a donjon. The coffer holding the relics of the Marys is kept here, except during the arcane *deus ex machina* rites unique to this church: during feast days the coffer is slowly lowered through a door over the altar after the singing of a special hymn, 'Les Saintes de Provence', the pilgrimage ends to the tune of 'Adieu aux Saintes', as the relics are slowly raised back into the chapel. In the 18th century this hocus-pocus had a reputation for curing madness, combined with the shock therapy of stripping the afflicted naked and throwing them in the sea. When Mistral attended the pilgrimage as a young man, a beautiful girl from Beaucaire abandoned by her fiancé dramatically flung herself across the altar just as the relics were being lowered, praying for the return of her lover. The girl made a considerable impression on Mistral and became the basis for his heroine Mireille, who arrives in Saintes-Maries-de-la-Mer to make a similar prayer and dies of too much sun and love in the upper chapel of this church, while the congregation in the lower church, like the chorus in a Greek tragedy, accuses the holy Marys: *Reino de Paradis, mestresso/De la Planuro d'amaresso* ('Queens of Paradise, mistresses/of the plain of bitterness').

Around Saintes-Maries-de-la-Mer

Mireille, in statue form at least, lives on in the main square north of the church, while to the south in Rue Victor Hugo the **Musée Baroncelli** (*t 04 90 97 87 60*) is devoted to zoology, archaeology and folklore. It is named after the Camargue's secular saint, the Félibre Marquis Folco de Baroncelli-Javon (1869–1943), a descendant of a Florentine merchant family in Avignon, who at the age of 21 abandoned everything to go and live the life of a *gardian*. Baroncelli spent the next 60 years herding bulls, writing poetry and doing all that he could to maintain the Camargue and its customs intact. Although he was by trade a cowboy, his heart was actually with the Native Americans and other oppressed minorities; Chief Sitting Bull, visiting France with Buffalo Bill and his Wild West Show, smoked the peace pipe with the marquis and named him 'Faithful Bird'.

St-Gilles

West of Arles, the N572 takes you through the drier parts of the Camargue. After crossing the Petit Rhône, you're in the **Petite Camargue**, in the *département* of the Gard, approaching **St-Gilles**, the only town for miles in any direction.

History

In medieval times and earlier, St-Gilles was a flourishing port, much nearer the sea than it is now. Remains have been found of a Phoenician merchant colony, and the Greek-Celtic *oppidum* that replaced it, but the place did not really blossom until the 11th century. The popes and the monks of Cluny, who owned it, conspired to make the resting place of Gilles, an obscure 8th-century Greek hermit, a major stop along the great pilgrim road to Compostela. The powerful counts of Toulouse helped too – the family originally came from St-Gilles. Soon pilgrims were pouring in from as far away as Germany and Poland, the port boomed with the onset of the Crusades, and both the Templars and Knights Hospitallers (who owned large tracts in the Camargue) built important *commanderies*. In 1116 the abbey church of St-Gilles was begun, one of the most ambitious projects ever undertaken in medieval Provence.

Destiny, however, soon began making it clear that this was not the place. As the delta gradually expanded, the canals silted up and St-Gilles could no longer function as a port (a major reason for the building of Aigues-Mortes; see p.448). The real disaster came with the Wars of Religion, when the town became a Protestant stronghold; the leaders of the Protestant army thought the church, that obsolete relic from the Age of Faith that took 200 years to build, would look much better as a fortress, and they demolished nearly all of it to that end. It was rebuilt, in a much smaller version, after 1650. What was left suffered more indignities during the Revolution – the loss of many of the figures' faces is nothing short of tragic – but it is a miracle that otherwise one of the greatest ensembles of medieval sculpture has survived more or less intact.

The Abbey of St-Gilles

This is the masterpiece of the Provençal school of 12th-century sculptors, the famous work that was copied, life-size, in the Cloisters Museum in New York. Created roughly at the same time as the façade of St-Trophime in Arles, it is likewise inspired by the ancient Roman triumphal arches. Instead of Roman worthies and battle scenes, the 12 Apostles hold place of honour between the Corinthian columns. This is a bold, confident sculpture, taking delight in naturalistic detail and elaborately folded draperies, with little of the conscious stylization that characterizes contemporary work in other parts of France. In this, too, the Romans were their masters. The scheme is complex, and worth describing in detail.

The Church Façade

Left portal: tympanum of the Adoration of the Magi (1); beneath it, Jesus' entry into Jerusalem (2); flanking the door, a beautiful St Michael slaying the dragon (3); and on the right the first four Apostles, SS Matthew and Bartholomew, Thomas and James the Lesser (4–7).

Tourist Information

St-Gilles: Pl Frédéric Mistral, **t** 04 66 87 33 75, www.ot-saint-gilles.fr. Open July and Aug Mon–Fri 9–7, Sat 9–12.30 and 3–7, Sun 10–12; Sept–June Mon–Sat 10–12 and 2–5.

Market Days
St-Gilles: Thurs and Sun am.

Where to Stay and Eat

St-Gilles ✉ 30800

During the Middle Ages scores of pilgrims (sometimes thousands of them), would stay over at St-Gilles every night; if you tried it today, even the innkeepers would wonder what you were thinking of.

* **★★★Héraclée**, 30 Quai du Canal, **t** 04 66 87 44 10, www.hotel-heraclee.com (inexpensive). An unexciting but well-run choice.
* **★★Le Cours**, 10 Av François Griffeuille, **t** 04 66 87 31 93, www.hotel-le-cours.com (moderate–inexpensive). A typically traditional Logis de France residence (you pay extra for air-conditioning), with a shady restaurant terrace (moderate) where you can try the likes of Camargue pilaf and frogs' legs. Closed Dec–Mar.

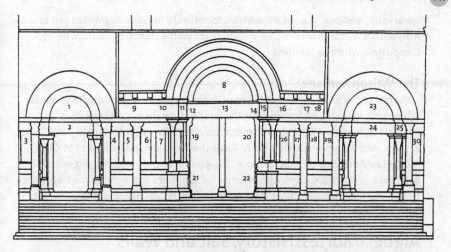

Central portal: tympanum of Christ in Majesty (8), with symbols of the Evangelists; underneath, a long frieze that runs from one side portal across to the other: from left to right, Judas with his silver (9); Jesus expelling the money-changers from the temple (10); the resurrection of Lazarus (11); Jesus prophesying the denial of Peter and the washing of the Apostles' feet (12); the Last Supper (13); the Kiss of Judas, a superb, intact work (14); the Arrest of Christ (15); Christ before Pilate (16); the Flagellation (17); Christ carrying the Cross (18). Left of the door, saints John and Peter (19); right of the door, saints James the Greater and Paul, with the soul-devouring Tarasque under his feet (20). Beneath these, at ground level, are small panels representing the sacrifices of Cain and Abel and the murder of Abel (21); a deer hunt and Balaam and his ass, and Samson and the Lion (22).

Right portal: tympanum of the Crucifixion (23); beneath it, two unusual scenes: the three Marys purchasing spices to anoint the body of Jesus, and the three Marys at the tomb. To the left of this, the Magdalen and Jesus (24); to the right, Jesus appearing to his disciples (25). Left of the door, four more unidentifiable Apostles (26–29; note how the 12 represented here are not the canonical list – better-known figures such as John the Evangelist and Paul were commonly substituted for the more obscure of the original Apostles). To the right of the door, Archangels combat Satan (30).

The Vis de St-Gilles

The 17th-century interior of the rebuilt church holds little of interest, but beneath it the original, wide-vaulted **crypt** or lower church (*adm*) survives (so many pilgrims came to St-Gilles that upper and lower churches were built to hold them). Behind the church, you can see the ruins of the **choir and apse** of the original, which was much longer than the present structure. Here is the *vis* or 'screw' of St-Gilles, a spiral staircase of 50 steps that once led up one of the bell towers. Built about 1142, it is a *tour de force*. The stones are cut with amazing precision to make a self-supporting spiral vault; medieval masons always tried to make the St-Gilles pilgrimage just to see it. Its author, Master Mateo of Cluny, also worked on the church of Santiago de Compostela, where he is buried.

The Maison Romane

The rest of the town shows few traces of its former greatness. The medieval centre is unusually large, if a bit forlorn. Near the façade of the church, on Place de la République, is a fine 13th-century mansion, claimed to be the birthplace of Guy Folques, who became Pope Clement IV. Today this 'Maison Romane' houses St-Gilles' **Musée Lapidaire** (*t 04 66 87 40 42; open Tues–Sun summer 9.30–12 and 3–7; winter 9–12 and 2–5; closed Jan; adm*), with a number of sculptures and architectural fragments from the church, and collections displaying the folk life and nature of the Camargue.

Aigues-Mortes: History, Salt and Walls

Every French history or geography textbook has a photo of Aigues-Mortes in it, and every French person, most likely, carries in their mind the haunting picture of the great walls of the port from which Saint Louis sailed off to the Crusades, now marooned in the muck of the advancing Rhône delta. It is as compelling a symbol of time and fate as any Roman ruin, and as evocative of medieval France as any Gothic cathedral.

In 1241 the Camargue was the only stretch of Mediterranean coast held by France. To solidify this precarious strip, Louis IX (Saint Louis) began construction of a new port and a town, laid out in an irregular grid to stop the wind from racing up the streets. In 1248 the port was complete enough to hold the 1,500 ships that carried Louis and his knights to the Holy Land on the Seventh Crusade, which was to bring Louis disasters both at home and abroad (the town was the last he saw of France – he died in Tunis of the plague in 1270). His successor, Philippe III, finished Aigues-Mortes and built its great walls. Being the only French Mediterranean port, by the late 13th century it was booming, with perhaps four times as many inhabitants as its present 4,800, its harbour filled with ships from as far away as Constantinople and Antioch.

Aigues-Mortes means 'dead waters', and it proved to be a prophetic name. The sea deserted Aigues and, despite efforts to keep the harbour dredged, the port went into decline after 1350. Attempts to revive it in the 1830s failed, ensuring Aigues' demise, but allowing the works of Louis and Philippe to survive undisturbed. Forgotten and nearly empty a century ago, Aigues now makes its living from tourists, and from salt; half of France's supply is collected here, at the 10,000-hectare **Salins-du-Midi** pans south of town in the Petite Camargue (*t 04 66 73 40 00, www.salins.com; open Mar–Oct, call for times*). Now the sea wants to return, and attempts to keep the tides from draining the lucrative salt pans could be futile, or at least very expensive.

Aigues-Mortes' **walls** are more than 1.5km in length, streamlined and almost perfectly rectangular. The highly impressive **Tour de Constance** (*entry inside the walls on Rue Zola, t 04 66 53 61 55; open daily 9.30–7, 10–5 in winter; adm*) is an enormous

Getting Around

For trains from Nîmes, contact **t** 08 92 35 35 35; the station is on the Route de Nîmes.

For buses to and from Montpellier and Nîmes, call **t** 08 25 34 01 34 and **t** 04 66 29 27 29 respectively.

Parking: There are signs around all the entrances to the town forbidding cars; ignore them (everyone else does). There is no problem driving around Aigues-Mortes or finding parking, except in July and August.

Tourist Information

Aigues-Mortes: Place Saint-Louis, **t** 04 66 53 73 00, *www.ot-aiguesmortes.fr*. *Open July and Aug Mon–Fri 9–8, Sat and Sun 10–8; Sept–June Mon–Fri 9–12 and 1–6, Sat and Sun 10–12 and 2–6*. Offers historical tours of the town, year-round.

Market Days

Aigues-Mortes: Av Frédéric Mistral: Wed and Sun am; flea market Sat am.

Where to Stay and Eat

Aigues-Mortes ✉ 30220

★★★**Le Saint-Louis**, 10 Rue de l'Amiral Courbet, **t** 04 66 53 72 68, *www.lesaintlouis.fr*

(*moderate*). A distinguished and beautifully furnished 18th-century building just off Place Saint-Louis, with gracious staff and a restaurant.

Hermitage de St-Antoine, 9 Bd Intérieur Nord, **t** 06 03 04 34 05, *www.hermitagesa.com* (*inexpensive*). A *chambre d'hôte* just inside the Porte St-Antoine in the medieval walls; all 3 rooms have en suite bathrooms. Added bonuses are a tranquil patio area and fantastic breakfasts.

La Camargue, 19 Rue de la République, **t** 04 66 53 86 88 (*moderate*). The place where the Gypsy Kings got their musical start, and still the liveliest and most popular place in town, with flamenco guitars strumming in the background. Eat in the garden in summer.

Activities and Entertainment

Like Saintes-Maries, Aigues-Mortes offers many guided tours of local flora and fauna: **Pescalune**, **t** 04 66 53 79 47, and **Isles de Stel**, **t** 04 66 53 60 70, offer barge tours of the Petite Camargue.

Four-wheel-drive safari tours are efficiently run out of Le Grau-du-Roi by **Le Gitan**, **t** 06 08 60 97 56, and **Pierrot le Camarguais**, **t** 04 66 51 90 90.

---

cylindrical defence tower that was used to guard the northeastern land approach to the town. After the Crusades, the tower was turned into a prison, first for Templars and later for Protestants. One of them, Marie Durand, spent a wretched 38 years here in unspeakable conditions. On her release in 1768, she left her credo, *register* ('resist' in Provençal) chiselled into the wall, where it can still be seen.

The tower situated to the south was used as a temporary mortuary in 1431, during the Hundred Years' War, when the Bourguignons, who held the city, were suddenly attacked and decimated by their arch-enemies, the Armagnacs. There were so many gruesome bodies lying around that the Armagnacs simply stacked them up in the tower, covering each of them with a layer of salt: hence the rather eloquent name – the **Tower of the Salted Bourguignons**.

Eight kilometres southwest of Aigues-Mortes, **Le Grau-du-Roi** doubles as France's most important fishing port (after Sète) and a charmless if hyperactive beach resort; the **Palais de la Mer** (*Av du Palais de la Mer*, **t** 04 66 51 57 57; *open May, June and Sept* *daily 9.30–8; July and Aug daily 10am–midnight; Jan–April and Oct–Dec daily 10–7; adm*), has a good aquarium, including tanks that pass right over your head, and a small museum on the town's history. Le Grau's **Port Camargue** is nothing less than Europe's largest marina, with 5,000 berths and a long waiting list. To the south of this stretches the **Plage de l'Espiguette**, a remarkable stretch of natural sand dunes that go on and on and on, the only building in sight a lighthouse (the road ends there, by the *phare*, in an enormous car park).

Nîmes, the Gard and Montpellier

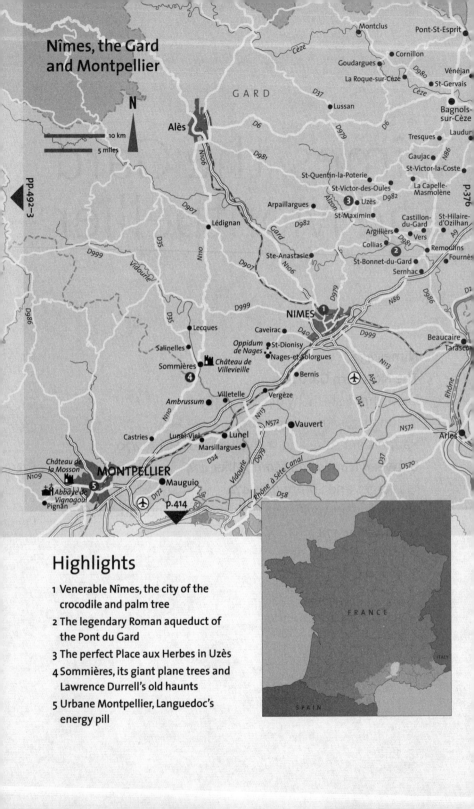

Nîmes, the Gard and Montpellier

GARD

Montclus
Pont-St-Esprit
Cornillon
Goudargues
Vénéjan
La Roque-sur-Cèze
St-Gervais
Cèze
Bagnols-sur-Cèze
Lussan
Tresques
Laudur
Gaujac
St-Victor-la-Coste
Alès
St-Quentin-la-Poterie
La Capelle-Masmolène
St-Victor-des-Oules
❸ Uzès
Arpaillargues
St-Maximin
Castillon-du-Gard
St-Hilaire-d'Ozilhan
Lédignan
Argilliers
Vers
Collias
Remoulins
Ste-Anastasie
❷
St-Bonnet-du-Gard
Fournè
Sernhac

pp.492-3
p.376

NÎMES ❶
Lecques
Caveirac
Beaucaire
Tarascc
Salinelles
Oppidum de Nages
St-Dionisy
Sommières ❹
Château de Villevieille
Nages-et-Solorgues
Bernis
Arles
Ambrussum
Villetelle
Vergèze
Castries
Lunel-Viel
Lunel
Vauvert
Marsillargues
Château de la Mosson
MONTPELLIER
Mauguio
❺
Abbaye de Vignogoul
Pignan
p.414

Highlights

1 Venerable Nîmes, the city of the crocodile and palm tree
2 The legendary Roman aqueduct of the Pont du Gard
3 The perfect Place aux Herbes in Uzès
4 Sommières, its giant plane trees and Lawrence Durrell's old haunts
5 Urbane Montpellier, Languedoc's energy pill

FRANCE
ITALY
SPAIN

Like most French *départements*, the Gard is named after a river – a river made famous by a feat of Roman engineering that symbolizes the Midi as boldly as the Eiffel Tower does Paris. Its spirit, or at least something intangibly Classical, lingers in the Gard's luminous, sun-blonde landscapes and clear air; note how often a solitary windswept pine or cypress dominates the view, as if lifted straight from a painting by Claude Lorraine. The Gard's capital, Nîmes, was especially coddled by Rome and still has a full share of grand monuments; Sommières, one of the *département*'s most charming (and most flooded) towns, stands by its Roman bridge. The Gard is also home to Uzès, *ville d'art* and the 'First Duchy of France', Bagnols-sur-Cèze, with its exceptional little museum of modern art, and the natural charms and vineyards of the lower valley of the Cèze.

Note that the towns on the Rhône – Beaucaire, Villeneuve lez Avignon, Aigues-Mortes, etc. – are covered in the two preceding chapters, and that this chapter also includes Montpellier, Nîmes' fierce rival in the Hérault; we've put them in the same chapter, just to tease.

Nîmes

Built of stone the colour of old piano keys, Nîmes disputes with Arles the honour of being the 'Rome of France' – the Rome of the Caesars, of course, not of the popes: neither the Church (nor, for that matter, bossy old Paris) have ever gone down well in this mercantile, Protestant town. But after the passions of the Wars of Religion, Nîmes fell into a doze that lasted for centuries. Travellers in the 19th century found it the quintessential dusty southern city; they came to marvel at the city's famous Maison Carrée, the best-preserved Roman temple in the world, and wrote that it was so neglected it looked as if it were dedicated to the goddess of sewage.

The city saw some spectacular change under dynamic Jean Bousquet, elected mayor in 1983. He was former head of Cacharel, Nîmes' fashionable *prêt-à-porter* firm, and he not only wakened Nîmes from its daydreams but, by devoting nearly 14 per cent of its budget to culture, urged it to echo the ambitious efforts of upstart Montpellier, its chief rival in Languedoc. The opening of the new Carré d'Art, designed by Sir Norman Foster, threw down the gauntlet to the former mayor of Montpellier, Georges Frêche. Bousquet then signed up Sir Norman to redevelop Nîmes' old centre, with plans for a '*Grand Axe*' running from the Jardin de la Fontaine to surrounding smaller villages. In addition, a university has been built, specializing in law, literature and medicine. Just like the one in Montpellier. The current mayor, Jean-Paul Fournier, was elected in 2001, and he isn't resting on his laurels either. At the time of writing, the town hall is proposing 32 separate building projects. Fournier has declared 2005 'protection of our architectural heritage' year, which will include the restoration of the Maison Carrée (*see* pp.459–60) on its 2,000th birthday.

Most Nîmois view the battle for avant-garde supremacy in this corner of France with detached amusement. For what really makes the juices flow in Nîmes is not modern architecture, but bulls. Nîmes is passionate about its *ferias*, featuring top

Getting There and Around

By Air

Nîmes-Garons airport is 8km from Nîmes along Rte de St-Gilles (A54). Call t 04 66 70 49 49 for flight information. Ryanair flies from the UK to Nîmes, *see* p.66. *Navettes* (shuttle buses) run between the airport and Nîmes (train station and other parts of town see *www.nimes.cci.fr* or call t 04 66 29 27 29).

By Train

Nîmes' train station, at the south end of Av Feuchères on Bd Sgt. Triaire, is a kind of arcaded train-aduct that perfectly suits *la Rome française*. There are direct trains (t 04 66 70 41 92) to Carcassonne, Montpellier, Arles and Marseille; and TGVs to Paris (4hrs) and Lille (5hrs).

By Bus

The *gare routière* is just behind the train station in Rue Ste Felicité, t 04 66 29 52 00; there are services to the Pont du Gard, Uzès, St-Gilles, Aigues-Mortes, Le Grau du Roi, La Grande Motte, Avignon and Montpellier.

Car and Bike Hire

Avis is at Rue du Maréchal Juan, t 04 66 29 05 33, and at the airport along with a selection of other companies. The baggage area at the train station has bicycle hire, as does **Cycles Passieu**, 2 Place Montcalm, t 04 66 21 09 16.

Tourist Information

Nîmes: 6 Rue Auguste, near the Maison Carrée, t 04 66 58 38 00, *www.ot-nimes.fr. Open July–Aug Mon–Fri 8.30–8, Sat 9–7, Sun 10–6; Easter–June and Sept Mon–Fri 8.30–7, Sat 9–7, Sun 10–6; Oct–Easter Mon–Fri 8.30–7, Sat 9–7, Sun 10–5.*

A tourist mini-train does the rounds of the sites between April and October, leaving from the Esplanade, opposite the Palais de Justice.

Market Days

Fri am: Av Jean Jaurès, organic and farmers' market.
Tues am: Chemin Bas d'Avignon, farmer's market.
Mon: Parking du Stade des Castières, flowers.
Mon am: Av Jean Jaurès, flea market.

Festivals

To find out what's going on in Nîmes, call the tourist office on t 04 66 58 38 00. There are usually a couple of bullfights each month in the summer, but to see the best *toreros* come for the *ferias* at **Carnival** time in February/early March or the third week of September, and especially the 6-day **Feria de Pentecôte** (Whitsun), which draws even bigger crowds than Munich's Oktoberfest. As in Seville, people open up their homes as *bodegas* to take the overflow of aficionados from the cafés, and the drinking and music go on until dawn. The Arènes come to life during July, with contemporary and popular music at the **Festival de Nîmes**.

Where to Stay

Nîmes ✉ 30000
Reservations are essential during the *ferias*, and prices may also be higher.

Expensive

★★★★**Hôtel Impérator Concorde**, Quai de la Fontaine, t 04 66 21 90 30, f 04 66 67 70 25. *www.hotel-imperator.com*. A 19th-century dowager with a facelift, a lovely garden, TVs, air-conditioning, and Nîmes' top restaurant to boot (*see* 'Eating Out'). *Open year round.*

matadors from France, Spain and Portugal and a beautiful blonde *torera*, a native of Nîmes who learned her art at the city's Ecole Française de Tauromachie.

History

Geography dealt Nîmes a pair of trump cards: first, a mighty spring, the **Fontaine**, whose god, Nemausus, was worshipped by the first known residents, the Celtic Volcae-Arecomici, and second, a position on the main route from Italy to Spain, a trail

***L'Hacienda**, Chemin du Mas de Brignon, Marguerittes ✉ 30320 (8km northeast on N86), **t** 04 66 75 02 25, **f** 04 66 75 45 58, *www.hotel-hacienda-nimes.com*. A large farmhouse in the *garrigue*, converted into a hotel with a spacious swimming pool, terraces and an excellent restaurant (*expensive; dinner only*), part of the Relais du Silence group. *Book out of season*.

***New Hotel La Baume**, 21 Rue Nationale, **t** 04 66 76 28 42, **f** 04 66 76 28 45, *www.new-hotel.com*. Stylish modern rooms in a 17th-century mansion with a garden terrace.

Moderate

***L'Orangerie**, 755 Rue de la Tour de l'Evêque, **t** 04 66 84 50 57, **f** 04 66 29 44 55, *www.orangerie.fr*. Just outside the centre with a garden, small pool and restaurant (*moderate*). *Open year-round*.

***Royal**, 3 Bd Alphonse-Daudet, **t** 04 66 58 28 27, **f** 04 66 58 28 28. A delightful Art Deco hotel with artistic rooms and a palm-fronded lobby and restaurant (*expensive*). Reserve early in the summer because it fills up fast. *Restaurant closed Sun and Mon*.

Kyriad, 10 Rue Roussy, **t** 04 66 76 16 20, **f** 04 66 67 65 99. An old house (with a private garage) converted into an air-conditioned hotel with attractive retro furnishings.

Inexpensive

Central Hotel, 2 Place du Château, **t** 04 66 67 27 75, **f** 04 66 21 77 79, *www.hotel-central.org*. A small, simple, unpretentious hotel, with several rooms looking out over the roofs of the old city.

Hotel de L'Amphithéâtre, 4 Rue des Arènes, **t** 04 66 67 28 51, **f** 04 66 67 07 79. Sweetly restored 18th-century building in the old town, with antique furniture and nice big bathrooms. *Closed Jan and early Nov*.

Hotel de la Mairie, 11 Rue des Greffes, **t** 04 66 67 65 91. Rugged, simple and in the historic centre.

*Hotel Brasserie d'Arenes**, 4 Bd des Arènes, **t** 04 66 67 23 05, **f** 04 66 67 76 93, *www.brasserie-arenes.com*. Not so quiet, but the brasserie within the hotel serves Provençal cuisine. *Restaurant closed Christmas*.

Auberge de Jeunesse, 257 Chemin de l'Auberge de Jeunesse, **t** 04 66 68 03 20, **f** 04 66 68 03 21, *www.fuaj.org*. On a hill 2km from the centre (bus I from the train station, direction Alès or Villeverte, get off at stop 'Stade' and follow the signs).

Eating Out

Nîmes isn't exactly famous for its restaurants, but it has some delicious specialities: *brandade de morue* (pounded cod mixed with fine olive oil), a recipe said to date back to Roman times, and *tapenade d'olives*, an appetizer made of olives, anchovies and herbs. Its *pélardons*, the little goat's cheeses from the *garrigues*, are among the best anywhere. In the sweet category, the city is proudest of its *croquants Villaret*, almond biscuits cooked by the same family in the same oven since 1775, available at Maison Villaret, 13 Rue de la Madeleine, **t** 04 66 67 41 79.

L'Enclos de la Fontaine, Hôtel Impérator (*see above*), **t** 04 66 21 90 30 (*expensive*). *Brandade* is often on the menu at one of Nîmes' top restaurants, and alongside the classics (*escalope de foie gras, rouget*) the chef cooks up imaginative, subtle dishes that melt in your mouth, like veal served with fresh fig *beignets*, which seem especially fresh served outside in the courtyard.

Magister, 5 Rue Nationale, **t** 04 66 76 11 00, *www.lemagister.com* (*expensive*). A smart Nîmes restaurant with good service and

blazed by Hercules himself during his Tenth Labour, as he herded Geryon's cattle back to Greece from the Pillars that bear his name. The Romans paved his route and called it the Via Domitia, and made Celtic Nîmes into their *Colonia Nemausensis*. The Volcae-Arecomici Celts, unlike Astérix and Obélix, thought the Romans were just swell, and Augustus reciprocated by endowing Nîmes with the Maison Carrée, a sanctuary for the Fontaine, an aqueduct (the Pont du Gard) to augment the spring, and four miles of walls. The Nîmois celebrated Augustus' conquest of Egypt, and the arrival of a

highly professional cooking (*brandade* and *taureau* – bull's meat – *au pistou* especially recommended), as well as a good local wine list. *Closed Mon lunch, Sat lunch and Sun.*

Jardin d'Hadrien, 11 Rue de l'Enclos Rey, t 04 66 21 86 65 (*expensive*). A favourite, with its beamed dining room and veranda; try the cod with olive oil, or courgette flowers stuffed with *brandade. Aug–July closed Sun and Mon, and Wed lunch; Sept–June closed Sun eve, Wed, and Tues eve.*

Le Lisita, 2 Bd des Arènes, t 04 66 67 29 15, f 04 66 67 25 32, *www.lelisitia.com* (*expensive*). Next to the amphitheatre, restaurant decorated with bullfighting memorabilia, serving regional cusine.

Aux Plaisirs des Halles, 4 Rue Littré, t 04 66 36 01 02 (*expensive–moderate*). Cosy little bistro near the market for *aïoli* with vegetables or *brandade* with truffles and black olives. *Closed Sun, Mon, early Nov and most of Feb.*

Nicolas, Rue Poise (off Bd Amiral Courbet), t 04 66 67 50 47 (*expensive–moderate*). One of the more affordable fine restaurants in town, and always busy. *Closed Sat lunch, Mon and July.*

Le P'tit Bec, 87 bis Rue de la République, t 04 66 38 05 83 (*moderate*). A tempting selection of seasonal dishes , which you can eat in the garden. *Closed Sun eve, Mon, and Wed eve, early Aug and most of Feb.*

La Fontaine du Temple, 22 Rue de la Curaterie, t 04 66 21 21 13 (*moderate*). Friendly bar and restaurant; a good place to try *taureau* or lamb with thyme. Takeaways available. *Closed Sun and Jan–Feb.*

Bistrot du Chapon Fin, Place du Château-Fadaise (behind St-Paul's church), t 04 66 67 34 73 (*moderate*). Serves local, filling dishes. *Closed Sat lunch, Sun.*

Au Flan Coco, 31 Rue du Mûrier d'Espagne, t 04 66 21 84 81 (*moderate*). A delightful tiny

restaurant run by two *traiteurs* alongside their shop; the food comes fresh from the market and is whipped up before your eyes. *Closed Sun and mid–end Aug.*

Entertainment and Nightlife

Clubs and Bars

Café Napoléon, **Bar de la Bourse** and several other bars are located on Bd Victor Hugo.

La Bodeguita, 3 Bd Alphonse Daudet, t 04 66 58 28 29. A *tapas* and music bar (jazz, tango, flamenco and salsa)in the Royal Hotel, especially popular during *feria* time.

Trois Maures, 10 Bd des Arènes, t 04 66 36 23 23. A big traditional brasserie hung with tributes to bullfighting and rugby. *Closed Sun in July and Aug.*

The Haddock Café, 13 Rue de l'Agau, t 04 66 67 86 57. Popular local club and café with food served late, music concerts and art exhibitions. *Closed Sat lunch and Sun except July and Aug.*

Classical Music and Theatre

Opera, **dance** and **concerts** take place throughout July, August and September. For events at Les Arènes, contact the tourist office.

Cinema

Le Sémaphore, 25a Rue Porte de France, t 04 66 67 83 11, *www.lesemaphore.fr.st*. Sometimes shows films in their original language (*v.o.*).

Leisure

Aquatropique, 39 Chemin de l'Hostellerie, near the *autoroute* exit Nimes-Ouest, t 04 66 38 31 00. Indoor/outdoor water park, with sauna, tennis and keep-fit centre.

---

colony of veterans from the Battle of Actium, by minting a coin with a crocodile chained to a palm, a striking image which François Ier adopted as the city's coat of arms in 1535.

Nîmes declined along with Rome; the city contracted and became a mere frontier post for the Visigothic kings of Toledo. After a brief Arab occupation in the 8th century, Nîmes was ruled by Frankish viscounts, who restored some of the town's former prestige in the 11th century by dominating Narbonne and Carcassonne; the Roman amphitheatre was transformed into a fort, the *castrum arenae*, whose knights played a major role in urban affairs. Nîmes, like much of Languedoc, got into trouble with the Church in the early 13th century by taking up the Cathar heresy, although at the approach of the terrible Simon de Montfort the city surrendered without a fight.

Catholicism never went down well in Nîmes, and when the Protestant alternative presented itself in the 16th century, three-quarters of the population took to the new religion immediately and bashed the other quarter's churches and prelates. The terror reached a peak with the 1567 massacre of 200 priests, monks and nuns, known as the *Michelade*, but continued off and on until the Edict of Nantes (1598); this brought Nîmes enough peace for its Protestants to set up a prosperous textile industry and the city seemed happy to settle down as the Huguenot capital of the south.

Louis XIV spoiled everything by revoking the Edict in 1685; troops were quartered in the Huguenots' homes, forcing them to abjure their faith or face exile or slavery aboard the king's galleys. Nîmes and the Cévennes, the wild hilly region to the north, responded with the desperate war of the Camisards, tying up an important part of the French army by inventing, or reinventing, many of the techniques used in modern guerrilla warfare. After the troubles, Nîmes went back to its second concern after religion: textiles. Its heavy-duty blue *serge de Nîmes* was reduced to the more familiar 'denim' in 1695, in London – where many of the Protestants went in exile – and it was exported widely. Some of it found its way to California, where in 1848 a certain Levi Strauss discovered it to be perfect for outfitting goldrushers. More recently, Nîmes made the headlines on 3 October 1988, when violent storms in the rocky hills of the *garrigues* brought down a torrent that engulfed the city in eight feet of mud. The victory of the French Davis Cup tennis team at Nîmes' Roman arena in 1991 and the opening in May 1993 of the Carré d'Art have done much to dispel this muddy memory.

Les Arènes

Open summer 9–7 (tickets until 6.30); winter 10–5 (tickets until 5.15); closed public holidays and events; adm.

Twentieth in size, but the best preserved of the 70 surviving amphitheatres of the Roman world, the arena at Nîmes (late 1st century AD) is just a bit smaller than its twin at Arles. Like the Maison Carrée, it escaped being cannibalized for its stone by being put to constant use: as a castle for the Visigoths and the knightly militia of the Frankish viscounts, who bricked up the arches facing the Palais de Justice and made them their headquarters; then, after union with France, as a slum, where some 2,000 people lived in shanties jammed into the arches, seats and vomitoria. When restorers came in 1809 to clear it out, they had to shovel 20ft of rubbish to reach the floor where the sands (*arènes*) were spread to soak up the blood of the men and animals who died here to amuse the crowd.

When new, the arena could accommodate 24,000 people, who were able to reach or leave their seats in only a few minutes thanks to an ingenious system of five concentric galleries and 126 stairways. Near the top of the arena are holes pierced in the stone for the supports of the canvas awning (*velum*) that sheltered the spectators from sun and rain – an idea that Mayor Bousquet revived in 1988, but with a

mobile plexiglass and aluminium roof that from the air looks like a giant toilet seat, but which allows the amphitheatre to host events year round. The event that has packed the crowds in since 1853 is the *corrida*, a sport always close to the hearts of the Nîmois – even in ancient times, judging by the two bulls carved over the main gate.

Wandering around the outside, note the curious Siamese-twin figure embedded in the wall of the Palais de Justice, known as the '**Four-Legged Man**', made of ancient sculptural fragments pieced together wrongly long ago. You may also notice Rue Bigot, named after a 19th-century fable writer from Nîmes. The name is particularly pertinent to local attitudes in the Wars of Religion. 'Bigot', after all, comes from the Old French and refers to the first religious intolerance to shake Nîmes – the conflict between the Catholicism of the Franks and the Arianism of the Visigoths, or *Bigothi*.

Crocodiles Galore, the Maison Carré and the Carré d'Art

The *hôtels particuliers* in the historic centre – the area between Les Arènes, the Maison Carrée and the cathedral – date mostly from the 17th and 18th centuries, when Nîmes' textile magnates and financiers enjoyed their greatest prosperity. Beginning at the Four-Legged Man, **Rue de l'Aspic** (which in French evokes vipers as well as jelly) is one of the candidates for the *cardo*, the shorter of the two main streets of a Roman town. Place du Marché opens up to the left, the city's most charming square and site of a fine new **crocodile fountain** designed by Martial Raysse. Four more examples of the city's saurian emblem (donated by well-wishers to the city between 1597 and 1703) can be seen stuffed and dangling over the stair in the high-tech designer interior of the 18th-century **Hôtel de Ville**, to the right of Rue de l'Aspic. Around the corner, at 16 Rue Dorée, Nîmes' very own Académie meets behind the elaborate portal of the 17th-century **Hôtel de l'Académie**. This body was granted the same privileges as the Académie Française in 1682 by Louis XIV, and even today the Académiciens of Nîmes may sit with their fellows in Paris.

To the south, the amphibian community is represented in **Place de la Salamandre**, named after François Ier's totem animal. Many Renaissance rulers had similar emblems, and used to represent them in works of art; François chose the salamander for the belief it could survive in fire – hence the first fabrics woven of asbestos were called 'salamander skins'. The salamander sculpture that once adorned this square now stands in the courtyard of the Archaeology Museum, but note the square's 17th-century **Hôtel de Chazelles**, another fine example of civic architecture.

To the north stands Nîmes' **Cathédrale Notre-Dame-et-St-Castor**, which was consecrated in 1096 but almost completely flattened by rampaging Huguenots in 1597 and 1622, who spared only the campanile to use as a watchtower. Across the façade runs a vigorous frieze of the Old Testament. Lower down, and sadly damaged, are reliefs of Samson and the lions, and Alexander the Great being pulled up to heaven by a pair of griffons, coaxed by a piece of liver dangled over their heads – a favourite medieval fancy. There's a Romanesque frieze nearby, on the corner of Place aux Herbes and Rue de la Madeleine, adorning a rare 12th-century house (the **Maison Romane**).

Of course, more remarkable still is the state of that graceful little 1st-century BC temple known as the **Maison Carrée**, just off the Via Domitia (*Place de la Maison*

Carrée; open summer 9–7; winter 10–5). The best-preserved Roman temple anywhere, it was built by the great General Agrippa (who also built the Pantheon in Rome) and was dedicated to the Imperial cult of Augustus' grandsons, Caius and Lucius, known as the 'Princes of Youth'—their 'deification' a form of flattery to the emperor. Called *Carrée*, or square, because of its right angles and 'long' square shape (85 by 50ft), it has a *cella* (or cult sanctuary) that is perfectly intact, as are the Corinthian columns of the porch. Nîmes always found it useful for something, most notably as the meeting hall of the consuls and least notably as a stable. The temple was originally surrounded by a colonnaded forum, similar to the Imperial Fora of Rome.

In his 1787 *Travels*, Englishman Arthur Young couldn't get enough of the Maison Carrée: 'What an infatuation in modern architects, that can overlook the chaste and elegant simplicity of taste manifest in such a work, and yet rear such piles of laboured foppery and heaviness as are to be met with in France.' One modern architect (and another Englishman), Sir Norman Foster, was given the chance to respond to Mr Young's gripe, on a site next to the Maison Carrée, now unimaginatively known as the **Carré d'Art**. Inaugurated in May 1993, this palace of glass and steel houses a modern art museum, audiovisual centre and extensive library, and cost 400 million francs to build. While many of ex-Mayor Bousquet's critics condemned the project as further evidence of his advanced megalomania, the mayor cheerfully pointed out that his own 'petits projets' in Nîmes were merely a response to President Mitterrand's '*Grands Projets*' in Paris. The ancient columns of the Maison Carrée are reflected in Sir Norman's own slender columns of steel; the walls and even the stairways are of glass to let light stream through the building. Inside, the **Musée d'Art Contemporain** (*t 04 66 76 35 70, http://musees.nimes.fr/carreart/ac-carre.htm; open 10–6; closed Mon; similar hours for the library; adm; guided tours Mon–Fri at 4.30, Sat, Sun and hols at 3 and 4.30*) on the first floor contains post-1960 works. The library has over 360,000 volumes and is especially strong in two local obsessions – Protestantism and bullfighting. The smaller library, part of the Musée d'Art, has 12,000 works dedicated to art post 1950.

Water and Other Mysteries

A block north of the Carré d'Art is another recent project, the **Place d'Assas**, designed by Martial Raysse as a kind of expiatory gesture, one imagines, to the two religions that went down in Nîmes without a fight: that of the Celts (the two figures in the central fountain represent the indigenous gods, 'Nemausa' and 'Nemausus') and the Cathars (the mysterious seven-pointed stars, the magic square Rotas Sator, and inscription '*Les Nuages Sont Sans Age*'). It's all a bit silly, and no one seems to pay much attention to it any more. The statue at the west end, on the other hand, is of Ernest Denis of Nîmes, whose writing championed the founding of Czechoslovakia in 1918. Just north, in the irregular polygonal Square Antonin, is a 19th-century statue of Emperor Antoninus Pius (whose family was from Nîmes), holding his hand out, as the Nîmois say, to see if it's raining.

A short stroll to the west down Quai de la Fontaine is Nemausus' first abode, the great spring that originates in the karst caverns of the *garrigue*, to gush out at the foot of Mont Cavalier. It was domesticated as the **Jardin de la Fontaine** in the 18th century, and the waters were marshalled to flow in a neo-Roman nymphaeum below a maze of balustrades and urns. Narrow, stone-walled canals surround the gardens and extend down the centre of the Quai de la Fontaine into the surrounding neighbourhoods; altogether, the ensemble is one of the loveliest city parks in France. In ancient times a complex of temples and sanctuaries stood here, of which only the so-called **Temple de Diane** remains.

Paths wind up among the flower beds and leafy arbours of Mont Cavalier to the oldest Roman monument in Gaul, the octagonal **Tour Magne**. No record of its origin or purpose has survived, though some speculate that it may have been a trophy dedicated to the opening of the Via Domitia, or a signal tower, or simply the mightiest of the 30 towers in the city wall – a sort of 'homage tower' like those of Aigues-Mortes and other medieval cities. Although 106ft high today, the tower was once half as big again; stairs spiral up to the viewing platform (*open summer 9–7; winter 10–5; adm*). The Tour Magne made news in 1601, when a gardener named François Traucat read Nostradamus' prediction that a gardener would uncover an immense buried treasure. As it was commonly believed that the Romans, like leprechauns, hid pots of gold in their ruins, Traucat decided the treasure must be buried under the Tour Magne. Henri IV gave him permission to dig (at his own expense, and with two-thirds of the loot going to the crown), but instead of finding gold, he found another pre-Roman tower around which the even larger Tour Magne had been built. No one could identify the rubble at the time, and the Consul of Nîmes, fearing that any more digging would undermine the Tour Magne, ordered the now bankrupt Traucat back to his garden.

Two hundred years later there was another discovery of something very rare, though not of gold, down below in Rue Lampèze: a round basin 18ft in diameter called the **Castellum**, where the water rushing in from the Pont du Gard was distributed to the city through 10 pipes of lead. The only other one to survive is at Pompeii. Like so many things in Nîmes it was built under Augustus, and to him was dedicated the city's east gate on the Via Domitia (Rue Nationale), the **Porte d'Auguste**. Built in 15 BC, it had two large entrances for vehicles, and two smaller ones for pedestrians.

Nîmes' Caesar from 1983 to 1995, Mayor Bousquet, hired Jean Nouvel (architect of Paris' Institut du Monde Arabe) to design a subsidized housing project known as **Nemausus I**. It's south of the station, off Avenue du Général Leclerc, and looks like a pair of beached ocean liners from the future. It isn't really a nice place to visit, and you wouldn't want to live there.

Museum-crawling

The former Jesuit college at 13 bis Boulevard Amiral Courbet was, after the Edict of Nantes, diplomatically divided into a Protestant half and a Catholic half. Nowadays, the division is between pot-shards and possums, the first half devoted to archaeology and the second to natural history (*both open 10–6; closed Mon; joint adm*). The **Musée Archéologique** (*t 04 66 76 74 80*) is filled with odds and ends for the expert, such as France's largest collection of ancient inscriptions, but there are some crowd-pleasers as well: the 4th- to 3rd-century BC figure of the *Guerrier de Grézen*, in his curved hood-helmet and belt, and nearby a rare Celtic lintel, the *Linteau de Nages*, found near

Wine: Costières-de-Nîmes

Covering 24 *communes* between Estézargues and Vauvert, the AOC Région des Costières-de-Nîmes (*www.espace-costieres.com*) rides the high terraces and hills of the Rhône, where the vineyards are planted amid round pebbles (*les grès*). Near Nîmes, the rough landscape is tempered by the sea, and although the district is best known for rosés, the reds (similar to Côtes du Rhône) and whites (made from clairette, grenache blanc, maccabéo and malvoisie) are good, inexpensive, fresh young wines; the reds are only aged two or three years at the most.

The easiest place to get acquainted with them is near Nîmes' airport at the **Château de la Tuilerie**, Rte de St-Gilles, **t** 04 66 70 07 52, *www.chateautuilerie.com*, which also sells rum from Martinique and olive oil. Or try the medal-winning reds and rosés from the **Domaine des Goubins** just outside Nîmes (*not open to the public*).

In Nîmes itself, try the **Maison des Costières**, 19 Place Aristide Briand, Quai de la Fontaine (near the Imperator Hotel), **t** 04 66 36 96 20, for tastings, information on local wines and, as an added bonus, a *bodega* at *feria* time. Maison des Costières does not sell to the public, but will direct you to local producers and *caves* in town.

the *oppidum*'s spring (*see* Nages, p.474). The lintel has a frieze of galloping horses and human heads – favourite Celtic motifs, but rarely carved with such pizazz. Upstairs is a fine collection of ancient glass and everyday Roman items, Greek vases, bronze figurines and miniature altars, some bearing the mallet of the Celtic god Sucellus, whom the Romans adapted to their Silvanus.

The other half of the college is the charmingly old-fashioned **Musée d'Histoire Naturelle** (**t** 04 66 76 73 45) home to a collection of those mysterious menhirs-with-personality, the statue-steles. Carved with stylized faces, and sometimes with arms, a knife and a belt (*c.* 2000 BC), they are similar to those found in the Hérault, and also in Tuscany and Corsica. Large glass cases of scary masks and spears and turn-of-the-last-century photographs fill the ethnographic hall, and beyond, a brave little natural history collection that may be the highlight of your trip to Nîmes. It features a 9ft stuffed moose, a beaver foetus, a wide selection of faded bats, two-headed lambs and deformed kittens, pine-cone-shaped animals called pangolins, stuffed *corrida* bulls from the 1890s, two baby rabbits in formaldehyde retrieved from the belly of a snake, and an armadillo 'captured near the Pont du Gard'.

Adjacent is the Jesuit church **St-Ignace** (1678), a fine piece of Baroque architecture with an unusual pattern of vaults and openings, now used for exhibitions.

For the **Musée de Vieux Nîmes** (**t** 04 66 76 73 70; *open 10–6; closed Mon; adm*), follow Grand' Rue behind the museums, north to Rue Lacroix. It has an exceptional collection of 19th-century textiles and 500 print designs from Nîmes' wool and silk industries – a real eye-opener for anyone who thought paisley was invented in the 1960s. There are 17th-century carved *armoires*, painted ones from Uzès, a Charles X billiard table, thousands of socks, a 19th-century bed supported by weightlifters and ceramics and an abundance of curios.

The **Musée des Beaux-Arts** (**t** 04 66 67 38 21; *open 10–6; closed Mon; adm*) is on the other side of Les Arènes, 440 yards along on Rue de la Cité-Foulc, in a charming 1907 building by a local architect, who chiselled the façade with the names of Nîmes' painters and sculptors, and optimistically left plenty of room for future geniuses. It was opulently restored by architect Jean-Michel Wilmotte in 1986–7. In the centre of the ground floor is an enormous Roman mosaic, *The Betrothal of Admetus*, surrounded by a frieze of scenes. Upstairs, look out for two Venetian paintings: an example of 15th-century retro in Michele Giambono's *Mystic Marriage of St Catherine*, and one of Jacopo Bassano's finest works, *Suzanna and the Elders* (1585), with a serene bunny rabbit in the corner. As usual, it's the Dutch paintings, with their buxom wenches and oyster-slurping sessions, that one would most like to be in. Of the French offerings, the outstanding painting is Paul Delaroche's *Cromwell Looking into the Coffin of Charles I*, an 18th-century painting as memorable as its subject is odd.

If you are tired of terrestrial culture, Nîmes' small **Planétarium** (*Av du Mont Duplan, t 04 66 67 60 94; public shows Wed, Sat and Sun 3 and 4.30pm, Fri 8.30pm; adm*) takes you to the stars with glittering displays of the universe. Finally, a forthcoming attraction is the **Musée des Cultures Taurines** (*6 Rue Alexandre Ducros, t 04 66 36 83 77; open mid-May–mid-Oct Tues–Sun 10–6; closed Mon*), which opened in 2002 but currently only has temporary exhibitions about bullfighting. It is due to open properly in 2006.

The Northern Gard

By 19 BC, the fountain of Nemausus could no longer slake Nîmes' thirst, and a search was on for a new source. The Romans were obsessed with the quality of their water, and when they found a crystal-clear spring called the Eure near Uzès, the fact that it was 48km away hardly posed an obstacle to antiquity's star engineers. The resulting aqueduct, built under Augustus' son-in-law Agrippa, was like a giant needle hemming the landscape, piercing tunnels through hills and looping its arches over the open spaces of the *garrigues*, and all measured precisely to allow a slope of .07 centimetres per metre. Where the water had to cross the gorge of the unpredictable river Gard (or Gardon, as it's usually called), the Roman engineers knuckled down, ordered a goodly supply of neatly dressed stone from the nearby quarries at Vers, and built the Pont du Gard, at 157ft the highest of all Roman aqueducts and, along with the span in Segovia, the best preserved in the world.

The Pont du Gard

No matter how many photos you've seen before, the aqueduct's three tiers of arches of golden stone without mortar makes a brave and lovely sight; since the 1920s the natural setting and river have been maintained as intact as possible. What the photos never show are the two million people who come to pay it homage every year – the Pont du Gard (*www.lepontdugard.com*) is the second most-visited site in France outside Paris – and you may well find it more evocative if you arrive very early in the morning or about an hour before sunset, when the site regains some of its ancient dignity. As you walk over it, note how it's slightly curved (the better to stand up to floods) and how the Roman engineers left cavities and protruding stones to

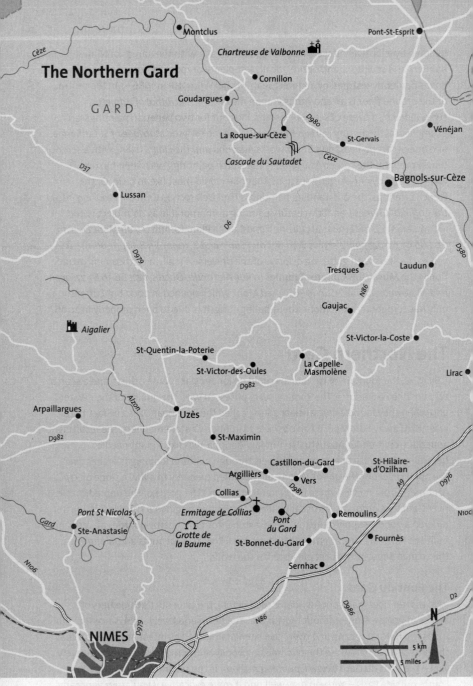

The Northern Gard

Montclus

Pont-St-Esprit

Chartreuse de Valbonne

Cornillon

GARD

Cèze

Goudargues

La Roque-sur-Cèze

St-Gervais

Vénéjan

Cascade du Sautadet

Cèze

Bagnols-sur-Cèze

D980

D37

Lussan

D6

D979

D580

Tresques

Laudun

Aigalier

Gaujac

N86

St-Quentin-la-Poterie

St-Victor-des-Oules

La Capelle-Masmolène

St-Victor-la-Coste

Lirac

Uzès

D982

Arpaillargues

Alzon

D982

St-Maximin

Castillon-du-Gard

St-Hilaire-d'Ozilhan

Argillièrs

Vers

A9

D976

Collias

D981

Pont St Nicolas

Ermitage de Collias

Remoulins

N100

Gard

Ste-Anastasie

Grotte de la Baume

Pont du Gard

St-Bonnet-du-Gard

Fournès

N106

Sernhac

D2

N86

D986

NIMES

D979

N

5 km

5 miles

support future scaffolding. In the 18th century, the bottom tier was expanded to take a road. This is now limited to pedestrians, due to the damaging vibrations caused by cars. A major renovation project has recently been completed, with new visitor's centres on either side of the bridge, an auditorium in the former quarry, a pedestrian-

Getting There and Around

STDG-Cevennes cars (**t** 04 66 29 27 29) **buses** from Nîmes, Uzès and Avignon pass frequently within a kilometre of the Pont du Gard. Note that you can no longer **drive** over the Pont du Gard, but will have to leave your car in one of the pay car parks on either side.

Canoe and **kayak hire** is available upstream at Collias: contact Kayak Vert, **t** 04 66 22 80 76, *www.canoe-france.com/gardon*.

Tourist Information

Pont du Gard: 200 yards from the aqueduct on the Remoulins side of the Pont du Gard, **t** 04 66 37 50 99, *www.ot-pontdugard.com*.
Remoulins: Place des Grands Jours (by the eastern roundabout), **t** 04 66 37 22 34. *Open summer Mon–Sat 9–1 and 3–6.30, Sun 9–1; winter Mon–Fri 9–12.30 and 2.30–6.*

Where to Stay and Eat

Castillon-du-Gard ✉ 30210
★★★★Le Vieux Castillon, Rue Turion Sabatier, **t** 04 66 37 61 61, **f** 04 66 37 28 17, *www.vieux castillon.com* (*luxury–expensive*). A Relais & Châteaux hotel in the heart of the medieval village. The rooms are scattered on several different levels in several different houses connected by patios; there are tennis courts,

a stunning swimming pool perched among the gardens, and an excellent restaurant (*very expensive*) featuring dishes with truffles (the Gard produces 15% of France's crop), *langoustines* and a wide variety of Côtes du Rhône wines. *Closed Jan and Feb; restaurant closed Mon, and Tues lunch.*

Remoulins ✉ 30210
★★Le Colombier, Rte du Pont du Gard, **t** 04 66 37 05 28, **f** 04 66 37 35 75 (*inexpensive*). With 10 comfortable rooms behind its broad awnings, and a restaurant (*moderate*).

Vers ✉ 30210
La Bégude St-Pierre, on the D981 at Les Coudoulières, **t** 04 66 63 63 63, **f** 04 66 22 73 73, *www.hotel-saintpierre.fr* (*expensive– moderate*). Luminous, air-conditioned rooms inside a 17th-century post station, with a quiet park and pool, restaurant (*expensive*) and terrace. *Restaurant closed Sun eve and Mon in winter.*

Collias ✉ 30210
★★★Le Castellas, Grand'Rue, **t** 04 66 22 88 88, **f** 04 66 22 84 28, *www.lecastellas.fr* (*expensive–moderate*). A friendly, Art Deco hotel spread out in two large houses, with a good and stylish restaurant (*expensive*), plus a very pretty garden and deep enclosed pool. *Closed Jan–Mar; restaurant closed Mon and Wed, and Fri lunch.*

ized promenade and restaurants and shops. **Le Portal** (**t** 04 66 37 50 99; *open daily June–Aug 9.30–10; Sept–May 9.30–6; adm*) presents archaeological and engineering projects for children, films and permanent exhibitions. In summer the site is lit up at night. For the restoration, the ancient quarries were reopened in Vers (*see* p.466), so the patches should blend right in. Some of the original blocks weigh 6 tonnes; many have inscriptions, a few left by the Roman builders, but most left by the *compagnons*, French journeymen masons who, as part of their training, travelled about France studying its most important monuments. On the Remoulins side, a palaeolithic shelter, the **Abri Préhistorique de la Salpêtrière**, is being excavated (*no visitors*).

Paddling down the gorge and under the Pont du Gard is great fun, especially if you can avoid peak periods and potential canoe jams (*see* above).

Around the Pont du Gard: Villages and More Aqueducts

Take time to visit the pretty wine villages around the aqueduct. Just north, hilltop **Castillon-du-Gard** exudes medieval atmosphere, even if it was mostly rebuilt in the

16th century. Other attractions include views down to the Pont du Gard and a Romanesque chapel, St-Caprais, a setting for summer concerts. East of Castillon, 11th-century **St-Hilaire-d'Ozilhan** is another charming village with an even older chapel, the Clastre, standing on its own just to the south. If it's *supermarchés* or bustling sprawl you're after, there's **Remoulins**, the area's market town and gateway to the **Fosses de Fournès**, a weirdly eroded lunar landscape to the east.

Southwest of Remoulins, you can explore traces of the aqueduct in the hills around **Sernhac** (the local IGN map may come in handy here). Here the Romans dug two impressive tunnels, one for the water and one for maintenance, still bearing the grooves left by the hammers that excavated them, stroke by stroke. The extraordinarily hard calcium deposits that accumulated in the water channels were chiselled out as a prized building material in the Middle Ages: some went into the walls of the fortified Romanesque church of **St-Bonnet-du-Gard**, near Sernhac.

Columns, Columns, Columns and a Bridge

Then there are the Roman (and later) stone quarries that produced the Pont du Gard, just off the Uzès road in **Vers**, another pleasant little village with another Romanesque church. Here, by the level crossing on the D227 and down the white road a couple of hundred yards to the south, stand a few aqueduct arches in a state of romantic abandon; other vestiges may be seen between Vers and Argilliers, just off the D3B, taking the side road that veers sharply to the left. At **Argilliers**, a Romanesque chapel and a neoclassical colonnaded funeral chapel dedicated to Saint Louis on the D981 mark the entrance to one of Languedoc's most curious follies, the **Château de Castille**, the private mania of Froment Fromentès, Baron de Castille (1747–1829). One of the great travellers of his day, the Baron was afflicted by a serious case of columnitis in Rome, and on his return to his estates in the Gard he erected over 200 pillars and columns, of which only some 50 survive, incorporated into garden follies, porticoes and hemicycles inspired by Bernini. Unfortunately, the estate isn't open, and you have to boldly trespass to peek into the Baron's magic garden.

South of Argilliers, down on the banks of the river, **Collias** has a popular beach, kayak rental and paths going up and down the river from the Pont du Gard to Pont St-Nicolas. The dramatic, wild beauty of the sheer walled Gardon gorge around Collias inspired an awe of religious proportions in the past, and there are several old hermitages in caves, one near the **Grotte de la Baume**, with an 11th-century chapel (an hour's walk), and another, the **Ermitage de Collias**, in a place so beautiful that it has been classed like a historic monument. People have worshipped here since prehistoric times – there's a little chapel by the cave, a Roman bridge and fountain dedicated to Minerva. Further west, the D112 will take you to **Pont St-Nicolas**, where an impressive 13th-century bridge, made of the same lovely and reliable stone as the Pont du Gard, takes the scenic old Nîmes–Uzès road over the Gardon gorge. Just above it to the west, the 12th-century church of **Ste-Anastasie** is all that survives of the Priory of St-Nicolas de Campagnac; built with exquisite care, the church is unusually large, sober, pure and empty.

Uzès, the First Duchy of France

Few towns of 8,000 souls have so bold a skyline of towers, or so little truck with the modern industrial world. Uzès seems to have been vacuum-packed when its wealthy, Protestant merchants of cloth and silk stockings packed their bags and left at the

Getting There and Around

Uzès is linked by frequent **buses** to Nîmes, Avignon, Alès and the Pont du Gard, t 04 66 22 17 75 or STD Gard, t 04 66 29 27 29.

Bike Hire

Ets Payan, 16 Av Gén. Vincent, t 04 66 22 13 94.

Tourist Information

Uzès: Chapelle des Capucins, Place Albert 1er, t 04 66 22 68 88, f 04 66 22 95 19, www.uzes-tourisme.com. Open Mon–Fri 9–6, Sat–Sun 10–1 and 2–5. Guided tours include a night-time one on summer.

Market Days

Wed, and a massive general one on Sat. Also a *marché aux truffes*, Sat Dec–Mar, Av de la Libération.

Where to Stay and Eat

Uzès ✉ 30700

★★★Hôtel d'Entraigues, Place de l'Echevé, t 04 66 22 32 68, f 04 66 22 57 01, www.lepontdu gard.com/entraigues (*moderate*). A fine old hotel fit for a duke in a 15th-century building opposite the cathedral, with a pool suspended over the dining room; try to get a room near the top for the view. The restaurant, **Les Jardins de Castille** (*moderate*) is elegant, with a classy lunch menu.

★★Le St Genies, Route de St-Ambroix, t 04 66 22 29 99, f 04 66 03 14 89, www.hotel-saint genies.com (*moderate*). An oasis of tranquillity half a mile from the centre, with a charming pool and three-star rooms. You can hire bikes here, too.

★★La Taverne, 7 Rue Sigalon (just off Place Albert Ier), t 04 66 22 13 10, f 04 66 22 45 90 (*moderate*). Renovated rooms in the centre of town, and the chance to dine on a pretty

garden terrace (*moderate*). *Closed last 2 weeks Jan.*

De l'Ancienne Gare, outside of Uzès on the Remoulins road, t 04 66 03 19 15 (*moderate*). In a former train station; the delicious, refined cooking keeps it full of happy customers. The menus change regularly, and specialities include *tête de veau*. *Closed Feb.*

La Boulangerie Uzetienne, Place des Herbes. The best bakery in town, famous for the local speciality, *fougasse*, a savoury flat bread made with bits of bacon.

Around Uzès ✉ 30700

★★★Hôtel Marie d'Agoult, 4km west of Uzès at Arpaillargues et Aureillac, t 04 66 22 14 48, f 04 66 22 56 10, www.lepontdugard.com/ agoult (*very expensive–expensive*). Sleep in an antique bed (or just dine) at this 18th-century hotel. Marie d'Agoult was Liszt's muse and Wagner's mother-in-law, and a frequent guest. There's a pool and tennis courts, and garden restaurant (*expensive*) serving truffles in season. *Closed Nov–Mar.*

Ferme-Auberge de Cruviers, Montée de Larnac, Route de St-Ambroix, t 04 66 22 10 89, f 04 66 22 06 76 (*inexpensive*). Orchards and views encompass this bed-and-breakfast place 5km north of Uzès. There's also a *table d'hôte* (*moderate*) for guests only, serving dishes based on asparagus, free-range chickens and ducks.

L'Auberge de St-Maximin, St-Maximin, 6km south of Uzès, t 04 66 22 26 41 (*expensive–moderate*). Some of the best food in the area is served on the garden terrace, where they specialize in *taureau* and other local products. *Closed Mon lunch and Tues lunch in summer, Mon and Tues in winter, and Nov.*

Table d'Horloge, Place de l'Horloge, St-Quentin-la-Poterie, t 04 66 22 07 01, www.table-horloge.fr (*expensive*). The single-price €45 menu changes with the seasons. *Closed Wed, Sun eve and Christmas. Book.*

Revocation of the Edict of Nantes. 'O little town of Uzès,' wrote André Gide (whose father was a Uzètien), 'were you in Umbria, the Parisians would flock to visit you!' Now they do, more or less, ever since 1962, when Uzès was selected as one of France's 50 *villes d'art*, entitling it to dig into the historical preservation funds set aside by De Gaulle's culture minister, André Malraux. Houses tumbling into ruin have been repaired, creating the perfect stage for films like *Cyrano de Bergerac*.

The Duché and Around

Café life in Uzès engulfs most of the available space in and around Place Albert Ier, just under the residence of the dukes, the **Duché** (*t 04 66 22 18 96, www.duche-uzes.fr; daily guided tours July–mid-Sept 10–1 and 2–6.30; mid-Sept–June 10–12 and 2–6; English translation available; adm exp*). The de Crussols of Uzès, claiming a family tree that sent out its first shoots under Charlemagne, became the first dukes and peers of the realm when the Duc de Montmorency forfeited the title (along with his head) in 1632. The current title-holders, a handsome young couple (he can often be spotted messing about with his car collection, she shopping with the kids in the local Carrefour supermarket), open their grand fortified home to visitors. The oldest section, the rectangular donjon called the **Tour Bermonde**, was built over a Roman tower in the 10th or 11th century; its crenellations were designed by the inevitable Viollet-le-Duc to replace the originals destroyed in the Revolution. The **Renaissance façade** in the central courtyard, a three-layered classical cake of Doric, Ionic and Corinthian orders, was constructed in 1550 and bears the motto of the dukes: *Ferro non auro* ('iron, not gold' – i.e. they were warriors, not financiers). This didn't keep the women of the family from sometimes donning the trousers: in 1565 the Duchess of Uzès became the first woman to be sent abroad as an ambassador, and then there's the amazing Duchess Anne, heiress to the Veuve Clicquot fortune, talented sculptress, enthusiastic huntress who rode until the age of 86, feminist, friend of anarchist Louise Michel (of Paris Commune fame) but still an ardent monarchist (she personally financed General Boulanger's attempt to overthrow the Republic to the tune of 3 million gold écus); the first woman in France to get a driving licence – and the first to get a speeding ticket. The tour of the Duché includes several furnished rooms.

Across Place du Duché is the attractive 18th-century **Hôtel de Ville**, while to the left of the Duché is a rock-cut **crypt** that lost its church (the Jesuits discovered it under their monastery); it is believed to date from the 4th century and has some primitive bas-reliefs of St John the Baptist and a convert. Uzès is a lot smaller than it seems, and a short wander will soon bring you to the irregular, arcaded, perfectly delightful **Place aux Herbes**, with its old plane trees, for centuries the centre of public life. The nearby church of **St-Etienne**, with an attractive Baroque façade, had to be rebuilt in the 18th century after the Wars of Religion and contains a handful of good paintings.

The Cathedral and Tour Fenestrelle

Set apart from the rest of the old town on a terrace, the 1671 **Ancien Palais Episcopal** was the seat of the powerful bishops of Uzès (64 bishops reigned here between the 5th century and the Revolution). A restoration attempt in the 1970s caused the interior to cave in behind the façade, although the right wing is in good enough nick to hold the eclectic collections of the **Musée Municipal** (*open July and Aug Tues–Sun 10–12 and 3–6; Mar–June and Sept–Oct Tues–Sun 3–6; Nov and Feb Tues–Sun 2–5; closed Dec–Jan*), with its fossils, ceramics, paintings, and memorabilia of the Gide family. Behind it stretches the pleasant **Promenade des Marronniers**, while adjacent, the **Cathédrale St-Théodorit** was built in 1663, the third to occupy the site after its predecessors were destroyed in the Albigensian Crusade and the Wars of Religion. The quaint neo-Romanesque façade was tacked on in 1875, with the idea of making a better partner to the stunning 12th-century **Tour Fenestrelle**, spared by the Protestants only because they found it useful as a watchtower. Unique in France, the 137ft tower is encircled by six storeys of double-lit windows, inspired by the Romanesque campaniles of Ravenna and Lombardy. The cathedral's interior was severely damaged during the Revolution, when it was converted into a Temple of Reason, leaving only the peculiar upper gallery with its wrought iron railing (erected right after the revocation of the Edict of Nantes, to make room for the former Protestants) and the cathedral's pride and joy: a splendid **organ** of 1670, the only one in France to have retained its original painted shutters. Restored, it is the centrepiece of the end-of-July/beginning of August festival, *Nuits Musicales d'Uzès*.

The odd building just below the terrace is the **Hôtel du Baron de Castille**, its façade adorned with – guess what – columns; tall slender ones that don't conform to any classical order but which have a charm all their own. There is also a lovely little herb garden in the Impasse Port Royal, the **Jardin Médiéval** (*t 04 66 22 38 21; open July and Aug daily 10.30–12.30 and 2–6; April–June and Sept Mon–Fri 2–6, Sat and Sun 10.30–12.30 and 2–6; Oct daily 2–5; closed Nov–Mar; adm*) with a collection of carefully labelled local plants, and medicinal and culinary herbs used since the Middle Ages.

The funny little domed building abutting the belvedere-cum-*pétanque* courts on the far side of the cathedral is the so-called **Pavillon Racine**, named after the play-wright and poet who, in spite of popular belief, never sat there because it was built a quarter of a century too late. In 1661, at the age of 22, Racine spent a year with his uncle, the Vicar-General of Uzès, during which time his family hoped he would forget his foolish love of poetry and turn to the priesthood. Just the opposite happened. The climate, the friendly welcome, the charming girls, the food and the inscrutable *patois* made a great impression on the young man.

Around Uzès: the Uzège

Close enough to walk to from Uzès (from Parc du Duché, follow the Chemin André Gide; the Uzès tourist office sells a map), the **Vallée de l'Alzon** is the arcadian setting of the **Fontaine d'Eure**, the spring where the Roman aqueduct to Nîmes began; you can see the large basin that regulated the flow down the canal, excavated in 1993.

If you have kids, the Haribo candy company runs a **Musée du Bonbon** south of town at Pont des Charrettes (*t 04 66 22 74 39; open July–Sept 10–7; the rest of the year 10–1 and 2–6; closed Mon and Jan*), where you can watch them make little jelly crocodiles and more. Horse-lovers can meet the 65 stallions at the national stud farm, **Les Haras Nationaux d'Uzès** (*Mas des Tailles, Route d'Alès, t 04 66 22 68 88; open mid-Mar–mid-June Mon–Sat 2–5.30; mid-June–mid-Sept guided visits only; contact the tourist office*).

The countryside around Uzès – where fields of asparagus, cherry orchards, forests of truffle oaks and vineyards alternate with *garrigues* – is dotted with attractive old villages. One, **Arpaillargues**, 4km west on the D982, has the added attraction of the **Musée 1900** at Moulin de Charlier (*t 04 66 22 58 64; open July and Aug daily 10–7; Sept–June 9–12 and 2–7; adm*), one man's amazing 30-year accumulation of period cars, motorcycles, gramophones, movie posters, locomotives and more; there is also a **Musée du Train et du Jouet**, with model trains and toys. Just west of Arpaillargues, the walled hilltop hamlet of **Aureilhac** has a superb view of Uzès' skyline.

Nine kilometres northwest of Uzès, off the road to Alès, **Aigalier**, with its medieval lanes, dungeons, Saracen wall and Romanesque church all piled under a ruined castle, has long been a favourite subject of local painters.

The clay-rich soil north of Uzès has provided **St-Quentin-la-Poterie** with its vocation since the cows came home, and in some strange tangential way inspired its most famous son, Joseph Monier (1823–1906), to invent reinforced concrete. After producing thousands of amphorae, roof tiles, all the glazed tiles for the floors of the Popes' Palace in Avignon, bricks and ceramic pipes, the last ceramic factory closed in 1974; but in 1983 the kilns were fired up again as the village made a concerted effort to bring the potters back. Fifteen now live in the village year-round; you can visit their workshops or get an overview of their work at the **Maison de la Terre** (*5 Rue de la Fontaine, t 04 66 03 65 86, open April–June and Oct–Dec Wed–Sun 10–1 and 3–7; July–Sept daily 10–1 and 3–7; closed Jan–Mar*). The adjoining **Musée de la Poterie Méditerranéenne** has a wonderful selection of examples of pottery from all over the Mediterranean, in a beautiful variety of glazes.

Lovely **Lussan** is 18km north of Uzés, but well worth the detour: a nearly perfect, unspoiled medieval *village perché* below a 13th-century château. Near Lussan, the sheer gorge of the river Aiguillon, **Les Concluses**, makes a magnificent and easy walk in the summer when the river is dry, with potholes (*marmites*) formed by the river, eagle's nests and a remarkable steep and narrow **Portail** that closes in on top. Leave your car in one of the car parks along the D643; the walk takes about 30 minutes.

Northeast of Uzès, towards Bagnols-sur-Cèze, strange sandstone formations and quarzite quarries mark the environs of **St-Victor-des-Oules**, 'of the pots', another pottery village, this one specializing in stoneware (*grès*). Paths lead up **Mont Aigu**, for scant ruins of a 5th-century BC *oppidum* and superb views of the Cévennes to the west. Further east, the 12th-century château in **La Capelle-Masmolène** was the summer palace of the bishops of Uzès.

Bagnols-sur-Cèze and the Valley of the Cèze

North of Uzès, where the river Cèze meets the Rhône, **Bagnols-sur-Cèze** is the traditional gateway – or exit – of Languedoc. The Romans named it for its sulphur baths, but these days Bagnols is more famous for its green beans (*les bagnolais*), and the nearby nuclear power plant at Marcoule, the construction of which saw Bagnols' population quadruple. In spite of all the new building, the narrow lanes of the old town have changed little; every now and then you'll see the city's quaint emblem of three golden pots.

The prettiest square in Bagnols, central, arcaded **Place Mallet**, has a tower, the **Tour de l'Horloge**, erected by Philippe le Bel, and an 18th-century Hôtel de Ville housing the only real reason for visiting Bagnols: the **Musée de Peinture Albert André** (*t 04 66 50 50 56; open summer 10–12 and 3–7; winter 10–12 and 2–6; closed Mon, Feb and hols; adm*). In 1854, Léon Alègre, a local humanist and Sunday painter, set up a museum to

Getting There and Around

The nearest passenger **train** stations are in Avignon and Nîmes. **Buses** link Bagnols with Uzès, Avignon and Nîmes.

Tourist Information

Bagnols-sur-Cèze ✉ 30200: Espace St-Gilles, Av Léon Blum, t 04 66 89 54 61, f 04 66 89 83 38, *www.ot-bagnolssurceze.com*. Open Mon–Fri 9–7, Sat 9–6, Sun 10–1.
Pont St-Esprit ✉ 30130: 1 Rue Kennedy, t 04 66 39 44 45, f 04 66 39 51 81, *www.ot-pont-saint-esprit.fr*. Open July and Aug Mon–Sat 9–7, Sun 9–12; Sept–June Mon–Fri 8–12 and 2–5.30, Sat 9–12.
Goudargues ✉ 30630: 4 Route de Pont Saint Esprit, t 04 66 82 30 02, f 04 66 82 29 63. Open Sept–June Mon–Fri 9–12 and 2–5; July–Aug Mon–Fri 9–1 and 3–7, Sat, Sun 9–1.

Market Days

Bagnols: Wed and Thurs.
Laudun: Mon.
Pont St-Esprit: Sat.
Goudargues: Wed.

Where to Stay and Eat

Bagnols-sur-Cèze ✉ 30200

★★★★**Château de Montcaud**, Rte d'Ales, in Sabran, t 04 66 89 60 60, f 04 66 89 45 04, *www.chateau-de-montcaud.com* (*luxury–very expensive*). Part of the Relais & Châteaux group, in a park, with extremely comfortable, air-conditioned rooms, a gym and Turkish bath, and an equally exquisite

restaurant (*expensive*) and cheaper bistrot. *Closed Nov–Mar; restaurant closed lunch, bistrot closed Sat and Sun..*
★★★**Le Château du Val de Cèze**, 69 Rte d'Avignon, t 04 66 89 61 26, f 04 66 89 97 37 (*expensive*). The most luxurious hotel in town. In a large park, with tennis courts and a pool, it has rooms in individual bungalows around a 13th-century château. No restaurant. *Closed weekends Nov–Feb.*
★★**Le St-Georges**, 210 Av Roger-Salengro, t 04 66 89 53 65, f 04 66 79 98 01 (*inexpensive*). A small, typical place; all rooms have bath. The restaurant (*moderate*) is the best in town, with local specialities served on a terrace. *Restaurant closed Sat lunch and Sun.*

Pont St-Esprit

L'Auberge Provençale, Av Général de Gaulle, t 04 66 39 08 79 (*inexpensive*). Simple *Logis de France* with a restaurant serving reasonably priced local cuisine.

Goudargues/Cornillon ✉ 30630

Mas Rodières, 7km north (take the D980 to the D141 towards Salazac), t 04 66 82 29 25, f 04 66 82 26 34, *www.masrodieres.ch* (*luxury*). A 17th-century building, beautifully restored to house four elegant suites (*from €580 for a week, €680 with cleaning*).
★★★**La Vieille Fontaine**, Cornillon, t 04 66 82 20 56, f 04 66 82 33 64, *www.vieillefontaine. net* (*expensive*). In the walls of the castle, with eight rooms, each furnished with antiques and Provençal fabrics. The garden terraces descend to a pool, with views all around. The restaurant (*expensive*) is just as delightful. *Closed Nov–early Mar; must reserve at restaurant out of season.*

instruct his fellow citizens, with everything from Roman pots to paintings to stuffed animals. In 1918, Albert André, a painter friend of Renoir's, was made volunteer curator and gave the museum the first provincial collection of contemporary art in France – only to have the whole thing go up in smoke in 1924, when the local fireman set it alight during their annual ball. It proved to be a blessing in disguise when Albert André sent out a message to France's artists: 'I am the curator of a museum of naked walls. Help me fill them!' They did. The eight rooms blaze with colour: Fauvist Albert Marquet's famous *14 Juillet au Havre* (1906); Pierre Bonnard's *Bouquet des fleurs des champs*; Matisse's *La Fenêtre ouverte à Nice* (1919); and other works by Renoir, Van Dongen, Paul Signac, Gauguin, Jongkind and Picasso, as well as a room of Albert André's own works.

Bagnols also has the **Musée Léon Alègre** (*24 Rue Paul Langevin; open Thurs–Sat 10–12 and 2–6; July–Aug till 7; closed Feb and hols*), with archaeological finds from the Iron Age to the Romans.

Many of the items in the archaeology museum were found at the lofty *oppidum* of **St-Vincent de Gaujac**, 13km south of Bagnols and a 2km walk up from the car park. Dating from the 5th century BC to the 6th century AD, it became a holy site in Gallo-Roman times, and has the foundations of temples and a bath complex from the 3rd century AD. If you're in the vicinity, don't miss medieval **St-Victor-la-Coste**, a picturesque village gathered around its ruined castle, with a pair of 11th-century chapels.

Laudun, between St-Victor-la-Coste and Bagnols, is another handsome medieval village, with a 14th-century church, Renaissance château and above, on a high plateau with superb views, the **Camp de César**, a 40-acre archaeological site. After its start as a Celtic *oppidum* in the 5th century BC, it grew into a Roman city and was abandoned in the 7th century: Cyclopean walls, Roman towers, Forum, houses and a basilica have so far been excavated (*t 04 66 39 88 22, www.ville-laudun.fr; call for guided tours*).

The Romans later built villas in the area: around **Tresques**, just west, many were converted into Romanesque chapels. One, **St-Martin de Jussan**, on the north end of Tresques, is Lombard in inspiration – companies of builders from the banks of Lake Como roved far and wide in the Middle Ages – and has a carved portal. Another church, **St-Pierre de Castres**, 4km northeast, is one of the oldest, with archaic chapels.

Five kilometres north of Bagnols, there are more views over the Rhône valley from **Vénejan**; and 2km northeast from there the charming 11th-century **Chapelle de St-Pierre** is decorated with Lombard-style bands of stone and a little square bell tower. If you're lucky enough to find it open, the interior has curious, primitive sculptural decoration: six pointed stars, concentric circles, solar discs, birds, animals and two praying figures.

Further north, **Pont St-Esprit** was named for its famous bridge over the Rhône, erected between 1265 and 1309 by a confraternity of builders called the Brothers of the Holy Ghost. Nineteen of the 25 arches are original, but the mighty towers that once controlled access from either bank are long gone. There are fine views of the bridge from the terrace by the 15th-century parish church, once part of the influential Clunisien abbey of St-Saturnin-du-Port. Pilgrims to Santiago de Compostela would cross the bridge, stop at the church and head down Rue St-Jacques, a street that has preserved many of its medieval houses. Appropriately enough for a town named Holy Ghost Bridge, one of these (No.2) now contains a museum of religious art, the **Musée d'Art Sacré du Gard** (*t 04 66 39 17 61; open Sept–Jan and Mar–June Tues–Sun 10–12 and 2–6; July and Aug Tues–Sun 10–7; closed Mon and Feb; adm*). The house itself, the Maison des Chevaliers, was built in the 12th century by a prosperous family of merchants, who kept right on enlarging and improving their home until the 18th century. The museum displays a wide range of works from the 15th to the 19th centuries, from paintings to *santons*. Just up the street, the **Musée Paul-Raymond** (*Place de l'Ancienne Mairie, t 04 66 39 09 98; open July–Aug Tues–Fri and Sun 10–12.30 and 3–6; Sept–June Tues–Fri and Sun 9–12 and 2–6*) has a collection of prehistoric finds, ceramics, a reconstruction of an 18th-century pharmacy and more religious art.

Bagnols is also a good base for exploring the scenic lower valley of the Cèze, beginning with **St-Gervais**, a wine village set under the steep cliffs. Further upstream, **La Roque-sur-Cèze** is piled on a hill opposite a 13th-century bridge, with streets so narrow that cars are forbidden. La Roque overlooks the **Cascade du Sautadet**, where the Cèze flows through a mini-canyon that looks as if it were clawed out of the rock by a giant bear.

Isolated in an oak forest to the north, the **Chartreuse de Valbonne** (*t 04 66 90 41 03, www.chartreusedevalbonne.com*) dates from 1203, and was rebuilt in a grand Baroque style with a beautiful varnished tile roof after the Wars of Religion, only to be abandoned again in 1901. In the 1920s it found a new lease of life as a hospital for tropical diseases: you can visit the church, with its stuccos and stone vaults, and the huge cloister. It has now been converted into a hotel complex; 13 of the monks' cells are now bedrooms. There is also a 16ha vineyard.

At the beginning of the 9th century, St Guilhem of Toulouse founded an abbey in **Goudargues**, which Louis the Pious gave to the abbey of Aniane: the ruins of St Guilhem's original Chapelle St-Michelet still stand over the village, while the later abbey church, built in the 12th century and remodelled in the 18th and 19th centuries, is particularly grand and spacious. The Benedictines drained the marsh that once surrounded Goudargues into a canal, to water their crops and make Goudargues,

---

Wine: Côtes du Rhône Gardoise

Bagnols is the centre of Languedoc's Côtes du Rhône production, while three villages, Chusclan, Laudun and St-Gervais, take pride in bottling their own Côtes du Rhône-Villages, as well as good red table wines. Try the **Cave des Vignerons de Chusclan**, at Chusclan, **t** 04 66 90 11 03, **f** 04 66 90 16 5 (*open 9–12 and 2–630*), for bottled or *en vrac* wines (Côtes du Rhône, Côtes du Rhône Villages, Côtes du Rhône Village Chusclan); and the exceptional wines of **Domaine Ste-Anne**, at Les Cellettes in St-Gervais, **t** 04 66 82 77 41 (*open 9–11 and 2–6; closed Sun and bank holidays*), especially the Cuvée Notre-Dame and their pure syrah Côtes du Rhône. One of the finest white Côtes du Rhône is made by Luc Pelaquie, at Laudun, *www.domaine-pelaquie. com*. Pelaquie's wine has a natural freshness that is unusual for such a hot area. It has great depth and will age well for several years. The domaine produces a good range of other wines too, including Tavel, Lirac red and rosé, and Côtes du Rhône red.

with no little exaggeration, 'the Venice of the Gard'; in high summer it often has more water in it than the Cèze.

Across the Cèze from Goudargues, **Cornillon** is a 17th-century village with a ruined château and a grand view. Little **Montclus**, further up, is prettily set in a tight loop of the Cèze, guarded by a ruined castle keep.

Between Nîmes and Montpellier

There are three routes to choose from between the two rival cities: the *autoroute*; its southern parallel, the N113; or the longest, prettiest and most interesting route, along the back roads through Sommières – the D40 from Nîmes to Sommières, then the N110 to Montpellier.

Via Nages and Sommières

Nages: A Celtic *Oppidum*

The D40 from Nîmes is a winding, pretty route that passes through lush, hilly country and slumberous villages like Caveirac and **St-Dionisy**.

Above the latter, off the D737, is the 3rd-century BC *oppidum* of **Nages**, one of the outstanding pre-Roman sites in the south (easy access on foot, signposted from the village of Nages-et-Solorgues). Like Nîmes, Nages was built around a spring, entirely of dry stone, with a temple, and walls punctuated by round towers; on top of the tallest, the **Tour Monumentale**, a cache of stones for slings was discovered. The streets, with their rectangular houses, were laid out in a tidy grid – long before the Romans introduced their waffle-shaped city plans. The first floor of Nages-et-Solorgues' *mairie* has been converted into a small **archaeology museum** (*t 04 66 35 05 26; open Tues, Thurs and Fri 8.30–11.45, Mon and Wed 8.30–11.45 and 2–6; Thurs 5–7*).

Sommières

Hidden under the cliffs of the river Vidourle, Sommières suffers only moderately from the usual plagues besetting picturesque southern villages: the Parisians, the English, the trinket shops – it even has to do without a famous writer, since long-time resident Lawrence Durrell died in October 1990. Its streets and squares could be paintings by Maurice Utrillo: soft and pastel, well worn and well lived-in, with faded shop signs of a century ago and flowers under every window. Huge plane trees, a little bull-ring and an enormous *boulodrome* (for *pétanque*) line the river, and swans and mallards float calmly by, one imagines, during the *vidourlades*, the local name for the Vidourle's seasonal floods, when it pours down from the Cevennes, hell for leather: recent measures have dampened some of its impetuosity, but the town is still badly flooded from time to time.

Before Sommières, there was Sommières' **bridge**, built by Tiberius between AD 19 and 31. Its 17 arches have withstood centuries of *vidourlades*; they carry road traffic to this day and still look in mint condition. The top was restored in 1715. Oddly, almost half of the bridge is now hidden inside the town; medieval Sommières expanded into the dry parts of the riverbed and eventually an embankment was built. The **Tour de l'Horloge**, the entrance to the town, was built over the bridge's fifth arch in 1659.

The other arches of the bridge lie under Rue Marx Dormoy, the street leading from the bridge to **Place des Docteurs Dax** (natives of Sommières who discovered the exact spot in the brain in charge of language), a lovely 12th-century market square that everyone in Sommières still calls by its old name, the **Marché-Bas**. It preserves the Pierre d'Inquant, where slaves were once made to stand when they were being sold. The houses are all built on stone arcades: in the old days, the square would be underwater every spring, forcing the market up two streets to the **Marché-Haut** (now Place Jaurès). The web of lanes radiating from these squares has its share of handsome *hôtels particuliers*. Sommières was an enthusiastically Protestant town and was destroyed during the Wars of Religion after two terrible sieges, in 1573 and 1575, then again in 1622, so most of what you see is from the 17th-century rebuilding, and little has changed since then. Rue de la Taillade, cut into the cliffs by the Romans for the Nîmes–Lodève road, is one of the most attractive streets, with its well-preserved old shops; the former Ursuline convent here, now the **Espace Lawrence Durrell**, is used for temporary exhibitions. From here, the Montée des Régordanes lead up to the half-ruined **Château de Sommières** and the **Tour Bermond** (*open July–Aug daily 4–7; adm*), worth the climb for its views up and down the valley of the Vidourle, as far as Pic St-Loup and Aigues Mortes.

Tourist Information

Sommières: 5 Quai Frédéric Gaussorgues, t 04 66 80 99 30, f 04 66 80 06 95, *www.ot-sommieres.fr. Open July–Aug daily 9–12.30 and 2–6; rest of year closed Sun.*

Market Days

Sommières: Sat.
Calvisson: Sun.
Castries: Tues and Fri.

Where to Stay and Eat

Sommières ✉ 30250
Hôtel de l'Orange, 7 Rue Beaumes, t 04 66 77 79 94, f 04 66 80 44 87, *www.hotel.delorange.free.fr (moderate)*. A 17th-century building, lovingly converted into a guesthouse, with a pool and garage but only five rooms, so book early in the summer; ask to see the *baume* (cave).
★★★**Auberge du Pont Romain**, 2 Rue E. Jamais, t 04 66 80 00 58, f 04 66 80 31 52, *www.aubergedupontromain.com (moderate)*.

Lovely, spacious rooms in a 19th-century herbal distillery close to the river, with a pool and a gourmet restaurant (*expensive*) serving the house *foie gras* and other delights on a peaceful garden terrace. *Closed Nov and mid-Jan–mid-Mar.*

L'Olivette, 11 Rue Abbe Fabre, t 04 66 80 97 71, f 04 66 80 39 28 (*moderate*). This restaurant in the centre is a local favourite, serving regional cuisine with an original twist, such as duck with balsamic vinegar and snails *à la sommiéroise. Closed Tues in summer, Tues eve and Wed in winter.*

L'Evasion, 6 Rue Paulin Capmal, t 04 66 77 74 64 (*cheap*). At lunchtime, watch the life of the Marché Bas pass by from an outdoor table; the menu includes pizza and mussels. *Closed Sun eve and Mon.*

Castries ✉ 34160
L'Art du Feu, 13 Av du 8 Mai 1945, t 04 67 70 05 97 (*moderate*). Offers refined cooking on bargain menus; the house speciality is thin-sliced *aiguillettes* of duck in delicate sauces. *Closed Sun eve, Tues eve and Wed, and one week Feb.*

Around Sommières

A mile away, on a hill above Sommières, the **Château de Villevieille** (*t 04 66 80 01 62; open June–Sept daily 2–7 and 2 weeks around Easter depending on number of visitors; adm*) was first built in the 11th century by the lords of Sommières, Bermond d'Anduze et Sauve, whose most famous scion was a Cathar and brother-in-law of Raymond VII of Toulouse – excuse enough for St Louis to confiscate their estate in 1243. He divided the vast property in two, leaving a bit for Bermond's daughter and trading the remainder to the monks of Psalmody in exchange for Aigues-Mortes – which Louis built into France's first Mediterranean port. In 1527 the château was ceded to the Pavée family, who have owned it ever since. It escaped being sold off in the Revolution, thanks to the Marquis de Villevieille's friendship with Mirabeau and Voltaire. You can count the châteaux in France that have preserved their original family furnishings on one hand – this is one of them.

Four kilometres northwest of Sommières, along a Roman road, you can visit a pretty country chapel, St-Julien-de-Montredon at **Salinelles**, in a lovely setting among the vines, with an ancient cemetery (*ring the keyholder, René Peyrolle, t 04 66 80 01 95, before setting out*). First mentioned in 813, it was rebuilt by the monks of Psalmody in the 11th century and decorated with archaic carvings of animals and birds. Salinelles also has a **beach** along the Vidourle; others are nearby at Lecques and Villetelle.

At **Calvisson**, 10km east of Sommières, is the **Maison du Boutis** (*t 04 66 01 63 75, www.la-maison-du-boutis.com; open Thurs–Sun 2.30–6.30*), a museum and shop dedicated to local embroidery.

Castries

Continuing towards Montpellier, Castries has a Renaissance-era **château** belonging to one of the 19 barons of Languedoc. Though it was wrecked in the Revolution, this castle came back into the possession of its original owners, the de Castries family, who restored it. It was once open to the public for visits, but now belongs to the Académie Française, which meets here once a year. It is also undergoing further restoration.

Nîmes to Montpellier by Way of Perrier and Lunel

This faster, southern route along the N113 isn't as scenic as the Sommières route but has its own rewards, especially if you combine it with a detour to Aigues-Mortes on the edge of the Camargue (*see pp.448–50*).

Fizzy Water and a Statue of Liberty

Bernis, 7km from Nîmes, offers the first potential stop, for the sake of its 12th-century church, once a possession of the abbey of St-Gilles. Although mostly rebuilt after the Wars of Religion, its façade is intact, carved in a style archaic back in the 12th century, especially the Carolingian-inspired decorations by the door. The capitals are carved with people, birds, animals, a dragon and a mermaid.

Just off the the N113 at **Vergèze**, trendies may make a pilgrimage to the **Source Perrier**. Surprisingly, the vast complex was established by an Englishman in 1903, and looks less like a natural spring than an obsessively tidy aeroplane factory; ring **t** 04 66 87 61 01 for the tour, to see the Indian-club-shaped green bottles come whizzing off the line in their billions, all guaranteed benzene-free.

The big town along this route is **Lunel**, and a peculiar place it is. Legend has it that Lunel was founded by Jews from Jericho under the reign of Vespasian – a story now dismissed as a play on words (Jericho was the city of the moon, the *ville de la lune*). Historians now say the first Jews probably settled in the 11th century and, until their expulsion in 1306, Lunel was their educational centre in France, with well-known schools of everything from medicine (predating even Montpellier's) to the Kabbala. Today, the town raises steers for bloodless *course libre* bullfights. Its landmark is a copy of the Statue of Liberty (erected in 1989 to commemorate the bicentenary of the French Revolution), its cops wear star-and-crescent badges just like those of New Orleans, and one of its biggest businesses is dog food research and development. Little remains of medieval Lunel: some bits of the Jewish schools on Rue Ménard, and a vaulted alley called the Passage des Caladons that once was part of a Templar commandery. In the 19th century the Lunel area was the holiday retreat of a man who hardly seemed the type to take a vacation in the south of France – Karl Marx. Marx suffered from asthma, and whenever he had a bad bout his wife Jenny sent him down to the Château de la Tour de Fages, owned by the husband of her best friend, opera diva Caroline Ungher.

South of Lunel, the sweet and shady village of **Marsillargues** has an elegant Renaissance château. The rooms, with their marble and plaster relief decoration of the 1570s and later, are lovely, but empty; it's sad that this château, one of the few

Tourist Information

Lunel: 16 Cours Gabriel Peri, **t** 04 67 71 01 37, **t** 04 67 87 83 97, *www.ot-paysdelunel.fr.* *Open July–Aug Mon–Sat 9–7, Sun 9.30–12.30; Sept–June 9–12 and 2–6, Sun 9.30–12.30.*

Market Days

Lunel: Thurs and Sun, food market; Sat am, flea market.
Marsillargues: Tues and Thurs.

Where to Stay and Eat

Vergèze ✉ 30310

La Passiflore, 11 Rue Neuve, **t** 04 66 35 00 00, **f** 04 66 35 09 21 (*inexpensive*). Well placed for the *autoroute* and the Camargue, this gorgeous little hotel with enclosed courtyard

in a small village is run by an English couple. It's beautifully decorated, the service is friendly, they like kids and the restaurant (*moderate*) is excellent, with a menu covering French classics to apple crumble. *Restaurant closed Sun and Mon.*

Lunel ✉ 34400

★★Les Mimosas, Av du Vidourle, **t** 04 67 71 25 40, **f** 04 67 83 20 81 (*inexpensive*). Just outside the centre. *Open daily, year round.*
Mas St-Félix, St-Séries, 7km north of Lunel, **t** 04 67 86 05 83 (*inexpensive*). A B&B in an old posthouse of the Knights Hospitallers (with use of the kitchen). *Closed Oct–April.*
Didier Chodoreille, 140 Rue Lakanal, **t** 04 67 71 55 77 (*expensive*). Dine well on French classics; it's by the station and has a pretty garden terrace that makes Lunel's traffic seem far away. *Closed Mon eve and Sun.*

undamaged in the Revolution, should have lost most of its furnishings in a fire in 1936. Recently, four of the rooms have been filled up with the contents of the villagers' attics to form a **Musée d'Arts et de Traditions Populaires** (*t 04 67 83 52 12; open April–Sept Tues–Sat 2–6; Oct–Mar Mon–Fri 2–5*). There are various events and theatre performances at the château throughout the year.

The **Château de Teillan**, at Aimargues, on an unpaved road across the river Vidourle from Marsillargues (*open by appt only, call the mairie on t 04 66 73 12 12*), has a large park with fragmentary Roman ruins, milestones, the largest *noria* in Languedoc and a gigantic *pigeonnier*, once part of a 7th-century military depot.

By the *autoroute* north of Lunel in **Villetelle**, a single arch of a Roman bridge stands in the middle of the Vidourle at **Ambrussum** (*tourist office organizes guided visits July–Sept Wed 3pm and Sat 10am, Oct–June Wed only, in English by appointment*), a Celtic *oppidum* from the same period as Nages (*see* p.474) and later way station on the Via Domitia. Archaeologists have uncovered 200 yards of paved Roman road (the deep grooves near the bridge mark the spot where the wagons and chariots stopped to pay their toll), as well as villas and public buildings.

Montpellier

If that town could suck as hard as it can blow, it could bring the ocean to it and become a seaport.

Although this old saying originally referred to the brash, booming, braggart Atlanta of the 1880s, it applies just as fairly to France's eighth city. The public relations geniuses in Montpellier have managed to outdo even Atlanta: their beloved city has been cockadoodled as the 'Technopole', the *Surdoué* (the Specially Gifted), the 'Synergetic Euro-cité', the 'Capital of Southern Europe', rightful 'heir to the Florence of the Medicis', the 'French California', and indeed nothing less than 'the Rome of Tomorrow'. Unlike Atlanta, Montpellier has actually sucked hard enough to get a port of its own (for sailing boats at least) by widening a puny river called the Lez, a feat that gave it a new horn to toot: *Montpellier la Méditerranée*! Today it is merely *'Montpellier, le sud que j'aime'*.

Until 1977 and the election of the irrepressible socialist Mayor Georges Frêche, Montpellier was a pleasant, sleepy university backwater of fawn-coloured stone with a population of 100,000, one that could put forth the modest claim that Stendhal found it the 'only French city of the interior that doesn't look stupid'. The population now approaches 300,000, making it the eighth biggest city in France, including the large staff of IBM and more than 60,000 university students from around the world who come to study where Rabelais and Nostradamus learned medicine. With his huge development projects, notably the monumental modern quarter called Antigone, Frêche made Montpellier a European model for innovative and effective city government. He stayed in charge for 27 years; the current mayor, Hélène Mandroux, elected in April 2004; will find it hard to come out from Frêche's shadow. This is one live wire of a city.

History

Compared with its venerable Roman neighbours, Narbonne, Béziers and Nîmes, Montpellier is a relative newcomer, tracing its roots back a mere thousand years, to 985, when the count of Mauguio bestowed a large farm at Monspestelarius on a certain Master Guilhem. It was a fortunate site, near the old Via Domitia and the newer Cami Salinié (salt route) and Cami Roumieu (the pilgrimage route between St-Gilles and Compostela), and it had access to the sea through the river Lez.

Guilhem's farm soon grew into a village of merchants, who made their fortunes by importing spices from the Levant, especially spices with medicinal uses taught to the merchants by their Arab and Jewish trading partners and by graduates of the medical school of Salerno; by the year 1000 they were training pupils in Montpellier. By the late 12th century, the town was big enough to need a wall with 25 towers, shaped like an escutcheon, or *écusson* (as the old town is still known). It lost its independence when Guilhem VIII failed to produce a son and gave his only daughter, Marie, to Pedro II of Aragon. Montpellier was her dowry, just in time to spare the town from the Albigensian Crusade. When Marie and Pedro's son, Jaime the Conqueror, divided Aragon between his two sons, Montpellier joined the kingdom of Majorca.

In 1220 the teachers of medicine formed a *Universitas Medicorum*, and began to attract students from all over Europe; in 1250 it was supplemented by a *studium* of law, both of which were given Pope Nicholas IV's seal of approval in 1289. Another impetus behind Montpellier's tremendous growth in the 13th and 14th centuries was dead bugs – dark red cochineal insects found on oaks in the surrounding *garrigues*, believed at the time to be grains and used for dying cloth scarlet. The spice and gold-working trades thrived, especially after those mega-consumers, the popes, moved to Avignon.

In 1349 the Kings of Majorca sold Montpellier to France for 120,000 golden écus. A period of relative peace and prosperity continued until the 1560s, when the university academics and tradesmen embraced the Reformation. For the next 70 years much of what Montpellier had achieved was wiped out; churches and suburbs were destroyed, building and art came to a halt. In 1622, Louis XIII came in person to besiege the rebellious city and reassert royal authority; he built a citadel to keep an eye on the Montpellerains, then transferred the States-General of Languedoc here from Pézenas, with all its nobles, prelates and deputies, who built themselves the patrician *hôtels particuliers* that still dominate the old city.

Putting its merchant republic days behind it, Montpellier settled down to the life of a university town and regional capital. The Revolution passed without kicking up much dust; a far bigger crisis for Montpellier occurred in the 1890s, when phylloxera knocked out the wine-making industry the city had come to depend on – an economic blow from which it only began to recover in the 1950s. With the French mania for categorizing, Montpellier now pigeonholes its economy into five 'poles': *Euromédecine*, including its numerous labs and pharmaceutical industries), *Héliopolis* (tourism), *Informatique* (IBM has been here since 1965), *Agropolis* (it boasts the first European research centre of agronomy in hot climates, among other institutes) and *Pole Antenna*, for its role as the telecommunications centre of Languedoc. Meanwhile,

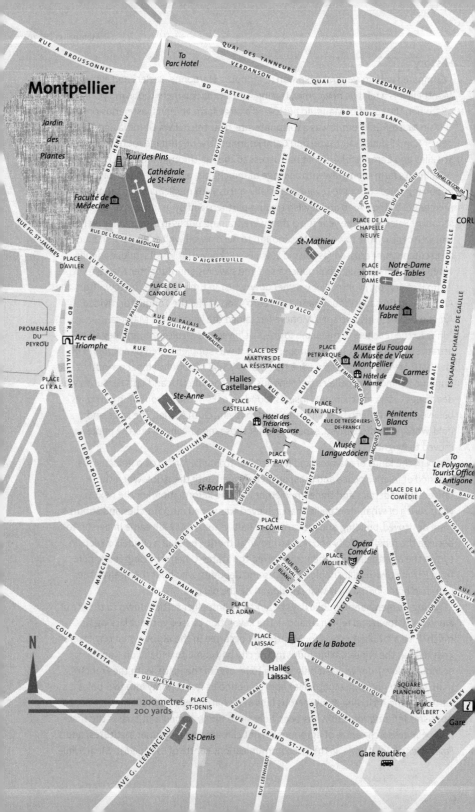

Getting There and Around

By Air

The airport, Montpellier-Méditerranée, is 8km southeast of the centre on the D21 (t 04 67 20 85 00, *www.montpellier.aeroport. fr*). British Airways flies direct to London Gatwick, Ryanair to London Stansted, and Air France serves Paris. The regular airport **shuttle bus** leaves from the *gare routière* at roughly one-hour intervals, t 04 67 92 01 43 or see the airport website.

By Train

The train **station** is in Place Auguste Gilbert, just south of the Ecusson, t 04 99 74 15 10. You can race there from Paris in 4hrs 40mins on the TGV, or catch direct trains to Avignon, Nîmes, Marseille, Nice, Perpignan, Béziers, Narbonne, Agde, Lunel, Sète and Carcassonne.

By Bus

The train station is linked by an escalator to the *gare routière* in nearby Rue du Grand St-Jean (t 04 67 92 01 43), which has buses to Nîmes, La Grande Motte, Béziers, Aigues-Mortes, etc. Every 30mins bus 17 trundles down to the sea at Palavas. In town the little **Petibus** vans can take you around the pedestrian zones of the Ecusson and Antigone.

By Tram

In summer 2000, Montpellier opened the first stage of its tram project. The first line crosses the city centre from northwest to southeast; a second line going northeast to southwest is due to open at the end of 2006. Information from TAM, t 04 67 22 87 87, *www.montpellier-agglo.com/tam*, or the tourist office.

Car and Bike Hire

Big-name car hire firms are at the airport, or try **Avis** at 900 Av Prés-d'Arènes (south of the centre), t 04 67 92 51 92, or **Hertz France**, Place Auguste Gilbert, t 04 67 06 87 90 (outside the station). You can also hire a less expensive used car from **A.D.A.**, 58 bis Av Clemenceau, t 04 67 58 34 35.

You can hire a bike at 27 Rue Maguelone (off Place Comédie), t 04 67 92 92 67 – worth looking into, since the entire historic centre is a pedestrian zone.

Tourist Information

Montpellier: Allée Jean de Latte de Tassigny, Esplanade de Comédie, t 04 67 60 60 60, f 04 67 60 60 61, *www.ot-montpellier.fr. Open Mon–Fri 9–7.30, Sat 9.30–6, Sun 2.30–6.* There are also offices in the station (Place Auguste Gilbert, t 04 67 92 90 03), and at Antigone, at the motorway exit, t 04 67 22 06 16, f 04 67 22 38 10. The offices have a hotel reservation service in season and offer tours of the city centre in English, every Wed and Sat in season.

Market Days

At Espace Mosson (La Paillade), there is a **flower** market on Tues and a **flea market** on Sun am. Daily **food** markets take place in Rue de la Loge, Halles Castellanes and Halles Laissac (Place A. Laissac); on Tues and Sat there's an **organic** market at Aux Arceaux, by Rue Mariage; and at Antigone a market of **farmers' produce** every Wed, Place du Nombre d'Or. Ask at the tourist office for others.

Festivals

The city hosts many festivals: among them are **theatre** in mid-June–beginning of July, during the *Printemps des Comédiens* at Château d'O, t 04 67 63 66 67, *www.printemps descomediens.com*; **dance** performances of all kinds, including whirling dervishes, films and workshops at the **Festival International Montpellier Danse**, t 04 67 60 83 60, *www. montpellierdanse.com*, also June and July; and all-star **music** from opera to Jazz at the **Festival Radio France et Montpellier**, t 04 67 60 60 60, in the last 3 weeks of July. The end of October sees the **Festival International du Cinéma Méditerranéen**, t 04 99 13 73 73, *www.cinemed.tm.fr*.

Shopping

The tourist office has a display of wine, *confits* and other regional products; antiques shops cluster around Place de la Canourgue and the district of Ste-Anne. For a special perfume, pick up a bottle of '*Eau de Montpellier*' (no kidding) for your sweetie-pie at G. de Guidais, 51 Rue de la Méditerranée.

The Bookshop, 6 Rue de l'Université, t 04 67 66 09 08. A good selection of reasonably priced English books and videos, and the latest lowdown on Montpellier. *Open Mon–Sat 9.30–1 and 2.30–7.*

Caves Notre Dame, 1348 Av de la Mer, on the other side of the river, t 04 67 64 48 00. An excellent source of local wines and information, including tastings. *Open Mon–Fri 9–12 and 3–7.30.*

Maison Regionale des Vins et des Produits du Terroir, 34 Rue St-Guilhem, t 04 67 60 40 41. A good range of local wines and food products from olive oil to caviar. *Open Mon–Sat 9.30–8.*

Where to Stay

Montpellier ✉ 30400

Montpellier is well endowed with hotels, especially two-star hotels for small business travellers that double well enough for pleasure travellers.

Very Expensive

****Holiday Inn Métropole, 3 Rue du Clos-René, t 04 67 12 32 32, f 04 67 92 13 02, *himontpellier.manager@alliance-hospitality. com*. Top of the line: antique-furnished, with a quiet garden courtyard, air-conditioning and restaurant (*moderate*), between the train station and Place de la Comédie.

Le Jardin des Sens, 11 Av St-Lazare (off the N113 towards Nîmes; bus 4), t 04 99 58 38 38, *www.jardin-des-sens.com*. Modern rooms, with restaurant. *See* 'Eating Out'.

Expensive–Moderate

***Demeure des Brousses, Rte des Vauguières (4km east of town on the D24 and D127E towards the Château de la Mogère), t 04 67 65 77 66, f 04 67 22 22 17, *www.demeure-des-brousses.fr*. If you have a car, the most charming place to stay is this 18th-century ivy-covered *mas* in a vast park of shady trees, a few minutes from the city or the sea.

Furnished with antiques; excellent restaurant (*expensive*).

Moderate

***La Maison Blanche, 1796 Av de la Pompignane (off the route to Carnon), t 04 99 58 20 70, f 04 67 79 53 39, *www. hotel-maison-blanche.com*. Another gem requiring your own transport: 35 rooms in a big, balconied house that looks as if it has escaped from the French quarter of New Orleans, surrounded by a 5-hectare park.

**Parc, 8 Rue Achille Bège, t 04 67 41 16 49, f 04 67 54 10 05, *www.hotelduparc-montpellier.com*. An 18th-century *hôtel particulier* fitted out with air-conditioning, TV, etc.

**Palais, 3 Rue du Palais (just off Rue Foch), t 04 67 60 47 38, f 04 67 60 40 23. Comfortable rooms in a recently restored building, with a charming breakfast room.

**Les Arceaux, 35 Bd Arceaux, t 04 67 92 03 03, f 04 67 92 05 09, *www.hoteldesarceaux. com*. Attractive, clean and comfortable, with a small garden and terrace.

Inexpensive

*Les Fauvettes, 8 Rue Bonnard, t 04 67 63 17 60, f 04 67 63 09 09. Good value for money near the Jardin des Plantes, with quiet rooms overlooking interior courtyards.

You'll find a choice on the side streets around Place de la Comédie:

Etuves, 24 Rue des Etuves, t 04 67 60 78 19, *www.hoteldesetuves.fr*. Cheap and comfortable.

Majestic, 4 Rue du Cheval Blanc, t 04 67 66 26 85, f 04 67 66 11 42. Around the corner from the Etuves, and similar.

Eating Out

Very Expensive

Le Jardin de Sens, 11 Av St-Lazare (off the N113 towards Nîmes; bus 4), t 04 99 58 38 38, *www.jardin-des-sens.com*. Montpellier, not formerly celebrated for its cuisine, is now home to one of the most celebrated restaurants in the southwest. It is run by local twins Jacques and Laurent Pourcel, who are devoted to the cuisine of Languedoc and the Mediterranean. Try the squid stuffed with ratatouille and crayfish tails, *bourride* soup, fish soup and traditional *oreillette* pastries. The restaurant has an exquisite garden, and now has its own vineyard, above Valmagne abbey. A few rooms are also available (*see above*). *Closed Sun, Mon lunch and Wed lunch in July and Aug, Sept–June Sun, Mon, Tues, and Wed lunch; also 2 wks Jan.*

Expensive

L'Arboisie, 12 bis Rue Jules Ferry, **t** 04 67 92 02 55, *www.arboisie.com*. An excellent restaurant preparing Mediterranean dishes from very fresh fish and meat. There is also an extensive wine list. *Closed Sun all day, Mon lunch.*

Cellier Morel, 27 Rue de l'Aiguillerie, **t** 04 67 66 46 36. Serves local produce in a 13th-century vaulted dining room, and sells it in the adjoining shop. *Closed Sun all day, Mon lunch and Wed lunch.*

Moderate

Le Petit Jardin, 20 Rue J Rousseau, **t** 04 67 60 78 78, **f** 04 67 66 16 79, *www.petit-jardin.com*. Remarkably quiet restaurant in the centre of town, with a delightful large shady garden with a view of the cathedral. Good local fish, salads and fresh pasta with vegetables. *Closed Mon lunch July–Sept, and Jan.*

L'Ollivier, 12 Rue Aristide Ollivier, **t** 04 67 92 86 28. A popular family restaurant bang on the new tramway; smooth service, classic cuisine and the best local wine, of course. *Closed Sun and Mon.*

Le Vieil Ecu, 1 Place de la Chapelle Neuve, **t** 04 67 66 39 44. Good French food, served in the old chapel or on the terrace. *Closed Sun lunch and Mon lunch in winter, and most of Feb.*

Cheap

Lively Rue des Ecoles Laïques and Place de la Chapelle Neuve make up Montpellier's Latin Quarter, where the colours, smells and live music from the Turkish, Greek, Spanish and Tunisian restaurants collide in gleeful culinary discord.

Tripti-Kulai, 20 Rue Jacques Cœur, **t** 04 67 66 30 51. A vegetarian restaurant and tea room near the Musée Languedocien that offers some exotic dishes: a good spot for a light lunch. *Closed Sun.*

Pizzeria du Palais, 22 Rue du Palais des Guilhem, **t** 04 67 60 67 97. Here you may safely break the Languedoc-Roussillon pizza rule (never order a pizza in Languedoc-Roussillon): it's Italian-run, with a wide choice of pizzas and other Italian dishes, and always crowded.

Entertainment and Nightlife

Montpellier is a great town for **cinema**, both recent releases and classics, some in English; complete listings for these, as well as clubs, theatre and music, can be found in the city weekly *La Gazette*. FNAC, in the Polygone, has tickets for most events.

CORUM, **t** 04 67 61 67 61, **f** 04 67 61 67 00, *www.corum-montpellier.fr*. Home of the Orchestre National de Montpellier (*www.orchestre-montpellier.com*) and the Opéra Berlioz.

Opéra Comédie, **t** 04 67 60 19 99. Opera and theatrical performances.

Most bars and clubs do not heat up until after 11pm, and the clubs rock until dawn.

Le Rockstore, down from Place de la Comédie at 20 Rue de Verdun, **t** 04 67 06 80 00. By the beach, and still Montpellier's leading place to be. A café, bar, concert hall and disco. *Open Mon–Sat till 4am.*

At weekends and often weekdays there's live jazz, blues or world music at:

Sax'Aphone, 24 Rue Ernest-Michel, **t** 04 67 58 80 90. The oldest music bar in the city.

Le Fil, 16 Rue du Pila St-Gély, **t** 04 67 66 20 67. A philosophy café, with French music and jazz. *Closed Sat and Sun.*

Villa Rouge, **t** 04 67 06 52 15, *www.villa-rouge.net*. Buzzy place on the beach front.

La Barberousse, 6 Rue Boussairolles, **t** 04 67 58 03 66. Montpellier's very popular rum bar, packed at weekends. Good cocktails are available too.

the city used to teasingly threaten to tax the balconies of its residents to pay for the ambitious 'follies' of Mayor Frêche, follies that are the envy of nearly every other city in France. One of the latest is a high-tech, ultramodern tramway, like those of Strasbourg and Nantes; even the stops are decorated with artworks and nicely landscaped.

A Place Named Comédie

The various personalities of Montpellier all come together in the lively, café-lined **Place de la Comédie**, locally known as *l'Œuf*, or the Egg, owing to the shape it had in the 18th century. Now flattened into an omelette, its centre is watered by the fountain of the *Three Graces* (1796), while along one side stretches the waist-level trough of a modern fountain, where three bronze stooges gesticulate frantically, presumably because they forgot their trousers. Other ornaments of the square include a doppelgänger of the Paris Opera, and various 19th-century larded bourgeois buildings with domes reminiscent of bathyspheres, while opposite the square looms a modern glass-and-steel semi-ziggurat, the **Polygone**, a shopping mall and town hall complex.

To the north of Place de la Comédie extends the **Esplanade Charles de Gaulle**, replacing the city walls demolished by Louis XIII after the siege of 1622, the better to keep Montpellier at the mercy of the cannons of his new citadel. In the 18th century the Esplanade was planted with rows of trees and became Montpellier's chief *promenade*; among its monuments is a rare survival of 1908, the Cinématographe Pathé, a little cockerel-emblazoned palace from the magical early days of cinema (now renamed the Rabelais Cultural Centre, it often shows foreign films). The north end of the Esplanade is flanked by the mastodontic **CORUM**, 'the House of Innovation' designed by Claude Vasconi, one of Georges Frêche's Euro-Cité showcases, which encompasses the Opéra Berlioz and two smaller congress halls.

Antigone

East of the Comédie lies another of the jewels in the Euro-Cité's crown: **Antigone**, a mostly moderate-income quarter with housing for 10,000 people, and shops and restaurants, all designed by Barcelona architect Ricardo Bofill in 1979 and spread along a huge formal axis down to the river Lez. Bofill understood just what a Rome of Tomorrow needs: 'a parody of neo-Classicism', as Robert Hughes wrote – Mannerist neo-Roman arches, cornices, pilasters, and columns as big as California redwoods, built around the **Place du Nombre d'Or** and the **Place du Millénaire**, the squares of the 'Golden Number' and the 'Millennium' that link Montpellier to its newly dredged-out Tiber, the Lez. Does Antigone work? Even though it stretches nearly to the centre of the city, there was no attempt to relate the project to the rest of town – as you'll discover when you try to find it (from Comédie, the only way to reach Antigone is to pass through the Polygone shopping mall and walk out the back door of the Galéries Lafayette department store). On a bad day, Antigone looks like the surreal background to a De Chirico painting, as troubling as the Antigone of myth; on a good day, it seems like a delightful place to live, especially for kids, who can play football in the monumental Place du Millennium and still hear their parents call them in for lunch.

The newest parts of the project lie along the Lez: a gargantuan semicircle of apartments with a vaguely Stalinist air called the **Esplanade d'Europe**, decorated with a huge blue 'M' for Montpellier on the pavement. This part of the river has been blocked off by two bridges that hug the waterline, forming a space for paddling canoes; opposite Antigone across the river, and closing the long axis, stands a sharp glass and stone castle housing the Hérault regional council, the **Hôtel de Région**.

Musée Fabre

2 Rue Montpelliéret, t 04 67 14 83 00; closed for renovation until 2006. Temporary exhibitions of some of its contents at the museum's pavilion on Esplanade Charles de Gaulle, t 04 67 66 13 46; open Tues–Fri 9.30–5.30, Sat and Sun 10–5.30; closed Mon; adm.

On Boulevard Sarrail, between the Cinématographe and CORUM, in the fastness of a former Jesuit College, the Musée Fabre was long the main reason for visiting Montpellier, with one of the most important collections of art in provincial France. In the front courtyard, a large arch built into the wall is decorated with two mossy look-alikes of Michelangelo's *Day* and *Night*, although instead of moping in opposite directions, these two statues lean amorously towards each other – fittingly enough, for this museum was founded on a Florentine romance.

François Xavier Fabre (1766–1837), a pupil of David, was in Florence at the outbreak of the French Revolution, where he became a close friend of the countess of Albany, the merry widow of Bonnie Prince Charlie, and her lover, the Italian dramatist Vittore Alfieri. When Alfieri died in 1805, he left the countess his library and paintings. Fabre in turn inherited the countess' affections, and when she died in 1824, she left everything to her young man from Montpellier. A year later, Fabre donated the lot to his native city; the valuable Alfieri and Albany libraries are now in the adjacent **Gutenberg Médiathèque**, in a building formerly (and more simply) known as the Hôtel de Massilian, where Molière played in the *Ballet des Incompatibles* in 1655.

The Musée Fabre has six levels. The penalty for touring it from the bottom up is to start with the compost of the 17th century, when sunlight was an abomination, and people who paid for paintings liked bloody hunting scenes of boars goring dogs, and only the hard-drinking Dutch seemed to have any fun (works by Ruysdael, Jan Steen, David Teniers, and a good Rubens portrait). The next floor up, formerly the Jesuits' kitchen, is devoted to ceramics: apothecary vases made in Montpellier in the 17th century, faïence portraits of the Caesars and, finest of all, a 16th-century plate by Orazio Fontana of Urbino.

The next floor up contains the bulk of Fabre's donation, and although much of it is overblown and unintentionally hilarious, there are some gems: a lush *Mystic Marriage of St Catherine* by Paolo Veronese that explains why 'Veronese green' is such a popular colour in France; a self-portrait by Bernini; Magnasco's *Fondaco dei Turchi*, set in Venice, where wraith-like creatures flit in the darkness; and a Florentine *tondo* of the *Virgin and Child* by a talented follower of Botticelli. From Naples, there's an anonymous Caravaggiesque *Ecce Homo*; from Spain, a Ribera and a pair of Zurbaráns, *St Agatha* carrying her breasts on a plate and the *Angel Gabriel*, who looks as if he can't find the right address; and from England, landscapes by Richard Parkes Bonington, and Joshua Reynolds' famous *Infant Samuel in Prayer*. Fabre himself (*St Sebastian* and *The Death of Narcissus*) proves to be a romantic in his art as in his life; more influential was Jean-Baptiste Greuze, who seems to have invented the simpering genre of big-eyed kid pictures sold in supermarkets. Fabre's *cabinet* on the fourth floor contains portraits of Alfieri, Canova, and of Fabre himself at the end of his life.

The Good Narcissist of Montpellier

The superb collection on **Floor 5** was donated by the museum's other great bene-factor, Alfred Bruyas (1821–77). Born into a Montpellier banking family, Bruyas resolved the frustration of not being able to paint himself by befriending many of the artists of his day and asking them to paint him – there are 24 portraits of the red-bearded patron in this museum alone, lined up one after another, including examples by Delacroix and Alexandre Cabanel of Montpellier (1823–89). Four are by Gustave Courbet (1819–77), who became Bruyas' friend and whose works are the highlight of the museum. Two paintings were pivotal in Courbet's proto-Impressionist discovery of light: the *Baigneuses*, which caused such a scandal in the Paris Salon of 1853 that Napoléon III ordered it to be removed, and the delightful, sun-drenched *Bonjour, Monsieur Courbet* (1854), in which the jaunty Courbet, strutting down a country lane with easel and paints strapped to his back, meets who else but Alfred Bruyas?

Other paintings on this floor cover the artistic movements on either side of Courbet: the earlier cold classicism of Ingres' *Stratonice* (1866) and David (the clean, unbloodied *Dead Hector*), paintings that stand as the antithesis of the warm exotic romanticism of Delacroix's *Mulatress and Algerian Odalisques* (1849), or the melting landscapes of Corot. From southern painters of the period there are big historical and exotic scenes and landscapes. The gloomy young romantic Théodore Géricault (1791–1824) is repre-sented by an unidealized *Portrait of Lord Byron* and a surreal *Study of Arms and Legs*, cannibal leftovers painted in a medical school while students dissected the corpses.

Floor 6 is dedicated to painters from Montpellier. Eugène Castelneau (1827–94) painted bright landscapes around Languedoc, like the *Vue du Pic St-Loup* (1859). Alexandre Cabanel (1823–89), who studied in Rome, left his best work in Montpellier, including the pre-Raphaelesque *Albaydé*, *La Chiarruccia* and *Self-portrait at Age 29*. Best of all is the short-lived early Impressionist Frédéric Bazille (1841–70), a friend of Renoir and Monet, whose best works glow with the strong sun of Languedoc: *Les Remparts d'Aigues-Mortes* and *La Vue du village* (Castelnau, now engulfed by Montpellier). Also here are the museum's more recent works, by Berthe Morisot, jolly Fauvist Desnoyer, Robert Delaunay, Kees Van Dongen, and Nicolas de Staël's painting of *Ménerbes*, which if it really looked like that wouldn't attract so many tourists or disciples of Peter Mayle.

Into the Ecusson

There is nothing as compelling as the Musée Fabre in Montpellier's historic centre; much was lost in the Wars of Religion, and even the many 17th- and 18th-century *hôtels particuliers*, as stuccoed and ornate as many of them are inside, show mostly blank walls to the street. But few cities in the south of France manage to be as pleasant and lively. Instead of gaggles of tourists, Montpellier has students to keep the city on its toes; this is the biggest university town in the south. Mayor Frêche made the entire Ecusson a pedestrian zone, and a delightful place for walking.

One of the major crossroads of the Ecusson is Place Notre-Dame, under the cool gaze of the neoclassical **Notre-Dame-des-Tables** (1748), originally the chapel connected to the Jesuit college that is now the Musée Fabre. In front passes the old pilgrims' route, the Cami Romieu, now Rue du l'Aiguillerie, where St Roch was arrested as a spy (see the plaque by Rue de Pila-St-Gély), and where Montpellier merchants and innkeepers cashed in on passing pilgrims. In the crypt is the **Musée de l'Histoire de Montpellier** (*open Tues–Sat 10.30–12.30 and 1.30–6*), with audiovisuals and other techniques telling the city's history. Residential *hôtels* went up later; nearby **Rue du Cannau** has some of the flashiest 17th-century models, while, in Place Pétrarque, the **Hôtel de Varennes'** façade (1758) conceals a pair of Gothic halls, one a depository for architectural fragments salvaged from medieval Montpellier. Upstairs, there's a pair of small museums devoted to the good old days. The **Musée du Fougau** ('the Foyer'; *open Wed and Thurs 3–6*) was founded by the local Félibres to preserve the arts and traditions of old Montpellier. The **Musée de Vieux Montpellier** (*open Tues–Sat 9.30–12 and 1.30–5; adm*) exhibits portraits of notables, and plans and views of the city from the 16th century on, along with some peculiar relics, such as the model of the Bastille carved from one of the fortress' stones soon after it was demolished in 1789.

Around the corner, at 4 Rue Embouque-d'Or, the 1670 **Hôtel de Manse** is famous for its richly decorated openwork staircase, designed by Italian architects – a stair that became the prototype for a score of others in Montpellier, including the one in the gorgeous Renaissance courtyard of the nearby **Hôtel de Lunaret**, at 5 Rue des Trésoriers-de-France. This, combined with the adjoining **Hôtel des Trésoriers de France**, around the block at 7 Rue Jacques Cœur, was the residence of the famous merchant and financier Jacques Cœur, whose motto was 'flies can't enter a closed mouth'. In 1441 he was appointed a treasurer of Charles VII, and charged with obtaining royal subsidies from Languedoc. Reasoning that the wealthier the land, the easier it is to tax, Cœur became one of Montpellier's greatest benefactors, among other things building a merchants' exchange and dredging the outlets of the Lez to make them navigable; this town house originally had a tower so high that he could scan the sea and its traffic. His career ended abruptly in 1451, when he was accused of poisoning the king's mistress, Agnès Sorel; he escaped prison in 1454 and died in Chios, fighting the Ottomans for the pope.

Although much renovated since Jacques Cœur's day, most of the contents of the *hôtel particulier* predate him, as it's now the **Musée Languedocien**. Although you may have to arrange your schedule to fit theirs (*open Sept–June Mon–Sat 2–5; July and Aug Mon–Sat 3–6; adm*), it has its rewards – Greek vases, dolmens, funeral steles and other prehistoric finds from the Hérault; an excellent collection of Romanesque sculpture salvaged from the 11th-century version of Notre-Dame-des-Tables and from surrounding abbeys; the rock-crystal seal of King Sancho of Aragon; and three 12th-century Islamic funeral steles discovered in Montpellier, a rare relic of the city's cosmopolitan spice-trading days. From Jacques Cœur's day there are two fine paintings, an anonymous Catalan *SS. Apolline and Guilhem* and, from the Clouets' workshop, *Gabrielle d'Estrées and her Sister in their Bath*. A major collection of 16th–18th-century faïence made in Montpellier rounds things off, together with a grand ceiling painting of 1660, *Justice discovering Truth with the help of Time* by Jean de Troy, the city's top interior decorator of the age. A plaque nearby in Rue des Trésoriers-de-France recalls that another of the city's colourful cast of characters lived here: that great wanderer Rabelais, who enrolled at Montpellier's medical school in 1530, at the age of 40, and became a doctor as well as a priest, although he later wrote that 'the calling was far too tiresome and melancholy a one', and that 'physicians always smelled of enemas, like old devils' (*Pantagruel*, 1532).

To the south, Rue Jacques Cœur becomes Grand Rue Jean Moulin, one of the city's most elegant streets. On weekdays you can drop in at the Chamber of Commerce and Industry to see the **Amphithéâtre Anatomique St-Côme**, built in 1757 with funds left by Louis XV's surgeon, François Gigot de Lapeyronie. Turn left at the foot of Grand Rue Jean Moulin for the **Tour de la Babote**, a recently restored medieval tower topped by an astronomical observatory in 1741.

Western Quarters: Rue Foch and the Promenade du Peyrou

Despite its Protestant leanings, Montpellier's fame in heaven's circle hinges on Roch, the pious son of a wealthy merchant, who was born around 1350 and abandoned all of his worldly goods to make the pilgrimage to Rome in 1367. On his way home, he came to an Italian village decimated by plague; after curing a number of victims with the sign of the Cross, Roch went down with the disease himself, and retreated to the country where no one could hear his groans. Nourished by a friendly dog who stole food for him from its master's table, Roch recovered and returned to Montpellier, so ravaged and changed by his illness that he wasn't recognized and was thrown into prison as a spy, where he died in 1379. Only then did his grandmother recognize him by a birthmark in the shape of a cross. News of Roch's reputation as an intermediary against the Black Death reached plague-torn Venice, and even though he had yet to be canonized, Venetians disguised as pilgrims stole his bones and built the magnificent Confraternity of San Rocco in his honour – one of the wonders of the lagoon city.

As patron saint of Montpellier, St Roch came through for his home town in the cholera epidemics of 1832 and 1849, and finally a church of **St-Roch** was built, in Viollet-le-Duc's Ideal Gothic, in the medieval quarter of the Ecusson. Rue Voltaire leads up to the socializing centre of the neighbourhood, Rue de l'Ancien Courrier and Place St-Ravy. Here, too, is one of the most handsome residences in old Montpellier, **Hôtel des Trésoriers-de-la-Bourse** (1631–93), on the street of the same name.

From the centre of the Ecusson, **Rue Foch** was sliced out in the 18th century as a grand formal boulevard, just missing a rare Jewish ritual bath, or **Mikveh**, at 1 Rue Barralerie (*to visit, contact the tourist office*). Dating from *c*. 1200, it was part of the synagogue in the midst of what was then a large, active Jewish quarter. Since the late 17th century, however, this loftiest edge of Montpellier has been devoted to tons of mouldy fol-de-rol glorifying Louis XIV, beginning with an **Arc de Triomphe** (the triumphs referred to include digging a canal, wrestling the English lion to the ground and conquering heresy – with the Revocation of the Edict of Nantes, a nasty piece of bigotry that went down like a lead balloon in Montpellier). You can climb its 103 steps on a guided visit from the tourist office. Beyond stretches the **Promenade du Peyrou**, a nice park spoiled by an equestrian statue of his megalomaniac majesty as big as the Trojan Horse. It was brought down laboriously from Paris in 1718, fell into the Garonne en route, whence it was rescued and brought here, only to be smashed to bits in the Revolution – a fact that didn't prevent the erection of the present copy in 1838. At the edge of the promontory stands the far more elegant **Château d'Eau**, one of Montpellier's landmarks, a neoclassical temple designed by Jean Giral to disguise the reservoir of the **Aqueduc St-Clément** (1771) snaking below in curious perspective, a triple-tiered work inspired by the Pont du Gard that brings in water from the river Lez. The Promenade has recently undergone an upheaval: American architect Richard Meier was charged with adding the **Espace Pitot** to the area, a complex including a swimming pool and car park. The huge **cross** you can see looking south of the Promenade was erected by a Catholic society in the 1820s.

The Cathedral and the Jardin des Plantes

The waters of the aqueduct feed the unicorn fountain in the nearby **Place de la Canourgue**, a charming 17th-century square shaded by nettle trees (*micocouliers*). It looks down on the medieval monastery college of St-Benoît, on Rue de l'Ecole de Médecine, built by papal architects from Avignon, currently (since 1795) the **Faculté de Médecine**, housing an enormous medical library (*can be visited on a tourist office tour*). Adjacent, the former monastic chapel has been Montpellier's **Cathédrale St-Pierre** ever since the see was transferred here from Maguelone in 1563, although its status didn't spare it the usual depredations in the Wars of Religion and the Revolution. The cathedral's greatest distinction is its unusual porch, supported by two conical turrets.

Boulevard Henri IV, running alongside the Faculté, descends to the tree-topped **Tour des Pins**, a last vestige of the medieval walls. Beyond lies the lovely **Jardin des Plantes** (*t 04 67 63 43 22; open June–Sept Tues–Sun 12–8; Oct–May Tues–Sun 12–6*), the oldest botanical garden in France, founded by a decree of Henri IV in 1593 to instruct students on native and exotic plants used for healing. It has several magnificent 400-year-old trees, exotic succulents, plants from the *garrigues*, and an *orangerie*; near the latter, in a spot celebrated for its exquisite melancholy, there's a marble plaque with the inscription *Placandis Narcissae Manibus*. The Narcissa in question is said to be the consumptive 18-year-old daughter of the poet Edward Young (best known for his *Night Thoughts*, illustrated by Blake). In 1734 he brought Narcissa to France, hoping the warm climate would cure her; instead the exertion of travelling killed her, and she was buried either in Lyon or here 'in the garden she loved' – a story that made this a favourite rendezvous for romantic students like Paul Valéry and André Gide. At the highest point of the garden is the Tree of Secrets, its trunk pitted with niches where lovers would leave *billets d'amour*.

The Montpellier Follies

Montpellier, one of the fastest growing cities in France, is spreading its tentacles to suck in all that surrounds it, and has already gobbled up a number of 18th-century châteaux and gardens that were the country retreats of its élite (*before setting out, check hours at the tourist office; some places can only be visited on the office's 'Les Folies' tour*). One of the oldest is 3km east of Antigone on the D24: the **Château de Flaugergues** (*t 04 99 52 66 37, www.flaugergues.com; guided tours July and Aug Tues–Sun 2.30–6.30, otherwise telephone; gardens open in summer daily 9–12.30 and 2.30–7, winter by appt only; closed Sun and public hols; adm*). Begun in the 1690s, the place is impressively filled with 17th- and 18th-century furnishings and tapestries, and a collection of optical instruments. A bit further east (take the D172), **Château de la Mogère** (*t 04 67 65 72 01, www.lamogere.com; guided tours June–Sept daily 2.30–6.30; Oct–May Sat, Sun and hols only, by appt; adm*) is a refined *folie* of 1716, with period furnishings, family portraits and, in the garden, a delightful Baroque *buffet d'eau*, a fountain built into a wall.

North of Montpellier, on the road to Mende, the **Parc Zoologique de Lunaret** (*open daily summer Mon–Sat 9–7, otherwise until dusk; adm*) has exotic and regional fauna, where you can wander amid woodlands and *garrigues*. The 1750 **Château d'O** (*northwest, on the road to Grabels*), now used for receptions, art exhibitions and theatrical performances, is famous for its park, decorated with statues taken from the gardens of the **Château de la Mosson** (1729), which lies to the south, just off the N109. La Mosson was the most opulent of all the follies until the Revolution and its conversion into a soap factory; after decades of neglect the city of Montpellier acquired it in 1982 and is still restoring it. It has a lovely oval, Venetian-style music chamber and a poignant seashell and pebble *buffet d'eau* in the garden, now stripped of all its ornaments.

From Mosson, take the D27E/D5E and turn towards Pignan for the remarkable 1250 church of the Cistercian **Abbaye St-Martin-du-Vignogoul** (*t 04 67 47 70 17; open Mon–Fri 10–12 and 2–6*). Believed to be the first attempt at Gothic in Languedoc, the church is small in size but grand in vision, a lofty, single-naved, pint-sized cathedral decorated with a trefoil arch, finely sculpted capitals (still more Romanesque than Gothic), and a unique polygonal choir, lit by a row of bull's-eye windows.

The Hérault

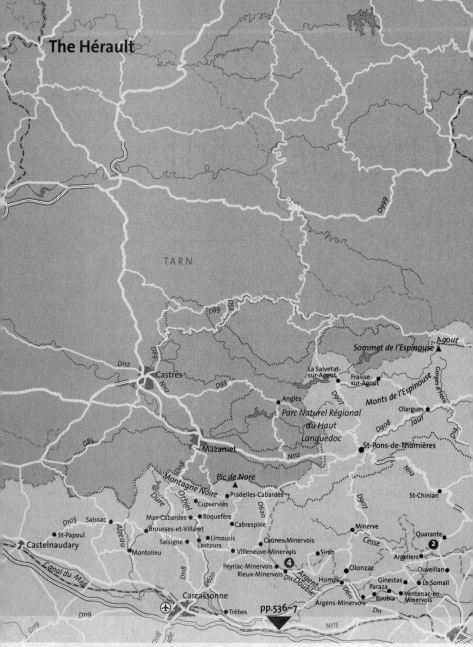

The Hérault

TARN

D112

Castres

D89

D53

D89

D93

Anglès

La Salvetat-sur-Agout

Fraisse-sur-Agout

Sommet de l'Espinouse ▲

Agout

D907

Monts de l'Espinouse

Parc Naturel Régional du Haut Languedoc

Olargues

D908

Jaur

Mazamet

N112

St-Pons-de-Thomières

N112

Gorges d'Héric

D85

Pic de Nore ▲

Montagne Noire

Pradelles-Cabardès

St-Chinian

Dure

Orbiel

Cupserviès

D620

Minerve

Quarante ②

D103

Saissac

Mas-Cabardès

Roquefère

Cesse

St-Papoul

Brousses-et-Villaret

Cabrespine

Caunes-Minervois

Argeliers

Alzeau

Salsigne

Limousis

Villeneuve-Minervois

Siran

Ouveillan

Castelnaudary

Montolieu

Lastours

Olonzac

Le Somail

Peyriac-Minervois ④

Ginestas

Canal du Midi

D18

D620

Rieux-Minervois

Homps

Paraza

Ventenac-en-Minervois

Argent-Double

Roubia

Carcassonne

Argens-Minervois

D119

Trèbes

pp.536–7 ▼

D11

N113

D119

Aude

N113

Highlights

1 Pézenas, scarcely changed since Molière's day

2 Boating down the Canal du Midi

3 Sète, a genuine fishing port with a sardine museum

4 The seven-sided medieval church of Rieux-Minervois

Getting Around

By Train

Except along the coast, public transport is rudimentary at best; the coastal SNCF line runs from Montpellier through Frontignan, Sète, Agde and Béziers on its way to Narbonne and Perpignan, with around 6 trains a day. For the interior there is a service from Béziers to Bédarieux, and trains from Béziers to Castres in the Tarn go via Toulouse.

By Bus

Olargues is connected by bus to Bédarieux, St-Pons, Montpellier, Béziers and Toulouse. From the *gare routière* in Montpellier there are regular bus services to Gignac, Clermont l'Hérault and Lodève, less regularly to other villages; there are buses to tourist attractions (like St-Guilhem-le-Désert) in the summer.

Beaches

The sand of the Camargue continues around the elbow of the French coast. The Golfe d'Aigues-Mortes washes against immense swathes of sand, much of which is being eaten up by concrete development, such as the resort of La Grande Motte. **Palavas** is Montpellier's summer cruising zone – trendy and overpopulated. For more space and fewer frills, head south past Sète, or stop at the tranquil **Plage des Aresquiers**, accessible only by a dead-end road from Frontignan.

Best Beaches

Palavas: wide sand, quite energetic.
Espiguette: this lovely beach, signposted from Grau-de-Roi, is wild, with dunes and plenty of sand grass. Try a picnic at disk for a breathtaking sunset.

France isn't the sort of country that allows itself to be neatly dissected for the benefit of geographers and travel writers. So it is only for convenience's sake that the rugged *garrigue* of the upper Hérault, the green hills of the Espinouse and the flat expanses of the Béziers coast are combined together in one chapter. In this *département*, some 150km across at the most, the diversity is tremendous: a microcosm of France, from mountain forests of oak and pine, and limestone cirques and *causses*, to the endless beaches of the coast and the rolling hills around the Canal du Midi.

For devotees of rural France, this seemingly innocuous area may be the ultimate find. Just enough tourists come for there to be plenty of country inns and *fermes-auberges*, though in some villages foreigners are still a novelty. The food is good, and there's enough wine to make anyone happy. That's an understatement – the Hérault is the most prolific wine-producing region in France. It can be a perfect alternative to overcrowded and overpraised Provence: just as beautiful, more real and relaxed, full of things to see – and considerably less expensive.

The Northern Hérault

North of Montpellier: the *Garrigue*

On a map, you'll notice lots of blank space in this region, a *pays* without a name. It is a geographer's textbook example of *garrigue*, a dry limestone plateau with sparse vegetation, where even sheep only just get by. *Garrigue* is an old Occitan word for the holly-oak, and these scrubby would-be trees grow everywhere, along with thyme and lavender-scented *maquis* and, increasingly, vines, which not only thrive but are quickly changing the local economy. The windblown landscapes are as romantic as anything

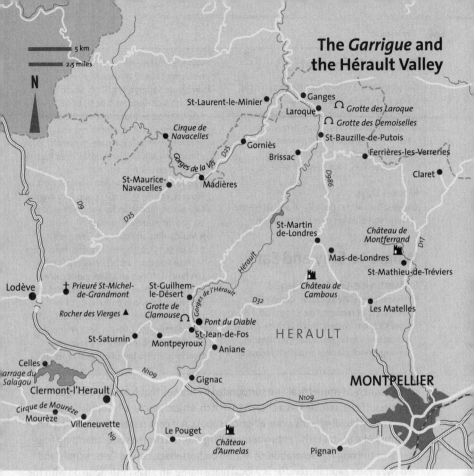

The Garrigue and
the Hérault Valley

5 km
2.5 miles

N

St-Laurent-le-Minier
Ganges
Laroque Ω Grotte des Laroque
Ω Grotte des Demoiselles
Cirque de Navacelles
Gorniès
Brissac
St-Bauzille-de-Putois
Ferrières-les-Verreries
Gorges de la Vis
D25
Claret
St-Maurice-Navacelles
Mâdières
D9
D986
St-Martin-de-Londres
Château de Montferrand
Mas-de-Londres
St-Mathieu-de-Tréviers
D17
Lodève
† Prieuré St-Michel-de-Grandmont
St-Guilhem-le-Désert
Grotte de Clamouse Ω
Pont du Diable
Gorges de l'Hérault
Hérault
D32
Château de Cambous
Les Matelles
Rocher des Vierges ▲
St-Jean-de-Fos
HÉRAULT
St-Saturnin
Montpeyroux
Aniane
Celles
Barrage du Salagou
N109
Gignac
MONTPELLIER
Clermont-l'Hérault
N109
Cirque de Mourèze
Mourèze
Villeneuvette
Le Pouget
Château d'Aumelas
Pignan
N9

in Provence, although a shade more sombre. The few villages seem huddled, closed in to themselves.

Pic St-Loup, St-Martin-de-Londres and Cambous

From Montpellier, the best approach to the *garrigue* is by way of the D17 to St-Mathieu-de-Tréviers, where you can pick up the D1/D122 west, a scenic high road that passes below the ruined **Château de Montferrand**, a long climb but one that offers a memorable view. Montferrand was one of the first castles to fall to the Albigensian Crusade, but the real damage was done by Louis XIV, as part of his general royal policy of cleaning up unnecessary and possibly dangerous castles. The view takes in **Pic St-Loup**, just up the road, a striking 2,110ft exclamation point of the *garrigue*. Along with the cliff-rimmed lump, the Montagne d'Hortus, it is the remnant of a volcanic crater.

The D122 passes through the typical *garrigue* village of **Le Mas de Londres** before arriving at **St-Martin-de-Londres** (25km direct on the D986 from Montpellier). St-Martin is a surprise package. Passing the tiny, densely built village on the road, you would never guess it conceals one of the most exquisite medieval squares anywhere,

Tourist Information

Ganges: Plan de l'Ormeau, **t** 04 67 73 00 56, **f** 04 67 73 63 24. *Open July–Aug Mon–Sat 10–7; Sept–June Mon–Sat 9–12 and 2–6.*
St-Martin-de-Londres: Place de la Mairie, **t** 04 67 55 09 59, *www.tourismed.com. Open July and Aug 9–12.30 and 2–7; Sept–June Tues, Thurs and Sat 9–12.30.*

Market Days

Ganges: Tues and especially Fri am, when the lively market takes over half the town.

Where to Stay and Eat

St-Martin-de-Londres ✉ 34380

Hostellerie le Vieux Chêne, Causse de la Selle, west of Frouzet, **t 04 67 73 11 00, **f** 04 67 73 10 54 (*inexpensive*). This has three double rooms and a good restaurant (*moderate*) serving French classics on a pretty terrace.

Closed early Jan–early Feb and 2 wks Oct; restaurant closed Wed, and Sun eve.
Auberge de Saugras, Argelliers, south of St-Martin-de-Londres, **t** 04 67 55 08 71, **f** 04 67 55 04 65 (*moderate–inexpensive*). A stone *mas* with several rooms and gourmet menus (*expensive–moderate*). Book ahead, and ask for directions! *Closed Tues and Wed excpet July and Aug.*
Bergerie du Bayle, in the *garrigue* just west of Frouzet, **t** 04 67 55 72 16 (€1,000 for 2 nights). *Gîte* accommodation for groups of around 29. You do your own cooking.
Les Muscardins, 19 Route des Cévennes, **t** 04 67 55 75 90, (*expensive*). Gourmets from Montpellier drive up especially to feast on the fancy terrines and pâté, game dishes, formidable desserts and a selection of the best regional wines on a choice of four menus. *Closed Feb and Mon and Tues.*
La Pastourelle, 350 Chemin de la Prairie, **t** 04 67 55 72 78 (*expensive–moderate*). Delicious dishes based on local *cèpes*, and

picturesquely asymmetrical and surrounded by houses that have not changed for centuries. The ensemble has a church to match, an architecturally sophisticated 11th-century building with a rare elliptical cupola. A recent restoration, clearing out the dross of a brutal 19th-century remodelling, has uncovered some charming fragments of the original decoration: St Martin on horseback, carved Celtic spirals, and neo-Byzantine capitals. *Londres* is a local place name, and has nothing to do with the big town on the island.

South of St-Martin, in a military zone just off the D32, a 5,000-year-old settlement was discovered at **Cambous** in 1967 (*visits May–Oct for groups only; call the Société Languedocienne de Préhistoire and St-Martin-de-Londres, **t** 04 67 55 70 57, for further information*). With considerable intelligence and dedication, the archaeologists have made the site into a veritable re-creation of ancient life. They have reconstructed a communal house of this 'Fontbouisse civilization' and gathered together enough artefacts to make you feel entirely at home among the Fontbouissians. These peaceful folk knew both farming and husbandry, and were just learning about copper tools. They also had a well-developed cultural life, as evidenced by their geometrically decorated pottery and stone statue steles.

In the 13th–18th centuries, the country north of the **Causse d'Hortus** was famous for its 'Gentlemen Glassblowers', who passed their secrets down through the generations. North of St-Martin, on the D107E, learn about their art at the Renaissance Verrerie de Couloubrines in **Ferrières-les-Verreries**, restored in 1989 (**t** 04 67 59 06 39; *open to groups only, by appt*). Living glassmakers ply their trade to the west at the *verrerie* in **Claret** (**t** 04 67 59 06 39; *open July–Aug daily 10–1 and 3–7;*

truffles in winter. *Closed Tues eve and Wed, plus Sun, and Mon eve, in Oct–Mar.*

Ganges ✉ 34190
★★Hôtel de la Poste, 8 Plan de l'Ormeau, t 04 67 73 85 88, f 04 67 73 83 79 (*inexpensive*). A prettily restored hotel.

Le Parc aux Cedres, Laroques, south of Ganges, t 04 67 73 82 63, f 04 67 73 69 85 (*inexpensive*). With a garden, pool and restaurant (*moderate*). *Closed Nov–April.*

Les Norias, 254 Av des 2 Ponts, to the east of Ganges on the D25, t 04 67 73 55 90, f 04 67 73 62 08, (*inexpensive*). The dining room and terrace overlook the Hérault river and the restaurant (*expensive–moderate*) features Mediterranean cooking. *Closed mid-Nov–early Dec and part of Feb; restaurant closed Mon eve and Tues exc. July and Aug*

Ferme-Auberge Domaine de Blancardy, Moules et Baucels, 7km east of Ganges on the D999, t 04 67 73 94 94, f 04 67 73 55 59, *www.blancardy.com* (*inexpensive*). Fourteen rooms in a distinctive old *mas* dating from the 12th century, where home-made *confits* and pâté accompany fine wine. There is also a *gîte*.

Chez Maurice, Pont d'Hérault, 11km north of Ganges, t 04 67 82 40 02 (*expensive*). The best *cuisine du terroir* around. Book early on the day you wish to eat; the number of non-residents allowed to dine depends on number of guests in the rooms (*moderate*). *Closed Sun eve and Oct–Easter.*

Gorniès ✉ 34190
★★★★Château de Madières, 7km west of Gorniès, t 04 6773 84 03, f 04 67 73 55 71 (*very expensive*). If you want to combine the austerity of the *garrigue* with style and creature comforts, this hotel has 13 super-luxurious rooms in a 14th-century fort. A park, swimming pool, fitness centre/gym and beautiful vaulted dining room (*expensive*) are some of the amenities available. *Closed Nov–Mar.*

June and Sept Thurs–Tues 10–12 and 2–6, closed Wed; Oct–Dec and Mar–May Thurs–Mon 2–6, closed Tues and Wed; closed Jan and Feb) where a centre dispenses information on the **Chemin des Verriers**, a route set up to explore the tiny villages once attached in some way to the trade. In Claret you can also visit Europe's only family-run cade oil mill, **La Distillerie des Cévennes** (*t 04 67 59 02 50, http://huilede cade.chez.tiscali.fr*); cade oil has been used for embalming since antiquity, and the mill offers a range of modern products made from the stuff.

Ganges, Caves and the Cirque de Navacelles

From St-Martin, the main D986 leads northwards towards the Cévennes. From the village of **St-Bauzille-de-Putois** (a *putois* is a skunk – St-Bauzille used to have more than its share) there is a steep side road to the **Grotte des Demoiselles** (*t 04 67 73 70 02, www.desmoiselles.com; open for guided visits July and Aug 9.45–6; April–June and Sept 10–12 and 1.30–5.30; Oct–Mar 10–11 and 2–4.30; adm*), an important Protestant hideout during the war of the Camisards (1702–04) which also has one of France's most spectacular displays of pipe-organ stalactites and stalagmites in the staggeringly enormous 'Cathedral of the Abysses'. Visits take an hour by subterranean funicular; bring a sweater.

Geologically, this is folded country; along the Hérault you can clearly see the lines of stratification of limestone and schist in the cliffs. See them from river level by floating down the Hérault in a canoe (*hire one at Canoë Le Moulin, at St-Bauzille-de-Putois, t 04 67 73 30 73, www.canoe-france.com/herault*) to **Brissac**, which is guarded by a ruined castle perched on a pinnacle of rock.

Wine: Coteaux du Languedoc

By the time Caesar conquered Gaul, the vineyards in the hills and the great plain of Languedoc (north and west of modern Montpellier) were already well established, thanks to the Greeks. Amphorae full of wine sent back to Rome met with such fervent demands for more that the wine-makers back in Italy went to court to curtail the competition – history's first round of the great French-Italian wine battle. The Gauls won this one, perhaps because they hired the oratory of Cicero.

Zoom ahead to the 18th century, when the Canal du Midi made it easy to ship wine to northern Europe and the New World through Bordeaux. The region boomed, but boom turned to bust in the phylloxera epidemics of the 1880s. In the subsequent depression, recovery was hastened by grafting, and vintners, in response to the increased demand of the new industrial society, set their sights on the mass production of a soulless wine dubbed *bibine du Midi*, competing with tankers of high-octane plonk from Algeria and graded, as if it were crude oil, by its alcohol content – as French rotgut is to this day.

All of this is only worth mentioning to help the newcomer better savour the revelation that now awaits in the bottles of Coteaux du Languedoc (AOC since 1963, *www.coteaux-languedoc.com*). The post-war return to Gallo-Roman techniques and craftsmanship have so improved matters that Coteaux du Languedoc has become one of the brightest stars in the French wine firmament. A huge, confusing region that takes in pockets from Lunel to Narbonne-Plage, it has been divided into 13 specialized micro-areas (*terroirs*) and three *crus*. The Pic St-Loup area produces red wines of character that can take considerable ageing (such as the 2000 of **Domaine de La Roque**, at Fontanès, **t** 04 67 55 34 47, *www.deveze.com* (*open July, Aug and hols Mon–Sat 9–12 and 3–7; Sept–June Mon, Wed and Sat 9–12 and 2–6*). The rising star in the area, the **Domaine de la Devèze**, at Montoulieu, 6km east of St-Bauzille-de-Putois towards La Cadière, **t** 04 67 73 70 21, has won prizes.

The region of La Clape, south-east of Narbonne (*see* p.546), is becoming an increasingly exciting area for wine lovers. An excellent estate to experience the quality of the wines is **Château de l'Hospitalet**, **t** 04 68 45 34 47, *www.domaine-hospitalet.com*.

Just west of Montpellier, at Lavérune, **Château L'engarran**, **t** 04 67 27 60 89, *www.chateau-engarran.com* (*open all year 9–7*), part of the *terroir* St-Georges d'Orques, produces fine red wines with a scent of dried herbs. The 2000 is highly recommended. In Jonquières, west of Gignac, the Julliens, father and son, have a fine array of wines at the **Mas Jullien**, **t** 04 67 96 60 04 (*open April–end Dec*).

Ganges is the only real town around, and quite a pleasant one, closed in between the river Hérault and *maquis*-carpeted hills. In the 18th century it was France's capital of silk stockings. Like most of the Cévennes, Ganges was and remains a mostly Protestant area; the old part of town is crisscrossed by *chemins de traverse*, labyrinthine passes laid out to confuse Catholic troops, and it has an imposing, peculiar seven-sided Protestant 'temple', built in 1850.

Ganges makes a good base for exploring this pretty region, between the *garrigue* and the Causse du Larzac. The **Gorges de la Vis** can be followed on the D25 west of town, passing a waterfall and a 17th-century château (at St-Laurent-le-Minier). The route through the gorges is 34km long (one-way only); the best parts, after Madières, can only be reached on foot. If you go the whole route, there's a real curiosity to be seen at the end, the famous **Cirque de Navacelles**. A *cirque* looks like a deep lunar crater, though it is in fact a loop dug deep into the limestone of the *garrigue* by the meandering river Vis long ago. There are many in the *garrigues* of the Midi, and this is the most striking, with steep walls and a rocky 'island' in the centre. You can spend a day walking through it by picking up the GR7 at **St-Maurice-de-Navacelles**.

A second popular excursion from Ganges is the 30km drive north to the **Observatoire Météorologique du Mont Aigoual** (5,141ft), in the northern Gard (*t 04 67 82 60 01, www.aigoual.asso.fr; open May–Sept 10–7*). Set on the summit of the Cévennes, this has been the training ground for France's weather forecasters since 1887, and you can see why: on a clear day the view encompasses all the territory covered in this book, from Mont Blanc and the Alps to Canigou in the Pyrenees, down to the Mediterranean. Inside, a museum has photos, information on the work of the observatory, and old and high-tech new weather instruments.

The Valley of the Hérault: the Haut Pays d'Oc

The Hérault slices dramatically through the *garrigue*, and the atmosphere is clear, luminous, otherworldly – the perfect landscape for saints and pilgrims, and wine.

St-Guilhem-le-Désert

'Desert' might seem a little unfair to this rosemary-scented jumble of *garrigue* around St-Guilhem northwest of Montpellier; there are plenty of green, shady spots for a picnic, and even forests of pines. But *desert*, in French or English, originally meant deserted, and this is still as lonely a region as it was when the hermit St Guilhem came here, in the reign of Charlemagne. Besides being a delightful place to visit, St-Guilhem is a living history lesson, evoking the time when the 'desert' was a troubled frontier between Frank and Saracen, and later, when it became a key cultural outpost in the process of making the Midi Christian and French.

The little village of St-Guilhem is stretched on the edge of a ravine. Its one street being too narrow for traffic, a parallel road and car park has been built on the other side; from here you'll have a good view of its rugged stone houses, their gardens and tiny bridges, little changed since medieval times. On the village's main street, some modest Romanesque palaces survive from the 13th century, an especially picturesque one housing the *mairie*; at the opposite end, facing the D4 at the entrance to the village, the church of **St-Laurent** (now the tourist office) has a fine apse like that of the abbey church of St-Guilhem.

The Abbaye de Gellone

*Open Mon–Sat 7.45–11.50 and 2–5.40, Sun and hols 8.30–10.30
and 2.30–5.40.*

Guilhem Court-Nez, the powerful Frankish count of Toulouse, Aquitaine and Orange, was a grandson of Charles Martel and a cousin, liegeman and friend to Charlemagne. For over 30 years he campaigned from the Atlantic to the Alps, mostly against the Arabs, whose wave of 8th-century expansion through Spain had washed up as far north as Narbonne. Another of Guilhem's friends was Benedict, the monastic reformer from Aniane; Benedict, too, had once been a warrior, and he convinced Guilhem to follow his example and renounce the world. Guilhem spent the last six years of his life in a humble cell here, at a place near the gorges of the Hérault, originally called Gellone, and was canonized soon after his death in 812.

And soon after that, pilgrims began to visit. St-Guilhem was a popular saint with the Spaniards, and with northerners on their way to Compostela. The original community of hermit cells grew into a wealthy monastery; construction of the great abbey church began about 1050. Already in decline during the Wars of Religion, it was sacked by the Protestants in 1569 – its celebrated library was burnt in the process. The final indignity came not during the Revolution, surprisingly, but a decade before,

The Abbaye de Gellone

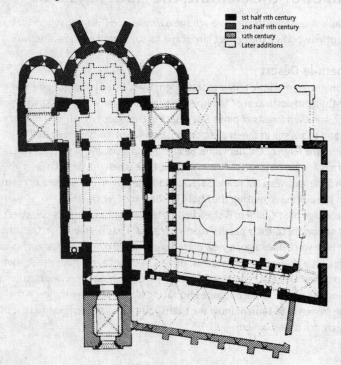

■ 1st half 11th century
▨ 2nd half 11th century
▧ 12th century
□ Later additions

when clerics from Lodève and other towns succeeded in having the monastery suppressed, apportioning its treasures and holy relics among themselves.

The abbey church (*open same hours*) is a remarkably grand and lovely specimen of Lombard architecture, with its blind arcading and trademark cross-shaped window. The best part, the broad, arcaded **apse**, recalls the contemporary churches of Milan or Pavia. The **façade**, facing an ancient, colossal plane tree in the village square, is somewhat blighted by an ungainly tower of cheap stone, built in the 14th century more for defence than for bell-ringing. The **interior**, lofty and dark, has lost almost all of its original decoration. Some fragments of frescoes survive in the side chapels, and niches in the pillars around the choir once held the relics of St-Guilhem and a bit of the True Cross, a gift from Charlemagne. The organ, built in 1782, is the focus of a summer series of Baroque concerts. The cloister is ruined, and most of its capitals have ended up at the Cloisters Museum in New York. There are sometimes exhibitions there.

Around St-Guilhem

More medieval relics can be seen along the Hérault: medieval mills, for grain and for oak bark (used in tanning leather), set near the modern trout hatcheries by the river. The hills around St-Guilhem make interesting exploring on foot – a ruined castle and other fortifications, and the **Rue du Bout du Monde** that leads from the back end of the village to a lovely spot with a flowing spring. The steep **Gorges de l'Hérault** extend on both sides of the village and can be followed on the D4.

With all this eroded limestone about, you would expect caves, and there are several. The most impressive, 3km south, is the **Grotte de Clamouse** (*t 04 67 57 71 05, f 04 67 57 78 00, www.grottedeclamouse.com; open July–Aug Sun–Fri 10–7; June and Sept Sun–Fri 10–6; Oct–May Sun–Fri 12–5; closed Sat; guided tour; adm*), one of the big tourist attractions of the Hérault, with its lovely aragonite crystals. Some 500 yards to the south, don't miss the massive stone bridge of 1030, the **Pont du Diable**.

Aniane and Gignac

Everyone who studies medieval history has trouble untangling the two Benedictine Benedicts. The first, Benedict of Norcia, founded the order. In the time of Charlemagne, Benedict of **Aniane**, St Guilhem's mentor, reformed it, forcing the poor Benedictines back to the original precepts of obedience, hard work and no fooling around. The abbey he built in his home town was thoroughly wrecked by the Protestants and rebuilt in the 17th century, and is now occupied by a school. The church, **St-Sauveur**, was rebuilt under Louis XIV, and in drab little Aniane it comes as quite a shock, with its glorious Baroque façade framed in big *volutes*, one of the best in the south. The interior is typically divided into two parts: one for the monks and one for the villagers. Nearby is a Romanesque church, 12th-century St-Jean-Baptiste des Pénitents.

South of Aniane on the D32, the bustling market town of **Gignac** enjoyed a period of prosperity in the 17th and 18th centuries, embellishing itself with an ensemble of Baroque churches and palaces to go with its pretty medieval **Tour de l'Horloge**; its best-known monument, however, is outside town, over the Hérault: the **Pont de**

Tourist Information

St-Guilhem-le-Désert: 2 Rue de la Font du Portal, t/f 04 67 57 44 33, *www.saint-guilhem-le-desert.com. Open daily 9.30–1 and 2–7.*

Gignac: Hôtel des Laurès, Pl Général Claparède, t 04 67 57 58 83, f 04 67 57 67 95. *Open July and Aug Mon–Sat 9–1 and 2–7, Sun 10–1 and 4–7; Sept–June Mon–Fri 9–12 and 2–5, Sat 10–12.*

Clermont-l'Hérault: 9 Rue Doyen Réné Gosse, t 04 67 96 23 86, f 04 67 96 98 58, *www.clermont-herault.com. Open Mon–Sat 9–12.30 and 2–7.*

Lodève: 7 Pl de la République, t 04 67 88 86 44, f 04 67 44 07 56, *www.lodeve.com. Open July–Aug Mon–Sat 9.30 –12.30 and 2.30–7, Sun 10–12.30; Sept–June Mon–Fri 9.30 –12.30 and 2.30–7, Sat 9.30–12.30.*

Market Days

Gignac: Sat.
Clermont-l'Hérault: Wed.

Where to Stay and Eat

St-Guilhem-le-Désert ✉ 34150

In St-Guilhem, rooms are scarce.

★La Taverne de l'Escuelle, Place de la Liberté, t/f 04 67 57 72 05 (*inexpensive*).

★★Hostellerie St-Benoît, Aniane, t 04 67 57 71 63, f 04 67 57 47 10 (*inexpensive*). A comfortable motel with a pool and a good restaurant (*moderate*) using local produce. *Closed mid-Dec–Feb; restaurant closed Sun eve except July and Aug.*

Auberge sur le Chemin, 38 Rue Fond de Portal, t 04 67 57 75 05 (*expensive*). A medieval inn serving tasty regional food.

Gignac ✉ 34150

★★Les Liaisons Gourmandes de Capion, 3 Bd de l'Esplanade, t 04 67 57 50 83, f 04 67 57 93 70 (*expensive–moderate*). This popular restaurant with an outdoor terrace is well worth a visit for its inventive regional and seasonal cooking such as chicken with truffles. *Closed Sat lunch, Sun and Mon.*

Ferme-Auberge Le Pélican, Domaine du Pélican, t 04 67 57 68 92 (*moderate*). This place (which also has rooms, *moderate*) has wonderful dishes on a single set menu with choices – *pintade* (guinea hen) stuffed with olives, duck in honey vinegar – and their own wines. *Rooms available all year; restaurant closed Sept and Oct.*

Gignac. This bridge, begun in 1776, is every inch a product of the Age of Enlightenment, strong and functional architecture without a trace of Bourbon curlicues. There is also a museum of the river at the **Barrage de la Meuse** (*t 04 67 57 99 00; open July and Aug Sun–Fri 10–12 and 2–6; April–June, Sept and Oct Wed, Sat and Sun 2–6; Nov and Jan–Mar Wed and Sun 2–6; closed Dec*), with information on the Hérault, its wildlife and economy. There is also an aquarium.

Mouldering Castles and a Rotten Borough

The monasteries of St-Guilhem and Aniane brought considerable prosperity to the surrounding areas. Villages like **St-Jean-de-Fos** and **St-Saturnin** have fine Romanesque churches and buildings. Near the latter, there are fine views from the ruined early 11th-century castle on the **Rocher des Vierges**. There are two other fascinating ruined castles in this region. **Montpeyroux,** a village between St-Jean and St-Saturnin, grew up around a mysterious abandoned pile called the Castel Viel, a long, impressive circuit of walls with nothing inside. Its history is utterly unknown; it may be from the 11th century, the 16th century or anywhere in between, and it was probably less a military post than a protection for livestock in times of war. Southeast of Gignac, off the main N109, the **Château d'Aumelas** occupies a romantically isolated hilltop. This castle, built some time before 1036 by the lords of Montpellier, is on a dirt track and

St Saturnin ✉ 34725

Ostalaria Cardabela, 10 Place de la Fontaine, t 04 67 88 62 62, f 04 67 88 62 82 (*moderate*). A gorgeous small hotel run by a British couple, all tastefully restored stones and tiles and modern furniture. Very comfortable bedrooms. No restaurant but excellent breakfast with fresh orange juice and home-made jam. *Closed Nov–mid-Mar*.

Le Mimosa, in the next village of St-Guiraud, t 04 67 96 67 96 (*expensive*). Run by the owners of the Ostalaria and long a pilgrim-age for *cognoscenti* from Montpellier. An 18th-century wine-grower's house, beauti-fully decorated and offering superb cuisine. Eat outside in summer. *Closed Mon, Tues–Sat lunch and Sun eve, plus Nov–mid-Mar*.

Auberge de Pressoir, Place de la Fontaine, t 04 67 88 67 89 (*moderate*). Offers good regional cooking such as fresh trout, *poulet fermier*, lamb and grills and 130 wines, in a friendly artistic atmosphere; regular art and photog-raphy exhibitions are held, as well as jazz and theatre evenings. *Closed Jan–mid-Feb*.

Clermont-l'Hérault ✉ 34800

Clermont-l'Hérault will be the most likely place to find a room if you haven't booked.

★★Sarac, Rte de Nebian, t 04 67 96 06 81, f 04 67 88 07 30 (*inexpensive*). A pleasant *Logis de France* overlooking the vineyards. *Closed Jan*.

★★La Source, Place Louis XIV, Villeneuvette, 4km southwest, t 04 67 96 05 07, f 04 67 96 90 09 (*inexpensive*). A charming rural retreat with a pool and tennis, and a restaurant serving salmon and truffles. *Closed Jan–mid-Feb; restaurant closed last 2 wks Nov, Jan and Feb; July and Aug half-board only*.

Ferme-Auberge de la Vallée du Salagou, at Salasc on the D8, t 04 67 88 13 39 (*inexpen-sive*). A comfortable B&B with lovely views; the restaurant (*moderate*) serves a filling menu, offering grilled lamb or steaks and wine from nearby Octon.

★★Les Hauts de Mourèze, 8km from Clermont, t 04 67 96 04 84, f 04 67 96 25 85 (*inexpensive*). Overlooking the *cirque*, with beautiful views. *Closed Nov–April*.

L'Arlequin, Place St-Paul, in the medieval centre of town, t 04 67 96 37 47 (*moderate*). The best of the restaurants, serving smoked and other sorts of fish, inventive duck dishes and lamb kebabs with thyme. Good Faugères wine in a refined candle-lit room. *Closed Sun eve, Mon, and Sat lunch*.

difficult to reach, but it's a wonderful place to explore; parts of the noble residence, chapels and other buildings are still substantially intact.

The castle is located in one of the biggest completely blank spots on the French map. It is part of a real, old-fashioned rotten borough, a *commune* without a town and hardly any inhabitants; it does have a mayor, who has a say in deciding represen-tatives to the French Senate – two centuries after the Revolution, such things are still common in rural France. Another attraction in this 'Commune d'Aumelas', south of the château on a rocky track, is a beautiful and austere Romanesque church, **St-Martin-de-Cardonnet**, set amidst the ruins of the monastery that once surrounded it. To the west, back towards civilization on the D139, the circular fortified village of **Le Pouget** is just north of the colossal **Dolmen Gallardet**.

Clermont-l'Hérault to Lodève

Clermont is a peacefully bovine and prosperous town, living off the wine and table grapes of this more fertile part of the Hérault valley. Its medieval centre, on a hill top, is large and well preserved, including a tall and graceful Gothic church, **St-Paul**, begun in 1276. The 10th–11th-century **castle** around which the town grew up is also in good shape, including the gates, prisons and keep. Clermont has the big weekly market in this region, every Wednesday, and has done since the year 1000.

West of Clermont, you leave the green valley for more peculiar landscapes around the **Lac du Salagou**, a man-made sheet of water surrounded by hills that is much more natural-looking and attractive than most artificial lakes. Circumnavigating it, you'll pass some singular cliffs and weirdly eroded rock formations, and also the village of **Celles**, on the water's edge, now almost completely abandoned. The oddest formations lie to the south, in the **Cirque de Mourèze**, a long, stretched-out *cirque* with the dusty village of Mourèze and its ruined castle at the centre.

Between the Cirque and Clermont lies **Villeneuvette**, founded only in 1670. The 'little new town' was a manufacturing centre for *londrins*, printed linen cloth. Though the works are now closed (since 1954), Villeneuvette is still the very picture of an old French paternalistic company town. The manufactories remain – behind the gate with the big inscription '*Honneur au Travail*' – along with some of the workers' housing, school, church, warehouses and gardens. Lately, artists and artisans have been re-colonizing the place, and there are art galleries and handicraft shops.

North of Clermont, the N9 heads into the *causses* of deepest France, passing **Lodève**, a comfortable, somewhat isolated town wedged between two rivers. Like Clermont-l'Hérault, Lodève has an impressive Gothic church with a lofty tower as its chief monument: **St-Fulcran** (*open summer 9–7; winter 9–5.30*), named after a 9th-century bishop who became the city's patron, was begun in 1280 and turned into a fortress during the Hundred Years' War. It is one of the few churches in France with a chandelier – a present from Queen Victoria to Napoléon III. Lodève's textile-manufacturing past is recalled in a local workshop of the famous Parisian tapestry factory, the **Atelier National de Tissage de Tapis de Lodève** (*48 Av Gén. de Gaulle*, *t 04 67 96 40 40; open Tues, Wed and Thurs 1.30–3.30 by appt only*). Lodève was a Roman town, and its **Musée Fleury** (*Square Georges-Avric*, *t 04 67 88 86 10; open Tues–Sun 9.30–12 and 2–6; closed Mon*) has finds from that age, along with dinosaur bones and footprints, and fossil trilobites, paintings and sculptures.

East of Lodève, a narrow but very pretty country road, the D153, takes you 9km to the **Prieuré St-Michel-de-Grandmont** (*t 04 67 44 09 31; open for guided tours June–Sept daily at 10.30, 3, 4 and 5; Oct–May Tues–Sun at 3; adm*). The Order of Grandmont, founded in the Limousin in the 12th century, was a monastic reform movement like that of Cluny or Cîteaux; it faded away five centuries ago and no one even remembers it today. This priory is its only surviving monument, gradually restored by private owners over the last century. The austere church and cloister, begun in the 12th century, are remarkably well preserved, and there are concerts and art exhibitions throughout spring and summer, but the real attraction here is a group of **dolmens** in the grounds, colossal works shaped like cèpe mushrooms, dating from c. 2000 BC.

The Northern Fringes: Monts de l'Espinouse

If you continue along the northern fringes of the Hérault, you'll get an idea of what France is like for the next hundred miles northwards, through Aveyron and Lozère into the Auvergne – rough canyons and rough villages, an occasional dusting of snow,

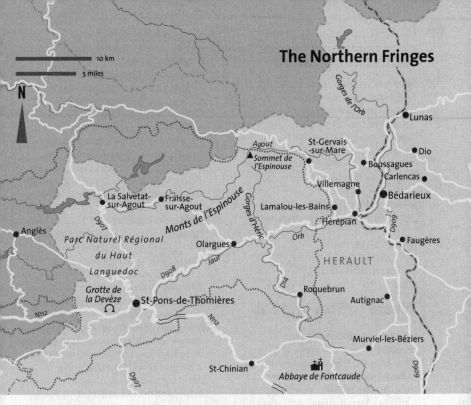

10 km
5 miles

N

Gorges de l'Orb

Lunas
Dio
Agout
St-Gervais-sur-Mare
Sommet de l'Espinouse
Boussagues
Carlencas
Villemagne
Bédarieux
La Salvetat-sur-Agout
Fraisse-sur-Agout
Monts de l'Espinouse
Lamalou-les-Bains
Gorges d'Héric
Hérépian
Anglès
D907
Parc Naturel Régional
Orb
Faugères
du Haut
Olargues
D909
Languedoc
Jaur
D908
HERAULT
Grotte de
la Devèze
St-Pons-de-Thomières
D14
Roquebrun
Autignac
N112
Murviel-les-Béziers
D907
St-Chinian
N112
Abbaye de Fontcaude
D909

trout streams and chestnut groves. The natural beauty of the Espinouse did it little good in former times; even 40 years ago, this was a poor area, losing its population to the cities. The creation of the Parc Naturel Régional du Haut Languedoc in the 1960s has made all the difference; *tourisme vert*, as the French call it – hiking and canoeing or just relaxing under the pines – increases every year. It's no strain on the kind and hospitable folk in the villages, and right now the Espinouse is as happy and content as a patch of mountains can be.

Bédarieux and Lamalou-les-Bains: the Pays d'Orb

The only big road in this region, the D908, runs west from Clermont-l'Hérault across the base of the mountains, following the valleys of the Orb and the Jaur. The first town on the way is **Bédarieux**, a humble enough agricultural centre and market town. Humility stops, however, with Bédarieux's famous son, Pierre-Auguste Cot, one of the 19th-century kitsch-realist artists so popular with the Academicians, the sort that made the Impressionist revolution necessary. They've named the main square after him, and you can see his work in the **Maison des Arts**, in the former poorhouse on Av Abbé Tarroux (*t 04 67 95 08 799; open Mon, Wed and Thurs 3–6; adm*), along with some fossils, railroad memorabilia and exhibits recreating country life and costumes in the old days.

Lamalou-les-Bains, 10km further west, is a sort of museum in itself. A thermal spa since the 17th century, Lamalou made it big when the railroad came through in 1868.

Tourist Information

Bédarieux: Place aux Herbes, **t** 04 67 95 08 79, **f** 04 67 95 39 69, www.bedarieux.fr.
Lamalou-les-Bains: 1 Av Capus, **t** 04 67 95 70 91, **f** 04 67 95 64 52, www.ot-lamaloulesbains.fr. Open June–mid-Sept Mon–Fri 9–12 and 2–7, Sat 9–12 and 2–5, Sun 10–12; mid-Sept–May Mon–Fri 9–12 and 2–6, Sat 9–12.
Olargues: Av de la Gare, **t** 04 67 97 71 26, www.olargues.org.
St-Pons-de-Thomières: Place du Foirail, **t** 04 67 97 06 65, www.saint-pons-tourisme.com.

Market Days
Lamalou-les-Bains: Tues.
La Salvetat: Thurs and Sun.

Where to Stay and Eat

Lamalou-les-Bains ✉ 34240
Belleville, 1 Av Charnot, **t 04 67 95 57 00, **f** 04 67 95 64 18, www.hotelbelleville.com (*inexpensive*). Excellent value for relative luxury: some bathrooms come with Jacuzzi and there's a restaurant (*moderate*).
L'Arboisier, 18 Av Daudet, **t 04 67 95 63 11, **f** 04 67 95 67 78 (*inexpensive*). This 100-year-old hotel has been prettily renovated; it serves old French favourites in the restaurant (*expensive–moderate*).

Villemagne ✉ 34600
Auberge de l'Abbaye, next to the church, **t** 04 67 95 34 84 (*moderate*). Dine in the garden or in the 12th-century dining room. Specialities include *profiteroles de foie gras*. Closed Mon, Tues lunch and Nov–early Feb.

Olargues ✉ 34390
***Domaine de Rieumégé, 3km out on the St-Pons road, **t** 04 67 97 73 99, www.tbs france.com/rieumege (*moderate*). Enchanting 17th-century building set in a 20-acre estate – peace guaranteed. Twelve nice rooms, two pools and tennis, and a separate farmhouse with its own pool for a big splurge. If you don't stay, at least eat in the superb restaurant (*moderate*) in the beautifully restored grange. Closed mid-Dec–Mar.

St-Pons-de-Thomières ✉ 34220
Le Somail, 2 Av de Castres, **t 04 67 97 00 12 (*inexpensive*). A simple place in town.
La Route du Sel, 15 Grand'Rue, **t** 04 67 97 05 14. A little restaurant (*moderate*) specializing in original, well-prepared dishes such as *foie gras* with jerusalem artichokes when they're in season (*topinambours*). Closed Sun.
Les Bergeries de Ponderach, about 1km outside St-Pons towards Narbonne, **t** 04 67 97 02 57, www.bergeries-ponderach.com (*moderate*). A haven of peace in the hills, with a charming owner. There is a rustic restaurant, rooms with terraces and country views, summer concerts and even an art gallery.
Le Cabaretou, on the D907 towards La Salvetat, **t 04 67 95 31 62, www.lecabaretou. com (*inexpensive*). Up in the heart of the mountains, 10km from St-Pons, is this plain but comfortable motel with a surprisingly ambitious restaurant (*moderate*), its cuisine based entirely on seasonal ingredients. *Restaurant closed Mon out of season.*
Ferme-Auberge du Moulin, 4km from La Salvetat, **t** 04 67 97 22 27 (*moderate*). Good farm cooking, specializing in cold meats, farm veal and mushrooms. Book ahead. Closed Dec–Easter and Wed.

The prosperity of the next three decades – dukes and counts, famous actresses, even a sultan of Morocco checked in for the cure – built it into a sweet little resort of Belle Epoque hotels and villas, cafés and a casino with a chocolate-box theatre. Today, Lamalou is bidding to become fashionable once again. Its restored 19th-century centre makes a perfect setting for the big event on its calendar, an important festival of operettas (and opera) that lasts throughout the summer. Inside the cemetery, on the eastern edge of town, is an exceptional 11th-century Romanesque church with a sculpted portal and apse, **St-Pierre-de-Rhèdes**.

The Eastern Espinouse

Either of the above towns is a good base for exploring the eastern half of the Espinouse. North of Bédarieux, the upper valley of the Orb starts out plagued by industry and power lines, but you can escape into the hills on either side, to **Dio** or to **Boussagues**, both delightful medieval villages with ruined castles; the latter's highly picturesque, stone-roofed Renaissance Maison du Bailli once belonged to Toulouse-Lautrec. Persevere northwards and you'll come to the **Gorges de l'Orb**, ending in a big dam and artificial lake at Avène. East of Bédarieux, there's another pretty village, **Carlencas**, famous for chickpeas; to the south is **Faugères**, centre of a small wine region.

Hérépian, between Bédarieux and Lamalou, has one of Europe's last bell foundries, the **Fonderie Bruneau-Garnier**, in business since 1605; it has created a **museum of bells** (*t 04 67 95 39 95; open June–Aug daily 10.30–12 and 2–7; Mar–May and Sept–Oct 10.30–12 and 2–6; Nov and Feb 10.30–12 and 2–5; Oct–Mar closed Tues, plus Dec and Jan; adm includes a guided tour of the foundry*). Hérépian offers another medieval detour, north on the D922 to **Villemagne**. Villemagne-l'Argentière it was in the 12th century, when a Benedictine abbey here looked after a rich silver mine owned by the Trencavels of Béziers and Carcassonne. Most of the abbey and its fortifications are in ruins, and the parts that are left are sadly neglected. There are two lovely churches, Romanesque **St-Grégoire**, which has an **archaeology museum** (*t 04 67 23 06 79; open May–Oct Wed, Sat and Sun 3–6*) and Gothic **St-Majan**, along with a richly decorated 13th-century building believed to have been the mint, the **Hôtel des Monnaies**.

Just to the north of Villemagne is a humpbacked medieval bridge called, like that of St-Guilhem and so many others, the **Pont du Diable** – it must have been hard for the medieval peasant imagination to see how such things could stand up without divine or infernal aid.

Continuing west from Lamalou, at Moulin the Orb turns south, away from the road; there's a choice of directions and of scenery: the **Gorges d'Heric** to the north, a hiker's paradise with no roads, and another gorge to the south, leading towards **Roquebrun**. Sheltered by the mountains, this village grows mimosas and likes to call itself the 'Little Nice'. South of Roquebrun, it's a clear shot along to Béziers and the sea, with nothing to detain you along the way.

The Parc Naturel Régional du Haut Languedoc

The loveliest village of the Espinouse, **Olargues**, is dominated by two medieval monuments, a striking 11th-century bell tower set up above on a hill, and a hump-backed bridge. Next, **St-Pons-de-Thomières** is the little capital of the Espinouse, surrounded by forests. St-Pons probably gets more snow than anywhere in Languedoc east of the Pyrenees, giving it a decidedly Alpine air. Its landmarks are a **cathedral**, with a Romanesque portal and a tremendous 18th-century organ, and its **Musée Municpal de Préhistoire Régionale** (*t 04 67 97 22 61; open daily 10–12 and 2–5; adm*). Never suspecting they were in a future Regional Park, Neolithic people made St-Pons and the Espinouse one of their favourite haunts in France; archaeologists go

Wine: Faugères and St-Chinian

It's the mix of limestone and schist in this beautiful, mountainous corner of Languedoc that creates the dark, beefy red wines of Faugères and St-Chinian. The French currently view these wines as the ascendant stars of the country's lesser-known regions, views borne out by the concentration of talented wine-makers to emerge from the area.

The wines require a few years in the cellar to reveal their true personalities; AOC Faugères, *www.faugeres.com*, has a high percentage of syrah, as well as grenache, old carignan stock and mourvèdre grapes – 2000s are excellent. Pick up a few bottles at **Domaine Gilbert Alquier**, Rte de Pézenas, in Faugères, **t** 04 67 23 07 89 (*open after-noons*); and **Château des Estanilles**, in Cabrerolles, **t** 04 67 90 29 25 (*call ahead*), **f** 04 67 90 10 99 (*closed Sun*), which produces delightful variations in all three colours (including a fine white Coteaux du Languedoc of macabeu and grenache).

St-Chinian, *www.saint-chinian.com*, encompasses 20 villages, but you can try nearly all the labels of fruity, dark, cherry-red St-Chinian (especially the 2000s and 2001s) at St-Chinian's **Cave des Vignerons de Saint-Chinian**, **t** 04 67 38 28 48, *info@vin-saint-chinian.com*. Or visit the **Château Cazals-viel**, in Cessenon, **t** 04 67 89 63 15.

so far as to speak of a *civilisation saintponienne*. This museum documents their career, but the star attractions are the statue menhirs, the true cultural totems of this part of the Mediterranean, similar to those found in the Gard, in Tuscany and in Corsica, from 3000 BC to Roman times.

St-Pons is the perfect base for visiting the **Parc Naturel Régional du Haut Languedoc** (*t 04 67 97 38 22, www.parc-haut-languedoc.fr*), spread over a wide area of the Espinouse on the borders of the Hérault, Tarn and Aveyron. It's an extremely well-organized park; all you need do is visit the Maison du Parc at the tourist office in St-Pons (see p.506). There is a wide choice of hiking trails in the mountains through wild areas that have, among other things, what is said to be the largest population of *mouflons* in Europe.

From Prat-d'Alaric, the valley of the Agout spreads across the heart of the park; the roads that follow it, the D14 and D53, make a delightful tour, through beautiful villages like **La Salvetat-sur-Agout** and **Fraisse-sur-Agout**, which has a curious statue-menhir *in situ*, carved with a serpent and egg, a universal symbol found as far afield as the prehistoric Indian mounds in Ohio. The D53 continues towards the summit of the Espinouse (3,652ft). A little further on – over the Lauze pass on the D180 – there is a stone enclosure, a vestige of a Roman army camp, and beyond – on the D922 – **St-Gervais-sur-Mare**, full of medieval and Renaissance buildings.

Much closer to St-Pons, there is the **Grotte de la Devèze** (*t 04 67 97 03 24; open July–Aug 10–6; April–June and Sept 2–5; adm*), another gorgeous cave of delicate stalactites and shining crystals. To climb down from the Espinouse, there is the choice of the D907 out of St-Pons towards Minerve, or the N112 for Béziers and the Canal du Midi (*see* pp.521–7). On this route, you'll pass through **St-Chinian** and its wine region; about 9km east of that village is the Romanesque **Abbey of Fontcaude**.

The Hérault Coast

West of the Camargue (*see* pp.438–50), the lagoons continue for another 80km, dotting the coast like beads on a string. Unlike the Camargue, almost all of this coast is easily accessible by car; there are beaches and resorts in abundance, and attractions like salty Sète and medieval Maguelone and Agde.

Only a few kilometres from the walls of Aigues-Mortes (*see* pp.448–50), the Hérault coast begins with a bang, with an uncanny skyline of tall holiday ziggurats, a resort town straight from science fiction.

La Grande Motte

At the same time as the Fos complex (see p.276) was going up on the eastern edge of the Camargue, something even stranger was happening on the west. It almost seems as if France's planners wanted an appropriate bookend to Fos's weird mill furnaces and refinery towers. Making the Languedoc resort plan in 1963, they decided that one of the new holiday towns was to be boldly modernist, and they picked the 'big lump', an empty swathe of sand on the Golfe d'Aigues-Mortes for the experiment.

Jean Balladur, the original architect, and his successors gave them more than they bargained for. La Grande Motte looks like no other resort in the world, its hotels and apartments rising in colourful triangles and roller-coaster curves, its public buildings in jarring, amoeboid shapes like a permanent 1960s World Fair. The 'modernism' of the Motte is more surface than substance; there are no real innovations in architecture or design. The buildings themselves, like all the experiments of the kitschy '60s, already look a bit dated. But La Grande Motte is a great success as a resort, a proper city with room for over 100,000 space-age holidaymakers. The complex has been so successful that it has expanded to envelop the old fishing village of **Le Grau-du-Roi**, just to the east.

The fun starts at **Point Zéro**, the name Balladur whimsically gave the central square on the waterfront. In season 'little train' tours around the town start from here. The first clutches of ziggurats (the Grande Mottois prefer to call them *pyramides*) rise to the west, around the marina; to the east are the outlandish buildings of the civic centre, including the *mairie* and congress hall. Beyond that, the planners ensure you will be entertained to death, with broad beaches, thalassotherapy, 39 tennis courts, golf courses (three, designed by Robert Trent Jones), marinas, windsurfing, diving, a big water park, Scrabble clubs, a casino and all the rest. Summer is packed with festivals, concerts and sporting events, and there are masses of opportunities to learn how to sail, to hire boats and take trips out to sea. The deep waters off La Grande Motte are frequented by fin whales (*rorquals*), the world's second largest mammal after the blue whale, measuring up to 70 feet in length. Many of the whales migrate in the autumn, which makes it the best time to spot one; Orphrys, a wildlife conservation agency, may relaunch its whale-spotting trips during September 2005 (adverse weather conditions led to their cancellation in 2004); call **t** 04 67 56 63 01.

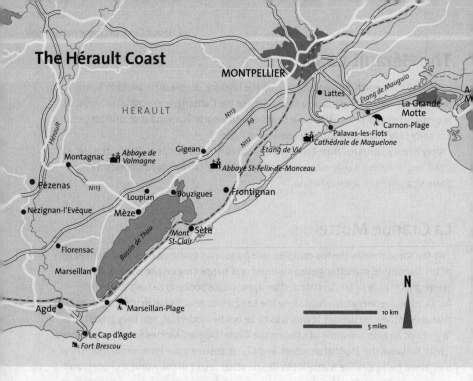

The Hérault Coast

MONTPELLIER

Lattes

Étang de Mauguio

La Grande-Motte

Carnon-Plage

HERAULT

N113

A9

N112

Palavas-les-Flots

Cathédrale de Maguelone

Étang de Vic

Hérault

Montagnac

Abbaye de Valmagne

Gigean

Abbaye St-Felix-de-Monceau

Pézenas

N113

Loupian

Bouzigues

Frontignan

Nézignan-l'Evêque

Mèze

Sète

Bassin de Thau

Mont St-Clair

Florensac

Marseillan

Agde

Marseillan-Plage

10 km

5 miles

N

Le Cap d'Agde

Fort Brescou

For you fogies, a more old-fashioned beach holiday can be spent at **Carnon-Plage** or
Palavas-les-Flots, 15km down the dune-lined coast. Built around a narrow canal full of
boats, Palavas is an endearing resort with some 8km of good beaches, where grocery
clerks from Montpellier come to flash their polyester in the frowzy waterfront casino.
The old centre has a wonderfully casual air about it, toured by a silly tourist train
dedicated to French humorist Albert Dubout, whose works, if you are at all curious,
are displayed in the **Musée Humoristique Albert Dubout**, in the 18th-century Redoute
de Ballestras, built to defend Palavas' fishermen (*t 04 67 68 56 41; open July–Aug daily
4pm–11pm; spring and autumn Wed–Mon 2–6, closed Tues; school holidays and weekends only in winter; adm*). Palavas is especially proud of its **Phare de la Méditerranée**,
a modern 45m tower (formerly a *château d'eau*) with panoramic views from the
restaurant at the top and the tourist office in the bottom. You can also see bullfights
in the arena.

Inland, towards Montpellier, in the village of **Lattes**, you can visit Roman necrop-
olises and the **Musée Archéologique Henri-Prades** (*390 Av de Pérols, t 04 67 99 77 20,
http://musee.lattes.free.fr; open 10–12 and 2–5.30; closed Tues*), with recent discoveries
from the ongoing excavations at the adjacent Bronze Age site of Lattara.

Maguelone

To balance La Grande Motte, a town without a history, here we have a history
without a town. Maguelone, 4km from Palavas, may have begun as a Phoenician or
Etruscan trading post. It prospered under the Romans and Visigoths, becoming the
seat of a bishop. After that the history is obscure. Old maps show the place as 'Port

Sarrasin', suggesting Arab corsairs were using it as a base in the 8th century, and there is a record of Charles Martel coming down from Paris to chase them out, destroying the town in the process.

Maguelone still had one attraction – salt – and the rights were owned by a powerful and progressive multinational, the Church. In the 1030s, when demand was high, a cleric named Arnaulf oversaw the town's rebuilding and added a monastery. The enterprise prospered; Urban II, the first of many popes to visit (1096), called Maguelone the 'second church of Rome', and gave its restored bishops special privileges. Later, Maguelone became a papal holding, a key base both politically and

Tourist Information

La Grande Motte: Allée des Parcs, **t** 04 67 56 42 00, **f** 04 67 29 91 42, *www.ot-lagrande motte.fr. Open April–June 9.30–7; July–Aug 9–8; Oct–Mar 9.30–12.30 and 2–6.*
Palavas-les-Flots: Phare de la Méditerranée, **t** 04 67 07 73 34, **f** 04 67 07 73 58, *www. palavaslesflots.com. Open July–Aug daily 10–8;April–June daily 10–1 and 2–6; Sept daily 10–1 and 2–6; Oct–Mar Mon–Fri 10–1 and 2–6, Sat–Sun 10–1 and 2–5.*

Market Days

Palavas-les-Flots: Sun am, Mon, Wed and Fri; Sat am, flower market and flea market.
La Grande Motte: Sun am, and Thurs am June–Sept.

Festivals

Palavas-les-Flots: Feria, first weekend of May and Oct.

Where to Stay and Eat

La Grande Motte ✉ 34280

The bad news about La Grande Motte is that you can't stay there; all the hotels in the centre are overpriced to the point of absurdity.
***Grand M'Hotel, Quartier Point Zero, **t** 04 67 29 13 13, **f** 04 67 29 14 74 (*very expensive*). The fanciest hotel, right on the front, with a thalassotherapy centre (*www. thalasso-grandemotte.com*) and balconied rooms with good sea views. *Thalassotherapy centre closed mid-Dec–mid-Jan.*
***Mercure, Rue du Port, **t** 04 67 56 90 81, **f** 04 67 56 92 29, *www.accorhotels.com/ mercure_la_grande_motte.htm*

(*expensive*). The splashy status address on the Big Lump, looming over the marina like a concrete refugee from Miami Beach; rather charmless, but a chance to meet that segment of the fast crowd who choose to avoid the Riviera, and it does have a nice terrace regional food restaurant.
Alexandre, Presqu'île du Port, **t** 04 67 56 63 63, *www.alexandre-restaurant.com* (*expensive*). A splurge for refined regional specialities in an especially elegant setting. *Closed Sun eve and Mon, also Tues in Oct–Mar, and Jan.*
La Cuisine du Marché, 89 Rue Casino, **t** 04 67 29 90 11 (*expensive*). Good fresh fish served in classic style. It's small, so you'll need to book. *Closed Mon and Tues.*

Palavas-les-Flots ✉ 34250

Palavas has plenty of inexpensive, undistin-guished hotels. The restaurants have few pretensions, but there are some gratifying, no-nonsense seafood joints.
L'Escale, 5 Bd Sarrail, north of the canal on the seafront, **t** 04 67 68 24 17 (*expensive*). Here you can have *sèche à la rouille* for starters, or extravaganzas like the mixed shellfish plate they call *panaché de coquil-lages* – the bill can skyrocket.
La Passerelle, Quai Paul-Cunq, **t** 04 67 68 55 80 (*inexpensive*). This couldn't be simpler, its menu limited to piles of fresh, inexpensive shellfish. *Closed Oct–April.*

Lattes ✉ 34250

Mas de Couran, Route de Fréjorgues, **t 04 67 65 57 57, **f** 04 67 65 37 56, *www.mas-de-couran.com* (*moderate*). It's worth coming inland to Lattes for this special place, set in a beautiful park, with pool and restaurant. *Closed Sun eve, Mon, and Sat lunch.*

ideologically in the difficult 12th century. It gradually dwindled after that, and the see moved to Montpellier in 1536.

Though almost no trace of the town remains today (its very stones were hauled off by the canal builders), the impressive **Cathedral St-Pierre** (*t 04 67 50 63 63, see Palavas website; open daily 9–7*) was saved from ruin and restored in the 1870s. Built, and built well, by Lombard masons in the 1170s, it is an austere building. The main decorative feature – reliefs around the main portal – show Christ in Majesty with the four Evangelists. Inside, there are fragments of the bishops' tombs, inscriptions and furnishings, and you may climb the surviving bell tower for views down the coast.

Except at the height of summer, Maguelone makes a peaceful place to escape to; there are plenty of beaches around it, a bit rocky but good for seashells. The lagoons in this stretch of coast, from La Grande Motte to Frontignan, are rich in waterfowl, especially pink flamingos, but little else. Most are stagnant and lack oxygen; decomposing water plants in hot summers cause a phenomenon called the *malaïgue*, making the air smell like rotten eggs. The vineyards (*vin de sable*, 'sand wine', and others, run by the Compagnons de Maguelone) don't mind the occasional pong; there's a *cave* for tasting next to the cathedral car park.

From Maguelone, you'll need to backtrack to Palavas and continue around the landward side of the lagoons, rejoining the coast at **Frontignan**, an industrial town with a good 12th-century church, **St-Paul**, with a frieze of fish and boats over the door. Frontignan claims to be nothing less than the world capital of muscat, beloved by the ancient Romans and Thomas Jefferson; it comes in a screwy bottle, in honour of Hercules, who stopped here for a drink while performing his Twelve Labours. The big fellow liked the wine so much that he twisted the bottle to squeeze out the last drop.

Sète

After the glitzy candy-land of the Côte d'Azur, and the empty spaces that follow, you may have despaired by now of finding anything really Mediterranean on these shores; you can find it almost anywhere along the coasts of Spain, Italy or Greece, but in southern France it is as rare as snowmen. Just in time, there's gritty, salty, workaday Sète, France's biggest Mediterranean fishing port. What could be more romantic? After the depressing town entrance, you can stroll along the Canal Maritime and watch businesslike freighters carrying French sunflower and rapeseed oil to every corner of the globe, along with dusty cement boats, gigantic tankers of Algerian natural gas (if one ever goes off, it will take the whole town with it) and Algerian wine (marginally less dangerous), and rusty trawlers jammed full of woebegone sardines or some of the 138 other fish caught by Sètois fishermen. After that, perhaps a leisurely tour of the city's historic monuments? Go ahead and try; in this infant city, younger even than Boston or New York, there isn't a single one.

For entertainment, there are the sailors' bars, or you might try one of the **boat tours** (*from along the Quai de la Résistance, www.sete-croisieres.com*) through the Bassin de Thau, with a stop at an oyster farm. The tourist office has plenty of information on

Tourist Information

Sète: 60 Grand'Rue Mario Roustan,
t 04 67 74 71 71, f 04 67 46 17 54, *www.ot-sete.fr. Open July–Aug daily 9–8; May–June and Sept daily 9–12 and 2–6; Oct–April Mon–Sat 9–12 and 2–6.* In the summer, the tourist office offers one-hour tours of the *Criée*, the extraordinary fish wholesale market on Quai Maximin-Licciardi.

Market Days

Daily: Les Halles, Rue Gambetta.
Wed am: Place A. Briand, Place Blum and Rue A. Lorraine.
Fri am: Av V. Hugo, opposite the train station.
Sun am: Place de la République, flea market.

Local Wine

For wine, head for the **Skalli Fortant de France** winery, 278 Av du Maréchal Juin, t 04 67 46 70 00, which produces excellent wines and has guided visits and tastings.

Where to Stay and Eat

Sète ☒ 34200

***Grand Hôtel, 17 Quai Lattre de Tassigny, t 04 67 74 71 77, f 04 67 74 29 27, *www.sete-hotel.com* (*expensive–moderate*). Right on Sète's 'Grand Canal', it almost deserves its name, with plenty of original décor from the 1920s. If you can't swing the Danieli in Venice, this will do fine: nice people and very reasonable rates. The hotel's **Rotonde** restaurant, t 04 67 74 86 14 (*expensive*) is refined and serves rewarding menus. *Closed mid-Dec–early Jan.*

**L'Orque Bleue, 10 Quai Aspirant-Herber, t 04 67 74 72 13, *www.setehotel.com* (*moderate*). Anyone who grew up in the 1970s will feel at home here.
**Les Abysses, 47 Grand'Rue Mario Roustan, t 04 67 74 37 73, f 04 67 74 24 82 (*inexpensive*). Small and central.
Terrasses du Lido, Rond-Point de Europe, along the Corniche road, t 04 67 51 39 60 (*expensive*). A pretty Provençal-style villa serving authentic Mediterranean dishes from *bourride* to *bouillabaisse*. *Closed Sun eve and Mon except in July and Aug.*
La Palangrotte, Rampe Paul Valéry, t 04 67 74 80 35 (*expensive–moderate*). Quality seafood on the lower end of the Canal de Sète: grilled fish and several styles of fish stew, including the local *bourride sètoise*. *Closed Sun eve and Mon, except in July and Aug.*
Le Chalut, 38 Quai Maximin Licciardi, t 04 67 74 81 52 (*expensive–moderate*). The seafood, including many Sètois specialities, is as tasty as the décor).
La Péniche, 1 Quai des Moulins, t 04 67 48 64 13 (*moderate–cheap*). For lunch with the dock-hands try this place serving simple stuff on an old barge in the harbour. *Closed Sat lunch and Sun eve.*

Bouzigues ☒ 34140

Côte Bleue, Av Louis-Tudesq, t 04 67 78 30 87 (*expensive*). A large family restaurant overlooking the Bassin de Thau which is the best place to sample a vast variety of shellfish, mussels, langoustines and the local Bouzigues oysters. *Closed Sun eve mid-Oct–Mar and Feb.*

boats to rent and opportunities to dive. Or take in an American football match and watch the Sète Praetorians joust with the dreaded Bastia Black Heads from Corsica. If you can stand a little modern madness, Sète will be great fun. It's an attractive town, laced with canals, and livelier and more colourful than any place on the coast, save only Marseille.

Along the Grand Canal

The city's arms show a field of *fleurs-de-lis* with a whale – *cetus* in Latin – one of the possible explanations for the name, which is first mentioned in a Carolingian document of 814. In 1666, Louis XIV's minister, Colbert, began construction of the port, the terminus for the Canal du Midi (*see* pp.523–7), which was begun in the same year. In 1673 the new town was declared a free port. The pesky English first came to visit in 1710, occupying the city during the War of the Spanish Succession; out in the harbour, you can see **Fort St-Pierre**, which failed to keep them out. Little has happened since. Despite its booming port, Sète never grew into a major city; hedged between Mont St-Clair, the lagoons and the sea, there simply isn't room.

Sète should be the twin city of Livorno (Leghorn) in Italy. Both grew up at the same time; both have canals (Sète likes to call itself the 'Venice of Languedoc') and a winsome architectural anonymity. And they have both made their offbeat contributions to modern culture; Livorno was the birthplace of Modigliani, Sète of the poet Paul Valéry, singer-composer Georges Brassens and Jean Vilar, father of the Avignon festival. The bustling centre of Sète is its 'Grand Canal', the **Canal de Sète**, lined with quays where the ambience ranges from boatyards and ship chandlers to banks and boutiques and waterside cafés. A block west, on Place Aristide Briand in front of the *mairie*, Sète has what is undoubtedly the world's biggest cast-bronze octopus, writhing over a modern fountain.

At the southern end of the canal, the **Vieux Port** handles most of the fishing fleet, as well as offering tourist fishing boats and excursions around the Thau lagoon. From the Vieux Port, it's a bit of a climb up to the **Cimetière Marin**, celebrated in a famous poem by Paul Valéry, who was buried here in 1945, his family tomb (under the name Grassi – like Brassens, his mother was Italian) bearing an inscription from the poem (*Ô récompense après une pensée/Qu'on long regard sur le calme des dieux*).

The adjacent **Musée Paul Valéry** (*t 04 67 46 20 98; open 10–12 and 2–6, closed Tues exc. July and Aug; adm*) contains exhibits on the poet, and on the history of Sète, as well as a good collection of modern paintings, older works by Courbet and even a minor Botticelli. Just below, the open-air **Théâtre de la Mer**, with a lively programme of summer concerts, is dedicated to Jean Vilar; just above begin a network of paths up to **Mont St-Clair** (600ft), once the Sunday promenade of the Sètois.

Sète's other contribution to French culture, Brassens (d. 1981) is buried in the **Cimetière de Py**, under the Pierres Blanches, overlooking the Etang de Thau; fans or the merely curious can learn much, much more in the nearby **Espace Georges Brassens** (*67 Bd Camille Blanc, t 04 67 53 32 77; open June–Sept daily 10–12 and 2–6; Oct–May closed Mon; adm*), where you'll not only see photos and exhibits relating to Brassens' life, but you can hear it as well on the headphones, accompanied by his hit songs and words of wisdom. There is also a **Musée International des Arts Modeste** (*23 Quai Maréchal de Lattre de Tassigny, t 04 67 18 64 00; open 10–12 and 2–6; closed Tues out of season; adm*), an eclectic collection of day-to-day items from over the past 50 years, imaginatively displayed.

Bassin de Thau

Sète's Bassin de Thau is one of the largest lagoons along the Mediterranean shore. There have always been salt pans here, though today most of the lagoon has found a more lucrative employment as a huge oyster and mussel farm, yielding incredibly tasty bivalves.

There are two roads south from Sète; taking the coastal route, passing quickly through the unhappy concrete piles of La Corniche, you'll pass 15km of narrow grey beach next to the road. Since there is no room for development, this is your best chance on the entire coast to find some empty beach space, even in the height of summer, if you don't mind the cars. At the southern end, the beach piles up into an expanse of partly overgrown dunes, near the small resort of **Marseillan-Plage**. **Marseillan** itself, another fishing/oyster port, was founded in the 6th century BC by the Greeks and is made of the same black basalt as Agde. By the port at 1 Rue Noilly (*t* 04 67 77 20 15) you can find out the secret ingredients of Marseillan's own aperitif, Noilly-Prat.

The other, longer route passes around the back of the lagoon. Along the way, it takes in the 11th–13th-century Benedictine (later Cistercian) **Abbaye St-Félix-de-Montceau** (*call t 04 67 43 34 81 to check opening hours, www.abbaye-st-felix.new.fr*), accessible on a white road from Gigean. Romantically ruined on its hilltop site, with a view over the lagoon, the abbey includes both a Romanesque and a Gothic church. Further south, the ancient lagoon port of **Mèze** still makes a go of it as a fishing village, though nowadays the money comes from the less romantic chores of oyster-farming.

If you want to know more about shellfish-breeding and -fishing, you can visit the **Musée de l'Etang de Thau**, at Bouzigues (*t 04 67 78 33 57; open July–Aug 10–12.30 and 2.30–7; Mar–June and Sept–Oct 10–12 and 2–6; Nov–Feb 10–12 and 2–5*). And just north of Mèze is a brilliant open-air dinosaur park, **La Plaine des Dinosaures**, on the N113 (*t 04 67 43 02 80, www.musee-parc-dinosaures.com; open daily July–Aug 10–7; Jan, Feb–June and Sept daily 2–6; closed Oct–Dec*), where in 1996 they found the biggest cache of dinosaur eggs ever discovered in Europe. Life-size models and skeletons can be glimpsed amongst the trees, including a complete skeleton of a brachiosaurus, and you can see the ongoing archaeological dig. There is also a new section on the evolution of Man.

Another possible distraction around the Bassin de Thau is in nearby Loupian: a **Gallo-Roman villa** (*t 04 67 18 68 18; site open for guided tours mid-June–mid-Sept daily, 11–5.45; otherwise school hols Sat 2–5, Sun 11–5*) which is being excavated and restored.

Abbaye de Valmagne

8km north of Mèze on the D161; t 04 67 78 06 09, www.valmagne.com; open mid-June–mid-Sept daily 10–11.45 and 2–5.50; mid-Sept–mid-June 2–5.40; closed Tues mid-Dec–mid-Feb; guided tours.

It might try the patience of some readers, dragging them on another detour to another ruined abbey – but this is the best one of all. Valmagne was an early Cistercian foundation, begun in 1138 and financed by Raymond Trencavel. Being one of the richest houses, it also gradually became one of the most decadent; the records mention a 16th-century Florentine abbot named Pietro da Bonzi, who built himself a palace on the site, plus a French garden with a statue of Neptune, and who threw the best dinner parties in Languedoc. Thoroughly trashed in the Revolution, the abbey has survived only by good luck; one owner proposed to dismantle it to provide building stone for a new church in Montpellier, but the canons there found the price too high. For the last century, the vast **church** has served as the biggest wine cellar in the Hérault, with some of the best fruity red AOC Coteaux de Languedoc, and a traditional lemon-coloured white and rosé (*open July–Sept daily 10–12 and 2.30–6.30; Oct–June 2–6, or ring **t** 04 67 78 47 32*).

Valmagne is not your typical Cistercian church. St Bernard would have frowned on architectural vanities like the porch, the big bell towers and the sculpted decoration – grapevines, representing less the scriptural 'labourer in the vineyard' than the real vineyards that made Valmagne so rich. Its size is astonishing: a 370ft nave, and great pointed arches almost as high as Narbonne cathedral's. Most of the work is 14th-century, in a straightforward but sophisticated Late Gothic; note how the nave columns grow slightly closer together towards the altar, a perspective trick that makes the church seem even longer (St Bernard wouldn't have fancied that either). The relatively few monks who lived here would hardly have needed such a church; here, too, architectural vanity seems to have overcome Cistercian austerity.

Both the chapter house and the refectory are well preserved, around a pretty **cloister** that contains the loveliest thing in the abbey, an octagonal Gothic pavilion with a tall flowing fountain inside, a fantasy straight from a medieval manuscript or tapestry; an 18th-century poet, Lefranc de Pompignan, named it right: a *fontaine d'amour*.

Agde, the 'Black Pearl of Languedoc'

If Sète is a brash young upstart, Agde has been watching the river Hérault flow down to the sea for some 2,500 years. Founded by Greeks from Phocis, not long after Marseille, its name was originally Agatha, after Agatha Tyche, the 'good spirit' of popular Greek religion, usually portrayed carrying a cornucopia; the people of Agde are still called Agathois. In medieval times it was an important port, despite occasional visits by Arab sea-raiders. The last few centuries have left Agde behind, but it is still a good town, and a grey one – built almost entirely of volcanic basalt from nearby Mont St-Loup. With the massive new tourist development at nearby Cap d'Agde, this lovely town does not get much peace in the summer; in parts of the old quarter there are almost as many restaurants as houses. Grau d'Agde, where the Hérault meets the sea, is pleasant along the riverbanks, with fishing boats, and seems more relaxed.

A Stroll Around Town

The tiny old quarter is defined by its walls, now largely demolished for a promenade; a bit of the old ramparts remains, near the river, resting on Greek foundations (now below street level). Overlooking the Hérault, Agde's stern basalt **Cathédrale St-Etienne** was begun about 1150. Its fortress-like appearance – it looks like a baddie's castle in a Hollywood movie – is no accident; Agde's battling bishops used it as their citadel (the outworks have been demolished). Previous cathedrals had been wrecked in battles, once at the hands of Charles Martel himself. It's open during mass; the only original feature is the 12th-century marble altar.

Tourist Information

Agde: Place Molière, **t** 04 67 94 29 68, **f** 04 67 94 03 50. *Open July and Aug daily 9–7; Sept–June Mon–Sat 9–12 and 2–6.*

Cap d'Agde: Rond-Point du Bon Accueil, **t** 04 67 01 04 04, **f** 04 67 26 22 99, *www.capdagde. com. Open July–Aug daily 8–8.30; Sept–June daily 9–12 and 2–6.*

Market Days

Agde: Thurs am, and a covered market Tues–Sun am.

Cap d'Agde: June–Sept Sat am, Mon am and Tues am, and a flea market Sun am.

Where to Stay and Eat

Agde ✉ 34300

You won't regret stopping over at Agde if you're passing anywhere nearby. It's a sweet town, and the hotels and restaurants are as good as you'll find on the coast, although parking can be difficult.

★★La Galiote, 5 Place Jean-Jaurès, **t** 04 67 94 45 58, **f** 04 67 94 41 33, *www.lagaliote.fr* (*moderate*). Some of the rooms in this old bishop's palace overlook the river; there's a bar full of English beer, and an excellent restaurant (*moderate*): seafood or roast lamb with thyme, and alcoholic sorbets between courses. *Closed 2 wks Nov, 2 wks Feb.*

★★Le Donjon, Place Jean-Jaurès, **t** 04 67 94 12 32, *www.hotelledonjon.com* (*moderate–inexpensive*). The second choice in town, with old-fashioned, comfortable rooms.

★★Le Château Vert, 25 Quai Commandant Méric, **t** 04 67 94 14 51, *www.extra2000.com/ le-chateau-vert* (*moderate*). Reasonable hotel in a good spot by the river and 150m from the beach. There's a restaurant (*moderate*) offering seafood and some surprises like kangaroo. *Closed Oct–Mar; restaurant closed Tues and Wed except July and Aug.*

From the quay along the Hérault, Rue Chassefière leads into the *bourg*, or medieval addition to the city. On Rue de la Fraternité, the **Musée Agathois** (*t 04 67 94 82 51; open 9–12 and 2–6; adm*) is one of the best of the south's town museums, encapsulating nearly everything about Agde's history and traditions in a few well-arranged rooms: archaeological finds, religious art, costume exhibits, dances and festivals, an old-fashioned kitchen and fishermen's gear. Behind the museum, Agde's market shares Place Gambetta with the church of **St-André**, where important Church councils were held in the days of the Visigoths; of the present building, though, the oldest part is the 12th-century tower.

Another church, **St-Sever** on Rue St-Sever, contains a fine Renaissance painting of Christ on wood, a little the worse for wear from having been thrown into the Hérault during the Revolution.

A Suspicious Saint and a Synthetic Resort

The road to Cap d'Agde, only 4km away, passes the ancient, extinct volcano **Mont St-Loup**, its top disfigured by communications pylons. Agde's black basalt comes from here. Whoever St Loup, or 'Holy Wolf', might have been is not clear (though there is a northern saint by that name, a 5th-century bishop of Troyes). *Loup* is also the name for sea bass, the favourite fish in Agde's restaurants. **Cap d'Agde**, built around a small harbour and a lovely black basalt sand beach and black cliffs, is the biggest beach playground in all Languedoc and another triumph of French holiday efficiency. Like La Grande Motte, it began in the 1960s as a planned resort fostered by the government, and it looks it: a freshly built 'traditional' centre, with plenty of parking, broad boulevards and everything in its place. The original plan even accommodated *naturistes*; the camp called **Héliopolis** on the northern edge of town, at Port-Ambone, has become the biggest nudist colony in Europe, with a futuristic semicircular central building that includes shops, banks and even a *naturiste* supermarket, where German has become the second language.

Cap d'Agde may not be what you came to Languedoc for, but there's plenty to do: a first-rate golf course (*t* 04 67 26 54 40), championship tennis courts and matches (*t* 04 67 01 03 60), and other sports facilities (they hosted the Mediterranean Games in 1993); a wildlife sanctuary at the nearby **Etang de Bagnas** (*t* 04 67 01 60 23) with rare waterfowl (purple heron, grand bittern); a casino; an **aquarium** specializing in live coral (*11 Rue des Deux Frères, t* 04 67 26 14 21, *www.aquariumagde.com*); a Luna Park; and the inevitable **Aqualand** with water-slides.

One surprising attraction is a fine, small archaeological collection at the **Musée de l'Ephèbe** (*t* 04 67 94 69 60; *open year-round daily 9–12 and 2–6; adm*), the star of which is the *Ephèbe d'Agde*, a Hellenistic bronze of a boy, discovered in 1964 in the bed of the Hérault.

The Southern Hérault

Pézenas

The area inland from Agde, behind the Bassin de Thau, is one of the duller stretches of the Hérault, a rolling plain dotted with a score of agricultural villages – up-to-date and businesslike rather than picturesque and cosy. Right in the centre is Pézenas. If Carcassonne is Languedoc's medieval movie set, this town has often been used for costume dramas set in the time of Richelieu or Louis XIV (most famously, *Cartouche*). Few cities have a better ensemble of buildings from what the French (rather over-enthusiastically) used to call the 'Golden Age'. Even when the cameras aren't rolling, it is all too easy to imagine moustachioed musketeers and *grandes dames* with laced bodices and perfumed gloves strolling its elegant streets. In summer, the Piscénois live out a lingering *ancien régime* fantasy, with a series of festivals, concerts and exhibitions called the *Mirondela dels Arts* in July and August (*www.mirondeladelsarts.com*).

History

Roman Piscenae was known for wool, the best in Gaul. In the 13th century, it became a possession of the French Crown and renewed its prosperity by royally chartered merchants' fairs. Later, the troubles of Béziers and Narbonne in the Albigensian Crusade and the Hundred Years' War would prove lucky for Pézenas. Besides draining off trade and commerce from those cities, the royal town replaced Narbonne as seat of the Estates-General of Languedoc after 1456. The royal governors of the region followed in 1526, bringing in their wake a whole wave of wealthy nobles, clerics and jurists, who rebuilt Pézenas in their own image with new churches, convents, government buildings and scores of refined *hôtels particuliers*. For the next two

Tourist Information

Pézenas: Place Gambetta, t 04 67 98
35 45/t 04 67 98 36 40, f 04 67 98 96 80,
www.paysdepezenas.net. *Open July–Aug
daily 9–7; Sept–June Mon–Sat 9–12 and 2–6,
Sun 2–5.*

Market Days

Pézenas: Sat.

Where to Stay and Eat

Pézenas ✉ 34120

***Hostellerie de St-Alban, 31 Rte d'Agde,
Nézignan l'Evêque, just south of Pézenas,
t 04 67 98 11 38, f 04 67 98 91 63, *www.saint
alban.com (expensive–moderate)*. A quiet
19th-century villa in the vines, with a pool,
tennis and restaurant (*expensive*). *Closed
mid-Nov–mid-Feb.*

**Genieys, 9 Av Aristide Briand, t 04 67 98
13 99, f 04 67 98 04 80 (*inexpensive*). Outside
the historic centre, but the only good hotel

in town. *Half-board only in July and Aug;
closed mid-Nov–early Dec.*

Le Pre St-Jean, 18 Av du Maréchal-Leclerc,
t 04 67 98 15 31 (*expensive*). Has a pretty
terrace and serves classics like stuffed squid
and *carré d'agneau en croute. Closed Sun eve,
Mon, and Thurs eve, and Feb.*

Côté Sud, Place 14 Juillet, t 04 67 09 41 74
(*moderate*). For a shellfish feast, this place
comes up with the goods. *Closed Mon and
Wed out of season and 3 wks Dec–Jan.*

La Tasca, Rue Anatole France, t 04 67 98 82 72
(*moderate*). Spanish and Mexican food.
Closed Sun and Mon.

Maison Alary, Rue St-Jean 9, t 04 67 98 13 13
This *boulangerie* makes Pézenas' claim to
culinary fame, its spool-shaped *petits pâtés.*
They often take French visitors by surprise
('what is this, half sweet and half mutton?'),
but if you're British you may not find them
that shocking: the recipe was introduced
in 1770 by the Indian chef of Lord Clive,
Governor of India, who spent a holiday in
Pézenas. They still make them here; enjoy
them warm. *Closed Mon in winter.*

centuries they remained, preferring their little aristocratic town to decaying
Narbonne or to Montpellier, full of untidy industry and Protestants.

All this came to an end with the Revolution, but meanwhile Pézenas has done its
best to keep up its monuments while making a living from agriculture and tourism.

A Walk Around Town

The tourist information office is the place to start. They offer a brochure with a
detailed walking tour of the town and its 70-odd listed historical buildings. From the
Renaissance through to the 18th century, Pézenas really did develop and maintain a
distinctive architectural manner; this can best be seen in the *hôtels particuliers*, with
their lovely arcaded courtyards and external staircases. It was an eclectic style, incorporating elements as diverse as Gothic vaulting and Italian Renaissance balustrades:
tasteful, if not ambitious.

The tourist office was also once the shop of a barber named Gély. Molière spent
some seasons in Pézenas in the 1650s, when his troupe was employed by the
governor, the Prince de Conti. He liked passing the afternoons in Gély's salon, doing
research for his comedies – watching the comings and goings and listening to the
conversations. Across Place Gambetta, the former government palace, the **Maison
Consulaire**, has been rebuilt so many times since the 13th century that it is in itself a
little museum of Pézenas architecture. Around the corner on Rue Alliès, the **Musée de
Vulliod-St-Germain** (*t 04 67 98 90 59; open May–Oct Tues–Sun 10–12 and 2–6;*

Wine: More Coteaux du Languedoc

One of the best pockets of this AOC label (*see* p.498) is here. Pézenas is the home of some excellent wines, especially those of the **Prieuré de St-Jean de Bebian**, t 04 67 98 13 60 (*ring in advance*), f 04 67 98 22 24. For a unique, golden-hued clairette wine from the fragrant, thyme-covered slopes to the north, try the **Château St-André**, Route de Nizas at Pézanas, t 04 67 98 12 58, f 04 67 98 33 46 (*open Mon–Fri 9–12 and 2–6*). The 2000 is good to lay down. Pomérols, near Pézenas, is the centre of a traditional but obscure, minuscule growing area on the west shore of the Bassin de Thau called Picpoul de Pinet, producing an unusual soft white wine with sea-green highlights that goes well with freshwater fish; try some at the **Cave Coopérative Les Costières**, in Pomérols, t 04 67 77 01 59, f 04 67 77 77 21, *www.cave-pomerols.com* (*open July and Aug Mon–Sat 8.30–1 and 2–7, Sun 10–1 and 4–7; Sept–June Mon–Sat 8.30–12 and 2–6*). In Lézignan-la-Cèbe, just north of Pézenas, the **Château d'Ormesson**, t 04 67 98 29 33 (*groups only; ring in advance*), is run by a count devoted to perfecting his white and red Vins de Pays d'Oc that have surpassed not a few proud AOC labels – especially a red called L'Enclos made of merlot and cabernet sauvignon.

Nov–April Tues–Sat 10–12 and 2–5, Sun 2–5; adm) contains memorabilia of Molière and his time in Pézenas, along with collections of tapestries, faïence, paintings and the bric-a-brac of Pézenas' past.

West of Place Gambetta are some of the best streets for peeking inside the courtyards of the *hôtels particuliers*: Rue Sabatini, Rue François-Oustrin (the **Hôtel de Lacoste**, with an elegant staircase, is at No.8), Rue de Montmorency, and especially **Rue de la Foire**, the status address of the old days, with a number of palaces, including the Renaissance **Hôtel de Carrion-Nizas** at No.10. Just down the street, note the charming relief of child musicians at No.22. At the northern end of the street, a left takes you into Rue Emile-Zola; the **Hôtel de Jacques Cœur** (the famous merchant of Montpellier; *see* p.487) is at No.7, with an interesting allegorical sculpted façade. It faces the **Porte Faugères**, a 1597 remnant of the town walls, and the nearby entrance to the small **Jewish Ghetto**, a single poignant lane closed in by two gates in the 14th century. At 517 Rue Montmorency, in keeping with the town's architectural heritage, there is a **museum of doors and ironwork** (*t 04 67 98 90 59; open mid-June–mid-Sept Mon–Fri 10.30–12.30 and 3–7, Sat 11–12.30 and 3–7, Sun 3–7; mid-Sept–mid-June Tues–Fri 10–12 and 2–5, Sat 11–12 and 2–5, Sun 2–5*).

The broad **Cours Jean-Jaurès**, site of the market, divides Pézenas in two. It, too, has its palaces: an especially good row of them at Nos.14–22, including the **Hôtel de Grasset**. The Cours leads into Place de la République, and the church of **St-Jean**, with profuse 17th- and 18th-century marble decoration that proves Pézenas' artistic instincts were much sounder in secular matters. South of the Cours, there are more palaces: the **Hôtel de Malibran** and **Hôtel de l'Epine**, with a lavish sculptural façade, both on Rue Victor Hugo; the **Hôtel Montmorency**, the Pézenas home of one of 16th-century France's most illustrious noble houses, on Rue Reboul; and, best of all, the **Hôtel d'Alfonse** on Rue Conti, which has a delightful courtyard loggia on three levels, built in the 1630s.

Béziers

This city's history is succinct: a rude interruption and a second chance. Béziers is older than the Romans; its site, a commanding, defensible hill on a key part of the Mediterranean coast, seems promising, but Béziers' long career has produced little distinction and only one famous anecdote. In 1209, at the beginning of the Albigensian Crusade, a large number of Cathars took refuge in the city and were besieged. When the besiegers offered the Cathars a chance to leave the city, they refused. The troops stormed the city and found that the entire population had taken refuge in the churches. The Crusaders' ayatollah, the Abbot of Cîteaux, had ordered the massacre of all the Cathars. Asked how to distinguish them from the Catholics, he replied 'Kill them all; God will know his own.' From all accounts, that is exactly what happened; in his report to Rome, the papal legate bragged that 20,000 people were put to death.

Not surprisingly, Béziers languished for centuries. The second chance came in the 1660s, with the building of the Canal du Midi (see p.523). A new Béziers has grown up since then, a busy port and industrial town of some 70,000, known best for its crack

Getting There and Around

By Train

Béziers is on the main coastal rail line and it's easy to get to Narbonne, Sète, Montpellier or points beyond, with trains never much more than two hours apart.

By Bus

The *gare routière* is on Place du Général de Gaulle, with regular connections to Pézenas , and less regular ones to villages of the eastern Hérault. City buses run from here to nearby Valras, the popular lido of the Biterrois.

Tourist Information

Béziers: Palais des Congrès, 29 Av St-Saëns, t 04 67 76 84 00, f 04 67 76 50 80, *www.ville-beziers.fr.* Open mid-June–mid-Sept Mon–Sat 9–7, Sun 9–12; mid-Sept–mid-June Mon–Fri 9–12 and 2–6.30, Sat 9–12 and 3–6.

Market Days

Fri: flowers, antiques, food and clothes in Allées Paul Riquet, Place David-d'Angers, and around.

Sat: Place de la Madeleine, flea and produce markets.

Where to Stay and Eat

Béziers ✉ 34500

★★★**Imperator**, 28 Allées Paul Riquet, t 04 67 49 02 25, f 04 67 28 92 30, *www.hotel-imperator. fr* (*moderate*). This has the best location in town, and there's a garage, too.

★★**Champ de Mars**, 17 Rue Metz, t 04 67 28 35 53, f 04 67 28 61 42 (*inexpensive*). A good-value place, nice and central but set on a quiet street.

★**Paul Riquet**, 46 Allées Paul Riquet, t 04 67 76 44 37 (*inexpensive*). Small and pleasant.

L'Ambassade, 22 Bd de Verdun, t 04 67 76 06 24 (*expensive–moderate*). You can dine well and elegantly while watching the progress of your meal (the kitchen has a large window in the wall) at L'Ambassade, with good-value menus. *Closed Sun and Mon.*

Le Jardin, 37 Av Jean Moulin, near Place 14 Juillet, t 04 67 36 41 31 (*expensive– moderate*). The finest local ingredients go into the wide-awake cuisine here. *Closed Sun eve and Wed.*

Café Mondial, 2 Rue Solférino, t 04 67 28 22 15. Packed most evenings, not so much for its food but for its free concerts (*several eves per month*). Open eves Tues–Sat.

rugby squad. Approaching it from the surrounding plains, you'll see its heroic hilltop skyline from miles away, crowned by its impressive cathedral; seen from inside, unfortunately, Béziers will not sustain your initial expectations, a pigeon-grey city with plenty of traffic, but also three good museums.

Allées Paul-Riquet and the Cathedral

Life in Béziers centres along the the **Allées Paul Riquet**, a broad promenade of plane trees named after the city's great benefactor, the builder of the Canal du Midi. Besides a statue of Riquet, there is a handsome 19th-century theatre, and a monument to Resistance hero Jean Moulin (another Bitérrois) at the top of the **Plateau des Poètes**, a romantic garden with ponds and swans and statues by local sculptor Jean-Antoine Injalbert that descends gracefully down to the train station. From the other end of the Allées Paul Riquet, any of the streets to the west will take you up to the top of the hill and the medieval centre.

Someone must have been left in Béziers after 1209, for the city spent the next two centuries working on its grandiose **cathedral**, replacing the original that was wrecked in the sack. Its grim, fortress-like exterior, similar to Narbonne's, seems a foreign presence, the citadel of an occupying force. The inside is more graceful, in clean, warm ashlar masonry with plenty of stained glass; it creates a light and airy effect, especially in the apse, where large windows of blue and white decorative glass (behind a dreadful Baroque altar) are the prettiest feature in the church. In two chapels (second right and second left) there are fragments of Giottoesque frescoes, and at the west front, a magnificent organ almost as good as the one in Narbonne, carved in walnut in 1623 by Guilhaume Martois, who is buried next to it. Architectural fragments from the earlier church can be seen in the beautiful vaulted **cloister**, a work of the late 14th century.

Behind the cathedral, the **Musée des Beaux Arts in the Hotel Fabregat** (*Place de la Révolution, t 04 67 28 38 78; open July–Aug daily 10–6; April–June and Oct 9–12 and 2–6; Nov–Mar 9–12 and 2–5; closed Mon; adm*) houses Béziers' fine arts museum, founded in 1859, with something for every taste: a 16th-century *Virgin and Child* by Martin Schaffner of Ulm, a portrait by Hans Holbein the Younger, 17th-century Italian works (including a Domenichino), a Richard Bonington *Storm*, and 18th- and 19th-century French paintings, by the likes of Géricault, Corot, Delacroix and Rousseau. Many of the fine modern works (de Chirico, Soutine, Friesz) were purchased by Jean Moulin; the great Résistance leader posed as a designer and art dealer under the name of Romanin.

Just north, the **Musée Fayet**, in a delightful 17th-century *hôtel particulier* (*9 Rue du Capus, t 04 67 49 04 66; open July–Aug daily 10–6; April–June and Oct 9–12 and 2–6; Nov–Mar 9–12 and 2–5; closed Mon; same adm*), contains several rooms of 18th- and 19th-century paintings and decorative arts, and several rooms dedicated to the sculptures of Injalbert.

If you have time for more churches, the Romanesque **Madeleine** (*open July and Aug Mon 4–6, Tues and Fri 10–6, Sat 10–12 and 4–6, Sun 10–12; Sept–June Tues 10–12, Thurs 2–6.30, Sat 10–12 and 2–7.30, Sun 10–12*), north of the cathedral and market on Place de la Madeleine, was one of the sites of the massacre of 1209, when the population sought to take refuge in its walls. **St-Aphrodise**, further north, hidden behind newer buildings in Place St-Aphrodise, was Béziers' cathedral in the 8th century. 'St Aphrodise', if it isn't Aphrodite herself, would be the legendary first bishop, who rode into Béziers one day on a camel (now the city's symbol). The Romans naturally chopped off his head and threw it into a well – but the water rose miraculously to the surface, floating the head with it. Aphrodise fished it out and carried it under his arm to the site of this church, and then disappeared into the ground. It's more likely that pagan Aphrodite had a temple on or near this site. Almost nothing remains of the original building, but a 4th-century sarcophagus has been recycled for use as a baptismal font.

A third Romanesque church, simple **St-Jacques**, is on a belvedere on the south side of Béziers, by a third museum, the **Musée du Biterrois**, or de **St-Jacques** (*t 04 67 36 71 01; open July and Aug Tues–Sun 10–6; Sept–June Tues–Sun 9–12 and 2–6; closed Mon; adm*), newly housed in an 18th-century barracks on Rampe du 96ème (from the top of Av Gambetta, turn down Av de La Marine). The museum divides its space between regional archaeological finds, medieval capitals and other bits (including St Aphrodise with his head), ethnography (especially wine-making), science and ceramics.

The Canal du Midi

The best thing to do in Béziers is go west for one of Languedoc's best-kept secrets. The waterways of other parts of France are well-enough known; this, one of very few in the south, remains serene and relatively unburdened by tourism, planted its entire length with parallel rows of plane trees (not just for decoration; they hold the soil and help keep the canal from silting up).

Shady and idyllic, Paul Riquet's canal is also an early monument of economic planning, from the days of Louis XIV's great minister Colbert, when everything in France was being reformed and modernized (and Louis was blowing the profits on Versailles and his endless wars). Riquet was a local baron, the state's tax farmer for Languedoc (*ancien régime* tax farmers bought rights to collect taxes in a region and got to keep any amounts above the sum expected by the government). He conceived the idea for the canal and sold it to Colbert, then saw through its construction with remarkable single-mindedness, inventing ingenious tricks to get the canal over the highest stretches, paying a third of the expenses himself, and even sacrificing his daughters' dowries to the cause. From 1666, as many as 12,000 men worked on the project, which required over 100 locks and runs for 145 miles. It was completed 39 years later; Riquet died a few months before the opening.

No one has shipped any freight on the Canal du Midi for years, but it is still kept up for the benefit of holidaymakers. Some of the locks are tended; at others you'll have to figure out the mechanism yourself. You can take a slow cruise from Béziers all the way to Toulouse, or just rent a rowing boat or canoe in one of the villages and spend a drowsy day under the plane trees.

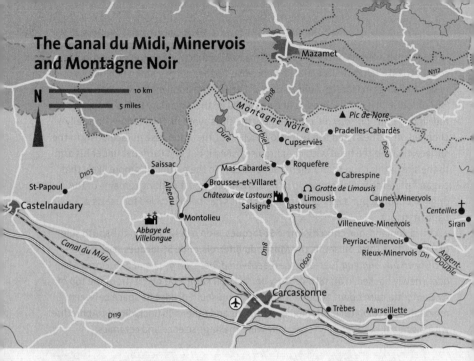

The Canal West of Béziers

The canal connects Sète, on the Mediterranean, with Toulouse – where it still flows right past the central railway station – and thence to the Atlantic, by way of the river Garonne. The best parts of it are west of Béziers, where it passes through a score of lovely old villages, fitting so well into the landscape that it seems to have been there all the time. Pick it up just outside Béziers at the **Ecluses de Fonséranes**, just off the N113 for Narbonne. This is a series of seven original locks, a watery stair that facilitated the biggest drop in altitude along the canal's length.

No one road follows the canal for long, but with a good map and some careful navigation you can stay close to it, on the back roads through **Colombiers**, first of the canal villages, then to **Nissan-lez-Ensérune**, a busy place with a 14th-century Gothic church. You will already have noticed this landmark in the flat countryside; signs from Nissan will lead you up to it, and to the remains of one of the most important pre-Roman towns of southern Gaul, the Oppidum d'Ensérune. The Canal du Midi passes right under it by way of the 567ft **Malpas tunnel** (1679), the first canal tunnel ever, dug by Riquet, who knew best, in spite of considerable controversy at the time.

Oppidum d'Ensérune

t 04 67 37 01 23, www.oppidumdenserune.com; open mid-May–mid-Sept 10–7; April–mid-May 10–12.30 and 2–6; mid-Sept–Mar 9.30–12.30 and 2–5.30; last entry 1 hour before closing; guided tours possible; adm.

The site is a relic of the time when these coasts were first coming into the mainstream of Mediterranean civilization. Initially settled in the 6th century BC, it began as a fortified trading village under Greek influence, closely connected to Marseille.

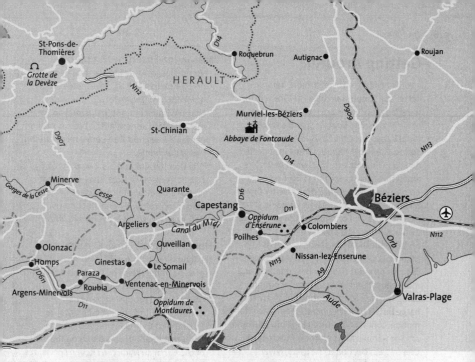

By 250 BC it may have had as many as 10,000 people, though later in that century it was wrecked, possibly by Hannibal on his way to Italy during the Punic Wars. Under Roman rule it revived again, refounded as a Roman colony, but in peaceful, settled times it could not survive. The cramped, difficult site was good for defence; when this was no longer necessary, people and trade gradually moved down to the plains and the coast, and Ensérune was largely abandoned by the 1st century AD.

Not much remains of the town: the foundations of the wall, cisterns and traces of habitations can be seen. The excellent **museum** in the centre of the excavations has a collection of ceramics, including some fine Greek and Etruscan works, along with local pieces that show the strong influence of the foreigners. Just outside the town, where an ancient column with an unusual, trapezoidal capital has been re-erected, you can take in one of the oddest panoramas in France, a gigantic surveyor's pie, neatly sliced. This was the **Etang de Montady**, a roughly circular swamp reclaimed in the 13th century, when the new fields were precisely divided by drainage ditches radiating from the centre.

Canal Villages

Most of these have at least one restaurant, some have guest houses and boat rentals; all of them are agreeable spots to while away an afternoon. From Nissan, the D37 takes you to **Poilhes**, a sleepy, lovely village built around one of Paul Riquet's graceful brick canal bridges. **Capestang**, the next one, has a landmark visible for miles around: the tall, unfinished Gothic Collégiale St-Etienne, a monument to unfulfilled ambition, like Narbonne cathedral, which indeed may have been the work of the same architect.

Getting Around

You'll need a car to get around here, or better still a **mountain bike** (VTT in French); the shady tow paths are lovely for cycling. Best of all, hire a small **boat**, or spend a week on a **canal barge** (*the canal is usually open to navigation Mar–Nov*). Reputed firms include **Rive du Sud** in Colombiers, southwest of Béziers along the canal, **t** 04 67 37 14 60, **f** 04 67 37 60 03, *www.rivedefrance.com*. Also try **Crown Blue Line**, in Castelnaudary, **t** 04 68 94 52 72, **f** 04 68 94 52 73; **Connoisseur Cruisers**, 7 Quai d'Alsace, Narbonne, **t** 04 68 65 14 55, **f** 04 68 90 66 72, or **Locaboat Plaisance**, in Argens-Minervois, **t** 04 68 27 03 33, *www.locaboat. com*. No previous experience is required, and most people bring bikes along for outings along the way. Most luxurious of all are the **barge hotels** (*péniches hôtels*). For more information, contact Comité Regional du Tourisme, 417 Rue Samuel Morse, 34000 Montpellier, **t** 04 67 22 81 00, **f** 04 67 64 47 48, *www. sunfrance.net/canal*.

Tourist Information

Nissan-lez-Ensérune: t 04 67 37 14 12. *Open Mon–Fri 9–12 and 2–5.30, Sat 9.30–12.*
Capestang: Bd Pasteur, **t** 04 67 93 34 23.

Market Days

Capestang: Wed and Sun am.

Where to Stay and Eat

Can you dine well under the *platanes* of the canal? Indeed; most of the villages have at least one place with a terrace overlooking it.

Nissan-lez-Ensérune ✉ 34440

- **★★Résidence**, 35 Av de la Cave, **t** 04 67 37 00 63, **f** 04 67 37 68 63, *www.hotel-residence.com* (*inexpensive*). Antiquated charm with restaurant (*moderate*) and a more modern annexe at the bottom of the garden. *Closed mid-Dec–early Jan; restaurant closed lunchtimes.*
- **★★Via Domitia**, Colombiers, **t** 04 67 35 62 63, **f** 04 67 35 62 00 (*inexpensive*). Hotel that is part of a medical clinic but takes healthy guests too; colour TV and air-conditioning. *Café open weekdays morning and lunch.*

Homps and Le Somail ✉ 11120

Les Tonnaliers, by the port in Homps, **t** 04 68 91 14 04 (*moderate*). The terrace is a favourite stop. *Closed mid-Dec–mid-Mar.*
- **★★Auberge de l'Arbousier**, 50 Av de Carcassonne, Le Somail, **t** 04 68 91 11 24, **f** 04 68 91 12 61 (*moderate*). A charming hotel-restaurant in an old *mas* on the banks of the Canal du Midi; the kitchen specializes in cooking with local Minervois wine. *Closed mid-Feb–mid-Mar and end Oct–Nov.*
Bed and breakfast, Le Somail, **t** 04 68 46 16 02 (*inexpensive*). In a charming 17th-century house. There is also a *gîte*. *Closed Oct–Mar.*

Trèbes ✉ 11800

- **★★★Château de Floure**, 1 Allée Gaston Bonheur, Floure, **t** 04 68 79 11 29, **f** 04 68 79 04 61, *www.chateau-de-floure.com* (*expensive*). Just east of Trèbes, this ivy-covered chateau was a Romanesque abbey converted into a home by writer Gaston Bonheur; now a Relais du Silence hotel, it has an elegant French garden, with pool and tennis, comfortable rooms and a good restaurant (*expensive*). *Closed Nov–1 April.*

A detour south of Capestang and just west of the village of Ouveillan will take you to an unusual and almost completely forgotten medieval monument, the **Grange de Fontcalvy**. A testament to the wealth of the Cistercian order, this was a key stronghold of Fontfroide Abbey (*see* pp.548–9), a fortified barn of considerable architectural sophistication, 66ft square, with ogival vaulting.

Quarante

All along, the lands around the canal have been packed full with vineyards. Further west, this continues but the countryside becomes greener and lusher, with some of the cosiest landscapes in the Languedoc. **Quarante** isn't on the canal (although there's an impressive aqueduct nearby, one of Vauban's last works (1693), over the river Quarante), but it is worth a 4km side trip, north on D36/D37E, for its severe and dignified Romanesque church, the Abbatiale Ste-Marie, built between 982 and 1053. The *trésor* contains a marble sarcophagus of the 3rd century, decorated with angels and portraits of the deceased, and a remarkable example of Montpellier silver-smithing from the 1440s, a very leonine bust of St John the Baptist with almond eyes and a Gallic nose. Quarante also has a pretty picnic-ground and park (with a pool), in the grounds of the Château de Rouière. Back on the canal, the string of villages continues: **Argeliers** and **Le Somail**, a sweet hamlet where the bargemen traditionally stop to take their afternoon naps. It has a great second-hand bookshop, an ice house, chapel and a quirky **Musée des Chapeaux** (*t 04 68 46 19 26; open summer Mon–Sat 9–12 and 2–7, Sun 2–7; winter 2–5; adm*), with thousands of hats.

Further west are **Ventenac-en-Minervois**, **Paraza**, **Roubia** and **Argens-Minervois**, a once-fortified village with a ruined castle. The canal at this point runs parallel to the river Aude, and in places the two are only a few hundred feet apart. Near Roubia, the canal passes over a small stream on the **Pont-Canal de Répudre**. Paul Riquet designed this, too; it is the oldest canal bridge in France. Further west comes **Homps**, with another ruined castle, built by the Knights Hospitallers, and then a long, empty, very scenic stretch leading towards **Marseillette** in the Minervois, followed by **Trèbes**, a fortified village with a triple set of locks and an impressive canal bridge over the Orb built by Vauban in 1686.

The Minervois

This is a *pays* with plenty of character, though not many people. With typical French irony, the Minervois suffered grievously from poverty and rural depopulation throughout the 20th century – then, just when everyone was gone, vintners improved the quality of their Minervois wines. They have become increasingly popular across France and the region's prosperity has returned. The Corbières, just over the Aude, tells much the same story. In other ways, too, the Minervois is a prelude to the Corbières: the sharp contrast of tidy vineyards with ragged country and outcrops of weird, eroded limestone, the sense of strangeness and isolation – in a region of France that has been inhabited for more or less 200,000 years.

From the Canal to Minerve

Olonzac, just north of the canal, is the centre of the wine district and the closest thing the eastern Minervois has to a town. It is an attractive place with cafés under the trees and a holiday feel on warm days. There is a collection of archaeological finds at the *mairie*. To the northwest, some of the most civilized landscapes in the Minervois lie around the village of **Siran**, with three little-known attractions: to the east, an impressive dolmen called the **Mourel des Fades** ('fairy dolmen') and the 12th-century country church of **St-Germain-de-Cesseras**, with a beautifully sculpted apse.

Tourist Information

Olonzac: Place de la Mairie, **t** 04 68 91 34 95. *Open Mon–Sat 10–12 and 4–6.*
Minerve: t 04 68 91 81 43. *Open Tues–Sat 9–12 and 2–6.*

Market Days
Olonzac: Tues.
Laure-Minervois: Sun.

Where to Stay and Eat

Siran ✉ 34210
★★★Villa d'Eléis, Av du Château, **t** 04 68 91 55 98, **f** 04 68 91 48 34 (*expensive–moderate*). Offers charming comfortable rooms and a good restaurant (*expensive*). *Closed Tues and Wed in winter and mid-Jan–mid-Feb.*

Olonzac and Minerve ✉ 34210
★Relais Chantovent, 17 Grande Rue, Minerve, **t** 04 68 91 14 18, **f** 04 68 91 81 99 (*inexpensive*). The only hotel in Minerve, with just seven rooms; also a fine restaurant with a terrace overlooking the gorges, serving truffles (*expensive– moderate*). *Closed mid-Dec–mid-Mar; restaurant closed Sun eve and Mon.*
Restaurant du Minervois, 2 Rue Ecoles, Olonzac, **t** 04 68 91 20 73 (*moderate*). *Closed Sat lunch, and eves in winter.*
Auberge de St-Martin, south of Minerve in Beaufort, **t** 04 68 91 16 18 (*moderate*). A sweet old *mas* with a shady terrace, offering wood-fire grilled meat and fish and a variety of regional dishes which change seasonally. *Closed Mon in April–Oct; Sun eve, Mon and Tues in Oct–Mar.*

Both are signposted off the D168. Another country church, the **Chapelle de Centeilles**, north of Siran, is a unique survival, entirely covered inside with frescoes from the 13th to the 15th centuries; there is also a fragment of Roman mosaic, found nearby.

From Olonzac, the narrow D10 will take you up into the heights of the Minervois, to **Minerve**, a town as old as any in Languedoc. Minerve is a natural place for a defensible settlement, on a steep rock between two rivers, but that does not explain why the area around it should have been so popular for so long. Traces of habitation dating back 170,000 years have been found in its caves, and Neolithic dolmens abound. The Celts and the Romans built the town itself, and in the Middle Ages it was a feudal stronghold with a Cathar slant. Minerve accepted refugees from the sack of Béziers in 1209; Simon de Montfort followed them and took the town after a two-month siege, followed by the usual butchery and burning of 140 Cathars at the stake.

Minerve today counts little over a hundred inhabitants; nothing has been done or built since Unspeakable Simon's visit, and the medieval relic on its dramatic site has become a peaceful and unambitious tourist attraction, with potters, artists and souvenir stands filling the spaces left by all the folks who have moved to the cities in the last 80 years. Parts of the walls are still in good nick, but all that is left of the château is a single, slender, octagonal tower; the Minervois call it the 'candela'. There are narrow medieval alleys, gates and cisterns, a simple 12th-century church with a white marble altar from 456, said to be the oldest in Europe, and a small **archaeology museum** (**t** 04 68 91 22 92; *open May–Nov daily; weekends only the rest of the year, call for opening times*) with some fossils and prehistoric finds, across from a *caveau de dégustation* of Minervois wines. The **Musée Hurepel** (*Rue des Martyrs,* **t** 04 68 91 12 26, www.ocmusic.org/liens/hurepel*) tells the Cathar story (*see pp.36–8*) with figurines.

The real attractions, however, are out in the country. A short walk from town, there are **'natural bridges'** – really more like tunnels, eroded through the limestone by streams. To the west extends the narrow, blushing pink **Canyon de la Cesse**, and determined hikers can seek out a collection of caves and dolmens north of this, at Bois Bas, off the D147.

The Seven-Sided Church of Rieux-Minervois

t 04 68 78 13 98; open 9–12 and 2–6.

West of Siran, the Minervois flattens out into the valley of the Argent-Double ('silver water'; *dubron* was a Celtic word for water, and the Romans made it *Argentodubrum*). A handsome old bridge spans it for the village of Rieux, built around one of the most uncanny medieval monuments in France.

The seven-pointed star is the recurring mystic symbol of the Midi. The Cathar castle at Montségur, in Ariège, was laid out subtly to fit inside its angles, the Félibres of Provence used it as part of their emblem, and it has been a recurring theme in folk art. Just what it means has never been adequately explained; neither has anyone ventured an explanation for the presence in this unremarkable Minervois village of what may be the only seven-sided church anywhere. Dedicated to the Virgin, the church was built some time in the late 12th century, exactly when, why and by whom no one knows. A medieval scholar would have cited Scripture: *Wisdom has built her house; she has set up her seven pillars* (Proverbs 1:9), also recalling that the Divine Wisdom was identified (at the time) with the Virgin Mary. Clearly, this temple opens a deep vein of intellectual medieval mysticism, full of geometry and allegory and not entirely recoverable by our minds. Its builders, pressed to explain why the central heptagon around the altar has four squat pilasters and three columns, might have mumbled something about the 'Marriage of Heaven and Earth' – the four-square world and the spiritual triangle. Modern investigators have also discovered various

Tourist Information

Rieux-Minervois: 1 Rue de République, **t** 04 68 78 13 98, **f** 04 68 78 32 32. *Open Jdaily 10–12 and 2–6.*

Market Days

Rieux-Minervois: Tues, Thurs and Sat.

Where to Stay and Eat

Rieux-Minervois ✉ **11160, and Around**

★★Logis de Merinville, Av Georges Clemenceau, **t** 04 68 78 12 49 (*inexpensive*). An atmospheric 19th-century stone inn in the village centre, with lovely rooms, 1930s furniture and a good restaurant. *Half-board only. Closed Oct–April.*

★★★Château de Violet, Route de Pepieux, outside Peyriac-Minervois, **t** 04 68 78 10 42, **f** 04 68 78 30 01, *www.chateau-de-violet. com* (*expensive–moderate*). The Minervois' luxury resort: a restored farmhouse, elegant and sumptuously furnished, with swimming pool and gardens and a restaurant (*moderate*). *Booking essential for restaurant.*

★★Hôtel d'Alibert, Place de la Mairie, Caunes-Minervois, **t** 04 68 78 00 54 (*moderate*). A sweet little place to stay or eat, with good regional food in the restaurant (*moderate*). *Closed mid-Dec–mid-Mar, and Sun eve and Mon.*

Rieux-Minervois

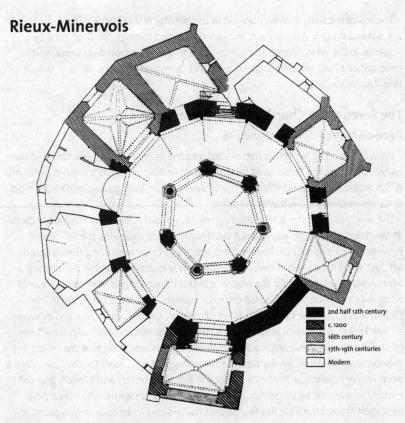

2nd half 12th century
c. 1200
16th century
17th-19th centuries
Modern

series of ley lines based on this site; according to them, the line of the midsummer sunrise passes from an altar inside the church through a (now closed-up) window and begins an alignment that goes as far as Minerve and St-Guilhem-le-Désert, passing several chapels dedicated to St John along the way.

The ambition of the builders of this church, and their resources, are seen in the sculptural detail inside, entrusted to the Master of Cabestany. Most of the capitals carved with fanciful foliage are by his workshop, while the Master himself is believed to have done the capitals with the reliefs of lions and the *Assumption of the Virgin*. Building in heptagons certainly must have tried the patience and mathematical know-how of a 12th-century mason; we can admire their careful work, especially the seven-sided belfry, directly over the altar, and the tricky toroid vaulting that connects the heptagon with the 14-sided exterior wall. Over the centuries, a number of chapels have been built along the edges of the church; its exterior aspect, along with the original portal, are now lost.

Caunes-Minervois

The marble for Rieux's church came from **Caunes-Minervois**, just up the Argent-Double, which is also the source of the marble for the Paris Opera and parts of

Wine: Minervois

Rough and arid, protected from the cold winds of the north by the mountains, the sun-bleached region of AOC Minervois stretches from Carcassonne almost to St-Chinian. Its glories are supple but powerful red wines, dominated by mourvèdre, grenache, syrah and carignan, and with a lingering bouquet reminiscent of the *maquis* that have long been one of the gems of Languedoc – the best wines may require several years in the cellar to reach their best. Along with Fitou, Minervois is the region's wine that has built the best reputation for itself in recent years; it can be found in shops all over France and is also widely available in British supermarkets. In particular, seek out wines from the new *appellation* **Minervois La Livinière**, where the *cave* cooperative is especially good.

Try the excellent wines produced by the **Château St-Eulalie** (which looks more like a farm than a château) at La Livinière (all first on **t** 04 68 91 42 72); or at Laure-Minervois taste the dark, exquisite Cuvée Alexandre at **Château Fabas**, on the Rieux road, **t** 04 68 78 17 82 (*open 8–12 and 2–7*); also try the **Cave Coopérative Tour St-Martin** at Peyriac, **t** 04 68 78 11 20, **f** 04 68 78 17 93. If you're passing by the Canal du Midi, you can stop to try some Minervois wines right by the canal at two spots: the **Domaine de Sérame**, **t** 04 68 27 59 00, an old *mas* just outside Argens, or the *cave cooperative* at the **Château de Ventenac**, Ventenac, **t** 04 68 43 25 10 (*ring in advance*). Another estate worthy of mention is **Château de Paraza**, high above the canal in Paraza, 11200 Lézignan, **t** 04 68 43 20 76, run by the Baronne Dominique de Girard Passerieux.

The white wines of Minervois are amongst the revelations of recent years, both clean and packed with character. Good examples are to be found at **Château La Grave** at Badens, **t** 04 68 79 16 00 (*open 9–12 and 2–6; closed Wed and Sun*), and Château de Paraza (*see above*).

In this area north of Carcassonne there is a relatively new *appellation* called **Cabardès**. Here, mainly red wines are produced from Bordeaux grape varieties, resulting in rounded, quite stylish wines. Producers to look out for in this area are Château de Ventenac (*see above*) and **Château Peannautier t** 04 68 72 65 29, *www.vignobles-lorgeril.com*. You can smaple the wines with food at the café in the wine shop.

One of the most innovative producers in Minervois is **Château Maris**, based at La Livinière and part of the Comte Cathare group, **t** 04 68 91 42 63, *www.comte cathare.com*. Their vineyards are all in conversion to organic viticulture and the wines are notable for their depth and purity of flavour.

Versailles. It is rare for good stone in so many tints, from green to pink to reddish-orange, to occur in one place. The quarries, neatly geometrical excavations around Caunes, make an unusual sight. There is a path along the edge of the quarries with huge chunks of marble left lying around (signposted from the village). Over the centuries they have made Caunes more prosperous and open to the world than its Minervois neighbours. Its streets show some modest palaces, such as the Hôtel d'Alibert on the main square, along with the former abbey church of **St-Pierre-et-**

St-Paul (*t 04 68 78 09 44; open 10–12 and 2–7; adm*), founded by Benedict of Aniane, a hotchpotch of Gothic, Romanesque and later styles, conserving some odd capitals from the Carolingian original and a good 13th-century portal. You can also visit the cloister. North of town, the D620 leads past the quarries into the narrow and scenic **Gorge de l'Argent-Double**.

The Montagne Noire

Even wilder than the Minervois, if not as unusual, the bleak, brooding Black Mountain is an 18-mile-wide stretch of peaks, taller than their neighbours and diffi-cult to access until modern times. The long ridge in fact divides two climates: its north face, looking towards the Massif Central (the Montagne Noire is the southern-most point of the range), has an Atlantic climate, while the south is Mediterranean. Its slate-roofed villages have a solemn air, and their people are bent to serious moun-tain pursuits – mining and quarrying, logging and paper-making. In the old days they scratched iron and copper out of the mountain; this still continues, along with a bit of silver and gold – the deposits at Salsigne, discovered a century ago, yield around a tonne of gold each year. The trees are even more important; you'll see chestnut groves, some planted in the Middle Ages when chestnuts were a mountain staple, and also stands of foreign intruders – Scots pine and Douglas fir, important to the lumber business.

All the routes into the mountains follow narrow parallel valleys leading up from the river Aude; the first is the Argent-Double, from Caunes (*see above*). Next comes the Clamoux (on the D112), with equally impressive gorges, north of Villeneuve-Minervois; 6km up the Clamoux is **Cabrespine** with its lofty castle (Simon de Montfort slept here) and deep abyss, the **Gouffre Géant de Cabrespine** (*t 04 68 26 14 22; open July–Sept 10–7; Mar–June and Oct–Nov 10–12 and 2–6; closed Dec–Feb*), part of it accessible to all, including wheelchairs, and part of it left as it was, explored in four- to five-hour excursions guided by Les Safaris Souterrains (*to book, t 04 67 66 11 11, f 04 67 66 27 27*). Further up is the Gorge de Clamoux in **Pradelles-Cabardès**, where the people used to make a living by shipping ice down to the cities of the valley. Their sunken ice cham-bers are still a feature of the landscape. Above Pradelles looms **Pic de Nore**, at 3,937ft the highest point of the Montagne Noire.

Châteaux de Lastours

The next valley, that of the Orbiel (D101), is the most populous of the region, and perhaps the most beautiful. It also contains the region's landmark, the **Châteaux de Lastours** (*t 04 68 77 56 02; open daily April, May, June and Sept 10–6; July and Aug 9–8; Oct 10–5; Feb, Mar, Nov and Dec weekends and hols only 10–5; closed Jan; adm*) – not one, but four castles, in various states of picturesque ruin, all on the same hilltop to defend the Montagne Noire's mineral richness. The lords of Cabardès, bosses of the Montagne Noire before the arrival of de Montfort in 1211, built the first of them, the castles of Cabaret and Quertinheux; the two between these, Surdespine and Tour

Where to Stay and Eat

Accommodation up here is rudimentary, partly because Carcassonne (*see* next chapter) is close enough for the Montagne Noire to be an easy day trip. But you'll always eat well.

Brousses et Villaret ✉ 11390
La Galaube, Lacombe-du-Sault, **t** 04 68 26 51 23 (*moderate*). Closest to Lastours is this simple but welcoming restaurant. There are also eight rooms (*inexpensive*). *Closed Oct–April.*

Saissac ✉ 11310
Montagne Noire, Av Maurice Sarrault, **t** 04 68 24 46 36 (*inexpensive*). Has rooms and serves tasty dishes with cèpes and freshwater crayfish under its century-old trees. *Closed Oct–April.*

Montolieu ✉ 11170
Abbaye de Villelongue, west of Montolieu, **t** 04 68 76 92 58 (*inexpensive*). Simple *chambres d'hôtes* rooms to rent. *Book at least 2 wks ahead in summer.*

Régine, were added by the French kings in the 13th century. Remember the Drac, in Beaucaire? (If not, *see* p.409.) Apparently, after his embarrassment there he took refuge in the Hérault. The legendary knight Roland himself was on his trail near Lastours, and his horse left a hoof-print in a great boulder near the Châteaux, a place still called the *Saut de Roland*.

Salsigne, with its gold mine, lies just to the west of Lastours. To the east is a remarkable cave, the **Grotte de Limousis** (*t 04 68 26 14 20; open July and Aug daily 10–6; April–June and Sept daily 10.30–5.30; Mar and Oct daily 2.30–5.30; Nov Sun and hols daily 2.30–4.30; closed Dec–Feb; adm*), with unique formations of gleaming white aragonite crystals, one of which, called the *Lustre* (chandelier), is over 30ft across. Further up the valley are two of the most beautiful and unspoiled villages of the region: **Roquefère** and Mas-Cabardès; north of Roquefère, a 5km detour will take you up to a high, lovely waterfall at a place called **Cupserviès**. **Mas-Cabardès** has some half-timbered houses and a 16th-century church with a rugged octagonal belfry. In the village centre, note the pretty, carefully carved stone cross, a typical decoration of Montagne Noire villages. This one was a 16th-century gift of the weavers' guild; with its abundance of water, this region had a thriving textile trade before the black-hearted English Industrial Revolutionaries started underselling them in the 18th century. Another water-powered trade was paper; in **Brousses-et-Villaret**, west of Mas-Cabardès, you can visit an 18th-century paper mill and learn the history of paper and how to make it by hand at the **Musée du Moulin à Papier** (*t 04 68 26 67 43, www.moulinapapier.com; open for guided tours July–mid-Sept daily at 11am and hourly from 3–6; mid-Sept–June Mon–Fri 11 and 3.30, Sat, Sun and hols 11am and hourly 2.30–5.30; adm*).

Further west, the crown of the Montagne Noire is dotted with artificial lakes, part of a big hydroelectric scheme. In the valley furthest west, that of the Vernassonne, **Saissac** is another lovely village, built over a ravine and surrounded by forests. Saissac, too, has its romantically ruined, overgrown fortress, and a 10ft menhir, just to the north off the D4.

To the south, **Montolieu** (*www.montolieu.net*), balanced over the gorges of the Alzeau and Dure, has become the 'Village du Livre', a centre of the local book-making trade: in the middle of this pretty floral village the **Musée Michel Braibant** (*t 04 68 24 80 04; open 10–12 and 2–6; adm*), traces the history of bookbinding and printing, and there are a dozen or so bookshops, and summer book fairs. West on the D64, the 13th-century **Abbaye de Villelongue** (*t 04 68 76 00 81; open May–Oct 10–12 and 2–6.30; rest of the year by appt; guided tours, English spoken; adm*) has little artistic interest, but is one of the best preserved monastic complexes in Languedoc.

For regions to the west and south, *see* the next chapter. North of Pic de Nore, the Montagne Noire descends to rolling hills, in a vast forested area that is part of the Parc Régional Naturel du Haut-Languedoc. Beyond the boundaries of this book, in the Tarn, **Castres** offers its **Musée Goya** (*t 05 63 71 59 30; open Tues–Sat 9–12 and 2–5; Sun 10–12 and 2–5; closed Mon except July and Aug; adm*), a small collection of paintings by the Spanish magician, and other minor works by Velázquez, Murillo, Valdes Leal and Alonso Cana. There's also a museum devoted to socialist hero Jean Jaurès (*2 Place Pélisson, t 05 63 72 01 01*)

Narbonne, the Corbières and the Aude

17

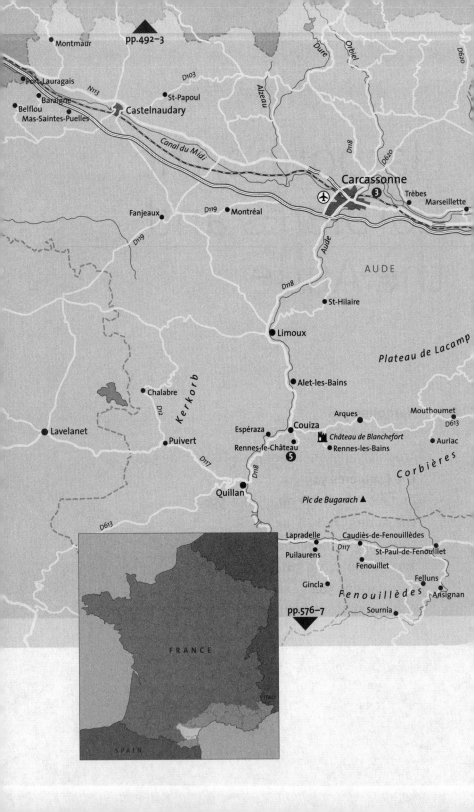

Montmaur

Port-Lauragais

Baraigne

Belflou

Mas-Saintes-Puelles

N113

Castelnaudary

D103

St-Papoul

Canal du Midi

Aizeau

Dure

Orbiel

D620

D118

D620

Carcassonne **3**

Trèbes

Marseillette

Fanjeaux

D119

Montréal

D119

Aude

AUDE

D118

St-Hilaire

Limoux

Plateau de Lacamp

Chalabre

K e r k o r b

D12

Lavelanet

Puivert

D117

Alet-les-Bains

Espéraza

Rennes-le-Château **5**

Couiza

Arques

Château de Blanchefort

Rennes-les-Bains

Mouthoumet

D613

Auriac

C o r b i è r e s

D118

Quillan

Pic de Bugarach ▲

D613

Lapradelle

Caudiès-de-Fenouillèdes

D117

St-Paul-de-Fenouillet

Puilaurens

Fenouillet

Felluns

Gincla

Ansignan

F e n o u i l l è d e s

Sournia

FRANCE

ITALY

SPAIN

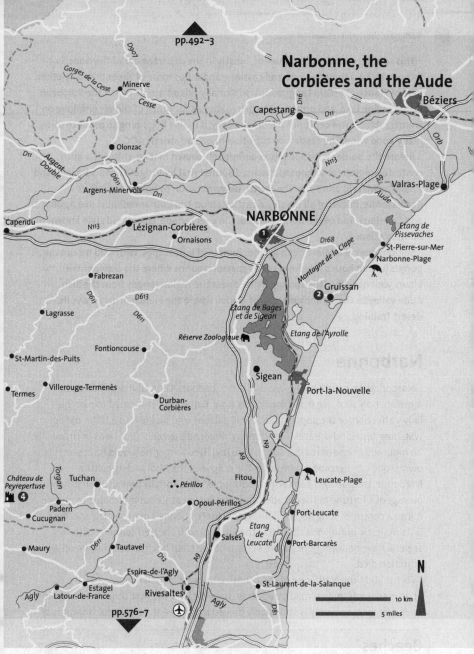

pp.492–3

Narbonne, the Corbières and the Aude

Béziers

Gorges de la Cesse
Minerve
Cesse

Capestang

Olonzac

Argens-Minervois

Valras-Plage

Aude

Capendu

NARBONNE

Lézignan-Corbières
Ornaisons

Étang de Pissevaches

St-Pierre-sur-Mer
Narbonne-Plage

Fabrezan

Montagne de la Clape

Gruissan

Lagrasse

Étang de Bages et de Sigean

Étang de l'Ayrolle

Fontioncouse

Réserve Zoologique

St-Martin-des-Puits

Termes
Villerouge-Termenès

Sigean

Port-la-Nouvelle

Durban-Corbières

Château de Peyrepertuse

Torgan

Tuchan

Périllos

Fitou

Leucate-Plage

Padern

Opoul-Périllos

Port-Leucate

Cucugnan

Maury

Tautavel

Salses

Étang de Leucate

Port-Barcarès

Espira-de-l'Agly

Agly

Estagel
Latour-de-France

Rivesaltes

St-Laurent-de-la-Salanque

Agly

N

10 km

5 miles

pp.576–7

Highlights

1 Narbonne, and the finest Gothic cathedral in the Midi
2 Gruissan, with its beach cottages on stilts
3 The walled vision of medieval Carcassonne
4 The vertiginous Château de Peyrepertuse
5 Rennes-le-Château, Languedoc's capital of Templar mysteries

This southern corner of Languedoc, mostly in the *département* of the Aude, is famous for two things – wine and castles – and it has more of them than any other part of France. Western Languedoc traditionally fills an ample bay of the European Union's wine lake, and provides the raw materials for much of the *vin ordinaire* on French tables. After centuries of complacency, it is also beginning to produce some really good wine. The castles, on the other hand, are strictly AOC.

Before the border with Spain was definitively drawn in 1659, this was a hotly contested region for a thousand years, disputed first by Visigoths and Saracens, and finally by Madrid and Paris. The French determination to hold it has left us Carcassonne, queen of all medieval castles, cloud-top Cathar redoubts like Aguilar and Quéribus, and over a hundred others, in every shape, colour and style known to military science.

Seldom does the Midi offer a greater jumble of landscapes, with wild mountain gorges just an hour's ride from sandy coastal lagoons where the *tramontane* blows your hat off in the spring; in greenness the region ranges from the lush Aude valley to the scrubby plateau of Opoul, where the French Army enjoys its desert training.

Narbonne

Narbonne gave birth to the last of the troubadours, Guiraut Riquier (d. 1292). A melancholy soul, like many men of his time, Riquier never seemed to earn his lady's affection, or the appreciation of his patrons, and he grew to a bitter old age watching his world unravel. '*Mas trop suy vingutz als derriers*' (but I was born too late) he mourned in one of his last songs. If he had lived longer, he would have seen his own proud city become a symbol for the eclipse of the Midi and its culture. Narbonne, Languedoc's capital and metropolis since Roman times, suffered some outrageous fortune in the decades after Riquier's death, enough trouble to plunge it into a centuries-long decline. The symbol for Narbonne's own particular eclipse is its majestic unfinished cathedral, the arches and truncated columns of its skeletal nave haunting the square in front of the plain brick façade thrown up when ambition died.

Fortunately, the Narbonne of today has no interest in melancholy whatsoever. Thanks to roads and railroads, trade has come back for the first time since the Middle Ages. The local economy is still largely fuelled by plonk – the bountiful vineyards of

Beaches

From Narbonne south into Spain is really just one long beach. The sand is perfect and the lagoons often give you the feeling of being isolated on a desert island, amongst sand dunes and flocks of summer flamingos.

Best Beaches

Gruissan Plage: setting for the cult film *Betty Blue*; a wide expanse of sand populated by curious raised houses on stilts.

Port-la-Nouvelle: un-chic; watch the tankers roll by.

La Frangui: a simple, old-fashioned family beach.

the Corbières and other nearby regions. The city is also finding a new vocation as an industrial centre, and its outskirts have developed accordingly. With a population of only 48,000, Narbonne can nonetheless sometimes fool you into thinking it a metropolis. With its impressive medieval monuments, boulevards and lively streets, it is quite a happy and contented town – one of the Midi's most agreeable urban destinations – with an excellent museum and the best cathedral in the south.

History

Colonia Narbo Martius, a good site for a trading port along the recently built Via Domitia, began by decree of the Roman Senate in 118 BC. The colony rapidly became the most important city of southern Gaul, renowned for its beauty and wealth. Under Augustus it was made the capital of what came to be known as the province of Gallia Narbonensis. After 410, it briefly became the headquarters of the Visigoths, and continued as their northernmost provincial capital until the Arab conquest of Spain in the 8th century; the Arabs took Narbonne but could not hold it, and Pépin the Short reclaimed it for the Frankish Kingdom in 759.

In the 12th century, Narbonne entered its second golden age. Under a native dynasty of viscounts the city maintained its independence for two centuries and began its great cathedral (1272). The famous Viscountess Ermengarde, who ruled for five decades after 1134, managed the ship of state with distinction while presiding over a 'court of love' graced by troubadours such as Bernart de Ventadorn. The troubled 14th century was murder on Narbonne, however. As if wars and plagues were not enough, the harbour began to silt up; finally, even the river Aude decided to change its course and desert the city, ruining its trade. By the end of the century, the city had shrunk to a mere market town, albeit one with an archbishop and a very impressive cathedral.

Stagnation continued until the 20th century, despite the efforts of the indefatigable Paul Riquet in the 1680s; though his Canal du Midi met the sea further north, Riquet began a branch canal, the Robine, that followed the old course of the river through Narbonne. Powerful interests in Béziers and Sète, however, kept it from being completed until 1786; the man who finally saw it through was Narbonne's last archbishop, an Irishman named Arthur Dillon, who played an important role in the city's history. Only in the last hundred years has Narbonne started to revive, thanks to industry and the wine trade; since the Second World War it has overtaken Carcassonne as the largest city of the Aude *département*.

The City Centre

Narbonne is a city of surprises. If you come by train or bus, the first thing you're likely to see is the gargantuan, horrific **Palais du Travail** on Bd Frédéric Mistral, a full-blown piece of 1930s Stalinist architecture with statuary to match. Turn the corner on to Rue Jean-Jaurès, though, and you'll be following the **Canal de la Robine** into the centre of the city, lined with a delightful park called the **Jardin Entre Deux Villes**. Behind the Hôtel de Ville, the **Pont des Marchands** is covered with shops, a charming miniature version of Florence's Ponte Vecchio.

Getting There and Around

By Train

Narbonne is an important rail junction, in the middle of the main Bordeaux–Toulouse–Nice route across the Midi; there are frequent connections (about 6 a day) to Perpignan, Toulouse, and to Béziers and the other coastal cities to the east.

The railway station is just north of the centre, on Bd Frédéric Mistral.

By Bus

The *gare routière*, on Av Carnot, offers coach services that largely duplicate the trains; there will also be a bus or two a day to Gruissan, Leucate and along the coast.

By Boat

If you haven't any particular destination in mind, take a trip on the **canal boat** (*coche d'eau*) that traverses the Canal de la Robine and the coastal lagoons; in season it leaves every morning except Monday from the Pont des Marchands, and goes as far as Port-la-Nouvelle on the coast (**t** 04 68 49 12 40). Otherwise rent a **boat**, on the Quai d'Alsace north of the railway bridge, **t** 04 68 65 14 55.

Tourist Information

Narbonne: Pl Roger Salengro, **t** 04 68 65 15 60, **f** 04 68 65 59 12, *www.mairie-narbonne.fr.*

Open mid-Sept–mid-June Mon–Sat 8.30–12 and 2–6; mid-June–mid-Sept Mon–Sat 8–7 and Sun 9.30–12.30.
Post office: 19 Bd Gambetta.

Market Days

Daily am: Les Halles.
Thurs: outdoor market.

Local Wine

For a wide selection of Languedoc wines, the **Palais du Vin** at Domaine de St-Crescent on the Route de Perpignan outside Narbonne, **t** 04 68 41 49 67, *www.lacavedupalais.com*, can't be beaten.

Where to Stay

Narbonne ✉ 11100

Most of the cheaper places are around the station, especially on or around Av Pierre Semard.

★★★**La Residence**, 6 Rue du 1er Mai, **t** 04 68 32 19 41, **f** 04 68 65 51 82 (*moderate*). Near the cathedral in an old *hôtel particulier*, with calm, well-equipped rooms and a garage. Closed mid-Jan–mid-Feb.

★★★**Languedoc**, 22 Bd Gambetta, **t** 04 68 65 14 74, **f** 04 68 65 81 48, *www.hoteldu languedoc.com* (*moderate–inexpensive*). A formerly gracious old establishment, now a little down-at-heel. It has a good restaurant and bar-crêperie.

Palais des Archevêques

Narbonne's centre is the busy **Place de l'Hôtel de Ville**; in the middle of the square a recently discovered section of the Via Domitia is cleverly displayed in its original bed and alignment. Standing over this countersunk exhibit and looking at the entrance to the Rue Droite on the northeast side of the square and the Pont des Marchands opposite, you see a pair of steel strips, set in the ground, tracing the edge of the old highway to the two streets. This gives the rather eerie feeling that only a dust cover has been thrown over ancient Narbo Martius. Facing the square, the twin façades of the **Palais des Archevêques** were blessed with a romantic Gothic restoration by the master himself, Viollet-le-Duc, in the 1840s; opinion has been divided ever since over whether this 19th-century fancy was an improvement on the austere 13th-century original it replaced. The passage between the two buildings (the Palais Neuf on the left, and the Palais Vieux on the right) leads to a small courtyard, and the

France, 6 Rue Rossini, t 04 68 32 09 75, f 04 60 65 50 30, *www.hotelnarbonne.com* (*moderate–inexpensive*). On a quiet side street near the covered market.

*La Dorade**, 44 Rue Jean-Jaurès, t 04 68 32 65 95, f 04 68 65 81 62 (*inexpensive*). But for the lack of parking and a bit of street noise, this would be perfect. Narbonne's old 'Grand Hôtel', with marble telamones holding up the balcony, this establishment is still well kept, centrally located overlooking the canal, and a good bargain. *Closed mid-Nov–mid-Dec.*

****Will's Hôtel**, 23 Av Pierre Semard, t 04 68 90 44 50, f 04 68 32 26 28, *http://willshotel-narbonne.com* (*inexpensive*). It's not run by a Will, and the present owners can't imagine who Will might have been, but it is still a comfortable and friendly place.

Hôtel du Lion d'Or, Av Pierre Semard, t 04 68 32 06 92, f 04 68 65 51 13 (*inexpensive*). Small family-run hotel with a good line in wine-tastings.

*Hôtel de la Gare**, 7 Av Pierre Semard, t 04 68 32 10 54 (*inexpensive*). Very nice for its price.

Eating Out

As you might expect after a tour of their wonderful market, the Narbonnais are a gastronomically fastidious lot; their restaurants reflect this, with a minimum of pretension.

Table St Crescent, Rte de Perpignan, t 04 68 41 37 37 (*expensive*). One of Narbonne's top restaurants is outside town at the Palais du Vin. A vine-covered terrace shelters a modern stylish establishment specializing, of course, in the best regional wines and dishes. *Book. Closed Sun eve and Mon.*

Le Petit Comptoir, 4 Bd du Maréchal Joffre, t 04 68 42 30 35 (*moderate*). For more adventurous dishes. *Closed Sun and Mon.*

Le Billot, 22 Rue de l'Ancienne Porte de Béziers, t 04 68 32 70 88 (*moderate*). East of the centre, near a delightful park called the Place Thérèse et Léon Blum. Specializes in meat dishes – beef, lamb, duck and pork. *Closed Mon, and Tues lunch.*

Alsace, 2 Av Pierre Semard, t 04 68 65 10 24 (*moderate*). This friendly brasserie with a veranda is a good source of fresh seafood. *Closed Tues and Wed.*

Le Castel, 26 Bd du Dr Lacroix, t 04 68 41 35 07 (*cheap*). A wide choice of pizzas; also steaks and chops with good salads. *Closed Mon.*

Activities

On a wet day in Narbonne, you could do worse than head out of town on the N9 towards Perpignan to **L'Espace de Liberté** (t 04 68 42 17 89, *www.espaceliberte.com*; *open daily*), a giant aquatic park with three huge swimming pools, slides, ten-pin bowling and ice skating.

entrances to Narbonne's two excellent museums, the Musée d'Art et d'Histoire and the Musée Archéologique.

The parts of the Archbishops' Palace not used for museums house Narbonne's **Hôtel de Ville**. In the Palais Neuf, the 1628 Hall of the Synods has original Aubusson tapestries. Now a reception room for the city, it was once the political centre of the region; Narbonne's archbishop had the right of presiding over the *Etats-Généraux*, or parliament, of Languedoc, though that body moved to Pézenas in 1456.

Musée d'Art et d'Histoire

t 04 68 90 30 54; open daily April–Sept 9.30–12.15 and 2–6; Oct–Mar Tues–Sun 10–12 and 2–5; joint adm with the Musée Archéologique, Musée de l'Horreum and Musée Lapidaire valid for three days.

This museum occupies the old archbishops' apartments; it is reached by an elegant stair from the 1620s, decorated with a bust of the Venetian historian Andrea Morosini and a bronze Capitoline Wolf, sent by the city of Rome for Narbonne's 2,000th birthday. These reminders of Italy are perfectly fitting, for this museum could easily pass for one of the great aristocratic galleries of Rome. Most of the collection belonged to the archbishops; they must have acquired a Roman taste on sojourns there. The sumptuous rooms of these princes of the Church have been well preserved, beginning with the chapter house, or **Salle des Audiences**, where there is a portrait of the redoutable Archbishop Dillon (the last of the line – his period of office was rudely interrupted by the Revolution in 1792), and an *Equestrian Louis XIV* by Van der Meulen – a pompous, quite offensive portrait, typical of the Sun King's use of art as political propaganda. Louis slept here in 1642, in the adjacent **Chambre du Roi**. The 1632 ceiling frescoes are by local talent, the Rodière brothers: harmless *Muses* that look more like nursery-school teachers. Note the floor, a restored Roman mosaic in a labyrinth pattern.

The third room, the **Grande Galerie**, contains some of the best paintings: a gloomy landscape by Gaspard Dughet and an intense *St Jerome* by Salvator Rosa (both artists were favourites in Rome), a Canaletto and, among many Dutch and Flemish pictures, *Wedding Dance* by Pieter Breughel the Younger. The 16th- and 17th-century enamelled plaques come from Limoges, with portraits of French kings. Opposite these, a collection of lovely faïence apothecary jars from Montpellier makes a proper introduction to the next room, the **Salle des Faïences**. These 18th-century painted ceramics come mostly from well-known French centres like Moustiers and Varange, though many are from cities such as Marseille and Montpellier, where the art has since died out.

The archbishops' chapel, the **Oratoire**, harbours a few surprises: 14th-century carved alabaster from Nottingham, an odd Byzantine icon from the Aegean, and a perfect, incandescent 15th-century Florentine *Madonna*; though anonymous (once falsely attributed to Piero della Francesca), it gracefully upstages everything else in the museum. The rest of the apartments are a grab bag: Archbishop Dillon's library, with his well-thumbed St Augustine, and his dining room. You will encounter an *azulejo* tile floor from Portugal, François Ier's vinegar pot, Beauvais tapestries with scenes from La Fontaine's fairy tales, and more good painting: a luscious Veronese (*The Anointing of King David*), portraits by Nattier and by Venice's favourite 18th-century celebrity portraitist Rosalba Carriera, a sprinkling of native and foreign followers of Caravaggio, and a tortured *St Andrew* by Ribera. There are also 19th-century works, and two new rooms showing works representing the Orient.

If you don't mind climbing 162 steps, they'll let you up into the 13th-century **Donjon Gilles Aycelin** (*open daily 10–12 and 2–5; adm*), a Gothic defence tower with a collection of medieval sculpture and good views from the top.

Musée Archéologique

Same opening hours as the Musée d'Art et d'Histoire.

It is only luck that made Nîmes the 'French Rome' while none of Narbonne's monuments have survived; the ambitious viscounts and archbishops of medieval Narbonne obviously had a greater appetite for recycling old building stone. There is, however, no shortage of remaining bits and pieces, and the best of them have been assembled here: reliefs from Narbonne's three triumphal arches and the gates of its walls, milestones from the Via Domitia, funeral monuments and a model of a Roman house. The **Chapelle de la Madeleine**, where Greek and pre-Greek ceramics are displayed, retains some fragments of its original 14th-century frescoes; it also offers the best view of the apse and buttresses of the adjacent cathedral, which is almost completely surrounded by buildings.

Christianity seems to have come late to Narbonne; the first bishop, Paul, is recorded in the 3rd century. Nevertheless, there are some Christian sarcophagi, and an unusual reliquary in the form of the Church of the Holy Sepulchre in Jerusalem. The products of other faiths here are more interesting: a Greek statue of a *Drunken Silenus*, altars dedicated to Cybele and Attis, and an image of Priapus, that mythological embarrassment, this time at least keeping it decently covered.

Cathédrale St-Just

This can be entered through the fine 14th-century **cloister**, near the entrance to the museums, a Gothic quadrangle with leering gargoyles. A better way, though, is to circumnavigate the huge bulk of the cathedral and palace complex towards the west front and the **Cour St-Eutrope**, a spacious square that occupies the unfinished two-thirds of the cathedral itself. On every side rise truncated pilasters, walls and bases of arches, witness to medieval Narbonne's ambition and the 14th-century disasters that stopped it cold.

This is the third church to occupy the site; the first was a basilica from the reign of Emperor Constantine, the second a Carolingian rebuilding of AD 890. The present church was begun in 1272, at the height of the city's fortunes. Funds were hardly lacking; the cornerstone was sent by Pope Clement IV, a former Archbishop of Narbonne, and he probably contributed a little more besides. To extend the new cathedral to its planned length, it would have been necessary to rebuild a section of the city wall; in 1340 a lawsuit over this broke out between the city and the Church, a good, old-fashioned French lawsuit – just what was needed in those bad times to put an end to construction forever.

Just the same, this one-third of a cathedral is by any measure the finest in the Midi, the only one comparable to the magnificent Gothic structures of the Ile-de-France. The short nave, in fact, heightens the exuberant verticality of the 130ft apse and choir, exceeded in height only by those of Amiens and Beauvais. Throughout, the structural lines are accented with ribbing or with protruding stone courses, as if the builders wanted to leave a gentle reminder of the extraordinary technical skill that made such a building possible. The whole is done in a clean and elegant stone, grey perhaps, but a grey that here bids to be included among the colours of the spectrum.

Inside, most of the best features are in the ambulatory and its chapels. Near the altar, facing the chapels, are two remarkable archiepiscopal tombs. The **tomb of Cardinal Briçonnet** (1514) is a decorative mix of Renaissance refinement and ghoulish, grinning skeletons, typical of that age. The other, the **tomb of Cardinal Pierre de Jugie**, is an exquisite Gothic work of 1376; though much damaged, some of the original paint remains. The ambulatory chapels are illuminated by lovely 14th-century glass: the *Creation* (left chapel), the *Infancy of Christ* in the centre, and *Sts Michael, Peter and Paul* (right chapels). Some faded original frescoes can be seen in the far right chapel, and also around the main altar. The central **Chapelle de la Vierge** has something really special: unique polychrome reliefs of the late 14th century. Ruined and covered in a Baroque remodelling of 1732, these were rediscovered in the 19th century, and currently they are being restored and replaced. On the upper band (left to right): an *Annunciation* and *Kings of France*, the *Presentation at the Temple*, *Palm Sunday* and *Crucifixion*. Lower band: *Purgatory*, *Hell* and *Limbo*.

The side chapels have little to see but tapestries; in the first right is a 16th-century polychrome *Entombment of Christ* from Bavaria. Almost the entire west wall is covered by a spectacular **organ**, a mountain of carved wood and statuary that took over a hundred years to complete (1741–1856).

Cathedral Treasury

Open July–Sept Mon and Tues 11–5, Wed–Sat 11–6, Sun 2–6; Oct–June daily 2–6; adm

Don't miss the entrance to the treasury, through a tiny door in the right ambulatory chapel. Arranged in a domed chamber with odd acoustics, formerly housing the cathedral archives, the collection includes medieval reliquaries, books and a 10th-century carved ivory plaque. Here also are the most outlandish of all Narbonne's surprises: two early 16th-century Flemish tapestries unlike any others you're ever likely to see. Originally a set of 10, belonging to Archbishop François Fouquet, eight and a half have disappeared, probably ending up as insulation, mattress-stuffing and a bed for the dog. The half-tapestry depicts Adversity, from an *Allegory of Prosperity and Adversity*. Amidst a landscape of shipwrecks and earthquakes you will notice Cleopatra, Antiochus Seleucis and other celebrities of antiquity who met bad ends (all conveniently labelled), while Vulcan grinds out strife on his forge and a grinning Penury exults over the unfortunates. Part of the centrepiece also survived (on the left), dominated by an uncanny Goddess of Fortune on horseback, her face veiled.

The other tapestry, much better preserved, is a strange account of the *Creation*. The seven days of Genesis are arranged in tableaux, each with figures of the Holy Trinity, represented as three crowned, bearded old men. The iconography is unorthodox in the extreme; the symbolism throughout seems to hint at some concealed vein of medieval mysticism. In any case, the artists who created it produced a true *tour de force*, filling every corner with delightful naturalistic detail – a forest, the firmament, spring flowers and the Kingdom of the Sea. Bring the children, and see if they can spot the elephant.

Roman Narbonne

There isn't much of it. The centre of the ancient city, north of the cathedral, is a dowdy, blank-faced quarter, with a neighbourhood development group trying to interest people in fixing up the many abandoned houses. Small signs on the street corners direct you to the only Roman monument left – a warehouse or **Horreum** (*Rue Lt. Col. Deygmes; open April–Sept 9.30–12.15 and 2–6; Oct–Mar 10–12 and 2–5; adm*). Typical of the state-run warehouses of any Roman city, this is the only complete one anywhere. Just a small part has been excavated, a maze of tiny chambers; the original structure was over 500 feet long. Among the ancient fragments displayed in the various rooms is a charming relief of bear trainers and their bears bathing together. To the west, on Rue de l'Ancienne Porte Neuve, there is a 17th-century powder-house converted into a centre for temporary exhibitions.

From the Place de l'Hôtel de Ville, Rue Droite runs northwards, roughly following the route of the Roman main street; it ends at **Place Bistan** – the former Forum, though nothing remains but some re-erected columns and a modern mural painting. One block east is the 15th-century Flamboyant church of **St-Sébastien**, built over the (apocryphal) birthplace of the saint himself. A favourite of artists across southern Europe (usually depicted stuck full of arrows), Sebastian was always a popular saint owing to the belief that he could intercede against the plague.

The Bourg

This is Narbonne's medieval extension across the river (now across the canal). Cross over by the bridge in the **Promenade des Barques**, the elegant park along the canal. On the other side, the city's covered **market** is a rare sensory experience even by French market standards. The Narbonnais take great pride in it, and it once won an annual award as the best in France. Behind it, the deconsecrated 13th-century church of Notre-Dame-de-Lamourguier now houses the **Musée Lapidaire** (*t 04 68 32 45 30; open April–Sept 9.30–12.15 and 2–6; Oct–Mar 10–12 and 2–5; adm*), a large collection of architectural fragments from ancient Narbonne, displayed more or less at random. The fragments are here thanks to François Ier; on a visit, he recommended to the Narbonnais that they incorporate the vast heaps of antique rubble lying about into the new walls they were building. The walls themselves thus became an open-air museum, much commented on by travellers, until they were demolished in the 19th century and the old bits assembled here.

Follow the boulevards west, along the course of the demolished medieval walls; the modern city hospital on Boulevard Dr Lacroix incorporates the old one, the **Hôtel-Dieu**, with a grand Baroque chapel decorated by Narbonnais painters of the 1780s. Behind this, the **Maison des Trois Nourrices**, on the street of the same name, is the best surviving example of a Renaissance palace in the city; the 'three nurses' are the three classical caryatids holding up the main window.

Narbonne's other ancient church, the **Basilique St-Paul-Serge**, was first built in the 5th century, and dedicated to the first bishop of Narbonne. The present building was begun in 1229, an imposing monument that was one of the first in the south to adopt the new Gothic architecture. Three early Christian sarcophagi remain from the first church, an introduction to the catacomb-like **cemetery-crypt** beneath (*ask for the key from the vestry*). This subterranean necropolis was begun in the time of Constantine. Such burials were not peculiar to the Christians. In Rome, pagan and Christian catacombs exist side by side; parts of this one are decorated with pagan symbols, raising the intriguing possibility that this cemetery was for a time non-denominational.

Narbonne's Coast

The coastal road, more or less along the path of the Roman Via Domitia, cannot follow this complicated shoreline, a miasma of marshes and lagoons; some detours on the back roads will be necessary to see it. One big obstacle is the mouth of the Aude, northeast of Narbonne; this pretty and amiable river comes all the way from the high Pyrenees to meet an inglorious end in a boggy landscape called (literally) 'Piss-cow Swamp'.

Tourist Information

Gruissan: 1 Bd Pech-Maynaud, t 04 68 49 09 00, f 04 68 49 33 12, www.gruissan-mediterranee.com.

Sigean: Place de la Libération, t 04 68 48 14 81, www.sigean.org. Includes a little museum with stuffed birds and archaeological titbits. Open Mon–Fri 10–12 and 2–5.

Local Wine

Coteaux de Languedoc-La Clape: Château Rouquette-sur-Mer, off the D168 southwest of Narbonne-Plage in Gruissan, t 04 68 49 90 41, http://chateaurouquette.com. They also rent out gîtes and an apartment.

Château de Pech Redon, Rte de Gruissan in Narbonne, t 04 68 90 41 22.

Domaine du Fraisse, at Autignac, t 04 67 90 23 40. For whites.

Quatourze: A noble variation on Corbières, www.vitis.org/QUATOURZE.html, made along the back roads around Bages and Peyriac-de-Mer.

Fitou: Coopérative de Fitou, on the N9, t 04 68 45 71 41, www.cavedefitou.com.

Where to Stay and Eat

Narbonne-Plage ✉ 11100

Domaine d'Hospitalet, Rte de Narbonne Plage, t 04 68 45 34 47, f 04 68 45 23 49, www.domaine-hospitalet.com (expensive–moderate). A wine domaine on the Clape Massif, this incorporates an auberge with 22 pretty rooms (t 04 68 45 28 50), 7 gîtes, a restaurant gastronomique, a traditional restaurant, caves and wine-tastings, a wine museum and other small museums devoted to the history of telephones, La Poste, and old cars and craft workshops, all in an idyllic setting of vineyards overlooking the sea. Restaurant gastronomique closed Mon and Tues; traditional restaurant closed Mon.

**Hôtel de la Clape, 4 Rue Fleurs, t 04 68 49 80 15, f 04 68 75 05 05 (inexpensive). Hardly upmarket, but a wonderful address from which to write home. Closed Jan–mid-Mar.

Gruissan ✉ 11430

**Hôtel Corail, Quai Ponant in Gruissan Port, t 04 68 49 04 43, f 04 68 49 62 89 (moderate). Has a fine restaurant specializing in bouillabaisse. Closed Nov–Jan.

**Les Trois Caravelles, Av Front de Mer, Gruissan Plage, t 04 68 49 13 87, www.3caravelles.com (inexpensive). Slightly better, with reasonably priced food. Closed Oct–Easter; half-board only July and Aug.

L'Estagnol, t 04 68 49 01 27 (moderate). A popular converted fisherman's cottage at the entrance to the village, offering sumptuous seafood and fish. Closed Oct–Mar.

Bages ✉ 11100

Bages is a tiny fishing villlage overlooking the Etang de Bages, now a fashionable haunt of art galleries and fish restaurants.

Portanel, Passage du Portanel, t 04 68 42 81 66 (moderate). One of the best fish restaurants here, Portanel specializes in serving eel in every imaginable way. Closed Tues eve, Wed, and Sun eve.

Narbonne-Plage to Port-la-Nouvelle

South of the Etang de Pissevaches, one of the rare fishing villages in these parts, St-Pierre-sur-Mer, has been swallowed up by the bright, modern, characterless resort of **Narbonne-Plage**, with plenty of sand and its full whack of seaside amusements. Just to the north, near Oustalet, is Languedoc's answer to the Fontaine de Vaucluse, a 'bottomless' pool called the **Gouffre de l'Œil Doux** – the 'sweet eye' – always full of pure, fresh water, though only a mile from the sea. Beyond Narbonne-Plage, the landscape rises into the **Montagne de la Clape**, once an island and still a world in itself. Parts are lush and pine-clad, others rugged and desolate, reminiscent of a Greek island; on the lower slopes are vineyards that produce small quantities of a very good Côteaux de Languedoc wine. Near the top, the chapel of **Notre-Dame-des-Auzils** has a fascinating collection of sailors' *ex votos* – ship models, paintings and the like, many over a century old (*get the key from the tourist office at Gruissan*).

Most of those sailors came from **Gruissan**, south of La Clape. One of Narbonne's ports in the Middle Ages, Gruissan today is surrounded by lagoons and salt pans; the charming village is set in concentric rings around a ruined 13th-century castle, built to defend the approaches to Narbonne. Its tower, the Tour de Barbarousse, possibly takes its name from a visit by the famous Turkish pirate-admiral Barbarossa; in the 1540s the Ottoman sultan's fleet was briefly based in Toulon, helping the French against the Holy Roman Emperor Charles V. To Gruissan's fine beaches the government has added a marina, resulting in one of the more agreeable resorts on these coasts.

Gruissan's other landmark is the Plage des Pilotis, where neat rows of beach cottages hang in the air. The sea regularly covers the sand here, and over a century ago people began the habit of building their holiday retreats on stilts. The houses and beach gained romantic notoriety as the setting for Jean-Jacques Beineix's cult film of love, lust and bowls of chilli – *Betty Blue*.

To go further south, you'll have to return to Narbonne and circle around the **Etang de Bages et de Sigean**. This broad lagoon, with its many islands and forgotten, half-abandoned hamlets, is especially rich in waterfowl, including flamingos, cormorants, egrets and herons. For the best view, drive across part of the Etang on the narrow D105 between Bages and Peyriac-de-Mer. Boat trips can be arranged through the Cercle Nautique des Corbières, t 04 68 48 44 52, starting from the dock of a vanished medieval village, Port-Mahon, near **Sigean**, a pleasant if rather forgotten village that began as a station on the Via Domitia. Wildlife of an entirely different sort co-exists peacefully nearby at the **Réserve Africaine** north of Sigean (*t 04 68 48 20 20, www.reserveafricainesigean.fr; open summer daily 9–6.30; winter daily 9–4; adm*), a big zoo and drive-through safari park with the only white rhinoceroses, most likely, in all Languedoc; if you like zoos, it's quite a good one.

When the builders of the Canal de la Robine laid out their coastal port in 1820, they gave it the strikingly original name of **Port-la-Nouvelle**. Now France's third-largest Mediterranean port, it is a gritty, no-nonsense town of Communist stevedores, where the most prominent restaurant is called 'Le Chicken Shack', and where the waterfront promenade takes in a panorama of shiny oil tanks. It has good beaches, and for a long time it was also a resort; there are, incredibly, still some holiday motels in town. If you didn't fancy the palms and ice-cream of La Grande Motte or Cap d' Agde, a day on the beach here, watching cement barges and tankers sail past, might be just the thing. If you're sticking around, don't miss **Le Domaine de Jugnes et sa Baleine** (*t 04 68 48 00 39; open daily 10–12 and 3–7*), a skeleton of a dead whale that washed up on the beach which has been carefully reconstructed in a wine ware-house. If you know your plants, cross the Canal de la Robine to the 250ha **Ile Ste-Lucie**, abandoned and overgrown with 100 rare specimens.

Around Narbonne: Abbaye de Fontfroide

Attractions within a short drive of the city include, 11km to the north, the **Oppidum de Montlaures**, the site of a pre-Roman town, similar to the Oppidum d'Ensérune (*see* pp.524–5) and set on the same sort of hilltop. Better still, take the N113 west from the city and turn south on the D613. The first sight, to the left, is the derelict, frequently overlooked castle of **St-Pierre-des-Clars**. In its grounds, Roman coins with the images of Pompey and Brutus have been found, but the present building probably dates from the late 12th or 13th centuries. The purpose of this ineffably romantic ruin was prob-ably to protect sheep in wartime. This is not as daft as it may sound; after iron, sheep were the most valuable commodity of the Middle Ages, the wool-on-the-hoof that made the banking fortunes of so many medieval cities.

Three kilometres further down the D613, you'll see another ruined castle in the distance, madly perched on a perpendicular cliff. A perfect introduction to the forti-fied wilderness of the Corbières (*see* below), **St-Martin-de-Toques** was gradually built between the 10th and 13th centuries, and occupied until the 17th century. Someone, somehow, has got a crane up to it, and restorations are under way.

A little further along, a marked side road leads to the **Abbaye de Fontfroide** (*t 04 68 45 11 08, www.fontfroide.com; open daily for guided tours only July and Aug 9.30–6, every half-hour except 1pm; April–June and Sept–Oct 10–5.30, every 45mins except 1pm; Nov–Mar 10–4, every hour except 1pm; adm*). When the tour reaches the monks' **refectory**, the guide will take pains to point out that the fireplace is a recent addition; heating of any kind was a little too posh for medieval Cistercians. On the other hand, after inspecting the lavish church and grounds it is hard to believe the monks were giving much away to the poor – a typical medieval enigma: power and wealth, without the enjoyment of them. One of the most important Cistercian abbeys in the south, Fontfroide was founded in 1145 on the site of an earlier Benedictine house. Until its suppression in 1791, it was one of the richest and most influential of all Cistercian houses. It was largely in ruins when a local family, the Fayets, bought it early in the 20th century; they have been fixing it up a little at a time ever since – an example of the kind of shoestring private restoration that has saved so many French monuments, neglected by a traditionally stingy national government.

The best part of the tour is Fontfroide's lovely 13th-century **cloister**; its style of broad arches, inset with smaller ones, was much copied in later cloisters in Languedoc. The

12th-century **church** impresses with its proportions and Romanesque austerity; following Cistercian custom simple floral patterns constitute the only decoration. The art of making stained glass, once one of France's proudest achievements, had nearly died out by the 19th century. There has been a modest revival in the last century; one of its first productions was the excellent set of windows here, a *Last Judgement* and signs of the zodiac done in the 1920s. More glass can be seen in the **dormitory** – fascinating abstract collages of old fragments, brought here from northern French churches wrecked during the First World War. Behind the cloister is a nursery of roses where medieval varieties are grown by a local firm.

To protect the produce of its vast estates, the abbey maintained a network of fortified farms and storehouses all over the region. The most impressive is near Capestang (*see* p.526); the closest, 8km west of Fontfroide, is the **Château de Gaussan** at Bizanet. Followers of Viollet-le-Duc restored it in the 19th century, with plenty of neo-Gothic ornament and frescoes inside. In 1994 it became the home of some Benedictine monks from the abbey of Fontgombault in Indre, who cultivate vines and sell honey.

The Corbières

Thanks to wine, the Corbières has finally found its vocation. This scrubby, mountainous area, where landscapes range from classic Mediterranean to rugged Wild West, has been the odd region out since ancient times. As a refuge for disaffected Gauls, it was a headache to the Romans. In the Middle Ages, sitting astride the boundaries of France and Aragon, it was a permanent zone of combat. Local *seigneurs* littered the landscape with castles in incredible, impregnable mountain-top sites. Some of these became the last redoubts of the persecuted Cathars; nearly all of them are ruined today. For anyone with clear lungs and a little spirit, exploring them will be a challenge and a delight. Amidst the lonely landscapes of limestone crags and hills carpeted in *maquis*, the vineyards advance tenaciously across every dusty, sun-bleached hectare of arable ground.

Lézignan-Corbières and Lagrasse

The Corbières' 'capital', Lézignan-Corbières, lies halfway between Carcassonne and Narbonne, and offers, besides a few places to flop, an introduction to what the *pays* does best: the **Musée de la Vigne et du Vin** (*3 Rue Tuegot, t 04 68 27 07 57; open daily 9–7; adm*). Just south of Lézignan, on the other side of the *autoroute*, Fabrezan remembers the Corbières' most famous son in the **Salle du Souvenir Charles Cros** (*in the mairie, t 04 68 27 81 44*). Cros (1842–88) was a poet and would certainly be better known had he not also been the unluckiest inventor ever. In 1869 he invented a process of colour photography at exactly the same time as Ducos de Hauron, who got the credit for it, and in 1877 he invented the phonograph and discovered how to record sounds at the same time as Edison, who beat him to the patent office.

This northern part of the Corbières has more monasteries than castles. The greatest of these was the Abbey de Fontfroide, just west of Narbonne (*see* left). Continuing in

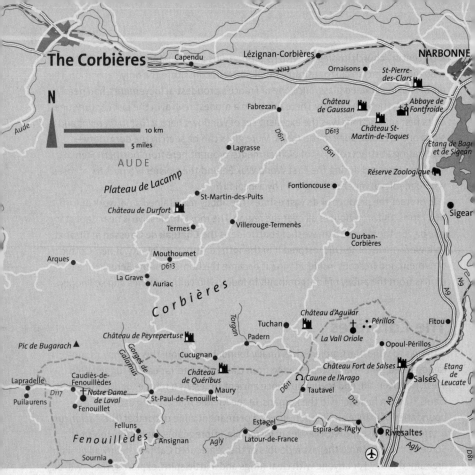

that direction on the D613/D3 takes you to **Lagrasse**, a walled medieval village that grew up around a Benedictine abbey founded in the 8th century and chartered by Charlemagne himself. Some of the houses date back to the 14th century, while the walls and the graceful arched Pont Neuf are from the 12th. The bridge leads to the **abbey** (*t 04 68 43 15 99; open July–Aug daily 10.30–6.15; May, June, Sept and Oct daily 10.30–11.45 and 2–5.30; Nov–mid-Dec daily 2–4.30; mid-Jan–mid-Feb Sat and Sun 2–4.30; mid-Feb–April daily 2–5; closed mid-Dec–mid-Jan; guided tours*), partly in ruins and partly the restored home of a Byzantine Catholic monastic community.

Southwest of Lagrasse, in one of the remotest corners of the Corbières, there is a remarkable country church at **St-Martin-des-Puits**. The oldest part, the choir, was built in the 10th century, and the nave has some still older capitals, recycled Merovingian pieces. The fanciful frescoes all around are 12th century (*ask at the mairie, t 04 68 43 11 66, for the key*).

Aguilar and Quéribus

The humble, two-lane D611 and D14 were the medieval main routes through the Corbières, connecting with the passes over the Pyrenees to Spain. Castles occur with

Getting Around

By Train

SNCF rail lines make a neat square around the Corbières – they define its boundaries almost exactly, but none of them ventures inside the region. The only useful one is from Carcassonne, following the Aude and then turning east through the Fenouillèdes, stopping at Limoux, Alet-les-Bains, Couiza and Quillan on its way to Perpignan.

By Bus

Don't count on buses either. There are some services from Perpignan's *gare routière* up the Agly valley to Maury, St-Paul and Quillan, t 04 68 35 29 02 for details or try Roussillon Voyages Autocars Cayrol, t 04 68 34 35 35.

By Car

If you're driving, keep the tank full. The Corbières is the badlands of France, and its unique fascination comes from traversing spaces as empty as central Anatolia with all the specific charms of France close at hand. There are few good roads.

Here are two possibilities for a quick tour: from Narbonne, the D613/D3 passing Fontfroide and Lagrasse, then south on the scenic D212, rejoining the D613 and ending up in Couiza. Alternatively, the N9/D611A/D611/D14/D10/D7 from south of Narbonne passes the best of the wine country, the castles of Aguilar, Peyrepertuse and Quéribus, and the Gorges de Galamus, ending up on the main D117 route for Perpignan.

Tourist Information

Lézignan-Corbières: 9 Cours de la République, t 04 68 27 05 42, *www.payscorbieresminer vois.com*. Open July and Aug Mon–Sat 9–7, Sun 10–12; Sept–June Mon–Sat 9–12 and 3–6.
Lagrasse: 6 Bd de la Promenade, t 04 68 43 11 56, f 04 68 43 16 34, *www.lagrasse.com*.

Open July and Aug 10.30–12.30 and 2.30–7; Sept–June 10.30–12.30 and 2.30.
St-Paul-de-Fenouillet ✉ 66220: 26 Bd Agly, t 04 68 59 07 57. *Open July–Aug Mon–Sat 10–12 and 3–7; Sept–June Tues–Sat 10–12 and 2–6.*

Market Days

Lézignan-Corbières: Wed.
Lagrasse: Mon.
Tuchan: Thurs.

Where to Stay and Eat

For tourism, the Corbières is virgin territory. Not only will you have trouble finding a petrol station, but accommodation has until recently been scarce – the price you pay for experiencing the least-touristy corner of the Midi. Most people make day trips, hopping between Carcassonne, Narbonne, Perpignan and Quillan. But if you want to spend some time exploring, here are most of the possibilities:

Lézignan-Corbières ✉ 11200

★★Le Tassigny, Place de Tassigny, t 04 68 27 11 51, f 04 68 27 67 31 (*inexpensive*). Has a restaurant, **Le Tournedos** (*moderate*). *Hotel closed late Jan–early Feb, and first 2 wks Oct; restaurant closed Sun eve and Mon.*
Le Patio, Bd Général Sarrail, on the outskirts, t 04 68 27 42 23 (*moderate*). Best for seafood. *Closed Sun eve and Mon.*
Stromboli, 43 Cours Lapeyrouse, t 04 68 27 00 81. A popular, better-than-average pizzeria, also with pancakes.

Ornaisons ✉ 11200

★★★Relais du Val d'Orbieu, on the D24, t 04 68 27 10 27, f 04 68 27 52 44 (*expensive*). A modernized *mas* among the fields north of the village, it has tennis, a pool and all amenities, including an excellent restaurant (*expensive*) serving fish baked with rosemary and other delicacies. *Closed Dec and Jan.*

the frequency of petrol stations on a motorway; before the kings of France asserted their authority, one wonders how many times the poor merchants had to pay tolls. Even the landscape is suggestive of castles, with limestone outcrops resembling ruined walls and bastions.

Auberge du Vieux Puits, Av St Victor, Fontjoncousse (off the D611, south of Thézan-des-Corbières), **t** 04 68 44 07 37 (*inexpensive*). Join the Narbonnais who make a special trip here to feast on the gorgeous cuisine of Gilles Goujon, who learned a trick or two at the Moulin de Mougins. There are also 8 rooms (*expensive*). *Closed Jan, Feb, Sun eve, Tues except June–mid-Sept, and Mon lunch.*

Lagrasse ✉ 11220

L'Hostellerie des Corbières, 9 Av de la Promenade, **t** 04 68 43 15 22, **f** 04 68 43 16 56 (*moderate*). A *Logis de France* hotel in a *maison de maître*, with a decent restaurant looking out over the vines (*moderate*). *Closed mid-Nov–mid-Feb; restaurant closed Wed.*

Villesque-des-Corbières ✉ 11360

Château Haut Gléon, **t** 04 68 48 85 95, **f** 04 68 48 46 20 (*moderate*). A wine estate in the Corbières hills that's worth seeking out, with comfortable stylish accommodation available in the renovated stable wing and works of art in the garden. There's no restaurant (most go to the Auberge du Vieux Puits, *see* above), but wine-tasting is, of course, offered and they sell olive oil.

Cucugnan ✉ 11350

★★Auberge du Vigneron, 1 Rue Achille-Mir, **t** 04 68 45 03 00, **f** 04 68 45 03 08 (*inexpensive*). The only hotel, but a good one, with just 6 cosy rustic rooms and a restaurant (*moderate*) in a former wine cellar with simple but fragrant dishes. *Closed mid-Nov–Feb.*

Tautavel ✉ 66720

Le Petit Gris, Route d'Estagel, **t** 04 68 29 42 42 (*expensive–moderate*). A very popular family restaurant with great views of the plain from big windows; they serve grilled dishes including an excellent Catalan *cargolade* of snails, pork, lamb and sausages cooked on your own personal grill. *Closed Mon.*

Maury ✉ 66460

★★Hôtel des Graves, 9 Bd Jean-Jaurès, Estagel, near Tautavel on the D117, **t** 04 68 29 00 84, **f** 04 68 29 30 26 (*moderate*). If you're passing by you can eat and/or sleep well and economically at this hotel owned by the local wine barons; Catalan specialities (*moderate–cheap*) served with wine from you know where.

L'Auberge du Grand Rocher, Rue Eloi Tresserres, Caramany, **t** 04 68 84 51 58 (*moderate*). This simply furnished restaurant in a pretty hill town is well worth the 20min drive from Maury; the terrace has lovely views over the valley. The husband-and-wife team prepare perfectly cooked local specialities such as roast lamb with thyme. Leave room for *crème brûlée* or home-made sorbet and a glass of Banyuls. *Book. July–Aug open every eve, otherwise lunch and Fri and Sat eves only; closed Jan and Feb.*

St-Paul-de-Fenouillet ✉ 66220

★★Le Chatelet, Rte de Caudies, **t** 04 68 59 01 20, **f** 04 68 59 01 29, *http://perso.wanadoo.fr/chatelet* (*inexpensive*). A *Logis de France* hotel, with a pool and restaurant. *Closed mid-Nov–mid-Mar; restaurant closed lunch.*

★La Garrigue, 10 Av Jean Moulin, **t** 04 68 59 23 89 (*inexpensive*). Smaller, central and also *Logis de France*, with restaurant (*moderate*). *Closed Sun eve and Mon except July and Aug.*

Gincla (near Puilaurens) ✉ 11140

★★Hostellerie du Grand Duc, 2 Rue de Boucheville, **t** 04 68 20 55 02, **f** 04 68 20 61 22 (*moderate–inexpensive*). A handsome old mansion with a shady garden; the restaurant serves tasty French classics. *Closed Nov–Mar; restaurant closed Wed lunch except July and Aug.*

All of the real strongholds are in ruins today. The first, one of the smaller models, is at **Durban-Corbières**, in the centre of the wine-growing region; it was built by the kings of Aragon.

Tuchan, another typically stark and dusty Corbières village, has no fewer than three ruined castles; the best of them, the impressive **Château d'Aguilar** (**t** *04 68 45 51 00,* *www.lescathares.free. fr/chateau/aguilar.html; open mid-June– mid–Sept 10–1 and 3–7; adm*) – one of the 'five sons of Carcassonne', along with Puilaurens, Quéribus, Peyrepertuse and Termes – saw plenty of action: Simon de Montfort stormed it in 1210, but the French had to take it again from rebellious barons 30 years later; over the next 200 years the Spaniards knocked at the gate with regularity.

West of Tuchan, the landscapes become higher and wilder. **Padern** has another castle, ruined despite rebuilding work in the 18th century, and so does **Cucugnan**, a colourful little village. Both these towns offer scenic detours – from Padern, north through the **Gorges du Torgan**, and from Cucugnan, south through the spectacular **Grau de Maury**, the Corbières' back door.

Cucugnan's landmark is obvious from a distance, the picture-postcard **Château de Quéribus** (*t 04 68 45 03 69; open July and Aug daily 9–8; April–June and Sept daily 9.30–7; Oct–Dec daily 10–5; Feb daily 10–5.30; Mar daily 10–6; closed Jan; adm*), balancing nonchalantly on a slender peak, half a mile in the air over the gorge. Quéribus was the last redoubt of the Cathars; a small band of bitter-enders held out against the French for months here in 1255. Probably the best maintained of the Corbières castles, it takes about 10 minutes to walk up to – watch your step. Admission includes an optional stop at the Achille Mir theatre to hear the famous speech of the parish priest of Cucugnan, from the story in Alphonse Daudet's *Lettres de Mon Moulin*. And who was Achille Mir? The local scribe who wrote the story that Daudet shamelessly plagiarized for his own.

Château de Peyrepertuse

t 06 71 58 63 36, www.chateau-peyrepertuse.com; open April–May and Oct 9–7; June–Sept 9–8; Oct–Dec and Feb–Mar 10–5; closed Jan.

Castles atop mountains will be nothing new by now, but nowhere else, perhaps, is there a bigger castle atop a taller, steeper mountain. If the air is clear, and you know where to look for it, you can see Peyrepertuse from any bit of high ground as far away as the coast. From Cucugnan it is an unforgettable sight, a white, limestone cliff rising vertically up to the clouds, crowned by a stretch of walls and towers over 777ft long. Close up, from the bottom of the cliff, you can't see it at all.

Probably begun in the 10th century, Peyrepertuse was expanded to its present dimensions by Saint Louis in the 1240s. As important to the defence of France's new southern border as Carcassonne, Peyrepertuse was intended as an unconquerable base, big enough to hold a large force that could come down and attack the rear of any Aragonese invader. As you will see when you climb up to it, attacking the place would be madness; no one ever tried. The vertiginous road to the castle starts from the village of Duilhac; from the car park, it's an exhausting 20-minute struggle up to the walls.

The entrance leads into the **Château Vieux**, the original castle, rebuilt by Saint Louis. Here you'll discover one of Peyrepertuse's secrets: the castle may indeed be long, but, conforming to its narrow site, in places it is only a few yards across. Nearly everything is in ruins; the keep is still in good shape, and a large cistern and the ruined chapel

Wine: Corbières, and Some Others

The Corbières has a singular microclimate, swept by the *tramontane* and with a sparse, irregular rainfall. Under its vines and *maquis* lies a geological jigsaw puzzle of Liassic, Triassic, Urgonian and who-knows-what-other kinds of rocks, not to mention the Urgo-Aptian debris and Villefranchean scree. There are as many variations of soil, often giving wine from one village a completely different character from that of its neighbour.

Wine has always been made here – the land isn't good for much else – but only recently have producers really tried to exploit its unique possibilities. The results have been more than encouraging. Corbières red (mostly carignan, grenache and cinsault) varies widely in price and quality: from some of the best 12 per cent *appellation contrôlée* plonk you'll ever taste, to truly excellent, estate-bottled wines costing seven times as much. Always, though, it will be dark ruby red, full-bodied and intense. There is also white and rosé Corbières, although you won't often see them; good rosé (as well as red) comes from **Château La Baronne**, near Fontcouverte, **t** 04 68 43 90 20.

The Corbières is a stronghold of the village co-operative cellar, and has been ever since the troubles in 1907. There are, nevertheless, a number of strictly private producers. Along the D611A, you may visit **Château Gléon**, west of Portel, **t** 04 68 48 28 25, *www.gleon-montaine.com*, a lovely estate behind an old stone bridge, which makes a fine, very traditional red and a striking Corbières white, based on 100% malvoisie as well as rosé.

Nearby, the vast **Château Lastours**, Portel-des-Corbières, **t** 04 68 48 29 17, **f** 04 68 48 29 14, is set among the *garrigues* and canyons where motor-heads train for the Paris-Dakar rally. Château Lastours has grown wine since the 12th century, and was revived in 1970 by a group in Marseille to produce Corbières and special *cuvées* according to the most modern methods, and at the same time to offer employment and independence to the mentally handicapped (try the excellent Cuvée en Fûts de Chêne or the extremely unusual Vendange Tardive 2000 harvested at the end of October, perfumed and rich).

One of the new superstars of Corbières is **Domaine de Cascadais**, at St-Laurent de la Cabrerisse, **t** 04 68 44 01 44, owned by a brilliant producer of Bordeaux, Philippe

can be seen directly behind it. Further up is a vast open space that held most of the barracks and stores; and above this, Louis added yet another citadel, the **Château St-Georges**, with another keep and chapel.

Do you need more castles? North of Peyrepertuse, in the wildest, least-travelled part of the Corbières, there are at least four more, starting with one at **Auriac**, an old copper-mining village; nearby, at **La Grave**, is an unusual 9th- to 12th-century country church, the Chapelle de St-André.

A bit further north, castles at **Termes** (**t** 04 68 70 09 20; *open July and Aug daily 10–8; April–June and Sept–mid-Oct daily 10–6; mid-Oct–Dec and Mar Sat, Sun and hols 10–5; closed Jan and Feb; adm*) and **Durfort** are less than 5km apart. Both the strongholds of local barons, both were besieged and taken by Simon de Montfort under the pretext

Courrian. The first vintage was 1992. He produces red only, from carignan, grenache, syrah and mourvèdre; you can visit by appointment.

The stretch of D611 between Villeneuve and Tuchan is the heartland of one of Languedoc's finest wines, Fitou; strong and fragrant with the scent of the *garrigue*, dominated by carignan (mixed with grenache and syrah), it was the first AOC-designated wine in the region (1948). It isn't sold until after a year or more of maturation, and after five years or longer in the bottle takes on a spicy, wild aroma.

At the **Château de Nouvelles**, on a side road north of Tuchan, **t** 04 68 45 40 03, *http://chateaudenouvelles.com*, try the delicious 2000 Fitous, drinking well now. They also produce Rivesaltes and Muscat.

One of the best of the bunch is **Château L'Espigne** in Villeneuve-les-Corbières, **t** 04 68 45 91 26, **f** 04 68 45 83 54. This ancient estate was originally a '*moulin à l'huile*'. It is planted with 80-year-old vines that produce tiny amounts of grapes, resulting in wines of enormous concentration and complexity.

The **Château de Boutenac**, Maison des Terroirs en Corbières, **t** 04 68 27 84 73, is the recently opened showcase for Corbières AOC wines, *www.aoc-corbieres.com*, with a wide range of wines to taste and buy, along with other local products.

In the valley of the Agly, just over the boundary between Languedoc and Roussillon, the wine scene changes completely. Like most of Roussillon, the area around Maury and Estagel produces sweet dessert and aperitif wines called VDNs, or *vins doux naturels* – but it makes what many consider the best of them, Maury. Like its chief rival Banyuls, Maury is made from grenache noir, but it has a distinctive character of its own, a more consistent colour and spicy, leathery aroma, especially as it ages (1994 was a great year); a fragrant well-aged Maury Chabert is one of the few French wines that goes well with curries. Most of the 40,000 hectolitres produced each year pass through Maury's village co-operative, the **Vignerons de Maury**, on Av Jean-Jaurès in Maury, **t** 04 68 59 00 95, **f** 04 68 59 02 88; there is a good selection of Maury and other wines. Also look out for wines from the excellent estate of **Mas Amiel**, **t** 04 68 29 01 02, isolated in the middle of the dry schist vineyards surrounded by cypress and olive trees under the grey jagged peaks. You can see the Maury being exposed to the sun in a collection of glass jars (*bonbonnes*). Call to visit and get directions from Maury.

---

of the Albigensian Crusade; Termes held out for four months, until a lack of water drove the defenders to surrender. Montfort also conquered the **Château de Villerouge-Termenès**, 14km to the east (**t** *04 68 70 09 11; open July and Aug daily 9.30–7.30; April–June and Sept daily 10–6; Oct daily 10–5; Feb–Mar Sat, Sun and hols 10–5; closed Nov–Jan; adm*). There is an audiovisual display, 'The World of Guilhem Bélibaste, the last Cathar *parfait*', evoking 13th-century life and Bélibaste's story.

There are no easy roads in any other direction from Peyrepertuse, but, if you're heading west, rejoin the main route by way of the D7 and the white cliffs of the **Gorges de Galamus**, the most impressive natural wonder of the Corbières, a deep gorge with wonderful stone pools for swimming and canyoning.

The Plateau d'Opoul

The southern border of the Corbières is a long rocky wall, crossed by the Gorges de Galamus and the Grau de Maury. Near the sea it spreads into a *petit plateau*, one of the most barren and isolated places in France. Don't be surprised to find tanks and suchlike growling across your path. The western half of the Plateau d'Opoul is one of the French Army's zones for manoeuvres, the closest France can get to desert conditions. Most of the time, however, you won't see anyone at all, save old farmers half-heartedly trying to keep their ancient Citroëns on the road, on their weekly trip to the village to get a goose or a haircut.

The village is **Opoul-Périllos**, a cosy place that shuts itself off from the surrounding void. It is a relatively new settlement; its predecessor, **Périllos**, is an eerie ruined village higher up on the plateau, now inhabited only by praying-mantises, with another castle nearby. Both castle and village have enormous stone cisterns. Water was always a problem here – indeed, everything was a problem, and the 14th-century Aragonese kings who built both village and castle had to bribe people with special privileges to live on the plateau. Today there are vineyards, but until very recently the only real occupation was smuggling.

Near the castle, a rocky side road leads west into the most desolate part of the plateau; at a spot called **La Vall Oriole** you'll see a massive, lonely limestone outcrop with a door at the bottom (locked). It seems that some time in the early Middle Ages, this rock was hollowed out by a community of cave-dwelling monks, like the famous ones of Cappadocia in Turkey.

Tautavel and the Fenouillèdes

Descending from Opoul to the southwest, the D9 passes through some romantically empty scenery towards **Tautavel**, a pretty village under a rocky escarpment. Throughout Europe, prehistoric man picked the unlikeliest places to park his carcass. Around Tautavel, human bones have been found from as far back as 450–680,000 BC, making 'Tautavel Man' a contender for the honour of First European; the only older finds come from Isernia, an equally unpromising spot in southern Italy. Back then, the climate was quite different, and Tautavel Man had elephants, bison and even rhinos to keep him company. Palaeolithic bones have become a cottage industry – over 430,000 have been found, especially in a cave called the **Caune de l'Arago**, north of the village (*open July and Aug to groups only*) – the best being displayed in the village's **Musée de la Prehistoire** (*t 04 68 29 07 76; open July and Aug daily 9–9; April–June and Sept daily 10–6; Oct–Mar 10–12.30 and 2–6; adm*), which shares a car park with the wine co-operative.

From Tautavel, the D9 continues south into the valley of the Agly, joining the D611 and finally the D117 west, the main route inland from the coast to Foix and the Ariège. This road passes **Maury**, famous for its dessert wines and its pottery of deep blues and greens, and **St-Paul-de-Fenouillet**, known for almond cookies. The next village, **Caudiès-de-Fenouillèdes**, has become something of an art centre, especially in summer.

To the north, you will see the **Pic de Bugarach**, the highest crag in the Corbières. Three kilometres to the south, the hamlet of **Fenouillet** is guarded by three more ruined castles, all within a few hundred yards of each other (for the crow, anyhow). Beneath them, the simple medieval chapel of **Notre-Dame-de-Laval** has a wonderful polychrome wooden altarpiece, dated 1428. Higher into the mountains, there's yet another mountain-top castle to climb (about 20 minutes): **Puilaurens** (*t 04 68 20 65 26, www.lapradelle-puilaurens.com; open daily April–June and Sept 10–6; July and Aug 9–8; Oct 10–5; the rest of the year open weekends and school hols only 10–5; closed Jan; adm*). Even Simon de Montfort couldn't get into this one; its fortifications were the most complete and sophisticated of any in the region. The Cathars who took refuge here only surrendered in 1256, after the fall of Montségur.

The Agly valley and the mountains around it make up the **Fenouillèdes** – Fenouillet in Catalan, the northernmost region of medieval Catalunya. Though equally mountainous, its scenery makes a remarkable contrast to the dry and windswept Corbières. Here, limestone gradually gives way to granite, the true beginning of the Pyrenees. Much of it is covered by ancient virgin forest, broken by quick-flowing streams and scenic ravines. The best parts are the **Forêt d'Ayguesbonnes-Boucheville**, southwest of Fenouillet, and the **Forêt des Fanges**, in the steep mountains behind Puilaurens castle.

The D619 south from St-Paul-de-Fenouillet is the only good road through the Fenouillèdes, passing through **Sournia**, on the Desix river, the only real town. Along the way, be sure to stop at **Ansignan** to see its Roman aqueduct, a rustic, seldom-visited version of the famous Pont du Gard. An arcade of 551ft, with 29 arches, carries it over the Agly; it is still in use, carrying water to the vineyards, and you can walk over it, or follow the channel towards the village. The question is why the Romans built it, with no nearby towns for it to serve. It is unlikely that agriculture on the coastal plains was ever so intensive as to merit such a work. One possibility is an important patrician villa – such things were often cities in themselves – but no traces of one have been discovered. Signs in Ansignan point the way up to a dolmen and to **Felluns**; there are wide-ranging views over the mountains just beyond, along the D7 south to Sournia.

The Aude

The Valley of the Upper Aude

Near the castle of Puilaurens, the D117 joins the course of the Aude, passing northwards through a spectacular canyon, the **Défilé de Pierre-Lys**. The *pays* that begins here is called the **Razès**, a sparse, scrubby, somewhat haunted region, the back door to the Corbières. As Rhedae, it has been known to history since the time of the Visigoths; according to author Henry Lincoln, the uncanniness begins with the Razès' sacred geometry: its five most prominent peaks, including the perch of Languedoc's conspiracy headquarters, Rennes-le-Château, describe a unique, perfect natural pentangle. The precise measurements were repeated in the Middle Ages, in the geomantic placing of churches around Espéraza. Even in the off season you'll see cars with number plates from far-away countries, cruising about, looking for goodness knows what.

Quillan, Espéraza and Couiza

Quillan, the first town after the Pierre-Lys canyon, makes its living from manufacturing shoes; it has an odd, perfectly square castle from the 1280s, a ball and three *quilles* (bowling pins) on its coat of arms. Dinosaurs were fond of the Aude valley and especially **Espéraza**, just north, where they left a nest of eggs, now displayed with fossils, skeletons, dioramas and more Jurassic-era souvenirs at **Dinosauria** (*Av de la Gare, t 04 68 74 26 88, www.dinosauria.org; open July and Aug daily 10–7; early Feb–June and Sept–early Nov daily 10–12 and 2–6; early Nov–Jan Mon–Fri 2–5, Sat and Sun 10–12 and 2–5; adm*). In later years the village was nothing less than 'the world's second-greatest maker of hats in the first half of the 20th century' and, like many a hat manufacturer, curses the day JFK set the fashion for going without. The village's glory days are recalled in the **Musée de la Chapellerie** (*t 04 68 74 00 75; open July and Aug 10–7; late Feb–June and Sept–Dec daily 10–12 and 2–6; Jan–late Feb 10–12 and 2–5; closed first 3 wks Jan; adm*).

The Razès' biggest town, gritty and peculiar **Couiza**, makes even more shoes, and plastic panelling, too. Its landmark is the imposing Renaissance château of the Ducs de Joyeuse, who made nuisances of themselves on the Catholic side during the Wars of Religion; their descendants have just turned the old homestead into a hotel (*see* box, below). To the east of Couiza are **Rennes-les-Bains**, a small spa in business since the time of the Romans (finds from the ancient baths are in the Villa Marie), and

Tourist Information

Quillan: Square André Tricoire, t 04 68 20 07 78, f 04 68 20 04 91, *www.ville-quillan.fr. Open June–mid-Sept Mon–Sat 8–12 and 2–7, Sun 8–12; mid-Sept–May Mon–Fri 9–12 and 2–6, Sat 9–12.*
Chalabre: Cours Colbert, t/f 04 68 69 26 28.

Market Days
Quillan: Wed.
Espéraza: Thurs and especially Sun.
Couiza: Tues and Sat.
Chalabre: Sat.

Where to Stay and Eat

Quillan ✉ 11500
★★★La Chaumière, 25 Bd Charles de Gaulle, t 04 68 20 17 90, f 04 68 20 13 55 (*inexpensive*). Cosy rooms and mountain cooking featuring trout. *Closed mid-Nov–Mar.*

★★Pierre Lys, Av de Carcassonne, t 04 68 20 08 65 (*inexpensive*). At the north end of town, this modern hotel offers comfort, quiet and the best meals in the town, with sea perch, *confits* and so on.
★★Hôtel Cartier, 31 Bd Charles de Gaulle, t 04 68 20 05 14, f 04 68 20 22 57, *www. hotelcartier.com* (*inexpensive*). Near the train station and Quillan's indoor pool, with restaurant (*moderate*). *Closed mid-Dec–mid-Mar; restaurant closed Dec–Mar.*
Terminus, 45 Bd Charles de Gaulle, t/f 04 68 20 93 33 (*cheap*). Inexpensive restaurant near the train station.

Couiza ✉ 11190
Château des Ducs Joyeuse, off the main road, set amid playing fields, t 04 68 74 23 50, f 04 68 74 23 36, *www.chateau-des-ducs.com* (*expensive*). A handsome 16th-century place with attractive rooms; the elegant restaurant (*expensive–moderate*) serves the best meals around. *Closed mid-Nov–Mar.*

Arques, where a few Cathars still go about their business. Arques has a tall, elegant, Gothic 13th-century **château** – or just the keep of one, framed in turrets, as Simon de Montfort took it from the Termes family in 1231 and gave it to one of his lieutenants (*t 04 68 69 84 77; open July and Aug daily 9.30–8; June and Sept daily 10–7; April and May daily 10.30–6.30; Mar and Oct daily 10.30–12 and 1.30–5.30; first half Nov daily 10.30–12; closed mid-Nov–Feb; adm*). The same ticket admits you to the **Maison de Déodat Roché** (*t 04 68 69 85 62; open mid-June–mid-Sept daily 10.30–8.30; Mar–mid-June and mid-Sept–Oct daily 100–6; closed Nov–Feb*); a famous Cathar historian, Roché (1877–1978) was born in Arques, and his house in the centre of the village has a permanent exhibition on Catharism in the 19th and 20th centuries.

Rennes-le-Château

This is a terrible place.
> Abbé Saunière's inscription over the door of Ste-Marie-Madeleine

Whatever is haunting the Razès, it resides here, in a woebegone mountain-top village above Couiza that is possibly familiar to more people in Britain and America than Carcassonne. The fun began in the 1890s, when the young parish priest, Bérenger Saunière, began spending huge sums of money on himself and on embellishing his church. The story, and the speculation, hasn't stopped unfolding since. In a nation addicted to secret conspiracies, preferably with a medieval pedigree, every sort of shadowy religious cult and fantastico-political faction has got its oar in, from neo-fascists to neo-Jews, along with monarchists, satanists, dilettante Cathars and dressed-up Templars.

With its few dusty streets, spectacular views over the Aude valley, and a superabundance of mangy dogs, Rennes-le-Château is an unsurpassed vortex of weirdness. Its one permanent business is an occult bookshop, where you can pick up a copy of the 1970s bestseller *Holy Blood, Holy Grail*, the first and best account in English that attracted international attention to Rennes, describing Jesus' problematical but well-publicized western European tour, an escape from Israel after a faked crucifixion. It has been a recurring theme in French and English legend from the beginning ('And did those feet in ancient time,' etc.). Here, the idea is that Jesus came to Gaul with his wife Mary Magdalene; both may have been buried in Rennes and their descendants were the Merovingian kings of France, deposed in the 8th century by a shady deal between the popes and Carolingians. Supposedly, the blood line has survived to this day.

Did Saunière discover proof of Jesus' tomb in Rennes and make his fortune by blackmailing the Vatican to keep his mouth shut? Or did he find the Holy Grail, or the treasure of the Visigoths, the Merovingians or the Templars? The most fashionable theory these days leans towards the fabulous treasure of the Jews, stolen from Jerusalem by Titus in AD 10 and pillaged in turn by the Visigoths, who carted it off from Rome to Carcassonne in the 5th century. When Clovis, King of the Franks, took the Visigoths' capital of Toulouse, the treasure was secretly removed further away for safekeeping in the impregnable fortress at Rennes. Rennes became the capital of the region when Amairic, a Visigothic prince, married a Frankish princess, and is claimed to have eventually had a population of 30,000 (3,000 would be closer to reality) before it was definitively sacked by the Aragonese in 1170, only to be destroyed again for good measure in Simon de Montfort's blitzkrieg.

When Bérenger Saunière was appointed parish priest of Rennes-le-Château, the village was in a sorry state; even the 12th-century church was falling over. During the repairs on the church in 1891, Saunière found, under a statue of the Virgin (she stands on a stone carved with a cross set upside down – perhaps a Visigothic altar?), a parchment in a glass phial. Not long after, Saunière was spotted by the villagers, digging furtively most evenings in the local cemetery. One of his activities was the systematic defacement of the inscription on the tomb of the last Lady of Rennes, Hautpoul de Blanchefort (d. 1781), not knowing that someone had already copied it out in the early 1820s (it had Greek letters reading 'Et in Arcadia ego', i.e. death is present, even in Arcadia). Hautpoul, who died without heirs, had in her last hours of life confided some great secret to the parish priest, who left the enigmatic epitaph on her tomb. The same inscription, by apparently no coincidence at all, appears on the tomb in one of Nicolas Poussin's best-known paintings. The background of his painting shows – surprise! – the distinctive profile of Rennes-le-Château.

After his nocturnal digs, Saunière began spending money like nobody's business, paving the road up to Rennes, and redoing the **church**, dedicated (naturally) to Mary Magdalene (*same hours as museum below*), in a style the French have labelled 'St-Sulpicien', or the 'last reaction against the separation of Church and state'. This hardly seems to have been Saunière's main concern in his decorative schemes; rather, the somewhat unorthodox imagery of his bevy of plaster statues apparently distils a secret message to the initiated (note, for instance, that in the Holy Family both Mary and Joseph hold babies). Even Saunière got into hot water with the Church over the demonic figure that supports the font by the door, representing not Satan, but Asmodeus, the guardian of the treasure of Solomon.

Outside the church, the statue of the Virgin still stands on her mysterious stone. An adjacent **museum** (*t 04 68 74 72 68; open May–mid-Sept daily 10–7; Mar, April, mid-Sept–Oct daily 10–6; Dec–Feb daily 10–5; adm*), relates some of this to the Cathars, who had a mysterious treasure of their own that they slipped out of Montségur and hid in parts unknown before the bitter end (*see pp.36–8*).

You can visit the **Domaine du l'Abbé Saunière** (*open May–mid-Sept daily 10–7; Mar, April, mid-Sept–Oct daily 10–6; Dec–Feb daily 10–5; adm*), the genteelly dilapidated bourgeois villa and garden that Saunière built for himself with his secret loot. A video by Henry Lincoln shown in the parlour tells the amazing tale (translated into French, though); under the Abbé's peculiar library-belvedere, the Tour Magdala, you'll find documents and photos relating to his doings and the whole history of Rennes. Saunière died in 1917, leaving everything to his housekeeper, Marie Dénaraud, who took the secret with her to the grave in 1953. From the top of the belvedere you can see a number of towers, fortresses and other ruins, their origin and purpose a matter of conjecture; the largest of them, the **Château de Blanchefort**, was probably wrecked by Simon de Montfort.

Further up the Aude, and Down into the Earth

The tourist office in Quillan can arrange visits to the **Grotte L'Agouzou**, 27km up the Aude on the D188 (*t 04 68 20 45 38; http://perso.wanadoo.fr/grotte.agouzou; visits strictly by appointment, with one-day tours, including lunch, for small groups, and half-day tours*). This is a spectacular stalactite cave, full of lovely delicate formations and crystals, but unlike others open to visitors. It hasn't been fitted out with walkways and lights; rather, small groups from eight to ten (children must be at least 10 years old) are taken in with lighted helmets, overalls, belts and lights to explore. Diehard couch potatoes should abstain.

Into the Limouxin

Before its right turn at Carcassonne, the Aude traverses a lovely, modest stretch of open rolling country, the Limouxin. Most of the roads here are still graced with their long arcades of plane trees – there isn't enough traffic yet to threaten them.

Alet-les-Bains

Continuing down the Aude from Couiza, Alet-les-Bains is one of the most beautiful and best-preserved medieval villages of Languedoc. A small spa since Roman times, Alet owes its prominence to the popes, who made it a bishopric in 1318. Its two jewels are the 14th-century church of **St-André**, with frescoes and a fine west portal, and the nearby impressive **Benedictine abbey** (*just reopened after renovation; call tourist office for opening times, see overleaf; adm*), founded in the 9th century and wrecked in the Wars of Religion. The narrow streets of the village itself are an equal attraction, with a score of 13th- and 14th-century buildings, such as the colonnaded house called the **Maison Romane**. Alet is still a thriving spa; it bottles its water to clean out your digestive tract and runs a casino to clean out your pockets.

Limoux and the Quercorb

Even before you notice the vineyards, the civilized landscapes suggest wine. Limoux, the capital, is an attractive town, with a medieval bridge across the Aude, the **Pont Neuf**; this meets the apse and steeple of **St-Martin**, a good piece of Gothic, if anachronistic – although the church was begun in the 14th century, most of the work is from three centuries later. The centre is the arcaded **Place de la République**. Like Carcassonne's Ville Basse, Limoux was a *bastide*, and this was its market square; the streets of the old town around it make a pleasant stroll. Rue Blanquerie, named for the tanneries that once were Limoux's main business, is one of the streets with 15th- and 16th-century houses, like the 1549 **Hôtel de Clercy**, with a lovely and unusual courtyard of interlocking arches.

On the Promenade du Tivoli, a broad boulevard that replaced the town walls, the tourist office shares the home of the Petiet family with the **Musée Petiet** (*t 04 68 31 85 03; open July–Aug daily 9–7; Sept–June Mon–Fri 9–12 and 2–6, Sat and Sun 10–12 and 2–5; adm*), which contains a collection of 19th-century paintings, and canvases by the museum's founder, Marie Petiet, a talented, neglected artist of the 1880s. A woman painter, and a woman's painter, her work brings a touch of magic to very domestic subjects, nowhere better than in the serene, luminous composition called *Les Blanchisseuses* (The Washerwomen). There is also a **Musée du Piano** (*Chapelle St-Jacques, Place du 22 Septembre, t 04 68 31 85 03; open July and Aug daily 10–12 and 2–5, otherwise call for times*), with 50 instruments. Limoux's other attraction sounds like something P. T. Barnum would think up: **Catha-Rama** (*47 Av F. d'Egaltine, t 04 68 31 48 42, www.catharama.d-av.com; open July–Aug 10–6; Easter–June and Sept–Oct 10–5; closed Nov–Easter; adm*), two 30-minute audiovisual spectaculars on the history of the Cathars, in a choice of languages from Catalan to Japanese.

In the sculpted countryside around Limoux, you can combine picnics and piety with a tour of three sites. The chapel of **Notre-Dame-de-Marceille**, just to the northeast, houses a 'Black Virgin', an icon from the 11th century. To the east, an exceptionally pretty side road (the D104) takes you to **St-Hilaire d'Aude** (*t 04 68 69 62 76; open July–Sept for guided tours*), an abbey founded in the 8th century; its Benedictine

Wine: Blanquette de Limoux

Available in many corner shops of London or New York, Blanquette de Limoux may already be familiar under the Aimery label and others, popularly recognized as the poor man's champagne. The Limouxins wouldn't care to hear it put that way; they would point out that their Blanquette was the world's first sparkling wine, produced at least since 1531, when it was first recorded – long before anyone ever heard of champagne. Blanquette, made from mauzac, chenin and chardonnay, may not have the depth or aging ability of its celebrated rival, but you should certainly give it a try while you're here, especially as it is excellent value. Locals like to drink it as an aperitif, with little cakes called *pebradous*, flavoured with pepper.

You'll have little trouble finding Blanquette (along with the other, non-classified *vins de pays*, white and red) on the roads around Limoux, starting with the big firm **Sieur d'Arques**, Av Mauzac (from Carcassonne, follow signs to Chalabre and you will see it indicated, t 04 68 74 63 00, *www.sieurdarques.com*). They have a big tasting room filled with local wines and offer tours to see how it is produced. They also produce an excellent, slightly-less-sparkling wine called Crémant de Limoux, such as the Grande Cuvée Renaissance. Among the best producers is the **Maison Antech**, at Domaine de Flaissian, on the D118 towards Carcassonne, t 04 68 31 15 88, f 04 68 31 71 61, *www.antech-limoux.com* (*closed weekends*). Maison Antech is a producer of several special *cuvées* and fine Crémants. Those interested in tasting some excellent organic Blanquette should visit **Cave Beirieu** at Roquetaillade, t 04 68 31 60 71, *beirieu@blanquette-bio.com* (*contact them first*).

Northwest of Limoux you'll find an estimable but little-known VDQS red wine called Côtes de la Malepère, produced in a small area, but the closest one in Languedoc to Bordeaux – hence the use of varieties like cot, merlot and cabernet franc. You'll find it around Malepère, Brugairolles, Malviès and Lauraguel: an estate to look out for is the **Château de Malviès**, 1 Bd Malviès, t 04 68 31 14 41, f 04 68 31 58 09.

Tourist Information

Alet-les-Bains: Av Nicolas Pavillon, **t** 04 68 69 93 56, **f** 04 68 69 98 29.
Limoux: Promenade du Tivoli, **t** 04 68 31 11 82, **f** 04 68 31 87 14, *www.limoux.fr*.

Market Day

Limoux: Fri, and flea market first Sun of month.

Where to Stay and Eat

Alet-les-Bains ✉ 11580

Hostellerie de l'Evêché, **t 04 68 69 90 25, **f** 04 68 69 91 94, *www.hotel-eveche.com* (*inexpensive*). The riverside former bishop's mansion; rather plain, it nevertheless has a huge garden with century-old cypresses. *Closed Oct–Mar*.

Limoux ✉ 11300

***Grand Hôtel Moderne et Pigeon, Place Général Leclerc, **t** 04 68 31 00 25, **f** 04 68 31 12 43 (*moderate–inexpensive*). The most luxurious choice. It has a history as strange as its name, having served as a convent, a *hôtel particulier* and a bank in the past. The restaurant (*expensive*) is good, appropriately serving *magret de pigeon*. *Closed first half Jan; restaurant closed Sat lunch and Sun eve except July and Aug*.

Hôtel des Arcades, 96 Rue St-Martin, just off Place de la République, **t 04 68 31 02 57, **f** 04 68 31 66 42 (*inexpensive*). With seven comfortable rooms and a restaurant (*cheap*). *Closed mid-Dec–mid-Jan; restaurant closed Wed*.

*Auberge de la Corneilla, just off the D118 at Cournanel, south of Limoux, **t** 04 68 31 17 84 (*inexpensive*). An unpretentious restored farmhouse with nice rooms, a restaurant (*moderate*) and a garden and pool. *Closed Oct; restaurant closed Sun eve out of season*.

Maison de la Blanquette, 46 Promenade du Tivoli, **t** 04 68 31 01 63 (*expensive–moderate*). Offering wine sampling and home cooking, with an emphasis on the local specialities, from Limoux's *charcuterie* to *confits* to the people's choice, a variation on *cassoulet* called *fricassée* (the Limouxins are very proud of it; Limoux even has an 'Association pour la Promotion de la Fricassée').

monks invented the bubbly Blanquette de Limoux. A graceful, double-columned Gothic cloister survives, along with the Romanesque abbey church, containing the white marble sarcophagus of St Sernin (d. 250), the patron of Toulouse, sculpted by the Master of Cabestany – one of his masterpieces.

South of St-Hilaire, the monastery of **St-Polycarpe** is just as old, though not as well preserved. Its Romanesque church retains some bits of early frescoes and Carolingian carved altars.

Southwest of Limoux, you may venture into one of the most obscure *pays* in all France. Very few French people, even, have heard of the **Kercorb** (or Quercorb), a sleepy region that has plenty of sheep and plenty of trees. **Kercorb** is known for its apple cider, and little else. **Chalabre**, an attractive village of old stone houses with overhanging windows, is its capital. Find out more at *www.quercorb.com*. At **Puivert**, 8km south, the **Musée du Quercorb** (**t** *04 68 20 80 98; open mid-July–Aug daily 10–7; April–mid-July and Sept daily 10–12.30 and 2–6; Oct daily 2–5; adm*) will tell you everything there is to know (a reconstructed kitchen, cow bell manufacturing, and other crafts). It also includes eight reconstructions of 14th-century musical instruments, based on the sculptures of musicians found in the donjon of the **Château de Puivert** (*www.chateau-de-puivert.com; open 9–8 in summer; 10–5 in winter; adm*); its lords were famous as patrons and protectors of the troubadours.

Carcassonne

Standing before the great eastern gate of the walled city, the writer had his note-book out and was scribbling furiously. It was market day, and rustic villeins in coarse wool tunics were offering hung pheasants and great round cheeses from their wooden carts. Geese honked from cages made of twigs and rushes, while pigs and hounds poked about in the cobbled gutters. 'This is medieval indeed,' the writer mused – and just then the director and his entourage appeared over the drawbridge. 'Lovely, everyone, but we'll want more sheep; lots more sheep!'

Plenty of obscure costume dramas have been shot here, drawn by Viollet-le-Duc's romantic restoration. Even without pigs in the gutters, Carcassonne is the Middle Ages come to life. The people of the city do their best to heighten the medieval atmosphere: every August there are various medieval-themed events with artisans in costume, music and jousts. Reality intrudes in the history of the place. Today a dour manufacturing town, Carcassonne was once the strategic key to the Midi; the castle built here by Saint Louis (Louis IX) was a barrier greater than the Pyrenees to invaders.

History

After running north down from the Pyrenees, the river Aude makes a sharp right turn for the sea, thus conveniently providing not only an easy natural route into the mountains, but also one across the 'French isthmus', between the Mediterranean and the Atlantic. The river's angle, one of the crossroads of France since prehistoric times, is an obvious site for a fortress; there seems to have been one nearby since the 8th century BC. The Tectosage Gauls occupied the site of the present Cité in the 3rd century BC; a century later the Romans established a fortified veterans' colony on it called Carcaso, which gradually grew into a town. With the coming of the Visigoths in the Germanic invasions of the 5th century AD, Carcassonne began to assume its historic role as a border stronghold between France and Spain – the Frankish and Visigothic kingdoms. The action started as early as AD 506, when the Frankish King Clovis unsuccessfully besieged the town.

Arabs from Spain arrived about 725, one of the high-water marks of the Muslim tide in Europe. Pépin the Short chased them out 30 years later. Not that the Franks could hold it either. With the collapse of the Carolingian Empire, local viscounts attained a *de facto* independence. From 1084 to 1209, Carcassonne enjoyed a glorious period of wealth and culture under the Trencavels, a family who were also viscounts of Béziers and Nîmes. Under them, the cathedral and the Château Comtal were begun. Simon de Montfort, realizing the importance of the town, made it one of his first stops in the Crusade of 1209. The last viscount, Raymond-Roger Trencavel, was no Cathar but a gentleman and a patriot, determined to oppose the planned rape of Languedoc by the northerners. His famous declaration is still remembered today: 'I offer a town, a roof, a shelter, bread and my sword to all the persecuted people who will soon be wandering in Provence.' Unfortunately, Trencavel allowed himself to be tricked outside the Cité walls on pretence of negotiation; he was put in chains and the leaderless town surren-dered soon after. Raymond-Roger died in prison three months later, probably poisoned by Montfort, who declared himself viscount and used Carcassonne as his base of operations until his death in 1218. His son, Amauri, ceded the town and the rest of Montfort's conquests to King Louis IX. The last of the Trencavels, Raymond-Roger's son and heir, also named Raymond, fought to reclaim his lands until 1240, without success despite popular revolts. Under Louis and his son, Philip III, the outer walls were built, making the entire town into the greatest fortress in Europe, the impregnable base of French power in the south. No attempts were ever made on it; even the Black Prince, passing through in 1355, declined to undertake a siege.

When France gobbled up the province of Roussillon in 1659, this mighty bastion no longer had any military purpose and it was allowed to fall into disrepair. While the lower town, with its large textile industries, prospered until English competition ruined the trade in the 19th century, the Cité gradually decayed into a half-abandoned slum. It was the writer Prosper Mérimée, France's Inspector-General of Historic Monuments in the 1830s, who called attention to this sad state of affairs. Viollet-le-Duc, fresh from sprucing up Narbonne, got the huge job of restoring the Cité in 1844; work continued, according to his plans, for the rest of the century.

Today's Carcassonne has a split personality: up on its hill, the pink towers of the lovingly restored Cité glitter like a dream. No longer impregnable, its few hundred inhabitants (all of whom, it seems, have opened Ye Olde tourist shops or snack bars) are invaded by over 200,000 visitors each year, while down below, the workaday Ville Basse gets on with the job. This is one place where you really should try to come outside of high season.

The Cité and its Walls

Most visitors come in through the back door, by the car parks and the bus stop at the **Porte Narbonnaise**. This is not the best introduction to the impressive military sophistication of Carcassonne's defences. It's probably the weakest point along the walls, though there may have been outworks that have since disappeared. Still, it looks strong enough, with two stout rounded bastions on the inner wall from which to mow down any attackers fortunate enough to have got through the outer wall.

Between the two walls, you can circumnavigate Carcassonne by the open space called **Les Lices**, the 'lists', where knights trained and where tournaments were held. The **outer wall** is the work of Louis IX; note how it is completely open on the inside, so that attackers who stormed it would have no protection from the defenders on the **inner wall**. Parts of this date back to the Romans – wherever you see large, irregular blocks without mortar, or layers of smaller stones interspersed with courses of thin brick. The ground level within the lists was slightly lowered by the French, so that you will often see their rectangular stones, either smooth or rusticated, beneath Roman work, where they had to underpin the towers.

To the right of the Porte Narbonnaise, the first large tower is the mighty **Tour du Trésau**. Beyond it, the northern side of the inner wall is almost completely Roman, begun in the 1st century and rebuilt in the Imperial decline of the 4th century, like the walls of Rome itself, with the characteristic rounded bastions used all over the

Getting There and Around

By Air

Ryanair has regular flights from London Stansted; a bus shuttle service links airport to Cité, Place Gambetta and the station.

By Train

From the train station, on Av du Maréchal Joffre at the northern edge of the Ville Basse, there are regular connections to Narbonne (17 a day), and from there to all the coastal cities; there are also trains down the Aude valley to Limoux and Quillan.

By Bus

There are several companies going to towns and villages outside Carcassonne; contact Cars Tessier, **t** 04 68 25 85 45, *www.tessier.fr*, or Trans Aude, 1 Place Davilla, **t** 04 68 25 13 74.

To get up to the Cité from the lower town, take the no.8 city bus from Place Gambetta.

By Car

There is a big car park outside Porte Narbonnaise, but expect to pay €3.50 a day. Otherwise, you need to be up at the crack of dawn to find a space in summer.

Bike, Scooter and Boat Hire

You can hire bicycles and scooters at **Espace 11**, 3 Route Minervois, **t** 04 68 25 28 18, *espace@wanadoo.fr*. You can hire a boat by the week at **Nautic**, 15 Quai Riquet, **t** 04 68 71 88 95, *www.nautic.fr*. If you prefer letting someone else do the work for a couple of hours, contact **Lou Gabaret**, for trips up and down the river from the port, April–Oct (*except Mon out of season*), **t** 04 68 71 61 26.

Other Ways of Seeing the Cité

Carriage rides leave from Porte Narbonnaise for a trot around the Lices April–early Nov, **t** 04 68 71 54 57; and a **tourist train** leaves from the same area for a visit of the towers and ramparts May–Sept, **t** 04 68 24 45 70.

Tourist Information

Carcassonne: 28 Rue de Verdun, in the centre of the Ville Basse, **t** 04 68 10 24 30, **f** 04 68 10 24 38, *www.carcassonne-tourisme.com*. *Open Sept–June daily 9–12.30 and 1.30–6; July–Aug 9–7*. There is also a tourist office in the Porte Narbonnaise in the Cité, **t** 04 68 10 24 36, **f** 04 68 10 24 37. *Open Sept–June daily 9–5; July–Aug 9–7*.

Post office: Rue Jean Bringer in the Ville Basse.

Market Days

Tues, Thurs and Sat: Place Carnot, flowers, fruit and veg, and Bd Barbès, clothes.

Where to Stay

Carcassonne ✉ 11000

Stay in the Cité if you can, though it won't be cheap. Otherwise, hotels are down in the Ville Basse, near the train station or around Bd Jean-Jaurès. There are some real dives, but most are respectable enough.

Luxury–Very Expensive

****Hôtel de la Cité**, Place de l'Eglise, **t** 04 68 71 98 71, **f** 04 68 71 50 15, *www.hoteldelacite. orient-express.com*. In a pretty garden beside the walls of the Cité, and next to the Basilique St-Nazaire this hotel occupies the former episcopal palace, grandly restored in 1909, with marble baths, a pool, and three restaurants. *Closed Dec–mid-Jan*.

****Domaine d'Auriac**, Rte St-Hilaire, south of town, **t** 04 68 25 72 22, **f** 04 68 47 35 54, *www.relaischateaux.fr/auriac*. A luxury alternative to staying in the Cité is this Relais & Châteaux hotel, a stately, ivy-covered 18th-century mansion set in a large, immaculately kept park. There's a pool, tennis, and even a golf course close by (preferential rates for hotel guests). Also an elegant and highly rated restaurant, featuring mostly traditional dishes of the Aude, such as pigeon, which you can get here with truffles. *Closed Jan; restaurant closed weekday lunch, and Sun eve and Mon in winter*.

Expensive

***Hôtel du Donjon**, Rue du Comte Roger, **t** 04 68 11 23 00, **f** 04 68 25 06 60, *www. hotel-donjon.fr*. In a charming and atmospheric old mansion of the Cité, with a small garden and a fine restaurant.

Expensive–Moderate

***Auberge du Château de Cavanac**, Cavanac, 4km south on the Rte St-Hilaire, **t** 04 68 79 61 04, **f** 04 68 79 79 67. A big old wine-maker's house in a quiet garden, with an excellent restaurant in the former stables which serves a unique four-course menu with wine and all the works, starting with a peach kir and a choice of starters. *Closed Jan–Feb; restaurant closed Mon.*

Moderate

***Trois Couronnes**, 2 Rue des 3 Couronnes, **t** 04 68 25 36 10, **f** 04 68 25 92 92 . A modern hotel by the river in the lower town, which makes up for its unprepossessing appearance with a stupendous view of the Cité, and a very good restaurant.

***Terminus**, 2 Av Maréchal Joffre (lower town), **t** 04 68 25 25 00, **f** 04 68 72 53 09. For a touch of class at economy prices; the building has been used as a set in a number of French films. Try to get one of the rooms that have not been 'renovated'. *Closed Nov–Mar.*

Moderate–Inexpensive

***Bristol**, 7 Av Foch, **t** 04 68 25 07 24, **f** 04 68 25 71 89. A grand 19th-century hotel near the station, with rooms overlooking the Canal du Midi. *Closed Dec–Feb; restaurant closed Sat lunch and Sun eve.*

****Hôtel du Pont Vieux**, 32 Rue Trivalle, **t** 04 68 25 24 99, **f** 04 68 47 62 71, *www.hoteldupont vieux.com*. One of the closest hotels to the Cité, and one of the best. No restaurant.

Inexpensive

****Hotel Royal**, 22 Bd Jean-Jaurès (lower town), **t** 04 68 25 19 12, **f** 04 68 47 33 01. Rather incongruously named. *Closed Dec–early-Jan.*

***Astoria**, 18 Rue Tourtel (lower town), **t** 04 68 25 31 38, **f** 04 68 71 34 14, *hotel-astoria@ wanadoo.fr*. A friendly, family-run place, with a comfy décor.

****Central**, 27 Bd Jean-Jaurès (lower town), **t** 04 68 25 03 84, **f** 04 68 72 46 41. One of the cheapest, but quite nice.

Auberge de Jeunesse, Rue Vicomte-Trencavel, **t** 04 68 25 23 16, **f** 04 68 71 14 84. In the Cité; fax or write to reserve in summer, or book online at *www.fuaj.org*. *Closed mid-Dec–Jan.*

Eating Out

Château St-Martin, Montredon (take Bd Jean-Jaurès to Rue A. Marty and follow the signs), **t** 04 68 71 09 53, *www.chateausaintmartin. net* (*expensive*). If you have a car, this is situated in a handsome *gentilhommerie* with a huge terrace over a park, offering a choice of traditional dishes and fresh market cuisine; delicious seafood salad, *cassoulet* and langoustines. *Closed Wed, and Sun eve in winter.*

Brasserie le Donjon, 4 Rue Porte d'Aude (Cité), **t** 04 68 25 95 72 (*moderate*). Dedicates itself to the best of Languedoc cooking – and here the humble *cassoulet* reaches new heights. *Closed Sun eve from Nov–Mar.*

Le Languedoc, Hôtel Montseguer, 32 Allée d'Iéna (lower town), **t** 04 68 25 22 17 (*moderate*). A popular restaurant with a patio, serving regional cuisine but particularly famed for its *cassoulet* with *confit de canard* and salad of *foie gras*. *Closed Sun eve and Mon.*

Jardins de la Tour, 11 Rue Porte d'Aude (Cité), **t** 04 68 25 71 24 (*moderate*). A pretty, idiosyncratic restaurant with garden dining and authentic regional dishes and fish. *Booking advised in high season. Closed Nov–mid Dec, lunch, and Sun and Mon.*

Escalier, 23 Bd Omer Sarraut (lower town), **t** 04 68 25 65 66 (*moderate*). Something of an institution in Carcassonne, where Tex Mex, pizza and moussaka share the menu.

Dame Carcas, 3 Place du Château, **t** 04 68 71 23 23 (*moderate*). Delicious wood-fired food, with Provençal options like grilled piglet with honey sauce. *Closed Jan, and Wed.*

Le St Jean, Place St-Jean (Cité), **t** 04 68 47 42 43 (*moderate–cheap*). A varied menu at this popular lunchtime restaurant serving *cassoulet*, meat and fish dishes. The *cassoulet* has hearty chunks of meat including sausages. *Closed Dec–mid-Jan.*

L'Oeil, 32 Rue de Lorraine, **t** 04 68 25 64 81 (*cheap*). You can also find wood-fired food down in the Ville Basse. *Closed most of Aug and Sun.*

In most of Carcassonne's *pâtisseries* you can satisfy your sweet tooth on the local favourite, *boulets de Carcassonne*, which are made with peanuts and honey.

Empire. Near the second-last of them is a Roman postern gate. The walls to the left of the Porte Narbonnaise were almost completely rebuilt under Philip III, a long stretch of impressive bastions culminating in the great **Tour St-Nazaire**.

Atop both the inner and outer walls, almost everything you see today – the crenellations, wooden galleries (*hourds*) and pointed turrets that make up Carcassonne's memorable skyline – is the work of Viollet-le-Duc. As in all his other works, the pioneer of architectural restoration has been faulted for not adhering literally to original appearances. This is true, especially concerning the pointed turrets and northern slate roofs, but Viollet-le-Duc worked in a time before anyone could have imagined our own rigorous, antiseptic approach to recreating the old. His romantic, 19th-century appreciation of the Middle Ages made possible a restoration that was not only essentially correct, but creative and beautiful.

Château Comtal

Approaching the Cité from the western side, above the river, you pass the Gothic church of **St-Gimer**, ascending to the **Porte d'Aude**. In the old days, you couldn't come empty-handed; the Cité has no natural source of water and commoners from the Ville Basse had to bring up two buckets each time to get in. The Porte d'Aude was the ultimate discouragement for an attacker, employing every trick in the medieval bag. Note, for example, how the approach comes from the right; to protect themselves, soldiers on the way up would have to keep their shields in their right hand, making it difficult to do anything else. The winding path made it impossible to use a battering ram on the gate, and attackers would be under fire from the walls the entire way; there is another gate inside, and if anyone got through the first they would find themselves trapped in a box, under fire from all sides.

The defences are strongest on the western side because here the Cité's three lines of defence are closely compressed – the outer and inner walls and the citadel, the **Château Comtal** (*t 04 68 11 70 73; open April–Sept 9.30–6.30; Oct–Mar 9.30–5; closed most public hols; adm*). Probably the site of the Roman governors' palace, the château was rebuilt by the Trencavels for their own palace, and expanded by King Louis IX. You have a choice of guided tours of the walls and towers (*40 or 90mins, usually on the hour, schedule posted at the entrance*), which begin with a room-sized model and continue, in fascinating, excruciating detail, through an advanced course in medieval military architecture. Louis' builders laid as many traps for invaders inside the walls as without – for example, the stairways where each riser is a different height. Be careful.

Your ticket also includes the **Musée Lapidaire**, which fills much of the château. The collection includes ancient and medieval fragments: from Roman inscriptions and milestones to Merovingian sarcophagi and country roadside crosses (in local folklore, erroneously believed to be tombstones of the Cathars). Old prints and paintings give an idea of the half-ruined state of the Cité before Viollet-le-Duc went to work on it, with houses half-filling Les Lices and windmills along the walls. Two medieval works saved from the town's churches are especially worth a look: an unusual 15th-century English alabaster of the *Transfiguration*, and an excellent sculpted altarpiece, with a host of expressive faces in attendance.

Basilique St-Nazaire

Open summer daily 9–11.45 and 1.45–6; winter daily 9–11.45 and 1.45–5.

In 1096 (the year after he declared the First Crusade), Pope Urban V visited here, giving his blessing to the beginning of the works. The building took shape as an austere, typically southern Romanesque cathedral, and stayed that way until 1270. The French conquerors had more ambitious plans and rebuilt the transepts and choir in glorious perpendicular Gothic. The best features can be seen from outside: two tremendous rose windows and a tall apse with acres of windows and gargoyles projecting like cannons, although these are now awaiting restoration.

The windows illuminate the interior with beautiful 16th- and 17th-century stained glass depicting the *Tree of Jesse* and *Life of Christ*. In the right aisle, pay your respects to the devil himself at the **tomb of Simon de Montfort**, marked by a small plaque. Understandably, Montfort is no longer present; six years after his death, his descendants took him back up north, where he would be less in danger of desecration.

The Ville Basse

Before Saint Louis, the Cité was surrounded by long-established suburbs. In 1240 these were occupied by Raymond Trencavel, son of the last viscount. With the help of the townspeople, he besieged the Cité and nearly took it back. Louis pardoned the rebels, but did find it necessary to knock their houses down, to deprive any future attackers of cover. To replace the old *bourg*, he laid out a new town across the river, in the strict (and here, rather drab) grid pattern of a *bastide*. Don't confuse this with the *bastides*, or old farmhouses, in Provence and Languedoc; as you approach the former English possessions of Aquitaine, *bastide* takes on the meaning of a medieval new town, one of hundreds constructed by the French and English rulers during the Hundred Years' War; this Ville Basse (or Bastide Saint-Louis, as it's sometimes called, especially by the tourist office) has gradually replaced the Cité as the centre of modern Carcassonne.

Descending from the Cité through the Porte d'Aude, you'll pass some streets of houses that managed to creep back despite the royal decree. Rue Trivalle, with a pair of elegant Renaissance *hôtels particuliers*, leads down to the long, 14th-century **Pont Vieux**. At the far end, there once was a sort of triumphal arch, as can be seen in the old prints in the Château Comtal. Now there remains only the chapel of **Notre-Dame-de-la-Santé**, built in 1538.

The Ville Basse proper begins two streets further down, with a circle of boulevards that replaced the old walls. In 1355, during the Hundred Years' War, the walls failed to keep out the Black Prince, who burned the *bastide* to the ground. Only the street plan survived and, at the north and south ends, two huge, mouldering Gothic churches: **St-Vincent** and **St-Michel**, both begun under Louis IX, both on Rue Dr Tomey. St-Michel was restored by Viollet-le-Duc and serves as co-cathedral with St-Nazaire.

A *bastide* was always built around a central market square (here, Place Carnot), while one street over, off Rue de Verdun, you can see the handsome 18th-century **Halles aux Graines**.

Museums and Sights

You can learn all about the famous heretics at the **Imaginarium** (*3–5 Rue St-Jean, Cité*, **t** *04 68 47 78 78, http://imaginarium.cathares.org; open July and Aug daily; June and early Sept Tues–Sun; late Sept, April and early May Wed–Sun; Oct–Mar school hols only; adm*) a mixture of theatre, museum and multi-media history of Catharism; or at **Catha-Rama**, Domaine de Sautés, towards Narbonne, **t** *04 68 78 77 98, www.catharama.d-av.com (open Easter–Oct; adm*), like the one in Limoux (*see* p.562) a surprisingly good video projection on big screens of the history of the Cathars and their castles in the area, also in English); or at the **Centre for Cathar Studies** in the **Maison des Mémoires** (*53 Rue de Verdun, Ville Basse*, **t** *04 68 72 45 55; open Tues–Sat 9–12 and 2–6*); this was the home of Carcassonne's contribution to Surrealism, Joë Bousquet, and there's a display about him, and another organization dedicated to the study of folk traditions in the Aude.

At 1 Rue de Verdun, the 17th-century Presidial houses the **Musée des Beaux Arts** (**t** *04 68 77 73 70; open mid-June–mid-Sept daily 10–6; mid-Sept–mid-June Tues–Sat 10–12 and 2–6; guided visits*), with paintings and decorative arts from the 16th century to the present. Museums dedicated to all things medieval include the **Musée de la Chevalerie, Armes et Archeries** (*in Place St-Jean, but is due to move to another address in the Cité*, **t** *04 68 72 75 51; open Easter–Nov Thurs–Tues 10–1 and 3–7; closed Wed; guided visits at 10.30 and 3.30; adm*) and **Musée Memoires du Moyen Age** (*just outside the Cité, near Porte Narbonnaise*, **t** *04 68 71 08 65; open all year except Christmas hols 10–7; adm*) with videos and models of the Cité, costumes, weapons and so on.

Between Easter and 1 November, you can watch an exhibition of falconry, **Les Aigles de la Cité**, at Colline Pech Mary, 1km from the Cité, signposted off the road to Narbonne (**t** *04 68 47 88 99; open 1 April–1 Nov, demonstrations in July and Aug at 11.15, 3, 4.15 and 6.30; otherwise phone for details; adm*). And finally, learn about animals, art and music from Down Under at the **Parc Australien**, Chemin des Bartavelles, on the way out to Lake Cavayere (**t** *04 68 25 05 07; open July–mid-Sept daily 2–7.30; April–June and mid-Sept–mid-Nov Wed, Sat, Sun and hols 2–6.30*).

The Aude's Northwest Corner: the Lauragais

West of Carcassonne and the Montagne Noire lies a region called the Lauragais, a mostly flat expanse of serious farming of the humbler sort: beans, of course, barley and pigs, and in some villages a substantial chicken-plucking trade. Windmills are a chief landmark, as is the shady, blue and nearly straight ribbon of the Canal du Midi en route to Toulouse. Rugby makes the juices flow in these parts, but in the old days it was religion: St-Felix-de-Caraman, where the doctrines of the Catharism (*see* pp.36–8) were formulated, is here.

Castelnaudary, Famous for Beans

To be authentic, a *cassoulet* requires four things: 'white beans from Lavelanet, cooked in the pure water of Castelnaudary, in a casserole made of clay from the Issel,

Tourist Information

Castelnaudary: Place de la République, **t** 04 68 23 05 73, **f** 04 68 23 61 40, *www.ville-castelnaudary.fr*. Open Mon–Sat 9–12 and 2–6.

Market Day

Castelnaudary: Mon.

Where to Stay and Eat

Castelnaudary ⊠ 11400 and Around

Centre et Lauragais, 31 Cours République, **t 04 68 23 25 95, **f** 04 68 94 01 66 (*inexpensive*). A family-run hotel in the centre, with nice big rooms, a terrace and a restaurant serving *cassoulet*, of course. *Closed most of Jan–early Feb.*

*Grand Hôtel Fourcade, 14 Rue des Carmes, **t** 04 68 23 02 08, **f** 04 68 94 10 67 (*inexpensive*). Family-run and remodelled but still a bit old-fashioned, this is the classic place to sleep in bean town. Even if you're not staying, its restaurant (*moderate*) is the best in town, the place to experience gourmet *cassoulet* with goose *confits* and many less folkloric treats. *Closed Sun eve and Mon out of season, and Jan.*

Aux Deux Acacias, Villepinte (11km southeast on the D113), **t** 04 68 94 24 67, **f** 04 68 94 21 28 (*inexpensive*). Another highly respected pot of beans is dished up here; they also have rooms. *Closed Fri.*

Hôtel Sanègre, Verdun-en-Lauragais ⊠ 11400, **t** 04 68 94 33 59 (*inexpensive*). A restored farmhouse 5km from St-Papoul, with a garden and a good, simple restaurant.

Auberge Le Cathare, Château de la Barthe, Belflou ⊠ 11410, **t** 04 68 60 32 49, *www.auberge-lecathare.com* (*inexpensive*). West of Castelnaudary, on an artificial lake off the D217, this offers home cooking, peace, and pleasant rooms at bargain rates. There is also a campsite and you can hire a mobile home. *Closed Fri eve and Sat lunch in winter.*

over a fire of furze from the Black Mountain'. Every French book ever written on the area mentions this, so we felt obliged to pass it on. The clay pot of *cassoulet* in Castelnaudary's kitchen is the town's Eiffel Tower, its Acropolis, its very identity. Having finally penetrated to deepest France, what you find is not always what you might expect. Here, the precious insight into the folk soul is a cherished mess of beans, lard, goose fat and miscellaneous pork parts. Back in the 1570s, Castelnaudary's *cassoulet* was prescribed to Queen Margot as a cure for sterility, unfortunately without success. Today, all over central France, housewives are torn between making their own, which takes hours, or succumbing to the allure of canned *cassoulet*; any good supermarket will stock at least six brands.

With *cassoulet*, the charms of Castelnaudary are nearly exhausted. There is the 14th-century church of **St-Michel**, with a tall steeple that dominates the city; the **Moulin de Cugarel** (*open mid-July–mid-Aug Tues–Sat 10–12 and 3–5.30, Sun and Mon 3–5.30*), a restored 17th-century windmill, one of over 30 that once spun in the vicinity, and the port and turning basin of the Canal du Midi. You can also visit an **archaeology museum** in the **Présidial** (*t* 04 68 23 00 42; *open July and Aug Tues–Sat 10–12 and 3–6.30, Sun and Mon 3–6.30*); in 1554, Catherine de Médicis, Queen of France and Countess of Lauragais, made Castelnaudary the main town of the senechalsy and the Présidial was a court.

The Medieval Lauragais

In the Middle Ages, **St-Papoul**, 8km east of Castelnaudary on the D103, was the centre of the Lauragais and the home of its bishop. An **abbey** (*t* 04 68 94 97 75; *guided* *tours April–Oct 10–12 and 2–6; July and Aug 10–7)* has been here since the time of Charlemagne; in 1317 Pope John XXII turned the abbot into a bishop and the monks into canons – the better to keep an eye on local heretics. In decline for centuries, this forgotten town still has some of its walls and half-timbered houses, as well as a fine Romanesque cathedral – from the 14th century, a typically archaic building in a region that disdained the imported Gothic of the hated northerners. Though remodelled in trashy Baroque inside, the exterior has remained largely unchanged, including a beautiful apse with carved capitals attributed to the Master of Cabestany. Other good Romanesque churches with carvings are west of Castelnaudary at **Mas-Stes-Puelles** and **Baraigne** (take the D33 and D218 from Castelnaudary), and at **Montmaur**, north of the D113 on the D58; the latter two preserve examples of small circular roadside crosses, like those in the Carcassonne museum. In medieval times this region had hundreds of them; almost all have been destroyed or moved.

West of Castelnaudary, the Canal du Midi loses most of its tranquillity, as both the *Autoroute des Deux Mers* and the N113 move in to keep it company on the way to Toulouse. On the borders of the *département*, at **Port-Lauragais**, the canal passes its highest point. Figuring out how to cross it was Paul Riquet's biggest challenge; he solved it with an elaborate system of smaller canals and reservoirs, carrying water to the locks from as far as 30 miles away, in the Montagne Noire. Near Port-Lauragais there is a large obelisk in Riquet's honour (erected by his descendants in 1825, the year the canal turned in a profit!) and a small museum-cum-information centre about the canal, accessible from the *autoroute*.

South of Castelnaudary are more reminders of the Cathars and their oppressors. **Fanjeaux**, on the D119, began its career as Fanum Jovis, from an ancient temple of Jupiter; from that you can guess that the town, like almost all the sites dedicated to the god of thunder and storms, is on a commanding height, with a wide view over the Lauragais plains. Fanjeaux was a hotbed of Catharism and gained its fame in 1206, when St Dominic himself came from Spain to live here as a missionary to the heretics – quite peacefully and sincerely, though his Dominican followers would be the Church's chief inquisitors and torture-masters for centuries to come. They bequeathed Fanjeaux a 14th-century Gothic church, in the former Dominican monastery; a better work, the parish church of 1278, has a *trésor* full of unusual old reliquaries.

St Dominic founded a monastery in nearby **Prouille**, after a vision in Fanjeaux, and it became a pilgrimage site. Unfortunately, it was wrecked in the Revolution and charm-lessly rebuilt in the 19th century.

South of Fanjeaux, on the way to Limoux, the villages are often laid according to a circular or even elliptical plan: Ferran, Brézilhac and La Digne, among others. They are medieval new towns, or *bastides* (*see* Carcassonne); no one knows exactly why the medieval planners decided to depart from their accustomed strict rectangularity here, but there are clusters of them in Languedoc. They even have their own associa-tion, so if you want to know more, contact Association des Villages Circulaires (*Maire de Paulhan* ✉ *34230, t 04 67 25 31 42, www.circulades.com*).

Roussillon

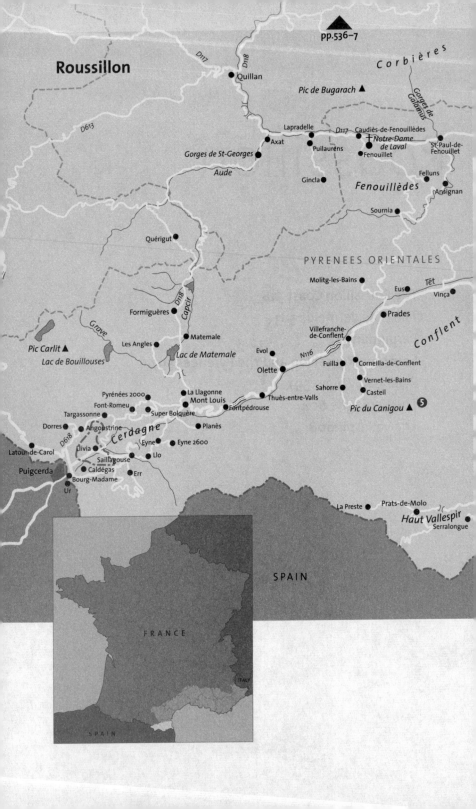

pp.536-7

Roussillon

Corbières

D117

D118

Quillan

Pic de Bugarach ▲

Gorges de Calamus

D613

Lapradelle

Caudiès-de-Fenouillèdes

D117

✝ *Notre-Dame de Laval*

St-Paul-de-Fenouillet

Axat

Puilaurens

Fenouillet

Gorges de St-Georges

Aude

Gincla

Fenouillèdes

Felluns

Ansignan

Sournia

Quérigut

PYRENEES ORIENTALES

Molitg-les-Bains

Eus

Têt

Vinça

D118

Capcir

Formiguères

Prades

Grave

Villefranche-de-Conflent

Conflent

Matemale

Evol

N116

Pic Carlit ▲

Les Angles

Lac de Matemale

Fuilla

Corneilla-de-Conflent

Lac de Bouillouses

Olette

Vernet-les-Bains

Sahorre

Casteil

Pyrénées 2000

La Llagonne

Mont Louis

Thuès-entre-Valls

Pic du Canigou ▲ ⑤

Font-Romeu

Super Bolquère

Fontpédrouse

Targassonne

Planès

Dorres

Angoustrine

Cerdagne

D618

Eyne

Eyne 2600

Latour-de-Carol

Llivia

Llo

Puigcerda

Saillagouse

Caldégas

Err

Bourg-Madame

Ur

La Preste

Prats-de-Molo

Haut Vallespir

Serralongue

SPAIN

FRANCE

ITALY

SPAIN

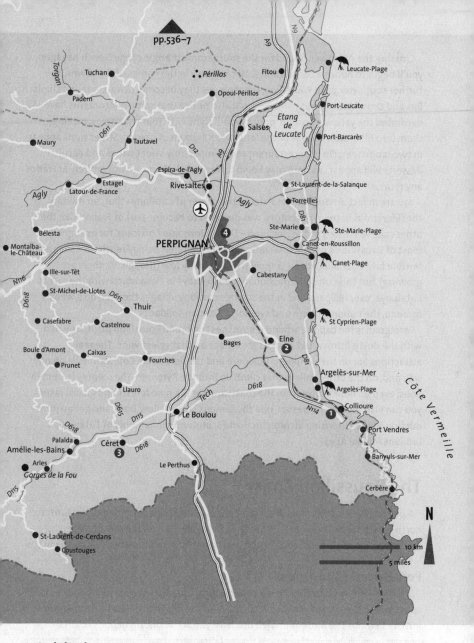

Torgan

Tuchan

Padern

Maury

Tautavel

Périllos

Opoul-Périllos

Fitou

Leucate-Plage

Port-Leucate

Salses

Etang de Leucate

Port-Barcarès

D611

Agly

Estagel

Latour-de-France

Espira-de-l'Agly

Rivesaltes

D12

A9

Agly

St-Laurent-de-la-Salanque

Torreilles

Bélesta

D618

Montalba-le-Château

Ille-sur-Têt

N116

St-Michel-de-Llotes

D615

Thuir

Casefabre

Castelnou

Boule d'Amont

Caixas

Prunet

Fourches

Ste-Marie

D81

Ste-Marie-Plage

Canet-en-Roussillon

PERPIGNAN **4**

Cabestany

Canet-Plage

St Cyprien-Plage

Bages

Elne **2**

D81

Argelès-sur-Mer

Argelès-Plage

Collioure **1**

Côte Vermeille

Llauro

D615

D115

Tech

D618

Le Boulou

N114

Port Vendres

Palalda

D618

Céret **3**

D618

Amélie-les-Bains

Arles

Gorges de la Fou

Le Perthus

Banyuls-sur-Mer

Cerbère

D115

St-Laurent-de-Cerdans

Coustouges

N

10 km

5 miles

Highlights

1 Colour-drenched Collioure, inspiration for Fauvist painters

2 Elne's Romanesque cloister, the best in the Midi

3 Céret and its delightful modern art museum

4 Perpignan, the hot spot of France, and its unnerving Dévôt Christ

5 Canigou, the holy mountain of the Catalans

Crossing the Agly river, bound for the southernmost angle of the French hexagon, you'll begin to notice a certain non-Gallic whimsy in the names of the towns. The further south you go in Roussillon, the stranger they become: Llivia, Llous and Llupia, Eus and Oms, Molitg, Politg and Py. You'll also notice that some malcontents have decorated the yellow diamond 'priority road' signs with four red stripes, making them into little escutcheons of the long-ago Kingdom of Aragon. Street signs appear in two languages. On your restaurant table, impossibly sweet wines and peculiar desserts will appear, and you may begin to suspect that you are not entirely in France any more.

You are in fact among the Catalans, in the corner of Catalunya that, for military considerations in the 17th century, was destined to become part of France. Like the other captive nations of the Hexagon – the Bretons and Corsicans, for example – most of Roussillon's people have rationally decided that being French isn't such a terrible fate after all. Catalan is spoken by relatively few (though numbers are growing), but this culturally passionate people stays in close touch with the rest of Catalunya, over in Spain, and in the squares of many villages they still do a weekly *sardana*, the national dance and symbol of Catalan solidarity.

Perpignan is the capital; around it stretches the broad Roussillon plain, crowded with the dusty, introverted villages that make all that sweet wine. The real attractions are on the periphery: Collioure and the delectable Côte Vermeille on one side and, on the other, valleys that climb up into the Pyrenees. The scenery is tremendous, even an hour's drive from the coast; among the pine forests and glacial lakes you can visit Vauban fortresses, ride the famous Little Yellow Train, and get an introduction to the surprising architectural and sculptural monuments of Catalunya's brilliant Middle Ages.

The Roussillon Coast

A geographical oddity, this run of coastline is nearly perfectly straight and runs due north–south for 40km, from Port-Barcarès to Argelès. It isn't the most compelling landscape, but it is almost solid beach, and has been much developed since the 1940s.

Port-Barcarès and Around

South of Port-la-Nouvelle, the hill of **Cap Leucate** anchors the northern end of this coast, with government-planned resorts at Leucate-Plage and Port-Leucate. These initiate perhaps the most animated but least attractive of Languedoc's resorts,

Beaches

The sand continues into Roussillon, to beaches favoured by beach bum Pablo Picasso. From Port-Barcarès southwards, beach follows beach, some less accessible than others (these tend to be haunted by overweight nudists).

Picasso's favourite was Collioure, with its three small stretches of sand.

Best Beaches

South of Port-Barcarès: empty miles of sand.
Collioure: because Picasso can't be wrong, but be prepared to share the space.

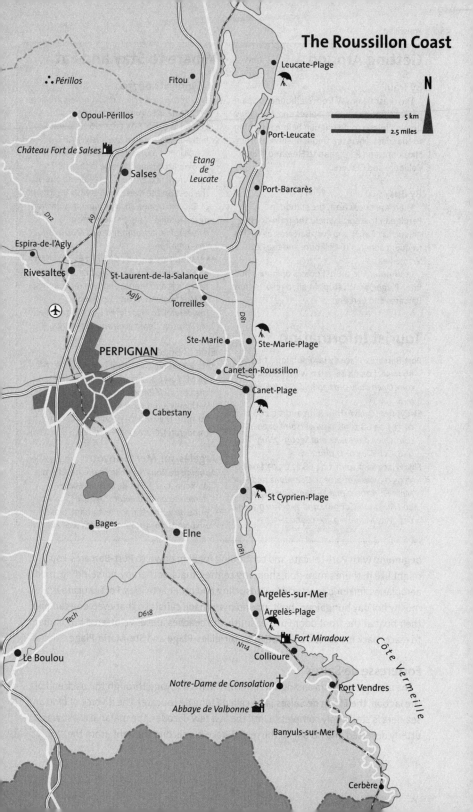

Getting Around

By Train

The coastal railway from Narbonne to Spain passes through Leucate, Salses and Rivesaltes, dipping inland for Perpignan before returning to the coast. There are frequent services from Narbonne and Perpignan to Elne, and then Collioure and Cerbère.

By Bus

There are buses from the station in Perpignan to resorts where the train doesn't go, such as Canet and Port-Barcarès, as well as frequent services to Collioure and the Côte Vermeille.

In summer, the tourist offices operate a Bus Inter-Plages, which stops at all 10 resorts, from Barcarès and Cerbère.

Tourist Information

Port-Barcarès: Place de la République, t 04 68 86 16 56, f 04 68 86 34 20, www.portbarcares. com. Open daily 9–12.30 and 2–6, July–Aug 9–8.

St-Cyprien: Quai Arthur Rimbaud, t 04 68 21 01 33, f 04 68 21 98 33, www.saint-cyprien. com. Open daily June and Sept 9–7; July–Aug 9–8; Oct–May 9–12 and 2–6.

Elne: Place Sant Jordi, t 04 68 22 05 07, f 04 68 37 95 05, www.ot-elne.fr. Open June and Sept Mon–Fri 9.30–12 and 2–5, Sat 9.30–12; July and Aug Mon–Sat 9–12 and 2–6, Sun 9.30–12; Oct–May Mon–Fri 9.30–12 and 2–5.

Where to Stay and Eat

St-Cyprien ✉ 66750

Two of the area's class resort hotels are here.
****L'Ile de la Lagune, Bd de l'Almandin, t 04 68 21 01 02, f 04 68 21 06 28, www. hotel-ile-lagune.com (expensive). Air-conditioned rooms, tennis and pool, all on its own little island, L'Ile de la Lagune. The restaurant (expensive) is considered one of the best on the coast, with stylish treatment of Catalan dishes, such as blinis aux anchois de Collioure à la tapenade et caviar d'aubergine. Restaurant closed Mon and Tues Oct–mid-April.
***Mas d'Huston, t 04 68 37 63 63, f 04 68 37 64 64 (expensive). By the golf course, with two pools and tennis, and two restaurants: **Le Mas** (expensive) and **Les Parasols** (moderate). Le Mas closed lunch in summer; Les Parasols closed eves, and Oct–May.

Elne ✉ 66201

**Le Weekend, 29 Av Paul Reig, t 04 68 22 06 68, f 04 68 22 17 16, www.hotel-weekend. chez.tiscali.fr (inexpensive). A delightful place with only eight rooms and a garden terrace far from the crowds; good home cooking, too (moderate). Closed Nov–mid-Feb.

Argelès-sur-Mer ✉ 66700

Auberge de Roua/La Belle Demeure, Chemin du Roua, t 04 68 95 85 85, www.belle-demeure.com (moderate). A little Catalan auberge with a terrace restaurant. Closed mid-Nov–Jan; restaurant closed Wed eve.

---

beginning with Port-Leucate and continuing for 8km down to **Port-Barcarès**. You might like it; there's mini-golf, shopping centres, thalassotherapy, horse-riding, model aeroplanes, folkloric spectacles, windsurfing and other activities. **Port-Leucate** is mostly holiday bungalows, built around man-made canals so that everyone can park their boat at the front door. Further south, the beaches are less cluttered but harder to reach; back roads lead off the D81 to **Torreilles-Plage** and **Ste-Marie-Plage**.

Forteresse de Salses

The alternative to traversing this inferno means a voyage through the back end of the lagoon, the **Etang de Salses** (also called Etang de Leucate). The divorce of land and sea here is startlingly complete. Until the last few decades, the malarial coast was utterly deserted and no one in the region gave it a second thought; from the landward side of the lagoon, in a few minutes you can be up in the rugged, dusty hills of the Corbières and Opoul (*see* previous chapter), where it is hard to believe any sea could be within a hundred miles. The only village on this side of the lagoon is **Fitou**, justifiably famous for one of the finest wines of Languedoc-Roussillon (though most Fitou wine comes from a nearby area of the Corbières).

After another 7km of total emptiness appears the last, lowest and least spectacular of all this region's many castles – but the **Forteresse de Salses** was the most important of them all (*t 04 68 38 60 13; guided tours on the hour until 1hr before closing; June–Sept 9.30–7; Oct–May 10–12.15 and 2–5; adm*). Built in 1497 by Ferdinand the Catholic, first king of united Spain, Salses was the last word in castles for its time, the masterpiece of a great military architect named Ramiro Lopez. Set squarely on the French–Spanish border, Salses was meant to guard Perpignan and the coastal road. It did not have a chance to do so until 1639, and sadly it was not up to the task. The Spaniards, caught by surprise, had only a small garrison at Salses; nevertheless, it required 18,000 Frenchmen and a month's siege to take it. The same year, a Spanish army spent three months winning it back. Both sieges were serious operations; the locals still go out cannonball-hunting for fun in the surrounding hills. When France acquired Roussillon in 1659, Salses no longer had a role to play.

At first glance, Salses looks strikingly streamlined and modern. It is a product of a transitional age, when defenders were coming to terms with the powerful new artillery that had made medieval castles obsolete. Salses is all curves and slopes, designed to deflect the cannonballs; its walls are not only incredibly thick (28ft on average, 50ft thick at the base), but also covered with heavy stone barrel vaulting to protect the walkway at the top.

The region around Salses and **Rivesaltes**, to the south, is famous for its inexpensive sweet wines, sold throughout France. Rivesaltes was the home of Marshal Joffre, now the small **Musée du Maréchal Joffre**, dedicated to the Battle of the Marne (*t 04 68 38 59 59; open Oct–May Mon–Fri 8–12 and 2–6; June–Sept Mon–Fri 8–12 and 2–6, Sat and Sun 2–6; adm*). In nearby **Espira-de-l'Agly** stands the impressive fortified Romanesque church of **Ste-Marie**, built in 1136 as part of a monastery by the bishops of Urgel in Spain (powerful Catalan clerics whose successors, along with the presidents of France, are still the joint tributary lords of Andorra). The businesslike exterior has one fine carved portal, but the lavish interior still comes as a surprise, with polychromed marbles and elaborate altarpieces from the 16th century.

Canet-en-Roussillon to Argelès

Back on the coast, **Canet-en-Roussillon** has long been the favourite resort of the Perpignanais. After taking a beating in the last war, it has been rebuilt without much distinction. There is an **Aquarium** by the port (*t 04 68 80 49 64; open 10–12 and 2–6, closed Mon; July and Aug daily 10–8; adm*), where the star attraction is that impossibly unlovely living fossil from the depths of the Indian Ocean, the coelacanth. You can also jetski, dive and do other water-based activities; see *http://aquatile.free.fr*. South, past a long stretch of wild beach, good for windsurfing and kite-flying, you'll find **St-Cyprien-Plage**, which looks just like Canet only more so, with fancier restaurants,

Wine: Rivesaltes and Côtes du Roussillon

Catalans have a notoriously sweet tooth, and some 90 per cent of the dessert wine (*vin doux naturel*) of France comes from this *département*, spilling over into the Corbières to the north. Mostly from grenache, muscat or maccabeu grapes, these wines are made simply by stopping the fermentation at the right moment, leaving more sugar in the wine; usually a small amount of pure alcohol is added at the same time. Since the 13th century, Rivesaltes, *www.rivesaltes.com*, has been known for its fruity Muscat, a wine to be drunk young, with sorbets or lemon tarts. Its AOC status, awarded in 1972 along with other Rivesaltes red and white aperitif wines, covers 99 *communes* in the eastern Pyrenees. Try some in Rivesaltes itself, at the Domaine Cazes, 4 Rue Francisco-Ferrer, **t** 04 68 64 08 26, **f** 04 68 64 69 79, *www.cazes-rivesaltes.com*; the talented brothers Bernard and André Cazes not only produce some of the finest Muscat but also AOC Côtes du Roussillon and Côtes du Roussillon Village, plus some excellent white, rosé and red *vin de pays*. In the past, few wine writers ever had anything good to say about this old *vin de pays* but, as in Languedoc, a number of producers like the Cazes brothers have been exerting themselves to create notable, individualistic wines from fine blends of syrah, carignan, grenache and mourvèdre.

Côtes du Roussillon is made all over the *département*, often in village co-operatives that also produce Rivesaltes or sweet Muscat, but there are a few good estates to visit. In the hot corner around Perpignan, **Domaine Sarda-Malet**, Chemin de Ste-Barbe, **t** 04 68 56 72 38, **f** 04 68 56 47 60, puts out three labels of red and a dry white, all of high quality. Or visit the **Château de Jau** on the D117 in Cases-de-Pène **t** 04 68 38 91 38, which produces Côtes du Rouissillon of surprisingly high quality. In summer they also host art exhibitions and have a restaurant that offers good value fixed-price menu lunches featuring local specialities and a wide range of wines. Some of the finest red and white wines can be found at **Domaine Gauby** in Calce, **t** 04 68 64 35 19: wines of rare concentration and full of local character.

two 27-hole golf courses, 21 tennis courts and a summer chamber music festival. It has two museums of its own, set back in St-Cyprien proper, 3km from the beach: the **Centre d'Art Contemporain** (*Rue J. Romains*, **t** *04 68 21 32 07; open mid-Sept–June Wed–Sat 10–12 and 2–6, Sun and Mon 2–6, closed Tues; July–mid-Sept daily 10–12 and 3–7; adm*), dedicated to Catalan artists such as Maillol, Delfau and Bonel; and the **Musée Desnoyer** (*Rue Emile Zola*, **t** *04 68 21 06 96; open same hours as art museum*), with a small collection of lesser works by Picasso, Dufy, Chagall, Miró and especially François Desnoyer, who spent time here. South of St-Cyprien, **Argelès-Plage**, the largest of the French Catalan resorts with 7km of sand and 3km of rocky shoreline, makes some claim as the European Capital of Camping, with 56 sites and a capacity for 100,000 happy campers.

Elne and its Cloister

Between these last two resorts, set a little way inland atop a steep hill, the citadel of Elne has guarded the Roussillon plain for at least 2,700 years. Its ancient name,

Illiberis, is said to come from the Iberians. Hannibal sojourned here on his way to Italy, waiting to negotiate an alliance with the Celts to guard his rear; the locals, apparently unimpressed even with the elephants, made him pay a toll to pass through. The name change came in the time of Constantine, to Castrum Helenae, after the Emperor's mother, St Helen, legendary discoverer of the True Cross. Through the Middle Ages, and until the 16th century, Elne remained the most important city in Roussillon and seat of the archbishops. The town is now reduced to some 6,000 souls (and 70,000 tourists a year), having lost all its honours and status to Perpignan.

But they couldn't take away its **cathedral**, a fortified church begun in 1069; it has a wonderful stage presence, with its crenellated roof-line and stout, arcaded tower. Inside, in a chapel on the right is an Italianate 14th-century altarpiece of St Michael and there are some fine tombs, especially that of Ramon de Costa (1310). The **cloister** (*t 04 68 22 70 90; open daily except during services April, May and Oct 9.30–6; June–Sept 9.30–7; Nov–Mar 9.30–12 and 2–5; guided visits July–Sept; adm*) is perhaps the best in the Midi, and also the best preserved. Capitals and pillars are decorated with imaginative, exquisitely carved arabesques and floral patterns. The four sides were completed in different periods, in roughly 50-year intervals; that closest to the cathedral is the earliest, from the 12th century, and its capitals show the influence of the sculptors of St-Michel-de-Cuxa (*see* pp.601–602). Oddly, each generation of sculptors chose to repeat the subjects of their predecessors: all but the north gallery have central pillars carved with serpentine dragons and mermaids spreading their forked tails; other capitals repeat scenes from the Old Testament. The little **history museum** tells the history of the cathedral and cloister, including its lost upper gallery, dismantled in 1827 and sold off at an auction in 1960. There is also a **museum of archaeology** in the cloister, with finds from the area dating from Neolithic times to the Middle Ages. Admission to the cloister includes the chance to climb the steps up to the terrace which dominates the cloister and admission to the **Musée Terrus** across the square (*t 04 68 22 88 88; open June–Sept 10–7; Oct 10–6; Nov–Mar 10–12 and 2–5; April–May 10–6*); the painter Terrus was a friend of Matisse and Derain and the museum contains mainly his works.

The Côte Vermeille

For anyone with the determination to follow France's long Mediterranean coast all the way to the end, there is a lovely surprise. After Argelès, the shoreline changes dramatically, climbing into the Pyrenees and a delicious southern world of crystalline rock, olive trees and uncanny sunlight, a 30km prelude to Spain's famous Costa Brava. Forgive yourself for cynically thinking that the name 'Vermilion Coast' might have been cooked up by tourist promoters – of course it was, just like the 'Côte d'Azur', 'Costa Smeralda' and all the rest. The red clay soil of the ubiquitous olive groves does lend the area a vermilion tint, but as far as colours go that is only the beginning. Every point or bend in the Mediterranean coast is a sort of meteorological vortex, given to strange behaviour: the Fata Morgana at the southern tip of Italy, the winds of the Mani in the Peloponnese or the glowing, subdued light of Venice. The Côte Vermeille gets a strong dose of the *tramontane* wind, but also a remarkable mix of light and air, inciting the coast's naturally strong colours into an unreasonably heady and sensual Mediterranean spectrum. Henri Matisse spent one summer here, at Collioure, and the result was a milestone in the artistic revolution known as Fauvism.

Collioure

If the tourists would only leave it in peace, Collioure would be quite happy to make its living in the old way, filling up barrels with anchovies. As it is, the town bears their presence as gracefully as possible. In a way, Collioure is unspoiled – if it has 17 hotels for its 2,700 inhabitants, it does not have a casino, a miniature golf course or a water slide, or all the hype projected on St-Tropez, that other unaffectedly beautiful resort discovered at the beginning of the 20th century by the Fauves. Instead, you'll find every other requisite for a civilized Mediterranean resort: a castle, a pretty church by the sea, three small beaches, a shady market square with cafés – and warehouses full of anchovies.

Tourist Information

Collioure: Place du 18 Juin, **t** 04 68 82 15 47, **f** 04 68 82 46 29, *www.collioure.com. Open July and Aug Mon–Sat 9–8, Sun 10–6; Sept–June Tues–Fri 9–12 and 2–6, Mon 2–6, Sat 9–12.*
Port-Vendres: Quai Forgas, **t** 04 68 82 07 54, **f** 04 68 82 53 48, *www.port-vendres.com. Open 9–12.30 and 2–5.30.*
Banyuls-sur-Mer: Av de la République, **t** 04 68 88 31 58, **f** 04 68 88 36 84, *www.banyuls-sur-mer.com. Open July–Aug 8–8; Sept–June Mon–Sat 9–12.30 and 2.30–7.*

Market Days

Collioure: Wed, and Sun am.
Port-Vendres: Sat am.

Where to Stay and Eat

Collioure ✉ 66190

★★★Casa Païral, Impasse des Palmiers, **t** 04 68 82 05 81, **f** 04 68 82 52 10, *www.hotel-casa-pairal.com (expensive–moderate).* The place for an agreeable stay in the centre; a dignified, Mansard-roofed palace a few streets from the shore. There is a wide choice of rooms, from the simple to the luxurious and expensive; also a pool and enclosed garden. *No restaurant; closed Nov–Mar.*

★★La Frégate, Av Camille Pelletan, **t** 04 68 82 06 05, **f** 04 68 82 55 00, *www.lafregate.fr (moderate–inexpensive).* This pink and jolly place is on the busiest corner of Collioure, but has been soundproofed and air-conditioned; it has a good restaurant (*moderate*), serving mostly seafood. *Closed Jan–Feb.*

★★Les Templiers, Quai de l'Amirauté, **t** 04 68 98 31 10, **f** 04 68 98 01 24, *www.hotel-templiers.com (inexpensive).* Picasso, Matisse, Dufy and Dalí all stayed here, and owner Réné Pous was friend to them all. Original works cover the walls of this unique hotel, although the Picassos have been locked away since several were stolen by a 'guest' a few years ago. Each room has its own charm; reservations are imperative. The bar is a friendly local hang-out, and the restaurant (*moderate*) is excellent, with a people-watching terrace and imaginative, good-value dishes like lamb on the bone with cinnamon-scented onion *confit*, or cod with aubergine caviar. *Closed Jan and early Feb.*

Boramar, 19 Rue Jean-Bart, on the Plage du Faubourg, **t** 04 68 82 07 06 (*inexpensive*). A simple budget hotel overlooking the busiest beach. *Closed Nov–Mar.*

Ermitage, Notre-Dame-de-Consolation, above Collioure on the D86, **t** 04 68 82 17 66

It's hard to believe, looking at the map, but in the Middle Ages this village was the port for Perpignan; with no good harbours on the dismal and (then) unhealthy coast to the north, Perpignan's fabrics and other goods had to come to the Pyrenees to go to sea. In the 14th century, Collioure was one of the biggest trading centres of Aragon, but nearly the whole town was demolished by the French after they took possession in 1659. They weren't angry with the Colliourencs; the town was merely in the way of modernizing its castle's fortifications. Our own century has no monopoly on twisted military logic. Collioure had to be razed in order that it could be better defended.

The population moved into the part that survived, the steep hillside quarter called the Mouré, where they have made the best of it ever since. Collioure was discovered in 1905 by Matisse and Derain. Many other artists followed, including Picasso, but these two were the most inspired by the place, and they put a little of Collioure's vermilion tint into the deep colours of their first Fauvist experiments. A couple of Matisses are in nearby Céret, but the best are in private collections, or in the Hermitage in St Petersburg. There is none in Collioure. To rectify the lack, the village has created the *Chemin du Fauvisme*, placing copies of Matisse and Derain's works on

---

(*inexpensive*). A pleasant B&B. *Closed mid-Nov–Mar.*

Dinner in Collioure need not necessarily include anchovies, but the rest of the local catch merits your attention.

Neptune, 9 Rte Port-Vendres, **t** 04 68 82 02 27 (*expensive*). One of the best restaurants in town, with wonderful canopied sea views and the full *nouvelle* Catalan *cuisine* – a *salade chemin des Fauves*, which combines eggs, artichokes, tapenade and tomato *confit* in highly decorative style, or lobster ravioli with cardamom vinaigrette. Ravishing desserts include poached figs and rosemary sorbet. *Closed Tues, Wed; July–Sept closed Tues only.*

La Marinade, 14 Place 18 Juin, **t** 04 68 82 09 76 (*moderate*). Delectable seafood from simple sardines *en papillote* to an elaborate Catalan *bouillabaisse. Closed Dec–Jan.*

Le Tremail, 16 bis Rue Mailly, **t** 04 68 82 16 10 (*moderate*). A small seafood restaurant just off the front, with a good reputation. Catalan specialities. *Closed Jan, and Mon and Tues out of seaon.*

Copacabana, Plage du Boramar, **t** 04 68 82 06 74 (*moderate*). A tourist option, admittedly, but with good views of the château and belltower from the terrace. *Closed mid-Jan–Feb.*

Banyuls-sur-Mer ✉ **66650**

Banyuls lacks Collioure's glamour, but also its high prices.

★★Les Elmes, Plages des Elmes, **t** 04 68 88 03 12, **f** 04 68 88 53 03, *www.hotel-des-elmes.com* (*moderate*). Pleasant seaside rooms and an excellent restaurant, **La Littorine**, serving Catalan dishes with *savoir faire;* half-board is excellent value.

★★La Pergola, 5 Av Fontaulé, by the port, **t** 04 68 88 02 10, **f** 04 68 88 55 45, *www.pergola.com* (*moderate–inexpensive*). Immaculate rooms and good fish in the restaurant (*moderate*). *Closed Oct–mid-Feb.*

La Plage, at the centre of the beach strip, **t** 04 68 88 34 90 (*expensive*). Serves satisfying seafood dinners.

Chez Rosa, 22 Rue St-Pierre, **t** 04 68 88 31 89 (*moderate*). A neighbourhood favourite for lunch; not much seafood, but tasty dishes such as roast pork, couscous, chicken and mushrooms. *Closed eves out of season.*

Cerbère ✉ **66290**

★★La Vigie, on the N114, **t** 04 68 88 41 84, **f** 04 68 88 48 87 (*moderate–inexpensive*). The choice spot in Cerbère, built on the sea cliffs, with a fine view; it also has a restaurant (*moderate–cheap*). *Closed mid-Nov–mid-April.*

the spots where the two set up their easels. The **Espace Fauve** is on Quai de l'Amirauté (*t 04 68 98 07 16, open June–Sept daily 10–12 and 3–7; Oct–May Tues–Fri 10–12 and 3–6, Sat and Sun 3–6*); there is also the **Musée d'Art Moderne** (*t 04 68 82 10 19; open July and Aug Wed–Mon 10–12 and 2–7; June and Sept Wed–Mon 10–12 and 2–6; Oct–May Wed–Mon 9–12 and 2–6; closed Tues; adm*), in a peaceful villa on the south edge of town with a terraced olive grove, which has works by lesser-known artists in the style of the Fauves, as well as an intriguing collection of Moorish ceramics.

Collioure (or as the locals call it, Cotllures) is a thoroughly Catalan town, and the red and yellow striped Catalan flag waves proudly over the **Château Royal** (*t 04 68 82 06 43; open daily June–Sept 10–6; Oct–May 9–5; adm*), which dominates the harbour. With its outworks it is nearly as big as the town itself. First built by the Templars in the 13th century, it was expanded by various Aragonese kings. The outer fortifications, low walls and broad banks of earth, were state-of-the-art in 1669. The great Vauban, Louis XIV's military genius, oversaw the works and the demolition of the old town. Collioure's fate could have been even worse; Vauban had wanted to level it completely and force everyone to move to Port-Vendres. The older parts of the castle have been restored and are open for visits, along with several small exhibitions on local specialities from whip-making to espadrilles.

From the castle, cross the small stream called the Douy (usually dry and used as a car park) into the **Mouré**, the old quarter that is now the centre of Collioure. There is an amiable shorefront, with a small beach from which a few anchovy fishermen still ply their trade; several brightly painted fishing smacks are usually pulled up to complete the effect.

At the far end you'll see Collioure's landmark, painted by Matisse and many others: the church of **Notre-Dame-des-Anges** (*open daily 9–12 and 2–6*). The Colliourencs built it in the 1680s to succeed the original church destroyed by Vauban; they chose the beach site to use the old cylindrical lighthouse as a bell tower. The best thing about the church is that you can hear the waves of the sea from inside, a profound *basso continuo* that makes the celebration of mass here a unique experience. The next best are the retables, five of them, done between 1699 and 1720 by Joseph Sunyer and others. Catalan Baroque at its eccentric best, influenced by the Spanish *churrigueresque*, often concentrated its finest efforts on these towering constructions of carved wooden figures, dioramas of scriptural scenes with intricately painted stage-drop backgrounds. Sunyer's are especially lifelike.

The second of Collioure's beaches lies right behind the church; really an old sand-bar that has become part of dry land, it connects the town with a former islet, the **Ilôt St-Vincent**, crowned with a tiny medieval chapel. A scenic footpath called the Sentier de la Moulade leads from near the church along the rocky shore north of Collioure. High above, you'll see **Fort Miradoux**, the Spanish King Philip II's addition to Collioure's defences, and still in military use.

If you want to see how all those anchovies are prepared, visit the Roque family anchovy business at 17 Route d'Argelès, **t** 04 68 82 22 30 (*call first*). There's also a shop selling the produce.

Port-Vendres and Banyuls-sur-Mer

Few of us, probably, give any thought to how anchovies are apprehended in the open sea. It isn't, in fact, a terribly difficult operation. The diabolical Catalans have boats called *lámparos*, with big searchlights. They sneak out on warm summer nights, when the normally shy anchovies are making their promenade, and nab the lot. After spending a few months in barrels of brine, the unfortunate fish reappear, only to be stuffed into olives, a Catalan favourite. More of this doubtful business goes on in **Port-Vendres**. This is a real port, modern-style, with none of the charm of Collioure. Louis XVI's government had big plans for developing Port-Vendres, all of which were scuppered with the Revolution; some grandiose neoclassical buildings remain from this programme, around the central **Place de l'Obélisque**, along with a 98ft obelisk decorated with propaganda reliefs celebrating poor Louis' glorious reign.

From here, the coast juts out eastwards, with a picturesque small promontory called **Cap Béar**, topped by another of this area's many Baroque-era fortresses. Its monument to Sidi-Ferruch was originally erected in Algiers in 1930 to celebrate the centenary of French colonization; after 1962, when the Algerians didn't want the thing anymore, it was set up here. There are many isolated **beaches** in the vicinity, though they are hard to reach; most are south of the cape, including the one at Paulilles, near an abandoned dynamite factory (a mildly historic one, because it belonged to Alfred Nobel, inventor of dynamite and plywood, who used the profits to finance his Prizes).

Banyuls-sur-Mer (Banyuls de la Marenda in Catalan) is the next town along the picturesque coastal N114, a sleepy resort with a beach and mini-golf right at the centre. The heart of the Banyuls wine region, it is also the home of the Fondation Arago, an oceanographic laboratory affiliated to the University of Paris. Their excellent **Aquarium of Mediterranean Species** (*t 04 68 88 73 39; open July and Aug daily 9–1 and 2–9; Sept–June daily 9–12 and 2–6.30; adm*) was built in 1883; don't miss the grand-daddy lobster and sea anemones and 250 kinds of birds. The coast between Banyuls and Cerebère forms a 650ha **Marine Reserve**, the oldest in France. You can visit some parts of it through organized driving trips; call t 04 68 88 09 11. As for art, Banyuls has a good 11th-century Romanesque church, **La Rectorie** (*Av du Puig-del-Mas; open Sat 9–11 only*), and takes credit for Aristide Maillol, perhaps the best-known French sculptor of the last century after Rodin, born here in 1861. He contributed the town's War Memorial, on the waterfront promontory, as well as many other monuments along the Côte Vermeille and in Perpignan; his tomb, documents tracing his life, and a few copies of works are in his old farmhouse, La Métairie, now the **Musée Aristide Maillol**, 4km up the Col de Banyuls road (*t 04 68 88 57 11; open daily May–Sept 10–12 and 4–7; Oct–April 10–12 and 2–5; adm*).

If you don't care to go to Cerbère, or to Spain, there is an alternative to retracing your steps along the coast – an extremely scenic route through the mountains back to Collioure, along the steep and narrow D86. It begins from the back of Banyuls, beyond the railway overpass, and climbs through ancient olive groves on the lower slopes of the Monts-Albères. Several abandoned fortresses come into view, though

Wine: Banyuls

A naturally sweet, spicy wine (AOC since 1936), fortified with a dollop of *eau de vie* prior to being aged for 3 to 15 years, Banyuls was first made by the Templars in the 11th century, from the dark grenache grapes grown on the rocky red terraces of the Côte Vermeille. A fine old Banyuls is claimed to be the only wine that can accompany chocolate desserts, but be warned: a cheap young bottle may hardly do justice to a Mars bar.

Collioure, Port-Vendres, Cerbère and Banyuls are the only places allowed to wear the AOC label, and 80 per cent of their wine, as well as the delightful dry red wines of Collioure, pass through the **Cellier des Templiers** co-operative, Route de Mas-Reig, t 04 68 98 36 92 (*open Nov–Mar 10.30–1 and 2.30–6.30; April–Oct 10.30–7.30*), a large concern happy to receive visitors for tastings and a tour at their magnificently vaulted 13th-century Cellier des Templiers; their *cave souterraine* just below (*open July and Aug only and by appt*) has enormous hundred-year-old oak barrels, and a film on the wine. The **Cave de l'Etoile**, 26 Av du Puig-del-Mas in Banyuls, t 04 68 88 00 10, f 04 68 88 15 10, *www.banyuls-etoile.com*, is a co-operative where everything is done lovingly in the old-fashioned way; up the same street, one can visit the excellent **Domaine de la Rectoire**, t 04 68 88 07 78, f 04 68 88 18 55, *www.la-rectoire.com*.

A good selection of Collioure wine can be found at **Domaine du Mas Blanc**, 9 Av Gén. de Gaulle, t 04 68 88 32 12, *www.domaine-du-mas-blanc.com*, and in Collioure at **Caves les Dominicains**, Place Orfila, t 04 68 82 05 63, *www.dominicain.com*. If you wish to try the local wines with local food in a delightful setting, book dinner (*June–Sept only*) at the *ferme-auberge* at **Les Clos de Paulilles**, Port Vendres, t 04 68 98 07 58 – different wines accompany each course.

none is especially easy to reach. This border region rivals even the Corbières for quantity of castles. There is also a ruined monastery, the **Abbaye de Valbonne**, on the heights to the west; the track to it begins at the pilgrimage chapel of **Notre-Dame-de-Consolation**. A little before this, the **Tour Madeloc** is the climax of the trip; it was a signal tower, part of the sophisticated communications network that kept the medieval kings of Aragon in close contact with their borders.

Cerbère and Beyond

You may well have already been here, but Cerbère won't bring back any pleasant memories – being herded from one train to another in the middle of the night (because Spanish railways still use a different track gauge) under the gaze of soldiers with sub-machine-guns and impossible customs men who do their best to make this seem like an old Hitchcock spy film instead of one of the busiest, most unexciting border rail-crossings in the EU. No one has ever seen Cerbère in daylight, but you might give it a try. The coast here is at its most spectacular (it's especially good for diving) and there are a few pebble beaches, never crowded. With its three small hotels, Cerbère is a minuscule resort, with a World's End air about it.

There is a lot to be said for pressing on even further, into Unoccupied Catalunya (the signs at the border still say 'Spain' for courtesy's sake). **Barcelona**, one of the most vibrant and creative cities in Europe today, is only two hours by train from Cerbère. **Girona**, with its exquisite medieval centre and unique cathedral, is half the distance. If you liked the Côte Vermeille, continue south for more of the same on the **Costa Brava**, often overcrowded though still nice (especially the northern parts). And if you can manage only one unambitious day trip into Spain, try **Figueras**, a short hop by train or a pleasant 50km drive along the C252; the Salvador Dalí Museum here, in the artist's home town, is an unforgettable attraction, the 'temple of Surrealism', where you can water the plants in the garden by feeding pesetas into a Cadillac.

Perpignan

There's a little craziness in every Catalan soul. In *Perpinyà* (as its residents call it), former capital of the kings of Majorca and the counts of Roussillon, this natural exuberance was until recently rather suppressed by French centralization, but the spate of building works, the busy calendar of festivals and activities and the lively outdoor cafés suggest that the city is now springing into life in its own way; the tourist office certainly wants it on the European cultural map, filling the streets with information panels pinpointing historical sites, sights, and even shops.

The king of kookiness himself, Salvador Dalí, set off the first sparks when he passed Perpignan's train station in a taxi, and 'it all became clear in a flash: there, right before me, was the centre of the universe!' The otherwise ordinary Gare SNCF has been a hot destination for Surrealist pilgrims ever since; the street leading to the station, Av du Général de Gaulle, has undergone a *traitement dalinien*, which includes the installation of benches shaped like Mae West's lips and a Dalinien railway carriage suspended in front of the station. The city worships Dalí like a hero.

History

Perpignan is named after Perperna, a lieutenant of the great 1st-century BC populist general Quintus Sertorius. While Rome was suffering under the dictatorship of Pompey, Sertorius governed most of Spain in accordance with his astonishing principle that one should treat Rome's provinces decently. The enraged Senate sent out five legions to destroy him, but his army, who all swore to die if he was killed, defeated each one until the villainous Perperna invited his boss to a banquet in the Pyrenees and murdered him.

In 1197, Perpignan became the first Catalan city granted a municipal charter, and governed itself by a council elected by the three estates or 'arms'. Its merchants traded as far abroad as Constantinople, and the city enjoyed its most brilliant period in the 13th century when Jaime I, king of Aragon and conqueror of Majorca, created the Kingdom of Majorca and County of Roussillon for his younger son, Jaime II. This little kingdom was absorbed by the Catalan kings of Aragon in the 14th century, but continued to prosper until 1463, when Louis XI's army came to claim Perpignan and Roussillon as payment for mercenaries sent to Aragon. Besieged, the Perpignanais ate rats rather than become French, until the king of Aragon himself ordered them to

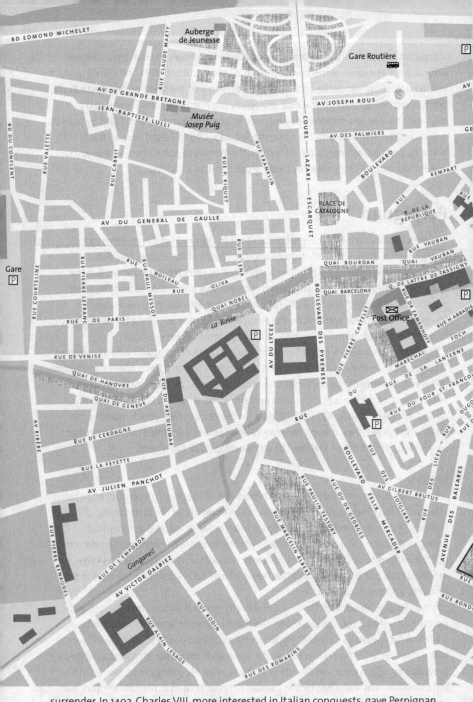

surrender. In 1493, Charles VIII, more interested in Italian conquests, gave Perpignan back to Spain. But in the 1640s Richelieu pounced on the first available chance to grab back this corner of the mystic Hexagon, and French possession of Roussillon and the Haute Cerdagne was cemented in the 1659 Treaty of the Pyrenees.

Le Castillet

When most of Perpignan's walls were destroyed in 1904, its easy-going river-cum-moat, La Basse, was planted with lawns, flowerbeds, mimosas and Art Nouveau cafés. The fat brick towers and crenellated gate of **Le Castillet** in Place du Verdun were left

Getting There and Around

By Air

Perpignan's airport, *www.perpignan.cci.fr*, is 5km northwest of the city and linked by shuttle bus *navettes* from the bus station an hour before each flight (info on t 04 68 55 68 00).

Ryanair has a daily flight from London Stansted and there are flights from Birmingham and Southampton with Flybe (*see* p.66).

By Train

The train station, Dalí's 'centre of the universe', is at the end of Av du Général de Gaulle and has frequent services down to the Spanish border at Port Bou and a TGV service to Paris in 6 hours.

By Bus

The *gare routière* is to the north of the city, on Av du Général Leclerc, t 04 68 35 29 02, *www.udsist.net*.

Car and Bike Hire

You can hire a **car** at the airport, or from **Europcar**, 1 Av Gén. de Gaulle, t 04 68 34 89 80, or **Avis**, 13 Bd du Conflent, t 04 68 34 26 71.

Bicycle hire is available at **Cycles Mercier**, 20 Av Gilbert-Brutus, t 04 68 85 02 71.

Tourist Information

Perpignan: Palais des Congrès, Place Armand Lanoux, t 04 68 66 30 30, f 04 68 66 30 26, *www.perpignantourisme.com*. Open mid-June–mid–Sept Mon–Sat 9–7, Sun 10–4; mid-Sept–mid-June Mon–Sat 9–6, Sun 9–12.

Post office: Rue Dr Zamenhof.

Market Days

Daily am: Place Cassanyes.

Sat am: Place de Catalogne, regional produce. *See www.mairie-perpignan.fr for a full list.*

Where to Stay

Perpignan ⊠ 66000

***Le Park, 18 Bd Jean-Bourrat, near the tourist office, t 04 68 35 14 14, f 04 68 35 48 18, *www.parkhotel-fr.com* (*luxury–expensive*). Plush, air-conditioned, soundproofed rooms and restaurant (*expensive; see 'Eating Out'*) with an old Spanish feel and flair.

****La Villa Duflot, Rond-Point Albert Donnezan, t 04 68 56 67 67, f 04 68 56 54 05, *www.villa-duflot.com* (*expensive*). The only 4-star hotel is near the Perpignan-Sud-Argelès motorway exit, in the middle of an industrial zone! However, you can pretend to be elsewhere in the comfortable air-conditioned rooms and garden, or in the popular restaurant overlooking the pool.

**Hôtel de la Loge, 1 Rue desFabriques d'en Nabot, t 04 68 34 41 02, f 04 68 34 25 13, *www. hoteldelaloge.fr* (*inexpensive*). Nicest in the centre, in a 16th-century building, this has pretty rooms, some with TV and air-conditioning, and a lovely inner courtyard.

**Le Maillol, 14 Impasse des Cardeurs, t 04 68 51 10 20, f 04 68 51 20 29 (*inexpensive*). In a 17th-century building: not too noisy, and convenient for the sights.

upright for memories' sake; built in 1368 by Aragon to keep out the French, it became a prison once the French got in, especially during the Revolution. In 1946 a mason broke through a sealed wall in Le Castillet and found the body of a child, which on contact with the air dissolved into dust; from the surviving clothing fragments the corpse was dated to the end of the 18th century. And ever since, people have wondered: could it have been Marie-Antoinette's son, the dauphin Louis XVII? After all, the child buried in the Temple in Paris was known to be a substitute, and there have always been rumours that the Revolutionaries used the dauphin as a secret bargaining chip in dealing with his Bourbon relatives in Spain.

Along with this mysterious ghost, Le Castillet houses a museum of Catalan art and traditions, the **Musée Pairal** (t *04 68 35 42 05; open May–Sept Wed–Mon 10–7;*

★★Le Helder, Av du Général de Gaulle, t 04 68 34 38 05 (*inexpensive*).

★Le Berry, 6 Av du Général de Gaulle, t 04 68 34 59 02 (*inexpensive*).

Auberge de Jeunesse, Parc de la Pépinère, Av de Grande-Bretagne, t 04 68 34 63 32, *perpignan@fuaj.org*. A small youth hostel, with breakfast available. *Book in summer. Closed mid-Dec–mid-Jan.*

Eating Out

Le Chapon Fin, Le Park (*see above*), t 04 68 35 14 14 (*expensive*). This has been Perpignan's finest restaurant for years, as well as one of the prettiest, with its Catalan ceramics. But it's the *tartare de saumon* and ravioli stuffed with scallops that keep its clients coming back for more, even all the way from Spain. *Closed Sun, and first 2 wks in Jan and 2 wks Aug.*

Casa Sansa, 3 Rue Fabriques Couvertes, near Le Castillet, t 04 68 34 21 84 (*expensive–moderate*). Lively, with excellent food served in a 14th-century cellar – with dishes ranging from Catalan *escargots* to rabbit with *aïoli*; occasional live music; and more than its share of Catalan flair. *Book Fri and Sat nights.*

Le France, Place de la Loge, t 04 68 51 61 71 (*expensive–moderate*). The bistro-grill under the Loge, a relaxed place with pink and white floor tiling to match the outside. Eat inside or on the terrace; there are good meat and fish menu choices. *Closed Sun and Mon eve, and early Jan–early Feb.*

Le Vauban, 29 Quai Vauban, t 04 68 51 05 10 (*moderate*). A sure bet, with well-prepared plats du jour and menus. *Closed Sun, and 2 wks May.*

Les Antiquaires, Place Desprès, t 04 68 34 06 58 (*moderate*). A local favourite for reliable classic French cooking. *Closed Sun eve and Mon.*

Brasserie l'Arago, Place Arago, t 04 68 51 81 96 (*cheap*). Packed day and night; good food and pizza – not always a strong point with the Catalans.

Les Expéditeurs, 19 Av du Général Leclerc, t 04 68 35 15 80 (*cheap*). Catalan cooking and paella on Wed. *Closed Sat eve, Sun, Mon eve and Aug.*

Entertainment and Nightlife

On evenings from June to September in Place de la Castillet, the Perpignanais come to dance *sardanas*, the national Catalan circle dance. Outside of summer, nightlife is mostly concentrated on students.

Le Zinc, 8 Rue Grande-des-Fabriques, t 04 68 35 08 80. Jazz and cocktails; especially animated during the Perpignan Jazz Festival in Oct, *Jazzèbre*.

Every year in September, Perpignan is host to **Visa pour Image**, *www.visapourlimage.com*, the annual world festival of photo-journalism, with exhibitions from top photographers in venues from churches to shops.

Cinemas

Cinéma Castillet, 1 Bd Wilson, t 04 68 51 25 47.

Cinéma Rive Gauche et Centre-Ville, 29 Quai Vauban, t 04 68 51 05 00.

Oct–April 11–5.30; *closed Tues; adm*), with items ranging from casts of Pau (Pablo) Casals' hands to a kitchen from a Catalan *mas*, complete with a hole in the door for the Catalan cat. Place du Verdun, by Le Castillet, is one of Perpignan's liveliest squares, while just outside the gate, the **Promenade des Platanes** is lined with rows of magnificent plane trees and palms.

Loge de Mer to the Musée Rigaud

From Le Castillet, Rue Louis Blanc leads back to Place de la Loge, where the cafés provide a grandstand for contemplating Aristide Maillol's voluptuous bronze *Venus* and Perpignan's most beautiful building, the Gothic **Loge de Mer**, or Llotja, built in 1397 by the king of Aragon to house the exchange and the Consolat de Mar, a branch of the Barcelona council founded by Jaime I to resolve trade and maritime disputes. This proud and noble building of ochre stone, with its Venetian arches and loggia and ship-shaped weathercock, fell on hard times – but Perpignan takes good care of its monuments. At one point the city rented the Llotja to a fast-food chain, but things have moved slightly upmarket and it is now a nice bistro-grill (see 'Eating Out').

The neighbouring 13th-century **Hôtel de Ville** has been spared the Llotja's humiliation, probably because it still serves its original purpose: on Saturday mornings, when its courtyard fills with blushing brides posing for photos by Maillol's allegory of the Mediterranean (as a naked woman, of course). It is built of rounded river pebbles and bricks in the curious layer-cake style of medieval Perpignan; three bronze arms sticking out of the façade are said to symbolize Perpignan's three estates, or *bras*. To the right, the **Palais de la Députation Provinciale** (1447) is a masterpiece of Catalan Renaissance, formerly the seat of Roussillon's parliament and now housing dismal municipal offices.

Rue Fabriques-Nabot, opposite the palace, was once the street of drapers: note the **Hôtel Julia** (No.2), a rare survival of a 15th-century town house, with a Gothic courtyard.

South of the Députation, in Rue de l'Ange, the **Musée Rigaud** (*t 04 68 35 43 40; open Wed–Mon 12–7; closed Tues; adm*) is named after Perpignan native Hyacinthe Rigaud (1659–1743), portrait painter to Louis XIV. Hyacinthe, master of raising the mediocre and unworthy to virtuoso heights of rosy-cheeked, debonair charm and sophistication, is well represented, most famously in his portrait of the Cardinal de Bouillon, who beams with self-satisfaction as chubby *putti* wallow in his worldly loot. All the hypersensitive alarms, however, are around the *Retable de la Trinité* (1489) by the Master of Canapost, painted for the 100th anniversary of the Consolat de Mar and showing, underneath, a fanciful scene of the sea lapping at the base of the Llotja. Works by Picasso, Dufy, Maillol, Miró and a score of others are upstairs. The tangle of narrow streets near here and around Place de la République are full of interesting stalls and small shops.

Cathédrale St-Jean and the Dévôt Christ

Just east of Place de la Loge unfolds Place Gambetta, site of Perpignan's pebble-and-brick **cathedral** (*open daily 8–11.45 and 3–6.15*), topped by a lacy 19th-century wrought-iron campanile. Begun in 1324 but not ready for use until 1509, the interior is a success because the builders stuck to the design provided in the 15th century by Guillem Sagrera, architect of the great cathedral of Palma de Majorca. Typical of Catalan Gothic, it has a single nave, 157ft long, striking for its spacious width rather than its soaring height.

The chapels, wedged between the huge piers, hold some unique treasures, the oldest of which is a mysterious marble **baptismal font** (first chapel on the left). Pre-Romanesque, perhaps even Visigothic in origin, and carved from the drum of a Roman column to look like a tub bound with a cable, it bears a primitive face of Christ over an open book. Further up the left aisle, the massive organ was decorated in the 15th century with painted shutters and sumptuous carvings. On the pendentive under the organ, note the Moor's head – a common Catalan conceit symbolizing wisdom, taken from the Templars, who exerted a powerful influence over the kings of Aragon. The jaw was originally articulated, to vomit sweetmeats on holidays; now it's stuck, gaping open. Beyond the Moor's head, in an 11th-century chapel from the original cathedral, is a pawnshop window of dingy reliquaries and the effigy of the cathedral's founder, Jaime's son Sancho, his feet resting on a Chinese lion.

The cathedral is proudest of its exquisite **retables**: on the high altar, the marble *Retable de St-Jean*, carved in a late Renaissance style in 1621 by Claude Perret; at the end of the left crossing, the *Retable des Stes Eulalie et Julie* (1670s); in the apsidal chapels, the painted wood *Retable de St-Pierre* (mid 16th century), and to the right, the lovely *Notre-Dame de la Mangrana* (1500) – its name, 'of the pomegranate', comes from an earlier statue of the Virgin, which held a pomegranate, a symbol of fertility.

A door in the right aisle leads out to a 16th-century chapel constructed especially to house an extraordinary wooden sculpture known as the **Dévôt Christ**. Carved in the Cologne region in 1307, this wasted Christ, whose contorted bones, sinews and torn flesh are carved with a rare anatomical realism, is stretched to the limits of agony on the Cross. Almost too painful to behold, it comes straight from the gloomy age when Christendom believed that pain, contemplated or self-inflicted, brought one closer to God. It is an object of great veneration, and the Perpignanais claim that when the Christ's bowed head sags another quarter inch to touch His chest, the world will end.

Nearby in Place Gambetta is the entrance to the cathedral's **Campo Santo** of 1300–1330 (*open April–Sept daily 12–7; Oct–Mar daily 11–5*), the only cloister-cemetery of its kind of France, the tombs decorated with fine bas reliefs; this being Perpignan, until the late 1980s it was used as offices by the local *gendarmerie*. A door from the cloister leads into the striking 15th-century **Salle Capitulaire**, its complex ogival vaulting attributed to Guillem Sagrera. To the left of the cathedral's façade is Perpignan's oldest church, **St-Jean-le-Vieux** (1025), converted into an electrical generating station in 1890. Its Romanesque portal offers a very different view of Jesus from the German Dévôt Christ: the imperious and typically Catalan *Majestat* (Christ in Majesty).

Quartier St-Jacques

The piquant neighbourhood south of the cathedral, built on the slopes of Puig des Lépreux (Lepers' Hill), was once the *aljama*, or Jewish quarter of Perpignan. In its happiest days, in the 13th century, it produced a remarkable body of literature – especially from the pen of the mathematician and Talmudic scholar Gerson ben Salomon (author of the philosophical *Gate of Heaven*) – as well as rare manuscripts and calligraphy, all now in Paris. After the Jews were exiled, the quarter was renamed St-Jacques, and inhabited by working men's families and Gypsies, and most recently by Algerians.

The 12th to 14th-century church of **St-Jacques** (*closed for renovation in 2005*) is opulent and rich inside: there's a 'Cross of Insults' as in Elne, a statue of St James in Compostela pilgrimage gear (1450), and more fine retables, especially the 15th-century *Notre-Dame de l'Espérance*, featuring a rare view of the pregnant Virgin.

In the early 15th century, while the fire-eating Dominican preacher St Vincent Ferrer was in Perpignan to advise in the dispute between Antipope Benedict XIII and Rome, he founded in this church the confraternity of the Holy Blood (*de la Sanch*) to bring religious comfort to prisoners condemned to death. As in Seville, the confraternity reaches a wider audience during Holy Week, when it dons spooky Ku Klux Klan-like hoods and bears a procession of holy floats (the *misteri*) while singers wail dirges from the crowd.

The Palace of the Kings of Majorca

Enclosed in a vast extent of walls, originally medieval and later enlarged by Vauban, the **Palais des Rois de Majorque** (*entrance in Rue des Archers, t 04 68 34 48 29; open daily June–Sept 10–6; Oct–May 9–5; adm*) is the oldest royal palace in France, begun in the 1270s by Jaime the Conqueror and occupied by his son Jaime II after 1283. Yet for all its grandeur, only three kings of Majorca were to reign here before Roussillon, Montpellier, the Cerdagne and the Balearic islands were reabsorbed by Aragon in 1349. The scale of magnificence that they intended to become accustomed to survives, but not much else.

A rectangle built around a mastodontic but elegant Romanesque–Gothic courtyard, the palace is now a favourite venue for events, exhibitions and dancing the *sardana*, the Catalan national dance.

The **Salle de Majorque**, or throne room, with its three vast fireplaces, and the double-decker chapels in the **Donjon**, with the queen's chapel on the bottom and the king's on top, both offer hints at the exotic splendour of the Majorcan court. The sacristy was the entrance to a network of underground passageways that connected the palace to its enormous 147ft-deep wells, which also afforded Jaime II an escape from his fierce and unwelcome older brother, Pedro III of Aragon. The palace once stood in the midst of what the archives call 'Paradise' – partly enclosed terraced gardens, inspired by Moorish gardens on Majorca. A few traces remain to the right of the mightiest tower, the **Tour de Homage**.

The narrow grid of streets below the palace, around the church of **St-Mathieu**, were designed by the Templar tutors of Jaime the Conqueror, although most of the buildings date from the 18th century.

Lastly, on the northwest side of town, the **Musée des Médailles et des Monnaies Puig** (*42 Av de Grande-Bretagne, t 04 68 66 24 86; open Tues–Sat 10–6; adm*), has an excellent collection of coins and medals from antiquity to modern times, with a section on Catalan money.

Cabestany

Of all the villages ingested by Greater Perpignan, none is as celebrated as Cabestany (Cabestanh), 4km to the southeast. It produced a highly original Romanesque sculptor known as the Master of Cabestany, who worked as far afield as Tuscany and left his home-town church a **tympanum** of the *Dormition and Assumption of the Virgin*, and a scene of the Virgin in heaven, handing her girdle down to St Thomas.

Cabestany was also the home of the troubadour Guilhem de Cabestanh, who wrote some of the most popular love poems of the Middle Ages. He is most famous for a legend that reached even Boccaccio (*Decameron*, Day 4: 9). Guilhem loved and was loved by the wife of a knight, one Raymond of Castel-Rossello. When Raymond learned of their affair, he ambushed Guilhem, murdered him and cut out his heart, which he gave to his cook to prepare with plenty of pepper. His wife ate it and praised the dish. 'I am not surprised,' said her husband, 'as you loved it so well when it was alive.' And he told her what she had eaten. But the lady kept her *sang-froid*. 'Sir,' she said, 'you have given me such an excellent thing to eat that God forbid any other food should again pass my lips.' And she leapt out the window to her death.

Southern Roussillon and the Pyrenees

Pyrenean Valleys

Two important valleys, the **Conflent** (the valley of the river Têt) and the **Vallespir** (of the river Tech), slope in parallel lines toward the Spanish border. Don't think that this butt end of the Pyrenees consists of mere foothills; in between the two valleys stands snow-capped **Canigou**, not the highest (a mere 9,134ft) but certainly one of the most imposing peaks of the chain, jauntily wearing a Phrygian cap of snow until late spring. The *muntanya regalada* ('fortunate mountain') of the Catalans is one of the symbols of the nation, the subject of one of the best-known Catalan folksongs. Every summer solstice Catalans from both sides of the frontier ceremoniously light a huge bonfire on its summit, the signal for surrounding villages to light their own, all at the exact same moment. Legends and apparitions abound on Canigou. Fairies and 'ladies of the waters' are said to frequent its forested slopes, and King Pedro of Aragon climbed it in 1285 and met a dragon near the top.

From Perpignan to Ille-sur-Têt

The fish-filled Têt, before passing through Perpignan, washes a wide plain packed full of vineyards and fat villages. The fattest, **Thuir**, puts up signs all over Roussillon inviting us over to see the World's Biggest Barrel, in the cellars of the famous aperitifs Byrrh and Dubonnet – wine mixed with quinine, invented here a little over a century ago (*www.byrrh.com; tours April–Sept 9–11.45 and 2.30–5.45; July and Aug 10–11.45 and 2–6.45; adm*).

After a few aperitifs, head 6km west for golden-hued **Castelnou**, a perfectly preserved medieval village on winding, pebble-paved lanes and steps under the 10th-century castle of the counts of Cerdagne (*t 04 68 53 22 91; open July and Aug 10–7; April–Sept 10.30–6; Oct–Mar 11–6; last ticket 1hr before closing; adm*). Restored after the roof caught fire in 1981, this castle, unlike most military castles in France, never graduated into a lordly residence, and the rooms are empty today.

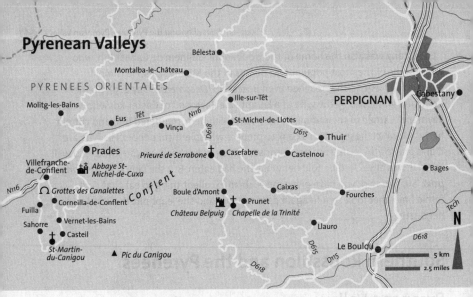

Pyrenean Valleys

The narrow D48 wiggling west of Castelnou is unabashedly beautiful: if you have a couple of hours to spare, you can circle around to the Prieuré de Serrabonne (*see below*) by way of the D2 to Caixas and Fourques, then on to the D13 for Llauro and **Prunet-et-Belpuig**, where the ruins of the Château de Belpuig offer a superb view and the 11th-century Chapelle de la Trinité has sculpture by the same school as Serrabonne.

In **Boule d'Amont**, just up the road, there's another charming church from the same century. A shorter alternative, but on even more dubious roads, is to take the D2 north to St-Michel-de-Llotes (site of the **Dolmen de la Creu de la Llosa** and with a museum on local agriculture and wine production) and turn back to Serrabonne by way of **Casefabre**, with its tremendous views.

At **Ille-sur-Têt**, an attractive old village at the gateway to the mountains, neglected art from the 11th to 19th centuries from churches all over Roussillon has been assembled in a 16th-century hospital, the **Centre d'Art Sacré**, with exhibitions on various themes and periods, changing every six months or so (*t 04 68 84 83 96; open mid-June–Sept Mon–Fri 10–12 and 2–7, Sat and Sun 2–7; Oct–Nov and Feb–mid-June Wed–Mon 2–6, closed Tues; closed Dec and Jan*).

The D2 northwest of Ille to Montalba-le-Château takes you very quickly to some surprising scenery: orange eroded 'fairy chimneys' called the **Orgues** (*t 04 68 84 13 13; site open July–Aug daily 9.30–8; April–June and Sept daily 10–6.30; Oct daily 10–12.30 and 2–6; Nov–Jan daily 2–5; Feb and Mar daily 10–12.30 and 2–5.30; adm*), with the forgotten ruin of a 12th-century tower perched on top, and the Pyrenees forming a magnificent backdrop.

The fortified church of **Régleille** (from Ille, take the D2 over the river and after a kilometre turn right on to a little road) looks like a castle – a typical example of a monastic church, in an area without any castles, that grew into a fortress to protect the monks and the village. Ille was here before its population drifted to the present site.

Six kilometres north on the D21, in little **Bélesta**, the **Château-Musée** (*t 04 68 84 55 55; open mid-June–mid-Sept Wed–Fri and Sun 2–7; mid-Sept–mid-June Wed–Fri and*

Sun 2–5.30; closed Tues and Sat; adm) holds the treasure found in a Neolithic tomb in 1983; the superbly restored castle itself is a 13th-century work built by Saint Louis.

Prieuré de Serrabonne

Seeing the finest medieval sculpture in Roussillon requires dedication: the most direct route (for others, *see* above) requires 13km of hairpin bends on a road where you dread oncoming traffic, starting from the D618 at Bouleternère, just west of Ille, and

Getting Around

The bus and train service is probably better here than in any other rural region in this book – only it won't help you see rural monuments like St-Michel or Serrabonne.

By Train

At Villefranche-de-Conflent you can pick up **Le Petit Train Jaune**, *www.traintouristiques-ter. com/train_jaune.htm*, a scenic narrow- gauge train that runs 6 times a day in July and August into the Cerdagne, unchanged since 1910. One of the most unlikely railways in France, it was entirely a political project, meant to bring some new life into the impoverished mountain valleys. It has kept puffing ever since – only tourism has saved it from closing: when checking the schedule, make sure you don't choose one of the departures taken over by buses. The scenery is striking, even more so in summer when viewed from topless carriages. The last station is Latour-de-Carol, where you can pick up a bus to Andorra and Spain, or a train to Toulouse or Barcelona.

By Bus

Using Perpignan as a base, it's possible to see quite a bit of the Conflent and Vallespir; from the *gare routière* there are 10 or 12 buses a day (**t** 04 68 35 29 02) to Prades and Villefranche-de-Conflent, and a few of these continue to Font-Romeu and Latour-de-Carol. For the Vallespir, there are frequent, convenient buses to Ceret, Arles-sur-Tech and Amélie-les-Bains-Palada, and a few press on further up the valley to Prats-de-Mollo.

Tourist Information

Ille-sur-Têt: Square de la Poste, **t** 04 68 84 02 62, **f** 04 68 84 02 62, *www.ille-sur-tet.com*.

Open Mon–Fri 9–12 and 2–6; July–Aug Mon–Sat 9–12 and 2–6, Sun 9–12.
Prades: 4 Rue des Marchands, **t** 04 68 05 41 02, **f** 04 68 05 21 79, *www.prades-tourisme.com. Open Mon–Thurs 9–12 and 2–6, Fri 9–12 and 2–5.*
Vernet-les-Bains: 6 Place de l'Ancienne Mairie, **t** 04 68 05 55 35, **f** 04 68 05 60 33, *www.ot-vernet-les-bains.fr. Open July–Aug Mon–Fri 9–12.30 and 3–6.30 and Sat 9–12; Sept–June Mon–Fri 9–12 and 2–6.*
Villefranche-de-Conflent: 32 bis Rue St-Jacques, **t** 04 68 96 22 96. *Open July–Aug daily 10–7.30; June and Sept daily 10–6.30; Oct–May daily 2–5; school hols daily 10–12 and 2–5; closed Jan.*

Market Days

Ille-sur-Têt: Wed and Fri; flea market on Sun.
Prades: Tues.

Where to Stay and Eat

Until recently this area has been a gastronomic desert, but it's improving, with imaginative Catalan cuisine and seafood.

Prades ✉ 66500

*Hostalrich, 156 Rue Général de Gaulle, **t** 04 68 96 05 38 (*inexpensive*). A big neon sign makes it easy to find the Hostalrich; all rooms have TV and showers and some have balconies. Avoid the restaurant if you can; the food is simple to the point of dullness. There's a wonderful chestnut-shaded garden as compensation.
Jardin de L'Aymeric, 3 Av du Général de Gaulle, **t** 04 68 96 53 38 (*moderate*). The best bet for stylish regional cooking, though the excess of neon detracts from the atmosphere. *Closed Sun, Mon, and Wed eve.*

ending in a lofty, remote, barren spot on the slopes of a mountain called Roque Rouge. The solemn, spare shape and dark schist of Serrabonne's church (*t 04 68 84 09 30; open daily 10–6; adm*) are not promising, making the surprise inside that much the greater. The best efforts of the 12th-century Catalan sculptors were concentrated in the single gallery of the cloister, and especially in the **tribune**, in rose marble from Canigou. Perfectly preserved in its isolated setting, this includes a fantastical bestiary, centaurs, a grimacing St Michael, reliefs of the four Evangelists and more. The style of

L'Hostal de Nogarols, Chem Nogarols, at Codalet, on the way to St-Michel-de-Cuxa, t 04 68 96 24 57 (*moderate*). A good stop before music concerts, serving excellent wood-fired pizzas, as well as Catalan classics like *petit gris* snails, in an airy dining room or pretty shady garden. *Closed Wed, and Tues eve.*

Vernet-les-Bains ✉ 66820

★★★Le Mas Fleuri, 25 Bd Clemenceau (the road up to St-Martin), t 04 68 05 51 94, f 04 68 05 50 77, *www.hotellemasfleuri.fr* (*expensive–moderate*). At the top of the list, this century-old hotel is set in a pretty park, with a pool; rooms are air-conditioned (no restaurant). *Closed mid-Oct–mid-April.*

★★Princess, Rue Lavandières, t 04 68 05 56 22, f 04 68 05 62 45 (*inexpensive*). A pleasant *Logis de France* with a better-than-average restaurant (*moderate*). *Closed Dec–mid-Mar.*

Comte Guilifred, t 04 68 05 51 37, f 04 68 05 64 11 (*moderate*). This modern restaurant is the training ground for the local hotel school. *Open lunchtimes Mon, Tues, Thurs and Fri; closed July.*

Molitg-les-Bains ✉ 66500

★★★★Château de Riell, t 04 68 05 04 40, f 04 68 05 04 37, *www.relaischateaux.fr/riell* (*luxury–expensive*). Molitg may have only 180 inhabitants, but it can claim Roussillon's top luxury hotel, the sumptuous Relais & Châteaux Château de Riell. This Baroque folly from the turn of the century is in a theatrically Baroque setting, perched on a rock with exquisite views of Canigou; it has elegant, luxurious Hollywoodian rooms in the château (€275) and maisonettes in the garden (€144) – both a contrast with the medieval *oubliettes*, which you can visit – and two pools, including one on top of the

tower, perhaps the best place in the world to watch the Catalan bonfires go up on the solstice (*see* p.597). Lots of extras, and a restaurant worthy of the décor. *Closed Nov–Mar.*

★★★Grand Hotel Thermal, t 04 68 05 00 50, f 04 68 05 02 91 (*expensive*). Less pricey, but almost as splendid, with marble spa rooms, swimming pool and marble terrace, glorious views and also a very good value restaurant (*moderate*). *Closed Dec–Mar; restaurant closed eves and weekends.*

Mas Lluganas, just outside Mosset, t 04 68 05 00 37, f 04 68 05 04 08, *www.maslluganas. com* (*inexpensive*). Offers rooms and *chambre d'hôte* meals (*moderate*) based on its own produce of ducks, guinea fowl, veal and *foie gras*. The same family also offers inexpensive *chambre d'hôte* accommodation at **La Forge**, a peaceful retreat by the river (t 04 68 05 04 84, f 04 68 05 04 08) *Closed mid-Oct–Mar.*

Villefranche-de-Conflent ✉ 66500

★★Auberge du Cèdre, Domaine Ste-Eulalie, outside the walls, t 04 68 96 05 05 (*inexpensive*). Nine comfortable rooms, an adequate restaurant and two fat, friendly cats in the garden. *Restaurant only open to residents.*

Auberge St-Paul, Place de l'Eglise, t 04 68 96 30 95, *http://perso.wanadoo.fr/auberge. stpaul* (*expensive*). The chef at this lovely restaurant fetches from Canigou all the basic ingredients for mountain surprises like *filet mignon de sanglier* (boar) and beef with morel mushrooms. *Closed Sun eve and Mon in summer, Sun eve, Mon and Tues in winter, and 3 wks Jan, 1 wk June and 1 wk Nov.*

Au Grill La Senyra, 81 Rue St-Jean, t 04 68 96 17 65. Solid traditional cuisine. *Closed Tues eve and Wed.*

these capitals will become familiar if you spend much time in the Conflent; like most of the works in the region, Serrabonne's was done by the school of artists that grew up at St-Michel-de-Cuxa. Note the small figure of the Virgin; a narrow window allows a ray of sunlight to illuminate it only one day each year – the Feast of the Assumption on 15 August.

Prades, St-Michel-de-Cuxa and Canigou

Prades is known around the world in connection with the music festival founded in 1951 by Pablo Casals, but few people could place it on a map. Casals, in exile after the Spanish Civil War, spent much of the 1940s and '50s here, in the one safe corner of his beloved Catalunya. From the beginning, his festival (*www.prades-festival-casals.com; late July–mid-Aug*) attracted many of the world's greatest musicians. Otherwise, Prades is a rather typical, stolid Catalan town with a rather worrying road system. There are a couple of things to see: the **Musée Pablo Casals** (*Médiathèque de Prades, 33 Rue de l'Hospice, t 04 68 96 52 37; open summer Mon–Sat 9–12 and 2–6; winter Tues 10–12 and 3–7, Wed 10–7, Fri 3–7 and Sat 10–1*) has a section dedicated to Casals – photos, his piano and pipes, records, letters, etc. In the heart of Prades, the church of **St-Pierre** has a fine Romanesque bell tower with a pyramid crown and, inside, an operatic Baroque retable in full 17th-century fig by Catalan chisel virtuoso Joseph Sunyer, along with an exhibition of church treasures. There is also a silk museum, the **Maison de Soie** (*Av Général Roques; open June–mid-Sept daily; Mar–May and mid-Sept–Nov Mon–Fri; closed Dec–Feb; adm*), with stories of the silk industry, important here in the 17th century; and you can see how garnets are made into jewellery at **Casa Perez** (*Place de l'Eglise; open daily*).

Best of all, it's only a few kilometres from Prades up through orchards to **St-Michel-de-Cuxa**, one of the most important monasteries of medieval Catalunya (*t 04 68 96 15 35 or t 04 68 96 02 40; open 9.30–11.50 and 2–6, to 5pm in winter; closed Sun am; adm*). Even in its reduced, semi-ruined state, the scale is impressive; this was one of the great monastic centres from which medieval Europe was planned and built.

The coming of the French Revolution found St-Michel already in a state of serious decay. Looted and abandoned, the abbey suffered greatly in the 19th century. One of the two bell towers collapsed, and much of the best sculptural work went 'into exile' as the Catalans put it, carted off to the Cloisters Museum in New York. When restoration began, the rest of the cloister was in a public bathhouse in Prades, while the altar top was found holding up a balcony in Vinça. Now restored, St-Michel is occupied once again by a small community of Benedictine monks from Montserrat, the centre of Catalan spiritualism and nationalism.

While much of the inspiration for early medieval architecture in Languedoc came from north Italy or France, Roussillon was heavily influenced by nearby Spain. Here, the obvious Spanish feature is the more-than-semicircular 'Visigothic' arches in the nave. This style, which goes back almost to Roman times, never became too popular in Christian Europe, though the Muslims of Spain adopted it to create the architectural fantasies of Seville and Granada.

Other notable features of St-Michel include the massive and extremely elegant bell tower, and an unusual circular crypt, built in the 11th century under a building that was later demolished. The crypt is covered by toroid barrel vaulting, with a mushroom-like central column almost unique in medieval architecture. Antonio Gaudí used similar columns in his work in Barcelona – a fascinating piece of Catalan cultural continuity, for Gaudí could not have got the idea here, since the crypt was discovered and excavated only in 1937. In the cloister, you can see the galleries and capitals that didn't go to Manhattan: monsters from the medieval bestiary in the corners, intertwined with men on the four faces. There is an obsession with lions, almost Chinese in their stylization, biting and licking each other.

If **Canigou**'s magnetism is working its juju on you, don't resist the call. You can make two-thirds of the climb – 7,053ft – by car, on a forest road that begins on the east end of Prades. This leaves you at the Chalet-Hôtel des Cortalets refuge (*open May–Sept; call* t *04 68 96 36 19 to book a bed; €28 a night, meals €13.80; half-board €31.30*). From here it's a fairly easy three- to four-hour walk to the summit, requiring only a decent pair of walking shoes and a windbreaker. There's a second, even more hair-raising forest road up to the refuge from the D27, practical only in a four-wheel drive. The Prades and Vernet-les-Bains tourist offices have lists of operators; leave the driving to them.

Vernet-les-Bains and St-Martin-du-Canigou

The D27, the narrow road that snakes around the lower slopes of Canigou, is an exceptional drive through the mountain forests, with grand views of the big mountain itself; after St-Michel-de-Cuxa, it meets **Vernet-les-Bains**, a bustling modern spa with most of the accommodation in the area and hot sulphuric waters that are good for your rheumatism and respiratory problems.

Three kilometres further up, **Casteil**, a little wooded resort with a small museum of mountain life and plenty of picnic grounds, is the base for visiting Canigou's other great medieval monument, the abbey of **St-Martin-du-Canigou** (t *04 68 05 50 03; open daily in summer, closed Tues Oct–April; call for hours of guided tours; adm*) – a taxing though lovely 40-minute walk up from the town.

A monkish architect named Sclua designed this complex, begun in the early 11th century by a count of the Cerdagne named Guifred Cabreta. Sclua was a designer ahead of his time; he made his monastery a rustic acropolis, spectacularly sited with views around Canigou and the surrounding peaks, and arranged as a series of courtyards and terraces on different levels. The church, with its immense, fortress-like bell tower, has two levels, an upper church dedicated to St-Martin and a lower crypt for a certain obscure subterranean Virgin Mary, Notre-Dame-sous-Terre. Some good white marble capitals can be seen in the cloister, heavily restored in the early 20th century, and medieval tombs, including Count Guifred's, survive in the upper church. But on the whole, St-Martin, damaged by an earthquake in 1428, abandoned after the Revolution, restored between 1952 and 1971 and reinhabited, retains relatively few of its former glories.

To complete the tour of Romanesque Canigou, there is another 11th- to 12th-century church in the village of **Corneilla-de-Conflent**, a former Benedictine priory full of good sculpture. Side roads to the west, in the valley of the Rotja, can take you to several more, including rare 10th-century churches in the tiny villages of **Fuilla** and **Sahorre**.

Not all the area's attractions are on Canigou. Five kilometres northeast of Prades, in the empty, largely forested Pyrenean foothills, **Eus**, 'one of the most beautiful villages in France,' is an ambitious place; it also claims to have 'the most sunshine of any *commune* in France'. Spilling down its steep hillside, as you see it from the Têt valley, it makes an elegant composition. The parish church has some elaborate 17th-century polychrome retables.

Heading up from Prades in the Castellare valley, on the D14, **Molitg-les-Bains**, on a hill in the forest, has been a spa (specializing in skin disorders) since the Belle Epoque, with a suitably grand hotel with a lake, river and lovely gardens open to the public. Beyond Molitg, the road climbs up to the **Col de Jau**, a pass with stunning views, once the border between France and Spain, and a route to the Aude valley. On the way, you pass the fortifed village of **Mosset**, a little haven of artists and potters, where there is a beautifully restored Romanesque chapel, the *capelletta*, in the old village.

At **Escaro** there is a **mining museum** (*t 04 68 97 15 34; open June–Sept 2–6; April–May and Oct–Nov Sat and Sun only 2–6*) with trains, tools, old equipment and photos, and organized walks around the mining area on Wed and Sat in summer, lasting 3hrs 30mins (*call the museum for details*).

Villefranche-de-Conflent

Some villages have their own ideas for welcoming visitors. This one casually points cannons down at you as you pass along the N116, by way of an invitation to drop in. Villefranche, the most logical place from which to defend the Têt valley, has had a castle at least since 1092. In the 17th century it took its present form, as a model Baroque fortress-town, rebuilt and refortified by Vauban. Almost nothing has changed since, and Villefranche remains as a fascinating historical record, a sort of stage set of that era.

Tours of Vauban's **ramparts**, with their walkway built through in the wall, are offered (*t 04 68 96 22 96; daily July and Aug 9–8; June and Sept 9–7; April and May 10.30–12.30 and 2–6; Feb, Mar, Oct and Nov 10.30–12.30 and 2–5; not Dec and Jan; adm*) and, if you have sufficient puff and military curiosity, there's a steep climb up the remarkable 1,000 subterranean rock hewn steps (at the end of Rue St-Pierre) to **Fort Liberia** (*t 04 68 96 34 01; open June–Sept daily 9–8; Oct–May daily 10–6; adm*), another Vauban opus, further fortified by Napoléon III, dominating the valley and long used as a prison, where you can 'meet the villainous female prisoners' (don't be alarmed – they're made of wax). There's a bus up from Villefranche's Café Canigou.

A survivor from the pre-Vauban Villefranche, the church of **St-Jacques** is a fine 12th-century building with the familiar capitals from the workshop of St-Michel-de-Cuxa; inside there's another retable by Sunyer and, by the door, note the measures engraved in the stone, used by drapers who had market stalls in the square. Vauban built its walls and tower into his wall to help with the defence. For all its grim purpose, Villefranche is a lovely town, lately attracting a number of crafty types, woodcarvers and potters.

One kilometre up the Vernet road, some of the Pyrenees' most peculiar stalactites await your inspection at the **Grotte des Canalettes** (*open July and Aug 10–6.30; adm*) and the **Grotte des Grandes Canalettes** (**t** *04 68 96 23 11, www.grottes-grandes-canalettes.com; open April–mid-June and mid-Sept–Oct 10–6; mid-June–Aug 10–6.30; Nov–Mar Sun and hols only 2–5; adm*), with a *son-et-lumière* show in July and August.

The Cerdagne

This is as close as we get, in this book, to the heart of the Pyrenees, but it's far enough for the real thing: mountain rhododendrons and blue gentians, hordes of skiers, herds of horses, and snow on top until May or June. The lofty plateau of the Cerdagne (Cerdanya in Catalan) was an isolated and effectively independent county in the Middle Ages; from the 10th century its counts gradually extended their power, eventually becoming counts of Barcelona – the founders of the Catalan nation. In spite of this heritage, the Cerdagne was split between Spain and France in the 1659 Treaty of the Pyrenees. The building of the Little Yellow Train, in 1911, brought the French Cerdagne into the modern world (*see* p.599); skiing has made it rather opulent today. And besides skiing, you can see some good Romanesque churches, warm up at the world's largest solar furnace, visit the highest railway station in France – and circumnavigate Spain in less than an hour.

To Mont-Louis and the Capcir

After Villefranche, the main N116 climbs dramatically into the mountains. There are a few possible stop offs on the way: at **Olette**, you can turn off to explore nearly abandoned old mountain villages like **Nyer** and **Evol**.

A bit further up, at **Thuès-entre-Valls**, you can stretch your legs in the beautiful Gorges de la Carança, then soak your weary bones in the natural hot springs at St-Thomas-les-Bains, **Fontpedrouse**, where no matter the weather you can take a dip outside, have a Jacuzzi, visit the hammam or have a massage (**t** *04 68 97 03 13; open daily 10–8, July and Aug 10–9; hammam closed Mon; adm*).

Climb, climb, climb, and at last you'll reach the gateway to the Cerdagne, **Mont-Louis**, another work of Vauban's and the highest fortress in France (5,250ft), named after Louis XIV. The army still resides here, though only to look after a pioneer **solar furnace** (**t** *04 68 04 14 89; guided tours only; documents available in English; open summer 9.30–12.30 and 2–7; spring and autumn 9.30–12.30 and 2–6; winter 2–5; visits leave every hour; closed first half of Dec; adm*), built in 1953 and used, not for generating power, but for melting substances for scientific experiments; the huge mirror generates temperatures up to 6,000 degrees. It shares the small space inside the walls with some 200 residents and a few cafés and shops. In the summer you can also

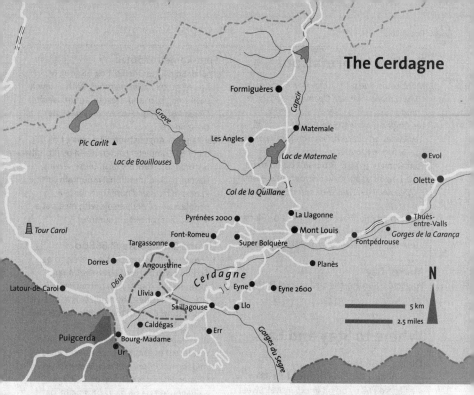

Formiguères

Matemale

Les Angles

Pic Carlit ▲

Lac de Matemale

Lac de Bouillouses

Evol

Olette

Col de la Quillane

Pyrénées 2000

La Llagonne

Thuès-
entre-Valls

Font-Romeu

Mont Louis

Tour Carol

Super Bolquère

Gorges de la Carança

Targassonne

Fontpédrouse

Dorres

Angoustrine

Cerdagne

Planès

Latour-de-Carol

Llívia

Eyne

Eyne 2600

Saillagouse

Llo

N

Caldégas

Err

Puigcerda

Bourg-Madame

Gorges du Segre

Ur

5 km

2.5 miles

visit the Puits des Forcats and see the 17th-century wheel which lifted water from the wells dug into the rock (*contact tourist office for times; adm*).

A 7km detour up into the mountains will take you to tiny **Planès** and its equally tiny and unique triangular 11th-century church. Like the seven-sided model at Rieux-Minervois, this one has occasioned much speculation; some have claimed it as the centre of a network of ley lines.

The road to Planès is a dead end, but there are better choices from the big cross-roads at Mont-Louis. To the north, the D118 carries you to the isolated plateau of the **Capcir**. It's a perfect place to get away from it all – after a road was built into the Capcir in the 19th century, almost the entire population deserted it, tired of scratching a living from land that would only support a few cows. They left behind beautiful pine forests and a score of little lakes carved out long ago by Pyrenean glaciers. Skiing has brought the Capcir back to life since the 1960s, and the government has transformed the landscape with a number of dams and artificial lakes.

On your way into the Capcir, don't miss the church of St-Vincent in **La Llagonne**, only 3km from Mont-Louis. The centuries have left it in peace, with a remarkable collection of medieval art, including an altarpiece and painted baldachin (12th- and 13th-centuries), and an excellent polychrome *Majestat*.

Further north, **Les Angles**, **Matemale** and **Formiguères** are the main ski centres. Les Angles has, as well as some 30 ski pistes and a whole range of winter sports, a **Parc Animalier** (*t 04 68 04 17 20, www.faunepyreneenne.com; open daily summer 9–6; winter 9–5; adm*), a free-range zoo with native fauna of the Pyrenees, both current

Tourist Information

Mont-Louis: Rue du Marché, **t** 04 68 04 21 97, *www.mont-louis.net. Open Tues–Sat 10–12 and 2–6.*

Les Angles: 2 Av de l'Aude, **t** 04 68 04 32 76, *www.les-angles.com; Open daily 9–12 and 2–6; to 7 in summer and hols.*

Font-Romeu: 38 Av E.-Brousse, **t** 04 68 30 68 30, **f** 04 68 30 29 70, *www.fontromeu.com. Open daily 9–12 and 2–6; summer and hols 8.30–7.*

Bourg-Madame: Place Catalogne, **t** 04 68 04 55 35. *Open winter Mon–Fri 9–12 and 2–6; summer Mon–Fri 9–7.30 and Sun 9.30–1.30.*

Market Day

Puigcerdà: Sun am, the best market in the area.

Where to Stay and Eat

Olette ✉ 66360

La Fontaine, 3 Rue de la Fusterie, **t** 04 68 97 03 67, **f** 04 68 97 00 98 *(inexpensive).* Sweet little hotel in a mountain village on the route to Font Romeu, with several pleasant rooms and hearty dishes. *Closed Tues eve, Wed, and Jan.*

Mont-Louis ✉ 66210

Le Clos Cerdan, t 04 68 04 23 29, **f 04 68 04 23 79 *(moderate).* Get a room with a view at this grey stone hotel on a cliff overlooking the valley; modern but very comfortable, with a restaurant *(moderate). Closed Nov–mid-Dec.*

Lou Rouballou, Rue des Ecoles-Laïques, **t** 04 68 04 23 26, **f** 04 68 04 14 09 *(inexpensive).* In the village, by the ramparts, the family-run Lou Rouballou is pleasant and serves delicious food specializing in mushrooms (including one called the *roubaIlou*) in various guises. *Closed mid-Oct–mid-Dec and May; restaurant closed Wed.*

Font-Romeu ✉ 66120

Clair Soleil, Rte Odeillo, **t 04 68 30 13 65, **f** 04 68 30 08 27 *(inexpensive).* With a view, a swimming pool and a restaurant *(moderate). Closed last wk April–1st wk May and late Oct–mid-Dec.*

Cal Xandera, Angoustrine, 8km away, **t** 04 68 04 61 67. Completely different – a beautifully restored 18th-century farmhouse serving flavour-packed traditional mountain cuisine. Rooms in *maison d'hôte* style, for 2–6 people: €23–26 per person, with meals at a set €15. Jazz concerts in summer.

Llo and Saillagouse ✉ 66800

***Auberge l'Atalaya, Llo, **t** 04 68 04 70 04, **f** 04 68 04 01 29 *(very expensive).* A rare example of a country inn unconcerned with the skiing business; tranquillity is assured in this setting, close to the wild flowers of the Vallée d'Eyne and infinitely far from anything else, with a pool and an excellent restaurant in summer *(expensive). Closed mid-Jan–mid-April and mid-Nov–mid-Dec.*

Planes, Place des Comtes-de-Cerdagne, Saillagouse, **t 04 68 04 72 08, **f** 04 68 04 75 93, *www.planotel.fr (inexpensive).* Planes has been hosting guests since 1895; the dining room, with its huge fireplace, is a great place to settle down to a plate of Catalan anchovies and red peppers. *Closed last 2 wks Mar, and Nov–mid-Dec.*

Planotel, Rue de la Poste, **t** 04 68 04 72 08, *www.planotel.fr (inexpensive).* Modern, with a heated pool and restaurant and run by the same family that runs Planes *(see above). Closed Oct–May except school hols.*

Valcebollère ✉ 66340

***Les Ecureuils, t 04 68 04 52 03, **f** 04 68 04 52 34 *(moderate).* Friendly, simple mountain *auberge* in the Cevennes, offering charming rooms and local produce. Proprietor Etienne Lafitte will take you on guided mountain walks following smugglers' paths. *Closed mid-Oct–mid-Dec and 2 wks May.*

and past residents, including bears, reindeer, wolves and bison. **Formiguères** (not the ski station, but the village, 4km away) is one of the prettiest and best-preserved villages in the region, hardly changed since the days when the kings of Majorca sojourned here to relieve their asthma. This region is great for hiking. The best parts lie to the west, on the slopes of the 9,584ft **Pic Carlit**; there you will find the sources of both the Têt and the Aude (above the D60, in the Forêt de Barrès).

Font-Romeu

The western road (D618) will take you through more pine forests to Font-Romeu; along with its new satellite towns, Super-Bolquère and Pyrénées 2000, this is one of the biggest ski resorts in France. Font-Romeu grew up after 1910, around a now-closed *'Grand Hôtel'*; it prospers today partly from its excellent sports facilities, often used for training France's Olympic teams. Stamped from the same mould as every other continental ski resort, it has plenty of fake Alpine chalets, innumerable pizzerias and 460 snow machines to help out when the weather isn't co-operating. But no other resort has the world's largest **solar furnace** (*t 04 68 30 77 86; open summer daily 10–7 to 7.30 July–Aug; winter 10–12.30 and 2–6; adm*), 'stronger than 10,000 suns!', the successor to the one in Mont-Louis. With its curved mirror, covering an entire side of the nine-storey laboratory building, it reflects the Pyrenees beautifully while helping scientists work out all sorts of high-temperature puzzles. Above the town, the pilgrimage chapel of **Notre-Dame-de-Font-Romeu** has an exuberant altarpiece by Joseph Sunyer and a 12th-century statue of the Virgin. There is a **reindeer park** at Bolquère/Pyrénées 2000 where in winter you can feel like Santa being pulled along on a sledge (*open Christmas–Easter and summer school holidays*).

Another solar experiment can be seen at **Targasonne**, west of Font-Romeu on the D618; this big mirror was built to generate electricity, but hasn't quite worked as well as intended. The glaciers that reshaped the Capcir were busy here too, leaving a strange expanse of granite boulders called the **Chaos**. The Cerdagne is famous for its Romanesque churches and chapels, testimony to the mountain Catalans' prosperity and level of culture even in the very early Middle Ages. One of the best of the churches is St-André, at **Angoustrine**, west of Targasonne, with fragments of 13th-century frescoes representing the months of the year.

To the west, **Dorres** is a lofty *village perché* with another church, this one from the 11th century, with another Romanesque Virgin inside and a chance to soak in a granite hot tub with a sulphurous pong (*t 04 68 04 66 87; open daily 8.30–7.30*).

The Vallée du Carol

From the village of **Ur** (with yet another richly decorated Romanesque church), you can make a northern detour into the Vallée du Carol, the western edge of Roussillon. **Latour-de-Carol** is a romantic name for another great border rail-crossing most of us have blinked at in the dark; the name does not come from Charlemagne, as most people think, but the Carol river. Latour's church has more work by Joseph Sunyer. The best church in the area, however, is the Chapelle St-Fructueux in the minuscule village of **Yravals**, above Latour-de-Carol – with a wealth of medieval art inside, and a magnificent mid 14th-century altarpiece of St Martha by a Catalan named Ramon Destorrents.

Further up this scenic valley, you'll pass the tower of the ruined 14th-century castle that gives Latour its name. The trees give out as the tortuous road climbs to the pass of Puymorens. From here, if you have a sudden hankering for some tax-free Havanas or a new phonograph, it's only 40km to the Pyrenean Ruritania, the principality of **Andorra**.

Llivia, Llo and Eyne

Bourg-Madame, 'the same latitude as Rome, but sunnier', as its brochure claims, is the crossing point for Spain; just across the border lies Puigcerdà, with a 14th-century church and the best ice-hockey squad on the Iberian peninsula.

The N116 will take you northeast from here back to Mont-Louis, completing your circumnavigation of Spain – or at least the tiny Spanish enclave of **Llivia**, marooned by accident in the Treaty of 1659. The treaty stipulated that Spain must give up the *villages* of the Cerdagne, and everyone had forgotten that Llivia had the legal status of a *ville*; it had been a Roman *municipium*, the capital of the Cerdagne in ancient times. Llivia's historic centre is clustered around a 15th-century fortified church, housing a superb 13th-century sculpture of Christ; opposite, in the Musée Municipal (*open Tues–Sat 10–1 and 3–7, Sun 10–2; closed Mon*), the unlikely attraction is a 16th-century pharmacy, one of the most beautiful, oldest and best preserved in Europe.

East of Bourg-Madame, more Catalan Romanesque churches can be visited: at **Hix**, an impressive edifice of 1177, built when the town was the residence of the counts of the Cerdagne and containing a majestic Romanesque Virgin with a little kingly Christ child on her lap, and at **Caldégas**, where the frescoes include a hunting scene with falcons.

Further east along the N116, road signs will startle you with town names like Llo and Err; linguists say they're Basque, evidence that the Basques lived here in remote times. **Llo** has a church with a lovely sculptured portal and an exceptionally sweet cemetery in nearby **Ste-Léocadie** (home of the highest vineyard in Europe). You can visit the **Musée de Cerdagne** (*t 04 68 04 08 05; open mid-June–mid-Sept 11–5*) in a 17th-century farm, dedicated to rural life including the pre-ski trades of the great plateau – shepherding and farming. The other half of the museum is at nearby **Eyne**, and focuses more on the natural history of the area, with a botanical garden; it also offers guided tours in summer through the Réserve Naturelle d'Eyne. Come in May, when it's late enough to avoid the skiers from the resort called Eyne 2600 and just in time for a spectacular display of wild flowers and medicinal herbs in the Vallée d'Eyne, climbing up to the Spanish border. There are opportunities for hiking, southwards into the narrow **Gorges du Sègre**.

The Vallespir

The valley of the Tech, the southernmost valley of Roussillon, and of France, winds a lonesome trail around the southern slopes of Canigou. Known for its mineral waters since Roman times, it traditionally made its living from these and from ironworking,

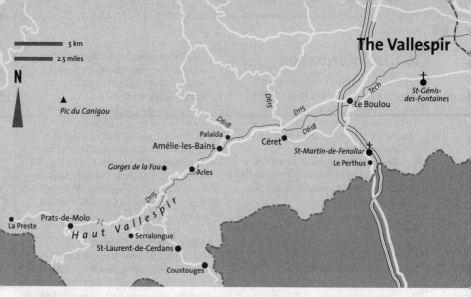

the basis of Catalan prosperity in the Middle Ages. When the iron gave out, there was smuggling.

Today, as smugglers have become superfluous, the Vallespir lives by tourism, with some euros on the side from cherries and cork oak – the *primeurs*, the first cherries in the French market each year, and the *grand cru* corks that have kept the best champagne bubbly for centuries.

Le Boulou and St-Martin-de-Fenollar

From Perpignan, you reach the Vallespir by the A9, getting off at **Le Boulou**, a truck-stop known to every European TIR jockey. The ancient Roman teamsters knew it, too. Le Boulou has been fated by geography as an eternal transit point, today jammed in summer with tourists heading up the N9 into Spain via La Perthus. It also has a casino and spa, and a fine Romanesque church with a superb white marble tympanum sculpted by the Master of Cabestany, portraying the *Resurrection of the Virgin*. The cornice shows scenes of the Nativity, the Christ Child's first bath (also rarely depicted in art), the *Shepherds*, *Magi* and *Flight into Egypt*.

East of Le Boulou, **St-Génis-des-Fontaines** (*t 04 68 89 84 33; open July and Aug daily 9.30–12.30 and 3–7; April–June and Sept 8.30–12 and 2–6; Oct–Mar 9.30–12 and 2–5*) was one of the important early medieval monasteries of Roussillon. Its church has a remarkable carved lintel dated 1020, with a *Majestat* and stylized apostles shaped like bowling-pins; the cloister was dismantled and sold off in 1924, one of the final scandals of France's traditional lack of concern for its medieval heritage. In 1988 it was rebuilt as it was, with originals and copies; restoration contiued until recently and there is now an art gallery to see as well.

The A9 and N9 continue south into Spain, passing **St-Martin-de-Fenollar** and its 9th-century **church** (*t 04 68 89 84 33; open mid-June–mid-Sept Wed–Mon 10.30–12 and 3.30–7; mid-Sept–mid-June Wed–Mon 2–5; closed Tues; adm*), with some of the most unusual and best-preserved 12th-century frescoes in the Midi. Nine-tenths of all early

Tourist Information

Céret: Av Clemenceau, **t** 04 68 87 00 53, **f** 04 68 87 00 56, *www.ot-ceret.fr. Open Mon–Sat 10–12 and 2–5.*

Arles-sur-Tech: Rue Barjau, **t** 04 68 39 11 99, **f** 04 68 39 11 99, *www.villes-arles-sur-tech.fr. Open Mon–Sat 9–12 and 2–6.*

Prats-de-Mollo: Place le Foiral, **t** 04 68 39 70 83, **f** 04 68 39 74 51, *www.pratsdemollola preste.com. Open Mon–Sat 9–12 and 2–6; July–Aug also Sun.*

Market Days

Céret: Sat.
Arles-sur-Tech: Wed.
Prats-de-Mollo: Wed and Fri.

Where to Stay and Eat

Céret ✉ 66400

****Terrasse au Soleil, Route Fontfrède, **t** 04 68 87 01 94, **f** 04 68 87 39 24, *www. la-terrasse-au-soleil.fr* (*luxury*). A restored, modernized *mas* on a hill above Céret, with a view, a heated pool and tennis court (a bit dear, especially on full board). Its restaurant, **Cerisaie**, is good. *Closed Jan–early Feb.*

Le Mas Trilles, Pont de Reynes, on the Céret–Amélie-les-Bains road, **t** 04 68 87 38 37, **f** 04 68 87 42 62 (*very expensive– moderate*). A tastefully renovated *mas* with a heated pool and a charming garden over-looking a trout stream. No restaurant, just snacks, but there are three very nearby. *Closed Oct–Easter.*

Les Arcades, 1 Place Picasso, **t 04 68 87 12 30, **f** 04 68 87 49 44, *www.hotel-arcades-ceret.*

com (*inexpensive*). Artistically decorated, with balconies overlooking the market square. You can rent rooms with a small kitchen for €360 per week.

*Vidal, 4 Place du 4 Septembre, **t** 04 68 87 00 85, **f** 04 68 87 62 33 (*inexpensive*). In a charming, if quirky, listed building, with restaurant (*moderate*). *Open year round.*

Les Feuillants, 1 Bd Lafayette, **t** 04 68 87 37 88, *www.feuillants.com.* Modern paintings on the walls and a varied choice of dishes, many Catalan-based. *Closed Mon all year, plus Sun eve except in July and Aug.*

Amélie-les-Bains ✉ 66110

La Pergola, 60 Av du Vallespir, **t 04 68 39 05 71, **f** 04 68 39 81 15 (*inexpensive*). A good choice which does not require full board. You can also rent rooms with a small kitchen and balcony for €45 per night. *Closed Jan.*

Castel Emeraude, Route de la Corniche, **t 04 68 39 02 83, **f** 04 68 39 03 09, *www. lecastelemeraude.com* (*inexpensive*). This is the place to get away from it all: a big white manor on the banks of the river, with a good restaurant (*moderate*). *Closed mid-Nov– mid-Mar.*

Arles-sur-Tech ✉ 66150

Les Glycines, Rue Jeu de Paume, **t 04 68 39 10 09, **f** 04 68 39 83 02 (*inexpensive*). Named for the ancient wisteria that shades the garden terrace, Les Glycines has modernized rooms, all with bath, and a wonderful restaurant (*moderate*) where the chef defies every snide remark we've ever made about Catalan cuisine: try his aubergine *tian* and delectable *panaché* of Mediterranean fish. *Closed mid-Nov–mid-Feb..*

---

medieval painting is lost to us, and this is a rare example of the best of what is left: brilliant colours and a confident stylization, with an imagery untroubled by the dogma of later religious painting, as in the *Nativity*, where Mary lies not in a stable but in a comfortable bed under a chequered baldachin. The scene from the Apocalypse, of Christ in Majesty with the four symbols of the Evangelists and the 24 elders, was a favourite 12th-century theme on both sides of the Pyrenees.

Hannibal entered Gaul through **Le Perthus**, the last, or first stop in France. As a fitting bookend to this long volume, archaeologists have recently uncovered, at Panisars, a monumental pedestal, identified as belonging to the **Trophée de Pompée**. Similar to La Turbie near the Italian border (*see* pp.117–18), this monument was erected by a victorious Pompey in 71 BC on the Gallo-Hispanic frontier. Part of the stone was used to build a priory in 1011 (the ruins are nearby); the rest was quarried by Vauban in the 17th century to build the **Fort de Bellegarde** (*t 04 68 83 60 15; open June–end Sept 10.30–6.30; adm*).

Céret: the 'Mecca of Cubism'

Back in the valley of the Tech, the D115 streaks from Le Boulou to Céret, centre of the optimal cherry-growing region suspended between the Pyrenees and the sea. Amid the orchards in the hills around town, Céret is a laid-back town under enormous plane trees, with perfect little squares (especially the **Plaça dels Nou Raigs**), medieval gates, the biggest Baroque church in Roussillon, **St-Pierre**, a war memorial by Maillol and an elegant 14th-century **bridge** over the Tech.

Have a look around Céret before visiting the **Musée d'Art Moderne** (*8 Bd du Maréchal Joffre, t 04 68 87 27 76, www.musee-ceret.com; open mid-June–mid-Sept daily 10–7; mid-Sept–mid-June 10–6; closed Tues Oct–April; adm*) and you'll be surprised at how many scenes you'll recognize. Céret found its artistic destiny at the turn of the century, thanks to Picasso, Braque, Gris, Manolo, Matisse, Soutine, Kisling, Masson, Tzara, Lhote, Marquet and others who spent time here up until 1940, and whose works fill the rooms. Best of all are the works donated by Picasso in 1953, among them 28 little plates painted in a five-day spurt of energy, all with variations on the *corrida* under a blasting sun.

Although not as dazzling, the **Maison de l'Archéologie** in the Tour Port d'Espagne (*t 04 68 87 31 59; open daily July–Aug 10–12 and 1–6; rest of the year Mon–Fri 10–12 and 2–5; closed Jan and Feb*) has well-arranged Neolithic, Classical and medieval finds from the Vallespir.

Amélie-les-Bains and Arles-sur-Tech

Sulphurous waters, good for your rheumatism, have been the fortune of **Amélie-les-Bains** since ancient times; a Roman swimming pool with a vaulted roof has been uncovered, and the spa, rising on either side of the river Tech, still does a grandstand business. Amélie's pretty medieval ancestor, **Palalda**, is piled on a nearby hill, and offers a small **Musée de la Poste** (*t 04 68 39 34 90; open summer Mon–Fri 10–12 and 2–5; adm*) for snail-mail nostalgia from the days of Louis XI to 1900; there's a collection of stamps, and telephones, too.

Just west, **Arles-sur-Tech**, the ancient capital of the Vallespir, is a curious old village built on a narrow maze of lanes and offering some even curiouser hagiography in its 11th- and 12th-century abbey of **Ste-Marie**, originally the centre of an important monastery. Dark Age Arles-sur-Tech got by with an anonymous saint – an empty 4th-century sarcophagus known as *Sainte-Tombe* – until the dreaded *simiots* came to town, ape-like monsters that trampled the crops and violated the women. In despair, the abbot of Ste-Marie went to the pope asking for some holy relics. This was in 957, when demand for saints' bones was at its historic high, and the best the pope could offer was a pair of Persian martyrs named Abdon and Sennen. The abbot brought them back in a false-bottomed water-barrel, to fool the Venetians and Germans and any other relic thieves, and they dealt with the *simiots* as efficiently as if they had been the bones of St Peter himself. The story is portrayed in a 17th-century retable, in the chapel where Abdon and Sennen's relics are kept. The *Sainte-Tombe* itself, once a major pilgrimage attraction, is kept in a little enclosure outside the front door. It fills continually with perfectly pure water – some 500 to 600 litres a year, ceremoniously pumped every 30 July.

Arles-sur-Tech is the home of Tissages Catalans, where they've been making cloth since 1900 (there's a little museum on Rue des Usines, **t** *04 68 39 10 07; open April–Oct Mon–Fri 10–12 and 2.30–5.30*), and it was the last redoubt of the valley's famous medieval iron industry; the last working mine in Roussillon, up at Batère, closed down in the early 1990s. There's also a museum on the history of the iron industry in the abbey's cloister.

Two kilometres northwest along the D44 you can go through the World's Narrowest Gorge, the **Gorges de la Fou** (**t** *04 68 39 16 21; open April–Sept daily 10–6; Oct and Nov daily 10–5; adm*), a giant crack in the rock with sides towering 650ft, with waterfalls and caves along the mile-long walkway. Legend made it the lair of witches, bogeymen and *traboucayres*, robbers who pounced on passing diligences. At Montferrer, just west of Arles-sur-Tech, there is a museum which, among other things, tells the story of the *traboucayres* (**t** *04 68 39 12 44; open Mon–Fri 2–6*).

Continuing up the valley, just south of the D115, the hill-top village of **Serralongue** has a church dating from 1018, with a fine portal and one of the only surviving examples of a Catalan *conjurador*; this is a small, square pavilion with a slate roof and statues of the four Evangelists facing the four cardinal directions. When a storm threatened, the priest would go up to the *conjurador* and perform certain rites facing the direction of the storm to avert its wrath.

A detour further south, on the D3, will uncover **St-Laurent-de-Cerdans**, famous for making espadrilles, and **Coustouges**, which has a lovely early 12th-century fortified church with a slate roof and two carved portals, one inside the other.

Some towns just ask for it. As if having a name like **Prats-de-Mollo** weren't enough, this tiny spa advertises itself as the 'European Capital of Urinary Infections'. Prats-de-Mollo's other claim to fame is a European record for rainfall, 33 inches in 16 hours on 15 October 1940. The baths are really at **La Preste**, 8km up in the mountains; Prats-de-Mollo itself is an attractive old village, with remains of its walls and medieval buildings that recall the days when it was a textile centre, specializing in Catalan bonnets. Don't miss the whale bone stuck in the church wall. This is as far as we go; the Spanish border is 14km away.

Language

A working knowledge of French will make your holiday more enjoyable, but is hardly essential on the Côte d'Azur, where you can always find someone working in a travel office, bank, shop, hotel or restaurant who speaks at least rudimentary English. Venturing into the less-travelled hinterlands may well require an effort to recall your school French; a small travel phrase book and English–French dictionary can come in handy.

Even if your French is brilliant, the soupy southern twang may throw you. Any word with a nasal *in* or *en* becomes something like *aing* (*vaing* for *vin*). The last vowel on many words that are silent in the north get to express themselves in the south (*encore* sounds something like *engcora*).

What remains the same as anywhere else in France is the level of politeness expected: use *monsieur, madame* or *mademoiselle* when speaking to everyone (and never *garçon* in restaurants!), from your first *bonjour* to your last *au revoir*.

See pages 85–91 for menu vocabulary.

Pronunciation

Vowels

a, à, â between *a* in 'bat' and 'part'
é, er ez at end of word as *a* in 'plate' but a bit shorter
e at end of word not pronounced
e at end of syllable or in one-syllable word pronounced weakly, like *er* in 'mother'
i as *ee* in 'bee'
o as *o* in 'pot'
ô as *o* in 'go'
u, û between *oo* in 'boot' and *ee* in 'bee'

Vowel Combinations

ai as *a* in 'plate'
aî as *e* in 'bet'
ail as *i* in 'kite'
au, eau as *o* in 'go'
ei as *e* in 'bet'
eu, œu as *er* in 'mother'
oi between *wa* in 'swam' and *u* in 'swum'
oy as 'why'
ui as *wee* in 'twee'

Nasal Vowels

Vowels followed by an *n* or an *m* have a nasel sound.

an, en as *o* in 'pot' + nasal sound
ain, ein, in as *a* in 'bat' + nasal sound
on as *aw* in 'paw' + nasal sound
un as *u* in 'nut' + nasal sound

Nasal Vowels

Many French consonants are pronounced as in English, but there are some exceptions:
c followed by *e, i* or *y* and *ç* as *s* in 'sit'
c followed by *a, o* or *u* as *c* in 'cat'
g followed by *e, i* or *y* as *s* in 'pleasure'
gn as *ni* in 'opinion'
j as *s* in 'pleasure'
ll as *y* in 'yes'
qu as *k* in 'kite'
s between vowels as *z* in 'zebra'
s otherwise as *s* in 'sit'
c followed by *e, i* or *y* and *ç* as *s* in 'sit'
w except in English words as *v* in 'vest'
x at end of word as *s* in 'sit'
x otherwise as *x* in 'six'

Stress

The stress usually falls on the last syllable except when the word ends with an unaccented *e*.

Vocabulary

General

hello *bonjour*
good evening *bonsoir*
good night *bonne nuit*
goodbye *au revoir*
please *s'il vous plaît*
thank you (very much) *merci (beaucoup)*
yes *oui*
no *non*
good *bon (bonne)*
bad *mauvais*
excuse me *pardon, excusez-moi*

Can you help me? *Pourriez-vous m'aider?*
My name is... *Je m'appelle...*
What is your name? *Comment t'appelles-tu?*
  (informal), *Comment vous appelez-vous?*
  (formal)
How are you? *Comment allez-vous?*
Fine *Ça va bien*
I don't understand *Je ne comprend pas*
I don't know *Je ne sais pas*
Speak more slowly *Pourriez-vous parler plus*
  lentement?
How do you say ... in French? *Comment dit-on*
  ... en français?
Help! *Au secours!*

Where is (the railway station)? *Où se trouve*
  (la gare)?
Is it far? *C'est loin?*
left *à gauche*
right *à droite*
straight on *tout droit*

entrance *l'entrée*
exit *la sortie*
open *ouvert*
closed *fermé*
WC *les toilettes*
men *hommes*
ladies *dames* or *femmes*

doctor *le médecin*
hospital *un hôpital*
emergency room *la salle des urgences*
police station *le commissariat de police*
tourist information office *l'office de tourisme*

How much is it? *C'est combien?*
Do you have...? *Est-ce que vous avez...?*
It's too expensive *C'est trop cher*
bank *une banque*
money *l'argent*
change *la monnaie*
traveller's cheque *un chèque de voyage*
post office *la poste*
stamp *un timbre*
postcard *une carte postale*
public phone *une cabine téléphonique*
shop *un magasin*
central food market *les halles*
tobacconist *un tabac*
pharmacy *la pharmacie*
aspirin *l'aspirine*
condoms *les préservatifs*
insect repellent *l'anti-insecte*
sun cream *la crème solaire*
tampons *les tampons hygiéniques*

Transport

airport *l'aéroport*
aeroplane *l'avion*
go on foot *aller à pied*
bicycle *la bicyclette/le vélo*
mountain bike *vélo tout terrain, VTT*
bus *l'autobus*
bus stop *l'arrêt d'autobus*
coach station *la gare routière*
railway station *la gare*
train *le train*
platform *le quai*
date-stamp machine *le composteur*
timetable *l'horaire*
left-luggage locker *la consigne automatique*
car *la voiture*
taxi *le taxi*
subway *le métro*
ticket office *le guichet*
ticket *le billet*
single to... *un aller* (or *aller simple*) *pour...*
return to... *un aller et retour pour...*
What time does the ... leave?
  A quelle heure part...?
delayed *en retard*
on time *à l'heure*

Accommodation

single room *une chambre pour une personne*
twin room *une chambre à deux lits*
double room *une chambre pour deux personnes*
bed *un lit*
blanket *une couverture*
cot (child's bed) *lit d'enfant*
pillow *un oreiller*
soap *du savon*
towel *une serviette*
booking *une réservation*
I would like to book a room *Je voudrais réserver une chambre*

Months

January *janvier*
February *février*
March *mars*
April *avril*
May *mai*
June *juin*
July *juillet*
August *août*
September *septembre*
October *octobre*
November *novembre*
December *décembre*

Days

Monday *lundi*
Tuesday *mardi*
Wednesday *mercredi*
Thursday *jeudi*
Friday *vendredi*
Saturday *samedi*
Sunday *dimanche*

Time

What time is it? *Quelle heure est-il?*
month *un mois*
week *une semaine*

day *un jour/une journée*
morning *le matin*
afternoon *l'après-midi*
evening *le soir*
night *la nuit*
today *aujourd'hui*
yesterday *hier*
tomorrow *demain*
day before yesterday *avant-hier*
day after tomorrow *après-demain*

Numbers

one *un*
two *deux*
three *trois*
four *quatre*
five *cinq*
six *six*
seven *sept*
eight *huit*
nine *neuf*
ten *dix*
eleven *onze*
twelve *douze*
thirteen *treize*
fourteen *quatorze*
fifteen *quinze*
sixteen *seize*
seventeen *dix-sept*
eighteen *dix-huit*
nineteen *dix-neuf*
twenty *vingt*
twenty-one *vingt et un*
twenty-two *vingt-deux*
thirty *trente*
forty *quarante*
fifty *cinquante*
sixty *soixante*
seventy *soixante-dix*
seventy-one *soixante-onze*
eighty *quatre-vingts*
eighty-one *quatre-vingt-un*
ninety *quatre-vingt-dix*
hundred *cent*
two hundred *deux cents*
thousand *mille*

Glossary

abbaye: abbey

anse: cove

arrondissement: a city district

auberge: inn

aven: natural well

bastide: taller, more elaborate version of a *mas*, with balconies, wrought-ironwork, reliefs, etc; also a medieval new town, fortified and laid out in a grid

beffroi: tower with a town's bell

borie: dry-stone shepherd's hut with a corbelled roof

buffet d'eau: in French gardens, a fountain built into a wall with water falling through levels of urns or basins

cabane: simple weekend or holiday retreat, usually near the sea; a *cabane de gardian* is a thatched cowboy's abode in the Camargue

calanque: narrow coastal creek, like a miniature fjord

capitelles: the name for *bories* in Languedoc

cardo: the main north–south street in a Roman *castrum* or town

caryatid: column or pillar carved in the figure of a woman

castrum: rectangular Roman army camp, which often grew into a permanent settlement

causse: rocky, arid limestone plateaus, north of Hérault and in the lower Languedoc

cave: (wine) cellar

château: mansion, manor house or castle

chemin: path

chevet: eastern end of a church, including the apse

cirque: round natural depression created by erosion at the loop of a river

cloître: cloister

clue: rocky cleft or transverse valley

col: mountain pass

commune: in the Middle Ages, the government of a free town or city; today, the smallest unit of local government, encompassing a town or village

côte: coast; on wine labels, *côtes*, *coteaux* and *costières* mean 'hills' or 'slopes'

cours: wide main street, like an elongated main square

couvent: convent or monastery

crèche: Christmas crib with *santons*

donjon: castle keep

ecluse: canal lock

eglise: church

etang: lagoon or swamp

Félibre: member of the movement to bring back the use of the Provençal language

ferrade: cattle branding

gardian: a cowboy of the Camargue

gare: train station (SNCF)

gare routière: coach station

garrigues: irregular limestone hills pitted with caves, especially those north of Nîmes and Montpellier

gisant: sculpted prone effigy on a tomb

gîte: shelter

gîte d'étape: basic shelter for walkers

grande randonnée (GR): long-distance hiking path

grau: a narrowing, either of a canyon or a river

halles: covered market

hôtel: originally the town residence of the nobility; by the 18th century the word became more generally used for any large, private residence

hôtel de ville: city hall

lavoir: communal fountain, usually covered, for the washing of clothes

mairie: town hall

manade: a *gardian*'s farm in the Camargue

maquis: Mediterranean scrub. Also used as a term for the French Resistance during the Second World War

marché: market

mas: a farmhouse and its outbuildings

mascaron: ornamental mask, usually one carved on the keystone of an arch

modillon: stone projecting from the cornice of a church, carved with a face or animal figure

motte: hammock, or a raised area in a swamp

oppidum: pre-Roman fortified settlement

Parlement: French juridical body, with members appointed by the king; by the late *ancien régime*, parlements exercised a great deal of influence over political affairs

pays: region or village

pont: bridge

porte: gateway

predella: small paintings beneath the main subject of a retable

presqu'île: peninsula

puy: hill

restanques: vine or olive terraces

retable: carved or painted altarpiece, often consisting of a number of scenes or sculpted ensembles

rez-de-chaussée (RC): ground floor

santon: figure in a Christmas nativity scene, usually made of terracotta and dressed in 18th-century Provençal costume

source: spring

tour: tower

transi: on a tomb, a relief of the decomposing cadaver

tympanum: sculpted semicircular panel over a church door

vieille ville: historic, old quarter of town

village perché: hill-top village

Chronology

BC

c. 1,000,000 First human presence, near Menton; use of bone as a tool

c. 450,000 Tautavel Man in northern Roussillon

c. 400,000 Discovery of fire, as at Terra Amata in Nice

c. 60,000 Neanderthal hunters on the Riviera and around Ganges

c. 40,000 Advent of *Homo sapiens*; invention of art

c. 3500 Development of Neolithic culture; first villages built

c. 2000 First metallurgy; copper and tin at Vence and Caussols

c. 1800–1000 Worship on Mont Bégo, at Tende, incisions made in the Vallée des Merveilles

c. 800 Celts begin to occupy Languedoc

c. 600 Greek traders found Marseille

c. 380 Celtic invasions in Provence

218 Hannibal and elephants pass through region on the way to Italy

125 Roman legions attack Celto-Ligurian tribes that threaten Marseille

122 Founding of Aquae Sextiae (Aix)

118 Founding of Narbonne and Provincia, the first Roman province in Gaul

102 Marius and his legionaries defeat the Teutones

49 Marius' nephew, Julius Caesar, punishes Marseille for supporting Pompey

14 Augustus defeats Ligurian tribes in the Alpes-Maritimes

AD

46 Arrival of the Boat of Bethany at Stes-Maries-de-la-Mer (trad.)

310 Emperor Maximilian captured at Marseille by son-in-law Constantine

314 Constantine calls Church Council at Arles

410 Honorat founds Lérins monastery

413 Visigoths conquer Languedoc

476 Formal end of Western Roman Empire

535 Provence and Languedoc ceded to the Franks

719 Arab invasions in Languedoc

737 Charles Martel defeats Arabs and crushes anti-Frank rebellions in Arles, Avignon and Marseille

759 Pépin the Short adds region to his Frankish empire

812 Canonization of St Guilhem, Languedoc's warrior saint

855 Creation of the kingdom of Provence for Charles the Bald

879 Duke Viennois Boson proclaims himself king of Provence

c. 890 More Arab raids and invasions

924 Magyars (Hungarians) sack Nîmes

946 Lords of Cerdagne become counts of Barcelona; beginning of Catalan nation

949 Conrad of Burgundy inherits Provence and divides it into four feudal counties

979 Count William defeats Saracens at La Garde-Freinet, proclaims himself marquis of Provence

985 Montpellier founded

1002 First written text in Occitan

1032 Death of Rudolph II, king of Burgundy and Provence; lands bequeathed to Holy Roman Emperor Conrad II

1084 Trencavels rule Carcassonne and Béziers

1095 Occitans join First Crusade under Raymond of St-Gilles, count of Toulouse and marquis of Provence; William of Aquitaine writes first troubadour poetry

1112 Marriage of Douce, duchess of Provence, with Raymond-Berenger III, count of Barcelona

1125 Provence divided between the houses of Barcelona and Toulouse

1137 Catalunya unified as Kingdom of Aragon

1176 Pierre Valdo of Lyon founds Waldensian (Vaudois) sect

1186 Counts of Provence make Aix their capital

1187 Discovery of relics of St Martha at Tarascon

1208 Albigensian Crusade begins

1209 Sack and massacre at Béziers by Simon de Montfort

1213 Battle of Muret; Montfort defeats count of Toulouse and king of Aragon

1229 French annex Carcassonne and eastern Languedoc

1246 Charles I of Anjou weds Béatrice, heiress of Provence, beginning the Angevin dynasty

1248 St Louis embarks on Seventh Crusade from Aigues-Mortes

1255 Fall of Quéribus, the last Cathar stronghold

1266 Battle of Benevento gives Charles of Anjou the Kingdom of Naples

1272 Narbonne Cathedral begun

1274 Papacy acquires Comtat Venaissin

1276 Division of Aragon; Kingdom of Majorca founded with capital at Perpignan

1280 Relics of Mary Magdalene 'discovered' at St-Maximin-la-Ste-Baume

1286 First meeting of the Etats de Provence

1289 The school of medicine in Montpellier becomes a university

1295 The death of the 'last troubadour', Guiraut Riquier

1297 Francesco Grimaldi the Spiteful, merchant-prince of Genoa, conquers Monaco (but is forced to abandon it in 1301)

1303 Boniface VIII founds University of Avignon

1309 Papacy moves to Avignon

1327 Petrarch first sees Laura

1340s Siennese painters bring International Gothic style to Avignon

1344 Kingdom of Aragon reunited

1348 Jeanne of Naples and Provence sells Avignon to the pope; the Black Death strikes the south

1349 Jews expelled from France and take refuge in the Comtat Venaissin

c. **1350** First paper mills in the Comtat Venaissin

1362 Election of abbot of St-Victor as Pope Urban V

1360s The Grandes Compagnies ravage the countryside

1363 The Grimaldis recover Monaco and hold it still

1377 Papacy returns to Rome

1380 Louis I d'Anjou adopted by Jeanne of Naples

1388 Regions of Nice, Barcelonnette and Puget-Théniers secede from Provence and join county of Savoy

1464 Founding of the Fair of Beaucaire

1481 Count of Provence leaves Provence to the king of France

1492 Union of Aragon and Castile (Ferdinand and Isabella); end of Catalan independence

1496 Military port founded in Toulon

1501 French create *Parlement* of Aix to oversee Provence

1524 Provence invaded by the imperial troops of Charles V

1525 Jews in the Comtat Venaissin compelled to wear yellow hats

1539 Edict of Villars-Cotterêts forces use of French as official language

1540 *Parlement* of Aix orders massacre of Waldensians in the Luberon

1559 Completion of the canal between the Durance and Salon

1560 First Protestant synod in Languedoc

1562 Beginning of Wars of Religion: Protestant assembly at Mérindol

1577 First soap factory (Prunemoyr) founded in Marseille

1590–2 Carlo Emanuele of Savoy invades Provence

1598 Edict of Nantes ends the Wars of Religion

1603 Royal college founded at Aix

1639 Last meeting of the Etats de Provence before the Revolution

1646 Jews confined to ghettos

1650 Molière moves to Pézenas

1659 Treaty of the Pyrenees; French annex Roussillon

1666 Digging begins on the Canal du Midi; founding of Sète

1680 Louis XIV enters rebellious Marseille

1685 Louis XIV revokes Edict of Nantes

1702–4 The War of the Camisards

1707 Toulon unsuccessfully besieged by the English and duke of Savoy

1720–1 100,000 die of plague, mostly in Marseille

1731 Principality of Orange incorporated into France

1752 Last Protestant persecutions

1766 Tobias Smollett publishes his *Travels*, enticing the British to Nice

1779 Roman mausoleum and palace of the counts demolished, at Aix

1784 Hot air balloon goes up in Marseille

1787 The Edict of Tolerance

1790 France divided into *départements*

1791 France annexes Comtat Venaissin

1792 Volunteers from Marseille sing La Marseillaise to Paris

1793 Revolutionary tribunal in Marseille; Siege of Toulon makes Bonaparte famous

1795 Massacres in Marseille and Tarascon

1800 Marseille population around 100,000

1815 Napoleon escapes Elba and pops up again near Juan-les-Pins

1820 First signs of tourist industry at Hyères

1830 Revolution brings Louis Philippe to power

1831 Lord Brougham begins the vogue for wintering in Cannes

1839 Inauguration of Marseille–Sète railroad; birth of Cézanne

1840–8 Prime Ministry of Guizot, Protestant liberal from Nîmes

1844 Viollet-le-Duc begins restoration of Carcassonne

1851 Louis Napoleon's coup ends Second Republic; armed resistance in the south

1854 Founding of the Félibrige at the Château de Fontségugne

1859 Mistral publishes *Miréio*

1860 Plebiscite in county of Nice votes for union with France

1861 The prince of Monaco sells Roquebrune and Menton to France

1865 Silkworm industry destroyed by disease

1868–90 Phylloxera epidemic devastates vines

1869 Opening of Suez Canal brings boom times to Marseille

1888 Stephen Liégeard gives the Côte d'Azur its name

1888–90 Van Gogh in Provence

1900 Population reaches 500,000 in Marseille, 20% of which is Italian

1904 Frédéric Mistral wins the Nobel Prize for Literature

1906 Colonial Exposition at Marseille

1907 Climax of farm protests; Languedoc occupied by the army

1911 Diaghilev signs contract to bring the Ballets Russes to Monte-Carlo

1924–5 Scott and Zelda Fitzgerald raise hell on the Riviera

1928 Creation of the Camargue Regional Park

1930 D. H. Lawrence dies in Vence

1930s Marcel Pagnol films his *Marius*, *Fanny* and *César* trilogy in Marseille

1939 Founding of the Cannes Film Festival

1942 Sinking of the fleet at Toulon

1943 Formation of the Maquis resistance cells

1944 American and French landings around St-Tropez; Provence liberated in two weeks

1945 Creation of the Institut d'Etudes Occitanes

1947 Val de Roya incorporated into France

1956 Bardot and Vadim make *And God Created Woman* in St-Tropez

1962 Independence of Algeria: tens of thousands of French North Africans (*pieds-noirs*) settle in the south

1965 Last silk weaving company closed

1966 Steelworks founded at Fos

1968 Big resort development plan begins in Languedoc

1970 Completion of Paris–Lyon–Marseille *autoroute*

1982 Regional governments created

1988 Floods in Nîmes

1992 30 die in Vaison-la-Romaine floods

1995 The election of Jacques Chirac as president ends 14 years of socialist presidency

1999 France joins Euro currency

2001 End of compulsory national service

2002 January: Euro replaces franc as national currency

2002 Strength of support for Jean-Marie Le Pen's National Front party in the first round of presidential elections leads to mass protest; in May Jacques Chirac is re-elected

2002 September: 8 die in floods in the Gard

Further Reading

Ardagh, John, *France Today* (Penguin, 1987). One in Penguin's informative paperback series on contemporary Europe.

Barr, Alfred, *Henri Matisse: his Art and his Public* (Museum of Modern Art, New York, 1951).

Bishop, Morris, *Petrarch and His World* (Chatto & Windus, 1964).

Bonner, Anthony, *Songs of the Troubadours* (Allen & Unwin, 1973). An introduction to the life and times of the troubadours, with translations of best-known verses.

Cézanne, Paul, *Letters* (London, 1941).

Cook, Theodore A., *Old Provence* (London, 1905). A classic traveller's account of the region, out of print and hard to find.

Daudet, Alphonse, *Letters from my Windmill* (Penguin, 1982). Bittersweet 19th-century tales of Midi nostalgia by Van Gogh's favourite novelist.

Dumas, Alexandre, *The Count of Monte Cristo*, many editions; romantic fantastical tale of revenge, much of it set in Marseille and the Château d'If.

Durrell, Lawrence, *The Avignon Quintet* (Faber, 1974–85); lush wartime sagas that take place in Avignon and around.

Fitzgerald, F. Scott, *Tender is the Night*, many editions. 1920s Riviera decadence based on personal research.

Ford, Ford Madox, *Provence: From Minstrels to the Machine* (Allen & Unwin, 1935). A lyrical pre-war view of the region.

Fortescue, Winifred, *Perfume from Provence* (1935). Poor, intolerable Lady Fortescue's misadventures with the garlicky peasants near Nice.

Giono, Jean, *To the Slaughterhouse, Two Riders of the Storm* (Peter Owen, 1988). Giono is a major 20th-century novelist of Provence, whose deep pessimism contrasts with the sunnier views of his contemporary Pagnol.

Goldring, Douglas, *The South of France* (Macdonald, 1952). Travels and comments by another English resident.

Gramont, Sanche de, *The French: Portrait of a People* (Putnam, New York, 1969). One of the funnier attempts at the favourite French pastime: national self-analysis.

Greene, Graham, *J'Accuse: The Dark Side of Nice* (Bodley Head, 1982). The late Graham Greene, resident of Antibes, discovers the mafia connections and graft in the government of discredited mayor Jacques Médecin.

Hugo, Victor, *Les Misérables*, many editions. Injustice among the galley-slaves and basis for the hit musical.

Ladurie, Emmanuel Leroi, *Love, Death and Money in the Pays d'Oc* (Scolar, 1982).

de Larrabeiti, Michael, *The Provençal Tales* (Pavilion, 1988). Troubadours' tales, legends and stories told by shepherds around the camp fire.

Lugand, Jacques, Robert St-Jean and Jean Nougaret, *Languedoc Roman* (Zodiaque, 1975). The best of Languedoc's Romanesque architecture, with plans, lots of photos and an English translation.

Lyall, Archibald, *Companion Guide to the South of France* (Collins, 1978). Personal, well-written but dated guide of the entire Mediterranean coast.

Mayle, Peter, *A Year in Provence* and *Toujours Provence* (Sinclair Stevenson/Pan, 1989 and 1991). The entertaining bestsellers on ex-pat life in the Luberon.

Mistral, Frédéric, *Miréio* and *Poème de la Rhône*, epic poems by the Nobel prize-winning Félibre, widely available in French or Provençal.

More, Carey and Julian, *A Taste of Provence* (Pavilion, 1987). Father and daughter team up to evoke the countryside and gastronomy of Provence in words and photographs.

Morris, Edwin T., *Fragrance: The Story of Perfume from Cleopatra to Chanel* (Charles Scribner & Sons, 1984).

Pagnol, Marcel, *Jean de Florette and Manon of the Springs, The Days were too Short* (Picador, 1960). Autobiography by Provence's most beloved writer.

Petrarch, Francesco, *Songs and Sonnets from Laura's Lifetime* (Anvil Press, 1985).

Pope Hennessy, James, *Aspects of Provence* (Penguin, 1952). A fussy but lyrical view of the region in the '40s and '50s.

Smollett, Tobias, *Travels through France and Italy* (London, 1776). The irrepressible, grouchy Tobias 'Smellfungus' makes modern travel writing look like advertising copy.

Stendhal, *Travels through the South of France* (London, 1971).

Süskind, Patrick, *Perfume* (Penguin, 1989). Thrilling and fragrant murder in the 18th-century perfume industry in Grasse.

Van Gogh, Vincent, *Collected Letters of Vincent Van Gogh* (New York, 1978).

Vergé, Roger, *Cuisine of the Sun* (London, 1979). The owner of the Moulin de Mougins tells some of his secrets of *nouvelle* Provençal cooking.

Whitfield, Sarah, *Fauvism* (Thames and Hudson, 1991). A good introduction to the movement that changed art history.

Worwood, Valerie, *Aromantics* (Pan, 1987). An amusing look at aromatherapy.

Wylie, L., *Village in the Vaucluse* (Harvard University Press, 1971). The third edition of a very readable sociologist's classic based on the village of Roussillon.

Zeldin, Theodore, *France 1845–1945* (Oxford University Press, 1980). Five well-written volumes on all aspects of the period.

Index

Main page references are in **bold**. Page references to maps are in *italics*.